Accounting for Governmental and Nonprofit Entities

D0068843

THE IRWIN SERIES IN UNDERGRADUATE ACCOUNTING

Barr and Morris
Short Audit Case
Seventh Edition

Bernstein
Financial Statement Analysis: Theory, Application and Interpretation
Fifth Edition

Bernstein and Maksy
Cases in Financial Statement Reporting and Analysis
Second Edition

Boatsman, Griffin, Vickrey, and Williams
Advanced Accounting
Seventh Edition

Boockholdt
Accounting Information Systems
Third Edition

Brownlee, Ferris, and Haskins
Corporate Financial Reporting: Text and Cases
Second Edition

Dalton
1994 Individual Tax Return
Ninth Edition

Dalton
1994 Corporate Tax Return
Ninth Edition

Danos and Imhoff
Introduction to Financial Accounting
Second Edition

Dyckman, Dukes, and Davis
Intermediate Accounting
Third Edition

Edwards, Hermanson, and Maher
Principles of Financial and Managerial Accounting
Revised Edition

Engler
Managerial Accounting
Third Edition

Engler, Bernstein, and Lambert
Advanced Accounting
Third Edition

Engstrom and Hay
Essentials of Governmental Accounting for Public Administrators

Epstein and Spalding
The Accountant's Guide to Legal Liability and Ethics

FASB 1994–1995 Editions
Current Text: General Standards
Current Text: Industry Standards
Original Pronouncements Volume I
Original Pronouncements Volume II
Financial Accounting Concepts

Ferris
Financial Accounting and Corporate Reporting: A Casebook
Third Edition

Garrison and Noreen
Managerial Accounting
Seventh Edition

Hay and Engstrom
Essentials of Accounting for Governmental Accounting and Not-for-Profit Organizations
Third Edition

Hay and Wilson
Accounting for Governmental and Nonprofit Entities
Tenth Edition

Hendrikson and Van Breda
Accounting Theory
Fifth Edition

Hermanson and Edwards
Financial Accounting: A Business Perspective
Sixth Edition

Hermanson, Edwards, and Maher
Accounting: A Business Perspective
Sixth Edition

Hermanson, Strawser, and Strawser
Auditing Theory and Practice
Sixth Edition

Hermanson, Walker, Plunkett, and Turner
Computerized Accounting with Peachtree Complete® Accounting, Version 6.0

Hoyle
Advanced Accounting
Fourth Edition

Jesser
Integrated Accounting Computer Applications

Koerber
College Accounting
Revised Edition

Larson and Miller
Financial Accounting
Sixth Edition

Larson and Miller
Fundamental Accounting Principles
Thirteenth Edition

Larson, Spoede, and Miller
Fundamentals of Financial and Managerial Accounting

Maher and Deakin
Cost Accounting
Fourth Edition

Marshall
A Survey of Accounting: What the Numbers Mean
Second Edition

Miller, Redding, and Bahnson
The FASB: The People, the Process, and the Politics
Third Edition

Mueller, Gernon, and Meek
Accounting: An International Perspective
Third Edition

Pany and Whittington
Auditing

Pratt and Kulsrud
Corporate, Partnership, Estate, and Gift Taxation, 1996 Edition

Pratt and Kulsrud
Federal Taxation, 1996 Edition

Pratt and Kulsrud
Individual Taxation, 1996 Edition

Rayburn
Cost Accounting: Using a Cost Management Approach
Fifth Edition

Robertson
Auditing
Seventh Edition

Schrader
Accounting for the Small Business
Second Edition

Schroeder and Zlatkovich
A Survey of Accounting

Short
Fundamentals of Financial Accounting
Seventh Edition

Smith and Wiggins
Readings and Problems in Accounting Information Systems

Whittington and Pany
Principles of Auditing
Eleventh Edition

Yacht and Terry
Computer Accounting for Windows

Accounting for Governmental and Nonprofit Entities

TENTH EDITION

Leon E. Hay, Ph.D., CPA
Distinguished Professor Emeritus
University of Arkansas–Fayetteville

Earl R. Wilson, Ph.D., CPA
KPMG Peat Marwick/Joseph A. Silvoso
  Distinguished Professor
University of Missouri–Columbia

IRWIN

Chicago • Bogota • Boston • Buenos Aires • Caracas
London • Madrid • Mexico City • Sydney • Toronto

IRWIN
Concerned About Our Environment

In recognition of the fact that our company is a large end-user of fragile yet replenishable resources, we at IRWIN can assure you that every effort is made to meet or exceed Environmental Protection Agency (EPA) recommendations and requirements for a "greener" workplace.

To preserve these natural assets, a number of environmental policies, both companywide and department-specific, have been implemented. From the use of 50% recycled paper in our textbooks to the printing of promotional materials with recycled stock and soy inks to our office paper recycling program, we are committed to reducing waste and replacing environmentally unsafe products with safer alternatives.

Material from Uniform CPA Examination, Questions and Unofficial Answers, copyright © 1983–1993 by American Institute of Certified Public Accountants, Inc., is reprinted (or adapted) with permission.

Portions of various GASB documents, copyright by Governmental Accounting Standards Board, 401 Merritt 7, P.O. Box 5116, Norwalk, Connecticut, 06856-5116, USA, are reprinted wih permission. Copies of the complete documents are available from the GASB.

© RICHARD D. IRWIN, INC., 1951, 1956, 1961, 1969, 1974, 1980, 1985, 1989, 1992, and 1995

All rights reserved. No part of this publication may be reproduced, stored in a retrieval system, or transmitted, in any form or by any means, electronic, mechanical, photocopying, recording, or otherwise, without the prior written permission of the publisher.

Senior sponsoring editor:	Ron M. Regis
Developmental editor:	Elaine Cassidy
Senior marketing manager:	Heather L. Woods
Project editor:	Karen M. Smith
Production manager:	Ann Cassady
Cover designer:	Pam Rice
Interior designer:	Mercedes Santos
Art coordinator:	Heather Burbridge
Art studio:	Wm. C. Brown, Inc.
Compositor:	Bi-Comp, Inc.
Typeface:	10/12 Times Roman
Printer:	R. R. Donnelley & Sons Company

Library of Congress Cataloging-in-Publication Data

Hay, Leon Edwards, 1923–
    Accounting for governmental and nonprofit entities / Leon E. Hay, Earl R. Wilson. — 9th ed.
      p. cm. — (The Irwin series in undergraduate accounting)
    Includes index.
    ISBN 0-256-13216-X
    1. Finance, Public—Accounting.   2. Nonprofit organizations—Accounting.   3. Nonprofit organizations—United States—Accounting.
    I. Wilson, Earl Ray, 1939–   II. Title. III. Series.
    HJ9733.H38   1995
    657'.95—dc20   93–43984

Printed in the United States of America
   4 5 6 7 8 9 0 DO 1 0 9 8 7 6

Preface

The first two editions of this text (published in 1951 and 1956) were written by Professor R. M. Mikesell of Indiana University–Bloomington. The senior author of this tenth edition joined Professor Mikesell as coauthor of the third and fourth editions (1961 and 1969). After Professor Mikesell's death in 1972, the senior author prepared the fifth (1974), sixth (1980), seventh (1985), and eighth (1989) editions with the help and suggestions of many good friends, but without a coauthor. Because of the rapid pace of change in financial reporting standards and auditing standards for state and local governments in the United States, the federal government, and not-for-profit organizations, Dr. Earl R. Wilson of the University of Missouri–Columbia became a coauthor beginning with the ninth edition of *Accounting for Governmental and Nonprofit Entities*.

The pace of change in financial reporting standards and in auditing standards for governments and for not-for-profit organizations is expected to be as rapid in the next three years as it has been during the past three years. Accordingly, it is anticipated that there will be a need for an eleventh edition of this text in 1997 or 1998. During the life of the tenth edition, the authors will prepare Update Bulletins as needed to inform adopters of this text of changes in the standards explained and illustrated in the tenth edition, as necessitated by new pronouncements of the Governmental Accounting Standards Board, the Financial Accounting Standards Board, federal government standards setters, and the American Institute of Certified Public Accountants.

As was true of each previous edition, the authors owe a debt of gratitude to the many professors, students, and governmental financial report users, preparers, and auditors who have shared their knowledge, experience, and views on governmental and not-for-profit organization accounting and financial reporting. In the preparation of this edition the authors are greatly indebted to the standards-setters themselves, especially to James F. Antonio, Chairman; Martin Ives, Vice-Chairman; and David Bean, Director of Research; all of the Governmental Accounting Standards Board.

Many professors who were thanked by name in the Prefaces to earlier editions have continued to give generously of their time and efforts in improving explanations in chapters of the text and improving the wording of questions, exercises, problems, and answers and solutions. In addition, a number of professors have provided valuable suggestions that have helped achieve significant improvements in the forthcoming Third Edition of the *City of Bingham Continuous Problem Adapted for Microcomputer Solution.*

Bruce K. Michelson of the U.S. General Accounting Office, J. Thomas Luter of the U.S. Department of Treasury, and Robert Bramlett of the Federal Accounting Standards Advisory Board were very helpful in reviewing drafts of Chapter 15 of the text and providing excellent suggestions for improvement. The authors also gratefully acknowledge the assistance of Bridget M. Anderson, KPMG Peat Marwick; Robert T. Forrester, Coopers & Lybrand; Tom Gray, Healthcare Financial Management Association; Wayne McDanal, Federal Energy Regulatory Commission; Ruth Ann Robinson, United Way of America; and David S. Smarr, University of Missouri, for providing advice and resource materials used in the text. Bobbye S. Hay, CPA, contributed greatly to this and previous editions, both technically and personally. Florence J. Wilson also provided significant administrative assistance as well as much needed moral support. Laura Gripka and Karen Staggs devoted many hours to helping prepare the manuscript and ancillary materials for this edition of the text.

The authors appreciate the courtesy of the Government Accounting Standards Board in giving permission to quote their pronouncements and reproduce illustrations from their publications. The Government Finance Officers Association of the United States and Canada generously gave permission to use its published materials. The American Institute of Certified Public Accountants has also been very helpful by allowing use of questions and problems from the Uniform Certified Public Accountant Examinations and permitting quotations from its publications, particularly in the accounting and audit guide series. The International City/County Management Association contributed significantly to the material now in Chapter 13 by granting permission for use of its materials on financial analysis. In Chapter 21, the United Way of America graciously allowed the use of illustrations from *Standards of Accounting and Financial Reporting: A Guide for United Ways and Not-for-Profit Human Service Organizations.*

Although a number of persons helped refine the explanations in the chapters and the wording of the questions, exercises, and problems, it is probable that errors, inconsistencies, and ambiguities remain in this edition. As readers encounter errors of omission or commission in this text, we urge them to let us know so that corrections can be made. Additionally, every user of this edition who has suggestions or comments about the material in the chapters—or the questions, exercises, or problems—is invited to share them with us.

Leon E. Hay
Earl R. Wilson

Brief Contents

Contents

CHAPTER 14   **Audits of Governmental Entities**   **434**

CHAPTER 15   **Accounting and Reporting for Federal Government Agencies**   **467**

CHAPTER 16   **Budgets for Resource Management**   **507**

CHAPTER 17   **Planning and Control of Cash and Temporary Investments**   **544**

CHAPTER 18

Cost Determination for Governmental and Nonprofit Entities   580

CHAPTER 19

College and University Accounting   609

Financial Reporting for Governmental and Not-for-Profit Entities

Sources of Financial Reporting Standards

Accounting and financial reporting standards for state and local governmental units are established by the Governmental Accounting Standards Board (GASB). Accounting and financial reporting standards for profit-seeking businesses are established by the Financial Accounting Standards Board (FASB). The GASB and the FASB are parallel bodies under the oversight of the Financial Accounting Foundation. The Financial Accounting Foundation appoints the members of the two Boards and supports the operating expenses of the Boards by obtaining contributions from business corporations; professional organizations of accountants, financial analysts, and other groups concerned with financial reporting; CPA firms; debt-rating agencies; and state and local governments (for support of the GASB). Because of the breadth of support and the lack of ties to any single organization or governmental unit, the Financial Accounting Foundation, the GASB, and the FASB are referred to as "independent standards-setting boards in the private sector." Before the creation of the GASB and the FASB, financial reporting standards were set by groups sponsored by professional organizations: The forerunners of the GASB (formed in 1984) were the National Council on Governmental Accounting (1973–84), the National Committee on Governmental Accounting (1948–73), and the National Committee on Municipal Accounting (1934–41). The forerunners of the FASB (formed in 1973) were the Accounting Principles Board (1959–73) and the Committee on Accounting Procedure (1938–59) of the American Institute of Certified Public Accountants.

The Council of the American Institute of Certified Public Accountants (AICPA) has formally designated the GASB and the FASB as the authoritative bodies to establish accounting principles for state and local governments and for business organizations, respectively. "Authority to establish accounting principles" is interpreted in practice to mean "authority to establish financial reporting standards." Federal statutes assign responsibility for establishing and maintaining a sound financial structure for the federal government to three officials: the Comptroller General, the Director of the Office of Management and Budget, and the

1

Secretary of the Treasury. These three officials have created the Federal Accounting Standards Advisory Board (FASAB) to recommend accounting principles and standards for the federal government and its agencies. It is understood that, to the maximum extent possible, federal accounting and financial reporting standards will be consistent with those established by the GASB and, where applicable, by the FASB.

Authority to establish accounting principles (financial reporting standards) for not-for-profit organizations is split between the GASB and the FASB because a sizable number of not-for-profit organizations (particularly colleges and universities, and hospitals) are governmentally related, but many others are independent of governmental units. Accordingly, the GASB has the responsibility for establishing accounting and financial reporting standards for not-for-profit organizations which are considered to be governmentally related; the FASB has the responsibility for establishing accounting and financial reporting standards for nongovernmental not-for-profit organizations.

Both the GASB and the FASB have issued concepts statements, which are intended to communicate the framework within which the two bodies strive to establish consistent financial reporting standards for entities within their respective jurisdictions. Both the GASB and the FASB are concerned with standards for financial reporting to external users—those who lack the authority to prescribe the information they want and who must rely on the information management communicates to them. The Boards do not set standards for reporting to managers, administrators, regulatory bodies, or others deemed to have the ability to enforce their demands for information. Financial reports to external users are called **general purpose financial reports.** General purpose financial reporting includes not only financial statements but all other means of communicating information that relates directly or indirectly to the information provided by the accounting system. The GASB specifies that governmental general purpose financial reporting includes "in addition to general purpose financial statements (GPFS), 'popular reports' and comprehensive annual financial reports (CAFRs)." The GPFS of a governmental reporting entity are the statements which an independent Certified Public Accountant audits and on which the CPA expresses the opinion that the statements are (or are not) in conformity with generally accepted accounting principles (GAAP). Popular reports, as such, are not audited but usually contain selected data from the audited financial statements, statistical data, graphic displays, and narrative explanations. Illustration 1–1 shows the GASB's view of the relation of the GPFS to other information financial report users are thought to need to assess accountability and make resource allocation, investment, and other economic, social, and political decisions. The GASB is encouraging state and local governments to experiment with reporting **service efforts and accomplishments** to provide more complete information about a governmental entity's performance than can be provided by one operating statement, balance sheet, and budgetary comparison statements and schedules. Indicators of service efforts include inputs of nonmonetary resources as well as inputs of dollars. Indicators of service accomplishments include both outputs and outcomes.

ILLUSTRATION 1–1   Information Used by Financial Report Users

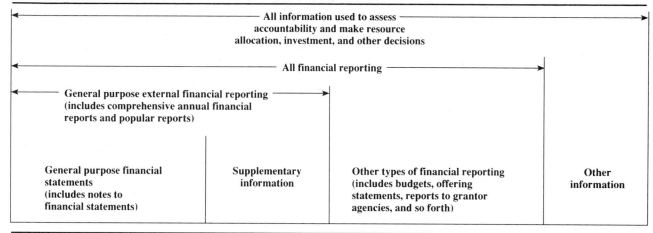

SOURCE: Adapted from GASB Codification Sec. 100, Figure 1.

Distinguishing Characteristics of Governmental and Not-for-Profit Entities

In its *Statement of Financial Accounting Concepts No. 4,* the Financial Accounting Standards Board noted the following characteristics the Board felt distinguished governmental and not-for-profit entities from business organizations:

> Receipts of significant amounts of resources from resource providers who do not expect to receive either repayment or economic benefits proportionate to the resources provided,
>
> Operating purposes that are other than to provide goods or services at a profit or profit equivalent, and
>
> Absence of defined ownership interests that can be sold, transferred, or redeemed, or that convey entitlement to a share of a residual distribution of resources in the event of liquidation of the organization.[1]

The Governmental Accounting Standards Board further distinguishes governmental entities in the United States from not-for-profit entities and from businesses by stressing that governments exist in an environment in which the power ultimately rests in the hands of the people. Voters delegate that power to public officials through the election process; the power is divided among the executive, legislative, and judicial branches of the government so that the actions, financial and otherwise, of governmental executives are constrained by legislative actions;

---

[1] Financial Accounting Standards Board, *Statement of Financial Accounting Concepts No. 4,* "Objectives of Financial Reporting by Nonbusiness Organizations" (Norwalk, Conn., 1980), p. 3. In 1985 the FASB decided to replace the term *nonbusiness* with the term *not-for-profit.* Other organizations use the term *nonprofit* as a synonym for not-for-profit. The terms are used interchangeably in this text.

and executive and legislative actions are subject to judicial review. Further constraints are imposed on state and local governments by the existence of the federal system in which higher levels of government encourage or dictate activities by lower levels and finance the activities (partially, at least) by an extensive system of intergovernmental grants and subsidies that require the lower levels to be accountable to the entity providing the resources, as well as to the citizenry. Revenues raised by each level of government come, ultimately, from taxpayers. Taxpayers are required to serve as providers of resources to governments even though they often have very little choice about which governmental services they receive and the extent to which they receive them. Since governments may have a monopoly on the services they provide to the public, the lack of a competitive marketplace makes it difficult to measure efficiency in the provision of the services. It is also extremely difficult to measure optimal quantity or quality for many of the services rendered by government—for example, how many police are "enough"? The Governmental Accounting Standards Board notes the determination of optimal quantity or quality of government services is complicated by the involuntary nature of the resources provided. "A consumer purchasing a commercial product can determine how much to purchase and may choose among 'good,' 'better,' or 'best' quality and pay accordingly. A group of individuals paying for governmental services (and paying in different proportions for services that some of them may not use or desire) presents a far more complex situation."[2]

Objectives of Financial Reporting

In its *Concepts Statement No. 1,* "Objectives of Financial Reporting," the Governmental Accounting Standards Board stated that "**Accountability** is the cornerstone of all financial reporting in government. . . . Accountability requires governments to answer to the citizenry—to justify the raising of public resources and the purposes for which they are used."[3] The Board elaborated:

> Governmental accountability is based on the belief that the citizenry has a "right to know," a right to receive openly declared facts that may lead to public debate by the citizens and their elected representatives. Financial reporting plays a major role in fulfilling government's duty to be publicly accountable in a democratic society.[4]

Financial reports of state and local governments, according to the Governmental Accounting Standards Board, are used primarily to (1) compare actual financial results with the legally adopted budget; (2) assess financial condition and results of operations; (3) assist in determining compliance with finance-related laws, rules, and regulations; and (4) assist in evaluating efficiency and effectiveness.

---

[2] Governmental Accounting Standards Board, *Codification of Governmental Accounting and Financial Reporting Standards as of June 30, 1993* (Norwalk, Conn., 1993), Sec. 100.117e.

[3] Ibid., Sec. 100.156.

[4] Ibid.

Closely related to the concept of accountability as the cornerstone of governmental financial reporting is the concept the GASB refers to as **interperiod equity.** The concept and its importance are explained as follows:

> The GASB believes that interperiod equity is a significant part of accountability and is fundamental to public administration. It therefore needs to be considered when establishing financial reporting objectives. In short, *financial reporting should help users assess whether current-year revenues are sufficient to pay for services provided that year and whether future taxpayers will be required to assume burdens for services previously provided.* (Emphasis added.)[5]

Financial reports of not-for-profit organizations—voluntary health and welfare organizations, colleges and universities, hospitals, religious organizations, and others—have similar uses but, in recognition of the fact that the financial operations of not-for-profit organizations are generally not subject to as detailed legal restrictions as are those of governments, the Financial Accounting Standards Board believes the financial reports for not-for-profit organizations should provide: (1) information useful in making resource allocation decisions; (2) information useful in assessing services and ability to provide services; (3) information useful in assessing management stewardship and performance; and (4) information about economic resources, obligations, net resources, and changes in them.[6]

Note the objectives of financial reporting for governments and not-for-profit entities stress the need for the public to understand and evaluate the financial activities and management of these organizations. All readers must already be aware of the impact on their lives, and on their bank accounts, of the activities of the layers of government they are obligated to support and of the not-for-profit organizations they voluntarily support. Since each of us is vitally affected, it is important that we be able to read intelligently the financial reports of governmental and not-for-profit entities. In order to understand the content of the financial reports it is necessary for the reader to make the effort to learn the accounting and financial reporting standards developed by authoritative bodies. The standards are explained and illustrated in Chapters 2 through 21 of this text. This chapter sets forth the distinguishing characteristics of governmental and not-for-profit entities and provides an overview of the objectives of accounting and financial reporting for these entities.

Governmental Financial Reporting

Serious users of governmental financial information have need for much more detail than is found in the audited general purpose financial statements. Much of that detail, as well as the auditor's report and the GPFS, is found in the governmental reporting entity's comprehensive annual financial report (CAFR), which

---

[5] Ibid., Sec. 100.161.

[6] Financial Accounting Standards Board, *Statement of Financial Accounting Concepts No. 4,* pp. 19–23.

is considered the entity's official annual report published as a matter of public record.

Comprehensive Annual Financial Report

Standards for the content of the CAFR are found in the GASB's *Codification of Governmental Accounting and Financial Reporting Standards*. Each CAFR should contain an introductory section, a financial section, and a statistical section.

Introductory Section.   Introductory material includes such items as title page and contents page, the letter of transmittal, and other material deemed appropriate by management.

The **letter of transmittal** may be literally that—a letter from the chief finance officer addressed to the chief executive and governing body of the governmental unit—or it may be a narrative over the signature of the chief executive. In either event, the letter or narrative material should cite legal and policy requirements for the report and discuss briefly the important aspects of the financial condition and financial operations of the reporting entity as a whole and of the entity's funds and account groups. Significant changes since the prior annual report and changes expected during the coming year should be brought to the attention of the reader of the report.

Financial Section.   The financial section of a comprehensive annual financial report should include: (1) an auditor's report, (2) general purpose financial statements, and (3) combining and individual fund and account group statements and schedules.

Laws relating to the audit of governmental units vary markedly from state to state. In some, all state agencies and all governmental units created pursuant to the state law are required to be audited by an audit agency of the state government. In others, local governmental units are audited by independent certified public accountants. In still others, some governmental units are audited by the state audit agency and some by independent certified public accountants. In any event, the auditor's opinion should accompany the financial statements reproduced in the report.

The financial section should contain sufficient information to disclose fully and present fairly the financial position and results of financial operations during the fiscal year. As noted previously, the financial operations of governmental units are constrained in considerable detail by laws of higher jurisdictions and by the actions of the legislative branch of the governmental unit itself. In addition, agreements with creditors and others provide constraints over financial activities and introduce financial reporting requirements. In order to make it possible to determine and demonstrate compliance with laws, regulations, and agreements, governmental units use **fund accounting.** The technical definition of fund is given in Chapter 2; the nature of each fund type and account group provided in GASB standards is also explained in Chapter 2. At this point it is sufficient to note that general purpose financial statements of state and local governments are **combined** statements in which financial data are presented in columnar form for each fund type and account group used by the reporting entity. The effects of interfund transactions are not eliminated; therefore the GPFS are **not** properly referred to as **consolidated.** The five combined statements that comprise the GPFS and that must be included in the financial section of a CAFR are:

1. Combined Balance Sheet—All Fund Types, Account Groups, and Discretely Presented Component Units. (See Illustration 2–1.)
2. Combined Statement of Revenues, Expenditures, and Changes in Fund Balances—All Governmental Fund Types and Discretely Presented Component Units. (See Illustration 3–1.)
3. Combined Statement of Revenues, Expenditures, and Changes in Fund Balances—Budget and Actual—General and Special Revenue Fund Types (and similar governmental fund types of the primary government for which annual budgets have been legally adopted). (See Illustration 3–2.)
4. Combined Statement of Revenues, Expenses, and Changes in Retained Earnings (or Equity)—All Proprietary Fund Types and Discretely Presented Component Units. (See Illustration 12–7.)
5. Combined Statement of Cash Flows—All Proprietary Fund Types and Discretely Presented Component Units. (See Illustration 12–8.)

The Notes to the Financial Statements are an integral part of the GPFS and are intended to be read with the GPFS. Accordingly, an independent auditor's report on the GPFS is a report on the five combined statements and on the notes that accompany them. GASB standards allow governments to "lift" the GPFS (including notes and auditor's report) from the CAFR and issue them separately for widespread distribution to users who require less detailed information than is contained in the CAFR. The CAFR must contain the GPFS, however, even if the GPFS are separately issued. Illustrations of the five combined statements, the GPFS, are presented in Chapters 2, 3, and 12, as noted in the preceding list of the GPFS.

Governments may have many different funds within each fund type; therefore persons with a depth of interest in the financial condition and financial operations of a governmental reporting entity will wish to refer to the "Combining and Individual Fund Statements," which follow the GPFS in the financial section of a CAFR. **Combining** statements are used to aggregate the financial data of all funds within each fund type. (Illustration 5–3 presents an example of a combining balance sheet.) If a reporting entity maintains only one fund within a given fund type it should be obvious that the financial data for that fund would be presented in **individual fund** statements, rather than in combining statements. Individual fund statements may be presented for one or more funds included in a fund-type combining statement where necessary to present prior year or budgetary comparisons. Combining and individual fund statements are not ordinarily audited, but if the reporting entity has need for an auditor's opinion on those statements the audit can be extended to cover the necessary additional work. Unaudited information often presented in the financial section of the CAFR following the combining and individual fund statements includes schedules necessary to demonstrate compliance with finance-related legal and contractual provisions; schedules to present comparative data on such items as tax collections, long-term debt, etc., and schedules to provide greater detail for information reported in the statements.

Statistical Section.   In addition to the introductory section (which presents the highlights of the CAFR) and the financial section (which presents the GPFS, combining and individual fund statements, and supplemental information), a CAFR should contain a statistical section, which presents tables and charts showing social and economic data, financial trends and the fiscal capacity of the government in detail needed by readers who are more than casually interested in the activities of the governmental unit. The GASB Codification suggests the content of the tables usually considered necessary for inclusion in a CAFR. The statistical section is discussed at greater length in Chapter 13 of this text.

Fund and Account Group Accounting and Reporting

The principles that underlie GASB accounting and financial reporting standards are introduced and discussed briefly in Chapter 2. Chapters 3 through 12 explain and illustrate the standards applicable to each of the fund types and account groups used by state and local governments. Chapter 13 reviews the essentials of Chapters 3 through 12, reviews and expands the discussion of the treatment of interfund transactions, reviews general purpose financial reporting of a governmental reporting entity, and discusses evaluation of governmental financial condition.

Analysis of Governmental Financial Statements; Independent Auditors' Reports

The characteristics that distinguish governmental and not-for-profit entities from business entities are identified in the section of this chapter headed "Distinguishing Characteristics of Governmental and Not-for-Profit Entities." Consideration of those characteristics should make it obvious that the majority of the ratios used in the analysis of the financial statements of business organizations have no relevance to the analysis of the financial statements of a governmental reporting entity or a not-for-profit entity. Similarly, the section on distinguishing characteristics and the section headed "Objectives of Financial Reporting" should indicate that the focus of independent audits of governmental financial statements logically differs from the focus of the independent audits of profit-seeking businesses. Governmental auditing objectives include reviews of the economy and efficiency with which governmental agencies manage and utilize resources, determination of whether results intended by those who authorized programs or activities are being achieved, as well as audits (similar to those of businesses) to determine whether financial statement presentations are in conformity with generally accepted accounting principles. In all cases auditors of governmental entities should ascertain that the entity has complied with relevant laws and regulations. Chapter 13 discusses financial ratios useful for the analysis of governmental financial statements.

Chapter 14 explains government auditing standards established by the Comptroller General of the United States and related publications issued by the American Institute of Certified Public Accountants for the guidance of auditors of governmental and not-for-profit entities.

Accounting and Reporting for Federal Agencies; Managerial Information

Accounting and financial reporting standards for federal government agencies are discussed in Chapter 15. Chapters 16 through 18 are concerned with information needed for financial management of governmental and not-for-profit entities: budgets for resource management, cash planning and control, and the determination of costs of services performed by governments and not-for-profit entities.

Financial Reporting of Not-for-Profit Entities

As noted in an earlier section, jurisdiction over financial reporting standards for not-for-profit entities (colleges and universities, hospitals, voluntary health and welfare organizations, religious organizations, and others) is divided between the FASB and the GASB. The FASB is following the approach of examining specific topics that have been treated differently by different categories of not-for-profit organizations and, after due process, issuing standards intended to force consistency among all not-for-profit organizations subject to the FASB's jurisdiction.[7] Similarly, Statements issued by the GASB which are applicable to proprietary funds and nonexpendable trust funds are also applicable to governmental entities that use proprietary fund accounting. Neither the FASB nor the GASB has issued a comprehensive set of financial reporting standards applicable to any specific category of not-for-profit entity, nor do they appear to intend to do so. Currently, the accounting and financial reporting structure utilized by the various categories of not-for-profit entities are found in AICPA accounting and audit guides, and in industry publications. Chapters 19 through 21 explain the accounting and financial reporting structure of colleges and universities, health care entities, and voluntary health and welfare organizations and other not-for-profit organizations, respectively.

A Caveat

The first edition of this text was written by the late Professor R. M. Mikesell. Some words of his bear thoughtful rereading from time to time by teachers and students in all fields, not just those concerned with accounting and financial reporting for governmental and not-for-profit entities:

> Even when developed to the ultimate stage of perfection, governmental accounting cannot become a guaranty of good government. At best, it can never be more than a valuable tool for promotion of sound financial management. It does not offer a panacea

---

[7] For example, *SFAS No. 93, Recognition of Depreciation by Not-for-Profit Organizations; SFAS No. 116, Accounting for Contributions Received and Contributions Made;* and *SFAS No. 117, Financial Statements of Not-for-Profit Organizations.*

for all the ills that beset representative government; nor will it fully overcome the influence of disinterested, uninformed citizens. It cannot be substituted for honesty and moral integrity on the part of public officials; it can help in resisting but cannot eliminate the demands of selfish interests, whether in the form of individual citizens, corporations, or the pressure groups which always abound to influence government at all levels.

It is difficult to strike a balance between the pursuit of perfection in a given field in isolation and the effort to improve the total system within which we live (which often involves settling for less than perfection in the elements of the system). The reader is urged to keep the ultimate goal of improving the system within which we live in mind throughout the period of time the text is being studied—and thereafter.

Selected References

Financial Accounting Standards Board. *Statement of Financial Accounting Concepts No. 4,* "Objectives of Financial Reporting by Nonbusiness Organizations." Norwalk, Conn., 1980.

Governmental Accounting Standards Board. *Codification of Governmental Accounting and Financial Reporting Standards as of June 30, 1993.* Norwalk, Conn., 1993.

Questions

1–1. GASB and FASB standards are concerned only with general purpose external financial reporting. To what users is such reporting directed? (In your answer explain what the acronyms GASB and FASB stand for.)

1–2. Why should persons interested in becoming able to read financial reports of governmental and not-for-profit entities intelligently be familiar with standards set by the GASB and the FASB?

1–3. What are the principal characteristics that distinguish governmental and not-for-profit entities from business enterprises?

1–4. Explain in your own words what is meant by "Accountability is the cornerstone of all financial reporting in government."

1–5. Explain how the concepts of accountability and interperiod equity relate to the objectives of financial reporting for governmental entities. Why is interperiod equity important in assessing accountability?

1–6. Why is it more difficult to measure the optimal quantity or quality of services rendered by a government than it is to measure optimal quantity or quality of the goods or services of a business enterprise?

1–7. In your own words state the primary uses the GASB believes external users have for financial reports of state and local governments. Compare and contrast these with the uses the FASB believes external users have for financial reports of not-for-profit entities.

1–8. According to the GASB, what statements are included in governmental general purpose financial statements? Contrast and compare general purpose financial reporting with all financial reporting.

1–9. What do the acronyms GPFS and CAFR stand for? List the statements and any other material that must be included in the GPFS by a governmental reporting entity intending to present financial statements in conformity with generally accepted accounting principles.

1–10. What is the significance of the GPFS to an independent auditor (CPA)?

1–11. What purposes are served by the following sections of a CAFR:

     a. Introductory section?
     b. Financial section?
     c. Statistical section?

1–12. What material should be included in the introductory section of a CAFR?

1–13. What material should be included in the financial section of a CAFR?

1–14. What material should be included in the statistical section of a CAFR?

1–15. Has the FASB or the GASB issued a comprehensive set of reporting standards for not-for-profit entities? If not, what approach is being followed by these standards-setting bodies?

Exercises and Problems

1–1. Obtain a copy of a recent comprehensive annual financial report (CAFR) of a governmental reporting entity (city, town, or county) and, if possible, the related budget.* Familiarize yourself with the organization of the comprehensive annual financial report—reread Chapter 1 of this text, particularly the section headed "Governmental Financial Reporting." Note particularly the items suggested below.

    A. Introductory Section.
    Read the Letter of Transmittal or any narrative that accompanies the financial statements. Does this material define the governmental reporting entity and name the primary government and all related component units included in the report? (If the reporting entity is not discussed in the Introductory Section, you should find this information in the Notes to the Financial Statements.) Is the explanation of the reporting entity understandable to you at this time? Does the Introductory Section discuss the financial condition of the reporting entity at balance sheet date? Does it discuss the most significant changes in financial condition that occurred during the year? Does it alert the reader to forthcoming changes in financial condition that are not as yet reflected in the financial statements? Do the amounts reported in the Letter of Transmittal or other narrative agree with amounts in the statements and

---

    * These may be obtained from the chief financial officer of the city, town, or county. If you do not know the exact title and address, you should write "Director of Finance, City of _____," and address it to the City Hall in the city and state of your choice. It is also acceptable, if you prefer, to obtain a copy of the comprehensive annual financial report of a state government. If you plan on studying Chapter 16 of this text, it would be convenient to request a copy of the most recent available operating budget document as well as the most recent available comprehensive annual financial report. Because some governmental units may not have any report available to send at the time of your request, it may be necessary to write a second or even a third request. The instructor may wish to obtain the reports and budgets before the term starts, or at least approve the selection of governmental units, so that every member of the class has a different report.

schedules in the Financial Section? (Specify any exceptions.) Does the Introductory Section define the generic fund types and individual funds and account groups included in the CAFR? Does the Introductory Section include a list of principal officials? An organization chart? Is a reproduction of a Certificate of Achievement for Excellence in Financial Reporting from the Government Finance Officers Association (GFOA) included in the Introductory Section?† Does the Introductory Section mention that the CAFR has been submitted to the GFOA for consideration for an award of the Certificate of Achievement?

B. **Financial Section.**
 1. *Audit Report.*   Are the financial statements in the report audited? By an independent CPA? By state auditors? By an auditor employed by the governmental unit being audited? Does the auditor express an opinion that the statements are: (*a*) "in conformity with generally accepted accounting principles," (*b*) "in conformity with generally accepted accounting principles applicable to governmental entities," (*c*) "in compliance with state laws," or (*d*) is the opinion qualified in some manner or disclaimed? Does the auditor clearly indicate the extent of any responsibility taken for other Financial Section contents? Does the auditor indicate specific responsibility for the general purpose financial statements?
 2. *General Purpose Financial Statements.*   Does the CAFR contain the five combined statements that must be included: (*a*) Combined Balance Sheet—All Fund Types, Account Groups, and Discretely Presented Component Units. (*b*) Combined Statement of Revenues, Expenditures, and Changes in Fund Balances—All Governmental Fund Types and Discretely Presented Component Units. (*c*) Combined Statement of Revenues, Expenditures, and Changes in Fund Balances—Budget and Actual—General and Special Revenue Fund Types, and similar fund types of the primary government for which annual budgets have been legally adopted. (*d*) Combined Statement of Revenues, Expenses, and Changes in Retained Earnings (or Equity)—All Proprietary Fund Types and Discretely Presented Component Units. (*e*) Combined Statement of Cash Flows—All Proprietary Fund Types and Discretely Presented Component Units. Does the report contain Notes to the Financial Statements? Notes are an integral part of the GPFS and are intended to be read with the GPFS.
 3. *Individual Fund and Combining Financial Statements.*   Following the notes to the GPFS, does the CAFR provide combining and individual fund statements? The combining statements should aggregate all the funds of a given fund type. For the general fund and other fund types containing one fund, individual fund statements should be provided.

C. **Statistical Tables.**
 Become familiar with the material presented in the statistical tables so that you can refer to these tables as needed in subsequent weeks.

---

† The Certificate of Achievement for Excellence in Financial Reporting (Certificate of Achievement) is recognized as the highest award in government financial reporting. The Government Finance Officers Association (GFOA) established the Certificate of Achievement Program in 1945 to encourage government units to publish excellent comprehensive annual financial reports (CAFRs) and to provide peer recognition and educational assistance to the *officials* preparing CAFRs. (Source: Government Finance Officers Association, 1993.)

Chapter 2

Principles of Accounting and Financial Reporting for State and Local Governments

The U.S. Bureau of the Census defines a government as:

> an organized entity which, in addition to having governmental character, has sufficient discretion in the management of its own affairs to distinguish it as separate from the administrative structure of any other governmental unit.[1]

In its most recent census of governments, the Bureau of the Census reports there are 86,692 local governmental units within the 50 states: 3,043 counties; 19,296 municipalities; 16,666 political townships; 14,556 independent school districts; and 33,131 special districts.[2] States, counties, municipalities, and political townships are general purpose governments—governments that provide many categories of services to their residents, such as police and fire protection; sanitation; construction and maintenance of streets, roads, and bridges; health and welfare; and others. Independent school districts and special districts are *limited purpose* governments—governments that provide only a single function, or a limited number of functions, such as education, drainage and flood control, irrigation, soil and water conservation, fire protection, water supply, and others. Limited purpose governmental units, as well as general purpose governmental units, have the power to levy and collect taxes and to raise revenues from other sources allowed by state laws to finance the services they provide.

The objectives of accounting and financial reporting for governmental units are summarized in Chapter 1. The objectives are those adopted by the Governmental Accounting Standards Board (GASB), the organization that establishes standards for accounting and financial reporting of states and local governments. The GASB's *Codification of Governmental Accounting and Financial Reporting*

---

[1] U.S. Department of Commerce, Bureau of the Census, *1987 Census of Governments,* vol. 1, no. 1 (Washington D.C.: U.S. Government Printing Office, 1988), p. B–1.

[2] 1992 census data, reported to authors by Marshall Moore, Government Division, Bureau of the Census.

Standards presents 12 principles of governmental accounting and financial reporting. It appears useful at this point to provide the reader with a statement of each principle and a brief explanation of the importance of the principle to persons who want to be able to read the financial reports of state and local governments intelligently.[3] Chapters 3 through 13 present more detailed explanations of the principles and illustrate their application to accounting and financial reporting of governmental units.

Summary Statement of Principles

Accounting and Reporting Capabilities
A governmental accounting system must make it possible both: (*a*) to present fairly and with full disclosure the financial position and results of financial operations of the funds and account groups of the governmental unit in conformity with generally accepted accounting principles; and (*b*) to determine and demonstrate compliance with finance-related legal and contractual provisions.

Adherence to generally accepted accounting principles (GAAP) is essential to ensuring a reasonable degree of comparability among the general purpose financial reports of state and local governmental units. The American Institute of Certified Public Accountants (AICPA) recognizes the GASB as the designated body to establish accounting principles for state and local governments under the AICPA Ethics Rule 203, *Accounting Principles*.[4]

In some states, however, laws require the state government and the local governments within the state to follow practices (such as cash basis accounting) not consistent with GAAP. In those cases, financial statements and reports prepared in compliance with state law are considered "special reports" or "supplemental schedules" and are **not** the basic general purpose financial statements discussed in Chapter 1. Governmental units may prepare two sets of financial statements: one set in compliance with legal requirements, and one set in conformity with GAAP.

Fund Accounting Systems
Governmental accounting systems should be organized and operated on a fund basis. A fund is defined as a fiscal and accounting entity with a self-balancing set of accounts

---

[3] It is assumed the reader of this text is familiar with principles of accounting for business entities, and therefore the text is focused on the differences between accounting for governmental and nonprofit entities and accounting for business enterprises rather than on the many similarities. Readers who are not familiar with basic accounting should study any contemporary introductory accounting text before attempting to understand the more technical portions of Chapters 3 through 21. Particular attention should be given to the discussion in the introductory text of financial statements and to the explanation of double-entry methodology (often called *the accounting cycle*).

[4] American Institute of Certified Public Accountants, *Statement on Auditing Standards No. 69, The Meaning of "Present Fairly in Conformity with Generally Accepted Accounting Principles" in the Independent Auditor's Report* (New York, 1991), par. 12.

recording cash and other financial resources, together with all related liabilities and residual equities or balances, and changes therein, which are segregated for the purpose of carrying on specific activities or attaining certain objectives in accordance with special regulations, restrictions, or limitations.

The definition of **fund** given above is mentioned in Chapter 1. The principle quoted below defines and categorizes the seven fund types that should be used, as needed, by state and local governments, both general purpose and limited purpose such as public school systems.

Types of Funds

The following types of funds should be used by state and local governments:

a. *Governmental Funds*
   (1) *The General Fund*—to account for all financial resources except those required to be accounted for in another fund.
   (2) *Special Revenue Funds*—to account for the proceeds of specific revenue sources (other than expendable trusts or for major capital projects) that are legally restricted to expenditures for specified purposes.
   (3) *Capital Projects Funds*—to account for financial resources to be used for the acquisition or construction of major capital facilities (other than those financed by proprietary funds and trust funds).
   (4) *Debt Service Funds*—to account for the accumulation of resources for, and the payment of, general long-term debt principal and interest.
b. *Proprietary Funds*
   (5) *Enterprise Funds*—to account for operations (*a*) that are financed and operated in a manner similar to private business enterprises—where the intent of the governing body is that the costs (expenses, including depreciation) of providing goods or services to the general public on a continuing basis be financed or recovered primarily through user charges; or (*b*) where the governing body has decided that periodic determination of revenues earned, expenses incurred, and/or net income is appropriate for capital maintenance, public policy, management control, accountability, or other purposes.
   (6) *Internal Service Funds*—to account for the financing of goods or services provided by one department or agency to other departments or agencies of the governmental unit, or to other governmental units, on a cost-reimbursement basis.
c. *Fiduciary Funds*
   (7) *Trust and Agency Funds*—to account for assets held by a governmental unit in a trustee capacity or as an agent for individuals, private organizations, other governmental units, and/or other funds. These include (*a*) expendable trust funds, (*b*) nonexpendable trust funds, (*c*) pension trust funds, and (*d*) agency funds.

Accounting for each of the fund types defined above is explained and illustrated in Chapters 3 through 13. Accounting characteristics common to each of the three categories of fund types—governmental funds, proprietary funds, and fiduciary funds—are set forth in the final section of this chapter.

Number of Funds
Governmental units should establish and maintain those funds required by law and sound financial administration. Only the minimum number of funds consistent with legal and operating requirements should be established, however, since unnecessary funds result in inflexibility, undue complexity, and inefficient financial administration.

The importance of the Number of Funds Principle is sometimes overlooked by academicians and, even, independent auditors. **The seven fund types defined in the Types of Funds Principle are to be used if needed by a governmental unit to demonstrate compliance with legal requirements or if needed to facilitate sound financial administration.** In rare instances the use of a certain fund type is required by GASB standards. If legal requirements, GASB standards, or sound financial administration do not require the use of a given fund type, it should not be used. In the simplest possible situation, a governmental unit could be in conformity with GAAP if it used a single fund, the General Fund, to account for all events and transactions. In addition to that one fund, however, it would need the two account groups for reasons set forth below:

Accounting for Fixed Assets and Long-Term Liabilities[5]
A clear distinction should be made between (*a*) fund fixed assets and general fixed assets and (*b*) fund long-term liabilities and general long-term debt.

   a. Fixed assets related to specific proprietary funds or trust funds should be accounted for through those funds. All other fixed assets of a governmental unit should be accounted for through the General Fixed Assets Account Group.
   b. Long-term liabilities of proprietary funds and trust funds should be accounted for through those funds. All other unmatured general long-term liabilities of the governmental unit, including special assessment debt for which the government is obligated in some manner, should be accounted for through the General Long-Term Debt Account Group.

General long-term obligations are those to be paid from general tax levies, specific debt service tax levies, or special assessments. Accounting and reporting for the General Long-Term Debt Account Group is explained and illustrated in Chapter 8.

General fixed assets include land, buildings, improvements other than buildings, and equipment used by activities accounted for by the four fund types classified as **governmental funds.** The two principles quoted below establish requirements that relate to fixed asset accounting.

Valuation of Fixed Assets
Fixed assets should be accounted for at cost, or, if the cost is not practicably determinable, at estimated cost. Donated fixed assets should be recorded at their estimated fair value at the time received.

---

[5] The GASB has been studying issues related to the financial reporting model for governments and expects to issue a Statement that may require revision of the Accounting for Fixed Assets and Long-Term Liabilities Principle, as well as other principles. When new standards are issued, the publisher will distribute to faculty members who have adopted this text an Update Bulletin describing the effect of the new standards on the explanations and illustrations in this text.

Depreciation of Fixed Assets

a. Depreciation of general fixed assets should not be recorded in the accounts of governmental funds. Depreciation of general fixed assets may be recorded in cost accounting systems or calculated for cost-finding analyses; and accumulated depreciation may be recorded in the General Fixed Assets Account Group.

b. Depreciation of fixed assets accounted for in a proprietary fund should be recorded in the accounts of that fund. Depreciation is also recognized in those trust funds where expenses, net income, and/or capital maintenance are measured.

Application of the three preceding principles to the General Fixed Assets Account Group is explained and illustrated in Chapter 6.

Accrual Basis in Governmental Accounting

The modified accrual or accrual basis of accounting, as appropriate, should be utilized in measuring financial position and operating results.

a. *Governmental fund* revenues and expenditures should be recognized on the modified accrual basis. Revenues should be recognized in the accounting period in which they become available and measurable.[6] Expenditures should be recognized in the accounting period in which the fund liability is incurred, if measurable, except for unmatured interest on general long-term debt, which should be recognized when due.

b. *Proprietary fund* revenues and expenses should be recognized on the accrual basis. Revenues should be recognized in the accounting period in which they are earned and become measurable; expenses should be recognized in the period incurred, if measurable.

c. *Fiduciary fund* revenues and expenses or expenditures (as appropriate) should be recognized on the basis consistent with the fund's accounting measurement objective. Nonexpendable trust and pension trust funds should be accounted for on the accrual basis; expendable trust funds should be accounted for on the modified accrual basis. Agency fund assets and liabilities should be accounted for on the modified accrual basis.

d. *Transfers* should be recognized in the accounting period in which the interfund receivable and payable arise.

The principle quoted above is not difficult to read, but its importance becomes evident to most students only after they have studied the chapters dealing with each fund type. Briefly, accrual accounting means that (1) revenues should be recorded in the period in which the service is given, although payment is received in a prior or subsequent period and (2) expenses should be recorded in the period

---

[6] GASB *Statement No. 11, Measurement Focus and Basis of Accounting—Governmental Fund Operating Statements,* drops the terms *modified accrual* and *available and measurable.* The Statement indicates that governmental funds use an accrual basis of accounting, and establishes criteria for the timing of recognition of governmental fund revenues and expenditures. The Statement was to have become effective for financial statements for periods beginning after June 15, 1994; but GASB *Statement No. 17* delays the effective date of *Statement No. 11* until related Statements are issued in final form. When the effective date of *Statement No. 11,* and related Statements, become definite an Update Bulletin will be distributed to faculty members who have adopted this text.

in which the benefit is received, although payment is made in a prior or subsequent period. In business enterprise accounting, the accrual basis is employed to obtain a matching of costs against the revenue flowing from those costs, thereby producing a more useful income statement. In governmental entities, however, even for those funds that do attempt to determine net income, only certain trust funds have major interest in the largest possible amount of gain. Internal service and enterprise funds are operated primarily for service; they make use of revenue and expense accounts to promote efficiency of operation and to guard against impairment of ability to render the services desired. For these reasons, operating statements of proprietary funds, nonexpendable trust funds, and pension trust funds are called statements of revenues and expenses rather than income statements.

Funds of other types (general funds, special revenue funds, capital projects funds, debt service funds, and expendable trust funds) are not concerned with income determination. As explained in Chapter 3, these funds are concerned with matching **expenditures** of legal appropriations, or legal authorizations, with revenues available to finance expenditures. Accordingly, GASB standards require that the "governmental" funds and expendable trust funds use the "modified accrual" basis. The modified accrual basis requires recognition of revenues in the period in which they become available and measurable. **Measurable** means capable of being expressed in monetary terms; **available** is defined as "collectible within the current period or soon enough thereafter to be used to pay liabilities of the current period."[7] GASB standards currently in effect require the accrual of revenue from property taxes. For other categories of revenue discussed in detail in following chapters, determination of the amount of revenue collectible is ordinarily made at the time of the collection, thus placing the fund partially on the cash basis in respect to revenue recognition. In respect to expenditure recognition, however, the modified accrual basis is almost identical to the accrual basis.

Budgeting, Budgetary Control, and Budgetary Reporting
   a. An annual budget(s) should be adopted by every governmental unit.
   b. The accounting system should provide the basis for appropriate budgetary control.
   c. Budgetary comparisons should be included in the appropriate financial statements and schedules for governmental funds for which an annual budget has been adopted.

Part *a* above is not an accounting or financial reporting principle, but it is a necessary precondition to parts *b* and *c*. A budget, when adopted according to procedures specified in state laws, is binding on the administrators of a governmental unit. Accordingly, a distinctive characteristic of governmental accounting resulting from the need to demonstrate compliance with laws governing the sources of revenues available to governmental units, and laws governing the utilization of those revenues, is the formal recording of the legally approved

---

[7] GASB Codification Sec. 1600.106.

budget in the accounts of funds operated on an annual basis. The nature and operation of budgetary accounts are explained in appropriate detail in following chapters. Briefly, budgetary accounts are opened as of the beginning of each fiscal year and closed as of the end of each fiscal year; therefore, they have no balances at year-end. During the year, however, the budgetary accounts of a fund are integrated with its proprietary (balance sheet and operating statement) accounts. In the governmental sense, proprietary accounts include accounts similar to the real and the nominal groups found in accounting for profit-seeking entities—that is, asset, liability, net worth, revenue, and expense (or expenditure) accounts. The nature and use of recommended proprietary accounts are explained in the appropriate chapters. The Combined Statement of Revenues, Expenditures, and Changes in Fund Balances—Budget and Actual, which is listed in Chapter 1 as one of the basic general purpose financial statements, is one of the budgetary comparisons required for conformity with GAAP. Budgetary accounting and budgetary reporting are explained in Chapter 3.

Transfer, Revenue, Expenditure, and Expense Account Classifications
a. Interfund transfers and proceeds of general long-term debt issues should be classified separately from fund revenues and expenditures or expenses.
b. Governmental fund revenues should be classified by fund and source. Expenditures should be classified by fund, function (or program), organization unit, activity, character, and principal classes of objects.
c. Proprietary fund revenues and expenses should be classified in essentially the same manner as those of similar business organizations, functions, or activities.

The principle quoted above elaborates on accounting and reporting requirements. The applications of this principle are illustrated and discussed at appropriate points in subsequent chapters.

Common Terminology and Classification
A common terminology and classification should be used consistently throughout the budget, the accounts, and the financial reports of each fund.

The Common Terminology and Classification Principle is simply a statement of the commonsense proposition that if the Budgeting, Budgetary Control, and Budgetary Reporting Principle is to be implemented, persons responsible for preparing the budgets and persons responsible for preparing the financial statements and financial reports should work with the persons responsible for designing and operating the accounting system. Agreement on a common terminology and classification scheme is needed to make sure the accounting system produces the information needed for budget preparation and for financial statement and report preparation.

Interim and Annual Financial Reports
a. Appropriate interim financial statements and reports of financial position, operating results, and other pertinent information should be prepared to facilitate management control of financial operations, legislative oversight, and, where necessary or desired, for external reporting purposes.

b. A comprehensive annual financial report should be prepared and published, covering all funds and account groups of the primary government (including its blended component units) and providing an overview of all discretely presented component units of the reporting entity—including introductory section; appropriate combined, combining, and individual fund statements; notes to the financial statements; required supplementary information; schedules; narrative explanations; and statistical tables. The reporting entity is the primary government (including its blended component units) and all discretely presented component units presented in accordance with Section 2100, ''Defining the Financial Reporting Entity.''

c. General purpose financial statements of the reporting entity may be issued separately from the comprehensive annual financial report. Such statements should include the basic financial statements and notes to the financial statements that are essential to the fair presentation of financial position and results of operations (and cash flows of those fund types and discretely presented component units that use proprietary fund accounting). Those statements may also be required to be accompanied by required supplementary information, essential to financial reporting of certain entities.

d. As discussed in Section 2100, the financial reporting entity consists of (1) the primary government, (2) organizations for which the primary government is financially accountable, and (3) other organizations for which the nature and significance of their relationship with the primary government are such that exclusion would cause the reporting entity's financial statements to be misleading or incomplete. The reporting entity's financial statements should present the fund types and account groups of the primary government (including its blended component units, which are, in substance, part of the primary government) and provide an overview of the discretely presented component units.

e. The nucleus of a financial reporting entity usually is a primary government. However, a governmental organization other than a primary government (such as a component unit, joint venture, jointly governed organization, or other stand-alone government) serves as the nucleus for its own reporting entity when it issues separate financial statements. For all of these entities, the provisions of Section 2100 should be applied in layers ''from the bottom up.'' At each layer, the definition and display provisions should be applied before the layer is included in the financial statements of the next level of the reporting government.

Interim financial statements of the various fund types are illustrated in the appropriate chapters. The content of a comprehensive interim financial report is explained in Chapter 13. The contents of the comprehensive annual financial report (CAFR) and of the general purpose financial statements (GPFS) are discussed briefly in Chapter 1; a more detailed explanation of each is given in appropriate chapters. Illustration 2–1 presents a Combined Balance Sheet, prepared in conformity with currently effective GASB standards to display financial data of a primary government and provide summary data for that government's component units. Concepts and terminology that readers of this text will encounter in state and local government financial reports are explained in the following section. Additional terms used in governmental and not-for-profit accounting are defined in Appendix 1 at the end of this book.

Governmental Financial Reporting Entity. A governmental reporting entity is defined as:

> The financial reporting entity consists of (*a*) the primary government, (*b*) organizations for which the primary government is financially accountable, and (*c*) other organizations for which the nature and significance of their relationship with the primary government are such that exclusion would cause the reporting entity's financial statements to be misleading or incomplete.[8]

A **primary government** is defined as ''a state government or general purpose local government. Also, a special purpose government that has a separately elected governing body, is legally separate, and is fiscally independent of other state or local governments.'' Note that each fund type and account group of the primary government is reported in a separate column of Illustration 2–1. The column to the right of the Totals—Memorandum Only Primary Government column is headed Component Units. **Component units** are legally separate organizations for which the elected officials of the primary government are financially accountable. In addition, a component unit can be another organization for which the nature and significance of its relationship with the primary government is such that exclusion would cause the reporting entity's financial statements to be misleading or incomplete. Reporting financial data of component units in the manner shown in Illustration 2–1 is called a **discrete presentation.** Discrete presentation should be used unless the financial activities of a component unit are so intertwined with those of the primary government that they are, in substance, the same as the primary government. In such cases the component unit's balances and transactions should be reported in a manner similar to the balances and transactions of the primary government itself; this method of inclusion is known as **blending.** Notes to the Financial Statements should contain a brief description of the component units of the financial reporting entity and their relationships to the primary government. This disclosure should include a brief discussion of the criteria for including the component units and how the component units are reported. Information about individual component units may be presented in condensed financial statements within the notes, or in combining statements. The notes should also include information about how separate financial statements for the individual component units may be obtained.[9]

The notion of financial accountability is basic to the definition of a governmental financial reporting entity. A primary government is, of course, financially accountable for the organizations that make up its legal entity. It is also financially accountable for legally separate organizations if its officials appoint a voting majority of an organization's governing body and either it is able to impose its will on that organization or there is a potential for the organization to provide specific

---

[8] GASB Codification Sec. 2100.111.

[9] All definitions in this paragraph are quoted or paraphrased from GASB Codification Sec. 2100.501.

ILLUSTRATION 2–1

NAME OF GOVERNMENTAL UNIT
Combined Balance Sheet—All Fund Types, Account Groups, and Discretely Presented Component Units
December 31, 19x2

| | Primary Government's Fund Types and Account Groups | | | | | |
| | Governmental Fund Types | | | | Proprietary Fund Types | |
	General	*Special Revenue*	*Debt Service*	*Capital Projects*	*Enterprise*	*Internal Service*
Assets:						
Cash	$258,500	$101,385	$ 598,366	$461,917	$ 257,036	$ 29,700
Investments	130,000	37,200	160,990	—	111,800	—
Receivables, net	155,300	77,760	264,666	213,540	161,985	12,000
Investment in joint venture	—	—	—	—	2,300,000	—
Due from component units	65,000	—	—	—	—	—
Lease receivable from primary government	—	—	—	—	—	—
Fixed assets, net	—	—	—	—	4,281,759	103,100
Amount available	—	—	—	—	—	—
Amounts to be provided	—	—	—	—	—	—
Total Assets	608,800	216,345	1,024,022	675,457	7,112,580	144,800
Liabilities:						
Accounts payable	50,512	15,380	—	29,600	57,000	15,000
Due to primary government	—	—	—	—	—	—
Lease payable to component unit	—	—	—	—	810,000	—
Revenue bonds payable	—	—	—	—	—	—
Tax-supported bonds payable	—	—	—	—	—	—
Total Liabilities	50,512	15,380	—	29,600	867,000	15,000
Equity:						
Investment in general fixed assets	—	—	—	—	—	—
Contributed capital	—	—	—	—	4,103,224	95,000
Retained earnings	—	—	—	—	2,142,356	34,800
Fund balances:						
Reserved	76,000	93,000	—	500,000	—	—
Unreserved	482,288	107,965	1,024,022	145,857	—	—
Total Equity	558,288	200,965	1,024,022	645,857	6,245,580	129,800
Total Liabilities and Equity	$608,800	$216,345	$1,024,022	$675,457	$7,112,580	$144,800

SOURCE: Based on Example 1, GASB Codification Sec. 2600.905.

Fiduciary Fund Types	Account Groups		Totals—Memorandum Only Primary Government	Component Units	Totals—Memorandum Only Reporting Entity
Trust and Agency	General Fixed Assets	General Long-Term Debt	December 31, 19x2	December 31, 19x2	December 31, 19x2
$ 216,701	—	—	$ 1,923,605	$ 1,656,960	$ 3,580,565
1,239,260	—	—	1,679,250	893,227	2,572,477
328,855	—	—	1,214,106	87,329	1,301,435
—	—	—	2,300,000	—	2,300,000
—	—	—	65,000	—	65,000
—	—	—	—	810,000	810,000
—	$7,326,500	—	11,711,359	19,191,577	30,902,936
—	—	$ 550,000	550,000	—	550,000
—	—	5,856,000	5,856,000	193,000	6,049,000
1,784,816	7,326,500	6,406,000	25,299,320	22,832,093	48,131,413
—	—	—	167,492	733,710	901,202
—	—	—	—	65,000	65,000
—	—	—	810,000	—	810,000
—	—	—	—	2,776,000	2,776,000
—	—	6,406,000	6,406,000	193,000	6,599,000
—	—	6,406,000	7,383,492	3,767,710	11,151,202
—	7,326,500	—	7,326,500	7,836,545	15,163,045
—	—	—	4,198,224	8,841,640	13,039,864
—	—	—	2,177,156	1,359,581	3,536,737
1,784,816	—	—	2,453,816	226,617	2,680,433
—	—	—	1,760,132	800,000	2,560,132
1,784,816	7,326,500	—	17,915,828	19,064,383	36,980,211
$1,784,816	$7,326,500	$6,406,000	$25,299,320	$22,832,093	$48,131,413

financial benefits to, or to impose specific financial burdens on, the primary government. A primary government may also be financially accountable for governmental organizations that are fiscally dependent on it.

A primary government has the ability to impose its will on an organization if it can significantly influence the programs, projects, or activities of, or the level of services performed or provided by, the organization. A financial benefit or burden relationship exists if the primary government (*a*) is entitled to the organization's resources; (*b*) is legally obligated or has otherwise assumed the obligation to finance the deficits of, or provide financial support to, the organization; or (*c*) is obligated in some manner for the debt of the organization.

Some organizations are included as component units because of their fiscal dependency on the primary government. An organization is fiscally dependent on the primary government if it is unable to adopt its budget, levy taxes or set rates or charges, or issue bonded debt without approval by the primary government.

A Summary of Accounting Characteristics of Fund Types

Information pertaining to accounting and financial reporting for governmental funds is given in a number of different contexts in the 12 principles discussed in the preceding section of this chapter. The same is true of information pertaining to accounting and financial reporting for proprietary funds and for fiduciary funds. Chapters following this one deal with individual fund types. In order to provide a framework for the student to keep the detailed discussion of fund types in perspective, this section presents the accounting characteristics common to each category of fund types: governmental, proprietary, and fiduciary.

Accounting Characteristics Common to Governmental Funds

All funds in any of the four types of funds classified by the GASB as governmental funds (the General Fund, Special Revenue Funds, Capital Projects Funds, and Debt Service Funds) have certain accounting characteristics that differentiate them from funds of types classified as proprietary funds or fiduciary funds:

1. Governmental funds are created in accord with legal requirements. Each fund has only those resources allowed by law—a local governmental unit may choose not to use a resource authorized by state law, but it may **not** choose to utilize an unauthorized resource. The resources may be expended only for purposes and in amounts approved by the legislative branch in accord with procedures detailed in laws of component jurisdictions. Therefore, the measurement focus of governmental fund accounting is on the flow of financial resources (as distinguished from a business organization's focus on the determination of net income). Governmental funds are said to be **expendable;** that is, resources are received and expended, with no expectation that they will be returned through user or departmental charges. Revenues and expenditures (**not** expenses) of governmental funds are recognized on the "modified accrual" basis of accounting. The meaning of the term **modified accrual** is explained further in Chapter 4.

2. Legal constraints on the raising of revenue and the expenditure of revenue are, in most jurisdictions, set forth in a legally adopted budget. Accordingly, it is a recognized principle of accounting and financial reporting for state and local governmental units that accounting systems of governmental funds should provide the basis for appropriate budgetary control. The nature and operation of budgetary accounts recommended for use by each of the fund types in the governmental funds category is explained in following chapters.

3. Governmental funds account only for financial resources: cash, receivables, marketable securities, and, if material, prepaid items and supplies inventories. They do not account for plant and equipment.

4. Funds in the governmental category account for only those liabilities to be paid from fund assets.[10]

5. The arithmetic difference between fund assets and fund liabilities is called the **Fund Equity.** Fund Equity may be reserved for reasons discussed in following chapters; the portion of Fund Equity that is not reserved is called **Fund Balance.** Residents of the governmental unit have no legal claim on any portion of the Fund Equity, so it is not equivalent to the capital section of an investor-owned entity.

Accounting Characteristics Common to Proprietary Funds

The definition of internal service funds, given in the Types of Funds Principle, states that these funds provide services to users on a "cost-reimbursement basis." The definition of enterprise funds, given in the same principle, states that they bear a "close resemblance to investor-owned enterprises" and that they are used in the event that the governmental body desires to compute revenues earned, costs incurred, or net income of certain activities. Proprietary funds are not subject to income taxation, nor do they have owners in the sense that business entities do, but in all other respects it follows that funds properly classified as proprietary funds should adhere to accounting practices deemed appropriate for business organizations:

1. Proprietary funds are established in accord with enabling legislation, and their operations and policies are subject to legislative oversight. Ordinarily, however, the purposes of legislative oversight are served by proprietary fund accounting and financial reporting that focuses on the matching of revenues and expenses (**not** expenditures) on the full accrual basis recommended for business organizations.

2. Funds classified as proprietary should prepare budgets as an essential element in the management planning and control processes. It is generally true, however, that proprietary funds do not have to adopt

---

[10] The GASB is considering alternative financial reporting models. When new standards are issued in final form, the publisher will distribute to faculty members who have adopted this text a bulletin setting forth the effect of the new standards on the explanations and illustrations in this text.

budgetary documents by law as governmental funds do. Therefore, standards established by the GASB state that accounting systems of proprietary funds do not need to provide for the integration of budgetary accounts.

3. Proprietary funds account for all assets used in fund operations—current assets, plant and equipment, and any other assets considered as belonging to the fund.

4. Proprietary funds account for current and long-term liabilities to be serviced from fund operations and/or to be repaid from fund assets.

Accounting Characteristics of Fiduciary Funds

Since the four types of fiduciary funds (agency funds, expendable trust funds, nonexpendable trust funds, and pension trust funds) all are used to account for assets held by a governmental unit as a trustee or agent, they have that characteristic in common. That characteristic, however, does not provide a basis for specifying a set of accounting characteristics that are appropriate for all fiduciary funds. On the contrary, the GASB has determined that the manner in which **agency funds** and **expendable trust funds** are created and operated is such that it is appropriate for these two types of fiduciary funds to be accounted for in essentially the same manner as the four types of governmental funds. The manner in which **nonexpendable trust funds** and **pension trust funds** are created and operated leads the GASB to conclude that these two types of fiduciary funds should be accounted for in essentially the same manner as the two types of proprietary funds.

Selected References

Governmental Accounting Standards Board. *Codification of Governmental Accounting and Financial Reporting Standards as of June 30, 1993.* Norwalk, Conn., 1993.

Questions

2–1. "The primary purpose of an accounting system for a state or a local governmental unit is to make it possible for financial statements to demonstrate compliance with finance-related legal and contractual provisions." Explain why you believe this statement to be correct or incorrect.

2–2. What is the technical meaning of the term *fund* in governmental accounting?

2–3. "In order for the general purpose financial statements of a governmental financial reporting entity to be in conformity with GAAP, the Combined Balance Sheet must provide a column for each of the seven fund types described in the GASB Types of Funds Principle." Do you agree or disagree? Explain the reasons for your answer.

2–4. The Combined Balance Sheet for the City of Briggs shows the following column headings: General Fund, Street and Bridge Fund, Capital Projects Fund, General Asset and Liability Fund, and Utility Fund. In what respects does the City of Briggs appear to follow recommended fund usage, and in what respects does it appear to differ?

2–5. "All unmatured general long-term liabilities of a governmental unit should be accounted for in a separate fund called the General Long-Term Debt Fund." Do you agree or disagree? Why?

2–6. "General fixed assets of a governmental unit should always be reported on the same basis as a business—depreciated historical cost." Do you agree? Why or why not?

2–7. "Governmental fund expenditures should be recognized in the accounting period in which the fund liability occurs." Is this statement true or false? Explain your answer.

2–8. "Proprietary funds do not have as their objective to make a profit; therefore, proprietary funds should not use the same accounting principles as a business enterprise." Do you agree or disagree? Why?

2–9. "Because budgetary accounts are used by governmental units, their financial statements can never be said to be in accord with generally accepted accounting principles." Comment.

2–10. "Interim financial statements are not required by GASB principles." Do you agree? Why or why not?

2–11. Explain in your own words what the term *governmental financial reporting entity* means.

2–12. "If a discrete presentation is used for the financial data of a component unit in the Combined Balance Sheet of a governmental financial reporting entity, there is no need for the component unit to issue a separate financial report." Is this statement true or false? In your answer explain what is meant by the term *discrete presentation*.

2–13. The four types of funds classified by the GASB as governmental funds have certain accounting characteristics in common that differentiate them from proprietary funds and fiduciary funds. In your own words state the accounting characteristics common to governmental funds.

2–14. The two types of funds classified by the GASB as proprietary funds have certain common accounting characteristics that differentiate them from governmental funds and fiduciary funds. In your own words, state the accounting characteristics common to proprietary funds.

2–15. Name the types of fiduciary funds that should be accounted for on the same basis as proprietary funds. Explain why this is the appropriate basis of accounting for those types of funds.

2–16. Name any of the types of funds classified as fiduciary funds that recognize revenues and expenditures on the basis of accounting used by governmental fund types. Explain why this is the appropriate basis.

Exercises and Problems

2–1. Utilizing the CAFR obtained for Exercise 1–1, examine the financial statements included in the Financial Section and answer the following questions.

    a. General Fund. (If necessary refer to the Individual Fund section of the CAFR for the General Fund balance sheet and other information.) What title is given the fund that functions as the General Fund of the reporting entity? Does the report specify that the General Fund of the reporting entity is the General Fund of the primary government? Does the report state the basis of accounting used for the General Fund? If so, is the financial statement presentation consistent with the stated basis (i.e., some reports claim the modified accrual basis was used but show no receivables in the balance sheet or any other evidence that measurable and available revenues are accrued)? If the basis of accounting is not stated, analyze the statements to determine what basis is used. Is the same basis used for both revenues and expenditures? Is the basis used consistent with GASB standards?

b. *Special Revenue Funds.*   What special revenue funds are included in the report? Are they described as special revenue funds, or only by a title such as "Library Fund," "School Fund," "Street Fund," etc.? Does the report specify why each special revenue fund was created (is there a reference to a state statute, local government ordinance, or other legislative or administrative action)? Is the basis of accounting for these funds stated, or must it be determined by analysis of the statements? Is the same basis used for all special revenue funds? Is it the same basis as used for the General Fund? If not, does the report explain why each basis is used? Is the basis of accounting for special revenue funds in conformity with GASB standards?

c. *Other Governmental Fund Types.*   List the names of governmental fund types, in addition to the General Fund and Special Revenue Funds, which are included in the combined balance sheet of the reporting entity. Are any governmental fund types included in other combined statements but not included in the balance sheet? If so, determine why.

d. *Proprietary Funds.*   List the names of the proprietary fund types included in the combined balance sheet. Do the balance sheet accounts evidence that all proprietary funds are accounted for on the full accrual basis?

e. *Fiduciary Funds.*   List the names of fiduciary fund types included in the combined balance sheet. (You may have to refer to a combining balance sheet for fiduciary funds, or to individual fund balance sheets, to determine the types of fiduciary funds used by this reporting entity.) For each fiduciary fund type identify the basis of accounting used.

f. *Account Groups.*   Does the combined balance sheet include a column for financial data of the General Fixed Assets Account Group? For the General Long-Term Debt Account Group?

g. *Notes to the Financial Statements.*   Read through the notes to the financial statements in order to become generally familiar with their content so that you can refer to the notes as needed in subsequent weeks. At this time determine whether the notes include a summary of significant accounting policies. Do the notes describe the criteria used in determining the scope of the entity for financial reporting purposes? Do the notes disclose which component units were included in the reporting entity and the key decision criteria considered? If there is a component unit disclosed in a separate column as a discrete presentation of the combined financial statements of the reporting entity, do the notes clearly disclose the accounting policies of the component unit and the relationship of the component unit to the primary government? Are there notes that disclose: (1) any material violations of legal provisions, (2) any deficit fund balance or retained earnings of individual funds, (3) any excess of expenditures over appropriations in individual funds, explanations therefor, and remedial action planned?

2–2. Write the numbers 1 through 10 on a sheet of paper. Beside each number write the letter corresponding with the *best* answer to each of the following questions:

1. An accounting system for a state or local governmental unit must make it possible:
   a. To prepare consolidated statements for the governmental reporting entity in conformity with FASB standards.
   b. To prepare financial statements as required by relevant laws.
   c. To present fairly the financial position and results of financial operations of the funds and account groups in conformity with GAAP and to demonstrate compliance with finance-related legal and contractual provisions.
   d. To demonstrate service efforts and accomplishments.

2. A fund is a(an):
   a. Accounting but not a fiscal entity.
   b. Self-balancing set of accounts recording cash and other financial resources, together with all related liabilities and residual equities or balances, and changes therein.
   c. Legal entity created only when authorized or required by law.
   d. All of the above are elements of the definition of a fund.

3. The governmental funds category is made up of:
   a. The General Fund, special revenue funds, trust funds, capital projects funds, and debt service funds.
   b. The General Fund, special revenue funds, capital projects funds, debt service funds, and enterprise funds.
   c. The General Fund, special revenue funds, capital projects funds, and debt service funds.
   d. The General Fund, special revenue funds, the General Fixed Assets Account Group, and the General Long-Term Debt Account Group.

4. Currently effective GASB standards require governmental funds to recognize revenues and expenditures on the:
   a. Full accrual basis.
   b. Modified accrual basis.
   c. Cash basis.
   d. There is no requirement; each government may choose whatever basis it wants, as long as it uses that basis consistently.

5. The proprietary funds category is made up of:
   a. Enterprise funds, nonexpendable trust funds, pension trust funds, and the General Fund.
   b. Enterprise funds and internal service funds.
   c. Internal service funds, special revenue funds, and enterprise funds.
   d. None of the funds; this term is not used in GASB standards.

6. Currently effective GASB standards require proprietary funds to recognize revenues and expenses on the:
   a. Full accrual basis.
   b. Modified accrual basis.
   c. Cash basis.
   d. Whatever basis is required by state law.

7. The fiduciary funds category is made up of:
   a. Expendable trust funds, agency funds, internal service funds, and general funds.

   b. Expendable trust funds, nonexpendable trust funds, agency funds, and pension trust funds.
   c. Expendable trust funds, nonexpendable trust funds, agency funds, and special revenue funds.
   d. None of the funds; this term is not used in GASB standards.
8. The General Fixed Assets Account Group should be used to account for fixed assets constructed or acquired to be used in the operations accounted for by:
   a. An internal service fund.
   b. An enterprise fund.
   c. A nonexpendable trust fund.
   d. A special revenue fund.
9. A governmental financial reporting entity consists of:
   a. The primary government.
   b. Organizations for which the primary government is financially accountable.
   c. Other organizations for which the nature and significance of their relationship with the primary government are such that exclusion would cause the reporting entity's financial statements to be misleading or incomplete.
   d. All of the above.
10. A primary government is defined as:
   a. A state government.
   b. A general purpose local government.
   c. A special purpose government that has a separately elected governing body, is legally separate, and is fiscally independent of other state or local governments.
   d. All of the above.

2–3. Write the numbers 1 through 10 on a sheet of paper. Beside each number write *T* if the corresponding statement is true. Write *F* if the corresponding statement is false. If the statement is false, state what changes should be made to make it true.

1. General funds, capital projects funds, and debt service funds are the only fund types that are classified as *governmental funds*.
2. Interfund transfers should be recognized in the period in which the interfund receivable and payable arise.
3. The measurement focus of governmental funds should be on the flow of financial resources, rather than on income determination.
4. The accounting system of the General Fund of a governmental reporting entity should incorporate budgetary accounts to assist administrators to achieve budgetary control.
5. The ''proprietary fund'' designation indicates that the funds operate in a manner similar to investor-owned enterprises.
6. Internal service funds and enterprise funds are the only fund types categorized as *proprietary funds*.
7. A governmental fund accounts for only liabilities to be paid from fund assets on hand at balance sheet date.
8. Depreciation should be reported for fixed assets accounted for in an internal service fund.

9. The accounting system for proprietary funds should provide for integration of budgetary accounts.
10. Enterprise fund accounting focuses on matching revenues and expenditures on the full accrual basis.

2–4. Write the numbers 1 through 10 on a sheet of paper. Beside each number write *T* if the corresponding statement is true. Write *F* if the corresponding statement is false. If the statement is false, state what changes should be made to make it true.

1. Funds used to account for transactions related to assets held by a governmental unit as a trustee or agent are known as *fiduciary funds*.
2. Trust funds appropriate for use by state and local governmental units are classified as expendable trust funds, nonexpendable trust funds, and pension trust funds.
3. Expendable trust funds are accounted for in essentially the same manner as pension trust funds.
4. Nonexpendable trust funds are accounted for in essentially the same manner as proprietary funds.
5. Interfund transfers and proceeds of general long-term debt need not be distinguished from a fund's revenues and expenditures or expenses for financial reporting purposes.
6. The term *CAFR* may be used correctly to refer to the comprehensive annual financial report of any governmental financial reporting entity.
7. The Combined Balance Sheet of a governmental financial reporting entity should display in separate columns the financial data for each fund type and account group used by the primary government of the reporting entity.
8. Financial data of component units of a governmental reporting entity are ordinarily not blended with the financial data of the primary government.
9. The notion of financial accountability is basic to the definition of a governmental financial reporting entity.
10. Since the government has no stockholders it need not prepare interim financial statements.

2–5. The City of Vermillion is financially accountable, as defined in GASB standards, for the Vermillion Water Utility, although the administrators of the Utility report to the Water Board.

The total assets of the City General Fund amount to $1,057,000. The assets of all the City's special revenue funds have a combined total of $2,024,000. Total assets of the City's capital projects funds equal $9,457,000. Total assets of the City's debt service funds equal $884,000. Total assets of the General Fixed Assets Account Group of the City equal $29,120,000. Total liabilities reported in the City's General Long-Term Debt Account Group equal $11,148,000. The City utilizes no other funds or account groups.

Total current assets of the Vermillion Water Utility amount to $895,000. Fixed assets of the Utility cost $20,000,000; accumulated depreciation on these assets totals $5,000,000. Current liabilities of the Utility total $600,000. Long-term bonds payable from revenues of the Utility total $10,000,000. Contributed capital of the Utility amounts to $4,900,000; Retained Earnings of the Utility total $395,000.

Required   *a.* Name the primary government of the City of Vermillion financial reporting entity. Explain your answer.

b. Should the balances of the Vermillion Water Utility be blended with the balances of the City, or should the balances of the Utility be shown in a discrete presentation? Explain your answer.

c. Should the fixed assets of the Utility be reported at cost, or at depreciated cost? Explain.

Continuous Problems

Note: Chapters 3 through 13 of this text deal with specific knowledge needed to understand the accounting for the funds recommended for use by state and local governmental units and with specific aspects of financial management. In order to help the student keep the entire accounting and financial management area in perspective, two series of related problems are presented. The first series covers representative activities of the City of Bingham; the problems in this series relate to all funds and account groups; they are designated 2–L, 3–L, 4–L, etc. The second series covers activities of the City of Smithville relating to only the General, capital projects, debt service, and Solid Waste Disposal funds, and the General Fixed Assets and General Long-Term Debt Account Groups; the problems in this series are designated 2–S, 3–S, 4–S, etc. The City of Smithville problem also illustrates the conversion of a budget for *functions* to a budget for *programs* (see Problem 16–S).

At the option of the instructor, students may be required to solve the City of Bingham problems manually, using journal paper and ledger paper available from college bookstores and from office supply stores, or students may be required to use microcomputers to maintain accounting records and produce financial statements. The instructions accompanying the L problems at the end of this chapter and the following chapters are presented on the assumption that the student is required to prepare solutions manually.*

2–L. 1. The City of Bingham has the following funds in addition to its General Fund; you are required to classify each in accordance with the types described in the GASB Types of Funds Principle quoted in this chapter.

> *City Hall Annex Construction Fund.* This fund was created to account for the proceeds of the sale of serial bonds issued for the construction and equipping of an annex to the city hall.
>
> *Debt Service Fund.* Nonactuarially determined contributions and earnings thereon, for the purpose of the payment of interest on and redemption of tax-supported and special assessment long-term debt issued by the City, are accounted for by this fund.
>
> *Stores and Services Fund.* This fund was established to account for centralized purchasing and management of inventories used by a number of departments of the city government.
>
> *Water Utility Fund.* The water utility serving the City of Bingham was originally constructed and operated by a private corporation. It was subsequently sold to the City, but it is still operated on a self-supporting basis under the regulations of the State Public Service Commission.

---

* Students whose instructors require the use of a microcomputer (IBM Personal Computer, or any compatible microcomputer) should purchase the *City of Bingham Continuous Problem Adapted for Microcomputer Solution,* 3rd ed., and its program diskette (Burr Ridge, Ill.: Richard D. Irwin, 1994). Be sure to purchase the 1994 edition, not an earlier edition.

Pass-Through Agency Fund. This fund is used to account for grants, entitlements, and shared revenues, which may be used in more than one fund at the discretion of the City Council of the City of Bingham; or which the City of Bingham receives as the primary recipient of grants, and which must be transmitted in whole or in part to other governmental units.

Employees' Retirement Fund. This fund was established to account for actuarially determined retirement contributions and earnings thereon, and for the payment of retirement annuities.

2. In addition to the funds described above, what account groups should be maintained by the City of Bingham? Why are these called **account groups** rather than "funds"?

3. For each of its funds and account groups, the City of Bingham maintains separate, manually kept books of original entry and ledgers.

Required

a. Open a *general journal* for the General Fund. Allow seven pages of 8½-by-11-inch loose-leaf journal paper, or its equivalent. (Do not open general journals for other funds until instructed to do so in subsequent L problems.) The form you use must allow for entry of subsidiary ledger accounts as well as general ledger accounts, and for entry of adequate explanations for each journal entry. (The form in which journal entries are illustrated in Chapter 3 is appropriate.) You will use the journal as your only posting medium; it should be complete.

b. Open a *general ledger* for the General Fund. Allow three pages of 8½-by-11-inch loose-leaf ledger paper, or its equivalent. On each page allow the number of lines shown below for each account.

Account No.	Title	Lines
1110	Cash	12
1111	Petty Cash	5
1130	Taxes Receivable—Current	5
1131	Estimated Uncollectible Current Taxes	5
1132	Taxes Receivable—Delinquent	5
1133	Estimated Uncollectible Delinquent Taxes	5
1134	Interest and Penalties Receivable on Taxes	5
1135	Estimated Uncollectible Interest and Penalties	5
1140	Advance to Stores and Services Fund	5
1210	Vouchers Payable	10
1211	Tax Anticipation Notes Payable	5
1212	Due to Federal Government	5
1213	Due to Other Funds	5
1300	Estimated Revenues	5
1400	Revenues	8
1500	Appropriations	5
1600	Expenditures—19x2	15
1650	Expenditures—19x1	5
1700	Encumbrances—19x2	5
1800	Reserve for Encumbrances—19x2	5
1801	Reserve for Encumbrances—19x1	5
1802	Reserve for Advance to Stores and Services Fund	5
1900	Fund Balance	8

c. The trial balance of the General Fund of the City of Bingham as of June 30, 19x1, the last day of the fiscal year prior to the year with which the L problems are concerned, is shown below.

(1) Prepare an entry in general journal form to enter the amounts shown in the trial balance in the proper general ledger accounts. Date the entry "July 1, 19x1." Note that no subsidiary ledger accounts are affected by this entry.

(2) Post the journal entry to the proper general ledger accounts opened in part 3b of this problem; each of the amounts entered should be dated "July 1, 19x1."

CITY OF BINGHAM
General Fund Trial Balance
As of June 30, 19x1

Account No.	Title	General Ledger Debits	General Ledger Credits
1110	Cash	$ 45,000	
1132	Taxes Receivable—Delinquent	244,000	
1133	Estimated Uncollectible Delinquent Taxes		$ 24,400
1134	Interest and Penalties Receivable on Taxes	13,376	
1135	Estimated Uncollectible Interest and Penalties		662
1210	Vouchers Payable		187,000
1213	Due to Other Funds		7,000
1801	Reserve for Encumbrances—19x1		14,000
1900	Fund Balance		69,314
		$302,376	$302,376

2–S. The City of Smithville maintains separate books of original entry and ledgers for each of its funds and account groups.

Required

a. Open a *general journal* for the General Fund. Allow five pages of 8½-by-11-inch loose-leaf journal paper, or its equivalent. (Do not open general journals for other funds until instructed to do so in subsequent S problems.) The form you use must allow for entry of subsidiary ledger accounts as well as general ledger accounts, and for entry of adequate explanations for each journal entry. (The form in which journal entries are illustrated in Chapter 3 is appropriate.) You will use the journal as your only posting medium; it should be complete.

b. Open a *general ledger* for the General Fund. Allow three pages of 8½-by-11-inch loose-leaf ledger paper, or its equivalent. On each page allow six lines for each of the following accounts:

> Cash
> Taxes Receivable—Current
> Estimated Uncollectible Current Taxes
> Taxes Receivable—Delinquent
> Estimated Uncollectible Delinquent Taxes
> Interest and Penalties Receivable on Taxes
> Estimated Uncollectible Interest and Penalties
> Due from Other Funds
> Due from State Government
> Estimated Revenues
> Revenues
> Vouchers Payable
> Tax Anticipation Notes Payable
> Due to Other Funds
> Due to Federal Government
> Due to State Government
> Appropriations
> Expenditures—19y1
> Encumbrances—19y1
> Reserve for Encumbrances—19y1
> Fund Balance

Note: If desired, a numerical classification system may be devised for the general ledger accounts to facilitate journalizing and posting transactions. The classification system should provide for subsidiary ledger accounts supporting Estimated Revenues, Revenues, Appropriations, Expenditures—19y1, and Encumbrances—19y1. Do *not* open subsidiary ledgers until instructed to do so in subsequent S problems.

c. The Trial Balance of the General Fund of the City of Smithville as of December 31, 19y0, is shown below. Enter the balance sheet amounts directly in the proper general ledger accounts; date each ''1/1/y1.''

CITY OF SMITHVILLE
General Fund Trial Balance
As of December 31, 19y0

Account Title	General Ledger Debits	Credits
Cash	$ 97,080	
Taxes Receivable—Delinquent	275,420	
Estimated Uncollectible Delinquent Taxes		$ 62,200
Interest and Penalties Receivable on Taxes	41,300	
Estimated Uncollectible Interest and Penalties		12,400
Due from Other Funds	21,200	
Due from State Government	500,000	
Vouchers Payable		330,500
Tax Anticipation Notes Payable		250,000
Due to Other Funds		18,900
Fund Balance		261,000
	$935,000	$935,000

CHAPTER

3

General Funds and Special Revenue Funds—Budgetary Accounting, Classification of Revenues and Expenditures

The General Fund of a state or local government unit is the entity that accounts for all the assets and resources used for financing the general administration of the unit and the traditional services provided to the people. General funds are sometimes known as operating funds or current funds; the purpose, not the name, is the true test of identity. The typical governmental unit now engages in many activities that for legal and historical reasons are financed by sources other than those available to the General Fund. Whenever a tax or other revenue source is authorized by a legislative body to be used for a specified purpose only, a governmental unit availing itself of that source may create a *special revenue* fund in order to be able to demonstrate that all revenue from that source was used for the specified purpose only. A common example of a special revenue fund is one used to account for state gasoline tax receipts distributed to a local government; in many states, the use of this money is restricted to the construction and maintenance of streets, highways, and bridges. The accounting structure specified for special revenue funds by the Governmental Accounting Standards Board (GASB) is identical with that specified for general funds.

In order to avoid excessive repetition of the phrase *general funds and special revenue funds,* the term **General Fund** is used in this chapter and in following chapters to include both categories of funds. General funds and special revenue funds are also referred to generically as revenue funds. In the GASB Types of Funds Principle, discussed in Chapter 2, the General Fund and special revenue fund types and two other fund types are classified by the GASB as governmental funds. Chapter 2 presents in brief the essential accounting characteristics common to all governmental funds. This chapter illustrates in greater depth the manner in which the body of generally accepted accounting principles (GAAP) is applied to general funds and to special revenue funds.

Proprietary (Balance Sheet and Operating Statement) Accounts

It should be emphasized that the General Fund, special revenue funds, and all other funds classified as governmental funds account for only financial resources (cash, receivables, marketable securities, and, if material, prepaid items and inventories). Assets such as land, buildings, and equipment utilized in fund operations are not accounted for by these funds because they are not normally converted into cash. Similarly, the same categories of funds account for only those liabilities incurred for normal operations that will be liquidated by use of fund assets.[1]

The arithmetic difference between the amount of financial resources and the amount of liabilities recorded in the fund is the Fund Equity. Residents of the governmental unit have no legal claim on any excess of liquid assets over current liabilities; therefore, the Fund Equity is not analogous to the capital accounts of an investor-owned entity. Accounts in the Fund Equity category of general funds and special revenue funds consist of **reserve** accounts established to disclose that portions of the equity are, for reasons explained later, not available for appropriation; the portion of equity available for appropriation is disclosed in an account called **Fund Balance.**

In addition to the Balance Sheet accounts described above, the General Fund and special revenue funds account for financial activities during a fiscal year in accounts classified as Revenues, Other Financing Sources, Expenditures, and Other Financing Uses. **Revenue** is defined as increases in fund financial resources other than from interfund transfers and debt issue proceeds. Operating transfers to a fund and debt issue proceeds received by a fund are classified as **Other Financing Sources** of the fund. Accounting standards specify that the revenues of all fund types classified as **governmental funds** (the General Fund, special revenue funds, capital projects funds, and debt service funds) be recognized on an accrual basis, designated in currently effective GASB standards as the modified accrual basis. Because the operations of governmental funds are subject to rather detailed legal restrictions, governmental fund revenues should be recognized in the fiscal year in which they are available to finance expenditures. (In a few jurisdictions laws provide that taxes must be collected in the year before the year in which they are available to finance expenditures. In such jurisdictions, tax collections should be credited to Deferred Revenues when cash is debited; in the following year Deferred Revenues should be debited and Revenues should be credited.)

Expenditure is a term which replaces both the terms **costs** and **expenses** used in accounting for profit-seeking entities. Expenditures are defined as decreases in fund financial resources other than through interfund transfers. Operating transfers out of a fund are classified as **Other Financing Uses.** Under the modified accrual basis an expenditure is recognized in the General Fund, or in special revenue funds, when a liability to be met from fund assets is incurred. It is important to note that an appropriation is considered to be expended in the amount of a liability incurred whether the liability is for salaries (an expense), for

---

[1] See footnote 10 of Chapter 2.

supplies (a current asset), or for a long-lived capital asset, such as land, buildings, or equipment.

An example of the use of transfer accounts occurs in those jurisdictions where a portion of the taxes recognized as revenue by the general fund of a unit is transferred to a debt service fund that will record expenditures for payment of interest and principal of general obligation debt. The General Fund would record the amounts transferred as Operating Transfers Out; the debt service fund would record the amount received as Operating Transfers In. Thus, use of the transfer accounts achieves the desired objective that revenues be recognized in the fund that levied the taxes and expenditures be recognized in the fund that expends the revenue. Other Financing Sources accounts and Other Financing Uses accounts are closed to Fund Balance in a manner identical with the closing of Revenues and Expenditures but are disclosed separately in the Statement of Revenues, Expenditures, and Changes in Fund Balances, as shown in Illustration 3–1.

Budgets and Budgetary Accounts

The fact that budgets are legally binding upon administrators has led to the incorporation of budgetary accounts in the General Fund and in special revenue funds and in all other funds required by state laws to adopt a budget. GASB standards require that, in addition to the statement shown as Illustration 3–1, a Combined Statement of Revenues, Expenditures, and Changes in Fund Balances—Budget and Actual be presented as one of the five combined statements required for conformity with generally accepted accounting principles. The budgetary comparison statement, shown as Illustration 3–2, must include the General Fund, special revenue funds, and all other governmental fund types for which annual budgets have been legally adopted. In this example, it is assumed that legal budgets are required for only the General Fund and all special revenue funds. The amounts in the Actual column are to be reported on the basis required by law for budget preparation, even if that basis differs from the basis provided in GASB financial reporting standards. For example, in some states revenues must be budgeted on the cash basis. If the Budget and Actual columns of the Combined Statement differ from GASB standards, the heading of the statement should so indicate. Budgetary practices of a government may differ from GAAP accounting practices in respects other than basis. GASB standards identify **timing, entity,** and **perspective** differences. Discussion of these differences is beyond the scope of this text; it is sufficient to emphasize that GASB standards require that the amounts shown in the Actual column of the Budget versus Actual statement conform in all respects with practices used to develop the amounts shown in the Budget column of the statement, so there is a true comparison. Standards further require that either on the face of the Budget versus Actual statement, or in the Notes to the Financial Statements the amounts in the Actual column of the Budget versus Actual statement (Illustration 3–2) must be reconciled with the amounts shown in the Combined Statement of Revenues, Expenditures, and Changes in Fund Balances (Illustration 3–1) prepared in conformity with GAAP. Reconciliation of the amounts

ILLUSTRATION 3–1

NAME OF GOVERNMENTAL UNIT

Combined Statement of Revenues, Expenditures, and Changes in Fund Balances—
All Governmental Fund Types and Discretely Presented Component Units
For the Fiscal Year Ended December 31, 19x2

	Primary Government's Fund Types							
	Governmental Fund Types				Fiduciary Fund Type	Totals— Memorandum Only Primary Government December 31, 19x2	Component Units	Totals— Memorandum Only Reporting Entity December 31, 19x2
	General	Special Revenue	Debt Service	Capital Projects	Expend- able Trust			
Revenues:								
Taxes	$ 881,300	$ 189,300	$ 380,587	—	—	$1,451,187	$ 675,327	$2,126,514
Intergovernmental	186,500	831,100	41,500	$1,250,000	—	2,309,100	233,474	2,542,574
Licenses and permits	191,700	—	—	—	—	191,700	13,942	205,642
Miscellaneous	—	—	—	—	$ 2,000	2,000	—	2,000
Total Revenues	1,259,500	1,020,400	422,087	1,250,000	2,000	3,953,987	922,743	4,876,730
Expenditures								
Current:								
General government	1,078,375	—	—	—	—	1,078,375	233,587	1,311,962
Public safety	204,095	534,200	—	—	—	738,295	—	738,295
Highways and streets	—	502,400	—	—	—	502,400	—	502,400
Education	—	—	—	—	—	—	658,923	658,923
Capital outlay	—	—	—	1,437,100	2,000	1,439,100	102,500	1,541,600
Debt service—								
Principal	—	—	315,500	—	—	315,500	33,400	348,900
Interest	—	—	368,420	—	—	368,420	14,800	383,220
Total Expenditures	1,282,470	1,036,600	683,920	1,437,100	2,000	4,442,090	1,043,210	5,485,300

Other Financing Sources (Uses):								
Proceeds of general obligation bonds	—	—	—	1,365,500	—	1,365,500	—	1,365,500
Operating transfers in	—	—	77,030	—	—	77,030	—	77,030
Operating transfers from primary government	—	—	—	—	—	—	100,000	100,000
Operating transfers out	(74,500)	—	—	—	—	(74,500)	—	(74,500)
Operating transfers to component units	(200,000)	(75,000)	—	—	—	(275,000)	—	(275,000)
Total Other Financing Sources (Uses)	(274,500)	(75,000)	77,030	1,365,500	—	1,093,030	100,000	1,193,030
Excess of Revenues and Other Sources over(under) Expenditures and Other Uses	(297,470)	(91,200)	(184,803)	1,178,400	—	604,927	(20,467)	584,460
Net income from golf course operations	—	—	—	—	—	—	2,350	2,350
Fund Balance—Beginning	855,758	292,165	1,208,825	(532,543)	33,163	1,857,368	1,352,056	3,209,424
(Increase) in Reserves	(76,000)	(93,000)	—	(500,000)	—	(669,000)	(226,617)	(895,617)
Fund Balance—Ending	$ 482,288	$ 107,965	$1,024,022	$ 145,857	$33,163	$1,793,295	$1,107,322	$2,900,617

Source: Based on Example 1, GASB Codification Sec. 2600.905.

ILLUSTRATION 3–2

NAME OF GOVERNMENTAL UNIT

Combined Statement of Revenues, Expenditures, and Changes in Fund Balances—
Budget and Actual—General and Special Revenue Fund Types of the Primary Government
Non-GAAP Presentation
For the Fiscal Year Ended December 31, 19x2

	General Fund			Special Revenue Funds			Totals (memorandum only)		
	Budget	Actual	Actual Over (Under) Budget	Budget	Actual	Actual Over (Under) Budget	Budget	Actual	Actual Over (Under) Budget
Revenues:									
Taxes	$ 882,500	$ 881,300	$ (1,200)	$ 189,500	$ 189,300	$ (200)	$1,072,000	$1,070,600	$ (1,400)
Intergovernmental	200,000	186,500	(13,500)	837,600	831,100	(6,500)	1,037,600	1,017,600	(20,000)
Licenses and permits	195,000	191,700	(3,300)	—	—	—	195,000	191,700	(3,300)
Miscellaneous	—	—	—	—	—	—	—	—	—
Total Revenues	1,277,500	1,259,500	(18,000)	1,027,100	1,020,400	(6,700)	2,304,600	2,279,900	(24,700)
Expenditures and Encumbrances									
Current:									
General government	1,150,000	1,148,375	(1,625)	—	—	—	1,150,000	1,148,375	(1,625)
Public safety	212,000	210,095	(1,905)	580,000	577,200	(2,800)	792,000	787,295	(4,705)
Highways and streets	—	—	—	555,000	552,400	(2,600)	555,000	552,400	(2,600)
Total Expenditures and Encumbrances	1,362,000	1,358,470	(3,530)	1,135,000	1,129,600	(5,400)	2,497,000	2,488,070	(8,930)
Other Financing Sources (Uses):									
Operating transfers out	(74,500)	(74,500)	—	—	—	—	(74,500)	(74,500)	—
Operating transfers to component units	(200,000)	(200,000)	—	(75,000)	(75,000)	—	(275,000)	(275,000)	—
Total Other Financing Sources (Uses)	(274,500)	(274,500)	—	(75,000)	(75,000)	—	(349,500)	(349,500)	—
Excess of Revenues over (under) Expenditures, Encumbrances, and Other Uses	(359,000)	(373,470)	(14,470)	(182,900)	(184,200)	(1,300)	(541,900)	(557,670)	(15,770)
Fund Balance—Beginning	855,758	855,758	—	292,165	292,165	—	1,147,923	1,147,923	—
Fund Balance—Ending	$ 496,758	$ 482,288	$(14,470)	$ 109,265	$ 107,965	$(1,300)	$ 606,023	$ 590,253	$(15,770)

SOURCE: Prepared by Authors in Conformity with GASB Codification Sec. 2600.905.

shown in the two statements is discussed and illustrated in a later section of this chapter.

In order to facilitate preparation of budgets and preparation of the Combined Statement of Revenues, Expenditures, and Changes in Fund Balances—Budget and Actual required for GAAP conformity, accounting systems of funds for which budgets are required by law should incorporate **budgetary accounts.** Only three general ledger control accounts are needed to provide appropriate budgetary control: **Estimated Revenues, Appropriations,** and **Encumbrances;** all three must be supported by subsidiary ledger accounts in whatever detail is required by law or by sound financial administration. Budgeted interfund transfers and debt proceeds may be recorded in **Estimated Other Financing Sources** and **Estimated Other Financing Uses** control accounts supported by subsidiary accounts as needed.

At the beginning of the budget period, the Estimated Revenues control account is debited for the total amount of revenues expected to be recognized, as provided in the Revenues budget. The amount of revenue expected from each source specified in the Revenues budget is recorded in a subsidiary ledger account, so that the total of subsidiary ledger detail agrees with the debit to the control account, and both agree with the adopted budget. If a separate entry is to be made to record the Revenues budget, the general ledger debit to the Estimated Revenues control account is offset by a credit to Fund Balance. Recall that the Fund Balance account, before the budget is recorded, would normally have a credit balance representing the excess of fund assets over the total of liabilities and reserved Fund Equity. (If fund liabilities and reserved Fund Equity exceed fund assets, the Fund Balance account would have a debit balance—referred to as a **deficit.**) After the revenues budget is recorded, Fund Balance represents the excess of fund assets *plus* the estimated revenues and other financing sources for the budget period over liabilities and reserves. The credit balance of the Fund Balance account, therefore, is the total amount available to finance appropriations. Consequently, the accounting entry to record the legally approved appropriations budget is a debit to Fund Balance and a credit to Appropriations for the total amount appropriated for the activities accounted for by the fund. The Appropriations control account is supported by a subsidiary ledger kept in the same detail as provided in the appropriations ordinance, so that the total of the subsidiary ledger detail agrees with the credit to the Appropriations control account, and both agree with the adopted budget. The use of the Encumbrances account is explained in a following section of this chapter.

Recording the Budget

The use of budgetary accounts is described briefly in the preceding section. In order to illustrate entries in journal form to record a budget, assume the amounts in the first money column of Illustration 3–2 are the amounts that have been legally approved as the budget for the General Fund of a certain governmental unit for the fiscal year ending December 31, 19x2. As of January 1, 19x2, the first day of the fiscal year, the total Estimated Revenues should be recorded in the General

Fund general ledger control account, and the amounts expected to be recognized during 19x2 from each revenue source specified in the budget should be recorded in subsidiary ledger accounts. An appropriate entry would be:

	General Ledger		Subsidiary Ledger	
	Debits	*Credits*	*Debits*	*Credits*
1. Estimated Revenues...................	1,277,500			
Fund Balance		1,277,500		
Revenues Ledger:				
Taxes..............................			882,500	
Intergovernmental Revenues			200,000	
Licenses and Permits................			195,000	

The total Appropriations and Other Financing Uses legally budgeted for 19x2 for the General Fund of the same governmental unit should also be recorded in the General Fund general ledger control accounts, and the amounts appropriated for each function itemized in the budget should be recorded in subsidiary ledger accounts. An appropriate entry would be:

	General Ledger		Subsidiary Ledger	
2. Fund Balance	1,636,500			
Appropriations		1,362.000		
Estimated Other Financing Uses......		274,500		
Appropriations ledger:				
General Government				1,150,000
Public Safety				212,000
Other Financing Uses ledger:				
Operating Transfers Out to				
Other Funds.....................				74,500
Operating Transfers Out to				
Component Units				200,000

It would, of course, be acceptable to combine the two entries illustrated above and make one General Fund entry to record Estimated Revenues, Appropriations, and Estimated Other Financing Uses; in this case there would be a debit to Fund Balance for $359,000 (the amount by which Appropriations and Estimated Other Financing Uses exceed Estimated Revenues). Even if a single combined entry is made in the General Fund general ledger accounts, that entry must provide for entry of the budgeted amounts in each individual subsidiary ledger account as shown in the illustrations of the two separate entries.

Accounting for Revenues

In the preceding section, entries to record the budget in general ledger accounts and in subsidiary ledger accounts are illustrated. During a fiscal year, actual revenues should be recognized in the general ledger accounts of governmental funds by credits to the Revenues account (offset by debits to receivable accounts for revenues that are accrued or by debits to Cash for revenues recognized on the cash basis). The general ledger Revenues account is a control account supported by Revenues subsidiary ledger accounts kept in exactly the same detail as kept for the Estimated Revenues subsidiary ledger accounts. For example, assume the General Fund of the governmental unit for which budgetary entries are illustrated in the preceding section collected revenues in cash during the month of January from Licenses and Permits, $13,200, and Intergovernmental Revenues, $61,900. In an actual case, entries should be made on a current basis and cash receipts should be deposited each working day; however, for the purpose of this chapter, the following entry illustrates the effect on the General Fund accounts of collections during the month of January:

	General Ledger		Subsidiary Ledger	
	Debits	*Credits*	*Debits*	*Credits*
3. Cash	75,100			
Revenues		75,100		
Revenues Ledger:				
Licenses and Permits..............				13,200
Intergovernmental Revenues				61,900

Comparability between Estimated Revenues subsidiary accounts and Revenues subsidiary accounts is necessary so that periodically throughout the fiscal year actual revenues from each source can be compared with estimated revenues from that source. Material differences between estimated and actual revenues should be investigated by administrators to determine whether (1) estimates were made on the basis of assumptions that may have appeared realistic when the budget was prepared but are no longer realistic (in that event, the budget needs to be revised so that administrators and legislators have better knowledge of revenues to be realized during the remainder of the fiscal year), or (2) action needs to be taken so that revenues estimated with reasonable accuracy are actually realized (i.e., one or more employees may have failed to understand that certain revenue items are to be collected). Illustration 3–3 shows a form of Revenues subsidiary ledger in which the debit column is subsidiary to the Estimated Revenues general ledger control account and the credit column is subsidiary to the Revenues general ledger control account. If the accounting system is computerized, as is often the case, the program should provide for screen displays and printouts that match Estimated Revenues and Revenues, by source, in a manner similar to Illustration 3–3.

A Statement of Actual and Estimated Revenues is illustrated in Chapter 4. Normally, during a fiscal year, the amount of revenue budgeted from each source will exceed the amount of revenue from that source realized to date; consequently, the Balance column will have a debit balance and may be headed Estimated Revenues Not Yet Realized. This amount is a **resource** of the governmental

---

ILLUSTRATION 3–3

Revenues Ledger
NAME OF GOVERNMENTAL UNIT
General Fund

Class: Licenses and Permits   Number: 351.1
Subclass: Title:

Date	Item	Reference	Estimated Revenues DR.	Revenues CR.	Balance DR. (CR.)
19x2					
January 1	Budget estimate	J1	$195,000		$195,000
31	Collections	CR6		$13,200	181,800

unit—legally and realistically budgeted revenues that will be recognized as assets before the end of the fiscal year.

Accounting for Encumbrances and Expenditures

When enacted into law, an appropriation is an authorization for administrators to incur on behalf of the governmental unit liabilities in the amounts specified in the appropriation ordinance or statute, for the purposes set forth in that ordinance or statute, during the period of time specified. An appropriation is considered **expended** when the authorized liabilities have been incurred. Because penalties are imposed by law on an administrator who incurs liabilities for any amount in excess of that appropriated, or for any purpose not covered by an appropriation, or who incurs liabilities after the authority to do so has expired, prudence dictates that each purchase order and each contract be reviewed before it is signed to determine that a valid and sufficient appropriation exists to which the expenditure can be charged when goods or services are received. If the review indicates that a valid appropriation exists and it has an available balance in excess of the amount of the purchase order or contract being reviewed, the purchase order or contract legally may be issued. When a purchase order or contract has been issued it is important to record the fact that the appropriation has been **encumbered** in the amount of the purchase order or contract. The word *encumbered* is used, rather than the word *expended,* because the amount is only an estimate of the liability that will be incurred when the purchase order is filled or the contract executed. (It is reasonably common for quantities of goods received to differ from quantities ordered, and it is not uncommon for invoice prices to differ from unit prices shown on purchase orders.) The use of appropriation authority is also somewhat tentative inasmuch as some suppliers are unable to fill orders or to perform as stipulated in a contract; in such cases, related purchase orders or contracts must be canceled.

Notice the issuance of purchase orders and/or contracts has two effects: (1) the encumbrance of the appropriation(s) that gave the governmental unit the authority to order goods or services and (2) the starting of a chain of events that will result in the government incurring a liability when the purchase orders are filled and the contracts executed. Both effects should be recorded in order to assist administrators to avoid overexpending appropriations and to plan to be able to pay liabilities on a timely basis. The accounting procedure used to record the two effects is illustrated by Entry 4. The first effect is recorded by the debit to the general ledger account **Encumbrances.** Encumbrances is a control account that is related to the **Appropriations** control account discussed previously and to the **Expenditures** control account discussed in relation to Entries 5a and 5b. In order to accomplish the matching of Appropriations, Expenditures, and Encumbrances necessary for budgetary control, subsidiary account classifications of all three must correspond exactly (see Illustration 3–4). The general ledger account credited in Entry 4, **Reserve for Encumbrances,** is used to record the second effect of issuing purchase orders and contracts—the creation of an expected liability. Reserve for Encumbrances, sometimes called Outstanding Encumbrances, is not a control account; the balance of the account at balance sheet date is reported as a reservation of Fund Equity, as illustrated in Chapter 4.

Entries 4, 5a, 5b, and 6 illustrate accounting for Encumbrances and Expenditures for the General Fund of the governmental unit for which entries are illustrated in previous sections of this chapter. Entry 4 is made on the assumption that early in January purchase orders are issued pursuant to the authority contained in the General Fund appropriations; assumed amounts chargeable to each function for which purchase orders are issued on this date are shown in the debits to the Encumbrances subsidiary accounts.

	General Ledger		Subsidiary Ledger	
	Debits	*Credits*	*Debits*	*Credits*
4. Encumbrances—19x2	45,400			
Reserve for Encumbrances—19x2 ..		45,400		
Encumbrances Ledger:				
General Government			38,000	
Public Safety			7,400	

When goods or services for which encumbrances have been recorded are received and the suppliers' invoices are approved for payment, the accounts should record the fact that appropriations have been **expended,** not merely encumbered, and that an actual liability, not merely an expected liability, exists. Entry 5a reverses Entry 4 to the extent that purchase orders are filled (ordinarily some of the purchase orders recorded in one encumbrance entry will be filled in one time period, and some in other time periods); it is important to note that since estimated amounts were used when encumbrances were recorded, the reversing entry must also use the estimated amounts. Thus the balance remaining in the Encumbrances control account, and in the Reserve for Encumbrances account, is the **total** estimated dollar amount of purchase orders and contracts outstanding. The estimated dollar amount of purchase orders outstanding against each appropriation is disclosed by the subsidiary accounts, as shown in Illustration 3–4.

	General Ledger		Subsidiary Ledger	
	Debits	*Credits*	*Debits*	*Credits*
5a. Reserve for Encumbrances—19x2	42,000			
Encumbrances—19x2		42,000		
Encumbrances ledger:				
General Government				35,000
Public Safety				7,000
5b. Expenditures—19x2.................	42,400			
Vouchers Payable...............		42,400		
Expenditures ledger:				
General Government			35,100	
Public Safety			7,300	

Expenditures and the liability account must both be recorded at the actual amount the governmental unit agrees to pay the vendors who have filled the purchase orders (see Entry 5b). The fact that estimated and actual amounts differ causes no accounting difficulties as long as goods or services are received in the same fiscal period as ordered. The accounting treatment required when encumbrances outstanding at year-end are filled, or canceled, in a following year is illustrated in Chapter 4.

The encumbrance procedure is not always needed to make sure that appropriations are not overexpended. For example, although salaries and wages of governmental employees must be chargeable against valid and sufficient appropriations in order to give rise to legal expenditures, many governmental units do not find it necessary to encumber the departmental personal services appropriations for estimated payrolls of recurring, relatively constant amounts. Departments having payrolls that fluctuate greatly from one season to another may follow the encumbrance procedure to make sure the personal service appropriation is not overexpended. Entry 6 shows the recording of expenditures of appropriations for salaries and wages not previously encumbered, assuming gross pay is vouchered.

6. Expenditures—19x2.................	67,600			
Vouchers Payable...............		67,600		
Expenditures ledger:				
General Government			57,000	
Public Safety			10,600	

From the foregoing discussion and illustrative journal entries, it should be apparent that administrators of governmental units need accounting systems designed to provide at any given date during a fiscal year comparisons for each item in the legal Appropriations budget of (1) the amount appropriated, (2) the amount of outstanding encumbrances, and (3) the cumulative amount of expenditures to this date. The net of the three items is accurately described as "Unencumbered Unexpended Appropriations" but can be labeled more simply as "Available Appropriations" or "Available Balance." Classification of appropriations, expenditures, and encumbrances is discussed in the following section of this chapter. In order to provide needed comparisons, classification of expenditures and encumbrances must agree with the classifications of appropriations mandated by law. In many jurisdictions, good financial management may dictate all three elements be classified in greater detail than required by law.

Illustration 3–4 shows a form of subsidiary ledger that supports all three general ledger control accounts: Appropriations, Expenditures, and Encumbrances.

At intervals during the fiscal year, a Statement of Budgeted and Actual Expenditures and Encumbrances should be prepared to inform administrators and members of the legislative branch of the data contained in the subsidiary ledger records. An example of such a statement is illustrated in Chapter 4 (see Illustration 4–3). Also in Chapter 4, the entry needed at year-end to close budgetary and nominal accounts is illustrated (Entry 22, Chapter 4).

ILLUSTRATION 3–4

NAME OF GOVERNMENT UNIT
Appropriations, Expenditures, and Encumbrances Ledger

Code No.: 0607–03
Fund: General
Function: General Government

Year: 19x2

Month and Day	Reference	Encumbrances			Expenditures		Appropriations	
		Debits	Credits	Open	Debits	Cumulative Total	Credits	Available Balance
Jan. 2	Budget (Entry 2)						$1,150,000	$1,150,000
3	Purchase orders issued (Entry 4)	$38,000		$38,000				1,112,000
17	Invoices approved for payment (Entries 5a, 5b)		$35,000	3,000	$35,100	$35,100		1,111,900
31	Payrolls (Entry 6)				57,000	92,100		1,054,900

Reconciliation of
Amounts Reported in
Illustration 3–1 with
Amounts Reported in
Illustration 3–2

As noted in a previous section of this chapter, GASB standards require that differences between amounts reported in the GAAP basis operating statement (Illustration 3–1) and those reported in conformity with budgetary practices (Illustration 3–2) be reconciled either on the face of the statements or in the notes to the financial statements. Readers will note that the amounts in the Revenues section of the Actual column of Illustration 3–2 are the same as the Revenues reported in Illustration 3–1 because in this example the budget for revenues is prepared on the same basis as is used in the accounts. The amounts in the Expenditures section of the Actual column of Illustration 3–2 differ from the Expenditures reported in Illustration 3–1, however, because the latter, in conformity with GASB standards, reports Expenditures chargeable to the prior year's appropriations as well as Expenditures chargeable to 19x2 appropriations and does not report Encumbrances as Expenditures. In contrast, Encumbrances outstanding at the end of fiscal year 19x2 are added to 19x2 Expenditures in Illustration 3–2 because both are uses of the 19x2 appropriation authority (reported in the Budget column). Expenditures chargeable to the prior year's appropriation are excluded from Illustration 3–2 because it relates only to the 19x2 Budget and Actual. Consequently, the Notes to the Financial Statements should include a reconciliation of the General Fund and Special Revenue Funds Expenditures reported in the two statements illustrated. One form of reconciliation appears below (the year-end Reserve for Encumbrances in each fund is taken from the Combined Balance Sheet shown as Illustration 2–1.

	General Fund	*Special Revenue Funds*
Expenditures of 19x2 appropriations, budgetary basis (Illustration 3–2)	$1,358,470	$1,129,600
Less: Increase in Reserve for Encumbrances, December 31, 19x2 (Illustration 3–1)	76,000	93,000
Expenditures for 19x2, GAAP basis (Illustration 3–1)	$1,282,470	$1,036,600

A second form of reconciliation sometimes found in practice is:

	General Fund	*Special Revenue Funds*
Excess of revenues over (under) expenditures and other uses, budgetary basis (Illustration 3–2)	$ (373,470)	$ (184,200)
Increase in Reserve for Encumbrances (Illustration 3–1)	76,000	93,000
Excess of revenues over (under) expenditures and other uses, GAAP basis (Illustration 3–1)	$ (297,470)	$ (91,200)

Accounting for Allotments

In some jurisdictions, it is necessary to regulate the use of appropriations so only specified amounts may be used from month to month or from quarter to quarter. The purpose of such control is to prevent expenditure of all or most of the authorized amount early in the year, without providing for unexpected requirements arising later in the year. A common device for regulating expenditures is the use of allotments. An *allotment* may be described as an internal allocation of funds on a periodic basis usually agreed upon by the department heads and the chief executive or his representative.

Allotments may be formally recorded in ledger accounts. This procedure might begin with the budgetary entry, in which Unallotted Appropriations would replace Appropriations. If this is desired, a combined entry to record the budget would be (using the numbers given in Entries 1 and 2, omitting entries in subsidiary accounts—which would be as illustrated previously, except the subsidiary ledger credits in Entry 2 would be designated as Unallotted Appropriations instead of Appropriations):

	General Ledger		Subsidiary Ledger	
	Debits	*Credits*	*Debits*	*Credits*
Estimated Revenues	1,277,500			
Fund Balance	359,000			
Unallotted Appropriations		1,362,000		
Estimated Other Financing Uses		274,500		

If it is assumed that $342,000 is the amount formally allotted for the first period, the following entry could be made (amounts allotted for each function are shown in the subsidiary ledger entries):

Unallotted Appropriations	342,000			
Allotments		342,000		
Allotments Ledger:				
General Government				289,000
Public Safety				53,000

Expenditures can be recorded periodically as reports are received from using departments or divisions. Under this procedure, Expenditures, Allotments, and Unallotted Appropriations are all closed to Fund Balance at year-end, usually in one combined entry.

Terminology and Classification for Governmental Fund Budgets and Accounts

Budgets as they are incorporated in legal documents and in financial reports required for conformity with GAAP may be described as legally approved plans of financial operations embodying the authorization of expenditures for specified purposes to be made during the budget period and the proposed means of financing them. The sequence of budget preparation in practice is often the same as the sequence in the preceding sentence: Expenditures are planned first; then plans are made to finance the expenditures. For that reason, the discussion in this chapter follows the same sequence.

Classification of Appropriations and Expenditures

Recall that an appropriation, when enacted into law, is an authorization to incur on behalf of the governmental unit liabilities for goods, services, and facilities to be used for purposes specified in the appropriation ordinance, or statute, in amounts not in excess of those specified for each purpose. When liabilities authorized by an appropriation have been incurred, the appropriation is said to be expended. Thus budgeted appropriations are often called **estimated expenditures,** and the appropriation budget is called the **Expenditures budget.** According to the GASB Transfer, Revenue, Expenditure, and Expense Account Classifications Principle, expenditures should be classified by (1) fund, (2) function or program, (3) organization unit, (4) activity, (5) character, and (6) object. The GASB Common Terminology and Classification Principle should also be recalled at this time. It provides that a common terminology and classification should be used consistently throughout the budget, the accounts, and the financial reports of each fund.

Classification by Fund

The primary classification of governmental expenditures is by fund, since funds are the basic fiscal and accounting entity of a governmental unit. Within each fund, the other five classifications itemized in the preceding paragraph are used to facilitate the aggregation and analysis of data to meet the objectives of financial reporting set forth in Chapter 1.

Classification by Function or Program

The GASB distinguishes between functions and programs in the following manner:

> *Functions* group related activities that are aimed at accomplishing a major service or regulatory responsibility. *Programs* group activities, operations, or organizational units that are directed to the attainment of specific purposes or objectives.[2] [Emphasis added.]

Examples of functional classifications commonly found are:

General government   Health and welfare
Public safety   Culture and recreation
Highways and streets

In one city in New England, the budget is summarized according to the following program classification:

Policy formulation and   Environmental protection
    administration   Transportation
Protection of persons and   Social enrichment opportunities
    property   Physical resource development

---

[2] GASB Codification Sec. 1800.117.

Classification by Organization Unit

Classification of expenditures by organization unit is considered essential to management control, assuming the organizational structure of a given governmental unit provides clear lines of responsibility and authority. Some examples of organization units that might be found in a city are:

Police Department	City Clerk
Fire Department	Personnel Department
Building Safety Department	Parks and Recreation
Public Works Department	Department
City Attorney	

The key distinction between classification of expenditures by organization unit and classification by program or function is that responsibility for a department is fixed, whereas a number of departments may be involved in the performance of a program or a function. Management control within a department, and rational allocation of resources within the governmental unit, both require much more specific identification of expenditures (and costs and expenses) than is provided by the major classifications illustrated thus far. The next step needed is classification by **activity.**

Classification by Activity

An activity is a specific and distinguishable line of work performed by an organizational unit. For example, within the Public Works Department, activities such as the following may be performed:

Solid waste collection—residential.
Solid waste collection—commercial.
Solid waste disposal—landfill.
Solid waste disposal—incineration.

Activity classification is more meaningful if responsibility for the performance of each activity is fixed, performance standards are established, and a good management accounting system is installed to measure input of resources (dollars, personnel time, equipment and facilities used) versus output of services.

The GASB recommends that expenditures also be classified by character.

Classification by Character

Classification by character, as defined by the GASB, is based on the fiscal period that benefits from a particular expenditure. A common classification of expenditures by character recognizes three groups:

Current expenditures
Capital outlays
Debt service

Current expenditures are expected to benefit the period in which the expenditure is made. Capital outlays are expected to benefit not only the period in which the capital assets are acquired but as many future periods as the assets provide service. Debt service includes payment of interest on debt and payment of debt principal; if the debt was wisely incurred, residents received benefits in prior periods from the assets acquired by use of debt financing, are receiving benefits currently, and will continue to receive benefits until the service lives of the assets expire.

Character classification of expenditures is potentially of great significance to taxpayers and other citizens. Properly used, it could give them valuable information for appraising the cost of government during a given period. Generally speaking, expenditures for debt service relate to actions incurred by previous administrations. Capital outlays are current expenditures expected to provide benefits in future periods; but the present statement of governmental accounting "principles" does not allow depreciation expense to be recorded in governmental funds in the periods that receive the benefits (see GASB, "Depreciation of Fixed Assets Principle" in Chapter 2). It appears, however, that expenditures in the current expenditures class are the most influential on the public mind, strongly influencing popular attitudes toward responsible officials.

A fourth character class, Intergovernmental, is suggested by the GASB for use by governmental units that act as an intermediary in federally financed programs or that transfer "shared revenues" to other governmental units.

Classification by Object

The **object** of an expenditure is the thing for which the expenditure was made. Object classes may be viewed as subdivisions of character classifications. One scheme of object classification includes the following major classes:

Personal services	Capital outlays
Supplies	Debt service
Other services and charges	

Many other object classifications are encountered in practice, generally more detailed than that listed above. Greater detail can, of course, be achieved by the utilization of subclasses under the major titles.[3] Thus personal services may be subdivided on the basis of permanence and regularity of employment of the persons represented; and each subclass may be further subdivided to show whether the services performed were regular, overtime, or temporary. Employee benefits may be recorded in as much detail as desired as subclasses of the personal services class. "Other services and charges" obviously must be subdivided if the class is to provide any useful budgeting and control information. Professional Services, Communication, Transportation, Advertising, Printing and Binding, In-

---

[3] Under an object classification literally followed, the cost of construction of fixed assets by employees of a governmental fund would be dispersed among the personal services, supplies, and other services and charges classes. That is, the cost of salaries, wages, and benefits would be charged to personal services; the cost of materials used, to supplies; the cost of transportation of materials, construction equipment rentals, etc., to other services and charges. From this, the reader can conclude that excessively detailed object classifications should be avoided.

surance, Public Utility Services, Repairs and Maintenance, Rentals, Aid to Other Governments, and Miscellaneous are possible subdivisions.

Capital outlays, which is listed as a title under both the character and object classifications, should be subdivided in order to provide information needed in accounting by the General Fixed Assets Account Group for the assets required. Titles such as Land, Buildings, Improvements Other than Buildings, and Machinery and Equipment are useful subclasses of the capital outlays class.

Debt service, also listed as both an object of expenditure and a character class, should be subdivided in as much detail as needed to provide evidence that all interest payments and principal payments that should have been made in a certain fiscal period were actually made (or the appropriate liability recorded).

Classification of Expenditures of Public School Systems

Approximately 1,500 public school systems are agencies or departments of general purpose governments—states, counties, municipalities, or townships. Because these "dependent" school systems are as heavily financed by federal and state governments as are the 14,556 school districts which are independent of general governments, all school systems are expected to follow the classification systems specified by the National Center for Education Statistics (NCES). The NCES system of expenditure classification combines several of the GASB classifications discussed above. In NCES terminology, a combination of classifications is called a **dimension.** Two groups of dimensions are provided in the expenditure classification system: (1) dimensions essential to meet reporting requirements at the federal level and (2) dimensions optionally available for management use. The dimensions essential to meet federal (and most state) reporting requirements are: Program, Function, Object, and Project/Reporting. In the optional group are: Level of Instruction, Operational Unit, Subject Matter, Job Classification, and Special Cost Center.

Essential Dimensions. *Program* dimensions provided in the NCES publication include Special Programs (such as Mentally Retarded, Physically Handicapped, or Gifted and Talented), Vocational Programs, Other Instructional Programs— Elementary/Secondary, Nonpublic School Programs, Adult/Continuing Education Programs, Community/Junior College Programs, Community Services Programs, and Enterprise Programs (Food Services, etc.). The *Function* dimension includes Instruction, Support Services such as Guidance Services, Health Services, or Psychological Services, Support Services—Instructional Staff, Support Services—General Administration, Support Services—School Administration, Support Services—Business, Operation and Maintenance of Plant Services, Student Transportation Services, Support Services—Central, Other Support Services, Operation of Non-Instructional Services (Food Services, Other Enterprise Services, Community Services), Facilities Acquisition and Construction Services, Other Outlays. *Object* classifications of a public school system are Personal Services—Salaries, Personal Services—Employee Benefits, Purchased Professional and Technical Services, Purchased Property Services, Other Purchased Services, Supplies and Materials, Property, Other Objects (Dues and Fees, Judgments, Interest, etc.), Other Uses of Funds (Redemption of Principal, Housing Authority Obligations, and Fund Transfers). The *Project/Reporting* code permits school systems to accumulate expenditures to meet a variety of specialized reporting requirements, such as Local Projects, State Projects, and Federal Projects.

Optional Dimensions. The optional dimensions are: Level of Instruction (Elementary, Middle, Secondary, Post-Secondary, and Districtwide), Operational Unit (possibly attendance centers, budgetary units, buildings, or location code for paycheck distribution), Subject Matter (i.e., Agriculture, Arts, Business, etc.), Job Classification (this dimension may be used to [1] classify payroll costs for personnel purposes, such as Official, Professional, Technical, Clerical, etc., and [2] to segregate certified and noncertified salaries and benefits or accumulate payroll costs by bargaining unit for purposes of labor negotiations); and Special Cost Centers such as Term, Course, Work Order, Bus Route or Vehicle, State Accounting Number, or Federal Common Accounting Number.

Classification of Estimated Revenues and Revenues

In order for administrators to determine that proposed expenditures presented in the Appropriations budget can be financed by resources available under the laws of the budgeting jurisdiction and higher jurisdictions, a Revenue budget should be prepared. "Revenue," in the sense in which it is customarily used in governmental budgeting, includes all financial resource inflows—all amounts that increase the net assets of a fund—interfund transfers and debt issue proceeds, as well as taxes, licenses and permit fees, fines, forfeits, and other revenue sources described in following sections of this chapter.

It should be emphasized that a governmental unit, and the funds thereof, may raise revenues only from sources available to them by law. Often, the law that authorizes a governmental unit to utilize a given revenue source to finance general governmental activities, or specific activities, also establishes the maximum rate that may be applied to a specified base in utilizing the source, or establishes the maximum amount that may be raised from the source during the budget period.

The primary classification of governmental revenue is by **fund.** Within each fund, the major classification is by **source.** Within each major source class, it is desirable to have as many secondary classes as needed to facilitate revenue budgeting and accounting. Secondary classes relating to each major source are discussed below under each source caption. Major revenue source classes commonly used are:

Taxes	Charges for Services
Special Assessments	Fines and Forfeits
Licenses and Permits	Miscellaneous Revenues
Intergovernmental Revenues	

The Revenues budget and the accounting system for each governmental fund should include all revenue sources available to finance activities of that fund. The General Fund of most governmental units will ordinarily need all seven major classes itemized above; in some units, additional major classes may be needed. Each special revenue fund will need to budget and account for only those revenues legally mandated for use in achieving the purpose for which the special revenue fund was created. Similarly, debt service funds budget and account for those sources of revenue that are to be used for payment of interest and principal of tax-supported and special assessment long-term debt. Revenues and other financing sources earmarked for construction or acquisition of general fixed assets are reported as being budgeted and accounted for by capital projects funds.

In order to determine during a fiscal year that revenues are being realized from each budgeted source in amounts consistent with the budget, actual revenues should be accounted for on the same classification system as used in the Estimated Revenues budget.

Taxes

Taxes are of particular importance because (1) they provide a very large portion of the revenue of governmental units on all levels and (2) they are compulsory contributions to the cost of government, whether the affected taxpayer approves or disapproves of the levy.

Ad valorem (based on value) **property taxes** are a mainstay of financing for many units of local government but are not used as a source of revenue by many states or by the federal government. Ad valorem taxes may be levied against real property and personal property. Some property taxes are levied on a basis other than property values, one illustration being the tax on some kinds of financial institutions in relation to the deposits at a specified date. Other kinds of taxes are sales taxes, income taxes, gross receipts taxes, death and gift taxes, and interest and penalties on delinquent taxes.

Ad Valorem Taxes. Revenues from ad valorem taxes should be recognized on the accrual basis in the fiscal period for which the taxes are levied, provided the taxes are due on or before the end of the period. In "available and measurable" terms, tax revenues are available during the period for which they are levied if they may be used to pay liabilities arising from expenditures of that period.[4] Also, the amount of revenue from this source is "measurable" because both the property valuation and the tax rate must be determined in advance of the time the taxes are to be collected. The valuation of each parcel of taxable real property, and of the taxable personal property owned by each taxpayer, is assigned by a process known as **property assessment.** The assessment process differs state by state, and

---

[4] The general definition of *available* is discussed in Chapter 2 in relation to the Accrual Basis in Governmental Accounting Principle. GASB Codification Sec. P70.103 tightens the definition with respect to recognition of property tax revenue by specifying that the taxes must be collected within 60 days after balance sheet date, unless because of unusual circumstances the facts justify a period greater than 60 days.

in some states by jurisdictions within the state. The tax rate is set by one of two widely different procedures: (1) the governmental body simply multiplies the assessed valuation of property in its jurisdiction by a flat rate—either the maximum rate allowable under state law or a rate determined by policy—or (2) the property tax is treated as a residual source of revenue. In the latter event, revenues to be recognized from all sources other than property taxes must be budgeted; the total of those sources must be compared with the total proposed appropriations in order to determine the amount to be raised from property taxes. Illustration 3–5 shows the computation of the total amount of revenues to be raised from property taxes under the assumption that property taxes are a residual source of revenues. The heading of Illustration 3–5 indicates that it is for the Town of Merrill's General Fund. A similar computation would be made for each other fund for which property taxes are levied. It is common for an elected county official to serve as collector for all property taxes levied for all the funds of all of the governmental units within the county (and, of course, for all the funds of the county government itself). As discussed in Chapter 11, in such cases the county official serves as an agent for all funds for which property taxes have been levied; the Taxes Receivable are properly accounted for as assets of the funds for which they are levied, and those funds recognize revenues from the taxes to the extent that the taxes are expected to be collectible.

Note that Illustration 3–5 is a computation of the amount of revenue to be raised from property taxes, which is one step in determining the tax levy for the year. A second step is the determination from historical data and economic fore-

---

ILLUSTRATION 3–5

TOWN OF MERRILL
General Fund
Statement of Amount to Be Raised
by Property Taxes for 19x6
July 31, 19x5

Requirements:		
Estimated expenditures, August 1–December 31, 19x5		$ 4,200,000
Proposed appropriations for 19x6		8,460,000
Estimated working balance required for beginning of 19x7		510,000
Estimated total requirements		13,170,000
Resources other than tax levy for 19x6:		
Actual balance, July 31, 19x5....................................	$ 654,000	
Amount to be received from second installment of 19x5 taxes........	2,430,000	
Miscellaneous receipts expected during balance of 19x5	1,960,000	
Revenue expected from sources other than property taxes		
during 19x6	4,544,000	
Estimated total resources other than property tax levy		9,588,000
Amount required from property taxes in 19x6		$ 3,582,000

casts of the percentage of the tax levy expected to be collectible. (Even though property taxes are a lien against the property, personal property may be removed from the taxing jurisdiction and some parcels of real property may not be salable enough for the taxing jurisdiction to recover accumulated taxes against the property.) Therefore, the levy must be large enough to allow for estimated uncollectible taxes. For example, assume the Town of Merrill can reasonably expect to collect only 96 percent of the 19x6 property tax levy for its General Fund. Thus, if tax revenue is to be $3,582,000 (per Illustration 3–5), the gross levy must be $3,582,000 ÷ .96, or $3,731,250.

When the gross levy is known, the tax rate may be computed on the basis of the assessed valuation of taxable property lying within the taxing jurisdiction. The term **taxable property** is used in the preceding sentence in recognition of the fact that property owned by governmental units and property used by religious and charitable organizations are often not taxable by the local government. In addition, senior citizens, war veterans, and others may have statutory exemption from taxation for a limited portion of the assessed valuation of property. Continuing the example, assume the net assessed valuation of property taxable by the General Fund of the Town of Merrill is $214,348,000. In that case, the gross property tax levy ($3,731,250) is divided by the net assessed valuation ($214,348,000) to determine the property tax rate. The rate would be expressed as "$1.75 per $100 assessed valuation," or "$17.41 per $1,000 assessed valuation"—rounding up the actual decimal fraction (.017407) to two places to the right of the decimal, as is customary.

Interest and Penalties on Delinquent Taxes. A **penalty** is a legally mandated addition to a tax on the day it becomes delinquent (generally, the day after the day the tax is due). Penalties should be recognized as revenue when they are assessed. **Interest** at a legally specified rate also must be added to delinquent taxes for the length of time between the day the tax becomes delinquent until the day it is ultimately paid or otherwise discharged; interest revenue should be accrued at the time financial statements are to be prepared.

Sales Taxes, Income Taxes, and Gross Receipts Taxes. Currently effective GASB standards provide that revenue from sales taxes, income taxes, and gross receipts taxes be recognized, net of estimated refunds, in the accounting period in which they become susceptible to accrual—measurable and available.

Special Assessments. Special assessments differ from ad valorem real property taxes in that the latter are levied against all taxable property within the geographic boundaries of the government levying the taxes, whereas the former are levied against certain properties to defray part or all of the cost of a specific improvement or service that is presumed to be of particular benefit to the properties against which the special assessments are levied. Briefly, when routine services (street cleaning, snow plowing, and so on) are extended to property owners outside the normal service area of the government, or are provided at a higher level or at more frequent intervals than for the general public, "service-type" special assessments are levied. Service-type special assessments are accounted for by the fund which accounts for similar services rendered to the general public—usually the General Fund or a special revenue fund. Special assessments for capital improvements should be accounted for by a capital projects fund during the construction phase, and by a debt service fund during the debt service phase.

Licenses and Permits

Licenses and Permits include those revenues collected by a governmental unit from individuals or business concerns for various rights or privileges granted by the government. Some licenses and permits are primarily regulatory in nature, with minor consideration to revenue derived, whereas others are not only regulatory but provide large amounts of revenue as well, and some are almost exclusively revenue producers. Licenses and permits may relate to the privilege of carrying on business for a stipulated period, the right to do a certain thing that may affect the public welfare, or the right to use certain public property. Vehicle and alcoholic beverage licenses are found extensively on the state level and serve both regulatory and revenue functions. States make widespread use of professional and occupational taxes for purposes of control. Local governments make extensive use of licenses and permits to control the activities of their citizens; and from some they derive substantial amounts of revenue. Commonly found among licenses and permits are building permits, vehicle licenses, amusement licenses, business and occupational licenses, animal licenses, and street and curb permits.

Regardless of the governmental level or the purpose of a license or permit, the revenue it produces is ordinarily accounted for on a cash basis. Applicable rates or schedules of charges for a future period may be established well in advance, and fairly reliable information may be available as to the number of licenses or permits to be issued; but the probable degree of fluctuation in the latter factor is so great as to prevent satisfactory use of the accrual basis.

Intergovernmental Revenue

Intergovernmental Revenues include grants, entitlements, and shared revenues. As defined by the GASB:

1. A *grant* is a contribution or gift of cash or other assets from another governmental unit to be used or expended for a specified purpose, activity, or facility. *Capital grants* are restricted by the grantor for the acquisition and/or construction of fixed (capital) assets. All other grants are *operating grants*.
2. An *entitlement* is the amount of payment to which a state or local government is entitled as determined by the federal government pursuant to an allocation formula contained in the applicable statutes.
3. A *shared revenue* is a revenue levied by one government but shared on a predetermined basis, often in proportion to the amount collected at the local level, with another government or class of government.[5]

---

[5] Paraphrased from GASB Codification Sec. G60.501–.505.

Some kinds of intergovernmental revenues can well be accounted for on the accrual basis while other kinds cannot. Grants by state and federal agencies ordinarily are announced somewhat in advance of their actual distribution, which makes it possible to record the revenue with a debit to Due from State Government or some such title, even to the extent of designating the agency or department from which the grant is forthcoming. Distributions of shared revenues, stating amounts, are frequently announced in advance of the actual disbursements and are obviously adapted to accrual.

Charges for Services

Charges for Services includes revenue from charges for all activities of a governmental unit, except the operations of enterprise funds. A few of the many revenue items included in this category are court costs; special police service; solid waste collection charges; street, sidewalk, and curb repairs; receipts from parking meters; library use fees (not fines); and tuition.

Classification of expenditures by function is discussed in an earlier section of this chapter. The grouping of Charges for Services revenue may be correlated with the functional classification of expenditures. For example, one functional group of expenditures is named General Government, another Public Safety, and so on. A governmental unit, in connection with providing general government service, collects some revenue such as court cost charges, fees for recording legal documents, and zoning and subdivision fees, and should relate the revenues to the expenditures.

Charges for Services should be recognized as revenue when earned, if that is prior to the collection of cash.

Fines and Forfeits

Revenue from Fines and Forfeits includes fines and penalties for commission of statutory offenses and for neglect of official duty; forfeitures of amounts held as security against loss or damage, or collections from bonds or sureties placed with the government for the same purpose; and penalties of any sort, except those levied on delinquent taxes. Library fines are included in this category. If desired, Fines and Forfeits may be the titles of two accounts within this revenue class, or they may be subgroup headings for more detailed breakdowns.

Revenues of this classification should be accrued to the extent practicable. In direct contrast with general property taxes, neither rates nor base or volume may be predetermined with any reasonable degree of accuracy for this type of revenue. Because of these uncertainties, it is often difficult to determine whether all amounts paid by transgressors have been accounted for, therefore revenues from fines and forfeits may be recognized on the cash basis if accrual is not practicable.

Miscellaneous Revenues

Although the word *miscellaneous* is not informative and should be used sparingly, its use as the title of a revenue category is necessary. It (1) substitutes for other possible source classes that might have rather slight and infrequent usage and (2) minimizes the need for forcing some kinds of revenue into source classifications in which they do not generically belong. While Miscellaneous Revenue in itself represents a compromise, its existence aids in sharpening the meanings of other source classes. The heterogeneous nature of items served by the title is indicated by the following listing: interest earnings (other than on delinquent taxes); rents and royalties; sales of, and compensation for loss of, fixed assets; contributions from public enterprises (utilities, airports, etc.); escheats (taking of property in default of legally qualified claimants); contributions and donations from private sources; and "other."

Some items of Miscellaneous Revenue, such as interest earnings on investments, might well be accrued, but mostly they are accounted for on the cash basis.

Classification of Revenues of Public School Systems

Revenues of public school systems, both those dependent upon a general purpose government and those independent entities, should be classified in the manner prescribed by the National Center for Education Statistics. As is true of the NCES expenditure classification, the NCES revenue classification system provides for a combination of classifications known as a **dimension.** Generally, public school revenues should be classified by fund, source, and project/reporting code. The NCES suggests the following revenue classification:

```
1000  Revenue from Local Sources
      1100  Taxes levied/assessed by the school system
      1200  Revenue from local governmental units other than the
               school system
      1300  Tuition
      1400  Transportation fees
      1500  Earnings on investments
      1600  Food services
      1700  Student activities
      1800  Community services activities
      1900  Other revenue from local sources
2000  Revenue from Intermediate Sources
      2100  Unrestricted grants-in-aid
      2200  Restricted grants-in-aid
      2800  Revenue in lieu of taxes
      2900  Revenue for/on behalf of the school system
3000  Revenue from State Sources
      3100  Unrestricted grants-in-aid
      3200  Restricted grants-in-aid
      3800  Revenue in lieu of taxes
      3900  Revenue for/on behalf of the school system
4000  Revenue from Federal Sources
      4100  Unrestricted grants-in-aid received directly
      4200  Unrestricted grants-in-aid received through state
      4300  Restricted grants-in-aid received directly
      4500  Restricted grants-in-aid received through state
      4700  Grants-in-aid received through other agencies
      4800  Revenue in lieu of taxes
      4900  Revenue for/on behalf of the school system
```

5000 Other Sources
    5100 Sale of bonds
    5200 Interfund transfers
    5300 Sale or compensation for loss of fixed assets

An additional level of detail provided in the NCES revenue source classification system is not illustrated above. The nature of the detail is readily apparent; for example, revenue account 1100, Taxes, comprehends account 1110, Ad Valorem Taxes levied by local school system; 1120, Sales and Use Taxes; 1130, Income Taxes; 1140, Penalties and Interest on Taxes; and 1190, other taxes.

"Intermediate" sources of revenue are administrative units or political subdivisions between the local school system and the state. "Grants-in-aid" from intermediate, state, or federal governments are contributions from general revenue sources of those governments, or, if related to specific revenue sources of those units, are distributed on a flat grant or equalization basis. "Revenue in lieu of taxes" analogous to payment from an enterprise fund to the General Fund discussed in Chapter 10 are payments made out of general revenues of intermediate, state, or federal governments to a local school system because the higher governmental units own property located within the geographical boundaries of the local unit that is not subject to taxation. "Revenue for/on behalf of the local school system" includes all payments made by intermediate, state, or federal governments for the benefit of the local system; payments to pension funds, or a contribution of fixed assets, are examples.

Interfund Transactions and Transfers

Quasi-External Transactions

Interfund transactions that would result in the recognition of revenues, expenditures, or expenses if the transactions involved organizations **external** to the governmental unit should be accounted for as revenues, expenditures, or expenses of the funds involved. For example, it is common for enterprise funds to remit to the General Fund a payment in lieu of taxes. If the enterprise had been investor owned, it would have paid taxes to the General Fund. Since taxes are an item of General Fund revenue, the payment in lieu of taxes is also considered General Fund revenue even though from the viewpoint of the governmental unit as a whole there is no increase in net assets because the enterprise fund records an expense equal in amount to the General Fund revenue.

Internal service fund billings to other funds, routine employer contributions from a General Fund to an employee retirement fund, and routine service charges for services provided by a department financed by one fund to a department financed by another fund are additional examples of "quasi-external" interfund transactions that properly result in the recognition of fund revenue, expenditures, or expenses, even though from the viewpoint of the governmental unit as a whole there is no net effect.

Reimbursements

Quasi-external transactions, described above, are the only form of interfund transaction that result in the recognition of revenue by the receiving fund. In certain instances, discussed at greater length in Chapter 13, one fund may record as an expenditure an item that should have been recorded as an expenditure by another fund. When the second fund reimburses the first fund, the first fund should recognize the reimbursement as a reduction of its Expenditures account, not as an item of revenue.

Interfund Transfers   **Operating Transfers.**   Operating transfers are generally periodic, routine transfers. State laws may require that taxes be levied by a General Fund or a special revenue fund to finance an expenditure to be made from another fund (such as a debt service fund). Since the general rule is that revenues should be recorded as such only once, the transfer of tax revenue to the expending fund is recorded by the transferor as Operating Transfers Out and by the transferee as Operating Transfers In. The transferee fund does not recognize the transfer as revenue. Operating transfers are often reported in the Other Financing Sources (Uses) section of the Statement of Revenues, Expenditures, and Changes in Fund Balances. An equally acceptable presentation, however, is to group Other Financing Sources with Revenues, and Other Financing Uses with Expenditures in the Statement of Revenues, Expenditures, and Changes in Fund Balances.

Equity Transfers.   Equity transfers are nonroutine transactions often made to establish or liquidate a fund. The creation of a fund by transfer of assets and/or resources from an existing fund to a new fund (remember, a fund is a fiscal entity as well as an accounting entity) does not result in the recognition of revenue by the new fund. Similarly, subsequent return of all or part of the contribution, or transfers of residual balances of discontinued funds, to another fund would not result in the recognition of revenue by the fund receiving the assets or resources. Transfers of equity should be accounted for as such and should be reported in the Changes in Fund Balances section of the Statement of Revenues, Expenditures, and Changes in Fund Balances.

Proceeds of Debt Issues; Capital Leases

General funds, special revenue funds, capital projects funds, and debt service funds report only current liabilities to be paid from fund assets. Tax-supported or special assessment capital debt that is not a current liability of these four fund types is reported in the General Long-Term Debt Account Group (GLTDAG). Accordingly, when a fund in any of these four fund types receives the proceeds of general long-term capital debt, it has an increase in assets not offset by an increase in liabilities; therefore, the Fund Equity is increased. An increase in Fund Equity arising from the receipt of proceeds of such debt is considered as an Other Financing Source and reported under that caption in the Statement of Revenues, Expenditures, and Changes in Fund Balances for the fund. Debt issue proceeds are reported in this manner, rather than as revenue, because the debt is a liability of the governmental unit even though not a liability of the fund.

General fixed assets acquired under capital lease agreements are reported in the General Fixed Assets Account Group (GFAAG); the offsetting liability under the lease is reported in the General Long-Term Debt Account Group. In addition, acquisition of a general fixed asset under a capital lease should be reflected as an expenditure and as an Other Financing Source of a governmental fund, just as if the general fixed asset had been constructed or acquired from debt issue proceeds.

Selected References

American Institute of Certified Public Accountants. *Audit and Accounting Guide. Audits of State and Local Governmental Units.* Revised. New York, 1993.

Governmental Accounting Standards Board. *Codification of Governmental Accounting and Financial Reporting Standards as of June 30, 1993.* Norwalk, Conn., 1993.

National Center for Education Statistics. *Financial Accounting for Local and State School Systems.* State Educational Records and Reports Series: Handbook II, Revision. Washington, D.C.: U.S. Government Printing Office, 1990.

Questions

3–1. How should you determine whether the routine activities of a city's Street Department ought to be accounted for in the General Fund or in a special revenue fund?

3–2. Governmental accounting gives substantial recognition to budgets, with those budgets being recorded in the accounts of the governmental unit.

   a. What is the purpose of a governmental accounting system, and why is the budget recorded in the accounts of a governmental unit? Include in your discussion the purpose and significance of appropriations.

   b. Describe when and how a governmental unit records its budget and closes it out.

(AICPA)

3–3. If Estimated Revenues and Estimated Other Financing Sources exceed Appropriations and Estimated Other Financing Uses when the budget of a special revenue fund is recorded, would you expect the balance of Fund Balance to increase, or to decrease, with respect to the balance displayed in the balance sheet of the special revenue fund prepared as of the end of the year preceding the budget year? Explain your answer.

3–4. Distinguish between:

   a. Expenditure and Encumbrance.

   b. Revenues and Estimated Revenues.

   c. Reserve for Encumbrances and Encumbrances.

   d. Reserve for Encumbrances and Fund Balance.

   e. Appropriations and Expenditures.

   f. Expenditure and Expense.

3–5. Why do GASB standards specify that the amounts in the Actual column of a budgetary comparison statement be reported on the basis required by law for budget preparation—even if that basis differs from GAAP?

3 6. Is there any necessity for a governmental unit to use the same expenditure classification system in its General Fund accounting system as in its budget? Why or why not?

3–7. Explain how legislative appropriations and the use of encumbrance accounting procedures achieve control over governmental fund expenditures. Do budgetary control procedures assure sound financial management? Why or why not?

3–8. On a sheet of paper list the letters *(a)* through *(j)* corresponding to the expenditure items listed below. Beside each letter indicate whether the expenditure item should be classified as a function, program, organization unit, activity, character, or object.

   a. County Treasurer's Office.
   b. Welfare.
   c. Solid waste disposal—landfill.
   d. Accident investigation.
   e. Supplies.
   f. Debt service.
   g. Environmental protection.
   h. Health.
   i. Department of Health.
   j. Personal services.

3–9. On a sheet of paper list the letters *(a)* through *(j)* corresponding to the revenue items listed below. Beside each letter state whether the item should be classified as Taxes, Licenses and Permits, Intergovernmental Revenue, Charges for Services, Fines and Forfeits, or Miscellaneous Revenue.

   a. Sales taxes levied by the governmental units.
   b. Receipts from county in payment for rural library service.
   c. Dog licenses.
   d. Traffic violation penalties.
   e. Federal grant for housing rehabilitation.
   f. Royalties from oil wells on city property.
   g. Charges for solid waste collection and disposal.
   h. Plumbers' registration fees.
   i. City's share of state severance tax.
   j. Charges for pumping basements.

3–10. Explain how expenditure and revenue classifications for public school systems differ from those for state and local governments.

Exercises and Problems

3–1. Utilizing the CAFR obtained for Exercise 1–1, review the combined, combining, and individual governmental fund financial statements and related data. Note particularly the items suggested below:

   a. **Combined Statement of Revenues, Expenditures, and Changes in Fund Balances— All Governmental Fund Types and Discretely Presented Component Units.**
      (1) **Revenues and Other Financing Sources.** What system of classification of revenues is used in the combined, combining, and individual fund statements? Do

the major classes used agree with the source classes listed in Chapter 3? If there are differences, are they minor differences of terminology, or major differences in system of classification? Are transfers, proceeds of debt issues, and assets acquired under capital lease agreements identified as described in Chapter 3?

List the three most important sources of General Fund revenues, and list the most important source of revenue of each special revenue fund. Is the reporting entity dependent upon any single source for as much as one third of its General Fund revenue? What proportion of revenues is derived from property taxes? Do the notes clearly indicate recognition criteria for primary revenue sources? Do the notes disclose details of the property tax calendar, including lien dates, levy (assessment) dates, due dates, and collection dates?

Are charts, graphs, or tables included that show the changes over time in reliance on each revenue source? Is the proper distinction made between operating transfers in and equity transfers in? Are operating transfers in reported in the same section of the statement as the revenues, or are they reported in an Other Financing Sources (Uses) section following the Expenditures section? Are proceeds of debt issues, and general fixed assets acquired under capital lease agreements, if any, reported in the same section as operating transfers in? Are equity transfers in reported in the Changes in Fund Balances section of the statement?

(2) **Expenditures and Other Financing Uses.** What system of classification of expenditures is used in the combined, combining, and individual fund statements? If the system of classification is not one discussed in Chapter 3, does it appear to be more or less informative than any of those discussed in the chapter? Are operating transfers out shown in the same section of the statement as expenditures, or are they reported in an Other Financing Sources (Uses) section following the Expenditures section? Are equity transfers out reported in the Changes in Fund Balances section of the statement? List the three categories that caused the largest General Fund expenditures; list the category of the largest expenditure of each of the special revenue funds.

Does the report contain, perhaps in the Introductory Section, any information that would enable the reader to determine what results were achieved for the expenditures?

Are charts, tables, or graphs presented to show the trend of General Fund expenditures, by category, for a period of 10 years? Is expenditure data related to population of the governmental unit, square miles within the governmental unit, or workload statistics (such as tons of solid waste removed and number of miles of street constructed)?

b. **Combined Statement of Revenues, Expenditures, and Changes in Fund Balances— Budget and Actual—General and Special Revenue Fund Types of the Primary Government.**
Note: In addition to reading Chapter 3, read the following before analyzing the budgetary comparisons in the CAFR you are using: The Budget versus Actual statement should include budgetary comparisons for the General Fund, the special revenue fund type, and *all other* fund types for which annual budgets have been legally adopted. The budgets adopted by the reporting entity whose CAFR you are reviewing may differ from the GAAP reporting model as to *basis, timing, perspective,* and *entity.* GASB standards define these differences as:

Basis differences arise through the employment of a basis of accounting for budgetary purposes that differs from the basis of accounting applicable to the fund type when reporting on the operations in accordance with GAAP.

Timing differences that can result in significant variances between budgetary practices and GAAP may include continuing appropriations, project appropriations, automatic reappropriations, and biennial budgeting.

Perspective differences result from the structure of financial information for budgetary purposes. The perspectives used for budgetary purposes include fund structure, organizational structure, or program structure. Additionally, some subsidiary perspective, such as nature of revenue source, special projects, or capital and operating budgets, may also be used. The fund structure and individual fund definitions establish which assets, liabilities, equities, and revenue and expenditure/expense flows are accounted for in a fund. In the traditional view, budgeting, accounting, financial reporting, and auditing would follow the fund perspective.

Entity differences are the fourth possible type of difference. Frequently, an "appropriated budget" may either include or exclude organizations, programs, activities, and functions that may or may not be compatible with the criteria defining the governmental reporting entity.

Actual data presented in budgetary comparison statements should be prepared on the same basis as the budgetary data (which may include encumbrances along with expenditures). If basis, timing, perspective, or entity differences exist between budgetary data and actual data reported in conformity with GAAP, the "actual" data reported in the budgetary comparison statement should be reconciled with the actual data reported in conformity with GAAP; the reconciliation may be made as a part of the budgetary comparison statement or in the notes to the financial statements. If the data reported in the Actual column of the budgetary comparison statement are not in conformity with GAAP, the heading of the statement should make clear that the data are "Non-GAAP."

Questions:

Are any fund types in addition to the General Fund and special revenue funds included in the budgetary comparison statement? If so, list the additional fund types included and attempt to determine whether the inclusion is mandated by state law, local ordinance, or custom.

Is the budgetary comparison presented only in the GPFS (the Combined Statement of Revenues, Expenditures, and Changes in Fund Balances—Budget and Actual), or are there also budgetary comparisons in the combining statements for each fund type, and budgetary comparisons in the individual fund statements? Do budgetary comparison statements show only the budget as originally enacted, the original budget plus or minus budget amendments made during the year, or only the budget as it existed at balance sheet date; or is the report unclear as to which budget is presented? If amendments to the budget are not shown in the financial statement are they shown in the Notes to the Financial Statements, or elsewhere in the CAFR? Is the legal procedure for budget adoption and budget amendment explained in the Notes or elsewhere in the CAFR?

Do the Notes state whether or not appropriations lapse at year-end? Do the

Notes disclose the level of control for each budget for which data are presented (the level at which expenditures may not legally exceed appropriations)?

Are the amounts in the Actual column clearly labeled (either in the heading of the statement or in the column heading) as being on the budgetary basis, or does the statement disclose that the budget is on the GAAP basis, or are the bases unclear? Are differences between budgeted amounts and actual amounts shown only in dollars, or are percentage differences shown? Is there any explanation in the Notes to the Financial Statements, the Introductory Section, or elsewhere in the CAFR, of material differences between budget and actual?

If the budget differs from the GAAP reporting model as to *basis, timing, perspective,* or *entity,* are the amounts in the Actual column reconciled with the amounts reported in the Combined Statement of Revenues, Expenditures, and Changes in Fund Balances (the statement you analyzed in part *a* of this Exercise)? One element which often appears in the reconciliation of Actual on the budgetary basis to Actual on the GAAP basis relates to the fact that encumbrances outstanding at year-end should not be considered as expenditures in GAAP-based statements, but should be added to expenditures in the Actual column of the budgetary comparison statement (unless, by law, encumbrances lapse at year-end). Also, expenditures made during one year which were authorized by appropriations (sometimes called *budgetary expenditures*) of a preceding year may not be distinguished in the GAAP basis statement from expenditures during the year authorized by appropriations for that year; whereas "actual" expenditures reported in the budgetary comparison statement should be only those authorized for the year for which the statement is prepared. Are these and other reconciling items disclosed within the budgetary comparison statement, within the Notes to the Financial Statements, or elsewhere in the CAFR? Is the reconciliation clear and understandable to you, or is it merely confusing?

Do all blended component units use the same budgetary practices as the oversight unit of the reporting entity? Does the CAFR state this explicitly, or does it indicate that budgetary practices differ by disclosures in the headings of statements, the headings of columns within statements, or by narrative and schedules within the Notes to the Financial Statements?

3–2. Write the numbers 1 through 10 on a sheet of paper. Beside each number write the letter corresponding with the best answer to each of the following questions.

1. The Estimated Revenues control account balance of a governmental fund type is eliminated when
   a. The budget is recorded.
   b. The budgetary accounts are closed.
   c. Appropriations are closed.
   d. Property taxes are recorded.
2. Encumbrances outstanding at year-end in a state's General Fund should be reported as a
   a. Liability in the General Fund.
   b. Fund Balance reserve in the General Fund.
   c. Liability in the General Long-Term Debt Account Group.
   d. Fund Balance designation in the General Fund.

3. Accounting for special revenue funds is most similar to which other type of fund?
   a. Capital Projects.
   b. Enterprise.
   c. General.
   d. Debt Service.

4. Which of the following will decrease the Fund Balance of a governmental unit at the end of the fiscal year?
   a. Appropriations are more than Expenditures and Reserve for Encumbrances—Prior Year.
   b. Appropriations are less than Expenditures and Encumbrances.
   c. Appropriations are more than Estimated Revenues.
   d. Appropriations are more than Expenditures and Encumbrances.

5. The following balances are included in the subsidiary records of Burwood Village's Parks and Recreation Department at March 31, 19x2:

Appropriations—Supplies	$7,500
Expenditures—Supplies	4,500
Encumbrances—Supplies Orders	750

   How much does the Parks and Recreation Department have available for additional purchases of supplies?
   a. $0.
   b. $2,250.
   c. $3,000.
   d. $6,750.

6. Which of the following steps in the acquisition of goods and services occurs first?
   a. Appropriation.
   b. Encumbrance.
   c. Disbursement.
   d. Expenditure.

7. Which of the following terms refers to an actual cost rather than an estimate?
   a. Expenditure.
   b. Appropriation.
   c. Budget.
   d. Encumbrance.

8. The Board of Commissioners of the City of Fulton adopted its budget for the year ending July 31, 19x2, which indicated revenues of $1,000,000 and appropriations of $900,000. If the budget is formally integrated into the accounting records, what is the required journal entry?

		Debits	Credits
a.	Memorandum entry only		
b.	Appropriations	900,000	
	General Fund	100,000	
	Estimated Revenues		1,000,000
c.	Estimated Revenues	1,000,000	
	Appropriations		900,000
	Fund Balance		100,000
d.	Revenues Receivable	1,000,000	
	Expenditures Payable		900,000
	Fund Balance		100,000

9. The City of Hinton incurred $150,000 of salaries and wages for the month ended May 31, 19x2. To record this transaction the City of Hinton should debit:

   a. Encumbrances.

   b. Expenditures.

   c. Reserve for Encumbrances.

   d. Both Expenditures and Reserve for Encumbrances.

10. An Expenditures account appears in:

    a. The General Fixed Assets Account Group.

    b. The General Long-Term Debt Account Group.

    c. A special revenue fund.

    d. An internal service fund.

                                                                   (AICPA, adapted)

3–3. Johnson County has budgeted the following General Fund revenues and appropriations for the fiscal year 19x6:

Estimated Revenues:	
Taxes	$12,000,000
Licenses and Permits	2,400,000
Fines and Forfeits	800,000
Intergovernmental Revenues	4,000,000
Total Estimated Revenues	$19,200,000
Appropriations:	
General Administration	$ 3,400,000
Police	4,100,000
Fire	4,500,000
Health and Welfare	3,600,000
Public Works	3,750,000
Total Appropriations	$19,350,000

a. Assuming a reasonably responsible level of financial management, what is the minimum figure the administration of Johnson County expects to have as the General Fund Fund Balance at the conclusion of fiscal year 19x5? Explain.

b. Show in general journal form the entry, or entries, that would be necessary to record the budget, assuming it is legally approved, at the beginning of the budget year, 19x6. Show entries in subsidiary ledger accounts as well as general ledger accounts.

3–4. Assume that Johnson County's (Problem 3–3) General Fund received revenues in cash from the following sources during the first month of 19x6:

Licenses and Permits	$ 200,000
Fines and Forfeits	60,000
Intergovernmental Revenues	600,000
Total	$ 860,000

a. Show the necessary entry in general journal form to record the revenue received. (Show entries in subsidiary ledger accounts as well as in general ledger accounts.)

b. Compute how much revenue Johnson County expects to realize from Licenses and Permits in the remainder of 19x6. Does the amount appear reasonable, considering that there are 11 months remaining in 19x6?

3–5. Assume purchase orders and contracts in the following estimated amounts were issued by Johnson County (Problem 3–3), chargeable against the 19x6 appropriations shown below:

General Administration	$ 200,000
Police	360,000
Fire	400,000
Public Works	270,000
Total	$1,230,000

a. Show the necessary entry in general journal form to record the issuance of purchase orders and contracts. (Show entries in subsidiary ledger accounts as well as general ledger accounts.)

b. Explain why GASB standards for state and local governmental units require that the estimated amount of purchase orders issued be recorded in the accounts of governmental fund types, whereas FASB standards for business organizations do not have a similar requirement.

3–6. Assume that purchase orders and contracts issued by Johnson County (see Problem 3–5 for the estimated liability for goods and services ordered) have now been filled and the actual liability of the General Fund is chargeable to the 19x6 appropriations as follows:

General Administration	$ 202,000
Police	363,000
Fire	400,000
Public Works	275,000
Total	$1,240,000

a. Show the necessary entry or entries in general journal form to record the fact that the purchase orders and contracts have been filled and vouchers payable have been issued in the amount of $1,240,000.

b. Assuming that Johnson County does not encumber appropriations for salaries of Police Department employees, show the entry needed to record the issuance of vouchers in the amount of $300,000 for salaries chargeable to the Police appropriation.

c. Compute the amount of the Police appropriation available for use during the remainder of 19x6, using data given in Problems 3–3, 3–5, and 3–6 as needed.

d. Under what circumstances would you expect a governmental unit to encumber appropriations for wages?

3–7. The common council of the City of Dexter adopted for the City General Fund a budget that is shown below in summary form:

Estimated Revenues:	
Taxes	$11,420,000
Licenses and Permits	2,740,000
Fines and Forfeits	3,790,000
Intergovernmental Revenue	3,010,000
Charges for Services	2,400,000
Total Estimated Revenues	$23,360,000

Appropriations:	
Personal Services	$10,540,000
Contractual Services	2,560,000
Commodities	5,435,000
Capital Outlays	4,639,000
Total Appropriations	$23,174,000

a. Assume that the City of Dexter employs a system of quarterly allotments to enhance expenditure control. Show in general journal form the entry to record the complete budget as of January 1, the first day of the fiscal year, in general ledger and subsidiary ledger accounts.

b. Assume allotments for the first quarter were as follows; make the journal entry as of January 1 to record the allotments in general ledger and subsidiary ledger accounts. Show subsidiary ledger accounts for both unallotted appropriations and allotments.

Personal Services	$2,660,000
Contractual Services	640,000
Commodities	1,350,000
Capital Outlays	1,400,000
Total	$6,050,000

3–8. The printout of the Estimated Revenues and Revenues subsidiary ledger accounts for the General Fund of a certain city as of February 28, 19x9 appeared as follows:

Property Taxes

Date	Tracer	Estimated Revenues	Revenues	Balance
01 01	45 1	9,600,000		9,600,000
02 28	45 6	(20,000)	9,580,000	–0–

Licenses and Permits

Date	Tracer	Estimated Revenues	Revenues	Balance
01 01	45 1	1,600,000		1,600,000
01 31	27 4		640,000	960,000
02 27	27 7		200,000	760,000

Intergovernmental Revenue

Date	Tracer	Estimated Revenues	Revenues	Balance
01 01	45 1	3,200,000		3,200,000
02 28	27 7		1,500,000	1,700,000

Charges for Services

Date	Tracer	Estimated Revenues	Revenues	Balance
01 01	45 1	600,000		600,000
02 28	27 7		160,000	440,000

Assuming the above printout is correct in all details and that there are no other General Fund revenue classifications, you are to answer the following questions. *Show all necessary computations in good form.*

    a. What should be the balance of the Estimated Revenues control account?

    b. What was the original approved budget for Estimated Revenues for 19x9?

    c. (1) Was the 19x9 Estimated Revenues budget adjusted during the year?
       (2) If so, when?
       (3) If so, how much?
       (4) If so, was the original budget increased or decreased?

    d. What should be the balance of the Revenues control account?

    e. If in the Tracer column of the accounts the numerals 45 stand for General Journal and the numerals 27 stand for Cash Receipts Journal, what is the most likely reason that revenues from Property Taxes are first recognized in a general journal entry, whereas revenues from the other three sources are first recognized in cash receipts journal entries?

3–9. Selected subsidiary accounts for the Town of Cook general fund appropriations, expenditures, and encumbrances are provided below for the month of January 19x8, the first month of the city's fiscal year.

TOWN OF COOK
General Fund

Account: **General Government**

| | | | | **Appropriations** | |
Date	Reference	Encumbrances Dr.(Cr.)	Expenditures Dr.(Cr.)	Cr.(Dr.)	Available Balance
Jan. 2	Budget Auth.			$180,000	$180,000
Jan. 5	P.O. No. 758	$9,500			170,500
Jan. 8	P.O. No. 843	6,800			163,700
Jan. 23	Invoice/P.O. No. 758	(9,500)	$9,760		163,440
Jan. 31	Payroll		9,400		154,040

Account: **Public Safety**

| | | | | **Appropriations** | |
Date	Reference	Encumbrances Dr.(Cr.)	Expenditures Dr.(Cr.)	Cr.(Dr.)	Available Balance
Jan. 2	Budget Auth.			$900,000	$900,000
Jan. 8	P.O. No. 845	$13,850			886,150
Jan. 12	P.O. No. 901	17,900			868,250
Jan. 17	Invoice/P.O. No. 901	(17,900)	$17,842		868,308
Jan. 22	Invoice/P.O. No. 845	(13,850)	14,050		868,108
Jan. 31	Payroll		39,900		828,208

				Account:	**Parks and Recreation**
				Appropriations	
Date	Reference	Encumbrances Dr.(Cr.)	Expenditures Dr.(Cr.)	Cr.(Dr.)	Available Balance
Jan. 1	Budget Auth.			$285,700	$285,700
Jan. 13	*Invoice/P.O. No. 543, for 19x7		$ 750		284,950
Jan. 24	P.O. No. 1078	$18,800			266,150
Jan. 31	Payroll		$14,470		251,680

* The balance of the Reserve for Encumbrances—19x7 account is also $750.

    a. For the three accounts shown, compute the amount of open encumbrances and total expenditures for the month of January.

    b. What are the total available appropriations for the three accounts?

    c. Assuming an informal (unrecorded) monthly allotment of one-twelfth of the annual appropriations, do any of the accounts appear to be spending at an excessive rate? Explain.

    d. What changes could be made to these accounts to improve the Town of Cook's budgetary control?

3–10. The Director of Finance of the City of Worth has asked you to determine whether the appropriation, expenditures, and encumbrances comparison for Office Supplies for a certain year (reproduced below) presents the information correctly.

    You determine that the General Fund manual of accounts describes Office Supplies as "tangible items of relatively short life to be used in a business office." You also determine that the transfer of stationery, at cost, to the city water utility was properly authorized; the Water Utility Fund is to pay the General Fund $330 for the supplies. The transfer of $46,000 from Office Supplies to Personal Services was made by an accounting clerk without knowledge of superiors to avoid reporting that the Personal Services appropriation had been overexpended.

    In order to determine whether the comparison shown above is correct you are required to compute each of the following. Organize and label your computations so the Director of Finance can understand them.

    a. The final amended amount of the appropriation for Office Supplies for the year.

    b. The valid amount of encumbrances outstanding against this appropriation at the end of the year.

    c. The net amount of expenditures made during the year that were properly chargeable to this appropriation.

    d. The unencumbered unexpended balance of this appropriation.

CITY OF WORTH
General Fund
Appropriation, Expenditures, and Encumbrances
Office Supplies

Purchase No.	Explanation	Appropriations	Encumbrances Debits	Encumbrances Credits	Expenditures	Available Balance
	Budget legally approved	62,200				62,200
350	Purchase order—computer paper		600			61,600
356	Purchase order—stationery			420		62,020
	Refund of prior year expenditure	30				62,050
370	Purchase order—filing supplies		400			61,650
350	Invoice			605	605	61,045
378	Purchase order—microcomputer		3,160			57,885
380	Contract for washing office windows		2,000			55,885
356	Invoice			420	420	55,885
	Cost of stationery issued to city water utility	330				56,215
	Refund on P.O. 350	10				56,225
370	Invoice			400	425	55,800
380	Invoice				2,000	53,000
385	Purchase order—furniture		7,000			46,000
	Transfer to Personal Services appropriation	(46,000)				–0–

Continuous Problems

3–L. The following budget for the General Fund of the City of Bingham (see Problem 2–L) was legally adopted for the fiscal year ended June 30, 19x2.

Estimated Revenues:

Property Taxes	$2,910,000
Interest and Penalties on Taxes	29,000
Licenses and Permits	443,000
Fines and Forfeits	336,000
Intergovernmental Revenue	531,000
Charges for Services	110,000
Miscellaneous Revenues	50,000
Total Estimated Revenues	$4,409,000

Appropriations:

General Government	$ 765,000
Public Safety	1,630,000
Public Works	710,000
Health	200,000
Public Welfare	300,000
Recreation	325,000
Contributions to Retirement Funds	344,000
Miscellaneous Appropriations	66,000
Total Appropriations	$4,340,000

Required   a. Record the budget in the general journal. Include the general ledger accounts, subsidiary ledger accounts, and adequate explanations for each entry (and for all journal entries in all L problems).

b. Post the entries to *general ledger* accounts.

c. (1) Open *revenues ledger* accounts for the seven sources of Estimated Revenues listed in the budget for the City of Bingham General Fund. (An appropriate form is illustrated in Chapter 3.) Allow five lines for each account.

(2) Post to the appropriate revenues ledger accounts the amounts shown in the general journal entry.

d. (1) Open *appropriations ledger* accounts for the eight classifications of appropriations shown in the budget for the General Fund. (An appropriate form is illustrated in Chapter 3.) Allow 10 lines for each account.

(2) Post the amounts shown in the general journal entry to the proper accounts in the appropriations ledger.

3–S. The following budget for the General Fund of the City of Smithville (see Problem 2–S) was legally adopted for the calendar year 19y1.

Estimated Revenues:	
Taxes:	
Real Property	$ 980,000
Sales	1,140,000
Interest and Penalties on Taxes	10,000
Licenses and Permits	350,000
Fines and Forfeits	250,000
Intergovernmental Revenue	200,000
Charges for Services	60,000
Miscellaneous Revenues	20,000
Total Estimated Revenues	$3,010,000
Appropriations:	
General Government	$ 326,000
Public Safety:	
Police	624,200
Fire	609,800
Building Safety	57,600
Public Works	501,400
Health and Welfare	353,500
Parks and Recreation	270,000
Contributions to Retirement Funds	278,000
Miscellaneous Appropriations	39,500
Total Appropriations	$3,060,000

Required   a. Record the budget in the general journal. Show general ledger accounts, subsidiary ledger accounts, and adequate explanations for each entry (and for all journal entries in all S problems).

b. Post the entries to the *general ledger* accounts.

c. (1) Open *revenues ledger* accounts for the eight sources of Estimated Revenues listed in the budget for the City of Smithville General Fund. (An appropriate form is illustrated in Chapter 3.) Allow five lines for each account.

(2) Post to the appropriate revenues ledger accounts the amounts shown in the general journal entry.

d. (1) Open *appropriations ledger* accounts for the nine classifications of appropriations shown in the budget for the General Fund. (An appropriate form is illustrated in Chapter 3.) Allow 10 lines for each account.

(2) Post the amounts shown in the general journal entry to the proper accounts in the appropriations ledger.

General Funds and Special Revenue Funds—Illustrative Transactions and Financial Statements

In Chapter 3, the use of general ledger budgetary control accounts (Estimated Revenues, Estimated Other Financing Sources, Appropriations, Estimated Other Financing Uses, and Encumbrances) and related operating statement accounts (Revenues, Other Financing Sources, Expenditures, and Other Financing Uses) is discussed and illustrated. The necessity for subsidiary ledgers supporting the budgetary control accounts and related operating statement accounts is also discussed in Chapter 3. In this chapter, common transactions and events in the operation of the General Fund of a hypothetical local governmental unit, the Town of Brighton, are discussed, and appropriate accounting entries and financial statements are illustrated. For the sake of completeness, entries in subsidiary ledger accounts as well as in general ledger accounts are illustrated. The accounting structure illustrated in this chapter is entirely applicable to special revenue funds of state and local governmental units as well as to general funds.

Illustrative Case

Assume at the end of a fiscal year, 19y0, the Balance Sheet shown on the next page is presented for the General Fund of the Town of Brighton.

Flow of Financial Resources Focus

Notice that the assets of the General Fund of the Town of Brighton illustrate the flow of financial resources measurement focus prescribed by GASB standards for all governmental funds. Financial resources include prepaid items and supplies inventories, if material, and marketable investments, as well as cash and receivables. Land, buildings, and equipment utilized in governmental fund operations are not accounted for by governmental funds because they are not financial resources, as defined by the GASB. Fixed assets used in governmental fund operations are accounted for by the General Fixed Assets Account Group (GFAAG), discussed in Chapter 6.

TOWN OF BRIGHTON
General Fund Balance Sheet
As of December 31, 19y0

Assets

Cash		$190,000
Taxes receivable—delinquent	$660,000	
Less: Estimated uncollectible delinquent taxes	50,000	610,000
Interest and penalties receivable on taxes	13,200	
Less: Estimated uncollectible interest and penalties	3,300	9,900
Total Assets		$809,900

Liabilities and Fund Equity

Liabilities:		
Vouchers payable	$320,000	
Due to federal government	90,000	
Total Liabilities		$410,000
Fund Equity:		
Reserve for encumbrances—19y0	127,000	
Fund balance	272,900	
Total Fund Equity		399,900
Total Liabilities and Fund Equity		$809,900

The arithmetic difference between total financial resources and total liabilities of the fund is the **Fund Equity.** Residents have no legal claim on any excess of liquid assets over current liabilities; therefore, the Fund Equity is not analogous to the Stockholders' Equity of an investor-owned entity. The Town of Brighton's General Fund Balance Sheet illustrates that at December 31, 19y0, a portion of Fund Equity is **reserved** because not all of the purchase orders issued in fiscal year 19y0 were filled by the end of that year. The liability that will result when goods or services are received in fulfillment of purchase orders outstanding on December 31, 19y0, is estimated to total $127,000, as shown by the Reserve for Encumbrances—19y0 in the Balance Sheet illustrated above. The portion of Fund Equity not reserved is shown as Fund Balance in the Balance Sheet illustrated. An alternate and more descriptive designation would be "Available for Appropriation" because this amount ($272,900 in the Town of Brighton General Fund Balance Sheet) is the excess of financial resources over actual liabilities and amounts expected to become liabilities when goods and services on order at balance sheet date are received.

Recording the Budget   As discussed in detail in Chapter 3, the budget should be recorded in the accounts of each fund for which a budget is legally adopted. Entry 1, below, illustrates an entry to record the budget for the General Fund of the Town of Brighton for fiscal year 19y1. (The entry is shown in combined form to illustrate that format. The detail shown is assumed to be the detail needed to comply with laws applicable to the Town of Brighton. Since both Estimated Revenues and Appropriations accounts refer only to the 19y1 budget and will be closed at the end of the year, it is not necessary to incorporate "19y1" in the title of either.)

	General Ledger		Subsidiary Ledger	
	Debits	*Credits*	*Debits*	*Credits*
1. Estimated Revenues..................	3,986,000			
Fund Balance	194,000			
Appropriations		4,180,000		
Revenues Ledger:				
Property Taxes			2,600,000	
Interest and Penalties on Delinquent				
Taxes..............................			13,000	
Sales Taxes			480,000	
Licenses and Permits.................			220,000	
Fines and Forfeits			308,000	
Intergovernmental Revenue			280,000	
Charges for Services			70,000	
Miscellaneous Revenues..............			15,000	
Appropriations Ledger:				
General Government				660,000
Public Safety				1,240,000
Public Works.....................				910,000
Health and Welfare				860,000
Parks and Recreation.............				315,000
Contributions to Retirement Plans ..				180,000
Miscellaneous Appropriations				15,000

Tax Anticipation Notes Payable

In the December 31, 19y0, Balance Sheet of the Town of Brighton, two items, Vouchers Payable and Due to Federal Government, are current liabilities. Assuming the Town Treasurer wishes to pay these in full within 30 days after the date of the Balance Sheet, he is forced to do some cash forecasting because the balance of Cash is not large enough to pay the $410,000 debt. In addition to this immediate problem, he and most other governmental treasurers are faced with the problem that cash disbursements during a fiscal year tend to be approximately level month by month, whereas cash receipts from major revenue sources are concentrated in just a few months. For example, property tax collections are concentrated in two separate months, such as May and November, when the installments are due; collections by a local government from the state or federal governments of revenues collected by superior jurisdictions for distribution to a local government are also usually concentrated in one or two months of the year. Therefore, the Treasurer of the Town of Brighton may forecast that he will need to disburse approximately one fourth of the budgeted appropriations before major items of revenue are received; one fourth of $4,180,000 is $1,045,000. This amount plus current liabilities at the beginning of the year, $410,000, equals $1,455,000 expected cash disbursements in the period for which the forecast is made. Experience may indicate that a conservative forecast of collections of delinquent taxes and interest and penalties thereon during the forecast period will amount to $425,000. Further, assume the Treasurer's review of the items in the Estimated Revenues budget indicates that at least $140,000 will be collected in the forecast period. Therefore, total cash available to meet the $1,455,000 disbursements is $755,000 ($190,000 cash as of the beginning of the period, plus the $425,000 and $140,000 items just described), leaving a deficiency of $700,000 to be met by borrowing. The taxing power of the government is ample security for short-term debt; local banks customarily meet the working capital needs of a governmental unit by accepting a "tax anticipation note" from the unit. If the amount of $700,000 is borrowed at this time, the necessary entry is:

	General Ledger		Subsidiary Ledger	
	Debits	*Credits*	*Debits*	*Credits*
2. Cash	700,000			
Tax Anticipation Notes Payable		700,000		

Encumbrance Entry

Purchase orders for materials and supplies were issued in the total amount of $306,450; amounts chargeable against the appropriations for 19y1 are shown as debits to Encumbrance Ledger accounts. The entry to record the encumbrance for the purchase orders is (since some encumbrance documents issued in 19y1 will likely not be filled until the following year, it is convenient to incorporate "19y1" in each general ledger account title):

3. Encumbrances—19y1	306,450			
Reserve for				
Encumbrances—19y1		306,450		
Encumbrances Ledger:				
General Government			28,000	
Public Safety			72,000	
Public Works........................			160,000	
Parks and Recreation..................			36,000	
Health and Welfare			10,000	
Miscellaneous Appropriations			450	

Payment of Liabilities as Recorded

Checks were drawn to pay the vouchers payable and the amount due to the federal government as of the end of 19y0:

4. Vouchers Payable..................	320,000			
Due to Federal Government.........	90,000			
Cash		410,000		

Notice it is not necessary in the above entry to know what appropriations were affected at the time goods and services giving rise to the liabilities were received, because under the accrual concept, the appropriations were considered expended in 19y0 when the goods and services were received.

Payrolls and Payroll Taxes

The gross pay of employees of General Fund departments amounted to $840,000. The Town does not use the encumbrance procedure for payrolls. Deductions from gross pay for the period amount to $64,260 for employees' share of FICA tax; $84,000, employees' federal withholding tax; and $16,800, employees' state withholding tax—the first two will, of course, have to be remitted by the Town to the federal government, and the last item will have to be remitted to the state government. The gross pay is chargeable to the appropriations as indicated by the Expenditures Ledger debits. Assuming the liability for net pay is vouchered, the entry is:

	General Ledger		Subsidiary Ledger	
	Debits	*Credits*	*Debits*	*Credits*
5a. Expenditures—19y1..................	840,000			
Vouchers Payable...............		674,940		
Due to Federal Government.......		148,260		
Due to State Government.........		16,800		
Expenditures Ledger:				
General Government			116,800	
Public Safety........................			520,400	
Public Works........................			97,200	
Health and Welfare			63,600	
Parks and Recreation.................			42,000	

Payment of the vouchers for the net pay results in the following entry:

5b. Vouchers Payable...................	674,940			
Cash		674,940		

Inasmuch as the Town is liable for the employer's share of FICA taxes ($64,260) and for contributions to additional retirement plans established by state law (assumed to amount to $18,000 for the pay period ended), it is necessary that the Town's liabilities for its contributions be recorded, as shown in Entry 6. These obligations were provided for in the Appropriations budget under the caption "Contributions to Retirement Plans."

6. Expenditures—19y1..................	82,260			
Due to Federal Government.......		64,260		
Due to State Government..........		18,000		
Expenditures Ledger:				
Contributions to Retirement Plans			82,260	

Recording Property Tax Levy

Entry 1 of this chapter shows that the estimated revenue for 19y1 from property taxes levied for the Town of Brighton General Fund is $2,600,000. If records of property tax collections in recent years, adjusted for any expected changes in tax collection policy and changes in local economic conditions, indicate that approximately 4 percent of the gross tax levy will never be collected, the gross tax levy must be large enough so that the collectible portion of the levy, 96 percent, equals the needed revenue from this source, $2,600,000. Therefore, the gross levy of property taxes for the General Fund of the Town of Brighton must be $2,708,333

($2,600,000 ÷ .96). In an actual situation, property situated in the Town of Brighton also would be taxed for other funds of that Town; for various funds of other general purpose governmental units, such as the township and the county in which the property in the Town of Brighton is located; the various funds of special purpose governmental units that have the right to tax the same property, such as one or more independent school districts or a hospital district; and perhaps the state in which the Town is located.

The gross property tax levies for each fund of the Town of Brighton, and for each other general purpose and special purpose governmental unit, must be aggregated, and the aggregate levy for that unit divided by the assessed valuation of property within the geographical limits of that unit, in order to determine the tax rate applicable to property within the unit. In many states, a county official prepares bills for all taxes levied on property within the county; the same official, or another, acts as collector of all property taxes levied for the county and all governmental units within the county. Although the billing and collecting functions may be centralized, the taxes levied for each fund must be recorded as an asset of that fund. If the accounts are to be kept in conformity with generally accepted accounting principles, the portion of the taxes expected to be collectible (.96 of the total levy, in this example) must be recorded as revenues of that fund, and the portion expected to be uncollectible (.04 of the total levy, in this example) recorded in a "contra-asset" account, as illustrated by Entry 7:

	General Ledger		Subsidiary Ledger	
	Debits	*Credits*	*Debits*	*Credits*
7. Taxes Receivable—Current	2,708,333			
Estimated Uncollectible Current				
Taxes		108,333		
Revenues		2,600,000		
Revenues Ledger:				
Property Taxes				2,600,000

As Entry 7 shows, since the general ledger control account, Revenues, is credited, an entry must also be made in the Revenues subsidiary ledger. Taxes Receivable—Current is also a control account, just as is the Accounts Receivable account of a business entity; each is supported by a subsidiary ledger that shows how much is owed by each taxpayer or customer. Ordinarily, the subsidiary ledger supporting the real property taxes receivable control is organized by parcels of property according to their legal descriptions, since unpaid taxes are liens against the property regardless of changes in ownership. Because of its conceptual similarity to accounting for business receivables, taxes receivable subsidiary ledger accounting is not illustrated in this text.

Recognition of Expenditures for Encumbered Items

When supplies and services ordered during the current year have been received and found to be acceptable, the suppliers' or contractors' invoices should be checked for agreement with purchase orders or contracts as to prices and terms, and for clerical accuracy. If everything is in order, the invoices are approved for payment. If, as is probable, the estimated liability for purchase orders and contracts was recorded in the Encumbrance account and in the appropriate subsidiary accounts, the encumbrance entry must be reversed, and expenditures must be recorded in the control account and appropriate subsidiary accounts in the amount of the actual liability for goods or services received. Assume goods and services ordered during 19y1 by departments accounted for by the Town of Brighton General Fund (see Entry 3) are received. Invoices for the items received totaled $269,450; related purchase orders totaled $269,775. (The appropriations assumed to be affected are shown in Entries 8a and 8b.)

	General Ledger		Subsidiary Ledger	
	Debits	*Credits*	*Debits*	*Credits*
8a. Reserve for Encumbrances—19y1	269,775			
Encumbrances—19y1		269,775		
Encumbrances Ledger:				
General Government				12,250
Public Safety				72,000
Public Works...................				150,900
Parks and Recreation............				30,000
Health and Welfare				4,175
Miscellaneous Appropriations				450
8b. Expenditures—19y1.................	269,450			
Vouchers Payable...............		269,450		
Expenditures Ledger:				
General Government			12,300	
Public Safety			72,000	
Public Works.......................			150,600	
Parks and Recreation................			30,000	
Health and Welfare			4,100	
Miscellaneous Appropriations			450	

*Revenue Recognized
on Cash Basis*

Revenue from licenses and permits, fines and forfeits, and other sources not previously accrued is recognized on the cash basis.[1] Collections to date in 19y1

[1] GASB *Statement No. 11,* "Measurement Focus and Basis of Accounting—Governmental Fund Operating Statements," established governmental fund revenue recognition standards, which provide for a much greater use of the accrual basis of accounting than is provided by standards currently in effect. The effective date of *Statement No. 11* has been deferred until related GASB projects are completed. When the effective date is set an Update Bulletin will be sent to instructors who have adopted this text.

are assumed to be as shown in Entry 9:

	General Ledger		Subsidiary Ledger	
	Debits	*Credits*	*Debits*	*Credits*
9. Cash	259,200			
Revenues		259,200		
Revenues Ledger:				
Licenses and Permits.............				100,000
Fines and Forfeits				151,000
Charges for Services				7,000
Miscellaneous Revenues...........				1,200

Collection of Delinquent Taxes

Delinquent taxes are subject to interest and penalties that must be paid at the time the tax bill is paid. It is possible for a government to record the amount of penalties at the time the taxes become delinquent. Interest may be computed and recorded periodically to keep the account on the accrual basis; it must also be computed and recorded for the period from the date of last recording to the date when a taxpayer pays his delinquent taxes. Assume taxpayers of the Town of Brighton have paid delinquent taxes totaling $440,000, on which interest and penalties of $8,800 had been recorded as receivable at the end of 19y0; further assume $600 additional interest was paid for the period from the first day of 19y1 to the dates on which the delinquent taxes were paid. Since it is common for the cashier receiving the collections to be permitted to originate source documents that result only in credits to Taxes Receivable—Current, Taxes Receivable—Delinquent, or Interest and Penalties Receivable on Taxes, it is necessary to record the $600 interest earned in 19y1 in a separate entry, such as the following:

10a. Interest and Penalties Receivable on				
Taxes...........................	600			
Revenues		600		
Revenues Ledger:				
Interest and Penalties on				
Delinquent Taxes				600

The collection of delinquent taxes and interest and penalties is summarized in Entry 10b.

10b. Cash	449,400		
Taxes Receivable—Delinquent ...		440,000	
Interest and Penalties Receivable			
on Taxes....................		9,400	

Correction of Errors

No problems arise in the collection of current taxes if they are collected as billed; the collections are debited to Cash and credited to Taxes Receivable—Current. Sometimes, even in a well-designed and well-operated system, errors occur and must be corrected. If, for example, the assessed valuation of a parcel of property were legally reduced but the tax bill erroneously issued at the higher valuation, the following correcting entry would be made when the error was discovered, assuming the corrected bill to be $364 smaller than the original bill. (The error also caused a slight overstatement of the credit to Estimated Uncollectible Current Taxes in Entry 7, but the error in that account is not considered material and, for that reason, does not require correction.)

	General Ledger		Subsidiary Ledger	
	Debits	*Credits*	*Debits*	*Credits*
11. Revenues	364			
Taxes Receivable—Current		364		
Revenues Ledger:				
Property Taxes				364

Postaudit may disclose errors in the recording of expenditures during the current year, or during a prior year. If the error occurred during the current year, the Expenditures account and the proper Expenditures subsidiary account can be debited or credited as needed to correct them. If the error occurred in a prior year, however, the Expenditures account in error has been closed to Fund Balance, so logically the correcting entry should be made to the Fund Balance account. The "all-inclusive income statement" practice that is considered appropriate for profit-seeking entities does not have equal acceptance in governmental accounting because of the greater importance of legal constraints on governmental actions. For example, if a governmental unit collects from a supplier an amount that was erroneously paid in a preceding year, the appropriation for the year of the collection is not increased by the amount collected; it remains as originally budgeted. As a practical matter, collections from suppliers of prior years' overpayments may be budgeted as Miscellaneous Revenues and recorded as credits to the Revenues account.

Interim Financial Statements

Periodically during a year it is desirable to prepare financial statements for the information of administrators and members of the legislative branch of the governmental unit. Illustration 4–1 shows how a Balance Sheet would look for the Town of Brighton if it were prepared in 19y1 after the entries numbered 1 through 11 above were made; the date is assumed to be March 31, 19y1.

The Interim Balance Sheet, Illustration 4–1, reflects the balances of both proprietary and budgetary accounts. Instead of Assets, which those familiar with accounting for profit-seeking entities would expect, the caption must be Assets and Resources, because the excess of Estimated Revenues over Revenues is not an asset as of balance sheet date but does indicate the amount that will be added to assets when legally budgeted revenues are recognized. Similarly, the caption is not Equities, or Liabilities and Capital, or another title commonly found in financial reports of profit-seeking entities, but Liabilities and Fund Equity. The Liabilities section is consistent with that of profit-seeking entities, but the next section discloses the three subdivisions of the Fund Equity. The first presents the amount

ILLUSTRATION 4–1   Interim Balance Sheet

TOWN OF BRIGHTON
General Fund Balance Sheet
As of March 31, 19y1

Assets and Resources

Assets:

Cash		$ 513,660
Taxes receivable—current	$2,707,969	
Less: Estimated uncollectible current taxes	108,333	2,599,636
Taxes receivable—delinquent	220,000	
Less: Estimated uncollectible delinquent taxes	50,000	170,000
Interest and penalties receivable on taxes	4,400	
Less: Estimated uncollectible interest and penalties	3,300	1,100
Total Assets		3,284,396

Resources:

Estimated revenues	3,986,000	
Less: Revenues	2,859,436	1,126,564
Total Assets and Resources		$4,410,960

Liabilities and Fund Equity

Liabilities:

Vouchers payable	$ 269,450	
Due to federal government	212,520	
Due to state government	34,800	
Tax anticipation notes payable	700,000	
Total Liabilities		$1,216,770

Fund Equity:

Appropriations		4,180,000	
Less: Expenditures—19y1	$1,191,710		
Encumbrances—19y1	36,675	1,228,385	
Available Appropriations		2,951,615	
Reserve for encumbrances—19y1		36,675	
Reserve for encumbrances—19y0		127,000	
Fund balance		78,900	
Total Fund Equity			3,194,190
Total Liabilities and Fund Equity			$4,410,960

appropriated for the year, less the amount of appropriations that have been expended during the year to date, and less the amount of appropriations that have been encumbered by purchase orders and contracts outstanding at balance sheet date; the net is the amount that legally may be expended or encumbered during the remainder of the budget year. In Illustration 4–1 only one item, Reserve for Encumbrances, is shown in the second subdivision. This subdivision discloses the portion of net assets and resources that is not available for appropriation because expected liabilities exist (or because, as discussed later in the Town of Brighton example, certain assets will not be converted into cash in the normal operations of the fund). The remaining subdivision, Fund Balance, discloses that portion of the taxpayers' equity available for appropriation. Accordingly, in financial statement presentation, the word *Unreserved,* or the phrase *Available for Appropriation,* is sometimes used in place of *Fund Balance.* Fund Balance, it should be emphasized, is the excess of the sum of actual assets and budgeted resources over the sum of actual liabilities, available appropriations, and reserves for assets not available for appropriation; in short, it has both proprietary and budgetary aspects.

Interim statements and schedules should be prepared to accompany the interim balance sheet to disclose other information needed by administrators and members of the legislative body; a statement comparing the detail of budgeted and actual revenues is shown as Illustration 4–2, and a statement comparing appropriations, expenditures, and encumbrances in detail is shown as Illustration 4–3. Interim Statements of Revenues, Expenditures, and Changes in Fund Balance are similar to the end-of-the-year statement (Illustration 4–6) on page 101.

Illustration of Events Subsequent to Date of Interim Statements

Transactions and events such as the collection of revenue and receivables, and the encumbering and expenditure of appropriations, would obviously occur frequently in a governmental unit of any appreciable size. Since entries for the recurring events would be similar to the entries illustrated above, it seems unnecessary to present entries for these events in the portion of 19y1 subsequent to the date of the Interim Balance Sheet shown as Illustration 4–1. Entries for common General Fund transactions and events not previously illustrated are shown in the following sections.

Revision of the Budget

Comparisons of budgeted and actual revenues, by sources, and comparisons of departmental or program appropriations with expenditures and encumbrances, as well as interpretation of information that was not available at the time the budgets were originally adopted, may indicate the desirability or necessity of legally amending the budget during the fiscal year. For example, the Statement of Actual and Estimated Revenues for the three months ended March 31, 19y1 (Illustration 4–2), shows that over 70 percent of the revenues budgeted for the General Fund of the Town of Brighton for 19y1 have already been realized—almost entirely because revenue from property taxes is recognized on the accrual basis, whereas in this illustrative case revenues from all other sources have been recognized on the cash basis during the three-month period for which entries are illustrated. Consequently, administrators of the Town must review the information shown in Illustration 4–2 and determine whether the budget that was legally approved before the beginning of 19y1 appears realistic or whether changes should be made in the

ILLUSTRATION 4–2

TOWN OF BRIGHTON
General Fund
Statement of Actual and Estimated Revenues
For the Three Months Ended March 31, 19y1

Sources of Revenues	Estimated	Actual	Estimated Revenues Not Yet Realized
Taxes:			
Property taxes	$2,600,000	$2,599,636	$ 364
Interest and penalties on taxes	13,000	600	12,400
Sales taxes	480,000	—	480,000
Total Taxes	3,093,000	2,600,236	492,764
Licenses and permits	220,000	100,000	120,000
Fines and forfeits	308,000	151,000	157,000
Intergovernmental revenue	280,000	—	280,000
Charges for services	70,000	7,000	63,000
Miscellaneous revenues	15,000	1,200	13,800
Total General Fund Revenue	$3,986,000	$2,859,436	$1,126,564

ILLUSTRATION 4–3

TOWN OF BRIGHTON
General Fund
Statement of Budgeted and Actual Expenditures and Encumbrances
For the Three Months Ended March 31, 19y1

Function	Appropriations	Expenditures of 19y1 Appropriations	Outstanding Encumbrances	Available Appropriations
General government	$ 660,000	$ 129,100	$15,750	$ 515,150
Public safety	1,240,000	592,400	—	647,600
Public works	910,000	247,800	9,100	653,100
Health and welfare	860,000	67,700	5,825	786,475
Parks and recreation	315,000	72,000	6,000	237,000
Contributions to retirement plans	180,000	82,260	—	97,740
Miscellaneous appropriations	15,000	450	—	14,550
Total General Fund	$4,180,000	$1,191,710	$36,675	$2,951,615

Revenues budget in light of current information about local economic conditions; possible changes in state or federal laws relating to grants, entitlements, or shared revenues; or other changes relating to license and permit fees, fines, forfeits, and charges for services. Similarly, revenue collection procedures and revenue recognition policies should be reviewed to determine if changes should be made in the remaining months of the year. Assume the Town of Brighton's General Fund Revenues budget for 19y1 has been reviewed as described and the budget is legally amended to reflect that revenues from Charges for Services are expected to be $5,000 more than originally budgeted, and Miscellaneous Revenues are expected to be $10,000 more than originally budgeted; revenues from other sources are not expected to be materially different from the original 19y1 budget. Entry 12 records the amendment of the Revenues budget, as well as the amendment of the Appropriations budget, as discussed below.

Information shown in Illustration 4–3 should be reviewed by administrators of the Town of Brighton to determine if the appropriations legally approved before the beginning of 19y1 appear realistic in light of expenditures of the 19y1 budget incurred in the first three months of 19y1 and encumbrances outstanding on March 31 of that year. Illustration 4–3 shows that total cumulative expenditures and outstanding encumbrances exceed 29 percent of the total appropriations by 19y1, which can be related to the fact that as of March 31, the year is almost 25 percent over. By function, however, cumulative expenditures and outstanding encumbrances range from 3 percent of the Miscellaneous appropriation to almost 48 percent of the Public Safety appropriation. Therefore, each appropriation should be reviewed carefully in whatever detail is available, in light of current information about expenditures needed to accomplish planned services during the remainder of 19y1. Assume the Town of Brighton's General Fund appropriations for 19y1 have been reviewed and are legally amended to reflect a $50,000 decrease in the appropriation for Public Works and an $80,000 increase in the appropriation for Public Safety. Entry 12 reflects the legal amendment of appropriations for 19y1, as well as the amendment of the Revenues budget. Note the net increase in Appropriations ($30,000) is larger than the net increase in Estimated Revenues ($15,000), requiring a decrease in Fund Balance.

	General Ledger		Subsidiary Ledger	
	Debits	*Credits*	*Debits*	*Credits*
12. Estimated Revenues.................	15,000			
Fund Balance	15,000			
Appropriations		30,000		
Revenues Ledger:				
Charges for Services			5,000	
Miscellaneous Revenues.............			10,000	
Appropriations Ledger:				
Public Works.......................			50,000	
Public Safety				80,000

Comparisons of Budget and Actual should be made periodically during each fiscal year. Generally, monthly comparisons are appropriate. In the Town of Brighton case, it is assumed that comparisons subsequent to the ones illustrated disclosed no further need to amend either the Revenues budget or the Appropriations budget for 19y1.

Collection of Current Taxes

Collections of property taxes levied in 19y1 for the General Fund of the Town of Brighton amount to $2,041,668. Since the revenue was recognized at the time the levy was recorded (see Entry 7), the following entry suffices at this time:

	General Ledger		Subsidiary Ledger	
	Debits	Credits	Debits	Credits
13. Cash	2,041,668			
Taxes Receivable—Current		2,041,668		

Repayment of Tax Anticipation Notes

As tax collections begin to exceed current disbursements, it becomes possible for the Town of Brighton to repay the local bank for the money borrowed on tax anticipation notes. Just as borrowing the money did not involve the recognition of revenue, the repayment of the principal is merely the extinguishment of debt of the General Fund and is not an expenditure. Payment of interest, however, must be recognized as the expenditure of an appropriation because it requires a reduction in the net assets of the fund. Assuming the interest to be $13,500, and the amount is properly chargeable to Miscellaneous Appropriations, the entry is:

14. Tax Anticipation Notes Payable	700,000			
Expenditures—19y1.................	13,500			
Cash		713,500		
Expenditures Ledger:				
Miscellaneous Appropriations				13,500

Procedures of some governmental units would require the interest expenditures to have been recorded as an encumbrance against Miscellaneous Appropriations at the time the notes were issued, and the liability for the principal and interest to have been vouchered before payment. Even if these procedures were followed by the Town of Brighton, the net result of all entries is achieved by Entry 14.

Encumbrances of Prior Year

As noted under the heading "Flow of Financial Resources Focus," purchase orders and other commitment documents issued in 19y0 and not filled or canceled by the end of that year total $127,000. This amount is designated as Reserve for Encumbrances—19y0 in the December 31, 19y0, General Fund Balance Sheet of the Town of Brighton. When the goods or services are received in 19y1 their actual cost is considered an Expenditure of the 19y0 Appropriations to the extent of the amount encumbered in 19y0; any additional amount must be charged to the 19y1 Appropriations. The Appropriations account for 19y0, however, was closed at the end of that year to Fund Balance, as were the other budgetary accounts for that year. Therefore, when goods or services ordered in 19y0 are received in 19y1 it is convenient to debit the Expenditures—19y0 account when the liability account is credited. When all encumbrance documents outstanding at the end of 19y0 have been filled, or canceled, the Expenditures—19y0 account is closed to the Reserve for Encumbrances—19y0 account, as shown by Entry 21.

Assuming that all goods and services for which encumbrances were outstanding at the end of 19y0 were chargeable to the Parks and Recreation appropriation, and that all were received in 19y1 at a total invoice cost of $127,250, Entry 15 is necessary. Notice that only the estimated amount, $127,000, may be charged to Expenditures—19y0 since this was the amount of the encumbrance against the 19y0 appropriation; the difference between the amount encumbered in 19y0 and the amount approved for payment in 19y1 must be charged against the 19y1 appropriation for Parks and Recreation.

	General Ledger		Subsidiary Ledger	
	Debits	*Credits*	*Debits*	*Credits*
15. Expenditures—19y0.................	127,000			
Expenditures—19y1.................	250			
Vouchers Payable...............		127,250		
Expenditures Ledger:				
Parks and Recreation—19y0			127,000	
Parks and Recreation—19y1			250	

Interfund Transactions

Water utilities ordinarily provide fire hydrants and water service for fire protection at a flat annual charge. A governmentally owned water utility accounted for by an enterprise fund should be expected to support the cost of its operations by user charges. Fire protection is logically budgeted for as an activity of the fire department, a General Fund department. Assuming the amount charged by the water utility to the General Fund for hydrants and water service is $30,000, and the fire department budget is a part of the Public Safety category in the Town of Brighton example, the General Fund should record its liability as:

16a. Expenditures—19y1.................	30,000	
Due to Other Funds............		30,000
Expenditures Ledger:		
Public Safety		30,000

Governmental utility property is not assessed for property tax purposes, but a number of governmental utilities make an annual contribution to the General Fund in recognition of the fact the utility does receive police and fire protection and other services. If the water utility of the Town of Brighton agrees to contribute $25,000 to the General Fund in lieu of taxes, the General Fund entry is:

	General Ledger		Subsidiary Ledger	
	Debits	*Credits*	*Debits*	*Credits*
16b. Due from Other Funds.................	25,000			
Revenues		25,000		
Revenues Ledger:				
Miscellaneous Revenues				25,000

Interfund transactions of the nature illustrated by Entries 16a and 16b are called **quasi-external transactions.** That is, transactions that are recognized as revenues and expenditures (or expenses, in the case of proprietary funds) of the funds involved because they would be recognized as revenues and expenditures (or expenses) if the transactions involved organizations external to the governmental unit. In addition to quasi-external transactions, interfund transactions that constitute reimbursements of one fund for expenditures (or expenses) initially recognized by it but that are properly applicable to another fund should be recognized as expenditures (or expenses) by the reimbursing fund and as reductions of the expenditure (or expense) in the fund that is reimbursed. Other types of interfund transactions are classified as transfers, or as interfund loans, and do not, in a strict sense, result in the recognition of revenues, expenditures, or expenses, as explained in Chapter 3.

Adjusting Entries

Physical Inventories. If a governmental unit is large enough to have sizable inventories of supplies that are used by a number of departments and funds, it is generally recommended that the purchasing function be centralized and the supply activity be accounted for by an internal service fund. For one reason or another, some governments have not created the appropriate internal service fund and account for the supply activity as a part of the General Fund. In either case, accountants would feel better control was provided if perpetual inventory accounts were kept; this procedure is illustrated in Chapter 9. Many small cities, such as the Town of Brighton, not only account for supply activity in the General Fund but do so only on the basis of periodic physical inventories. (If only minor amounts are involved, no accounting records at all may be kept.)

The purchase of supplies must be authorized by an appropriation; therefore, when supplies are received the Expenditures account is debited. If the dollar amount of the physical inventory at the end of a fiscal year is larger than the dollar amount of the inventory at the end of the preceding fiscal year, it is obvious that Expenditures for the year includes the cost of supplies added to inventory. Therefore, the Inventory of Supplies account should be debited and the Expenditures account should be credited for the dollar amount of the increase in physical inventory. (If the dollar amount of the physical inventory at year-end is smaller than the dollar amount of the inventory at the end of the prior year, the Expenditures account should be debited, and the Inventory of Supplies account credited, for the amount of the decrease in inventory.) This procedure is called the **consumption** method of accounting for inventory. Since the inventory will not be converted into cash in the normal operations of a governmental fund, it is not a liquid asset whose carrying cost should be reflected in Fund Balance. Rather, the Inventory account should be offset by a Reserve for Inventory account that is classified for balance sheet purposes in the same manner as discussed for Reserve for Encumbrances under the heading "Interim Financial Statements" in this chapter—both represent elements of Fund Equity not available for appropriation. If a governmental unit uses the consumption method of inventory accounting, the Reserve for Inventory account is credited, and the Fund Balance account is debited, for the increase in the dollar amount of the physical inventory at the time the entries are made in the Inventory and Expenditures accounts. (If the dollar amount of the physical inventory has decreased, Reserve for Inventory should be debited and Fund Balance credited for the amount of the decrease.)

Assuming that the dollar amount of the physical inventory of the Town of Brighton General Fund, as of the end of 19y1, is $61,500, and that the inventory at the end of 19y0 was such a small amount that it was not recorded, the increase in both the Inventory account and the Reserve for Inventory Account is $61,500. Entry 17 illustrates the consumption method of accounting for inventories (for the sake of simplicity it is assumed that all items in inventory were acquired by expenditure of the Public Works appropriation):

	General Ledger		Subsidiary Ledger	
	Debits	*Credits*	*Debits*	*Credits*
17. Inventory of Supplies	61,500			
Fund Balance	61,500			
Expenditures		61,500		
Reserve for Inventory of				
Supplies		61,500		
Expenditures Ledger:				
Public Works....................				61,500

An alternative method of accounting for inventories of governmental funds—equally acceptable under present GASB standards—is known as the **purchases** method. Under the purchases method the Expenditures account is **not** credited for the increase in the dollar amount of the physical inventory, nor is the Fund Balance account debited. The only entry required is the debit to the asset account, Inventory, with offsetting credit to the Reserve for Inventory account, for the amount of the increase in the dollar amount of the physical inventory (or the reverse in the event that the dollar amount of the physical inventory decreased).

Write-Off of Uncollectible Delinquent Taxes. Just as officers of profit-seeking entities should review aged trial balances of receivables periodically in order to determine the adequacy of allowance accounts and authorize the write-off of items judged uncollectible, so should officers of a governmental unit review aged trial balances of taxes receivable and other receivables. Although the levy of property taxes creates a lien against the underlying property in the amount of the tax, accumulated taxes may exceed the market value of the property, or, in the case of personal property, the property may have been removed from the jurisdiction of the governmental unit. When delinquent taxes are deemed uncollectible, the related interest and penalties must also be written off. If the Treasurer of the Town of Brighton receives approval to write off delinquent taxes totaling $26,300 and related interest and penalties of $1,315, the entry would be:

	General Ledger		Subsidiary Ledger	
	Debits	*Credits*	*Debits*	*Credits*
18. Estimated Uncollectible Delinquent Taxes	26,300			
Estimated Uncollectible Interest and Penalties	1,315			
Taxes Receivable—Delinquent		26,300		
Interest and Penalties Receivable on Taxes		1,315		

When delinquent taxes are written off, the tax bills are retained in the files, although no longer subject to general ledger control, because changes in conditions may make it possible to collect the amounts in the future. If collections of written-off taxes are made, it is highly desirable to return the tax bills to general ledger control by making an entry that is the reverse of the write-off entry, so that the procedures described in connection with Entries 10a and 10b may be followed.

Reclassification of Current Taxes.   Assuming all property taxes levied by the Town of Brighton in 19y1 were to have been paid before the end of the year, any balance of taxes receivable at year-end is properly classified as "delinquent" rather than "current." The related allowance for estimated uncollectible taxes should also be transferred to the delinquent classification. An entry to accomplish this, using amounts assumed to exist in the accounts at year-end, is:

19. Taxes Receivable—Delinquent	666,301	
Estimated Uncollectible Current Taxes	108,333	
Taxes Receivable—Current		666,301
Estimated Uncollectible Delinquent Taxes.		108,333

Accrual of Interest and Penalties.   Delinquent taxes are subject to interest and penalties, as discussed previously. If the amount of interest and penalties earned in 19y1 by the General Fund of the Town of Brighton and not yet recognized is $13,320, but it is expected that only $10,800 of that can be collected, the following entry is necessary:

20. Interest and Penalties Receivable on Taxes	13,320		
Estimated Uncollectible Interest and Penalties		2,520	
Revenues		10,800	
Revenues Ledger:			
Interest and Penalties on Delinquent Taxes.			10,800

Pre-Closing Trial Balance

Assuming the illustrated entries for the transactions and events pertaining to the year 19y1 for the Town of Brighton have been made and posted, and a number of other entries—not illustrated because they pertain to similar transactions and events—have been made and posted, the trial balance below shows the General Fund general ledger accounts before closing entries:

TOWN OF BRIGHTON
Pre-Closing Trial Balance
As of December 31, 19y1

	Debits	Credits
Cash...	$ 145,800	
Taxes Receivable—Delinquent	666,300	
Estimated Uncollectible Delinquent Taxes		$ 88,000
Interest and Penalties Receivable on Taxes	3,085	
Estimated Uncollectible Interest and Penalties........................		1,985
Due from Other Funds...	25,000	
Inventory of Supplies..	61,500	
Estimated Revenues...	4,001,000	
Revenues..		4,015,000
Vouchers Payable		396,800
Due to Federal Government..		126,520
Due to State Government		39,740
Due to Other Funds		30,000
Expenditures—19y0	127,000	
Appropriations...		4,210,000
Expenditures—19y1	4,069,260	
Encumbrances—19y1..	70,240	
Reserve for Encumbrances—19y1....................................		70,240
Reserve for Encumbrances—19y0....................................		127,000
Reserve for Inventory of Supplies...................................		61,500
Fund Balance..		2,400
	$9,169,185	$9,169,185

Closing Entries

The essence of the closing process for a governmental fund is the transfer of the balances of the operating statement accounts and the balances of the budgetary accounts for the year to the Fund Balance account. Individual accountants have preferences as to the sequence in which this is done, and as to the combinations of accounts in each closing entry. Any sequence and any combination, however, should yield the same result that closing entries for a profit-seeking entity do: All financial events in the history of the organization are summarized in the balance sheet accounts. This effect is achieved by Entries 21 and 22. Entry 21 is made to close the Expenditures—19y0 account and the Reserve for Encumbrances—19y0 account since those are the only accounts relating to that year.

	General Ledger		Subsidiary Ledger	
	Debits	Credits	Debits	Credits
21. Reserve for Encumbrances—19y0	127,000			
Expenditures—19y0..............		127,000		

	General Ledger		Subsidiary Ledger	
	Debits	*Credits*	*Debits*	*Credits*
22. Revenues	4,015,000			
Appropriations	4,210,000			
Estimated Revenues.............		4,001,000		
Expenditures—19y1.............		4,069,260		
Encumbrances—19y1		70,240		
Fund Balance		84,500		

Although Entry 22 affects five General Fund general ledger control accounts, it is not considered necessary to make closing entries in their subsidiary ledger accounts because separate subsidiary ledgers are kept for each budget year.

It is important to notice the closing entry has the effect of reversing the entry made to record the budget (Entry 1) and the entry made to amend the budget (Entry 12). Therefore, after the closing entry is posted, the Fund Balance account is purely a balance sheet account and not one in which historical and expected effects are mixed, as is true during a year. That is, it again represents the net amount of financial resources available for appropriation for fund purposes.

Year-End Financial Statements

The Balance Sheet for the General Fund of the Town of Brighton as of the end of 19y1 is shown as Illustration 4–4. Since only balance sheet accounts are open, the captions "Assets" and "Liabilities and Fund Equity" are used instead of the captions in the Interim Balance Sheet, Illustration 4–1. The amount due from the Water Utility Fund is offset against the amount due to the same fund, and only the net liability is shown in the balance sheet, in conformity with GASB standards. It should be emphasized that it is **not** acceptable to offset a receivable from one fund against a payable to a different fund. The General Fund balance sheet would be presented in columnar form in the Combined Balance Sheet, one of the five general purpose financial statements required for conformity with generally accepted accounting principles. In addition, GASB standards require disclosures in the notes to the financial statements of a number of details regarding deposits with financial institutions, investments, property taxes, receivables, and other assets.

A second financial statement that should be presented in the year-end comprehensive annual financial report is a Statement of Revenues, Expenditures, and Changes in Fund Balance (see Illustration 4–5). Illustration 4–5 presents the actual revenues and actual expenditures that resulted from transactions illustrated in this chapter and other transactions not illustrated because they were similar in nature. If the General Fund of the Town of Brighton had had any financial inflows or outflows resulting from operating transfers, the receipt of debt issue proceeds, or other transactions not strictly defined as resulting in revenues or expenditures, their effects should be reported as Other Financing Sources or Other Financing Uses.

The Other Financing Sources (Uses) section in Illustration 4–5 shows a common means of disclosure of nonrevenue financial inflows and nonexpenditure financial outflows. Information shown here as Illustration 4–5 would be presented

ILLUSTRATION 4–4

TOWN OF BRIGHTON
General Fund Balance Sheet
As of December 31, 19y1

Assets

Cash		$145,800
Taxes receivable—delinquent	$666,300	
Less: Estimated uncollectible delinquent taxes	88,000	578,300
Interest and penalties receivable on taxes	3,085	
Less: Estimated uncollectible interest and penalties	1,985	1,100
Inventory of supplies		61,500
Total Assets		$786,700

Liabilities and Fund Equity

Liabilities:		
Vouchers payable	396,800	
Due to federal government	126,520	
Due to state government	39,740	
Due to other funds	5,000	
Total Liabilities		$568,060
Fund Equity:		
Reserve for encumbrances—19y1	70,240	
Reserve for inventory of supplies	61,500	
Fund balance	86,900	
Total Fund Equity		218,640
Total Liabilities and Fund Equity		$786,700

in columnar form in the Combined Statement of Revenues, Expenditures, and Changes in Fund Balances—All Governmental Fund Types, one of the five general purpose financial statements required for conformity with generally accepted accounting principles.

A third statement that should be prepared at year-end is the Statement of Revenues, Expenditures, and Changes in Fund Balance—Budget and Actual (Illustration 4–6). This information should be included in columnar form, as shown in Illustration 3–2, in the Combined Statement of Revenues, Expenditures, and Changes in Fund Balances—Budget and Actual, one of the five general purpose financial statements required for conformity with GAAP.

The amounts in the Revenues section of the Actual column in Illustration 4–6 present the same information as shown in the Revenues section of Illustration 4–5 because in the Town of Brighton example the General Fund revenues budget is on the same basis as the Revenues account. However, the amounts in the Expenditures section of the Actual column of Illustration 4–6 differ from the Expenditures shown in Illustration 4–5 because Illustration 4–5, in order to conform with GASB

ILLUSTRATION 4–5

TOWN OF BRIGHTON
General Fund
Statement of Revenues, Expenditures, and
Changes in Fund Balance
For the Year Ended December 31, 19y1

Revenues:		
Property taxes	$2,599,636	
Interest and penalties on delinquent taxes	11,400	
Sales taxes	485,000	
Licenses and permits	213,200	
Fines and forfeits	310,800	
Intergovernmental revenue	284,100	
Charges for services	82,464	
Miscellaneous revenues	28,400	
Total Revenues		$4,015,000
Expenditures:		
19y1:		
General government	649,400	
Public safety	1,305,435	
Public works	778,300	
Health and welfare	850,325	
Parks and recreation	292,500	
Contributions to retirement plans	179,100	
Miscellaneous appropriations	14,200	
Expenditures—19y1	4,069,260	
19y0 Expenditures		
Parks and recreation	127,000	
Total Expenditures		4,196,260
Excess of Expenditures over Revenues		(181,260)
Other Financing Sources (Uses):		
Operating transfers in	–0–	
Operating transfers out	–0–	
Total Other Financing Sources		–0–
Excess of Expenditures and Other Uses over Revenues and Other Sources		(181,260)
Increase in Reserve for Inventory of Supplies		(61,500)
Decrease in Reserve for Encumbrances during 19y1		56,760
Change (Decrease) in Fund Balance for Year		(186,000)
Fund Balance, January 1, 19y1		272,900
Fund Balance, December 31, 19y1		$ 86,900

standards, reports Expenditures chargeable to 19y0 appropriations ($127,000) as well as Expenditures of the 19y1 appropriations ($4,069,260) and does not report Encumbrances in the Expenditures section of the statement. In contrast, GASB standards require the amounts in the Actual column of Illustration 4–6 to conform with budgetary practices; therefore in that statement Encumbrances outstanding at the end of fiscal 19y1 are added to 19y1 Expenditures because both are uses of the 19y1 appropriation authority. Note that in Illustration 4–6 Expenditures (Public Works) is not adjusted for the inventory of supplies at year-end because the

---

ILLUSTRATION 4–6

TOWN OF BRIGHTON
General Fund
Statement of Revenues, Expenditures, and
Changes in Fund Balance—Budget and Actual
(Non-GAAP Presentation)
For the Year Ended December 31, 19y1

	Budget	Actual	Actual Over (Under) Budget
Revenues:			
Taxes:			
Property taxes	$2,600,000	$2,599,636	$ (364)
Interest and penalties on taxes	13,000	11,400	(1,600)
Sales taxes	480,000	485,000	5,000
Total Taxes	3,093,000	3,096,036	3,036
Licenses and permits	220,000	213,200	(6,800)
Fines and forfeits	308,000	310,800	2,800
Intergovernmental revenue	280,000	284,100	4,100
Charges for services	75,000	82,464	7,464
Miscellaneous revenues	25,000	28,400	3,400
Total Revenues	4,001,000	4,015,000	14,000
Expenditures and Encumbrances:			
General government	660,000	658,850	(1,150)
Public safety	1,320,000	1,318,500	(1,500)
Public works	860,000	859,200	(800)
Health and welfare	860,000	858,650	(1,350)
Parks and recreation	315,000	312,500	(2,500)
Contributions to retirement plans	180,000	179,100	(900)
Miscellaneous appropriations	15,000	14,200	(800)
Total Expenditures	4,210,000	4,201,000	(9,000)
Excess of Expenditures over Revenues	209,000	186,000	(23,000)
Other Financing Sources (Uses)	–0–	–0–	–0–
Decrease in Fund Balance for Year	(209,000)	(186,000)	(23,000)
Fund Balance, January 1, 19y1	272,900	272,900	–0–
Fund Balance, December 31, 19y1	$ 63,900	$ 86,900	$ 23,000

purchase of supplies was a use of 19y1 appropriation authority whether or not the supplies were used in 19y1. Expenditures for 19y0 are excluded from the Budget and Actual statement because that statement relates only to the 19y1 budget. GASB standards require differences between the amounts reported in the two statements to be reconciled in the notes to the financial statements if not reconciled on the face of a statement. For example, the notes to the financial statements for the Town of Brighton might include the following reconciliation of General Fund Expenditures reported in the two operating statements illustrated:

Expenditures for 19y1, budgetary basis	$4,201,000
Less: Reserve for Encumbrances as of December 31, 19y1	(70,240)
Reserve for Inventory of Supplies as of December 31, 19y1	(61,500)
Expenditures for 19y1, GAAP basis	$4,069,260

The presentation of Reserve for Encumbrances in Illustrations 4–4, 4–5, 4–6, and in the illustrative reconciliation, is based on the assumption that amounts encumbered at year-end do not need to be appropriated for the following year. The amounts shown in Illustration 4–6 in the Expenditures section in the Actual Over (Under) Budget column, however, disclose the portion of each appropriation for 19y1 that was neither expended nor encumbered during that year; those amounts, totaling $9,000, are said to *lapse*, that is, become unavailable for expenditure or encumbrance in the year following 19y1.

Special Revenue Funds

As noted in Chapter 2, special revenue funds are needed when legal or policy considerations require separate funds to be created for current purposes other than those served by proprietary or fiduciary funds. An example of a special revenue fund created to demonstrate legal compliance is a Street Fund, which is largely financed by a local government's share of the motor fuel tax levied by the state to be used only for maintenance and construction of streets, roads, and bridges. A second example of a special revenue fund is a Library Operating Fund created to account for a special tax levy or simply the desire of the governing board to have a separate fund to account for an activity that differs from other governmental activities. A third example is a fund to account for grants received from a higher jurisdiction; grant accounting is discussed briefly in the following paragraph.

Accounting for Operating Grants.[2]　Grants received by a local government from the state or federal government—or received by a state from the federal government—are often restricted for specified operating purposes. Consequently, revenues of such grants are frequently accounted for by use of a special revenue fund.

---

[2] Accounting for capital grants is discussed in Chapter 5, "Capital Projects Funds."

A number of grants provide that the grantor will pay the grantee on a reimbursement basis. In such instances, GASB standards require that the grant revenue not be recognized until the expenditure has taken place (because the grant revenue has not been "earned" until the terms of the grant have been met through the required expenditure). As an example of appropriate accounting procedures, assume a local government has been awarded a state grant to finance a fine arts program, and a special revenue fund is created. When the grant receivable is recognized, an offsetting credit is made to Deferred Revenues, a liability account, to disclose that no revenue has yet been earned. Therefore, the entry would be:

	General Ledger		Subsidiary Ledger	
	Debits	*Credits*	*Debits*	*Credits*
Grants Receivable—State	150,000			
Deferred Revenues		150,000		

When expenditures for the purposes specified by the grant have taken place, it is appropriate to recognize revenues in the amount of the expenditures, as illustrated by the following entries:

Expenditures...........................	50,000	
Vouchers Payable (or Cash)		50,000
Deferred Revenues	50,000	
Revenues...........................		50,000

Accounting and Financial Reporting. Special revenue fund accounting and financial reporting are exactly parallel to that described for the General Fund in this chapter. Along with the General Fund, the total of the special revenue funds would be included in the Combined Balance Sheet; the Combined Statement of Revenues, Expenditures, and Changes in Fund Balances (All Governmental Fund Types); and the Combined Statement of Revenues, Expenditures, and Changes in Fund Balances—Budget and Actual. In addition, when more than one special revenue fund exists, *combining* balance sheets, operating statements, and budget-actual statements are required for the Comprehensive Annual Financial Report. Combining statements for capital projects funds are illustrated in Chapter 5; combining statements for special revenue funds would be similar.

Alternatives Sometimes Encountered in General Fund and Special Revenue Fund Accounting

In addition to the method of accounting for encumbrances outstanding at the end of a fiscal year illustrated earlier and assumed to this point, other methods exist in practice. In at least one state, the law requires outstanding encumbrances to be added to the appropriations budgeted for the following year. In this case, the Reserve for Encumbrances account, as well as the Encumbrances account, may be closed at year-end because in essence the encumbered amount is reappropriated for the following year and is not carried forward as a reservation of Fund Balance. Thus at the beginning of the following year it is necessary to debit

Other Treatments of Encumbrances Outstanding at Year-End

Encumbrances and credit Reserve for Encumbrances for the amount of purchase orders, contracts, or other commitment documents carried over from the prior year. From that point on no distinction need be made in the accounting records between expenditures arising from encumbrances of the prior year and those arising from encumbrances of the current year.

Cash Basis Recognition of Tax Revenue

Even though taxes become liens on the underlying property, collections in a given period sometimes fall substantially short of the amount levied. If expenditure commitments are based on the amount levied but actual collections fall short of anticipations, the result may be a condition of financial stringency for the taxing unit. Accordingly, *laws of some states require local governments to record all revenue*, including tax revenue, *on the cash basis*. Such laws are, of course, in conflict with GAAP, which require revenues to be recognized on the modified accrual basis. It is possible to keep the accounting system in conformity with GAAP and to adjust the data to the basis required by law when reporting to the state. Alternatively, it is possible to keep the accounting system in compliance with state law and adjust the data to conform with GAAP when preparing general purpose financial statements.

If the cash basis is applied strictly, the receivable from billed taxes cannot be recorded as an asset even though by all accounting criteria it should be. A procedure that permits placing the receivable under accounting control but defers recognition of the revenue until it is collected is illustrated below:

	General Ledger		Subsidiary Ledger	
	Debits	*Credits*	*Debits*	*Credits*
Taxes Receivable—Current................	1,000,000			
Estimated Uncollectible Current Taxes		20,000		
Reserve for Uncollected Taxes........		980,000		

The entry above records the levy of property taxes assumed to be in the amount of $1,000,000 with 2 percent estimated as uncollectible. The account titles of the debit and the first credit agree with those of Entry 7 above. The second credit, however, is to Reserve for Uncollected Taxes instead of to Revenues. The nature of Reserve for Uncollected Taxes is consistent, under cash basis theory, with that of other reserves discussed earlier. The balance of the Reserve for Uncollected Taxes would be deducted from the net Taxes Receivable on the balance sheet, so that the net noncash item does not add to the asset total (and, obviously, does not add to Fund Equity).

When some of the taxes are collected, the following two entries are necessary (amounts assumed):

Cash....................................	365,000	
Taxes Receivable—Current...........		365,000
Reserve for Uncollected Taxes............	365,000	
Revenues...........................		365,000
Revenues Ledger:		
Property Taxes......................		365,000

The two entries are illustrated because the first one summarizes entries that would be made from source documents originated by the cashier each time taxes are collected. The second entry shows that the Reserve for Uncollected Taxes account must be adjusted periodically to reflect the collection of taxes and the consequent cash basis recognition of revenue.

If financial statements were prepared on the legally required basis after the entries illustrated above, the Statement of Revenues, Expenditures, and Changes in Fund Balance would report revenues from current taxes of $365,000, the amount collected in cash. In the Balance Sheet, full disclosure would be achieved by reporting:

Taxes Receivable—Current		$635,000
Less: Estimated Uncollectible		
Current Taxes	$ 20,000	
Reserve for Uncollected		
Taxes	615,000	635,000

Statements presented on the legally required basis illustrated are, of course, **not** in conformity with GASB standards and would not be considered general purpose financial statements; under AICPA auditing standards they would be considered special reports.

Discounts on Taxes Some governmental units utilize a cash discount system to encourage early payment of property taxes. Although a small amount of revenue is lost from discounts taken, the practice minimizes the use of short-term borrowing or, another alternative, carrying over a sizable available cash balance from the preceding period. If not prohibited by law, discounts are best accounted for as reductions of the amount of revenue to be derived from a given tax levy. Thus, if a tax levy totals $2,000,000 and the estimated discounts that will be taken amount to $18,000, the latter figure may be subtracted from the amount of the levy, along with the estimated loss from uncollectible taxes, to give the net estimated revenue. Assuming an estimated loss from uncollectible taxes of $31,000, the $2,000,000 levy, with discount provision, would be recorded as follows:

	General Ledger		Subsidiary Ledger	
	Debits	*Credits*	*Debits*	*Credits*
Taxes Receivable—Current..............	2,000,000			
Estimated Uncollectible Current Taxes		31,000		
Estimated Discounts on Taxes		18,000		
Revenues..........................		1,951,000		
Revenues Ledger:				
Property Taxes.....................				1,951,000

Payment of taxes within the discount period requires a debit to the Estimated Discounts on Taxes accounts of the amount earned, in the following manner, using assumed amounts:

	General Ledger		Subsidiary Ledger	
	Debits	*Credits*	*Debits*	*Credits*
Cash	197			
Estimated Discounts on Taxes	3			
Taxes Receivable—Current		200		

If discounts are taken in excess of the amount of allowance created, the excess will be debited to Revenues—Property Taxes. Any balance remaining in the allowance after the close of the discount period should be transferred to Revenues—Property Taxes by a credit to that account and a debit to the Estimated Discounts on Taxes account.

As a device for closer control against unwarranted granting of discounts, some governmental units may require discounts on taxes to be covered by an appropriation. Under this method the allowance for discounts is not established when the tax levy is recorded. Discounts granted are debited to Expenditures in the following manner, assuming an entry for one month's collection of taxes:

Cash	23,640	
Expenditures—Discounts on Taxes	360	
Taxes Receivable—Current		24,000

Selected References

American Institute of Certified Public Accountants. *Audit and Accounting Guide. Audits of State and Local Governmental Units.* Revised. New York, 1993.

Governmental Accounting Standards Board. *Codification of Governmental Accounting and Financial Reporting Standards as of June 30, 1993.* Norwalk, Conn., 1993.

Questions

4–1. In the preparation of balance sheets for business organizations it is considered essential to classify liabilities as *current* or *long term*. Is it also essential in the balance sheet of a governmental unit General Fund to classify liabilities as current or long term? Why or why not? Would it be essential to classify the liabilities of a special revenue fund? Explain.

4–2. Explain why it is often necessary to reserve a portion of the fund equity of the General Fund or a Special Revenue Fund.

4–3. "Fund Equity of a governmental fund is directly analogous to Owners' Equity of a commercial entity." Do you agree or disagree? Explain.

4–4. Explain why a city, even a well-managed one, may find it necessary to issue "tax anticipation notes."

4–5. "Tax anticipation notes" generally require the issuing government to pledge specific assets as security. True or false? Explain.

4–6. "If the actual liability for goods or services received in one fiscal year but ordered in a prior fiscal year differs from the estimated liability recorded in the prior year, the actual liability should be reported as an Expenditure of the prior year." Do you agree? Why or why not?

4–7. If the General Fund of a certain city needs $5,760,000 revenue from property taxes to finance estimated expenditures of the forthcoming year, and historical experience and forecasts indicate 4 percent of the gross levy will not be collected, how much should the gross levy of General Fund property taxes for the forthcoming year be? Show all computations in good form.

4–8. Explain the relationship between proprietary accounts and budgetary accounts in an interim balance sheet prepared for the general fund.

4–9. Is it ever permissible to write off uncollectible delinquent property taxes? If so, explain the accounting procedures involved.

4–10. Grant A from the federal government will reimburse the city for allowable costs incurred for authorized operating purposes; grant B is also restricted for a specified operating purpose, but the full amount under the grant is provided to the city at the beginning of the fiscal year in which the grant monies will be used. Explain the difference in revenue recognition procedures for these two grants.

4–11. Since all funds of a governmental unit are part of the same reporting entity, why are certain interfund transactions recorded as Expenditures and liabilities of one fund, and as assets and Revenues of another fund?

4–12. "If a budget is prepared on the cash basis, in order to comply with state law, it should be adjusted to the modified accrual basis in order that financial statements may be prepared in conformity with generally accepted accounting principles." Do you agree? Why or why not?

4–13. State law requires a governmental unit to follow the cash basis of accounting for revenues, yet the finance officer of that unit feels taxes receivable should be placed under accounting control. Suggest a procedure to accomplish both objectives.

4–14. A governmental fund may charge materials and supplies to Expenditures when the items are purchased (the purchases method) or when the items are used (the consumption method). In either case, significant amounts of inventories should be reported in the balance sheet. If administrators are interested in computing and reporting the cost of services rendered, would you recommend the purchases method or the consumption method?

Exercises and Problems

4–1. Utilizing the comprehensive annual financial report obtained for Exercise 1–1, follow the instructions below:

    a. General Fund. What statements and schedules pertaining to the General Fund are presented? In what respects (headings, arrangements, items included, etc.) do they seem similar to the year-end statements illustrated or described in the text? In what respects do they differ?

        What purpose is each statement and schedule intended to serve? How well, in your reasoned opinion, does each statement and schedule accomplish its intended purpose? (After reading the first four chapters of this text carefully and solving assigned problems, you have a much greater understanding of the purposes of General Fund accounting and reporting than most other citizens, and even than nonaccountants in elective or appointive governmental positions.)

        Are any noncurrent or nonliquid assets included in the General Fund balance sheet? If so, are they offset by "Reserve" accounts in the Fund Equity section?

Are any noncurrent liabilities included in the General Fund balance sheet? If so, describe them and attempt to determine why they are included in this statement rather than in the Statement of General Long-Term Debt.

b. *Special Revenue Funds.*   What statements and schedules pertaining to the special revenue funds are presented? Are these only combining statements, or are there also statements for individual special revenue funds?

Refer to *a* above—answer questions from the perspective of the special revenue funds. Review your answers to Exercises 1–1, 2–1, and 3–1 in light of your study of Chapter 4. If you feel your earlier answers were not entirely correct, change them to conform with your present understanding of GASB financial reporting standards.

4–2. Write the numbers 1 through 10 on a sheet of paper. Beside each number write the letter corresponding with the best answer to each of the following questions:

1. Oro County's Expenditures control account at December 31, 19y9, had a balance of $9,000,000. When Oro's books were closed, this $9,000,000 Expenditures control balance should have
   a. Been debited.
   b. Been credited.
   c. Remained open.
   d. Appeared as a contra account.

2. At December 31, 19x9, Alto Township's encumbered appropriations that had not been expended in 19x9 totaled $10,000. Encumbered appropriations do not lapse at year-end. Alto reports on a calendar-year basis. On its December 31, 19x9, balance sheet, the $10,000 should be reported as
   a. Vouchers Payable—Prior Year.
   b. Deferred Expenditures.
   c. Fund Balance Reserved for Encumbrances.
   d. Budgetary Fund Balance—Encumbrances.

3. When Rolan County adopted its budget for the year ending June 30, 19y0, $20,000,000 was recorded in Estimated Revenues. Actual revenues for the year ended June 30, 19y0, amounted to $17,000,000. In closing the budgetary accounts at June 30, 19y0,
   a. Revenues should be debited for $3,000,000.
   b. Estimated Revenues should be debited for $3,000,000.
   c. Revenues should be credited for $20,000,000.
   d. Estimated Revenues should be credited for $20,000,000.

4. Property taxes levied in fiscal year 19x1 to finance the general fund budget of fiscal year 19x2 should be reported as general fund revenues in fiscal year 19x2
   a. Regardless of the fiscal year in which collected.
   b. For the amount collected in fiscal year 19x2 only.
   c. For the amount collected before the end of fiscal year 19x2 only.
   d. For the amount collected before the end of fiscal year or within 60 days thereafter.

5. When equipment was purchased with general fund resources, an appropriate entry was made in the General Fixed Assets Account Group. Which of the following accounts would have been increased in the General Fund?
   a. Due from General Fixed Assets Account Group.
   b. Expenditures.

    c. Appropriations.

    d. No entry should be made in the General Fund.

6. The City of Thomasboro uses the consumption method for recording its inventory of supplies in the general fund. Physical inventories of supplies were $100,000 and $85,000 at December 31, 19x9, and December 31, 19y0, respectively. The adjusting journal entry on December 31, 19y0, will include a:

    a. Debit to Expenditures in the amount of $15,000.

    b. Credit to Expenditures in the amount of $15,000.

    c. Debit to Inventory of Supplies in the amount of $15,000.

    d. Credit to Reserve for Inventory of Supplies in the amount of $85,000.

7. Goods costing $62,000 were received early in 19y0. The estimated liability for these goods had been recorded in 19x9 as $60,000. The journal entry to record these goods in 19y0 will include a:

    a. Debit to Expenditures—19x9 in the amount of $62,000.

    b. Debit to Expenditures—19x9 in the amount of $60,000.

    c. Debit to Expenditures—19y0 in the amount of $62,000.

    d. Debit to Expenditures—19y0 in the amount of $60,000.

8. If a city legally adopts its annual General Fund budget on the modified accrual basis of accounting, its estimated revenues should be

    a. Reported on the modified accrual basis of accounting in the General Fund Statement of Revenues, Expenditures, and Changes in Fund Balance—Budget and Actual.

    b. Converted to the cash basis of accounting and reported in the General Fund Statement of Revenues, Expenditures, and Other Changes in Fund Balance—Budget and Actual.

    c. Reported as current assets in the General Fund Balance Sheet.

    d. Reported as noncurrent assets in the General Fund Balance Sheet.

9. Gold County received goods that had been approved for purchase but for which payment had not been made. Should the accounts listed below be increased?

	Encumbrances	*Expenditures*
a.	No	No
b.	No	Yes
c.	Yes	No
d.	Yes	Yes

10. In which of the following fund types of a city government are revenues and expenditures recognized on the same basis of accounting as the General Fund?

    a. Nonexpendable Trust.

    b. Internal Service.

    c. Enterprise.

    d. Debt Service.

(AICPA, adapted)

4–3. At the end of fiscal year 19y0, budgetary and operating statement control accounts in the general ledger of the General Fund of the City of Adams had the following balances: Appropriations, $5,224,000; Estimated Other Financing Uses, $2,776,000; Estimated Revenues, $7,997,000; Encumbrances, $0; Expenditures, $5,182,000; Other Financing Uses, $2,780,000; and Revenues, $8,022,000. Appropriations included an authorization to order a certain item at a cost not to exceed $64,700; this was not ordered during 19y0 because it will not be available until late in the following year, 19y1. Show in general journal form the entry needed to close all of the accounts listed above that should be closed as of the end of the fiscal year 19y0.

4–4. The following is a list of the ledger accounts of the General Fund of Quincy as of June 30, 19y3 (the fiscal year ends on December 31):

Accounts Payable	$ 352,600
Appropriations	2,663,400
Cash	284,600
Due to Other Funds	16,800
Encumbrances	117,000
Estimated Revenues	2,670,000
Estimated Uncollectible Current Taxes	69,000
Expenditures—19y3	1,385,900
Reserve for Encumbrances—19y3	117,000
Revenues	1,420,400
Tax Anticipation Notes Payable	540,000
Taxes Receivable—Current	898,500
Fund Balance	?

Required

a. Determine the balance of the Fund Balance account as of June 30, 19y3, without preparing a balance sheet or closing entries. Show computations.

b. Prepare in good form an Interim Balance Sheet as of June 30, 19y3.

c. If the only entry recorded in the Fund Balance account during the first six months of 19y3 was to record the original budget for the year, compute the balance of the Fund Balance account that would have been reported in the General Fund Balance Sheet as of December 31, 19y2.

4–5. As of December 31, 19y3, Quincy's General Fund (see Problem 4–4) had the following account balances:

	Debits	Credits
Accounts Payable		$ 209,700
Appropriations		2,678,400
Cash	$ 152,400	
Due to Other Funds		19,000
Encumbrances	34,300	
Estimated Revenues	2,670,000	
Estimated Uncollectible Delinquent Taxes		62,000
Expenditures—19y3	2,581,600	
Inventory of Supplies	60,000	
Reserve for Encumbrances—19y3		34,300
Reserve for Inventory of Supplies		60,000
Revenues		2,627,100
Taxes Receivable—Delinquent	294,000	
Fund Balance		101,800
	$5,792,300	$5,792,300

Required

a. The General Fund trial balance shown above is presented as of the last day of the fiscal year of Quincy. Inspect the trial balance, and the trial balance as of June 30, 19y3 (see Problem 4–4), and answer the following questions. Explain the reason for each of your answers. Assume that the consumption method of recording inventories is used.

(1) Have closing entries been recorded?

(2) Have adjusting entries been recorded?

b. Have any amendments to the General Fund budget been recorded during the six months ended December 31, 19y3? If so, state which budgetary accounts were amended, and whether the amendments represented increases, or decreases, to the budget (state the amount of each increase or decrease). Show in good form all computations needed to support your answers.

4–6. Refer to the December 31, 19y3, trial balance of the General Fund of Quincy (see Problem 4–5) and answer the following questions. Explain each of your answers and show all necessary computations in good form.

a. In the Quincy General Fund Statement of Revenues, Expenditures, and Changes in Fund Balance for the year ending December 31, 19y3, how much should be reported as the Excess of Revenues over Expenditures (or Excess of Expenditures over Revenues, if that is the case)?

b. In the Quincy General Fund Statement of Revenues, Expenditures, and Changes in Fund Balance—Budget and Actual for the year ended December 31, 19y3, how much should be reported as:

(1) The *budgeted* Excess of Revenues over Expenditures (or Excess of Expenditures over Revenues)?

(2) The *actual* Excess of Revenues over Expenditures (or Excess of Expenditures over Revenues)?

c. Explain why your answer to b1 differs from your answer to a, if it does.

d. Explain why your answer to b2 differs from your answer to a, if it does.

e. Compute the Fund Balance that should be reported in the General Fund Balance Sheet for Quincy as of December 31, 19y3. (There are several ways you can compute this amount correctly. It is suggested that you make the computation at least two different ways and prove that the answer is the same in each case.)

4–7. Many years ago, Washington County accounted for revenue on the accrual basis. After it incurred serious financial difficulty because collections of property taxes fell far short of the amount of revenue shown when the tax levy was recorded, the use of accrual basis for revenue was officially prohibited, but recording of the tax levy as charges against property owners was approved.

At June 30, the end of a fiscal year, Washington County's General Fund ledger showed the following names and balances of accounts related to property taxes:

Estimated Uncollectible Taxes—Current Year	$ 30,000
Estimated Uncollectible Taxes—Prior Years	78,000
Estimated Revenues—Current Year's Taxes	835,000
Estimated Revenues—Prior Years' Taxes	58,000
Reserve for Uncollected Taxes—Current Year	56,000
Reserve for Uncollected Taxes—Prior Years	31,000
Revenue—Current Year's Taxes	811,000
Revenue—Prior Years' Taxes	65,000
Taxes Receivable—Current Year	66,000
Taxes Receivable—Prior Years	107,000

It is the practice to transfer at the end of each month the amount collected during the month from Reserve for Uncollected Taxes to Revenue. This had not yet been done at the end of June, as evidenced by the fact that the sum of Reserve for Uncollected Taxes and Estimated Uncollectible Taxes for both this and prior years exceeded the balances of the related taxes receivable accounts.

For the forthcoming year, the town board approved a tax rate that would produce a total levy of approximately $1,000,000 of which 5 percent was expected to be uncollectible.

Required

a. Make all entries required at June 30. Use Fund Balance as the balancing account for the Estimated Revenue and Revenue accounts. Accounts related to the current year's taxes receivable may be transferred to prior years' classification at this time.

b. Record the tax levy for the new fiscal year.

4–8. For budgetary purposes the City of Trenton reports encumbrances in the Expenditures section of its Statement of Revenues, Expenditures, and Changes in Fund Balance—Budget and Actual. Expenditures chargeable to a prior year's appropriation are excluded from the current year budgetary comparison statements. From the following information prepare:

a. Entries in general journal form to record the transactions for fiscal year 19x5 given below.

b. A Statement of Revenues, Expenditures, and Changes in Fund Balance—Budget and Actual for the General Fund of the City of Trenton for the fiscal year ending December 31, 19x5.

(1) The budget prepared for the fiscal year 19x5 was as follows:

Estimated Revenues:	
Taxes	$1,943,000
Licenses and Permits	372,000
Intergovernmental Revenue	297,000
Miscellaneous Revenues	62,000
Total Estimated Revenues	$2,674,000
Appropriations:	
General Government	$ 471,000
Public Safety	786,000
Public Works	650,000
Health and Welfare	600,000
Miscellaneous Appropriations	86,000
Total Appropriations	$2,593,000
Budgeted Increase in Fund Balance	$ 81,000

(2) Encumbrances issued against the appropriations during the year were as follows:

General Government	$ 58,000
Public Safety	201,000
Public Works	392,000
Health and Welfare	160,000
Miscellaneous Appropriations	71,000
Total	$882,000

(3) A current-year tax levy of $2,005,000 was recorded; uncollectibles were estimated as $62,000.

(4) Tax collections from prior years' levies totaled $132,000; collections of the current year's levy totaled $1,459,000.

(5) Personnel costs during the year were charged to the appropriations shown below in the amounts indicated. Encumbrances were not recorded for personnel costs.

General Government	$ 411,000
Public Safety	584,000
Public Works	254,000
Health and Welfare	439,000
Miscellaneous Appropriations	11,100
Credit to Vouchers Payable	$1,699,100

(6) Invoices for all items ordered during the prior year were received and approved for payment in the amount of $14,470. Encumbrances had been recorded in the prior year for these items in the amount of $14,000. The amount chargeable to 19x5 appropriations should be charged to the Public Safety appropriation.

(7) Invoices were received and approved for payment for items ordered in documents recorded as encumbrances in transaction 2 of this problem. The following appropriations were affected:

	Actual Liability	Estimated Liability
General Government	$ 52,700	$ 52,200
Public Safety	187,800	189,700
Public Works	360,000	357,000
Health and Safety	130,600	130,100
Miscellaneous Appropriations	71,000	71,000
	$802,100	$800,000

(8) Revenue other than taxes collected during the year consisted of: licenses and permits, $373,000; intergovernmental revenue, $299,000; and $66,000 of miscellaneous revenues.

(9) Payments on vouchers payable totaled $2,475,000.

The General Fund Fund Balance account had a credit balance of $62,700 as of December 31, 19x4; no entries other than the entry at the beginning of 19y5 to record the budgeted increase have been made in the Fund Balance account during 19x5.

4-9. The City of Warren's General Fund had the following after-closing trial balance at April 30, 19x2, the end of its fiscal year:

	Debits	Credits
Cash	$ 93,000	
Taxes Receivable—Delinquent	583,000	
Estimated Uncollectible Delinquent Taxes		$189,000
Interest and Penalties Receivable	26,280	
Estimated Uncollectible Interest and Penalties		11,160
Inventory of Supplies	16,100	
Vouchers Payable		148,500
Due to Federal Government		59,490
Reserve for Inventory of Supplies		16,100
Fund Balance		294,130
	$718,380	$718,380

During the six months ended October 31, 19x2, the first six months of fiscal year 19x3, the following transactions, in summary form, with subsidiary ledger detail omitted, occurred:

1. The budget for fiscal 19x3 provided for General Fund estimated revenues totaling $3,170,000 and appropriations totaling $3,100,000.

2. The City Council authorized a temporary loan of $300,000 in the form of a 120-day tax anticipation note. The loan was obtained from a local bank at a discount of 6 percent per annum (debit Expenditures for discount).

3. The property tax levy for fiscal 19x3 was recorded. Net assessed valuation of taxable property for the year was $43,000,000, and the tax rate was $5.00 per hundred. It was estimated that 4 percent of the levy would be uncollectible. Classify this tax levy as current.

4. Purchase orders, contracts, and so on, in the amount of $1,027,000 were issued to vendors and others.

5. $1,034,000 of current taxes, $340,000 of delinquent taxes, and interest and penalties of $13,240 were collected. Because of taxpayers' delinquencies in payment of the first installment of taxes, additional penalties of $15,230 were levied.

6. Total payroll during the first six months was $481,070. Of that amount, $36,800 was withheld for employees' FICA tax liability, $61,200 for employees' federal income tax liability, and $20,000 for state taxes; the balance was paid in cash.

7. The employer's FICA tax liability amounted to $36,800.

8. Revenues from sources other than taxes were collected in the amount of $339,000.

9. Amounts due the federal government as of April 30, and amounts due for FICA taxes and state and federal withholding taxes during the first six months of fiscal 19x3, were vouchered.

10. Purchase orders and contracts encumbered in the amount of $890,800 were filled at a net cost of $894,900, which was vouchered.

11. $1,099,060 cash was paid on vouchers payable and credit for purchases discount earned was $8,030 (credit Expenditures).

12. The tax anticipation note of $300,000 was repaid.

Required
a. Record in general journal form the effect on the General Fund of the transactions for the six months ended October 31. You need not record subsidiary ledger debits and credits.

b. Prepare a City of Warren General Fund Interim Balance Sheet as of October 31, 19x2.

4–10. This problem continues Problem 4–9. During the second six months of fiscal 19x3, the following transactions that affected the City of Warren's General Fund occurred:

1. Because of a change in a state law, the City is informed it will receive $100,000 less revenue from the state than was budgeted. Make the entry to amend the Estimated Revenues account accordingly. Do not amend the Appropriations account.

2. Purchase orders and other commitment documents in the amount of $1,032,000 were issued during the six months ended April 30, 19x3.

3. Property taxes of $6,500 and interest and penalties receivable of $1,340, which had been written off in prior years, were collected. Additional interest of $270 that had accrued since the write-off was collected at the same time.

4. Personnel costs, excluding the employer's share of the FICA tax, totaled $338,420 for the second six months. Withholdings amounted to $25,890 for FICA; $42,510 for employee's federal income tax liability, and $14,400 for state withholding tax; the balance was paid in cash.

5. The employer's FICA tax of $25,890 was recorded as a liability.

6. The County Board of Review discovered unassessed properties of a total taxable value of $500,000 located within the City boundaries. The owners of these properties were charged with taxes at the City General Fund rate of $5.00 per hundred dollars assessed value. (Do not adjust the Estimated Uncollectible Current Taxes Account.)

7. The following were collected in cash: Current taxes of $927,000; delinquent taxes of $43,270; interest and penalties of $7,330; and revenues of $593,700 from a number of sources. (No part of any of these amounts is included in any other transaction given above.)

8. Accrued interest and penalties, estimated to be 30 percent uncollectible, was recorded in the amount of $23,200.

9. All unpaid current year's taxes became delinquent. The current taxes and related estimated uncollectibles were transferred to the delinquent classification.

10. All amounts due to the federal government and state government were vouchered.

11. Invoices and bills for goods and services that had been encumbered at $1,097,240 were received in the amount of $1,092,670 and were vouchered.

12. Personal property taxes of $39,940 and interest and penalties of $4,180 were written off because of inability to locate the property owners.

13. A physical inventory of materials and supplies at April 30, 19x3, showed a total of $19,100. Inventory is recorded on the consumption method.

14. Payments made on vouchers during the second half-year totaled $1,202,600.

Required

a. Record in general journal form transactions for the second half of fiscal 19x3.

b. Record in general journal form entries to close the budgetary accounts and operating statement accounts.

c. Prepare a Balance Sheet as of April 30, 19x3, for the City of Warren General Fund.

d. Prepare a Statement of Revenues, Expenditures, and Changes in Fund Balance for the fiscal year ended April 30, 19x3, in as much detail as is possible from the data given in Problems 4–9 and 4–10.

Continuous Problems

4–L. Presented below are a number of transactions of the General Fund of the City of Bingham that occurred during the first six months of the fiscal year for which the budget given in Problem 3–L was prepared, i.e., July 1, 19x1, through December 31, 19x1. You are required to:

a. Record in the general journal the transactions given below. Make any computations to the nearest dollar. For each entry affecting budgetary accounts or operating statement accounts, show subsidiary account titles and amounts as well as general ledger control account titles and amounts.

(1) A general tax levy in the amount of $3,000,000 was made. It is estimated that 3 percent of the tax will be uncollectible.

(2) Tax anticipation notes in the amount of $250,000 were issued.

(3) Purchase orders, contracts, and other commitment documents were issued against appropriations in the following amounts:

General Government	$116,000
Public Safety	158,000
Public Works	342,000
Health	112,000
Public Welfare	125,000
Recreation	108,000
Miscellaneous Appropriations	24,000
Total	$985,000

(4) The General Fund collected the following in cash: Delinquent Taxes, $212,000; Interest and Penalties Receivable on Taxes, $10,720; Licenses and Permits, $188,000; Fines and Forfeits, $153,000; Charges for Services, $24,500; and Miscellaneous Revenues, $27,000.

(5) A petty cash fund was established for general operating purposes in the amount of $6,000.

(6) General Fund payrolls totaled $1,033,000. Of that amount, $147,450 was withheld for employees' income taxes and $79,000 was withheld for employees' FICA tax liability; the balance was paid in cash. The encumbrance system is not used for payrolls. The payrolls were for the following departments:

General Government	$ 316,233
Public Safety	467,771
Public Works	111,732
Health	22,066
Public Welfare	33,653
Recreation	81,545
Total	$1,033,000

(7) The liability for the City's share of FICA taxes, $79,000, was recorded. The amount was budgeted as part of the Contributions to Retirement Funds appropriation.

(8) Invoices for some of the services and supplies ordered in transaction (3) were received and approved for payment; departments affected are shown below:

	Actual	*Estimated*
General Government	$109,300	$109,100
Public Safety	144,375	138,500
Public Works	300,000	298,500
Health	111,700	112,000
Public Welfare	120,100	119,800
Recreation	92,125	95,000
Miscellaneous Appropriations	20,400	20,000
Totals	$898,000	$892,900

(9) Delinquent taxes receivable in the amount of $11,683 were written off as uncollectible. Interest and penalties accrued on these taxes amounting to $584 were also written off.

(10) Collections of the first installment of the current year's taxes totaled $1,530,000.

(11) Payments on General Fund vouchers amounted to $1,080,000.

(12) Collections on delinquent taxes written off in a prior year amounted to $438. Interest and penalties on the taxes written off amounted to $30. Interest accrued since the date of write-off amounted to $14 (this is Revenue of fiscal year 19x2). All interest and penalties were collected at the time delinquent taxes were collected.

(13) The General Fund vouchered its required contributions to the Employees' Retirement Fund, $56,490, its liability for employees' income taxes withheld; the total amount of FICA tax liability; and the amount due other funds on July 1. Checks were drawn for all these vouchers.

b. Post each entry to the general ledger accounts and to all subsidiary ledger accounts required. (If you used the subsidiary ledger forms illustrated in Chapter 3, the Revenues ledger debit column supports the Estimated Revenues control account in the general ledger and the credit column supports the Revenues general ledger control account. Similarly, Chapter 3 illustrates how a single account in a subsidiary ledger can support three general ledger control accounts: Appropriations, Encumbrances, and Expenditures. Note the subsidiary ledger form provides only a debit column for Expenditures, so if a general journal entry indicates a credit to Expenditures, the amount must be entered in the subsidiary ledger account as a negative item in the Expenditures debit column. Since only a credit column is provided for Appropriations, if a general journal entry indicates a debit to Appropriations, the amount must be entered as a negative item in the Appropriations credit column of the subsidiary ledger account.)

c. Prepare a trial balance of the General Fund general ledger as of December 31, 19x1, the end of the first six months of the fiscal year.

d. Prepare in good form an Interim Balance Sheet for the General Fund as of December 31, 19x1. (See Illustration 4–1.)

e. Prepare in good form a Statement of Actual and Estimated Revenues for the six months ended December 31, 19x1. (See Illustration 4–2.) Make sure the total Estimated Revenues and total Revenues shown on this statement agree with the same items shown on the December 31 Balance Sheet.

f. Prepare in good form a Statement of Budgeted and Actual Expenditures and Encumbrances for the six months ended December 31, 19x1. (See Illustration 4–3.) Make sure the total Appropriations, Expenditures, and Encumbrances shown on this statement agree with the same items shown on the December 31 Balance Sheet.

g. Below are described the transactions during January 1–June 30, 19x2, the second six months of the fiscal year. Record each in the general journal for the General Fund. For each entry affecting budgetary accounts or operating statement accounts, show subsidiary ledger account titles and amounts as well as general ledger control account titles and amounts.

(1) In view of the information shown in the Statement of Actual and Estimated

Revenues and the Statement of Budgeted and Actual Expenditures and Encumbrances, each for the first six months of the fiscal year, the City Council revised the budgets for the current year as shown below:

	Budget Adjustments Inc. (Dec.)
Estimated Revenues:	
Taxes	$ –0–
Licenses and Permits	3,000
Fines and Forfeits	4,000
Intergovernmental Revenue	(11,000)
Charges for Services	–0–
Miscellaneous Revenue	5,000
Appropriations:	
General Government	50,000
Public Safety	(12,000)
Public Works	–0–
Health	–0–
Public Welfare	14,000
Recreation	–0–
Contributions to Retirement Funds	–0–
Miscellaneous Appropriations	(6,000)

(2) Purchase orders, contracts, and other commitment documents totaling $813,000 were issued against the following appropriations:

General Government	$ 68,490
Public Safety	416,000
Public Works	120,710
Health	40,000
Public Welfare	104,800
Recreation	42,000
Miscellaneous Appropriations	21,000

(3) Invoices for services and supplies were received and approved for payment: Actual, $898,500; and Estimated, $893,000.

	Expenditure	Encumbrance
General Government	$ 77,390	$ 75,390
Public Safety	431,300	429,300
Public Works	161,810	160,310
Health	40,000	40,000
Public Welfare	110,000	110,000
Recreation	53,000	53,000
Miscellaneous Appropriations	25,000	25,000

(4) Payrolls were computed, liabilities for withholdings were recorded, and the net paid in cash, as follows: General Fund—Gross Pay, $1,157,500; Income Tax Withheld, $170,800; and FICA Tax Withheld, $88,500. Payrolls are not encumbered. The distribution was:

General Government	$301,800
Public Safety	551,700
Public Works	132,000
Health	26,000
Public Welfare	50,000
Recreation	96,000

(5) The City's liability for FICA tax, $88,500, was recorded as an expenditure of the Contributions to Retirement Funds appropriation.

(6) Collections of the second installment of the current year's taxes were $1,300,000.

(7) The General Fund collected the following revenue in cash: Licenses and Permits, $259,000; Fines and Forfeits, $185,000; Intergovernmental Revenues, $520,000; Charges for Services, $84,000; and Miscellaneous Revenues, $27,500.

(8) A taxpayer who had been classified as delinquent proved he had paid general taxes of $8,440 when due. Audit disclosed that a former employee had embezzled $8,440—through oversight of the Treasurer, the employee had not been bonded. Interest and penalties in the amount of $845 had been recorded as receivable on the $8,440 "delinquent" tax bill at the end of the prior year. Since neither the $8,440 taxes nor the $845 interest and penalties are actually receivable, the total of the two, $9,285, was by resolution of the City Council charged as an expenditure of the current year's Miscellaneous Appropriations.

The audit also disclosed that tax bills totaling $2,586 on several pieces of property had been sent to both the present and the prior owner, and no tax bills at all had been prepared for several pieces of property—general taxes of $2,250 should have been charged. (Correct all accounts affected; do not adjust the Estimated Uncollectible Taxes account.)

(9) Tax anticipation notes issued by the General Fund were paid at maturity at face amount plus interest of $5,000. (Charge Miscellaneous Appropriations for the expenditure.)

(10) Invoices for all items encumbered in the prior year were received and approved for payment in the amount of $14,180. (Charge the amount encumbered in 19x1 to Expenditures of the 19x1 Public Works Appropriation. Charge the excess of the amount approved for payment over the Reserve for Encumbrances—19x1 balance to Expenditures of the 19x2 Public Works Appropriation.)

(11) The petty cash fund was reimbursed for $4,810. (Charge General Government for the entire expenditure.)

(12) The General Fund vouchered and paid its liability for employees' income taxes withheld, the total liability for FICA taxes, and the required contribution to the Employees' Retirement Fund, $119,900.

(13) The General Fund recorded its liabilities to other funds for services received during the year, $20,000. ($15,300 should be charged to the Public Safety appropriation and $4,700 to the General Government appropriation.)

(14) The General Fund paid vouchers in the amount of $870,000.

(15) The General Fund made a long-term advance of $30,000 cash to the Stores and Services Fund.

(16) Current taxes receivable and related estimated uncollectibles were transferred to the delinquent category. Interest and penalties accrued on delinquent taxes amounted to $31,240; of this amount it is estimated that $9,360 is uncollectible.

h. Post to the general ledger and prepare a trial balance before adjustment of the accounts of the General Fund. Post to the subsidiary ledgers and make sure the totals of the subsidiary ledger columns agree with the balances of their respective control accounts.

i. Prepare and post the necessary closing entries for the General Fund.

j. Prepare in good form a Balance Sheet as of the end of the fiscal year, June 30, 19x2.

k. Prepare in good form a Statement of Revenues, Expenditures, and Changes in Fund Balance for the General Fund for the year ended June 30, 19x2. (See Illustration 4–5. Classify 19x1 expenditures as Public Works.)

l. Prepare in good form a Statement of Revenues, Expenditures, and Changes in Fund Balance—Budget and Actual for the year ended June 30, 19x2. Use the final adjusted budget figures. (See Illustration 4–6.)

4–S. Presented below are a number of transactions of the General Fund of the City of Smithville that occurred during the year for which the budget given in Problem 3–S was prepared, the calendar year 19y1.

a. Record in the general journal the transactions given below. Make all computations to the nearest dollar. For each entry affecting budgetary accounts or operating statement accounts, show subsidiary account titles and amounts as well as general ledger control titles and amounts.

(1) The real property tax levy for the year was made to yield the budgeted amount ($980,000), assuming 98 percent of the levy would be collectible.

(2) Encumbrances in the following amounts were recorded against the appropriations indicated:

General Government	$ 59,700
Public Safety—Police	52,420
Public Safety—Fire	50,980
Public Safety—Building Safety	5,760
Public Works	147,420
Health and Welfare	103,050
Parks and Recreation	78,000
Miscellaneous Appropriations	24,750
	$522,080

(3) Cash collections during the year totaled: Current Property Taxes, $750,000; Delinquent Property Taxes, $210,000; Interest and Penalties Receivable on Taxes, $35,088—of which $29,643 had been accrued as of the first of the year and $5,445 was revenue of the current year (make the entry to record this revenue); the amounts due from other funds and from the state government at the beginning of the year; Licenses and Permits, $347,500; Fines and Forfeits,

$252,000; Intergovernmental Revenue, $100,000; Charges for Services, $55,000; Miscellaneous Revenues, $19,500; and Sales Taxes, $1,136,000. (Additional sales taxes susceptible to accrual were deemed to be immaterial and were not recorded as a receivable or as revenue in 19y1.)

(4) General Fund payrolls for the year totaled $2,270,000. Of that amount, $316,300 was withheld for employees' federal income taxes; $173,700 for employees' share of FICA taxes; $60,000 for employees' state income taxes; and the balance was paid in cash. The City of Smithville does not record encumbrances for payrolls. The payrolls were chargeable against the following departmental appropriations:

General Government	$271,750
Public Safety—Police	587,520
Public Safety—Fire	563,930
Public Safety—Building Safety	46,080
Public Works	363,810
Health and Welfare	236,710
Parks and Recreation	192,000
Miscellaneous Appropriations	8,200

(5) The City's share of FICA taxes, $173,700, and the City's contribution to other retirement funds administered by the state government, $116,300, were recorded as liabilities. These items were budgeted as part of the Contributions to Retirement Funds appropriation.

(6) Invoices for some of the services and supplies recorded as encumbrances in transaction (2) were received and approved for payment as listed below. Related encumbrances were canceled in the amounts listed below:

	Expenditures	*Encumbrances*
General Government	$ 54,656	$ 55,200
Public Safety—Police	53,240	52,420
Public Safety—Fire	44,364	45,000
Public Safety—Building Safety	5,760	5,760
Public Works	113,490	113,400
Health and Welfare	105,000	103,050
Parks and Recreation	72,000	75,000
Miscellaneous Appropriations	24,700	24,750
	$473,210	$474,580

(7) Checks were drawn in payment of vouchers totaling $680,000; in payment of the tax anticipation notes and the amount due other funds as of December 31, 19y0; in payment of $5,000 interest on the notes; $653,700 of the amount due to the federal government for withholding taxes and FICA taxes; and $175,000 of the amount due to the state government for state withholding tax and contributions to the state retirement funds. Interest expense is budgeted in Miscellaneous Appropriations.

(8) The Appropriations budget was legally amended as follows:

	Decreases	Increases
General Government		$ 5,000
Public Safety—Police		16,600
Public Safety—Fire		4,500
Public Safety—Building Safety	$ 5,700	
Public Works		10,000
Health and Welfare	11,700	
Parks and Recreation	3,000	
Contributions to Retirement Funds		12,000
Miscellaneous Appropriations	1,600	
	$22,000	$48,100

(9) The City of Smithville received notification that the state government would remit $98,000 to it early in the next fiscal year; this amount had been included in the budget for the current year as "Intergovernmental Revenue."

(10) Interest and penalties receivable on delinquent taxes was increased by $15,000; $6,000 of this was estimated as uncollectible.

(11) Current taxes receivable uncollected at year-end, and the related estimated uncollectible current taxes account, were both transferred to the delinquent category.

(12) Delinquent taxes receivable in the amount of $16,247 were written off as uncollectible. Interest and penalties already recorded as receivable on these taxes, amounting to $14,302, was also written off. Additional interest on these taxes that had legally accrued was not recorded since it was deemed uncollectible in its entirety.

(13) Postaudit disclosed that $9,760, which had been recorded during the year as an encumbrance and, later, as an expenditure in the same amount, of the General Government appropriation of the General Fund should have been charged to the Water Utility Fund. An interfund invoice was prepared for $9,760 by the General Fund.

(14) Services received by the general government departments of the General Fund from other funds amounted to $9,800; the liability was recorded by the General Fund.

b. Post each entry to the general ledger accounts and to all subsidiary ledger accounts required. If you used the subsidiary ledger forms illustrated in Chapter 3, the Revenues ledger debit column supports the Estimated Revenues control account in the general ledger and the credit column supports the Revenues general ledger control account. Similarly, Chapter 3 illustrates how a single account in a subsidiary ledger can support three general ledger control accounts: Appropriations, Encumbrances, and Expenditures. Note that the subsidiary ledger form provides only debit column for Expenditures, so if a general journal entry indicates a credit to Expenditures, the amount must be entered in the subsidiary ledger account as a negative item in the Expenditures debit column. Since only a credit column is provided for Appropriations, if a general journal entry indicates a debit to Appropriations, the amount must be entered as a negative item in the Appropriations credit column of the subsidiary ledger account.

c. Prepare a trial balance of the General Fund general ledger as of December 31, 19y1, the end of the fiscal year. Make sure the totals of the subsidiary ledger columns agree with the balances of their respective control accounts.

d. Prepare and post the necessary entries to close the Estimated Revenues, Revenues, Appropriations, Expenditures, and Encumbrances accounts to Fund Balance.

e. Prepare in good form a Balance Sheet for the General Fund as of December 31, 19y1.

f. Prepare in good form a Statement of Revenues, Expenditures, and Changes in Fund Balance for the General Fund for the year ended December 31, 19y1.

g. Prepare in good form a Statement of Revenues, Expenditures, and Changes in Fund Balance—Budget and Actual for the General Fund for the year ended December 31, 19y1. Use the final adjusted budget figures.

h. Prepare in good form a reconciliation of total Expenditures reported in your solution to part *f* of this problem with the total Expenditures and Encumbrances reported in your solution to part *g* of this problem.

CHAPTER
5

Capital Projects Funds

Chapters 3 and 4 illustrate that long-lived assets such as office equipment, police cruisers, and other items may be acquired by a governmental unit by expenditure of appropriations of the General Fund or one or more of its special revenue funds. Long-lived assets used by activities accounted for by governmental fund types are called **general fixed assets.** Acquisitions of general fixed assets that require major amounts of money ordinarily cannot be financed from General Fund or special revenue fund appropriations. Major acquisitions of general fixed assets are commonly financed by issuance of long-term debt to be repaid from tax revenues, or by special assessments against property deemed to be particularly benefited by the long-lived asset.[1] Other sources of financing the acquisition of long-lived assets include grants from other governmental units, transfers from other funds, gifts from individuals or organizations, or by a combination of several of these sources. If money received from these sources is restricted, legally or morally, to the purchase or construction of specified capital assets, it is recommended that a capital projects fund be created to account for resources to be used for such projects. Capital projects funds are also used to account for the acquisition by a governmental unit of general fixed assets under a capital lease agreement.

Illustration 5–1 summarizes the information in the paragraph above. It shows that general fixed assets may be acquired from expenditures of the General Fund, special revenue funds, and capital projects funds. The cost or other carrying value of general fixed assets is accounted for in the General Fixed Assets Account Group (GFAAG), and long-term debt related to general fixed asset acquisition is accounted for in the General Long-Term Debt Account Group (GLTDAG). Debt service funds are used to account for resources to be used for payment of matured general debt principal and interest. This chapter focuses on capital projects funds

---

[1] Debt to be serviced from tax revenue or from special assessments is explained in some detail in Chapter 7. Debt backed by the "full faith and credit" of the issuing government is known as general obligation debt or, for short, G.O. debt.

ILLUSTRATION 5–1   Interrelationships among Governmental Fund Types and Account Groups—Fixed Asset Acquisition

General Fund and/or Special Revenue Funds	*Capital Projects Funds*	*Debt Service Funds*
Account for acquisition of general fixed assets from expenditures of annual appropriations. Cost of assets acquired is recorded in the GFAAG.	Account for acquisition of general fixed assets from expenditures of debt proceeds, capital grants, special assessments, and other sources restricted for fixed asset acquisition. Cost of assets acquired is recorded in the GFAAG. Long-term debt to be serviced from tax revenues, or from special assessments, is recorded in the GLTDAG.	Account for accumulation of resources for, and the payment of, matured debt principal and interest, except that being repaid from revenues of Enterprise Funds. Resources generally include taxes levied for debt service or operating transfers from other funds, accrued interest and premium on tax-supported long-term debt issued, and accrued interest and premium on special assessment long-term debt issued.

General Fixed Assets Account Group	*General Long-Term Debt Account Group*
Accounts for cost of general fixed assets acquired by expenditures of the General Fund, Special Revenue Funds, and Capital Projects Funds. Also accounts for GFA acquired under capital leases and for GFA acquired by gift.	Accounts for all unmatured long-term debt except debt being repaid from revenues of Enterprise Funds. Long-term debt includes present value of rentals under capital leases.

---

accounting and financial reporting. Chapters 3 and 4 discuss accounting and financial reporting for the General Fund and for special revenue funds. Subsequent chapters discuss accounting and financial reporting of the other fund types and the account groups shown in Illustration 5–1.

The reason for creating a fund to account for capital projects is the same as the reason for creating special revenue funds: to provide a formal mechanism to enable administrators to ensure revenues dedicated to a certain purpose are used for that purpose and no other, and to enable administrators to report to creditors, and other grantors of capital projects fund resources, that their requirements regarding the use of the resources were met.

Capital projects funds differ from general and special revenue funds in that the latter categories have a year-to-year life, whereas capital projects funds have a project-life focus. In some jurisdictions governments are allowed to account for all capital projects within a single Capital Projects Fund. In other jurisdictions laws are construed as requiring each project to be accounted for by a separate capital projects fund. Even in jurisdictions which permit the use of a single fund, managers may prefer to use separate funds in order to enhance control over each project. In such cases a fund is created when a capital project or a series of related projects is legally authorized; it is closed when the project or series is completed. Budgetary accounts need not be used because the legal authorization to engage in the project is in itself an appropriation of the total amount that may be obligated for the construction or acquisition of the capital asset specified in the project authorization. Estimated revenues need not be recorded because few contractors will start work on a project until financing is ensured through the sale of bonds or the receipt of grants or gifts. To provide control over the issuance of contracts and purchase orders, which may be numerous and which may be outstanding for several years in construction projects, it is recommended that the encumbrance procedure described in Chapter 3 be used. Since the purpose of the Capital Projects Fund is to account for the acquisition and disposition of revenues for a specific purpose, it (as is true for general and special revenue funds) contains balance sheet accounts for only financial resources and for the liabilities to be liquidated by those resources. Neither the capital assets acquired nor any long-term debt incurred for the acquisition is accounted for by a Capital Projects Fund; the General Fixed Assets Account Group and the General Long-Term Debt Account Group account for these items, as discussed in Chapter 6 and Chapter 8, respectively.

In some jurisdictions, annual revenues are raised for the expressed purpose of financing major repairs to existing capital assets, or for replacement of components of those assets (e.g., furnaces, air conditioning systems, roofs). Revenues of the nature described are accounted for by a **capital improvements fund,** sometimes called a *cumulative building fund*. The specific repairs and replacements to be undertaken in a given year are not necessarily known at the time the revenues are budgeted. The appropriation process described in previous chapters is used to authorize expenditures from capital improvement funds when the nature and approximate cost of needed repairs and replacements become known. Necessary expenditures that cannot be financed by appropriation of the Fund Balance of a capital improvement fund, nor from the General Fund or special revenue funds, may occasion the establishment of a capital projects fund.

Legal Requirements

Since a governmental unit's power to issue bonds constitutes an ever-present hazard to the welfare of its property owners in particular,[2] and its taxpayers in general, the authority is ordinarily closely regulated by legislation. The purpose of

---

[2] An issue of bonds to be repaid from tax revenues is virtually a mortgage on all taxable property within a governmental unit's jurisdiction. Responsibility for payments of principal and interest on general bonded debt provides for no consideration of a property owner's financial condition, his ability or inability to pay.

legislative regulation is to obtain a prudent balance between public welfare and the rights of individual citizens. In some jurisdictions, most bond issues must be approved by referendum; in others, by petition of a specified percentage of taxpayers. Not only must bond issues be approved according to law but other provisions, such as method and timing of payments from the proceeds, and determination of validity of claims for payment, must be complied with. A knowledge of all details related to a bond issue is prerequisite to the avoidance of difficulties and complications that might otherwise occur.

Participation of state and federal agencies in financing capital acquisitions by local government adds further complications to the process. Strict control of how such grants are used is imperative for ensuring proper use of the funds. This necessitates more or less dictation of accounting and reporting procedures to provide information necessary for proving or disproving compliance with terms of the grants. Details of the fund structure and operation should provide for producing all the required information when it is needed, in the form in which it is needed.

Accomplishment of a capital acquisition project may be brought about in one or more of the following ways:

1. Outright purchase from fund cash.
2. By construction, utilizing the governmental unit's own working force.
3. By construction, utilizing the services of private contractors.
4. By capital lease agreement.

General Outline of Capital Projects Fund Accounting

GASB standards require use of the same basis of accounting for capital projects funds as for general and special revenue funds. Proceeds of debt issues should be recognized by a capital projects fund at the time the issue is sold, rather than the time it is authorized, because authorization of an issue does not guarantee its sale. Proceeds of debt issues should be recorded as Proceeds of Bonds or Proceeds of Long-Term Notes rather than as Revenues, and they should be reported in the Other Financing Sources section of the Statement of Revenues, Expenditures, and Changes in Fund Balance. Similarly, tax revenues raised by the General Fund, or a special revenue fund, and transferred to a capital projects fund are recorded as Operating Transfers In and reported in the Other Financing Sources section of the operating statement. Taxes raised specifically for a capital projects fund would be recorded as Revenues of that fund, as would special assessments to be used for the construction of assets deemed to be of particular benefit to certain property owners. Grants, entitlements, or shared revenues received by a capital projects fund from another governmental unit are considered Revenues of the Capital Projects Fund, as would be interest earned on temporary investments of the Capital Projects Fund if the interest is available for expenditure by the Capital Projects Fund (if, by law, the interest must be used for service of long-term capital debt the interest should be transferred to the appropriate Debt Service Fund).

In the following illustration of accounting for representative transactions of a capital projects fund, it is assumed the Town Council of the Town of Brighton authorized an issue of $1,200,000 of 6 percent bonds as partial financing of a fire station expected to cost approximately $1,500,000; the $300,000 additional was to be contributed by other governments. The project, to utilize land already owned by the Town, was done partly by a private contractor and partly by the Town's own working force. Completion of the project was expected within the current year. Transactions and entries were as shown below, all of which are assumed to occur in fiscal year 19y1. For economy of time and space, vouchering of liabilities will be omitted, as will entries in subsidiary ledger accounts.

The $1,200,000 bond issue, which had received referendum approval by taxpayers, was officially approved by the town council.

> No formal entry is required by GASB standards. A memorandum entry may be made to identify the approved project and the means of financing it.

The sum of $50,000 was borrowed from the National Bank for defraying engineering and other preliminary expenses. Security for this note is the expectation that the approved bond issue can be sold.

1. Cash	50,000	
Bond Anticipation Notes Payable		50,000

The receivable from the other governments was recorded:

2. Due from Other Governmental Units	300,000	
Revenues...		300,000

Total purchase orders and other commitment documents issued for supplies, materials, items of minor equipment, and labor required for the part of the project to be performed by the Town's employees amounted to $443,000. (Since the authorization is for the **project,** not for a budget year, it is unnecessary to include "19y1," or any other year, in the account titles.)

3. Encumbrances	443,000	
Reserve for Encumbrances		443,000

A contract was let for certain work to be done by a private contractor in the amount of $1,005,000.

4. Encumbrances	1,005,000	
Reserve for Encumbrances		1,005,000

Special engineering and miscellaneous costs that had not been encumbered were paid in the amount of $48,000.

5. Construction Expenditures	48,000	
Cash		48,000

When the project was approximately half finished, the contractor submitted billing for a payment of $495,000.

| 6a. Reserve for Encumbrances | 495,000 | |
| Encumbrances | | 495,000 |

| 6b. Construction Expenditures | 495,000 | |
| Contracts Payable | | 495,000 |

(This entry records conversion of an estimated liability to a firm liability, eligible for payment upon proper authentication. Contracts Payable records the status of a claim under a contract between the time of presentation and verification for vouchering or payment.)

Payment in full was received from the other governmental units that had agreed to pay part of the cost of the new fire station.

| 7. Cash | 300,000 | |
| Due from Other Governmental Units | | 300,000 |

The National Bank Loan was repaid with interest amounting to $1,000.

8. Interest Expenditures	1,000	
Bond Anticipation Notes Payable	50,000	
Cash		51,000

The bond issue was sold at par, on June 15, 19y1, the date of the bonds.

| 9. Cash | 1,200,000 | |
| Proceeds of Bonds | | 1,200,000 |

The contractor's initial claim was fully verified and paid.

| 10. Contracts Payable | 495,000 | |
| Cash | | 495,000 |

Total disbursements for all costs encumbered in Transaction 3 amounted to $440,000.

| 11a. Reserve for Encumbrances | 443,000 | |
| Encumbrances | | 443,000 |

| 11b. Construction Expenditures | 440,000 | |
| Cash | | 440,000 |

Billing for the balance due on his contract was received from the contractor.

| 12a. Reserve for Encumbrances | 510,000 | |
| Encumbrances | | 510,000 |

| 12b. Construction Expenditures | 510,000 | |
| Contracts Payable | | 510,000 |

Inspection revcaled only minor imperfections in the contractor's performance, and on correction of these, his bill was paid.

| 13. Contracts Payable | 510,000 | |
| Cash | | 510,000 |

All requirements and obligations related to the project having been fulfilled, the operating statement accounts were closed.

14. Revenues	300,000	
Proceeds of Bonds	1,200,000	
Construction Expenditures		1,493,000
Interest Expenditures		1,000
Fund Balance		6,000

Since the project has been completed, it is appropriate to close the Capital Projects Fund. The only asset of the fund remaining after the 14 transactions illustrated is Cash in the amount of $6,000. State laws customarily require that assets no longer needed in a capital projects fund be transferred to the fund that will service the debt incurred for this project, a debt service fund. Transfers of this nature are called **Equity Transfers** and are reported in the Changes in Fund Balance section of the Statement of Revenues, Expenditures, and Changes in Fund Balance, as shown in Illustration 5–2. The entries to record the transfer and the closing of the Capital Projects Fund accounts are:

15a. Equity Transfer Out	6,000	
Cash		6,000
15b. Fund Balance	6,000	
Equity Transfer Out		6,000

The cost of the fire station constructed by the Town of Brighton is recorded in the General Fixed Assets Account Group; the necessary entry is illustrated in

ILLUSTRATION 5–2

TOWN OF BRIGHTON
Fire Station Capital Projects Fund
Statement of Revenues, Expenditures, and
Changes in Fund Balance
For the Year Ended December 31, 19y1

Revenues:		
From other governmental units		$ 300,000
Expenditures:		
Construction	$1,493,000	
Interest on short-term debt	1,000	
Total Expenditures		1,494,000
Excess of Revenues over (under) Expenditures		(1,194,000)
Other Financing Sources (Uses):		
Proceeds of bonds		1,200,000
Excess of Revenues and Other Financing Sources over Expenditures		6,000
Fund Balance, January 1, 19y1		–0–
Equity transfer out		(6,000)
Fund Balance, December 31, 19y1		$ –0–

Chapter 6. The liability for the bonds sold for the benefit of this fund is recorded in the General Long-Term Debt Account Group, as illustrated in Chapter 8.

Illustrative Financial Statements for a Capital Projects Fund

Inasmuch as all balance sheet accounts of the Town of Brighton Fire Station Capital Projects Fund are closed in the case illustrated in the preceding section of this chapter, there are no assets, liabilities, or fund equity to report in a balance sheet. The operations of the year, however, should be reported in a Statement of Revenues, Expenditures, and Changes in Fund Balance, as shown in Illustration 5–2.

Consistent with the illustrative entries for this case, it is assumed the Town of Brighton is not required to adopt a legal budget for this, or any other, capital projects fund. Accordingly, GASB standards do not require the inclusion of a Statement of Revenues, Expenditures, and Changes in Fund Balance—Budget and Actual for the capital projects fund type.

Alternative Treatment of Residual Equity or Deficits

In the example presented above, a modest amount of cash remained in the Capital Projects Fund after the project had been completed and all liabilities of the fund liquidated. If necessary expenditures and other financing uses are planned carefully, and controlled carefully so that actual does not exceed plans, revenues and other financing sources of the Capital Projects Fund should equal, or slightly exceed, the expenditures and other financing uses, leaving a residual equity. If, as in the example presented above, long-term debt had been incurred for the purposes of the Capital Projects Fund, the residual equity is ordinarily transferred to the fund that is to service the debt. If the residual equity were deemed to have come from grants or shared revenues restricted for capital acquisitions or construction, legal advice may indicate that any residual equity must be returned to the source(s) of the restricted grants or restricted shared revenues.

In some situations, in spite of careful planning and cost control, expenditures and other financing uses of a Capital Projects Fund may exceed its revenues and other financing sources, resulting in a negative Fund Balance, or deficit. If the deficit is a relatively small amount, the legislative body of the governmental unit may be able to authorize transfers from one or more other funds to cover the deficit in the Capital Projects Fund. If the deficit is relatively large, and/or if intended transfers are not feasible, the governmental unit may seek additional grants or shared revenues from other governmental units to cover the deficit. If no other alternative is available, the governmental units would need to finance the deficit by issuing debt in whatever form is legally possible and salable under market conditions then existing.

Bond Premium, Discount, and Accrued Interest on Bonds Sold

Governments that issue bonds, or long-term notes, to finance the acquisition of capital assets commonly sell the entire issue to an underwriter, or a syndicate of underwriters, on the basis of bids. The underwriters then "retail" the bonds or notes to institutions or individuals. Statutes of approximately half of the states prohibit the initial sale of an issue of local government bonds at a discount.

Accordingly, it is usual to set the interest rate high enough to enable the under-writers to pay the issuer at least the par, or face, value of the bonds; it is not unusual for underwriters to pay issuers an amount in excess of par, known as premium. State statutes, local ordinances, or bond indentures often require that premiums be used for debt service. In such cases only the par value of the bonds is considered as an Other Financing Source of the Capital Projects Fund; the premium is considered as an Other Financing Source of the Debt Service Fund. Therefore, the sale of bonds at a premium would require an entry in the Capital Projects Fund for the face of the bonds (as shown in Entry 9 of this chapter) and an entry in the Debt Service Fund for the premium. Similarly, when bonds are sold between interest payment dates the amount of accrued interest is included in the total selling price. Conceptually, accrued interest sold is an offset to the interest expenditure on the first interest payment date following the sale of the bonds. Generally, in practice, however, accrued interest sold is recorded as a Revenue of the Debt Service Fund.

It may happen that the issuing government receives one check from the under-writers for the total amount of the par plus the premium. If procedures of that government indicate that it is desirable to record the entire amount in the Capital Projects Fund, the following entry is currently considered to be appropriate (using assumed amounts):

Cash...	1,509,000	
Proceeds of Bonds		1,500,000
Due to Debt Service Fund		9,000

The entry accounts for bond premium as a liability of the Capital Projects Fund because it must be remitted to the Debt Service Fund. Some accountants use Premium on Bonds as the liability account title, rather than Due to Debt Service Fund; the accounting treatment is the same, however. (In the event that the entire proceeds of the bond sale are, in fact, available for expenditure for construction, the amount of premium should be included in the credit to Proceeds of Bonds.)

In those jurisdictions in which it is legal for bonds to be sold initially at a discount, using the amounts assumed in the entry above, the entry might be:

Cash...	1,491,000	
Discount on Bonds	9,000	
Proceeds of Bonds		1,500,000

Crediting Proceeds of Bonds for $1,500,000 carries the implication that, if neces-sary, the discount is expected to be counterbalanced at a future date by receipt of money from another source. When money from another source has been pro-vided, or it has been determined that no money from another source will be provided, the discount would be written off against Proceeds of Bonds. When it is known in advance that the discount will not be made up by transfers from other sources, a debit to Cash and a credit to Proceeds of Bonds, each for par value less discount, would suffice.

Profit-seeking entities amortize bond premium and accumulate bond discount in order to state bond interest expense at its "true" amount (as defined in generally accepted accounting principles). Capital projects funds are concerned with accounting for the receipt and expenditure of financial resource inflows designated for the construction or purchase of capital facilities; they are not concerned with income determination. Accordingly, bond premium is **not** amortized and bond discount is not accumulated by capital projects funds. Other funds and account groups affected by the bond sale and debt service are discussed in following chapters; none of these funds or groups record amortization of premium or accumulation of discount on tax-supported bonds payable or special assessment bonds payable.

Sale of bonds to finance a capital project is sometimes avoided, in whole or in part, through an agreement by the contractor to accept bonds in full or part payment for his services. This arrangement is common in some states and unused in others. It forces the financing onto the contractor. Not being a specialist in finance, his costs are likely to be above those of an expert, thus increasing the amount he must bid on the project.

Retained Percentages
It is common to require contractors on large-scale contracts to give performance bonds, providing for indemnity to the governmental unit for any failure on the contractor's part to comply with terms and specifications of the agreement. Before final inspection of a project can be completed, the contractor may have moved his working force and equipment to another location, thus making it difficult for him to remedy possible objections to his performance. Also, the short-coming alleged by the governmental unit may be of a controversial nature, with the contractor unwilling to accede to the demands of the governmental unit; and results of legal action in such disagreements are not predictable with certainty.

To provide more prompt adjustment on shortcomings not large or convincing enough to justify legal action, and not recoverable under contractor's bond, as well as those the contractor may admit but not be in a position to rectify, it is common practice to withhold a portion of the contractor's remuneration until final inspection and acceptance have come about. The withheld portion is normally a contractual percentage of the amount due on each segment of the contract.

In the Town of Brighton illustration, the contractor submitted a bill for $495,000, which, on preliminary approval, was recorded in Entry 6 as:

Construction Expenditures	495,000	
Contracts Payable		495,000

Assuming the contract provided for retention of 5 percent, current settlement on the billing would be recorded as follows:

Contracts Payable	495,000	
Cash		470,250
Contracts Payable—Retained Percentage		24,750

Alternatively, the intention of the government to retain the percentage stipulated in the contract could be recorded at the time the progress billing receives preliminary approval. In that event, the credit to Contracts Payable in the first entry in this section would be $470,250, and the credit to Contracts Payable—Retained Percentage in the amount of $24,750 is made at that time. The second entry, therefore, would be a debit to Contracts Payable and a credit to Cash for $470,250.

On final acceptance of the project, the retained percentage is liquidated by a payment of cash. In the event the governmental unit that made the retention finds it necessary to spend money on correction of deficiencies in the contractor's performance, the payment is charged to Contracts Payable—Retained Percentage.

Claims and Judgments Payable

Claims and judgments often, although not always, relate to construction activities of a government. If a claim has been litigated and a judicial decision adverse to the governmental unit has been rendered, there is no question as to the amount of the liability that should be recorded. If claims have not been litigated, or judgments have not been made, as of balance sheet date, liabilities may be estimated through a case-by-case review of all claims, or the application of historical experience to the outstanding claims, or a combination of these methods.[3]

GASB standards currently specify that the amount of claims and judgments recognized as expenditures and liabilities of governmental funds is limited to the amount that would normally be liquidated with expendable resources then in the fund; any liability for claims and judgments payable that exceeds the amount recognized in the governmental fund must be recognized in the General Long-Term Debt Account Group. (Accounting and financial reporting for the GLTDAG is illustrated in Chapter 8.)

Bond Anticipation Notes Payable and the Problem of Interest Expenditures

Bond Anticipation Notes Payable is a liability resulting from the borrowing of money for temporary financing before issuance of bonds. Delay in perfecting all details connected with issuance of bonds and postponement of the sale until a large portion of the proceeds is needed are the prevailing reasons for preliminary financing by use of bond anticipation notes. The "bond anticipation" description of the debt signifies an obligation to retire the notes from proceeds of a proposed bond issue. The account is increased and decreased for the same reasons and in the same manner employed for Tax Anticipation Notes Payable, discussed in Chapter 4.

Interest almost always must be paid on Bond Anticipation Notes Payable. Both practical and theoretical problems are involved in the payment of interest on liabilities. Practically, payment of interest by the Capital Projects Fund reduces the amount available for construction or acquisition of the assets, so the administrators of the Capital Projects Fund would wish to pass the burden of interest payment to another fund. Logically, the Debt Service Fund set up for the bond

---

[3] GASB standards (GASB Codification Sec.C50.110–.111) require governmental units to use the criteria of FASB *SFAS No. 5* as guidelines for recognizing a loss liability. That is, if information available prior to issuance of the financial statements indicates it is probable that an asset has been impaired or a liability has been incurred at the date of the financial statements and the amount of the loss can be estimated with a reasonable degree of accuracy, the liability should be recognized.

issue should bear the burden of interest on bond anticipation notes, and possibly on judgments, but at the time this interest must be paid the Debt Service Fund may have no assets. It would also appeal to the Capital Projects Fund's administrators that interest on the bond anticipation notes and judgments should be paid by the General Fund (or any other fund with available cash). If such interest payments had been included in the appropriations budget by the General Fund (or other fund), the payment would be legal; if not, the legislative body might authorize the other fund to pay the interest.

If the Capital Projects Fund bears the interest on bond anticipation notes or other short-term debt, either initially or ultimately, an expenditure account must be debited. In Entry 8 in the series of Capital Projects Fund entries illustrated earlier in this chapter, interest paid on Bond Anticipation Notes was debited to Interest Expenditures rather than to Construction Expenditures. The illustrated procedure would be used by governmental units that choose not to capitalize interest payments by capital projects funds. GASB standards allow each governmental unit to choose whether or not it wishes to capitalize net interest incurred in the construction or acquisition of **general** fixed assets as a part of the cost of the asset, as long as the policy is consistently applied and is disclosed in the notes to the financial statements.[4] If a governmental unit chooses to capitalize interest on short-term debt of the Capital Projects Fund, it is logical to debit that item to Construction Expenditures and not create a separate Interest Expenditures account.

If any governmental fund other than a capital projects fund pays interest on Bond Anticipation Notes, it is simpler for the governmental unit to choose not to capitalize the interest, otherwise the accountants will have to analyze all the funds in order to determine the amount of interest to be capitalized. Similarly, since debt service funds routinely pay interest on long-term debt incurred on capital projects, the interest on long-term debt during the period of construction presents the same problem as interest on short-term debt. GASB standards provide that interest expenditures for short-term debt or for long-term debt incurred for the construction or acquisition of general fixed assets should be offset by any interest earned by the governmental unit on investment by a capital projects fund of debt proceeds. (In some jurisdictions, any such revenue may not be used by the Capital Projects Fund but must be transferred to a Debt Service Fund.) The provisions of the relevant standards are more complex than is appropriate for discussion here. Since capitalization of net interest is optional in the case of general fixed assets, the great majority of governmental units choose the simpler option: noncapitalization.

Depreciation on general fixed assets is not recorded by state and local governments, and there is no determination of governmental net income for financial reporting or for federal income tax purposes; therefore, the inclusion or exclusion of interest as an element of asset cost is largely a matter of theoretical concern at this time.

---

[4] GASB Codification Sec. 1400.111.

Investments

Interest rates payable by governmental units on general long-term debt have been lower than interest rates the governmental units can earn on temporary investments of high quality, such as U.S. Treasury bills and notes, bank certificates of deposit, and government bonds with short maturities. Consequently, there is considerable attraction to the practice of selling bonds as soon as possible after a capital project is legally authorized, and investing the proceeds to earn a net interest income. (This practice also avoids the problems and costs involved in financing by Bond Anticipation Notes Payable, described in the preceding section.) Arbitrage rules under the Internal Revenue Code, particularly after the Tax Reform Act of 1986 became effective, however, constrain the investment of bond proceeds to securities whose yield does not exceed that of the new debt. Application of these rules to state and local governmental units is subject to continuing litigation and legislative action, so competent legal guidance must be sought by governmental units wishing to invest bond proceeds in a manner that will avoid difficulties with the Internal Revenue Service.

Interest earned on temporary investments is available for use by the Capital Projects Fund in some jurisdictions; in others, laws or local practices require the interest income to be transferred to the Debt Service Fund or to the General Fund. If interest income is available to the Capital Projects Fund, it should be recognized on the accrual basis as a credit to Revenues. If it will be collected by the Capital Projects Fund but must be transferred, the credit for the income earned should be to Due to Other Funds; if the interest will be collected by the Debt Service Fund, or other fund that will recognize it as revenue, no entry by the Capital Projects Fund is necessary.

Multiple-Period and Multiple-Project Bond Funds

Thus far, discussion of capital projects fund accounting has proceeded on the tacit assumption that initiation and completion of projects occur in the same fiscal year. Many projects large enough to require a capital projects fund are started in one year and ended in another. Furthermore, a single comprehensive authorization may legalize two or more purchase or construction projects as segments of a master plan of improvements. Both multiple-period and multiple-project activities require some deviations from the accounting activities that suffice for one-period, one-project accounting.

The first difference appears in the budgeting procedure. Whereas for a one-period operation a single authorization might adequately cover the project from beginning to end, annual budgets, in one form or another, may be desirable or even required for those extending into two or more periods. This practice is resorted to as a means of keeping the project under the legislative body's control and preventing the unacceptable deviations that might result from lump-sum approval, in advance, of a long-term project. Likewise, a large bond issue, to be supplemented by grants from outside sources, may be authorized to cover a number of projects extending over a period of time but not planned in detail before initiation of the first project. Such an arrangement requires the fund administration to maintain control by giving final approval to the budget for each project only as it comes up for action.

For a multiple-projects fund, it is necessary to identify encumbrances and expenditures in a way that will indicate the project to which each encumbrance and expenditure applies, in order to check for compliance with the project budget. This can be accomplished by adding the project name or other designation (e.g., "City Hall," or "Project No. 75") to the encumbrance and expenditure account titles. This device is almost imperative for proper identification in the recording of transactions, and it facilitates preparation of cash and expenditure statements for multiproject operations.

In accounting for encumbrances for multiperiod projects, there is some difference of opinion as to the desirable procedure to follow in relation to encumbrances outstanding at the end of a period. In the management of a General Fund, for example, operations in terms of amounts of revenues and expenditures during a specified standard period of time (quarter, half year, etc.) provide measures of accomplishment. Because capital projects are rarely of the same size and may be started and ended at any time of year, periodic comparisons are of little significance. Furthermore, although the personnel of a legislative body may change at the beginning of a year during which a capital project is in progress, the change is unlikely to affect materially the project's progress. Although the operations of a capital projects fund are project-completion oriented, with slight reference to time, GASB standards require Encumbrances, Expenditures, Proceeds of Bonds, and Revenues accounts to be closed to Fund Balance at year-end in order to facilitate preparation of capital projects fund financial statements for inclusion in the governmental unit's annual report on a basis consistent with year-end statements of other funds.

The required procedure does produce year-end capital projects fund balance sheets that appear similar to those of general and special revenue funds illustrated in preceding chapters. The similarity of appearance and terminology may be misleading, however. The Fund Balance account of a general or special revenue fund represents net financial resources available for appropriation, whereas the Fund Balance account of a multiple-period capital projects fund represents net assets already set aside for the acquisition of specified capital facilities. The Fund Balance of a multiple-period capital projects fund is comparable to the unexpended unencumbered appropriation item on an interim balance sheet of a general or special revenue fund; it is *not* comparable to the year-end Fund Balance of such funds.

Reestablishment of Encumbrances

The year-end closing procedure required by GASB standards for use by capital projects funds artificially chops the Construction Expenditures pertaining to each continuing project into fiscal-year segments, rather than allowing the total cost of each project to be accumulated in a single Construction Expenditures account. Similarly, closing the Encumbrance account of each project to Fund Balance at year-end creates some procedural problems in accounting in the subsequent year. The procedure illustrated for general and special revenue funds (using separate Encumbrances, Reserve for Encumbrances, and Expenditures accounts for each year) could be followed. The procedure illustrated for general and special revenue funds is logical in that case because each appropriation expires at year-end, and yearly Expenditure and Encumbrance accounts are needed to match with the yearly Appropriations account. The authorization (appropriation) for a capital project, however, does not expire at the end of a fiscal year but continues for the life of the project. Accordingly, it appears desirable to reestablish the Encumbrance account at the beginning of each year in order to facilitate accounting for expenditures for goods and services ordered in one year and received in a subsequent year. Reestablishment of the Encumbrance account may be accomplished as shown by the following entry (amount assumed):

Encumbrances	210,000	
Fund Balance		210,000

If the Encumbrance account is reestablished, subsequent receipt of goods or services entered as encumbrances in a prior year may be accounted for in the same manner as if they had been ordered in the current year:

Reserve for Encumbrances	210,000	
Construction Expenditures	210,000	
Vouchers Payable		210,000
Encumbrances		210,000

Capital Projects Financed by Special Assessments

In the first paragraph of this chapter it is noted that one common source of financing major acquisitions of general fixed assets is by issuance of long-term debt to be repaid by special assessments. A **special assessment** is a compulsory levy made against certain property to defray part or all of the cost of a specific improvement or service that is presumed to be of general benefit to the public and of particular benefit to the property against which the special assessment is levied. Special assessment financing is allowed under the laws of many states. Generally, a majority of owners of the property that will be assessed must agree to the formation of a special assessment district, sometimes called a *local improvement district*. A special assessment district may be an independent special purpose governmental unit created under the laws of the state in which it is located; or it may be a component unit of a county, city, or other general governmental unit; or in some cases, special assessment transactions are administered directly by a general governmental unit.

If a special assessment district is an independent special purpose governmental unit it will need to account for the construction phase of a capital project in the manner described in this chapter, the debt service phase of the project in the manner described in Chapter 7, and to account for the resulting fixed assets and related long-term debt as described in Chapters 6 and 8, respectively. The same observations apply to a special assessment district that is a component unit of a primary government, which should be reported in a discrete presentation in the general purpose financial statements of the governmental financial reporting entity, as discussed in relation to Illustration 2–1.

If the financial activities of a special assessment district are so intertwined with those of the primary government that the balances and transactions meet the criteria for blending (see discussion related to Illustration 2–1), it is logical that special assessment transactions be administered directly by the primary government. In that event the accounting and reporting standards set forth in this chapter apply to capital projects financed in whole, or in part, by special assessments, with the following modifications and additions:

The total dollar amount of a capital project to be financed by special assessments must be paid by owners of real property within the special assessment district. Accordingly, the portion of the total to be borne by each parcel of property within the district must be determined in whatever manner is specified by laws of the relevant jurisdiction. It is often true that the amount to be paid by each owner is large enough that laws will provide that the total special assessment against each parcel may be paid in equal installments over a specified period of years. Commonly, the first installment is due within a relatively short period of time (say, 60 days after the assessment is levied) and, if paid by the due date, is noninterest bearing. The remainder of the installments are due annually thereafter, and are interest bearing. Assume, for example, that the final installment is due five years after the levy of the special assessment. Contractors cannot be expected to wait five years to be paid for work done on the project; therefore, an issue of long-term debt is authorized in the amount of installments due in future years. The first installment and the proceeds of the long-term debt would be used to finance the capital project and would be accounted for by a capital projects fund. GASB standards provide that the first installment should be recognized as Revenue of the Capital Projects Fund at the time of the levy—providing, of course, for any estimated uncollectibles.

Long-term debt proceeds would be considered an Other Financing Source—Proceeds of Bonds (or Notes) of the capital projects fund if the primary government has an obligation to assume debt service in the event that collections of remaining installments are insufficient. If the primary government has *no* obligation for debt service and the creditors are payable solely from collections of the special assessment installments and interest thereon, the proceeds of special assessment long-term debt should be credited to a capital projects fund equity account such as Contribution from Property Owners, rather than as Proceeds of Bonds (or Notes).

Installments of special assessments and interest thereon, which are to be used to service long-term debt, and are not available for expenditure by a Capital Projects Fund, should be accounted for as described in Chapter 7, "Debt Service Funds." General fixed assets financed wholly or partially, through collections of special assessments are accounted for in the same manner as any other general fixed assets (see Chapter 6); special assessment long-term debt accounting is discussed in Chapter 8.

Acquisition of General Fixed Assets under Lease Agreements

FASB *SFAS No. 13* defines and establishes accounting and financial reporting standards for a number of forms of leases, only two of which, **operating** leases and **capital** leases, are of importance in governmental accounting. GASB standards accept the *SFAS No. 13* definitions of these two forms of leases and prescribe accounting and financial reporting for lease agreements of state and local governmental units.[5] If a particular lease meets any *one* of the following classification criteria, it is a *capital* lease.

1. The lease transfers ownership of the property to the lessee by the end of the lease term.
2. The lease contains an option to purchase the leased property at a bargain price.
3. The lease term is equal to or greater than 75 percent of the estimated economic life of the leased property.
4. The present value of rental or other minimum lease payments equals or exceeds 90 percent of the fair value of the leased property less any investment tax credit retained by the lessor.

If none of the criteria is met, the lease is classified as an **operating** lease by the lessee. Rental payments under an operating lease for assets used by governmental funds are recorded by the using fund as expenditures of the period. In many states, statutes prohibit governments from entering into obligations extending beyond the current budget year. Because of this legal technicality, governmental lease agreements typically contain a "fiscal funding clause," or cancellation clause, which permits governmental lessees to terminate the agreement on an annual basis if funds are not appropriated to make required payments. GASB standards specify that lease agreements containing fiscal funding or cancellation clauses should be evaluated. If the possibility of cancellation is judged remote, the lease should be disclosed in financial statements and accounts in the manner specified for **capital** leases.[6]

As an example of accounting for the acquisition of general fixed assets under a capital lease agreement, assume a governmental unit signs a capital lease agreement to pay $10,000 on January 1, 19y0, the scheduled date of delivery of certain equipment to be used by an activity accounted for by a special revenue fund. The lease calls for annual payments of $10,000 at the beginning of each year thereafter; that is, January 1, 19y1, January 1, 19y2, etc., through January 1, 19y9. There are 10 payments of $10,000 each, for a total of $100,000, but GASB standards require entry in the accounts of the **present value** of the stream of annual payments, not their total. Since the initial payment of $10,000 is paid at the inception of the lease, its present value is $10,000. The present value of the remaining nine payments must be determined from present value tables, using the rate "the lessee would have incurred to borrow over a similar term the funds necessary to purchase the

---

[5] GASB Codification Sec. L20.107.
[6] GASB Codification Sec. L20.119–122.

leased asset.''[7] Assuming the rate to be 10 percent, tables show that the present value of payments 2 through 10 is $57,590. The present value of the 10 payments is, therefore, $67,590. GASB standards require a governmental fund (ordinarily a capital projects fund) to record the following entry at the inception of the capital lease:

Expenditures	67,590	
Other Financing Sources—Capital Lease Agreements		67,590

Related entries in the General Fixed Assets Account Group, the Debt Service Fund, and the General Long-Term Debt Account Group are illustrated and discussed in Chapters 6, 7, and 8, respectively.

Combining Financial Statements for Capital Projects Funds

To give protection against unintended uses of their grants for capital improvements, it is common practice for state and federal governmental agencies to require reports of how their money is being used. Required reports may be conventional financial statements or reports in a form specified by the grantor. Some grantors require the statements or reports to be accompanied by the opinion of an independent Certified Public Accountant, or by the report of auditors employed by a state audit agency. In other instances, the statements or reports need not be accompanied by an auditor's opinion but are merely subject to audit by the grantor agency or its designated auditors.

As noted in Chapter 1, the general purpose financial statements of a state or local government reporting entity are combined statements in which the financial data for each fund type used by the primary government are shown in separate columns. If, as is usually true except for the General Fund, the governmental unit has several funds within each type, it is necessary to present a **combining** statement for each fund type. In a combining statement, the financial data for each fund within that type are shown in columnar form. The data displayed in the Total column of the **combining** statement should be identical with the data shown in the column for that fund type in the **combined** statement. If the combining statement does not present sufficient information to make the statements not misleading, financial statements for individual funds within the fund type must be included in the government's comprehensive annual financial report. Illustration 5–3 shows the Combining Balance Sheet for all capital project funds of a certain city in Texas. Illustration 5–4 presents the accompanying Combining Statement of Revenues, Expenditures, and Changes in Fund Balances. In this case, disclosure is deemed sufficient, so individual fund statements are not presented. It should be noted that although the statements are year-end statements in terms of the fiscal year of the city, they are interim statements in terms of the life of the capital project.

---

[7] Financial Accounting Standards Board, *Statement of Financial Accounting Standards No. 13,* "Accounting for Leases, as Amended and Interpreted through January 1990" (Norwalk, Conn., 1990), L10.510.

ILLUSTRATION 5–3

SOUTHWESTERN CITY, TEXAS
All Capital Projects Funds
Combining Balance Sheet
As of September 30, 19x6
With Comparative Totals for September 30, 19x5
(in thousands of dollars)

	Parks	Streets and Drainage	Buildings	Neighborhood Projects	Totals 9/30/x6	9/30/x5
Assets						
Cash and certificates of deposit	$9,499	$34,482	$14,526	$9,411	$67,918	$63,526
Due from other funds	—	—	243	—	243	300
Notes receivable—current	—	1,350	—	35	1,385	—
Total Assets	$9,499	$35,832	$14,769	$9,446	$69,546	$63,826
Liabilities and Fund Balances						
Current Liabilities:						
Accounts payable	$ 203	$ 767	$ 264	$ 127	$ 1,361	$ 1,600
Due to other funds	14	62	454	—	530	380
Total Current Liabilities	217	829	718	127	1,891	1,980
Fund Balances:						
Encumbered	3,362	14,641	3,319	2,338	23,660	20,440
Not encumbered	5,920	20,362	10,732	6,981	43,995	41,406
Total Fund Balances	9,282	35,003	14,051	9,319	67,655	61,846
Total Liabilities and Fund Balances	$9,499	$35,832	$14,769	$9,446	$69,546	$63,826

The statements illustrated present adequate detail for published reports. For internal management purposes, and for external review of project management, additional information is needed as to whether the work accomplished to statement date is commensurate with expenditures to date and whether the remaining work can be accomplished with the available assets and resources.

Selected References

Financial Accounting Standards Board. *Statement of Financial Accounting Standards No. 5*, "Accounting for Contingencies." Norwalk, Conn., 1975.

———. *Statement of Financial Accounting Standards No. 13*, "Accounting for Leases, as Amended and Interpreted through January 1990." Norwalk, Conn., 1990.

Governmental Accounting Standards Board. *Codification of Governmental Accounting and Financial Reporting Standards as of June 30, 1993*. Norwalk, Conn., 1993.

ILLUSTRATION 5–4

SOUTHWESTERN CITY, TEXAS
All Capital Projects Funds
Combining Statement of Revenues, Expenditures, and Changes in Fund Balances
For the Year Ended September 30, 19x6
With Comparative Totals for the Year Ended September 30, 19x5
(in thousands of dollars)

	Parks	Streets and Drainage	Buildings	Neighbor-hood Projects	Flood Control	Totals 9/30/x6	Totals 9/30/x5
Revenues:							
Federal grants	$ —	$ 300	$ —	$ —	$ —	$ 300	$ 2,000
Interest earned	581	1,834	788	538	—	3,741	2,390
Other	19	1,312	54	11	—	1,396	400
Total Revenues	600	3,446	842	549	—	5,437	4,790
Expenditures:							
Capital outlays	4,437	17,068	4,150	635	45	26,335	20,510
Excess of Revenues over (under) Expenditures	(3,837)	(13,622)	(3,308)	(86)	(45)	(20,898)	(15,720)
Other Financing Sources (Uses):							
Proceeds of bonds	3,600	17,610	4,490	800	—	26,500	8,000
Operating transfers in	—	—	243	—		243	500
Total Other Financing Sources	3,600	17,610	4,733	800	—	26,743	8,500
Excess of Revenue and Other Sources over (under) Expenditures and Other Uses	(237)	3,988	1,425	714	(45)	5,845	(7,220)
Fund Balances, October 1	9,519	31,015	12,626	8,605	81	61,846	69,066
Residual Equity Transfer to Debt Service Fund	—	—	—	—	(36)	(36)	—
Fund Balances, September 30	$9,282	$35,003	$14,051	$9,319	$ —	$67,655	$61,846

Questions

5–1. Under what conditions should a state or local governmental unit utilize the capital projects fund type? If a unit does utilize the capital projects fund type, should it create a separate capital projects fund for each project? Why or why not?

5–2. How does an outlay for a capital *project* differ from a capital *outlay* of a general or special revenue fund? Give an example of a capital project and an example of a capital outlay.

5–3. How does a *capital projects* fund differ from *general* and *special revenue* funds?

5–4. How does a *capital projects* fund differ from a *capital improvements* fund?

5–5. Why is encumbrance accounting recommended for capital projects funds even though it is not considered necessary to record Estimated Revenues or Appropriations?

5–6. How should the residual equity or deficit existing at the completion of a capital project be treated?

5–7. If bonds sold to finance a project for the construction of general fixed assets are sold at a premium, what legal question arises? Discuss the accounting treatment appropriate to two of the common answers to the legal question.

5–8. Should interest expenditures during the period of construction be capitalized as a part of the cost of general fixed assets? Explain your answer.

5–9. If bond proceeds are not needed immediately to finance construction expenditures, what restrictions are imposed by the Internal Revenue Code on the governmental unit's earnings on temporary investments?

5–10. If a capital project is incomplete at the end of a fiscal year, why is it considered desirable to close Encumbrances and all operating statement accounts at year-end? If these accounts are closed, why is it desirable to reestablish the Encumbrances account as of the first day of the following year?

5–11. If a capital project is financed partially by use of special assessments, should the capital projects fund recognize revenue from the assessments at the time of the levy or at the time that the assessments are collected? Explain your answer.

5–12. If a capital projects fund receives the proceeds of a long-term debt issue that is backed primarily by collections of special assessments, but which is also backed by a primary government in the event that collections of special assessments are insufficient to pay debt service on time, what account should be credited for the debt proceeds, and how should that account be reported in the capital projects fund Statement of Revenues, Expenditures, and Changes in Fund Balance?

5–13. "If general fixed assets are acquired under a capital lease agreement, no entry at all needs to be made in any governmental fund at the inception of the lease." Do you agree or disagree? Explain.

5–14. If one capital projects fund is used to account for multiple capital projects, how can adequate control and accountability for individual projects be maintained?

5–15. "If all the capital projects funds of a governmental reporting entity have no assets, no liabilities, and no Fund Equity at balance sheet date, no columns need be provided for the Capital Projects Fund type in any of the general purpose financial statements." Explain why you agree, or disagree, with this statement.

Exercises and Problems

5–1. Utilizing the CAFR obtained for Exercise 1–1, follow the instructions below:

   a. Title and Content. What title is given the funds that function as capital projects funds, as described in Chapter 5? (Bond Funds and Capital Improvement Funds are common titles.)

   Does the report state the basis of accounting used for capital projects funds? If so, is the financial statement presentation consistent with the stated basis? (That is, the report may state that the modified accrual basis was used, but no receivables are shown, or there is a "Reserve for Receivables," or the report refers to "disbursements" rather than "expenditures.")

   If the basis of accounting is not stated, analyze the statements to determine which basis is used—full accrual, modified accrual, or cash basis. Is the same basis used for both revenues and expenditures? Is the basis used consistent with GASB standards discussed in Chapter 5? Are there separate capital projects funds for each project; or are there several funds, each of which accounts for related projects; or is only one fund used for all projects?

b. *Statements and Schedules.* What statements and schedules pertaining to capital projects funds are presented? In what respects (headings, arrangement, items included, etc.) do they seem similar to statements illustrated or described in the text? In what respects do they differ? Are any differences merely a matter of terminology or arrangement, or do they represent significant deviations from GASB accounting and reporting standards for capital projects funds?

c. *Financial Resource Inflows.* Describe the nature of the financial resource inflows utilized by the capital projects funds. If tax-supported bonds, or special assessment bonds, are a source, have any been sold at a premium? At a discount? If so, what was the accounting treatment of the bond premium or discount?

d. *Fund Expenditures.* How much detail is given concerning capital projects fund expenditures? Is the detail sufficient to meet the information needs of administrators? Legislators? Creditors? Grantors? Interested residents? For projects that are incomplete at the date of the financial statement, does the report compare the percentage of total authorization for each project expended to date with the percentage of completion? For those projects completed during the fiscal year does the report compare the total expenditures for each project with the authorization for each project? For each cost overrun, how was the overrun financed?

e. *Assets Acquired under Capital Leases.* Were any general fixed assets acquired by the primary government or one or more component units under a capital lease agreement during the year for which you have statements? If so, was the present value of minimum lease rentals recorded as an Expenditure and as an Other Financing Source in a capital projects fund (or in any other governmental fund)? If the primary government or one or more component units leased assets from another component unit, how are the assets, related liabilities, expenditures, and other financing sources reported in the general purpose financial statements, or in another section of the CAFR of the reporting entity?

5–2. Write the numbers 1 through 10 on a sheet of paper. Beside each number write the letter corresponding with the best answer to each of the following questions.

1. A capital projects fund of a municipality is an example of what type of fund?
   a. Internal Service (Intragovernmental Service).
   b. Proprietary.
   c. Fiduciary.
   d. Governmental.

Items 2 and 3 are based on the following:

On December 31, 19x7, Vane City paid a contractor $3,000,000 for the total cost of a new municipal annex built in 19x7 on city-owned land. Financing was provided by a $2,000,000 general obligation bond issue sold at face amount on December 31, 19x7, with the remaining $1,000,000 transferred from the General Fund.

2. What account and amount should be reported in Vane's 19x7 financial statements for the General Fund?
   a. Other Financing Uses control, $1,000,000.
   b. Other Financing Sources control, $2,000,000.
   c. Expenditures control, $3,000,000.
   d. Other Financing Sources control, $3,000,000.

3. What accounts and amounts should be reported in Vane's 19x7 financial statements for the Capital Projects Fund?
    a. Other Financing Sources control, $2,000,000; General Long-Term-Debt, $2,000,000.
    b. Revenues control, $2,000,000; Construction Expenditures control, $2,000,000.
    c. Other Financing Sources control, $3,000,000; Construction Expenditures control, $3,000,000.
    d. Revenues control, $3,000,000; Construction Expenditures control, $3,000,000.

4. In what fund type should the proceeds from special assessment bonds issued to finance construction of sidewalks in a new subdivision be reported? Assume that the city agreed to pay debt service if collections of assessments are insufficient.
    a. Agency Fund.
    b. Special Revenue Fund.
    c. Enterprise Fund.
    d. Capital Projects Fund.

5. In 19x6, Menton City received $5,000,000 of bond proceeds to be used for capital projects. Of this amount, $1,000,000 was expended in 19x6. Expenditures for the $4,000,000 balance were expected to be incurred in 19x7. These bond proceeds should be recorded in capital projects funds for.
    a. $5,000,000 in 19x6.
    b. $5,000,000 in 19x7.
    c. $1,000,000 in 19x6 and $4,000,000 in 19x7.
    d. $1,000,000 in 19x6 and in the general fund for $4,000,000 in 19x6.

6. When Calumet City realized $2,020,000 from the sale of a $2,000,000 bond issue, the entry in its Capital Projects Fund was:

Cash	2,020,000	
Proceeds of Bonds		2,000,000
Premium on Bonds		20,000

Recording the transaction in this manner indicates that:
    a. A safety factor is being set to cover possible contract defaults on the construction.
    b. The nominal rate of interest on the bonds is below the market rate for bonds of such term and risk.
    c. The full $2,020,000 can be used by the Capital Projects Fund to accomplish its purpose.
    d. The $20,000 cannot be used for the designated purpose of the fund but must be transferred to another fund.

7. If general fixed assets are acquired by a governmental unit under a lease agreement, it is appropriate to record in a Capital Projects Fund as an Expenditure and as an Other Financing Source:
    a. The lesser of the present value of the rental and other minimum lease payments, or the fair value of the leased property, if the lease agreement meets all of the criteria for capital leases set forth in FASB's *SFAS No. 13*.
    b. The amount recorded at the inception of a capital lease agreement as a liability in the General Long-Term Debt Account Group.
    c. The amount of lease rentals or other minimum lease payments due during the year under operating lease agreements.

    d. The amount of lease rentals or other minimum lease payments paid during the year under capital lease agreements.

8. As of the first day of a fiscal year it is normally desirable to enter in a Capital Projects Fund account:
   a. The amounts of bonds expected to be sold during the year.
   b. The reestablishment of Encumbrances closed to Fund Balance as of the end of the preceding year.
   c. The amount of grants expected to be received during the year.
   d. Both *a* and *c*.

9. On July 1, 19x6, Randal City borrowed $500,000 as temporary financing for construction of a new city office building until bonds could be issued for the project. On October 1, 19x6, Randal City repaid the short-term notes for temporary financing, including interest of $10,000 which was paid from resources of the Capital Projects Fund. The journal entry to record repayment of the note and interest should include debits to:
   a. Construction Expenditures and Interest Expenditures.
   b. Bond Anticipation Notes Payable and Construction Expenditures.
   c. Bond Anticipation Notes Payable and Interest Expenditures.
   d. Either *b* or *c*, depending on whether the interest is to be capitalized.

10. Final inspection of a construction site revealed minor discrepancies which were corrected by employees of the Town of Quincy. An adequate amount had been retained from contractor billings to cover this contingency. The costs of correcting these discrepancies should be recorded in the Capital Projects Fund as a debit to:
   a. General Fixed Assets.
   b. Reserve for Encumbrances.
   c. Construction Expenditures.
   d. Contracts Payable—Retained Percentage.

(Items 1 through 6, AICPA, adapted)

5–3. The proceeds of the sale of special assessment bonds issued to finance the acquisition of capital facilities amounted to $8,120,000. The face amount of the bond issue was $8,000,000; $40,000 of the proceeds represented interest accrued on the bonds to date of sale.

    a. Assuming both the premium on bonds sold and the interest accrued on the bonds to date of sale must be recorded directly in a Debt Service Fund, show in general journal form the entry made by the Capital Projects Fund for the receipt of the $8,000,000 face amount.

    b. If several months are expected to elapse between receipt of bond proceeds and payment for the capital assets being acquired, what action should be taken by the governmental finance officer?

    c. What are the accounting and financial implications of the course of action you recommended in part *b*?

5–4. The post-closing trial balance of the City of Dudley's Capital Projects Fund, as of December 31, 19x2, listed Fund Balance in the amount of $1,500,000.

The project had been authorized early in 19x2 in the total amount of $4,000,000, to be financed $800,000 by the federal government, $200,000 by the state government, and the remainder by a bond issue. Most of the work was to be done by various private contractors.

Cash from the state grant was received in full during 19x2. The entire bond issue was sold at par early in 19x2. The federal government is expected to pay its grant in full before March 1, 19x3. Cash not disbursed during 19x2 was invested on December 31, 19x2.

  a. Assuming GASB standards discussed in Chapter 5 were followed:
- (1) How much Revenue was recognized by the Capital Projects Fund in 19x2? How much should this fund report as Other Financing Sources for 19x2?
- (2) How much did 19x2 expenditures total?
- (3) What was the balance of the Investments account on December 31, 19x2, assuming all 19x2 expenditures were paid in cash?

  b. During 19x3, the following events occurred:
- (1) Expenditures of the fund totaled $1,350,000 on construction contracts.
- (2) Interest on temporary investments totaled $16,000.

Prepare a Statement of Revenues, Expenditures, and Changes in Fund Balance for the City of Dudley's Capital Projects Fund for the year ended December 31, 19x3.

5–5. The following information pertains to Eden Township's construction and financing of a new administration center:

Estimated total cost of project	$9,000,000
Project financing:	
State grant	3,000,000
General obligation bonds:	
Face amount	6,000,000
Stated interest rate	6%
Issue date	December 1, 19x0
Maturity date	December 1, 20a0

During Eden's year ended June 30, 19x1, the following events occurred that affect the Capital Projects Fund established to account for this project:

July 1, 19x0—The Capital Projects Fund borrowed $300,000 from the General Fund for preliminary engineering and planning costs.

July 9, 19x0—Engineering and planning costs of $200,000, for which no encumbrance had been recorded, were paid to Napp Associates.

December 1, 19x0—The bonds were sold at 101. Total proceeds were retained by the Capital Projects Fund. (The premium is available for expenditure for the project.)

December 1, 19x0—The grant was formally approved by the state. The grant was to be used only for financing construction of the new administration center.

April 30, 19x1—A $7,000,000 contract was executed with Caro Construction Corp., the general contractors, for the major portion of the project. The contract provides that Eden will withhold 4 percent of all billings pending satisfactory completion of the project.

May 9, 19x1—$1,000,000 of the state grant was received.

June 10, 19x1—The $300,000 borrowed from the General Fund was repaid.

June 30, 1991—Progress billing of $1,200,000 was received from Caro.

Eden uses encumbrance accounting for budgetary control.

Required

  a. Prepare journal entries in the Administration Center Capital Projects Fund to record the foregoing transactions.

b. Prepare the June 30, 19x1, closing entries for the Administration Center Capital Projects Fund.

c. Prepare the Administration Center Capital Projects Fund balance sheet at June 30, 19x1.

(AICPA, adapted)

5–6. During fiscal year 19x8, the voters of the City of Ashland approved the construction and equipping of a recreation center to be financed by tax-supported bonds in the amount of $5,000,000. During 19x8, the following events and transactions occurred:

1. Preliminary planning and engineering expenses were incurred in the amount of $125,000. No money was immediately available for paying these costs (credit Vouchers Payable).

2. Supplies to be used by the city's own working force in connection with the project were ordered in the amount of $50,000.

3. A contract was let under competitive bids for a major segment of the construction project in the amount of $4,000,000.

4. All the supplies referred to in item 2 were received at a net cost of $50,500. This amount was approved for payment.

5. An interfund invoice (not encumbered) was received from the Street Fund for work done on the project in the amount of $60,000. The invoice was approved for payment.

6. An invoice for $2,100,000 was received from a contractor for a portion of work that had been completed under the general contract.

7. The bond issue was sold at par plus accrued interest (the accrued interest was deposited in the fund which will service the bonded debt).

8. The amount due the Street Fund was paid.

9. The contractor's bill, less a 5 percent retention, was vouchered for payment.

10. All vouchers payable, except $1,300 (about which there was some controversy), were paid.

11. Cash in the amount of $2,500,000 was invested in short-term marketable securities.

12. Fiscal year-end closing entries were prepared.

Required

a. Prepare journal entries to record the above information in the general ledger accounts of the Recreation Construction Fund (you may omit subsidiary ledger accounts.)

b. Prepare a City of Ashland Recreation Center Construction Fund Balance Sheet for the year ended December 31, 19x8.

c. Prepare a Recreation Center Construction Fund Statement of Revenues, Expenditures, and Changes in Fund Balance for the year ended December 31, 19x8.

5–7. In 19x5, Wye City began the work of improving certain streets, to be financed by a bond issue supplemented by a federal grant. Estimated total cost of the project was $3,000,000; $2,500,000 was to come from the bond issue, and the balance from a federal grant. The Capital Projects Fund to account for the project was designated as the Street Improvement Fund.

The following transactions occurred in 19x5:

1. Issued $80,000 of 6 percent bond anticipation notes maturing in 180 days.

2. The federal grant was recorded as receivable; half of the grant is to be paid to Wye City in 19x5, and the remainder late in 19x6.

3. A contract was let to Rogers Construction Company for the major part of the project on a bid of $2,700,000.

4. An invoice received from the City's Stores and Services Fund for supplies provided to the Street Improvement Fund in the amount of $40,000 was approved for payment. (This amount had not been encumbered.)

5. Preliminary planning and engineering costs of $59,000 were paid to the Midwest Engineering Company. There had been no encumbrance for this cost.

6. A voucher payable was recorded for a $14,500 billing from the local telephone company for the cost of moving some of its underground properties necessitated by the street project.

7. An invoice in the amount of $1,000,000 was received from Rogers for progress to date on the project. The invoice was consistent with the terms of the contract and a liability was recorded in the amount of $1,000,000.

8. Cash received during 19x5 was as follows:

From federal government	250,000
From sale of bonds at par	2,500,000

9. Repaid bond anticipation notes and interest thereon (see Transaction 1). Interest is an expenditure of the Capital Projects Fund and is not intended to be capitalized as part of the cost of street improvements.

10. The amount billed by the contractor (see Transaction 7), less 5 percent retainage was paid.

11. Temporary investments were purchased at a cost of $1,700,000.

12. Closing entries were prepared as of December 31, 19x5.

Required

a. Prepare journal entries to record the above information in the general ledger accounts of the Street Improvement Fund.

b. Prepare a Balance Sheet as of December 31, 19x5.

c. Prepare a Statement of Revenues, Expenditures, and Changes in Fund Balance for the period, assuming the date of authorization was July 1, 19x5.

5–8. This problem presents the transactions of the Wye City Street Improvement Fund (see Problem 5–7) for 19x6:

1. Encumbrances in effect on December 31, 19x5, were reestablished on January 1, 19x6.

2. The City Board of Works decided on further street improvements and, after necessary legal actions, awarded the addition to the original contractor at $500,000. Additional bonds were authorized in that amount.

3. An additional billing submitted by the contractor in the amount of $1,700,000 was recorded as a liability.

4. Investments were disposed of for cash totaling $1,732,000, which included $32,000 accrued interest sold (all of which is revenue of the Street Improvement Fund).

5. Bonds authorized this year were sold at 102, but the premium was paid directly to the Street Improvement Debt Service Fund.

6. The contractor's second billing, less 5 percent retention, was paid.

7. The contractor reported the project completed, including the work authorized in 19x6, subject to final inspection and approval by the supervising engineers, and submitted his invoice for the balance of the contract. The final invoice was recorded as a liability.

8. The balance due from the federal government was received.

9. The amount due on the contractor's last billing, less 5 percent retained, was paid.

10. The vouchers payable and the amount due to the Stores and Services Fund was paid.

11. On final inspection, a defect was discovered and reported to the contractor. Having moved his working force and equipment to another job, he authorized correction of the defect at a cost not to exceed $50,000. The correction was made at a cost of $49,700, which was paid from the project Cash account.

12. The balance due to the contractor was paid.

13. All operating statement accounts were closed.

14. The balance of cash was transferred to the Street Improvement Debt Service Fund (debit Equity Transfer Out, then close that account to Fund Balance) on December 31, 19x6.

Required

a. Prepare journal entries to record the above information in the general ledger accounts of the Street Improvement Fund.

b. Prepare a Statement of Revenues, Expenditures, and Changes in Fund Balance for inclusion in the City's Financial Report for the year ended December 31, 19x6.

c. What is the total cost of the street improvement projects for which data are given in Problems 5–7 and 5–8? Show computations. Is this amount reported in any of the financial statements prepared for Problems 5–7 or 5–8? Explain why or why not.

d. Compare the total cost computed in requirement *c* with estimated cost of the projects (the estimated cost was the basis for bond issues and grant applications). If Transaction 14 had not been given above, explain what alternative disposition might have been made of the cash remaining in the fund after all liabilities had been paid.

5–9. The City Council of the City of Berryville approved a $5,000,000 issue of 6 percent bonds to help finance a general improvement program estimated to cost a total of $6,000,000. Action of the Council was approved by vote of property owners in the city. Based on estimated cost of projects included in the improvement program, the City Council formally allocated $1,250,000 to an office building and the remainder to an addition to the jail. A federal grant of $1,000,000, to be used for the jail addition, was applied for.

For control purposes, Encumbrances, Reserve for Encumbrances, Interest Expenditures, and Construction Expenditures are to be identified as to whether they relate to the office building or to the jail project, by use of the following account titles:

Encumbrances—Jail Addition
Reserve for Encumbrances—Jail Addition
Construction Expenditures—Jail Addition
Encumbrances—Office Building
Reserve for Encumbrances—Office Building
Construction Expenditures—Office Building
Interest Expenditures—Office Building

The following transactions occurred during the year ended December 31, 19x7:

1. An advance of $50,000 cash was received from the General Fund for preliminary expenditures related to the office building project.

2. $8,000 was paid, without prior encumbrance, for preliminary expenditures related to the office building project.

3. Half of the bonds were sold for 102 plus accrued interest from January 1 to April 30, date of the sale; money from premium and accrued interest was recorded directly in the Debt Service Fund for these bonds.

4. The advance from the General Fund was repaid with interest amounting to $2,500.

5. Materials for work to be done on the office building by the City's work force were ordered in the amount of $100,000.

6. A contract was let for a major portion of the office building construction at a total price of $1,000,000.

7. All materials ordered for the office building were received at a total cost of $101,200 (credit Vouchers Payable).

8. Prior to completion of the office building, changes in plans and specifications were requested by the City. By agreement of the two parties involved, the changes were incorporated in the contract at an additional cost of $80,000.

9. Payrolls for work done by the City's work force on the office building totaled $54,100 (do not voucher) and were paid, as were the invoices for materials, previously vouchered.

10. The remainder of the bonds were sold on August 31, they yielded 101 and accrued interest from July 1; premium and accrued interest were recorded directly in the Debt Service Fund.

11. An invoice was received from the construction company for the amount of the office building contract as revised.

12. The amount of the grant from the federal government was recorded as a receivable upon notice that the grant was approved in the amount applied for.

13. The face amount of the second bond sale was invested in marketable securities.

14. The claim of the office building contractor was paid less a retained percentage amounting to $54,000.

15. Land needed for the jail addition was acquired at a cost of $600,000, paid in cash. This amount had not been encumbered.

16. A contract was let for construction of a jail addition at an estimated cost of $4,000,000.

17. $500,000 of the amount due from the federal government was received; it is expected that the remainder of the grant will be received in January 19x8.

18. The office building project having been found acceptable, the balance due the contractor was paid.

19. Various general construction expenses incurred on the jail addition were paid at a cost of $77,600. These amounts had not been encumbered.

20. An invoice based upon 25 percent of the jail construction contract was received; the liability was recorded.

Required   The period ended at this stage of the project, and you are required to do the following things:

a. Record the foregoing transactions in general journal form in the general ledger accounts of the General Improvement Fund.

b. Prepare a pre-closing trial balance as of December 31, 19x7.

c. Prepare in general journal form an entry to close operating statement and budgetary accounts.

d. Prepare a Statement of Revenues, Expenditures, and Changes in Fund Balances for the year ended December 31, 19x7, showing columns for the Office Building, the Jail Addition, and the Total.

5–10. The case described here illustrates how political factors can be as important as, or even more important than, economic factors in planning and financing major capital projects. Often the political dimension clouds the issues and makes it difficult for even knowledgeable citizens to determine the best course of action. After reading the case, you will be asked to "cast your vote" on the proposed financing plan and explain why you voted as you did. Although the names of the governments described in the case are fictitious, the case is adapted from an actual case that has come to the authors' attention. Similar jurisdictional tax disputes are not uncommon.

Background.   Brown County is a rural county with a well-diversified economy, mainly institutional (educational and medical), commercial and light manufacturing, and agricultural. The county has a population of about 125,000, which for the last decade has been growing at nearly 5 percent a year. The County's largest city and the County Seat is Brownville, with a population of about 75,000. The County is governed by three elected commissioners and most key County functions are managed by elected officials. The City has a Council-Manager form of government under which the Chief Executive Officer, the City Manager, is appointed by and serves at the pleasure of the City Council. The governments are "overlapping" in the sense that taxpayers who reside in Brownville pay property and sales taxes to both the City and County. However, except for the court system, the County mainly provides services for persons who live outside incorporated cities and towns. Historically, relationships between the County and City governments have been strained, with each government being suspicious of the motives of the other. As a result, regional planning has generally suffered and agreements, when they have occurred, have related to narrow issues or projects rather than long-range plans.

Situation and Facts.   To cope with rapid population growth, the County has developed a five-year plan which includes paving and upgrading 55 miles of heavily traveled roads at a cost of $7,000,000; upgrading about 150 miles of substandard roads using "chip-and-seal overlay," $2,000,000; eliminating 10 "safety hazard areas," $210,000; and acquiring right of way, $500,000; for a total estimated cost of $9,710,000 over five years. Financing for the plan would come from the following sources:

Half-cent sales tax	$5,400,000
Increase in property tax of 5 cents per $100 of assessed valuation	400,000
Gasoline taxes	500,000
Motor vehicle sales tax	200,000
Annual Revenues	$6,500,000

The gasoline taxes and motor vehicle sales taxes are already being collected and distributed to localities by the state government. The property tax increase requires no special approval since the Road and Bridge property taxes are currently below the limit imposed by state statutes. The half-cent sales tax, however, requires approval by a simple majority of registered voters in the County, including those who reside in Brownville and other incorporated cities and towns. Accordingly, a special election has been called to schedule a vote on the proposed sales tax.

Even a casual look at the financing plan shows that $6,500,000 × 5 years will produce at least $32,500,000 in revenues (excluding probably investment earnings) whereas the required capital outlay will be only $9,710,000 over the five years. The remainder is intended to provide for expanded operations of the County Road and Bridge Department.

In the weeks before the special election, the Brownville City Council and Finance Director have strongly opposed the proposed sales tax on the grounds that it is unfair to expect taxpayers in the cities and towns to pay for road improvements that mainly benefit rural county residents. They argue that special assessment debt financing should be used, with the debt to be repaid by residents receiving the benefit. They further complain that the County's planning process was flawed and that joint planning with the City is needed to coordinate the five-year plan of both governments. City officials are also concerned that the County's proposed sales tax increase would eliminate the City's ability to raise sales taxes during the next five years if a need should arise. To mute some of the opposition, the County has amended the original plan and proposes to cut in half the Road and Bridge property taxes paid by taxpayers in the cities and towns. The property tax rollback would reduce revenues from $32,500,000 to about $27 million over the next five years. However, since property in that state is assessed at different levels for different classes of property (32 percent of market value for commercial and manufacturing property, 19 percent for residential property, and 12 percent for agricultural property), only the larger (mainly commercial and manufacturing) property owners stand to gain if the proposed sales tax increase is approved. For most taxpayers the sales tax increase will still be greater than the property tax decrease. Thus, while some large property owners might now support the sales tax, the majority of Brownville voters view the proposed rollback as regressive and only worsening the inequity for most property owners in the cities and towns.

Advocates for the sales tax argue that the cities and towns will benefit from improved transportation throughout the county. Further, nearly a quarter of the people who work in Brownville live in the unincorporated subdivisions surrounding the City. Advocates also point out that Brownville is a regional shopping center that draws shoppers from a 50-mile radius. Thus, one attractive feature of the proposed sales tax is that it would be borne, in part, by people who neither live nor work in the County.

Required After weeks of heavy media coverage, both for and against the proposed sales tax, voters have become extremely interested in this issue but thoroughly confused. Election day has finally arrived and turnout is expected to be heavy. Imagine yourself as a voter in the City of Brownville and answer the following questions.

a. Would you vote "yes" for the proposed half-cent sales tax or "no" in opposition? Explain the rationale for your vote, being sure to analyze factors pertinent to your voting decision.

b. Would your vote have changed under different assumed scenarios (e.g., if you were a large commercial or manufacturing property owner versus a residential or agricultural property owner, or renter)?

    c. Do you think special assessment financing would be more appropriate than general sales taxes for the proposed projects? Explain.

    d. Are there any significant accounting issues related to the financing alternatives? Explain.

Continuous Problems

5–L. The voters of the City of Bingham approved the issuance of 8 percent tax-supported bonds in the face amount of $3,000,000 for the construction and equipping of an annex to the City Hall. The bonds are to mature in blocks of $150,000 each year over a 20-year period commencing July 1, 19x2.

Required

a. Open a general journal for the City Hall Annex Construction Fund. Record the transactions below, as necessary. Use account titles listed under requirement *b.*

    (1) On the first day of the fiscal year (July 1, 19x1), the bond issue was sold at 101. Cash in the face amount of the bonds, $3,000,000, was deposited in the City Hall Annex Construction Fund; the premium was deposited in the Debt Service Fund, as required by state law.

    (2) The City Hall Annex Construction Fund purchased land needed for the site for the annex for $165,000; this amount was paid.

    (3) Legal and other costs of the bond issue were paid in the amount of $40,000.

    (4) Architects were engaged at a fee of 6 percent of the bid of the contractors. It is estimated that the architect's fee will be $150,000.

    (5) Preliminary plans were received, and the architects were paid $20,000.

    (6) The detailed plans and specifications were received, and a liability in the amount of $100,000 to the architects was recorded.

    (7) Advertisements soliciting bids on the construction were run at a cost of $450. This amount was paid.

    (8) Construction bids were opened and analyzed. A bid of $2,400,000 was accepted, and the contract let.

    (9) The contractor requested a partial payment of $1,400,000. This amount was vouchered for payment.

    (10) Vouchers payable to the contractor and to the architects were paid.

    (11) Furniture and equipment for the annex were ordered at an estimated total cost of $247,000.

    (12) The contractor completed the construction and requested payment of the balance due on the contract. After inspection of the work, the amount was vouchered and paid.

    (13) Furniture and equipment were received at a total actual installed cost of $248,560. Invoices were approved for payment.

    (14) The remainder of the architect's fee was approved for payment.

    (15) The City Hall Annex Construction Fund paid all outstanding liabilities on June 30, 19x2.

b. Open a general ledger for the City Hall Annex Construction Fund. Use the account titles shown below. Allow five lines unless otherwise indicated. Post the entries to the City Hall Annex Construction Fund general ledger.

        Cash—12 lines

        Proceeds of Bonds

Vouchers Payable—12 lines

Construction Expenditures—15 lines

Encumbrances—18 lines

Reserve for Encumbrances—18 lines

Equity Transfers Out

Fund Balance

c. Prepare a City Hall Annex Construction Fund trial balance as of June 30, 19x2.

d. The City Hall Annex Construction Fund was closed. Remaining assets were transferred to the Debt Service Fund. Record the proper journal entries in the City Hall Annex Construction Fund and post to its general ledger. All transactions and events were as of June 30, 19x2.

e. Prepare a Statement of Revenues, Expenditures, and Changes in Fund Balance for the year ended June 30, 19x2.

5–S. Early in 19y1, the voters of the City of Smithville authorized tax-supported bond issues totaling $6,400,000 as partial financing for a series of projects to construct or reconstruct streets, curbs, sidewalks, bridges, culverts, and storm sewers in various parts of the City. The estimated total cost of the series of projects was $7,000,000. In addition to the proceeds of the bonds, special assessments totaling $600,000 were levied against property owners deemed to be particularly benefited by one of the projects, designated the "Springer Street Project." All special assessments were due December 1, 19y1, without interest. Any special assessments unpaid on December 1 were subject to a 10 percent penalty, plus interest at the rate of 1 percent per month until paid.

Required

a. Open a general journal for the Street Improvement Fund. Record the transactions below, as necessary. Use account titles listed under requirement b.

(1) Plans and specifications for the first project, to be known as "Springer Street Project," were prepared by a consulting engineer's office. The engineer sent the Street Improvement Fund an invoice for $18,000; the Street Improvement Fund recorded the liability as "Vouchers Payable."

(2) Special assessments in the amount of $600,000 were recorded as receivable; revenue in that amount was recognized.

(3) Advertisements soliciting bids for the first project were published at a cost of $200; this amount was vouchered.

(4) Bonds in the amount of $1,000,000 were sold at $1,037,500, $17,500 of which was interest accrued from the date of the bonds to date of sale. Cash in the amount of the premium and accrued interest was deposited in the Street Improvement Bond Debt Service Fund. Cash in the amount of $1,000,000 was deposited in the Street Improvement Fund; $500,000 of the bond proceeds was invested in 90-day, 6 percent certificates of deposit.

(5) Construction bids were opened and analyzed. A bid of $1,200,000 was accepted, and the contract let. The contract called for a 5 percent retention from each progress payment, and from the final payment, until final inspection and acceptance by the consulting engineers.

(6) The contractor requested a progress payment of $400,000. This amount was paid, less the agreed 5 percent retention.

(7) The total amount of Vouchers Payable was paid.

(8) Two property owners along Springer Street claimed the new sidewalk was not where they had given easements. A resurvey proved the sidewalk was laid erroneously, but the City did not feel the property owners were entitled to damages. The property owners brought suit and were awarded a total of $10,000, which was recorded as a liability. The amount will be borne by the Street Improvement Fund; it will not be recoverable from the contractor.

(9) Plans and specifications for the second street improvement project, to be known as the "Alzmann Street Project," were prepared by the consulting engineer's office. The engineer's invoice in the amount of $16,500 was vouchered.

(10) Advertisements soliciting bids for the Alzmann Street Project were published at a cost of $225. The amount was paid by the Street Improvement Fund.

(11) The contractor for the Springer Street Project requested a progress payment of $600,000. This amount was recorded as a liability.

(12) Construction bids for the Alzmann Street Project were opened and analyzed. A bid in the amount of $980,000 was accepted, and the contract, bearing a 5 percent retention clause, was let.

(13) The certificates of deposit matured; the face amount plus interest was collected. The interest is considered revenue of the Street Improvement Fund.

(14) The amount due the contractor, less the agreed retainage (see Transactions 5, 6, and 11), was paid, as were outstanding vouchers. The judgments, including interest of $500, were paid. The interest is to be borne by the Street Improvement Fund and is not to be capitalized.

(15) Special assessments in the amount of $600,000 were collected before December 1, 19y1. The amount was invested in U.S. Treasury notes at par; no interest was accrued on the notes at date of purchase.

(16) $3,000 interest was accrued on Treasury notes at year-end. The accrual and all year-end closing entries were recorded.

b. Open a general ledger for the Street Improvement Fund. Use the account titles shown below. Allow 12 lines for Cash and 6 lines for each other account. Post the entries made in requirement *a* to the general ledger.

Cash

Investments

Special Assessments Receivable—Current

Interest Receivable on Investments

Contracts Payable

Contracts Payable—Retained Percentage

Judgments Payable

Vouchers Payable

Encumbrances—Springer Street Project

Encumbrances—Alzmann Street Project

Reserve for Encumbrances—Springer Street Project

Reserve for Encumbrances—Alzmann Street Project

Construction Expenditures—Springer Street Project

Interest Expenditures—Springer Street Project
Construction Expenditures—Alzmann Street Project
Proceeds of Bonds
Revenues
Fund Balance

c. Prepare a Balance Sheet for the Street Improvement Fund as of December 31, 19y1.
d. Prepare a Statement of Revenues, Expenditures, and Changes in Fund Balance for the year ended December 31, 19y1.

CHAPTER 6

General Fixed Assets Account Group

Only enterprise and internal service funds routinely account for property, plant, and equipment used in their operations. Trust funds that use fixed assets for the production of income also account for property, plant, and equipment. All other funds account only for financial resources. Thus, property, plant, ∴ equipment acquired by general, special revenue, and capital projects funds are brought under accounting control by the creation of a General Fixed Assets Account Group (GFAAG).[1]

Accounting control of fixed tangible assets is generally deemed superior to that provided by a record system not formally integrated with the accounting information system. Records of individual assets of significant value or groups of assets of lesser unit value should include all information needed for planning an effective maintenance program, preparing budget requests for replacements and additions, providing an adequate insurance coverage, and fixing the responsibility for custody of the assets.

In conformity with generally accepted accounting principles, general fixed assets are recorded at acquisition cost (or fair value at time of receipt if assets are received by donation). If the cost of fixed assets was not recorded when the assets were acquired and is unknown when accounting control over the assets is established, it is acceptable to record them at estimated cost. The General Fixed Assets Account Group is only an accounting entity, not a fiscal entity (therefore, not a fund). It records no current assets and no liabilities of any kind. The offset to the fixed asset accounts is the set of equity accounts that indicate the sources from

---

[1] Accounting and financial reporting for capital assets is under study by the GASB at the present time. Some consideration is being given to a number of possible changes in current GASB standards relating to general fixed assets. If standards discussed in this chapter are changed, the publisher will distribute to faculty members who have adopted this text a bulletin describing the effect of the new standards on the explanations and illustrations in this chapter, and in any other chapters affected.

which the fixed assets were acquired. "Investment in General Fixed Assets from Capital Projects Funds—General Obligation Bonds" or "Investment in General Fixed Assets from General Fund Revenues" are examples of typical equity accounts of a General Fixed Assets Account Group. Balance sheets of this account group (sometimes called Statements of General Fixed Assets) display to interested parties the total cost of each category of general fixed assets and the total amount contributed by each source used for the acquisition of these assets. Customarily, a balance sheet is supplemented by a schedule showing the description of and dollar amount of additions to and deductions from each fixed asset category during the year.

The cost of fixed assets used by funds that are expected to cover their full costs by sale of products or services would be depreciated, just as is done by profit-seeking businesses. **General** fixed assets are acquired for the production of general governmental services, however, not for the production of services that are sold. Therefore, the GASB Depreciation of Fixed Assets Principle states that:

> Depreciation of general fixed assets should not be recorded in the accounts of governmental funds. Depreciation of general fixed assets may be recorded in cost accounting systems or calculated for cost finding analyses; and accumulated depreciation may be recorded in the General Fixed Assets Account Group.[2]

The provision for the computation of depreciation for unit cost purposes is in recognition of the fact that general fixed assets may be used for activities financed by grants from other governmental units, and that depreciation may be an allowable cost under the terms of the grant. In addition, unit costs stated on an accrual basis, including depreciation on general fixed assets, is considered by some to be useful information to provide administrators and legislators concerned with the allocation of resources to programs, departments, and activities. To a limited extent, a comparison of the accumulated depreciation on an asset with the cost of the asset may be relevant to the process of budgeting of outlays for replacement of capital assets. For these reasons, the GASB sees no objection to recording accumulated depreciation in the General Fixed Assets Account Group and reporting it in the Statement of General Fixed Assets.[3] Since depreciation expense cannot be recorded in the General Fixed Assets Account Group, credits to Accumulated Depreciation accounts must be offset by debits to those Investment in General Fixed Assets accounts that were credited when the depreciating asset was first recorded in the GFAAG.

General fixed assets may be thought of as those not used exclusively in the operations of any one fund nor belonging to any one fund. They include courthouses and city halls, public buildings in general, the land on which they are situated, highways, streets, sidewalks, equipment, and other tangible assets with a life longer than one fiscal year that are not used by an enterprise, nonexpendable trust, or internal service fund. Formerly, general fixed assets and general fixed

---

[2] GASB Codification Sec. 1100.107.
[3] GASB Codification Sec. 1400.118.

ILLUSTRATION 6–1

CITY OF SMALLVILLE
Statement of General Fixed Assets—By Source
June 30, 19x8

General Fixed Assets:

Land	$2,455,033
Buildings	3,549,352
Improvements other than buildings	939,068
Equipment	2,355,114
Total General Fixed Assets	$9,298,567

Investment in General Fixed Assets from:
Capital projects funds:

Tax-supported bonds	$1,553,611
Federal grants	942,504
State grants	26,441
General fund revenues	6,679,409
Special revenue fund revenues	96,602
Total Investment in General Fixed Assets	$9,298,567

---

liabilities were sometimes merged in a group under the heading of "Capital Fund" or "General Property Fund," but this practice is not currently recommended. A Statement of General Fixed Assets might appear as shown in Illustration 6–1.

General Fixed Assets

The asset accounts shown in Illustration 6–1 are those commonly found in Statements of General Fixed Assets. Additional or substitute accounts may be used as needed to present information relating to general fixed assets of a given governmental unit. As in accounting for businesses, cost is the generally accepted basis of accounting for governmental fixed assets. Determination of what constitutes cost of a governmental fixed asset follows the criteria specified in intermediate financial accounting texts for the determination of cost of fixed assets of a profit-seeking entity, except governments are not required to capitalize net interest cost during the period of construction of general fixed assets, but may do so if they wish. Similarly, the kinds of items reported in each fixed asset account are the same whether the reporting entity is a governmental body or a profit-seeking entity. Also, as is true in profit-seeking entities, the test of materiality is applied and items costing below an established minimum amount are not recorded in the asset accounts no matter how long their estimated useful lives, but are merely accounted for as expenditures of the acquiring fund. The following paragraphs are presented as a brief review of generally accepted principles of accounting for fixed assets.

Land

The cost of land acquired by a governmental unit through purchase should include not only the contract price but also such other related costs as taxes and other liens assumed, title search costs, legal fees, surveying, filling, grading, drainage, and other costs of preparation for the use intended. Governments are frequently subject to damage suits in connection with land acquisition, and the amounts of judgments levied are considered capital costs of the property acquired. Land acquired through forfeiture should be capitalized at the total amount of all taxes, liens, and other claims surrendered, plus all other costs incidental to acquiring ownership and perfecting title. Land acquired through donation should be recorded on the basis of appraised value at the date of acquisition; the cost of the appraisal itself should not be capitalized, however. Valuation of land obtained by donation is of importance chiefly for report, statistical, and other comparative purposes.

Buildings and
Improvements Other
than Buildings

The nature of assets to be classified as Buildings is a matter of common knowledge; but if a definition is needed, they may be said to consist of those structures erected above ground for the purpose of sheltering persons or property. "Improvements Other than Buildings" consists of land attachments of a permanent nature, other than buildings, and includes, among other things, roads, bridges, tunnels, walks, walls, and parking lots.

The determination of the cost of buildings and improvements acquired by purchase is relatively simple, although some peripheral costs may be of doubtful classification. The price paid for the assets constitutes most of the cost of purchased items; but legal and other costs, plus expenditures necessary to put the property into acceptable condition for its intended use, are proper additions. The same generalizations may be applied to acquisitions by construction under contract; that is, purchase or contract price, plus positively identified incidentals, should be capitalized. The determination of the cost of buildings and improvements obtained through construction by some agency of the governmental unit (sometimes called **force account** construction) poses slightly more difficulty. In these cases, costs should include not only all the direct and indirect expenditures (including net interest during the period of construction on debt incurred for the purpose of financing construction of fixed assets of proprietary funds—and of general fixed assets if the government chooses to capitalize interest on construction of GFA) of the fund providing the construction but also materials and services furnished by other funds as well. The valuation of buildings and improvements acquired by donation should be established by appraisal. As in the case of land, one reason for setting a value on donated buildings and improvements is to aid in determining the total value of fixed property used by the government, and for reports and comparisons. However, more compelling reasons exist for setting a value on buildings and certain improvements: the need for obtaining proper insurance coverage and the need for being able to substantiate the insurance claim if loss should occur.

Current GASB standards allow governmental units the option of not capitalizing the cost of infrastructure assets such as roads, bridges, curbs and gutters, streets, sidewalks, drainage systems, and lighting systems because such assets are immovable, and generally of value only to the governmental unit. If improvements are omitted from financial statements, the annual report should contain statistical data relative to them that would be of interest to residents, creditors, and other readers of the annual report. It is probable that GASB standards will be changed in the future to require the capitalization of the cost of infrastructure assets.

Equipment, or Machinery and Equipment

Machinery and equipment are most likely acquired by purchase, although construction financed by an internal service fund may be the source in some instances, in which case the same rules will apply as for buildings and improvements constructed by the governmental employees. The cost of machinery and equipment purchased should include items conventional under business accounting practice: purchase price, transportation costs if not included in purchase price, installation cost, and other direct costs of readying for use. Cash discounts on governmental fixed assets purchased should be treated as a reduction of costs. Donated equipment should be accounted for in the same manner, and for the same reasons, as donated buildings and improvements.

Construction Work in Progress

Construction Work in Progress, as an account classification of an enterprise fund, is discussed in Chapter 10. As a fixed asset classification in the General Fixed Assets Account Group, it is needed to account for construction expenditures accumulated to balance sheet date on projects financed by capital projects funds. As described in the appropriate chapters, construction expenditures by capital projects funds are ordinarily closed to Fund Balance at the end of each year, but the amounts are not capitalized in the funds doing the construction: The amounts are set up under the caption of Construction Work in Progress in the General Fixed Assets Account Group.

Assets Acquired under Capital Lease Agreements

As explained in some detail in Chapter 8, state and local governmental units generally are subject to constitutional or statutory limits on the amount of long-term debt they may issue. Consequently, it has been customary for governmental units that have reached their legal debt limit, or nearly done so, to acquire the use of capital assets through a lease agreement. In Chapter 5, under the heading "Acquisition of General Fixed Assets under Lease Agreements," a brief example is given of the computation of the amount to be recorded in a capital projects fund under the provisions of GASB standards if a general fixed asset is acquired under a capital lease. In a governmental fund, usually a capital projects fund, an entry is made to record an expenditure offset by a credit to Other Financing Sources, in the amount of the present value at the inception of the lease of the stream of lease payments.[4] That amount (or the fair value of the leased property, if less)

---

[4] Intermediate accounting texts generally discuss at length the computation of amounts to be capitalized under capital lease agreements. Appendix 2 of this text presents present value tables and a brief discussion of their use.

is recorded in the GFAAG as the cost of the leased property. Continuing the example introduced in Chapter 5, the appropriate entry in the GFAAG is:

Equipment 67,590
     Investment in General Fixed Assets—Capital Leases   67,590

Source Accounts or "Investment in General Fixed Assets"

Since the General Fixed Assets Account Group is only a self-balancing set of accounts, not a fiscal entity, the self-balancing feature is achieved by the creation of a series of credit-balance accounts to record the sources from which general fixed assets were acquired. The Investment in General Fixed Assets accounts shown in Illustration 6–1 are examples. If the accounts illustrated do not adequately describe the source of certain general fixed assets of a given governmental reporting entity, other appropriately named accounts should be used.

Cost after Acquisition

Governmental accounting procedures should include clear-cut provisions for classifying cost incurred in connection with fixed assets after the acquisition cost has been established. Outlays closely associated with fixed assets will regularly occur in amounts of varying size, and responsible persons will be charged with deciding whether these should be recorded as additions to assets.

In general, any outlay that definitely adds to a fixed asset or enhances the value of an integral part of it may be classified as a capital item. Thus, drainage of land, addition of a room to a building, and changes in equipment that increase its output or reduce its cost of operation are clearly recognizable as additions to assets. Special difficulty arises in the case of large-scale outlays that are partly replacements and partly additions or betterments. An example would be replacement of a composition-type roof with a roof of some more durable material. To the extent that the project replaces the old roof, outlays should not be capitalized unless cost of the old roof is removed from the accounts; and to the extent that the project provides a better roof, outlays should be capitalized. The distribution of the total cost in such a case is largely a matter for managerial determination. Consistent with policy in recording original acquisition costs, some outlays unquestionably representing increases in permanent values may not be capitalized if the amount is less than some specified minimum or on the basis of any other criterion previously decided on.

Outlays that are partly replacements and partly additions or betterments occasion some accounting difficulty. The distribution of the outlay having been decided on, the estimated amount of addition or betterment might be added to the asset. Perhaps better results might be obtained by crediting the appropriate asset account for the cost of the replaced part, thus removing the amount, and then debiting the asset account for the total cost of the replacing item.

Reduction of Cost

Reductions in the cost of fixed assets may relate to the elimination of the total amount expended for a given item or items, or they may consist only of removing the cost applicable to a specific part. Thus, if an entire building is demolished, the total cost of the structure should be removed from the appropriate accounts; but if the separation applies only to a wing or some other definitely identifiable portion, the cost eliminated should be the amount estimated as applying thereto. Reductions in the recorded cost of fixed assets may be brought about by sale, retirement from use, destruction by fire or other casualty, replacement of a major part, theft, or loss from some other cause, and possibly other changes. The cost of fixed assets held by a fund or the General Fixed Assets Account Group may sometimes be reduced by the transfer of a unit to another fund or to the General Fixed Assets Account Group.

Accounting for cost reductions consisting of entire units is a relatively simple matter if adequate records have been kept. Entries must be made in both controlling accounts and subsidiary ledger records to show the fact of the reduction. If a separate subsidiary ledger record is kept for the unit in question, that record should be removed from the ledger and stored in a file with other similar inactive records. If the reduction is only partial, the cost as shown by the subsidiary record must be modified to reflect the change, with a complete description of what brought about the change.

Since, under GASB standards, depreciation of general fixed assets does not have to be formally recorded in the general ledger, the removal may be accomplished by crediting the ledger account recording its cost and debiting the source account(s) that were credited when the asset was acquired. If a government follows the option allowed by GASB standards and records accumulated depreciation of general fixed assets, the Accumulated Depreciation account must also be debited to remove the amount related to the asset disposed of.

Governments sometimes trade fixed assets for new items. In the general fixed assets accounts, the total cost of the old item should be removed and the total cost (not merely the cash payment) of the new one set up.

Illustrative Entries

Acquisition of general fixed assets requires a debit to the appropriate General Fixed Assets general ledger asset account and a credit to an equity account indicating the source from which the asset was provided. Thus, if office equipment is purchased for the treasurer's office from General Fund resources, the **General Fixed Assets Account Group** entry should be as follows:

Equipment	450	
Investment in General Fixed Assets—General Fund Revenues ..		450

Although purchased for the immediate use of one department, the equipment belongs to the general government and could, if desired, be transferred to other use. On the **General Fund** books, the foregoing transaction would appear as an appropriation expenditure, which would be recorded as follows, passing over reversal of the encumbrance.

Expenditures	450	
Vouchers Payable		450

General fixed assets acquired by use of Capital Projects Fund resources would be recorded in the same manner as if acquired from the General Fund, the difference in entries being that the credits should show not only that the Investment in General Fixed Assets came from a Capital Projects Fund but also, to the extent practicable, the specific sources of Capital Projects Fund resources (tax-supported bonds, federal grants, state grants, private gifts, etc.). For example, the set of 15 illustrative entries in Chapter 5 shows that the Town of Brighton utilized a Capital Projects Fund to account for the construction of a fire station on land already owned by the Town. Total construction expenditures amounted to $1,493,000; the project was financed by a $1,200,000 bond issue and $300,000 contributed by other governmental units. In addition to the construction expenditures, the Capital Projects Fund expended $1,000 for interest on short-term financing and transferred the remaining $6,000 to a Debt Service Fund. Assuming the cost of the land on which the fire station was constructed is already recorded in the accounts of the General Fixed Assets Account Group, and assuming interest expenditures are not to be capitalized, the required entry in the GFAAG to record the cost of the new fire station is (interest expenditures and the residual equity transfer are both assumed to have come from bond proceeds):

Buildings	1,493,000	
Investment in General Fixed Assets—Capital Projects Funds		
—General Obligation Bonds		1,193,000
—Contributions by Other Governmental Units		300,000

If construction of a general fixed asset is in progress at the end of a fiscal year, Chapter 5 stresses that the Construction Expenditures and Encumbrances accounts of the Capital Projects Fund are closed at year-end so that financial data for that fund may be included in the comprehensive annual financial report and general purpose financial statements of the governmental unit. For disclosure to be complete, construction expenditures to the date of the financial report should be capitalized in the General Fixed Assets Account Group. Assuming construction expenditures of $250,000 (financed by a federal grant) had been made on a building project during a given year, the information would be recorded in the General Fixed Assets Account Group by the following entry:

Construction Work in Progress	250,000	
Investment in General Fixed Assets—Capital Projects		
Fund—Federal Grant		250,000

Following through from the foregoing entry, assume the completion of construction in the next year entailed additional expenditures of $275,000 (also provided by a federal grant), which would have been accounted for by the Capital Projects Fund in the normal manner. The additional expenditure would be recorded in the General Fixed Assets Account Group as part of the cost of the completed project; and the previously suspended cost would be converted from its temporary account to the permanent one, as illustrated in the following entry:

Buildings	525,000	
Construction Work in Progress		250,000
Investment in General Fixed Assets—Capital Projects		
Fund—Federal Grant		275,000

The net effect of the two entries is, of course: Buildings, $525,000; Investment in General Fixed Assets—Capital Projects Fund—Federal Grant, $525,000.

A question arises if fixed assets constructed or acquired by a proprietary fund are later transferred to an activity accounted for by a governmental fund: If the asset is of depreciable nature, at what figure should it be recorded in the accounts of the General Fixed Assets Account Group—book value as shown by the transferor, original cost, or fair value at date of transfer? The answer at present seems to be book value. In the event fair value differs greatly from book value, a minority of authorities recommend that fair value should be used. Assuming a building carried on the books of a proprietary fund at $200,000 cost less accumulated depreciation of $150,000 is permanently surrendered to the general government, the following entry would be made in the **General Fixed Assets Account Group:**

Buildings	50,000	
Investment in General Fixed Assets—Electric Utility Fund		50,000

The proprietary fund's accounting treatment of this transaction would be as shown below:

Accumulated Provision for Depreciation of Utility Plant	150,000	
Loss on Disposal of Buildings	50,000	
Utility Plant in Service		200,000

Disposal of general fixed assets involves no accounting problem if no cash or other extraneous assets are involved in the liquidation. The requirement is elimination of the fixed asset and reduction of the equity account that records its source. Assuming a building that cost $100,000, provided by a capital projects fund, is retired without revenue or expenditure to the governmental unit, the following entry in the **General Fixed Assets Account Group** would suffice:

Investment in General Fixed Assets—Capital		
Projects Fund—Federal Grant	100,000	
Buildings		100,000

The subsidiary record or account for the building should receive appropriate notations about the transaction and thereafter be transferred to an inactive file.

In the event cash is disbursed or received in connection with the disposal of general fixed assets, that fact would have no bearing on the entry to be made in the GFAAG. Cash disbursements in connection with the removal of an item from the GFAAG should appear among the transactions of the disbursing fund and be classified according to the nature of the charge. Assuming the General Fund pays

$3,000 for the demolition of the building, an entry in the following form should be made on the **General Fund** books:

Expenditures	3,000	
Vouchers Payable (or Cash)		3,000

If cash is received from the disposal of a general fixed asset, some question may arise as to its disposition. Theoretically, it should be directed to the fund that provided the asset; but this may not always be practicable. If the asset was provided by a capital projects fund, the contributing fund may have been liquidated before the sale occurs. Unless prescribed by law, disposition of the results of sale will be handled as decided by the legislative body having jurisdiction over the asset and will be accounted for in the manner required by the accounting system of the recipient fund. Commonly, proceeds of sales of general fixed assets are budgeted as Miscellaneous Revenue by the General Fund. In such cases, when sales actually occur, the General Fund debits Cash (or a receivable) for the selling price and credits Revenues and the appropriate revenues ledger subsidiary account.

Detailed Property Accounts

Governmental organizations should keep both general and subsidiary records for fixed assets owned. General records consist primarily of general ledger accounts operated for control over groups of subsidiary records. Subsidiary records consist of the detailed records kept for individual items of fixed assets.

One or more of a number of purposes are served by the use of adequate fixed property records. The most important of these purposes are as follows:

1. As suggested elsewhere, fixed property records, properly kept, furnish information about the investment that taxpayers and others in the past have made for the benefit of future citizens and other users of government property, in contrast with expenditures for current purposes.
2. They provide a basis for adequate insurance coverage on insurable fixed assets. Although cost is not the major determinant of insurable value, it would be given consideration.
3. Properly kept records, providing for information on care and maintenance, assist in the budgeting of such costs and perhaps in singling out items on which current expenditures are abnormally high or possibly some that require minimum outlays for upkeep and maintenance.
4. They assist in fixing accountability for the custody of individual items and in determining who is responsible for seeing that care and maintenance requirements receive the attention to which they are entitled.
5. Since capital budgets are best developed on a long-term basis, reliable information about fixed assets now owned should be of material assistance in approximating future requirements.

6. Complete fixed assets records are indispensable for proprietary funds as a basis for computing depreciation. For utility funds, they are absolutely essential in establishing the base that should be used in fixing charges for service or in judging the reasonableness of rate schedules already in effect.

The main classifications of fixed assets are shown in Illustration 6–1 and discussed in related paragraphs. The names of these classifications may be used as general ledger account titles; or, more specific account titles may be used, with a code to designate the general classifications to which the account belongs.

Subsidiary ledger accounts for fixed assets may be kept in the form indicated by the data processing system in use. Whatever the form of the subsidiary record, it should provide for showing, among other things, a complete description of the asset, including the formal title and the serial number or other objective information for positive identification of the asset; complete data on increases and decreases in cost, including amounts, dates, and sources from which posted; and provision for memorandum entries related to depreciation, repairs, and maintenance. (See Illustrations 6–2 and 6–3.)

Classification of Subsidiary Accounts

Subsidiary fixed asset accounts should be maintained in a manner that facilitates shifting items from one group to another. This is important because accountability and responsibility for general fixed assets may be indicated by a significant grouping of the accounts. Thus ledger accounts for all property in the custody of a given department may be grouped together in the ledger. Within the departmental group, individual records will be organized according to the standard groups of Land, Buildings, Improvements Other than Buildings, and Machinery and Equipment (or Equipment), or other general ledger titles. If subdivisions are recognized under the main classes, such as different subclasses of Machinery and Equipment (or Equipment), subsidiary accounts may be so grouped.

In order to ensure accurate records of accountability and responsibility for property, standard forms should be utilized for recording transfers. Such forms should provide a complete description of the property transferred; the names of the transferor and the transferee; financial data, including cost and accumulated depreciation (for assets used by proprietary funds); and blanks for the necessary authentication of the transfer. The transfer document should be prepared in at least three copies: one for the accounting office, one for the transferor department, and one for the transferee. The accounting department copy provides the basis for taking a subsidiary account from the section for one department and putting it in the section for the other department, thus effecting a change in the record of responsibility. The transferor's copy is his receipt to show that the department should no longer be charged. The transferee's copy serves as the fixed asset record. If desired, the transfer form may be used to record abandonment,

ILLUSTRATION 6–2

TOWN OF DENTON

EQUIPMENT LEDGER*

Property Code No. E 413

Description Tractor
Manufacturer J.I. Case & Co.
Manufacturer's Serial No. 3796465   **Model** 4 NB
Date of Purchase June 20, 19x5   **Reference** V.R., 19x5, p. 34
Cost Total $ 67,460   **Fund** General
Invoice Price $ Same   **Freight $** None
Installation $ None   **Other $** 400, painting
Estimated Life (Years) 8   **Estimated Salvage Value $** 2500.00
Location City Garage

DISPOSAL

Disposal Approved by _____   **Reference** _____
Reason _____   **Date** _____
How Disposed of (Sold, Scrapped, etc.) _____
Age at Date of Disposal _____   **Amount Realized** _____

Date	Reference	Additions, Betterments, Major Repairs	Amount

* If used for a depreciable asset of a proprietary fund, this form should be modified to provide for entering periodic depreciation thereof and for adjustments of recorded depreciation, if any need to be made.

retirement, or other permanent reduction in fixed assets; or, if preferred, a special form may be devised for this purpose.

Inventories of Fixed Assets

All fixed property should be inventoried periodically. This checks against losses not previously revealed and brings to light errors in records of accountability; that is, having one department charged with an item that is actually in the custody of another. Furthermore, a systematic physical inventory of fixed assets gives an opportunity for surveying their physical condition, with respect to their need for

ILLUSTRATION 6–3

TOWN OF DENTON

LAND LEDGER

Property Code No. __L-34__

Location of Property __309 W. Third__

Legal Description __Huntington's Addition__

Dimensions __60' x 200'__   **Area** __12,000 sq. ft.__

How Acquired __Donation__   **Fund** __None__

Date Acquired __Aug. 6, 19x4__   **Reference** __Journal, 19x4, p. 71__

Original Cost or Appraised Value $ __60,000__   **Use of Property** __Recreation__

Appraised by __R. R. Mills & Co.__

ADDITIONAL COSTS

Amount	Reference	Description
$ 25	W.R., p. 91	Examination of title
190	W.R., p. 93	Clearing

Deed:

  Kind __Quit claim__ **Date** __Aug. 6, 19x4__ **Where Recorded** __Deed Record 96, p. 7__

Abstract of Title (by Whom): __Monroe County Abstract Co.__

Date __July 21, 19x4__ **Where Filed** __Safe, Town Treasurer's Office__

Disposal Record: _____

  Date of Disposal _____

  Manner of Disposal _____

  Amount Received $ _____

Remarks __Donated by Alfred Huntington__

---

repairs, maintenance, or replacement. Property inventories need not be taken simultaneously in all departments but may be spread over a period of time, with due consideration for departmental or other transfers or changes during the period. As suggested elsewhere, government fixed assets, especially those that are movable, should be marked by a numerical or other form of code so that each item may be positively identified. The marking may be accomplished by the use of labels or tags, by the use of indelible ink, by stamping, or by other permanent methods. To save time in locating markings, rules should be established and observed concerning the exact points where they will be affixed on different types of equipment. Assets that cannot be located after diligent search should be written off in a prescribed manner, which should include approval by responsible persons.

ILLUSTRATION 6–4

TOWN OF DENTON

FIXED ASSET INVENTORY

Sheet No. ___1___

No. of Sheets ___1___

Taken by ___M. Kerr___

Class of Property ___Furniture___
Department ___Treasurer's Office___
Date ___December 29, 19x5___

Description	Manufacturer's No.	Serial No.	No. of Units	Unit Cost	Total
Tables, wooden	None	T7-11	5	$120	$600
Desk, wooden	"	T12	1	195	195
Chairs, wooden, office	"	T1-6	6	35	210
Chairs, metal, swivel	"	T13	1	90	90
Note: One wooden chair charged to office could not be located.					

Property inventories may follow the general plan pursued in checking mercantile and manufacturing inventories, with considerably less detail than in the latter types. Provisions should be made for accurate description of the items listed and for showing the departments or units charged for each group of assets (see Illustration 6–4).

Statements of General Fixed Assets

For general fixed assets, the basic exhibit is the Statement of General Fixed Assets or, as it is sometimes captioned, the General Fixed Assets Balance Sheet. Its special contribution is to show the total cost of assets of the various groups in use by the general government and the sources from which they were derived. This statement is shown in Illustration 6–1.

The purposes for which, and by whom, fixed assets were being used at a given date, ordinarily the end of a fiscal period, are set forth in a Schedule of General Fixed Assets classified by functions and activities. Illustration 6–5 is an example of a Statement of General Fixed Assets—by Function and Activities.

Another schedule that should be of interest to taxpayers and citizens generally shows changes in general fixed assets during a period of time (see Illustration 6–6). The value of this schedule is that it not only accounts systematically for changes between one date and another but also shows the extent to which responsible officials are investing for future requirements, in contrast to spending primarily for current requirements. In addition, the statement of changes serves as a reconcilement or transition between Statements of General Fixed Assets for the ends of consecutive years.

ILLUSTRATION 6–5

CITY OF SMALLVILLE
Schedule of General Fixed Assets—By Function and Activity
As of June 30, 19x8

Function and Activity	Total	Land	Buildings	Improvements Other than Buildings	Machinery and Equipment
General government:					
Control:					
Legislative	$ 2,825	$ —	$ —	$ —	$ 2,825
Executive	600	—	—	—	600
Judicial	5,070	—	793	—	4,277
Total control	8,495	—	793	—	7,702
Staff agencies:					
Purchasing	10,245	—	—	—	10,245
Finance	3,268	—	—	—	3,268
Data processing	179,875	—	—	—	179,875
Treasurer	1,475	—	—	—	1,475
Recorder	1,366	—	—	—	1,366
Attorney	1,924	—	—	—	1,924
Community development	592,991	237,364	351,888	—	3,739
Taxi	5,300	—	—	—	5,300
Garage	12,188	—	—	—	12,188
Personnel	1,330	—	—	—	1,330
Government buildings	1,640,862	525,113	1,025,569	6,153	84,027
Billing	12,013	—	—	—	12,013
Total staff agencies	2,462,837	762,477	1,377,457	6,153	316,750
Public safety:					
Police department	341,067	—	1,665	676	338,726
Fire department	940,715	—	444,541	92,427	403,747
Total public safety	1,281,782	—	446,206	93,103	742,473
Public works:					
Streets and highways	1,458,257	—	51,463	553,985	852,809
Engineering	93,554	—	—	—	93,554
Planning and zoning	5,050	—	—	—	5,050
Total public works	1,556,861	—	51,463	553,985	951,413
Mosquito abatement	8,588	—	—	—	8,588
Parks	1,872,919	1,612,402	22,299	39,889	198,329
Recreation	2,005,988	66,550	1,619,236	235,416	84,786
Cemetery	20,414	—	—	—	20,414
Library	71,079	4,000	30,320	10,980	25,779
Airport	9,604	9,604	—	—	—
Total General Fixed Assets	$9,298,567	$2,455,033	$3,547,774	$939,526	$2,356,234

ILLUSTRATION 6–6

CITY OF SMALLVILLE
Schedule of Changes in General Fixed Assets—By Function and Activity
Year Ended June 30, 19x8

Function and Activity	General Fixed Assets June 30, 19x7	Additions	Deductions	General Fixed Assets June 30, 19x8
General government:				
Control:				
Legislative	$ 1,430	$ 1,395	$ —	$ 2,825
Executive	600	—	—	600
Judicial	5,070	—	—	5,070
Total control	7,100	1,395	—	8,495
Staff agencies:				
Purchasing	10,245	—	—	10,245
Finance	2,493	775	—	3,268
Data processing	67,371	112,504	—	179,875
Treasurer	700	775	—	1,475
Recorder	1,366	—	—	1,366
Attorney	1,924	—	—	1,924
Community development	592,991	—	—	592,991
Taxi	5,300	—	—	5,300
Garage	12,188	—	—	12,188
Personnel	1,330	—	—	1,330
Government buildings	777,814	865,515	(2,467)	1,640,862
Billing	12,013	—	—	12,013
Total staff agencies	1,485,735	979,569	(2,467)	2,462,837
Public safety:				
Police department	340,222	39,712	(38,867)	341,067
Fire department	923,056	17,659	—	940,715
Total public safety	1,263,278	57,371	(38,867)	1,281,782
Public works:				
Streets and highways	1,349,142	109,189	(74)	1,458,257
Engineering	89,221	4,333	—	93,554
Planning and zoning	5,050	—	—	5,050
Total public works	1,443,413	113,522	(74)	1,556,861
Mosquito abatement	8,588	—	—	8,588
Parks	1,845,283	28,446	(810)	1,872,919
Recreation	1,981,573	24,415	—	2,005,988
Cemetery	20,414	—	—	20,414
Library	23,191	49,080	(1,192)	71,079
Airport	9,604	—	—	9,604
Total General Fixed Assets	$8,088,179	$1,253,798	$(43,410)	$9,298,567

Selected References	American Institute of Certified Public Accountants. *Audit and Accounting Guide, Audits of State and Local Governmental Units.* Revised. New York, 1993. Governmental Accounting Standards Board. *Codification of Governmental Accounting and Financial Reporting Standards as of June 30, 1993.* Norwalk, Conn., 1993.

Questions	**6–1.** Explain how an accountant or administrator would be able to determine whether the cost of a certain piece of equipment purchased by a governmental unit should be recorded in the General Fixed Assets Account Group or in an enterprise fund.

6–2. What sources are often used to finance the acquisition of general fixed assets of governments?

6–3. Below are stated several transactions related to fixed assets of a governmental unit. Which should be debited to asset accounts of the General Fixed Assets Account Group? Which should not? Explain your answers.

   a. Contract price of land purchased for the use of a government-owned utility.

   b. Cost of land title abstract (paid by the utility for the land referred to in item *a* above).

   c. Cost of securing an easement for right-of-way over an adjoining property for a new entrance to the employees' parking lot next to City Hall.

   d. Cost of demolishing and removing an old building from a site to be used for construction of a new City Hall.

   e. Contract price of new building constructed for use as a fire station.

   f. Interest during the period of construction on money borrowed for construction of the new City Hall.

   g. Cost of a set of building plans followed in construction of the new City Hall.

   h. Cost of assembling and testing a piece of complicated machinery purchased for a government-owned utility.

   i. Freight on equipment purchased for use by the Street Department.

   j. Mowing grass and weeds, and other care and maintenance activities, for the grounds around City Hall.

6–4. Below are stated three major expenditures relating to the Town of Renton's general fixed assets. Which expenditures should be debited to asset accounts of the General Fixed Assets Account Group? Which should not? Explain your answers.

   a. Replaced an old boiler in the Town Hall with a new model having twice the capacity of the old model.

   b. Added a new wing to the Town Hall.

   c. Renovated the Town Council Chambers (replaced carpeting, painted walls, and upgraded the sound system).

6–5. GASB standards do not allow depreciation of general fixed assets to be recorded in the accounts of any governmental fund, but do allow accumulated depreciation to be recorded in the General Fixed Assets Account Group. (1) Explain how accumulated depreciation can be recorded if depreciation expense cannot. (2) Explain why it is *not* in conformity with GASB standards to record depreciation in the accounts of governmental funds.

6–6. The finance officer of a certain city instructed his staff to analyze the Construction Work in Progress account at the end of each year to determine the amounts that should be debited to each general fixed asset account and the amounts that should be credited to Construction Work in Progress. Explain what records or documents should be utilized to support the General Fixed Assets general ledger accounts.

6–7. "If a governmental unit acquires computer hardware for use by the City Comptroller's Office under a capital lease agreement, the cost of the system is defined for the purposes of recording in the General Fixed Assets Account Group as the total of the lease rentals to be paid by the City over the term of the lease." Is this statement true or false? Explain the reason for your answer.

6–8. What considerations should be kept in mind when developing a classification system for subsidiary fixed asset accounts?

6–9. A certain city finance officer instructed his staff:

  a. To ignore capital projects fund expenditures for items costing under $1,000 each when preparing entries to record the cost of general fixed assets.
  b. To ignore all special assessment expenditures for street paving, curbs, gutters, and sidewalks when preparing entries to record the cost of general fixed assets.
  c. To ignore all assets acquired under lease agreements.

For each of the three practices enumerated above, state whether or not you believe the practice to be in conformity with generally accepted accounting principles. Defend your answers.

6–10. Why is a periodic physical inventory of general fixed assets necessary? Is a physical inventory more useful for some classes of general fixed assets than others? Explain.

6–11. To avoid unusually heavy expenditures in some fiscal periods, governments often prepare a Capital Improvement Program, or Capital Expenditure Budget, for a period of several years.

  a. What is the significance of buildings and equipment records in connection with such a budget?
  b. Would you recommend that infrastructure asset records be maintained in the GFAAG? Why or why not?

6–12. What are the benefits of accounting for general fixed assets in the General Fixed Assets Account Group rather than in a record system not formally integrated with the accounting system?

Exercises and Problems

6–1. Utilizing the CAFR obtained for Exercise 1–1, follow the instructions below:

  a. Reporting of Fixed Assets. Does the Combined Balance Sheet contain a column reporting the General Fixed Asset Account Group data? Are fund fixed assets reported only in appropriate columns (Enterprise, Internal Service, and Trust and Agency Fund Types and the General Fixed Assets Account Group)? Is a Statement of General Fixed Assets included in the Individual Funds section? Does this statement, or one or more schedules, disclose the function or activity that uses the assets? What categories of fixed assets are shown in the statement? Are Improvements Other than Buildings separately disclosed and described? Do the

Notes describe the accounting treatment accorded general fixed assets and fixed assets accounted for by proprietary funds? If donated fixed assets are reported, are they stated at their fair value on the date donated? Are purchased fixed assets stated at historical cost, if known, or estimated historical cost if actual cost is unknown? Has the government refrained from using terms like *appraised values* or *estimated values* without indicating whether they involve historical cost, replacement cost, or market value appraisals or estimates? Do the Notes specify capitalization policies for "public domain" (infrastructure) fixed assets? Are commitments under capital leases and operating leases disclosed? Are assets being acquired under capital leases reported in the GFAAG as specified in Chapter 6? (See also Exercise 5–1, part *e*, for related questions relating to assets acquired under capital leases.)

b. *Sources of Fixed Asset Financing.* Does the Statement of General Fixed Assets disclose the sources from which acquisitions or construction of fixed assets were financed? If not, is the information disclosed elsewhere in the report? If so, are the sources for all general fixed assets disclosed, or only those assets acquired since a certain date? Do the source accounts agree with those discussed in Chapter 6? What three sources account for the major portion of fixed asset acquisitions? What percentage of the total cost, or other carrying value, of fixed assets is accounted for by each of the three major sources?

c. *Changes in General Fixed Assets.* Does the report contain a Schedule (or Statement) of Changes in General Fixed Assets? If so, does the schedule disclose the sources from which fixed asset acquisitions and construction were financed? Does the schedule disclose changes by function and activity, or merely by asset category?

d. *Other.* Compare the general fixed asset information disclosed in the report with related information disclosed in statements of general and special revenue funds, capital projects funds, or elsewhere in the report. Is the accumulated cost of construction work in progress recorded as an asset in the GFAAG? If not, is the information disclosed adequately, in your opinion? Is net interest during the period of construction on debt incurred to finance construction capitalized? Is this true for just tax-supported debt, or for both tax-supported debt and special assessment debt? Which fund, or funds, account for cash received, or receivables created, from sales of general fixed assets? Which fund, or funds, account for cash received, or receivables created, as a result of charging depreciation on general fixed assets as a cost of grants?

6–2. Write the numbers 1 through 10 on a sheet of paper. Beside each number write the letter corresponding with the best answer to each of the following questions:

1. Fixed assets donated to a governmental unit should be recorded
   a. At estimated fair value when received.
   b. At the lower of donor's carrying amount or estimated fair value when received.
   c. At the donor's carrying amount.
   d. As a memorandum entry only.

2. The following are Boa City's fixed assets:

Fixed assets used in proprietary fund activities	$1,000,000
Fixed assets used in expendable trust funds	1,800,000
Fixed assets used by governmental funds	9,000,000

What aggregate amount should Boa account for in the General Fixed Assets Account Group?

  a. $ 9,000,000.
  b. $10,000,000.
  c. $10,800,000.
  d. $11,800,000.

3. One feature of state and local government accounting and financial reporting is that fixed assets used for general government activities

  a. Often are **not** expected to contribute to the generation of revenues.
  b. Do **not** depreciate as a result of such use.
  c. Are acquired only when direct contribution to revenues is expected.
  d. Should **not** be maintained at the same level as those of businesses so that current financial resources can be used for other government services.

4. Old equipment, which is recorded in the General Fixed Assets Account Group, is sold for less than its carrying amount. The sale reduces the Investment in General Fixed Assets' balance by the

  a. Difference between the cost of the equipment and the sales price.
  b. Difference between the carrying amount of the equipment and the sales price.
  c. Selling price of the equipment.
  d. Carrying amount of the equipment.

5. The General Fixed Assets Account Group is:

  a. An accounting entity.
  b. A fiscal entity.
  c. A legal entity.
  d. All of the above.

6. If $2,200,000 of the proceeds from the sale of tax-supported bonds were expended by a capital projects fund during the fiscal year 19x8 on a street-paving project not complete at the end of that year, the General Fixed Assets Account Group should:

  a. Make no entry at all; infrastructure assets are never capitalized.
  b. Make no entry until the project is complete.
  c. Debit Improvements Other than Buildings, $2,200,000; credit Investments in General Fixed Assets—Capital Projects Funds, $2,200,000.
  d. Debit Construction Work in Progress, $2,200,000; credit Investment in General Fixed Assets—Capital Projects Funds—Tax-Supported Bonds, $2,200,000.

7. Accumulated depreciation of general fixed assets:

  a. *Should* be recorded in the accounts of governmental funds.
  b. May *optionally* be recorded in the accounts of governmental funds.
  c. May *optionally* be recorded in the accounts of the General Fixed Assets Account Group.
  d. Either *b* or *c* is permitted by GASB standards.

8. General fixed assets should be recorded at:

  a. Cost.
  b. Estimated cost, if cost is not practically determinable.
  c. Fair value, if the fixed assets were donated.
  d. Either *a*, or *b*, or *c*, as appropriate.

9. Since general fixed assets are not assets of any fund, generally accepted accounting principles provide that:

  a. A column should be provided in all general purpose financial statements to report GFAAG financial data.

b. A column should be provided in the Combined Balance Sheet, but not in any other of the combined statements, to report GFAAG financial data.

c. They need not be reported at all in any of the general purpose financial statements, or in the notes to the financial statements.

d. The carrying value of the GFAAG should be disclosed in the notes to the financial statements, but not on the face of any of the statements.

10. General fixed assets acquired under a capital lease:
   a. Should not be capitalized.
   b. Should be capitalized at the lower of cost or market.
   c. Should be capitalized under the same rules as proprietary fund fixed assets acquired under an operating lease.
   d. Should be capitalized at the lesser of (1) the present value of rental and other minimum lease payments, or (2) the fair value of the leased property.

(Items 1 through 4, AICPA, adapted.)

6–3. The statement and two schedules shown in the annual report of Prairie City for the year ended June 30, 19x5, which present information about general fixed assets are shown below and on the following page.

PRAIRIE CITY
Statement of General Fixed Assets
June 30, 19x5
(000 omitted)

General Fixed Assets

Land	$13,186
Building and structures	17,492
Machinery and equipment	2,384
Streets, sidewalks, and other infrastructure	7,692
Total General Fixed Assets	$40,754

Investment in General Fixed Assets

General obligation bonds	$19,700
Special assessment bonds	4,625
General Fund revenues	12,829
Capital leases	3,600
Total Investment in General Fixed Assets	$40,754

PRAIRIE CITY
Schedule of General Fixed Assets—
By Function and Activity
June 30, 19x5
(in thousands)

Function	Total	Land	Buildings	Machinery and Equipment	Streets and Other
General Government Equipment	$10,076			$2,384	$7,692
General Government Buildings	19,492	$ 2,000	$17,492		
Parks and Recreation	11,186	11,186			
Total General Fixed Assets	$40,754	$13,186	$17,492	$2,384	$7,692

PRAIRIE CITY
Schedule of Changes in General Fixed Assets—
By Function and Activity
For the Year Ended June 30, 19x5
(in thousands)

	General Fixed Assets 6/30/x4	Additions	Deductions	General Fixed Assets 6/30/x5
General Government Equipment	$ 9,135	$1,172	$231	$10,076
General Government Buildings	19,057	502	67	19,492
Parks and Recreation	10,425	761		11,186
Total General Fixed Assets	$38,617	$2,435	$298	$40,754

Required

a. To what extent does the information about general fixed assets satisfy the information needs of (1) a new member of the City Council, and (2) a resident interested in the financial management of fixed assets of the city?

b. If you were a CPA auditing the city, should you give a clean opinion on the statements as they exist? If not, are there any changes that the client could make that would enable you to give a clean opinion?

6–4. Below are described a number of transactions, each of which had an effect on the General Fixed Assets Account Group of a certain city. You are required to make an entry or entries for each transaction as it should have been recorded in the General Fixed Assets Account Group.

1. During the year, a Capital Projects Fund completed a building project initiated in the preceding year. The total cost of the project was $6,780,000, of which $4,130,000 had been expended in the two preceding years. Current-year expenditures on the project were reported to have consisted of $650,000 from a federal grant, with the balance coming from proceeds of a tax-supported bond issue.

2. A tract of land held for future development as a city park was, by resolution of the City Council, transferred to the City Water Utility. The Utility agreed to pay the City General Fund $200,000 for the land, which was carried in the GFAAG at its estimated cost of $50,000. The land had been purchased from General Fund revenues.

3. An electric typewriter was traded in on a personal computer. List price of the personal computer was $3,500; $100 allowance was received for the old machine. The old typewriter had been purchased from General Fund revenue for $500. Cash for the new computer was furnished by a special revenue fund.

4. A piece of heavy equipment was purchased by the Street Fund, a special revenue fund. Catalog price of the equipment was $150,000. Terms of payment quoted by the manufacturer were 2/10, n/30. Payment for the equipment was made within the cash discount period.

5. The cost of remodeling of the interior of the City Hall was $514,700; $38,400 of this amount was classified as maintenance rather than improvement. In the remodeling process, walls, partitions, floors, and so on, estimated to have cost $76,600 were

removed and replaced. Cost of the remodeling was financed by a current appropriation of the General Fund. The original construction had been financed by a tax-
supported bond issue accounted for by a capital projects fund.

6. A subdivision annexed by the City contained privately financed streets and sidewalks and a system of sewers. The best available information showed a cost of
$1,400,000 for the sewer system and $1,550,000 for the streets and sidewalks, of
which $150,000 was the estimated cost of the land. Both types of improvements
were provided by the developers. The City *does* record infrastructure assets in the
GFAAG.

6–5. Early in 19y6, the City Manager of the City of Charlesville decided to bring the City's
financial reports into conformity with GASB standards by bringing the general fixed assets
of the City under accounting control in a General Fixed Assets Account Group. Fortunately, a considerable portion of the general fixed assets had been acquired in rather recent
years, after installation of a fairly complete accounting system. All available records were
scanned for expenditures of $1,000 or more, and responsible officials determined which of
these expenditures resulted in the acquisition of general fixed assets and whether each
asset should be reported as Land, Buildings, Improvements Other than Buildings, Equipment, or Construction Work in Progress. Insofar as possible, the sources that had financed
the acquisition of general fixed assets were identified and recorded. By December 31, 19y6,
the following summary of information about general fixed assets had been developed:

Fixed Assets	*Amount*	*Sources of Acquisition*	*Amount*
Land	$ 2,156,000	General Fund	$ 2,770,000
Buildings	6,837,000	Special Revenue Funds	1,399,000
Improvements other		Capital Projects Funds—	
than buildings	4,914,000	Tax-Supported Bonds	8,200,000
Equipment	2,623,000	Special Assessment	
Construction work		Bonds	1,230,000
in progress	406,000	Federal Grants	1,200,000
		State Grants	802,000
		Private Gifts	73,000
		Capital Leases	1,300,000
Total	$16,936,000	Total	$16,974,000

After preparation of the list of general fixed assets as identified from examining the
records of expenditures, a physical inventory was taken to determine the location and
condition of each asset. Because of retirements, abandonments, destruction, and other
forms of loss, properties supposed to have had the following total costs could not be
located for inventory: buildings, $116,000; improvements other than buildings, $223,000;
equipment, $311,000. However, assets not listed in the examination of expenditure records
were found and the costs of these assets were estimated to be: land, $7,000; buildings,
$60,000; equipment, $81,000.

The following amounts of the sources of acquisition listed above could not be associated with any general fixed asset included in the December 31, 19y6, inventory: General
Fund, $821,000; special revenue funds, $76,000; capital projects funds—tax-supported
bonds, $513,000; capital projects funds—state grants, $34,000; and private gifts, $11,000.

From the foregoing collection of information, you are required to prepare in good form
a Statement of General Fixed Assets for the City of Charlesville at December 31, 19y6.

6–6. Information in the CAFR of the Town of Rodham reported general fixed assets in the following amounts as of April 30, 19x8:

Land	$1,326,780
Buildings	6,984,430
Improvements other than buildings	3,027,790
Equipment	1,622,310
Construction work in progress	401,130

During fiscal year 19x9 the following changes in general fixed assets took place:

1. A project started during fiscal 19x9 was being financed by a tax-supported bond issue of $3,000,000 sold at par during the year and a federal grant of $500,000, both accounted for through a capital projects fund. By the end of fiscal 19x9, $30,000 of the federal grant had been received and expended for planning and engineering for a project in progress. Bond proceeds expended during the year totaled $900,000 ($300,000 for land, and $600,000 for the building under construction).

2. Records of capital projects funds reported that construction work in progress at the end of fiscal 19x8 was completed during fiscal 19x9 at a total cost of $799,066, all financed from special assessment bonds. All of the construction resulted in additions to Improvements Other than Buildings.

3. Special revenue fund expenditures during the year added equipment costing $152,700.

4. General Fund expenditures during the year for equipment amounted to $306,000.

5. Annexation added buildings for which the estimated cost was $301,600, and land for which the estimated cost was $75,000.

6. Land having an appraised value of $750,000 was donated to the City, and additional land with an appraised value of $15,000 was received in settlement of delinquent General Fund property taxes.

7. Land acquired at an estimated cost of $12,000, on which an $80,000 building was located, was sold to the State Highway Department for a right-of-way at a price of $119,700.

8. Construction activities during fiscal 19x9 required demolition of a building that had cost $33,600 and a bridge for which the estimated cost was $119,200. Equipment that had cost $19,300 could not be located and was presumed to have been stolen.

Required   Prepare in good form a Schedule of Changes in General Fixed Assets during the fiscal year ended April 30, 19x9. Show the sources of assets acquired and the causes of reduction.

6–7. At June 30, 19x8, the fixed property schedule of the City of Glezen was as follows:

General Government:	
Land	$ 110,320
Buildings	1,070,000
Improvements other than buildings	263,500
Equipment	718,570
Fire protection:	
Land	60,500
Buildings	310,000
Equipment	501,850
Police protection:	
Equipment	245,000

Recreation:

Land	618,770
Buildings	62,000
Improvements other than buildings	281,500
Equipment	109,000

Health and Welfare Department:

Land	115,930
Buildings	92,410
Improvements other than buildings	301,250
Equipment	64,980

Purchases of equipment during the year ended June 30, 19x9, were as follows:

General Government	$ 29,020
Fire Department	407,300
Police Department	81,700
Recreation Department	48,000
Health and Welfare Department	18,020

Also, during the year ended June 30, 19x9:

1. A piece of equipment appraised at $57,100 was received from a federal agency for general governmental use.
2. The cost of equipment sold during the year included $10,800 of equipment used by the General Government; $39,000 by the Fire Department; and $2,100 by Health and Welfare. Equipment traded in during the year included $4,700 of equipment used by the Police Department; and $680, by the Health and Welfare Department.
3. Buildings demolished during the year had cost $4,120 (assigned to the Recreation Department), and $12,860 (assigned to the Health and Welfare Department).
4. Reductions from abandonment on account of obsolescence (all equipment) were $18,640 by the General Government; $9,200 by the Fire Department; $4,300 by the Police Department; $2,700 by the Recreation Department; and $1,310 by the Health and Welfare Department.

Required Prepare in good form a schedule for the year ended June 30, 19x9, showing the beginning balance of each class of fixed assets, the causes of change (purchases, received from other governmental units, sales, demolition and abandonment, trade-ins), and the amounts thereof, and the ending balance. Show totals for each function, considering fire protection and police protection as separate functions.

6–8. A Statement of General Fixed Assets of the Town of Smithton showed the following departmental balances for December 31, 19y0:

Clerk-Treasurer	$ 114,800
Fire Department	1,863,170
Health Department	324,100
Inspector of Weights and Measures	122,600
Mayor's office	68,000
Parks Department	1,397,600
Police Department	1,255,140
General Government	4,642,930
Street Department	2,638,720
City Attorney	86,760
Total	$12,513,820

During 19y1, the following changes occurred:

1. The Clerk-Treasurer's office traded $980 of equipment on new equipment costing $2,070, and purchased additional equipment for $2,230.

2. The Fire Department acquired $362,950 of new equipment, partly by outright purchase and partly by trading $97,390 of old property.

3. The Street Department acquired new equipment for a cash outlay of $131,040 and a trade-in of old equipment on which an allowance of $15,030 was received. The equipment traded in had cost $68,730. Equipment that had cost $7,890 was scrapped.

4. The Inspector of Weights and Measures succeeded in getting new equipment that cost $12,000. One piece of office equipment that had cost $500 was transferred from this office to that of the Mayor.

5. The Mayor's office acquired new equipment by purchase at a cost of $8,000.

6. The Parks Department acquired $186,120 of new property by purchase, and property appraised at $21,040 by donation. Property that had cost $25,190 was worn out and retired. In addition, property that had cost $46,380 was stolen or destroyed by vandals.

7. $189,650 cash was spent on property for the Police Department. $21,830 was for major overhaul of various kinds of property, which did not add anything to its value, and $8,440 was for betterments to old equipment. The balance was for purchase of new property. Old property was traded on some of the new, and allowances totaling $9,610 were received. The property traded in had cost $41,620. Other property that had cost $4,630 was scrapped, with no residual value.

8. The total outlay on buildings for general government for the year was $766,190, of which $463,040 was for maintenance and upkeep; $86,470 was for remodeling the interior of one building. An architect estimated the cost of the part remodeled and removed at approximately $37,180. The remainder of the $766,190 was for additions. Structures that had cost $20,190 were demolished for various reasons.

9. New furniture for the City Attorney's office was purchased at a cost of $1,200; furniture from that office that had cost $360 was junked.

10. Total outlay for Health Department equipment during the year was $19,010, of which $370 was for items costing less than the minimum amount to be capitalized. Health Department equipment that had cost $2,330 was disposed of during the year, with no salvage value.

Required   Prepare in good form a Schedule of Changes in the General Fixed Assets of the Town of Smithton for the year ended December 31, 19y1, with the information classified by function and department. The main classification is by function, with departments listed under the function that each serves. Include columns for Balance, December 31, 19y0; 19y1 Increases; 19y1 Decreases; and Balance, December 31, 19y1.

Continuous Problems

6–L. The Controller of the City of Bingham assigned you, and other top personnel on his staff, to audit the General Fixed Assets Account Group—a task that had not been done in many years. The bookkeeper had been a marketing major at the university but had never succeeded in getting his grade average high enough to allow him to graduate. He was able to show you the records he had been keeping but was not able to give you a very clear explanation as to why he kept them that way. The auditors found the following General Fixed Assets control account balances as of the audit cutoff date, June 30, 19x2. (No source amounts had been kept.)

Land	$ 600,000
Buildings	5,200,000
Improvements Other than Buildings	16,560,000
Equipment and Miscellaneous	3,930,000
Fund Balance	$26,290,000

Required

a. Open a general journal for the General Fixed Assets Account Group and make the entries necessary to state the accounts in accord with GASB standards. Additional information disclosed by your audit is presented below:

(1) Analysis of the Land account disclosed that the balance was comprised of: *(a)* An amount of $100,000 entered in 1968 when the General Fixed Assets group was established; this amount was the estimated cost of the City Hall site, the fire station sites, and city park land. The unimproved park land had been acquired as a gift from a citizen and was estimated in 1968 to be worth $12,000; the building sites had been acquired from the proceeds of tax-supported bond issues. *(b)* An amount of $160,000 entered in 1978 as the cost of two houses and lots. The houses were torn down, and an addition to City Hall was erected on one lot; the remainder was used as a parking lot for city-owned cars and for the private cars of city employees. This amount was financed under a grant from the federal government. *(c)* An amount of $240,000, dated 1984, which was financed by tax-supported bonds issued for the purchase of land used as a public park. The former property owners received $200,000; the Mayor, who was a real estate dealer, $20,000 commission for arranging the transaction; and the Mayor's brother, an attorney, $20,000 for handling the legal details. *(d)* An amount of $100,000 entered in 1985 as the cost of land purchased by the Water Utility from current operating funds; the land is being held by the Water Utility as the site of a projected new pumping station.

(2) Analysis of the Buildings account disclosed that the balance was comprised of: *(a)* An amount of $2,600,000 entered in 1968 as the estimated cost of City Hall and the fire stations, constructed from the proceeds of tax-supported bond issues. *(b)* Charges of $16,000 for demolishing the houses purchased in 1978, and grading the land to the level of City Hall; $1,200,000 for the addition to City Hall; and $104,000 for paving the parking lot—all of which were financed from a grant by the federal government. *(c)* $400,000 for a golf clubhouse in the park, constructed from part of the proceeds of a tax-supported bond issue. (The golf course is not operated as an enterprise fund.) *(d)* $880,000 for a 240-acre estate to be used as a park. The mansion was appraised at $400,000; the unimproved land at $960,000; and the gardens, artificial lakes, and other improvements at $2,000,000. The entire purchase price was charged to Buildings; the amount had been paid over three years out of General Fund appropriations for public works. The City's independent auditors agreed that Land, Buildings, and Improvements Other than Buildings should be recorded at appraised amounts and the source accounts should recognize that the former owner had made a substantial gift to the city.

(3) The following items had been entered in the Improvements Other than Buildings account: *(a)* Estimated cost of streets, curbs, and sidewalks as of July 1,

1968, $5,250,000—$2,250,000 had been financed from annual General Fund appropriations during the years; the balance had been financed from various special assessment funds. *(b)* $600,000, the cost of constructing a municipal golf course on city park land, financed from a tax-supported bond issue. *(c)* An aggregate of $10,710,000 spent for street paving and widening, curbs, sidewalks, bridges, and culverts—$5,350,000 of this was from the General Fund appropriations, and the remainder from special assessment funds.

(4) *(a)* "Equipment and Miscellaneous" supporting data was in such an incomplete and obviously inaccurate state that the auditors secured permission to have an appraisal made. The cost of the appraisal was charged to a supplemental appropriation made under the General Government classification of the General Fund. The appraisal cost $30,000; it was a thorough job and showed location, and condition, as well as appraised value of items classifiable as "Equipment and Miscellaneous." The total appraised value of owned equipment and miscellaneous was $6,300,000. The auditors could identify the sources of financing for only a portion of the equipment; therefore, it was decided to assume the sources to have contributed the following percentages of appraised value: General Fund, 65 percent; special revenue funds, 15 percent; capital projects funds, 5 percent; special assessment funds, 5 percent; and grants from the federal government, 10 percent. *(b)* In addition to equipment owned by the City of Bingham, certain equipment was held under capital lease agreements. The present value of lease rentals, not previously capitalized, amounted to $948,000. The fair value of the leased equipment as of June 30, 19x2, was $960,000.

b. None of the information presented in Problems 2–L through 5–L has been recorded by the General Fixed assets bookkeeper. Record the applicable information in the General Fixed Assets general journal. (Expenditures of the City Hall Annex Construction Fund for Land and for Equipment are given in Problem 5–L; assume the expenditures of that fund for Improvements Other than Buildings amount to $80,260, and the remainder of expenditures are proper charges to Buildings. Interest on City Hall annex bonds during the period of construction is not to be capitalized.)

c. Open a general ledger for the General Fixed Assets Account Group and post your journal entries.

d. Prepare a Statement of General Fixed Assets as of June 30, 19x2.

6–S. As of December 31, 19y0, the City of Smithville presented the following Statement of General Fixed Assets:

CITY OF SMITHVILLE
Statement of General Fixed Assets—By Source
As of December 31, 19y0

General Fixed Assets:	
Land	$ 618,000
Buildings	3,006,000
Improvements other than buildings	4,197,000
Equipment	928,000
Total General Fixed Assets	$8,749,000

Investment in General Fixed Assets from:	
Capital Projects Funds:	
Tax-supported bonds	$4,000,000
Federal grants	1,236,000
State grants	431,000
General Fund revenues	2,089,000
Special Revenue Fund revenues	364,000
Special assessments	629,000
Total Investment in General Fixed Assets	$8,749,000

1. Subsidiary records of the General Fixed Assets Group of accounts showed that as of December 31, 19y0, the assets were assigned to functions and activities as shown below:

Function and Activity	Total	Land	Buildings	Improve-ments	Equip-ment
General Government	$1,922,000	$ 50,000	$1,504,000	$ 140,000	$228,000
Public safety:					
Police	501,000	35,000	420,000	8,000	38,000
Fire	636,000	41,000	309,000	20,000	266,000
Building safety	38,000	3,000	22,000	5,000	8,000
Public works	4,425,000	370,000	301,000	3,448,000	306,000
Health and welfare	97,000	9,000	40,000	16,000	32,000
Parks and recreation	1,130,000	110,000	410,000	560,000	50,000
Total	$8,749,000	$618,000	$3,006,000	$4,197,000	$928,000

2. Changes in general fixed assets resulting from General Fund activities in 19y1 were as follows:

Function and Activity	Improvements		Equipment	
	Cost of Additions	Cost of Assets Retired	Cost of Additions	Cost of Assets Retired
General Government			$ 40,000	$ 10,000
Public safety:				
Police			42,000	19,000
Fire			36,000	24,000
Building safety			3,000	
Public works	$30,000	$ 8,000	53,000	30,000
Health and welfare			16,000	8,000
Parks and recreation	24,000	6,000	18,000	10,000
Total	$54,000	$14,000	$208,000	$101,000

3. Changes in general fixed assets occurred during 19y1 as a result of activities of the Street Improvement Fund (see Problem 5–S). Assume $990,925 of the construction expenditures was financed from tax-supported bond proceeds, and the remainder from special assessments.

Required   *a.* Open a general journal for the General Fixed Assets Account Group and record the changes resulting from activities of the General Fund and activities of the Street Improvement Fund.

b. Prepare a Statement of General Fixed Assets—by Source as of December 31, 19y1.

c. Prepare a Schedule of General Fixed Assets—by Function and Activity as of December 31, 19y1.

d. Prepare a Schedule of Changes in General Fixed Assets—by Function and Activity for the year ended December 31, 19y1.

CHAPTER 7

Debt Service Funds

Long-term debt incurred to provide money to pay for the construction or purchase of fixed assets, or for any other purposes, can be repaid only from revenue raised in subsequent years to service the debt. The Accounting for Fixed Assets and Long-Term Liabilities Principle, discussed briefly in Chapter 2, provides that long-term liabilities to be serviced from the revenues of a proprietary fund should be accounted for by that proprietary fund and the service of such debt is also accounted for by the proprietary fund. *Debt service* includes both the payment of interest and the repayment of principal when due. Long-term debt serviced by tax levies, or by special assessments, however, is accounted for by the General Long-Term Debt Account Group (discussed in Chapter 8). Revenue raised from taxes or from special assessments for debt service, and expenditures for debt service, are commonly accounted for by use of a **debt service fund,** the subject of this chapter.

Types of Debt Service Funds

Earlier in this century, governmental issues of long-term debt commonly matured in total on a given date. In that era, bond indentures often required the establishment of a "sinking fund," sometimes operated on an actuarial basis. Some sinking fund term bond issues are still outstanding, but they are dwarfed in number and amount by serial bond issues, in which the principal matures in installments. Four types of serial bond issues are found in practice: regular, deferred, annuity, and irregular. If the total principal of an issue is repayable in a specified number of equal annual installments over the life of the issue, it is a **regular** serial bond issue. If the first installment is delayed for a period of more than one year after the date of the issue, but thereafter installments fall due on a regular basis, the bonds are known as **deferred** serial bonds. If the amount of annual principal repayments is scheduled to increase each year by approximately the same amount that interest payments decrease (interest decreases, of course, because the amount of outstanding bonds decreases) so that the total debt service remains reasonably level over the term of the issue, the bonds are called **annuity** serial bonds. **Irregular** serial bonds may have any pattern of repayment that does not fit the other three categories.

Budgeting for
Debt Service

Whether or not additions to debt service funds are required by the bond indenture to be approximately equal year by year, good politics and good financial management suggest that the burden on the taxpayers be spread reasonably evenly rather than lumped in the years that issues or installments happen to mature. If taxes for payment of interest and principal on long-term debt are to be raised directly by the debt service fund, they are recognized as **Revenues** of the debt service fund. If the taxes are to be raised by another fund and transferred to the debt service fund, they must be included in the Revenues budget of the fund that will raise the revenue (often the General Fund) and also budgeted by that fund as *operating transfers* to the debt service fund, and reported as an Other Financing Use. Since the debt service fund is a budgeting and accounting entity, it should prepare a Revenues and Other Financing Sources budget that includes operating transfers from other funds as well as revenues it will raise directly or earn on its investments. Although the items may be difficult to budget accurately, debt service funds can often count on receiving premium on debt issues sold and accrued interest on debt issues sold. Accrued interest on debt sold is considered Revenues of the recipient debt service fund; premium on debt sold is an Other Financing Source. Similarly, as illustrated in Chapter 5, if capital projects are completed with expenditures less than revenues and other financing sources, the residual equity is ordinarily transferred to the appropriate debt service fund. Persons budgeting and accounting for debt service funds should seek competent legal advice on the permissible use of both premium on debt sold and residual equity transfers-in. In some cases, one or both of these items must be held for eventual debt repayment and may not be used for interest payments; in other cases, both premiums and residual equity transfers-in may be used for interest payments.

The Appropriations budget of a debt service fund must provide for the payment of all interest on general long-term debt that will become legally due during the budget year, and for the payment of any principal amounts that will become legally due during the budget year. GASB standards currently require debt service fund accounting to be on the same basis as is required for general and special revenue funds. One peculiarity of the modified accrual basis used by governmental fund types (which is not discussed in Chapter 3 because it relates only to debt service funds) is that interest on long-term debt is not accrued. For example, if the fiscal year of a governmental unit ends on December 31, 19x5, and the interest on its bonds is payable on January 1 and July 1 of each year, the amount payable on January 1, 19x6, would not be considered a liability in the balance sheet of the debt service fund prepared as of December 31, 19x5. The rationale for this recommendation is that the interest is not legally due until January 1, 19x6. (See Illustration 7–1.) The same reasoning applies to principal amounts that mature on the first day of a fiscal year; they are not liabilities to be recognized in statements prepared as of the day before. In the event 19x5 appropriations include January 1, 19x6, interest and/or principal payment, the appropriation expenditures (and resulting liabilities) should be recognized in 19x5.

ILLUSTRATION 7–1 **Modified Accrual Basis of Recognition of Expenditures for Long-Term Debt Interest and Principal**

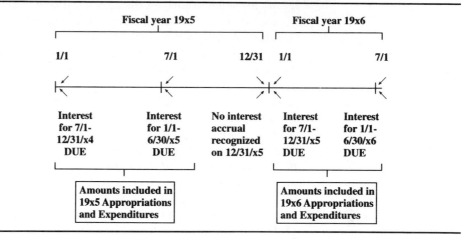

Bearer Bonds and Registered Bonds

Federal law requires tax-exempt bonds issued after June 30, 1983, to be *registered* instead of being *bearer* bonds, as the vast majority of issues were until that date. Many issues of bearer bonds are still outstanding and will continue to be for a number of years—for example, the final maturity of bonds issued as of June 30, 1983, may be June 30, 2013. Bearer bonds have some advantage for issuers in that bondholders receive payment for interest by presenting to their local banks (or other paying agent) on the interest payment date the coupon dated that day. Since the interest payment date may fall on a Saturday, Sunday, or holiday, even an alert bondholder may not collect the interest until two or more days after it is due. On any given interest payment date, some bondholders may not find it convenient to clip their coupons or may forget about it. Even if the coupons are paid on the due date by banks where bondholders reside, bondholders may live in locations distant from the issuing government, so coupons take a number of days to work their way through banking channels to the issuer's paying agent. The same is true of matured bearer bonds; they may not actually be presented to the issuer's paying agent for payment until long after maturity. Consequently, issuers of bearer bonds, and their paying agents, often have the use of a portion of their cash designated for interest and bond redemption long enough after maturity of coupons and bonds to earn significant amounts of interest.

Issuance of bonds that are registered as to interest and principal, however, requires the issuer, or its agent, to write a check as of each interest payment date, and as of the date of maturity of the bonds, to the registered owner of the bonds. Checks are commonly put in the mail in time to be delivered to the payee by the payment date. The fact that checks are written and mailed in advance of the interest or bond payment date makes it prudent for governmental units to raise and collect revenues in one fiscal year in the amount of interest and bonds that will legally be payable early in the next fiscal year. Failure to pay interest, or matured bonds, when due is called a *default*. A default would be viewed seriously by all creditors of the governmental unit or agency that defaulted, not just the bondholders who did not receive the amount of interest and principal when due. News of defaults reaches debt-rating agencies and newspapers and television financial reporters rapidly. Even if the default is cured promptly there is damage to the reputation of the defaulter, and probably to the ratings of all its debt issues, which will make it more difficult and more expensive for that government to borrow in the future. Of more immediate concern, however, is the fact that bond indentures commonly provide that the entire principal of the issue would be deemed to mature at the time any interest payment is defaulted. The prospect of having to pay in the current period the holders of all outstanding bonds of that issue should impress even the least financially knowledgeable administrators with the need for being meticulous about paying interest when due, as well as paying the principal of debt at maturity. Registered bonds may be issued in much the same form as bearer bonds (i.e., engraved on paper of bank note quality to make it difficult for counterfeiters to issue spurious bonds), or they may be in "book entry" form. In the latter case, issuers deposit a single certificate for each issue of term bonds, or each maturity of serial bonds, with a designated depository. Purchasers of bonds receive only a confirmation of the purchase and periodic statements of their accounts. Similarly, when a bondholder sells one or more bonds, the seller receives a confirmation of the sale, and the new owner receives a confirmation of the purchase.

Number of Debt Service Funds

In addition to term bonds and serial bonds, debt service funds may be required to service debt arising from the use of notes or warrants having a maturity more than one year after date of issue. In addition, debt service funds may be used to make periodic payments required by capital lease agreements. Although each issue of long-term or intermediate-term debt is a separate obligation and may have legal restrictions and servicing requirements that differ from other issues, GASB standards provide that, if legally permissible, a single Debt Service Fund be used to account for the service of all issues of tax-supported and special assessment debt. Subsidiary records of that fund can provide needed assurance that restrictions and requirements relating to each issue are properly budgeted and accounted for. If legal restrictions do not allow the service of all issues of tax-supported and special assessment debt to be accounted for by a single debt service fund, as few additional debt service funds as is consistent with applicable laws should be created. In this chapter, a separate debt service fund for each bond issue is illustrated simply as a means for helping the reader focus on the different accounting procedures considered appropriate for each kind of bond issue encountered in practice.

Use of General Fund to Account for Debt Service

In some jurisdictions, laws do not require the debt service function to be accounted for by a debt service fund. Unless the debt service function is very simple, it may be argued that good financial management would dictate the establishment of a debt service fund even though not required by law. If neither law nor sound financial administration require the use of debt service funds, the function may be performed within the accounting and budgeting framework of the General Fund. In such cases, the accounting and financial reporting standards discussed in this chapter should be followed for the debt service activities of the General Fund.

Debt Service Accounting for Regular Serial Bonds

Accounts recommended for use by debt service funds created to account for revenues to be used for the payment of interest and principal of serial bond issues are similar to those recommended for use by general and special revenue funds, but not exactly the same. Serial bond debt service funds should record the budget in Estimated Revenues and Appropriations control accounts and subsidiary accounts (and Estimated Other Financing Sources and Estimated Other Financing Uses control accounts and subsidiary accounts, if needed) just as general and special revenue funds should, but their operations do not involve the use of purchase orders and contracts for goods and services, so the Encumbrance account is not needed. Proprietary accounts of a serial bond debt service fund include Revenues and Expenditures control and subsidiary accounts (and Other Financing Sources and Other Financing Uses control and subsidiary accounts, if needed); and liquid asset, current liability, and Fund Balance accounts. Liquid assets of a serial bond debt service fund are held for the purpose of paying interest on outstanding bonds and retiring the principal installments as they fall due; for the convenience of bondholders, the payment of interest and the redemption of matured bonds is ordinarily handled through the banking system. Usually the government designates a bank as Paying Agent or Fiscal Agent, to handle interest and principal payments for each issue whether the issue is in registered or bearer form. The assets of a debt service fund may, therefore, include "Cash with Paying Agent," and the appropriations, expenditures, and liabilities may include amounts for the service charges of paying agents. Investment management may be performed by governmental employees or by banks, brokers, or others who charge for the service; investment management fees are a legitimate charge against investment revenues.

Accounting for debt service of regular serial bonds furnishes the simplest illustration of recommended debt service fund accounting. Assume the bonds issued by the Town of Brighton as partial financing for the fire station construction project (discussed in Chapter 5, under the heading "General Outline of Capital Projects Fund Accounting") are regular serial bonds maturing in equal annual amounts over 20 years and are registered as to interest and principal. The total face value of the issue was $1,200,000; all bonds in the issue bear interest of 6 percent per year, payable semiannually on June 15 and December 15. The bonds were dated June 15, 19y1, and sold on that date at par. During 19y1 the only expenditure the Debt Service Fund will be required to make will be the interest payment due December 15, 19y1, in the amount of $36,000 ($1,200,000 × .06 × ½ year). Assuming revenues to pay the first installment of bonds on June 15, 19y2, and both interest payments due in 19y2, will be raised in 19y2, the budget for 19y1 need only provide revenues in the amount of the 19y1 expenditure. The entry to record the budget for the year ended December 31, 19y1, would be:

1. Estimated Revenues	36,000	
Appropriations		36,000

If revenues in the amount of $30,000 were collected in cash from various sources available for debt service, the entry would be:

2. Cash	30,000	
Revenues		30,000

As illustrated in Chapter 5, the $6,000 residual equity of the Fire Station Capital Projects Fund was transferred to the Debt Service Fund. The entry required in the latter fund is:

3. Cash	6,000	
Equity Transfer In.................................		6,000

On December 15, 19y1, when the first interest payment is legally due, the Debt Service Fund records the expenditure of the appropriation:

4. Expenditures—Bond Interest	36,000	
Interest Payable		36,000

Checks totaling $36,000 are written to the registered owners of these bonds:

5. Interest Payable	36,000	
Cash		36,000

As of December 31, 19y1, the Debt Service Fund has no assets and no liabilities, therefore no need to prepare a balance sheet; but the budgetary and operating statement accounts have balances, which are closed by the following entry:

6. Revenues	30,000	
Appropriations	36,000	
Fund Balance	6,000	
Estimated Revenues		36,000
Expenditures—Bond Interest		36,000

The Equity Transfer In must be reported in the Changes in Fund Balance section of the operating statement. Accordingly, it is closed in the following manner:

7. Equity Transfer In.....................................	6,000	
Fund Balance		6,000

The Regular Serial Bonds Debt Service Fund Statement of Revenues, Expenditures, and Changes in Fund Balance for the year ended December 31, 19y1, and the budgetary comparison statement for this fund for the year are illustrated in the combining statements for all debt service funds, Illustrations 7–3 and 7–4.

Debt Service Accounting for Deferred Serial Bonds

If a government issues bonds other than regular serial bonds, debt service fund accounting is somewhat more complex than that illustrated above. In the entries below, it is assumed the Town of Brighton issued a total of $2,000,000 face value of deferred serial bonds on January 1, 19x0. Each installment is in the amount of $200,000. The first installment matures on January 1, 19y1; the final installment on January 1, 19z0. Interest is payable on January 1 and July 1 of each year at the nominal annual rate of 10 percent. Debt service is financed from taxes levied by the Debt Service Fund and from net earnings on Debt Service Fund investments. Taxes for this Debt Service Fund are levied in an amount equal to interest to be paid during the budget year, plus a level amount of $80,000 to be invested by the Debt Service Fund and used for principal repayment when the principal installments fall due. The trial balance of the Town of Brighton's Deferred Serial Bonds Debt Service Fund at the end of the 10th year (19y0) following the date of the deferred serial bond issue showed:

	Debits	Credits
Cash	$ 300,000	
Investments	830,625	
Interest Receivable	26,750	
Fund Balance	—	$1,157,375
Totals	$1,157,375	$1,157,375

Notice the trial balance shows Cash in the exact amount of interest on this bond issue due on January 1, 19y1 ($2,000,000 × .10 × ½ year = $100,000), plus $200,000 for the bonds that mature on January 1, 19y1. As noted in a preceding section of this chapter, checks totaling $300,000, dated January 1, 19y1, have been written and are in the mail to the registered bondholders; since the checks are dated the day after balance sheet date, they will not be credited to Cash until that date. Similarly, the $300,000 liability does not legally exist until January 1, 19y1; therefore, it is not reported in the December 31, 19y0, trial balance.

The budget for this fund for fiscal 19y1 includes the appropriations for payment of the interest of $100,000 on January 1, the payment of matured bonds of $200,000 on January 1, and the payment of interest of $90,000 on bonds outstanding on July 1, 19y1 ($1,800,000 × .10 × ½ year). It is assumed, for the sake of simplicity, that the Town will not incur any fees for paying agents or for investment management; therefore, the total of the **Appropriations budget** for 19y1 is $390,000. As noted in the description of this deferred serial bond issue, taxes are levied each year to allow for collection of cash in the amount of interest checks to be written that year, plus an amount of $80,000 to be invested for use for bond principal payment; earnings on the investments are also accumulated for bond principal repayment. Therefore, the **Revenues budget** for 19y1 for this fund for revenues from taxes totals $260,000 ($90,000 for the interest payment due July 1, 19y1; $90,000 for the interest payment due January 1, 19y2; and the $80,000 level amount to be invested); revenues from earnings on investments during 19y1 are budgeted at $98,600. Total Estimated Revenues for 19y1, therefore, amounts to $358,600. The entry to record the 19y1 budget is:

1. Estimated Revenues	358,600	
Fund Balance	31,400	
Appropriations		390,000

Subsidiary records, as needed, would be kept in the manner illustrated in Chapters 3 and 4. Since the records, and their use, are the same, they are omitted from this chapter.

Also, as of January 1, 19y1, the bond payment and interest payment due on that date should be recognized as expenditures of 19y1 appropriations (Entry 2a), and the fact that checks dated January 1, 19y1, have been issued in payment of the interest and bond principal should be recorded (Entry 2b):

2a. Expenditures—Bond Principal	200,000	
Expenditures—Bond Interest	100,000	
Interest Payable		100,000
Bonds Payable		200,000
2b. Interest Payable	100,000	
Bonds Payable	200,000	
Cash		300,000

In an actual case it would, of course, simplify the accounting to make one entry for the net effect of Entries 2a and 2b: a debit to Expenditures and a credit to Cash. As shown in Illustrations 7–3 and 7–4, however, the expenditures for bond interest and the expenditures for the redemption of matured bonds should be separately reported in the operating statements.

Taxes levied for debt service on the deferred serial bond issue are levied in the amount of $268,000; $8,000 of the levy is expected to be uncollectible:

3. Taxes Receivable—Current.............................	268,000	
Estimated Uncollectable Current Taxes		8,000
Revenues		260,000

Entry 4a summarizes the collection of taxes during the first half-year (assumed to amount to $120,000), the collection of interest receivable as of December 31, 19y0 ($26,750, per the trial balance), and the collection of $49,250 interest earned during the first half-year on investments of this fund. Cash in the amount of $106,000 was promptly invested, as shown by Entry 4b.

4a. Cash	196,000	
Taxes Receivable—Current...........................		120,000
Interest Receivable on Investments....................		26,750
Revenues		49,250
4b. Investments...	106,000	
Cash		106,000

Interest payable July 1 is recorded as an expenditure, and checks are written and mailed in the amount of interest payable July 1:

5a. Expenditures—Bond Interest	90,000	
Interest Payable		90,000
5b. Interest Payable	90,000	
Cash		90,000

Tax collections during the second half of 19y1 totaled $138,000; interest earnings received in cash during that period amounted to $24,000. Cash in the amount of $162,000 was invested:

6a. Cash	162,000	
Taxes Receivable—Current		138,000
Revenues		24,000
6b. Investments	162,000	
Cash		162,000

Taxes not collected during 19y1 must be classified as delinquent, as required by the laws of the state in which the Town of Brighton is located. Administrators estimate that at least $4,000 of taxes levied in 19y1 will be collected early in 19y2, and the remainder of that levy, $6,000, will be uncollectible. Since the original estimate of uncollectible taxes was $8,000 ($2,000 too much), Revenues should be credited for $2,000. Entry 7 accomplishes the necessary reclassifications:

7. Taxes Receivable—Delinquent	10,000	
Estimated Uncollectible Current Taxes	8,000	
Taxes Receivable—Current		10,000
Estimated Uncollectible Delinquent Taxes		6,000
Revenues		2,000

Bonds in the amount of $200,000 will mature on January 1, 19y2, and interest in the amount of $90,000 will be payable on that date. Investments in the amount of $290,000 are converted to cash as of December 31, 19y1, so that checks dated January 1, 19y2, may be mailed.

8. Cash	290,000	
Investments		290,000

Interest receivable on investments accrued at year-end is computed as $25,000; this accrual is recorded:

9. Interest Receivable on Investments	25,000	
Revenues		25,000

Budgetary and operating statement accounts for 19y1 are closed:

10. Revenues	360,250	
Appropriations	390,000	
Estimated Revenues		358,600
Expenditures—Bond Interest		190,000
Expenditures—Bond Principal		200,000
Fund Balance		1,650

After recording the entries for 19y1, the Town of Brighton Deferred Serial Bonds Debt Service Fund Balance Sheet would be as presented in Illustration 7–2, the Combining Balance Sheet for all debt service funds of the Town of Brighton. In addition to the Balance Sheet, the revenues, expenditures, and changes in fund balance during the fiscal period should be reported for each debt service fund. Illustration 7–3 presents the Combining Statement of Revenues, Expenditures, and Changes in Fund Balances for the Town of Brighton Deferred Serial Bonds Debt Service Fund for the year ended December 31, 19y1, and all other debt service funds of the Town. Since the funds are assumed to operate under legally required budgets, a Combining Statement of Revenues, Expenditures, and Changes in Fund Balances—Budget and Actual for the year is required. Illustration 7–4 presents the budgetary comparison for all debt service funds of the Town of Brighton.

Debt Service Accounting for Term Bonds

Term bond issues mature in their entirety on a given date, in contrast to serial bonds, which mature in installments. Required revenues of term bond debt service funds may be determined on an "actuarial" basis or on less sophisticated bases designed to produce approximately level contributions during the life of the issue. If an actuarial basis is not used, accounting procedures and statements illustrated for the deferred serial bond issue of the Town of Brighton are appropriate for use by term bond debt service funds. In order to illustrate the differences that exist when an actuarial basis is used, the following example is based on the assumption that the Town of Brighton has a term bond issue amounting to $1,500,000 with a 20-year life. The term bonds bear semiannual interest coupons with a nominal annual rate of 5 percent, payable on January 1 and July 1. Revenues and other financing sources of this particular debt service fund are assumed to be taxes levied directly for this debt service fund and earnings on investments of the debt service fund. The amount of the tax levy is computed in accord with annuity tables on the assumption that revenues for principal repayment will be invested and will earn 6 percent per year, compounded semiannually. (Actuaries are usually very conservative in their assumptions because they are concerned with a long time span.) Annuity tables are illustrated in Appendix 2. Table D in Appendix 2 shows that an annuity of $1 invested at the end of each period will amount to $75.4012597 at the end of 40 periods, if the periodic compound interest is 3 percent (as specified in the Town of Brighton example). Since the amount needed for bond repayment at the end of 40 six-month periods is $1,500,000, the tax levy for bond principal repayment must yield $1,500,000 ÷ 75.4012597, or $19,893.57 at the end of each six-month period throughout the life of the bonds. Revenue for each bond interest payment must be $37,500 ($1,500,000, the face of the bonds, × 5 percent, the annual nominal interest rate, × ½ year).

Assuming the bonds were issued on January 1, 19y0, and actual additions and actual earnings were both exactly as budgeted, the Town of Brighton Term Bonds

Debt Service Fund would have the following trial balance as of December 31, 19y0:[1]

	Debits	*Credits*
Investments	$40,383.95	—
Fund Balance	—	$40,383.95
Totals	$40,383.95	$40,383.95

For every year of the life of the issue, the budget for the Term Bonds Debt Service Fund of the Town, reflecting the conditions described above, will include two required additions of $19,893.57 each for investment for eventual principal repayment, and two amounts of $37,500 each for interest payment, for a total of $114,787.14. The budget will also include earnings on debt service fund investments computed in accord with actuarial requirements. For 19y1, the second year of the Term Bonds Debt Service Fund's operation, the actuarial assumption is that the fund will earn 6 percent per year, compounded semiannually; the required earnings for the year amount to $3,056.19.[2] Therefore, Estimated Revenues is debited for $117,843.33 ($114,787.14 + $3,056.19). The Appropriations budget would include only the amounts becoming due during the budget year, $75,000 (two interest payments, each amounting to $37,500). The entry to record the budget is shown below.

1. Estimated Revenues	117,843.33	
Fund Balance		42,843.33
Appropriations		75,000.00

If the debt service fund is to accumulate the amount needed to retire the term bond issue at maturity, both additions and earnings must be received, and invested, in accord with the actuarial assumptions. Therefore, the tax levy for this fund must yield collections in the first six months totaling $57,393.57, at least, so

---

[1] The computation is:

Year	Period	Addition at End of Period	3 Percent Interest per Period	Balance at End of Period
19y0	1	$19,893.57	$ —0—	$19,893.57
	2	19,893.57	596.81	40,383.95
19y1	3	19,893.57	1,211.52	61,489.04
	4	19,893.57	1,844.67	83,227.28

The balance at the end of period 2 is the total of Investments, and the total of Fund Balance, in this case since actuarial assumptions were met exactly in 19y0.

The sum of the interest for period 3 and period 4 is $3,056.19, the required earnings for the second year.

[2] See footnote 1 for the computation.

that $19,893.57 can be invested and $37,500 interest paid to bondholders, both as of the end of the first six-month period. Collections during the second six months must also total $57,393.57, for the same reason. In the real world it is unlikely that collections would ever total $57,393.57, to the penny, in either six-month period. If collections are less than that amount in either period, it should be obvious that this fund would have to borrow enough to make the required investments—there is no question that the interest would have to be paid when due, as discussed in an early section of this chapter. Assuming collection experience of the Town of Brighton indicates that a tax levy in the amount of $120,000 is needed in order to be reasonably certain that collections during each six-month period will equal the needed amount, the entry to record the levy and the expected uncollectibles amounting to $3,000 is:

2.	Taxes Receivable—Current...............................	120,000.00	
	Estimated Uncollectible Current Taxes		3,000.00
	Revenues		117,000.00

If actual collections during the first six months of 19y1 were $57,400, Entry 3 records that fact.

3.	Cash	57,400.00	
	Taxes Receivable—Current...........................		57,400.00

Entry 4 records the investment of the required $19,893.57 and the payment of interest of $37,500.

4.	Expenditures—Bond Interest	37,500.00	
	Investments...	19,893.57	
	Cash		57,393.57

Entry 5 records the addition of interest on June 30 in the amount of $1,261.99 to the investments of $40,383.95 invested for the entire first six months of 19y1. Note the actual interest for this period is $50.47 greater than the required earnings of $1,211.52 for the period, because the actual rate was slightly greater than the rate used in actuarial computations.

5.	Investments...	1,261.99	
	Interest Earnings		1,261.99

During the second six months, tax collections for the Term Bonds Debt Service Fund totaled $58,000 (Entry 6a). The required addition to the Investment account was made, and interest of $37,500 was paid, both actions as of December 31, 19y1 (Entry 6b).

6a.	Cash	58,000.00	
	Taxes Receivable—Current...........................		58,000.00
6b.	Expenditures—Bond Interest	37,500.00	
	Investments...	19,893.57	
	Cash		57,393.57

Interest earnings during the last six months on the $61,539.51 invested since July 1, 19y1, totaled $1,883.10; this amount was added to the Investment account:

7. Investments...	1,883.10	
Interest Earnings		1,883.10

Taxes levied for 19y1 but not collected during the year are recorded as delinquent; the amount in the related Estimated Uncollectible account is reviewed and determined to be reasonable.

8. Taxes Receivable—Delinquent..........................	4,600.00	
Estimated Uncollectible Current Taxes	3,000.00	
Taxes Receivable—Current..........................		4,600.00
Estimated Uncollectible Delinquent Taxes..............		3,000.00

As of December 31, 19y1, the budgetary accounts and operating statement accounts were closed.

9. Appropriations	75,000.00	
Revenues...	117,000.00	
Interest Earnings	3,145.09	
Estimated Revenues		117,843.33
Expenditures—Bond Interest		75,000.00
Fund Balance		2,301.76

Assets, liabilities, and Fund Balance of the Term Bonds Debt Service Fund as of December 31, 19y1 (all rounded to the nearest dollar), are shown in one column of the Combining Balance Sheet of all debt service funds of the Town of Brighton, Illustration 7–2. Similarly, revenues, expenditures and changes in fund balance of the Term Bonds Debt Service Fund are shown in the Combining Statement of Revenues, Expenditures, and Changes in Fund Balances, Illustration 7–3, and the Budget and Actual comparison in Illustration 7–4.

Disclosures in Notes to the Financial Statements

Any information in addition to the financial statements shown as Illustrations 7–2, 7–3, and 7–4 that would be helpful to administrators, members of the legislative body, interested residents, creditors, or any other category of person who uses the financial reports of a governmental reporting entity should, of course, be provided. GASB standards require disclosure in the notes to the financial statements (the notes are an integral part of the general purpose financial statements and are covered by the auditor's report) of specific data about deposits with financial institutions and investments. Disclosures are required for the entity as a whole, not just for debt service funds. However, since the Town of Brighton's debt service funds hold almost $1.2 million in cash and investments, it is appropriate to mention required note disclosures at this point.

GASB standards require disclosure in the notes of the types of deposits and investments authorized by legal and contractual provisions. Any significant violations during the period of legal or contractual provisions should, of course, be disclosed. If bank balances as of balance sheet date are entirely insured or collateralized with securities held by the entity or its agent in the entity's name,

ILLUSTRATION 7–2

TOWN OF BRIGHTON
Debt Service Funds
Combining Balance Sheet
As of December 31, 19y1

	Deferred Serial Bonds	Term Bonds	Total Debt Service Funds
Assets			
Cash	$ 290,000	$ 613	$ 290,613
Investments	808,625	83,316	891,941
Taxes receivable net	4,000	1,600	5,600
Interest receivable	25,000	–0–	25,000
Total Assets	$1,127,625	$85,529	$1,213,154
Fund Equity			
Fund Equity			
Fund Balance	1,127,625	85,529	1,213,154
Total Fund Equity	$1,127,625	$85,529	$1,213,154

ILLUSTRATION 7–3

TOWN OF BRIGHTON
Debt Service Funds
Combining Statement of Revenues, Expenditures,
and Changes in Fund Balances
For the Year Ended December 31, 19y1

	Regular Serial Bonds	Deferred Serial Bonds	Term Bonds	Total Debt Service Funds
Revenues:				
Taxes	$ –0–	$ 262,000	$117,000	$ 379,000
Miscellaneous sources	30,000	–0–	–0–	30,000
Interest on investments	–0–	98,250	3,145	101,395
Total Revenues	30,000	360,250	120,145	510,395
Expenditures:				
Interest on bonds	36,000	190,000	75,000	301,000
Redemption of matured bonds	–0–	200,000	–0–	200,000
Total Expenditures	36,000	390,000	75,000	501,000
Excess of Revenues over (under) Expenditures	(6,000)	(29,750)	45,145	9,395
Fund Balance, January 1, 19y1	–0–	1,157,375	40,384	1,197,759
Equity Transfer In	6,000	–0–	–0–	6,000
Fund Balance, December 31, 19y1	$ –0–	$1,127,625	$ 85,529	$1,213,154

ILLUSTRATION 7–4

TOWN OF BRIGHTON
Debt Service Funds
Combining Statement of Revenues, Expenditures, and Changes in Fund Balances—Budget and Actual
For the Year Ended December 31, 19y1

	Regular Serial Bonds			Deferred Serial Bonds			Term Bonds			Total Debt Service Funds		
	Budget	Actual	Actual over (under) Budget	Budget	Actual	Actual over (under) Budget	Budget	Actual	Actual over (under) Budget	Budget	Actual	Actual over (under) Budget
Revenues:												
Taxes	$ -0-	$ -0-	$ -0-	$ 260,000	$ 262,000	$2,000	$114,787	$117,000	$2,213	$ 374,787	$ 379,000	$4,213
Miscellaneous sources	36,000	30,000	(6,000)	-0-	-0-	-0-	-0-	-0-	-0-	36,000	30,000	(6,000)
Interest on investments	-0-	-0-	-0-	98,600	98,250	(350)	3,056	3,145	89	101,656	101,395	(261)
Total Revenues	36,000	30,000	(6,000)	358,600	360,250	1,650	117,843	120,145	2,302	512,443	510,395	(2,048)
Expenditures:												
Interest on bonds	36,000	36,000	-0-	190,000	190,000	-0-	75,000	75,000	-0-	301,000	301,000	-0-
Redemption of bonds	-0-	-0-	-0-	200,000	200,000	-0-	-0-	-0-	-0-	200,000	200,000	-0-
Total Expenditures	36,000	36,000	-0-	390,000	390,000	-0-	75,000	75,000	-0-	501,000	501,000	-0-
Excess of Revenues over (under) Expenditures	-0-	(6,000)	(6,000)	(31,400)	(29,750)	1,650	42,843	45,145	2,302	11,443	9,395	(2,048)
Fund Balance, January 1, 19y1	-0-	-0-	-0-	1,157,375	1,157,375	-0-	40,384	40,384	-0-	1,197,759	1,197,759	-0-
Equity Transfer In	-0-	6,000	6,000	-0-	-0-	-0-	-0-	-0-	-0-	-0-	6,000	6,000
Fund Balance, December 31, 19y1	$ -0-	$ -0-	$ -0-	$1,125,975	$1,127,625	$1,650	$ 83,227	$ 85,529	$2,302	$1,209,202	$1,213,154	$3,952

that fact should be mentioned. If not, the amount of the total bank balance should be classified and reported in the three categories of credit risk specified in the standards. Similarly, the carrying amount and market value of investments as of balance sheet date should be disclosed in total and for each type of investment. The disclosure of carrying amounts by type of investment should be classified in the three categories of credit risk specified in the standards.[3]

GASB standards apply to all state and local governmental reporting entities' financial reports that are intended to conform with generally accepted accounting principles. A number of states have established by law reporting requirements for the state government itself and for local governments within the state. It is common for financial reports prepared in compliance with state laws to include a list of the amounts on deposit in named banks; a list of securities held, their cost, and their market value as of balance sheet date; and, perhaps, a schedule of realized gains and losses on investments sold during the year. Supplementary schedules presented in order to conform with laws, or presented because administrators feel the disclosures should be made, are not covered by the independent auditor's report unless the audit engagement specifically extends the scope of the audit to the supplementary schedules.

Amortization of Premium and Discount on Investments

The Deferred Serial Bond Debt Service Fund and the Term Bond Debt Service Fund examples in this chapter do not illustrate the purchase of investments at a premium or discount, a common occurrence in practice. If the expectation is that investments may be held until maturity, at which time the face value would be received, amortization of premium or discount is necessary. Amortization is discussed at length in intermediate accounting texts, and therefore it is treated here only briefly. As an example, if a Term Bond Debt Service Fund purchases investments with a face value of $24,000 at 102, and $300 accrued interest, the entry to record the purchase might be:

Investments	24,000	
Unamortized Premium on Investments	480	
Interest Earnings	300	
Cash		24,780

Assuming $600 interest on the investments is received, the entry is:

Cash	600	
Interest Earnings		600

Either at the time interest is received, or at year-end as a part of the adjusting and closing process, the amortization of the premium should be computed and recorded. Intermediate financial accounting texts discuss the amortization computation in the context of profit-seeking entities; the discussion is equally applicable to nonprofit-seeking entities. Assuming the amount of amortization of premium on

---

[3] GASB Codification Sec. I50.163–.171.

the investments of the Term Bond Debt Service Fund of the Town of Brighton for the period under consideration is $18, the entry is:

Interest Earnings	18	
Unamortized Premium on Investments		18

Amortization of premium and discount on investments, discussed here in the context of term bond debt service fund accounting, should also be a part of the accounting plan for a serial bond debt service fund, which expects to hold investments until maturity.[4]

Debt Service Accounting for Special Assessment Debt

Special assessment projects, as discussed in Chapter 5, typically follow the same pattern as transactions of other capital projects. Specifically, construction activities are usually completed in the first year or so, using either interim financing from the governmental unit or proceeds of special assessment debt issuances (bonds or notes) to pay construction costs to contractors. Either at the beginning of the project or, more commonly, when construction is completed, assessments for debt service are levied against property owners in the defined special benefit district. Annual assessment installments receivable, and interest on deferred installments, usually approximate the amount of debt principal and interest payable during the same year. If the governmental unit is obligated in some manner to make the debt service payments in the event amounts collected from benefited property owners are insufficient, the debt should be recorded in the General Long-Term Debt Account Group (GLTDAG) and a debt service fund should be used to account for debt service activities. If the governmental unit is not obligated in any manner for special assessment debt, the debt should **not** be recorded in the GLT-DAG. In the latter case, which is relatively rare, debt service transactions should be accounted for in an **agency fund,** as explained in Chapter 11.

Assume that special assessment bonds, secondarily backed by the general taxing authority of the City of X, were issued to complete a street-widening project. Upon completion of the project the City levied assessments amounting to $480,000, payable in 10 equal installments with 5 percent interest on deferred installments, on owners of properties fronting on the improved streets. As shown by Entry 1, all receivables are recorded at the time of the levy, but Revenues is credited only for the amount expected to be collected within one year from the date of the levy; Deferred Revenues is credited for the amount of deferred installments. Required budgetary entries, as shown earlier in this chapter for serial bond and term bond debt service funds, are omitted for the sake of brevity.

---

[4] The reader should note this discussion refers to amortization of premium and discount on investments purchased with the expectation of holding them until maturity. Premium or discount on bonds payable sold by a governmental unit is *not* amortized; premium on bonds sold is considered as an Other Financing Source of the debt service fund if it must be used for debt service, as discussed in Chapter 5. Accrued interest sold should be recorded as revenue of the debt service fund.

1. Assessments Receivable—Current.........................	48,000	
Assessments Receivable—Deferred.......................	432,000	
Revenues...		48,000
Deferred Revenues		432,000

All current assessments receivable, due at year-end, were collected along with interest of $24,000 (see Entry 2). Any amounts not collected by the due date should be reclassified by a debit to Assessments Receivable —Delinquent and a credit to Assessments Receivable—Current.

2. Cash	72,000	
Assessments Receivable—Current....................		48,000
Revenues...		24,000

Matured special assessment bond principal in the amount of $48,000 and matured bond interest of $24,000 payable were recorded and paid on schedule.

3a. Expenditures—Bond Principal	48,000	
Expenditures—Bond Interest	24,000	
Bonds Payable		48,000
Interest Payable		24,000
3b. Bonds Payable	48,000	
Interest Payable	24,000	
Cash		72,000

The second installment of assessments receivable was reclassified from the Deferred category to the Current category. A corresponding amount of Deferred Revenues was reclassified as Revenues.

4a. Assessments Receivable—Current........................	48,000	
Assessments Receivable—Deferred....................		48,000
4b. Deferred Revenues	48,000	
Revenues...		48,000

This pattern of journal entries will be repeated during each of the remaining nine years until all special assessment bonds are retired.

Use of Debt Service Funds to Record Capital Lease Payments

In Chapter 5, under the heading "Acquisition of General Fixed Assets under Lease Agreements," an example is given of the computation of the amount to be recorded in a governmental fund, usually a capital projects fund, at the inception of a capital lease. In Chapter 6, under the heading "Assets Acquired under Capital Lease Agreements," the example is continued to illustrate the entry required in the General Fixed Assets Account Group when an asset is acquired by a capital lease agreement. The example presented in Chapter 5 specified that the first payment of $10,000 was due on January 1, 19y0, the inception of the lease. Governmental units commonly use a Debt Service Fund to record capital lease payments because the annual payments are merely installment payments of general long-term debt. The first payment, since it is on the first day of the lease, is entirely a payment on the principal of the lease obligation. Accordingly, the payment would be recorded as:

Expenditures—Principal of Capital Lease Obligation	10,000	
Cash...		10,000

The Expenditures detail record would show that the entire amount of the first payment was a payment on the principal. The payment due on January 1, 19y1, and the payment due each year thereafter, however, must be considered a partial payment on the lease obligation and a payment of interest on the unpaid balance of the lease obligation. GASB standards are consistent with the FASB's *SFAS No. 13;* both specify that a constant periodic rate of interest must be used. In the example started in Chapter 5, the present value of the obligation is computed using the rate of 10 percent per year. It is reasonable to use the same interest rate to determine what part of the annual $10,000 payment is payment of interest, and what part is payment of principal. The following table shows the distribution of the annual lease rental payments:

Payment Date	Amount of Payment	Interest on Unpaid Balance at 10 Percent	Payment on Principal	Unpaid Lease Obligation
				$67,590
1/1/y0	$10,000	$ –0–	$10,000	57,590
1/1/y1	10,000	5,759	4,241	53,349
1/1/y2	10,000	5,335	4,665	48,684
1/1/y3	10,000	4,868	5,132	43,552
1/1/y4	10,000	4,355	5,645	37,907
1/1/y5	10,000	3,791	6,209	31,698
1/1/y6	10,000	3,170	6,830	24,868
1/1/y7	10,000	2,487	7,513	17,355
1/1/y8	10,000	1,736	8,264	9,091
1/1/y9	10,000	909	9,091	–0–

As shown by the table above, although the total expenditure recorded each year, January 1, 19y0, through January 1, 19y9, is $10,000, the detail records for each year should show how much of the expenditure was for interest on the lease obligation and how much was payment on the obligation itself. As noted in Chapter 8, the unpaid balance of the capital lease obligation is carried in the General Long-Term Debt Account Group.

Accounting for Debt Refunding

If debt service fund assets accumulated for debt repayment are not sufficient to repay creditors when the debt matures, or if the interest rate on the debt is appreciably higher than the governmental unit would have to pay on a new bond issue, or if the covenants of the existing bonds are excessively burdensome, the governmental unit may issue refunding bonds.

The proceeds of refunding bonds issued at the maturity of the debt to be refunded are accounted for as Other Financing Sources of the debt service fund that is to repay the existing debt. The appropriation for debt repayment is accounted for as illustrated in the Town of Brighton Deferred Serial Bond Debt Service Fund example (see Entries 1, 2a, and 2b).

If a governmental unit has accumulated no assets at all for debt repayment, it is probable that no debt service fund exists. In such a case, a debt service fund should be created to account for the proceeds of the refunding bond issue and the repayment of the old debt. When the debt is completely repaid, the debt service fund relating to the liquidated issue should be closed, and a debt service fund for the refunding issue should be created and accounted for as described in this chapter. If the refunding bond issue is not sold but is merely given to the holders of the matured issue in an even exchange, the transaction would not require entries in a debt service fund but could be disclosed adequately in statements and schedules prepared for the General Long-Term Debt Account Group (discussed in Chapter 8) and in the notes to the financial statements.

Advance Refunding of Debt

Advance refundings of tax-exempt debt are common during periods when interest rates are falling sharply. Complex accounting and reporting issues have surfaced relating to legal questions such as, "Are both issues still the debt of the issuer?" "If the proceeds of the new issue are to be held for the eventual retirement of the old issue, how can the proceeds be invested to avoid conflict with the Internal Revenue Service over the taxability of interest on the debt issue?" (Compliance with the arbitrage rules under Section 148 of the Internal Revenue Code, and related regulations, is necessary for the interest to be exempt from federal income tax and, possibly, from state and local taxes.) Full consideration of the complexities of accounting for advance refundings resulting in defeasance of debt is presented in the GASB Codification Section D20. Defeasance of debt can be either "legal" or "in substance." **Legal defeasance** occurs when debt is legally satisfied based on certain provisions in the debt instrument even though the debt is not actually paid. **In-substance defeasance** occurs when debt is considered defeased for accounting and financial reporting purposes even though legal defeasance has not occurred. The GASB Codification Section D20.103 sets forth in detail the circumstances for in-substance defeasance. Briefly, the debtor must irrevocably place cash or other assets in trust with an escrow agent to be used solely for satisfying scheduled payments of both interest and principal of the defeased debt. The amount placed in escrow must be sufficiently large so that there is only a remote possibility that the debtor will be required to make future payments on the defeased debt. The trust is restricted to owning only monetary assets that are essentially risk-free as to the amount, timing, and collection of interest and principal.

To illustrate accounting for advance refundings resulting in defeasance of debt reported in the GLTDAG, assume the proceeds from the sale of the refunding issue amount to $2,000,000, and assume debt to be defeased amounted to $2,500,000. The proceeds are recorded in the fund receiving the proceeds (normally, a **debt service fund**) by an entry such as:

Cash	2,000,000	
Other Financing Source—Proceeds of Refunding Bonds		2,000,000

Payments to the escrow agent from resources provided by the new debt should be recorded in the debt service fund as an Other Financing Use; payments to the escrow agent from other resources are recorded as debt service expenditures. Therefore, assuming $500,000 has previously been accumulated in the debt service fund for payment of the $2,500,000 bond issue, the entry to record the payment to the escrow agent would be:

Other Financing Use—Payment to Refunded Bond Escrow Agent...	2,000,000	
Expenditures—Payment to Refunded Bond Escrow Agent . . .	500,000	
Cash		2,500,000

Disclosures about Advance Refundings

The **disclosure** guidance in GASB Codification Section D20 is applicable to state and local governments, public benefit corporations and authorities, public employee retirement systems, and governmental utilities, hospitals, colleges and universities, and to all funds of those entities.

Detailed disclosure guidance is set forth in Section D20.111-.114. Briefly, all entities subject to GASB jurisdiction are required to provide in the notes to the financial statements in the year of the refunding a general description of any advance refundings resulting in defeasance of debt. At a minimum the disclosures must include *(a)* the difference between the cash flows required to service the old debt and the cash flows required to service the new debt and complete the refundings, and *(b)* the economic gain or loss resulting from the transaction. Economic gain or loss is the difference between the **present value** of the old debt service requirements and the **present value** of the new debt service requirements, discounted at the effective interest rate and adjusted for additional cash paid. Section D20.601-.616 provides examples of effective interest rate and economic gain calculations and of note disclosures.

Selected References

American Institute of Certified Public Accountants. *Audit and Accounting Guide. Audits of State and Local Governmental Units*. Revised. New York, 1993.
Governmental Accounting Standards Board. *Codification of Governmental Accounting and Financial Reporting Standards as of June 30, 1993*. Norwalk, Conn., 1993.

Questions

7–1. "Debt service funds are established to account for long-term debt issued by state or local governments and for assets held to pay interest and matured debt principal." Is this statement true or false? Explain.

7–2. "All taxes raised for payment of interest and principal on general long-term debt are recognized as Other Financing Sources of the Debt Service Fund." Do you agree? Why or why not?

7–3. What revenue sources and other financing sources are commonly utilized for service of types of debt discussed in Chapter 7?

7–4. What basis of accounting is used for expenditures of a debt service fund? What exception is usually followed in recognizing expenditures for matured bond principal and interest?

7–5. What are the primary differences between bearer bonds and registered bonds? What implications do these differences have for bond issuers? For bondholders?

7–6. "If a certain city has six tax-supported bond issues and three special assessment bond issues outstanding, it would be preferable to operate nine separate debt service funds or, at a minimum, one debt service fund for tax-supported bonds and one for special assessment bonds." Do you agree? Explain.

7–7. If the city described in Question 7–6 does operate nine debt service funds, and statutes require debt service funds for tax-supported bonds to be operated under legal budgets (debt service funds for special assessment bonds are not required to operate under legal budgets), describe the financial statements that should be prepared for the debt service funds in order for that fund type to be presented in the GPFS in conformity with GASB standards.

7–8. It is conceivable that a debt service fund for an issue of regular serial bonds might have no assets or liabilities and, necessarily, no fund balance at the ends of some fiscal years. If this is true why should the fund be created at all? Explain your answer.

7–9. What asset and liability accounts would you expect to find in the statements for a deferred serial bond debt service fund? Why would you expect deferred serial bonds to create a more complex accounting situation than regular serial bonds?

7–10. One argument advanced in favor of financing with term bonds secured by some sort of a sinking fund is that earnings on investments held by the debt service fund will reduce the amount of support required from other sources. What is your opinion of the validity of this argument?

7–11. Briefly describe the note disclosures GASB standards require with respect to deposits with financial institutions and with respect to investments.

7–12. If general fixed assets are being acquired by a government under a capital lease agreement, describe the entries that should be recorded in a governmental fund (logically, a debt service fund) for each lease payment.

7–13. "Premiums and discounts on bond investments of the Debt Service Fund should not be amortized since the Debt Service fund is not a profit-seeking entity." Do you agree or disagree? Explain your answer.

7–14. During periods of low interest rates, governmental units often refund outstanding bonds in advance of their maturity. Explain the different ways of treating advance refundings that will permit, under GASB standards, removal of the liability for the refunded bonds from the General Long-Term Debt Account Group.

7–15. Referring to Question 7–14, what disclosures are required by GASB standards about advance refundings resulting in defeasance of debt?

Exercises and Problems

7–1. Utilizing the CAFR obtained for Exercise 1–1, follow the instructions below:

    a. Debt Service Function. How is the debt service function for tax-supported debt and special assessment debt handled—by the General Fund, by a Special Revenue Fund, or by one or more Debt Service Funds? If there is more than one Debt Service Fund, what kinds of bond issues or other debt instruments are serviced by each fund? Is debt service for bonds to be retired from enterprise revenues accounted for by enterprise funds?

Does the report state the basis of accounting used for debt service funds? If so, is the financial statement presentation consistent with the stated basis? If the basis of accounting is not stated, analyze the statements to determine which basis is used—full accrual, modified accrual, or cash basis. Is the basis used consistent with the standards discussed in Chapter 7?

b. *Investment Activity.* Compare the net assets of each debt service fund at balance sheet date with the amount of interest and the amount of debt principal the fund will be required to pay early in the following year (you may find debt service requirements in supplementary schedules following the individual fund and account group statements in the Financial Section of the CAFR). If debt service funds have accumulated assets in excess of amounts needed within a few days after the end of fiscal year, are the excess assets invested? Does the CAFR contain a schedule or list of investments of debt service funds? Does the report disclose gains and losses on investments realized during the year? Does the report disclose net earnings on investments during the year? What percentage of revenue of each Debt Service Fund is derived from earnings on investments? What percentage of the revenue of each Debt Service Fund is derived from taxes levied directly for the Debt Service Fund? What percentage is derived from transfers from other funds? List any other sources of debt service revenue and other financing sources, and indicate the relative importance of each source.

Are estimated revenues for term bond debt service budgeted on an actuarial basis? If so, are revenues received as required by the actuarial computations?

c. Considering the debt maturity dates as well as the amount of debt, and apparent quality of debt service fund investments, does the debt service activity appear to be properly managed? Does the report disclose whether investments are managed by a corporate fiduciary, another outside investment manager, or by governmental employees? If outside investment managers are employed, is the basis of their fees disclosed? Are the fees accounted for as additions to the cost of investments, or as expenditures?

Is one or more paying agents, or fiscal agents, employed? If so, does the report disclose if the agents keep track of the ownership of registered bonds, write checks to bondholders for interest payments and matured bonds (or, in the case of coupon bonds, pay matured coupons and matured bonds presented through banking channels)? If agents are employed, does the balance sheet, or notes to the financial statements, disclose the amount of cash in their possession? If so, does this amount appear reasonable in relation to interest payable and matured bonds payable? Do the statements, schedules, or narratives disclose for how long a period of time debt service funds carry a liability for unpresented checks for interest on registered bonds, for matured but unpresented interest coupons, and for matured but unpresented bonds?

If agents are employed, do they charge fees? If so, is the basis of the fee disclosed? What percentage of interest and principal payments is the fiscal agent's fee? Are fees accounted for as expenditures of debt service fund appropriations? If not, how are they accounted for, and by which fund?

d. *Capital Lease Rental Payments.* If general fixed assets are being acquired under capital lease agreements, are periodic lease rental payments accounted for as

Expenditures of a debt service fund (or by another governmental fund)? If so, does the report disclose that the provisions of *SFAS No. 13* are being followed (see the Use of Debt Service Funds to Record Capital Lease Payments section of Chapter 7) to determine the portion of each capital lease payment considered as interest and the portion considered as payment on the principal.

7–2. Write the numbers 1 through 10 on a sheet of paper. Beside each number write the letter corresponding with the best answer to each of the following questions:

1. Central County received proceeds from various towns and cities for capital projects financed by Central's long-term debt. A special tax was assessed by each local government, and a portion of the tax was restricted to repay the long-term debt of Central's capital projects. Central should account for the restricted portion of the special tax in which of the following funds?

   a. Internal Service Fund.

   b. Enterprise Fund.

   c. Capital Projects Fund.

   d. Debt Service Fund.

2. Tott City's serial bonds are serviced through a debt service fund with cash provided by the General Fund. In a debt service fund's statements, how are cash receipts and cash payments reported?

	Cash Receipts	*Cash Payments*
a.	Revenues	Expenditures
b.	Revenues	Operating Transfers
c.	Operating Transfers	Expenditures
d.	Operating Transfers	Operating Transfers

3. Interest expenditures relating to tax-supported bonds payable should be recorded in a debt service fund:

   a. At the end of the fiscal period if the interest due date does *not* coincide with the end of the fiscal period.

   b. When bonds are issued.

   c. When the interest is legally payable.

   d. When the interest checks are written.

Items 4 and 5 are based on the following information: The following events relating to the City of Albury's Debt Service Fund occurred during the year ended December 31, 19x1.

Debt principal matured	$2,000,000
Unmatured (accrued) interest on outstanding debt at January 1, 19x1	50,000
Matured interest on debt	900,000
Unmatured (accrued) interest on outstanding debt at December 31, 19x1	100,000
Interest revenue from investments	600,000
Cash transferred from General Fund for retirement of debt principal	1,000,000
Cash transferred from General Fund for payment of matured interest	900,000

All principal and interest due in 19x1 were paid on time.

4. What is the total amount of expenditures that Albury's Debt Service Fund should record for the year ended December 31, 19x1?
   a. $2,950,000.
   b. $2,900,000.
   c. $950,000.
   d. $900,000.

5. How much should Albury's Debt Service Fund report as Revenues for the year ended December 31, 19x1?
   a. $2,500,000.
   b. $1,900,000.
   c. $1,600,000.
   d. $600,000.

6. A debt service fund should be used to account for the payment of interest and principal on:
   a. Debt recorded in the General Long-Term Debt Account Group.
   b. Debt secured by the revenues of a governmentally owned enterprise.
   c. Debt recorded as a liability of the General Fund.
   d. All of the above.

7. Debt Service Fund financial statements that should be included in the Comprehensive Annual Financial Report of a state or local governmental unit are:
   a. Combining Balance Sheet; Combining Statement of Revenues, Expenditures, and Changes in Fund Balances; and Schedule of Investments.
   b. Combining Balance Sheet; Combining Statement of Revenues, Expenditures, and Changes in Fund Balances; and Combining Statement of Revenues, Expenditures, and Changes in Fund Balances—Budget and Actual for all Debt Service Funds for which annual budgets have been legally adopted.
   c. Combining Balance Sheet; Combining Statement of Cash Flows, and Combining Statement of Revenues and Expenses.
   d. The following statements for each individual Debt Service Fund: Balance Sheet; Statement of Revenues, Expenditures, and Changes in Fund Balances; and Statement of Revenues, Expenditures, and Changes in Fund Balances—Budget and Actual.

8. Debt service funds may be used to account for:
   a. Lease payments under capital lease agreements.
   b. Repayment of bond principal.
   c. The proceeds of refunding bond issues.
   d. All of the above.

9. Which of the following accounts is *least* likely to appear in a debt service fund?
   a. Estimated Revenues.
   b. Encumbrances.
   c. Appropriations.
   d. Matured Bonds Payable.

10. If a governmental unit has issued refunding bonds in advance of the maturity of a noncallable general obligation debt issue:
    a. The liability for both bond issues must be reported in the body of the financial statements.
    b. The liability for the old issue should be shown in the notes to the financial

statements, and the liability for the new issue should be shown in the body of the financial statements.

c. The liability for the new debt should be reported in the statements if the old debt is defeased and the criteria set forth in GASB standards are met.

d. The liability for neither issue should be shown in the financial statements until the old issue has matured.

(Items 1 through 5, AICPA, adapted)

7–3. The Debt Service Fund Combining Balance Sheet found in an annual report of Northeast City is reproduced below. Study the balance sheet and list *(a)* the items that appear to be in accord with GASB standards discussed in Chapter 7, and *(b)* the items that appear to differ from GASB standards.

NORTHEAST CITY
Combining Balance Sheet
All Debt Service Funds
June 30, 19y5

	General Obligation Bonds	Urban Renewal Tax Increment Notes	Totals June 30, 19y5	Totals June 30, 19y4
Assets				
Cash and pooled cash investments	$237,376	$500,580	$ 737,956	$3,530,016
Taxes receivable	164,976	3,051	168,027	135,791
Due from other funds	—	423,944	423,944	423,944
Total Assets	$402,352	$927,575	$1,329,927	$4,089,751
Liabilities and Fund Balances				
Liabilities:				
Warrants payable	$ —	$494,493	$ 494,493	$2,872,846
Matured bonds payable	5,000	—	5,000	250,000
Matured interest payable	67,171	—	67,171	367,034
Total Liabilities	72,171	494,493	566,664	3,489,880
Fund Balance:				
Unreserved:				
Designated for debt service	330,181	433,082	763,263	599,871
Total Fund Balance	330,181	433,082	763,263	599,871
Total Liabilities and Fund Balance	$402,352	$927,575	$1,329,927	$4,089,751

7–4. The only other combining statement for Northeast City's Debt Service Fund in addition to the balance sheet (Exercise 7–3) is the Combining Statement of Revenues, Expenditures, and Fund Balances—Budget and Actual, reproduced on page 215. Study this statement and comment on the extent to which the City appears to adhere to GASB standards for debt service fund accounting and reporting.

NORTHEAST CITY
Combining Statement of Revenues, Expenditures, and Changes in Fund Balances—Budget and Actual— Debt Service Fund Types
For the Fiscal Year Ended June 30, 19y5

	General Obligation Bonds			Urban Renewal Tax Increment Notes			Totals (Memorandum Only)		
	Budget	Actual	Variance— Favorable (Unfavorable)	Budget	Actual	Variance— Favorable (Unfavorable)	Budget	Actual	Variance— Favorable (Unfavorable)
Revenues:									
Taxes	$6,216,292	$6,154,601	$ (61,691)	$677,121	$673,170	$ (3,951)	$6,893,413	$6,827,771	$ (65,642)
Expenditures:									
Principal retirement	4,539,000	4,129,000	410,000	249,901	249,901	—	4,788,901	4,378,901	410,000
Interest and fiscal charges	2,225,292	1,858,258	367,034	427,220	427,220	—	2,652,512	2,285,478	367,034
Total Expenditures	6,764,292	5,987,258	777,034	677,121	677,121	—	7,441,413	6,664,379	777,034
Excess of Revenues over (under) Expenditures	(548,000)	167,343	715,343	—	(3,951)	(3,951)	(548,000)	163,392	711,392
Fund Balances—July 1, 19y4	657,170	162,838	(494,332)	—	437,033	437,033	657,170	599,871	(57,299)
Fund Balances—June 30, 19y5	$ 109,170	$ 330,181	$221,011	$ —	$433,082	$433,082	$ 109,170	$ 763,263	$654,093

7–5. The debt service fund statements in an annual report of Northeast City are reproduced in connection with Exercises 7–3 and 7–4.

    a. If you were considering the purchase of several Urban Renewal Tax Increment notes of Northeast City, would the statements serve your information needs? Why or why not? What additional information, if any, would you want before you made your final decision on the note purchase?

    b. If you were a resident of Northeast City interested in evaluating the manner in which the City administration performs the debt service function, would the statements serve your information needs? Why or why not? What additional information, if any, would you want?

7–6. A governmental unit is planning a sinking fund to retire $10,000,000 of term bonds that mature in 20 years. Semiannual additions will be made to the sinking fund for the next 20 years at the end of each period. It is estimated that a net return of 6 percent per annum, compounded semiannually, can be realized on the average.

    a. Compute the necessary periodic additions for debt repayment. (Annuity tables are provided in Appendix 2.)

    b. What information would you need, in addition to the results of your computation in part *a*, in order to be able to prepare the revenue budget for debt service for the term bond issue?

7–7. The Heinz Township has agreed to acquire a new fire truck under a capital lease agreement. At the inception of the lease a payment of $50,000 is to be made; nine annual lease payments, each in the amount of $50,000, are to be made at the end of each year after the inception of the lease. The total amount to be paid under this lease, therefore, is $500,000. The City could borrow this amount for 9 years at the annual rate of 8 percent. Assume that the fair value of the fire truck at the inception of the lease is $370,000. **Show all computations in good form.**

    a. Show the entry that should be made in a **capital projects fund** at the inception of the lease.

    b. Show the entry that should be made at the inception of the lease in the **GFAAG.**

    c. Show the entry which should be made in the **debt service fund** at the end of the first year after the inception of the lease.

7–8. The Town of Shropshire Serial Bond Debt Service Fund Balance Sheet as of December 31, 19x6, is presented below:

TOWN OF SHROPSHIRE
Serial Bond Debt Service Fund—Balance Sheet
As of December 31, 19x6

Assets		Fund Equity	
Cash	$ 1,500	Fund Balance	$514,000
Investments	500,000		
Interest receivable on investments	12,500		
Total Assets	$514,000	Total Fund Equity	$514,000

Required   *a.* Prepare entries in general journal form to reflect, as necessary, the following information:

(1) The Revenues budget for serial bond debt service for 19x7 consists of estimated revenues of $330,000 to be raised from a debt service tax levy, and estimated revenues of $30,000 from earnings on investments. The Appropriations budget consists of bond interest to be paid on January 1, $100,000, and bond interest to be paid on July 1, $100,000.

(2) Taxes receivable in the amount of $340,000 and estimated uncollectible taxes in the amount of $10,000 are recorded.

(3) Half of the gross levy of taxes is collected in cash.

(4) Checks are written and mailed for the interest payment due on January 1, 19x7.

(5) Cash in the amount of $70,000 is invested.

(6) Interest receivable as of December 31, 19x6, is collected and invested.

(7) Taxes in the amount of $160,000 are collected in cash.

(8) Checks are written and mailed for the interest payment due on July 1, 19x7.

(9) Interest on investments is received in cash in the amount of $15,000; cash in the amount of $75,000 is invested.

(10) Accrued interest receivable on investments at year-end is computed as $13,000.

(11) Budgetary and operating statement accounts are closed, and Taxes Receivable and the related Estimated Uncollectible accounts are designated as Delinquent.

b. Prepare a Balance Sheet for the Town of Shropshire Serial Bond Debt Service Fund as of December 31, 19x7.

c. Prepare a Statement of Revenues, Expenditures, and Changes in Fund Balance for the fund for the year ended December 31, 19x7.

d. Prepare a Statement of Revenues, Expenditures, and Changes in Fund Balance—Budget and Actual for the year ended December 31, 19x7.

7–9. On July 1, 19x3, the City of Melton issued $2,000,000 of 6 percent term bonds maturing in five years on July 1, 19x8. Interest on the bonds is payable semiannually on January 1 and July 1, with the first interest payment falling due on January 1, 19x4.

A sinking fund is to be established, with equal additions to be made semiannually on December 31 and June 30 each year. The first addition will be made on December 31, 19x3. Sinking fund investments are expected to yield a return of 6 percent per annum, compounded semiannually. Investment earnings are added to the sinking fund principal.

Required   *a.* Prepare a schedule in good form showing the required additions to the sinking fund, the expected semiannual earnings, and the end-of-period balance in the sinking fund for each of the 10 periods.

b. Prepare entries in general journal form to reflect the following transactions or information for the fiscal year ended June 30, *19x8* only. Disregard any entries that should be made in the General Fund.

(1) On July 1, 19x7, the budget for fiscal year 19x8 was enacted approving operating transfers from the General Fund totaling $468,922.02. In addition, the budget provides appropriations for the interest payments due on July 1, 19x7, and January 1, 19x8. (Record only the budget entry at this time.)

(2) The semiannual interest payment due on July 1, 19x7, was made using cash transferred at the end of the prior fiscal year.

(3) On December 31, 19x7, operating transfers of $234,461.01 were made from the General Fund to the Term Bond Debt Service Fund. Of this amount, $60,000 is for the semiannual interest payment due on January 1, 19x8, and $174,461.01 is for the December 31 addition to the sinking fund. The latter amount was invested immediately in approved sinking fund investments.

(4) Sinking fund investments earned $47,500 for the six months ending December 31, 19x7.

(5) The interest payment due on January 1, 19x8, was made on schedule.

(6) On June 30, 19x8, another $234,461.01 was transferred from the General Fund for the final (July 1, 19x8) interest payment and the final addition to the sinking fund. The final addition to the sinking fund is not invested since the bond principal is to be retired the next day on July 1, 19x8.

(7) Sinking fund investments earned $53,500 for the six months ending June 30, 19x8.

(8) Prepare necessary closing entries as of June 30, 19x8.

c. Prepare entries in general journal form to reflect the final transaction for the Term Bond Debt Service Fund on July 1, 19x8, the date the bonds are retired and the last semiannual interest is due.

(1) The budget for fiscal year 19x9 approved appropriations in the amount of $2,060,000; $2,000,000 to retire the bonds and $60,000 for the final interest payment.

(2) All sinking fund investments are sold on July 1, 19x8, for $1,826,826.95, the sum of the 10 additions plus accumulated investment earnings.

(3) On July 1, 19x8, the City retired the bonds in the amount of $2,000,000 and paid the last semiannual interest of $60,000 on the bonds.

(4) Prepare the necessary journal entries to close the Term Bond Debt Service Fund and transfer any remaining equity to the General Fund.

7–10. The City of Arnold had outstanding 5 percent term bonds, scheduled to mature July 1, 19x8, in the amount of $4,000,000. Early in 19x8, only $500,000 had been accumulated in a Term Bonds Debt Service Fund to apply on retirement of the bonds so a proposal was made to refund the remainder with 6 percent registered serial bonds, to mature at the rate of $500,000 every year, beginning July 1, 19x9. Interest on the new issue is to be paid semiannually—on January 1 and July 1. Enough of the present bondholders accepted the proposal to make it feasible, and the budget for the fiscal year ending June 30, 19x9, was set up to pay all the semiannual interest due on July 1 and $500,000 to bondholders. The $500,000 in the Term Bonds Debt Service Fund was in a noninterest-bearing Cash account.

a. The following transactions occurred in the Term Bonds Debt Service Fund during the year ended June 30, 19x9. Record them in general journal form.

(1) The Revenues budget for the year provided for an operating transfer from the General Fund in the amount of the interest due July 1 on the entire $4,000,000 worth of term bonds. The Appropriations budget authorized the July interest payment and the payment of $500,000 for bonds to be redeemed. Record the budget.

(2) The General Fund transferred enough cash to the Term Bonds Debt Service Fund to pay interest due July 1 on the entire $4,000,000 worth of term bonds.

(3) The $500,000 worth of bonds to be redeemed and the interest due on July 1 were recorded as liabilities.

(4) Interest for the year and the bond liability were paid.

(5) All remaining open accounts were closed.

b. A Serial Bond Debt Service Fund was created to account for debt service activities related to the new issue. During the year ended June 30, 19x9, the following transactions occurred. Record them in general journal form:

(1) The budget for the year was recorded. Estimated revenues, to be raised from taxes levied directly for this fund, were in the amount of one year's interest payments and the first serial bond repayment. Appropriations were budgeted only for the interest legally due during the fiscal year.

(2) Taxes receivable were levied to yield the amount of estimated revenues, assuming 3 percent of the taxes would be uncollectible. Round computation of the levy to the nearest $10.

(3) Ninety percent of the gross levy of taxes was collected. The remainder of the taxes receivable and the related Estimated Uncollectible Current Taxes Account were classified as delinquent.

(4) Cash in the amount of the January 1, 19x9, interest payment was paid to bondholders; remaining cash was invested.

(5) Interest on investments collected in cash during the year totaled $9,300; interest on investments accrued at year-end was $2,900. Interest and penalties receivable on taxes totaled $2,840, of which $600 is estimated to be uncollectible.

(6) Budgetary and operating statement accounts for the year were closed.

c. Prepare a Serial Bond Debt Service Fund Balance Sheet as of June 30, 19x9.

d. Prepare a Serial Bond Debt Service Fund Statement of Revenues, Expenditures, and Changes in Fund Balance for the year ended June 30, 19x9.

e. Prepare a Serial Bond Debt Service Fund Statement of Revenues, Expenditures, and Changes in Fund Balance—Budget and Actual for the year ended June 30, 19x9.

Continuous Problems

7–L. The City of Bingham utilizes a single debt service fund to account for the service of all issues of tax-supported and special assessment long-term debt. As of June 30, 19x1, one issue of tax-supported serial bonds and one issue of special assessment term bonds were outstanding. The post-closing trial balance of the Debt Service Fund as of June 30, 19x1, is shown on the next page.

The issue of tax-supported serial bonds outstanding on June 30, 19x1, amounted to $6,000,000; bonds of this issue in the amount of $300,000 mature on July 1, 19x1, and on each July 1 thereafter. This bond issue bears interest at the annual rate of 6 percent, payable on January 1 and July 1 of each year. The cash balance of the debt service fund on June 30, 19x1, is to be used for the repayment of tax-supported bonds maturing on July 1, 19x1, and for the interest on those bonds due on July 1, 19x1.

The issue of special assessment term bonds outstanding on June 30, 19x1, amounted to $600,000; it bears interest at the annual rate of 8 percent, payable on January 1 and July 1 of each year. The bonds will mature on July 1, 19y1. As of June 30, 19x1, investments in the amount of $260,000 are being held for payment of the special assessment bonds at maturity.

CITY OF BINGHAM
Debt Service Fund
Trial Balance
As of June 30, 19x1

	Debits	Credits
Cash	$ 505,000	
Taxes Receivable—Delinquent	42,000	
Estimated Uncollectible Delinquent Taxes		$ 38,000
Special Assessments Receivable—Current	66,000	
Special Assessments Receivable—Deferred	594,000	
Investments for Special Assessment Bond Payment	260,000	
Deferred Revenues		594,000
Fund Balance		835,000
Totals	$1,467,000	$1,467,000

In order to add to investments held to pay the bonds at maturity and to pay interest due in fiscal year 19x2, the City of Bingham Debt Service Fund must budget revenues from special assessments during fiscal year 19x2 in the amount of $66,000.

Capital lease obligations outstanding have a present value on June 30, 19x1, of $1,020,000. Collections of delinquent taxes receivable plus revenues to be raised in fiscal year 19x2 will be used to make required lease payments during fiscal year 19x2.

On July 1, 19x1, the City of Bingham sold an issue of tax-supported serial bonds to finance the construction and equipping of an annex to City Hall. As described in Problem 5–L, the total amount of bonds sold on that date was $3,000,000. The issue bears interest at the annual rate of 8 percent, payable on January 1 and July 1 of each year; bonds in the amount of $150,000 will mature on July 1, 19x2, and each July 1 thereafter.

In addition to the accounts listed in the trial balance, general ledger accounts provided for the debt service fund are:

Investments—Temporary

Taxes Receivable—Current

Estimated Uncollectible Current Taxes

Interest and Penalties Receivable

Estimated Uncollectible Interest and Penalties

Estimated Revenues

Revenues

Appropriations

Expenditures—19x2

Equity Transfer In

Subsidiary ledger accounts for the debt service fund are:

Revenues—Subsidiary Ledger Accounts
Property Taxes
Interest and Penalties on Taxes
Special Assessments
Premium on Bonds Sold
Interest on Investments

Appropriations and Expenditures—Subsidiary Ledger Accounts
Interest on Bonds Payable
Principal of Matured Bonds
Interest on Capital Lease Obligations
Principal of Capital Lease Obligations

Required

a. Prepare general journal entries to record the following transactions in the general ledger accounts and in subsidiary ledger accounts.

(1) From the data given about the two bond issues outstanding on June 30, 19x1, and the bond issue sold on July 1, 19x1, record the adoption of the legal budget for the fiscal year ended June 30, 19x2. (The budget provided estimated revenues from property taxes, $1,182,000; from special assessments, $66,000; from premium on bonds sold, $30,000; and from earnings on investments, $28,000. Appropriations were provided for the payment of bonds maturing on July 1, 19x1, for bond interest payments due on July 1, 19x1, for bond interest payments due on January 1, 19x2; $108,000, for interest payments on capital lease obligations, and $72,000 for payments on the principal of capital lease obligations.)

(2) Taxes were levied by the Debt Service Fund in the amount of $1,218,000. Of this amount, $36,000 was expected to be uncollectible.

(3) Cash in the amount of the premium on the bonds sold on July 1, 19x1 (see Problem 5–L, requirement *a*, Transaction 1) was received and deposited by the Debt Service Fund. The premium is not to be amortized; credit Revenues for the entire $30,000.

(4) Temporary investments in the amount of $30,000 were purchased.

(5) Checks were written and mailed to pay holders of bonds maturing on July 1, 19x1, and to pay all bond interest due that day.

(6) Delinquent taxes receivable were collected in the amount of $4,000. Taxes Receivable—Current were collected in the amount of $620,000. Special Assessments in the amount of $66,000 were collected.

(7) Investments to be held for repayment of special assessment bonds at maturity were purchased in the amount of $18,000. Temporary investments in the amount of $610,000 were purchased.

(8) Information was received that interest in the amount of $8,300 had been added to investments held for repayment of special assessment bonds. Interest on temporary investments was received in cash in the amount of $8,000.

(9) Temporary investments amounting to $425,000 were sold at par.

(10) Checks were written and mailed to holders of all three issues of bonds for the interest payments due January 1, 19x2. Payments on capital lease obligations totaled $180,000—$108,000 interest and $72,000 on the principal.

(11) Current taxes receivable were collected in the amount of $550,000. The balance of taxes receivable, and the related estimated uncollectible account, were classified as delinquent.

(12) Information was received that interest in the amount of $8,800 had been added to investments held for repayment of special assessment bonds. Interest on temporary investments was received in cash in the amount of $4,600.

(13) Cash to close the City Hall Annex Construction Fund was received (see Problem 5–L, requirement *d*).

(14) Special assessments receivable in the amount of $66,000 were transferred

from the deferred category to the current category; an equivalent amount was transferred from Deferred Revenues to Revenues.

(15) Interest and penalties on delinquent taxes as of year-end was computed as $9,200, of which $4,200 was expected to be uncollectible.

(16) All temporary investments were converted into cash.

(17) Budgetary and operating statement accounts for the year were closed.

b. Prepare a Balance Sheet for the Debt Service Fund as of June 30, 19x2.

c. Prepare a Statement of Revenues, Expenditures, and Changes in Fund Balance for the Debt Service Fund for the year ended June 30, 19x2.

d. Prepare a Statement of Revenues, Expenditures, and Changes in Fund Balance—Budget and Actual for the year ended June 30, 19x2.

7–S. The City of Smithville created a Street Improvement Bond Debt Service Fund to be used to retire the bonds issued for the purposes described in Problem 5–S, and to pay the interest on the bonds. The $1,000,000 worth of bonds issued during 19y1 were dated January 1, 19y1, and were each in the denomination of $5,000, bearing the nominal annual interest rate of 7 percent. The first interest payment was due July 1, 19y1. Subsequent semiannual interest payments were to be made January 1 and July 1 of each following year until the maturity of the bond. Forty bonds are to mature 10 years after date of issue, and 40 bonds are to mature each year thereafter until all the bonds issued in 19y1 have matured.

Required

a. Open a general journal for the Street Improvement Bond Debt Service Fund. Record the transactions below, as necessary. Use account titles illustrated in Chapter 7.

(1) The budget for 19y1 was legally adopted. Since the bond issue was authorized after the General Fund budget for 19y1 was legally adopted, the Debt Service fund budget provided Estimated Revenues of $20,000 premium on bonds sold and $17,500 accrued interest on bonds sold; and appropriations in the amount of the interest payment to be made during 19y1.

(2) Premium and accrued interest on bonds sold were received and deposited (see Transaction 4, Problem 5–S).

(3) The July 1, 19y1, interest payment was made.

(4) Budgetary and operating statement accounts for the year were closed.

b. The City of Smithville had a Term Bond Debt Service Fund in addition to the Street Improvement Bond Debt Service Fund, for which you have made entries in part *a* of this problem. The financial statements of the Term Bond Debt Service Fund as of December 31, 19y1, and for the year then ended, appear below.

CITY OF SMITHVILLE
Term Bond Debt Service Fund
Balance Sheet
As of December 31, 19y1

Assets

Cash	$ 133,250
Investments	1,430,000
Total Assets	$1,563,250

Fund Equity

Fund Balance	$1,563,250
Total Fund Equity	$1,563,250

CITY OF SMITHVILLE
Term Bond Debt Service Fund
Statement of Revenues, Expenditures,
and Changes in Fund Balance
For the Year Ended December 31, 19y1

Revenues:	
Taxes	$ 153,450
Interest on Investments	79,800
Total Revenues	233,250
Expenditures:	
Interest on Bonds	133,250
Excess of Revenues over Expenditures	100,000
Fund Balance, January 1, 19y1	1,463,250
Fund Balance, December 31, 19y1	$1,563,250

CITY OF SMITHVILLE
Term Bond Debt Service Fund
Statement of Revenues, Expenditures, and
Changes in Fund Balance—Budget and Actual
For the Year Ended December 31, 19y1

	Budget	Actual	Actual Over (Under) Budget
Revenues:			
Taxes	$ 154,000	$ 153,450	$(550)
Interest on Investments	80,000	79,800	(200)
Total	234,000	233,250	(750)
Expenditures:			
Interest on Bonds	133,250	133,250	–0–
Excess of Revenues over Expenditures	100,750	100,000	(750)
Fund Balance, January 1, 19y1	1,463,250	1,463,250	–0–
Fund Balance, December 31, 19y1	$1,564,000	$1,563,250	$(750)

Prepare (1) a Combining Balance Sheet for the Term Bonds Debt Service Fund and the Street Improvement Debt Service Fund as of December 31, 19y1; (2) a Combining Statement of Revenues, Expenditures, and Changes in Fund Balances for the two debt service funds for the year ended December 31, 19y1; and (3) a Combining Statement of Revenues, Expenditures, and Changes in Fund Balances—Budget and Actual for the two debt service funds for the year ended December 31, 19y1.

c. It is expected that additional Street Improvement Bonds in the total amount of $2,000,000 will be issued in 19y2. It is expected that the additional bonds will be of the $5,000 denomination and will bear interest at the nominal annual rate of 7.2 percent. The additional bonds will be dated January 1, 19y2.

The first interest payment will be made July 1, 19y2; interest will be payable January 1 and July 1 of each following year until maturity. Forty bonds of the 19y2 issue will mature 10 years after date of issue, and 40 bonds will mature each year thereafter until all bonds of the 19y2 issue have matured. Record the following events and transactions for 19y2, as necessary.

(1) The budget for 19y2 was legally adopted. The budget provided estimated Other Financing Sources to be transferred from the General Fund in an amount equal to the appropriations for interest for the year on all Street Improvement Bonds expected to be outstanding during the year, plus an amount of $150,000 to be invested by the Debt Service Fund for eventual bond redemption. The budget also provided for earnings of $9,500 on Debt Service Fund investments. No premium or accrued interest on bonds sold is included in the 19y2 estimated revenues; if the Debt Service Fund does receive such items from the Street Improvement Fund, they will be invested and used for eventual bond redemption.

(2) On January 1, 19y2, the General Fund transferred $35,000 in cash to the Debt Service Fund; the remainder due from the General Fund was recorded as a receivable.

(3) Bond interest due January 1, 19y2, was paid.

(4) The fund received $43,000 from the Street Improvement Fund as premium and accrued interest on the $2,000,000 face value of bonds sold on March 1, 19y2. This amount is invested in 6 percent U.S. Treasury notes purchased at par. The notes mature March 1, 19y4; interest dates are March 1 and September 1.

(5) The amount due from the General Fund is received on June 30.

(6) Bond interest due July 1, 19y2, is paid; on July 1, the remainder of the cash transferred from the General Fund (see Transaction 5) is invested in long-term certificates of deposit at 8 percent per annum, compounded semiannually.

(7) Semiannual interest on Treasury notes is received on September 1.

(8) Necessary adjusting and closing entries were made as of December 31, 19y2.

d. Prepare a Balance Sheet for the Street Improvement Bond Debt Service Fund as of December 31, 19y2.

e. Prepare a Statement of Revenues, Expenditures, and Changes in Fund Balance for the Street Improvement Bond Debt Service Fund for the year ended December 31, 19y2.

f. Prepare a Statement of Revenues, Expenditures, and Changes in Fund Balance— Budget and Actual for the Street Improvement Bond Debt Service Fund for the year ended December 31, 19y2.

CHAPTER
8

General Long-Term Debt Account Group

The management of state and local governmental debt requires good legal advice and good understanding of the principles of public finance, both backed by competently designed and operated financial management information systems. Accounting aspects of the financial management information systems for four types of funds recommended for use by state and local governmental units are discussed in preceding chapters. The reader should recall that general and special revenue funds, capital projects funds, and debt service funds account for only short-term debt to be paid from fund assets. Enterprise funds, internal service funds, and nonexpendable trust funds account for long-term debt serviced by the fund, as well as short-term debt to be paid from fund assets.

General Long-Term Debt Account Group

Debt instruments backed by the "full faith and credit" of a governmental unit are known as *general obligation debt;* they are obligations of the unit and not of the individual funds. In order to bring such debt under accounting control, the General Long-Term Debt Account Group (GLTDAG) was created. Since the account group was named it has become common for governments to issue debt secured by a pledge of the collections of a certain specified tax (called *limited obligation debt*), or even a certain portion of a tax—for example, 1 cent of a 5 cent sales tax levied by a government (called *tax increment debt*); all debt secured by pledges of tax revenues is known as **tax-supported debt.** In addition to tax-supported long-term debt, GASB standards currently provide that the GLTDAG account for debt backed by special assessments (if the general government is obligated to assume debt service in the event that collections of special assessments are not sufficient to pay debt service); time warrants; notes having a maturity of more than one year from date of issuance; the present value of capital lease payments; the noncurrent portion of claims, judgments, and compensated absences to be paid when due by use of resources of governmental funds; and any unfunded liability for pensions of employees of activities accounted for by governmental funds. In short, all long-term debt not being serviced by the revenues of a proprietary fund or nonexpendable trust fund is accounted for by the GLTDAG under current standards.

Liability accounts have credit balances; in order for the GLTDAG to be self-balancing, it is necessary to create accounts that have debit balances even though no assets are assigned to the group (it is an account group, not a fund). The debit balance accounts that offset the long-term liabilities are of two categories: (1) amounts accumulated in debt service funds for repayment of general long-term debt and (2) amounts that must be provided in future years for repayment of long-term debt accounted for by the GLTDAG. The sum of the two categories of debit balance accounts, therefore, equals the total amount of outstanding "general" long-term debt.

Debt of enterprise funds may be issued with covenants that give it the status of general obligation debt, although the intent is for the debt to be serviced from the resources of the issuing fund. As discussed in subsequent chapters, the liability should be displayed on the face of the statement of the issuing fund, if that fund may realistically be expected to finance the debt service; the contingent liability should be disclosed in a note to the financial statements, such as:

> In addition to the long-term debt exhibited in this statement, the City of _____ has a contingent liability against its full faith and credit on $_____ of revenue bonds recorded in the Water Utility Fund. The general credit of the City is obligated only to the extent that revenues of that utility are insufficient to pay interest on matured bonds when due.

A similar note should be included in the event that the government has a contingent obligation to assume debt service of long-term debt backed primarily by special assessments.

Bonds and other debt of enterprise funds issued with covenants that give the debt the status, even contingently, of tax-supported debt may affect the governmental unit's ability to issue additional tax-supported debt. The reason for this is discussed under the heading "Debt Limit and Debt Margin" in this chapter. If the contingency clause becomes effective because resources of the enterprise fund are insufficient for debt service, the unpaid portion of the debt is assumed by the government as a whole and the liability is accounted for by the General Long-Term Debt Account Group. The enterprise fund that is relieved of the liability then removes the unpaid debt from its liability accounts and credits a Contributed Equity account for the amount of debt assumed by the government as a whole. Similarly, in some instances tax-supported debt is issued for the benefit of enterprise funds with no intent that the beneficiary service the debt. In such instances, the debt proceeds are in the nature of an equity contribution to the fund that receives the benefit of the proceeds, and the liability is properly accounted for by the GLTDAG.

The first paragraph of this section gives a lengthy list of the kinds of liabilities that should be recorded in the General Long-Term Debt Account Group of a state or local government. From this list and from the discussions in earlier chapters, it should be evident that entries are ordinarily made in the accounts of the GLTDAG only as a result of transactions and events that also require entries in the accounts of one or more of the funds; and, as Illustration 5–1 shows, if the incurrence of long-term debt is for the purpose of acquisition of general fixed assets, related entries are required in the General Fixed Assets Account Group. The following section illustrates the entries required in the GLTDAG of the Town of Brighton to correspond with the net effect of the Debt Service Fund entries illustrated in Chapter 7. A subsequent section illustrates the entries required in the General Long-Term Debt Account Group to correspond with the entries in the General Fixed Assets Account Group, a Capital Projects Fund, and a Debt Service Fund for obligations arising under a capital lease agreement.

Illustrative Case

At the end of fiscal year 19y0, the Town of Brighton had outstanding two issues of long-term debt that would properly have been reported in the Statement of General Long-Term Debt (the name generally given to the GLTDAG balance sheet). Data given in Chapter 7 are used in Illustration 8–1 to show the status of GLTDAG accounts as of December 30, 19y0.

Entries in General Long-Term Debt accounts may be made on a current basis throughout the fiscal period as long-term debt is issued, as it is repaid, and as assets are added to debt service funds; or, all the events of the period may be cumulated and appropriate entries made at period-end for the net effect of all events. The latter procedure appears more common. Note that the GLTDAG is

---

ILLUSTRATION 8–1

TOWN OF BRIGHTON
Statement of General Long-Term Debt
As of December 31, 19y0

Amount Available and to Be Provided for Payment of
General Long-Term Debt

Deferred serial bonds:		
Amount available in debt service fund	$1,157,375	
Amount to be provided	842,625	
Total Deferred Serial Bonds		$2,000,000
Term bonds:		
Amount available in debt service fund	40,384	
Amount to be provided	1,459,616	
Total Term Bonds		1,500,000
Total Available and to Be Provided		$3,500,000

General Long-Term Debt Payable

Deferred serial bonds	$2,000,000
Term bonds	1,500,000
Total General Long-Term Debt Payable	$3,500,000

---

concerned only with the principal of general long-term debt, not with transactions involving interest on that debt.

For the sake of the reader's convenience, the effect on the GLTDAG of entries in the three debt service funds of the Town of Brighton is shown separately for each of the three funds for 19y1.

Regular Serial Bond Issue.   As of June 15, 19y1, regular serial bonds in the amount of $1,200,000 were sold at par as partial financing for construction of a fire station. At that time, the entry in the **Capital Projects Fund** was:

Cash	1,200,000	
Proceeds of Bonds		1,200,000

The corresponding entry in the **General Long-Term Debt Account Group** should be:

Amount to Be Provided for Payment of Regular Serial Bonds	1,200,000	
Regular Serial Bonds Payable		1,200,000

During 19y1 no assets were provided to the **Regular Serial Bonds Debt Service Fund** for payment of the principal of these bonds; accordingly, no further entry in the GLTDAG is needed in 19y1.

Deferred Serial Bond Issue.   The deferred serial bonds in the Town of Brighton case were issued on January 1, 19x0. The first installment of these bonds matured on January 1, 19y1. As shown in the illustrative entries for the **Deferred Serial Bonds Debt Service Fund,** the Appropriations, Expenditures, and Fund Balance accounts were affected; however, the net effect on the accounts of that debt service fund is:

Fund Balance	200,000	
Bonds Payable		200,000

Cash in the Deferred Serial Bonds Debt Service Fund is used to pay the liability, as shown in Chapter 7; therefore, assets of that fund were decreased in the same amount as the decrease, illustrated above, in the Fund Balance. The effect on the **GLTDAG** of recording the liability in the Debt Service Fund, and extinguishing the liability, is:

Deferred Serial Bonds Payable	200,000	
Amount Available in Debt Service Fund for Payment of		
Deferred Serial Bonds		200,000

Revenues of the Deferred Serial Bonds Debt Service Fund for 19y1 were $262,000 from taxes and $98,250 from interest on investments, a total of $360,250. Since $190,000 was raised for the payment of interest, the remainder, $170,250, was dedicated for bond repayment. The effect on the **GLTDAG** of the Deferred Serial Bonds Debt Service Fund activity is:

Amount Available in Debt Service Fund for Payment of Deferred		
Serial Bonds	170,250	
Amount to Be Provided for Payment of Deferred Serial Bonds		170,250

The net effect of the two GLTDAG entries illustrated above is a $29,750 decrease in Amount Available in Debt Service Funds for Payment of Deferred Serial Bonds, which agrees with the decrease in the Fund Balance of that fund, shown in Illustrations 7–3 and 7–4.

Term Bond Issue. Information given in Chapter 7 with regard to the **Term Bonds Debt Service Fund** discloses that Revenues totaling $120,145 were raised during 19y1, and $75,000 was expended for interest; the difference between the two ($45,145) should be reported in the **GLTDAG,** as shown below:

Amount Available in Debt Service Fund for Payment of Term Bonds	45,145	
Amount to Be Provided for Payment of Term Bonds...........		45,145

The increase in Amount Available shown in the above entry agrees with the increase in the Fund Balance of the Term Bonds Debt Service Fund, as reported in Illustrations 7–3 and 7–4.

The status of the GLTDAG as of December 31, 19y1, is reported in Illustration 8–2.

Notice that the Amount Available in each debt service fund reported in Illustration 8–2 agrees with the Fund Balance of the respective debt service fund

---

ILLUSTRATION 8–2

TOWN OF BRIGHTON
Statement of General Long-Term Debt
As of December 31, 19y1

Amount Available and to Be Provided for Payment
of General Long-Term Debt

Regular serial bonds:		
Amount to be provided		$1,200,000
Deferred serial bonds:		
Amount available in debt service fund	$1,127,625	
Amount to be provided	672,375	
Total Deferred Serial Bonds		1,800,000
Term bonds:		
Amount available in debt service fund	85,529	
Amount to be provided	1,414,471	
Total Term Bonds		1,500,000
Total Available and to Be Provided		$4,500,000

General Long-Term Debt Payable

Regular serial bonds	$1,200,000
Deferred serial bonds	1,800,000
Term bonds	1,500,000
Total General Long-Term Debt Payable	$4,500,000

reported in Illustrations 7–2, 7–3, and 7–4. This agreement would be true in all cases, unless assets dedicated only for the payment of interest were held by a debt service fund; in that event, **only** the net assets available for payment of debt principal by the debt service fund would be reported by the GLTDAG as an Amount Available.

Changes in Long-Term Debt

The reasons why the amounts of the items in Illustration 8–2 are not the same as the amounts of the same items in Illustration 8–1 are clear to those who have access to the underlying records (here illustrated in journal entry form), but readers of the Annual Report of the Town of Brighton would not have access to the underlying records and should be furnished with a schedule summarizing the reasons for the changes during the year. In the illustrative case, all changes in General Long-Term Debt result from activities summarized in capital projects fund and debt service fund statements; therefore, adequate disclosure may be made by reference to those statements. In any given year, it is common for debt issues to be authorized, for previously authorized debt to be issued, and for older issues to be retired. When a combination of events takes place, a schedule detailing changes in long-term debt is desirable.

Illustration 8–3 presents a schedule taken from the annual report of the City of Gainesville, Florida, which summarizes, by cause, the changes in Long-Term Debt for the year ended on the date shown. Note that, consistent with current GASB standards, Gainesville reports both the liability for compensated absences and for capital lease obligations payable from resources to be provided in years subsequent to balance sheet date.

General Long-Term Debt Arising from Capital Lease Agreements

In Chapter 5, under the heading "Acquisition of General Fixed Assets under Lease Agreements," a brief example is given of the computation of the present value of rentals under a capital lease agreement. The entry necessary in a governmental fund at the inception of the lease is illustrated in Chapter 5. The corresponding entry in the General Fixed Assets Account Group is illustrated in Chapter 6, and the entries required in a Debt Service Fund for payment of annual lease rentals in the same example are illustrated and discussed in Chapter 7. At the inception of a capital lease for a general fixed asset, it is necessary to record a lease obligation in the GLTDAG at the present value of the stream of annual payments. Continuing the example given in Chapters 5, 6, and 7, the entry needed in the GLTDAG on January 1, 19y0, is:

Amount to Be Provided for Payment of Capital Lease Obligations . . .	57,590	
Capital Lease Obligations Payable		57,590

The entry above is appropriate because, in this particular example, $10,000 is paid on January 1, 19y0, all of which was applied to the principal of the obligation; therefore, only the present value of payments 2 through 10 need be recorded in the GLTDAG.

On January 1, 19y1, the second lease rental payment of $10,000 is made. As the table given in Chapter 7 (page 207) shows, only $4,241 of that payment applies to

ILLUSTRATION 8–3

CITY OF GAINESVILLE, FLORIDA
Notes to Financial Statements
September 30, 1992

NOTE 4—Long-Term Debt

(A) A summary of changes in long-term debt for the year follows:

	Balances 10/01/91	*Additions*	*Deletions*	*Balances 09/30/92*
General Obligation Bonds	$ 510,000	$ —	$ 140,000	$ 370,000
Public Improvement Revenue Certificates 1975	250,000	—	250,000	0
Public Improvement Revenue and Refunding Bonds 1987	9,940,000	—	580,000	9,360,000
First Florida Financing Commission Loan 1987	520,000	—	75,000	445,000
First Florida Financing Commission Loan 1988	410,000	—	410,000	0
First Florida Financing Commission Loan 1992	—	15,830,000	—	15,830,000
Promissory Note	213,016	—	17,917	195,099
Capital Leases	155,084	41,702	76,047	120,739
Compensated Absences	1,296,122	77,864	—	1,373,986
TOTAL GENERAL LONG-TERM DEBT	13,294,222	15,949,566	1,548,964	27,694,824
ENTERPRISE LONG-TERM DEBT:				
Utility Revenue Bonds	356,053,692	134,920,000	67,017,331	423,956,361
Utility Notes	71,361,000	—	1,700,000	69,661,000
	427,414,692	134,920,000	68,717,331	493,617,361
Less unamortized discount	⟨7,024,095⟩	⟨2,357,438⟩	—	⟨9,381,533⟩
TOTAL ENTERPRISE LONG-TERM DEBT	420,390,597	132,562,562	68,717,331	484,235,828
INTERNAL SERVICE LONG-TERM DEBT:				
Capital Leases	—	54,110	—	54,110
TOTAL LONG-TERM DEBT	$433,684,819	$148,566,238	$70,266,295	$511,984,762

the principal of the lease obligation, so the following entry is required:

Capital Lease Obligations Payable	4,241	
Amount to Be Provided for Payment of Capital Lease		
Obligations...		4,241

The credit in the entry above would have been to Amount Available in Debt Service Funds if that account had been debited and the Amount to Be Provided account had been credited when resources were made available in a Debt Service Fund for payment of the lease rental.

Principal and Interest Payable in Future Years   Some years ago, accounting standards for state and local governments provided a "General Bonded Debt and Interest Group." The essential difference between the former recommendation and the current one discussed in this chapter is that in the

General Bonded Debt and Interest Group, interest on long-term debt to date of maturity was computed and recorded in a credit-balance account called Interest Payable in Future Years. Offsetting the credit-balance account were two debit-balance accounts: Amount Available in Debt Service Funds for Payment of Interest and Amount to Be Provided for Payment of Interest.

The idea of trying to emphasize to readers of the financial statements the magnitude of the claim on municipal resources resulting from interest that will become payable in future years is appealing to fiscal conservatives. However, disclosure of the total amount of future interest (not the present value of the

---

ILLUSTRATION 8–4

CITY OF GAINESVILLE, FLORIDA
Notes to Financial Statements
September 30, 1992

Aggregate annual debt service requirements (excluding the Commercial Paper Notes) including maturities of principal and payment of current interest are as follows:

Debt Service Requirements

Fiscal Year(s)	General	Enterprise(1)	Internal Service	Total
1993	$ 2,815,299	$ 30,499,026	$22,273	$ 33,336,598
1994	2,838,305	34,499,804	22,273	37,360,382
1995	2,751,053	36,805,138	14,849	39,571,040
1996	2,693,201	39,340,417	—	42,033,618
1997	2,698,904	39,344,076	—	42,042,980
1998–2002	12,294,623	195,959,406	—	208,254,029
2003–2007	11,306,314	203,342,022	—	214,648,336
2008–2012	11,308,384	244,763,213	—	256,071,597
2013–2017	4,115,205	109,164,138	—	113,279,343
2018–2022	—	28,912,475	—	28,912,475
	52,821,288	962,629,715[1]	59,395	1,015,510,398
Less Interest	26,500,450	538,673,354[1]	5,285	565,179,089
Total Principal	$26,320,838	$423,956,361	$54,110	$ 450,331,309

[1] Excludes principal of $69,661,000 and undeterminable amount of interest. See prior description of the Utility System Commercial Paper Notes.

Included in the above tabulation are debt service requirements for the City's capital lease obligations as follows:

Fiscal year end September 30:

1993	65,577
1994	64,016
1995	54,955
1996	15,632
Net minimum lease payments	$200,180
Less amount representing interest	(25,331)
Present value of net minimum lease payments	$174,849

interest) in a manner that makes it appear to be a present liability is not considered in conformity with generally accepted principles of accounting. In order to disclose the future demands on resources resulting from the maturing of debt principal and the payment of interest, a schedule showing this information is often included in the annual report. One form this schedule may take is shown as Illustration 8–4, taken from the Notes to the Combined Financial Statements of the City of Gainesville, Florida.

Debt Limit and Debt Margin

The debt statements already illustrated in this chapter are primarily useful for the information of administrators, legislative bodies, and others concerned with the impact of long-term debt on the financial condition and activities of the governmental unit, particularly with reference to the resulting tax rates and taxes. Another matter of importance in relation to long-term indebtedness is the legal limit on the amount of long-term indebtedness that may be outstanding at a given time, in proportion to the assessed value of property within the jurisdiction represented. This type of restriction is of importance as a protection of taxpayers against possible confiscatory tax rates. Even though tax-rate limitation laws may be in effect for a governmental unit, the limitation on bonded indebtedness is usually needed because the prevailing practice is to exempt the claims of bondholders from the barrier of tax-rate restrictions. This is to say that, even though a law establishing maxima for tax rates is in the statutes, it will probably exclude debt service requirements from the restrictions of the law. This exclusion would be reiterated, in effect, in the bond indentures.

Before continuing a discussion of debt limitation, it seems well to clarify the meaning of the terms **debt limit** and **debt margin**. Debt **limit** means the total amount of indebtedness of specified kinds that is allowed by law to be outstanding at any one time. The limitation is likely to be in terms of a stipulated percentage of the assessed valuation of property within the government's jurisdiction. It may relate to either a gross or a net valuation. The latter is logical, but probably not prevalent, because debt limitation exists as a device for protecting property owners from confiscatory taxation. For that reason, tax-paying property **only** should be used in regulating maximum indebtedness. In many governmental jurisdictions, certain property is legally excluded even from **assessment.** This includes property owned by governments, churches, charitable organizations, and some others, depending on state laws. **Exemptions,** which apply to property subject to assessment, are based on homestead or mortgage exemption laws, military service, economic status, and possibly some others. Both exclusions and exemptions reduce the amount of tax-paying property.

Debt **margin,** sometimes referred to as "borrowing power," is the difference between the amount of debt limit calculated as prescribed by law and the net amount of outstanding indebtedness subject to limitation. The net amount of outstanding indebtedness subject to limitation differs from total general long-term indebtedness because certain debt issues may be exempted by law from the limitation, and the amount available in Debt Service Funds for debt repayment is

ILLUSTRATION 8–5

CITY OF GAINESVILLE, FLORIDA
FY92 Comprehensive Annual Financial Report
Statistical Section
Legal Debt Margin and
Ratio of City's Gross Bonded Debt to Taxable Value
and Bonded Debt per Capita

<u>Legal Debt Margin</u>

<u>Taxable Value</u> = $1,591,052,836

Legal Debt Limit = None(1)

NOTE: (1) Chapter 200.181, Florida Statutes, allows unrestricted Ad Valorem tax rate levies for debt service requirements for General Obligation Bonds approved by voter referendum.

Tax Roll Year	Taxable Value (January 1)	Bonded Debt (September 30)	Bonded Debt Ratio	City Population (April 1)	Bonded Debt per Capita
1983	$ 928,103,688	$1,885,000	0.20%	81,614	23.10
1984	1,003,863,526	1,305,000	0.13%	82,124	15.89
1985	1,068,009,730	1,210,000	0.11%	82,882	14.60
1986	1,190,125,000	1,110,000	0.09%	83,060	13.36
1987	1,256,295,392	1,005,000	0.07%	83,980	11.97
1988	1,281,612,508	890,000	0.06%	84,815	10.49
1989	1,307,412,913	770,000	0.06%	85,663	8.99
1990	1,349,653,947	645,000	0.05%	84,770	7.61
1991	1,345,552,130	510,000	0.04%	84,544	6.03
1992	1,591,052,836	370,000	0.02%	85,587	4.32

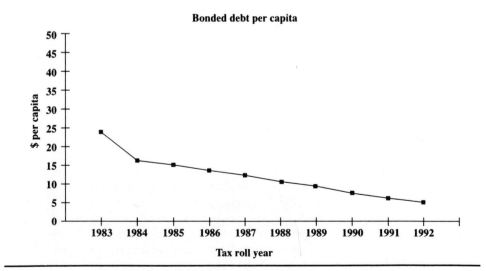

Bonded debt per capita

deducted from the outstanding debt in order to determine the amount subject to the legal debt limit. Total general long-term indebtedness must, in some jurisdictions, include debt serviced by special assessment funds and by enterprise funds if such debt was issued with covenants that give the debt tax-supported status in the event that collections of special assessments or enterprise fund revenues are insufficient to meet required interest or principal payments. Debt authorized but not issued as of the end of a fiscal year should be added to outstanding debt because it may be sold at any time. Although it would be in keeping with the purpose of establishing a legal debt limit to include the present value of capital lease obligations along with bonded debt in the computation of legal debt margin, state statutes at present generally do not specify that the liability for capital lease obligations is subject to the legal debt limit. The computation of legal debt margin for the City of Gainesville, Florida, is shown in Illustration 8–5.

ILLUSTRATION 8–6

CITY OF GAINESVILLE FLORIDA
FY92 Comprehensive Annual Financial Report
Statistical Section
Statement of Direct and Overlapping Bonded Debt (5)

Taxing Authority	Taxable Property Value (2)	General Obligation Bonded Debt (3)	Percent of Debt Applicable to City	City's Share of Debt (4)
City of Gainesville	$1,591,052,836	$ 370,000	100.00%	$ 370,000
Alachua County	3,478,806,917	16,930,000	45.74	7,743,782
Alachua County Schools	3,478,806,917	69,723,480	45.74	31,891,520
		$87,023,480	45.74%	$40,005,302

NOTES:
(1) The above information on Bonded Debt does not include Self Supporting and Non-self-Supporting Revenue Bonds, Certificates, and Notes as follows (Reserves and/or Sinking Fund balances have *not* been deducted).
(2) As of January 1, 1983 homestead property of certain qualified residents is eligible for up to $25,000 value exemption.
(3) Reserves and Sinking Fund Balances have *not* been deducted.
(4) Chapter 200.181, Florida Statutes, allows unrestricted Ad Valorem Tax rate levies for debt service for General Obligation Bonds approved by citizen referendum. See page 119 for history of debt ratios.
(5) Includes $14,735,000 in Alachua County Library District Serial & Term Bonds.

Taxing Authority	Self-Supporting	Non-self-Supporting	Totals
Alachua County	$ 60,220,000	$ —	$ 60,220,000
Alachua County Schools	—	—	—
City of Gainesville:			
Utilities	423,956,361	—	423,956,361
Other Than Utilities	—	16,275,000	16,275,000
	$ 484,176,361	$16,275,000	$500,451,361

Overlapping Debt

Debt limitation laws ordinarily establish limits that may not be exceeded by each separate governmental unit affected by the laws. This means the county government may incur indebtedness to the legal limit, a township within that county may do likewise, and a city within the township may become indebted to the legal limit, with no restriction because of debt already owed by larger territorial units in which it is located. As a result, a given parcel of real estate or object of personal property may be the basis of debt beyond the so-called legal limit and also may be subject at a given time to assessments for the payment of taxes to retire bonds issued by two or more governmental units. When this situation exists, it is described as "overlapping debt."

The extent to which debt may overlap depends on the number of units represented within an area that are authorized to incur long-term indebtedness. These may include the state, county, township, city, school board, library board, hospital board, and probably others. To show the total amount of fixed debt against property located within a given jurisdiction, a statement of direct and overlapping debt should be prepared. To this direct debt are added amounts owing by other units and authorities that levy taxes against the same property on which the direct debt is based. A Statement of Direct and Overlapping Debt is shown in Illustration 8–6. Notes included as a part of Illustration 8–6 disclose the relation of direct debt and overlapping debt to assessed valuation of real property within the City of Gainesville.

Information shown in this chapter as Illustrations 8–3, 8–4, 8–5, and 8–6 may be disclosed in the Notes to the Financial Statements or in supplementary schedules. GASB standards require that the following be disclosed for long-term debt in whatever manner the issuer deems to be the most meaningful presentation:

LONG-TERM DEBT

a. Description of individual bond issues and leases outstanding.

b. Changes in general long-term debt.

c. Summary of debt service requirements to maturity.

d. Disclosure of legal debt margin.

e. Bonds authorized but unissued.

f. Synopsis of revenue bond covenants.

Selected References

American Institute of Certified Public Accountants. *Audit and Accounting Guide. Audits of State and Local Governmental Units.* Revised. New York, 1993.

Governmental Accounting Standards Board. *Codification of Governmental Accounting and Financial Reporting Standards as of June 30, 1993.* Norwalk, Conn., 1993.

Questions

8–1. Describe the interrelationship between a debt service fund and the General Long-Term Debt Account Group. What is the relationship between a capital projects fund that receives the proceeds of tax-supported bonds and the General Long-Term Debt Account Group?

8–2. Under current GASB standards, long-term debt that is due the day after the date of the statement may properly be shown in the Statement of General Long-Term Debt. What is the rationale for this situation?

8–3. How does "tax-increment debt" differ from "general obligation debt"?

8–4. What provision in a bond indenture or bond ordinance is necessary for long-term debt to be classified as "general obligation"? Are all obligations properly reported as general long-term debt evidenced by bonds or notes? If not, give several examples of general long-term debt not evidenced by bonds or notes.

8–5. *a.* When general obligation bonds are issued at a premium that is recorded in a debt service fund and is to be used for eventual retirement of that bond issue, what is the effect on the amount of liability to be shown in the Statement of Long-Term Debt?

b. If a general obligation bond issue were sold at a premium that is required to be set aside for payment of bond interest, what is the effect upon the accounts in the General Long-Term Debt Account Group?

8–6. Explain the nature and purpose of the debit balance accounts used in the GLTDAG. Are these accounts informative to financial statement users?

8–7. "The entire debt arising from the acquisition of general fixed assets under a capital lease agreement should be reported as debt of the fund that accounts for the activities of the department or function using the leased asset. Only debt arising from the lease of equipment used by a number of departments should be reported in the GLTDAG, rather than a fund." Do you agree? Why or why not?

8–8. If a bond ordinance provides for regular and recurring payments of interest and principal payments on a general obligation bond issue of a certain government to be made from earnings of an enterprise fund, and these payments *are* being made by the enterprise fund, how should the bond liability be disclosed in the comprehensive annual financial report of the government?

8–9. Bonds and other debt of enterprise funds may legally, at least contingently, have the status of tax-supported debt. In the event that enterprise fund resources are insufficient for debt service on such debt, why might the government as a whole find it necessary or desirable to assume responsibility for debt service? How would assumption of responsibility for such debt by the government as a whole be accounted for in the GLTDAG? In the enterprise fund?

8–10. Why should a governmental annual report include a Schedule of Changes in Long-Term Debt?

8–11. The calculation of debt margin should take into account the amount of bonds authorized but not issued. This reduces borrowing power at a given date. What is the most logical reason for including authorized but unissued bonds?

8–12. In many jurisdictions, the statutory debt limit rate is relatively low, but overlapping debt is *not* prohibited. From the standpoint of the property owner and taxpayer, how does that situation compare with a relatively high total statutory debt limit?

Exercises and Problems

8–1. Utilizing the CAFR obtained for Exercise 1–1, follow the instructions below:

a. *Disclosure of Long-Term Debt.* Does the report contain evidence that the governmental unit maintains a General Long-Term Debt Account Group? What evidence is there? If the unit does not have a general long-term debt group, does the report specify that no such debt is outstanding, or does the report include a list of outstanding tax-supported debt issues; capital lease obligations; claims, judgments, and compensated absence payments to be made in future years; and the unfunded pension obligations?

   If the report contains a Statement of General Long-Term Debt, do the amounts shown in this statement as being available for payment of long-term debt agree with amounts of Fund Balance held for repayment of debt principal reported in statements of funds that perform the debt service function? If not, can you reconcile the differences?

   How does the "amount available" for payment of each issue relate to the "amount to be provided" for payment of each issue? How does the total amount available relate to the total amount to be provided? Has the government refrained from reporting nonasset "other debits" on fund-type balance sheets? (They should be reported only in the General Long-Term Debt Account Group.) Are all nonasset "other debits" referred to as "amounts available" and/or "amounts to be provided," so that it is clear that they do not represent assets? Has the government refrained from reporting interest payable in future years in the Combined Balance Sheet and the Statement of General Long-Term Debt? (It may properly be reported on a schedule such as the one shown as Illustration 8–4.)

   Refer to the Enterprise Funds balance sheets as well as to the Statement of General Long-Term Debt (or list of general debt outstanding): Are any enterprise debt issues backed by the full faith and credit of the general governmental unit? If so, how are the primary liability and the contingent liability disclosed?

b. *Changes in Long-Term Debt.* How are changes in long-term debt during the year disclosed? If there is a schedule of changes, does the information in that schedule agree with the statements presented for capital projects funds and debt service funds?

   Are interest payments and principal payments due in future years disclosed? If so, does the report relate these future payments with resources to be made available under existing debt service laws and covenants?

c. *Debt Limitations.* Does the report contain information as to legal debt limit and legal debt margin? If so, is the information contained in the report explained in enough detail so that an intelligent reader (you) can understand how the limit is set, what debt is subject to it, and how much debt the governmental unit might legally issue in the year following the date of the report?

d. *Overlapping Debt.* Does the report disclose direct debt and overlapping debt of the reporting entity? What disclosures are made of debt of the primary government in distinction to debt of component units? Is debt of component units reported as "direct" debt of the reporting entity, or as "overlapping debt"?

8–2. Write the numbers 1 through 10 on a sheet of paper. Beside each number write the letter corresponding with the best answer to each of the following questions.

   1. The following obligations were among those reported by Fern Village at December 31, 19x1:

Vendor financing with a term of 10 months when incurred, in connection with a capital asset acquisition that is not part of a long-term financing plan $ 150,000

Long-term bonds for financing of capital asset acquisition 3,000,000

Bond anticipation notes due in six months, issued as part of a long-term financing plan for capital purposes 400,000

What aggregate amount should Fern report as general long-term capital debt at December 31, 19x1?

a. $3,000,000.
b. $3,150,000.
c. $3,400,000.
d. $3,550,000.

Items 2 through 5 are based on the following:

On March 2, 19y0, Finch City issued 10-year general obligation bonds at face amount, with interest payable March 1 and September 1. The proceeds were to be used to finance the construction of a civic center over the period April 1, 19y0, to March 31, 19y1. During the fiscal year ended June 30, 19y0, no resources had been provided to the Debt Service Fund for the payment of principal and interest.

2. On June 30, 19y0, Finch's Debt Service Fund should include interest payable on the general obligations bonds for
   a. 0 months.
   b. 3 months.
   c. 4 months.
   d. 6 months.

3. Proceeds from the general obligation bonds should be recorded in the
   a. General Fund.
   b. Capital Projects Fund.
   c. General Long-Term Debt Account Group.
   d. Debt Service Fund.

4. The liability for the general obligation bonds should be recorded in the
   a. General Fund.
   b. Capital Projects Fund.
   c. General Long-Term Account Group.
   d. Debt Service Fund.

5. On June 30, 19y0, Finch's combined balance sheet should report the construction in progress for the civic center in the

	Capital Projects Fund	General Fixed Assets Account Group
a.	Yes	Yes
b.	Yes	No
c.	No	No
d.	No	Yes

6. The General Long-Term Debt Account Group should reflect in its accounts:
   a. Net assets set aside for redemption of bonds and for interest.
   b. Net assets in debt service funds for payment of utility revenue debt at maturity.

   c. Net assets in debt service funds for payment of interest due subsequent to the date of the Combined Balance Sheet.

   d. None of the above.

7. The General Long-Term Debt Account Group should be used to account for:

   a. All tax-supported bonds and government-commitment special assessment bonds and notes not yet legally due; the noncurrent portion of claims, judgments, and compensated absences; and the unfunded liability for pensions.

   b. General obligation bonds and notes that will mature in more than one year from balance sheet date.

   c. All bonds and notes that will mature in more than one year from balance sheet date.

   d. General obligation bonds and notes not yet legally due.

8. The General Long-Term Debt Account Group should be used to account for:

   a. The present value of the lease rentals for assets capitalized in the General Fixed Assets Account Group.

   b. The long-term debt resulting from all leases.

   c. The noncurrent portion of operating lease payments.

   d. The noncurrent portion of lease payments recorded in all funds as expenditures and expenses.

9. In addition to reporting general long-term debt in the combined balance sheet, information about the general long-term debt should be provided in the:

   a. Statement of General Long-Term Debt.

   b. Schedule of Changes in General Long-Term Debt.

   c. Computation of Legal Debt Margin (if applicable).

   d. All of the above.

10. Under current GASB standards, the General Long-Term Debt Account Group is used:

   a. As a group of credit balance liability accounts, the total of which offsets the total of the debit balance asset accounts of the General Fixed Assets Account Group.

   b. To place under accounting control long-term debt not properly recorded and reported by any of the types of funds.

   c. To place under accounting control all long-term debt issued with covenants that, either primarily or secondarily back the debt with the full faith and credit of the governmental unit.

   d. As an alternative to reporting general long-term debt in the General Fund.

(Items 1–5, AICPA, adapted)

8–3. Below are stated a number of unrelated transactions, some of which affect a General Long-Term Debt Account Group; none of the transactions have been recorded in that group.

(1) The tax levy for the General Fund included $650,000 to be transferred to the Debt Service Fund; $400,000 of this amount is designated for eventual retirement of outstanding serial bonds; the remainder is to be expended for interest on long-term debt. The transfer was made as planned, and the interest was paid.

(2) A $5,000,000 issue of serial bonds to finance a capital project was sold at 102, plus accrued interest in the amount of $50,000. The accrued interest was recorded as revenues of the Debt Service Fund and the premium was recorded as an Other

Financing Source. Accrued interest on bonds sold must be used for interest payments; premium is designated by state law for eventual payment of bond principal.

(3) A summary of Debt Service Fund operations during the year showed receipt of interest on investments in the amount of $180,000; this amount is to be used for payment of interest on long-term debt.

(4) $2,800,000 par value of tax-supported serial bonds were issued in partial refunding of a $3,500,000 par value issue of term bonds. The difference was settled with $700,000 that had been accumulated in prior years in a Debt Service Fund.

Required

a. Prepare in general journal form the necessary entry in the General Long-Term Debt Group for each transaction. Explanations may be omitted.

b. Prepare in general journal form all necessary entries in each fund (including budgetary entries to the extent information is available in this problem), and/or in the GFAAG, for each transaction. For each entry you prepare name the fund or account group in which the entry should be made.

8–4. Refer to Problem 7–7 for data pertaining to Heinz Township; prepare in general journal form the entry which should be made in the GLTDAG at the inception of the lease, and the entry which should be made one year later. Even if you had previously prepared the entries required by parts *a, b,* and *c* of Problem 7–7, prepare them again now, in addition to the entries in the GLTDAG.

8–5. At April 30, 19x6, all property inside the limits of the City of Marksville was situated within four additional governmental units, each authorized to incur long-term debt. At that date, net long-term debt of the five was as follows:

Florence County	$40,000,000
Florence Library District	2,000,000
City of Marksville	8,000,000
Marksville School District	17,000,000
Marksville Hospital District	13,600,000

Assessed values of property at the same date were: County and Library District, $900,000,000; City, $360,000,000; School District, $450,000,000; and Hospital District, $720,000,000.

Required

a. Prepare a statement of direct and overlapping debt for the City of Marksville. (Carry percentages to tenths.)

b. Compute the actual ratio (in percent carried to tenths) of total debt applicable to the City of Marksville property to assessed value of property within the city limits.

c. Compute the share of the City's direct and overlapping debt that pertained to the Reliable Manufacturing Company, having assessed valuation of $3,600,000 at April 30, 19x6.

8–6. In preparation for a proposed bond sale the city manager of the City of Edwardsville requested you to prepare a statement of legal debt margin for the City as of December 31, 19y5. You ascertain that the following bond issues are outstanding on that date:

Convention Center bonds	$3,600,000
Electric utility bonds	2,700,000
General obligation serial bonds	3,100,000
Tax increment bonds	2,500,000
Water utility bonds	1,900,000
Transit authority bonds	2,000,000

Other information obtained by you included the following items:

1. Assessed valuation of real and taxable personal property in the City totaled $240,000,000.
2. The rate of debt limitation applicable to the City of Edwardsville was 8 percent of total real and taxable personal property valuation.
3. Electric utility, water utility, and transit authority bonds were all serviced by enterprise revenues, but each carries a full-faith-and-credit contingency provision and by law is subject to debt limitation.
4. The convention center bonds and tax increment bonds are subject to debt limitation.
5. The amount of assets segregated for debt retirement at December 31, 19y5, is $1,800,000.

8–7. From records available in various offices of Leigh County, you find the following information about changes in long-term debt of the County during the year ended June 30, 19y6:

1. At the end of the 19y5 fiscal year, $500,000 was still outstanding on an issue of a 3 percent serial bond that matures at the rate of $250,000 per year. The payment during fiscal year 19y6 has been made by the Debt Service Fund.
2. The Leigh County Council decided to fund the General Fund deficit with an issue of four-year notes totaling $480,000. The notes were issued on July 1, 19y5, and were to be retired at the rate of $120,000 per year; the first payment was to be made on July 1, 19y6, by the Debt Service Fund.
3. At the end of the 19y5 fiscal year, $100,000 par value of general obligation serial bonds were outstanding, from an original amount of $400,000. Annual maturities of $25,000 had been paid on December 31 of each year.
4. In fiscal year 19y5, an issue of 7 percent serial bonds was sold in the amount of $6,000,000. The issue matures at the rate of $300,000 per year. The first payment was made in fiscal year 19y6.
5. On June 30, 19y5, the County had outstanding $200,000 of 4 percent serial bonds that had been issued to finance a revenue-producing recreation facility. On June 1, 19y6, bonds in the amount of $50,000 were paid. The bonds are being paid from enterprise revenues; they carry a covenant that obligates the County to levy taxes to service the debt if enterprise revenues are insufficient. It is expected that enterprise revenues will be sufficient to retire the bonds on schedule.
6. During fiscal year 19y6, a $300,000 issue of 6 percent term bonds matured, with little provision having been made for their payment. The bonds were closely held, and arrangements were made with holders of all but $25,000 to accept 8 percent refunding serial bonds. Cash was paid to creditors who declined to accept refunding bonds.

Required Prepare a Schedule of Changes in General Long-Term Debt for Leigh County for the year ended June 30, 19y6.

8–8. You have just accepted accounting responsibility for the City of Sellers. As of the end of the preceding fiscal year, your predecessor had prepared the following trial balance:

CITY OF SELLERS
General Long-Term Debt Account Group
Trial Balance, December 31, 19x5

	Debits	Credits
Amount Available in Debt Service Fund for Payment of Term Bonds...	$ 850,000	
Amount to Be Provided for Payment of Term Bonds.................	11,000,000	
Amount to Be Provided for Payment of Special Assessment Bonds....	75,000	
6% Term Bonds Payable		$ 6,000,000
7% Term Bonds Payable		5,600,000
3.5% Term Bonds Payable		250,000
10% Special Assessment Bonds Payable		75,000
	$11,925,000	$11,925,000

Required

a. Prepare in general journal form an entry for each of the following events that occurred in 19x6 to record the effects on the accounts of the General Long-Term Debt Account Group.

(1) $300,000 par value of the 6 percent term bonds were purchased on February 1, 19x6 and retired. The retirement was accomplished with a cash payment of $300,000 from the amount available in the Debt Service Fund.

(2) A $3,000,000 issue of five-year notes payable was sold on March 1. The rate of interest was 7 percent, payable March 1 and September 1.

(3) $2,000,000 par value of serial bonds were sold at par. The date of issue was May 1, 19x6, with final retirement on May 1, 19z6. The rate of interest was 6.5 percent per year, payable November 1 and May 1.

(4) $3,000,000 par value of serial bonds were issued on October 1, 19x6; $600,000 par value of the issue was scheduled to mature each year beginning October 1, 19x7. Interest at 7 percent per year on the issue is payable semiannually on April 1 and October 1.

(5) Records of the City Treasurer showed additions of $1,050,000 to debt service funds during 19x6, of which $830,000 was for principal of term bonds and the remainder for interest.

b. Prepare a Statement of General Long-Term Debt as of December 31, 19x6.

c. Prepare a Schedule of Changes in Long-Term Debt for the year ended December 31, 19x6.

Continuous Problems

8–L. The June 30, 19x1, trial balance of the City of Bingham General Long-Term Debt Account Group follows.

CITY OF BINGHAM
General Long-Term Debt Account Group
Trial Balance
As of June 30, 19x1

	Debits	Credits
Amount Available in DSF—6% Tax-Supported Serial Bonds...........	$ 300,000	
Amount to Be Provided—6% Tax-Supported Serial Bonds.............	5,700,000	
Amount Available in DSF—8% Special Assessment Term Bonds.......	260,000	
Amount to Be Provided—8% Special Assessment Term Bonds.........	340,000	
Amount to Be Provided—Capital Lease Obligations	1,020,000	
Tax-Supported Serial Bonds Payable—6%		$6,000,000
Special Assessment Term Bonds Payable—8%		600,000
Capital Lease Obligations Payable		1,020,000
Totals...	$7,620,000	$7,620,000

In addition to the accounts listed in the trial balance, general ledger accounts provided for the GLTDAG are (subsidiary ledger accounts are not required for this problem):

Amount Available in DSF—8% Tax-Supported Serial Bonds
Amount to Be Provided—8% Tax-Supported Serial Bonds
Tax-Supported Serial Bonds Payable—8%

Required

a. Prepare general journal entries to record in the General Long-Term Debt Account Group the sale of 8% tax-supported serial bonds on July 1, 19x1, in the amount of $3,000,000 as described in Problems 5–L and 7–L.

b. Review your solutions to Problems 2–L through 7–L and prepare general journal entries to record in the GLTDAG all information which should affect the accounts of the General Long-Term Debt Account Group. (Recall that assets held by the Debt Service Fund to be used to pay interest due on July 1, 19x2, are *not* reported as "Amount Available in Debt Service Funds for Retirement of Bonds.")

c. Prepare a Statement of General Long-Term Debt as of June 30, 19x2.

8–S. As of December 31, 19y0, the City of Smithville presented the following Statement of General Long-Term Debt:

CITY OF SMITHVILLE
Statement of General Long-Term Debt
December 31, 19y0

Amount Available and to Be Provided for the
Payment of General Long-Term Debt

Term Bonds:	
Amount available in debt service funds	$1,330,000
Amount to be provided	670,000
Total Available and to Be Provided	$2,000,000

General Long-Term Debt Payable

Term Bonds Payable:	
5⅝%, due 1/1/y4	$ 600,000
6¾%, due 1/1/y5	400,000
7¼%, due 1/1/z0	1,000,000
Total General Long-Term Debt Payable	$2,000,000

Required

a. Record in general journal form the effect of the following events and transactions on the accounts of the General Long-Term Debt Account Group:

(1) During 19y1, the Term Bond Service Fund raised sufficient revenues to pay the interest on all general obligation term bonds and to increase Fund Balance available for repayment of bonds by $100,000. No term bonds were issued or repaid in 19y1.

(2) Problems 5–S and 7–S provide information about the issuance of general obligation serial bonds during 19y1 and about the activities of the Street Improvement Bond Debt Service Fund during 19y1. (It will be necessary to create accounts since all existing accounts relate to term bonds, as shown in the December 31, 19y0, Statement of General Long-Term Debt.)

b. Prepare a Statement of General Long-Term Debt as of December 31, 19y1.

c. If the assessed valuation of property within the City of Smithville is $60,000,000, and the legal general obligation debt limit is 12 percent of assessed valuation, compute the legal debt *margin* of the City as of December 31, 19y1. (Bonds authorized but unissued [Problem 5–S] must be included, as well as bonds outstanding.)

d. Prepare a schedule showing the amount of interest and principal payments on outstanding general long-term debt for each year until all debt outstanding on December 31, 19y1, matures.

CHAPTER 9

Internal Service Funds

All of the funds discussed in previous chapters (general, special revenue, capital projects, and debt service funds) owe their existence to legal constraints placed on the raising of revenue and/or the use of resources for the provision of services to the public or segments thereof, and for the acquisition of facilities to aid in the provision of services. As governmental units became more complex, it became apparent that efficiency should be improved if services used by the several departments or funds, or even several governmental units, were combined in a single administrative unit. Purchasing is a common example, as is a motor pool. A logical name for a fiscal and accounting entity created to account for resources used for providing centralized services is Internal Service Fund. Traditionally, the reason for the creation of funds in this category was to improve the management of resources. In recent years, large numbers of governmental units have experienced a shortfall of revenues with an increase in the demand for governmental services. Consequently, many governmental units have turned to user charges as a means of financing operations formerly financed by tax revenues and intergovernmental revenues. In order to determine whether user charges are commensurate with operating costs, and to improve the ability of administrators and governing bodies to determine that costs are reasonable in relation to benefits, it is desirable for the activities to be operated and accounted for on a business basis. Thus many activities formerly operated on a purely noncommercial basis and accounted for by governmental funds are now accounted for by proprietary funds: **enterprise funds** and **internal service funds.** Activities that produce goods or services to be sold to the general public are accounted for by enterprise funds, discussed in Chapter 10. Activities that produce goods or services to be provided to departments or agencies of a governmental unit, or to other governmental units, on a cost-reimbursement basis are accounted for by internal service funds. (Internal service funds are also called *intragovernmental service funds, working capital funds, revolving funds,* and other similar names.)

The phrase **cost-reimbursement basis** is to be interpreted broadly. User charges need not cover the full cost of providing the goods or services; transfers from other funds or units to subsidize in part the operations of an internal service fund do not negate the use of this fund type.

Proprietary funds are accounted for in a manner similar to investor-owned business enterprises. Accordingly, such funds recognize revenues and **expenses (not expenditures)** on the accrual basis. They account for all fixed assets used in their operations and for long-term debt to be serviced from revenues generated from their operations, as well as for all current assets and current liabilities. Distinction should be made in the equity accounts of proprietary funds between equity contributed to the fund and retained earnings resulting from operations of the fund. Also, as is true of businesses, proprietary funds differ from governmental fund types discussed in preceding chapters in that proprietary funds are not required by GASB standards to record their budgets in their accounting systems. (Although a few states do require all funds of all local governments within the state to operate under legally adopted budgets. In such cases, GASB standards allow the integration of budgetary accounts in the manner described in Chapters 3 and 4 for general and special revenue funds.)

Establishment and Operation of Internal Service Funds

Although the reason for the establishment of an internal service fund is to improve financial management of scarce resources, it should be stressed that a fund is a fiscal entity as well as an accounting entity; consequently, establishment of a fund is ordinarily subject to legislative approval. The ordinance, or other legislative action, that authorizes the establishment of an internal service fund should also specify the source, or sources, of financial resources to be used for fund operations. The original allocation of resources to the fund may be derived from a transfer of assets of another fund, such as the General Fund or an Enterprise Fund, intended as a **contribution** not to be repaid, or a transfer in the nature of a long-term **advance** to be repaid by the internal service fund over a period of years. Alternatively, or additionally, the resources initially allocated to an internal service fund may be acquired from the proceeds of a tax-supported bond issue or transfer from other governmental units that anticipate utilizing the services to be rendered by the internal service fund. Since internal service funds are established to improve the management of resources, it is generally considered that they should be operated, and accounted for, on a business basis. Application of this general truth to a specific case can lead to conflict between managers who wish the freedom to operate the fund in accord with their professional judgment, and legislators who wish to exercise considerable control over the decisions of the internal service fund managers.

For example, assume that administrators request the establishment of a fund for the purchasing, warehousing, and issuing of supplies used by a number of funds and departments. At the time of the request, since no internal service fund exists, each fund or department must include in its budget its requested appropriation for supplies, its requested appropriation for salaries and wages of personnel engaged in purchasing and handling the supplies, and its requested appropriation for any operating expense or facility costs associated with the supply function. Accordingly, legislators tend to feel that through their control over budgets they are controlling the investment in supplies and the use of supplies by each fund and department. Legislators may feel that if they approved the establishment of an internal service fund that had authority to generate operating revenues sufficient to perpetuate the fund without annual appropriations, the supply function would no longer be subjected to annual legislative budget review, and the legislature would "lose control" after the initial allocation of resources to the fund. Administrators are more likely to feel that if an internal service fund did not have authority to generate operating revenues sufficient to perpetuate the fund, and to spend those revenues at the discretion of fund management rather than at the discretion of persons possibly more concerned with reelection than with financial management, there would be little gained by establishment of the internal service fund.

The two opposing views should be somewhat balanced by the fact that, as shown in Illustration 9–1, the customers of an internal service fund are, by definition, other funds and departments of the governmental entity, or of other governmental entities; therefore, each using fund and department must include in its Appropriations budget request justification for the amount to be spent (i.e., paid to the internal service fund) for supplies, so the legislative branch continues to exercise budgetary review over the amount each fund and department budgets for supplies. As shown in Illustration 9–1, departments and programs that require legislative appropriations to expend resources for goods and services should ac-

---

ILLUSTRATION 9–1

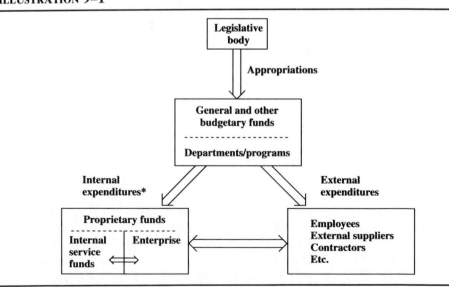

* Internal expenditures are more formally referred to as quasi-external transactions. (See Chapter 3 for a discussion of this term.)

count for purchases of goods or services from internal suppliers (i.e., internal service funds or enterprise funds) in essentially the same manner as goods and services purchased from external suppliers. If the legislative branch were to set pricing policies for the service fund, and policies governing the use of current earnings, and retention of earnings, and require the submission of periodic financial statements to evidence that its policies were followed, the legislature would be able to maintain considerable control over the function performed by the service fund, yet leave the fund managers freedom to operate at their discretion within the policies set by the legislative branch.

One of the more difficult problems to resolve to the satisfaction of persons with opposing views is the establishment of a pricing policy. "Cost" is obviously an incomplete answer: Historical cost of the supplies themselves, whether defined as FIFO, LIFO, average, or specific identification, will not provide sufficient revenue to replace supplies issued if replacement prices have risen since the last purchase, or to increase the inventory quantities if the scale of governmental operations is growing. Payroll and other cash operating expenses of the internal service fund must be met; and if the internal service fund has received a loan from another fund or another governmental unit, prices must be set at a level that will generate cash needed for debt retirement. If the internal service fund is to be operated on a true business basis, it must also be able to finance from its operations replacement, modernization, and expansion of plant and equipment used in fund operations. Prices charged by the internal service fund, however, should be less than the using funds and departments would have to pay outside vendors for equivalent products and services, if the existence and continued operation of the internal service fund is to be justified.

Because of the considerations mentioned in preceding paragraphs, many different approaches to internal service fund operations may be found in practice. Since accounting systems should give appropriate recognition to operating policies, as well as to legal requirements, practices vary from those of profit-seeking businesses at one extreme, to those discussed in this text in the chapters relating to general and special revenue funds at the other extreme. In the illustrations given in following sections of this chapter, it is assumed the financial objective of an internal service fund is to recover from operating revenues the full cost of operations, with enough net income to allow for replacement of inventories in periods of rising prices, and enough increase in inventory quantities to meet the needs of using funds and departments whose scale of operations is increasing. Similarly, it is assumed net income should be sufficient to allow for replacement of fixed assets used by the internal service fund, but expansion of the facilities must be financed through contributions from other funds authorized in their Appropriations budgets. Managers of internal service funds must prepare operating plans—budgets—as a management tool. In the illustrations it is assumed budgets of internal service funds are submitted to the legislative body, or bodies, and to the public for information but not for legal action, and therefore the budget is not formally recorded in internal service fund accounts. Similarly, managers of businesses must be kept informed of the status of outstanding purchase orders and contracts, but encumbrances need not be recorded in the accounts in order to accomplish this.

Accounting for an internal service fund concerned with the functions of purchasing, warehousing, and issuing supplies is illustrated in the following section of this chapter.

Illustrative Case—Supplies Fund

Assume that the administrators of the Town of Brighton obtain approval from the Town Council to centralize the purchasing, storing, and issuing functions as of January 1, 19y2, and to administer and account for these functions in a Supplies Fund. The town's General Fund is to transfer to the new fund its December 31, 19y1, inventory of supplies ($61,500) and $30,000 in cash to be used for working capital; these transfers are intended as contributions to the Supplies Fund and are **not** to be repaid. Transfers of this nature are initially accounted for by the recipient fund as **equity transfers in,** as shown in Entry 1. The Equity Transfers In account is closed at the end of the fiscal period to an appropriately named Fund Equity account—Contribution from General Fund, in this case—and reported in the Changes in Fund Equity section of the operating statement. General Fund entries for the transfer out of cash and inventory are illustrated in Chapter 13.

1. Cash	30,000	
Inventory of Supplies	61,500	
Equity Transfers In		91,500

In order to provide cash to be used for acquisition of a building and equipment needed to handle the supply function efficiently, the town's Water Utility Fund is to advance $130,000 to the Supplies Fund. The advance is to be repaid by the Supplies Fund in 20 equal annual installments. Entry 2 illustrates the entry to be made by the Supplies Fund for the receipt of the advance; Water Utility Fund entries for this transaction are illustrated in Chapter 10.

2. Cash	130,000	
Advance from Water Utility Fund		130,000

Assume that a satisfactory warehouse building is purchased for $95,000; $25,000 of the purchase price is considered a cost of the land. Necessary warehouse machinery and equipment is purchased for $25,000. Delivery equipment is purchased for $10,000. If the purchases are made for cash, the acquisition of the assets would be recorded in the books of the Supplies Fund as:

3. Land	25,000	
Building	70,000	
Machinery and Equipment—Warehouse	25,000	
Equipment—Delivery	10,000	
Cash		130,000

Additional supplies would need to be ordered to maintain inventories at a level commensurate with expected usage. Encumbrances need not be recorded for purchase orders issued, and so information about the dollar value of purchase orders is omitted from this illustration. During 19y2, it is assumed supplies are received and related invoices are approved for payment in the amount of $192,600; the entry needed to record the asset and the liability is:

4. Inventory of Supplies	192,600	
Vouchers Payable...		192,600

The General Fund of the Town of Brighton (see Chapter 4) accounted for supplies on the physical inventory basis. The Supplies Fund, however, should account for its inventories on the perpetual inventory basis since the information is needed for proper performance of its primary function. Accordingly, when supplies are issued the inventory account must be credited for the cost of the supplies issued. Since the using fund will be charged an amount in excess of the inventory carrying value, the receivable and revenue accounts must reflect the selling price. The markup above cost should be determined on the basis of budgeted expenses and other items to be financed from net income, in relation to expected requisitions by using funds. If the budget for the Town of Brighton's Supplies Fund indicates a markup of 35 percent on cost is needed, issues to General Fund departments of supplies costing $185,000 would be recorded by the following entries:

5a. Cost of Supplies Issued..	185,000	
Inventory of Supplies		185,000
5b. Due from General Fund	249,750	
Billings to Departments....................................		249,750

If collections from the General Fund during 19y2 totaled $231,000, the entry should be:

6. Cash	231,000	
Due from General Fund		231,000

Assuming that payrolls and fringe benefits during the year were all paid in cash and were distributed to the functional expense accounts in the amounts shown below, Entry 7 is appropriate.

7. Administrative Expenses	11,000	
Purchasing Expenses..	19,000	
Warehousing Expenses.......................................	12,000	
Delivery Expenses	13,000	
Cash		55,000

If payments on vouchers during the year totaled $164,000, the entry is made:

8. Vouchers Payable..	164,000	
Cash		164,000

The advance from the Water Utility Fund is to be repaid in 20 equal annual installments; repayment of one installment at the end of 19y2 is recorded as:

9. Advance from Water Utility Fund	6,500	
Cash		6,500

It is assumed the building used as a warehouse was estimated at the time of purchase to have a remaining useful life of 20 years; the warehouse machinery and equipment was estimated to have a useful life of 10 years, and the delivery equipment to have a useful life of 5 years. If the administrative and clerical office space occupies 10 percent of the area of the warehouse, 10 percent of the depreciation of the warehouse, $350, may be considered administrative expense; similarly, if the purchasing office occupies 10 percent of the space in the warehouse building, 10 percent of the building depreciation, $350, may be considered purchasing expense. The remainder of the building is devoted to warehousing; therefore, 80 percent of the total building depreciation, $2,800, is to be charged to warehousing expense. The latter account is also charged $2,500 for machinery and equipment depreciation expense. Delivery expense is charged $2,000 for depreciation of equipment during the year.

10. Administrative Expenses	350	
Purchasing Expenses	350	
Warehousing Expenses	5,300	
Delivery Expenses	2,000	
Allowance for Depreciation—Building		3,500
Allowance for Depreciation—Machinery and Equipment—Warehouse		2,500
Allowance for Depreciation—Equipment—Delivery		2,000

Organizations that keep perpetual inventory records must adjust the records periodically to reflect shortages, overages, or out-of-condition stock disclosed by physical inventories. Adjustments to the Inventory account are also considered adjustments to the warehousing expenses of the period. In this illustrative case, it is assumed no adjustments were found necessary at year-end.

Assuming all revenues and expenses applicable to 19y2 have been properly recorded by the entries illustrated above, the operating statement accounts should be closed as of December 31, 19y2:

11. Billings to Departments	249,750	
Cost of Supplies Issued		185,000
Administrative Expenses		11,350
Purchasing Expenses		19,350
Warehousing Expenses		17,300
Delivery Expenses		15,000
Excess of Net Billings to Departments over Costs		1,750

"Excess of Net Billings to Departments over Costs" (or "Excess of Costs over Net Billings to Departments," if operations resulted in a loss) is the account title generally considered more descriptive of the fund's results than "Income Summary" or "Current Earnings"—the titles commonly found in profit-seeking businesses. Whatever title is used for the account summarizing the results of operations for the period, the account should be closed at year-end. The title of the account that records earnings retained in an internal service fund is the same as the title commonly used for profit-seeking businesses: Retained Earnings.

12. Excess of Net Billings to Departments over Costs	1,750	
Retained Earnings		1,750

The Equity Transfer In account represents contributed equity and should be closed to an appropriately named account:

13. Equity Transfer In 91,500
      Contribution from General Fund............................   91,500

Illustrative
Statements

Balance Sheets.   As one would expect of funds accounted for in a manner similar to profit-seeking businesses, balance sheets of proprietary funds are *classified;* that is, current assets are segregated from fixed assets and other assets, and current liabilities are segregated from long-term debt. The balance sheet of the Supplies Fund of the Town of Brighton as of December 31, 19y2, is shown as Illustration 9–2.

ILLUSTRATION 9–2

TOWN OF BRIGHTON
Supplies Fund
Balance Sheet as of December 31, 19y2

Assets

Current Assets:			
Cash			$ 35,500
Due from General Fund			18,750
Inventory of supplies, at average cost			69,100
Total Current Assets			123,350
Fixed Assets:			
Land		$25,000	
Building	$70,000		
Less: Allowance for depreciation	3,500	66,500	
Machinery and equipment—			
warehouse	25,000		
Less: Allowance for depreciation	2,500	22,500	
Equipment—delivery	10,000		
Less: Allowance for depreciation	2,000	8,000	
Total Fixed Assets			122,000
Total Assets			$245,350

Liabilities and Fund Equity

Current Liabilities:	
Vouchers payable	$ 28,600
Total Current Liabilities	28,600
Long-Term Debt:	
Advance from water utility	123,500
Total Liabilities	152,100
Fund Equity:	
Contribution from General Fund	91,500
Retained earnings	1,750
Total Fund Equity	93,250
Total Liabilities and Fund Equity	$245,350

Operating Statements. The results of operations of an Internal Service Fund should be reported periodically in a Statement of Revenues, Expenses, and Changes in Retained Earnings, which is the equivalent of an income statement for a profit-seeking entity. Illustration 9–3 presents a Statement of Revenues, Expenses, and Changes in Retained Earnings for the year ended December 31, 19y2, for the Town of Brighton Supplies Fund. Inasmuch as there was a change in the Contributed Equity during the year, this change is disclosed in the same statement.

Statement of Cash Flows. GASB financial reporting standards require the preparation of a Statement of Cash Flows as a part of a full set of financial statements for all proprietary funds and nonexpendable trust funds and governmental entities that use proprietary fund accounting (hospitals, utilities, and public benefit corporations and authorities). Categories of cash flows provided by FASB *Statement No. 95* were deemed insufficient to meet the needs of users of governmental financial reports. Consequently, GASB standards provide four categories of cash flows: Operating, Noncapital Financing, Capital and Related Financing, and Investing. In each category, the term **cash** includes **cash equivalents** (defined as short-term, highly liquid investments).

Cash flows from **operating activities** include receipts from customers, receipts from quasi-external operating transactions with other funds, payments to suppli-

---

ILLUSTRATION 9–3

TOWN OF BRIGHTON
Supplies Fund
Statement of Revenues, Expenses, and Changes
in Retained Earnings and Contributed Equity
For the Year Ended December 31, 19y2

Billings to departments		$249,750
Less: Cost of supplies issued		185,000
Gross Margin		64,750
Less: Purchasing expenses	$19,350	
Administrative expenses	11,350	
Warehousing expenses	17,300	
Delivery expenses	15,000	
Total Operating Expenses		63,000
Excess of Net Billings to Departments over Costs for the Year		1,750
Retained Earnings, January 1, 19y2		–0–
Retained Earnings, December 31, 19y2		1,750
Equity Transfer In from General Fund		91,500
Contributed Equity, January 1, 19y2		–0–
Contributed Equity, December 31, 19y2		$ 91,500

ers of goods or services, payments to employees for services, payments for quasi-external operating transactions with other funds (including payments in lieu of taxes), and other operating cash receipts and payments. The transactions of the Town of Brighton's Supplies Fund recorded in Entries 6, 7, and 8 are classified as operating activities and are reported in the first section of the Statement of Cash Flows (see Illustration 9–4). As required by GASB standards the Statement of

---

ILLUSTRATION 9–4

TOWN OF BRIGHTON
Supplies Fund
Statement of Cash Flows
For the Year Ended December 31, 19y2

Cash flows from operating activities:		
Cash received from customers	$231,000	
Cash paid to employees for services	(55,000)	
Cash paid to suppliers	(164,000)	
Net cash provided by operating activities		$ 12,000
Cash flows from noncapital financing activities:		
Equity transfer from General Fund	30,000	
Net cash provided by noncapital financing activities		30,000
Cash flows from capital and related financing activities:		
Advance from Water Utility Fund	130,000	
Partial repayment of advance from Water Utility Fund	(6,500)	
Acquisition of capital assets	(130,000)	
Net cash used for capital and related activities		(6,500)
Net Increase in Cash and Cash Equivalents		35,500
Cash and Cash Equivalents, 1/1/y2		–0–
Cash and Cash Equivalents, 12/31/y2		$ 35,500

Reconciliation of Excess of Net Billings
to Departments over Costs to Net Cash
Provided by Operating Activities

Excess of Net Billings to Departments over Costs		$ 1,750
Adjustments:		
Depreciation expense		8,000
Increase in receivables from other funds		(18,750)
Increase in inventory	$ 69,100	
Less contributed inventory	61,500	(7,600)
Increase in vouchers payable		28,600
Net Cash Provided by Operating Activities		$ 12,000

Cash Flows is accompanied by a reconciliation of operating income (called Excess of Net Billings to Departments over Costs for the Year in Illustration 9–3) with the net cash flow from operating activities.

Cash flows from **noncapital financing** activities include proceeds from debt not clearly attributable to acquisition, construction, or improvement of capital assets; receipts from grants, subsidies, or taxes other than those specifically restricted for capital purposes or those for specific operating activities; payment of interest on, and repayment of principal of, noncapital financing debt; grants or subsidies paid to other governments, funds, or organizations, except payments for specific operating activities of the grantor government. The contribution from the General Fund to the Supplies Fund of the Town of Brighton (see Entry 1) is reported in the cash flows from noncapital financing activities section of the Statement of Cash Flows (Illustration 9–4).

Cash flows from **capital and related financing** activities include proceeds of debt and receipts from special assessments and taxes specifically attributable to acquisition, construction or improvement of capital assets; receipts from capital grants; receipts from the sale of capital assets; proceeds of insurance on capital assets that are stolen or destroyed; payments to acquire, construct, or improve capital assets; payment of interest on, and repayment or refunding of, capital and related financing debt. The transactions of the Town of Brighton's Supplies Fund recorded in Entries 2, 3, and 9 are classified as capital and related financing activities and are reported in that section of the Statement of Cash Flows (Illustration 9–4).

Cash flows from **investing** activities include receipts from collection of loans; interest and dividends received on loans, debt instruments of other entities, equity securities, and cash management and investment pools; receipts from the sales of debt or equity instruments; withdrawals from investment pools not used as demand accounts; disbursements for loans; payments to acquire debt or equity instruments; and deposits into investment pools not used as demand accounts. None of the transactions of the Town of Brighton's Supplies Fund during 19y2 are in the nature of investing activities.

Combining Statements

If a reporting entity operates more than one internal service fund, it is necessary to present a Combining Balance Sheet; a Combining Statement of Revenues, Expenses, and Changes in Retained Earnings; and a Combining Statement of Cash Flows for all Internal Service Funds in order to disclose the detail supporting the Internal Service Funds column in the combined statements.

Acquisition of Assets by Contributions or Grants

The fixed assets used by the Supplies Fund of the Town of Brighton were purchased for that fund from cash advanced by the Water Utility Fund. In other situations, the fixed assets themselves may have been contributed to the Supplies Fund (or any other Internal Service Fund) by another fund of the same governmental unit or by another governmental unit, may have been purchased from one or more capital grants, or may have been purchased from revenues generated by operations of the Internal Service Fund. Fixed assets purchased for an Internal

Service Fund from operating revenues would be accounted for and depreciated in the same manner as illustrated for the Town of Brighton Supplies Fund. If fixed assets are contributed to an Internal Service Fund (or Enterprise Fund) or are acquired from the proceeds of a capital grant, some accounting questions arise, as discussed below.

Fixed assets acquired as a gift, or contribution, should be capitalized at fair value at date of receipt; the offsetting credit is to an appropriately named Fund Equity account, such as Contributions from City or Contributions from Private Citizens. Similarly, grants, entitlements, or shared revenues that are restricted for capital acquisitions or construction by an internal service fund or an enterprise fund are reported as additions to a Fund Equity account, such as Contributions from State. (Note that the preceding sentence refers to capital grants to proprietary funds. GASB standards provide that operating grants to proprietary funds and grants that may be used for either operations or capital outlays of the proprietary fund should be recognized as nonoperating revenues on the accrual basis, not as contributed equity. In comparison, *all* grants to governmental funds should be recognized as *revenue,* on the accrual basis used by governmental fund types.)[1] Fixed assets acquired from proceeds of capital grants, entitlements, or shared revenues are recorded at cost.

Depreciation of Contributed Assets or Assets Acquired from Capital Grants

The accounting treatment of depreciation of fixed assets contributed to an Internal Service Fund, or assets constructed or acquired by an Internal Service Fund from capital grants, need not differ from the accounting treatment of depreciation illustrated in the Town of Brighton Supplies Fund case. However, GASB standards allow the option of closing the depreciation expense on contributed assets or assets acquired from capital grants to the appropriate contributed equity account, rather than to Retained Earnings. If that option is elected, the Statement of Revenues, Expenses, and Changes in Retained Earnings would be presented as shown in Illustration 9–5, and the equity section of the Internal Service Fund Balance Sheet would be presented as shown in Illustration 9–6. Both illustrations are taken from the GASB Codification.

Assets Acquired under Lease Agreements

The acquisition of general fixed assets under lease agreements is discussed in Chapter 5. Assets for use by proprietary funds may also be acquired under lease agreements. The criteria set forth in FASB *SFAS No. 13* (these criteria are itemized in Chapter 5) are used to determine whether the lease is an operating lease or a capital lease.

---

[1] GASB has issued an exposure draft of a proposed standard on accounting for grants and other forms of financial assistance. GASB has also placed on its agenda a project to reexamine the accounting and reporting of contributed capital. If either of these projects result in a new standard, the publisher will provide an update bulletin to adopters of the Tenth Edition. For additional information, see Governmental Accounting Standards Board, *Exposure Draft*, "Accounting and Financial Reporting for Certain Grants and Other Financial Assistance" (Norwalk, Conn.: 1994).

ILLUSTRATION 9–5

Statement of Revenues, Expenses, and Changes in Retained Earnings
For the Fiscal Year Ended (Date)

Operating Revenues:	
(Detailed)	$XX
Operating Expenses:	
(Detailed—includes depreciation on *all* depreciable fixed assets)	(XX)
Operating Income (Loss)	XX
Nonoperating Revenues (Expenses):	
(Detailed—nonoperating revenues include grants, entitlements, and shared revenues received for operations and/or such resources that may be used for either operations or capital outlay at the discretion of the recipient)	XX
Income (Loss) before Operating Transfers	XX
Operating Transfers:	
(Detailed)	XX
Net Income (Loss)	XX
Add depreciation on fixed assets acquired by grants, entitlements, and shared revenues externally restricted for capital acquisitions and construction that reduces contributed capital [Optional]	XX
Increase (Decrease) in Retained Earnings	XX
Retained Earnings—Beginning of Period	XX
Retained Earnings—End of Period	$XX

SOURCE: GASB Codification Sec. G60.116.

ILLUSTRATION 9–6

Proprietary Fund Balance Sheet
Equity Section

Fund Equity:			
Contributed capital:			
Capital grants	$XX		
Less amortization [Optional]	XX	$XX	
Government's contribution		XX	$XX
Retained earnings			XX
Total Fund Equity			$XX

SOURCE: GASB Codification Sec. G60.114.

Assets acquired under an operating lease belong to the lessor and not to the Internal Service Fund; accordingly, the annual lease payment is recorded as a rental expense of the Internal Service Fund,[2] and there is no depreciation expense on the assets acquired under an operating lease agreement. Assets acquired under a capital lease agreement by an Internal Service Fund, or an Enterprise Fund, should be· capitalized by that fund (*not* by the General Fixed Assets Account Group, as is true of assets acquired under a capital lease for use by any of the "governmental" funds). The amount to be recorded by a "proprietary" fund as the "cost" of the asset acquired under a capital lease, and as the related liability, is the lesser of *(a)* the present value of the rental and other minimum lease payments or *(b)* the fair value of the leased property. The amount recorded as the "cost" of the asset is amortized in a manner consistent with the government's normal depreciation policy for owned assets of proprietary funds. The amortization period is restricted to the lease term, unless the lease *(a)* provides for transfer of title or *(b)* includes a bargain purchase option, in which case the economic life of the asset becomes the amortization period.

During the lease term, each minimum lease payment by an internal service fund is to be allocated between a reduction of the obligation under the lease and as interest expense in a manner illustrated in Appendix A of *SFAS No. 13* (January 1990), so as to produce a constant periodic rate of interest on the remaining balance of the obligation. This allocation and other complexities that arise in certain events are described and illustrated in various paragraphs of *SFAS No. 13* (January 1990) and in many intermediate accounting texts. These complexities are beyond the scope of this text.

Internal Service Funds with Manufacturing Activities

The Supplies Fund of the Town of Brighton, for which journal entries and statements are illustrated in a preceding section of this chapter, is responsible for purchasing, storing, and issuing supplies used by other funds and departments of the town. Many states and local governmental units have funds similar to that of the Town of Brighton. It is also common to find printing shops, asphalt plants, or other service units that produce a physical product to be used by funds and departments, or that facilitate the operations of the other funds and units by performing maintenance or repair jobs, or even perform a temporary financing function.

If an internal service fund performs a continuous process manufacturing operation, its accounting system should provide process cost accounts. If a service fund performs a manufacturing, maintenance, or repair operation on a job-order basis, the fund's accounting system should provide appropriate job-order cost accounts. To the extent that operations, processes, or activities are capable of being standardized, cost standards for materials, direct labor, and overhead

---

[2] GASB Codification Sec. L20.109–.112 establishes measurement criteria and recognition criteria for revenues and expenditures/expenses relating to operating leases with scheduled rent increases. This situation is deemed to be beyond the scope of this text.

should be established; in such cases, the accounting system should provide for the routine measurement and reporting of significant variances from the standards. Cost determination for governmental and nonprofit entities is discussed in Chapter 18 of this text.

Internal Service Funds as Financing Devices

Governmental units may utilize internal service funds as devices to finance risk management, equipment purchases and operations (including centralized computer operations), and other functions that are facilitated by generating revenues from user charges to cover costs and expenses computed on a full accrual basis. In the case of funds to finance equipment purchases and operations, including the operations of computers owned by the governmental unit, an internal service fund can include depreciation and, perhaps, expected increases in the cost of replacing assets, in the charge to the using funds—thus incorporating these costs in current appropriations of governmental funds, rather than budgeting the estimated cost of equipment expected to be replaced. If internal service funds are used to finance equipment purchases and operations, therefore, the appropriations and expenditures of governmental funds more nearly approximate costs that would be reported by entities using full accrual accounting than is true under the procedures discussed in Chapters 3 and 4.

GASB has issued accounting and financial reporting standards for risk financing and related insurance activities.[3] Government entities that use internal service funds to account for risk financing activities are required to recognize revenues and claims expenses and liabilities in essentially the same manner as public entity risk pools (cooperative groups of governmental entities joined together to finance risks of loss to property, workers' compensation, employee health care, and similar risks or exposures). Briefly, the internal service fund should recognize claims expense and liability when a claim is asserted, it is probable that an asset has been impaired or a liability has been incurred, and the amount of the loss is reasonably estimable; or if an estimable loss has been incurred and it is probable that a claim will be asserted. Reasonably possible (but not probable) loss contingencies, probable losses which are not reasonably measurable, and loss exposure in excess of the accrued liability should be disclosed in the Notes to the Financial Statements. The disclosure should explain the nature of the contingency and an estimate of the possible loss or range of the loss, or a statement that the amount is not estimable.

Internal service fund charges to other funds for risk financing activities should be sufficient to recover the total amount of claim expenses recognized for the period or, alternatively, may be based on an actuarial method so that internal service fund revenues and expenses over time are approximately equal. Charges to other funds may also include a reasonable provision for expected future catastrophe losses. Internal service fund charges to other funds are recognized as revenues by the internal service fund and as expenditures by governmental funds

---

[3] GASB Codification Sec. Po20.

or expenses by proprietary and nonexpendable trust funds. Internal service fund charges in excess of the full cost amount determined as above should be reported as an other financing source by the internal service fund and an other financing use by the other funds. If the internal service fund fails to recover the full cost of claims over a reasonable period of time, the accumulated fund deficit should be charged to the other funds and reported by the other funds as an expenditure or expense, as appropriate.

Dissolution of an Internal Service Fund

When an internal service fund has completed the mission for which it was established, or when its activity is terminated for any other reason, dissolution must be accomplished. Liquidation may be accomplished in any one of three ways or in combinations thereof. The three ways are: (1) transfer of the fund's assets to another fund that will continue the operation as a subsidiary activity, for example, a supply fund becoming a **department** of the General Fund; (2) distribution of the fund's assets in kind to another fund or to another governmental unit; (3) conversion of all its noncash assets to cash and distribution of the cash to another fund or other funds. Dissolution of an internal service fund, as for a private enterprise, would proceed by prior payments to outside creditors, followed by repayment of long-term advances not previously amortized, and, finally, liquidation of Residual Equity. The entire process of dissolution should be conducted according to pertinent law and the discretion of the appropriate legislative body. Fund Equity contributed by another fund or governmental unit logically would revert to the contributor fund or governmental unit, but law or other regulations may dictate otherwise. If fund equity has been built up out of charges in excess of costs, then liquidation will follow whatever regulations may govern the case; and if none exist, then the appropriate governing body must decide on the recipient or recipients.

Selected References

Financial Accounting Standards Board. *Statement of Financial Accounting Standards No. 13,* "Accounting for Leases, as Amended and Interpreted through January 1990." Norwalk, Conn., 1990.

Governmental Accounting Standards Board. *Codification of Governmental Accounting and Financial Reporting Standards as of June 30, 1993.* Norwalk, Conn., 1993.

Questions

9–1. What are the benefits of establishing internal service funds? What kinds of activities are typically accounted for in internal service funds?

9–2. "Since the reason for the establishment of internal service funds is to facilitate management of resources, and not primarily to demonstrate compliance with law, they may be established at the discretion of governmental administrators." Comment.

9–3. Depreciation of general fixed assets is not recorded in the accounts of any of the governmental funds or in the account groups. If a building is transferred from the General Fixed Assets Account Group to an Internal Service Fund because the character of its use changes, should the internal service fund record building depreciation expense each year after the transfer? Explain.

9–4. Since internal service funds are expected to cover the cost of their operations by charges to departments or agencies using their services, they should use the accrual basis of accounting for both revenue recognition and expenditure recognition. Discuss.

9–5. What are some of the more important considerations in establishing a pricing policy for an internal service fund?

9–6. The Supplies Fund of Springfield is an internal service fund. It issues supplies to other funds of the city on a cost-reimbursement basis, as described in Chapter 9. During a certain year, billings to departments totaled $850,740. The same year, the operating statement showed a loss of $787. Based on those facts, was the fund, in your opinion, well managed? Explain your answer.

9–7. The laws in some states require all funds of local governmental units within those states to be operated under legal budgets. GASB accounting and financial reporting standards specify that internal service funds should be accounted for in the same manner as business organizations—which neither incorporate budgetary accounts in their accounting systems, nor present Budget versus Actual operating statements. Should a city in a state which requires all funds to be operated under a legal budget include the internal service fund type in its Combined Statement of Revenues, Expenditures, and Changes in Fund Balances in its GPFS? Explain your answer.

9–8. A governmental unit provided original financing for its Materials and Supplies Fund by transfer of $30,000 cash from its General Fund. The transferee fund credited the amount to Advance from General Fund. Assuming that the terminology is correct, how should the Advance account be classified in the statements of the Materials and Supplies Fund? Suggest an appropriate name for the corresponding account in the General Fund; how should the corresponding account be shown in the statements of the General Fund?

9–9. If the transfer referred to in Question 9–8 had been credited to Contribution from General Fund, how should the latter account be classified in the statements of the Material and Supplies Fund (again assuming that the account used fits the facts of the transfer)? Suggest an appropriate name for the corresponding account in the General Fund; how should the corresponding account be shown in the statements of the General Fund?

9–10. What are the categories of cash flows required in a proprietary fund statement of cash flows prepared in conformity with GASB standards? What kinds of transactions are reported in each category?

9–11. Name the financial statements required in the governmental entity's CAFR if more than one internal service fund is used.

9–12. Under the GASB accounting and financial reporting standards for risk financing activities, how does an internal service fund used for risk financing determine the appropriate claims expense and liability to be recognized for a period?

9–13. "Internal service funds used for risk financing should recognize as revenues the full charges billed to other departments even if those charges substantially exceed the full cost of providing risk financing service." Do you agree? Why or why not?

9–14. What are the alternative methods of dissolving an internal service fund? What factors should be considered in choosing the appropriate method?

Exercises and Problems

9–1. Utilizing the annual report obtained for Exercise 1–1, follow the instructions below:

  a. *Internal Service Funds.* What activities of the governmental unit are reported as being administered by internal service funds (working capital funds, revolving funds, rotary funds, industrial funds, and intragovernmental service funds are other names used for funds of the type discussed in Chapter 9)? If internal service funds are not used by the reporting entity, does the report disclose how activities such as purchasing, motor pools, printing, data processing, and other activities commonly used by more than one fund are financed and accounted for? Does the report state the basis of accounting used for the internal service funds? (Are all funds in this category accounted for on the same basis?) If so, is the financial statement presentation consistent with the stated basis? If the basis of accounting is not stated, analyze the statements to determine which basis is used—full accrual, modified accrual, or cash basis. Is the basis used consistent with the standards discussed in Chapter 9?

  b. *Fund Disclosure.* In the balance sheet(s) of the internal service fund(s), are assets classified in accord with practices of profit-seeking businesses, or are current, fixed, and other assets not separately displayed? If there are receivables other than from other funds or other governmental units, are allowances for estimated uncollectibles provided? Are allowances for depreciation deducted from related fixed-asset accounts?

  Are current liabilities and long-term debt properly distinguished in the balance sheet? Are long-term advances from other funds properly distinguished from capital contributions received from other funds? Are retained earnings (or deficits) from operations clearly distinguished from contributed equity?

  Are budgetary accounts (Estimated Revenues, Appropriations, Encumbrances) used by the internal service funds? From what sources were revenues actually obtained by each internal service fund? How are costs and expenses of each fund classified: by character, object, function, or activity (see Chapter 3 for definitions of these terms)? Are noncash expenses, such as depreciation, separately disclosed? Do the revenues of each fund exceed the costs and expenses of the period? Compute the net income (or net loss) of each fund in this category as a percentage of its operating revenue for the period. Does the net income (or net loss) for any fund exceed 5 percent of operating revenues? If so, do the statements, or the accompanying text, explain what the excess is being used for, or how the deficiency is being financed?

  c. *Statement of Cash Flows.* Is a Statement of Cash Flows presented for internal service funds? If so, how does the cash provided by operations shown in this statement relate to the revenues and expenses shown in the Statement of Revenues, Expenses, and Changes in Retained Earnings? Are cash flows from financing activities presented separately for noncapital- and capital-related activities? Is there a section for cash flows from investing activities?

9–2. Write the numbers 1 through 10 on a sheet of paper. Beside each number write the letter corresponding with the best answer to each of the following questions:

  1. Which of the following is *not* an appropriate reason to establish an internal service fund?
    a. To improve the management of resources.
    b. To develop a cash reserve to meet future contingencies.

    c. To determine whether user charges are sufficient to cover operating costs.

    d. To determine whether costs are reasonable in relation to benefits.

2. If an internal service fund is intended to operate on a "cost-reimbursement basis," then user charges should:

    a. Cover the full costs, both direct and indirect, of operating the fund.

    b. Cover at a minimum the direct costs of operating the fund.

    c. Cover the full costs of operating the fund *and* provide for future expansion and replacement of fixed assets.

    d. Any of the above could be an appropriate basis for establishing user charges, depending on the policy followed by a particular government.

3. Which of the following is a correct statement of the role of budgeting in internal service funds?

    a. Internal service fund managers should have discretion to operate within a flexible budget, consistent with pricing and other policies established by the legislative body.

    b. Expenditures from internal service fund resources require legislative appropriations.

    c. To ensure appropriations are not overspent, all internal service funds should use encumbrance procedures.

    d. Internal service fund managers should ensure that goods and services are not provided to other funds or departments unless a valid appropriation exists for the goods or services ordered.

4. Wood County operates a centralized data processing center as an internal service fund to provide services to other funds and departments. In 19y9, this fund billed the Parks and Recreation Fund $75,000 for data processing services. What account should Wood's internal service fund credit to record the billing to the Parks and Recreation Fund?

    a. Interfund Exchanges.

    b. Billings to Departments.

    c. Operating Transfers In.

    d. Data Processing Expenses.

5. The financial statements required by current GASB standards for an internal service fund are:

    a. A Balance Sheet and a Statement of Revenues, Expenditures, and Changes in Fund Balance.

    b. A Balance Sheet, Statement of Revenues, Expenditures, and Changes in Fund Balance, and a Statement of Cash Flows.

    c. A Balance Sheet, Statement of Revenues, Expenses, and Changes in Retained Earnings, and a Statement of Cash Flows.

    d. A Balance Sheet and a Statement of Revenues, Expenses, and Changes in Retained Earnings.

6. An equity transfer from the General Fund to an internal service fund will be reported in the balance sheet of the internal service fund as a (an):

    a. Contributed capital item in the Fund Equity section.

    b. Retained earnings item in the Fund Equity section.

    c. Long-term liability.

    d. None of the above. It would only be reported in the bottom section of the operating statement.

7. Which of the following would be reported as a "cash flow from investing activities?"
   a. Purchase of land.
   b. Repayment of a mortgage note issued to purchase a building.
   c. Interest received on U.S. government securities held by the fund.
   d. Advance from the General Fund to finance purchase of equipment.

8. Under current GASB standards fixed assets received by gift or contribution, or acquired from grants, entitlements, and shared revenues restricted for acquisition of fixed assets, should:
   a. Not be depreciated.
   b. Be depreciated in the normal manner.
   c. Be depreciated or not be depreciated at the option of the governmental unit, provided a consistent policy is followed.
   d. Be depreciated in the normal manner, but Depreciation Expense may optionally be closed to a contributed equity account rather than Retained Earnings.

9. GASB accounting and financial reporting standards for risk financing activities provide that an internal service fund should recognize claims expense and a related liability when a claim has been asserted and:
   a. It is reasonably possible that a loss has been incurred and the amount can be reasonably estimated.
   b. It is probable that a loss has been incurred and the amount can be reasonably estimated.
   c. A loss has been incurred, but the amount cannot be reasonably estimated.
   d. A municipal court has awarded a judgment to a claimant fund (e.g., the General Fund).

10. Which of the following is a feasible means of dissolving an internal service fund that the governmental unit no longer needs or wants?
    a. Conversion of the fund's noncash assets to cash and distribution of the cash to another fund or funds.
    b. Transfer the fund's assets to another fund that will continue the same or similar operating activities.
    c. Distribute the fund's assets in kind to another fund or funds which will not continue the same or similar operating activities.
    d. Any of the above, in any combination, would be feasible.

(Item 4, AICPA, adapted)

9–3. The formal financial objectives and funding policies for internal service funds of the City of Columbia, Missouri, are stated in the box on the following page.

Required Do the City of Columbia's financial objectives and funding policies appear to promote sound resource management? From the viewpoint of a council member, mayor or city manager, and department head, discuss the reasonableness of the factors used to determine billing rates/revenue requirements. Is this uniform policy for all internal service funds desirable, or would it be better to tailor the revenue requirements to the needs of each individual fund?

A Resolution
establishing a formal policy with respect to the financial objectives for internal
service funds; and establishing a policy regarding generation of funds required
for capital outlay.

BE IT RESOLVED BY THE COUNCIL OF THE CITY OF COLUMBIA, MISSOURI AS
FOLLOWS:

SECTION 1. That internal service funds such as Data Processing, Vehicle Maintenance, Utilities Accounts and Billing, Public Buildings, and Printing are funds whose financial objective should be to only recover the complete cost of operations without producing
any significant amount of profit in excess of the fund's requirements.

SECTION 2. That Section 1 is consistent with practices of "Governmental Accounting, Auditing, and Financial Reporting."

SECTION 3. That in computing an internal service funds revenue requirement for rate
setting purposes, the rate base should include such items as debt expense, interest expense,
operating expense, prorated reserve (accumulated over time to allow for purchase option
under lease/purchase arrangements), and either depreciation expense or estimated capital
outlay, either of which are usually financed 100% internally through rates.

SECTION 4. That since working capital in different funds varies because of many
factors it should be reviewed more closely with the budgetary process to assure captive
users that the cash account is not a result of billings in excess of revenue requirements.

SECTION 5. That if it appears that cash buildup has occurred in excess of reasonable
revenue requirements, rates should be adjusted; in the budgetary process cost recoveries
either over or under, should be rolled forward.

SECTION 6. That generation of funds for capital outlay be allowed either 100% internally through rates or through budgeted depreciation expense when lease/purchase agreements are used, in which case, an amount should be included in the rate base for a prorated
reserve which, accumulated over time, will enable purchase of such capital outlay at some
future date.

Allowable costs used in determining revenue requirements for the City of Columbia's
internal service funds are diagrammed in the next box.

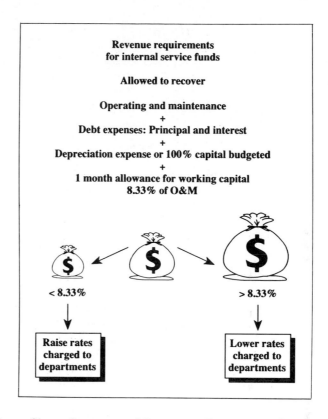

9-4. The Balance Sheet, Statement of Revenues, Expenses, and Changes in Retained Earnings, and Statement of Cash Flows for the Vehicle Maintenance Fund, an internal service fund of Bay City, are reproduced below. No further information about the nature or purposes of this fund is given in the annual report.

Required   Judging from the information presented, does the Vehicle Maintenance Fund appear to be accounted for and operated, financially, as an internal service fund should be? If you were the manager of a City department that uses the services of the Vehicle Maintenance Fund, what would you want to know in addition to the information disclosed in the financial statements?

BAY CITY
Vehicle Maintenance Fund
Balance Sheet
As of December 31, 19x9

Assets

Assets:	
Cash and investments	$ 152,879
Accounts receivable	2,116
Inventory	779,000
Prepaid expenses	19,854
Property, plant, and equipment	1,512,880
Total Assets	$2,466,729

Liabilities and Fund Equity

Liabilities:

Accounts payable	$ 35,675
Other accrued liabilities	109,099
Accrued annual leave	227,369
Total Liabilities	372,143

Fund equity:

Contributed capital	1,498,035
Retained earnings	596,551
Total Fund Equity	2,094,586
Total Liabilities and Fund Equity	$2,466,729

BAY CITY
Vehicle Maintenance Fund
Statement of Revenues, Expenses, and
Changes in Retained Earnings
Year Ended December 31, 19x9

Operating revenues:	
Charges for services	$10,774,781
Miscellaneous	100,344
Total operating revenues	10,875,125
Operating expenses:	
Salaries and employee benefits	3,353,413
Supplies	3,409,096
Operating services and charges	68,897
Maintenance and repairs	3,536,443
Interfund charges	426,246
Total operating expenses	10,794,095
Operating income	81,030
Other income:	
Interest income	–0–
Income before operating transfers	81,030
Operating transfers in	–0–
Operating transfers out	–0–
Net income	81,030
Retained earnings at beginning of year	515,521
Retained earnings at end of year	$ 596,551

BAY CITY
Vehicle Maintenance Fund
Statement of Cash Flows
Year Ended December 31, 19x9

Cash flows from operating activities:	
Cash received from customers	$10,875,938
Cash paid to:	
Employees	(3,306,086)
Other funds	(426,246)
Suppliers and vendors	(7,048,240)
Cash provided by operating activities	95,366
Cash flows from noncapital financing activities:	
Contributions from General Fund	59,860
Cash flows from capital and related financing activities:	
Acquisition of fixed assets	(163,050)
Net decrease in cash and investments	(7,824)
Cash and investments, January 1, 19x9	160,703
Cash and investments, December 31, 19x9	$ 152,879

Reconciliation of Operating Income
to Net Cash Provided by Operations

Operating Income	$ 81,030
Adjustments:	
Decrease in accounts receivable	813
Decrease in inventories and prepaid expenses	85,173
Decrease in accounts payable	(43,805)
Decrease in other accrued liabilities	(47,327)
Increase in accrued annual leave	19,482
Net cash provided by operations	$ 95,366

9–5. Your examination of the accounts of your new client, the City of Delmas, as of June 30, 19x1, revealed the following:

1. On December 31, 19x0, the City paid $115,000 out of General Fund revenues for a central garage to service its vehicles, with $67,500 being applicable to the building, which has an estimated life of 25 years; $14,500 to land; and $33,000 to machinery and equipment, which has an estimated life of 15 years. A $12,200 cash contribution was received by the garage from the General Fund on the same date.

2. The garage maintains no records, but a review of deposit slips and canceled checks revealed the following:

Collections for services to General	
Fund departments	$30,000
Office salaries	6,000
Utilities	700
Mechanics' wages	11,000
Materials and supplies	9,000

3. The garage had uncollected billings of $2,000, accounts payable for materials and supplies of $500, and an inventory of materials and supplies of $1,500 at June 30, 19x1.

Required   Prepare journal entries that should be made to establish an Internal Service Fund for the City of Delmas and to record the events for the period given. Also prepare any necessary adjusting and closing entries as of June 30, 19x1, the end of the fiscal year.

(AICPA, adapted)

9–6. The City of Kent operates a central garage through an Internal Service Fund to provide garage space and repairs for all city-owned-and-operated vehicles. The Central Garage Fund was established by a contribution of $300,000 from the General Fund on July 1, 19x3, at which time the land and building were acquired. The after-closing trial balance at June 30, 19x5, was as follows:

	Debits	Credits
Cash	$110,000	
Due from Other Funds	20,000	
Inventory of Materials and Supplies	90,000	
Land	50,000	
Building	250,000	
Allowance for Depreciation—Building		$ 20,000
Machinery and Equipment	65,000	
Allowance for Depreciation—Machinery and Equipment		12,000
Vouchers Payable		42,000
Contribution from General Fund		325,000
Retained Earnings		186,000
	$585,000	$585,000

The following information applies to the fiscal year ended June 30, 19x6:

1. Materials and supplies were purchased on account for $92,000; the perpetual inventory method is used.

2. The cost of materials and supplies used during the year ended June 30, 19x6, was $110,000. A physical count taken as of that date showed materials and supplies on hand totaled $72,000 at cost.

3. Salaries and wages paid to employees totaled $235,000, including related costs.

4. A billing was received from the Enterprise Fund for utility charges totaling $30,000, and was paid.

5. Depreciation of the building was recorded in the amount of $10,000; depreciation of the machinery and equipment amounted to $9,000.

6. Billings to other departments for services rendered to them were as follows:

General Fund	$270,000
Water and Sewer Fund	87,000
Special Revenue Fund	40,000

7. Unpaid interfund receivable balances at June 30, 19x6, were as follows:

General Fund	$10,000
Special Revenue Fund	17,000

8. Vouchers payable at June 30, 19x6, were $16,000.

9. Closing entries for the Central Garage Fund at June 30, 19x6, were prepared.

Required   *a.* Prepare journal entries to record all of the transactions for this period in the Central Garage Fund accounts.

b. Assuming that the City of Kent has no other internal service funds, name the general purpose financial statements in which the financial data of the Central Garage Fund should be reported.

9–7. As of the beginning of a certain year, the Automotive Service Fund of the City of Clarkton had the following post-closing trial balance as of September 30, 19y2:

	Debits	Credits
Cash	$ 11,000	
Due from Other Funds	20,200	
Service Supplies Inventory	35,300	
Machinery and Equipment	90,000	
Allowance for Depreciation—Machinery and Equipment		$ 18,000
Buildings	210,000	
Allowance for Depreciation—Buildings		70,000
Land	37,000	
Due to Federal Government		1,500
Due to Other Funds		800
Accounts Payable		12,700
Contribution from General Fund		250,000
Retained Earnings		50,500
	$403,500	$403,500

During the fiscal year ended September 30, 19y3, the following transactions (summarized) occurred:

1. Employees were paid $290,000 wages in cash; additional wages of $43,500 were withheld for federal income and social security taxes. The employer's share of social security taxes amounted to $23,375.
2. Cash remitted to the federal government during the year for withholding taxes and social security taxes amounted to $65,500.
3. Utility bills received from the City's Utility Fund during the year amounted to $23,500.
4. Office expenses paid in cash during the year amounted to $10,500.
5. Service supplies purchased on account during the year totaled $157,500.
6. Parts and supplies used during the year totaled $152,300 (at cost).
7. Charges to departments during the fiscal year were as follows:

    General Fund $294,000
    Street Fund 266,000

8. Unpaid balances at year-end were as follows:

    General Fund $10,000
    Street Fund 20,000

9. Payments to the Utility Fund totaled $21,800.
10. Accounts Payable at year-end amounted to $13,250.
11. Annual depreciation is recorded at the following rates:

    Machinery and Equipment 10%
    Buildings 3

12. Revenue and expense accounts for the year were closed.

Required   *a.* Prepare a Statement of Revenues, Expenses, and Changes in Retained Earnings for the year. Classify expenses as to direct and indirect costs. Wages and payroll taxes are considered to be 90 percent direct and 10 percent indirect. Utility services are estimated to be 80 percent direct and 20 percent indirect. Parts and supplies used, and depreciation of machinery and equipment are considered direct costs; all other costs are considered indirect costs.

b. Comment on the evident success of the pricing policy of this fund, assuming that user charges are intended to cover all operating expenses, including depreciation, but are not expected to provide a net income in excess of 3 percent of billings to departments.

9–8. Using the data given in Problem 9–7:

Required   *a.* Prepare a Balance Sheet for the Automotive Service Fund as of September 30, 19y3.

b. Prepare a Statement of Cash Flows for the Automotive Service Fund for the year ended September 30, 19y3.

9–9. From the following information concerning the City of Hilton, you are to prepare:

a. A Statement of Revenues, Expenses, and Changes in Retained Earnings for the Custodial Service Fund for the year ended December 31, 19x7.
b. A Balance Sheet for the Custodial Service Fund as of December 31, 19x7.
c. A Statement of Cash Flows for the Custodial Service Fund for the year ended December 31, 19x7:

The following transactions occurred during 19x7, the first year of operation.

1. The Custodial Service Fund received $250,000 cash as a contribution from the General Fund, of which $150,000 is designated for purchase of capital assets.
2. The following cash disbursements were made by the Custodial Service Fund.

Purchase of equipment (estimated useful life 10 years)	$150,000
Purchase of materials and supplies	300,000
Salaries, wages, and fringe benefits:	
Direct labor	60,000
Office	30,000
Superintendent	40,000
Heat, light, and power	25,000
Office expenses	10,000

3. Services rendered by the Custodial Service Fund to other departments resulted in charges as follows: General Fund, $294,600; Street Fund, $184,000. The cost of supplies used was $292,000.
4. The Custodial Service Fund received $226,500 cash from the General Fund and $156,000 cash from the Street Fund as partial payment on billings during the year.
5. Adjusting and closing entries were made at year-end; depreciate equipment for the entire year.

9–10. The City of Dalton operates an Internal Service Fund to manage and contract for the various kinds of insurance carried by the City. It pays all premiums to the insurers; then, as premiums expire, they are charged to the specific funds to which they pertain. Operating costs, consisting of personnel, rent, utilities, and miscellaneous other expenses, are charged to the insured funds by adding an "operating charge" to expired premium charges.

For the current year, the operating charge is 10 percent of premium expirations billed. Operating surpluses or deficits are usually small in amount and are closed at year-end to Retained Earnings. Insurers pay directly to insured funds and all losses are borne by the applicable funds; neither are recorded in the Insurance Fund. At June 30, 19y4, the trial balance of the Insurance Fund was as follows:

Cash	$ 5,650	
Due from Other Funds	29,000	
Prepaid Insurance Premiums	236,945	
Vouchers Payable		$105,945
Contribution from General Fund		120,000
Contribution from Water Fund		45,000
Retained Earnings		650
	$271,595	$271,595

During the year ended June 30, 19y5, the following transactions, in summary form, occurred:

1. The fund was billed by insurance companies for $132,625 premiums falling due on insurance coverage for the various funds of the city.
2. A total of $216,700 was charged to various funds on account of premiums that expired during the year in the amount of $197,000 and $19,700 of operating charges thereon.
3. Operating Expenses paid in cash during the year were:

Salaries and Wages	$12,400
Rent	4,800
Utilities	860
Miscellaneous	1,200
Total	$19,260

   The rent and the utilities were paid to other funds; Miscellaneous was paid to external suppliers.
4. A total of $3,000 was received from insurance companies as premium adjustments during the year. This amount, plus $300 billed previously for operating charges, was credited to the amount owed by various funds for the current year's expirations.
5. $127,000 was paid on amounts owed to insurance companies, for the benefit of funds and agencies of the City of Dalton.
6. Additional permanent financing for the fund was received in the form of a $60,000 contribution of cash from the General Fund.
7. $170,500 was collected from the various funds. Of this amount, $155,000 was for expirations of premiums and $15,500 was for the related operating charge, both previously billed.

Required

a. State what you consider to be the justification for operation of a separate fund for accounting for insurance premium payments and expirations.
b. In the fund described above there are no transactions related to settlement of losses. State the reason why.
c. Is the use of the account Retained Earnings appropriate for this fund? Why or why not?

9–11. Using the accounts given in the June 30, 19y4, trial balance and the transaction data from Problem 9–10 for the City of Dalton:

    a. Prepare entries in general journal form to record the transactions of the Insurance Fund, including closing entries, for the fiscal year ended June 30, 19y5.

    b. Prepare a Balance Sheet as of June 30, 19y5.

    c. Prepare a Statement of Revenues, Expenses, and Changes in Retained Earnings for the fiscal year ended June 30, 19y5.

    d. Prepare a Statement of Cash Flows for the fiscal year ended June 30, 19y5.

Continuous Problems

9–L. The City of Bingham established a Stores and Services Fund to be operated as an internal service fund to improve purchasing procedures and facilitate inventory management.

Required

    a. Open a general journal for the Stores and Services Fund; enter the following transaction:

        In June 19x2, the Stores and Services Fund recorded the receipt of the advance from the General Fund (see Transaction 15 of part *g* of Problem 4–L).

    b. Although no further transactions took place in the year ended June 30, 19x2, the Stores and Services Fund was required to prepare (1) a Balance Sheet as of that date and (2) a Statement of Cash Flows for the year ended June 30, 19x2, for inclusion in the City of Bingham's annual report.

    c. In order to put the Stores and Services Fund on a completely self-sustaining basis, it was decided to charge using departments for the stores plus a markup sufficient to recover expected cash expenses plus depreciation of equipment. Stores issues for one year were forecast to be $300,000 at cost. Compute the markup rate based on cost from the following information:

        In addition to rent of $500 per month, the estimated expenses were $3,600 a year for utilities; $46,800 for salaries and fringe benefits; and $2,400 a year for operation and maintenance of warehouse equipment. The warehouse equipment was in the basement of City Hall; nobody was quite clear as to when it had been purchased, for what purpose, by whom, or how much it had cost. It was usable, however; and after it was cleaned and minor repairs were made by the Department of Public Works employees, the equipment was turned over to the Stores and Services Fund. The fair value of the equipment is estimated to be $12,000; its remaining useful life is estimated at 10 years.

    d. Record in the Stores and Services Fund general journal all of the following transactions, which took place in July 19x2. Use account titles and practices illustrated in Chapter 9.

      (1) Warehouse and office space was not available in city-owned buildings; space was rented in a privately owned building for $500 a month. Five percent of the space is assigned to Purchasing, 5 percent to Administration, and 90 percent to Warehousing. Six months' rent was paid in advance. (Charge Prepaid Rent.)

      (2) Record the fair value of the equipment contributed to the Stores and Services Fund. Assume the General Fund was given credit for the contribution.

      (3) Invoices for stores received were approved for payment in the amount of $30,000.

(4) Vouchers amounting to $20,000 were paid, as was payroll totaling $3,600. (For the payroll, charge Purchasing Expenses, $800; Administrative Expenses, $800; and Warehousing Expenses, $2,000.)

(5) Invoices for utilities for the month were approved for payment in the amount of $300. (Charge to Warehousing Expenses.)

(6) Stores costing $25,000 were issued to the General Fund; an interfund invoice in the proper amount was prepared.

(7) Expenses for operation and maintenance of warehouse equipment totaled $200. This amount was approved for payment.

(8) The Stores and Services Fund used stores of its own that had cost $100. (Charge Administrative Expenses.)

(9) Adjusting and closing entries were recorded as of the end of the first month of operations.

  e. Prepare a Statement of Revenues and Expenses and Changes in Retained Earnings of this fund for July 19x2.

9–S. The City of Smithville does not have an internal service fund.

CHAPTER 10

Enterprise Funds

Enterprise funds and internal service funds are both classified by the GASB as "proprietary funds." Internal service funds, discussed in Chapter 9, are used to account for services provided by one department or agency of a governmental unit **to other departments** or agencies, **or to other governmental units** on a user charge basis. Enterprise funds are used by governmental units to account for services provided **to the general public** on a user charge basis. Enterprise funds may also be used to account for any operations "where the governing body has decided that periodic determination of revenues earned, expenses incurred, and/or net income is appropriate for capital maintenance, public policy, management control, accountability, or other purposes."[1] From this description, and from the fact that the word **enterprise** is often used as a synonym for "business," it may be apparent that enterprise funds should use full accrual accounting and account for all assets used in the production of goods or services offered by the fund. Similarly, if long-term debt is to be serviced by the fund, it is accounted for by the fund. Distinction should be made in fund equity accounts between equity contributed to the fund and earnings resulting from operations of the fund.

The most common examples of governmental enterprises are public utilities, notably water and sewer utilities. Electric and gas utilities, transportation systems, airports, ports, hospitals, toll bridges, produce markets, parking lots, parking garages, liquor stores, and public housing projects are other examples frequently found. Services of the kinds mentioned are generally accounted for by enterprise funds because they are intended to be largely self-supporting. However, they are properly accounted for by a general or special revenue fund by those governments that support the activities largely from general or special revenue sources other than user charges and are not concerned with measuring the costs of the activities.

---

[1] GASB Codification Sec. 1100.103b(1).

Almost every kind of enterprise operated by a government has its counterpart in the private sector. In order to take advantage of the work done by regulatory agencies and trade associations to develop useful accounting information systems for the investor-owned enterprises, **it is recommended that governmentally owned enterprises use the accounting structures developed for investor-owned enterprises of the same nature.**[2] Budgetary accounts should be used only if required by law. Debt service and construction activities of a governmental enterprise are accounted for within the enterprise fund, rather than by separate debt service and capital projects funds. Thus, the financial statements of enterprise funds are self-contained; and creditors, legislators, or the general public can evaluate the performance of a governmental enterprise on the same bases as they can the performance of investor-owned enterprises in the same industry.

By far the most numerous and important enterprise services rendered by local governments are public utilities. In this chapter, therefore, the example used is that of a water utility fund.

Illustrative Case—Water Utility Fund

The Balance Sheet as of December 31, 19y0, for the Town of Brighton Water Utility Fund is shown in Illustration 10–1. While the Balance Sheet appears fairly conventional, terminology peculiar to utilities warrants discussion prior to proceeding to the illustrative transactions for the year ending December 31, 19y1.

Current and Accrued Assets

Cash and Materials and Supplies shown in Illustration 10–1 in the Current and Accrued Assets section are not peculiar to utilities and need not be discussed here. The other two asset accounts in this section—Customer Accounts Receivable and Accrued Utilities Revenues—are related. The former represents billings

---

[2] GASB *Statement No. 20* provides interim guidance on business-type accounting and financial reporting for proprietary activities until GASB addresses these issues more fully as part of its reporting model project. Interim guidance is needed to clarify the authoritative status of FASB pronouncements in determining generally accepted accounting principles (GAAP) for proprietary activities given the GAAP hierarchy provided for in *Statement on Auditing Standards No. 69, The Meaning of "Present Fairly in Conformity with Generally Accepted Accounting Principles" in the Independent Auditor's Report* (AICPA, 1992). GASB *Statement No. 20* gives governments an option between two accounting and financial reporting approaches for proprietary funds. The first approach would require consistent use of all GASB pronouncements and applicable pronouncements of FASB and its predecessors (Accounting Principles Board and Committee on Accounting Procedure) issued on or before November 30, 1989, unless those pronouncements conflict with or contradict GASB pronouncements. The second approach requires consistent use of all GASB pronouncements and all applicable pronouncements (both before and after November 30, 1989) of FASB and its predecessors, unless those pronouncements conflict with or contradict GASB pronouncements. Thus, under the first approach, unless GASB directs otherwise, governments are not required to change their accounting procedures if FASB issues a standard that supersedes or amends a standard issued on or before November 30, 1989. This date (November 30, 1989) is significant as the date the Financial Accounting Foundation resolved a conflict over jurisdiction of the FASB and GASB.

ILLUSTRATION 10-1

TOWN OF BRIGHTON
Water Utility Fund
Balance Sheet
As of December 31, 19y0

Assets

Current and Accrued Assets:			
Cash		$ 126,000	
Customer accounts receivable	$ 69,000		
Less: Accumulated provision for uncollectibles	2,900	66,100	
Accrued utilities revenues		14,800	
Materials and Supplies		28,700	
Total Current and Accrued Assets			$ 235,600
Restricted Assets:			
Cash		6,600	
Investments		556,000	562,600
Utility Plant:			
Utility plant in service		3,291,825	
Less: Accumulated depreciation		440,325	
Utility Plant—Net		2,851,500	
Construction work in progress		125,000	
Net Utility Plant			2,976,500
Total Assets			$3,774,700

Liabilities and Fund Equity

Current Liabilities:			
Accounts payable	$ 33,200		
Customers advances for construction	21,000		
Total Current Liabilities			$ 54,200
Liabilities Payable from Restricted Assets:			
Customer Deposits			23,700
Long-Term Debt:			
Revenue bonds payable (net of unamortized discount of $5,300)			1,744,700
Total Liabilities			1,822,600
Fund Equity:			
Contribution from Town		$1,000,000	
Contributions from customers		252,000	
Retained Earnings:			
Reserved for payment of revenue bonds	538,900		
Unreserved	161,200	700,100	
Total Fund Equity			1,952,100
Total Liabilities and Fund Equity			$3,774,700

to customers that are outstanding at year-end (and are reduced, as one would expect, by an Accumulated Provision for Uncollectibles). The latter results from the fact that utilities generally prepare billings to customers on the basis of meter readings, and it is not practical for utilities to read all meters simultaneously at year-end and bill all customers as of that time. Utilities that meter their service make extensive use of cycle billing, which, in substance, consists of billing part of their customers each day, instead of billing by calendar months. Under this plan, meter reading is a continuous day-by-day operation, with billings following shortly after the filing of the meter readers' reports. Individual meters are read on approximately the same day each month, or every other month, in order that each bill cover approximately the same number of days usage. Cycle billing eliminates the heavy peak load of accounting and clerical work that results from uniform billing on a calendar month basis. It does, however, result in a sizable amount of unbilled receivables on any given date, thus requiring accrual of unbilled receivables (Accrued Utilities Revenues, in regulatory terminology) as of financial statement date in order to state assets and sales properly.[3]

Restricted Assets

The section below Current and Accrued Assets in Illustration 10–1 is captioned Restricted Assets, the caption most commonly used when the use of assets is restricted by contractual agreements or legal requirements. Some governments that use regulatory terminology report restricted assets of utilities under the broader caption, Other Property and Investments. Other Property and Investments may include, in addition to restricted assets, the carrying value of property not being used for utility purposes or being held for future utility use.

Cash and Investments are the only two items reported under the Restricted Assets caption of the balance sheet shown in Illustration 10–1. Those items are restricted for return of customer deposits and for retirement of revenue bonds pursuant to the bond covenants. The amount of assets segregated, $562,600, is offset by liabilities currently payable from restricted assets (in the case of the Town of Brighton, Customer Deposits of $23,700) and reservations of Retained Earnings (in this case, Reserved for Repayment of Revenue Bonds, $538,900). This **funds within a fund** approach permits segregation of assets, related liabilities, and reserved fund equity within a single enterprise fund. Retained earnings should be reserved in the amount of the net assets of each restricted "fund" within the enterprise fund, as shown in Illustration 10–1. Other items commonly reported in Restricted Assets include assets set aside to fund depreciation for capital improvements or grants and contributions restricted for capital acquisition or improvement.

---

[3] Most governments use the same or similar chart of accounts for utilities as those of regulated profit-seeking enterprises in the same industry. The principal regulatory bodies are the National Association of Regulatory Utility Commissioners (NARUC), an association of state regulatory utility commissioners, and the Federal Energy Regulatory Commission (FERC) which has jurisdiction over utilities in interstate commerce.

Utility Plant

Utility Plant in Service is a control account, supported in whatever detail is required by regulatory agencies and by management needs. For example, water utilities commonly have six subcategories of plant assets: Intangible plant, source of supply plant, pumping plant, water treatment plant, transmission and distribution plant, and general plant. Each of the six subcategories is supported by appropriate subsidiary accounts. For example, intangible plant consists of the costs of organization, franchises and consents, and any other intangible costs "necessary and valuable in the conduct of utility operations." Source of supply plant consists of land and land rights; structures and improvements; collecting and impounding reservoirs; lake, river, and other intakes; wells and springs; infiltration galleries and tunnels; supply mains; and other water source plant. Each of the accounts within each subcategory is supported by necessary subsidiary records for each individual asset detailing its description, location, cost, date of acquisition, estimated useful life, salvage value, depreciation charges, and any other information needed for management planning and control, regulatory agency reports, financial statements, or special reports to creditors.

Construction Work in Progress.   The other Utility Plant item shown on the Balance Sheet, Illustration 10–1, is Construction Work in Progress. This account represents the accumulated costs of work orders for projects that will result in items reportable as Utility Plant when completed and is, of course, supported by the work orders for projects in progress. Each work order, in turn, is supported by documents supporting payments to contractors and to suppliers, or supporting charges for materials, labor, and overhead allocable to the project.

The Uniform Systems of Accounts for water, sewer, gas, and electric utilities published by NARUC all contain a section on Utility Plant Instructions that, among other items, specifies the components of construction cost. Generally, the components are in agreement with those listed in any intermediate accounting text. One item long recognized in utility accounting but only recently specifically accepted by the FASB is the Allowance for Funds Used During Construction (AFUDC).[4]

AFUDC includes the net cost for the period of construction of borrowed funds used for construction purposes **and a reasonable rate on other funds so used.** Thus, interest paid, accrued, or imputed during the period of construction of a utility plant asset is included as a cost of the asset. Interest paid or accrued, known as the **debt component** of AFUDC, is deducted from Interest on Long-Term Debt in the Other Income and Deductions section of the utility's operating statement (see Illustration 10–3). This practice accomplishes two things: (1) it discloses to financial statement readers the amount of interest that was capitalized during the year, and (2) it reduces the reported interest expense, thus increasing

---

[4] Financial Accounting Standards Board, *Statement of Financial Accounting Standards No. 71*, "Accounting for the Effects of Certain Types of Regulation" (Norwalk, Conn., 1982), par. 15, as amended by *Statement of Financial Accounting Standards No. 90* (Norwalk, Conn., 1986), par. 8, and *Statement of Financial Accounting Standards No. 92* (Norwalk, Conn., 1987), pars. 8 and 9.

reported net income for the period (presumably slowing down utilities' requests for rate increases). If construction is financed, in part, by use of resources generated by operations of the utility, regulatory authorities allow interest to be imputed on these "equity" funds and capitalized. Since imputed interest is not viewed by accountants as an expense, it is offset by reporting the *equity component* of AFUDC as nonoperating income.

Current Liabilities

Items commonly found in the Current Liabilities section of a Utility Balance Sheet are shown under that caption in Illustration 10–1. Accounts Payable needs no comment here. The other item, **Customers Advances for Construction,** results from the practice of utilities of requiring customers to advance to the utility a sizable portion of the estimated cost of construction projects to be undertaken by the utility at the request of the customer. If the advances are to be refunded, either wholly or in part, or applied against billings for service rendered after completion of the project, they are classified as shown in Illustration 10–1. When a customer is refunded the entire amount to which he is entitled according to the agreement or rule under which the advance was made, the balance, if any, is transferred to Contributions from Customers, a Fund Equity account. Other items commonly reported under Current Liabilities include accrued expenses, amounts due to other funds, and current portions of long-term liabilities. Some governments also report customer deposits under the Current Liabilities caption.[5]

Liabilities Payable from Restricted Assets

Liabilities payable from restricted assets should be displayed separately from current liabilities as shown in Illustration 10–1. In addition to customer deposits, the current portion of revenue bonds payable, if any, would be reported here since restricted assets have been set aside for that purpose. The Town of Brighton follows the common practice of most utilities and requires all new customers to deposit a sum of money with the utility as security for the payment of bills. In many, but not all, jurisdictions utilities are required to pay interest on customer deposits at a nominal rate. Regulatory authorities or local policy may require utilities to refund the deposits, and interest, after a specified period of time if the customer has paid all bills on time. The utility may be required, as was the Town of Brighton Water Fund, to segregate cash or investments in an amount equal to the liability for Customer Deposits. Customers Advances for Construction are contractually different from Customer Deposits and are less likely to be reported separately as restricted assets and liabilities, unless agreements with developers make it necessary to restrict assets for this purpose.

---

[5] Generally, customer deposits should be reported as "Liabilities Payable from Restricted Assets," a special category of current liabilities, as explained in the following section. Although customer deposits may be held for an extended period, possibly for as long as customers receive metered service, the AICPA audit and accounting guide, "Audits of State and Local Governmental Units" states (par. 13.13): "Customer deposits remain in current liabilities until applied against billings or refunded to customers." Reporting customer deposits in this manner seems overly conservative since only a small portion are likely to be refunded in any given year.

Long-Term Debt

Bonds are the customary form of long-term debt. Bonds issued by a utility are usually secured by the pledge of certain portions of the utility's revenue, the exact terms of the pledge varying with individual cases; bonds of this nature are called **revenue bonds.** Some utility bonds are secured not only by a pledge of a certain portion of the utility's revenues but also by an agreement on the part of the town's or city's general government to subsidize the utility in any year in which its normal revenue is inadequate for compliance with the terms of the bond indenture. Other utility bonds carry the pledge of the governmental unit's full faith and credit, although the intent is to service them from utility revenues rather than general taxes. The latter are, therefore, technically **general obligation bonds.** GASB standards provide that general obligation bonds intended to be serviced from utility revenues be reported as a liability of the enterprise fund. Similarly, special assessment debt may be assumed by an enterprise fund if the assets constructed by special assessment financing are used in enterprise fund operations. The General Long-Term Debt Account Group should disclose the contingent liability by note rather than in the body of the Statement of General Long-Term Debt. An example of such a note is presented in Chapter 8 of this text.

Governmentally owned utilities may have received advances from the government's General Fund or other funds. Also, enterprises may acquire assets under a capital lease arrangement. The portion of advances, required lease payments, or bond or other debt issues to be paid within one year from balance sheet date should be reported as a current liability; the remainder is properly reported in the Long-Term Debt section of the Utility Balance Sheet. Long-term bonds payable should be reported net of unamortized discount or premium, as shown in Illustration 10–1, or else unamortized discount or premium can be reported as an offset against bonds payable at par on the Balance Sheet.

Fund Equity

Contributed Equity. The equity of an enterprise fund consists of **contributed equity** and **retained earnings.** Equity that results from the contribution of assets by a governmental unit requires no explanation here, although readers should recall that the proceeds of capital grants are to be recorded as contributed equity, as are the proceeds of debt that is to be repaid from tax revenue or special assessment revenue rather than from enterprise revenues.

In the case of utilities, equity may also be contributed by customers, as noted in the discussion of Customers Advances for Construction in the section on Current Liabilities. The treatment of Contributions from Customers as an item in Fund Equity is consistent with the uniform system of accounts published by the National Association of Regulatory Utility Commissioners. Utilities in interstate commerce, which are subject to regulation by the Federal Energy Regulatory Commission, are required to account for contributions from customers as credits to the *asset* accounts that were charged for the cost of such construction. From a regulatory viewpoint, the prescribed treatment reduces the carrying value of the assets to the cost borne by the utility and, therefore, presumably lowers the rate base. From an accounting viewpoint, the FERC requirement results in an understatement of both the costs of the assets and the amount of contributed equity.

Retained Earnings.   Although it is generally true that governmental units own utilities in order to have the capacity to render services to residents, rather than as a device to earn revenues, it is obviously in the best interests of taxpayers that the utility be self-supporting. Operating revenues, therefore, must be set at a level expected to cover operating expenses, provide for debt service, and finance routine capital projects. For these reasons, it is customary for governmentally owned utilities to accumulate retained earnings just as investor-owned utilities do—although perhaps not to the same extent.

Illustrative Accounting for a Water Utility Fund

The discussion in preceding pages of the balance sheet accounts of a water utility includes by implication the essential characteristics of accounting necessary for both governmentally owned utilities and investor-owned utilities. In this section, accounting for characteristic transactions of a utility fund is illustrated in general journal entry format for the year following the balance sheet presented in Illustration 10–1.

It is assumed the Town of Brighton is located in a state that permits enterprise funds to operate without formal legal approval of their budgets. Utility, or other enterprise, management must prepare operating budgets and capital expenditure budgets as management tools. For the illustrative case, it is assumed the budgets are submitted to the Town administrators, to the Town legislative body, and to the public, for information, not for legal action. Accordingly, the budget is not formally recorded in enterprise fund accounts. Similarly, utility management must be informed periodically of the status of outstanding construction contracts and purchase orders, but encumbrances need not be recorded in the accounts in order to accomplish this.

The nature of the Accrued Utilities Revenues account is explained above in the section on Current and Accrued Assets. In the year following the one for which the balance sheet is shown, it is not feasible when customers' bills are prepared to determine whether a portion of the bill has been accrued and, if so, how much. The simplest procedure, therefore, is to reverse the accrual entry as of the start of the new fiscal year. Assuming the entire December 31, 19y0, Town of Brighton Water Utility Fund revenues accrual has been credited to Sales of Water, the following entry is appropriate as of January 1, 19y1:

1. Sales of Water	14,800	
Accrued Utility Revenues		14,800

When utility customers are billed during the year, appropriate revenue accounts are credited. Assuming during 19y1 the total bills to nongovernmental customers amounted to $696,000, bills to the Town of Brighton General Fund amounted to $30,000, and all revenue was from sales of water, the following entry summarizes the events:

2. Customer Accounts Receivable	696,000	
Due from General Fund	30,000	
Sales of Water		726,000

If collections from nongovernmental customers totaled $680,000 for water billings, Entry 3 is needed:

3. Cash	680,000	
Customer Accounts Receivable............................		680,000

Materials and supplies in the amount of $138,000 were purchased during the year by the Water Utility Fund. The liability is recorded as:

4. Materials and Supplies	138,000	
Accounts Payable..		138,000

Materials and supplies chargeable to the accounts itemized in the entry below were issued during the year.

5. Source of Supply Expenses	18,000	
Pumping Expenses..	21,000	
Water Treatment Expenses	24,000	
Transmission and Distribution Expenses.......................	13,000	
Construction Work in Progress	66,000	
Materials and Supplies		142,000

Payrolls for the year were chargeable to the accounts shown in the entry below. Tax Collections Payable is the account provided in the NARUC and FERC systems to report "the amount of taxes collected by the utility through payroll deductions or otherwise pending transmittal of such taxes to the proper taxing authority." Taxes Accrued is the account provided in the NARUC and FERC systems to report the liability for taxes that are the expense of the utility, such as the employer's share of social security taxes. In the entry below, it is assumed that the employer's share of social security taxes is charged to the same accounts that the employees' gross earnings are; it is also assumed that checks have been issued for employees' net earnings.

6. Source of Supply Expenses	8,200	
Pumping Expenses..	15,700	
Water Treatment Expenses	17,500	
Transmission and Distribution Expenses.......................	76,250	
Customer Accounts Expenses.................................	96,550	
Sales Expenses...	17,250	
Administrative and General Expenses..........................	83,150	
Construction Work in Progress	30,400	
Taxes Accrued		13,800
Tax Collections Payable		51,750
Cash		279,450

Bond interest in the amount of $105,000 was paid; the bonds were issued to finance the acquisition of utility plant assets. Amortization of debt discount and expense amounted to $530.

7. Interest on Long-Term Debt	105,000	
Amortization of Debt Discount and Expense.....................	530	
Unamortized Debt Discount and Expense		530
Cash		105,000

Bond interest in the amount of $12,900 was properly capitalized as part of construction work in progress during the year. (The Town of Brighton does not impute interest on its own resources during construction.)

8. Construction Work in Progress	12,900	
Allowance for Funds Used During		
Construction		12,900

Construction projects on which costs totaled $220,000 were completed and the assets placed in service:

9. Utility Plant in Service	220,000	
Construction Work in Progress		220,000

Collection efforts were discontinued on bills totaling $3,410. The customers owing the bills had paid deposits to the water utility totaling $2,140; the deposits were applied to the bills, and the unpaid remainder was charged to Accumulated Provision for Uncollectible Accounts (Entry 10a). Restricted assets (cash) is reduced by $2,140, the amount of the decrease in Customer Deposits (Entry 10b).

10a. Customer Deposits	2,140	
Accumulated Provision for Uncollectible		
Accounts	1,270	
Customer Accounts Receivable		3,410
10b. Cash	2,140	
Cash—Customer Deposits		2,140

Customers deposits amounting to $1,320 were refunded by check to customers discontinuing service (see Entry 11a). Deposits totaling $2,525 were received from new customers (see Entry 11b).

11a. Customer Deposits	1,320	
Cash—Customer Deposits		1,320
11b. Cash—Customer Deposits	2,525	
Customer Deposits		2,525

Customers advances for construction in the amount of $14,000 were applied to their water bills; in accord with the agreement with the customers and NARUC recommendations, the remainder of the advances were transferred to Contributions from Customers.

12. Customers Advances for Construction	21,000	
Customer Accounts Receivable		14,000
Contributions from Customers		7,000

Payments of Accounts Payable for materials and supplies used in operations totaled $67,200, and payment of Accounts Payable for materials used in construction totaled $66,000. Payments of Taxes Accrued amounted to $13,500, and payments of Tax Collections Payable amounted to $50,000.

13. Accounts Payable	133,200	
Taxes Accrued	13,500	
Tax Collections Payable	50,000	
Cash		196,700

The Water Utility Fund agreed to pay $25,000 to the Town General Fund as a contribution in lieu of property taxes. The entry in the General Fund is illustrated in Chapter 4 (see Chapter 4, illustrative Entry 16b). The following entry records the event in the accounts of the Water Utility Fund:

| 14. Contribution in Lieu of Taxes | 25,000 | |
| Due to General Fund | | 25,000 |

During the year interest in the amount of $44,500 was received in Cash on restricted investments. The amount of $1,375 is allocable to investments of customer deposit assets and is unrestricted as to use; the remaining $43,125 adds to the amount restricted for revenue bond repayment.

15a. Cash	1,375	
Cash—Bond Repayment	43,125	
Interest and Dividend Income		44,500
15b. Unreserved Retained Earnings	43,125	
Retained Earnings Reserved for Bond Repayment		43,125

At year-end, entries to record depreciation expense, the provision for uncollectible accounts, and unbilled customers accounts receivable should be made as illustrated by Entry 16. In accord with regulatory terminology, Customer Accounts Expense, instead of Bad Debts Expense, is debited for the amount added to Accumulated Provision for Uncollectible Accounts. Amounts are assumed.

16. Depreciation Expense	102,750	
Customer Accounts Expenses	3,980	
Accrued Utility Revenues	15,920	
Accumulated Provision for Depreciation of Utility Plant		102,750
Accumulated Provision for Uncollectible Accounts		3,980
Sales of Water		15,920

In accord with the revenue bond indenture, $100,000 unrestricted cash was invested in U.S. Government Securities for eventual retirement of revenue bonds. Retained earnings is reserved in an amount equal to the increase in restricted assets. In addition, investments from restricted cash for bond repayment amounted to $40,000.

17a. Investments—Bond Repayment	140,000	
Cash		100,000
Cash—Bond Repayment		40,000
17b. Unreserved Retained Earnings	100,000	
Retained Earnings Reserved for Bond Repayment		100,000

Nominal accounts for the year were closed:

18. Sales of Water.. 727,120
    Allowance for Funds Used During Construction   12,900
    Interest and Dividend Revenue.............................. 44,500

Source of Supply Expenses	26,200
Pumping Expenses	36,700
Water Treatment Expenses	41,500
Transmission and Distribution Expenses	89,250
Customer Account Expenses	100,530
Sales Expenses	17,250
Administrative and General Expenses	83,150
Interest on Long-Term Debt	105,000
Amortization of Debt Discount and Expense	530
Contribution in Lieu of Taxes	25,000
Depreciation Expense	102,750
Unreserved Retained Earnings	156,660

Illustrative Statements

Balance Sheet. The balance sheet for a water utility, and definitions of certain balance sheet categories and items peculiar to regulated utilities, are explained at length in the sections of this chapter preceding the illustrative entries. The Balance Sheet of the Town of Brighton Water Utility Fund as of December 31, 19y1, is shown as Illustration 10–2. Note the amount due to the General Fund is offset against the amount due from that fund, and only the net amount of the receivable, $5,000, is shown as an asset.

Operating Statement. The results of the operations of the Town of Brighton's Water Utility Fund for the year ended December 31, 19y1, are shown in Illustration 10–3, the Statement of Revenues, Expenses, and Changes in Retained Earnings. The classifications used in the statement are consistent with NARUC and FERC recommendations.

Statement of Cash Flows. GASB standards require that a Statement of Cash Flows be prepared for all proprietary funds as a part of a full set of annual financial statements. As discussed at length in Chapter 9, GASB standards for preparation of a cash flow statement differ from FASB standards; the main difference being that GASB standards specify four major categories of cash flows rather than three. The Statement of Cash Flows for the Town of Brighton for the year ended December 31, 19y1 (Illustration 10–4) utilizes only three of the four categories of cash flows since the Town had no cash flows from noncapital financing activities. **Cash flows from operating activities** (Illustration 10–4) were provided by receipts from customers (Entry 3) and the net increase in refundable customer deposits (Entries 11a and 11b). Note that the application of customer deposits to pay overdue bills (Entries 10a and 10b) has no effect on total cash and cash equivalents. Cash from operating activities was used to pay employees (Entries 6 and 13). As suggested in the GASB *Implementation Guide* on reporting cash flows,[6] all

---

[6] Governmental Accounting Standards Board, *Implementation Guide,* "Guide to Implementation of GASB Statement 9 on Reporting Cash Flows of Proprietary and Nonexpendable Trust Funds and Governmental Entities That Use Proprietary Fund Accounting," (GASB, 1992), p. 23.

ILLUSTRATION 10–2

TOWN OF BRIGHTON
Water Utility Fund
Balance Sheet
As of December 31, 19y1

Assets

Current and Accrued Assets:			
Cash		$ 128,365	
Customer accounts receivable	$ 67,590		
Less: Accumulated provision for uncollectibles	5,610	61,980	
Accrued utilities revenues		15,920	
Due from General Fund		5,000	
Materials and supplies		24,700	
Total Current and Accrued Assets			$ 235,965
Restricted Assets:			
Cash		8,790	
Investments		696,000	704,790
Utility Plant:			
Utility plant in service		3,511,825	
Less: Accumulated depreciation		543,075	
Utility Plant—Net		2,968,750	
Construction work in progress		14,300	
Net Utility Plant			2,983,050
Total Assets			$3,923,805

Liabilities and Fund Equity

Current Liabilities:			
Accounts payable		$ 38,000	
Taxes accrued		300	
Tax collection payable		1,750	
Total Current Liabilities			$ 40,050
Liabilities Payable from Restricted Assets:			
Customer deposits			22,765
Long-Term Debt:			
Revenue bonds payable (net of unamortized discount of $4,770)			1,745,230
Total Liabilities			1,808,045
Fund Equity:			
Contribution from Town		1,000,000	
Contributions from customers		259,000	
Retained Earnings:			
Reserved for repayment of revenue bonds	$682,025		
Unreserved	174,735	856,760	
Total Fund Equity			2,115,760
Total Liabilities and Fund Equity			$3,923,805

ILLUSTRATION 10–3

TOWN OF BRIGHTON
Water Utility Fund
Statement of Revenues, Expenses, and Changes in Retained Earnings
For the Year Ended December 31, 19y1

Utility Operating Revenue:		
Sales of water		$727,120
Operating Expenses:		
Source of supply expenses	$ 26,200	
Pumping expenses	36,700	
Water treatment expenses	41,500	
Transmission and distribution expenses	89,250	
Customer account expenses	100,530	
Sales expenses	17,250	
Administrative and general expenses	83,150	
Depreciation expense	102,750	
Contribution in lieu of taxes	25,000	
Total Operating Expenses		522,330
Utility Operating Income		204,790
Other Income and Deductions:		
Interest and dividend revenue	(44,500)	
Interest on long-term debt	105,000	
Amortization of debt discount and expense	530	
Allowance for funds used during construction	(12,900)	
Total Other Income and Deductions		48,130
Net Income		156,660
Unreserved Retained Earnings, January 1, 19y1		161,200
Total		317,860
Less: Reservations of Retained Earnings		143,125
Unreserved Retained Earnings, December 31, 19y1		$174,735
Reserved Retained Earnings, January 1, 19y1		$538,900
Add: Reserved during Year		143,125
Reserved Retained Earnings, December 31, 19y1		$682,025

employee-related items (in this case Taxes Accrued and Tax Collections Payable) have been added to the amount actually paid to employees. Payroll taxes and fringe benefits may be included in a separate line "cash payments for taxes, duties, fines, and other fees or penalties," if significant in amount. "Cash paid to employees for services" in the amount of $312,550 is calculated as the net cash paid directly to employees, $279,450, less $30,400 capitalized as construction work in Progress (Entry 6) plus $63,500 paid for Taxes Accrued and Tax Collections Payable (Entry 13). Finally cash from operating activities was used to pay suppliers (Entry 13). Although suppliers were paid $133,200 in total, only $67,200 of this amount applied to operating activities.

Cash flows from capital and related activities in Illustration 10–4 show two uses of cash. The first item, acquisition and construction of capital assets, is calculated as the sum of $30,400 (Entry 6) and $66,000 (Entry 13). The other item, interest paid on long-term bonds, reflects bond interest in the amount of $105,000 paid in cash (Entry 7).

Cash flows from investing activities show cash provided by interest and dividend income (Entry 15a) and cash used by purchase of investments (Entry 17a).

As shown in Illustration 10–4, two reconciliations are required. The first reconciliation is necessary because the Town of Brighton's Statement of Cash Flows reports changes in **total** cash and cash equivalents, whereas the Balance Sheet shows two components of cash and cash equivalents: that included in Current and Accrued Assets and that included in Restricted Assets, respectively.[7] GASB standards also require a reconciliation of operating income to net cash provided by operating activities.

Combining Statements

If a reporting entity operates more than one enterprise fund, it is necessary to present a Combining Balance Sheet; a Combining Statement of Revenues, Expenses, and Changes in Retained Earnings; and a Combining Statement of Cash Flows for all Enterprise Funds in order to disclose the detail supporting the Enterprise Funds column in each of the Combined Statements. An illustrative Combining Balance Sheet for the enterprise funds of the City of Rock Island, Illinois, is shown as Illustration 10–5.

Events in Following Year

In Chapter 9, the establishment of a Supplies Fund by the Town of Brighton as of January 1, 19y2, is illustrated. The Water Utility Fund advanced $130,000 to the Supplies Fund as a long-term loan. The entry by the Supplies Fund is illustrated in Chapter 9 (Entry 2); the corresponding entry in the Water Utility Fund would be:

Long-Term Advance to Supplies Fund	130,000	
Cash		130,000

Toward the end of 19y2, the Supplies Fund paid its first installment of $6,500 to the Water Utility Fund as a partial repayment of the long-term advance. Entry 9 in Chapter 9 illustrates the effect on the accounts of the Supplies Fund. The effect on the accounts of the Water Utility Fund is recorded by the following entry:

Cash	6,500	
Long-Term Advance to Supplies Fund		6,500

Regulatory Accounting Principles (RAP)

Investor-owned utilities, and governmentally owned utilities in several states, are required to report in a prescribed manner to state regulatory commissions. Electric and certain other utilities subject to the Federal Power Act must also file reports with the FERC. As mentioned at several points in this chapter, both NARUC and FERC prescribe charts of accounts and uniform financial statement formats for reporting to regulatory agencies. Even though the Town of Brighton follows GAAP rather than RAP in preparing its financial statements, the Town

---

[7] Ibid, p. 28.

ILLUSTRATION 10–4

TOWN OF BRIGHTON
Water Utility Fund
Statement of Cash Flows
For the Year Ended December 31, 19y1

Cash flows from operating activities:	
Cash received from customers	$680,000
Cash provided from customer deposits	1,205
Cash paid to employees for services	(312,550)
Cash paid to suppliers	(67,200)
Net cash provided by operating activities	301,455
Cash flows from capital and related financing activities:	
Acquisition and construction of capital assets	(96,400)
Interest paid on long-term bonds	(105,000)
Net cash used for capital and related financing activities	(201,400)
Cash flows from investing activities:	
Interest and dividend income	44,500
Purchases of restricted investments	(140,000)
Net cash used for investing activities	(95,500)
Net increase in cash and cash equivalents	4,555
Cash and cash equivalents, January 1, 19y1	132,600
Cash and cash equivalents, December 31, 19y1	$137,155

Reconciliation of Cash and Cash Equivalents to the Balance Sheet

	End of Year	Beginning of Year
Cash and cash equivalents in current and accrued assets	$128,365	$126,000
Restricted cash and cash equivalents	8,790	6,600
Total cash and cash equivalents	$137,155	$132,600

Reconciliation of Utility Operating Income to Net Cash Provided by Operating Activities

Utility operating income		$204,790
Adjustments:		
Depreciation expense	$102,750	
Increase in accounts payable	4,800	
Increase in accrued liabilities	2,050	
Decrease in customer deposits	(935)	
Decrease in inventories	4,000	
Increase in interfund receivables	(5,000)	
Increase in accrued receivables	(1,120)	
Decrease in customer accounts receivable	4,120	
Customer advances applied to customer receivables	(14,000)	
Total adjustments		96,665
Net cash provided by operating activities		$301,455

ILLUSTRATION 10–5

CITY OF ROCK ISLAND, ILLINOIS
Enterprise Funds
Combining Balance Sheet
March 31, 1992

	Community Assistance Fund	Sunset Marina Fund	Waterworks Fund
Assets			
Current Assets:			
Cash and investments	$ —	$ 216,581	$ 259,789
Receivables, net of allowance for collection losses:			
Accrued interest	—	—	—
Accounts	—	1,602	222,615
Estimated unbilled usage	—	—	375,147
Current portion of notes	293,580	—	—
Other	—	—	—
Due from other funds	—	—	—
Inventories	—	5,000	—
Prepaid expenses	—	—	—
Total current assets	$ 293,580	$ 223,183	$ 857,551
Restricted Assets:			
Cash	$ —	$ —	$ —
Investments	—	—	—
Notes Receivable (net of current portion, net of allowance for uncollectibles of $978,025)	4,897,590	—	—
Property, Plant and Equipment:			
Land	—	—	41,976
Buildings	—	—	—
Equipment	—	—	96,946
Waterworks system	—	—	14,156,593
Wastewater system	—	—	—
Bridge and approaches	—	—	—
Marina facilities	—	1,649,033	—
Construction in progress	—	233,007	284,902
Accumulated depreciation	—	(848,908)	(9,960,418)
Net property and equipment	$ —	$1,033,132	$ 4,619,999
Total assets	$5,191,170	$1,256,315	$ 5,477,550

uses the chart of accounts and some of the financial statement captions provided for in regulatory publications. The illustrative financial statements shown earlier in this chapter are typical of those for water funds included in comprehensive annual financial reports.

For utilities which are required to report to a state rate regulatory commission or the FERC, accounting and reporting procedures under RAP are quite different

Wastewater Treatment Fund	Motor Vehicle Parking System Fund	Rock Island Centennial Bridge Fund	Housing and Community Development Loan Fund	Total
$ 1,005,973	$ 244,604	$ 2,293,343	$ 443,980	$ 4,464,870
—	—	5,435	—	5,435
146,705	10,042	—	—	380,964
283,240	—	—	—	658,387
—	—	—	207,388	500,968
6,904	—	—	—	6,904
—	36,689	—	—	36,689
—	—	3,000	—	8,000
—	—	20,229	—	20,229
$ 1,442,822	$ 291,335	$ 2,322,607	$ 651,368	$ 6,082,446
$ 223,151	$ —	$ —	$ —	$ 223,151
655,167	—	—	—	655,167
—	—	—	1,594,943	6,492,533
94,450	1,050,068	2,714,607	—	3,901,101
—	2,802,612	—	—	2,802,612
3,376	—	—	—	100,322
—	—	—	—	14,156,593
19,791,991	—	—	—	19,791,991
—	—	12,615,305	—	12,615,305
—	—	—	—	1,649,033
2,436,031	385,306	708,685	—	4,047,931
(10,744,709)	(1,231,216)	(7,074,754)	—	(29,860,005)
$11,581,139	$3,006,770	$ 8,963,843	$ —	$29,204,883
$13,902,279	$3,298,105	$11,286,450	$2,246,311	$42,658,180

from GAAP. Because plant assets and long-term debt are customarily a dominant share of the total assets and total debt of utilities, and current assets and current liabilities are relatively insignificant in amount, the regulatory balance sheet format displays plant assets before current assets and long-term debt before current liabilities. In Illustration 10–1, for example, Net Utility Plant amounts to almost 91 percent of total assets, and long-term debt is almost 96 percent of total debt.

ILLUSTRATION 10–5 (*concluded*)

CITY OF ROCK ISLAND, ILLINOIS
Enterprise Funds
Combining Balance Sheet
March 31, 1992

	Community Assistance Fund	Sunset Marina Fund	Waterworks Fund
Liabilities and Fund Equity			
Current Liabilities:			
Accounts and contracts payable	$ —	$ 10,014	$ 77,861
Accrued liabilities	141,230	29,568	144,133
Due to other funds	9,556	583	6,358
Deferred revenue	—	—	—
Current portion of capitalized lease obligations	—	—	—
Current portion of bonds payable	155,000	40,000	159,690
Total current liabilities	$ 305,786	$ 80,165	$ 388,042
Long-Term Liabilities:			
Bonds payable (net of current portion)	$4,785,000	$ 560,000	$ 118,310
Total liabilities	$5,090,786	$ 640,165	$ 506,352
Fund Equity:			
Contributed capital	$ —	$ 116,353	$2,188,370
Retained earnings (deficit):			
Reserved for bond ordinance	—	—	—
Unreserved	100,384	499,797	2,782,828
Total retained earnings	$ 100,384	$ 499,797	$2,782,828
Total fund equity	$ 100,384	$ 616,150	$4,971,198
Total liabilities and fund equity	$5,191,170	$1,256,315	$5,477,550

Under regulatory reporting Utility Plant in Service is stated at **original cost.** Original cost is a regulatory concept that differs from historical cost, a concept commonly used in accounting for assets of nonregulated businesses. In essence, **historical cost** is the amount paid for an asset by its present owner. In contrast, **original cost** is **the cost to the owner who first devoted the property to public service.** When a regulated utility purchases plant assets from another utility, it must record in its accounts the amounts shown in the accounts of the seller for the Utility Plant purchased and for the related accumulated depreciation. Any premium paid by the present owner over and above such cost less depreciation is in the general nature of payments for goodwill by nonutility enterprises. But utilities enjoy monopoly privileges and are subject to corresponding restrictions. One of

Wastewater Treatment Fund	Motor Vehicle Parking System Fund	Rock Island Centennial Bridge Fund	Housing and Community Development Loan Fund	Total
$ 53,387	$ 209,353	$ 16,228	$ 59,042	$ 425,885
127,286	20,464	92,358	11,420	566,459
25,469	14,560	—	—	56,526
11,206	—	18,598	—	29,804
—	—	89,663	—	89,663
165,000	—	260,000	—	779,690
$ 382,348	$ 244,377	$ 476,847	$ 70,462	$ 1,948,027
$ 2,345,000	$ 555,000	$ —	$ —	$ 8,363,310
$ 2,727,348	$ 799,377	$ 476,847	$ 70,462	$10,311,337
$ 9,975,121	$2,458,173	$ —	$2,706,976	$17,444,993
701,122	—	—	—	701,122
498,688	40,555	10,809,603	(531,127)	14,200,728
$ 1,199,810	$ 40,555	$10,809,603	$ (531,127)	$14,901,850
$11,174,931	$2,498,728	$10,809,603	$2,175,849	$32,346,843
$13,902,279	$3,298,105	$11,286,450	$2,246,311	$42,658,180

the restrictions is that earnings shall not exceed a fair rate of return. Since goodwill is the capitalized value of excess earnings, utilities can have no goodwill (in the accounting sense). Premium on plant purchased is therefore accounted for as **Utility Plant Acquisition Adjustments.** The amount of acquisition adjustment capitalized is amortized over a period of time determined by the appropriate regulatory body; accumulated amortization is disclosed in the Accumulated Provision for Amortization of Utility Plant Acquisition Adjustments account.

Other asset sections of balance sheets prepared in the regulatory format are Other Property and Investments and Deferred Debits. One item usually reported in the former section is Special Funds, which is similar to the Restricted Assets section of the GAAP-format balance sheet shown in Illustrations 10–1 and 10–2.

Thus, as mentioned previously, Other Property and Investments is broader in scope than Restricted Assets and may contain items other than restricted assets. One item typically reported under the Deferred Debits caption is Unamortized Debt Discount and Expense which under GAAP is reported as an offset to the related long-term debt.

Accounting for Nonutility Enterprises

Early in this chapter it is stressed that each governmentally owned enterprise should follow the accounting and financial reporting standards developed for investor-owned enterprises in the same industry. Generally, the standards developed by the Financial Accounting Standards Board, and its predecessors, have been accepted by the GASB as applying to Internal Service Funds and Enterprise Funds.[8] Consequently, many sections in Chapter 9—which discuss generally accepted accounting principles applicable to Internal Service Funds (such as the sections captioned "Acquisition of Assets by Contributions or Grants," "Depreciation of Contributed Assets or Assets Acquired from Capital Grants," and "Assets Acquired under Lease Agreements")—apply equally to enterprise funds accounting for activities other than utilities.

Accounting for Municipal Solid Waste Landfills

According to Environmental Protection Agency (EPA) estimates there are approximately 6,000 municipal solid waste landfills (MSWLF) in the United States, of which about 80 percent are owned by state or local general purpose or special purpose governments.[9] An EPA Rule, "Solid Waste Disposal Facility Criteria" (40 *Code of Federal Regulations*, parts 257 and 258), establishes certain closure requirements for MSWLFs and imposes stringent criteria for location, design, and operation of landfills, groundwater monitoring and corrective action, postclosure care, and financial assurance. State governments are assigned primary responsibility for implementing and enforcing the EPA rule, and may increase or reduce its provisions based on site conditions existing within their states.

MSWLF (municipal solid waste landfills) owners and operators may incur a variety of costs, both during the period of operation and after closure. These costs include the cost of equipment and facilities (including final covering of the MSWLF upon closure) and cost of services for such items as postclosure maintenance and monitoring for a period of 30 years after closure. The EPA requires owners and operators to estimate in detail the current dollar cost of hiring a third party to close the largest area of an MSWLF expected to require a final cover and to care for the MSWLF over the 30-year postclosure period. Each year the closure and postclosure cost estimates must be adjusted for inflation and revised as necessary to reflect changes in plans or conditions. Owners and operators of MSWLF must provide assurances that adequate financial resources will be available to cover the estimated costs of closure, postclosure care, and remediation or

---

[8] See Footnote 2.

[9] Governmental Accounting Standards Board, *Statement of Governmental Accounting Standards No. 18,* "Accounting for Municipal Solid Waste Landfill Closure and Postclosure Costs" (Norwalk, Conn.: 1993), par. 24.

containment of environmental hazards when the landfill has been filled to capacity. Several forms of financial assurance are acceptable, including third-party trusts, surety bonds, letters of credit, insurance, or state-sponsored plans.

GASB standards provide guidance both for measuring and reporting estimated total closure and postclosure costs. Although the detailed cost estimation procedures are beyond the scope of this chapter, reporting requirements for MSWLFs that use proprietary fund accounting are described briefly. An expense and liability should be recognized each period for a portion of the estimated total current cost of MSWLF closure and postclosure care. The portion of total cost to be recognized is based on the units of production method so that estimated total current cost is assigned to periods on the basis of landfill usage rather than the passage of time. Recognition begins in the period in which the MSWLF first accepts solid waste and continues each period until closure. Estimated total closure and postclosure costs should be reevaluated each year during operation of the landfill and the cumulative effect of changes in the estimated costs, if any, should be reported in the period of the change. Costs of equipment, facilities, services, or final cover acquired during the period are reported as a reduction of the accrued liability and not as capital assets. Equipment and facilities installed prior to commencement of operation of the landfill should be fully depreciated by the closure date.

Assets held by third-party trustees or in surety standby trusts to meet financial assurance requirements should be reported as "amounts held by trustee" in the restricted assets section of the balance sheet and as reservations of retained earnings. Earnings on such investments should be reported as revenue.

GASB standards also provide guidance for reporting of MSWLFs in governmental fund types or by other entities such as colleges and universities. Accounting for MSWLFs in the General Fund, for example, requires that an expenditure and fund liability be reported for the current closure and postclosure costs to the extent that an accrued liability would be settled with available fund resources; any remaining liability would be reported in the General Long-Term Debt Account Group discussed in Chapter 8. Regardless of the fund type or entity reporting the MSWLF activities, GASB standards require the following note disclosures:[10]

1. The nature and source of landfill closure and postclosure care requirements (federal, state, or local laws or regulations).
2. That recognition of a liability for closure and postclosure care costs is based on landfill capacity used to date.
3. The reported liability for closure and postclosure care at the Balance Sheet date (if not apparent from the financial statements) and the estimated total current cost of closure and postclosure care remaining to be recognized.
4. The percentage of landfill capacity used to date and approximate remaining landfill life in years.
5. How closure and postclosure care financial assurance requirements, if any,

---

[10] Ibid., par. 17.

ILLUSTRATION 10–6

Illustrative Segment Information Disclosure

.601   The following example of Notes to the Financial Statements disclosure of segment information is presented for illustrative purposes only. Alternative presentation formats may be acceptable. This illustration assumes that there were no other material facts necessary to make the GPFS not misleading.

Note (X)—Segment Information for Enterprise Funds

The City maintains five Enterprise Funds which provide water, sewer, airport, golf and parking services. Segment information for the year ended December 31, 19x2, was as follows:

	Water Fund	Sewer Fund	Airport Fund	Other Enterprise Funds	Total Enterprise Funds
Operating Revenues	300,000	20,000	300,000	52,150	672,150
Depreciation, Depletion, and Amortization Expense	70,000	10,000	60,000	4,100	144,100
Operating Income or (Loss)	130,000	5,000	(35,000)	7,970	107,970
Operating Grants, Entitlements, and Shared Revenues	—	—	55,000	—	55,000
Operating Transfers:					
In	—	20,000	—	—	20,000
Out	(30,000)	—	—	—	(30,000)
Tax Revenues	—	10,000	—	—	10,000
Net Income or Loss	42,822	10,000	10,000	15,990	78,812
Current Capital:					
Contributions	682,666	—	—	—	682,666
Transfers	(10,000)	—	—	—	(10,000)
Plant, Property and Equipment:					
Additions	180,000	25,000	125,000	24,453	354,453
Deletions	(30,000)	—	—	—	(30,000)
Net Working Capital	167,491	35,812	43,187	41,773	288,263
Bonds and Other Long-Term Liabilities:					
Payable from Operating Revenues	1,598,000	—	—	—	1,598,000
Payable from Other Sources	200,000	—	—	—	200,000
Total Equity	2,900,000	150,000	400,000	110,002	3,560,002

SOURCE: GASB Codification Sec. 2500.901.

are being met. Also, any assets restricted for payment of closure and postclosure care costs (if not apparent from the financial statements).

6. The nature of the estimates and the potential for changes due to inflation or deflation, technology, or applicable laws or regulations.

While municipal solid waste landfills may seem to be a dull topic, the costs of improving landfills to meet increased EPA standards, providing financial assurance, and complying with accounting and reporting requirements may be significant for many governmental units.

Required Segment Information

Revenue bonds and other debt instruments are secured by the revenues of individual enterprise funds, not by the aggregate revenues of all enterprise funds. Similarly, rate regulatory bodies and other oversight bodies require information about individual enterprises, rather than aggregated information for all enterprise funds.

GASB standards require, therefore, that general purpose financial statements include certain "segment information for major non-homogeneous enterprise funds." The presentation of segment information in the Notes to the Financial Statements section of the annual report is considered preferable, although some of the information may be included in the body of the combined statements or in the combining statements if the latter are included with the combined statements as part of the General Purpose Financial Statements. Segment information that should be presented for Enterprise Funds is that deemed essential to make the General Purpose Financial Statements not misleading. The following types of information are specified:

a. Material *inter*governmental operating subsidies to an enterprise fund.

b. Material *intra*governmental operating subsidies to or from an enterprise fund.

c. Material enterprise fund tax revenues.

d. A material enterprise fund *operating* income or loss.

e. A material enterprise fund *net* income or loss.

Materiality should be evaluated in terms of the individual enterprise funds, not in terms of the total enterprise fund type taken as a whole.

Illustration 10–6 presents an example of suggested segment information disclosure.

Selected References

American Institute of Certified Public Accountants. *Audit and Accounting Guide.* "Audits of State and Local Governmental Units." Revised. New York, 1993.

Federal Energy Regulatory Commission. *Accounting and Reporting Requirements for Public Utilities and Licensees,* Publication No. FERC-0114, Washington, D.C.: FERC, 1985 (with loose-leaf revisions).

————. "FERC Form No. 1: Annual Report of Major Electric Utilities, Licensees and Others." Washington, D.C.: FERC, December 1992.

Financial Accounting Standards Board. *Statement of Financial Accounting Standards No. 71,* "Accounting for the Effects of Certain Types of Regulation." Norwalk, Conn., 1982.

Governmental Accounting Standards Board. *Codification of Governmental Accounting and Financial Reporting Standards as of June 30, 1993.* Norwalk, Conn., 1993.

Grinnell, D. J., and Richard F. Kochanek. *Water Utility Accounting.* 2nd ed. Denver: American Water Works Association, 1980.

National Association of Regulatory Utility Commissioners. *Uniform System of Accounts for Water Utilities.* Washington, D.C., 1972, with 1973 and 1976 revisions.

————. *Uniform System of Accounts for Class A and B Water Utilities.* Washington, D.C., 1973, with 1976 revisions.

_____. *Uniform System of Accounts for Class C Water Utilities*. Washington, D.C., 1973, with 1976 revisions.

_____. *Uniform System of Accounts for Class D Water Utilities*. Washington, D.C., 1973, with 1976 revisions.

_____. *Uniform System of Accounts for Class A and B Sewer Utilities*. Washington, D.C., 1976.

_____. *Uniform System of Accounts for Class A and B Electric Utilities*. Washington, D.C., 1972, with 1976 revisions.

_____. *Uniform System of Accounts for Class C and D Electric Utilities*. Washington, D.C., 1973, with 1976 revisions.

_____. *Uniform System of Accounts for Class A and B Gas Utilities*. Washington, D.C., 1976.

_____. *Uniform System of Accounts for CATV*. Washington, D.C., 1978.

Questions

10–1. What factors should be considered in determining whether an activity or operation should be accounted for as an Enterprise Fund or as a governmental fund? As an Internal Service Fund?

10–2. In general, how may an administrator or accountant determine the accounting and financial reporting standards applicable to a nonregulated governmental enterprise? A governmental enterprise in a regulated industry?

10–3. Explain why utilities customarily need to present an Accrued Utilities Revenues account in their Balance Sheet. How should the amount of the accrual be determined?

10–4. What is the purpose of the Restricted Assets section of an Enterprise Fund Balance Sheet used to account for a utility? Provide examples of items that might be reported in the Restricted Assets section.

10–5. For items reported in the Restricted Assets section of an Enterprise Fund Balance Sheet, how are the items reported in the liability and fund equity sections of the balance sheet?

10–6. "Reporting 'utility plant in service' as a single line on the balance sheet provides adequate information for regulatory purposes and/or sound management." Do you agree with this statement? Explain why or why not.

10–7. What is the meaning of Allowance for Funds Used During Construction? What does this term include that is not includable as an element of the cost of fixed assets constructed by a nonutility enterprise?

10–8. If a governmental unit issues tax-supported bonds or special assessment bonds that are to be serviced by enterprise fund revenues, what treatment should be given to the bonds in the Enterprise Fund Balance Sheet? In the GPFS?

10–9. What is the meaning of original cost as used in public utility accounting? In your answer make clear how *original cost* differs from *historical cost*.

10–10. Explain what should be recorded in the Utility Plant Acquisition Adjustments account of a regulated utility, and why this account is used rather than a Goodwill account.

10–11. What is meant by "segment information for enterprise funds"? To what source should persons concerned with governmental financial report preparation go to determine the required disclosures?

10–12. Explain how the expense and liability of a period for the estimated current cost for closure and postclosure of a municipal solid waste landfill accounted for in a proprietary fund should be determined. Does this appear rational? Explain.

10–13. What disclosures are required in the Notes to the Financial Statements for a municipal solid waste landfill, regardless of the fund type or entity used to account for it?

Exercises and Problems

10–1. Utilizing the annual report obtained for Exercise 1–1, follow the instructions below:

a. Enterprise Funds. What activities of the governmental unit are reported as being administered by enterprise funds? Does the governmental unit own and operate its water utility? Electric utility? Gas utility? Transportation system? Are combining statements presented for all enterprise funds, or are separate statements presented for each enterprise fund? Are all enterprise funds accounted for on the full accrual basis? Are all funds in this category earning revenues at least equal to costs and expenses? If not, how is the operating deficit being financed? What sources furnished the original investment in fund assets? Do the notes include segment information on individual enterprise funds where applicable (see "Required Segment Information" section of Chapter 10)?

Are sales to other funds or other governmental units separately disclosed? Are there receivables from other funds? Other governmental units? How are receivables from component units, if any, disclosed? Is there any evidence that enterprise funds contribute amounts to the General Fund in lieu of taxes to help support services received by the enterprise? Is there any evidence that enterprise funds make excessively large contributions to the General Fund or any other funds?

b. Utility Funds. Is it possible to tell from the report whether utilities of this governmental unit are subject to the same regulations as investor-owned utilities in the same state? (If the utility statements follow the format of the NARUC and the FERC, as described in Chapter 10, there is a good chance the governmentally owned utilities are subject to at least some supervision by a regulatory agency.) What rate of return on sales (or operating revenues) is being earned by each utility fund? What rate of return on total assets is being earned by each utility fund?

Is depreciation taken on utility plant? Are accounting policies and accounting changes properly disclosed? If so, what method of depreciation is being used? Is the *original cost* basis used for plant assets—is a plant acquisition adjustment account shown? If so, over what period is the acquisition being amortized?

Does each utility account for its own debt service and construction activities in the manner described in Chapter 10? What Special Funds, or Restricted Assets, are utilized by each utility? Is Retained Earnings reserved in an amount equal to or exceeding Special Funds, or Restricted Assets?

c. Nonutility Enterprise Funds. Are nonutility enterprise funds accounted for in the same manner as investor-owned enterprises in the same industries? (In order to answer this, you may need to refer to publications of trade associations or to handbooks or encyclopedias of accounting systems found in business libraries.) If you cannot find information about investor-owned counterparts of the governmental nonutility enterprise funds, do the statements of the latter evidence that generally accepted accounting principles devised for profit-seeking businesses were used?

10–2. Write the numbers 1 through 10 on a sheet of paper. Beside each number write the letter corresponding with the best answer to each of the following questions:

1. Governmentally owned utilities should be accounted for:
   a. In the same manner as any governmentally owned nonregulated enterprise.
   b. In the same manner as investor-owned utilities, without creating separate general funds, debt service funds, and capital projects funds for the utility.
   c. In the same manner as investor-owned utilities, but in separate funds to account separately for general operations, capital projects, and debt service.
   d. In the same manner as all other governmental funds.

2. Which of the following assets is least likely to be reported as a Restricted Asset of a governmentally owned utility accounted for in an enterprise fund?
   a. Investments of idle cash held for working capital.
   b. Investments for retirement of revenue bonds.
   c. Investments purchased from customer deposits.
   d. Cash from customer deposits.

3. Which of the following accounts should be included in the balance sheet of an enterprise fund?

	Reserve for Encumbrances	*Revenue Bonds Payable*	*Retained Earnings*
a.	No	No	Yes
b.	No	Yes	Yes
c.	Yes	Yes	No
d.	No	No	No

4. Fixed assets utilized by a city-owned utility should be accounted for in which of the following?

	Enterprise Fund	*General Fixed Assets Account Group*
a.	No	No
b.	No	Yes
c.	Yes	No
d.	Yes	Yes

5. During 19x9 Spruce City reported the following operating receipts from self-sustaining activities paid for by users of the services rendered:

Operations of water supply plant	$5,000,000
Operations of bus system	900,000

What amounts should be reported as operating revenues of Spruce's enterprise funds?

a. $0.
b. $900,000.
c. $5,000,000.
d. $5,900,000.

6. The following cash transactions were among those reported by Cliff County's Water and Sewer Enterprise Fund for 19y1:

Proceeds from sale of revenue bonds for construction	$5,000,000
Cash received from customers	3,000,000
Capital contributed by subdividers	1,000,000

In the Water and Sewer Enterprise Fund's Statement of Cash Flows for the year ended December 31, 19y1, what amount should be reported as cash flows from capital and related financing activities?

a. $9,000,000.
b. $8,000,000.
c. $6,000,000.
d. $5,000,000.

7. Interest capitalized as a part of the cost of assets constructed by a governmentally owned utility properly consists of:

a. Net interest paid and accrued during the period of construction on money borrowed for construction purposes.
b. Net interest paid and accrued during the period of construction on money borrowed for construction purposes, and interest imputed on other money used for construction.
c. Only net interest actually paid during the period of construction.
d. None of the above.

8. The proceeds of tax-supported bonds issued for the benefit of an Enterprise Fund and being serviced by a Debt Service Fund:

a. Should not be reported by the Enterprise Fund at all.
b. Should be reported in the notes to Enterprise Fund statements, but not in the body of any of the statements.
c. Should be reported in the Enterprise Fund as Long-Term Debt.
d. Should be reported in the Enterprise Fund as Contributed Equity.

9. Sales revenues of a utility for a certain fiscal period:

a. Are equivalent to total debits to Customer Accounts Receivable for that period.
b. Include receivables billed during a fiscal period, plus receivables billed early in the next year if meters were read before year-end.
c. Should be reported on the cash basis for the sake of conservatism.
d. Include billed receivables and an accrual for unbilled receivables as of balance sheet date.

10. Financial statements that should be included in the comprehensive annual financial report of a government that has several enterprise funds are:

a. Combining Balance Sheet; Combining Statement of Revenues, Expenses, and Changes in Retained Earnings; Combining Statement of Cash Flows; and

Notes to the Financial Statements to ensure that required segment information is disclosed.

b. Combining Balance Sheet; Combining Statement of Revenues, Expenditures, and Changes in Retained Earnings; Combining Statement of Cash Flows.

c. Separate statements for each individual enterprise fund to ensure that all segment information is properly presented.

d. Separate combining statements for utility funds and for enterprise funds in organizational industries.

(Items 3, 4, 5, and 6, AICPA, adapted)

10–3. The City of Dixon operates a mass transit system (DTS) consisting of a network of bus and trolley routes. The following information is provided about the operations and financing of the mass transit system.*

1. Operating revenues for the most recent fiscal year amounted to $549,420; operating expenses for the same year amounted to $1,011,843. Operating revenues have covered only 45 to 50 percent of operating expenditures since DTS was established five year ago.

2. The operating deficit (from part 1) of $462,423 was financed jointly by $362,423 from the City's General Fund and $100,000 in operating grants from the Urban Mass Transit Administration (UMTA). Capital contributions over the past five years have amounted to $3,334,286 divided about evenly between the City and capital grants from the UMTA.

3. Transit system managers have been pressured at times by City officials to increase bus and trolley fares but are strongly opposed because they believe DTS ridership would drop significantly. Advocates for disadvantaged groups have also lobbied hard to keep the current fares. Thus, for at least the next several years, the City plans to provide an annual operating subsidy to DTS to cover its operating deficit, less any operating grants received from UMTA or other sources.

4. Until now DTS has been accounted for and reported as an enterprise fund of the City. The City Finance Director and the head of the mass transit system would like to continue to use enterprise fund accounting; however, influential members of the Finance Committee of the City Council are insisting that, since DTS is never expected to break even, it should be accounted for and reported as a special revenue fund. Changing to a special revenue fund also means that DTS will require Council-approved appropriations for its expenditures.

Required Based on the information provided for the City of Dixon mass transit system, should the activities of DTS be accounted for in an enterprise fund or as a special revenue fund? Explain fully.

10–4. The State Gas Company follows the practice of cycle billing in order to minimize peak workloads for its clerical employees. All customers are billed monthly on various dates, except in those cases when the meter readers are unable to enter the premises to obtain a reading.

The following information for the year ended September 30, 19x6, is presented by the company:

---

* The authors are indebted to Charles M. Hicks for providing the information from which this problem was adapted.

Cycle	Billing Period	Customers Billed		Customers Not Billed
		Number	Amount	
1	Aug. 7–Sept. 5, inclusive	2,760	$27,600	324
2	Aug. 12–Sept. 10, inclusive	3,426	27,408	411
3	Aug. 17–Sept. 15, inclusive	3,265	29,385	335
4	Aug. 22–Sept. 20, inclusive	2,630	24,985	370
5	Aug. 27–Sept. 25, inclusive	3,132	26,622	468

You are further advised all customers have been billed for prior periods and the company's experience shows that charges for those customers whose meters were not read average the same amount as the charges for the customers billed in their cycle. In addition, the company assumes the customers' usage will be uniform from month to month.

From the above information, compute the unbilled revenues of the company as of September 30, 19x6, arising from cycles 1 and 4. (Do not compute revenues from cycles 2, 3, and 5.)

(AICPA, adapted)

10–5. The Council of the City of Kentwood directed that $1,000,000 cash be transferred from the City's General Fund as a permanent contribution to a newly created Water Utility Fund. The Water Utility Fund is **not** regulated by any regulatory agency. The cash is intended to cover the purchase price of the Valley Water Company, plus an additional amount to serve as initial working capital for the new activity. At June 30, 19y3, the effective date of purchase, the Valley Company had the following after-closing trial balance:

	Debits	Credits
Utility Plant in Service	$2,195,000	
Allowance for Depreciation-Utility Plant		$1,357,000
Cash	29,000	
Accounts Receivable	64,000	
Estimated Uncollectible Receivables		26,000
Materials and Supplies	66,000	
Vouchers Payable		99,000
Miscellaneous Accruals		28,000
Capital Stock		1,000,000
Retained Earnings	156,000	
	$2,510,000	$2,510,000

The acquisition occurred as follows:

1. The General Fund contribution was received on June 27, 19y3.

2. As of June 30, 19y3, the City of Kentwood Water Utility Fund acquired the assets of the Valley Water Company, excluding cash. Receivables were purchased at half of their face value. When the purchased assets were recorded, the allowance for uncollectible receivables was increased to establish the new book value of receivables. The vendor's liabilities were assumed. A cash payment of $900,000 was made for the net assets of the water utility. (Hint: Record Accounts Receivable, Materials and Supplies, Accounts Payable, and Miscellaneous Accruals at the amounts shown in the trial balance. Increase Estimated Uncollectible Receiv-

ables to $32,000. Amounts shown for Valley Water Company's Cash, Capital Stock, and Retained Earnings accounts should not be recorded by the Water Utility Fund.)

Required

a. Record in general journal form the entries that should be made in the Water Utility Fund for the events of June 27 and June 30, 19y3.

b. Prepare in conformity with GAAP a balance sheet for the City of Kentwood Water Utility Fund as of June 30, 19y3.

10–6. This problem continues the preceding problem. During the year ended June 30, 19y4, the following transactions and events occurred in the City of Kentwood Water Utility Fund:

1. On July 1, 19y3, to finance needed plant improvements, the Water Utility Fund borrowed $500,000 from a local bank on notes secured by a pledge of water utility revenues. The notes mature in five years and bear interest at the annual rate of 8 percent.

2. Accrued expenses at June 30, 19y3, were paid in cash.

3. Billings to nongovernmental customers for water usage during the year totaled $632,000; billings to the General Fund totaled $40,000.

4. Liabilities for the following were recorded during the year:

Materials and supplies	$ 88,000
Source of supply expenses	32,000
Pumping expenses	40,500
Water treatment expenses	51,500
Transmission and distribution expenses	68,000
Customer accounts expenses	93,000
Administrative and general expenses	76,000
Construction work in progress	357,000
Total	$806,000

5. Materials and supplies were used by the following departments in the following amounts: Source of Supply, $10,800; Pumping, $6,500; Treatment, $34,500; Transmission and Distribution, $32,200; total, $84,000.

6. On July 2, 19y4, utility plant assets that had a historical cost of $25,000 were sold for $15,000 cash.

7. $28,000 of old accounts receivable were written off.

8. During fiscal 19y4, the utility instituted a program of deposits to reduce meter damage and customer defaults on water bills. Cash amounting to $15,000 was collected during the year. (Debit Cash–Customer Deposits)

9. Account receivable collections totaled $460,000 for the fiscal year from nongovernmental customers and $38,000 from the General Fund.

10. $800,000 of accounts payable were paid in cash.

11. $500 was recorded as interest expense accumulated on customers' deposits (credit Customer Deposits).

12. Depreciation expense for the year of $47,050 was recorded.

13. Bills for materials and supplies, $7,000, were received and approved for payment on June 30, 19y4.

14. One year's interest on notes payable was paid.

15. Interest on long-term notes was charged to Construction Work in Progress.

16. The provision for uncollectible accounts was increased by an amount equal to 1 percent of the sales of water to nongovernmental customers for the year.

17. Cash in the amount of $100,000 was transferred to Restricted Assets—Cash for eventual redemption of five-year notes. As required by the loan agreement, retained earnings in the same amount was reserved.

18. Operating statement accounts for the year were closed.

Required

a. Record the transactions for the year in general journal form.

b. Prepare a Balance Sheet as of June 30, 19y4.

c. Prepare a Statement of Revenues, Expenses, and Changes in Retained Earnings for the year ended June 30, 19y4.

10–7. a. From your solutions to Problems 10–5 and 10–6, prepare a Statement of Cash Flows for the City of Kentwood Water Utility Fund for the fiscal year ended June 30, 19y4, assuming that cash outflows for operating activities included $310,000 for wages and salaries.

b. On the basis of your analysis of the financial statements prepared for Problems 10–5, 10–6, and 10–7, comment on any matters that should be brought to the attention of the management of the City of Kentwood Water Utility Fund. What actions do you suggest management should take?

10–8. Carver City issued bonds for the construction of an addition to its utility plant that totaled $7,200,000 and bore interest at the rate of 6 percent per year. The bonds were sold at par on January 15, 19x8, the day the construction contract was signed; proceeds were invested on that date at the rate of 6 percent per year. On March 15, investments in the face amount of $1,200,000 plus accrued interest, were sold, in order to make a progress payment to the contractor. Investments in the face amount of $1,200,000, plus accrued interest, were sold on May 15 in order to make the second progress payment to the contractor. On July 15, semiannual bond interest due was paid. Also on July 15, semiannual interest on investments on hand on that date was collected, then investments in the face amount of $2,400,000 were sold in order to make a progress payment to the contractor. On September 15, investments in the face amount of $2,400,000, plus accrued interest, were sold in order to make a progress payment to the contractor. On November 15, 19x8, cash in the amount of $2,400,000 derived from operations of the utility was used for the final payment to the contractor; the utility plant addition was deemed completed on that date.

Required

a. From the information above:

(1) Compute the bond interest paid or accrued during the period of construction, January 15–November 15.

(2) Compute interest earned during the period of construction on the investment of the bond proceeds.

(3) Show in general journal form the entry to capitalize the net interest cost as a part of the cost of the plant addition, as required by GASB standards.

b. Assuming the amount of interest on utility resources generated from operations and used for construction that is to be capitalized as a part of the cost of the addition to the utility plant is $161,800, show in general journal form the entry to capitalize the imputed interest.

c. State, or illustrate, how the debt component of the Allowance for Funds Used During Construction (see your answer to part *a* (3) of this problem) should be reported in the utility's operating statement for the fiscal year ended December 31, 19x8.

d. State, or illustrate, how the equity component of the Allowance for Funds Used During Construction (see your answer to part *b* of this problem) should be reported in the utility's operating statement for the fiscal year ended December 31, 19x8.

10–9. From the following information about the Water Department, an enterprise fund of the City of X, prepare in proper form a Balance Sheet as of December 31, 19x6, and a Statement of Revenues, Expenses, and Changes in Retained Earnings for the year ended December 31, 19x6, using the regulatory format discussed under the heading "Regulatory Accounting Principles" in Chapter 10.

Ledger Balances December 31, 19x6

Cash	$ 605,800
Prepaid Expenses	1,000
Accounts Receivable	82,700
Due from Other Funds	—
Supplies Inventory	140,000
Investments	50,000
Utility Plant	6,000,000
Warrants Payable	50,100
Due to Other Funds	56,000
Customers Advances for Construction	—
Accounts Payable—Trade	47,000
Revenue Bonds Payable	300,000
Accumulated Depreciation	1,200,000
Retained Earnings, 1/1/x6	4,561,400
Sales of Water	1,500,000
Expense:	
Production	340,000
Distribution	151,000
Office	90,000
Administrative and General	105,000
Maintenance	140,000
Interest on Bonds	9,000

Examination of the records discloses the following data:

1. Erroneously included in Accounts Payable—Trade:
   a. For reimbursement of metered postage (should be credited to Prepaid Expenses) — $ 500
   b. Due to Other Funds — 28,500
2. Items included in book inventory that were shipped f.o.b. destination and were not received until 19x7 — 2,000
3. Computation of inventory items charged to distribution expense was understated by — 1,000
4. 19x7 expense purchases erroneously recorded as 19x6 Accounts Payable—Trade and charged to expense as follows:
   a. Production Expense — 500
   b. Distribution Expense — 500

    c. Office Expense   500

    d. Administrative and General Expense   500

5. Included in Accounts Receivable, but actually Due from Other Funds   500

6. Credit balances included in Accounts Receivable should be classified as Customers' Advances for Construction   1,000

7. Unrecorded receivable from General Fund for water used   5,000

(AICPA, adapted)

10–10. The Comparative Balance Sheet, the Statement of Revenue, Expenses, and Changes in Retained Earnings, and the Statement of Cash Flows for the Water Utility Fund of River City are shown below and on the following pages.

Required

    a. In what respects do the statements evidence that the Water Utility Fund is being operated and accounted for in the manner described in Chapter 10? In what respects is there evidence to the contrary?

    b. The statements disclose that $7,000,000 was received as Proceeds from the Sale of Bonds, yet General Obligation Bonds retired amounted to only $1,615,000, and Notes retired amounted to $500,000. What happened to the rest of the money?

RIVER CITY
Water Utility Fund
**Statement of Revenue, Expenses, and
Changes in Retained Earnings
For the Year Ended December 31**

	19x9	19x8
Operating Revenue:		
Charges for Services	$ 32,269,002.68	$ 29,864,447.31
Total Operating Revenue	32,269,002.68	29,864,447.31
Operating Expenses:		
Personal Services	14,608,420.10	13,497,586.71
Contractual Services	3,142,867.43	3,280,573.49
Materials and Supplies	2,522,556.77	2,434,132.73
Heat, Light, and Power	4,280,077.87	3,976,906.17
Rent	900.00	1,650.00
Depreciation	2,952,170.00	2,830,801.61
Bad Debt Expense	15,239.97	29,303.46
Total Operating Expenses	27,522,232.14	26,050,954.17
Operating Income	4,746,770.54	3,813,493.14
Nonoperating Revenue (Expenses):		
Interest Revenue	1,989,744.60	1,221,102.86
Rent	3,493.00	2,262.59
Interest Expenses and Charges	(1,734,253.47)	(1,280,975.00)
Total Nonoperating Revenue (Expenses)	258,984.13	(57,609.55)
Net Income	5,005,754.67	3,755,883.59
Retained Earnings—January 1	116,425,503.70	115,686,902.39
Restatement (Prior Period Adjustments)	—	(3,017,282.28)
Restated Retained Earnings—January 1	116,425,503.70	112,669,620.11
Retained Earnings—December 31	$121,431,258.37	$116,425,503.70

RIVER CITY
Water Utility Fund
Comparative Balance Sheet
As of December 31

	19x9	19x8
Assets		
Assets:		
Equity in City Treasury Cash	$ 10,859,601.38	$ 6,881,383.80
Receivables:		
Accounts	6,934,836.49	6,293,408.36
Others	185,905.12	243,829.82
Advances to Internal Service Funds	50,000.00	50,000.00
Inventory	2,981,897.96	2,840,368.94
Prepaid Expense	83,529.88	30,543.42
Restricted Assets:		
Equity in City Treasury Cash	5,860,306.59	4,391,750.30
Due from Other Governments	—	126,061.00
Land	2,846,039.12	2,846,039.12
Buildings	36,026,049.69	35,997,383.31
Accumulated Depreciation	(10,433,473.92)	(9,834,522.30)
Improvements Other than Buildings	83,779,585.18	82,047,092.31
Accumulated Depreciation	(24,064,680.41)	(23,069,396.69)
Machinery and Equipment	33,340,543.18	32,857,061.37
Accumulated Depreciation	(9,838,520.58)	(8,623,852.10)
Construction in Progress	23,414,432.00	19,348,944.45
Total Assets	$162,026,051.68	$152,426,065.11
Liabilities and Fund Equity		
Liabilities:		
Accounts Payable	$ 705,416.89	$ 1,150,091.37
Accrued Payroll	478,028.59	373,389.03
Accrued Interest on Notes Payable	44,492.00	108,333.33
Accrued Interest on General Obligation		
Bonds Payable	175,906.00	129,093.75
Payable from Restricted Assets:		
Construction Contracts	841,001.30	876,555.80
Deposits for Services	266,120.39	213,698.58
Deferred Revenue	969.83	2,980.42
Bond Anticipation Notes Payable	9,500,000.00	10,000,000.00
General Obligation Bonds Payable	21,300,000.00	15,915,000.00
Total Liabilities	33,311,935.00	28,769,142.28
Fund Equity:		
Contributed Capital:		
City Contribution	7,282,858.31	7,231,419.13
Retained Earnings:		
Reserve for Federal Capital Grant	1,754,757.92	1,828,202.74
Reserve for Capital Improvements	4,753,184.90	3,299,284.95
Unreserved	114,923,315.55	111,298,016.01
Total Fund Equity	128,714,116.68	123,656,922.83
Total Liabilities and Fund Equity	$162,026,051.68	$152,426,065.11

RIVER CITY
Water Utility Fund
Statement of Cash Flows
For the Year Ended December 31

	19x9	*19x8*
Cash flows from operating activities:		
Cash received from customers	$ 31,610,323.99	$ 30,018,819.07
Cash paid to employees for services	(14,503,780.54)	(13,428,409.18)
Cash paid to suppliers	(10,585,592.03)	(9,437,133.58)
Net Cash provided by Operating Activities	6,520,951.42	7,153,276.31
Cash flows from noncapital financing activities:		
Capital contributed by other funds and governments	51,439.18	85,023.09
Cash flows from capital and related financing activities:		
Proceeds from sale of bonds and notes	7,000,000.00	10,000,000.00
Retirement of bonds and notes	(2,115,000.00)	(1,615,000.00)
Acquisition of property, plant and equipment	(6,453,424,79)	(11,413,781.06)
Interest paid on bonds and notes	(1,751,282.55)	(1,184,162.50)
Net transfer to restricted assets	(1,325,627.98)	(1,860,358.70)
Net cash provided by capital related activities	(4,645,335.32)	(6,073,302.26)
Cash flows from investing activities:		
Rent	3,493.00	2,262.59
Interest on investments	2,047,669.30	1,130,840.90
Net cash provided by investing activities	2,051,162.30	1,133,103.49
Net increase in equity in City Treasury cash	3,978,217.58	2,298,100.63
Equity in City Treasury cash, Jan. 1	6,881,383.80	4,583,283.17
Equity in City Treasury cash, Dec. 31	$ 10,859,601.38	$ 6,881,383.80

Reconciliation of Net Operating Income
to Net Cash Provided by Operating Activities

	19x9	*19x8*
Utility Operating Income	$ 4,746,770.54	$ 3,813,493.14
Adjustments:		
Depreciation expense	2,952,170.00	2,830,801.61
Increase in accrued payroll	104,639.56	69,177.53
Increase (decrease) in accounts payable	(444,674.48)	18,638.74
Decrease in deferred revenues	(2,010.59)	(2,687.09)
Decrease (increase) in customers accounts receivable	(641,428.13)	186,362.31
Increase in prepaid expenses	(52,986.46)	(14,066.53)
Decrease (increase) in inventories	(141,529.02)	251,556.60
Total Adjustments	1,774,180.88	3,339,783.17
Net Cash Provided by Operating Activities	$ 6,520,951.42	$ 7,153,276.31

Continuous Problems

10–L. The city water utility is owned and operated by the City of Bingham. The water utility was originally constructed and operated by a private corporation, but it was sold to the City 30 years before the year for which transactions are given. The post-closing trial balance of the Water Utility Fund, as of June 30, 19x1, is shown below.

CITY OF BINGHAM
Water Utility Fund
Trial Balance
As of June 30, 19x1

	Debits	*Credits*
Cash	$ 144,952	
Customer Accounts Receivable	77,720	
Accumulated Provision for Uncollectible Accounts		$ 2,360
Due from Other Funds	7,000	
Inventory of Supplies	47,073	
Restricted Cash—Customer Deposits	27,638	
Utility Plant in Service	9,500,695	
Accumulated Depreciation—Utility Plant		2,006,139
Property Held for Future Use	100,000	
Construction Work in Progress	594,700	
Accounts Payable		39,210
Matured Interest		217,050
Customer Deposits		27,638
Revenue Bonds Payable, 6%		7,235,000
Unamortized Bond Discount	32,600	
Contributions from Customers		163,210
Contributions from City		425,000
Retained Earnings		416,771
Totals	$10,532,378	$10,532,378

You will need the following additional information about accounts shown on the June 30, 19x1, trial balance:

Matured Interest represents six months accrual of interest on the 6 percent Revenue Bonds. Interest is payable annually on January 1 of each year. Unamortized Bond Discount is credited once a year for the amortization applicable to the year. Amortization is computed by the straight-line method. The balance of $32,600 is to be amortized over 20 years commencing July 1, 19x1.

Required

a. Open a general journal for the Water Utility Fund and enter the transactions shown, as necessary. All transactions occurred during the year ended June 30, 19x2. Use the account titles shown in Chapter 10.

   (1) Billings to nonmunicipal customers for water service for the year totaled $1,468,368. Billings to the City of Bingham for water service totaled $20,000.

   (2) Collections from customers totaled $1,445,568; from the City, $7,000.

   (3) Construction work authorized amounted to $234,000. As a part of this, a contract for $112,000 was signed with a private firm; the remainder of the work was to be done by water utility employees.

   (4) Materials and supplies in the amount of $260,800 were ordered. All of these were received during the period. The invoices agreed with the purchase orders and receiving reports and were approved for payment. A perpetual inventory system is used for all materials and supplies.

(5) Payrolls totaling $289,765 for operations; $83,210 for maintenance; and $36,000 for construction were paid.

(6) Materials and supplies issued during the period amounted to $120,000 for operations; $52,000 for maintenance; and $84,000 for construction.

(7) All bond interest due during the year was paid. Debt discount was amortized on the straight-line basis.

(8) Interest of $14,500 was charged to Construction Work in Progress.

(9) A progress billing for $56,000 was received from the construction contractor and paid.

(10) Certain assets under construction at the start of the year and certain of those started during the year were completed and placed in service. The costs incurred on this construction totaled $456,350.

(11) The water utility paid $178,342 to the general fund as a contribution in lieu of property taxes.

(12) Collection efforts were discontinued on bills amounting to $1,965; the customers owing the bills had paid deposits and interest to the water utility in the amount of $672.

(13) Customer deposits and interest thereon amounting to $1,274 were applied to the final bills of customers discontinuing service. Additional deposits and interest amounting to $1,510 were refunded by check to customers discontinuing service. Deposits totaling $3,427 were received from new customers.

(14) Accounts payable paid during the year amounted to $167,600 for operating supplies, and $84,000 for materials used in construction.

(15) Interest on deposits amount to $628 (charge Operation Expense). Depreciation on utility plant was 2 percent of the beginning balance (round charge to the nearest dollar). The Accumulated Provision for Uncollectible Accounts should equal $2,910 at year-end. Make these and all other adjusting and closing entries necessary at year-end, including the entry for accrual of six months' interest on bonds payable.

b. Prepare a balance sheet for the Water Utility Fund as of the end of the year, June 30, 19x2.

c. Prepare a Statement of Revenue, Expenses, and Changes in Retained Earnings for the Water Utility Fund for the year ended June 30, 19x2.

d. Prepare a Statement of Cash Flows for the Water Utility Fund for the year ended June 30, 19x2.

10–S. The City Council of the City of Smithville decided in late 19y0 that the solid waste collection and disposal activities then financed by General Fund revenues would, effective January 1, 19y1, be financed by user charges. Accordingly, an enterprise fund, the Solid Waste Disposal Fund, was created to account for the assets used in the solid waste collection and disposal activities, and for related liabilities. In late December 19y0, cash in the amount of $150,000 was contributed to the Solid Waste Disposal Fund by the General Fund, so the fund could pay accrued salaries and other liabilities existing at the end of 19y0 and to provide working capital until customer billing and collections were regularized. Accounting responsibility for fixed assets used in solid waste removal and disposal activities was transferred from the GFAAG to the Solid Waste Disposal Fund before the end of 19y0, so the activities could be accounted for as an enterprise fund as of January 1, 19y1. The balance sheet of the new fund as of December 31, 19y0, appears below:

CITY OF SMITHVILLE
Solid Waste Diposal Fund
Balance Sheet
As of December 31, 19y0

Assets

Current Assets:		
Cash		$150,000
Property, Plant, and Equipment:		
Land	$ 94,000	
Buildings	324,000	
Equipment	57,000	
Total Property, Plant, and Equipment		475,000
Total Assets		$625,000

Liabilities and Fund Equity

Current Liabilities:	
Accrued payroll and fringe benefits	$ 46,300
Fund Equity:	
Contributions from City	578,700
Total Liabilities and Fund Equity	$625,000

Required

a. Open a general journal for the Solid Waste Disposal Fund and record the following events and transactions, which occurred during the year ended December 31, 19y1. Use account titles shown in part *b* of this problem.

(1) Billings to residential, commercial, and industrial customers of the Solid Waste Disposal Fund totaled $1,420,300 for the year ended December 31, 19y1.

(2) Collections from customers totaled $1,271,800 during 19y1.

(3) Payrolls and fringe benefits paid in cash during the year totaled $785,500, including the amount accrued as of December 31, 19y0.

(4) Equipment costing $103,000 was purchased on April 1, 19y1. Cash in the amount of $13,000 was paid at the time of purchase, and revenue anticipation notes were issued in the amount of $90,000. Notes in the amount of $40,000 will be payable on April 1, 19y2; notes in the amount of $50,000 will be payable on April 1, 19y3. All notes bear interest at the rate of 6 percent per year.

(5) Vouchers for materials and supplies to be used in the operations of the fund were issued in the total amount of $596,700 (charge Inventories).

(6) Vouchers in the amount of $497,650 were paid during the year.

(7) Accrued salaries and fringe benefits as of December 31, 19y1, amounted to $43,560. Materials and supplies used in operations during the year amount to $575,700, at cost.

(8) The City Council approved the following annual straight-line depreciation rates: Buildings, 8 percent; Equipment, 20 percent (equipment purchased during the year is to be depreciated for one-half year).

(9) Bad debts expense for the year is estimated to be $14,800.

(10) Interest accrued on revenue anticipation notes as of December 31, 19y1, was recorded.

(11) The City of Smithville estimates the total current cost for closure and postclosure compliance with the EPA rule discussed in Chapter 10 will be $900,000.

Based on the ratio of the amount of solid waste received in the current period to the total estimated capacity of the landfill, the current period expense and liability for future closure and postclosure costs is $70,000.

(12) All operating statement accounts for the year were closed.

b. Open a general ledger for the Solid Waste Disposal Fund. Use the account titles shown below; allow five lines for each account. Enter the balances shown in the Balance Sheet as of December 31, 19y0, designating each with the date "1/1/y1." Post the entries made in part *a* of this problem to the general ledger.

Cash

Customer Accounts Receivable

Allowance for Doubtful Accounts

Inventories

Land

Buildings

Accumulated Depreciation—Buildings

Equipment

Accumulated Depreciation—Equipment

Vouchers Payable

Accrued Payroll and Fringe Benefits

Accrued Interest Payable

Accrued Liability for Estimated Closure and Postclosure Costs

Revenue Anticipation Notes—Current

Revenue Anticipation Notes—Long-Term

Contributions from City

Retained Earnings

Payroll and Fringe Benefits Expense

Materials and Supplies Expense

Depreciation Expense

Provision for Closure and Postclosure Costs

Bad Debts Expense

Interest Expense

Charges for Services

c. Prepare a Balance Sheet for the Solid Waste Disposal Fund as of December 31, 19y1.

d. Prepare a Statement of Revenues, Expenses, and Changes in Retained Earnings for the Solid Waste Disposal Fund for the year ended December 31, 19y1.

e. Prepare a Statement of Cash Flows for the Solid Waste Disposal Fund for the year ended December 31, 19y1.

CHAPTER 11

Fiduciary Funds: Agency Funds and Cash and Investment Pools

Fiduciary funds are used to account for assets held by a governmental unit acting as a trustee or agent for individuals, organizations, other governmental units, or other funds of the same governmental unit. For that reason, fiduciary funds are often identified in governmental financial reports as Trust and Agency Funds. In law, there is a clear distinction between an agency relationship and a trust relationship. In accounting practice, the legalistic distinctions between trust funds and agency funds are not of major significance. The important and perhaps the sole consideration from an accounting standpoint is: What can and what cannot be done with the fund's assets in accordance with the laws and other pertinent regulations?

The name of a particular fund is not a reliable criterion for determining the correct accounting basis for trust and agency funds. Merely calling a fund by one name or another has no influence on the transactions in which it may engage. In fact, the words *trust* and *agency* are frequently omitted from the titles of funds in this classification. Examples are ''public employees' retirement system'' and ''condemnation and grading fund'': the former a trust fund, the latter an agency fund, each classified according to the circumstances under which its assets are held. It is sometimes said that a practical basis for distinguishing between the two types is the length of time specific assets are held. But this is not a wholly reliable guide, since there is no generally recognized pronouncement stating the maximum time restriction for holding assets to constitute an agency fund; nor is there a minimum time to constitute a fund of the trust variety. As suggested earlier, if not explicitly stated, the exact name or designation of a given fund is of little significance in establishing its accounting procedures and limitations; these depend on the enactment that brought about creation of the fund, plus all other regulations under which it operates. Regulations include pertinent statutes, ordinances, wills, trust indentures, and other instruments of endowment, resolutions of the governing body, statements of purposes of the fund, kinds and amounts of assets held, and others. This aggregate of factors, or such as are applicable to a given fund, determines the transactions in which it may and should engage.

In this chapter, several important agency relationships appropriately accounted for as agency funds are discussed. Chapter 12 discusses accounting for Expendable Trust Funds, Nonexpendable Trust Funds, and Public Employee Retirement Systems.

Agency Funds

GASB standards provide as one of the four types of fiduciary funds **agency funds.** Agency funds are used to account for assets held by a governmental unit acting as agent for one or more other governmental units, or for individuals or private organizations. Similarly, if a fund of a governmental unit regularly receives assets that are to be transmitted to other funds of that unit, an agency relationship exists. Assets accounted for in an agency fund belong to the party or parties for which the governmental unit acts as agent. Therefore, **agency fund assets are offset by liabilities equal in amount; no fund equity exists.** GASB standards require agency fund assets and liabilities to be recognized on the modified accrual basis used by governmental funds. In the typical case, revenues, expenditures, and expenses are not recognized in the accounts of agency funds.

Unless use of an agency fund is mandated by law, by GASB standards, or by decision of the governing board of a governmental unit, an agency relationship may be accounted for within governmental and/or proprietary funds. For example, local governmental units must act as agent of the federal and state governments in the collection of employees' withholding taxes, retirement contributions, and (in many instances) social security taxes. In the absence of contrary legal requirements or administrative decisions, it is perfectly acceptable to account for the withholdings, and the remittance to federal and state governments, within the funds that account for the gross pay of the employees, as is shown by the illustrative entries in Chapter 4. In general, if an agency relationship is incidental to the primary purposes for which a given fund exists, the relationship is ordinarily discharged on a rather current basis, and the amounts of assets held as agent tend to be small in relation to fund assets, there is no need to create an agency fund unless required by law or administrative decision.

IRC Section 457 Deferred Compensation Plans

Only rarely is the use of a certain fund type mandated by GASB standards, rather than by law or by decision of the governing board of a government. However, GASB standards require governmental units that provide deferred compensation plans for their employees to "display" in an agency fund the amount of IRC Section 457 deferred compensation plan asset balances. Total plan assets are, of course, offset by the liability to employees for deferred compensation and accumulated net earnings thereon. (Deferred compensation plans offer employees the opportunity to defer receipt of a portion of their salary and, consequently, to defer the related liability for federal income taxes. IRC Section 457 authorizes state and local governments to establish eligible deferred compensation plans for their employees, if the plans meet requirements set forth in Section 457.)

Readers of Chapters 2 through 10 of this text would assume the agency fund structure would be used to account for deferred compensation plan assets and liabilities pertaining to employees of governmental activities accounted for by funds classified as **governmental funds.** However, GASB standards specify that if employees of activities accounted for by proprietary funds are not covered by a separate deferred compensation plan, a single agency fund should be used to account for IRC Section 457 plan assets and liabilities.[1]

GASB standards require the use of an agency fund whether the assets are held by the employer, a public employee retirement system, a "nongovernmental third party" (such as an insurance company), or another governmental unit under a multiple-jurisdiction plan.

Agency Fund for Special Assessment Debt Service

Readers of Chapters 5 and 7 of this text should recall that GASB standards specify that a governmental unit which has **no** obligation to assume debt service on special assessment debt in the event of property owners' default, but does perform the functions of billing property owners for the assessments, collecting installments of assessments and interest on the assessments, and *from the collections* paying interest and principal on the special assessment debt, should account for those activities by use of an agency fund.

To illustrate **agency fund** accounting for special assessment debt service activities, assume the same information used in Chapter 7 for the City of X except that the governmental unit is not obligated in any manner for the special assessment debt. When the assessments in the amount of $480,000, payable in 10 equal installments, were levied on benefited property owners, the following journal entry was made in the agency fund.

1. Assessments Receivable—Current............................	48,000	
Assessments Receivable—Deferred...........................	432,000	
Due to Special Assessment Bondholders—Principal.......		480,000

All current assessments receivable were collected (see Entry 2) along with $24,000 interest (5 percent on the previous unpaid principal). As indicated in Chapter 7, any amounts not collected by the due date should be reclassified as Assessments Receivable—Delinquent.

2. Cash	72,000	
Assessments Receivable—Current.......................		48,000
Due to Special Assessment Bondholders—Interest........		24,000

Special assessment bond principal in the amount of $48,000 and interest in the amount of $24,000 were paid during the current year.

---

[1] GASB Codification Sec. D25.110 provides that if employees of "separately constituted governmental public utilities and public authorities" are covered by a separate plan, balance sheets of those entities should display the deferred compensation liability with a corresponding asset identified as "designated for deferred compensation benefits." (This disclosure is consistent with the disclosure of restricted assets of utilities, illustrated in Chapter 10.)

3. Due to Special Assessment Bondholders—Principal	48,000	
Due to Special Assessment Bondholders—Interest	24,000	
Cash		72,000

The second installment of assessments receivable was reclassified at year-end from the Deferred category to the Current category.

4. Assessments Receivable—Current.	48,000	
Assessments Receivable—Deferred.		48,000

This pattern of journal entries will be repeated during each of the remaining nine years until all special assessment bonds are retired.

Tax Agency Funds

An agency relationship that does, logically, result in the creation of an agency fund is the collection of taxes, or other revenues, by one governmental unit for several of the funds it operates and for other governmental units. State governments commonly collect sales taxes, gasoline taxes, and many other taxes that are apportioned to state agencies and to local governmental units within the state. At the local government level, it is common for an elected county official to serve as collector for all property taxes owed by persons or corporations owning property within the county. Taxes levied by all funds and units within the county are certified to the County Collector for collection. The County Collector is required by law to make periodic distributions of tax collections for each year to each fund or unit in the proportion the levy for that fund or unit bears to the total levy for the year. In many jurisdictions, the law provides that units may request advances or "draws" from the tax agency fund prior to regular distributions; advances are usually limited by law to a specified percentage, often 90 percent, of collections for the period from the last distribution until the date of the advance.

Tax agency fund accounting would be quite simple if all taxes levied for a given year were collected in that year. It is almost always true, however, that collections during any year relate to taxes levied in several prior years as well as taxes levied for the current year, and sometimes include advance collections of taxes for the following year. In many jurisdictions, not only does the total tax rate vary from year to year but the proportion that the rate of each unit (and each fund) bears to the total rate also varies from year to year. Additionally, interest and penalties on delinquent taxes must be collected at statutory rates or amounts at the time delinquent taxes are collected; interest and penalties collected must be distributed to participating funds and units in the same manner that tax collections are distributed.

Illustration of Composition of Total Tax Rates

Assume that the County Collector of Campbell County is responsible for collecting the taxes due in 19x8 for the funds and units located within the County. Ordinarily, the taxes levied for each fund and unit within the County are shown in columnar form in a newspaper advertisement as legal notice to taxpayers. In order to keep the illustrations in this text legible and comprehensible, Illustration 11–1 shows two columns of such a legal advertisement. Real property tax statements are prepared for each parcel of property located within the jurisdiction for which a

ILLUSTRATION 11–1

COMPOSITION OF TAXES TO BE COLLECTED
by County Collector of Campbell County
for Certain Units within the County
for the Year 19x8

	Washington Township	City of Washington
Total State Rate	$0.01	$ 0.01
County Funds:		
General..............................	1.08	1.08
Capital Projects........................	0.09	0.09
Debt Service	0.20	0.20
Welfare...............................	0.11	0.11
Total County Rate	1.48	1.48
Library Fund...........................	0.25	0.25
Township Funds:		
General...............................	0.07	0.07
Fire Protection	0.23	—
Total Township......................	0.30	0.07
School Funds:		
General..............................	4.50	4.50
Capital Projects.......................	0.18	0.18
Debt Service	0.38	0.38
Total School Rate....................	5.06	5.06
City Funds:		
General..............................		2.53
Street		0.33
Pension..............................		0.25
Debt Service		0.08
Total City Rate......................		3.19
Total Tax Rates per $100 Assessed Valuation	$7.10	$10.06

tax agency fund is operated. Whether each statement discloses the amount of tax that will be distributed to all of the entities that levy taxes on that parcel, or whether the statement shows only the total tax payable to the County Collector, the Collector's Office must be able to compute and distribute all taxes collected to the appropriate units and funds.

For example, Illustration 11–1 shows that a parcel of property located in Washington Township outside the City of Washington would be taxed at the rate of $7.10 per $100 of assessed valuation; whereas if the parcel were inside the city limits, the tax rate would be $10.06. Therefore, if a parcel of property located in Washington Township outside the City had an assessed valuation of $10,000, the total real property tax payable in 19x8 would be $710, but a parcel with the same assessed valuation located within the City would be taxed at $1,006. The total of each of these tax statements is comprised of the taxes levied for each unit, as shown in Illustration 11–1. In turn, the taxes levied for each unit are comprised of the taxes levied for funds of that unit, as shown in Illustration 11–1. The relationship between direct and overlapping debt is discussed in Chapter 8. Note that Illustration 11–1 shows that a person or organization owning property within the City of Washington is required to pay 66 cents of the total rate for debt service (20 cents to Campbell County, 38 cents to the school district, and 8 cents to the City of Washington). Illustration 11–2 summarizes the composition of each tax statement by governmental unit.

In those states in which taxes are levied on personal property, the funds and units that levy the personal property taxes are generally assumed to be the ones that levy taxes on the residence of the owner, unless there is convincing evidence that the situs of the personal property is at another location. Inasmuch as the tax rate levied for each unit and each fund often varies from year to year, it is necessary that all tax collections be identified with the year for which the taxes were levied as well as with the particular parcels of property for which taxes were collected.

Operation of the Collector's Office often requires the use of substantial administrative, clerical, and computer time and provision of extensive building and computer facilities. Accordingly, it is common for the Collector to be authorized to withhold a certain percentage from the collections for each unit, and to remit to the County General Fund (or other fund bearing the expenditures for operating the Tax Agency Fund) the total amount withheld from the collections of other funds.

Accounting for Tax Agency Funds

Taxes levied each year should be recorded in the accounts of each fund of each governmental unit in the manner illustrated in preceding chapters. Although an allowance for estimated uncollectible current taxes would be established in each

---

ILLUSTRATION 11–2

19x8 TAXES PAYABLE
To Campbell County Collector for
Parcel with Assessed Valuation of $10,000

	Parcel Located	
Amount Levied by	*Outside City*	*In City*
State	$ 1.00	$ 1.00
County	148.00	148.00
Library.................	25.00	25.00
Township..............	30.00	7.00
School.................	506.00	506.00
City...................	—	319.00
Total	$710.00	$1,006.00

fund, the **gross** amount of the tax levy for all funds should be recorded in the Tax Agency Fund as a receivable. Note the receivable is designated as belonging to other funds and units, and the receivable is offset in total by a liability. Assuming total real property taxes certified for collection during 19x8 amounted to $10,516,400, the Tax Agency Fund entry would be:

1. Taxes Receivable for Other Funds
    and Units—Current.................................... 10,516,400
        Due to Other Funds and Units   10,516,400

It would be necessary, of course, for the County Collector to keep records of the total amount of 19x8 taxes to be collected for each of the funds and units that participate in the Tax Agency Fund in order to distribute tax collections properly. Assume that the 19x8 taxes were levied for the following units (in order to reduce the detail in this example, a number of the units are combined):

State	$ 10,400
Campbell County	1,480,000
Washington School Corporation	5,060,000
City of Washington	2,400,000
Other units (should be itemized)	1,566,000 (total)
	$10,516,400

If collections of 19x8 taxes during a certain portion of the year amounted to $5,258,200, the Tax Agency Fund entry would be:

2. Cash 5,258,200
        Taxes Receivable for Other Funds and
        Units—Current.....................................   5,258,200

The tax collections must in an actual case be identified with the parcels of property against which the taxes were levied, because the location of each parcel determines the governmental units and funds that should receive the tax collections. Assuming for the sake of simplicity that the collections for the period represent collections of 50 percent of the taxes levied against each parcel in Campbell County, and that the County General Fund is given 1 percent of all collections for units other than the County as reimbursement for the cost of operating the Tax Agency Fund, the distribution of the $5,258,200 collections would be:

	Taxes Collected (50% of Levy)	*Collection Fee (Charged) Received*	*Cash to Be Distributed*
State	$ 5,200	$ (52)	$ 5,148
Campbell County	740,000	45,182	785,182
Washington School Corporation	2,530,000	(25,300)	2,504,700
City of Washington	1,200,000	(12,000)	1,188,000
Other units (should be itemized)	783,000	(7,830)	775,170
	$5,258,200	$ –0–	$5,258,200

If cash is not distributed as soon as the above computation is made, the entry by the Tax Agency Fund to record the liability would be:

3. Due to Other Funds and Units	5,258,200	
Due to State		5,148
Due to Campbell County		785,182
Due to Washington School Corporation		2,504,700
Due to City of Washington		1,188,000
Due to Other Units		775,170

If, as is likely, collections during 19x8 include collections of taxes that were levied for 19x7, 19x6, and preceding years, computations must be made to determine the appropriate distribution of collections for each tax year to each fund and unit that levied taxes against the property for which collections have been received.

When cash is distributed by the Tax Agency Fund, the liability accounts shown in Entry 3 should be debited and Cash credited. If cash is advanced to one or more governmental units or funds prior to a regular periodic distribution, the debits to the liability accounts may precede the credits. By year-end, all advances should be "cleared-up," all distributions computed and recorded, and all cash distributed to the units and funds for which the Tax Agency Fund is being operated. Therefore, if all those events have taken place, the year-end balance sheet for the Tax Agency Fund would consist of one asset: Taxes Receivable for Other Funds and Units—Delinquent; and one liability: Due to Other Funds and Units.

Required Financial Statement

GASB standards require that the comprehensive annual financial report of a governmental unit include a Combining Statement of Changes in Assets and Liabilities—All Agency Funds. This statement is shown as Illustration 11–3. Note the agency fund combining statement is not an operating statement; it is a required part of the CAFR, however, because it discloses changes in the government's custodial responsibilities.

Entries Made by Funds and Units Participating in Tax Agency Funds

Each unit that receives a distribution must record the appropriate portion of it in each of the funds it maintains. In each fund it must also record the fact that cash received differs from the amount of taxes collected by the fee paid to the County General Fund. The fee paid is, of course, recorded as an Expenditure. For example, the computation for the entries to be made by the various funds of Washington School Corporation would be (using the rates shown in Illustration 11–1):

	19x8 Rate	Collections of 19x8 Taxes	Collection Fee Paid	Cash Received
School Funds:				
General	$4.50	$2,250,000	$22,500	$2,227,500
Capital Projects	0.18	90,000	900	89,100
Debt Service	0.38	190,000	1,900	188,100
Total	$5.06	$2,530,000	$25,300	$2,504,700

ILLUSTRATION 11–3

NAME OF GOVERNMENTAL UNIT
Combining Statement of Changes in Assets and
Liabilities—All Agency Funds
For Fiscal Year Ended December 31, 19x2

SPECIAL PAYROLL FUND	Balance January 1, 19x2	Additions	Deductions	Balance December 31, 19x2
ASSETS				
Cash	$ 6,000	$ 40,900	$ 43,550	$ 3,350
LIABILITIES				
Vouchers payable	$ 6,000	$ 40,900	$ 43,550	$ 3,350
PROPERTY TAX FUND				
ASSETS				
Cash	$ 25,800	$ 800,000	$ 725,000	$100,800
Taxes receivable	174,200	1,205,800	800,000	580,000
Total Assets	$200,000	$2,005,800	$1,525,000	$680,800
LIABILITIES				
Due to Other Taxing Units:				
County	$180,000	$1,085,220	$ 652,500	$612,720
Special District	20,000	120,580	72,500	68,080
Total Liabilities	$200,000	$1,205,800	$ 725,000	$680,800
STUDENT ACTIVITY FUND				
ASSETS				
Cash	$ 1,600	$ 1,900	$ 1,650	$ 1,850
LIABILITIES				
Due to student groups	$ 1,600	$ 1,900	$ 1,650	$ 1,850
TOTALS—ALL AGENCY FUNDS				
ASSETS				
Cash	$ 33,400	$ 842,800	$ 770,200	$106,000
Taxes receivable	174,200	1,205,800	800,000	580,000
Total Assets	$207,600	$2,048,600	$1,570,200	$686,000
LIABILITIES				
Vouchers payable	$ 6,000	$ 40,900	$ 43,550	$ 3,350
Due to other taxing units	200,000	1,205,800	725,000	680,800
Due to student groups	1,600	1,900	1,650	1,850
Total Liabilities	$207,600	$1,248,600	$ 770,200	$686,000

SOURCE: GASB Codification Sec. 2200.910.

From the computations it can be seen that the entry made in the Washington School Corporation General Fund for the 19x8 collections distributed should be:

Cash..	2,227,500	
Expenditures	22,500	
Taxes Receivable—Current		2,250,000

Similar entries would be made in the other two funds of the Washington School Corporation and in all the funds of units that paid a tax collection fee to the County General Fund. Collection by the County General Fund of taxes collected for it and the fee collected for it is computed as follows.

	19x8 Rate	Collections of 19x8 Taxes	Collection Fee	Cash Received
County Funds:				
General	$1.08	$540,000	$45,182	$585,182
Capital Projects...........................	.09	45,000	–0–	45,000
Debt Service	.20	100,000	–0–	100,000
Welfare	.11	55,000	–0–	55,000
Total	$1.48	$740,000	$45,182	$785,182

The entry to be made in the General Fund of Campbell County for the 19x8 collections distributed should be:

Cash..	585,182	
Taxes Receivable—Current		540,000
Revenues...		45,182

"Pass-Through" Agency Funds

The receipt of grants, entitlements, and shared revenues that may be used in more than one fund at the discretion of the recipient should be accounted for in an Agency Fund.[2] Assuming the grant, entitlement, or shared revenue to have been received in cash, the "Pass-Through" Agency Fund entry would be (amount assumed):

Cash..	500,000	
Due to Other Funds		500,000

In the event that it is likely that some of the cash will be distributed to individuals, to other governmental units, or to nongovernmental organizations, the title of the liability account should be modified accordingly.

---

[2] GASB has issued an exposure draft of a proposed standard that, if adopted in final form, will restrict the use of "pass-through" agency funds to only those cases in which a government serves as a "cash conduit." Under the proposal, any administrative or direct involvement in the program will require the grant to be accounted for in a governmental, proprietary, or trust fund, with appropriate recognition of revenues and expenditures (or expenses). (See *Exposure Draft*, proposed Statement of the Governmental Accounting Standards Board, "Accounting and Financial Reporting for Certain Grants and Other Financial Assistance" (Norwalk, Conn., 1994).) If a final statement is issued, the publisher will provide an update bulletin to adopters of this text.

When the decision is made about amounts to be transferred to funds (units, etc.) that will use the grant, entitlement, or shared revenue, and the transfers are made, the "Pass-Through" Agency Fund entry would be (amount assumed):

Due to Other Funds	450,000	
Cash		450,000

The receipt of Cash or other assets from a Pass-Through Agency Fund should be accounted for by the recipient in conformity with GASB standards discussed previously: Governmental fund types are to recognize all grants as revenue when the grant proceeds are available for use for the purposes of the fund. If grant proceeds are available immediately, the Revenues account is credited; if some action prescribed by the conditions of the grant must be taken, the Deferred Revenues account should be credited at the time the grant proceeds are recognized as assets, and amounts transferred from Deferred Revenues to Revenues as grant conditions are met. Proprietary fund types recognize as nonoperating revenues the proceeds of grants for operating purposes, or that may be expended at the discretion of the recipient government; if the terms of the grant restrict the use of the proceeds to the acquisition or construction of capital assets, the proceeds must be recorded as contributed equity.

GASB standards provide that "assets being held in Agency Funds pending a determination of the fund(s) to be financed should be disclosed in the Notes to the Financial Statements."

Cash and Investment Pools

Although GASB standards require cash and investments of each fund to be accounted for by those funds, effective management of cash and investments is ordinarily enhanced by putting the cash and investments of the funds in a pool under the control of the Treasurer of the governmental unit or other official. Although the funds may continue to report cash and investments as fund assets, the asset title "Equity in Pooled Cash and Investments" is more descriptive. The cash and investments in the pool may properly be placed under accounting control by use of an agency fund.

Creation of a Cash and Investment Pool

Earnings on pooled investments and gains or losses on sales of investments are allocated to the funds having an equity in the pool in proportion to their relative contributions to the pool. To ensure an equitable division of earnings, gains, and losses, it is customary to revalue all investments in the pool, and all investments being brought into the pool or removed from the pool, to market value as of the time that investments of a fund are being brought into or removed from the pool. Each fund that contributes investments to the pool should debit Equity in Pooled Cash and Investments for the market value of the investments, credit the Investments account for the carrying value (cost or amortized cost), and either debit Expenditures or credit Revenues, depending on whether market value is lower

ILLUSTRATION 11–4

DREW COUNTY
Cash and Investment Pool
Balance Sheet
As of March 31, 19x3
(before admission of Capital Projects Fund)

Assets		*Liabilities*	
Cash	$ 1,000,000	Due to General Fund	$ 9,900,000
Investments:		Due to Debt Service Funds	14,850,000
U.S. Treasury Bills	9,545,000	Due to Enterprise Funds	4,950,000
U.S. Agency Obligations	16,385,000		
Repurchase Agreement	2,060,000		
Accrued Interest	710,000		
Total Assets	$29,700,000	Total Liabilities	$29,700,000

than or higher than carrying value, respectively. (Some pools carry investments at market, revaluing them daily.) For example, the balance sheet in Illustration 11–4 presents the condition of a Cash and Investment Pool as of March 31, 19x3.

On March 31, 19x3, tax-supported bonds in the amount of $15,000,000 are sold to finance the construction of roads and bridges. The proceeds of the bonds are added to the pool for investment until such time as they are needed for Capital Projects Fund disbursements. As of March 31, 19x3, the U.S. Treasury bills in the pool have a market value of $9,535,000 ($10,000 less than the book value reported in the balance sheet shown in Illustration 11–4), and the U.S. Agency Obligations in the pool have a market value of $16,695,000 ($310,000 more than the book value reported in the balance sheet); the market value of the repurchase agreement is the same as reported in the balance sheet. Therefore, total assets of the pool revalued to market as of March 31, 19x3, amount to $30,000,000 (a net increase of $300,000 over the book values previously reported). The increase in carrying value of assets should be credited to the liability accounts in proportion to the equity of each fund as of March 31 before asset revaluation. The liability to the General Fund, therefore, is increased by $100,000 (300,000 × 9,900/29,700); the liability to the Debt Service Funds is increased by $150,000 (300,000 × 14,850/29,700); and the liability to the Enterprise Funds is increased by $50,000 (300,000 × 4,950/29,700). Note that the equity of each of the funds in the pool remains proportionately the same (i.e., the amount due to the General Fund is $10,000,000 after revaluing the investments to market; total liabilities of the pool are $30,000,000; 10,000/30,000 = 9,900/29,700, etc.).

After revaluation of investments in the pool and receipt of $15,000,000 cash from proceeds of bonds sold to finance road and bridge construction, the Balance Sheet of the Cash and Investment Pool becomes as shown in Illustration 11–5.

ILLUSTRATION 11–5

DREW COUNTY
Cash and Investment Pool
Balance Sheet
As of March 31, 19x3
(after admission of Capital Projects Fund)

Assets		*Liabilities*	
Cash	$16,000,000	Due to General Fund	$10,000,000
Investments		Due to Capital Projects	
U.S. Treasury Bills	9,535,000	Fund	15,000,000
U.S. Agency Obligations	16,695,000	Due to Debt Service Funds	15,000,000
Repurchase Agreement	2,060,000	Due to Enterprise Funds	5,000,000
Accrued Interest	710,000		
Total Assets	$45,000,000	Total Liabilities	$45,000,000

Operation of a Cash and Investment Pool

Although the Capital Projects Fund invested $15,000,000 cash in the pool, upon admission to the pool that Fund no longer has a specific claim on the cash of the pool; rather, it (and each other Fund that is a member of the pool) has a proportionate interest in each of the assets of the pool, and will share in earnings, gains, and losses of the pool in that proportion. Ordinarily, it is inconvenient and unnecessary to apportion to liability accounts each receipt of dividends or interest, and the gain or loss realized on each sale of investments. It is simpler to accumulate the earnings in an **Undistributed Earnings on Pooled Investments** account and the gains and losses in a **Reserve for Realized Gains and Losses on Pooled Investments** account and to make periodic distributions to the liability accounts. The frequency of distributions depends on whether **all** cash of all funds is pooled, or whether each fund retains an operating cash account. In the former case, the pool would have frequent receipts attributable to collections of revenues and receivables of the funds, and would have daily disbursements on behalf of the funds; in this case, the interest of each fund in the pool would have to be recomputed each day. If, however, a working cash balance is retained in each active fund, the receipts and disbursements of pool cash would be much less frequent, and the distribution of gains and losses, and earnings, and recomputation of the interest of each fund in the pool would be correspondingly less frequent.

As an example of accounting for earnings on investments of a pool, assume the pool shown in Illustration 11–5 collects interest of $1,610,000, including $710,000 accrued as of March 31, 19x3. An appropriate entry would be:

Cash...	1,610,000	
Accrued Interest		710,000
Undistributed Earnings on Pooled		
Investments		900,000

By the time the earnings are to be distributed, the market value of all investments may have changed. Even if this is true, the proportionate interest of each fund will not have changed because each fund bears gains and losses proportionately. Therefore, in this example, when earnings are distributed, the shares apportioned to the funds are: General Fund, 10/45 or 2/9; Capital Projects Fund, 15/45 or 3/9; Debt Service Funds, 15/45 or 3/9; and Enterprise Funds, 5/45 or 1/9. The **agency fund** entry to distribute $900,000 earnings would be:

Undistributed Earnings on Pooled Investments	900,000	
Due to General Fund		200,000
Due to Capital Projects Fund		300,000
Due to Debt Service Funds		300,000
Due to Enterprise Funds		100,000

After the distribution, each fund has the same proportionate interest in the assets of the pool as it had before the distribution.

It should be obvious that each fund that is a member of the pool should maintain an asset account with a title such as Equity in Pooled Cash and Investments. The balance of this account in each member fund should be the reciprocal of the agency fund account that reports the Pool's liability to that member fund. Thus, in the Drew County example, the Drew County General Fund's Equity in Pooled Cash and Investments had a debit balance amounting to $10,000,000 as of March 31, 19x3. At the time the distribution of earnings on pooled investments was made, the following entry should be made in the **General Fund** accounts:

Equity in Pooled Cash and Investments	200,000	
Revenues		200,000

Interest and dividends earned on pooled investments would, of course, increase the equity of the funds that are members of the pool, as would realized gains on the sales of investments and unrealized gains resulting from periodic revaluation of the pooled investment portfolio to market in times of rising market values of securities held in the portfolio. Realized losses on securities sold, and unrealized losses resulting from periodic revaluation of the portfolio in times of falling market values, both decrease the equity of funds that are members of the pool. In the Drew County Cash and Investments Pool example, each member fund maintains an operating cash account. Consequently, the Pool does not need to distribute gains and losses daily, so it accumulates realized gains and losses in a Reserve for Realized Gains and Losses on Pooled Investments account and accumulates unrealized gains and losses in a Reserve for Unrealized Gains and Losses on Pooled Investments account. This procedure allows a netting of gains and losses in each account, so that only the net realized gain (or loss) and the net unrealized gain (or loss) need be distributed to the member funds, thus saving some clerical or computer time.

Assuming that during a certain time period the realized gains on sales of pooled investments of the Drew County Cash and Investments Pool, all credited to the Reserve for Realized Gains and Losses on Pooled Investments, amounted to $235,000 and, during the same period, realized losses (all debited to the Reserve account) totaled $50,000, the account has a net credit balance of $185,000. Similarly, assume the net effect of marking the portfolio to market is an unrealized gain of $265,000, which is reflected in the credit balance of the Reserve for Unrealized Gains and Losses on Pooled Investments account. Assuming no funds have joined the pool or withdrawn from the pool, and the four funds that have continued to be members of the pool have not transferred additional assets to the pool, nor withdrawn any, the realized and unrealized net gains should be distributed to the member funds in the proportions used for the distribution of earnings (2/9, 3/9, 3/9, and 1/9). The distribution is shown in the following **agency fund** entry:

Reserve for Unrealized Gains and Losses on Pooled Investments......................................	265,000	
Reserve for Realized Gains and Losses on Pooled Investments......................................	185,000	
Due to General Fund		100,000
Due to Capital Projects Fund		150,000
Due to Debt Service Funds.................................		150,000
Due to Enterprise Funds..................................		50,000

Assuming all earnings, gains, and losses have been accounted for by the entries illustrated, the interests of the fund are the same as previously:

General Fund	$10,300,000, or 2/9 of total
Capital Projects Fund	15,450,000, or 3/9 of total
Debt Service Funds	15,450,000, or 3/9 of total
Enterprise Funds	5,150,000, or 1/9 of total
Total	$46,350,000

Withdrawal from Pool

If distributions from a pool are not in proportion to the interest of each fund in the pool, the proportionate shares of each fund will change because there is, in effect, a partial withdrawal from the pool of the fund or funds receiving a larger than proportionate distribution. Therefore, prior to such a distribution there should be an apportionment of earnings, gains, and losses to date. The same is true in the event of complete withdrawal of one or more funds from the pool.

Continuing with the Drew County Cash and Investment Pool example, assume the Debt Service Funds need to withdraw $5,000,000 from the pool to retire matured bonds. The entry in the **agency fund** for the withdrawal would be:

Due to Debt Service Funds..................................	5,000,000	
Cash..		5,000,000

After withdrawal of $5,000,000 by the Debt Service Funds, the interests become:

General Fund	$10,300,000, or 24.9% of total
Capital Projects Fund	15,450,000, or 37.3% of total
Debt Service Funds	10,450,000, or 25.3% of total
Enterprise Funds	5,150,000, or 12.5% of total
Total	$41,350,000

Selected References	Governmental Accounting Standards Board. *Codification of Governmental Accounting and Financial Reporting Standards as of June 30, 1993.* Norwalk, Conn., 1993.

Questions

11–1. Explain the distinction(s) between *agency funds* and *trust funds*.

11–2. Why are *fiduciary funds* used by governmental units?

11–3. Must an agency fund be used to account for withholding taxes, retirement contributions, and (if applicable) social security taxes of general fund employees?

11–4. "If a governmental unit is not required by law to use the agency fund type to account for an agency relationship, it need not use the agency fund type for GAAP conformity either." Do you agree? Explain your answer.

11–5. Why do agency funds have no fund equity?

11–6. It is possible for a permanent agency fund to have no assets or liabilities at the end of a fiscal period. How?

11–7. Why should a governmental unit use an agency fund to account for the assets of an employees' deferred compensation plan established under the provisions of IRC Section 457?

11–8. Under what circumstances should a governmental unit use an agency fund to account for special assessment debt service? What is the rationale for using an agency fund for these transactions?

11–9. What are the most important factors that cause tax agency fund accounting to be complex?

11–10. Why is it considered reasonable for a governmental unit that operates a tax agency fund to charge other governmental units a fee for collecting their taxes, if state law permits such a charge?

11–11. What is a "Pass-Through" Agency Fund? How does such a fund differ from a Tax Agency Fund?

11–12. What information is shown in a Combining Statement of Changes in Assets and Liabilities—All Agency Funds? Why should that statement be included in the comprehensive annual financial report for a state or local governmental unit?

11–13. Why would an agency fund be created to account for pooled cash and investments?

11–14. Why would pooled investments be revalued to market value when a fund is added to the pool, or when a fund withdraws from the pool?

Exercises and Problems

11–1. Utilizing the annual report obtained for Exercise 1–1, follow the instructions below:

a. *Agency Funds.* Are employees' and employer's FICA tax contributions and contributions to other retirement funds accounted for by the General Fund, by an agency fund, or in some other manner (describe)?

Does the governmental unit operate a tax agency fund? Participate in a tax agency fund operated by another governmental unit?

Does the government operate an agency fund to account for employees' contributions to an IRC Section 457 deferred compensation plan? Does the government act as trustee for assets held under this plan, or are the assets held by another government, a Public Employees Retirement System, or an insurance company or other corporate fiduciary?

Does the government act as agent for owners of property within a special assessment district, and for the creditors of those property owners? Do the Notes to the Financial Statements disclose the agency relationship clearly and fully?

Does the governmental unit operate one or more "pass-through" agency funds? If so, describe. If not, is there any evidence that the governmental unit received grants, entitlements, or shared revenues that might properly have been accounted for by a pass-through agency fund?

 b. Cash and Investment Pools. Does the governmental unit operate, or participate in, a cash and investments pool? If so, is the pool accounted for as an agency fund? If there is a cash and investment pool and it is not accounted for as an agency fund, how is it accounted for? Explain.

 c. Financial Statements. Are agency funds properly disclosed in combined and combining financial statements? Explain the reasons for your answer.

11–2. Write the numbers 1 through 10 on a sheet of paper. Beside each number write the letter corresponding with the best answer to each of the following questions:

1. Which of the following accounts of an agency fund is (are) closed at the end of the fiscal year?
   a. The budgetary accounts.
   b. The operating statement accounts.
   c. Both *a* and *b*.
   d. None of the above.

2. Taxes collected by the County Collector for distribution to other funds of the County and/or to governmental units within the County should be accounted for in an:
   a. Enterprise Fund.
   b. Internal Service Fund.
   c. Expendable Trust Fund.
   d. Agency Fund.

3. Taxes certified to the County Collector of Leigh County by other County funds and by other governmental units within the County should be recorded by the Collector by a debit to:
   a. Taxes Receivable—Current and a credit to Revenues.
   b. Taxes Receivable—Current and a credit directly to Fund Balance.
   c. Taxes Receivable for Other Funds and Units—Current and a credit to Due to Other Funds and Units.
   d. Taxes Receivable—Current and a credit to Due to County General Fund.

4. Currently effective GASB standards require each state and local governmental unit to display in an agency fund
   a. IRC Section 457 Deferred Compensation Plan asset balances.
   b. Collections of special assessments and interest thereon, and from those collections payment of interest on and principal of special assessment debt for which the government has *no* obligation.

    c. Both *a* and *b*.

    d. All agency relationships in which the government is the principal.

5. Agency fund financial data should be displayed in the GPFS in:

    a. The same combined operating statements as the governmental funds of the primary government.

    b. The same combined operating statements as the proprietary funds of the primary government.

    c. The same combined operating statements as the Account Groups of the primary government.

    d. None of the combined operating statements.

6. Changes in agency fund assets and liabilities during a fiscal year should be displayed in the CAFR in the:

    a. Combined Statement of Changes in Assets and Liabilities—All Agency Funds.

    b. Combining Statement of Changes in Assets and Liabilities—All Agency Funds.

    c. Individual statements of each agency fund.

    d. Statistical section of the CAFR.

Items 7 through 10 all relate to the following information:

    The City Council of the City of Earlville decided to pool the investments of its General Fund, its Debt Service Fund, and the Capital Projects Fund, each of which had accounted for its investments at cost. At the date of the creation of the pool the cost and market value of the investments of each of the three funds were as follows:

	Investments	
	Cost	*Market*
General Fund	$ 600,000	$ 590,000
Debt Service Fund	3,600,000	3,640,000
Capital Projects Fund	1,800,000	1,770,000
Total	$6,000,000	$6,000,000

7. At the date of the creation of the pool each of the three funds should:

    a. Debit its Fund Balance account and credit its Investments account for the cost of the assets transferred to the pool.

    b. Debit or credit its Investments account as needed to adjust its carrying value to market, the offsetting entry in each fund should be to Fund Balance.

    c. Debit Equity in Pool for the market value of investments pooled, credit Investments for the cost of investments pooled, and debit Expenditures (or credit Revenues) for the difference.

    d. Only a memorandum entry need be made.

8. At the date of creation of the pool the City of Earlville should account for all pooled investments in:

    a. Its General Fund at market value.

    b. Its General Fund at cost.

    c. An agency fund at market value.

    d. An agency fund at cost.

9. One day after creation of the pool, investments that had belonged to the Capital Projects Fund were sold for $1,760,000.

   a. The loss of $40,000 is considered to be a loss borne by the Capital Projects Fund.

   b. The loss of $10,000 is considered to be a loss borne by the Capital Projects Fund.

   c. The loss of $40,000 is borne by each underlying fund in proportion to its equity in the pool.

   d. The loss of $10,000 is borne by each underlying fund in proportion to its equity in the pool.

10. One month after creation of the pool, earnings on pooled investments totaled $59,900. It was decided to distribute the earnings to the underlying funds, rounding the distribution to the nearest dollar. The Debt Service Fund should receive:

   a. $36,000.

   b. $35,940.

   c. $36,339.

   d. $37,000.

11–3. The Statement of Changes in Assets and Liabilities of the Deferred Compensation Agency Fund of the City of Disneyville for the fiscal year ended June 30, 19x2, is shown below. Information about the deferred compensation plan, taken from the Notes to the Financial Statements, is also reproduced.

CITY OF DISNEYVILLE
Agency Fund
Statement of Changes in Assets and Liabilities
Year Ended June 30, 19x2

Cash and Investments		$4,049,952
Deferred Compensation Payable		
Beginning Balance		$2,868,658
Add: Employee Contributions	$1,028,195	
Income on Investments	404,094	
Less: Withdrawals and Terminations	(250,995)	$1,181,294
Total Deferred Compensation Payable		
Ending Balance		$4,049,952

Extract from Notes to Financial Statements:

Deferred Compensation. The City offers its employees a deferred compensation plan created in accordance with Internal Revenue Code Section 457. The plan, available to all City employees, permits them to defer a portion of their salary until future years. The deferred compensation is not available to employees until termination, retirement, death, or unforeseeable emergency.

All amounts of compensation deferred under the plan, all property and rights purchased with those amounts, and all income attributable to those amounts, property, or rights are (until paid or made available to the employee or other beneficiary) solely the property and rights of the City (without being restricted to the provisions of benefits under the plan), subject only to the claims of the City's general creditors. Participants' rights under the plan are equal to those of general creditors of the City in an amount equal to the fair market value of the deferred account for each participant.

It is the opinion of the City's legal counsel that the City has no liability for losses under the plan but does have the duty of due care that would be required of an ordinary prudent investor. The City believes it is unlikely that it will use the assets to satisfy the claims of general creditors in the future.

Pursuant to the GASB Codification Section D25, the City has reclassified its Deferred Compensation Fund (previously a nonexpendable trust fund) as an Agency Fund. The assets are stated at the market value, which is represented by the contract value provided by the City's third-party administrator.

Required Judging from the statement illustrated, and the information given in the notes, does the City of Disneyville appear to conform with GASB standards for financial reporting of deferred compensation plans, as set forth in this chapter? Explain the reason for your answer.

11–4. The City of Fayette agreed to bill each owner of each parcel of property within Special Assessment District No. 21 for each installment of the owner's share of the total assessment for the construction project being undertaken by that Special Assessment District. The City agreed to collect the installments and interest thereon, and agreed to use the collections to pay interest and principal due on debt incurred for the construction project, although the City is not obligated in any manner for the special assessment debt.

Required

a. Name the fund type that should be used by the City of Fayette to record the activities described above. Explain the reason for your answer.

b. If the total assessment for the project to be undertaken by the Special Assessment District is $3,600,000, to be collected in three equal annual installments, show in general journal form the entry that should be made for the total assessment, assuming all installments are to be used for service of debt incurred for this project.

c. Show in general journal form the entry that should be made for collections from owners of property within Special Assessment District No. 21 of the first installment amounting to $1,276,000 ($1,160,000 for principal and $116,000 for interest).

d. Show in general journal form the entry that should be made to record the payment of interest amounting to $110,000 and principal amounting to $1,150,000 on debt incurred for the Special Assessment District No. 21 project.

e. Assuming all transactions described above occurred in the fiscal year ended June 30, 19x8, and the City of Fayette had no other transactions during that year with the property owners or creditors of Special Assessment District No. 21:
  (1) Name the general purpose financial statement, or statements, of the City of Fayette in which the results of the transactions described above should be reported, and state which information about the transactions should be reported in each statement you name.
  (2) If the effects of the transactions described above should be reported in a statement included in the CAFR, but not in the GPFS, name the statement and describe its purpose.

11–5. For the three years indicated, the rates applicable to real property within the Town of Clarkton were as shown below (rates are in terms of dollars and cents per $100 assessed valuation):

Fund or Unit	*19x2*	*19x3*	*19x4*
Town General Fund	$3.12	$ 3.18	$ 3.30
Town Debt Service Fund	.44	.50	.60
Total Town Rate	3.56	3.68	3.90
Clarkton School Corp.	4.70	4.90	5.00
Clarkton County Library	.13	.20	.30
Clarkton County	1.54	1.65	1.80
Total Rate	$9.93	$10.43	$11.00

Taxes on all real property located within Clarkton County are collected by the County Collector, who then distributes collections to the County funds and to governmental units located within the County. Collections during the second half of 19x4 totaled $6,800,000 from property located within the Town of Clarkton, which represented collections of the following levies in the following amounts:

From 19x2 levy	$ 72,000
From 19x3 levy	360,000
From 19x4 levy	6,368,000

Required

    a. Assuming state law prohibits the County Collector from charging funds and units for the collection service, how much of the $6,800,000 collected in the second half of 19x2 should be remitted by the County Collector to the Clarkton Town Treasurer? Show computations in good form.

    b. How much of the Town's share of collections of the 19x4 levy, as computed in part *a* of this problem, should be remitted to the Town's Debt Service Fund? Show computations in good form.

11–6. The County Collector of Springer County is responsible for collecting all property taxes levied by funds and units within the boundaries of the County. In order to reimburse the County for estimated administrative expenses of operating the Tax Agency Fund, the agency fund deducts 1 percent from the collections for the Town, the School District, and the townships. The total amount deducted is added to the collections for the County and remitted to the County General Fund.

The following events occurred in 19y1:

    1. Current-year tax levies to be collected by the agency fund were:

County General Fund	$1,420,000
Town of Cronan General Fund	2,287,100
Springer Co. Consolidated	
School District	3,920,000
Various Townships	960,000
Total	$8,587,100

    2. $15,100 was charged back to the Town of Cronan because of errors in the computation of that unit's current taxes.

    3. $4,190,000 of current taxes were collected during the first half of 19y1.

    4. Liabilities to all funds and units as the result of the first half-year collections were recorded. (A schedule of amounts collected for each participant, showing amount withheld for the County General Fund and net amounts due the participants, is recommended for determining amounts to be recorded for this transaction. Round computation of the final amounts to the nearest dollar.)

    5. All money in the Tax Agency Fund was distributed.

Required

    a. Make journal entries for each of the foregoing transactions that affected the Tax Agency Fund.

    b. Make journal entries for each of the foregoing transactions that affected the County General Fund. Begin with the tax levy entry, assuming 3 percent of the gross levy will be uncollectible.

    c. Make journal entries for each of the foregoing entries that affected the Town of Cronan General Fund. Begin with the tax levy entry, assuming 3 percent of the gross levy will be uncollectible.

11–7. Macon County customarily receives from various federal government agencies resources that are designated for the use of the governmental units within the County. These resources are accounted for by the County in a Pass-Through Agency Fund.

Required

a. Show in general journal form the entries in the Pass-Through Fund for the following events and transactions, which occurred in 19y6:
   (1) The County received in cash a grant of $38,000,000, which is to be distributed to various units within the County in a manner not yet specified.
   (2) Official word was received that $16,500,000 of the above grant is to be distributed to the City of Canterville for public improvements. The distribution was made.
   (3) Official word was received that $15,000,000 was to be distributed to the County Road and Bridge Fund. The distribution was made. Remaining cash was invested in marketable securities.
   (4) The County received in cash a grant of $3,000,000, to be distributed to law enforcement agencies throughout the County in a manner yet to be specified. The cash was invested in marketable securities.

b. Show in general journal form the entries that should be made in a Capital Projects Fund of the City of Centerville for the following:
   (1) $16,500,000 was received from the Macon County Pass-Through Agency Fund.
   (2) A construction contract in the amount of $6,000,000 was signed.

c. Assuming Macon County operated a Federal Payroll Tax Agency Fund in addition to the Pass-Through Agency Fund, and the cash balance of the Federal Payroll Tax Agency Fund on January 1, 19y6, was $125,800, additions during the year were $850,000, disbursements during the year were $815,500, and the ending balance was held in Cash, prepare a Combining Statement of Changes in Assets and Liabilities—All Agency Funds for Macon County for the year ended December 31, 19y6.

11–8. The City Council of the City of Liberty decided to pool the investments of its General Fund, its Capital Projects Fund, and its Debt Service Fund, each of which had accounted for its investments at cost. At the date of the creation of the pool, the cost and market value of the investments of each of the three funds were as follows:

	Investments	
	Cost	*Market*
General Fund	$ 800,000	$ 790,000
Capital Projects Fund	4,600,000	4,740,000
Debt Service Fund	3,000,000	3,060,000
Total	$8,400,000	$8,590,000

Required

a. Show the entry that should be made by (1) the General Fund, (2) the Capital Projects Fund, and (3) the Debt Service Fund, to do the following: open a new asset account, Equity in Investment Pool, in the amount of the market value of the investments transferred to the pool; close the existing Investments account; and debit the Expenditures account or credit the Revenues account of each fund as needed to balance the entry.

b. Show in general journal form the entries to be made in the accounts of the Investments Pool Agency Fund to record the following transactions of the first year of its operations:

(1) Record at market value the investments transferred to the pool; assume the investments of the General Fund were in U.S. Treasury bills, and the investments of both the Capital Projects Fund and the Debt Service Fund were in certificates of deposit.

(2) Certificates of deposit that had been recorded at a market value of $1,000,000 matured. The pool received $1,050,000 in cash ($1,000,000 for the face of the CDs and $50,000 interest). The entire amount was reinvested in a new issue of certificates of deposit.

(3) Interest on Treasury bills was collected in the amount of $50,000, and interest on certificates of deposit was collected in the amount of $300,000. These amounts were reinvested in Treasury bills.

(4) Interest on certificates of deposit accrued at year-end amounted to $28,250.

(5) At the end of the year, it was decided to compute and record the pool's liability to each of the three member funds for its proportionate share of earnings on the pooled investments. Carry your computation of each fund's proportionate share to four decimal places. Round the amount of the distribution to each fund to the nearest dollar.

c. Record in each of the three member funds the increase in its Equity in Investment Pool.

11–9. This problem continues the City of Liberty Investment Pool Agency Fund (Problem 11–8).

Required Show in general journal form the entries for the following transactions by the Investments Pool in the second year of its existence.

(1) It was decided that the Debt Service Fund should withdraw $2,000,000 from the Investments Pool because of the imminent need for cash to redeem matured bonds. Accordingly, the investments of the pool were revalued at market—U.S. Treasury bills, $1,200,000; and certificates of deposit, $7,900,000. The current market values are recorded by the Investments Pool, and the liability to each of the three funds for its proportionate share of the unrealized increase in the market values of investments is recorded.

(2) Cash in the amount of interest accrued at the end of the prior year is received.

(3) U.S. Treasury bills carried at the amount of $500,000 are sold for $500,000. Certificates of deposit in the amount of $1,500,000 matured, and the face amount was collected in cash.

(4) The amount the Debt Service Fund wished to withdraw, $2,000,000, is paid in cash.

(5) Interest collected in cash during the remainder of the year amounted to $26,000; $3,840 of interest was accrued at year-end.

(6) At the end of the year, it was decided to compute and record the liability to each member fund for its shares of earnings on pooled investments for the second year. (Compute the distribution on the basis of the proportionate share of each fund in the pool after the Debt Service Fund's withdrawal of $2,000,000.)

Continuous Problems

11–L. The City of Bingham utilizes a Pass-Through Agency Fund to account for grants, entitlements, and shared revenues which may be used in more than one fund at the discretion of the City Council of the City of Bingham, or which the City of Bingham receives as primary recipient of grants, and which must be transmitted in whole or in part to other governmental units.

The Pass-Through Agency Fund had disbursed all cash received during the fiscal year ended June 30, 19x1, and had no assets or liabilities on that date.

Required

a. Open a general journal for the City of Bingham Pass-Through Agency Fund and record the following events and transactions that occurred during the fiscal year ended June 30, 19x2:

(1) The City of Bingham is designated as the primary recipient of a grant from a federal agency. The City must remit 30 percent of the grant proceeds to the Bingham School Corporation and 10 percent of the grant proceeds to Bingham Township, both of which are governmental units independent of the City of Bingham. The remaining 60 percent of the grant proceeds may be spent by the City of Bingham for "ordinary and necessary maintenance and operating expenses" at the discretion of the City of Bingham City Council. In January 19x2, the grantor agency informed the City of Bingham that the total amount of the grant is to be $800,000; the entire amount is to be paid to the City within 60 days of notification.

(2) The City receives cash in the full amount of the grant, $800,000.

(3) The City remits the amounts due to the secondary recipients of the grant: Bingham School Corporation and Bingham Township. Remaining cash is invested in short-term certificates of deposit until the City Council determines the proper disposition of the City's share of the grant.

(4) The certificates of deposit matured and were converted into cash. Interest in the amount of $4,000 is received in cash on the certificates of deposit; this amount must, under terms of the grant, be added to the amount of the grant to be used at the discretion of the City Council.

(5) The City Council determined that the entire amount of the City's share of the grant should be expended by the General Fund for purposes included in General Fund appropriations recorded in Problem 3–L, as amended in Problem 4–L. (You may assume the City's share of grant proceeds, plus interest, is included in transaction 7 of Problem 4–L*g*, as a part of Intergovernmental Revenue.)

b. Prepare a Statement of Changes in Assets and Liabilities for the Pass-Through Agency Fund for the year ended June 30, 19x2. You may use the form shown as Illustration 11–3.

11–S. The City of Smithville did not have any agency funds in 19y1 or 19y2.

CHAPTER 12

Fiduciary Funds: Trust Funds and Public Employee Retirement Systems

In addition to agency funds discussed in Chapter 11, the Fiduciary Fund classification includes Expendable Trust Funds, Nonexpendable Trust Funds, and Pension Trust Funds (also referred to as Public Employee Retirement Systems).

Trust funds differ from agency funds principally in degree: Frequently a trust fund is in existence over a longer period of time than an agency fund; it represents and develops vested interests to a greater extent; and it involves more complex administrative and financial problems. In both trust and agency funds, the governmental unit has a fiduciary relationship with the creators and beneficiaries of the trust or agency. A historically important reason for the creation of a trust fund is the acceptance by a governmental unit of trusteeship over assets to be invested to produce income to be used for specified purposes (generally cultural or educational). The fair value of the assets placed in trust under such an agreement is referred to as the principal, or corpus, of the trust. Since the principal of this form of trust must be held intact in order to produce income, the trust is called **nonexpendable**. Nonexpendable trust funds are often called **endowment funds.** The income from the assets of a nonexpendable trust may be used only for the purposes specified by the trustor; therefore, the income is **expendable**. Separate funds should be established to account for expendable and nonexpendable assets. Nonexpendable trust funds should be accounted for in essentially the same manner as proprietary funds (Internal Service Funds, discussed in Chapter 9, and Enterprise Funds, discussed in Chapter 10). Expendable trust funds should be accounted for in essentially the same manner as the governmental funds discussed in Chapters 3 through 8.

Not all trust funds require the historic distinction between corpus and income; loan funds operated as trust funds are usually nonexpendable both as to principal and income, whereas public employee retirement systems are funds whose principal and income are **both** expendable for specified purposes. Accounting for public employee retirement systems follows the general pattern of accounting for proprietary funds, but there are many accounting problems not yet settled, as discussed in the final section of this chapter.

In addition to the nonexpendable versus expendable classification, trust funds may also be classified as **public** or **private**. Public trust funds are those whose principal or income, or both, must be used for some public purpose; the beneficiaries of private trust funds are private individuals or organizations. The preceding definition should not be taken too literally because public employee retirement systems are classified as public trust funds even though the beneficiaries are individuals. Funds established for the purpose of holding performance deposits of licensees under a governmental unit's regulatory activities are examples of private trust funds.

Accounting for Trust Funds—General Recommendations

The rules of law pertaining to testamentary and intervivos trusts are applicable to trusts in which a government acts as trustee; trust fund accounting information systems are therefore constrained by the trust laws of the several states. A primary problem is the distinction between transactions that affect the trust principal, or corpus, and transactions that relate to trust income. A case in point is the accounting treatment of depreciable assets. Governmental funds discussed in Chapters 3 through 8 do not account for fixed assets. However, if fixed assets are included in the principal of a trust fund, they obviously must be accounted for; therefore, GASB standards specify that nonexpendable trust funds follow the accounting practices recommended for proprietary funds discussed in Chapters 9 and 10. However, under the older rules of trust law that govern many trusts now in existence, cash basis accounting is assumed, which means the principal of the fund would record the fair value of the fixed assets at date of creation of the trust and carry that value until the assets were disposed of; no depreciation during that time would be recognized, nor would any difference between par and the fair value of securities held as part of the principal be amortized.

Trust laws adopted in many states make it possible for a trustor to specify that the income of the fund be computed on the accrual basis. If that is done, depreciation would be recognized as an expense and cash retained in the nonexpendable fund, or transferred to it, in the amount of depreciation and amortization taken—thus maintaining the fund principal at its original dollar amount. Accrual accounting, accompanied by "funding the depreciation" (as the retention of cash to offset depreciation expense is called), enables the administrators to maintain the principal intact, in the sense of maintaining the original dollar amount, which the older rules of trust law and cash basis accounting do not do. More important than maintaining fund principal at its original dollar amount is maintaining or enhancing the earning power of the assets placed in trust. Cash basis accounting offers no help in the measurement of the degree of success of trust fund administrators in maintaining or improving the earning power of the assets comprising the fund principal. Accordingly, GASB standards require nonexpendable trust funds to be kept on the full accrual basis. This requirement assumes an objective of trust funds is the production of net income to be used to support the purposes for which the trust was created. If interested persons are to be able to determine how effectively trust fund administrators have managed the assets, it is obvious that trust fund annual reports should include comparative accrual-based income statements, as well as a detailed listing of trust fund investments as of the end of the fiscal year. The lists of trust fund assets should show both cost (or fair value at date of acquisition) and market value as of the date of the statement. The transactions by the trustee during the year are of interest also; in recognition of this it is common for trust fund administrators to report purchases and sales of investments during the year, disclosing gains and losses on the sales. (It is a general rule of law that gains and losses on sales of principal assets serve to increase or decrease the principal rather than affect the income.[1] If transactions in principal investments are made for the purpose of maximizing earnings rather than for the purpose of maintaining the safety of the principal, a good case can be made that the gains or losses should increase or decrease the income. In many jurisdictions, a trustor can specify how the gains and losses are to be considered.)

Budgetary Accounts. Budgetary accounts generally are not needed for nonexpendable trust funds because transactions of the fund result in changes in the fund principal only incidentally; by definition, the principal cannot be appropriated or expended. Expendable trust funds, on the other hand, may be required by law to use the appropriation procedure to ensure adequate notice to parties at interest as to the expenditure of fund assets. If the appropriation procedure is required, the use of budgetary accounts by expendable trusts is recommended for reasons discussed at length in preceding chapters of this text.

Illustrative Case—Nonexpendable Trust Funds and Expendable Trust Funds

As an illustration of the nature of accounting for nonexpendable trust principal and expendable trust revenue, assume on November 1, 19x5, James Smith died, having made a valid will that provided for the gift of various securities to the City of Columbia to be held as a nonexpendable trust; the net income from the securities is to be computed on the full accrual basis. Income received in cash, less any amount needed to amortize bond premium or discount on a straight-line basis, is to be transferred to the City's Library Operating Fund. In this jurisdiction, the latter fund is operated as a budgetary fund on the modified accrual basis described in Chapters 3 and 4. The gift was accepted by the City of Columbia and a Library Endowment Fund established to account for the nonexpendable trust. The following securities were received by the Library Endowment Fund:

[1] William L. Cary and Craig B. Bright observe in *The Developing Law of Endowment Funds* (New York: Ford Foundation, 1974) that this is the position taken in the Uniform Principal and Income Acts that have been adopted by a majority of the states, but that the acts have no direct application to endowment funds of charitable corporations or of educational institutions.

	Interest Rate per Year	Maturity Date	Face Value	Fair Value as of 11/1/x5	Fair Value over (under) Face
Bonds:					
AB Company	10%	1/1/y0	$330,000	$340,000	$10,000
C & D Company	9	7/1/x7	110,000	112,000	2,000
D & G Company	9	1/1/z9	200,000	200,000	—
Total			$640,000	$652,000	$12,000

	Number of Shares	Fair Value as of 11/1/x5
Stocks:		
M Company, common	2,400	$126,000
S Company, common	10,000	96,000
K Company, common	3,000	129,000
GF Company, common	2,000	145,000
Total		$496,000

Illustrative Entries—
Nonexpendable
Trust Fund

The receipt of the securities by the Library Endowment Fund is properly recorded at the fair value of the securities as of the date of the gift because this is the amount the trustees are responsible for. Inasmuch as the trustees will receive the face of the bonds on maturity (if the bonds are held until maturity), accrual accounting theory dictates that the difference between fair value of the bonds and their face value be amortized over the period from date of receipt by the fund to date of maturity of the bonds. Thus the entry in the Library Endowment Fund to record the receipt of the securities must disclose both the par of the bonds held as investments and the difference between the fair market value and par. Interest accrued on the bonds as of the date of their transfer to the Endowment Fund is a part of the trust corpus. Therefore, the entry as of November 1, 19x5, is:

1. Bonds, at Par	640,000	
Unamortized Bond Premium	12,000	
Stocks	496,000	
Accrued Interest Receivable	20,300	
Fund Balance		1,168,300

[Interest accrued is AB ($330,000 × 10% × 4/12 = $11,000), C&D ($110,000 × 9% × 4/12 = $3,300), and D&G ($200,000 × 9% × 4/12 = $6,000)]

As of January 1, 19x6, interest is received on all bonds—$16,500 from AB Company; $4,950 from C&D Company; and $9,000 from D&G Company. The AB Company bonds were worth $340,000 when received by the Library Endowment Fund; when they mature, they will be worth $330,000. Therefore, the $10,000 difference between value on November 1, 19x5, and on January 1, 19y0, should be amortized over the 50 months intervening. Customarily, amortization is recorded as an adjustment of interest earnings (see Appendix 2 for a more detailed discussion) when the earnings are received or accrued. As of January 1, 19x6, 2 of the 50 months between receipt of the bonds and their maturity have expired; therefore, amortization of premium is $400 ($10,000 ÷ 50 × 2). Similarly, C&D Company bonds were worth $112,000 when received but will be worth $110,000 20 months later; therefore, on January 1, 19x6, amortization should be $200 ($2,000 ÷ 20 × 2). D&G Company bonds were worth par when received; therefore, there is no discount or premium to be amortized. The total bond premium to be amortized as of January 1, 19x6, therefore, is $600; this amount is treated as an adjustment of interest earnings, and therefore results in retention in the Library Endowment Fund of cash in the amount of premium amortized (because only the net earnings for the two months since the Library Endowment Fund was established are to be transferred to the Library Operating Fund). The entry for the receipt of bond interest in January 19x6, the amortization of premium, and the revenue earned for transfer to the Library Operating Fund is:

2.	Cash	30,450	
	Unamortized Bond Premium		600
	Accrued Interest Receivable		20,300
	Revenues—Bond Interest		9,550

Stock does not mature; therefore, its fair value at date of receipt need not be adjusted in any manner, and the stock may be carried at fair value as of the date of donation (11/1/x5) until sold, subject to adjustment for market value declines judged to be other than temporary. When sold, the gain or loss on sale would belong to the Endowment Fund under accounting principles currently regarded as generally accepted. Some accountants believe the carrying value of stock should be increased if the market value on balance sheet date is above the amount at which it was originally recorded. However, in the case of trust fund accounting, change in market value from date of acquisition to balance sheet date has not been converted into cash, so could not be transferred to the Library Operating Fund, so it is difficult to justify recognizing unrealized market fluctuations in the accounts.

Dividends on stock do not accrue. They become a receivable only when declared by the corporation issuing the stock. Ordinarily the receivable is not recorded because it is followed in a reasonably short time by issuance of a dividend check. Assuming dividends on the stock held by the Library Endowment Fund were received early in January 19x6, in the amount of $9,800, Entry 3 is appropriate:

3.	Cash	9,800	
	Revenues—Dividends		9,800

The Library Endowment Fund has sufficient cash to pay the amount owed to the Library Operating Fund for bond interest during the two months since the bonds were received, less the net amortization of premium and discount, and for dividends received. Assuming cash is transferred as of January 3, 19x6, Entry 4 is:

4.	Operating Transfers Out	19,350	
	Cash		19,350

On the advice of an investment manager, 1,000 shares of GF Company stock were sold for $78,750; this amount and cash of $19,000 was invested in 2,000 shares of LH Company common stock. The GF Company stock sold was half the number of shares received when the trust was established; therefore, it was recorded at its fair value then of $72,500; the difference between its book value and the proceeds is generally considered to belong to the corpus and does not give rise to gain or loss that would adjust the net income to be transferred to the Library Operating Fund.[2] Therefore, the sale of GF Company stock and the purchase of LH Company stock should be recorded in the Library Endowment Fund as shown in Entries 5a and 5b:

5a. Cash	78,750	
Stocks		72,500
Fund Balance		6,250
5b. Stocks	97,750	
Cash		97,750

Assuming there were no further purchases or sales of stock and that dividends received on April 1, 19x6, amounted to $9,920, Entry 6 is necessary, assuming that the cash is transferred to the Library Operating Fund promptly.

6a. Cash	9,920	
Revenues—Dividends...............................		9,920
6b. Operating Transfers Out.................................	9,920	
Cash		9,920

Interest accrued on June 30, 19x6, amounted to $30,450, the same amount received early in January 19x6. Inasmuch as all bonds had been held for six months, the amortization of premium on AB Company bonds is $1,200 ($10,000 ÷ 50 × 6), and the amortization of premium on C&D Company bonds is $600 ($2,000 ÷ 20 × 6). Therefore, the total amortization of premium, $1,800, is treated as an adjustment of interest earnings and is retained by the Library Endowment Fund. Entry 7a records the accrual of interest, the amortization of premium, and the revenue earned for transfer to the Library Operating Fund. Entry 7b records the liability to the Library Operating Fund.

7a. Accrued Interest Receivable	30,450	
Unamortized Bond Premium..........................		1,800
Revenues—Bond Interest		28,650
7b. Operating Transfers Out.................................	28,650	
Due to Library Operating Fund		28,650

---

[2] See material cited in footnote 1 for an alternative approach.

Illustrative Financial Statements— Nonexpendable Trust Fund

If June 30 is the end of the City of Columbia's fiscal year, the Library Endowment Fund should prepare financial statements for inclusion in the City's annual report, even though the fund was created on November 1, 19x5, and has been in operation only eight months. No adjustments in addition to Entries 7a and 7b are necessary as of June 30 because dividends on stock are not accrued. The financial statements required for this nonexpendable trust fund for inclusion in the City's report for the period ended June 30, 19x6, are shown in Illustrations 12–1, 12–2, and 12–3.

An unusually observant reader will notice that the equity account of a nonexpendable trust fund is called *Fund Balance* instead of *Contribution from Trustor,* although the fund is said to be accounted for in a manner similar to proprietary funds. Since no earnings are retained by the nonexpendable trust fund, there is no need for a Retained Earnings account, and the name given to the single equity account is moot.

Illustrative Entries—Expendable Trust Fund

In the case of the gift of James Smith to the City of Columbia, the trust corpus, or principal, was nonexpendable. Accounting for the nonexpendable trust fund, the Library Endowment Fund, which was established to account for the gift, is illustrated in the preceding sections. By the terms of James Smith's will, the income from the nonexpendable trust, after amortization of bond premium, is to be transferred to the City's Library Operating Fund. It is assumed the library had been established some time prior to Mr. Smith's demise, and consequently, its operating fund was in existence at the date of the establishment of the endowment. The Library Operating Fund is similar in nature to the general and special revenue funds described in Chapters 3 and 4, so the only entries illustrated below are those relating to the Library Endowment Fund entries for the period November 1, 19x5,

---

ILLUSTRATION 12–1

CITY OF COLUMBIA
Library Endowment Fund
Balance Sheet
As of June 30, 19x6

Assets			Liabilities and Fund Equity	
Cash		$ 1,900	Due to Library Operating Fund	$ 28,650
Accrued interest receivable		30,450	Fund Balance	1,174,550
Investments:				
Bonds, at par	$640,000			
Unamortized bond premium	9,600	649,600		
Stock		521,250	Total Liabilities and	
Total Assets		$1,203,200	Fund Equity	$1,203,200

ILLUSTRATION 12–2

CITY OF COLUMBIA
Library Endowment Fund
Statement of Revenues, Expenses, and Changes in Fund Balance
Eight Months Ended June 30, 19x6

Revenues earned for transfer to Library Operating Fund:	
Interest on bonds, net of amortization of bond premium	$ 38,200
Dividends on stock	19,720
Total Revenue	57,920
Expenses:	–0–
Income before operating transfers	57,920
Other Financing Sources (Uses):	
Operating transfers to Library Operating Fund	(57,920)
Increase in Fund Balance	–0–
Fund Balance received from Executor, November 1, 19x5	1,168,300
Realized gain on sale of stock	6,250
Fund Balance, June 30, 19x6	$1,174,550

ILLUSTRATION 12–3

CITY OF COLUMBIA
Library Endowment Fund
Statement of Cash Flows
For Eight Months Ended June 30, 19x6

Cash flows from investing activities:	
Interest and dividends on investments	$ 50,170
Proceeds of sale of investments	78,750
Purchase of investments	(97,750)
Net cash provided by investing activities	31,170
Cash flows from noncapital financing activities:	
Operating transfers to expendable trust	(29,270)
Net cash increase in cash and cash equivalents	1,900
Cash and cash equivalents, November 1, 19x5	–0–
Cash and cash equivalents, June 30, 19x6	$ 1,900

Reconciliation of Net Income to Net Cash
Provided by Investing and Noncapital Financing Activities

Net income		$ –0–
Adjustments:		
Amortization of bond premium	$ 2,400	
Increase in accrued interest receivable	(10,150)	
Increase in investments	(19,000)	
Increase in interfund liability	28,650	
Total adjustments		1,900
Net cash provided by investing and noncapital financing activities		$ 1,900

to June 30, 19x6. Fiscal year 19x6 of the City of Columbia started on July 1, 19x5; at the time the budget was originally recorded, the income from Mr. Smith's substantial endowment was not foreseen. After the securities were transferred to the Library Endowment Fund and an estimate could be made of the additional revenues to be made available to the Library Operating Fund, the Library Board approved an amended budget to record the additional estimated revenues of $56,000 and to appropriate them for subscriptions to periodicals ($6,000) and purchases of books ($50,000). Entry 1 is required to record the amended budget of the Library Operating Fund (subsidiary ledger detail should be recorded, as described in Chapters 3 and 4; the detail is omitted from the illustration in this chapter):

1.	Estimated Revenues	56,000	
	Appropriations		56,000

The Library Operating Fund received $19,350 from the Library Endowment Fund:

2.	Cash	19,350	
	Operating Transfers In		19,350

The Library Operating Fund ordered subscriptions for periodicals expected to cost $6,030 and ordered books expected to cost $12,000:

3.	Encumbrances—19x6	18,030	
	Reserve for Encumbrances—19x6		18,030

The Library Operating Fund received $9,920 from the Library Endowment Fund. It also received and approved for payment invoices from magazine publishers ($6,050) and book publishers ($12,160), fulfilling all purchase orders recorded in Entry 3.

4a.	Cash	9,920	
	Operating Transfers In		9,920
4b.	Reserve for Encumbrances—19x6	18,030	
	Expenditures—19x6	18,210	
	Encumbrances—19x6		18,030
	Vouchers Payable		18,210

The Library ordered books expected to cost $37,000 in anticipation of receiving further distributions from the Library Endowment Fund.

5.	Encumbrances—19x6	37,000	
	Reserve for Encumbrances—19x6		37,000

The Library Operating Fund recorded a receivable in the amount of $28,650 from the Library Endowment Fund for bond interest earned, less amortization of bond premium.

6.	Due from Library Endowment Fund	28,650	
	Operating Transfers In		28,650

Although in an actual situation the entries illustrated above would be incorporated with entries recording other transactions and events affecting the Library Operating Fund, for the purposes of this chapter only the effect of illustrated entries on the closing process is shown below:

7. Appropriations	56,000	
Operating Transfers In	57,920	
Estimated Revenues		56,000
Expenditures—19x6		18,210
Encumbrances—19x6		37,000
Fund Balance		2,710

Financial statements prepared for the Library Operating Fund for inclusion in the City of Columbia's annual report for the period ending June 30, 19x6, would be similar in content and format to those illustrated in Chapters 3 and 4. For that reason, and because events and transactions not related to the interrelationships of the Library Operating Fund and the Library Endowment Fund are omitted from this illustration, no financial statements for the Library Operating Fund are presented here.

Accounting for Public Employee Retirement Systems

Assets held by public employee retirement systems (PERS) were estimated recently to amount to over $800 billion and are expected to total over $1 trillion before the end of this decade. PERS are sometimes called **pension trust funds.** When a PERS is considered to be part of a governmental reporting entity, its financial data are included in the combined financial statements and in the combining financial statements prepared for fiduciary funds accounted for on the full accrual basis.

Accounting for pension trust funds should be distinguished from the governmental unit's responsibility as an employer to account for expenditures, expenses, and liabilities related to pension plans, and to disclose in the Notes to the Financial Statements a long list of items specified in GASB statements. Reporting requirements are complex and are in a process of change. Further, reporting requirements vary depending on whether the plan is administered by a unit of the reporting entity or by another entity. Full treatment of accounting and reporting requirements for both governmental employers and PERS is considerably beyond the scope of this book. This section is intended to introduce the topic and present a general overview of current standards.

GASB *Statement No. 1,* issued in 1984, provides that pension accounting and reporting standards set forth in the NCGA *Statement 1,* NCGA *Statement 6,* or in FASB *Statement No. 35* may be used pending the issuance by the GASB of a statement or statements on pension accounting and financial reporting. GASB *Statement No. 5,* ''Disclosure of Pension Information by Public Employee Retirement Systems and State and Local Governmental Employers,'' issued in late 1986, superseded the disclosure requirements of NCGA *Statement 1,* NCGA *Statement 6,* and FASB *Statement No. 35.* GASB disclosure standards may be found in the GASB's *Codification of Governmental Accounting and Financial Reporting Standards* in Sections Pe5, Pe6, and P20. Accounting and financial reporting standards for PERS and governmental employers have not yet been issued in final form by the GASB. Those standards are expected to be similar to those set forth in GASB Codification Sections Pe5 and Pe6, which are the accounting and financial reporting standards presented in NCGA *Statement 6*. Accordingly, the illustrative case in this section of this chapter is based on Sections Pe5 and Pe6.

Summary of Requirements for PERS Financial Reporting

Objectives of PERS and Government Employer Financial Reporting. The GASB's disclosure standards are based on the conclusion that the primary objective of pension disclosures by PERS and governmental employers is to provide users with information needed to assess:

a. Funding status of a PERS on a going-concern basis.
b. Progress made in accumulating sufficient assets to pay benefits when due.
c. Whether employers are making actuarially determined contributions.

Requirements for PERS General Purpose Financial Statements. PERS annual financial statements should include:

a. A balance sheet showing total assets, liabilities, and the total actuarial present value of credited projected benefits (see Illustration 12–4).
b. A Statement of Revenues, Expenses, and Changes in Fund Balance (see Illustration 12–5).
c. Notes to the Financial Statements necessary for fair presentation, including information regarding the actuarially determined funding requirement and the actual contribution made.

Required Balance Sheet Disclosures

In the balance sheet, PERS investments in equity securities are required to be reported at cost, and investments in fixed-income securities are required to be reported at amortized cost. In each case, market values of investments are to be disclosed parenthetically (whereas *SFAS No. 35* requires pension plan investments to be reported at fair value at the reporting date). Depreciable assets of a PERS should be reported at cost less accumulated depreciation. Cash, accrued interest on investments, investments, and depreciable assets are shown in the assets section of a PERS balance sheet; assets are **not** classified as current and fixed. PERS liabilities, usually short term (benefits due but unpaid, other vouchers payable, accrued expenses, and payroll taxes payable), are reported as a deduction from PERS assets; the difference is captioned "Net Assets Available for Benefits." Total Fund Balance of a PERS is equal to the Net Assets Available for Benefits. GASB standards require the Fund Balance of a PERS to be segregated to show the (1) actuarial present value of projected benefits payable to current retirants and beneficiaries, (2) actuarial present value of projected benefits payable

---

ILLUSTRATION 12–4

NAME OF GOVERNMENT EMPLOYEE RETIREMENT SYSTEM
Illustrative Financial Statements
Balance Sheet
June 30, 19x1

Assets:
Cash		$ 30,849
Accrued interest and dividends		4,822,076
Investments:		
Bonds, at amortized cost (market value $85,492,049)	$105,591,446	
Common stocks, at cost (market value $30,206,177)	27,199,702	
Commercial paper and repurchase agreements, at cost (market value $11,264,000)	11,215,833	
Total investments		144,006,981
Equipment and fixtures, net of accumulated depreciation of $24,673		19,585
Total assets		148,879,491

Liabilities:
Accounts payable and accrued expenses		251,650
Net assets available for benefits		$148,627,841

Fund balance:
Actuarial present value of projected benefits payable to current retirants and beneficiaries	$ 32,240,515
Actuarial present value of projected benefits payable to terminated vested participants	3,610,310
Actuarial present value of credited projected benefits for active employees:	
Member contributions	38,786,483
Employer-financed portion	92,945,781
Total actuarial present value of credited projected benefits	167,583,089
Unfunded actuarial present value of credited projected benefits	(18,955,248)
Total fund balance	$148,627,841

See accompanying Notes to Financial Statements.

SOURCE: GASB Codification Sec. Pe5.902, Example 1.

to terminated vested participants, and (3) actuarial present value of credited projected benefits payable to active employees; any unfunded actuarial present value of credited **projected** benefits is to be shown in the Fund Balance section as a deduction from the total of items (1), (2), and (3). This required disclosure is in distinction to that of *SFAS No. 35*, which requires disclosure of only the actuarial present value of **accumulated** plan benefits. Illustration 12–4 shows a balance sheet designed to conform with GASB requirements.

In addition to the items described above, which are disclosed in the body of PERS financial statements, GASB standards require the following additional information to be disclosed in the notes to PERS financial statements[3]:

a. Plan Description.

b. Summary of Significant Accounting Policies and Plan Asset Matters.

c. Funding Status and Progress.

d. Contribution Required and Contribution Made.

e. Location of Required 10-Year Historical Trend Information.

Items *a, b, c,* and *d* above are reasonably self-explanatory; item *e* refers to the following 10-year historical trend information, which is required to be presented as supplementary information. (The distinction between display on the face of financial statements or disclosure in the Notes to the Financial Statements and disclosure as supplementary information is that the statements and notes are covered by the auditor's report, whereas supplementary information is ordinarily unaudited.)

Requirements for PERS Comprehensive Annual Financial Report.   In addition to the financial statements (Illustrations 12–4 and 12–5) and notes, comprehensive annual financial reports of a PERS should include as "required supplementary information" the 10-year trend information described below. The GASB defines required supplementary information as "statements, schedules, statistical data, or other information that are necessary to supplement, although not required to be a part of, the general purpose financial statements."[4] Ten-year historical trend information should be included in separately issued PERS reports immediately after the Notes to the Financial Statements. If 10 years of information is unavailable, information should be presented for as many years as are available. Required trend information is:

a. Net assets available for benefits (as of the same date as the pension benefit obligation and as valued for PERS balance sheet purposes), the pension benefit obligation, and the former expressed as a percentage of the latter; also unfunded [assets in excess of] pension benefit obligation, annual covered payroll, and the former expressed as a percentage of the latter.

b. Revenues by source (employer contributions, employee contributions, investment income, and other income) and expenses by type (benefit payments, administrative expenses, refunds of employee contributions, and other expenses). Except for agent multiple-employer PERS, employer contributions should be expressed both as dollar amounts and as percentages of annual covered payroll. The disclosure should state whether contributions were made in accordance

---

[3] GASB Codification Sec. P50 requires similar disclosures in the financial statements of all governmental employers that provide postemployment benefits, the cost of which is borne by the employer in whole or in part.

[4] GASB Codification Sec. Pe6.107, footnote 2.

ILLUSTRATION 12–5

NAME OF GOVERNMENT EMPLOYEE RETIREMENT SYSTEM
Illustrative Financial Statements
Statement of Revenues, Expenses, and
Changes in Fund Balance
For the Fiscal Year Ended June 30, 19x1

Operating revenues:	
Member contributions	$ 8,009,400
Employer contributions	14,126,292
Investment income	14,262,845
Total operating revenues	36,398,537
Operating expenses:	
Annuity benefits	3,134,448
Disability benefits	287,590
Refunds to terminated employees	2,057,265
Administrative expenses	580,219
Total operating expenses	6,059,522
Net operating income	30,339,015
Fund balance, July 1, 19x0	118,288,826
Fund balance, June 30, 19x1	$148,627,841

See accompanying Notes to Financial Statements.

SOURCE: GASB Codification Sec. Pe5.902, Example 2.

with actuarial requirements. If contributions actually made for particular years differed from actuarial or legal requirements, both the contribution made and the contribution requirement should be presented for those years.

The timing, nature, and total dollar effect of any changes in actuarial assumptions, benefit provisions, actuarial funding methods, accounting policies, or other factors that significantly affect the information presented in *a* and *b* should be disclosed for the year in which the changes are made.[5]

PERS—Illustrative Case

Assume the Government Employee Retirement System whose financial statements for the year ended June 30, 19x1, are shown as Illustrations 12–4 and 12–5, started that year with the Balance Sheet shown as Illustration 12–6. During the year ended June 30, 19x1, the following events and transactions are assumed, for the sake of illustration, to have taken place:

---

[5] GASB Codification Sec. Pe6.132.

ILLUSTRATION 12–6

GOVERNMENT EMPLOYEE RETIREMENT SYSTEM
Balance Sheet
June 30, 19x0

Assets:
Cash	$ 28,569
Accrued Interest Receivable	2,507,612

Investments:
Bonds at amortized cost (market value $66,347,590)	71,603,976
Common stocks at cost (market value $33,703,650)	31,957,205
Commercial paper and repurchase agreements, at cost (market value $12,660,205)	12,570,401
Equipment and fixtures, net of accumulated depreciation of $17,673	22,644
Total Assets	118,690,407

Liabilities:
Accounts Payable and Accrued Expenses	401,581
Net Assets Available for Benefits	$118,288,826

Fund Balance:
Actuarial present value of projected benefits:
Payable to current retirants and beneficiaries	$ 26,492,185
Payable to terminated vested participants	2,980,295

Actuarial present value of credited projected benefits for active employees:
Member contributions	31,841,283
Employer-financed portion	76,241,701
Total Actuarial Present Value of Credited Projected Benefits	137,555,464
Unfunded actuarial present value of credited projected benefits	(19,266,638)
Total Fund Balance	$118,288,826

Accrued interest receivable as of June 30, 19x0, was collected:

1. Cash	2,507,612	
Accrued Interest Receivable		2,507,612

Member contributions in the amount of $8,009,400 and employer contributions in the amount of $14,126,292 were received in cash:

2. Cash	22,135,692	
Revenues—Member Contributions		8,009,400
Revenues—Employer Contributions		14,126,292

Annuity benefits in the amount of $3,134,448 and disability benefits in the amount of $287,590 were recorded as liabilities:

3. Annuity Benefits	3,134,448	
Disability Benefits	287,590	
Accounts Payable and Accrued Expenses		3,422,038

Accounts payable and accrued expenses paid in cash amounted to $3,571,969:

4. Accounts Payable and Accrued Expenses	3,571,969	
Cash		3,571,969

Terminated employees whose benefits were not vested were refunded $2,057,265 in cash:

5. Refunds to Terminated Employees	2,057,265	
Cash		2,057,265

Investment income received in cash amounted to $9,440,769; in addition, $4,822,076 interest income was accrued at year-end:

6. Cash	9,440,769	
Accrued Interest Receivable	4,822,076	
Investment Income		14,262,845

Commercial paper and repurchase agreements carried at a cost of $1,354,568 matured, and cash in that amount was received:

7. Cash	1,354,568	
Commercial Paper and Repurchase Agreements		1,354,568

Common stocks carried at a cost of $6,293,867 were sold for that amount; $1,536,364 was reinvested in common stocks and the remainder in bonds. An additional amount of $29,229,967 was also invested in bonds:

8a. Cash	6,293,867	
Common Stocks		6,293,867
8b. Bonds	33,987,470	
Common Stocks	1,536,364	
Cash		35,523,834

Administrative expenses for the year totaled $568,219 all paid in cash:

9. Administrative Expenses	568,219	
Cash		568,219

Equipment costing $11,059, on which depreciation in the amount of $5,000 had accumulated, was sold for $6,059 cash:

10. Accumulated Depreciation—Equipment	5,000	
Cash	6,059	
Equipment		11,059

Equipment costing $15,000 was purchased:

11. Equipment	15,000	
Cash		15,000

Depreciation expenses for the year amounted to $12,000 (charge to Administrative Expenses):

12. Administrative Expenses	12,000	
Accumulated Depreciation—		
Equipment		12,000

Nominal accounts for the year were closed:

13. Revenues—Member Contributions 8,009,400
    Revenues—Employer Contributions 14,126,292
    Investment Income 14,262,845
        Annuity Benefits 3,134,448
        Disability Benefits 287,590
        Refunds to Terminated Employees 2,057,265
        Administrative Expenses 580,219
        Net Operating Income 30,339,015

Information from the actuary indicated that the following changes in the components of Fund Balance as of June 30, 19x1, should be recorded:

14. Net Operating Income 30,339,015
    Actuarial Present Value of Projected Benefits Payable
        to:
            Current Retirants and
                Beneficiaries 5,748,330
            Terminated Vested Participants 630,015
    Actuarial Present Value of Credited
        Projected Benefits for Active
        Employees:
            Member Contributions 6,945,200
            Employer-Financed Portion..................... 16,704,080
    Unfunded Actuarial Present Value of Credited Projected
        Benefits 311,390

Entries 1 through 14 result in the financial statements shown as Illustrations 12–4 and 12–5, when applied to the accounts existing at the beginning of the period as shown in Illustration 12–6.

Summary of GASB Requirements for Government Employers' Financial Reporting

Requirements If PERS Is Component of Employer Reporting Entity. GASB standards require government employer entities to incorporate in their annual financial statements the financial statements of a PERS if the PERS is considered part of the reporting entity pursuant to GASB Codification Section 2100. The nature and extent of the employer's obligation to provide resources for PERS contributions may have a significant impact on the employer's financial position.[6] The note and statistical requirements enumerated in the paragraphs above are also

---

[6] The GASB has issued two exposure drafts of proposed statements that would establish revised standards for accounting for pensions by state and local governmental employers and financial reporting for defined benefit pension plans, respectively. The latter proposed statement also specifies certain note disclosures for defined contribution plans. The controversial nature of some provisions of these proposals could lead to further changes, as well as further delay, in issuing final statements. When final statements have been issued the publisher will provide an update bulletin to adopters of the Tenth Edition of this text. For further information, see *Exposure Draft*, Proposed Statement of Governmental Accounting Standards Board, "Accounting for Pensions by State and Local Governmental Employers" (Norwalk, Conn., 1994), and *Exposure Draft*, Proposed Statement of Governmental Accounting Standards Board, "Financial Reporting for Defined Benefit Pension Plans and Note Disclosures for Defined Contribution Plans" (Norwalk, Conn., 1994).

applicable to employer reporting, except note disclosure may be somewhat less detailed.

When PERS financial statements are incorporated in the employer's combined statements, PERS balance sheets should be formatted in the same manner as those of the other funds and component units. In the combined balance sheet, the PERS Fund Balance is to be shown as a single figure (captioned Reserved for Employees' Retirement System). Details required to be shown in the Fund Balance section of a PERS balance sheet are to be shown in the notes to the employer's GPFS (and in the PERS statements included in the employer's CAFR).

Requirements If PERS Is Not Component of Employer Reporting Entity. State and local government employers liable for making contributions to a single-employer PERS not considered to be a part of the employer reporting entity pursuant to GASB Codification Section 2100 are required to report in their GPFS all the note disclosures previously described and to report in their CAFRs all the statistical data previously itemized.

Employer Reporting of Contributions. Employers shall report as an expenditure of governmental funds and as an expense of proprietary funds the employer contribution amount developed by one of the actuarial cost methods specified in GASB Codification Section Pe6.511–.519, regardless of whether such amount has actually been contributed. To the extent the amount has not been or will not be funded by a governmental fund, the unfunded amount shall be reported in the General Long-Term Debt Account Group; amounts that have not been or will not be funded by proprietary funds or nonexpendable trust funds shall be shown as liabilities of those funds.[7]

Exchanges of Fixed-Income Securities

Because of legal restrictions on the nature of investments that may be made by governmental entities and the huge amounts of money flowing into PERS each year, their investments tend to be invested in much larger blocks of securities than are commonly traded. Accordingly, it is common for blocks of securities to be exchanged by pension fund investment managers for other blocks of securities in order to improve yields, change maturities, or change the quality of a portion of the investment portfolio. Notably absent from the list of reasons for exchanges of blocks of securities is the attempt to realize a gain or loss on the investments traded. The general rule in accounting is that gains or losses on sales of assets should be recognized at the time of sale in conformity with the completed transaction method of accounting. Pension fund investment managers argue, however, that application of this rule to their transactions does not reflect the reasons for the transactions. In recognition of this argument, GASB standards include the provision that if the four criteria listed below are met, a PERS may elect to use the deferral and amortization method of accounting for gains and losses on the exchange of fixed-income securities (frequently called *bond swaps*) instead of the completed transaction method. The deferral and amortization method defers the

---

[7] See footnote 6 of this chapter.

gain or loss at the time of sale and amortizes the deferral over the remaining time until maturity of the security sold or the security purchased, whichever is shorter. As an alternative to immediate amortization, the cost of the security sold may be passed through to the security purchased. If the cost pass-through method is elected, only two exchanges in a stream may be deferred. The third exchange in a stream must be accounted for on the completed transaction method or on the strict deferral and amortization method. The four criteria that define an exchange are:

1. Both the sale and the purchase must be planned simultaneously and each half executed conditioned on execution of the other.
2. Both the sale and the purchase must be made on the same day, although settlement of the two transactions may occur on different dates.
3. The sale and purchase must result in an increase in the net yield to maturity and/or an improvement in the quality of the bond held.
4. The purchase must involve an investment-graded bond that is better rated, equally rated, or rated no worse than one investment grade lower than the bond sold.

Required Disclosures for Other Postemployment Benefits (OPEB)

Rapid escalation of health care costs over the last two decades has created a significant unfunded obligation for many governmental units that provide postemployment health benefits for retirees. Unlike pension plans that are funded and accounted for actuarially, other postemployment benefits (OPEB) traditionally have been funded and accounted for on a pay-as-you-go-basis. Nevertheless, a minority of governmental employers advance fund their postemployment health care benefits on an actuarially determined basis, either separately or through a defined benefit pension plan or other plan that provides retirement income. Others set aside assets for future OPEB benefits but do not fund them on an actuarially determined basis.

Since unfunded OPEB benefits may represent a material liability, GASB standards require certain disclosures by governmental employers that provide OPEB.[8] The Notes to the Financial Statements should provide, at a minimum, the following disclosures, either separately for each OPEB or in the aggregate for all OPEB provided.[9]

---

[8] GASB Codification Secs. P50.105-.107. The GASB has also initiated a project on recognition and measurement of OPEB expenditures/expenses and related liabilities. Although this project is continuing, GASB has issued an exposure draft of an interim statement that would require defined benefit pension plans that administer postemployment healthcare plans to present certain financial statements for these plans. See *Exposure Draft*, Proposed Statement of the Governmental Accounting Standards Board, "Financial Reporting for Postemployment Healthcare Plans Administered by Defined Benefit Pension Plans" (Norwalk, Conn., 1994). If a standard on OPEB recognition and measurement is issued, the publisher will provide an update to adopters of the Tenth Edition of this text.

[9] GASB Codification Sec. P50.105.

a. Description of the OPEB; employee groups covered; eligibility requirements; and the employer and participant obligations to contribute, quantified in some manner.

b. Description of the statutory, contractual, or other authority under which OPEB provisions and obligations to contribute are established.

c. Description of the accounting and financing or funding policies followed.

d. Expenditure/expense information. If OPEB are financed on a pay-as-you-go basis, the employer should disclose expenditures/expenses recognized during the period by the employer (net of participant contributions) and the number of participants currently eligible to receive benefits. If OPEB are advance funded on an actuarially determined basis, the employer should disclose the number of active plan participants, the employer's actuarially required and actual contributions for the period (net of participant contributions), the amount of net assets available for the OPEB, and the actuarial accrued liability and unfunded actuarial accrued liability.

e. Description (and dollar effect, if measurable) of any significant matters that affect the comparability of the disclosures with those for the previous period.

f. Any additional information that the employer believes will help users assess the nature and magnitude of the cost of the employer's commitment to provide OPEB.

Employers that advance fund an OPEB through a pension plan have the option of following required employer pension disclosures, discussed previously in this chapter, or the OPEB disclosures just listed.

Illustrative Combined Financial Statements

The five combined financial statements required by GASB standards are listed in Chapter 1. A Combined Balance Sheet—All Fund Types and Account Groups and Discretely Presented Component Units is presented in Illustration 2–1. Combined Statements of Revenues, Expenditures, and Changes and Fund Balances, both GAAP basis and budget and actual, for governmental funds (and expendable trust funds) are illustrated in Chapter 3 (Illustrations 3–1 and 3–2). The two required combined financial statements for proprietary funds and nonexpendable trust funds are the Combined Statement of Revenues, Expenses, and Changes in Fund Equity—All Proprietary Fund Types, Similar Trust Funds, and Discretely Presented Component Units (Illustration 12–7), and the Combined Statement of Cash Flows—All Proprietary Fund Types, and Discretely Presented Component Units (Illustration 12–8). The GASB's requirement that proprietary and certain trust funds report their operating activities and cash flows in the statements shown in Illustrations 12–7 and 12–8 is consistent with FASB standards that require similar business enterprises to provide an income statement and a statement of cash flows. It will be noted that pension funds are included along with nonexpendable trust funds in the combined operating statement (Illustration 12–7), but are excluded from the statement of cash flows (Illustration 12–8). GASB standards do

ILLUSTRATION 12–7

NAME OF GOVERNMENTAL UNIT
Combined Statement of Revenues, Expenses, and Changes in Fund Equity—All Proprietary Fund Types, Similar Trust Funds, and Discretely Presented Component Units
Year Ended December 31, 19x2

Primary Government

	Proprietary Fund Types		Fiduciary Fund Types		Totals—Memorandum Only	Component Units	Totals—Memorandum Only
	Enterprise	Internal Service	Nonexpendable Trust	Pension Trust	Primary Government	Component Units	Reporting Entity
Operating Revenues:							
Charges for Services	$ 650,333	$109,817	—	—	$ 760,150	$1,189,631	$ 1,949,781
Interest	—	—	—	$ 20,150	20,150	—	20,150
Contributions	—	—	—	60,686	60,686	—	60,686
Total Operating Revenues	650,333	109,817	—	80,836	840,986	1,189,631	2,030,617
Operating Expenses:							
Cost of Services	357,305	72,999	—	—	430,304	1,018,008	1,448,312
General and Administrative	91,226	6,350	—	2,500	100,076	181,856	281,932
Depreciation	123,500	25,050	—	—	148,550	460,102	608,652
Benefit Payments	—	—	—	21,000	21,000	—	21,000
Refunds	15,225	—	—	10,520	25,745	—	25,745
Total Operating Expenses	587,256	104,399	—	34,020	725,675	1,659,966	2,385,641
Operating Income (Loss)	63,077	5,418	—	46,816	115,311	(470,335)	(355,024)

Nonoperating Revenues (Expenses):							
Operating Grants	55,000	—	—	—	55,000	410,000	465,000
Net Income from Joint Venture	145,000	—	—	—	145,000	—	145,000
Interest Revenue	8,830	—	10,790	—	19,620	82,522	102,142
Interest Expense and Fiscal Charges	(62,988)	—	—	—	(62,988)	(248,320)	(311,308)
Tax Revenues	—	—	—	—	—	100,000	100,000
Total Nonoperating Revenue (Expenses)	145,842	—	10,790	—	156,632	344,202	500,834
Income (Loss) before Operating Transfers	208,919	5,418	10,790	46,816	271,943	(126,133)	145,810
Operating Transfers In	—	65,000	—	—	65,000	—	65,000
Operating Transfers from Primary Government	—	—	—	—	—	175,000	175,000
Operating Transfers Out	(56,740)	—	(10,790)	—	(67,530)	—	(67,530)
Net Income	152,179	70,418	—	46,816	269,413	48,867	318,280
Fund Equity—Beginning	5,420,735	59,382	296,198	1,408,639	7,184,954	9,445,032	16,629,986
Contributions—Capital Grants	672,666	—	—	—	672,666	400,000	1,072,666
Fund Equity—Ending	$6,245,580	$129,800	$296,198	$1,455,455	$8,127,033	$9,893,899	$18,020,932

SOURCE: Based on Example 4, GASB Codification Sec. 2200.906.

ILLUSTRATION 12–8

NAME OF GOVERNMENTAL UNIT
Combined Statement of Cash Flows—All Proprietary Fund Types, and Discretely Presented Component Units
Year Ended December 31, 19x2

| | Primary Government | | | | | |
| | Proprietary Fund Types | | Fiduciary Fund Type | Totals—Memorandum Only | | Totals—Memorandum Only |
	Enterprise	Internal Service	Nonexpendable Trust	Primary Government	Component Units	Reporting Entity
Cash Flows from Operating Activities:						
Cash Received from Customers	$ 605,000	$110,410	—	$ 715,410	$ 1,220,000	$ 1,935,410
Cash Paid to Suppliers and Employees	(450,000)	(95,000)	—	(545,000)	(1,150,000)	(1,695,000)
Net Cash Provided by Operating Activities	155,000	15,410	—	170,410	70,000	240,410
Cash Flows from Noncapital Financing Activities:						
Operating Grants	55,000	—	—	55,000	410,000	465,000
Operating Transfers in from Other Funds	—	65,000	—	65,000	—	65,000
Operating Transfers out to Other Funds	(56,740)	—	$(10,790)	(67,530)	—	(67,530)
Operating Transfer from Primary Government	—	—	—	—	175,000	175,000
Net Cash Provided (Used) by (for) Noncapital Financing Activities	(1,740)	65,000	(10,790)	52,470	585,000	637,470
Cash Flows from Capital and Related Financing Activities:						
Purchase of Capital Assets	(700,000)	(70,000)	—	(770,000)	(200,000)	(970,000)
Principal Payments—Capital Leases	(81,000)	—	—	(81,000)	—	(81,000)
Interest Payments—Capital Leases	(62,988)	—	—	(62,988)	—	(62,988)
Interest Payments—Revenue Bonds	—	—	—	—	(248,320)	(248,320)
Contributions from State Government	672,666	—	—	672,666	400,000	1,072,666
Net Cash Provided (Used) by (for) Capital and Related Financing Activities	(171,322)	(70,000)	—	(241,322)	(48,320)	(289,642)

Cash Flows from Investing Activities:

Receipt of Interest	8,830	—	10,790	19,620	82,522	102,142
Net Income from Joint Venture	145,000	—	—	145,000	—	145,000
Net Cash Provided by Investing Activities	153,830	—	10,790	164,620	82,522	247,142
Net Increase (Decrease) in Cash and Cash Equivalents	135,768	10,410	—	146,178	689,202	835,380
Cash and Cash Equivalents at Beginning of Year	121,268	19,290	15,300	155,858	440,798	596,656
Cash and Cash Equivalents at End of Year	$ 257,036	$ 29,700	$ 15,300	$ 302,036	$ 1,130,000	$ 1,432,036
Reconciliation of Operating Income to Net Cash Provided by Operating Activities:						
Operating Income (Loss)	$ 63,077	$ 5,418	-0-	$ 68,495	$ (470,335)	$ (401,840)
Adjustments to Reconcile Operating Income to Net Cash Provided by Operating Activities:						
Depreciation	123,500	25,050	—	148,550	460,102	608,652
Decrease (Increase) in Investments	(9,812)	—	—	(9,812)	62,115	52,303
Decrease (Increase) in Accounts Receivable	(15,315)	(7,795)	—	(23,110)	29,116	6,006
Increase (Decrease) in Accounts Payable	(6,450)	(7,263)	—	(13,713)	(10,998)	(24,711)
Total Adjustments	91,923	9,992	-0-	101,915	540,335	642,250
Net Cash Provided by Operating Activities	$ 155,000	$ 15,410	-0-	$ 170,410	$ 70,000	$ 240,410

Source: Format based on GASB Codification Sec. 2450.901.

not require PERS to present a statement of cash flows, but do not preclude them from doing so.[10]

Selected References

American Institute of Certified Public Accountants. *Audits of State and Local Governmental Units,* revised. New York, 1993.

Cary, William L., and Craig B. Bright. *The Developing Law of Endowment Funds: "The Law and the Lore" Revisited.* New York: The Ford Foundation, 1974.

Financial Accounting Standards Board. *Statement of Financial Accounting Standards No. 35,* "Accounting and Reporting by Defined Benefit Pension Plans." Norwalk, Conn., 1980, as amended by *SFAS No. 59* (1982) and *SFAS No. 75* (1983).

Governmental Accounting Standards Board. *Codification of Governmental Accounting and Financial Reporting Standards as of June 30, 1993.* Norwalk, Conn., 1993.

Questions

12–1. Four types of funds are classified as "fiduciary funds." *(a)* Two of the four are to be accounted for in a manner similar to governmental funds. Name these two fund types, and explain why the modified accrual basis is appropriate for their use. *(b)* Two of the four are to be accounted for on the full accrual basis in a manner similar to proprietary funds. Name these two fund types, and explain why the full accrual basis is appropriate for their use.

12–2. Why should a fund be established to account for trust principal and a separate fund established to account for trust income? Is this primarily to create employment for accountants?

12–3. If Nonexpendable Trust Funds are accounted for in a manner similar to proprietary funds, why is the Fund Balance account used as the equity account rather than the Contributions from Trustor and Retained Earnings accounts?

12–4. Why are assets received by a governmental unit to be held as the principal, or corpus, of a nonexpendable trust recorded at fair value rather than historical cost?

12–5. Why is it not appropriate to classify a public employee retirement system (PERS) as either a nonexpendable trust fund or an expendable trust fund?

12–6. "Budgetary accounts generally are needed for both expendable and nonexpendable trust funds." Do you agree or disagree? Why?

12–7. In accounting for a testamentary trust, there is a problem of separating the items that should be charged against principal from the items that should be charged against income. You are to state whether each of the following items should be charged against principal or against income, assuming the older rule of law (cash basis) is to be followed. Give any explanation you may consider necessary in connection with your answers.

    a. Federal estate taxes paid by trustee.

    b. Interest paid by trustee on mortgage on real estate owned by trust.

    c. Depreciation of building owned by trust.

    d. Legal fees for collection of rent on building owned by trust.

    e. Special assessment for street improvement levied on real estate belonging to trust.

    f. Amortization of premium on bonds that have been purchased by the testator.

---

[10] GASB Codification Sec. 2450.102.

    g. Loss on sale of trust investments.

    h. Taxes on vacant city lots held by trustee as part of trust principal.

(AICPA, adapted)

12–8. Refer to Question 12–7. Classify each of the eight items as to whether it should be charged against principal or against income, assuming the applicable trust law allows the use of full accrual accounting.

12–9. What is the distinction between the actuarial present value of *projected benefits* and the actuarial present value of *accumulated benefits?* If you were a member of a public employee retirement system, which figure would you find more useful in determining the ability of the PERS to meet future pension obligations?

12–10. In addition to the items required to be disclosed in the body of PERS financial statements, what additional information is required by GASB standards to be disclosed in the notes to the PERS financial statements?

12–11. Explain the differences in GASB financial reporting requirements for *government employers* (not the PERS) if *(a)* the PERS is a component of the employer reporting entity and *(b)* the PERS is not a component of the employer reporting entity.

12–12. If a government has not contributed to a PERS the entire amount developed by an accepted actuarial cost method but has contributed the entire amount appropriated by the governing body, is there any liability to be disclosed in the financial statements? If not, why not? If so, in what statement or statements should the liability be disclosed?

12–13. Is it ever in conformity with generally accepted accounting principles to defer a loss on the exchange of fixed-income securities? Explain your answer.

12–14. What disclosures are employers who provide postemployment health care benefits required to make in the notes to their financial statements?

Exercises and Problems

12–1. Utilizing the annual report obtained for Exercise 1–1, follow the instructions below and on the next page.

    a. General. Are all fiduciary funds shown in a single combining statement in the annual report, or are nonexpendable trust funds and retirement systems reported with proprietary funds and other fiduciary funds reported with governmental funds?

        Does the report state the basis of accounting used for trust and agency funds? Are all funds in this category accounted for on the same basis? If so, is the financial statement presentation consistent with the stated basis? If the basis is not stated, analyze the statements to determine which basis is used—full accrual, modified accrual, or cash basis. Are the bases used consistent with those required by GASB standards discussed in the text? Are nonexpendable assets and expendable assets accounted for in separate funds? If not, are Fund Balance accounts for each category kept separate?

    b. Trust Funds. Does the report contain a schedule or list of investments of trust funds? Are the investments identified as belonging to specific trust funds or merely to "trust funds"? Does the report disclose gains or losses realized on sales of investments during the year? Does the report disclose net earnings on investments during the year?

        If nonexpendable trust funds own depreciable assets, is depreciation taken? If so, is depreciation considered a charge against principal or against income? Are any trust funds operated as profit-seeking businesses? If so, does the annual report contain income statements for the businesses?

c. *Pension Trust Funds, or PERS.* Are the government employees covered by a retirement fund operated by a local government, by the state, by the federal Social Security Administration, or by two or more of these?

     If the government operates one or more retirement funds, or retirement systems, are the retirement fund financial statements accompanied by a separate audit report, or are they included in the auditor's opinion accompanying the other funds? Are the retirement fund statements accompanied by an actuary's report? If not, is reference made to the actuary's report in the balance sheet, in notes to the financial statements, or in the auditor's report? Does the retirement fund have an "actuarial deficiency" or an "unfunded prior service liability"? If so, is this condition explained in the notes accompanying the statement?

     Are the financial statements in the format shown in Illustrations 12–4, 12–5, and 12–6? Is all the pension information specified in GASB standards discussed in Chapter 12 presented in the notes to the financial statements? Are the required 10-year comparative summaries presented as supplementary information in the comprehensive annual financial report?

12–2. Write the numbers 1 through 10 on a sheet of paper. Beside each number write the letter corresponding with the best answer to each of the following questions.

     1. Which of the following is *not* a fiduciary fund?
        a. Nonexpendable trust fund.
        b. Expendable trust fund.
        c. Internal service fund.
        d. Pension trust fund.

     2. Which of the following trust funds requires a careful distinction between principal (or corpus) and income in accounting for investment income and gains and losses?
        a. Expendable trust funds.
        b. Nonexpendable trust funds.
        c. Pension trust funds.
        d. All of the above are correct; that is, all of the above require a distinction between principal and income.

     Items 3 and 4 are based on the following information for the Arts Endowment Fund (a nonexpendable trust fund) of the Town of Braxton.

Dividend income from stock investments	$25,000
Interest received in cash from bond investments	24,000
Amortization of bond premium during the period	800
Realized gains on sale of stocks and bonds	1,200

3. Under current GAAP, which of the following represents the amount of *change* in the Fund Balance account of the Arts Endowment Fund for the period assuming, as shown in item 4 below, all appropriate transfers out were made to the Arts Acquisition Fund—an expendable trust fund?
   a. Increase of $800.
   b. Increase of $1,200, if realized gains must be retained in the Endowment Fund.
   c. Increase of $2,000, if realized gains must be retained in the Endowment Fund.
   d. Increase of $51,000, if realized gains must be retained in the Endowment Fund.

4. What amount would be debited to Operating Transfers Out for the period, assuming realized gains must be retained in the Endowment Fund?
   a. $51,000.
   b. $49,800.
   c. $48,200.
   d. Some other amount.

5. Which of the following fiduciary fund types is most likely to require formal legislative approval (appropriation procedures) for expenditures?
   a. Expendable trust funds.
   b. Nonexpendable trust funds.
   c. Pension trust funds.
   d. Agency funds.

6. A Statement of Cash Flows is required by current GASB standards for which of the following fiduciary fund types?
   a. Expendable trust funds.
   b. Nonexpendable trust funds.
   c. Pension trust funds.
   d. Agency funds.

7. Regarding financial reporting by governmental employers and public employee retirement systems (PERS), which of the following is a correct statement?
   a. Expenditures and/or expenses incurred by governmental unit employers need not be reported separately in governmental and proprietary funds if the PERS is determined to be a part of the governmental reporting entity.
   b. Expenditures and/or expenses incurred by governmental unit employers, and other pension-related financial information pertaining to employers, should be distinguished from financial information required to be reported by the PERS.
   c. When a PERS is considered to be part of a governmental reporting entity, its financial information need not be reported in the Fiduciary Funds column of the Combined Balance Sheet.
   d. Disclosure of PERS financial information is required only if the net assets available for benefits are less than the pension benefit obligation.

8. GASB's disclosure standards assume that the primary objective of pension disclosures by PERS and governmental employers is to provide users with which of the
following information?

   a. Funding status of a PERS on a going-concern basis.

   b. Progress made in accumulating sufficient assets to pay benefits when due.

   c. Whether employers are making actuarially determined contributions.

   d. All of the above are correct.

Items 9 and 10 are based on the following information:

Elm City contributes to and administers a single-employer defined benefit pension plan
on behalf of its covered employees. The plan is accounted for in a pension trust fund.
Actuarially determined employer contribution requirements and contributions actually
made for the past three years, along with the percentage of annual covered payroll, were as
follows:

	Contribution Made		Actuarial Requirement	
	Amount	*Percent*	*Amount*	*Percent*
19x9	$11,000	26	$11,000	26
19x8	5,000	12	10,000	24
19x7	None	None	8,000	20

9. What account should be credited in the pension trust fund to record the 19x9
employer contribution of $11,000?

   a. Revenues Control.

   b. Other Financing Sources Control.

   c. Due from Special Revenue Fund.

   d. Pension Benefit Obligation.

10. To record the 19x9 pension contribution of $11,000, what account would be debit-
ed in the governmental fund used in connection with employer pension contributions?

    a. Other Financing Uses Control.

    b. Expenditures Control.

    c. Expenses Control.

    d. Due to Pension Fund.

(Items 9 and 10, AICPA, adapted)

12–3. A description of the "Fiduciary Funds" taken from a recent annual report of the
City of Eugene, Oregon, are shown below; and the "Combining Balance Sheet—All Trust
and Agency Funds," "Combining Statement of Revenues, Expenditures and Changes in
Fund Balances—All Expendable Trust Funds," "Combining Statement of Revenues, Ex-
penses, and Change in Fund Balances—All Nonexpendable Trust Funds," "Combining
Statement of Cash Flows—Nonexpendable Trust Funds," and "Deferred Compensation
Agency Fund, Statement of Changes in Assets and Liabilities," taken from that report are
reproduced on the following pages.

Required

a. Review the statements for the City of Eugene. Do the statements appear to conform with GASB standards discussed in Chapter 12? Explain your answer.

b. Do all the funds classified as "Nonexpendable Trust Funds" and "Expendable Trust Funds" appear to be properly classified? Why or why not? Discuss any alternative classifications that appear reasonable to you, based on the information in Chapters 2 through 12.

FIDUCIARY FUNDS

Expendable Trust Funds

Library Trust Fund

To account for contributions from private donors to support the public library.

Parks and Recreation Trust Fund

To account for contributions from private donors to support City-owned parks and recreation facilities.

Low Income Housing Trust Fund

To account for contributions from private and public donors and proceeds from the sale of existing property holdings to support the public interest housing acquisition program.

Municipal Arts Trust Fund

To account for funds provided by private and public donors for the acquisition of works of art.

Nonexpendable Trust Funds

Community Development Trust Fund

To account for monies provided by grants from the U.S. Department of Housing and Urban Development, including the Community Development Block Grant, to be used for the purpose of subsidizing loans to individuals and businesses.

Housing Rehabilitation Trust Fund

To account for monies provided by grants from the U.S. Department of Housing and Urban Development to be used for the purpose of rehabilitating residential real property.

Urban Renewal Agency Trust Fund

To account for development loans to revitalize downtown Eugene.

Urban Renewal Agency Riverfront Trust Fund

To account for development loans to construct the Riverfront Research Park.

Agency Fund

Deferred Compensation

To account for assets and liabilities of the City's deferred compensation plan.

CITY OF EUGENE, OREGON
Combining Balance Sheet
All Trust and Agency Funds
June 30, 1992
(amounts in dollars)

	Expendable Trust					Nonexpendable Trust		Agency	
	Library	Parks and Recreation	Municipal Arts	Low Income Housing	Housing Rehabilitation	Community Development	Urban Renewal Agency	Deferred Compensation	Total
Assets									
Cash and investments	416,516	238,615	33,386	113,737	36,867	2,064,224	873,368	0	3,776,713
Investment in deferred compensation benefits	0	0	0	0	0	0	0	18,331,787	18,331,787
Receivables:									
Interest	355	188	30	96	30	3,915	734	0	5,348
Loans:									
Current	0	0	0	0	8,496	422,926	32,141	0	463,563
Noncurrent	0	0	0	0	88,790	6,518,311	795,869	0	7,402,970
Allowance for uncollectibles	0	0	0	0	(2,103)	(364,947)	(24,602)	0	(391,652)
Due from other funds	0	0	0	0	0	83,955	0	0	83,955
Land	0	0	0	368,435	0	0	0	0	368,435
Total assets	416,871	238,803	33,416	482,268	132,080	8,728,384	1,677,510	18,331,787	30,041,119
Liabilities and Fund Balances									
Liabilities									
Accounts payable	1,437	35,961	0	0	0	0	0	0	37,398
Wages payable	0	302	0	0	0	0	0	0	302
Deposits	0	0	0	0	0	4,923	0	0	4,923
Due to other governments	0	0	0	0	0	8,924	0	0	8,924
Deferred revenue	0	0	0	0	0	1,139,162	0	0	1,139,162
Deferred compensation benefits payable	0	0	0	0	0	0	0	18,331,787	18,331,787
Total Liabilities	1,437	36,263	0	0	0	1,153,009	0	18,331,787	19,522,496
Fund Balances									
Reserved for loans	0	0	0	0	0	7,575,375	1,677,510	0	9,252,885
Unreserved	415,434	202,540	33,416	482,268	132,080	0	0	0	1,265,738
Total Fund Balances	415,434	202,540	33,416	482,268	132,080	7,575,375	1,677,510	0	10,518,623
Total Liabilities and Fund Balances	416,871	238,803	33,416	482,268	132,080	8,728,384	1,677,510	18,331,787	30,041,119

CITY OF EUGENE, OREGON
Combining Statement of Revenues, Expenditures, and Changes in Fund Balances
All Expendable Trust Funds
For the Fiscal Year-End June 30, 1992
(amounts in dollars)

	Library	Parks and Recreation	Municipal Arts	Low Income Housing	Total
Revenues					
Charges for services	0	1,304	1,300	550	3,154
Miscellaneous revenues	66,040	66,090	2,197	6,299	140,626
Total revenues	66,040	67,394	3,497	6,849	143,780
Expenditures					
Current—departmental:					
Planning and development	0	0	0	25,000	25,000
Library	58,277	0	0	0	58,277
Parks, recreation and cultural services	0	16,021	11,218	0	27,239
Capital outlay	0	130,574	0	0	130,574
Total expenditures	58,277	146,595	11,218	25,000	241,090
Excess (deficiency) of revenues over expenditures	7,763	(79,201)	(7,721)	(18,151)	(97,310)
Fund balances, June 30, 1991	407,671	281,741	41,137	500,419	1,230,968
Fund balances, June 30, 1992	415,434	202,540	33,416	482,268	1,133,658

CITY OF EUGENE, OREGON
Combining Statement of Revenues, Expenses and Changes in Fund Balances
All Nonexpendable Trust Funds
For Fiscal Year-End June 30, 1992
(amounts in dollars)

	Housing Rehabilitation	Community Development	Urban Renewal Agency	Total
Operating revenues				
Intergovernmental revenue	0	669,838	0	669,838
Charges for services	5,727	256,050	42,224	304,001
Miscellaneous	0	74,560	0	74,560
Total operating revenues	5,727	1,000,448	42,224	1,048,399
Operating expenses				
Loans forgiven	0	12,671	0	12,671
Bad debts	0	0	14,786	14,786
Total operating expenses	0	12,671	14,786	27,457
Operating income	5,727	987,777	27,438	1,020,942
Nonoperating revenues				
Interest revenue	2,510	62,649	48,354	113,513
Total nonoperating revenues	2,510	62,649	48,354	113,513
Income before operating transfers	8,237	1,050,426	75,792	1,134,455
Operating transfers in	0	112,989	304,100	417,089
Operating transfers out	0	(219,722)	0	(219,722)
Net Income	8,237	943,693	379,892	1,331,822
Fund balances, June 30, 1991	123,843	6,631,682	1,297,618	8,053,143
Fund balances, June 30, 1992	132,080	7,575,375	1,677,510	9,384,965

CITY OF EUGENE, OREGON
Combining Statement of Cash Flows
Nonexpendable Trust Funds
For the Fiscal Year-End June 30, 1992
Increase (Decrease) in Cash and Cash Equivalents
(amounts in dollars)

	Housing Rehabilitation	Community Development	Urban Renewal Agency	Total
Cash flows from operating activities				
Operating grant received from Economic Development Department for regional strategies program	0	1,809,000	0	1,809,000
Principal received on program loans	21,515	711,883	47,597	780,995
Interest and penalties received on program loans	5,801	256,049	42,224	304,074
Disbursements for program loans	(42,381)	(1,744,162)	(550,044)	(2,336,587)
Net cash provided by (used for) operating activities	(15,065)	1,032,770	(460,223)	557,482
Cash flows from noncapital financing activities				
Operating transfers in from other funds	0	112,989	304,100	417,089
Operating transfers out to other funds	0	(219,722)	0	(219,722)
Net cash provided by (used for) noncapital financing activities	0	(106,733)	304,100	197,367
Cash flows from investing activities				
Interest revenue	2,552	60,279	49,106	111,937
Net cash provided by investing activities	2,552	60,279	49,106	111,937
Net increase (decrease) in cash and cash equivalents	(12,513)	986,316	(107,017)	866,786
Cash and investments, July 1, 1991	49,380	1,077,908	980,385	2,107,673
Cash and investments, June 30, 1992	36,867	2,064,224	873,368	2,974,459
Reconciliation of operating income to net cash provided by (used for) operating activities				
Operating income	5,727	987,777	27,438	1,020,942
Adjustments to reconcile operating income to net cash (used for) operating activities				
Allowance for uncollectibles	74	(74,561)	14,786	(59,701)
Changes in assets and liabilities				
(Increase) in loans receivable	(20,866)	(1,013,578)	(502,447)	(1,536,891)
(Increase) in due from other funds	0	(3,691)	0	(3,691)
(Decrease) in due to other funds	0	(1,533)	0	(1,533)
(Decrease) in due to other governments	0	(806)	0	(806)
Increase in deferred revenue	0	1,139,162	0	1,139,162
Net cash provided by (used for) operating activities	(15,065)	1,032,770	(460,223)	557,482

CITY OF EUGENE, OREGON
Deferred Compensation Agency Fund
Statement of Changes in Assets and Liabilities
For the Fiscal Year Ended June 30, 1992
(amounts in dollars)

	Balance June 30, 1991	Additions	Deductions	Balance June 30, 1992
Assets				
Investment in deferred compensation benefits	16,300,047	3,733,312	(1,701,572)	18,331,787
Total assets	16,300,047	3,733,312	(1,701,572)	18,331,787
Liabilities				
Deferred compensation benefits payable	16,300,047	3,733,312	(1,701,572)	18,331,787
Total liabilities	16,300,047	3,733,312	(1,701,572)	18,331,787

12–4. The City of Bryan has three fiduciary funds: Cemetery Trust Principal Fund, Cemetery Trust Income Fund, and City Employees' Retirement Fund. Below are several paragraphs of financial information as of June 30, 19x6, about the funds:

1. Total cash and temporary investments of the three funds aggregated $697,918, distributed: $178,667 to the Cemetery Trust Principal Fund; $475,492 to City Employees' Retirement Fund; and $43,759 to the Cemetery Trust Income Fund.

2. City Employees' Retirement Fund members owed contributions in the amount of $62,401.

3. Various City funds owed the Retirement Fund contributions in the amount of $89,078.

4. The City Employees' Retirement Fund owned U.S. Treasury bonds of $8,998,000 at amortized cost.

5. U.S. Treasury notes having a current redemption value of $4,899,462, owned by the funds, were distributed: $2,861,026 to the City Employees' Retirement Fund; $1,992,003 to the Cemetery Trust Principal Fund; and the remainder to the Cemetery Trust Income Fund.

6. Accrued interest receivable at June 30, 19x7, consisted of $469 for the Cemetery Trust Income Fund; $46,942 for the Cemetery Trust Principal Fund; and $161,918 for the City Employees' Retirement Fund. The accrued interest of the Cemetery Trust Principal Fund is due to the Cemetery Trust Income Fund.

7. Annuities payable by the City Employees' Retirement Fund to members and beneficiaries totaled $52,875.

8. The Cemetery Trust Income Fund had Vouchers Payable of $60,161.

Required

a. Prepare a trial balance for each of the funds at June 30, 19x7. The Fund Balance of each fund will have to be derived. If desired, all trial balances may be shown in combined columnar form.

    b. Under what assumption was it in conformity with generally accepted accounting principles to record accrued interest receivable in the accounts of the Cemetery Trust Income Fund?

    c. What additional information would you need in order to prepare a balance sheet for the Retirement Fund in conformity with GASB standards for an individual pension fund, or PERS, balance sheet?

12–5. The City of Malcolm has a recreation center that is partially supported by the earnings from a nonexpendable trust, the Joshua Malcolm Endowment Fund (named after its benefactor). The principal of the trust consists largely of an office building. By terms of the trust, all cash operating expenses, necessary maintenance, and improvements to keep the building attractive to desirable tenants, depreciation, and debt service are deducted from gross rentals to determine the net income to be transferred to the Recreation Center Operating Fund. The fiscal year of the City ends on March 31; the Balance Sheet of the nonexpendable trust fund as of March 31, 19x4, was as follows:

CITY OF MALCOLM
Joshua Malcolm Endowment Fund
Balance Sheet
As of March 31, 19x4

Assets

Current Assets:			
Cash		$ 20,000	
Rents Receivable		40,000	
Total Current Assets			$ 60,000
Property and Equipment:			
Land		240,000	
Building	$2,600,000		
Less: Accumulated Depreciation	300,000	2,300,000	
Equipment	60,000		
Less: Accumulated Depreciation	5,000	55,000	
Total Property and Equipment			2,595,000
Total Assets			$2,655,000

Liabilities and Fund Equity

Liabilities:		
Current Liabilities:		
Due to Recreation Center Operating Fund	$ 17,000	
Accrued Supplies Expenses	11,000	
Deferred Rent Revenue	30,000	
Current Portion of Mortgage Payable	46,000	
Total Current Liabilities		$ 104,000
Long-Term Debt:		
Mortgage Payable		1,254,000
Total Liabilities		1,358,000
Fund Equity:		
Fund Balance		1,297,000
Total Liabilities and Fund Equity		$2,655,000

During fiscal year 19x5, the following transactions and events, stated in summary form, occurred.

1. Rentals collected in cash during the year totaled $480,000 ($40,000 of the total represented collection of rents receivable as of April 1, 19x4; $48,000 of the total represented rentals applicable to fiscal year 19x6). Rentals amounting to $30,000 that had been collected in fiscal 19x4 were earned in fiscal 19x5. In addition, rents amounting to $20,0000 that should have been collected in fiscal 19x5 were still receivable at year-end.
2. The accrued expenses as of April 1, 19x4, were paid in cash. Other cash disbursements during the year were for wages and salaries expense, $105,000; supplies and other operating expenses, $78,000 (all paid to external suppliers); and payments to the Recreation Center Operating Fund, $66,000 (this included the liability as of April 1, 19x4, and an advance on anticipated net income for fiscal 19x5). Payment was made during the year for mortgage interest (8% per annum) in the amount of $104,000 and mortgage principal in the amount of $46,000. Inventories of supplies are deemed immaterial and thus are not reported.
3. Accrued as of March 31, 19x5, were supplies and other operating expenses of $14,000. Depreciation on the building amounted to $78,000; depreciation on the equipment amounted to $5,000.
4. Closing entries were made in order to determine the liability to Recreation Center Operating Fund for net income for fiscal 19x5. An entry was also made to reclassify the current portion of Mortgage Payable as a current liability, assuming the total payment for principal and interest in fiscal 19x6 will be $150,000—the same as fiscal 19x5.

Required

a. Prepare the financial statements as of March 31, 19x5, and for the year then ended for the Joshua Malcolm Endowment Fund. Prepare all statements required for conformity with generally accepted accounting principles, assuming the City of Malcolm has no other nonexpendable trust funds.

b. If you were Director of the Recreation Center, would you be satisfied with the net income earned by the Joshua Malcolm Endowment Fund? Explain. If you think you would be satisfied, what criteria did you use for determining adequacy of income? If you would not be satisfied, what questions would you raise with the Endowment Fund administrator or City chief executive?

12–6. The Town of Benton received a cash contribution in the amount of $500,000 from Annabelle Benton, great-granddaughter of the town's founder, Alex Benton, which is to be held as a nonexpendable trust. Under terms of the agreement, the Town must invest and conserve the principal in perpetuity. Earnings, measured on the full accrual basis, must be used to maintain Alex Benton Town Park, including Alex Benton's gravesite, in an "attractive manner." Gains or losses realized on sale of Endowment Fund investments must be used to adjust the fund balance of the Endowment Fund and do not affect earnings. Information pertaining to transactions of the funds for the fiscal year ended June 30, 19x5, is given as follows:

1. The contribution of $500,000 was received and recorded on December 31, 19x4.
2. On December 31, 19x4, bonds having a face value of $400,000 were purchased for $406,300, plus accrued interest of $6,000. A certificate of deposit with a face and fair value of $70,000 was also purchased on this date. Bonds mature on October 1, 19y3 (105 months from date of purchase) and pay interest of 6 percent per annum

semiannually on April 1 and October 1. The certificate of deposit pays interest of 4 percent per annum payable on March 31, June 30, September 30, and December 31.

3. On January 2, 19x5, the Town Council approved a budget for the Benton Park Expendable Trust Fund for estimated other financing sources of $13,040 and appropriations of $12,900.

4. On March 31, 19x5, interest on the certificate of deposit was received and transferred in cash to the Expendable Trust Fund.

5. The April 1, 19x5, bond interest payment was received and transferred in cash to the Expendable Trust Fund.

6. On June 30, 19x5, interest on the certificate of deposit was received and transferred in cash to the Expendable Trust Fund.

7. For the year ended June 30, 19x5, maintenance expenditures from the Expendable Trust Fund amounted to $2,700 for materials and contractual services, and $10,150 for wages and salaries. All expenditures were paid in cash except for $430 of accounts payable as of June 30, 19x5. Inventories of materials are deemed immaterial in amount.

8. On June 30, 19x5, bonds with face value of $100,000 were sold for $102,000, plus accrued interest of $1,500. On the same date, 2,000 shares of ABC Corporation's stock were purchased at $52 per share. Appropriate adjusting and closing entries were made in order to prepare financial statements as of the end of the town's fiscal year. The amount due to the Expendable Trust Fund for accrued bond interest, net of amortization of premium, was paid in advance on June 30, 19x5.

Required

a. Prepare in general journal form the entries required in the Benton Park Endowment Fund to record the transactions occurring during the fiscal year ending June 30, 19x5.

b. Prepare in general journal form the entries required in the Benton Park Expendable Trust Fund to record the transactions above.

c. Prepare for the Benton Park Endowment Fund:
   (1) Balance Sheet as of June 30, 19x5.
   (2) A Statement of Revenues, Expenses, and Changes in Fund Balance for the fiscal year ended June 30, 19x5.
   (3) A Statement of Cash Flows for the year ended June 30, 19x5.

d. Prepare for the Benton Park Expendable Trust Fund:
   (1) A Balance Sheet as of June 30, 19x5.
   (2) A Statement of Revenues, Expenditures, and Changes in Fund Balance for the fiscal year ended June 30, 19x5.

12–7. The City of Big Spring accepted a gift of cash and securities to be held as a nonexpendable trust; the net income from the trust investments is to be computed on the full accrual basis. Income received in cash, less any amount needed to amortize premium on fixed-income securities, is to be transferred to an expendable trust fund operated on a budgetary basis for the purchase of works of art for display in public buildings. The nonexpendable trust fund, to be known as the Art Endowment Fund, received the following as trust principal on July 1, 19y3: cash, $525,000; XY bonds (face value, $1,000,000; fair value on July 1, 19y3, $1,040,000; interest rate 8 percent per year payable on March 1 and September 1; 50 months until maturity); and one certificate of deposit ($100,000 face and fair value; interest rate 7 percent per year payable on August 1, November 1, February 1, and May 1; 48 months until maturity). Accrued interest receivable on XY bonds, $26,667; accrued interest receivable on certificate of deposit, $1,167.

Required

a. Show in general journal form the entries required in the Art Endowment Fund to record the following:

(1) The receipt of the trust principal on July 1, 19y3, as itemized above.

(2) On July 1, 19y3, the following common stocks were purchased: LM Company, 2,000 shares, cost $255,000; NO, Inc., 1,000 shares, cost $65,000; PQ Company, 800 shares, $200,000.

(3) The August 1, 19y3, interest on the certificate of deposit was received. The portion that was accrued when the Endowment Fund was established is retained; the portion subsequently earned is transferred in cash to the Artworks Expendable Trust Fund.

(4) The September 1, 19y3, interest payment on XY bonds was received. Interest accrued at date of establishment of the Endowment Fund and amortization of premium for two months were retained in the Endowment Fund; the remainder was transferred in cash to the Artworks Expendable Trust Fund.

(5) On October 1, cash dividends were received from LM Company common stock, $5,000; NO, Inc., common stock, $1,500; and PQ Company common stock, $2,000. All cash received was transferred to the Artworks Expendable Trust Fund.

(6) On November 1, interest on the certificate of deposit was received and transferred to the Artworks Expendable Trust Fund.

(7) In order to prepare financial statements as of the end of the City's fiscal year, December 31, 19y3, appropriate adjusting and closing entries were made.

b. Show in general journal form the entries required in the Artworks Expendable Trust Fund to record the following:

(1) On July 1, 19y3, a budgetary entry was made to record as Estimated Other Financing Sources six months' interest on the XY bonds, net of premium amortization; six months' interest on the certificate of deposit; and an estimated amount of $8,300 from dividends on common stock. It was decided that Appropriations for the period should be $27,000.

(2) Cash transferred from the Art Endowment Fund on August 1, 19y3, was received.

(3) Cash transferred from the Art Endowment Fund on September 1, 19y3, was received.

(4) A portrait of the Mayor was commissioned on September 15; the artist is to receive $6,800 when the portrait is completed. He was given an advance of $1,900 cash.

(5) Cash transferred from the Art Endowment Fund on October 1, 19y3, was received.

(6) Cash transferred from the Art Endowment Fund on November 1, 19y3, was received.

(7) The accrued interest receivable (net of premium amortization) from the Art Endowment Fund was recorded as of December 31, 19y3.

(8) In order to prepare financial statements as of year-end, December 31, 19y3, appropriate closing entries were made.

    c. Prepare for the Art Endowment Fund:
       (1) A Balance Sheet as of December 31, 19y3.
       (2) A Statement of Revenues, Expenses, and Changes in Fund Balance for the six months ended December 31, 19y3.
       (3) A Statement of Cash Flows for the six months ended December 31, 19y3.
    d. Prepare for the Artworks Expendable Trust Fund:
       (1) A Balance Sheet as of December 31, 19y3.
       (2) A Statement of Revenues, Expenditures, and Changes in Fund Balance for the six months ended December 31, 19y3.

12–8. The State of Arkoma operates a Public Employee Retirement System for all employees of the state. The trial balance of the PERS as of June 30, 19x1, follows (in thousands of dollars):

	Debits	Credits
Cash	$ 6,254	
Accrued Interest Receivable	32,955	
Investments, at Cost or Amortized Cost	2,054,586	
Equipment and Fixtures	15,200	
Accumulated Depreciation—Equipment and Fixtures		$ 3,110
Accounts Payable and Accruals		33,396
Fund Balance, July 1, 19x0		1,647,748
Member Contributions		112,126
Employer Contributions		197,768
Investment Income		199,679
Annuity Benefits	43,882	
Disability Benefits	4,026	
Refunds to Terminated Employees	28,801	
Administrative Expenses	8,123	
	$2,193,827	$2,193,827

Required

    a. Prepare a Statement of Revenues, Expenses, and Changes in Fund Balance for the State of Arkoma Public Employee Retirement System for the year ended June 30, 19x1, in as much detail as possible.

    b. Prepare a Balance Sheet as of June 30, 19x1, for the State of Arkoma Public Employee Retirement System. Assume the Fund Balance is composed of the actuarial present value of:

       (1) Projected benefits payable to current retirants and beneficiaries $ 401,360
       (2) Projected benefits payable to terminated vested participants   50,540
       (3) Credited projected benefits for active employees   1,685,959.

    Any difference between the total of (1), (2), and (3) and the Net Assets Available for Benefits is to be shown in the Fund Balance section as the Unfunded Actuarial Present Value of Credited Projected Benefits (see Illustration 12–4). The market value of the investments totaled $2,092,600 as of June 30, 19x1.

Continuous Problems

12–L. The City of Bingham (see Problems 2–L through 11–L) has had an Employees' Retirement Fund for many years. The fund is financed by actuarially determined contributions from the City's General Fund; the employees make no contribution. Administration of the retirement fund is handled by General Fund employees, and the retirement fund does not bear any administrative expenses.

The Balance Sheet of the Employees' Retirement Fund as of the end of the fiscal year prior to the one with which this problem is concerned is shown below:

CITY OF BINGHAM
Employees' Retirement Fund
Balance Sheet
As of June 30, 19x1

Assets

Cash	$ 8,360
Accrued interest receivable	15,000
Investments, at cost or amortized cost (market value $753,640)	750,840
Total Assets	$774,200

Liabilities

Accounts payable and accrued expenses	6,000
Net Assets Available for Benefits	$768,200

Fund Balance:	
Actuarial present value of projected benefits to current retirants and beneficiaries	$142,600
Actuarial present value of credited projected benefits for active employees	632,300
Total actuarial present value of credited projected benefits	774,900
Unfunded actuarial present value of credited projected benefits	(6,700)
Total Fund Balance	$768,200

Required

a. Record in the general journal for the Employees' Retirement Fund the following events and transactions, which occurred during the year ended June 30, 19x2:

(1) The interest receivable on investments as of the beginning of the year was collected in cash.

(2) A liability for annuities payable was recorded in the amount of $75,000.

(3) Contributions from the General Fund in the amount of $176,390 were received in cash.

(4) Interest earnings received in cash amounted to $30,000; additional interest earnings were accrued in the amount of $16,000.

(5) Accounts Payable for Annuities in the amount of $78,000 were paid.

(6) Investments that were carried at amortized cost, $80,840, were exchanged for similar securities with a face value of $80,000. The criteria that make deferral of the loss permissible (see Chapter 12) were met, and it was decided to amortize the loss over a period of six years—the remaining time until maturity of the

security sold (i.e., one sixth of the total loss, $840, was charged against Investment Income for the year).

(7) Additional investments were purchased at a cost of $150,000.

(8) Nominal accounts for the year were closed. Information from the actuary indicated that as of June 30, 19x2, the actuarial present value of projected benefits to current retirants and beneficiaries increased by $27,800, and the actuarial present value of credited projected benefits for active employees increased by $119,400.

b. Prepare a Balance Sheet as of June 30, 19x2, for the Employees' Retirement Fund. (Market value of investments held by the fund at year-end amounted to $906,300.)

c. Prepare a Statement of Revenues, Expenses, and Changes in Fund Balance for this fund for the year ended June 30, 19x2.

12–S. The City of Smithville does not have any trust funds.

CHAPTER 13

Review and Evaluation of Financial Reports of State and Local Governmental Units

Chapters 2 through 12 present extended discussions of the nature of fund types and account groups provided in Governmental Accounting Standards Board pronouncements. The reasons why each fund type and account group exists are set forth and the essential characteristics of accounting for typical transactions of the funds and groups are discussed in those chapters. In the first section of this chapter, the nature, purposes, and accounting characteristics of each fund type and account group are summarized and interfund transactions are reviewed. The second section of this chapter presents a brief discussion of the complexities of defining the governmental reporting entity. The third section reviews and describes general purpose financial statements and the comprehensive annual financial report. The fourth section describes the complex process of using financial statement and other data to evaluate the financial condition of a governmental entity. The final section discusses recent developments in financial reporting and unresolved reporting issues.

Summary of the Nature and Accounting Characteristics of Funds and Account Groups

A fund is an independent fiscal and accounting entity with a self-balancing set of accounts recording assets and resources, and related liabilities, reserves, and equities, segregated for the purpose of carrying on specific activities or attaining certain objectives in compliance with legal restrictions or agreements. Fund types are classified in three major categories—governmental funds, proprietary funds, and fiduciary funds—and two account groups. Four types of funds are classified as **governmental funds:** general funds, special revenue funds, capital projects funds, and debt service funds. Internal service funds and enterprise funds are classified as **proprietary funds. Fiduciary funds** is the generic name for all trust and agency funds. The two account groups are the General Fixed Assets Account Group and the General Long-Term Debt Account Group.

Classification of funds by major category is helpful because the principal accounting recommendations differ by category: **Governmental** fund revenues and expenditures should be recognized on the "**modified** accrual" basis of accounting. Governmental fund operating statements have a flow of financial resources measurement focus. Governmental funds do not account for fixed assets used in their operations, nor for long-term debt. **Proprietary** fund revenues and expenses should be recognized on the **full** accrual basis. Proprietary fund operating statements have an income determination focus. Proprietary funds account for fixed assets used in their operations and for long-term debt serviced by revenues from their operations. **Fiduciary** funds consist of Nonexpendable Trust Funds and Public Employee Retirement Systems, both of which are accounted for in a manner similar to proprietary funds; and Expendable Trust Funds and Agency Funds, both of which are accounted for in a manner similar to governmental funds. The two account groups exist to account for fixed assets and long-term debt not accounted for by the governmental funds. Illustration 13–1 presents a comparison of the principal accounting characteristics of funds and account groups provided for use by state and local governmental units by GASB standards. The following sections of this chapter summarize the nature, purposes, and accounting characteristics of each fund and group.

Governmental Funds

General Funds and Special Revenue Funds

The **General Fund** is the name given to the entity that accounts for all the assets and resources used for financing the general administration of the governmental unit and the traditional services provided to its residents. Operating funds and current funds are names sometimes given to funds that function as a general fund.

The typical governmental unit now engages in many activities financed by revenues designated by law for a particular operating purpose. In order to demonstrate compliance with such laws, it is recommended that a **Special Revenue Fund** be used to account for the receipt and use of each such restricted category of revenue.

Both general funds and special revenue funds are sometimes known as **revenue funds**. In terms of accounting characteristics, both types are alike. The effect of the budget when it becomes a legal document is recorded in the accounts of each type. Estimated Revenues, a control account for all sources of revenues available to the fund and to be utilized during the budget period, is debited for the total amount of revenues expected to be recognized during the budget period; Estimated Other Financing Sources, a control account for all sources of financial resource inflows not classified by the GASB as revenues, is debited for the total other financing sources expected to be recognized during the budget period. Appropriations, a control account for all categories of expenditures authorized in the legally approved budget, is credited; Estimated Other Financing Uses, a control account for all categories of financial resource outflows not classified by the GASB as expenditures, is credited for the total other financing uses authorized for the budget period. Fund Balance, the account that is similar to a capital account of a profit-seeking entity, is debited or credited for the difference between Estimated Revenues plus Estimated Other Financing Sources less Appropriations and Estimated Other Financing Uses.

Accounting for general and special revenue funds differs from accounting for profit-seeking entities in more respects than just the obvious one of formally recording the budget in the accounts. Two principal differences are:

1. Expenditures are made for the purposes specified in the Appropriations Budget and are not made in the hope of generating revenue (as is true of profit-seeking entities); therefore, income determination, which is the principal focus of accounting for profit-seeking entities, is of no concern in accounting for general and special revenue funds.

2. The sources and amounts of revenues and other financing sources relate to a budget for a particular time period, generally one year, so general and special revenue funds can be said to have a year-to-year life rather than an indefinite life, as is true of a profit-seeking entity. Thus, the going-concern assumption that is basic to accounting for profit-seeking entities is not applicable to accounting for revenue funds; flow of financial resources is the focus of general and special revenue funds.

Legally approved appropriations are authorizations to incur liabilities for specified purposes in specified amounts during a specified time period. Penalties provided by law may be imposed on governmental administrators who expend governmental resources in a manner in any way contrary to that authorized in appropriation ordinances or statutes. For that reason, it is recommended that Encumbrances, a control account supported by the appropriations expenditures subsidiary ledger, be debited, and Reserve for Encumbrances, a Fund Equity account, be credited when purchase orders, contracts, or other commitment documents are issued. When goods or services have been received, a liability is incurred and an appropriation is deemed to have been expended (under accrual accounting theory); thus, if the appropriation has previously been encumbered, it is necessary to reverse the encumbrance entry at the time the Expenditure account is debited and the liability account is credited.

Revenues of a general or special revenue fund are to be recognized on the modified accrual basis. That is, those items of revenue that are "susceptible to accrual" (measurable and available), such as property taxes, are recorded on the accrual basis; other items of revenue are generally recorded on the cash basis. Revenues and Expenditures are operating statement accounts and are closed to Fund Balance at the end of a fiscal period. Estimated Revenues, Estimated Other Financing Sources, Appropriations, Estimated Other Financing Uses, and Encumbrances, all referred to as **budgetary** accounts, are also closed to Fund Balance at the end of a fiscal period. Therefore, when budgetary and operating statement accounts have been closed, the balance sheet accounts remain open and their balances are reported in a balance sheet for the General Fund and in a combining balance sheet for the special revenue fund type. The balance sheet accounts of a general or special revenue fund consist of accounts for financial resources available for fund operations, current liabilities to be paid from fund assets, and Fund Equity. If prepaid items and/or inventories of materials and supplies are owned by a revenue fund, they should be included as an asset, but

ILLUSTRATION 13–1   Comparison of Characteristics of Funds and Account Groups of State and Local Governmental Units under Currently Effective GASB Standards

Characteristic	Governmental Funds			
	General	Special Revenue	Capital Projects	Debt Service
Focus	Liquidity	Liquidity	Liquidity	Liquidity
Length of Life	Year to year	Year to year	From approval of project until completion	From issue of general debt until final liquidation
Balance Sheet Accounts:				
Current Assets	Yes	Yes	Yes	Yes
Fixed Assets	No	No	No	No
Assets Available and to Be Provided	—	—	—	—
Current Liabilities	Yes	Yes	Yes	Yes
Fixed Liabilities	No	No	No	No
Fund Equity:				
Fund Balance—Reserved	Yes	Yes	Yes	No
Fund Balance—Available	Yes	Yes	Yes	Yes
Contributed Capital	—	—	—	—
Retained Earnings	—	—	—	—
Invested in G.F.A.	—	—	—	—
Operating Statement Accounts—Basis of Recognition:				
Revenues	Modified Accrual	Modified Accrual	Modified Accrual	Modified Accrual
Expenditures	Full Accrual	Full Accrual	Full Accrual	Modified Accrual
Expenses	—	—	—	—
Budgetary Accounts:				
Estimated Revenues	Yes	Yes	No	Yes
Appropriations	Yes	Yes	No	Yes
Encumbrances	Yes	Yes	Yes	No

Notes: 1. An agency fund recognizes, on the modified accrual basis, assets to be collected on behalf of the funds and units that are parties to the agency relationship. Since all assets belong to other funds and units, the assets are offset by liabilities to other funds and units.

2. Long-term debt of an internal service fund is usually owed to another fund rather than to external creditors.

3. Accumulated depreciation may be recorded in this group; related expense should *not* be recorded in any governmental fund.

SOURCE: Adapted from a comparative chart prepared by Professor W. David Brooks, CPA, of Chemeketa Community College, Salem, Oregon.

	Fiduciary Funds			Proprietary Funds		Account Groups	
Agency	*Expendable Trust*	*Nonexpendable Trust*	*Internal Service*	*Enterprise*	*General Fixed Assets*	*General Long-Term Debt*
Liquidity Duration of agency	Liquidity Duration of trust	Going concern Duration of trust	Going concern Decision of governing board	Going concern Decision of governing board	— As long as general fixed assets exist	— As long as unmatured long-term general debt exists
(Note 1) No	Yes No	Yes Yes	Yes Yes	Yes Yes	No Yes	No No
— (Note 1) No	— Yes No	— Yes Yes	— Yes (Note 2)	— Yes Yes	— No No	Yes No Yes
—	Yes	No	—	—	—	—
—	Yes	Yes	—	—	—	—
—	—	—	Yes	Yes	—	—
—	—	—	Yes	Yes	—	—
—	—	—	—	—	Yes	—
—	Modified Accrual	Full Accrual	Full Accrual	Full Accrual	—	—
—	Full Accrual	—	—	—	—	—
—	—	Full Accrual	Full Accrual	Full Accrual	(Note 3)	—
—	Yes	—	—	—	—	—
—	Yes	—	—	—	—	—
—	Yes	—	—	—	—	—

Fund Equity should be **reserved** in an equivalent amount. Unreserved Fund Balance, therefore, represents the net amount of financial resources available for appropriation and expenditure for legally approved purposes or for authorized other financing uses.

Capital Projects Funds

The receipt and disbursement of all moneys from the sale of tax-supported or special assessment bonds issued for the construction or acquisition of capital facilities, along with the receipt and disbursement of all moneys from other sources (such as grants from governmental units, special assessments, transfers from other funds, or gifts from citizens for the construction or acquisition of capital facilities), are accounted for by capital projects funds. The acquisition of general fixed assets under a capital lease is also recorded in a governmental fund, usually a capital projects fund.

A capital projects fund exists because certain resources are dedicated to a given capital purpose; all activities of the fund have the objective of accomplishing that purpose. Therefore, it is not considered necessary for budgetary accounts other than Encumbrances to be used. Encumbrances and Reserve for Encumbrances are considered desirable because of the large number of commitment documents that are issued for a typical governmental capital project. The encumbrance entry is reversed and Construction Expenditures of a capital projects fund are recognized when goods and services are received and the corresponding liability is recorded. Revenues of a capital projects fund are recognized on the same accrual basis as general and special revenue funds. The life of a capital projects fund is the length of time from legal approval of the project until completion of the project and formal acceptance of the capital assets by the governmental unit. The life of a capital projects fund generally does not coincide with a fiscal period; therefore, operating statement accounts and encumbrances are ordinarily closed at year-end to facilitate preparation of annual statements. Neither the fixed assets nor any long-term liabilities resulting from the project are accounted for by a capital projects fund. Only assets that will be converted into cash and disbursed for the project are to be accounted for by a fund of this type. Similarly, only liabilities that are to be paid out of fund assets are accounted for by capital projects funds. Fund Balance of a capital projects fund represents the excess of current assets over the sum of current liabilities and expected liabilities (Reserve for Encumbrances) or, therefore, the amount available for expenditure for the approved purposes of the fund.

Debt Service Funds

Tax-supported long-term debt issued and the interest thereon must be serviced primarily from revenue raised in years subsequent to the issue. Special assessment long-term debt for which a general government is obligated in some manner is expected to be serviced from collections of assessments and interest thereon. Laws of superior jurisdictions and bond indentures commonly require local governmental units to establish funds to account for debt service revenue.

It is recommended that debt service funds record Estimated Revenues and Appropriations (and Estimated Other Financing Sources and Estimated Other

Financing Uses, if needed). Encumbrance accounting is ordinarily not needed for debt service funds because the only appropriations for these funds are for the payment of interest and the payment of principal of matured debt.

Although a major portion of the revenues of a debt service fund for tax-supported bonds arises from taxes, a portion of the revenues arises from interest on investments. Special assessments against property benefited by a special assessment project, and interest on the assessments, furnish revenues for debt service of special assessment bonds. Since the fund must stay in existence until all general long-term debt is repaid, in most cases the fund may be said to have an unlimited life.

The accrual basis of accounting specified for debt service funds has the same meaning for the revenues of debt service funds as it has for general and special revenue funds, but whereas the expenditures of a general or special revenue fund are to be accounted for on the full accrual basis, the expenditures of a debt service fund for interest and matured bonds are to be accounted for in the fiscal year in which appropriations for the payment of interest and principal are made—generally, the year in which the items become due.

As is true of general and special revenue funds and capital projects funds, a regular serial bond debt service fund accounts for only current assets and current liabilities (matured interest and matured principal payments), and the Fund Balance represents the excess of current assets available for fund purposes. A term bond debt service fund or a deferred serial bond debt service fund ordinarily is expected to accumulate assets over the life of the bonds; it is prudent for the assets to be held in the form of high-quality investments that are readily marketable or that will mature by the time cash is needed. The debt to be retired by the debt service fund is recorded by the general long-term debt group, not the debt service fund (until maturity).

Proprietary Funds

Internal Service Funds

If governmental resources are segregated for the purpose of providing services to several departments or funds of the same governmental unit or to other governmental units, the resources are accounted for by an Internal Service Fund. The internal service fund type may be operated under many different levels of legislative supervision; in this summary it is assumed the financial objective of the fund is to recover through user charges the full cost of operations and to earn enough net income to allow for replacement of inventories and facilities in periods of rising prices. Accordingly, although budgets should be prepared for managerial use, it is not necessary to record the budget in the accounting system. Full accrual accounting should be used for revenues and for *costs* and *expenses* (these terms are used rather than *expenditures* because the latter refers to appropriation accounting). The life of an internal service fund is indefinite, so the going-concern assumption should be applied to accounting decisions. Current assets and fixed assets used in internal service fund operations should be accounted for by the internal service fund. Long-term debt to be repaid from earnings of the fund should also be accounted for by the internal service fund, as should all other liabilities to be paid from fund assets. Since net income is retained in the fund, a Retained Earnings account is needed as well as accounts that disclose the amount and source of the permanent equity of the fund.

Enterprise Funds

In contrast with internal service funds, resources utilized by a governmental unit to provide services on a user-charge basis to the general public are accounted for by an Enterprise Fund. Governmentally owned utilities are common examples of activities accounted for by enterprise funds. Almost any form of business engaged in by individuals, partnerships, and corporations may also be owned and operated by a governmental unit, however, and would be accounted for by an enterprise fund. Utilities or other enterprises that would be regulated if they were investor-owned should use the charts of accounts and accounting and statistical definitions required of investor-owned enterprises in the same industry. Other governmentally owned enterprises should use charts of accounts and definitions established by trade associations for the appropriate industry. In general, principles of accounting established for profit-seeking entities apply. Differences between regulatory accounting and accounting for nonregulated industries are discussed in Chapter 10.

In addition to operations financed primarily through user charges, the enterprise fund structure may be used to account for any other operations for which the governing body of the governmental unit desires a periodic determination of revenues earned, expenses incurred, and/or net income.

The life of an enterprise is assumed to be indefinite. Full accrual accounting is used. All assets used in fund operations and all debt to be serviced from fund earnings are included in enterprise fund accounts. A Retained Earnings account as well as accounts that disclose the amount and source of the contributed equity of the fund are utilized.

Fiduciary Funds

Trust and Agency Funds

Trust and agency funds are used to account for assets held by a state or local government in a fiduciary capacity. A governmental unit that collects taxes for other units would have need for an agency fund, for example. Employees' retirement funds, often called *Public Employee Retirement Systems* (PERS), are a very common form of trust fund.

Agency Funds. An agency relationship may be accounted for satisfactorily within the accounting structure of the General Fund, or other fund, if the amounts collected pursuant to the agency are small in relation to total fund assets, and if the amounts are remitted to the owner without an appreciable lapse of time. If the amounts collected are relatively large, however, or if they are held for an appreciable time, or if the law or GASB standards (discussed in Chapter 11) require it, agency funds should be established. A very simple set of proprietary accounts ordinarily suffices for an agency fund because all fund assets are held as agent and are entirely offset by a liability to the owner. At year-end, if all assets have been collected and have been remitted to the owner, the agency fund would have no balances to report in the annual statements. GASB standards provide that agency fund assets and liabilities are to be accounted for on the basis used by governmental fund types.

Trust Funds. Trust funds differ from agency funds in that a trust fund generally holds assets and manages them for the beneficiaries over a substantial period of time. As discussed in Chapter 12, trust fund accounting problems often relate to the distinction between trust principal and trust income, and to the distinction between expendability and nonexpendability. **Expendable trust funds**, in general, are those that are created to account for trust income expendable for purposes specified by the trustor. Thus, expendable trust funds are similar in nature to special revenue funds, and GASB standards provide that the measurement focus and basis of accounting for expendable trust funds be the same as for governmental funds.

Nonexpendable trust funds are created to account for trust principal, or corpus, held for purposes specified by the trustor—often, the generation of net income to be transferred to an expendable trust. If the generation of net income is the objective of a trust fund, it seems obvious that accounting principles derived for profit-seeking entities and proprietary funds are applicable. Thus, fixed assets given by the donor as a part of the trust principal, or acquired in pursuit of the trust objectives, and long-term debt related to trust assets are accounted for by the trust fund, as well as current assets and current liabilities of the trust.

Public Employee Retirement Systems, or pension trust funds, are accounted for as explained in Chapter 12. Since this type of trust fund generally has an objective of maximizing earnings from its investments (although the nature of investments that may be held is usually subject to legal restriction), GASB standards require that pension trusts be accounted for in a manner similar to proprietary funds.

Account Groups

General Fixed Assets

Only proprietary funds and fiduciary funds similar to proprietary funds routinely account for property, plant, and equipment used in their operations. All other funds account only for assets that will be turned into cash during the regular operations of the fund. Thus, property, plant, and equipment acquired by governmental funds and fiduciary funds similar to governmental funds are brought under accounting control by the creation of a General Fixed Assets Account Group. No other assets are recorded in the General Fixed Assets Account Group. No liabilities at all are recorded in the accounts of this group. The credit-balance accounts that offset the fixed assets accounts to create a self-balancing group show the source of the investment in general fixed assets.

Depreciation of *general* fixed assets is not recorded by any fund. It is permissible, but not required, for depreciation to be recorded in the General Fixed Assets Account Group as a deduction from the Investment in General Fixed Assets accounts. Accumulated depreciation accounts would then be deducted from related assets in the Statement of General Fixed Assets.

General Long-Term Debt

Debt instruments backed by the taxing power of a governmental unit are obligations of the governmental unit as a whole and not of the individual funds. The General Long-Term Debt Account Group (GLTDAG) was created to account for such debt. The GLTDAG is also used to account for special assessment long-term debt for which the government is obligated in some manner; the present value of capital lease payments; the noncurrent portions of claims, judgments, and compensated absences to be paid when due by use of the resources of governmental funds; and any unfunded liability for pensions of employees of activities accounted for by governmental funds. No assets are recorded in the group. The amount of long-term (and intermediate-term) debt is offset by accounts entitled "Amounts Available in Debt Service Funds for Payment of _____" and "Amounts to Be Provided for Payment of _____."

Summary of Interfund Transactions

Transactions, or events, that affect the accounts of more than one fund or account group of a single governmental unit have been noted in the discussions and illustrative entries of preceding chapters. A brief review of interfund transactions and events at this point should aid the reader in reinforcing his or her understanding of the relationships that exist among the funds and groups.

Each fund is (1) a fiscal entity, (2) an accounting entity and, in a sense, (3) a legal entity. Each account group is only an accounting entity, not a fiscal entity nor, in any sense, a legal entity. Events and transactions that must be recognized in more than one accounting entity of a single governmental unit may be classified in the following manner:

I. Transactions and Transfers between Funds
   A. Interfund loans and advances
   B. Transactions that would be treated as revenues, expenditures, or expenses if they involved organizations external to the governmental unit (quasi-external transactions)
   C. Transactions that reimburse a fund for expenditures made by it on behalf of another fund
   D. Recurring periodic transfers made primarily for the purpose of shifting resources from one fund to another (operating transfers)
   E. Nonrecurring transfers made in compliance with special statutes or ordinances that do not qualify as revenues or expenditures to the receiving or disbursing funds (equity transfers)
II. Events Requiring Recognition in More than One Accounting Entity
   A. Acquisition of general fixed assets

B. Creation of tax-supported and special assessment long-term debt, or repayment of principal of such long-term debt

Examples of each of the seven classes of interfund events or transactions, and entries that record them in each affected fund or group, are illustrated in the following paragraphs.

Transactions and Transfers between Funds

Interfund Loans and Advances

The terms *loans* and *advances* are used to indicate amounts that are temporarily transferred from one fund to another but that will have to be repaid in due time.

Since each fund is a fiscal entity, the interfund receivables and payables resulting from loans and advances must be disclosed in a combined balance sheet. They may not be eliminated, as would be proper in the preparation of consolidated statements for parent and subsidiary profit-seeking corporations.

Interfund loans and advances are discussed and illustrated in Chapters 9 and 10. The Supplies Fund of the Town of Brighton received a $130,000 long-term advance from the Water Utility Fund of the town. (The Supplies Fund also received a contribution from the General Fund, which is reviewed below under the Nonrecurring Transfers heading.) The effect of the advance on each fund is:

Supplies Fund

Cash..	130,000	
Advance from Water Utility Fund............................		130,000

Water Utility Fund

Long-Term Advance to Supplies Fund..........................	130,000	
Cash..		130,000

Partial repayment of the advance was made at year-end:

Supplies Fund

Advance from Water Utility Fund..............................	6,500	
Cash..		6,500

Water Utility Fund

Cash..	6,500	
Long-Term Advance to Supplies Fund......................		6,500

Transactions to Be Reported as Revenues and Expenditures

Interfund transactions that would result in the recognition of revenues, expenditures, or expenses if one of the parties were external to the governmental unit are called **quasi-external** transactions. One of the most common examples of this type of interfund transaction, which properly results in the recognition of revenue by one fund and the recording of an expenditure by another fund, is the provision to the General Fund of fire hydrants and water for fire protection by a municipally owned water utility; illustrative entries are given in Chapters 4 and 10 for this type of interfund transaction. The effect on the general ledger accounts of the Town of

Brighton's General Fund and Water Utility Fund for fire protection service provided by the utility is:

General Fund

Expenditures	30,000	
Due to Other Funds		30,000

Water Utility Fund

Due from Other Funds...	30,000	
Sales of Water		30,000

The Water Utility Fund of the Town of Brighton received services from General Fund departments, as is also common. The entries to record the resulting expense and revenues, as given in Chapters 4 and 10, are:

General Fund

Due from Other Funds...	25,000	
Revenues..		25,000

Water Utility Fund

Contribution in Lieu of Taxes	25,000	
Due to Other Funds		25,000

The net effect of the transactions between the two funds of the Town of Brighton is that the General Fund owes the Water Utility Fund $5,000. It is considered proper for the balance sheet of each fund, and the combined balance sheet for all funds, to display this net amount as a receivable or payable. It should be stressed, however, that it is **not** acceptable to offset a receivable from one fund against a payable to a different fund.

Transactions in the Nature of Reimbursements of Expenditures

If one fund performs services for another fund on an incidental rather than recurring basis, administrators and accountants may consider it more reasonable for the fund receiving the services to reimburse the fund rendering the services for their cost (or estimated cost) rather than to treat the transaction as a quasi-external transaction in the manner described above. For example, if the city engineers' office, a General Fund department, performed services of an incidental nature for the Street Fund (assumed to be a special revenue fund in this example), the following entries would reflect the reimbursement given to the General Fund by the Street Fund (assuming $2,600 is thought to reflect fairly the expenditure the city engineers' office incurred for the benefit of the Street Fund):

General Fund

Cash..	2,600	
Expenditures .•...		2,600

Street Fund

Expenditures	2,600	
Cash..		2,600

Similarly, it is not uncommon for an amount to be recorded as an expenditure, or expense, of one fund which, in fact, should have been recorded as an expenditure, or expense, of another fund. This may occur because of incorrect account coding, data entry error, or lack of adequate information at the time the transaction was recorded. Since the general rule is that revenues, expenditures, and expenses should be reported as such only once, it is considered proper for the fund that should have borne the expenditure, or expense, to debit the appropriate expenditure, or expense, account when it recognizes its liability to the fund that first recorded the expenditure. Similarly, the fund that erroneously recorded the expenditure should debit a receivable from the fund that should have recognized the expenditure, or expense, and should credit the expenditure, or expense, account originally debited.

Recurring Periodic Shifts of Resources (Operating Transfers)

A common example of a transfer of resources which would occur at regular periodic intervals, but which would not result in a true expenditure to the fund raising the revenue, or true revenue to the fund receiving the transfer, is the situation in which revenue to be used for debt service is raised by the General Fund and transferred to a debt service fund. The entry in the General Fund for the shift of resources from the General Fund to the debt service fund would be (amount assumed):

General Fund

Operating Transfers Out	128,000	
Cash..		128,000

The corresponding entry in the debt service fund would be:

Debt Service Fund

Cash..	128,000	
Operating Transfers In.....................................		128,000

The transfer illustrated above also has an effect on the General Long-Term Debt Account Group if a portion of the transfer is to be used for payment of debt principal. Assuming $50,000 of the $128,000 is to be used for debt principal payment, the entry in the GLTDAG would be:

General Long-Term Debt Account Group

Amount Available in Debt Service Fund for Payment of Regular Serial Bonds...	50,000	
Amount to Be Provided for Payment of Regular Serial Bonds ...		50,000

Nonrecurring Transfers Made in Compliance with Special Statutes (Equity Transfers)[1]

In Chapter 9, the first entry in the illustrative case of the Town of Brighton Supplies Fund reflects the transfer of inventory and cash from the General Fund of that town as a contribution of working capital that is not expected to be repaid. This transfer would have to have been authorized by appropriate legal action and therefore is an example of a nonrecurring transfer made in compliance with special statutes or ordinances that does not result in revenues or expenditures to the

---

[1] The GASB Codification continues the use of the NCGA's term *residual equity transfer,* which is appropriate to describe the transfer of the residual equity of a capital projects fund to a debt service fund (illustrated in Chapters 5 and 7, respectively) but not appropriate to describe equity transfers in general.

receiving or disbursing fund. The transfer is stated to have taken place in the year following the year for which illustrative entries are shown for the Town of Brighton General Fund, so the entries in that fund are not shown in Chapter 4. The entries to be made by both funds at the time of the transfer are:

General Fund

Equity Transfers Out*	91,500	
Cash..		30,000
Inventory of Supplies.......................................		61,500

Supplies Fund

Cash..	30,000	
Inventory of Supplies..	61,500	
Equity Transfers In†.......................................		91,500

* In the General Fund the Equity Transfers Out account would be closed to Fund Balance; the Reserve for Inventory of Supplies account would also be closed to Fund Balance since the General Fund no longer accounts for the inventory.

† In the Supplies Fund the Equity Transfers In account would be closed to the Contribution from General Fund account.

An example similar to the one discussed above is the contribution of equity by a general fund to a utility fund. The return of part or all of such contributions would also be a transfer of the nature comprehended in this category. A further example would be the transfer of residual equity balances of discontinued funds to general or debt service funds, normally required by statute.

Events Requiring Recognition in More than One Accounting Entity

Acquisition of General Fixed Assets

Preceding discussions of the General Fixed Assets Account Group emphasized that the group was created to place under accounting control assets acquired through expenditures of general funds, special revenue funds, and capital projects funds, none of which account for fixed assets. Chapter 6 illustrates several sets of entries in funds financing the acquisition of general fixed assets and corresponding entries in the General Fixed Assets Account Group. For review purposes, one set of entries involving the purchase of office equipment by the General Fund of a state or local governmental unit is shown below:

General Fund

Expenditures	1,450	
Vouchers Payable		1,450

General Fixed Assets Account Group

Equipment	1,450	
Investment in General Fixed Assets—General Fund Revenues ..		1,450

The acquisition of general fixed assets by use of a capital lease agreement results in three sets of entries at the inception of the lease: the assets must be recorded in the General Fixed Assets Account Group, the related liability must be recorded in the General Long-Term Debt Account Group, and an Expenditure and an Other Financing Source must be recorded in a governmental fund (ordinarily a Capital Projects Fund). Entries at the inception of one hypothetical capital lease are illustrated in Chapters 5, 6, and 8.

Creation or Repayment of General Long-Term Debt

One event that must be recorded in both a fund and in the General Long-Term Debt Account Group is the issuance of tax-supported bonds so that the proceeds may be used for the acquisition of capital facilities. In the Town of Brighton case presented in Chapter 7, the town has outstanding a deferred serial bond issue in the amount of $2,000,000 as of December 31, 19y0. At the time the bonds were sold, assuming they were sold at par for the acquisition of capital facilities, the following entries were necessary:

Capital Projects Fund

Cash	2,000,000	
Proceeds of Bonds		2,000,000

General Long-Term Debt Account Group

Amount to Be Provided for Payment of Deferred Serial Bonds	2,000,000	
Deferred Serial Bonds Payable		2,000,000

Later, after cash for bond repayment has been received by the debt service fund and the GLTDAG has recorded that amount in the Amount Available account, and removed it from the Amount to Be Provided account, assume the first $200,000 of bonds matures and the liability is transferred from the General Long-Term Debt Account Group to the Debt Service Fund for payment, as shown in the following entries:

Debt Service Fund

Expenditures—Bond Principal	200,000	
Bonds Payable		200,000

General Long-Term Debt Account Group

Deferred Serial Bonds Payable	200,000	
Amount Available in Debt Service Fund for Payment of Deferred Serial Bonds		200,000

General long-term debt arising from a capital lease agreement is recorded at the inception of the lease, as noted in the section above. The payment of rentals during the term of the lease requires entries in a governmental fund (ordinarily a Debt Service Fund) and in the General Long-Term Debt Account Group, as illustrated in Chapters 7 and 8.

The Governmental Reporting Entity

The objectives of accounting and financial reporting for governmental units set forth in the GASB's *Concepts Statement No. 1* are discussed in Chapter 1. *Concepts Statement No. 1* does not deal with the practical problem of deciding what a "governmental unit" is. The average citizen—including accountants whose only experience has been with business organizations—has only a vague knowledge, and little understanding, of the overlapping layers of general purpose and limited-purpose governmental organizations that have some jurisdiction over us wherever we may live and work. Illustration 11–1 indicates the layers of general purpose governments that levy taxes on property. The School Funds in that illustration show that taxes are also levied by limited-purpose governmental units (an independent school district, in that illustration). Omitted from that illustration, for the sake of brevity, are taxes levied by any special districts. Special districts are defined by the Bureau of the Census as "independent limited-purpose governmental units (other than school districts) that exist as separate entities and have substantial administrative and fiscal independence from general purpose local governments."[2] Over 38 percent of the local governments in the United States are classified as special districts.[3]

Although the Census definition stresses the independence of special districts, in many instances they were created to provide a vehicle for financing services demanded by residents of a general purpose governmental unit that could not be financed by the general purpose unit because of constitutional or statutory limits on the rates or amounts it could raise from taxes, other revenue sources, and debt. Building authorities are an example of special districts created as a financing vehicle.

In addition to special districts, defined by the Bureau of the Census as independent entities, but whose financial activities are often closely related to those of one or more general governmental units, it is common for certain governmental activities to be carried on by commissions, boards, and other agencies that are not considered as independent of a general governmental unit by the Bureau of the Census but that may have some degree of fiscal and administrative independence from the governing board of the general governmental unit. In past years, some governments have included in their annual reports the financial statements of such semi-independent boards and commissions, and even certain of the special districts, whereas other governments have excluded from their reports the financial data of semi-independent and independent entities.

In order to reduce disparity in reporting and to promote the preparation of financial reports consistent with GASB *Concepts Statement No. 1,* GASB Codification Section 2100 provides authoritative guidance on Defining the Reporting Entity, and Section 2600 presents guidance on Reporting Entity and Component Unit Presentations and Disclosure.

Entity Definition Criteria

GASB Codification Section 2100 notes that all government organizations are ultimately responsible to elected governing officials at the federal, state, or local level. Elected officials of the primary government are accountable to the citizens

---

[2] U.S. Department of Commerce, Bureau of the Census, *1987 Census of Governments* 1, no. 1 (Washington D.C.: U.S. Government Printing Office, 1988), p. B–2.

[3] 1992 census data, reported to authors by Marshall Moore, Government Division, Bureau of the Census.

for those organizations that are financially dependent on the primary government, or for which the primary government can impose its will. Thus, Section 2100 takes the position that governmental financial reporting should report the elected officials' accountability for such organizations. It should be emphasized that Section 2100 deals only with criteria for defining a governmental reporting entity; it does not establish standards for the incorporation of financial data of component units in the financial statements of the reporting entity. Standards for the incorporation of financial data are set forth in Section 2600.

Definitions of key terms and concepts needed to understand and apply reporting entity criteria are given in Section 2100.501, from which selected terms and concepts are provided here:

Financial Reporting Entity.   A primary government, organizations for which the primary government is financially accountable, and other organizations for which the nature and significance of their relationship with the primary government are such that exclusion would cause the reporting entity's financial statements to be misleading or incomplete. The nucleus of a financial reporting entity usually is a primary government. However, a governmental organization other than a primary government (such as a component unit, a joint venture, a jointly governed organization, or other stand-alone government) serves as the nucleus for its own reporting entity when it issues separate financial statements.

Primary Government.   A state government or general purpose local government. Also, a special purpose government that has a separately elected governing body, is legally separate, and is fiscally independent of other state or local governments.

Component Units.   Legally separate organizations for which the elected officials of the primary government are financially accountable. In addition, a component unit can be another organization for which the nature and significance of its relationship with a primary government is such that exclusion would cause the reporting entity's financial statements to be misleading or incomplete.

Blending (Blended).   The method of reporting the financial data of a component unit that presents the component unit's balances and transactions in a manner similar to the presentation of the balances and transactions of the primary government.

Discrete Presentation (Discretely Presented).   The method of reporting financial data of component units in a column(s) separate from the financial data of the primary government. An integral part of this method of presentation is that individual component unit supporting information is required to be provided either in condensed financial statements within the notes to the reporting entity's financial statements, or in combining statements in its general purpose financial statements (GPFS).

Financial Accountability (Financially Accountable).   The level of accountability that exists if a primary government appoints a voting majority of an organization's governing board and is either able to impose its will on that organization or there is a potential for the organization to provide specific financial benefits to, or impose specific financial burdens on, the primary government. A primary government may also be financially accountable for governmental organizations with a separately elected governing board, a governing board appointed by another government, or a jointly appointed board that is fiscally dependent on the primary government.

Jointly Governed Organizations.   A regional government or other multigovernmental arrangement that is governed by representatives from each of the governments that create the organization, but that is not a joint venture because the participants do not retain an ongoing financial interest or responsibility.

Joint Venture.   A legal entity or other organization that results from a contractual arrangement and that is owned, operated, or governed by two or more participants as a separate and specific activity subject to joint control, in which the participants retain (a) an ongoing financial interest or (b) an ongoing financial responsibility.

Legally Separate Organization (Separate Legal Standing).   An organization created as a body corporate or a body corporate and politic or otherwise possessing similar corporate powers. An organization that has separate legal standing has an identity of its own as an "artificial person" with a personality and existence distinct from that of its creator and others.

Other Stand-Alone Government.   A legally separate governmental organization that (a) does not have a separately elected governing body and (b) does not meet the definition of a component unit. Other stand-alone governments include some special purpose governments, joint ventures, jointly governed organizations, and pools.

The definition of the reporting entity is based primarily on the notion of financial accountability. A primary government is financially accountable for the organizations that make up its legal entity. It is also financially accountable for legally separate organizations if its officials appoint a voting majority of an organization's governing body and either it is able to impose it will on that organization or there is a potential for the organization to provide specific financial benefits to, or to impose specific financial burdens on, the primary government.

A primary government has the ability to impose its will on an organization if it can significantly influence the programs, projects, or activities of, or the level of services performed or provided by, the organization. A financial benefit or burden relationship exists if the primary government (a) is entitled to the organization's resources; (b) is legally obligated or has otherwise assumed the obligation to finance the deficits of, or provide financial support to, the organization; or *(c)* is obligated in some manner for the debt of the organization.

Some organizations are included as component units because of their fiscal dependency on the primary government. An organization is fiscally dependent on the primary government if it is unable to adopt its budget, levy taxes, or set rates or charges, or issue bonded debt without approval by the primary government.[4]

The flowchart in Illustraton 13–2 (taken from Codification Section 2100.901) shows the decision process for inclusion or exclusion of a potential component unit (PCU) and how the PCU should be presented in the financial statements or the notes thereto. Codification Section 2100.902–920 provides several examples of the application of the reporting entity criteria in specific circumstances.

GASB standards require that most component units be **discretely presented** (as defined previously) since they are legally separate organizations.[5] If, however, a component unit is, in substance, a part of the primary government, **blended** reporting is required. An example of the latter is a building authority established to finance and construct public facilities for the primary government, with debt service provided by lease payments made by the primary government. Blended reporting is accomplished by including component units' financial data for particular fund types and account groups with that for the same fund types and account groups of the primary government (e.g., special revenue fund data of the component unit included along with that of the primary government in the Special Revenue Funds column of combined financial statements). One exception in blended reporting is that component unit General Fund data is included in the Special Revenue Funds column of combined financial statements rather than the General Fund column.[6] Thus, the General Fund column presents only the data for the primary government's General Fund.

Governmental Financial Reports

Once the reporting entity has been determined in accord with the criteria discussed in the preceding section, persons responsible for preparing financial reports for the reporting entity should follow the guidance given in currently effective authoritative literature to determine the content of financial reports to be issued for external users. Chapter 2 contains a summary of the standards the GASB Codification sets forth for the content of the comprehensive annual financial report (CAFR) of a state or local governmental reporting entity. Chapters 3 through 12 elaborate on the application of those standards to accounting and financial reporting for each of the fund types and account groups provided in the GASB Codification and subsequent GASB Statements and Interpretations. Although much of the discussion in preceding chapters is concerned with general purpose external financial reporting, the needs of administrators, legislators, and

---

[4] GASB Codification Sec. 2100.
[5] GASB Codification Sec. 2600.107–114.
[6] GASB Codification Sec. 2600.117.

ILLUSTRATION 13–2   Decision Process for Inclusion or Exclusion of PCU

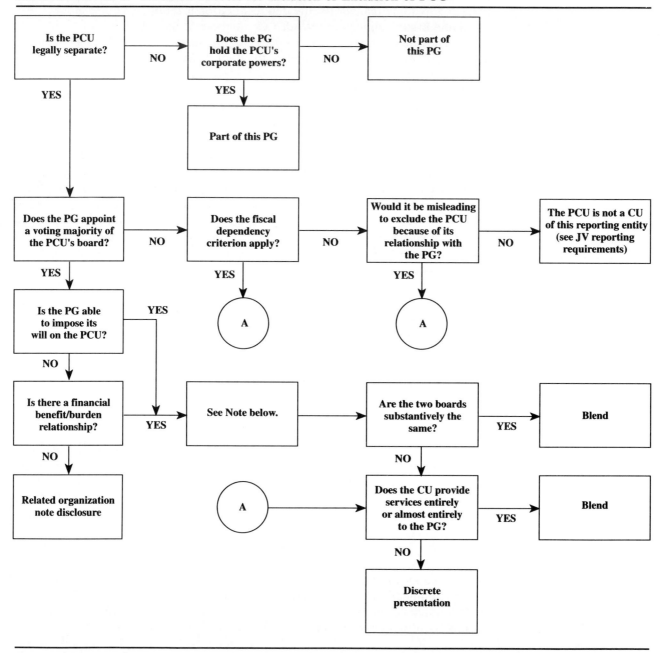

NOTE: A potential component unit for which a primary government is financially accountable may be fiscally dependent on another government. An organization should be included as a component unity of only one reporting entity. Professional judgment should be used to determine the most appropriate reporting entity. A primary government that appoints a voting majority of the governing board of a component unit of another government should make the disclosures required for related organizations.

SOURCE: GASB Codification Sec. 2100.901. Used with permission.

other users not properly classifiable as "external" have been given some attention. In the following paragraphs, the discussion in preceding chapters is briefly summarized and placed in perspective.

Need for
Periodic Reports

Persons concerned with the day-to-day operations and activities accounted for by governmental funds and groups should be familiar with much of the data processed by the accounting information system because it results from the events and transactions with which they are involved. It is easy for these persons to become overconfident of the intuitive "feel" they develop from their daily involvement. Past events were not always as remembered, and the relative significance of events changes over time. Similarly, administrators at succeedingly higher levels in the organization may feel that participation in decision making and observation of the apparent results of past decisions obviate the necessity for periodic analysis of accounting and statistical reports prepared objectively and with neutrality. However, the memory and perceptions of administrators at higher levels are also subject to failure. Therefore, it is generally agreed that it is useful for financial reports to be prepared and distributed at intervals throughout a fiscal period as well as at period-end.

Interim Financial
Reports

Administrators of a governmental unit have greatest need for interim financial reports, although members of the legislative branch of the governmental unit (particularly those on its finance committee) should also find them of considerable use. Other users of interim reports are news media and residents who are particularly concerned with aspects of the financial management of the unit.

A complete interim financial report should include at least the following statements and schedules:

1. Statement of Actual and Estimated Revenue (for the general and special revenue funds and each other fund type for which budgets have been legally adopted).
2. Statement of Actual and Estimated Expenditures (for the general and special revenue funds and for each other fund type for which budgets have been legally adopted).
3. Comparative Statement of Revenue and Expense (for each enterprise and internal service fund and for similar fiduciary funds).
4. Combined Statement of Cash Receipts, Disbursements, and Balances—All Funds.
5. Forecast of Cash Positions—All Funds.

Statements and schedules in addition to those listed above are needed by governmental units with varied and complex activities. A statement of investments held and their cost and market values is an example of an additional statement that is of wide utility.

Schedules of past-due receivables from taxes, special assessments, and utility customers may also be needed at intervals.

Complete interim reports should be prepared and distributed at regular intervals throughout a fiscal period, generally monthly, although small governmental units that have little financial activity may find a bimonthly or quarterly period satisfactory. Partial interim reports dealing only with those items of considerable current importance should be prepared and distributed as frequently as their information would be of value. For example, reports of market values of investments and of purchases and sales may be needed by a relatively small number of users on a daily basis during certain critical periods.

Annual Financial Reports

Governmental annual financial reports are needed by the same individuals and groups who should receive interim reports. They are also often required to be distributed to agencies of higher governmental jurisdictions and to major creditors. Other users include financial underwriters; debt insurers; debt rating agencies; debt analysts; libraries; other governmental units; associations of governmental administrators, accountants, and finance officers; and college professors and students.

A comprehensive annual financial report should be prepared and published by each state and local governmental unit as a matter of public record. The comprehensive annual financial report is the governmental unit's official annual report prepared and published as a matter of public record. GASB standards make it clear that a primary government is the nucleus of a financial reporting entity for which a CAFR is prepared. However, a governmental organization other than a primary government (e.g., a component unit, joint venture, jointly governed organization, or other stand-alone government) serves as the nucleus of its own reporting entity. The separately issued financial statements of such a reporting entity should follow the same reporting entity standards as those for a primary government and its component units. Specifically, Codification Section 1100.112 requires that the Section 2100 criteria for defining a reporting entity be applied in layers "from the bottom up." For each layer, reporting entity definition and display requirements must be applied before the layer is included in the financial statements for the next higher layer.

In addition to the general purpose financial statements (GPFS, in GASB nomenclature), the CAFR should contain introductory material, schedules necessary to demonstrate legal compliance, and statistical tables.

Introductory Section.   The introductory section of a CAFR should include the title page and contents page, the letter of transmittal, and other material deemed appropriate by management.

The letter of transmittal may be a letter from the chief finance officer addressed to the chief executive and governing body of the governmental unit, or it may be a narrative over the signature of the chief executive. In either event, the letter or narrative material should cite legal and policy requirements for the report and discuss briefly the important aspects of the financial condition and financial operations of the governmental unit as a whole and of the unit's funds and account groups. Significant changes since the prior annual report and changes expected during the coming year should be brought to the attention of the reader of the report.

Financial Section.   The financial section of a comprehensive annual financial report should include: (1) an auditor's report, (2) general purpose financial statements, or component unit financial statements, (3) required supplementary information, and (4) combining and individual fund and account group statements and schedules.

Laws relating to the audit of governmental units vary markedly from state to state. In some, all state agencies and all governmental units created pursuant to the state law are required to be audited by an audit agency of the state government. In others, local governmental units are audited by independent Certified Public Accountants. In still others, some governmental units are audited by the state audit agency and some by independent Certified Public Accountants. In any event, the auditor's report should accompany the financial statements reproduced in the CAFR. Chapter 14 illustrates auditors' reports and explains their significance.

The financial section should contain sufficient information to disclose fully and present fairly the financial position and results of financial operations during the fiscal year. GASB Codification Section 2200.108 lists the five combined statements that are the basic general purpose financial statements of a state or local government and stresses that these statements and notes thereto are required for conformity with GAAP. The GPFS, therefore, consists of the:

1. Combined Balance Sheet—All Fund Types, Account Groups, and Discretely Presented Component Units. (See Illustration 2–1.)
2. Combined Statement of Revenues, Expenditures, and Changes in Fund Balances—All Governmental Fund Types and Discretely Presented Component Units. (See Illustration 3–1.)
3. Combined Statement of Revenues, Expenditures, and Changes in Fund Balances—Budget and Actual—General and Special Revenue Fund Types (and similar governmental fund types of the primary government for which annual budgets have been legally adopted). (See Illustration 3–2.)
4. Combined Statement of Revenues, Expenses, and Changes in Retained Earnings (or Equity)—All Proprietary Fund Types, Similar Trust Funds, and Discretely Presented Component Units. (See Illustration 12–7.)
5. Combined Statement of Cash Flows—All Proprietary Fund Types and Discretely Presented Component Units. (See Illustration 12–8.)
6. Notes to the Financial Statements.

The general purpose financial statements are a necessary part of an official comprehensive annual financial report, but GASB standards specifically provide that the GPFS may also be issued separately for widespread distribution to users requiring less detailed information than is contained in the complete CAFR. A

Combined Statement of Revenues, Expenditures, and Changes in Fund Balances—Budget and Actual—General and Special Revenue Fund Types is illustrated in Chapter 3 (see Illustrations 3–1 and 3–2) as a means of introducing the reader to budgetary accounting and reporting. Each subsequent chapter illustrates individual fund and account group statements and combining statements needed to support the fund-type column in combined statements when a reporting entity has more than one fund in a given fund type.

Statistical Tables. In addition to the output of the accounting information system presented in the financial section of the governmental annual report, statistical tables reflecting social and economic data, financial trends, and the fiscal capacity of the government are needed by the reader who is more than casually interested in the activities of the governmental unit. Tabulations required by the GASB for inclusion in a CAFR are:

1. General Governmental Expenditures by Function—Last Ten Fiscal Years.
2. General Revenues by Source—Last Ten Fiscal Years.
3. Property Tax Levies and Collections—Last Ten Fiscal Years.
4. Assessed and Estimated Actual Value of Taxable Property—Last Ten Fiscal Years.
5. Property Tax Rates—All Overlapping Governments—Last Ten Fiscal Years.
6. Special Assessment Billings and Collections—Last Ten Fiscal Years (if the government is obligated in some manner for related special assessment debt).
7. Ratio of Net General Bonded Debt to Assessed Value and Net Bonded Debt per Capita—Last Ten Fiscal Years.
8. Computation of Legal Debt Margin (if not presented in the financial section).
9. Computation of Overlapping Debt (if not presented in the financial section).
10. Ratio of Annual Debt Service for General Bonded Debt to Total General Expenditures—Last Ten Fiscal Years.
11. Revenue Bond Coverage—Last Ten Fiscal Years.
12. Demographic Statistics.
13. Property Value, Construction, and Bank Deposits—Last Ten Fiscal Years.
14. Principal Taxpayers.
15. Miscellaneous Statistics.

Classification of governmental expenditures by function, classification of revenues by source, and other meaningful classifications of revenues and expenditures are discussed at some length in Chapter 3. Assessment of property and the levy and collection of property taxes are discussed in Chapter 4 and in subsequent chapters as appropriate. Reporting of the ratio of net general bonded debt to assessed valuation and the ratio per capita, as well as the computation of legal debt limit, legal debt margin, and direct and overlapping debt and future debt service requirements, are all illustrated and discussed in Chapter 8. Information about investments held for the various funds is often presented in the statistical section of a CAFR, although, as shown in Chapter 7, the information may also be presented in other sections of the report. Additional information listed by the GASB as desirable for presentation in the statistical section of the CAFR is generally self-explanatory. The demographic statistics and miscellaneous statistics often presented are those that are of interest to debt insurers, debt rating agencies, creditors and potential creditors, and organizations considering locating in the area included in the reporting entity, such as population, per capita income, unemployment rate, average education of the work force, fire protection data, police protection data, information about public schools and colleges and universities, recreation and cultural facilities, and parking facilities. Additionally, it seems to be common for state laws to require local governments to list administrators and their salaries, and to list property, casualty, and fidelity insurance coverage carried by the reporting entity.

Evaluating Financial Condition

GASB defines one objective of financial reporting as follows:

> Financial reporting should assist users in assessing the level of services that can be provided by the governmental entity and its ability to meet its obligations as they become due. (GASB Codification Sec. 100.179)

This paragraph further states:

> Financial reporting should provide information about the financial position and condition of a governmental entity. . . .

GASB has identified citizens, legislative and oversight bodies, and investors and creditors as the primary users of external financial reports. Clearly, all three user groups have a need to assess financial condition. Citizens need to know if their government has the ability to continue to provide services at an adequate level. Legislative and oversight officials have a burden to monitor the fiscal performance of their government and that of lower-level governments for which they have statutory oversight responsibility. Investors and creditors must assess the "credit risk" of the governmental entity; that is, its ability to pay principal and interest when due. Government administrators (preparers) and auditors of governmental financial statements also have a need to evaluate financial condition: administrators as part of their accountability to elected officials and the public, and auditors as required by audit standards to assess the ability of the government to continue as a going concern.

Despite the obvious need for user groups and others to assess governmental financial condition, there is surprisingly little agreement about what financial condition is and how it should be measured. The remaining discussion examines these questions briefly and presents a framework for evaluating financial condition.

What Is Financial Condition?

A recent GASB research study defines financial condition as:

> . . . [T]he probability that a government will meet both its financial obligations to creditors, consumers, employees, taxpayers, suppliers, constituents, and others as they become due and its service obligation to constituents, both currently and in the future.[7] (p. 17)

The GASB study distinguishes **financial condition** from the short-term concept **financial position**, which focuses on the relationship between liquid assets (i.e., cash and assets expected to be converted to cash in the near future) and liabilities that will be settled with liquid assets. As the definition implies, assessing financial condition requires judgment about the future as well as evaluation of current financial position. The GASB study definitions are consistent with the International City/County Management Association's concepts of short-term solvency, long-term solvency, and service-level solvency,[8] and the credit evaluation guidelines used by the major debt rating agencies.[9] Further, the definition of financial condition appears sufficiently broad to encompass the information needs of user groups, preparers, and auditors.

Measuring Financial Condition

The GASB study points out that financial condition is a complex, multidimensional concept whose measurement requires analysis of a multitude of factors. The study identifies the major categories of factors as economy and demographics, revenue base, current and capital expenditures, debt, pensions and other postemployment benefits, internal resources, management capabilities, infrastructure, and willingness to raise revenues and to provide needed public services.[10] Perusal of this list suggests that evaluation of some categories such as management capabilities, infrastructure, and willingness to raise revenues and provide services are largely qualitative judgments. Even the economic and financial quantitative factors will require a great deal of judgment to form a conclusion about financial condition.

The factor categories listed in the GASB study illustrate that, unlike the rather straightforward evaluation of the financial condition of a business entity based on

---

[7] R. Berne, *Research Report*. "The Relationship between Financial Reporting and the Measurement of Financial Condition" (Norwalk, Conn.: GASB, 1992).

[8] See S. M. Groves, *Evaluating Financial Condition: An Executive Overview for Local Governments,* Handbook No. 1 (Washington, D.C.: International City/County Management Association, 1980).

[9] See, for example, Moody's Investors Service, *Moody's on Municipals* (New York, 1991), and Standard & Poor's Corporation, *S&P's Municipal Finance Criteria* (New York, 1989).

[10] Berne, *Research Report*, p. 25.

analysis of profitability and well-understood financial ratios, evaluation of governmental financial condition demands attention to the interplay of environmental, organizational, and financial factors. Illustration 13–3 shows the framework developed by the International City/County Management Association (ICMA) for evaluating financial condition. Environmental factors such as population characteristics, economic conditions, employment base, political culture, intergovern-

---

ILLUSTRATION 13–3   Factors Affecting Financial Condition

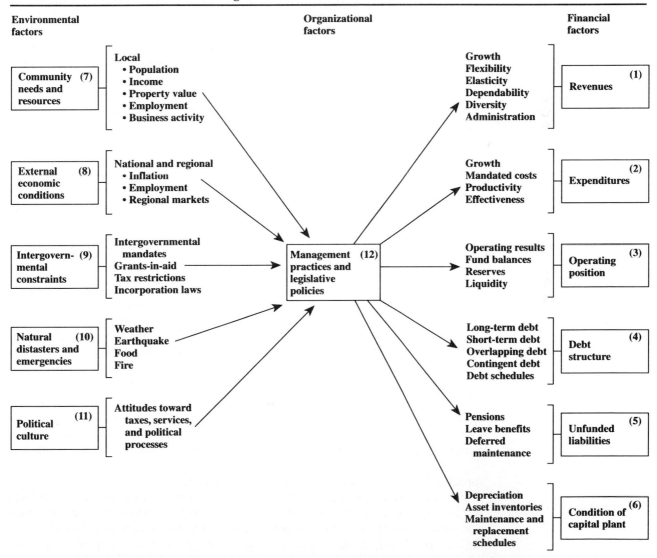

SOURCE: S. M. Groves and M. G. Valente, *Evaluating Financial Condition: A Handbook for Local Government* (Washington, D.C.: International City/County Management Association, 1986), p. 4.

mental relations, climate and natural disasters largely determine revenue capacity and demand for services. How fiscal policy within the governmental unit responds to environmental demand and changes in the environment is a major factor determining how environmental factors are translated into financial factors. Financial factors (identified in Illustration 13–3 as revenues, expenditures, operating position, debt structure, unfunded liabilities, and condition of capital plant) are the result of management and legislative policies in response to environmental demands and resources. Measures of financial condition include ratios consisting of one financial amount divided by another financial amount (such as fund balance divided by revenues) and ratios consisting of financial amounts divided by demographic or economic measures (such as debt divided by population).

Although identifying financial indicators and interpreting them is more of an art than a science, the ICMA provides a large number of potentially useful indicators grouped into 12 categories or factors corresponding to the environmental, organizational, and financial dimensions shown in Illustration 13–3. Examining changes in indicators over time and the relationships among indicators can yield useful information on financial issues such as whether revenue trends are adequate to meet expenditure trends, adequacy of financial reserves to withstand revenue shortfalls or unforeseen expenditure requirements, current debt burden and future debt capacity, future service demands and ability of the governmental unit to meet those demands, adequacy of enterprise fund revenues to meet debt covenant requirements, and what portions of operating costs could be met by user charges rather than by taxes.

Using Financial Reports in Evaluating Financial Condition

Given the complex analytical framework just discussed, one might question the usefulness of the comprehensive annual financial report in evaluating financial condition. A common complaint is that fund-based financial statements in the typical CAFR do not portray a clear picture of the governmental entity's financial condition. In fact, many trained analysts find the introductory and statistical sections of the CAFR, and the Notes to the Financial Statements, to be more useful than the financial statements for assessing financial condition. This is not surprising since the introductory and statistical sections of the CAFR and the Notes to the Financial Statements provide important information on environmental and organizational factors (such as those shown in Illustration 13–3), and how they relate to financial factors. Many governments further enhance understandability by providing excellent narrative and graphical explanation of economic and financial factors, including trend data, comparisons with other governments, and forecasts in the introductory section of their CAFR.

In the authors' view, the fact that many find the introductory and statistical sections to be more useful than financial statements for evaluating financial condition is more a reflection of the complex nature of financial condition itself than an indictment of financial statements. These complexities and the lack of a "bottom-line" performance measure (profit) may also explain why the CAFR has evolved to its present form, and provides justification for publishing a complete CAFR rather than just general purpose financial statements. Further, the combined general purpose financial statements (illustrated in Chapters 2 and 3) are not useless; they provide information for calculating financial ratios essential to understanding the entity's financial condition.

Examples of governmental fund financial ratios typically used in assessing financial condition are shown in Illustration 13–4. It should be noted that the ratios listed in Illustration 13–4 cover all of the financial factor categories shown at the right-hand side of Illustration 13–3, except for condition of capital plant. Many, if not most, governmental entities do not include information on the condition of capital plant in their CAFR. Descriptive information on miles of street, miles of sewer, number of fire and police stations, number of employees, and so on, are often provided, but seldom is any information provided about the *condition* of capital plant. Such disclosures are needed and are being studied by GASB.

ILLUSTRATION 13–4   Financial Ratios Based on CAFR Governmental Funds Information

Financial Ratios	Explanation for Ratio
Revenue measures:	
1. $\dfrac{\text{Total revenues}}{\text{Population}}$	Indicates demand for resources and the entity's ability and willingness to provide resources. Over time shows how revenues are changing relative to population changes. A high ratio, and increasing trend, in relation to ratio 3 below, is desirable. However, a high ratio may also suggest less flexibility for obtaining additional revenues.
2. $\dfrac{\text{Own source revenues}}{\text{Total revenues}}$	Indicates extent of fiscal self-reliance; a high ratio is viewed as a positive characteristic.
Expenditure measures:	
3. $\dfrac{\text{Total expenditures}}{\text{Population}}$	Indicates cost of providing services per capita. Over time it reflects changes in expenditures relative to changes in population. A high ratio may indicate inefficiency or that cost of services may eventually exceed residents' ability to pay for services.
4. $\dfrac{\text{Operating expenditures}}{\text{Total expenditures}}$	Operating Expenditures = Total Expenditures − Capital Expenditures. May indicate inadequate financial capacity to maintain infrastructure. Capital expenditures are often one of the first discretionary expenditures cut when fiscal stress occurs. Deferred capital expenditures create a need for increased capital expenditures in the future.
Operating position liquidity measures:	
5. $\dfrac{\text{Total revenues}}{\text{Total expenditures}}$	Indicates relationship of inflow from revenues to outflow for expenditures; a high ratio is viewed as a positive characteristic.
6. $\dfrac{\text{Unreserved fund balance(s)}}{\text{Operating revenues}}$	Indicates availability of "financial reserves" to meet unforeseen contingencies and for appropriation for future operations. A ratio below 5 percent is generally regarded by the debt rating agencies as a red flag indicating probable fiscal stress.

ILLUSTRATION 13–4 *(concluded)*

Financial Ratios	Explanation for Ratio
7. $\dfrac{\text{(Cash + Short-term investments)}}{\text{Current liabilities}}$	Indicates liquidity or "cash position"; a ratio of less than one is considered as a negative factor, particularly if it occurs in consecutive years.
8. $\dfrac{\text{Current liabilities}}{\text{Operating revenues}}$	Indicates the ability of the government to meet its current liabilities.

Debt structure measures:

9. $\dfrac{\text{Net tax-supported long-term debt}}{\text{Net assessed valuation}}$	Net tax-supported debt is direct tax-supported debt less amount available in debt service funds. Indicates the government's ability to repay its net general long-term debt; a ratio of 10 percent or more is viewed as a negative factor. This may not be a valid benchmark in some states which have extremely low assessment ratios, such as Missouri which averages 24 percent.
10. $\dfrac{\text{Net tax-supported long-term debt}}{\text{Population}}$	An alternative indicator measure of general long-term debt burden is debt per capita. A debt burden greater than $1,200 per capita or level of debt exceeding 90 percent of amount authorized by law is considered a warning signal.
11. $\dfrac{\text{Debt Service}}{\text{Operating revenues}}$	Indicates extent of the government's fixed costs for paying principal and interest on its direct tax-supported debt. A ratio of 20 percent or more is considered a warning signal; 10 percent or below is considered good.

Unfunded liabilities:

12. $\dfrac{\text{Unfunded pension liability}}{\text{Net assessed valuation}}$	When compared with ratio 9 above, this ratio indicates the level of unfunded liabilities relative to net tax-supported bonded debt. Other useful ratios would be unfunded "other postemployment benefits" or unfunded accrued vacation and sick leave divided by net assessed valuation.
13. $\dfrac{\text{Pension plan assets}}{\text{Benefits paid}}$	Indicates the amount of accumulated cash and investments relative to annual benefits paid. Over time, a decline in this ratio may indicate serious problems in the management or design of the pension plan.

SOURCE: These ratios are adapted from S. M. Groves and M. G. Valente, *Evaluating Financial Condition: A Handbook for Local Government* (Washington, D.C.: International City/County Management Association, 1986).

The data to calculate all 13 financial ratios are readily obtainable from most CAFRs. Except for population, which is usually disclosed in the statistical section, data for the first 8 ratios and ratio 11 can be obtained from the Combined Statement of Revenues, Expenditures, and Changes in Fund Balances—All Governmental Fund Types and Discretely Presented Component Units (see Illustration 3–1). Data for the remaining ratios are found in Notes to the Financial Statements.

In calculating ratios 1 through 8, some analysts will prefer to utilize General Fund data only, whereas others will utilize combined data for all governmental fund types. This decision will depend, in part, on how large the General Fund is relative to all governmental fund types. In calculating "operating revenues," capital project fund revenues should be excluded since the capital project fund is not an operating fund. For purposes of calculating revenues and expenditures in these ratios, revenues usually include other financing sources and expenditures usually include other financing uses.

Regardless of how the ratios are calculated, the more difficult task is how to interpret them to make an informed judgment about financial condition. Checking each ratio against the applicable "red flag" level shown in Illustration 13–4 may provide warning signals about low liquidity, overreliance on intergovernmental revenues, an imbalance between revenues and expenditures, excessive debt burden, and poor management of retirement plans. Five or 10-year trends in these ratios are essential in pinpointing emerging or existing problem areas.

No red flag levels are shown for several ratios. In those cases, analysts can compare specific ratios to national and state medians published by Moody's Investors Service.[11] One caveat to keep in mind, however, is that local government organizational structure differs significantly from state to state, and these differences may have a large effect on some ratios. A good example is that in a few states local school districts are legally part of the government of the city in which they are located, whereas in most states the school districts are independent governmental units. In those states in which schools are part of the city government, per capita measures such as ratios 1, 3, and 10 will generally be much larger than in the other states.

In addition to analyzing ratios, one should evaluate the stability, flexibility, and diversity of revenue sources, budgetary control over revenues and expenditures, adequacy of insurance protection, level of overlapping debt, and growth of unfunded employee-related benefits. Socioeconomic and demographic trends should also be analyzed, including trends in employment, real estate values, retail sales, building permits, population, personal income, and welfare. Much of this information is contained in the statistical section of the CAFR; the remainder can be obtained from U.S. Bureau of the Census publications available in most libraries.

Despite the complexity of evaluating governmental financial condition, there are recognizable signals of fiscal stress.[12] These include: (1) a decline or inadequate growth in revenues relative to expenditures, (2) declining property values, (3) declining economic activity (such as increasing unemployment, declining retail sales, and declining building activity), (4) erosion of capital plant, particularly

---

[11] Moody's Investors Service, Inc., *1993 Medians: Selected Indicators of Municipal Performance* (New York: Moody's 1993).

[12] See, for example, S. M. Groves, *Evaluating Financial Condition*; and J. R. Miller and M. H. Granof, *Governmental Accounting and Auditing Update* 1, no. 3 (Boston, Mass.: Warren, Gorham & Lamont, Inc., March 1990).

infrastructure, (5) increasing levels of unfunded pension and other postemployment obligations, and (6) inadequate capital expenditures. Warning signals such as these, particularly if several exist simultaneously, may indicate a potential fiscal crisis unless the government takes action to increase revenues or decrease spending.

Recent Developments in Financial Reporting and Unresolved Issues

GASB reporting objectives emphasize the role of accountability in external financial reporting. Indeed, accountability is considered to be "the paramount objective from which all other objectives must flow."[13] GASB *Concepts Statement No. 1* expands the definition of accountability beyond the traditional notion of accountability for expenditures of financial resources in conformity with the legally adopted budget. GASB's concept of accountability includes also accountability for the efficient and effective use of resources in providing government services and for interpersonal equity, or the extent to which current-year revenues are sufficient to pay for current-year services.[14] It follows that the boundaries of external general purpose financial reporting may need to be expanded to meet the objectives implied by the broader concept of accountability. The GASB, accordingly, has established several projects aimed at meeting these broader objectives. Not all constituents agree with the objectives GASB has established and their implications for financial reporting. Thus, some projects have been highly controversial. Some of GASB's key financial reporting projects are discussed briefly below.

Measurement Focus and Basis of Accounting— Governmental Fund Types (MFBA)

In May 1990, after extensive due process, the GASB issued Statement No. 11, *Measurement Focus and Basis of Accounting—Governmental Fund Operating Statements,* which was to have become effective for fiscal years beginning after June 15, 1994. This Statement would have shifted the measurement focus for governmental fund revenues and expenditure from flow of *available* financial resources to the flow of financial resources, regardless, of when cash is received or paid. Thus, revenues and expenditures would have been recognized on an accrual basis (revenues when earned or demanded and expenditures when incurred) rather than on the modified accrual basis required by current GAAP. GASB believed that use of the accrual basis for governmental funds would achieve better reporting on interperiod equity by including in governmental fund operating statements changes in noncurrent assets and noncurrent liabilities relating to operating activities. Early implementation of Statement No. 11 was not permitted since the Statement dealt only with measurement, recognition, and display of operating statement accounts; subsequent guidance on balance sheet display was to have been provided prior to implementation as part of GASB's financial reporting project.

---

[13] GASB Codification Sec. 100.176.
[14] GASB Codification Sec. 100.177.

Some constituent organizations strongly opposed issuance of Statement No. 11 prior to resolving related financial reporting (especially balance sheet display) issues. Their opposition continued after Statement No. 11 was issued, perhaps encouraged by inability of the GASB Board Members to reach agreement on a reporting model and the manner of reporting long-term accruals and operating debt in balance sheets, among other unresolved reporting issues. In 1992 GASB issued a Preliminary Views document designed to gather constituent's reaction to alternative views within the GASB about implementation of Statement No. 11. A majority of the Board, the "preliminary view," believed that operating debt and long-term accrued obligations related to operations should be reported as liabilities of governmental funds. The minority, or "alternative view," held that, pending completion of the full financial reporting model project, such liabilities should continue to be reported in the GLTDAG. Subsequent hearings found no consensus among constituents for either approach. After further due process input indicated that a number of constituents opposed implementation of Statement No. 11, as scheduled, prior to completion of the financial reporting model project, GASB issued Statement No. 17 in June 1993 that delayed indefinitely the implementation of Statement No. 11. The GASB, however, issued a standard that requires accrual recognition of revenues from taxpayer-assessed taxes (such as income and sales taxes) when the amount is known or reasonably determinable.

Financial Reporting Model

As discussed in the preceding section, the structure of the financial reporting model, particularly the form and content of financial statements, must now be determined before Statement No. 11 can be implemented. Although one major part of the reporting model project has been completed and implemented, the governmental reporting entity, much remains to be done. The GASB has tentatively adopted a "top-down" approach to resolving reporting model issues. It has identified seven financial data categories that are intended to constitute the building blocks of the reporting model. For each of the seven categories—financial resources, budgetary resources, capital resources, cash flows, service efforts and accomplishments (SEA) data, interperiod equity, and financial condition—definitions are being developed by considering how the category relates to the GASB's objectives of financial reporting, what elements of financial reporting would achieve the reporting objectives, what reporting alternatives are available for each category, and what definitions will achieve a common understanding of the reporting objectives and elements. As the model develops, GASB is expected to develop core financial statements that will meet these reporting objectives.

Numerous issues must be resolved, including the appropriate level of aggregation in financial statements, at what level of aggregation to apply accruals, whether budgetary and financial resources data should be reported at the same financial statement level (e.g., at the fund level or some higher level of aggregation), or on different levels, and whether to report capital assets and liabilities differently from noncurrent operating assets and liabilities, and, if so, how. If the reporting model that evolves differs significantly from the current model, GASB intends to field-test the new model prior to issuing a final standard. Considering the complex issues remaining to be resolved, the likely need for field testing, and time-consuming due process requirements, it seems unlikely a new model will be implemented within the next few years.

Service Efforts and Accomplishments (SEA)

GASB, as mentioned previously, has expanded the accountability reporting objective to include reporting on the efficient and effective use of resources. GASB Codification Section 100.177c states:

> Financial reporting should provide information to assist users in assessing the service efforts, costs, and accomplishments of the governmental entity.

The lack of a bottom-line measure of performance for a governmental entity, such as profit for a for-profit entity, means that *nonfinancial* measures of service efforts and accomplishments, and related costs, are necessary for informed decision making by citizens, elected officials, appointed officials, investors and creditors, and others having an interest in the government's performance. Advances in information technology, a growing number of highly qualified public managers, and increasing public demand for accountability now make feasible more sophisticated performance measurement and reporting systems than in the past. Thus, the GASB has sponsored and conducted extensive research on SEA measures for several service areas, including, among others, elementary and secondary education, higher education, fire departments, police departments, hospitals, public health, mass transit, road maintenance, and sanitation collection and disposal.

GASB issued a Preliminary Views document on SEA concepts in December 1992 and an exposure draft of a Concepts Statement on SEA measures and reporting in September 1993.[15] GASB's research has identified three broad categories of SEA measures: (1) those that measure service efforts, (2) those that measure service accomplishments, and (3) those that relate efforts to accomplishments. Measures of service efforts relate to the amount of financial and nonfinancial resources (such as money and materials) used in a program or process.[16] Measures of service accomplishments are of two types: outputs and outcomes. Output measures are quantity measures that reflect either the quantity of a service provided, such as the number of lane-miles of road repaired, or the quantity of service provided that meets a specified quality requirement, such as the number of lane-miles of road repaired to a specified minimum condition. Outcome measures gauge accomplishments, or the results of services provided, such as the percentage of lane-miles of road in excellent, good, or fair condition. Such measures are particularly useful when compared with established objectives or norms, or with results from previous years. Finally, measures that relate efforts to accomplishments are essential to assessing efficiency and effectiveness. Efficiency measures relate the quantity or cost of resources used per unit of output (e.g., cost per lane-

---

[15] Governmental Accounting Standards Board, *Preliminary Views of the Governmental Accounting Standards Board on Concepts Related to Service Efforts and Accomplishments Reporting* (Norwalk, Conn., 1992); and Governmental Accounting Standards Board, Exposure Draft, *Concepts Statement*, "Service Efforts and Accomplishments Reporting" (Norwalk, Conn., 1993).

[16] The discussion of SEA measures is paraphrased from pars. 57–58 of the GASB's Preliminary Views document.

mile of road repaired). Measures that relate resource costs to outcomes are useful in evaluating how effectively service objectives are being met and at what cost (e.g., the cost per lane-mile of road maintained in excellent, good, or fair condition). Additional quantitative and narrative explanation may be necessary to help users fully assess the entity's performance.

The authors believe that some form of SEA reporting, possibly as required supplemental disclosure in the CAFR, or perhaps in a separately issued "performance" report, will eventually be required by GASB. However, there is currently little consensus as to what kinds of measures should be reported, and even whether setting standards for SEA reporting is within the scope of GASB's mandate. Thus, considerable experimentation and deliberation will be required before GASB can issue a standard on SEA reporting.

Other Reporting Issues

GASB has established a number of other projects on reporting issues. These include accounting for pensions and other postemployment benefits, definition and measurement focus for the government's business-type activities, and accounting for government-owned or affiliated colleges and universities.[17] It should be obvious from the preceding discussion that governmental accounting has changed rapidly in the past 10 or 15 years. Developments in this area are expected to continue at a rapid pace for the forseeable future.

Popular Reporting

Although the CAFR has evolved to meet the diverse information needs of financial report users (i.e., citizens, legislative and oversight bodies, and investors and creditors), it is widely recognized that most citizens are incapable of reading and comprehending the CAFR. Indeed, only a relatively few sophisticated analysts with taxpayer associations, citizen watchdog groups, and the media find the CAFR to be useful. To better communicate financial results to citizens, a growing number of governments prepare and distribute "popular reports" that provide highly condensed financial information, budget summaries, and narrative descriptions. They are usually short in length and employ a variety of graphical techniques to enhance understandability. Popular reports are intended to supplement the CAFR, not replace it. Since they do not present minimum data required for complete and fair presentation, popular reports are considered "summary data" and are unaudited.[18] Both GASB and the Government Finance Officers Association (GFOA), however, recognize the value of popular reports. GASB has published a commissioned research report on popular reporting,[19] and the GFOA has

---

[17] As standards are issued in these areas, the publisher will provide updates to adopters of the Tenth Edition of this text.

[18] The American Institute of Certified Public Accountants issued in February 1993 an Exposure Draft of a proposed Statement of Position, *Reporting on Separately Issued Summary Financial Information Prepared by State or Local Governmental Units*, which would permit auditors to express their opinion that a popular report is fairly stated in relation to the general purpose financial statements from which it is derived. Current AICPA guidance does not permit auditors to express an opinion on popular reports. However, if this document is issued in final form, some popular reports likely will contain an auditor's opinion.

[19] Frances H. Carpenter and Florence C. Sharp, *Research Report*, "Popular Reporting: Local Government Financial Reports to the Citizenry" (Norwalk, Conn.: GASB 1992).

established an award program for excellence in popular reporting. As citizens continue to demand greater accountability from their elected and appointed officials, popular reporting is likely to become more common.

Persons concerned with decision making for governmental bodies, auditors, bond analysts and investors, and others have a need to understand and evaluate both financial and nonfinancial information not incoporated in the comprehensive annual financial report. Chapter 16 introduces the subject of budgeting as a means of aiding administrators and legislators to evaluate alternative plans and, after plans are decided on, to evaluate whether activities are conducted according to plan.

Chapter 17 introduces the important topics of cash budgeting and cash management. Chapter 17 also discusses accounting and reporting requirements for deposits with financial institutions and investments. Chapter 18 introduces the subject of cost finding as a means of translating data developed for use in financial statements into data needed for management of scarce resources, and in developing cost data needed for management of programs funded by federal grants.

Selected References

American Institute of Certified Public Accountants. *Audit and Accounting Guide. Audits of State and Local Governmental Units.* Revised, New York, 1993.

Brown, Ken W. "The 10-Point Test of Financial Condition: Toward an Easy-to-Use Assessment Tool for Smaller Cities." *Government Finance Review,* December 1993, pp. 21–26.

Governmental Accounting Standards Board. *Codification of Governmental Accounting and Financial Reporting Standards as of June 30, 1993.* Norwalk, Conn., 1993.

Questions

13–1. What is the minimum number of funds a government could keep if it were attempting to adhere to GASB standards? Explain.

13–2. *a.* State the principal reasons for the use of several funds in the accounts of governmental units.

b. List five kinds of funds frequently found in the accounting system of a municipality, and briefly discuss the content of each.

(AICPA)

13–3. William Bates is executive vice president of Mavis Industries, Inc., a publicly held industrial corporation. Bates has just been elected to the City Council of Gotham City. Prior to assuming office as a City Councilman, he asks you as his CPA to explain the major differences that exist in accounting and financial reporting for a large city when compared to a large industrial corporation.

Required
a. Describe the major differences that exist in the purpose of accounting and financial reporting and in the types of financial reports of a large city when compared to a large industrial corporation.

b. Why are inventories often ignored in accounting for local governmental units? Explain.

c. Under what circumstances should depreciation be recognized in accounting for local governmental units? Explain.   (AICPA)

13–4. Under what conditions may interfund receivables and payables properly be offset against each other? Under what conditions would it be improper to offset interfund receivables and payables?

13–5. Identify and describe the five classes of interfund transactions or transfers between funds. How do interfund loans and advances differ from the other four categories of interfund transactions?

13–6. The Mayor of a city contends that since he is the elected head of all city activities, he has authority to transfer assets from one fund to another on a temporary basis because "it is all in the family." What is the merit, if any, of the Mayor's contention?

13–7. A single balance sheet in which like items of all funds are consolidated into single figures has the valuable attribute of being very compact. Why, then, does the GASB require a combined balance sheet, rather than a consolidated balance sheet, in the GPFS?

13–8. What are the three major sections of a CAFR and what are the contents of each?

13–9. Listed below are four independent transactions or events that relate to a local government.

1. $25,000 was disbursed from the General Fund (or its equivalent) for the cash purchase of new equipment.
2. An unrestricted cash gift of $100,000 was received from a donor.
3. Listed common stocks with a total carrying value of $50,000, exclusive of any allowance, were sold by an endowment fund for $55,000, before any dividends were earned on these stocks. There are no restrictions on the gain.
4. $1,000,000 face amount of general obligation bonds payable were sold at par, with the proceeds required to be used solely for construction of a new building. This building was completed at a total cost of $1,000,000, and the total amount of bond issue proceeds was disbursed in connection therewith. Disregard interest capitalization.

Required For each of the above-listed transactions or events, prepare journal entries, without explanations, specifying the affected funds and account groups and showing how these transactions or events should be recorded by a local government whose debt is serviced by general tax revenues.

13–10. Explain the criteria currently prescribed by GASB standards for determining whether an organization is a primary government and whether it is financially accountable for another organization. Assuming a decision has been made to include a component unit in the reporting entity, how does one determine whether to report the component unit by discrete presentation or by blending?

Exercises and Problems

13–1. Utilizing the CAFR obtained for Exercise 1–1 and your answers to the questions asked in Exercise 1–1, and the corresponding exercises in Chapters 2 through 12, comment on the following:

a. Analysis of Introductory Section. Does the report contain all introductory material specified by the GASB (see Chapter 13)? Is the introductory material presented in such a manner that it communicates significant information effectively—do you understand what they are telling you and why they are telling it to you? On the basis of your study of the entire report, list any additional information you feel should have been included in the introductory section and explain why you feel it should have been included. On the basis of your study of the entire report, do you think the introductory material presents the information fairly? Comment on any information in the introductory section you feel is superfluous, and explain why.

b. *Analysis of Financial Statements.*
1. Do the statements, notes, and schedules in the financial section present the information required by the GASB (see Chapter 13)? Are Total columns provided in the combined statements and schedules for the primary government and the reporting entity? If so, are the Total columns for the current year compared with Total columns for the prior year? Are the combined statements, combining statements, and notes cross-referenced to each other? Are they cross-referenced to the statements and schedules of individual funds and account groups?
2. Review your answers to the questions asked in Exercises 3–1 and 4–1 in light of your study of subsequent chapters of the text and your analysis of all portions of the annual report. If you feel your earlier answers were not entirely correct, change them in accord with your present understanding of generally accepted accounting principles and proper disclosure of the financial position and financial operations of a governmental reporting entity.
3. Review your answers to Exercise 5–1 and all subsequent exercises in this series in light of knowledge you have gained since you prepared the answers. If any of your earlier answers should be changed, change them.

c. *Analysis of Statistical Section.* Are statistical tables presented in the annual report in conformity with GASB standards (see Chapter 13)? Make note of any data omitted. Make note of any additional data presented. If data have been omitted, to what extent does each omission impair your ability to understand the report? To what extent does each additional table, chart, graph, or other statistical presentation add to your understanding of the governmental reporting entity, its problems, its financial position, past and probable future changes in its financial position, financial operations, or past and probable future changes in financial operations?

d. *GFOA Certificate of Achievement.* Does the report include a copy of a GFOA Certificate of Achievement in Financial Reporting or refer to the fact that the governmental unit has received one? If the report has been awarded a certificate, does your review indicate it was merited? If the report has not been awarded a certificate, does your review indicate that the report should be eligible for one?

e. *Service Potential of the CAFR.* Specify the most important information needs that a governmental annual report should fulfill for each of the following:
(1) Administrators.
(2) Members of the legislative branch.
(3) Interested residents.
(4) Creditors or potential creditors.
In what ways does the CAFR you have analyzed meet the information needs you have specified for each of the four groups, assuming members of each group make an effort to understand reports equivalent to the effort you have made? In what way does the report fail to meet the information needs of each of the four groups?

f. Does your CAFR present any service efforts and accomplishments (SEA) data in the introductory section, statistical section, or elsewhere in the CAFR? If so, are measures provided for both service efforts and service accomplishments? From the data and/or narrative provided can you infer whether major service functions of the governmental unit were carried out efficiently and economically, and that program activities are having the desired effects?

g. Using the data in your CAFR, calculate insofar as possible the 13 financial ratios shown in Illustration 13–4. Evaluate the ratios in terms of the benchmarks provided in Illustration 13–4 and long-term trend data for each ratio, if available. In your opinion, is the governmental entity whose CAFR you have analyzed in sound financial condition? Explain your rationale. What other information would have helped your analysis?

13–2. Write the numbers 1 through 10 on a sheet of paper. Beside each number write the letter corresponding with the best answer to each of the following questions:

1. Which of the following funds of a governmental unit integrates budgetary accounts into the accounting system?
   a. Enterprise.
   b. Internal Service.
   c. Special Revenue.
   d. Nonexpendable Trust.

2. One of the differences between accounting for a governmental unit and accounting for a business is that a government should:
   a. *Not* record depreciation expense in any of its funds.
   b. Use only the modified accrual basis of accounting.
   c. Always establish and maintain complete self-balancing accounts for each fund.
   d. Use only the cash basis of accounting.

3. Cook County received goods that had been approved for purchase but for which payment had not yet been made. Should the accounts listed below be increased?

	Encumbrances	Expenditures
a.	No	No
b.	No	Yes
c.	Yes	No
d.	Yes	Yes

4. Which of the following items would generally be recognized as revenue in the General Fund of a governmental unit?
   a. Receipts from a city-owned parking structure that is operated on a business basis.
   b. Property taxes.
   c. Interest earned on investments held to finance pension payments to retired employees.
   d. Revenues from internal service funds.

5. Proceeds of General Obligation Bonds is an account of a governmental unit that would be included in the:
   a. Enterprise Fund.
   b. Nonexpendable Trust Fund.

    c. Capital Projects Fund.

    d. Debt Service Fund.

  6. Which of the following funds ordinarily should account for the payment of interest and principal on *revenue* bond debt?

    a. Debt Service.

    b. Enterprise.

    c. Expendable Trust.

    d. Capital Projects.

  7. What journal entry should be made at the end of the fiscal year to close Encumbrances?

    a. None. The account is only closed when no encumbrance documents are outstanding.

    b. Debit Reserve for Encumbrances and credit Encumbrances.

    c. Debit Fund Balance and credit Encumbrances.

    d. Debit Encumbrances and credit Reserve for Encumbrances.

  8. Equipment in general governmental service that had been constructed 10 years before by the Capital Projects Fund was sold. The receipts were accounted for as unrestricted revenue. Entries are necessary in the:

    a. General Fund and Capital Projects Fund.

    b. General Fund and General Fixed Assets Account Group.

    c. General Fund, Capital Projects Fund, and Enterprise Fund.

    d. General Fund, Capital Projects Fund, and General Fixed Assets Account Group.

  9. The Appropriations Control account of a governmental unit is debited when:

    a. Supplies are purchased.

    b. Expenditures are recorded.

    c. The budgetary accounts are closed.

    d. The budget is recorded.

  10. The members of the Library Board of the City of Fayetteville are appointed by the City Council of the City of Fayetteville, and the City Council has agreed to finance any operating deficits of the Library. Under these conditions:

    a. The Library is a primary government.

    b. The City is a primary government.

    c. Financial data of the Library should be included in the financial statements of the reporting entity, in the manner specified in GASB standards.

    d. Both *b* and *c.*

(AICPA, adapted)

13–3. Write the numbers 1 through 10 on a sheet of paper. Beside each number write the letter corresponding with the best answer to each of the following questions:

  1. Which of the following is an appropriate basis of accounting for a proprietary fund of a governmental unit?

	Cash Basis	*Accrual Basis*
a.	Yes	Yes
b.	Yes	No
c.	No	No
d.	No	Yes

2. Which of the following amounts are included in a general fund's Encumbrance account?

   I. Outstanding vouchers payable amounts.
   II. Outstanding purchase order amounts.
   III. Excess of the amount of a purchase order over the actual expenditure for that order.

   > *a.* I only.
   > *b.* I and III.
   > *c.* II only.
   > *d.* II and III.

3. Property taxes levied in fiscal year 19x1 to finance the General Fund budget of fiscal year 19x2 should be reported as General Fund revenues in fiscal year 19x2:

   a. Regardless of the fiscal year in which collected.
   b. For the amount collected in fiscal year 19x2 only.
   c. For the amount collected before the end of fiscal year 19x2 only.
   d. For the amount collected before the end of fiscal year 19x2 or shortly thereafter.

4. The comprehensive annual financial report (CAFR) of a governmental reporting entity should contain a Combined Statement of Cash Flows for:

	Governmental Funds	*Account Groups*
a.	Yes	No
b.	Yes	Yes
c.	No	Yes
d.	No	No

5. Repairs that have been made for a governmental unit, and for which a bill has been received, should be recorded in the General Fund as a debit to an:

   a. Expenditure.
   b. Encumbrance.
   c. Expense.
   d. Appropriation.

6. The budget of a governmental unit, for which the appropriations exceed the estimated revenues, was adopted and recorded in the general ledger at the beginning of the year. During the year, expenditures and encumbrances were less than appropriations; whereas revenues equaled estimated revenues. The Budgetary Fund Balance account is:

   a. Credited at the beginning of the year and debited at the end of the year.
   b. Credited at the beginning of the year and *not* changed at the end of the year.
   c. Debited at the beginning of the year and credited at the end of the year.
   d. Debited at the beginning of the year and *not* changed at the end of the year.

7. Brockton City serves as collecting agency for the local independent school district and for a local water district. For this purpose, Brockton has created a single agency fund and charges the other entities a fee of 1 percent of the gross amounts collected. (The service fee is treated as General Fund revenue.) During the latest fiscal year, a gross amount of $268,000 was collected for the independent school

district and $80,000 for the water district. As a consequence of the foregoing, Brockton's General Fund should:

a. Recognize receipts of $384,000.

b. Recognize receipts of $344,520.

c. Record revenue of $3,480.

d. Record encumbrances of $344,520.

Items 8 and 9 are based on the following information:

    During the year ended December 31, 19x1, Leyland City received a state grant of $500,000 to finance the purchase of buses and an additional grant of $100,000 to aid in the financing of bus operations in 19x1. Only $300,000 of the capital grant was used in 19x1 for the purchase of buses, but the entire operating grant of $100,000 was spent in 19x1.

8. If Leyland's bus transportation system is accounted for as part of the City's General Fund, how much should Leyland report as grant revenues for the year ended December 31, 19x1?

a. $100,000.

b. $300,000.

c. $400,000.

d. $500,000.

9. If Leyland's bus transportation system is accounted for as an Enterprise Fund, how much should Leyland report as grant revenues for the year ended December 31, 19x1?

a. $100,000.

b. $300,000.

c. $400,000.

d. $500,000.

10. The comprehensive annual financial report (CAFR) of a governmental reporting entity should contain a Combined Statement of Revenues, Expenses, and Changes in Retained Earnings for:

	Governmental Funds	Proprietary Funds
a.	No	Yes
b.	No	No
c.	Yes	No
d.	Yes	Yes

(AICPA, adapted)

13–4. Write the numbers 1 through 10 on a sheet of paper. Beside each number write the letter corresponding with the best answer to each of the following questions:

1. Self-supporting activities provided to the public on a user-charge basis are accounted for in what fund type?

a. Agency.

b. Enterprise.

c. Internal Service.

d. Special Revenue.

2. The activities of a central data processing department that offers data processing services at a discount to other departments of a certain city should be accounted for in:
   a. An Enterprise Fund.
   b. An Internal Service Fund.
   c. A Special Revenue Fund.
   d. The General Fund.

3. The initial contribution of cash from the General Fund in order to establish an Internal Service Fund would require the General Fund to credit Cash and debit:
   a. Accounts Receivable—Internal Service Fund.
   b. Equity Transfers Out.
   c. Operating Transfers Out.
   d. Long-Term Advance to Internal Service Fund.

4. The premium received at the time an issue of general obligation bonds is sold is usually considered an other financing source of what fund or account group?
   a. Debt Service.
   b. General Long-Term Debt.
   c. General.
   d. Special Revenue.

5. What would be the effect on the General Fund Fund Balance in the current fiscal year of recording a $15,000 purchase for a new automobile out of General Fund resources, for which a $14,600 encumbrance had been recorded in the General Fund in the previous year?
   a. Reduce the Fund Balance $15,000.
   b. Reduce the Fund Balance $14,600.
   c. Reduce the Fund Balance $400.
   d. Have no effect on the Fund Balance.

6. Brockton City's Debt Service Fund (for term bonds) recorded estimated other financing sources and estimated revenues for the current fiscal year of $15,000 and $7,000, respectively. The actual transfers in and interest earnings for future repayment of principal were $16,000 and $6,500, respectively. What are the necessary amounts to record the year's actual transfers and earnings in the Debt Service Fund and in the General Long-Term Debt Account Group, respectively?
   a. $22,500 and $22,000.
   b. $22,000 and $22,000.
   c. $22,500 and $22,500.
   d. $22,500 and no entry.

Items 7 through 10 are based on the following information:

   The following related entries were recorded in sequence in the General Fund of a city:

1. Encumbrances...	12,000	
Reserve for Encumbrances................................		12,000
2. Reserve for Encumbrances....................................	12,000	
Encumbrances...		12,000
3. Expenditures	12,350	
Vouchers Payable..		12,350

7. The sequence of entries indicates that:
   a. An adverse event was foreseen, and a reserve of $12,000 was created; later the reserve was canceled, and a liability for the item was acknowledged.
   b. An order was placed for goods or services estimated to cost $12,000; the actual cost was $12,350, for which a liability was acknowledged on receipt.
   c. Encumbrances were anticipated but later failed to materialize and were reversed. A liability of $12,350 was incurred.
   d. The first entry was erroneous and was reversed; a liability of $12,350 was acknowledged.

8. Entries similar to those for the General Fund may also appear on the books of the City's:
   a. General Fixed Assets Account Group.
   b. General Long-Term Debt Account Group.
   c. Nonexpendable Trust Fund.
   d. Special Revenue Fund.

9. Assuming GASB standards were followed, the entries:
   a. Occurred in the same fiscal period.
   b. Did not occur in the same fiscal period.
   c. Could have occurred in the same fiscal period.
   d. Reflect the equivalent of a "prior period adjustment" had the entity concerned been operated for profit.

10. Immediately after Entry 1 was recorded, the city had a balanced General Fund budget for all transactions. What would be the effect of recording Entries 2 and 3?
   a. Not change the balanced condition of the budget.
   b. Cause the city to show a surplus.
   c. Cause the city to show a deficit.
   d. Not affect the current budget but would affect the budget of the following fiscal period.

(AICPA, adapted)

13–5. The following example of application of reporting entity criteria is based on an example contained in GASB Codification Section 2100.

a. The Greater Metropolis Urban Development Authority (GMUDA) was authorized as a nonprofit corporation by the state legislature and created by the City of Metropolis Council to attract new industry and participate in long-range planning of the City. Although the City Council appoints GMUDA's governing board, the board has complete authority to hire management and all other employees. The City has no role in monitoring or participating in the day-to-day operating activities of GMUDA.

Per its State charter, GMUDA has separate taxing powers and levies taxes on all commercial and industrial properties located within the designated development district. GMUDA's tax levies are completely independent of the City's, other than they are levied on some of the same taxpayers. GMUDA performs some services for the Chamber of Commerce and other local business organizations for a fee. However, its primary source of revenues is property taxes. GMUDA receives no financial subsidies of any kind from the City and the City is not obligated in any manner for the authority's debt. Even though GMUDA does not require the City's approval of its operating budget, it routinely sends the budget to the City Council for review. The City Attorney has ruled that the City Council has no option but to approve the budget as submitted.

Required Using the reporting entity flow chart presented in Illustration 13–2, and the reporting entity definitions and criteria discussed in Chapter 13, determine whether or not the Greater Metropolis Urban Development Authority should be included in the reporting entity of which the City of Metropolis is the primary government? If so, should GMUDA be reported by blending or by discrete presentation? Explain your rationale for the inclusion/exclusion decision and, if applicable, method of display.

      b. Assume the same facts as in Part *a* above except that the City Council has the power to remove members of GMUDA's board for cause. Also, the City must approve all debt issuances and all expenditures in excess of $100,000.

Required Do your conclusions made in Part *a* above change in light of the different facts in Part *b*? Explain fully.

13–6. The letter of transmittal to the Mayor and Council accompanying the annual financial statements of the Town of Stevens is presented below. (Note: This case is based on an actual letter of transmittal and financial statements received by one of the authors quite some time ago; however, the name of the Town and certain other facts have been changed.)

LETTER OF TRANSMITTAL

To the Honorable Mayor and Town Council
Town of Stevens

Gentlemen:

We are attaching the financial report for the Town of Stevens for the year 19x9. The statements and organization of this report are designed to conform to generally accepted principals [sic] and standards of government accounting and reporting. A review of this report will reveal much information about the financial position and movements of the Town, some of which it is hoped will be valuable and some of which we fear will be tiresome and redundant.

Plans and performance for 19x9 did not exactly match. Hopes for major street repair and water line replacement on Castle Avenue were frustrated by the need to follow the county engineering and road department on its Jones Street relocation project. This meant relocating 300 feet of 6-inch main line, the rebuilding of two laterals, 12 services and the digging out and adjusting of 10 valve covers a number of times. This work, which was not anticipated, occupied most of the summer and partly explained why the water line maintenance cost was $97,418 for 19x9 as compared with $46,554 for 19x8. It is hoped that this deferred work can be accomplished in 19y0.

For the first time in a number of years the streets were hand-cleaned of old dirt and the remains of the winter debris. Although a new and richer layer of gum wrappers, beer cans, and cigarette packs corrected this condition, the Town's purchase of a Wayne sweeper in August puts the Town temporarily one up in its long struggle for clean streets. An additional help is that a tough antilitter ordinance was passed.

The new Town Hall was purchased on a contract for $90,900 payable at $30,000 per year, the first installment of which was met in 19x9. We thus own outright the Town Hall from the front door to the west end of the fireplace. A new roof was installed and arrangements made to have part of the interior repaired in 19y0.

At the moment the Town's financial position is not too grim. This may be changed in attempting to solve the remaining problems of sewage disposal and providing additional water to the areas the Town is required to serve.

/s/ Treasurer-Clerk

THE TOWN OF STEVENS
General Fund

Balance Sheet—December 31, 19x9   Form A-1

Assets:
Petty cash	500.00
Cash on deposit with treasurer	(16,404.70)
Temporary investments (S–9)	100,000.00
Inventory of supplies	3,800.00
Total Assets	87,895.30

Liabilities, reserves, and surplus:
Warrants payable	8,586.70
Contract payable—new town hall	60,900.00
Cumulative reserve fund	53,298.80
Deficit (A–2)	(34,890.20)
	87,895.30

Analysis of Changes in Fund Balance   Form A–2

	Estimated	Actual	Excess or Deficiency
Surplus—Jan. 1, 19x9	43,030.90	43,030.90	
Add: Revenues (A–3)	288,200.00	303,879.50	15,679.50
Total	331,230.90	346,910.40	15,679.50
Less: Town hall contract		90,900.00	(90,900.00)
Expenditures (A-4)	310,200.00	290,900.60	19,299.40
Deficit—Dec. 31, 19x9	21,030.90	(34,890.20)	55,921.10

Statement of Revenues—Estimated and Actual   Form A–3

	Estimated	Actual	Difference
General property tax	140,000.00	94,635.60	45,364.40
Special tax—utilities	33,000.00	31,400.00	1,600.00
Licenses and permits	10,000.00	8,145.60	1,854.40
Fines and penalties	9,000.00	21,275.00	(12,275.00)
Rental income	7,200.00	6,700.00	500.00
Revenue from other agencies:			
Aid to Cities	7,000.00	23,457.40	(16,457.40)
State liquor tax	39,000.00	38,795.30	204.70
Motor vehicle excise tax	35,000.00	38,373.90	(3,373.90)
Expense sharing—Fire district 2	8,000.00	4,852.70	3,147.30
Interest income		4,750.00	(4,750.00)
Other income		31,494.00	(31,494.00)
	288,200.00	303,879.50	15,679.50

THE TOWN OF STEVENS
General Fund
Statement of Expenditures Compared with Authorizations   Form A–4

	Appropriated	Expended	Actual Under (Over) Estimate
Police:			
Salaries	123,000.00	123,482.20	(482.20)
FICA tax	5,500.00	5,495.30	4.70
Retirement	7,400.00	7,228.80	171.20
Industrial insurance	3,000.00	1,666.70	1,333.30
Hospital insurance	3,000.00	2,644.30	355.70
Vehicle care	1,500.00	4,763.10	(3,263.10)
Police bond	700.00	550.00	150.00
Motor fuel	8,000.00	11,641.10	(3,641.10)
Supplies	2,000.00	2,892.80	(892.80)
Total	154,100.00	160,364.30	(6,264.30)
Clerk:			
Salaries	21,000.00	21,335.40	(335.40)
FICA tax	1,000.00	1,067.40	(67.40)
Retirement	2,300.00	2,345.40	(45.40)
Hospital	1,200.00	527.60	672.40
Bond	150.00	140.00	10.00
Office supplies	2,500.00	2,997.70	(497.70)
Total	28,150.00	28,413.50	(263.50)

	Appropriated	Expended	Actual Under (Over) Estimate
Fire Department:			
Salaries	12,000.00	8,120.00	3,880.00
Pensions	6,000.00	2,655.00	3,345.00
Hydrant rental	12,000.00	12,000.00	0
Vehicle care	2,000.00	240.80	1,759.20
Equipment repair		511.80	(511.80)
Heat and lights		5,102.20	(5,102.20)
Motor fuel	1,500.00	272.80	1,227.20
Supplies	1,000.00	1,252.80	(252.80)
Total	34,500.00	30,155.40	4,344.60
General Government:			
Census	1,000.00	897.00	103.00
Elections	800.00		800.00
Attorney fees	10,000.00	1,500.00	8,500.00
Police judge	9,000.00	6,000.00	3,000.00
Councilmen:			
Salaries (Ord. #581)		3,666.30	(3,666.30)
Retirement		374.40	(374.40)
FICA tax		171.60	(171.60)
Heat and lights	8,000.00	4,762.10	3,237.90
Telephone	1,500.00	1,687.10	(187.10)
Building repair	5,000.00	6,356.30	(1,356.30)
Audit fee	4,000.00		4,000.00
Printing	2,000.00	302.50	1,697.50
Advertising	2,850.00	2,256.10	593.90
Postage	500.00	468.80	31.20
Surety bonds and insurance	15,000.00	12,850.00	2,150.00
Janitor service	1,800.00	1,440.40	359.60
Library	19,000.00	15,110.00	3,890.00
Travel and subsistence	2,000.00	1,975.20	24.80
Association dues	2,000.00	1,875.10	124.90
Planning commission	3,000.00		3,000.00
Miscellaneous	3,500.00	3,948.40	(448.40)
Supplies	1,000.00	1,030.90	(30.90)
Household supplies	1,500.00	525.20	974.80
Driver education		4,770.00	(4,770.00)
Total	93,450.00	71,967.40	21,482.60
Combined totals—General Fund	310,200.00	290,900.60	19,299.40

Required The remainder of the report deals with other funds and account groups of the Town of Stevens; those statements are not reproduced because they are similar to the General Fund statements above. On the basis of the material given you, prepare a written evalution of the information produced by the Town's accounting system from the standpoint of its usefulness to:

    a. Town administrators.

    b. The Town Council (the legislative body).

    c. Taxpayers and citizens of the town.

    d. Creditors of the town.

13–7. The following transactions represent practical situations frequently encountered in accounting for state and local governments. Each transaction is independent of the others.

1. The City Council of Bernardville adopted a budget for the general operations of the government during the new fiscal year. Revenues were estimated at $695,000. Legal authorizations for budgeted expenditures were $650,000.

2. Taxes of $160,000 were levied for the Special Revenue Fund of Millstown. One percent was estimated to be uncollectible.

3. *a.* On July 25, 19x3, office supplies estimated to cost $2,390 were ordered for the City Manager's office of Bullersville. Bullersville, which operates on the calendar year, does not maintain an inventory of such supplies.

    b. The supplies ordered July 25 were received on August 9, 19x3, accompanied by an invoice for $2,500.

4. On October 10, 19x3, the General Fund of Washingtonville repaid to the Utility Fund a loan of $1,000 plus $40 interest. The loan had been made earlier in the fiscal year.

5. A prominent citizen died and left 10 acres of undeveloped land to Harper City for a future park site. The donor's cost of the land was $55,000. The fair value of the land was $85,000 at the time its ownership was transferred to the City.

6. *a.* On March 6, 19x3, Dahlstrom City issued 9 percent special assessment bonds payable March 6, 19x8, at face value of $90,000. Interest is payable annually. Dahlstrom City, which operates on the calendar year, will use the proceeds to finance a curbing project. In case of default by property owners, the City agreed to assume debt service.

    b. On October 29, 19x3, the full $84,000 cost of the completed curbing project was recorded as a liability. Also, appropriate closing entries were made with regard to the project. Cash in the amount of the residual equity was transferred to the Debt Service Fund to be used for interest payments.

7. *a.* Conrad Thamm, a citizen of Basking Knoll, donated common stock valued at $22,000 to the City under a trust agreement. Under the terms of the agreement, the principal amount is to be kept intact; use of revenue from the stock is restricted to financing academic college scholarships for needy students.

    b. On December 14, 19x3, dividends of $1,100 were received on the stock donated by Mr. Thamm.

8. *a.* On February 23, 19x3, the Town of Lincoln, which operates on the calendar year, issued 9 percent general obligation bonds with a face value of $3,000,000 payable February 23, 19y3, to finance the construction of an addition to the city hall. The bonds were sold for $3,080,000. The premium was recorded directly in the Debt Service Fund and is to be held for bond repayment at maturity.

    b. On December 31, 19x3, the addition to the city hall was officially approved, the full cost of $2,970,000 was paid to the contractor, and appropriate closing entries were made with regard to the project. (Assume no entries have been made with regard to the project since February 23, 19x3.) The residual equity of the construction fund was transferred to the Debt Service Fund to be held for bond repayment at maturity.

Required   For each transaction, prepare the necessary journal entries for *all* of the funds and account groups involved. No explanation of the journal entries is required. Use the following headings for your workpaper:

Trans- action Number	Journal Entries	Dr.	Cr.	Fund or Account Group

In the far right column, indicate in which fund or account groups each entry is to be made, using the coding below:

Funds:
General	G
Special Revenue	SR
Capital Projects	CP
Debt Service	DS
Enterprise	E
Internal Service	IS
Nonexpendable Trust	NT
Expendable Trust	ET

Account Group:
General Fixed Assets	GFA
General Long-Term Debt	LTD

(AICPA, adapted)

13–8. The Village of Dexter was recently incorporated and began financial operations on July 1, 19x8, the beginning of its fiscal year.

The following transactions occurred during this first fiscal year, July 1, 19x8, to June 30, 19x9:

1. The Village Council adopted a budget for general operations during the fiscal year ending June 30, 19x9. Revenues were estimated at $2,000,000. Legal authorizations for budgeted expenditures were $1,970,000.

2. Property taxes were levied in the amount of $1,950,000; it was estimated that 2 percent of this amount would prove uncollectible. These taxes are available as of the date of levy to finance current expenditures.

3. During the year, a resident of the Village donated marketable securities valued at $250,000 to the Village under the terms of a trust agreement. The terms of the trust agreement stipulated that the principal amount is to be kept intact; use of revenue generated by the securities is restricted to financing college scholarships for needy students. Revenue earned and received on these marketable securities amounted to $27,500 through June 30, 19x9.

4. A General Fund transfer of $100,000 was made to establish an Internal Service Fund to provide for a permanent investment in inventory.

5. The Village decided to install lighting in a subdivision of the Village; a special assessment project was authorized to install the lighting at a cost of $375,000. Assessments were levied for $360,000; the Village's share of cost was $15,000. All assessments were collected during the year, as was the transfer from the Village's General Fund.

6. A contract for $375,000 was let for the installation of the lighting. At June 30, 19x9, the contract was completed. The contractor was paid all but 5 percent, which was

retained to ensure compliance with the terms of the contract. Encumbrance accounting is used.

7. During the year, the Internal Service Fund purchased various supplies at a cost of $95,000.

8. Cash collections recorded by the General Fund during the year were as follows:

Property taxes	$1,930,000
Licenses and permits	35,000

9. The Village Council decided to build a village hall at an estimated cost of $2,500,000 to replace space occupied in rented facilities. In order to finance the project, 6 percent bonds were sold at their face value of $2,500,000. No contracts have been signed for this project, and no expenditures have been made.

10. A purchase order in the amount of $100,000 was issued for a truck for use by the street department, a General Fund department. The truck was received, and a voucher in the amount of $102,500 was approved and paid.

Required Prepare journal entries to properly record each of the above transactions in the appropriate fund(s) or group of accounts of Dexter Village for the fiscal year ended June 30, 19x9. Use the following funds and account groups, as necessary;

General Fund
Capital Projects Fund
Internal Service Fund
Nonexpendable Trust Fund
Scholarship Fund
General Long-Term Debt Account Group
General Fixed Assets Account Group

Each journal entry should be numbered to correspond with the transactions described above. Do *not* prepare closing entries for any fund.

Your answer sheet should be organized as follows:

		Account	*Amounts*	
Transaction	*Fund or*	*Title and*		
Number	*Account Group*	*Explanation*	*Debits*	*Credits*

(AICPA, adapted)

13–9. You have been engaged by the Town of Rego to examine its June 30, 19x8, balance sheet. You are the first CPA to be engaged by the Town and find that employees of the Town are unaware of governmental accounting and financial reporting standards. The Town clerk stated that the books had not been closed and presented the following preclosing trial balance of the General Fund as of June 30, 19x8:

	Debits	Credits
Cash...	$ 550,000	
Taxes Receivable—Current Year	159,200	
Estimated Losses—Current-Year Taxes Receivable..................		$ 18,000
Taxes Receivable—Prior Year......................................	28,000	
Estimated Losses—Prior-Year Taxes Receivable		30,200
Estimated Revenues...	1,310,000	
Appropriations...		1,348,000
Donated Land	127,000	
Expenditures—Building Addition Constructed.......................	250,000	
Expenditures—Serial Bonds Paid	56,000	
Other Expenditures...	1,005,000	
Special Assessment Bonds Payable................................		500,000
Revenues..		1,354,000
Accounts Payable		126,000
Fund Balance..		109,000
	$3,485,200	$3,485,200

Additional information

1. The estimated losses of $18,000 for current-year taxes receivable were determined to be a reasonable estimate.
2. Included in the Revenues account is a credit of $127,000 representing the value of land donated by the state to be used for a town park.
3. The Expenditures—Building Addition Constructed account balance is the cost of an addition to the Town Hall building. This addition was constructed and completed in June 19x8. The General Fund recorded the payment as authorized.
4. The Expenditures—Serial Bonds Paid account reflects the annual retirement of general obligation bonds issued to finance the construction of the Town Hall. Interest payments of $24,000 for this bond issue are included in the Other Expenditures account.
5. Operating supplies ordered in the prior fiscal year and chargeable to that year were received, recorded, and consumed in July 19x7. The outstanding purchase orders for these supplies, which were not recorded in the accounts at June 30, 19x7, amounted to $28,800. The vendors' invoices for these supplies totaled $30,400. Appropriations lapse one year after the end of the fiscal year for which they are made.
6. Outstanding purchase orders at June 30, 19x8, for operating supplies totaled $10,100. These purchase orders were not recorded on the books.
7. The special assessment bonds were sold in June 19x8 to finance a street paving project. No contracts have been signed for this project, and no expenditures have been made.
8. The balance in the Revenues account includes credits for $100,000 for a note issued to a bank to obtain cash in anticipation of tax collections and for $5,000 for the sale of scrap iron from the Town's water plant. The note was still outstanding at June 30, 19x8. The operations of the water plant are accounted for in the Water Fund.

Required

a. Prepare the formal adjusting and closing journal entries for the General Fund for the fiscal year ended June 30, 19x8. Assume capital projects and debt service legally may be accounted for in the General Fund.

    b. The foregoing information disclosed by your examination was recorded only in the General Fund even though other funds or account groups were involved. Prepare the formal adjusting journal entries for any other funds or account groups involved, assuming that financial statements are to be prepared in conformity with GAAP.

(AICPA, adapted)

Continuous Problems

13–L. *a.* Assemble all statements and schedules prepared for your solutions to Problems 2–L through 12–L.

    b. From your solutions to Problems 2–L through 12–L, prepare:

      (1) A Combined Balance Sheet for All Funds and Account Groups of the City of Bingham as of June 30, 19x2.

      (2) A Combined Statement of Revenues, Expenditures, and Changes in Fund Balances—All Governmental Fund Types for the fiscal year ended June 30, 19x2.

      (3) A Combined Statement of Revenues, Expenditures, and Changes in Fund Balance—Budget and Actual for the General Fund and the Debt Service Fund for the year ended June 30, 19x2.

      (4) A Combined Statement of Revenues, Expenses, and Changes in Retained Earnings/Fund Balances—All Proprietary Fund Types and Similar Fiduciary Funds for the year ended June 30, 19x2.

      (5) A Combined Statement of Cash Flows—All Proprietary Fund Types and Nonexpendable Trust Funds for the year ended June 30, 19x2.

      (Note: The City of Bingham is a primary government and has no other organizations for which it is accountable as component units.)

13–S. *a.* Assemble all statements and schedules prepared for your solutions to Problems 2–S through 12–S.

    b. Prepare the general purpose financial statements that must be presented by the City of Smithville in order for its annual report to be in conformity with generally accepted accounting principles. (Since the Solid Waste Disposal Fund is the only fund in the proprietary funds category, and there are no fiduciary funds, you may use the Statement of Revenues, Expenses, and Changes in Retained Earnings and the Statement of Cash Flows prepared for the Solid Waste Disposal Fund as two of the five required general purpose financial statements.)

    (Note: The City of Smithville is a primary government and has no other organizations for which it is accountable as component units.)

CHAPTER 14

Audits of Governmental Entities

Financial statements of governmental entities, colleges and universities, hospitals and other health care entities, voluntary health and welfare organizations, and other nonprofit entities are the representations of the officials responsible for the financial management of the entity. In order for users of the financial statements to have the assurance that the statements are prepared in conformity with accounting and financial reporting standards established by authoritative bodies, and that all material facts are disclosed, the statements should be accompanied by the report of an independent auditor. Audits for this purpose are called *financial audits,* or attest audits.

Financial Audits by Independent CPAs

Audits of State and Local Governments

In the case of state and local governmental units, audits may be made by independent Certified Public Accountants or by state audit agencies. The American Institute of Certified Public Accountants (AICPA) has developed standard wording for the auditor's reports to make clear the responsibility the auditor is accepting in his or her report. In the case of governmental units, the auditor's report to accompany the general purpose financial statements should be worded as shown in Illustration 14–1 if the auditor's opinion on the general purpose financial statements is "unqualified."

The first paragraph of the auditor's report is known as the **opening paragraph.** In the first sentence of that paragraph, the auditor specifies the financial statements on which the opinion is being expressed. Since 1986, GASB standards (Codification Section 2200.136) have stated that the general purpose financial statements (GPFS—illustrated and discussed in Chapters 2, 3, and 12, and reviewed in Chapter 13) are the statements that must be presented for conformity with generally accepted accounting principles (GAAP). The comprehensive annual financial report (CAFR) should include combining and individual fund and account group financial statements, as well as the general purpose financial statements; but in the auditor's report shown in Illustration 14–1, the auditor accepts responsibility only for the combined statements, not for the combining statements or for the individual fund and account group financial statements. This is also clear from the second sentence of the fourth paragraph of the auditor's report. Inasmuch as combined statements are prepared from combining and individual fund and account group statements, the auditor would apply auditing procedures to

---

ILLUSTRATION 14–1 **Unqualified Opinion on General Purpose or Component Unit Financial Statements Submitted Together with Combining and Individual Fund and Account Group Financial Statements and Supporting Schedules as Supplementary Data***

Independent Auditor's Report

We have audited the accompanying general-purpose financial statements of City of Example, Any State, as of and for the year ended June 30, 19x1, as listed in the table of contents. These general-purpose financial statements are the responsibility of City of Example, Any State, management. Our responsibility is to express an opinion on these general-purpose financial statements based on our audit.

We conducted our audit in accordance with generally accepted auditing standards. Those standards require that we plan and perform the audit to obtain reasonable assurance about whether the general-purpose financial statements are free of material misstatement. An audit includes examining, on a test basis, evidence supporting the amounts and disclosures in the general-purpose financial statements. An audit also includes assessing the accounting principles used and significant estimates made by management, as well as evaluating the overall general-purpose financial presentation. We believe that our audit provides a reasonable basis for our opinion.

In our opinion, the general-purpose financial statements referred to above present fairly, in all material respects, the financial position of City of Example, Any State, as of June 30, 19x1, and the results of its operations and cash flows of its proprietary fund types and nonexpendable trust funds for the year then ended in conformity with generally accepted accounting principles.

Our audit was made for the purpose of forming an opinion on the general-purpose financial statements taken as a whole. The combining and individual fund and account group financial statements and schedules listed in the table of contents are presented for purposes of additional analysis and are not a required part of the general-purpose financial statements of City of Example, Any State. Such information has been subjected to the auditing procedures applied in the audit of the general-purpose financial statements and, in our opinion, is fairly presented in all material respects in relation to the general-purpose financial statements taken as a whole.

[Signature]

[Date]

---

* If a schedule of federal assistance is reported on as supplementary data, *Government Auditing Standards*, issued by the Comptroller General of the United States, should be referenced in the second paragraph. See example 16.

SOURCE: American Institute of Certified Public Accountants, Statement of Position 92–7, *Audits of State and Local Governmental Entities Receiving Federal Financial Assistance* (New York: AICPA, 1992), App. D, Example 2. Copyright © 1992 by the American Institute of Certified Public Accountants, Inc.

financial data reported in combining and individual fund and account group statements from which the combined statements were derived. If the auditor is expressing an opinion on the GPFS, and they are issued separately from a CAFR, then the fourth paragraph is not required. If the government officials desire an audit report on combining statements, or on individual fund or account group statements, that fact should be made explicit, in writing, before the start of the audit so the auditor can modify the scope of the examination appropriately. The opening paragraph also states that the financial statements are the responsibility of the entity's management.

The first sentence of the second or **scope paragraph** of the auditor's report (Illustration 14–1) states that the examination was made "in accordance with generally accepted auditing standards." That phrase has a definite meaning to professional auditors—a meaning they have been trying for many years to communicate to clients, bankers, judges, legislators, and every other group with a need to understand what an auditor's report means. Generally accepted auditing standards (GAAS) have been summarized by the AICPA in the three General Standards, three Standards of Field Work, and four Standards of Reporting shown in Illustration 14–2.

The scope paragraph also includes a statement that generally accepted auditing standards require that the auditor plan and perform the audit to obtain reasonable assurance as to whether the financial statements are free of material misstatements. In addition, the scope paragraph includes a statement that an audit includes: (1) examining, on a test basis, evidence supporting the amounts and disclosures in the financial statements, (2) assessing the accounting principles used and significant estimates made by management, and (3) evaluating the overall financial statement presentation. Finally, the scope paragraph includes a statement that the auditor believes that the audit provides a reasonable basis for the opinion rendered.[1]

The third paragraph of the auditor's report (Illustration 14–1) is referred to as the **opinion paragraph.** In that paragraph, the financial statements on which the auditor is expressing an opinion are identified as presenting fairly in conformity with generally accepted accounting principles the financial position of the reporting entity as of a certain date; the results of its operations for the fiscal year ended on that date; and, in the case of proprietary fund types and nonexpendable trust funds, cash flows during the fiscal year. The auditor states a professional opinion that the financial statements described in the report are fairly presented in conformity with GAAP.

The introductory, scope, and opinion paragraphs would be sufficient if the independent auditor's report accompanied separately issued GPFS. If the auditor's report is associated with the GPFS in the financial section of a CAFR, however, as is customary, a fourth paragraph, known as the **explanatory para-**

---

[1] American Institute of Certified Public Accountants, Inc., *Statement on Auditing Standards No. 58,* par. 8 (New York: AICPA, 1988).

ILLUSTRATION 14–2   Generally Accepted Auditing Standards—AICPA

General Standards
1. The audit is to be performed by a person or persons having adequate technical training and proficiency as an auditor.
2. In all matters relating to the assignment, an independence in mental attitude is to be maintained by the auditor or auditors.
3. Due professional care is to be exercised in the performance of the audit and the preparation of the report.

Standards of Field Work
1. The work is to be adequately planned and assistants, if any, are to be properly supervised.
2. A sufficient understanding of the internal control structure is to be obtained to plan the audit and to determine the nature, timing, and extent of tests to be performed.
3. Sufficient competent evidential matter is to be obtained through inspection, observation, inquiries, and confirmations to afford a reasonable basis for an opinion regarding the financial statements under audit.

Standards of Reporting
1. The report shall state whether the financial statements are presented in accordance with generally accepted accounting principles.
2. The report shall identify those circumstances in which such principles have not been consistently observed in the current period in relation to the preceding period.
3. Informative disclosures in the financial statements are to be regarded as reasonably adequate unless otherwise stated in the report.
4. The report shall either contain an expression of opinion regarding the financial statements, taken as a whole, or an assertion to the effect that an opinion cannot be expressed. When an overall opinion cannot be expressed, the reasons therefor should be stated. In all cases where an auditor's name is associated with financial statements, the report should contain a clear-cut indication of the character of the auditor's work, if any, and the degree of responsibility the auditor is taking.

SOURCE: *AICPA Professional Standards,* AU 150.02.

---

graph is added. The purpose of the explanatory paragraph is to make clear that the combining, individual fund, and individual account group financial statements and schedules are not a required part of the GPFS, but that such information has been subjected to auditing procedures applied in the audit of the GPFS, and, in the auditor's opinion, is fairly presented in all material respects in relation to the GPFS taken as a whole.

If the auditor determines the financial statements contain a departure from GAAP, the effect of which is material; or there has been a material change between periods in accounting principles or in the method of their application; or there are significant uncertainties affecting the financial statements, he may not express an unqualified opinion (as shown in Illustration 14–1).

One example that precludes an unqualified opinion is a stand-alone consolidated report that some governments have issued on an experimental basis. If an audit opinion is to be rendered on such a report, it must be an adverse opinion stating the report does not present fairly in conformity with GAAP.[2] It is also possible that the auditor cannot express an unqualified opinion because the scope of the examination was affected by conditions that precluded the application of one or more auditing procedures the auditor considered necessary in the circumstances. If it is not appropriate for the auditor to express an unqualified opinion, the auditor should consult relevant authoritative pronouncements to determine if a qualified opinion (see Illustration 14–3) should be issued, or if an opinion should be disclaimed. Expanded discussion of the nature of each of these types of opinions, and the conditions that would warrant the use of each, is beyond the scope of this text. Interested readers are referred to current collegiate auditing texts and to the pronouncements of the AICPA.[3]

Before any audit work is done, there should be a clear understanding of the scope of each engagement by all interested parties. A written memorandum of the engagement, or engagement letter, specifying the scope of the work to be done should be prepared in advance and copies retained by both the auditor and auditee. A written record of the agreement is essential for the protection of both parties. Independent public accountants have had the need for specific, written memorandums of the scope of engagements forcefully pointed out to them by a number of well-known liability cases.

Governmental units often engage more than one audit firm to conduct annual audits. Some component units such as airports, hospitals, and utilities may have their own governing boards and select their own auditor, yet meet the criteria discussed in Chapters 2 and 13 for inclusion in the governmental reporting entity. The principal auditor for the governmental unit (the auditor of the General Fund of the primary government) must in this case decide whether to make reference to the other auditor in his or her audit report or to assume responsibility for the work performed by the other auditor without reference in the audit report. If reference is made to the other auditor, the principal auditor's report should disclose the magnitude of the portion of the financial statements audited by the other auditor. An audit report making reference to another auditor is not a qualified report, unless some other reason exists for qualification.

Auditing procedures deemed particularly applicable to audits of state and local governments by independent CPAs are published in the AICPA audit and accounting guide, *Audits of State and Local Governmental Units*. The audit guide and other authoritative auditing literature provide guidance to all auditors, not just

---

[2] As noted in Chapter 13, footnote 17, the AICPA has issued an exposure draft of a proposed Statement of Position that would permit auditors to express their opinion that condensed summary information, such as consolidated financial information, is fairly stated in relation to the general purpose financial statements from which it is derived. If this document is issued in final form, then the current prohibition on rendering an unqualified audit opinion on consolidated statements may be eliminated.

[3] A convenient source of information on currently effective pronouncements is a book published annually by the American Institute of Certified Public Accountants: *AICPA Professional Standards*.

ILLUSTRATION 14–3 **Qualified Opinion on General Purpose Financial Statements that Omit One or More, but Not All, Component Units of the Reporting Entity***

Independent Auditor's Report

We have audited the accompanying general-purpose financial statements of City of Example, Any State, as of and for the year ended June 30, 19X1. These general-purpose financial statements are the responsibility of City of Example, Any State, management. Our responsibility is to express an opinion on these general-purpose financial statements based on our audit.

We conducted our audit in accordance with generally accepted auditing standards. Those standards require that we plan and perform the audit to obtain reasonable assurance about whether the general-purpose financial statements are free of material misstatement. An audit includes examining, on a test basis, evidence supporting the amounts and disclosures in the general-purpose financial statements. An audit also includes assessing the accounting principles used and significant estimates made by management, as well as evaluating the overall general-purpose financial statement presentation. We believe that our audit provides a reasonable basis for our opinion.

The general-purpose financial statements referred to above do not include financial activities of the [identify the component unit omitted], which should be included in order to conform with generally accepted accounting principles. If the omitted component unit had been included,** the assets and revenues of the [identify fund type(s)—for example, special revenue fund type—or component unit(s)] would have been increased by $XXX,XXX and $XXX,XXX, respectively, there would have been an excess of expenditures over revenues in that fund type [or component unit(s)] of $XXX,XXX for the year, and the [identify fund type(s) or component unit(s)] fund balance would have been a deficit of $XXX,XXX.

In our opinion, except for the effects on the financial statements of the omission described in the preceding paragraph, the general-purpose financial statements referred to above present fairly, in all material respects, the financial position of City of Example, Any State, as of June 30, 19X1, and the results of its operations and cash flows of its proprietary fund types and nonexpendable trust funds for the year then ended in conformity with generally accepted accounting principles.

[Signature]
[Date]

* If the omission was sufficiently material, the auditor should express an adverse opinion on the general-purpose financial statements. In such a case, a separate explanatory paragraph should state all the substantive reasons for the adverse opinion and the principal effects of those matters. If an adverse opinion is to be rendered, the last two paragraphs of this report should be replaced with the following paragraphs:

> The general-purpose financial statements referred to above do not include financial activities of the [identify the component unit omitted], which should be included in order to conform with generally accepted accounting principles.
>
> Because of the departure from generally accepted accounting principles identified above, as of June 30, 19X1, the assets and revenues of the [identify fund type(s)—for example, special revenue fund type—or component unit(s)] would have increased by $XXX,XXX and $XXX,XXX, respectively, there would have been an excess of expenditures over revenues in the fund type [or component unit(s)] for the year of $XXX,XXX, and the [identify fund type(s) or component unit(s)] fund balance would have been a deficit of $XXX,XXX.
>
> In our opinion, because of the effects of the matters discussed in the preceding paragraphs, the general-purpose financial statements referred to above do not present fairly, in conformity with generally accepted accounting principles, the financial position of City of Example, Any State, as of June 30, 19X1, or the results of its operations or the cash flows of its proprietary fund types or nonexpendable trust funds for the year then ended.

** If the amounts applicable to the omitted component unit have not been audited, insert the phrase *based on unaudited information.*

SOURCE: American Institute of Certified Public Accountants, Statement of Position 92–7, *Audits of State and Local Governmental Entities Receiving Federal Financial Assistance* (New York: AICPA, 1992), Appendix D, Example 5. Copyright © 1992 by the American Institute of Certified Public Accountants, Inc.

independent CPAs, whose function it is to examine financial statements, and the underlying records, for the purpose of determining whether the statements present fairly the financial position as of a certain date, and the results of operations and cash flows for a fiscal period, in conformity with generally accepted accounting principles. The audit guide emphasizes that all audits of governmental units must include tests of compliance with laws and regulations sufficient to determine whether there have been events of noncompliance that may have a material effect on the financial statements. Noncompliance may include: (1) expending funds in excess of authorized limits, (2) expending funds for unauthorized purposes, and (3) failing to file reports required by the state and federal government accurately, completely, and on time.[4] The latter instance leads into the manifold reporting requirements placed on persons conducting an audit under the provisions of the federal Single Audit Act and related regulations. A brief discussion of Single Audits is given in a later section of this chapter.

Government Auditing Standards

Audit standards that are to be followed by auditors of federal organizations, programs, activities, functions, and funds received by contractors, nonprofit organizations, and other nonfederal organizations are much broader in scope than the audits discussed in the first section of this chapter. The standards are also recommended for audits of state and local governments performed by state or local government auditors or by public accountants. Government auditing standards have been developed by the General Accounting Office under the direction of the Comptroller General of the United States. Government auditing standards are set forth and explained in the *Government Auditing Standards*—because of the color of its cover, the document is generally referred to as "the yellow book." Generally accepted auditing standards (GAAS) shown as Illustration 14–2 were used as a basis for federal auditing standards. Reasons why the standards established by the AICPA were deemed to be too narrow in scope for audits of governmental entities are expressed in the Introduction of the yellow book.

> Our system of government today rests on an elaborate structure of interlocking relationships among all levels of government for managing public programs. Those officials and employees who manage the programs must render a full account of their activities to the public. While not always specified by law, this accountability is inherent in the governing processes of this Nation.
>
> The requirement for accountability has caused a demand for more information about government programs. Public officials, legislators, and private citizens want and need to know not only whether *government funds are handled properly and in compliance with laws and regulations,* but also whether government *organizations and pro-*

---

[4] American Institute of Certified Public Accountants, Audit and Accounting Guide, *Audits of State and Local Governmental Units,* Revised (New York: AICPA, 1993), p. 22.

grams are achieving the purposes for which programs were authorized and funded and are *doing so economically and efficiently.*[5] [Emphasis added.]

The italicized phrase above illustrates that the scope of audits of governmental entities is significantly broader than audits of business entities. The Comptroller General provides that in any given audit, auditors may perform a combination of financial statement audits, finance-related audits, economy and efficiency audits, and program audits; or, may perform only one or more aspects of one of the type of audits. Accordingly, the Planning Fieldwork Standards place on officials who authorize and prescribe the scopes of governmental audits the responsibility for planning audit work that is broad enough to help fulfill the reasonable needs of potential users of audit results.[6]

The term *audit* in the yellow book refers to both financial and performance audits. **Financial audits** provide an auditor's opinion that financial statements present fairly an entity's financial position and results of operations in conformity with GAAP or that other financial reports comply with other finance-related criteria. **Performance audits** provide an auditor's independent determination (but not an opinion) of the extent to which government officials are efficiently, economically, and effectively carrying out their responsibilities. Illustration 14–4 contrasts and compares the objectives and characteristics of financial and performance audits.

The first edition (1972) of the yellow book presented a single set of auditing standards that were similar to the AICPA statement of generally accepted auditing standards (GAAS) shown in Illustration 14–2. The revised edition of the yellow book, issued in 1981, however, presented a statement of standards that differed so much from GAAS that the Comptroller General referred to them as generally accepted *government* auditing standards, abbreviated to GAGAS.[7] Illustration 14–4, excerpted from the 1988 revision of the yellow book, should be compared with the scope of auditing as presented in AICPA literature and discussed in relation to Illustration 14–1. The statement of GAS contains the General Standards shown in Illustration 14–2. The three Standards of Field Work and the four Standards of Reporting shown in Illustration 14–2 are incorporated but not restated in GAS as Field Work and Reporting Standards for Financial Audits; also in that category are additional standards of field work reporting thought to be necessary "to satisfy the unique needs of government." The unique needs of government identified in the yellow book relate to the distinguishing characteristics of

---

[5] Comptroller General of the United States. *Government Auditing Standards* (Washington, D.C.: U.S. General Accounting Office, 1988), pp. 1-3, 1-4. An exposure draft (ED) of a revised edition of *Government Auditing Standards* was issued in July 1993. If a final version is issued, the publisher will provide an update bulletin to adopters of the Tenth Edition of this text.

[6] Ibid., p. 3-2.

[7] Although the acronym GAGAS is still in common usage, the acronym more frequently used in the recent authoritative literature is GAS, government auditing standards. Thus, in the remainder of this chapter we use the more abbreviated term GAS.

ILLUSTRATION 14–4   Types of Government Audits

A. Financial Audits
  1. Financial statement audits determine *(a)* whether the financial statements of an audited entity present fairly the financial position, results of operations, and cash flows in accordance with generally accepted accounting principles, and *(b)* whether the entity has complied with laws and regulations for those transactions and events that may have a material effect on the financial statements.
  2. Financial-related audits include determining *(a)* whether financial reports and related items, such as elements, accounts, or funds are fairly presented, *(b)* whether financial information is presented in accordance with established or stated criteria, and *(c)* whether the entity has adhered to specific financial compliance requirements.
B. Performance Audits
  1. Economy and efficiency audits include determining *(a)* whether the entity is acquiring, protecting, and using its resources (such as personnel, property, and space) economically and efficiently, *(b)* the causes in inefficiencies or uneconomical practices, and *(c)* whether the entity has complied with laws and regulations concerning matters of economy and efficiency.
  2. Program audits include determining *(a)* the extent to which the desired results or benefits established by the legislature or other authorizing body are being achieved, *(b)* the effectiveness of organizations, programs, activities, or functions, and *(c)* whether the entity has complied with laws and regulations applicable to the program.

SOURCE: *Government Auditing Standards* (Washington, D.C.: U.S. General Accounting Office, 1988), p. A–1.

government identified by the GASB and noted in Chapter 1 of this text, and to subsequent discussions of state and local governments in Chapter 13 and federal government in Chapter 15. Additional wording was added to GAS in its 1988 revision in order to provide more specific guidance to auditors performing examinations required by the Federal Single Audit Act of 1984 and OMB *Circulars A-128* and *A-133* (both documents are discussed later in this chapter).

Since the scope of government auditing encompasses performance audits, described in Illustration 14–4, GAS includes five Field Work Standards—Performance Audits and three Reporting Standards—Performance Audits. The yellow book devotes an explanatory chapter to each category of standards. It makes clear that all elements of government auditing must be concerned with a determination that the entity has complied with laws and regulations. Audits that focus on efficiency and economy and/or on program results with a view to future improvement of operations are sometimes called *operational audits* or *management audits,* in addition to the yellow book term, *performance audits.*

Government auditing standards are to be adhered to in all audits of federal grants and contracts received by state and local governments, nonprofit entities, and business organizations. Therefore, auditors who are employed by federal, state, or local governments, or nonprofit entities, and independent public auditors who audit government clients or who audit federal grants and contracts should be thoroughly familiar with the standards set forth in *Government Auditing Standards* and related governmental auditing literature.

Single Audit

Federal grants-in-aid to state and local governments grew from $2.2 billion in 1950 to over $100 billion in 1990. Federal grants-in-aid have originated from more than 1,100 different programs administered by the Department of Health and Human Services, Department of Transportation, Department of Labor, Department of Housing and Urban Development, Environmental Protection Agency, and 47 other federal departments, agencies, and commissions. Until the mid-1980s each agency established accounting, reporting, and auditing requirements for each program it administered, and these requirements differed from agency to agency. The requirements for programs administered by a given agency might differ from program to program, and requirements for grants made in different fiscal years often differed. Furthermore, each agency had the right to make on-site audits of grant funds, and usually did. Since even a relatively small local governmental unit might have during any given fiscal year several dozen active federal grants (each with different accounting, reporting, and auditing requirements) the amount of time spent in keeping track of conflicting requirements, and in providing facilities for a succession of different groups of auditors, became extremely burdensome. Efforts were made in the 1960s to standardize grant accounting, reporting, and auditing requirements, but with only modest success. In 1979, the Office of Management and Budget (OMB) issued Attachment P, *Audit Requirements,* to OMB *Circular A-102, Uniform Administrative Requirements for Grants-in-Aid to State and Local Governments*. Attachment P was intended to ensure that audits were made on an organizationwide basis, rather than on a grant-by-grant basis. This concept has generally been called the **single audit.**

Experience with Attachment P led to the enactment of the *Single Audit Act of 1984*. The purpose of the Act is:

(1) to improve the financial management of state and local governments with respect to federal financial assistance programs;
(2) to establish uniform requirements for audits of federal financial assistance provided to state and local governments;
(3) to promote the efficient and effective use of audit resources; and
(4) to ensure that federal departments and agencies, to the maximum extent practicable, rely upon and use audit work done pursuant to chapter 75 of title 31, United States Code (as added by this Act).

The Act is applicable to fiscal years of state and local governments beginning after December 31, 1984. OMB *Circular A-128* was issued in 1985 to facilitate implementation of the Single Audit Act. Each state and local government that receives a total amount of federal financial assistance equal to or in excess of $100,000 in any of its fiscal years is required to have an audit made for such fiscal year in accordance with the provisions of the Single Audit Act and OMB *Circular A-128*. It should be emphasized that this requirement relates to **total federal financial assistance,** which includes all federal assistance received indirectly through another state or local government (''pass-through'' grants, as discussed in Chapter 11 of this text) as well as assistance received directly from a federal agency. Contracts, loans, loan guarantees, property, cooperative agreements, interest subsidies, insurance, and direct appropriations, as well as grants-in-aid, are included in federal financial assistance. Federal cash assistance given directly to individuals is not, however, counted as assistance to a state or local governmental unit. Because of the definition of the audit requirement in terms of **total** federal financial assistance, not in terms of assistance under any one grant or contract, over 15,000 governmental units are required by this act to have **annual** audits. Governmental units receiving total federal financial assistance equal to or in excess of $25,000, but less than $100,000, in any fiscal year have the option of (1) having an audit for such fiscal year in accordance with the requirements of the Act or (2) complying with audit requirements contained in federal statutes and regulations governing programs under which such federal financial assistance is provided to that government. Governmental units receiving total federal financial assistance in any fiscal year of less than $25,000 are exempt for such fiscal year from compliance with audit requirements, but they must maintain records concerning federal financial assistance and permit grantor federal agencies or the Comptroller General access to such records.

Public hospitals, public colleges and universities, and other nonprofit organizations may be excluded from state and local government audits performed under *Circular A-128.* However, if such entities are excluded and their federal awards meet the criteria specified in OMB *Circular A-133, Audits of Institutions of Higher Education and Other Nonprofit Institutions,* audits of these entities must be made in accordance with the provisions of *Circular A-133. Circular A-133's* audit requirements agree in all major respects with those of the Single Audit Act and *Circular A-128,* so, in effect, public colleges and universities, hospitals associated with public colleges and universities and other nonprofit organizations receiving federal assistance are subject to essentially the same single audit requirements as state and local governments. Public hospitals **not** affiliated with an institution of higher learning, and that have been excluded from *Circular A-128,* do not fall under the requirements of *Circular A-133.* Instead, these entities must meet statutory audit requirements of the federal Medicare and Medicaid programs. Finally, it should be noted that even for-profit entities which receive federal assistance to conduct some aspect of a governmental program (but not as a vendor) may require audits conducted in accordance with GAS.

Audits under the provisions of the Single Audit Act of 1984 are to be conducted in accordance with generally accepted **government** auditing standards applicable to financial audits, as explained in the preceding section of this chapter. A recent interpretation of the AICPA Auditing Standards Board requires that if the independent auditor becomes aware that the audit should be performed under GAS when the engagement calls for generally accepted auditing standards (GAAS), the auditor must communicate with the governmental unit that an audit performed in accordance with GAAS will not satisfy the legal, regulatory, or contractual requirements of an audit under GAS. The Single Audit Act does not require performance audits or program evaluations of total federal financial assistance—however, such audits or evaluations may be required under laws or regulations applying to certain grants or contracts. Audits are to be conducted by "an independent auditor." The Act defines an independent auditor as:

(A) an external state or local government auditor who meets the independence standards included in generally accepted government auditing standards, or

(B) a public accountant who meets such independence standards.

The following requirements have been established for audits conducted under provisions of the Act:

Each audit shall encompass the entirety of the financial operations of such government or of such department, agency, or establishment, whichever is applicable, and shall determine and report whether—

(A) (i) the financial statements of the government, department, agency, or establishment present fairly its financial position and the results of its financial operations in accordance with generally accepted accounting principles; and

(ii) the government, department, agency, or establishment has complied with laws and regulations that may have a material effect upon the financial statements;

(B) the government, department, agency, or establishment has internal control systems to provide reasonable assurance that it is managing federal financial assistance programs in compliance with applicable laws and regulations; and

(C) the government, department, agency, or establishment has complied with laws and regulations that may have a material effect upon each major federal assistance program.

The preceding summary points out key dimensions of audits conducted under the Single Audit Act of 1984. First, the components of a single audit are an audit of the financial statements **and** an audit of federal financial assistance. Second, GAS imposes expanded requirements for evaluating the internal control structure **and** determining compliance with applicable laws and regulations. Extensive guidance on evaluating internal controls and compliance auditing is provided by the GAO yellow book, the OMB *Compliance Supplement for Single Audits of State and Local Governments,* the AICPA audit and accounting guide for state and local governmental units, AICPA Statement of Position 92–7, and several recent Statements on Auditing Standards (SASs) issued by the AICPA.[8]

AICPA Statement of Position 92–7 identifies two key factors that determine the scope of the auditor's work in auditing federal financial assistance (FFA): size—whether the program is major or minor—and applicable compliance requirements. Planning the scope of audit work requires that all federal assistance programs first be identified, that they be classified as major or nonmajor, and that the compliance requirements applicable to those programs be determined. These issues, and the required study and evaluation of the internal control structure, are

---

[8] Relevant SASs include SAS No. 55, *Consideration of the Internal Structure in a Financial Statement Audit*, SAS No. 60, *Communication of Internal Control Structure Related Matters Noted in an Audit*, and SAS No. 68, *Compliance Auditing Applicable to Governmental Entities and Other Recipients of Governmental Financial Assistance*.

discussed briefly before taking up the reporting requirements of the Single Audit Act.

Schedule of Federal Financial Assistance.   Audits conducted under the Single Audit Act of 1984 require the auditor to report on the Supplementary Schedule of Federal Financial Assistance prepared by management. This schedule should

---

ILLUSTRATION 14–5   Illustrative Supplementary Schedule of Federal Financial Assistance for the Year Ended June 30, 19x1—Minimum Data Required by OMB Circular A-128 Only

Federal Grantor/Pass-Through Grantor Program Title*	Federal CFDA Number	Pass-Through Grantor's Number	Expenditures†
U.S. Department of Education Direct Programs:			
Impact aid	84.041‡	N/A	$XXX
Bilingual education	84.003	N/A	XXX
			XXX
Pass-through State Department of Education:			
Chapter 1	84.011	XXXXX	$XXX
Chapter 2	84.151	XXXXX	XXX
Vocational education—basic grants to states	84.048	XXXXX	XXX
			XXX
Total Department of Education			XXX
U.S. Department of Housing and Urban Development Direct Programs:			
Community development block grant—entitlement	14.218	N/A	XXX
Urban development action grant	14.221	N/A	XXX
			XXX
Pass-through State Department of Community Development:			
Community development block grant—states program	14.219	XXXXX	XXX
Total U.S. Department of Housing and Urban Development			XXX
Other Federal Assistance§			
Department of Defense Engineering study contract	—	—	XXX
TOTAL FEDERAL ASSISTANCE EXPENDED			$XXX

CFDA = Catalog of Federal Domestic Assistance.

* All major and nonmajor programs should be individually identified, including those completed or terminated during the audit period.

† If the schedule is prepared on a basis of accounting other than GAAP, the basis should be disclosed. A reconciliation to the general-purpose financial statements may be provided.

‡ Major program as defined by OMB Circular A-128.

§ Significant programs or grants that have not been assigned a CFDA number should be identified separately.

SOURCE: American Institute of Certified Public Accountants, Statement of Position 92–7, *Audits of State and Local Governmental Entities Receiving Federal Financial Assistance* (New York: AICPA, 1992), Exhibit 3.1. Copyright © 1992 by the American Institute of Certified Public Accountants, Inc.

provide, as shown in Illustration 14–5, the program title, the Catalog of Federal Domestic Assistance (CFDA) number, pass-through grantor's number (if applicable), total expenditures for each program, total federal financial assistance expenditures, and identification of major programs. Statement of Position 92–7 also provides an example of an expanded Schedule of Federal Financial Assistance, required for some engagements, which provides additional financial details of each program. The more detailed schedule is beyond the scope of this text.

Major Programs. The Single Audit Act of 1984 uses a sliding scale to define a **major program;** the larger the entity's total expenditures of federal financial assistance, the larger the expenditure amount required for a program to be classified as a major program. The criteria for determining a major federal assistance program are given in Illustration 14–6.

Determination of major programs is fundamental to the single audit since much of the audit effort focuses on major programs, as discussed in the following two sections.

Study and Evaluation of Internal Control Structure. For federal financial assistance program purposes the Single Audit Act and OMB Circular A–128 define internal controls as the plan of organization and methods and procedures designed to ensure that:

1. Resource use is consistent with laws, regulations, and policies.
2. Resources are safeguarded against waste, loss, and misuse.
3. Reliable data are obtained, maintained, and fairly disclosed in reports.

ILLUSTRATION 14–6   Criteria for Determining a Major Federal Assistance Program

Total Expenditures of Federal Financial Assistance (FFA) for All Programs		Major Federal Assistance Program Is Any Program that Exceeds
More than $100,000	*But Less than $100 Million*	*Larger of $300,000 or 3% of Total FFA Expenditures*
100 million	1 billion	3 million
1 billion	2 billion	4 million
2 billion	3 billion	7 million
3 billion	4 billion	10 million
4 billion	5 billion	13 million
5 billion	6 billion	16 million
6 billion	7 billion	19 million
Over 7 billion		20 million

The Single Audit Act requires that auditors determine and report on whether the entity's internal control systems provide reasonable assurance that: (1) financial statements are not misleading, and (2) federal assistance programs are being managed in compliance with applicable laws and regulations. SOP 92–7 provides several examples of each of these reports, including cases in which no **reportable conditions** or **material weaknesses** are detected and cases in which they are detected. A reportable condition is a significant deficiency in the design or operation of the internal control structure that could adversely affect the entity's ability to administer federal financial assistance programs in accordance with laws and regulations. A material weakness is a reportable condition of such magnitude that the internal control structure elements do not reduce the risk of material noncompliance to an acceptably low level.

Study and evaluation of the internal control structure is required for each *major* financial assistance program. In the event the amount of major federal assistance program expenditures is less than 50 percent of the total amount of expenditures for all federal assistance programs, tests of internal controls should extend to all programs, both major and nonmajor, until at least 50 percent of total expenditures for all programs have been tested. An acceptable method is to select the largest nonmajor program, next largest, and so on until 50 percent of total program expenditures have been tested. Recently, however, Statement No. 6 of the President's Council on Integrity and Efficiency Standards Subcommittee took the position that nonmajor programs should be selected on a rotating basis so that all but insignificant nonmajor programs are covered at least once every three years.

Compliance Audits.   Every audit conducted under *Government Auditing Standards* requires the auditor to test for compliance with laws and regulations. For each major program the auditor is required to express an *opinion* on **specific requirements** applicable to that program. The auditor provides limited assurance (positive assurance for compliance on items tested; negative assurance for those not tested) on **general requirements** applicable to all programs. Specific requirements are described for most major programs in the OMB's A–128 Compliance Supplement and usually deal with such matters as types of services allowed or unallowed; eligibility of program beneficiaries; entities' own contributions to programs in terms of matching and level of effort; and reporting requirements imposed on organizations that received financial assistance. To support the required opinion for major programs the auditor must perform procedures to test specific requirements applicable to each program. General requirements applicable to all programs include the following nine requirements:

1. **Political Activity**—No program funds may be used for partisan political activity (Hatch Act and the Intergovernmental Personnel Act of 1970).
2. **Davis-Bacon Act**—wages of laborers and mechanics employed on projects financed by federal assistance must be paid at least the prevailing regional wage as established by the Secretary of Labor.

3. **Civil Rights**—prohibits discrimination on the basis of race, color, national origin, age, or handicap.

4. **Cash Management**—recipients of federal assistance should minimize the time between receipt of cash from grantor and disbursement of funds by recipient, in conformity with the Federal Cash Management Improvement Act.

5. **Relocation Assistance and Real Property Acquisition**—specifies systematic procedures to be followed to ensure property owners receive a fair price for their property and, if necessary, relocation assistance when a program requires acquisition of property.

6. **Federal Reports**—requires that information in financial reports submitted to grantors be supported by the books and records used to prepare the general purpose or basic financial statements.

7. **Allowable Costs/Cost Principles**—requires that both direct and indirect costs charged to federal assistance programs conform to the eligibility requirements of OMB Circular A–87, *Cost Principles for State and Local Governments*.

8. **Drug-Free Workplace**—requires recipients to certify they will provide a drug-free workplace as a precondition of receiving a federal grant.

9. **Administrative Requirements**—requires recipients of grants and cooperative agreements to comply with all administrative requirements of the "Common Rule," *Uniform Administrative Requirements for Grants and Cooperative Agreements to State and Local Governments*, Office of Management and Budget, March 1988. For entitlement programs the administrative requirements specified by the federal agency providing the assistance should be followed.

Single Audit Reports

Illustration 14–7 shows the three levels of reporting required for single audits by OMB Circular A–128. The top two levels, comprising three required reports, relate to the audit of the financial statements and require compliance with both AICPA (GAAS) and GAO (GAS) auditing standards. Often, however, the auditor's report on the audit of the financial statements (top level of Illustration 14–7) states that the audit was conducted in accordance with generally accepted auditing standards rather than both GAAS and GAS. The bottom level of Illustration 14–7 requires five reports related to the audit of federal financial assistance. As shown, the bottom level reports emphasize compliance with the general and specific requirements discussed in the preceding sections. Some auditors combine certain of the eight reports shown in Illustration 14–7. SOP 92–7 cautions against this practice, however, because of the varying levels of materiality in different reports and the need to show that the many unique audit requirements have been met.

The audit reports required for a single audit are briefly described as follows:

For the entity:

A report on an examination of the general purpose or basic financial statements of

ILLUSTRATION 14–7   **Levels of Reporting in Governmental Single Audits—GAAS Audit versus Government Auditing Standards Audit versus Single Audit**

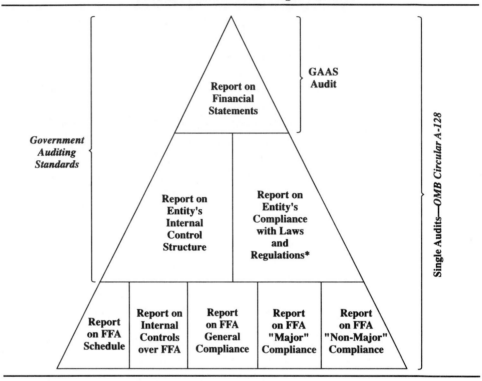

* See Chapter 6, paragraph 6.15 [of SOP 92–7] for a discussion of the report on illegal acts, which may also be required.

SOURCE: American Institute of Certified Public Accountants, Statement of Position 92–7, *Audits of State and Local Governmental Entities Receiving Federal Financial Assistance* (New York: AICPA, 1992), Exhibit 1.1. Copyright © 1992 by the American Institute of Certified Public Accountants, Inc.

the entity as a whole, or the department, agency, or establishment covered by the audit.

A report on internal accounting control based solely on a study and evaluation made as a part of the audit of the general purpose or basic financial statements.

A report on compliance with laws and regulations that may have a material effect on the financial statements.

For its federal financial assistance programs:

A report on a supplementary schedule of the entity's federal financial assistance programs, showing total expenditures for each federal assistance program.

A report on the internal control structure used in administering federal financial assistance programs.

A report on compliance with general requirements applicable to federal financial assistance programs. This report provides positive assurance on items tested and negative assurance on items not tested.

A report on compliance with specific requirements applicable to major federal financial assistance programs. The auditor is required to express an opinion on whether the entity complied with all specific requirements that could materially affect any major program.

A report on compliance with requirements applicable to nonmajor federal financial assistance programs. Requires that the auditor give positive assurance on items tested and negative assurance on items not tested.

OMB Circular A–128 requires one additional report, a Schedule of Findings and Questioned Costs, if there are findings of noncompliance with general or specific requirements or questioned costs, even if they are immaterial.

Reports of audits conducted pursuant to the Act are to be transmitted within 30 days after the completion of the report to the appropriate federal officials and made available by the state and local government for public inspection. If an audit conducted pursuant to the Act finds any material noncompliance with applicable laws and regulations, or material weakness in the internal controls of the auditee, the Act requires the auditee to submit to appropriate federal officials a plan for corrective action to eliminate such material noncompliance or weakness, or a statement describing the reasons corrective action is not necessary. The plan for corrective action must be consistent with the internal control standards established by the Comptroller General under 31 U.S.C. 3512, the Federal Managers' Financial Integrity Act, discussed in Chapter 15 of this text.

The Single Audit Act requires the auditor to state whether the financial statements of the governmental entity are expressed in accordance with GAAP. Some governments, however, prepare their financial statements on a legal or regulatory basis other than GAAP. The AICPA state and local government audit guide requires that the auditor issue a *Special Report* if the financial statements are prepared on a comprehensive basis other than GAAP. The auditor's special report should state, or refer to a note to the financial statements that states, the basis of presentation and how it differs from GAAP. The auditor's report should also state that the financial statements are not intended to conform to GAAP.

The Single Audit Act continues the **cognizant agency** approach established by Attachment P to OMB *Circular A-102*. The cognizant agency is the federal agency designated by the Director of the Office of Management and Budget to be responsible for implementing the requirements of the Act with respect to a particular state or local government. Each cognizant agency is charged with the responsibility of (1) ensuring that audits are made in a timely manner and in accordance with the requirements of the Act, (2) ensuring that audit reports and corrective action plans are transmitted to appropriate federal officials, and (3) coordinating, to the extent practicable, audits done by or under contract with federal agencies that are in addition to audits required by this Act, and ensuring that such additional audits build on the audits conducted pursuant to the Act.

Audit Committees

An audit committee is typically a committee of the governing board whose function it is to help select the auditor, monitor the audit process, review results of the audit, assist the governing board in understanding the results of the audit, and to participate with both management and the independent auditor in resolving internal control or other deficiencies identified during the audit. Audit committees usually consist of selected members of the governing board (e.g., the city council or school board) and sometimes outside members in order to increase the independence of the committee.

Audit committees, when properly organized and utilized, can provide substantial benefit to all concerned parties. The audit committee can strengthen the stewardship reporting function of the governing board; it can improve communication between the independent auditor and management and enhance the auditor's independence by serving as an objective buffer between the auditor and management. For taxpayers and creditors, audit committees help ensure maximum value and benefit from the audit.

Although most major corporations now consider an audit committee to be an important aspect of corporate governance, governmental units have been slow to establish audit committees. The U.S. General Accounting Office advocates the use of audit committees in government and, as the benefits become apparent, we can anticipate greater use of these committees in the future.

Selected References

American Institute of Certified Public Accountants. *Audit and Accounting Guide. Audits of State and Local Governmental Units.* Revised, New York: AICPA, 1993.
_____. *Statement on Auditing Standards, No. 1,* et seq. New York, 1973 to date.
_____. Statement of Position 92–7. *Audits of State and Local Governmental Entities Receiving Federal Financial Assistance.* New York, 1992.
Comptroller General of the United States. *Government Auditing Standards: Standards for Audit of Governmental Organizations, Programs, Activities, and Functions.* Washington, D.C.: Superintendent of Documents, U.S. Government Printing Office, 1988 revision.
Office of Management and Budget. *Circular A-128. Audits of State and Local Governments.* Washington, D.C.: Superintendent of Documents, U.S. Government Printing Office, 1985.
_____. *Circular A-133. Audits of Institutions of Higher Education and Other Nonprofit Organizations.* Washington, D.C.: Superintendent of Documents, U.S. Government Printing Office, 1990.
_____. *Compliance Supplement for Single Audits of State and Local Governments.* Washington, D.C.: Superintendent of Documents, U.S. Government Printing Office, 1985.

Questions

14–1. What assurance does the independent auditor provide users of financial statements of governmental and nonprofit entities?

14–2. What information is contained in the *opening paragraph* of an auditor's report prepared in conformity with the AICPA's standard wording?

14–3. What is the meaning of the term *scope paragraph* (of an auditor's report prepared in conformity with the AICPA's standard wording)? The term *opinion paragraph*?

14-4. What is the meaning of the term *unqualified opinion* as used in auditing literature?

14-5. The standard report used by Certified Public Accountants sets forth that the financial statements are presented in conformity with "generally accepted accounting principles." How may an auditor determine the meaning of this phrase in the case of a state or local government?

14-6. What are the two major types of audits described in the General Accounting Office's *Government Auditing Standards,* and how do they differ?

14-7. Define GAS. How do GAS differ from GAAS?

14-8. Does *Government Auditing Standards* apply to any audits except those made by General Accounting Office auditors? If so, to what others is it applicable?

14-9. Describe briefly the single audit concept set forth in the Single Audit Act of 1984 and OMB *Circulars A-128* and *A-133.*

14-10. What are the two key factors which determine the scope of the auditor's work in auditing federal financial assistance programs? How do these factors affect planning the scope of audit work to be performed?

14-11. What are the criteria prescribed by the Single Audit Act of 1984 for determining a *major* program?

14-12. What is the difference between a *reportable condition* and a *material weakness* detected during the study and evaluation of the internal control structure?

14-13. Describe the audit reports required for a single audit?

Exercises and Problems

14-1. Write the numbers 1 through 10 on a sheet of paper. Beside each number, write the letter corresponding with the best answer to each of the following questions:

1. The scope paragraph of an independent auditor's report on a financial audit of a local governmental unit:
   a. States that generally accepted auditing standards require that the auditor plan and perform the audit to obtain reasonable assurance as to whether the financial statements are free of material misstatement.
   b. Identifies the financial statements on which the auditor is expressing an opinion.
   c. States whether, in the auditor's opinion, the financial statements present fairly in conformity with generally accepted accounting principles the financial position of the reporting entity.
   d. All of the above.
2. An unqualified opinion paragraph of an independent auditor's report on a financial audit of a local governmental unit:
   a. States that, in the auditor's opinion, the combined financial statements present fairly the financial position, results of operations, and cash flows in conformity with generally accepted accounting principles.
   b. States that, in the auditor's opinion, the financial statements of the individual funds and account groups accurately present the financial condition as of a certain date, and the results of operations for the year then ended.

     c. States that the combining financial statements fairly present the financial condition as of a certain date, the results of operations for the year then ended.

     d. None of the above.

3. Which of the following best describes what is meant by generally accepted auditing standards?

     a. Pronouncements issued by the Auditing Standards Board of the AICPA.

     b. Procedures to be used to gather evidence to support financial statements.

     c. Rules acknowledged by the accounting profession because of their universal compliance.

     d. Measures of the quality of the auditor's performance.

4. Which of the following best describes the relationship between GAAS and GAS?

     a. GAAS does not apply to audits subject to the GAO yellow book.

     b. Independent CPAs must follow GAAS; governmental auditors must follow GAS.

     c. Auditors who perform audits in accordance with GAS automatically comply with GAAS.

     d. Auditors who perform audits in accordance with GAAS automatically comply with GAS.

5. Financial audits, as defined in the GAO's *Government Auditing Standards,* may include determining

     a. Whether the financial statements present fairly the entity's financial position, results of operations, and cash flows in conformity with GAAP.

     b. Whether the entity has complied with laws and regulations for those transactions and events that may have a material effect on the financial statements.

     c. Whether financial information is presented in accordance with established or stated criteria.

     d. All of the above.

6. Performance audits, as defined in the GAO's *Government Auditing Standards*:

     a. Provide a basis for an auditor's opinion as to whether the entity is acquiring, protecting, and using its resources economically and efficiently.

     b. Include determining whether or the extent to which government officials are efficiently, economically, and effectively carrying out their responsibilities.

     c. Provide assurance that operations are in compliance with *all* applicable laws and regulations that may have a material effect on the financial statements.

     d. Are performed by the internal audit staff to assist the entity's independent auditor.

7. When performing an audit of a city that is subject to the requirements of the Single Audit Act of 1984, an auditor should adhere to:

     a. Governmental Accounting Standards Board *General Standards*.

     b. Governmental Finance Officers Association *Governmental Accounting, Auditing, and Financial Reporting Principles*.

     c. General Accounting Office *Government Auditing Standards*.

     d. Securities and Exchange Commission *Regulation S-X*.

8. When engaged to audit a governmental entity in accordance with *Government Auditing Standards*, an auditor prepares a written report on the internal control structure:

     a. In all audits, regardless of circumstances.

     b. Only when the auditor has noted reportable conditions.

      c. Only when requested by the governmental entity being audited.

      d. Only when requested by the federal government funding agency.

9. Kent is auditing an entity's compliance with requirements governing a major federal financial assistance program in accordance with the Single Audit Act. Kent detected noncompliance with requirements that have a material effect on that program. Kent's report on compliance should express a(an):

      a. Unqualified opinion with a separate explanatory paragraph.

      b. Qualified opinion or an adverse opinion.

      c. Adverse opinion or a disclaimer of opinion.

      d. Limited assurance on the items tested.

10. What is an auditor's responsibility for supplementary information required by GASB that is placed outside the basic financial statements?

      a. Label the information as unaudited and expand the auditor's report to include a disclaimer on the information.

      b. Add an explanatory paragraph to the auditor's report and refer to the information as "required supplementary information."

      c. Apply limited procedures to the information and report deficiencies in, or the omission of, the information.

      d. Audit the required supplementary information in accordance with generally accepted government auditing standards.

(Items 3, 7–10, AICPA, adapted)

14–2. On September 23, 19x5, the CPA firm of Green and Jones completed its audit of the City of Deerfield's general purpose financial statements (GPFS) for the year ended June 30, 19x5. The City presents its financial position, results of operations, and cash flows using the financial statements prescribed by generally accepted accounting principles. However, Green and Jones believe that the Deerfield Cultural Center, a theater for the performing arts and financially subsidized by the City, meets the criteria specified by GASB for inclusion as a component unit in Deerfield's GPFS. Deerfield's finance director has steadfastly refused to include the cultural center in Deerfield's GPFS on the basis that it would cause the financial statements to be misleading. Green and Jones feel compelled to issue an "except for" qualified audit opinion to bring attention to this departure from GAAP, although they believe the financial statements present fairly in all other respects. Green and Jones have determined that the effect of including the cultural center in Deerfield's GPFS would have been to increase the reported assets and revenues of the enterprise funds by $450,000 and $127,000, respectively, and increase the excess of revenues over expenses in that fund type by $5,200 for the year ended June 30, 19x5.

Required Prepare the qualified audit report that Green and Jones, CPAs, should render on the City of Deerfield's GPFS for the year ended June 30, 19x5.

14–3. Jones and Todd, a local CPA firm, received an invitation to bid for the audit of a local, federally assisted program. The audit is to be conducted in accordance with the audit standards published by the General Accounting Office (GAO). Jones and Todd has become familiar with the GAO standards and recognizes that the GAO standards are not inconsistent with generally accepted auditing standards (GAAS). The GAO standards, unlike GAAS, are concerned with more than the financial aspects of an entity's operations. The GAO standards broaden the definition of auditing by defining two types of audits, financial audits and performance audits. Jones and Todd has been engaged to perform the following specific audits:

1. An examination of *financial* transactions, accounts, and reports, including an evaluation of *compliance* with applicable laws and regulations.
2. A review of *efficiency* and *economy* in the use of resources, such as personnel and equipment.
3. A review to determine whether desired results are effectively achieved (*program results*).

Jones and Todd has been engaged to perform the audit of the program, and the audit is to encompass all three elements.

Required

a. Jones and Todd should perform sufficient audit work to satisfy the *financial* and *compliance* element of the GAO standards. What should such audit work determine?
b. After making appropriate review and inquiries, what uneconomical practices or inefficiencies should Jones and Todd be alert to, in satisfying the *efficiency* and *economy* element encompassed by the GAO standards?
c. After making appropriate review and inquiries, what should Jones and Todd consider to satisfy the *program results* element encompassed by the GAO standards?

(AICPA, adapted)

14–4. The report of the independent auditors that appeared in an annual financial report for Prairie City is reproduced below. Compare this report with the one shown in Illustration 14–1 and discuss the likely reasons for the different wording. (The exhibits and tables referred to in the report are not included here.)

INDEPENDENT AUDITORS' REPORT

The Honorable Mayor and Members of the City Council
Prairie City

We have audited the general-purpose financial statements of Prairie City as of and for the year ended December 31, 19x9, as listed in the table of contents. These general-purpose financial statements are the responsibility of Prairie City management. Our responsibility is to express an opinion on these general-purpose financial statements based on our audit.

We conducted our audit in accordance with generally accepted auditing standards. Those standards require that we plan and perform the audit to obtain reasonable assurance about whether the general-purpose financial statements are free of material misstatement. An audit includes examining, on a test basis, evidence supporting the amounts and disclosures in the general-purpose financial statements. An audit also includes assessing the accounting principles used and significant estimates made by management, as well as evaluating the overall general-purpose financial statement presentation. We believe that our audit provides a reasonable basis for our opinion.

In our opinion, the general-purpose financial statements referred to above present fairly, in all material respects, the financial position of Prairie City at December 31, 19x9, and the results of its operations and cash flows of its proprietary fund types and nonexpendable trust funds for the year then ended, in conformity with generally accepted accounting principles.

Our audit was made for the purpose of forming an opinion on the general-purpose financial statements of Prairie City taken as a whole. The combining and individual fund financial statements and supplementary information in Exhibits A–1 through G–4, the schedule of Federal financial assistance, and Table 5 are presented for purposes of additional analysis and are not a required part of the general-purpose financial statements of Prairie City. Such information has been subjected to the auditing procedures applied in the audit of the general-purpose financial statements and, in our opinion, is fairly presented in all material respects in relation to the general-purpose financial statements taken as a whole.

Tables 1 through 4 on pages 105 through 108 are not a required part of the general purpose financial statements but are supplementary information required by the Governmental Accounting Standards Board. We have applied certain limited procedures which consisted principally of inquiries of management regarding the methods of measurement and presentation of the supplementary information. However, we did not audit the information in Tables 1 through 4, and express no opinion on it.

/s/ Firm Name

[Date]

14–5. The City of Granville receives grants from various state agencies as well as grants from several federal government agencies.

The City engaged Hall & Hall, CPAs to audit its financial statements for the year ended July 31, 19x5, in accordance with *Government Auditing Standards*. Accordingly, the auditor's reports are to be submitted by the City of Granville to granting government agencies, which make the reports available for public inspection.

The auditor's separate report on compliance with laws and regulations that was drafted by a staff accountant of Hall & Hall at the completion of the engagement contained the statements below. It was submitted to the engagement partner who reviewed matters thoroughly and properly concluded that no material instances of noncompliance were identified.

1. A statement that the audit was conducted in accordance with generally accepted auditing standards and with *Government Auditing Standards* issued by the Comptroller General of the United States.
2. A statement that the auditor's procedures included tests of compliance.
3. A statement that the standards require the auditors to plan and to perform the audit to detect all instances of noncompliance with applicable laws and regulations.
4. A statement that management is responsible for compliance with laws, regulations, contracts, and grants.
5. A statement that the auditor's objective was to provide an opinion on compliance with the provisions of laws and regulations equivalent to that to be expressed on the financial statements.
6. A statement of positive assurance that the results of the tests indicate that, with respect to the items tested, the entity complied, in all material respects, with the provisions of laws, regulations, contracts, and grants.
7. A statement of negative assurance that, with respect to items tested, nothing came to the auditors' attention that caused the auditors to believe that the entity had not complied, in all material respects, with the provisions of laws, regulations, contracts, and grants.
8. A statement that the report is intended only for the information of the specific legislative or regulatory bodies, and that this restriction is intended to limit the distribution of the report.

Required For each of the above statements indicate whether each is an appropriate or inappropriate element within the report on compliance with laws and regulations. If a statement is **not** appropriate, explain why.

(AICPA, adapted)

14–6. You are auditing the accounts of the clerk-treasurer of the Town of Franklin. You find, in the ledger, accounts for a General Fund, a Street Fund, and a Capital Projects

Fund. The legally approved budget for the Street Fund for the year you are examining consisted of the following three appropriations only:

Labor	$60,000
Materials	66,000
Equipment	24,000

In the appropriation and disbursement ledger accounts, you find the record of transactions for the Street Fund shown as follows:

Labor Account

Date	Description	Warrant	Appropriation	Disbursements	Appropriation Balance
Jan. 1	From advertised budget		$60,000		$60,000
31	Street labor	115–142		$ 6,000	54,000
Feb. 28	Street labor	219–241		7,000	47,000
Mar. 31	Street labor	252–263		6,000	41,000
Apr. 30	Street labor	274–294		5,000	36,000
June 30	Labor on municipal parking lots	371–388		8,000	28,000
Aug. 31	Street labor	400–424		10,000	18,000
Oct. 31	Street labor	510–523		10,000	8,000
Dec. 31	Street labor	600–621		8,000	–0–

Materials Account

Date	Description	Warrant	Appropriation	Disbursements	Appropriation Balance
Jan. 1	From advertised budget		$66,000		$66,000
20	Asphalt mix for street repair	109		$ 6,000	60,000
Feb. 21	Repair of truck used on streets	217		2,000	58,000
Mar. 12	Purchased used truck for street department	268		12,000	46,000
Apr. 15	Auditor of State, gasoline tax distribution		4,920		50,920
May 31	Gas and oil for street trucks	301		3,000	47,920
June 6	Tile	367		4,000	43,920
July 14	Concrete for building fireplaces in park	425		6,900	37,020
Aug. 7	Street lights (utility bill)	451		7,220	29,800
Sep. 29	Refund received on tile purchased by warrant No. 367		100		29,900
Oct. 18	Labor on streets	524–532		12,000	17,900
Nov. 2	Reimbursement for cutting weeds on private property		640		18,540
Dec. 11	To contractor for paving street	622		20,000	(1,460)
Dec. 31	Additional appropriations as advertised on this date		1,460		–0–

Equipment Account

Date	Description	Warrant	Appropriation	Disbursements	Appropriation Balance
Jan. 1	From advertised budget		$24,000		$24,000
9	Grading equipment			$16,000	8,000
Feb. 10	Fire hydrants	189		6,000	2,000
19	Shovels, picks, and hand tools	208		1,420	580

Required

1. Comment on whether accounting for the Street Fund appears in conformity with generally accepted accounting principles. Explain fully.

2. As the auditor, would you be able to render an unqualified opinion on the financial statements of the Town of Franklin? Would your answer depend on whether you are engaged to report on the financial statements at the individual fund level rather than at the combined level (general purpose financial statements)?

14–7. The Town of Arnold Balance Sheet as of December 31, 19x4, is shown below. The *Annual Report* for 19x4 also includes a Statement of Changes in Cash for that year and an Operating Statement for that year. No Auditor's Report is associated with these three financial statements. Assuming you made an audit for 19x4 and found no material errors in the amounts presented in the statements, could you express the opinion that the statements present fairly the financial position of the Town at December 31, 19x4, and the results of its operations for the year then ended in conformity with generally accepted accounting principles? Why or why not? Be explicit.

TOWN OF ARNOLD
Balance Sheet
As of December 31, 19x4

Assets

Cash	$ 155,155	
Accounts Receivable:		
Current-Year Property Taxes	58,792	
Prior-Year Property Taxes	2,921	
Other Taxes	514	
Municipal Services—Usage	71,861	
Municipal Services—Tap Fees	9,077	
Toll Bridges	30,598	
School District	5,242	
Other	173	
Total Current Assets		$ 334,333
Property, Plant, and Equipment:		
Library—Building and Equipment	$ 16,550	
Storage Shed	14,742	
Public Safety Dept.—Building and Equipment	266,317	
Municipal Services Dept.—Land, Building, and Equipment	2,325,893	
Highway Department	28,755	
Cemetery	21,595	
Town Office—Equipment	4,369	
Land	12,000	
Toll Bridges	22,500	
Total Property, Plant, and Equipment	2,712,721	
Less: Accumulated Amortization	(283,357)	2,429,364
Total Assets		$2,763,697

Liabilities and Equity

Accounts Payable	$ 1,725	
Tax Anticipation Notes	250,000	
Current Portion—Long-Term Debt		
Bonds	85,000	
Notes	84,304	
Due School District	46,089	
Total Current Liabilities	467,118	
Long-Term Debt—Bonds	1,395,000	
Notes	373,416	
Total Liabilities		$2,235,534
Equity	850,421	
Less: Wind Recovery Costs	(322,258)	528,163
Total Liabilities and Equity		$2,763,697

14–8. The Executive Summary appearing in the United States General Accounting Office *Report to Selected Agencies, Employee Benefits: Improved Plan Reporting and CPA Audits Can Increase Protection under ERISA*, is presented on pages 461–65. Comment on the report from the viewpoint of its apparent adherence to government auditing standards as discussed in this chapter. How well are CPA firms meeting their responsibilities for performing quality audits of private employee benefit plans covered by ERISA?

Executive Summary

Purpose

In November 1989, the Department of Labor's Office of Inspector General (IG) identified significant deficiencies in audits of private employee benefit plans. These findings generated congressional concerns about the protection of American workers' benefits and the risks associated with inadequate plan audits. As a result, the chairmen of the House Subcommittee on Oversight, Committee on Ways and Means, and the House Subcommittee on Labor-Management Relations, Committee on Education and Labor, asked GAO to identify problems in the performance of plan audits. In so doing, GAO also identified various ways to improve plan reporting and audits and, thus, further protect the interests of plan participants.

Background

The Employee Retirement Income Security Act of 1974 (ERISA) established various safeguards to protect the assets of private employee benefit plans and to ensure that plan participants receive benefits to which they are entitled. Under ERISA, the Department of Labor requires that an employee benefit plan (plan) having 100 or more participants obtain an annual financial statement audit by an independent public accountant. Audits of employee benefit plans are a key safeguard for protecting much of about $1.75 trillion in assets held by plans. Also, ERISA established the Pension Benefit Guarantee Corporation which insures about 95,000 defined benefit pension plans.

ERISA established fiduciary standards for plans and required that annual reports on plan operations, including an annual audit, be furnished to the Department of Labor and made available to plan participants. According to Labor's Office of Inspector General, ERISA cannot be materially enforced without plan audits.

In November 1989, the Labor IG reported that 64 of 279 plan audits it reviewed violated at least one auditing standard. Labor referred 14 of these 64 plan audits to the American Institute of Certified Public Accountants (AICPA), a voluntary professional association which provides guidance on auditing, for investigation of serious audit deficiencies. GAO reviewed 25 plan audits randomly selected from the remaining 50 in order to assess the reasonableness of the IG's criticisms.

In the last several years, GAO has become increasingly concerned about the inadequacies of audits which do not specifically address an entity's internal controls and compliance with applicable laws and regulations. Legislation enacted at the end of 1991 adopted GAO recommendations to require reforms to deal with inadequacies in financial statement audits of insured depository institutions, thereby helping to protect the government in its capacity as insurer of deposits in such institutions.

Results in Brief

Over a third of the 25 plan audits reviewed by GAO had audit weaknesses so serious that their reliability and usefulness were questionable. In some cases, the auditors failed to adequately test investments amounting to millions of dollars or test the appropriateness of millions of dollars in payments to insurance companies. These deficiencies indicate that auditors were sometimes unfamiliar with ERISA requirements and the special considerations associated with auditing employee benefit plans. Although the AICPA revised its guidance for performing plan audits in 1991, additional changes in the guide are needed.

Further action is needed to adequately protect the interests of plan participants. Legislation should be enacted to eliminate limited scope audits, which are presently permitted by ERISA. Legislation should also adopt, with appropriate modifications, the model reforms recently enacted for federally insured depository institutions. The legislation should require reporting on the adequacy of internal controls by plan administrators and auditors, provide for direct reporting to the Department of Labor of fraud and serious ERISA violations, and require peer review for plan auditors. These changes would enhance the value of plan audits, encourage better plan management, and, ultimately, better protect the interests of plan participants and the government.

Principal Findings

Failures by Auditors to Properly Audit

GAO evaluated 25 of the plan audits previously reviewed by the IG to determine if they were properly performed and if the IG's criticisms were reasonable. GAO found that nine of the plan audits did not satisfactorily comply with auditing standards because they had problems that were so severe that their reliability and usefulness were seriously diminished. The AICPA identified many of the same types of violations during its investigation of the 14 plan audits referred by Labor. For these reasons, GAO concluded that the IG's findings were generally reasonable.

The predominant problems in the plan audits were insufficient audit work or the lack of working paper evidence to prove that audit work was sufficient to support the unqualified opinions expressed by some auditors. In one case, for example, the working papers showed no evidence of tests for virtually all plan disbursements used to purchase insurance policies for plan participants. Many deficiencies involved the specialized auditing procedures intended to provide evidence about assets held by plan trustees, actuarial valuations, or the appropriateness of plan participant benefits. GAO concluded that these problems demonstrated that some auditors lacked industry knowledge and were not aware of ERISA requirements. The November 1989 IG study noted a similar problem of limited understanding.

Initiatives Taken to Improve Audit Quality

In response to the IG study, the AICPA has initiated various actions to publicize plan audit problems and better educate auditors about the audit procedures and requirements for plan audits. The AICPA also expanded its guidance on conducting plan audits. GAO believes that these initiatives are important steps toward ensuring that auditors have the expertise needed to improve the usefulness and reliability of future plan audits. However, additional changes need to be made to the audit guide to, among other things, clarify audit requirements and emphasize the need for specialized industry knowledge.

Reporting and Auditing Requirements Under ERISA Need Strengthening

GAO believes that legislation is needed to strengthen reporting and auditing requirements for plans and to further protect the interests of plan participants. Legislation should include several provisions.

First, the legislation should eliminate the limited scope audit provision from ERISA. This provision allows plan administrators to exclude from the scope of the audit investments held by certain regulated institutions, such as banks and insurance companies. Eliminating the limited scope provision from ERISA would subject all plan assets to audit and decrease vulnerabilities associated with plan assets. GAO found that over 25 percent of the total $126 million in plan assets covered by the 25 plan audits it reviewed were excluded from examination under ERISA's limited scope provision.

Second, the legislation should require reports on the effectiveness of internal controls by the plan administrator and the auditor. Plan administrators have a fiduciary responsibility to operate plans in the best interest of plan participants. Requiring plan administrators to prepare and sign reports on the effectiveness of the internal control structure, including controls for compliance with laws and regulations, and then providing the reports to regulators, participants, and others, would help ensure that adequate controls are established and maintained.

Requiring auditors to review plan administrators' reports on internal controls would help protect plan participants' interests by helping to ensure that plans maintain strong internal controls, adhere to laws and regulations, and properly report their financial condition. Such reviews could also provide early warnings of potential problems. Similarly, reviews of internal control reports would benefit the federal government, which, as insurer of defined benefit pension plans, faces a significant liability if plans with large unfunded liabilities terminate.

Further, GAO believes that auditors have a basic public responsibility and must consider the government's interests when auditing federally insured employee benefit plans. Auditors should be required to play a more active role in assisting regulators and plan administrators in identifying, preventing, and correcting problems in financial reporting and internal controls. This expansion of the auditor's role is in keeping with GAO's belief that auditors must recognize that they have greater responsibilities when accepting audit engagements for federally insured entities. Similar provisions, which are important reforms in auditing and reporting for federally insured financial institutions, were recently enacted in the Federal Deposit Insurance Corporation Improvement Act of 1991 (Public Law 102-242).

Third, legislation should require auditors to report fraud and serious ERISA violations directly to the Department of Labor. While both plan participants and Labor have significant interests in ERISA violations, there is no requirement in ERISA or Labor's implementing regulations that either be promptly and directly informed by the auditor when fraud or serious fiduciary breaches are discovered. Such a provision would increase protection of plan participants.

Fourth, legislation should require all audit firms which audit employee benefit plans to obtain a peer review. Peer review programs essentially entail the verification by other audit firms that the firm reviewed has a system of quality controls that reasonably ensures that audits meet established standards. Requiring all audit firms which audit employee benefit plans to participate in a peer review program that includes at least one plan audit would help ensure that audit firms performing plan audits adhere to auditing standards and perform quality audits.

Recommendations

GAO makes recommendations to the Department of Labor, the AICPA, and the Congress in chapters 2, 3, and 4. Of particular importance are the legislative recommendations that the Congress amend ERISA to: (1) eliminate the provision that permits limited scope audits, (2) require reports by plan administrators and auditors on internal controls, (3) require reporting by auditors of fraud and serious ERISA violations, and (4) require peer review of auditors conducting plan audits.

Agency Comments

Both the Secretary of Labor and the Chairman of the Board of the American Institute of Certified Public Accountants commented on a draft of this report. (See appendixes II and III.)

Labor agreed with many of GAO's recommendations but expressed concerns with the recommendations on internal control reporting and direct reporting to Labor of serious ERISA violations. However, Labor did agree that significant internal control weaknesses can lead to fraud and abuse of plan assets. Labor stated that it is currently assessing alternative approaches for the identification and reporting of significant internal control weaknesses. With respect to direct reporting, Labor is considering whether plan administrators should be required to report to Labor information related to certain criminal acts involving employee benefit plans covered by ERISA. However, this does not utilize the resource of the independent auditor to help protect against criminal acts by plan administrators.

The AICPA stated that it is considering many of GAO's recommendations. It also stated that it supports cost beneficial efforts and suggestions to increase the protection of plan participants but has concern about creating unrealistic expectations relative to the role and work of independent accountants. GAO believes implementing its recommendations would allow the profession to better meet the public's existing expectations. The AICPA expressed serious concerns with direct reporting of fraud and serious ERISA violations to Labor because of its view of client confidentiality. GAO disagrees with this view and believes the auditor should be required to report fraud and serious ERISA violations when the plan administrator fails to do so.

Continuous Problems

14–L. *a.* After calculating the financial ratios presented in Illustration 13–3 and examining the financial statements and schedules prepared for 13–L *a* and *b*, prepare a letter of transmittal to accompany the general purpose financial statements and the individual fund and account group statements. Your letter of transmittal should be addressed to the Honorable Mayor, City Council, and City Manager of the City of Bingham and should inform them of the accounting and budgeting policies employed by the City and explain in some detail which financial statements and schedules are enclosed. Your letter should also summarize the financial condition of the City and its funds, and, in general, note significant changes since the end of the prior year. (Trial balances and balance sheets as of June 30, 19x1, given at the beginning of each "L" problem, as needed, give you information about the financial condition of funds at the end of the prior year.)

b. Prepare the audit report you believe would be appropriate for a certified public accountant to express on the *general purpose financial statements* of the City of Bingham. Explain the rationale for the nature of the audit report (qualified or unqualified) rendered.

14–S. *a.* Calculate the financial ratios presented in Illustration 13–3 and examine the financial statements and schedules prepared for 13–S *a* and *b*, then briefly itemize the points you feel the City finance director should cover in his/her letter of transmittal to accompany the financial report for the City of Smithville. What is your assessment of the current financial condition of the City and its funds? What are the significant changes that have occurred since the end of the prior year? (Trial balances and balance sheets as of December 31, 19y0, given at the beginning of each "S" problem, as needed, give you information about the financial condition of funds at the end of the prior year.)

b. Prepare the audit report you believe would be appropriate for a certified public accountant to express on the financial statements of the City of Smithville. Explain the rationale for the nature of the audit report (qualified or unqualified) rendered.

CHAPTER 15

Accounting and Reporting for Federal Government Agencies*

An accounting structure has been provided for the federal government of the United States of America by statutes since 1789. The professional accounting consultants to the first and second Hoover Commissions generally are given credit for giving early direction to the effort to improve federal government accounting. Recent years have seen major institutional change that is providing the impetus for even greater change in federal accounting. Among these changes are the Chief Financial Officers Act of 1990, the creation of the Federal Accounting Standards Advisory Board (FASAB) in 1990, and the Government Performance and Results Act of 1993. Federal accounting standards are similar in many respects to those developed for state and local governments, as discussed in Chapters 1–13 of this text. Important differences do exist, however. This chapter is focused on the aspects of accounting for federal agencies that differ from the concepts for state and local governments.

Federal Government Financial Management Structure

The United States Code (31 U.S.C. 3512) requires the head of each executive agency to establish, evaluate, and maintain adequate systems of accounting and internal control within their agencies. Federal statutes, however, assign responsibility for establishing and maintaining a sound financial management structure for the federal government as a whole to three principal officials: the Comptroller General, the Director of the Office of Management and Budget (OMB), and the

* The authors are indebted to Bruce K. Michelson, Assistant Director, Accounting and Auditing Standards Group, U.S. General Accounting Office; J. Thomas Luter, Technical Director, Department of Treasury Financial Management Services; and Robert Bramlett, Assistant Director of the Federal Accounting Standards Advisory Board, for their technical guidance on this edition and prior editions of the text. Although their suggestions were of major assistance in revising the chapter, any errors or omissions are those of the authors. We would also like to thank Bruce Michelson for providing resource materials used in Chapter 14, Audits of Governmental Entities.

Secretary of the Treasury. Responsibilities assigned to each of these officials and others are discussed briefly, after which recent cooperative efforts of these officials to enhance the quality of federal financial management under the auspices of the Joint Financial Management and Improvement Program (JFMIP) will be examined.

Comptroller General

The Comptroller General of the United States is the head of the General Accounting Office (GAO), an agency of the legislative branch of the government. He is appointed by the President with the advice and consent of the Senate for a term of office of 15 years. Since 1950, the United States Code (31 U.S.C. 3511) has assigned to the Comptroller General responsibility for prescribing the accounting principles, standards, and related requirements to be observed by each executive agency in the development of its accounting system. The Chief Financial Officers Act of 1990, however, assigns significant responsibility for establishing policies and procedures for approving and publishing accounting principles and standards (particularly as regards agency financial reporting) to the Director of the Office of Management and Budget. Thus, both under the law and in fact, the responsibility for prescribing accounting principles and standards is now a joint responsibility.

Just as the appropriational authority of state and local governments rests in their legislative bodies, the appropriational authority of the federal government rests in the Congress. The Congress is, therefore, interested in determining that financial and budgetary reports from executive, judicial, and legislative agencies are reliable; that agency financial management is intelligent, efficient, and economical; and that legal requirements have been met by the agencies. Under the assumption that the reports of an independent audit agency would aid in satisfying these interests of the Congress, the General Accounting Office was created as the audit agency of the Congress itself. The standards of auditing followed by the GAO are discussed in some detail in Chapter 14. Briefly, the standards are set forth in the publication, *Government Auditing Standards*, often referred to as the "yellow book," and are usually followed by independent CPAs as well as by state audit agencies, programs, activities, and functions.

Secretary of the Treasury

The Secretary of the Treasury is the head of the Department of the Treasury, a part of the executive branch of the federal government. The Secretary of the Treasury is a member of the Cabinet of the President, appointed by the President with the advice and consent of the Senate to serve an indefinite term of office. The Department of the Treasury was created in 1789 to receive, keep, and disburse monies of the United States, and to account for them. From the beginning, the word **receive** was construed as **collect,** and the Internal Revenue Service, Bureau of Customs, and other agencies active in the enforcement of the collections of revenues due the federal government are parts of the Department of the Treasury, as are the Bureau of the Mint, the Bureau of Engraving and Printing, the Bureau of Public Debt, the Office of Treasurer of the United States, and the Bureau of Government Financial Operations. Although there is no complete centralized accounting system for the federal government at this time, the Secretary of the

Treasury, in coordination with the Director of OMB and the Comptroller General, has for several years published prototype consolidated financial statements for the United States Government as a whole.

The Secretary of the Treasury is responsible for the preparation of reports that will inform the President, the Congress, and the public on the financial condition and operations of the government (31 U.S.C. 3513). An additional responsibility of the Secretary of the Treasury is the maintenance of a system of central accounts of the public debt and cash to provide a basis for consolidation of the accounts of the various executive agencies with those of the Department of the Treasury.

Statutes provide that the reports of the Secretary of the Treasury shall include financial data needed by the Office of Management and Budget, and that the Department of the Treasury system of central accounting and reporting shall be consistent with the principles, standards, and related requirements prescribed for federal agency accounting systems. Instructions and requirements relating to central accounting, central financial reporting, and various other fiscal matters have been codified by the Department of the Treasury in the *Treasury Financial Manual* for guidance of departments and agencies.

The Department of the Treasury (Financial Management Service) also provides support for the interagency Standard General Ledger Board which maintains the *U.S. Government Standard General Ledger,* subject to the approval of the OMB. The *Standard General Ledger* was developed by an interagency task force under the direction of the OMB and was originally published by the OMB in 1986. The *Standard General Ledger* is intended to (1) provide an accounting structure that will standardize financial information accumulation and processing, (2) enhance financial control, and (3) support budget reporting and external financial reporting. Implementation of the *Standard General Ledger* has enhanced the ability of central agencies to more accurately consolidate accounting data derived from individual agency accounting records. The chart of accounts presented in the *Standard General Ledger* is based on a standardized coding system for asset, liability, equity, budgetary, revenue, expense, and "gains/losses/extraordinary items, etc." accounts and provides flexibility so that agency-specific accounts may be incorporated. In addition to the chart of accounts, the *Standard General Ledger* publication provides account descriptions; illustrates the manner in which accounting transactions should be recorded; discusses data elements, subaccounts, and definitions; and illustrates crosswalks to external reports. Accounting for typical transactions of a federal agency illustrated in a later section of this chapter is based on the *Standard General Ledger* structure.

Director of the Office of Management and Budget

The Director of the Office of Management and Budget is appointed by the President and is a part of the Executive Office of the President. As the direct representative of the President with the authority to control the size and nature of appropriations requested of each Congress, it is obvious that the Director of the Office of Management and Budget is an extremely powerful figure in the federal government.

Congressional requirements for the budget have a number of accounting implications in addition to the explicit historical comparisons that necessitate cooperation among the Office of Management and Budget, the Department of the Treasury and the General Accounting Office. Implicit in the requirements for projections of revenues and receipts is the mandate that the Office of Management and Budget coordinate closely with the Council of Economic Advisers in the use of macroeconomic (the study of the economic system in its aggregate) and macroaccounting (accounting for the economy in the aggregate) forecasts. Macroaccounting is beyond the scope of this text, yet the subject is of great, and increasing, importance in the financial management of the federal government; and the reader who desires an understanding of federal financial policies and their integration with political, social, and economic policies should be knowledgeable in the macroeconomic and macroaccounting areas.

The OMB is assigned major responsibilities under the Chief Financial Officers Act of 1990 for establishing policies and procedures for approving and publishing financial accounting principles and standards to be followed by executive branch agencies. Pursuant to the Act, an Office of Federal Financial Management has been established within the OMB, headed by a controller appointed by the President. The Act also authorizes each major department or agency of the federal government to have a Chief Financial Offier (CFO) and a deputy CFO. Under the Act, the Director of the OMB is required to prepare and update each year a five-year financial plan for the federal government.

Director of the Congressional Budget Office

The Congressional Budget and Impoundment Control Act of 1974 established House and Senate budget committees, created the Congressional Budget Office, structured the congressional budget process, and enacted a number of other provisions to improve federal fiscal procedures. The Director of the CBO, as the Congressional Budget Office is known, is appointed for a four-year term by the Speaker of the House of Representatives and the President pro tempore of the Senate. The CBO gathers information for the House and Senate budget committees with respect to the budget (submitted by the executive branch), appropriation bills, and other bills providing budget authority or tax expenditures.[1] The CBO also provides the Congress with information concerning revenues, receipts, estimated future revenues and receipts, changing revenue conditions, and any related information-gathering and analytic functions assigned to the CBO; its Director is responsible for working with the Comptroller General, the Secretary of the Treasury, and the Director of the Office of Management and Budget in developing central files of data and information to meet the recurring requirements of the Congress.

Illustration 15–1 shows in chart form the interrelationships among the officials and organizations whose accounting and financial management responsibilities are discussed above.

---

[1] A tax expenditure is a revenue loss attributable to provisions of federal tax laws which allow a special exclusion, exemption, or deduction from gross income, or which provide a special credit, a preferential rate of tax, or a deferral of tax liability.

ILLUSTRATION 15–1   **Federal Government Financial Management Structure**

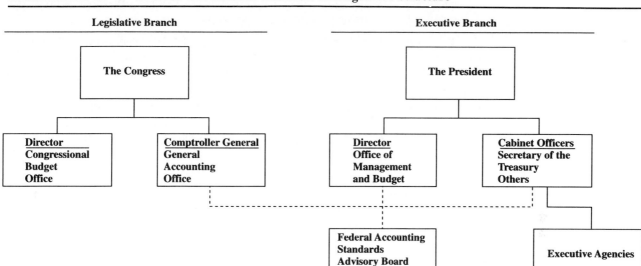

Structure for Establishing Accounting and Financial Reporting Standards for Federal Agencies

As noted previously, three officials or "principals" of the Joint Financial Management Improvement Program (JFMIP)—the Comptroller General, the Director of OMB, and the Secretary of the Treasury—have joint statutory responsibilities for improving financial management in the federal government. Although accounting principles and standards were prescribed for many years by *Title 2* of the *General Accounting Office Policy and Procedures Manual for Guidance of Federal Agencies,* not all federal agencies complied with the guidance contained in *Title 2*. The diverse financial systems used among and within federal departments and agencies made it difficult to achieve uniform financial reporting and to educate and train federal financial managers.

To establish an improved, and more generally accepted, structure for setting accounting principles and standards, the three principal sponsors of the JFMIP signed a memorandum of understanding in October 1990 creating the **Federal Accounting Standards Advisory Board (FASAB).** The nine member board utilizes a due process similar to that of FASB and GASB. The new board is comprised of one member from each of the three principal sponsors; one member from each of the following federal constituencies: the Congressional Budget Office, defense and international agencies, and civilian agencies; and three members from the nonfederal "general financial community" (defined as the accounting and auditing community and academia). According to OMB *Circular A-134*, "Financial Accounting Principles and Standards" (par. 2):

> The role of the FASAB is to deliberate upon and make recommendations to the Principals on accounting principles and standards for the Federal Government and its

agencies. The MOU [memorandum of understanding] states that if the Principals agree with the recommendations, the Comptroller General and the Director of OMB will publish the accounting principles and standards.

To date, three Statements of Federal Financial Accounting Standards (SFFASs) have been issued that collectively provide general and specific standards on a variety of topics, including assets (cash, fund balance with Treasury, accounts receivable, interest receivable, advances and prepayments, and investments in Treasury securities), liabilities (accounts payable, interest payable, and other current liabilities), direct loans and loan guarantees, and inventory and related property.[2] The authoritative status of SFFASs is made clear by OMB *Circular A–134* (par. 5.b.):

> SFFASs shall be considered generally accepted accounting principles (GAAP) for Federal agencies. Agencies shall apply the SFFASs in preparing financial statements in accordance with the requirements of the Chief Financial Officers Act of 1990. Auditors shall consider SFFASs as authoritative references when auditing financial statements.

Conceptual Framework

Accounting standards recommended by the FASAB, and issued by the Comptroller General and OMB for federal agencies, are intended to be consistent with a conceptual framework it is developing. In this respect, it is following the general pattern established by the FASB, which attempts to issue standards consistent with its several *Statements of Financial Accounting Concepts;* and the GASB, which looks to its *Concepts Statement No. 1,* ''Objectives of Financial Reporting (see Chapter 1 of this text). To date, however, only one concepts statement, *Statement of Accounting and Reporting Concepts No. 1,* ''Objectives of Federal Financial Reporting'' has been issued. FASAB *Concepts Statement No. 1* is considerably broader in scope than either the FASB's or GASB's concepts statements. The FASAB, for example, intends to set standards for internal management accounting and service efforts and accomplishments, as well as for external financial reporting. The FASAB objectives are described briefly in the next section.

Objectives

Statement of Accounting and Reporting Concepts No. 1 (Chapter 4) identifies four objectives of federal financial reporting, all of which rest on the foundation of accountability. The objectives in brief are to assist report users in evaluating **budgetary integrity, operating performance, stewardship,** and adequacy of **systems and controls. Budgetary integrity** pertains to accountability for raising monies through taxes and other means in accordance with appropriate laws, and expenditures of these monies in accordance with budgetary authorization. Accountability for **operating performance** is accomplished by providing report users information on service efforts and accomplishments—how well resources have been managed

---

[2] If additional SFFASs are issued the publisher will provide updates to adopters of the Tenth Edition of this text.

in providing services efficiently and economically, and effectively, in attaining planned goals. **Stewardship** relates to the federal government's accountability for the general welfare of the nation. To assess stewardship, report users need information about the "impact on the country of the government's operations and investments for the period and how, as a result, the government's and the nation's financial conditions have changed and may change in the future" (par. 134). Finally, financial reporting should help users assess whether financial management **systems and controls** (internal accounting and administrative controls) "are adequate to ensure that (1) transactions are executed in accordance with budgetary and financial laws and other requirements, are consistent with the purposes authorized, and are recorded in accordance with federal accounting standards, (2) assets are properly safeguarded to deter fraud, waste, and abuse, and (3) performance measurement information is adequately supported" (par. 146).

Unlike the FASB and the GASB, which focus their standards on external financial reporting, FASAB and its sponsors are concerned with both internal and external financial reporting. Accordingly, FASAB has identified four major groups of users of federal financial reports: citizens, Congress, executives, and program managers. Given the broad role FASAB has been assigned, future standards recommended by the board are likely to focus on cost accounting and service efforts and accomplishments measures as well as on financial accounting and reporting. The Memorandum of Understanding among the sponsors provides, however, that FASAB jurisdiction does not extend to agency budgetary accounting and the manner of controlling expenditures of budgetary resources.

The Reporting Entity The criteria to be used for defining a state or local government reporting entity are discussed in Chapter 13 of this text. Some federal government agencies are not financially accountable for other agencies, departments, or units and thus may present less difficulty than state and local governmental units in determining the reporting entity. Defining the reporting entity for the government as a whole or for certain major agencies, however, may be more difficult. It appears, for example, that federal reporting entities may have to be defined variously as organizational units (e.g., agencies and departments), related groups of budget accounts, or service delivery programs and activities to meet the reporting objectives established in FASAB *Concepts Statement No 1*. An interim definition of "entity" is defined in SFFAS *No. 1* (par. 17) as simply:

> . . . [A] unit within the federal government, such as a department, agency, bureau, or program, for which a set of financial statements will be prepared.

The term *entity* also may include: (par. 17)

> a group of related or unrelated commercial functions, revolving funds, trust funds [defined in the next section], and/or other accounts for which financial statements are prepared. . .

Finally, SFFASs are applicable as well to financial reporting by the U.S. Government as a whole, although, as noted previously, these financial statements are currently prepared on a prototype basis and are not audited. At this time, nonuniform agency financial accounting and reporting makes it difficult to compile governmentwide financial statements that can be audited. In the not too distant future, audited governmentwide financial statement should become routine.

Funds Used in
Federal Accounting

Fund accounting is required for federal agencies to demonstrate compliance with requirements of legislation for which federal funds have been appropriated or otherwise authorized to carry out specific activities, and also for financial reporting.

Two general types of funds are found in federal government accounting: (1) those used to account for resources derived from the general taxation and revenue powers or from business operations of the government and (2) those used to account for resources held and managed by the government in the capacity of custodian or trustee. Six kinds of funds are specified within the two general types:

1. Funds derived from general taxing and revenue powers and from business operations.
   A. General fund accounts.
   B. Special fund accounts.
   C. Revolving fund accounts.
   D. Management fund accounts.
2. Funds held by the government in the capacity of custodian or trustee.
   A. Trust fund accounts.
   B. Deposit fund accounts.

General Fund.   The General Fund is credited with all receipts that are not dedicated by law and is charged with payments out of appropriations of "any money in the Treasury not otherwise appropriated" and out of general borrowings.

Strictly speaking, there is only one General Fund in the entire federal government. The Bureau of Government Financial Operations of the Department of the Treasury accounts for the centralized cash balances (the cash is under the control of the Treasurer of the United States; cash accounts subsidiary to those of the Bureau of Government Financial Operations are maintained by the Treasurer), the appropriations control accounts, and unappropriated balances. On the books of an agency, each appropriation is treated as a fund with its own self-balancing group of accounts; these agency "appropriation funds" are subdivisions of *the* General Fund.

Special Funds.   Receipt and expenditure accounts established to account for receipts of the government that are earmarked by law for a specific purpose, but that are not generated from a cycle of operations for which there is continuing authority to reuse such receipts (as is true for revolving funds), are classified as *special fund accounts* in federal usage. The term and its definition are very close to that of the classification "special revenue funds" used in accounting for state and local governments.

Revolving. A revolving fund is credited with collections, primarily from other agencies and accounts, that are earmarked by law to carry out a cycle of business-type operations, in which the government is the owner of the activity. This type of fund is quite similar to the type of fund discussed in the chapter on internal service funds.

Management (including Working Funds). These are funds in which there are merged monies derived from two or more appropriations, in order to carry out a common purpose or project, but not involving a cycle of operations. Management funds include consolidated working funds that are set up to receive (and subsequently disburse) advance payments, pursuant to law, from other agencies or bureaus.

Trust Funds. Trust funds are established to account for receipts that are held in trust for use in carrying out specific purposes and programs in accordance with agreement or statute. In distinction to revolving funds and special funds, the assets of trust funds are frequently held over a period of time and may be invested in order to produce revenue. For example, the assets of the Federal Old Age and Survivors Insurance Trust Fund are invested in U.S. securities.

The corpus of some trust funds is used in business-type operations. In such a case, the fund is called a *trust revolving fund*. In general, the discussion of trust funds in Chapter 12 is applicable in principle to federal trust funds.

Deposit Funds. Combined receipt and expenditure accounts established to account for receipts held in suspense temporarily and later refunded or paid to some other fund, or receipts held by the government as a banker or agent for others and paid out at the discretion of the owner, are classified within the federal government as "deposit fund accounts." They are similar in nature to the "agency funds" established for state and local governmental units.

Elements of Financial Statements

The trial balance of the appropriated General Fund for a hypothetical federal agency as of the last day of a certain fiscal year, 19y6, is shown in Illustration 15–2. The fiscal year in the U.S. government is the 12-month period from October 1 through the following September 30.

Statement of Federal Financial Accounting Standards (SFFAS) No. 1 sets forth both general and specific standards for assets and liabilities. The general standards distinguish between **intragovernmental assets and liabilities** and **governmental assets and liabilities.** Intragovernmental assets and liabilities are claims by and against a federal entity that arise from transactions between that entity and other *federal* entities. Governmental assets and liabilities are claims by and against the federal government (or an entity within the federal government) that arise from transactions between the federal government (or federal entity) and *nonfederal* entities. The general standards also distinguish between **entity assets** and **nonentity assets.** Entity assets are assets the entity has authority to use in its operations whereas nonentity assets are assets being held by an entity but which

ILLUSTRATION 15–2

FEDERAL AGENCY
Post-Closing Trial Balance
As of September 30, 19y6

	Debits	Credits
Proprietary Accounts:		
Fund Balance with Treasury—19y6	$ 675,000	
Operating Materials and Supplies	610,000	
Equipment	3,000,000	
Accumulated Depreciation on Equipment		$ 600,000
Accounts Payable		275,000
Appropriated Capital—19y6		400,000
Invested Capital....................................		3,010,000
Cumulative Results of Operations		–0–
	$4,285,000	$4,285,000
Budgetary Accounts:		
Other Appropriations Realized—19y6	$ 400,000	
Undelivered Orders—19y6		$ 400,000
	$ 400,000	$ 400,000

are not available for use in its operations. An example of the latter is federal income taxes collected by the Internal Revenue Service for the U.S. government. Nonentity assets should be reported separately in the balance sheet from entity assets, offset by a liability (due to other entities) in the same total amount.

Specific standards issued in *SFFAS No. 1* are described briefly in the following discussions of assets and liabilities.

Assets. *SFFAS No. 1* provides specific standards relating to Cash, Fund Balance with Treasury, Accounts Receivable, Interest Receivable, and various other asset categories. In most federal agencies, "Fund Balance with Treasury" is used, rather than "Cash," to indicate that this agency has a claim against the U.S. Treasury on which it may draw to pay liabilities. Only a few large federal departments and agencies, such as the Department of Defense, are authorized to write and issue checks directly against their balances with the Treasury. Most departments and agencies must request that the Treasury issue checks to pay their liabilities. If a federal agency does have the right to maintain one or more bank accounts, bank balances would be reported as "Cash."

Consistent with the manner in which business entities report inventories, SFFAS No. 3, *Accounting for Inventory and Related Property*, distinguishes inventory from consumable supplies. Inventory is defined (p. 4) as "tangible personal property that is (1) held for sale, (2) in the process of production for sale, or (3) to be consumed in the production of goods for sale or in the provision of services for a fee." Inventory may be valued at either historical cost or latest acquisition cost. Supplies to be consumed in normal operations are reported as

operating materials and supplies. The federal agency whose trial balance is presented in Illustration 15–2 reports only "Operating Materials and Supplies," indicating that the agency does not sell goods or services as part of its normal operations. SFFAS No. 3 also defines several additional types of inventory or related property: (1) stockpile materials, (2) seized and forfeited property, (3) foreclosed property, and (4) goods held under price support and stabilization programs. Discussion of these other types is beyond the scope of this text.

Liabilities. *SFFAS No. 1* provides specific standards for Accounts Payable, Interest Payable, and Other Current Liabilities. Accounts Payable, the only liability account listed in the trial balance shown in Illustration 15–2, are defined in *SFFAS No. 1* as amounts owed by a federal entity for goods and services received from other entities, either federal or nonfederal. OMB *Bulletin No. 94–01*, "Form and Content of Agency Financial Statements," provides additional guidance on reporting liabilities. For example, it requires separate balance sheet reporting of **funded liabilities** and **unfunded liabilities.** Funded liabilities are those for which monies have been made available either through Congressional appropriations or current earnings of the entity. Unfunded liabilities result from the receipt of goods or services in the current or prior periods but for which monies have not yet been made available through Congressional appropriations or current earnings of the entity. Examples of the latter are liabilities for accrued leave, capital leases, and pensions. Accrued leave, in particular, would be found on nearly every agency's balance sheet; it has been omitted from the trial balance shown in Illustration 15–2 for simplicity.

Net Position. OMB *Bulletin No. 94–01* requires that the fund balances of the entity's funds be reported in the balance sheet as **Net Position.** An analysis of the fund balance for each fund classification reported in the balance sheet must also be provided in the Notes to the Financial Statements. In the trial balance displayed in Illustration 15–2, the federal agency is assumed to have only one fund, an appropriated fund functioning as a "General Fund," although, as mentioned previously, the fund is technically a subfund of the Treasury's General Fund.

The components of Fund Balance to be included in the defined required analysis of fund balances are as follows:

> **Unexpended Appropriations.** The amount of unexpended budget authority appropriated by Congress, both available and unavailable. Includes amounts transferred to and from the entity. [Note: the U.S. Standard General Ledger account corresponding to this component is **Appropriated Capital.**]
>
> **Invested Capital.** The net investment of the Government in the reporting entity. Includes the acquisition cost of capitalized fixed assets financed by appropriations; the additional investment in a revolving fund to commence operations or begin a new activity; less the reduction in investment due to depreciation, amortization, sales or exchanges, donations, other disposals, the return of initial investment to an investor, or transfer to another entity or revolving fund.
>
> **Cumulative Results of Operations.** The net difference between (1) expenses and

---

ILLUSTRATION 15–3   Analysis of Fund Balances

	Revolving Funds	Trust Funds	Appropriated Funds	Total
Unexpended Appropriations:				
(1) Unobligated				
(a) Available	$ XX	$ XX	$ XX	$ XX
(b) Unavailable	XX	XX	XX	XX
(2) Undelivered Orders	XX	XX	XX	XX
Invested Capital	XX	XX	XX	XX
Cumulative Results of Operations	XX	XX	XX	XX
Other	XX	XX	XX	XX
Future Funding Requirements	(XX)	(XX)	(XX)	(XX)
Total	$XXX	$XXX	$XXX	$XXX

SOURCE: OMB *Bulletin No. 94–01*, "Form and Content of Agency Financial Statements," p. 78.

losses and (2) financing sources, including appropriations, revenues, and gains, since the inception of the activity.

Other.   Any other components of net position not specifically identified above. Other components include the fair market value of donated assets, plus any costs incurred to place the donated assets in use, and assets (net of liabilities) transferred to or from other federal entities without reimbursement.

Future Funding Requirements.   Liabilities reported in the Statement of Financial Position which are not covered by available budgetary resources.

Total Net Position.   Sum of the above five components.[3]

Total amounts must be provided in the analysis of fund balances for each component of fund balance summed across all fund categories as well as for the fund balance of each fund category summed across components. An example of an analysis of fund balances is presented in Illustration 15–3. The subcomponents (1) Unobligated and (2) Undelivered Orders under Unexpended Appropriations are explained later in this chapter under the heading "Illustrative Transactions and Entries."

FASAB has not yet issued standards for elements of federal operating statements. OMB *Bulletin 94–01,* however, provides interim guidance for these elements. **Revenues and Financing Sources** include **Appropriated Capital Used; Revenues from Sales of Goods and Services to the Public; Revenues from Sales of Goods and Services, Intragovernmental; Interest and Penalties, Nonfederal; Interest, Federal; Taxes; Other Revenues and Financial Sources;** and **Taxes and Receipts Transferred to the Treasury or Other Agencies.** The latter is a revenue

---

[3] OMB *Bulletin No. 94–01*, pp. 28–29.

deduction account for taxes and other receipts that may not be retained for use of the reporting entity. It offsets amounts reported in one or more of the preceding accounts. Appropriations Expensed represents current and prior-year appropriations used for goods and services received in the current year.

OMB *Bulletin No. 94–01* also describes several expense classifications used in federal agency operating statements. The major classifications are **Program or Operating Expenses; Cost of Goods Sold to the Public; Cost of Goods Sold, Intragovernmental; Depreciation and Amortization; Bad Debts and Write-offs; Interest—Federal Financing Bank/Treasury Borrowing; Interest—Federal Securities; Interest—Other;** and **Other Expenses.** Most of the expenses incurred in conducting the normal activities of the entity, classified either by program or by object class, are reported in the first classification listed: Program or Operating Expenses.

Two-Track Accounting System

Financial reports of federal agencies must be based on historical costs to indicate whether an entity has complied with laws and regulations (e.g., 31 U.S.C. 1341). Congressional policy, as expressed in 31 U.S.C. 1108, calls for using cost information in budgeting and in managing operations. This law also provides for using cost-based budgets, at such time as may be determined by the President, in developing requests for appropriations. All departments and agencies, therefore, must have budget and accounting systems that have the capability to produce cost-based budgets. In this context, cost is the value of goods and services used or consumed by a government agency within a given period, regardless of when they were ordered, received, or paid for. In any given year, the obligations incurred may be less than, equal to, or greater than the costs recognized for that period, due to changes in inventories, obligations, etc. At the completion of a program, however, obligations and costs are identical.[4]

The accounting system of a federal agency must provide information needed for financial management as well as information needed to demonstrate that agency managers have complied with budgetary and other legal requirements. Accordingly, federal agency accounting is based on a **two-track system;** one track being a self-balancing set of **proprietary** accounts intended to provide information for agency management, and the other track being the self-balancing set of **budgetary** accounts needed (1) to assure that available budgetary resources and authority are not overexpended or overobligated and (2) to facilitate standardized budgetary reporting requirements. The two-track system is not likely to change in the near future since the FASAB's role specifically excludes budgetary accounting. Illustration 15–4 summarizes key differences between budgetary and proprietary track accounting in terms of timing of the recognition of events and transactions. The use of the two-track system is illustrated in the next section, "Illustrative Transactions and Entries."

---

[4] *Accounting Principles and Standards* (Appendix I of *Title 2 of GAO Policy and Procedures Manual for Guidance of Federal Agencies*), p. 11.

ILLUSTRATION 15–4   **Summary of Key Differences between Budgetary and Proprietary Accounting in Recognition of Events Which Constitute Transactions**

Budgetary Accounting	*Proprietary Accounting*
Entries are made for commitment of funds in advance of preparing orders to procure goods and services.	Entries are not made for commitments.
Entries are made for obligation of funds at the time goods and services are ordered.	Entries are not made for obligations.
Entries are made to expend appropriations when goods and service chargeable to the appropriation are received, regardless of when they are used and regardless of when they are paid for.	Goods and services which will last more than a year and otherwise meet the criteria to qualify as assets are capitalized and expensed when consumed, regardless of what appropriation funded them and when they are paid for.
Entries are only made against an appropriation for transactions funded by the appropriation.	Goods and services consumed in the current period for which payment is to be made from one or more subsequent appropriations is recognized as an expense in the current period.
Entries are not made against an appropriation for transactions not funded by the appropriation.	Goods and services consumed in the current period but paid for in prior periods are expensed in the current period.

SOURCE: U.S. General Accounting Office, *GAO Accounting Guide: Basic Topics Relating to Appropriations and Reimbursables* (Washington, D.C.: GAO, 1990), p. 3–2.

Illustrative Transactions and Entries[5]

The basic budgetary authority for a federal agency can come from many different sources. Only one of those sources is illustrated here—basic operating appropriations. The flow of budget authority generally follows a sequence of events described as follows:

1. The congressional **appropriation** is enacted into law and provides budget authority to fund an agency's operations for the year.
2. An **apportionment,** usually quarterly, is approved by the Office of Management and Budget which may be used by the agency to procure goods and services for the quarter.
3. The head of the agency or his designee authorizes an **allotment** of the apportionment for procurement of goods and services.

---

[5] The illustrative journal entries shown here use the account titles prescribed by the U.S. Government Standard General Ledger, except that we have added fiscal year designations after certain accounts for instructional purposes. The financial statements that follow are based on those specified by OMB *Bulletin No. 94–01.*

4. Authorized agency employees reserve allotted budget authority in the estimated amount of an order as a **commitment** prior to the actual ordering of goods and services.

5. **Obligation** of the allotment occurs when a formal order is placed for acquisition of goods and services, charging the allotment with the latest estimate of the cost of goods or services ordered.

6. An **expended appropriation** occurs when goods or services have been received.

It should be noted that the term *expended appropriation* means the budget authority has been used and is no longer available to provide for goods and services. It does not necessarily mean that cash has been disbursed; it may be that only a liability has been incurred. A **commitment** (item 4 above) does not legally encumber an appropriation, but its use is recommended in the GAO's *Title 2* for effective planning and fund control. Some agencies, however, use commitments only for certain spending categories.[6]

As shown in Illustration 15–5, the full amount of an agency's appropriation for the year is reported as a budgetary resource which, at a given point during the period, is distributed among the budgetary accounts shown under "Status of Resources." As discussed above, and in the following illustrative transactions, budgetary authority normally flows down the accounts, culminating ultimately in the expending of authority.

If the agency whose September 30, 19y6 Post-Closing Trial Balance is shown in Illustration 15–2 receives from the Congress a one-year appropriation for fiscal year 19y7 in the amount of $3,000,000, the Treasury's Bureau of Government Financial Operations would prepare a formal notice to the agency after the appropriation act has been signed by the President. The following entries would be made in the agency accounts:

1a. *Budgetary:*

Other Appropriations Realized—19y7	3,000,000	
Unapportioned Authority—19y7		3,000,000

1b. *Proprietary:*

Fund Balance with Treasury—19y7	3,000,000	
Appropriated Capital—19y7		3,000,000

The account entitled "Other Appropriations Realized—19y7" is used in the U.S. Standard General Ledger to distinguish basic operating appropriations from specific appropriation authority which earmarks appropriations for specific purposes.

---

[6] For a discussion of commitments, see U.S. General Accounting Office, *GAO Accounting Guide: Basic Topics Relating to Appropriations and Reimbursables* (Washington, D.C.: GAO, 1990), p. 2–3.

ILLUSTRATION 15–5   Relationship among Budgetary Accounts

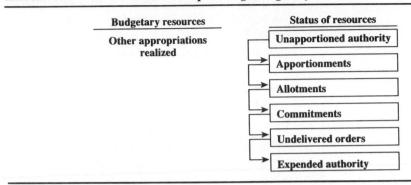

When the Office of Management and Budget approves the quarterly apportionment, the agency would be notified. Assuming the OMB approved apportionments of $700,000 for each quarter and withheld $200,000, the agency would record the apportionments as follows:[7]

2. *Budgetary:*		
Unapportioned Authority—19y7	2,800,000	
Apportionments—19y7...............................		2,800,000

If, upon notification of the apportionments, the agency head had allotted the entire first-quarter apportionment, the event would be recorded in the agency accounts in the following manner:

3. *Budgetary:*		
Apportionments—19y7..................................	700,000	
Allotments—19y7		700,000

All three entries—for the annual appropriation, for the apportionment by the OMB, and for the first-quarter allotment—would be made as of October 1, the first day of fiscal year 19y7, although in some years the appropriation bill might not have been actually enacted by that date. The substance of the three entries is that agency managers have new obligational authority totaling $700,000 for the operations of the first quarter, and so must manage the activities of the agency accordingly, even though the Congress did appropriate $3,000,000 for the year. It should also be noted that if the OMB does not release the $200,000 of appropriations withheld, that amount is not available to the agency. Similarly, apportionments and allotments not expended or obligated ordinarily must be returned to the U.S. Treasury at the end of the fiscal year. Again, for purposes of simplicity, all

---

[7] OMB ordinarily does not have authority to withhold appropriations. If OMB does withhold a portion of an appropriation, special accounts would be used. Our example here is intended to leave a balance in the Unapportioned Authority account for illustrative purposes.

apportioned amounts are assumed to have been expended or obligated in the illustrated transactions presented here.

Operations of the agency during the first quarter (October–December) of fiscal year 19y7 are accounted for in the following entries:

Commitments were recorded during the first quarter in the amount of $298,000.

> 4. *Budgetary:*
> Allotments—19y7 298,000
>   Commitments—19y7....................................   298,000

Purchase orders and contracts for goods and services were issued in the amount of $286,000 during the first quarter.

> 5. *Budgetary:*
> Commitments—19y7.................................... 286,000
>   Undelivered Orders—19y7   286,000

Checks for Accounts Payable as of October 1 were requested from the Treasury. The Accounts Payable were for materials received in fiscal year 19y6 in the amount of $90,000 and equipment received in the amount of $185,000. This event does not reduce the agency's Fund Balance with Treasury until the checks are actually issued by the Treasury. Instead, most agencies would credit the account Disbursements in Transit until notified by the Treasury that the requested checks have been issued. This account is a current liability account since liabilities to vendors and creditors cannot be considered settled until the checks have actually been issued. If this agency had been one of the few with authority to issue checks directly, then Fund Balance with Treasury would have been credited immediately. Since this agency is not assumed to have check-writing authority, the following entry would be made:

> 6. *Proprietary:*
> Accounts Payable 275,000
>   Disbursements in Transit—19y6........................   275,000

The agency received notification from the Treasury that the checks requested in Transaction 6 had been issued. This notification would be recorded as:

> 7. *Proprietary:*
> Disbursements in Transit—19y6.......................... 275,000
>   Fund Balance with the
>   Treasury—19y6   275,000

Goods and equipment ordered in 19y6 are reported in Illustration 15–2 in the Net Position account, Appropriated Capital—19y6, a proprietary account, as amounting to $400,000. A budgetary account in the same amount, Undelivered Orders—19y6 also exists, as does its offsetting account, Other Appropriations Realized—19y6 (all other budgetary accounts for 19y6 were closed at the end of that fiscal year because all unobligated appropriation authority expires at year-end). Assuming all the goods and equipment ordered in 19y6 were received during the first quarter of fiscal year 19y7, one entry is necessary in the budgetary accounts to show that fiscal 19y6 obligations are now liquidated and that the prior-year appropriation is expended in the same amount. Entries in proprietary accounts are required to record the debit to Appropriated Capital—19y6, the offsetting credit to the Invested Capital equity account,[8] and debits to asset accounts and a credit to Accounts Payable. These entries are:

8a. *Budgetary:*
Undelivered Orders—19y6	400,000	
Expended Authority—19y6		400,000

8b. *Proprietary:*
Operating Materials and Supplies	150,000	
Equipment	250,000	
Accounts Payable		400,000
Appropriated Capital—19y6	400,000	
Invested Capital		400,000

Payrolls for the first quarter amounted to $297,000. Utilities in the amount of $30,000 were also approved for payment. (The agency does not record commitments for payrolls and other recurring operating expenses.) Checks totaling $327,000 were requested from the Treasury for these expenses. The debit in the first proprietary track entry is to the control account Operating/Program Expenses. Obviously, each agency would have a subsidiary expense ledger tailored to its specific needs. Note in the second entry in the proprietary track that the account Appropriated Capital Used is credited instead of Invested Capital as in Entry 8b, because in this case no assets were acquired. The entry would be:

9a. *Budgetary:*
Allotments—19y7	327,000	
Expended Authority—19y7		327,000

9b. *Proprietary:*
Operating/Program Expenses	327,000	
Disbursements in Transit—19y7		327,000
Appropriated Capital—19y7	327,000	
Appropriated Capital Used		327,000

Materials and supplies used in the operating activities amounted to $405,000. Since Invested Capital was credited when materials and supplies were acquired (Entry 8b), the use of inventory must result in a debit to Invested Capital and a credit to Appropriated Capital Used. Thus, in the proprietary track, Appropriated Capital Used reflects the consumption of goods or services on an accrual basis.

10. *Proprietary:*
Operating/Program Expenses	405,000	
Operating Materials and Supplies		405,000
Invested Capital	405,000	
Appropriated Capital Used		405,000

[8] Technically, the account Invested Capital is a summary account in which routine transactions are not posted. The Standard General Ledger specifies the use of an account Capital Investments which is closed at year-end to Invested Capital. We use Invested Capital for simplicity.

Accounts Payable in the amount of $400,000 (see Entry 8b) were approved for payment and checks were requested from the Treasury. These checks will be charged against 19y6 Fund Balance with Treasury as shown in Illustration 15–2.

11. *Proprietary:*

Accounts Payable	400,000	
Disbursements in Transit—19y6		400,000

The agency was notified by the Treasury that checks in the amount of $700,000 (including $400,000 for Accounts Payable arising from fiscal 19y6—see Entry 11) had been issued. Of the $300,000 charged against the 19y7 Fund Balances with Treasury, $270,000 was for payrolls and $30,000 was for utilities expense.

12. *Proprietary:*

Disbursements in Transit—19y6	400,000	
Disbursements in Transit—19y7	300,000	
Fund Balance with Treasury—19y6		400,000
Fund Balance with Treasury—19y7		300,000

Adjusting Entries

In order to prepare accrual-based financial statements for the quarter, the following items were taken into account: (1) payroll accrued for the last week of the quarter is computed to be $27,000 and (2) invoices or receiving reports for goods received, but for which payment has not yet been approved, totaled $105,000, of which $36,000 worth has been used in operations and $69,000 is in ending inventory. Because the obligations for the items in parts (1) and (2) have become certain in amount and relevant expense accounts or inventory accounts can be charged, as illustrated below, the amounts should be shown in the financial statements as current liabilities. It is assumed that the goods received had been previously obligated in the amount of $105,000, but no commitment or obligation had been recorded for the accrued payroll. The required entries are:

13a. *Budgetary:*

Allotments—19y7	27,000	
Undelivered Orders—19y7	105,000	
Expended Authority—19y7		132,000

13b. *Proprietary:*

Operating/Program Expenses	63,000	
Operating Materials and Supplies	69,000	
Accounts Payable		105,000
Accrued Funded Payroll and Benefits		27,000
Appropriated Capital—19y7	132,000	
Appropriated Capital Used		63,000
Invested Capital		69,000

Depreciation of equipment was computed as $75,000 for the quarter. Inasmuch as depreciation is not an expense chargeable against the appropriation, the accrual of depreciation expense does not affect any of the appropriation, allotment, or obligation (budgetary) accounts but is recorded as in business accounting to measure the cost of activities on an accrual basis. Since the debit to Accumulated Depreciation reduces the book value of the equipment, Invested Capital must also be reduced. The reduction (debit) to Invested Capital is offset by a credit to Appropriated Capital Used, a financing sources account, since the accrual basis used in the proprietary track focuses on goods or services consumed. Conceptually, the depreciation of equipment is treated identically to the consumption of inventory (see Entry 10).

14. *Proprietary:*

Depreciation and Amortization.............................	75,000	
Accumulated Depreciation on Equipment		75,000
Invested Capital...	75,000	
Appropriated Capital Used		75,000

Although not illustrated here, federal agencies also accrue some expenses such as accrued annual leave which will be funded by future period appropriations. These unfunded accrued expenses require entries in the proprietary track, but require no entries in the budgetary track. The effect of these unfunded expenses is to reduce the balance of Cumulative Results of Operations since the expenses are not offset by a financing source.

End-of-Quarter Financial Statements

After entries illustrated above have been made, the federal agency Statement of Financial Position at the end of the first quarter in fiscal year 19y7 and the other required statements for the quarter can be prepared. OMB *Bulletin 94–01* prescribes the form and content of financial statements required to be prepared under the Chief Financial Officers (CFO) Act of 1990 by most executive agencies and departments. Each agency's "annual financial statement" should contain: (1) an overview of the reporting entity, (2) principal statements and related notes, (3) combining statements, and (4) supplemental financial and management information. In short, the required "annual financial statement" is quite similar to the comprehensive annual financial report (CAFR) issued by state and local governments and discussed in Chapter 13 of this text.

The required overview of the reporting entity is similar to the introductory section of a CAFR in that it should include a narrative overview and description of the reporting entity, a narrative discussion and analysis of financial condition, and performance data on the entity's programs, activities, and funds. Relevant financial trends should be pointed out and, if possible, financial data should be related to other measures of performance on a program-by-program basis. Finally, the overview should identify program and administrative highlights and critical areas for management improvement.

Simplified examples of the principal statements required by OMB *Bulletin 94–01* (i.e., Statement of Financial Position, Statement of Operations and Changes in Net Position, Statement of Cash Flows, and Statement of Budgetary Resources and Actual Expenses) are shown in Illustrations 15–7 through 15–10.

For the example agency used in this chapter no combining statements or supplemental financial and management information are provided. In the case of an actual federal entity, such as the Department of Defense, for example, there would be numerous funds, programs, and organizational units. The need for combining statements and supplemental information in such a case would be obvious.

In implementing financial reporting requirements mandated by the CFO Act of 1990, questions have arisen about which accounting principles and standards should govern preparation of agency financial statements. OMB *Bulletin 94–01*, pp. 6–7, provides the following interim guidance:

> Until a sufficiently comprehensive set of accounting standards are agreed to and published by the Joint Financial Management Improvement Program (JFMIP) principals, which will constitute "generally accepted accounting principles for the federal government," the following hierarchy shall constitute an "other comprehensive basis of accounting" and shall be used for federal agency financial statements:
>
> 1. Individual standards agreed to and published by the JFMIP Principals.
> 2. Form and Content requirements included in OMB *Bulletin 93–02,* dated October 22, 1992, and subsequent issuances [including OMB *Bulletin 94–02*].
> 3. Accounting standards contained in agency accounting policy, procedures manuals, and/or related guidance as of March 29, 1991, so long as they are prevalent practices. [By March 29, 1991 most agencies had adopted in their manuals and related guidelines the requirements of Title 2.]
> 4. Accounting principles published by authoritative standard-setting bodies and other authoritative sources (1) in the absence of other guidance in the first parts of this hierarchy, and (2) if the use of such accounting standards improve the meaningfulness of the financial statements.
>
> Disclosing differences between the accounting standards followed and Title 2 of GAO's *Policy and Procedures Manual for Guidance of Federal Agencies* is no longer required. Federal agencies will instead fully describe in the footnotes to their financial statements the accounting standards in the above hierarchy followed in preparing the statements.

As the preceding hierarchy makes clear, financial statements prepared using the accounting principles prescribed in the GAO's Title 2 are now considered to be prepared on "an other comprehensive basis" rather than GAAP. Nevertheless, until a comprehensive body of FASAB-recommended standards have been adopted, Title 2 will continue to be a primary source of accounting guidance since many agencies' accounting systems are based on Title 2.

Prior to preparing the illustrative principal financial statements, as of and for the quarter ended December 31, 19y6, a pre-closing general ledger trial balance should be prepared such as that presented in Illustration 15–6. This trial balance provides the information needed to prepare the principal statements (see Illustration 15–7 through 15–10). Although these financial statements are required only at year-end, it is useful to illustrate them at the end of the first quarter.

ILLUSTRATION 15–6

FEDERAL AGENCY
End-of-Quarter Trial Balance
As of December 31, 19y6

	Debits	*Credits*
Proprietary Accounts:		
Fund Balance with Treasury—19y7	$2,700,000	
Operating Materials and Supplies	424,000	
Equipment	3,250,000	
Accumulated Depreciation on Equipment		$ 675,000
Disbursements in Transit—19y7		27,000
Accounts Payable		105,000
Accrued Funded Payroll and Benefits		27,000
Appropriated Capital—19y7		2,541,000
Invested Capital		2,999,000
Cumulative Results of Operations		–0–
Appropriated Capital Used—19y7		870,000
Operating/Program Expenses	795,000	
Depreciation and Amortization	75,000	
	$7,244,000	$7,244,000
Budgetary Accounts:		
Other Appropriations Realized—19y6	$ 400,000	
Other Appropriations Realized—19y7	3,000,000	
Unapportioned Authority—19y7		$ 200,000
Apportionments—19y7		2,100,000
Allotments—19y7		48,000
Commitments—19y7		12,000
Undelivered Orders—19y7		181,000
Expended Authority—19y6		400,000
Expended Authority—19y7		459,000
	$3,400,000	$3,400,000

In Illustration 15–2, it was assumed that all of the fiscal 19y6 appropriations had been apportioned, allotted, and obligated; this assumption was made at that point in order to focus the attention of the reader upon major differences between balance sheets for federal agencies and those for state and local governments. The assumption was realistic, however, because the agency's authority to obligate a one-year appropriation expires at the end of the year for which the appropriation was made.[9] Fund Balance with Treasury pertaining to a one-year appropriation

---

[9] Federal government agencies may also receive multi-year appropriations or even "no year" appropriations. In such event, the budgetary account balances would not be closed at year-end, and the Net Position section of the year-end statement of financial position would appear as shown in Illustration 15–7.

remains available for payment of liabilities and obligations incurred under that appropriation for a limited period of time; unneeded balances should be returned to the General Fund control promptly without waiting for expiration of the time limit.

Illustration 15–7, the Statement of Financial Position, reveals several interesting relationships. Note that the sum of Appropriated Capital—19y7 ($2,541,000) plus total liabilities ($159,000) equals the amount of Fund Balance with Treasury—19y7 ($2,700,000), verifying that the federal agency can legally call on the Treasury to pay the current liabilities and, also, the remaining unexpended 19y7 appropriation when it is expended and converted into current liabilities. Similarly, the total of Operating Materials and Supplies ($424,000) and net fixed assets ($2,575,000) agrees with the total of the two equity accounts, Invested Capital ($2,999,000) and Cumulative Results of Operations ($0). Finally, the amount of Appropriated Capital—19y7 (a proprietary account, as are all of the accounts reflected in the Statement of Financial Position) equals the total of unused appropriations, which can be computed from the budgetary accounts (see Illustration 15–6) as follows:

Other Appropriations Realized—19y7	$3,000,000
Less: Expended Authority—19y7	459,000
Appropriations not used	$2,541,000

ILLUSTRATION 15–7

FEDERAL AGENCY
Statement of Financial Position
December 31, 19y6

Assets

Fund balance with Treasury—19y7		$2,700,000
Operating materials and supplies		424,000
Equipment	$3,250,000	
Less: Accumulated depreciation	675,000	2,575,000
Total Assets		$5,699,000

Liabilities and Net Position

Liabilities:		
Disbursements in transit—19y7	$ 27,000	
Accounts payable, nonfederal	105,000	
Accrued funded payroll and benefits	27,000	
Total Liabilities		$ 159,000
Net Position:		
Appropriated capital—19y7	2,541,000	
Invested capital	2,999,000	
Cumulative results of operations	–0–	
Total Net Position		5,540,000
Total Liabilities and Net Position		$5,699,000

Alternatively, unused appropriations can be computed as the sum of its components:

Unapportioned Authority—19y7	$ 200,000
Apportionments—19y7	2,100,000
Allotments—19y7	48,000
Commitments—19y7	12,000
Undelivered Orders—19y7	181,000
Appropriations not used	$2,541,000

The Net Position section of the Statement of Financial Position presented in Illustration 15–7 displays the components of fund balance on the face of the statement. Recall that in the Statement of Financial Position of an actual agency net position would be comprised of the total fund balances of each fund group of the agency, so the components of fund balance for each fund group would be presented in the Notes to the Financial Statements in the manner shown previously in Illustration 15–3.

The federal agency whose Statement of Financial Position is presented in Illustration 15–7 is assumed to be quite small and therefore does not engage in the diversity and complexity of transactions that a larger agency would. All resources are assumed to be provided by budgetary appropriations, and transactions are assumed to involve assets arising primarily from intragovernmental operations that can be used by the entity. Accordingly, the agency's Statement of Financial Position (Exhibit 15–7) omits certain classifications that would be required by *OMB Bulletin 94–01* for most federal agencies. *OMB Bulletin 94–01* requires that the assets section of the Statement of Financial position be classified into *Entity Assets* and *Non-Entity Assets*. Within each of those classifications, assets should be further subclassified into *Intragovernmental Assets* and *Governmental Assets*. Each of these categories is defined in SFFAS No. 1 and discussed earlier in this chapter under the heading, "Elements of Financial Statements." Liabilities should be classified according to those covered by budgetary resources and those not covered by budgetary resources. Within each of these classifications, liabilities should be further subclassified as to whether they are intragovernmental or governmental.

The Statement of Operations and Changes in Net Position (Illustration 15–8) shows that financing sources for the quarter equaled total expenses for the period. Thus, there was no change in Net Position from operations. It should be noted that in an operating statement for an actual federal agency, the first three expense items shown in Illustration 15–8 would likely be reported as a combined amount on a single line as "Operating/Program Expenses," the control account used in several of the journal entries illustrated previously in this chapter. Detail for the expenses, classified either by program or object class would be provided in the Notes to the Financial Statements. *OMB Bulletin 94–01* requires depreciation and amortization to be reported separately from operating/program expenses. Finally, the amounts shown for financing sources and expenses ($870,000) exceed the amount of expended appropriations ($459,000) because some expenses of the current period (consumption of materials and supplies and depreciation of fixed

---

ILLUSTRATION 15–8

FEDERAL AGENCY
Statement of Operations and Changes in Net Position
For the Quarter Ended December 31, 19y6

Financing Sources:		
Appropriated Capital Used		$ 870,000
Expenses:		
Payroll and Benefits	$ 324,000	
Cost of Materials Used	441,000	
Utilities	30,000	
Depreciation and Amortization	75,000	
Total Expenses		870,000
Excess of Financing Sources over		
Total Expenses		–0–
Net Position, Beginning of Quarter		3,410,000
Plus Net Nonoperating Changes:		
Increase in Appropriated Capital	2,141,000	
Decrease in Invested Capital	(11,000)	2,130,000
Net Position, End of Quarter		$5,540,000

---

assets) were financed by previous years' appropriations and some current year appropriations were used for purchase of materials and supplies that is still on hand at the end of the quarter.

If the only financing source available to an agency is appropriations, and all expenses of the current and prior periods have been funded, Cumulative Results of Operations will always have a zero balance. As shown in several of the entries illustrated in this chapter, the single financing source, Appropriated Capital Used, is credited when goods and services are consumed, including consumption of inventories of supplies and materials and depreciation of property, plant, and equipment financed by prior years' appropriations. Many agencies, however, will have revenues from sales of goods and services (i.e., from revolving funds), interest, and other sources; or unfunded accrued expenses, such as unfunded leave expense, which will require future appropriations. Items such as these result in a nonzero balance (either surplus or deficit) for Cumulative Results of Operations.

The required Statement of Cash Flows (Illustration 15–9) is similar to that required by FASB standards for business entities. Consistent with FASB and GASB Standards, OMB *Bulletin 94–01* permits use of either the direct or indirect method. The authors believe the direct method provides better information on operating cash flows; therefore, the direct method is used in the cash flow statement presented in Illustration 15–9. Even though the federal agency used in this example has only Fund Balance with Treasury rather than "cash," note that cash, in the context of the cash flow statement, is interpreted as "cash and cash equivalents." Since Fund Balance with Treasury is a cash equivalent, the terminology in

ILLUSTRATION 15–9

FEDERAL AGENCY
Statement of Cash Flows
For the Quarter Ended December 31, 19y6

Cash Used for Operating Activities:		
Personal services and benefits	$270,000	
Supplies and materials	240,000	
Utilities	30,000	
Net Cash Used for Operating Activities		$ (540,000)
Cash Used for Investing Activities:		
Purchase of equipment		(435,000)
Cash Provided by Financing Activities:		
Appropriations		3,000,000
Net Cash provided during period		2,025,000
Fund Balance with Treasury, October 1, 19y6		675,000
Fund Balance with Treasury, December 31, 19y6		$2,700,000

Illustration 15–9 is appropriate. Finally, one should verify that the beginning balance of Fund Balance with Treasury agrees with the amount reported for that account on the preceding period's Statement of Financial Position (see Post-Closing Trial Balance in Illustration 15–2) and the ending balance agrees with the amount reported on the end-of-quarter Statement of Financial Position (Illustration 15–7).

The final required statement, the Statement of Budgetary Resources and Actual Expenses, is presented in Illustration 15–10. For the simple example used in this chapter, the budget and actual comparison (upper section of the statement) is shown as one line for the General Fund. OMB *Bulletin 94–01* requires, however, that agencies report on separate lines the budget resources, budget obligations, and actual expenses for each program or functional activity. Alternatively, the budget and actual amounts can be reported for organizational components such as bureaus or services. The budget resources reported in the upper section is the sum of obligated budget authority carried over from the prior year ($400,000) (see Illustration 15–2) plus allotments for the current quarter ($700,000, Entry 3). Budget obligations are those from the prior period ($400,000) plus orders placed ($286,000, Entry 5), contracts awarded (none), services received ($327,000, Entry 9a; $27,000, Entry 13a), and similar transactions (none in this case), that expend budget authority. The amount in the Actual Expenses column is the Total Expenses amount displayed in Illustration 15–8.

A reconciliation of accrual-based expenses to accrual-based expenditures is provided in the lower section of the statement shown in Illustration 15–10. The bottom line—**Accrued Expenditures**—is the term used in OMB *Bulletin 94–01*,

---

ILLUSTRATION 15–10

FEDERAL AGENCY
Statement of Budgetary Resources and Actual Expenses
For the Quarter Ended December 31, 19y6

	Budget		
	Resources	*Obligations*	*Actual Expenses*
General Fund	$1,100,000	$1,040,000	$ 870,000
Budget Reconciliation:			
Total Expenses			$ 870,000
Add:			
Capital acquisitions			250,000
Less:			
Decrease in inventory			(186,000)
Depreciation on equipment			(75,000)
Accrued Expenditures			$ 859,000

---

but might more appropriately be termed *Expended Authority*, since the amount ($859,000) represents expenditures incurred against both current-year appropriations ($459,000) and prior-year appropriations ($400,000) (see Entry 15a).

Closing Entries

In addition to the adjusting entries, illustrated above, closing entries should be made at *year-end* to remove expired budget authority and expended authority from the accounts. Expired (unobligated) budget authority is removed by debiting the balances of Commitments, Allotments, Apportionments, and Unapportioned Authority, and crediting Other Appropriations Realized for the total unobligated balance. No entry is needed at this time to remove expired budget authority since none has expired as of the end of the quarter. Illustrative entries to remove expended authority and to close financing source and expense accounts are shown below as Entries 15a and 15b, respectively. (For quarterly statements, the following entries would be made only in worksheet form.)

15a. Budgetary:

Expended Authority—19y6	400,000	
Expended Authority—19y7	459,000	
Other Appropriations Realized—19y6		400,000
Other Appropriations Realized—19y7		459,000

ILLUSTRATION 15–11 **Comparison of Accounting for State and Local Governmental Fund Types and Accounting for Federal Agencies (journal entries)**

Item	State and Local Governmental Funds — Compliance Track Only	Federal Agency — Budgetary Track	Federal Agency — Proprietary Track
1. Passage of appropriations (and for state and local governments, revenue) bills	Estimated Revenues / Appropriations / Fund Balance	Other Appropriations Realized / Unapportioned Authority	Fund Balance with Treasury / Appropriated Capital
2. Revenues accrued (at expected collectible amount)	Taxes Receivable / Estimated Uncollectible Taxes / Revenues	No equivalent for taxes; user charges, if any, recognized as billed	No entry*
3. Apportionment by OMB	No equivalent	Unapportioned Authority / Apportionments	No entry
4. Allotment by agency head	No equivalent†	Apportionments / Allotments	No entry
5. Budget authority reserved prior to ordering goods or services	No equivalent	Allotments / Commitments	No entry
6. Goods or services ordered	Encumbrances / Reserve for Encumbrances	Commitments / Undelivered Orders‡	No entry
7. Goods or services received	Reserve for Encumbrances / Encumbrances / Expenditures / Accounts Payable	Undelivered Orders / Expended Authority	Expense or asset account / Accounts Payable / Appropriated Capital / Appropriated Capital Used or Invested Capital
8. Liability paid (expenditure recorded in 7 above)	Accounts Payable / Cash	No entry	Accounts Payable / Fund Balance with Treasury§

(Transaction)			
9. Supplies used	No entry	No entry	Operating/Program Expenses Inventory for Agency Operations Invested Capital Appropriated Capital Used
10. Physical inventory (consumption method assumed for state and local governments)	Inventory Expenditures Fund Balance Reserve for Inventory	No entry	Entry for (7) assumes perpetual inventory; would need entry for (10) if physical inventory and book inventory differed
11. Depreciation computed	No entry (computation used for cost reimbursements and management information)	No entry (Not an expenditure of appropriations; will never require a check to be drawn on U.S. Treasury)	Depreciation and Amortization Accumulated Depreciation Invested Capital Appropriated Capital Used
12. Closing entries	Appropriations Revenues Estimated Revenues Encumbrances Expenditures Fund Balance	Expended Authority Other Appropriations Realized; (Also must close any budgetary accounts associated with expired budget authority)	Cumulative Results of Operations Operating/Program Expenses Appropriated Capital Used Cumulative Results of Operations

* Prototype consolidated financial statements of federal government do include an accrual for taxes, fines, and other revenue categories.

† As discussed in Chapter 3, some local governmental units utilize allotment accounting. In such cases, the credit in Entry 1 would be to Unallotted Appropriations, and an Entry 4 would be necessary to record the debit to that account and the credit to Allotments.

‡ As illustrated by Entry 4 earlier in this chapter, and by entry 5, some agencies opt to use the interim account Commitments to improve planning for procurement of goods and services. If Commitments are not recorded in advance of placing orders the debit for the budgetary track entry would be "Allotments."

§ As indicated in this chapter, the account credited here might be Disbursements in Transit rather than Fund Balance with Treasury.

15b. Proprietary:

Appropriated Capital Used—19y7	870,000	
Cumulative Results of Operations		870,000
Cumulative Results of Operations	870,000	
Operating/Program Expenses		795,000
Depreciation and Amortization.........................		75,000

Illustration 15–11 provides a summary comparison of budgetary and proprietary accounting procedures for state and local governments as compared with federal agencies. Although some similarities exist, there are areas specific to each level of government. As shown in Illustration 15–11, state and local governments do not account for apportionments and most do not account for allotments. Federal Agency accounting takes into consideration certain accruals (supplies used and depreciation) generally ignored in state and local government accounting, although as mentioned in several earlier chapters, changes in the reporting model being considered by the GASB may lead to greater use of accrual accounting by state and local governments.

Summary of Accounting and Reporting for Federal Government Agencies

The head of each agency in the executive branch of the federal government has the statutory responsibility for the establishment and maintenance of systems of accounting and internal control in conformity with principles, standards, and requirements established by the Comptroller General, the Secretary of the Treasury, and the Director of OMB. Federal agency accounting is directed at providing information for intelligent financial management of agency activities and programs to the end they may be operated with efficiency and economy, as well as providing evidence of adherence to legal requirements. As emphasized by the headings of the illustration, and by the discussions in earlier chapters, accounting for governmental funds is presently focused on legal compliance. The focus of federal agency accounting, in contrast, is broadened to include information needed for the management of agency resources (the **proprietary** track) as well as for compliance with Fund Control requirements (the **budgetary** track).

Selected References

Publications of U.S. Government:

Department of the Treasury. *Treasury Financial Manual,* 1986.

General Accounting Office. *GAO Policy and Procedures Manual for Guidance of Federal Agencies, Title 2—Accounting,* 1984.

General Accounting Office. *Accounting Guide: Basic Topics Relating to Appropriations and Reimbursables,* 1990.

Office of Management and Budget. *U.S. Government Standard General Ledger,* 1986.

_____. *Bulletin 94–01, Form and Content of Agency Financial Statements,* 1993.

_____. *Circular A–134, Financial Accounting Principles and Standards,* 1993.

Questions

15–1. Describe the institutional framework for establishing accounting and financial reporting standards for the federal government.

15–2. Identify which of the following are part of the legislative branch of the federal government and which are part of the executive branch:
  a. Secretary of the Treasury.
  b. Director of the Office of Management and Budget.
  c. Director of the Congressional Budget Office.
  d. Comptroller General.

15–3. Discuss the conceptual framework of accounting for federal agencies and compare it to the conceptual framework established by the FASB for business organizations.

15–4. Identify and explain the elements of federal financial statements at their present state of development, as discussed in Chapter 15.

15–5. Discuss the "two-track system" used in federal agency accounting.

15–6. Compare and contrast the federal term *Fund Balance with Treasury* with the term *Fund Balance* used in state and local government accounting.

15–7. What accounts are used to describe the *net position* of a federal agency?

15–8. Identify the budgetary accounts used in federal agency accounting and explain the sequential flow of budgetary authority through the accounts.

15–9. Distinguish between a *commitment* and an *obligation* in budgetary track accounting for a federal agency.

15–10. Should the accounts Expended Authority and Appropriated Capital Used have the same pre-closing balance at year-end? Why or why not?

15–11. Name the financial statements that should be prepared for each federal agency at year-end and, if needed, on an interim basis.

15–12. What are the function and contents of each of the two sections of the Statement of Budgetary Resources and Actual Expenses?

Exercises and Problems

15–1. Write the numbers 1 through 10 on a sheet of paper. Beside each number write the letter corresponding with the best answer to each of the following questions.

  1. Federal statutes assign responsibility for establishing and maintaining a sound financial structure for the federal government to the:
    a. Comptroller General.
    b. Director of the OMB.
    c. Secretary of the Treasury.
    d. All of the above.

  2. Which of the following is a true statement about the process of setting accounting standards for the federal government?
    a. The FASAB issues accounting standards.
    b. The FASAB recommends accounting standards.

    c. GASB has primary responsibility for issuing federal government accounting standards; FASAB has secondary responsibility for federal standards.

    d. Each federal agency is responsible for setting its own accounting standards; those standards take precedence over standards developed by FASAB.

3. In the GAAP hierarchy for federal agency accounting and financial reporting, the highest level GAAP is (are):

    a. Title 2 of the *GAO Policy and Procedures Manual for Guidance of Federal Agencies*.

    b. *OMB Bulletin 94-01, Form and Content of Agency Financial Statements*.

    c. The *Treasury Financial Manual*.

    d. Statements of Federal Financial Accounting Standards (SFFASs).

4. Which of the following is *not* an objective of federal financial reporting?

    a. Assist report users in evaluating budgetary integrity.

    b. Assist report users in evaluating operating performance.

    c. Assist report users in evaluating the reliability of financial information.

    d. Assist report users in evaluating stewardship.

5. Which of the following is *not* one of the principals of the Joint Financial Management Improvement Project?

    a. Director of the FASAB.

    b. Comptroller General.

    c. Director of the OMB.

    d. Secretary of the Treasury.

6. The Invested Capital account will be decreased by which of the following transactions or events?

    a. Purchase of materials and supplies.

    b. Expiration of budget authority.

    c. Recording depreciation of fixed assets.

    d. Both *b* and *c* are correct.

7. Assuming that an agency's unused appropriations expire at year-end, but appropriations continue in effect for obligated amounts (purchase orders, etc.), which of the following *budgetary* accounts would likely be found in the agency's post-closing trial balance at year-end?

    a. Commitments and Undelivered Orders.

    b. Expended Authority and Undelivered Orders.

    c. Commitments and Other Appropriations Realized.

    d. Undelivered Orders and Other Appropriations Realized.

8. Which of the following correctly states a mathematical relationship among proprietary account balances?

    a. Fund Balance with Treasury equals the sum of funded liabilities plus Appropriated Capital.

    b. Invested Capital equals Fund Balance with Treasury.

    c. Cumulative Results of Operations equals Revenues and Financing Sources plus Operating/Program Expenses.

    d. Disbursements in Transit equals Fund Balance with Treasury minus Accounts Payable and other current liabilities.

9. If an agency has no authorization to disburse cash, and must utilize Fund Balance with Treasury to pay its liabilities, which of the following statements is correct?

    a. No Statement of Cash Flows is required for this agency.

    b. A Statement of Cash Flows is required since Fund Balance with Treasury is a "cash equivalent."

    c. A Statement of Cash Flows is required, but the term "cash" should be replaced by "funds" or "financial resources."

    d. A Statement of Cash Flows is required, but a Cash Flows from Financing Sources section is not needed since the agency's cash is held by the Treasury rather than by the agency.

10. In a Statement of Budgetary Resources and Actual Expenses prepared in conformity with OMB *Bulletin 94–01,* the amount shown for Accrued Expenditures at the bottom of the statement represents the:

    a. Amount of expended budgetary authority for the period.

    b. Amount of expenditures accrued but unpaid at the end of the period.

    c. Amount of appropriations obligated during the period.

    d. None of the above.

15–2. One amount is missing in the following trial balance of proprietary accounts and one amount is missing from the trial balance of budgetary accounts of a certain agency of the federal government, and the debits are not distinguished from the credits.

Required   *a.* Compute each missing amount in the pre-closing trial balance below.

FEDERAL AGENCY
Pre-Closing Trial Balance
September 30, 19x8

Proprietary Accounts:

Accounts Payable	$ 400,000
Accumulated Depreciation— Plant and Equipment	2,600,000
Appropriated Capital Used	3,300,000
Fund Balance with Treasury—19x8	?
Operating Materials and Supplies	1,000,000
Invested Capital	7,300,000
Cumulative Results of Operations—10/1/x7	–0–
Operating/Program Expenses	3,150,000
Depreciation and Amortization	150,000
Plant and Equipment	8,900,000
Appropriated Capital—19x8	1,200,000

Budgetary Accounts:

Other Appropriations Realized—19x8	?
Expended Authority—19x8	4,000,000
Undelivered Orders—19x8	1,200,000

b. Assuming Invested Capital, as of October 1, 19x7, amounted to $6,600,000, compute the net additions to assets other than Fund Balance with Treasury during fiscal year 19x8. Label and organize your computations so the grader can understand them.

15–3. Using the data from Problem 15–2:

a. Prepare in general journal form entries to close the budgetary accounts as needed, and to close the operating statement proprietary accounts.

b. Prepare in good form a Statement of Financial Position for the Federal Agency as of September 30, 19x8.

c. Prepare in good form a Statement of Operations and Changes in Net Position of the Federal Agency for the year ended September 30, 19x8 assuming Appropriated Capital, as of October 1, 19x7, amounted to $1,300,000.

15–4. The trial balance as of August 31, 19y7, of the Federal Science Administration, of the executive branch of the federal government, is shown below.

	Debits	*Credits*
Proprietary Accounts:		
Fund Balance with Treasury—19y7	$ 1,635,772	
Operating Materials and Supplies	942,000	
Plant and Equipment	7,651,633	
Accumulated Depreciation—Plant and Equipment		$ 2,332,628
Construction Work in Progress	581,818	
Accounts Payable		328,123
Advances from Other Federal Agencies . .		43,518
Appropriated Capital Used		2,388,538
Appropriated Capital		1,264,131
Invested Capital		6,842,823
Cumulative Results of Operations—10/1/y6		–0–
Production Expenses	1,502,496	
Development Expenses	507,343	
Research Expenses	286,866	
Small Program Expenses	91,833	
Total Proprietary Accounts	$13,199,761	$13,199,761
Budgetary Accounts:		
Other Appropriations Realized—19y7	$ 3,894,855	
Unapportioned Authority—19y7		$ 100,000
Apportionments—19y7		150,000
Allotments—19y7		600,000
Commitments—19y7		50,000
Undelivered Orders—19y7		364,131
Expended Authority—19y7		2,630,724
Total Budgetary Accounts	$ 3,894,855	$ 3,894,855

Required

a. Prepare a Statement of Financial Position for the Federal Science Administration, as of August 31, 19y7.

b. Prepare a Statement of Operations and Changes in Net Position for the 11 months ended August 31, 19y7, assuming the following account balances as of October 1, 19y6:

Invested Capital 6,726,800
Appropriated Capital 1,210,210
Cumulative Results of Operations . . . . –0–

15–5. A comparative statement of financial position for the Urban Studies Agency of the federal government for the years ended September 30, 19x5 and 19x6 is provided as follows:

URBAN STUDIES AGENCY
Statement of Financial Position
As of September 30, 19x5 and 19x6
($000s)

Assets

	September 30	
	19x6	*19x5*
Fund balance with Treasury	$2,226	$2,164
Land	500	500
Building and improvements, net of accumulated depreciation of $970 and $1,230 at September 30, 19x5 and 19x6, respectively	5,570	5,630
Furniture and equipment, net of accumulated depreciation of $820 and $1,010 at September 30, 19x5 and 19x6, respectively	715	705
Operating Materials and Supplies	340	325
Total Assets	$9,351	$9,324

Liabilities and Net Position

Liabilities:		
Accounts payable	$ 265	$ 240
Accrued payroll and benefits	60	55
Accrued annual leave	350	340
Total liabilities	675	635
Net Position:		
Appropriated capital	1,901	1,869
Invested capital	7,125	7,160
Cumulative results of operations	(350)	(340)
Total Net Position	8,676	8,689
Total Liabilities and Net Position	$9,351	$9,324

Additional Information

1. Appropriations for fiscal year ending September 30, 19x6, totaled $15,513,000.

2. Materials and supplies ordered in fiscal 19x5 were received in early fiscal year 19x6 in the amount of $1,869,000, the same amount as reported for Appropriated Capital on the Statement of Financial Position as of September 30, 19x5. All materials and supplies are credited to Accounts Payable upon receipt.

3. Additional materials supplies were ordered and received during fiscal year 19x6 in the amount of $2,050,000. Buildings and Improvements in the amount of $200,000 and Furniture and Equipment in the amount of $200,000 were also purchased during fiscal year 19x6. Upon the agency's request the Treasury paid $400,000 for the fixed assets. (Note: the $2,050,000 for purchases of materials and supplies was credited to Accounts Payable.)

4. Operating/program expenses for fiscal year 19x6 totaled $15,076,000. This amount excluded depreciation expense on fixed assets but included accruals at fiscal year-

end in the amounts of $5,000 for accrued payroll and benefits and $10,000 for accrued annual leave. (Recall that accrued annual leave is unfunded and therefore does not reduce the balance of Appropriated Capital.) Except for materials and supplies consumed in operations and the two accrued items, all other operating/program expenses were paid in cash during the fiscal year.

5. There were no fixed assets sold or otherwise disposed of during fiscal year 19x6.

Required   *a.* Prepare a Statement of Operations and Changes in Net Position for the Urban Studies Agency for the year ended September 30, 19x6.

     b. Prepare a Statement of Cash Flows for the Urban Studies Agency for the year ended September 30, 19x6, assuming cash used for operating activities was distributed as follows:

Personal services and benefits	$9,125,000
Supplies and materials	3,894,000
Contractual services	1,842,000
Utilities	190,000

15–6. The Statement of Financial Position of the Throttlebottom Commemorative Commission, of the United States Department of Culture, is given as follows:

THROTTLEBOTTOM COMMEMORATIVE COMMISSION
Statement of Financial Position
September 30, 19y8

Assets

Fund Balance with Treasury—19y8		$1,650,000
Operating Materials and Supplies		365,000
Equipment	$600,000	
Less: Accumulated Depreciation	60,000	540,000
Total Assets		$2,555,000

Liabilities and Net Position

Liabilities:		
Accounts Payable		$ 850,000
Total Liabilities		850,000
Net Position:		
Invested Capital	905,000	
Cumulative Results of Operations	–0–	
Appropriated Capital—19y8	800,000	
Total Net Position		1,705,000
Total Liabilities and Net Position		$2,555,000

Required   *a.* Prepare entries in general journal form for the following transactions, which summarize all financial transactions for fiscal year October 1, 19y8—September 30, 19y9. Use expense accounts named to describe the nature of each expense.

     (1) An appropriation for fiscal year 19y9 in the amount of $12,000,000 is authorized by Congress, and the bill is signed by the President.

     (2) The Office of Management and Budget apportioned $11,000,000 to the agency and withheld $1,000,000.

     (3) The agency head allotted $11,000,000 to subordinates.

(4) Commitments are recorded in the amount of $10,300,000.
(5) Obligation documents totaling $10,000,000 are recorded for those commitments that had been previously recorded.
(6) Goods and services were received and liabilities recorded for: Payroll, $6,500,000; equipment, $600,000; and materials and supplies, $2,000,000. The equipment and $200,000 worth of the materials and supplies had been ordered in the prior year; the remainder of the materials and the payroll relate to obligations of the current year.
(7) Materials and supplies issued during the period and used in operations, $1,200,000.
(8) Liabilities paid totaled $8,950,000.
(9) Depreciation is recorded at the rates of 10 percent on the beginning balance and 5 percent on the additions during the year.
(10) Accruals as of September 10, 19y9, are recorded for payroll, $350,000; and materials and supplies, $68,000. Obligations had been previously recorded for these amounts.
(11) The withheld and unobligated portions of the appropriation lapsed at year-end.
b. Prepare a trial balance as of September 30, 19y9.
c. Prepare closing entries as of September 30, 19y9.
d. Prepare a Statement of Financial Position as of September 30, 19y9.
e. Prepare a Statement of Operations and Changes in Net Position for 19y9.

15–7. The River Basin Commission was authorized by Congress to start operations on October 1, 19x6.

Required

a. Record the following transactions in general journal form as they should appear in the accounts of the River Basin Commission. Use expense accounts named to describe the nature of each expense.
(1) The River Basin received official notice that the one-year appropriation passed by Congress and signed by the President amounted to $7,000,000 for operating expenses.
(2) The Office of Management and Budget notified the Commission of the following schedule of apportionments: first quarter, $2,000,0000; second quarter, $2,000,000; third quarter, $1,500,000; and fourth quarter, $1,500,00.
(3) The River Basin Commissioner allotted $1,000,000 for the first month's operations.
(4) Obligations were recorded for salaries and fringe benefits, $400,000; furniture and equipment, $270,000; materials and supplies, $250,000; rent and utilities, $50,000. The River Basin Commission does not record commitments prior to recording obligations.
(5) Payroll for the first two weeks in the amount of $170,000 was paid.
(6) Invoices approved for payment totaled $395,000; of the total, $180,000 was for furniture and equipment, $175,000 for materials and supplies, and $40,000 for rent.
(7) Liability was recorded for the payroll for the second two weeks, $160,000; and for the employer's share of FICA taxes for the four weeks, $31,000.
(8) Accounts payable totaling $380,000 were paid which included liabilities for Payroll and FICA Taxes, $191,000; materials and supplies, $149,000; and Rent, $40,000.

(9) Accruals recorded at month-end were salaries, $30,000, and utilities, $10,000. Materials and supplies costing $60,000 were used during the month. No depreciation is to be charged by this agency, since the amount is deemed immaterial.

(10) Necessary closing entries were prepared as of October 31, 19x6.

   b. Prepare a Statement of Financial Position for the River Basin Commission as of October 31, 19x6.

   c. Prepare a Statement of Operations and Changes in Net Position for the River Basin Commission for the month ended October 31, 19x6.

   d. Prepare a Statement of Cash Flows for the River Basin Commission for the month ended October 31, 19x6.

   e. Prepare a Statement of Budgetary Resources and Actual Expenses for the River Basin Commission for the month ended October 31, 19x6.

15–8. The following trial balances were prepared for a federal agency at the end of its first month of existence by a new accountant, whose only prior experience had been as a bookkeeper in the accounting department of a large city.

INTERSTATE PARKS COMMISSION
Trial Balance
October 31, 19x1

	Debits	*Credits*
General Fund:		
Accounts Payable		$1,200,000
Allotments		1,600,000
Due from U.S. Treasury	$3,140,000	
Encumbrances	50,000	
Estimated Revenues	3,500,000	
Expenditures	1,410,000	
Fund Balance	50,000	
Inventory of Supplies	50,000	
Reserve for Encumbrances		50,000
Reserve for Inventory		50,000
Revenues		3,400,000
Unallotted Appropriations		1,900,000
	$8,200,000	$8,200,000
General Fixed Assets Account Group:		
Buildings	$ 720,000	
Equipment	180,000	
Improvements Other than Buildings	45,000	
Investment in General Fixed Assets—General Fund Revenues		$1,000,000
Land	55,000	
	$1,000,000	$1,000,000

Early in the second month of the agency's existence (before any transactions of the second month have been posted), you are sent to the agency to see how the new accountant is getting along. After looking over the trial balances, you ask to see the underlying accounts. (These are reproduced below. Related debits and credits are indicated by the same number. Explanations appear with the debit member of each entry.)

General Fund Accounts

Accounts Payable

Checks requested from U.S. Treasury	(7)	260,000	(5)	1,150,000
			(6)	310,000

Allotments

	(3)	1,600,000

Due from U.S. Treasury

OMB Apportionment	(2)	3,400,000	(7)	260,000

Encumbrances

Option to purchase land, building, and equipment—1,000,000; supplies ordered—200,000	(4)	1,200,000	(5)	1,150,000

Estimated Revenues

Congressional appropriation	(1)	3,500,000

Expenditures

Title taken to land, etc., 1,000,000; supplies received, 150,000	(5)	1,150,000	(8)	50,000
Salaries and wages	(6)	310,000		

Fund Balance

To set up Reserve for inventory	(8)	50,000

Inventory of Supplies

Month-end physical inventory	(8)	50,000

Reserve for Encumbrances

See explanation in Expenditures account	(5)	1,150,000	(4)	1,200,000

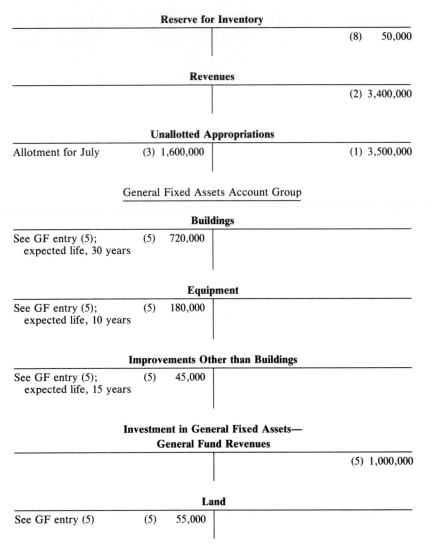

Reserve for Inventory

		(8)	50,000

Revenues

		(2)	3,400,000

Unallotted Appropriations

Allotment for July	(3) 1,600,000	(1)	3,500,000

General Fixed Assets Account Group

Buildings

See GF entry (5); expected life, 30 years	(5)	720,000	

Equipment

See GF entry (5); expected life, 10 years	(5)	180,000	

Improvements Other than Buildings

See GF entry (5); expected life, 15 years	(5)	45,000	

Investment in General Fixed Assets—
General Fund Revenues

		(5)	1,000,000

Land

See GF entry (5)	(5)	55,000	

Required   *a.* Prepare entries in general journal form to state the accounts of the Interstate Parks Commission correctly as of October 31, 19x1.

b. Prepare a Statement of Financial Position for the Interstate Parks Commission as of October 31, 19x1.

c. Prepare a Statement of Operations and Changes in Net Position for the Interstate Parks Commission for the month ended October 31, 19x1.

CHAPTER

16 Budgets for Resource Management

The GASB *Budgeting, Budgetary Control, and Budgetary Reporting* Principle provides that:

a. An annual budget(s) should be adopted by every governmental unit.

b. The accounting system should provide the basis for appropriate budgetary control.

c. Budgetary comparisons should be included in the appropriate financial statements and schedules for governmental funds for which an annual budget has been adopted.

The *Budgeting* Principle is directly related to the *Accounting and Reporting Capabilities* Principle, which specifies that a governmental accounting system must make it possible for a governmental unit (1) to prepare financial reports in conformity with generally accepted accounting principles (GAAP) and (2) to determine compliance with finance-related legal provisions. Chapter 3 is concerned with budgets as legal documents binding on the actions of administrators and with budgetary accounting needed to make it possible to prepare budgetary reports to demonstrate legal compliance. It is also concerned with budgetary comparisons required for inclusion in general purpose financial statements in conformity with GASB standards.

Budgeting is also an important tool for achieving efficient and effective management of resources. Because of growing public demand for improved government performance, innovative performance measurement systems are being developed at all levels of government. In 1993, for example, the U.S. Congress passed the Government Performance and Results Act which mandates the development of strategic plans and performance measures for all federal agencies. At least one state has passed similar legislation. Numerous state and local governments are experimenting with innovations such as total quality management (TQM), activity-based costing (ABC), and service efforts and accomplishments (SEA) measures. The Governmental Accounting Standards Board (GASB), as discussed in Chapter 13, has conducted extensive research into appropriate SEA measures for a variety of state and local government service functions. Clearly, budgeting can play a major role in developing effective performance measurement systems, and that role of budgeting is the focus of this chapter.

Rational Budgeting Approaches

The legalistic view is that a budget is a plan of financial operation embodying an estimate of proposed expenditures for a given period of time and the proposed means of financing them. In a much more general sense, budgets may be regarded as devices to aid management to operate an organization more effectively. In the general sense, budgets are the financial expression of plans prepared by managers for operating an organization during a time period and for changing its physical facilities and its capital structure.

A simplistic, and often used, approach to budgeting is called *incremental budgeting*. In essence, an incremental budget is derived from the current-year's budget by adding amounts expected to be required by salary and wage increases and increases in the cost of supplies and equipment to be purchased; decreases would result from shrinkage in the scale of operations forced by pressures such as spending limitations mandated by the electorate (e.g., California's Proposition 13) or cuts in capital equipment purchases. Incremental budgeting focuses largely on resource inputs and typically uses the "line-item" budget format in which the focus is on departmental expenditures for specified purposes, or objects, such as personnel, supplies, equipment, and travel. Rational budgeting approaches, discussed below, stress the relation of inputs to outputs (quantities of work accomplished) and outcomes (impacts on goals and objectives). Rational budgeting approaches, as they have evolved, attempt to identify fundamental objectives of the governmental unit, estimate future-year costs and benefits, and systematically analyze alternative ways of meeting the governmental unit's objectives.

The evolution of the concept of a budget from "an estimate of proposed expenditures and the proposed means of financing them" to an "operating plan" was a natural accompaniment to the development of the concept of professional management. In public administration, as in business administration, the concept of professionalism demanded that administrators, or managers, attempt to put the scarce resources of qualified personnel and money to the best possible uses. The legal requirement that administrators of governmental units and agencies submit appropriate requests to the legislative bodies in budget format provided a basis for adapting required budgetary estimates of proposed expenditures to broader management use. The legislative appropriation process has traditionally required administrators to justify budget requests. A logical justification of proposed expenditures is to relate the proposed expenditures of each governmental subdivision to the programs and activities to be accomplished by that subdivision during the budget period. **The type of budgeting in which input of resources is related to output of services is sometimes known as performance budgeting.** Performance budgeting is linked conceptually with *performance auditing* as defined in Chapter

14 of this text. Performance budgeting is a plan for relating resources inputs to the efficient production of outputs; performance auditing is the subsequent evaluation to determine that resources were in fact used efficiently and effectively in accordance with the plan.

Program budgeting is another term sometimes used synonymously with performance budgeting. However, the term is more generally used to refer to a budget format that discloses the full costs of programs or functions without regard to the number of organizational units that might be involved in performing the various aspects of the program or functions. Performance budgeting, at least in its earlier forms, focuses on the relation between inputs and outputs of each organizational unit rather than programs.

The use of performance budgeting in governmental units received significant impetus from the work of the first Hoover Commission for the federal government. The report of this commission, presented to the Congress in 1949, led to the adoption in the federal government of budgets then known as *cost-based budgets* or *cost budgets*. The use of these designations suggests that a governmental unit desiring to use performance budgeting must have an accrual accounting system, rather than a cash accounting system, in order to routinely ascertain the costs of programs and activities. The recommendations of the second Hoover Commission led to the statutory requirement of both accrual accounting and cost-based budgeting for agencies of the executive branch of the federal government. Federal statutes also require the synchronization of budgetary and accounting classifications and the coordination of these with the organizational structure of the agencies. Subsequently it was realized that the planning and programming functions of federal agencies were not performed by the same organizational segments that performed the budgeting and accounting functions and that plans and programs were thus often not properly related to appropriation requests.

The integration of planning, programming, budgeting, and accounting has considerable appeal to persons concerned with public administration because an integrated system should, logically, provide legislators and administrators with much better information for the management of governmental resources than has been provided by separate systems. In the late 1960s, there was a concentrated effort to introduce a planning-programming-budgeting system, called PPBS, throughout the executive branch of the federal government, and to adapt the concept to state and local governmental units and to other complex organizations.

In the 1970s, the wave of interest in PPBS receded and was replaced by widespread discussion of another approach to wedding the legally required budget process to a rational process of allocating scarce resources among alternative uses: the 1970s approach was called *zero-based budgeting* or ZBB. As the name indicates, the basic concept of ZBB is that the very existence of each activity be justifed each year, as well as the amounts of resources requested to be allocated to each activity.

Many governmental units of various sizes have experimented with performance budgeting, program budgeting, PPBS, ZBB, and mixed approaches to rational budgeting.[1] Successful implementation of these approaches, particularly PPBS, requires formulation of the governmental unit's fundamental objectives and identification and evaluation of alternative ways of achieving the objectives. Techniques used to evaluate alternatives are sometimes referred to as *systems analysis, cost/benefit analysis,* and *cost-effectiveness analysis.* Techniques for "productivity measurement" or "productivity evaluation" are also often utilized by administrators who use the budgeting process as an aid in the allocation of scarce resources among competing demands for services. Quantitative techniques such as model building and simulation studies are utilized as aids in evaluating alternative allocations of governmental resources just as they are for evaluating business alternatives.

However simple or however sophisticated the methods used to develop information to aid in the resource allocation process, any method can produce useful output only if the data input are sufficiently reliable. Chapters 2 through 13 are intended to provide the reader with the background needed to understand data produced in conformity with GASB standards. Modifications that would facilitate rational budgeting are discussed in Chapter 18.

Interrelation of Policysetting, Service Delivery, and Evaluation Activities

Illustration 16–1 is a graphic representation of the interrelations among the processes of policysetting, service delivery, and evaluation in one city. Illustration 16–1 shows that budget preparation is constrained by evaluation of prior years' action plans and accomplishments, generation of data about the city, and adjustment of goals and policies. Not specifically presented in the chart is the necessity of recognizing the impact on the city's action plans of changes in federal and state policies, programs, and revenues and expenditures structures.

Budgeting Procedures

Budgeting Governmental Appropriations

Appropriations budgets are an administration's requests for authorization to incur liabilities for goods, services, and facilities for specified purposes. In practice, the preparation of appropriations budgets for any one year is related to the administration's budget of revenues since the revenues budget is the plan for financing the proposed appropriations. If the program, or performance, budget concept is followed, appropriations budgets are prepared for each existing and continuing work

---

[1] A research study by Robert D. Lee, Jr. found that 95 percent of state governments included program effectiveness estimates in budget requests for new or revised programs in 1990 compared with only 24 percent reported for 1970 in an earlier survey. Similarly, 86 percent included productivity data in 1990 compared with 29 percent in 1970. Source: Robert D. Lee, Jr., "Developments in State Budgeting: Trends of Two Decades," *Public Administration Review,* May/June 1991, pp. 254–62. O'Toole and Stipak's survey of local governments found that 30 percent of the 526 local governments in their survey used a hybrid program/performance budget structure, compared with only 14 percent five years earlier. Source: Daniel E. O'Toole, and Brian Stipak, "Patterns and Trends in Budget Format Innovation among Local Governments," *Public Budgeting & Finance* 4, no. 2 (1992).

ILLUSTRATION 16–1   Integrated Budgeting Planning System

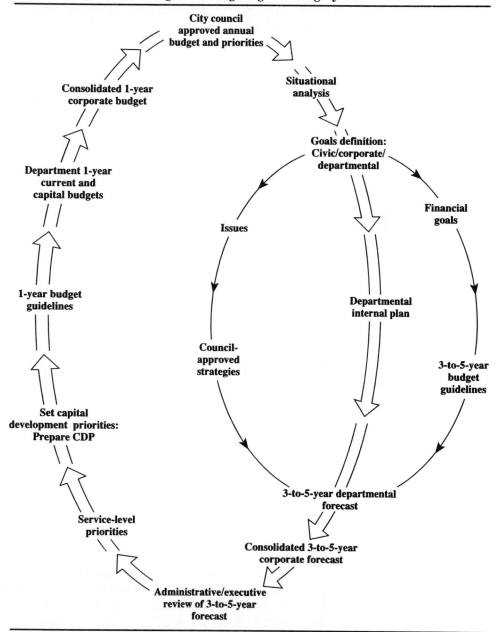

SOURCE: Adapted from Peter P. Fernandes and Myriam P. Laberge, "Setting Local Government Priorities through the Budget Process," *Government Finance Review* April 1986, p. 23. Reprinted with permission of the Government Finance Officers Association.

program or activity of each governmental subdivision; for each program authorized or required by action of past legislative bodies but not yet made operative; and for each new program the administration intends to submit to the legislative body for approval.

In business budgeting, each ongoing program should be subjected to rigorous management scrutiny at budget preparation time to make sure there is a valid reason for continuing the program at all: This is the fundamental idea of zero-based budgeting. If the program should be continued, then management must decide whether the prior allocation of resources to the program is optimal, or whether changes should be made in the assignment of personnel, equipment, space, and money. In a well-managed governmental unit, the same sort of review is given to each continuing program. The mere fact that the program was authorized by a past legislative body does not mean the administration may shirk its duty to recommend discontinuance of a program that has ceased to serve a real need. If the program should be continued, in the judgment of the administration, the appropriate level of activity and the appropriate allocation of resources must be determined; this determination takes far more political courage and management skill than the common practice of simply extrapolating the trend of historical activity and historical cost.

If the administration is convinced that a program should be continued and the prior allocation of resources is relatively appropriate, the preparation of the appropriations budget is delegated to the persons in charge of the program. In the case of a new program, the administration states the objectives of the program and sets general guidelines for the operation of the program, then delegates budget preparation to individuals who are expected to be in charge of the program when legislative authorization and appropriations are secured. State laws or local ordinances typically require that certain steps be followed in the budgeting process and may prescribe dates by which each step must be completed. These requirements are referred to as the **budget calendar.** A budget calendar for a small city is presented in Illustration 16–2.

In order to ensure that administrative policies are actually used in budget preparation and that the budget calendar and other legal requirements are met, it is customary to designate someone in the central administrative office as budget officer. In addition to the responsibilities enumerated, the budget officer is responsible for providing technical assistance to the operating personnel who prepare the budgets. The technical assistance provided may include clerical assistance with budget computations as well as the maintenance of files for each program containing: (1) documents citing the legal authorization and directives, (2) relevant administrative policies, (3) historical cost and workload data, (4) specific factors affecting program costs and workloads, and (5) sources of information to be used in projecting trends.

Budgets prepared by departmental administrators should be reviewed by the central administration before submission to the legislative branch because the total of departmental requests frequently exceeds the total of estimated revenues, and it is necessary to trim the requests in some manner. Central review may also

ILLUSTRATION 16–2

SAMPLE CITY
Budget Calendar
FY 19x5–x6

Date	Event	Requirement or Action
July 20	1st Budget Workshop	Draft budget and documentation.
August 4	2nd Budget Workshop	Draft budget and documentation.
August 11	Regular Council Meeting/3rd Budget Workshop	Long-term GF projections, capital outlay and analysis of budget increases.
August 25	Regular Council Meeting/4th Budget Workshop	Budget presentations by County Health District, Chamber of Commerce, and other organizations.
September 1	Special Council Meeting/5th Budget Workshop	Water/Sewer budget presentation. Call for public hearing to be held September 8.
September 3	Newspaper Publication	Publish notice of public hearing on budget to be held on September 8.
September 8	Regular Council Meeting	Public hearing on proposed budget.
September 15	Special Council Meeting	First reading of budget ordinance.
September 22	Regular Council Meeting	Second reading and vote on adoption of budget ordinance.

be necessary to make sure enough is being spent on certain programs. Good financial management of the taxpayers' dollars is a process of trying to determine the optimum dollar input to achieve the desired service output, not a process of minimizing input. Even though the appropriations budget is a legally prescribed document, the administration should not lose sight of its managerial usefulness.

It should be emphasized that governmental budgets submitted to the legislative branch for action must be made available for a certain length of time for study by interested citizens, and one or more public hearings must be held before the legislative branch takes final action. Ordinarily, few citizens take the trouble to study the proposed budgets in detail; however, newspaper and television reporters often publicize proposed appropriations, especially those for programs, activities, and functions deemed particularly newsworthy. News reporters also publicize increases in taxes and fees proposed to finance budgeted appropriations. Representatives of such organizations as the state or local Chamber of Commerce and League of Women Voters analyze the budgets in detail and furnish analyses to their members, the public, and news media. Generally, such broadly based organizations attempt to be even-handed in their budget analyses. In many instances, however, members of special interest groups also sift through the proposed budget to determine the proposed allocation of resources to the programs, activities, and functions of interest to the groups they represent; budget analyses of special interest groups are not intended to be even-handed. If the proposed budget does not meet the interests of the group as well as they think they can expect realistically, the groups may be counted on to attempt to influence the votes of the members of the legislative branch to change the budget before it is enacted into law. Thus it is evident that the governmental process involves political and social considerations and, at higher levels of government, aggregate economic considerations, all of which may be more important to many voters, administrators, and legislators than financial considerations. This process is presented graphically in Illustration 16–3. Governmental budgeting considerations are consistent with the overall goal of governmental accounting and financial reporting, discussed in Chapter 1.

Comparable considerations exist for business enterprises. A profit-seeking business will succeed in the long run only if it serves the needs of its customers and of society in general: The financial managers of a business must budget within this framework. In business budgeting, revenues and expenses of any year are interrelated; expenses are incurred in the effort to produce revenue, and the production of revenue enables the further incurring of expenses and the further production of revenue. Revenue and expense are interdependent variables in business budgeting.

Business budgeting concepts are appropriate for governmental activities run on a business basis. A similar interrelationship may be said to exist at the federal government level in the cases of certain General Fund expenditures made in order to stimulate segments of the economy; the costs of increasing economic activity tend to be recouped by increased tax revenue. For general governmental activities, however, revenues and expenditures are not interdependent variables. Expenditures are made in order to render a service to the citizens, and not in order to

ILLUSTRATION 16–3   The Governmental Budget Decision Process

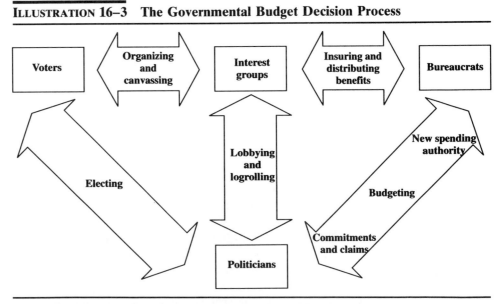

SOURCE: Ann Robinson and Bengt-Christer Ysander, "Re-Establishing Budgetary Flexibility," *Public Budgeting and Finance,* Autumn 1982, p. 23.

generate revenue. Similarly, although revenues may vary from month to month, the variation of revenues has little direct effect on the incurring of expenditures.

Budgeting Governmental Revenues

Although governmental revenues and expenditures are not interdependent variables as business revenues and expenses are, the availability of revenues is a necessary prerequisite to the incurring of expenditures. Some states and local governments may operate at a deficit temporarily, but it is generally conceded that they may not do so indefinitely. Thus, wise financial management calls for the preparation of revenues budgets, at least in rough form, prior to the preparation of detailed operating plans and finalizing appropriations budgets.

Revenues is a term that has a precise meaning in governmental accounting. The GASB states that the term *revenues* "means increases in sources of fund financial resources other than from interfund transfers and debt issue proceeds."[2] For purposes of budgeting inflows of financial resources of a fund, it does not seem particularly valuable to distinguish among "revenues," as defined by the GASB, interfund transfers, and debt issue proceeds, other than to keep budgeting terminology consistent with accounting and financial reporting terminology.

Sources of revenue and other financial inflows available to a given local governmental unit are generally closely controlled by state law; state laws also establish procedures for the utilization of available sources and may impose ceilings on the amount of revenue a local government may collect from certain sources. Sources generally available for financing routine operations include property taxes, sales taxes, income taxes, license fees, fines, charges for services, grants or allocations from other governmental units, and revenue from the use of money or property. Chapter 3 of this text describes revenue sources and discusses revenue accounting in some detail. The present discussion is, therefore, limited to the broad aspects of governmental revenue budgeting.

Within the framework set by legal requirements and subject to the approval of the legislative body (which, in turn, reacts to the electorate), the determination of revenue policy is a prerogative of the administration. Major considerations underlying the policy formulation are set forth in the preceding section of this chapter. After policies are established, the technical preparation of the revenues budget is ordinarily delegated to the budget officer. In order to facilitate budget preparation, experienced budget officers generally keep for each revenue source a file containing (1) a copy of legislation authorizing the source and any subsequent legislation pertaining to the source; (2) historical experience relative to collections from the source, including collections as a percentage of billings, where applicable; (3) relevant administrative policies; and (4) specific factors that affect the yield from the source, including for each factor the historical relationship of the factor to revenue procedures to be used in projecting the trend of factors affecting yield, and factors affecting collections. Graphic presentations of these factors are also frequently included in the file. Finance officers of large governmental units use

---

[2] GASB Codification Sec. 1800.114.

more sophisticated statistical and econometric methods of revenue forecasting, particularly to evaluate alternative assumptions, but the method described here is generally used for preparation of a legal revenues budget.

Program Budget Example

Illustration 16–4 presents a summary of the Expenditures budget requests for the eight categories of programs of governmental services offered by a medium-sized city. In addition to the total amount requested, the summary provides a brief description of each program. Detail supporting the total requested for each program is presented in the city's budget document. Illustration 16–5 presents the

---

ILLUSTRATION 16–4

Budget by Programs

I. DEVELOPMENT OF HUMAN RESOURCES	$ 317,281
To provide materials and programs to enable the educational development and improvement of all citizens and to attempt to motivate maximum utilization of their opportunities.	
II. TRANSPORTATION	2,706,519
To enable the movement of persons and goods within the City in an efficient, safe, and environmentally acceptable manner.	
III. PHYSICAL ENVIRONMENT AND ECONOMIC BASE	1,329,831
To achieve the best possible physical environment throughout the community, to stabilize and preserve property values, and to establish and maintain a sound economic base.	
IV. HOUSING	15,657
To ensure that those desiring to live in this town, regardless of race, creed, or socioeconomic standing, will find available housing that meets minimum safety and health standards, and that they will have some choice of housing types and location within the community.	
V. HEALTH, SAFETY, AND GENERAL WELL-BEING...........................	630,024
To conserve the mental and physical health of and to ensure the safety of all citizens, to eliminate unjust discrimination of all kinds, and to stimulate and facilitate maximum citizen participation in government.	
VI. CULTURE AND RECREATIONAL...	1,174,937
To provide opportunities for citizens to relax, to enjoy nature; to exercise; to socialize; to learn or practice artistic, social, or athletic skills; and to witness or participate in cultural events.	
VII. SERVICES TO PROPERTY	5,691,504
To make available the services essential for the operation and use of real property and to prevent damage to or the destruction or loss of real property.	
VIII. GENERAL MANAGEMENT AND SUPPORT..................................	1,055,093
To provide all management and support activities necessary to achieve the City's objectives.	
Total All Programs	12,920,846
Less: Interfund Transfer Included in Program Structure	(183,413)
Total Budget by Programs...	12,737,433

ILLUSTRATION 16–5

Detail Budget of Program V

	V. HEALTH, SAFETY, AND GENERAL WELL-BEING		$630,024
	A. Conservation of Health		180,565
5110	1. Public Health	$64,640	
5120	2. Hospital Treatment	30,000	
	3. Animal Control	44,211	
5131	A′. Dog Control	33,596	
5132	B′. Other Animals	1,992	
5133	C′. Records + Court	7,390	
5134	D′. Support	1,233	
	4. Resuscitator + Rescue Calls	41,714	
5141	A′. Volunteer Groups	1,800	
5142	B′. Public Safety—Calls	19,426	
5143	C′. Public Safety—Assemblies	5,806	
5144	D′. Public Safety—Training	12,082	
5145	E′. Ambulance	2,600	
	B. Crime Prevention		268,051
	1. Patrol	99,429	
5211	A′. Mobile	61,174	
5212	B′. Foot		
5213	C′. On-Site Arrests		
5214	D′. Dispatch	9,376	
5215	E′. Support	2,136	
	2. Investigation + Apprehension	893	
5221	A′. Intelligence Gathering	8,555	
5222	B′. Crime Investingation	0	
5223	C′. Records +	0	
		8,555	
	G. Inner-Group Relations		15,449
5710	1. Discrimination Cases	2,801	
5720	2. Education Programs	7,125	
5730	3. Support	5,523	
5740	4. Transient Youth Program	0	
	H. Citizen Participation		25,759
5810	1. Voter Registration	0	
5820	2. Elections	7,071	
5830	3. Public Information	13,030	
5840	4. Financial Reporting	884	
5850	5. Legal Notice Administration	2,796	
5860	6. Special Citizen Committees	1,978	

detail supporting Program V, Health, Safety, and General Well-Being; it shows that although Health, Safety, and General Well-Being is a program category, it is not a single program but an umbrella for programs, activities, and functions of a number of departments of the city. The same is true for each of the other program categories shown in Illustration 16–4.

Whatever theory of management is followed, responsibility for the performance of activities must be clearly fixed. In order to accomplish this, personnel, equipment, and facilities are assigned to organizational subentities. For management purposes, therefore, a budget must be prepared for each organizational subentity and related to the program budget. The four-digit number in the left margin of Illustration 16–5 is a program element number that cross references the detailed budget of the program category to the budgets for the organizational subentities; Illustration 16–6 shows the budget for the City Fire Department. The left-hand portion of Illustration 16–6 shows the proposed budget for the forthcoming year for personal services, nonpersonal expense, and capital outlay, each compared with the approved budget for the year in progress at the time the proposed budget is prepared, and with the actual expenditures for the most recent year completed. Underneath the dollar comparisons a brief explanation of the major functions served by the department is presented along with comments intended to answer questions administrators expect City Council members and interested residents to raise.

The right-hand portion of Illustration 16–6 indicates the amounts of the Fire Department budget that relate to each program element in which the department is involved. Note, for example, that the first four lines, 5141, 5142, 5143, and 5144, list programs included in section A4 of Illustration 16–5. Only in the case of the Public Safety—Assemblies program, 5143, does the Fire Department have sole responsibility. The Police Department budget, not reproduced here, includes the amount of $4,567 for Program 5142, Public Safety—Calls, and the amount of $390 for Program 5144, Public Safety—Training; these amounts, when added to the amounts shown for those programs in Illustration 16–6, verify that the Police and Fire Departments are the only city departments involved in these programs. The City Council budget, not reproduced here, shows that the Council supports the Volunteer Groups program, 5141, to the extent of $1,050; thus the Council and the Fire Department share responsibility for that program.

The budgets for each organizational subentity are summarized as shown by Illustration 16–7. The total Fire Department budget, $690,174 per Illustration 16–6, is shown on the second line under the Public Safety caption in Illustration 16–7. The departments and activities listed in Illustration 16–7 under the General Fund caption are largely those commonly financed by general funds. The Open Space and Major Thoroughfare Fund, Library Fund, and Permanent Parks and Recreation Fund are special revenue funds; the Public Improvement Fund is a capital projects fund; and the General Obligation Debt Retirement Fund is a debt service fund in GASB terminology. The total proposed expenditures from all funds shown in Illustration 16–7 account for approximately two thirds of the total proposed expenditures for all programs shown in Illustration 16–4; the remainder

ILLUSTRATION 16–6

Fire Department Budget

Summary

Activity 15 Fire	Division	Department Fire	Fund General Operating	
Classification		Actual Expenditures Prior Year	Current Budget	Proposed Budget
Personal Services		$467,897	$543,126	$613,066
Nonpersonal Expense		55,681	61,715	69,299
Capital Outlay		2,751	4,680	7,809
Total		$526,329	$609,521	$690,174

Function. The Fire Department has three major functions: First, to prevent fires; second, when fires occur, to prevent loss of life and to minimize property damage; third, in response to emergency calls, to dispatch a resuscitator or other appropriate equipment for rescue operations.

Budget Comments. Most of the increase in the Fire Department budget results from Personal Services. The increase in this area reflects general pay increases of $45,727 and the addition of new firefighters at a cost of $24,213. These latter will complete the implementation of the three-year program of reducing the workweek from 67½ hours to 56 hours. In Nonpersonal Expense, the increase is accounted for by uncontrollable increases in rentals and insurance, along with $2,500 for overhauling the motor and pump on Engine #11. The Capital Outlay expense consists of the following items: heart-lung resuscitator ($1,800); camera for fire investigation ($140); dictation equipment ($565); miscellaneous equipment ($986); miscellaneous construction items ($968); underwater rescue equipment ($350); and replacement of fire hose and nozzles ($3,000). The last item is a recurring expense in accordance with a programmed replacement of fire nozzles.

Budget by Programs

	Budget by Programs	Personal Services	Non-personal Expense	Capital	Total
5141	Volunteer Groups	$ 00	$ 750	$ 00	$ 750
5142	Public Safety—Calls	11,721	988	2,150	14,859
5143	Public Safety—Assemblies	5,806	00	00	5,806
5144	Public Safety—Training	11,642	50	00	11,692
7111	Evacuation Planning and Civilian Training	335	55	00	390
7112	Education—School Children	9,380	50	00	9,430
7113	Lectures and Demonstrations	6,330	221	00	6,551
7114	Public Assemblies	5,915	00	00	5,915
7121	Inspections (Construction)	7,248	00	00	7,248
7122	Adjudication (Construction)	335	00	00	335
7131	Inspections (Complaints)	40,937	3,538	00	44,475
7132	Adjudication (Complaints)	335	00	00	335
7140	Investigation of Fires	1,880	1,175	140	3,195
7151	Classroom (Training)	71,333	333	00	71,666
7152	Field (Training)	31,479	1,638	00	33,117
7153	Special Schools	13,775	1,550	00	15,325
7155	Facilities—Maintenance	00	125	00	125
7161	Surveys	11,818	00	00	11,818
7162	Plan Preparation and Instruction	14,307	00	00	14,307
7171	Answering Alarms	68,233	6,063	00	74,296
7172	Dispatching	27,128	00	00	27,128
7173	Equipment Acquisition and Maintenance	25,570	7,606	3,986	37,162
7174	Equipment Testing and Operation	12,505	1,966	00	14,471
7175	Building Construction and Modification	5,580	1,580	968	8,128
7176	Building Operation and Maintenance	41,630	8,955	00	50,585
7178	Standby (Firefighting)	121,686	00	00	121,686
7182	Hydrant Testing and Records	16,447	00	00	16,447
7184	Hydrant Rental	00	29,813	00	29,813
7190	Support	49,711	2,843	565	53,119
	Program Total	$613,066	$69,299	$7,809	$690,174

ILLUSTRATION 16–7

Summary Expenditure Budget
All Governmental Funds
Expenditures by Activity

Funds and Activities	Prior-Year Actual	Current Budget	Proposed Budget
GENERAL FUND			
General government:			
City council	$ 77,750	$ 49,738	$ 51,548
Municipal court	52,304	62,567	67,552
City attorney	52,210	80,855	83,332
City manager	65,724	72,946	80,746
Total General Government	247,988	266,106	283,178
Administrative services:			
Finance	196,597	226,570	255,197
Budget and research	27,688	37,162	44,994
Personnel	35,005	43,772	54,597
Data processing	15,812	15,751	59,877
Land acquisition	12,642	11,759	13,959
Total Administrative Services	287,744	335,014	428,624
Community development:			
Housing	10,350	10,072	12,436
Planning	85,489	96,776	109,335
Zoning and building inspection	97,127	110,300	125,894
Total Community Development	192,976	217,148	247,665

Funds and Activities	Prior-Year Actual	Current Budget	Proposed Budget
Parks and recreation:			
Administration	$ 36,557	$ 42,551	$ 47,317
Park maintenance	235,987	263,023	404,825
Recreation	125,481	151,581	186,871
Swimming pools	45,459	48,274	57,526
Reservoir	29,383	29,203	34,572
Concessions	8,698	11,950	12,552
Reservoir concessions			31,909
Total Parks and Recreation	481,565	546,582	775,572
Health and welfare:			
Human relations			15,449
Health	51,804	59,216	64,640
Animal control	24,029	38,123	39,886
Ambulance	1,999	2,600	2,600
Hospital	30,000	30,000	30,000
Noise abatement			14,818
Total Health and Welfare	107,832	129,939	167,393
Contingency:	25,794	51,864	73,000
Adjustments:	18,066		
TOTAL GENERAL FUND	$3,829,146	$4,091,643	$5,088,118

Public safety:			
Police	737,789	875,930	1,059,667
Fire	526,329	609,521	690,174
Civil defense	26,119	28,058	32,648
Total Public Safety	1,290,237	1,513,509	1,782,489
Public facilities:			
Administration	33,095	25,085	25,084
Engineering—design	71,294	104,407	115,182
Transportation	105,032	113,785	398,709
Street lighting	112,895	131,244	134,454
Operations:			
Administration	21,666	23,986	32,490
Operations	417,567	538,194	417,469
Flood Control	—	—	90,969
Building maintenance	84,646	94,780	107,240
Disaster relief	330,749	—	—
Airport	—	—	8,600
Total Public Facilities	1,176,944	1,031,481	1,330,197
OPEN SPACE AND MAJOR THOROUGHFARE FUND			
Open space	455,244	557,700	976,760
Major thoroughfares	746,126	749,600	1,300,000
Total Open Space and Major Thoroughfare Fund	1,201,370	1,307,300	2,276,760
PUBLIC IMPROVEMENT FUND	373,570	275,000	769,500
LIBRARY FUND			
Library operations	207,305	241,105	281,158
Gifts and grants	52,482	60,000	60,000
Total Library Fund	259,787	301,105	341,158
PERMANENT PARKS AND RECREATION FUND			
Projects from .9 mill	104,916	105,000	116,250
Gifts, grants, and fees	19,727	80,335	110,748
Total Permanent Parks and Recreation Fund	124,643	185,335	226,998
GENERAL OBLIGATION DEBT RETIREMENT FUND	98,761	96,514	96,358
TOTAL GOVERNMENTAL FUNDS	$5,887,277	$6,256,897	$8,798,892

ILLUSTRATION 16–8

Summary General Fund Revenue Budget

General Fund	Prior-Year Actual	Current Budget	Proposed Budget
Fund balance—beginning of year	$ 784,446	$ 778,960	$ 647,068
Taxes:			
Property taxes	601,369	642,700	746,968
Less: Property tax deferral	—	—	(40,000)
Franchise taxes:			
Gas and electric	161,879	210,000	274,000
Telephone and telegraph	108,682	115,000	170,000
Television cable	1,400	2,000	2,500
Contribution in lieu of taxes:			
Water utility	118,600	128,000	128,000
Sewer utility	19,500	25,600	25,600
Cigarette taxes	128,232	150,000	170,000
Sales and use tax	1,858,474	2,050,000	2,521,314
Public accommodations and admissions tax	—	—	187,500
Total taxes	2,998,136	3,323,300	4,185,882
Licenses and fees:			
Bicycle licenses	590	600	600
Alcoholic beverage fees	27,304	30,900	35,000
Health Department licenses	10,238	7,000	8,000
Police and protective licenses	1,612	1,600	1,600
Amusement licenses	835	900	900
Merchandising licenses	785	800	800
Occupational licenses	5,004	5,000	5,000
Dog licenses	15,288	15,500	32,500
Total licenses	61,656	62,300	84,400
Parking meter fees	13,179	13,000	13,000
Court fines and costs	129,469	120,000	156,500
Revenues from use of money and property	155,745	120,000	120,000
Revenues from other agencies:			
Highway users tax—State	238,356	284,000	317,000
Auto registration—$1.50 special	55,472	62,000	68,000
Auto registration—$2.50 special fee—State	—	—	102,000

General Fund	Prior-Year Actual	Current Budget	Proposed Budget
Road and bridge fund—County	—	—	245,000
Specific ownership tax—County	65,025	74,000	80,000
Highway aid—State	14,140	14,000	14,000
Civil defense—Federal	12,425	13,700	16,300
Civil defense—County	6,718	7,000	8,000
Dog control—County	3,120	3,000	3,000
Disaster grant—Federal	364,872	—	—
Total Other Agencies	760,128	457,700	853,300
Revenue from parks and recreation:			
Reservoir	22,355	24,000	26,000
Swimming pools	36,553	39,990	46,660
Athletics	29,918	41,465	51,057
Crafts	18,290	18,823	22,971
Social activities	14,235	14,082	20,976
Concessions	10,732	13,800	14,800
Reservoir concessions	—	—	22,200
Miscellaneous revenue	883	—	—
Total Revenue from Parks and Recreation	132,966	152,160	204,664
Other revenues:			
Annexation fees	417	3,500	3,500
Sale of city property	4,671	4,000	4,000
Building inspection revenues	63,348	75,000	80,000
Street department revenues	12,101	13,000	13,000
Engineering department revenues	6,516	6,000	6,000
Miscellaneous receipts and services	16,148	10,000	10,000
Airport revenues	—	—	10,500
Total Other Revenues	104,201	111,500	127,000
General Fund Revenue	4,355,480	4,359,960	5,744,746
Less: Operating transfers out	(531,820)	(400,209)	(925,838)
Total General Fund Revenue	3,823,660	3,959,751	4,818,908
Amount Available	$4,608,106	$4,738,711	$5,465,980

of the proposed expenditures for programs are found in the expenditures budgets for the Water Utility Fund and Sewer Utility Fund, not reproduced here.

Illustration 16–8 presents the summary General Fund revenues budget for the city whose appropriations budgets are presented in Illustrations 16–4 through 16–7. The sources of revenue shown in the illustrations are typical of many governmental units. Presentation of data comparing estimates for the budget year with the budget for the current year, and the actual revenues of the immediately prior year, is also typical. If estimates differ markedly from current and recent experience, explanations are sometimes made a part of the budget presentation by a note, sometimes by supplementary schedules, and other times are omitted from the formal presentation with the thought that the explanations may be given orally, if called for.

Note that the final item in Illustration 16–8, Amount Available, is the total of General Fund revenues budgeted for the year plus the expected Fund Balance at the beginning of the year. (Since the budget must be prepared several months before the beginning of the budget year in order to allow for legally mandated periods of time for inspection of the budget by interested residents, public hearings, and review by agencies of the state, it is necessary to compute what the Fund Balance should be at the beginning of the budget year based on expected revenues and expenditures of the current year.) The Amount Available for the General Fund should be compared with the budgeted Total General Fund Expenditures (see Illustration 16–7). The budgeted Amount Available exceeds the budgeted Expenditures by approximately $378,000, which, if actual revenues are reasonably close to budgeted revenues and if expenditures are kept within the budget, is considered a reasonable figure.

Budgeting Capital Expenditures

One feature of Illustration 16–6 to which the reader's attention has not been previously directed is the Capital Outlay line. Accounting principles for business enterprises and for proprietary funds of governmental units require the cost of assets expected to benefit more than one period to be treated as a balance sheet item, rather than as a charge against revenues of the period. No such distinction exists for governmental fund types. As Illustration 16–6 indicates, expenditures for long-lived assets to be used in the general operations of a governmental unit are treated in the appropriations process in the same manner as are expenditures for salaries, wages, benefits, materials, supplies, and services to be consumed during the accounting period. Accounting control over long-lived assets used in general operations is established, however, as described in Chapter 6 of this text.

In Illustration 16–6 the Capital Outlay item consists of equipment, as described in the Budget Comments section. Proposed major construction or acquisition projects are included in the Public Improvements Fund budget for legislative approval.

Effective financial management requires the plans for any one year to be consistent with intermediate- and long-range plans. Governmental projects such as the construction or improvement of streets; construction of bridges and buildings; acquisition of land for recreational use, parking lots, and future building

ILLUSTRATION 16–9

CITY OF FARMINGTON
Classification of Revenues by Project Area—CIP
Traffic Construction
FY 19x3 thru FY 19x8

Project Number	Project	Total Estimated Cost	Revenue Source		Recommended Scheduling					
			Source*	Amount	FY 19x3	FY 19x4	FY 19x5	FY 19x6	FY 19x7	FY 19x8
E-01	Flashing Signals—21st Street S.W.	$ 142,674	RUT	$ 16,000	$ 16,000	$ —	$ —	$ —	$ —	$ —
			PC	126,674	126,674	—	—	—	—	—
E-02	Ped. Overpass, 1st Ave. & 27th St. East	1,425	FG-USTEP	1,425	1,425	—	—	—	—	—
E-03	Project CR-16-81-229 (Overpass)	395	FG-USTEP	395	395	—	—	—	—	—
E-04	1st Ave. Computer Traffic Control Upgrade	2,291	FG-USTEP	2,291	2,291	—	—	—	—	—
E-05	Upgrading Computer Control	12,190	FG-USTEP	12,190	12,190	—	—	—	—	—
E-06	Computer Expansion	3,000	FG-USTEP	3,000	3,000	—	—	—	—	—
E-07	Mast Arm Upgrading	300,000	GOB-TS	159,500	—	159,500	—	—	—	—
			FG-USTEP	140,500	80,000	60,500	—	—	—	—
E-08	16th Ave., Edgewood, Wiley, Williams	200,000	GOB-TS	90,000	—	90,000	—	—	—	—
			FG-USTEP	110,000	—	110,000	—	—	—	—
E-09	1st Avenue East & Cottage Grove	85,000	GOB-TS	42,000	—	42,000	—	—	—	—
			FG-USTEP	43,000	—	43,000	—	—	—	—
E-10	8th Avenue S.E.	200,000	GOB-TS	200,000	—	200,000	—	—	—	—
E-11	E Avenue & Edgewood Road N.W.	30,000	GOB-TS	30,000	—	30,000	—	—	—	—
E-12	GTC Signals	120,000	GOB-TS	120,000	—	120,000	—	—	—	—
E-13	Controllers Upgrading	120,000	GOB-TS	120,000	—	30,000	30,000	30,000	30,000	—
E-14	Blairs Ferry & Center Point & North Towne	90,000	FG-FAUS	90,000	—	—	90,000	—	—	—
E-15	12th Street S.E., 2nd & 3rd Avenue	120,000	GOB-TS	120,000	—	—	30,000	90,000	—	—
E-16	2nd Avenue, 7th & 8th Street S.E.	120,000	GOB-TS	120,000	—	—	30,000	90,000	—	—
E-17	CBD Rewiring, Phase I & II	110,000	FG-FAUS	110,000	—	—	110,000	—	—	—
E-18	15th Avenue & 6th Street S.W.	60,000	GOB-TS	60,000	—	—	—	15,000	45,000	—
E-19	42nd Street & Council Street N.E.	60,000	GOB-TS	60,000	—	—	—	15,000	45,000	—
E-20	Signal Upgrading	155,000	GOB-TS	155,000	—	—	—	60,000	70,000	25,000
E-21	E Avenue N.W. & Edgewood Road	60,000	GOB-TS	60,000	—	—	—	60,000	—
E-22	1st Avenue Widening	100,000	GOB-TS	45,000	—	—	—	—	—	45,000
			FG-USTEP	55,000	—	—	—	—	—	55,000
E-23	Mt. Vernon Road at 34th Street S.E.	60,000	GOB-TS	60,000	—	—	—	—	—	60,000
E-24	15th Street S.E., 2nd & 3rd Avenue	120,000	GOB-TS	120,000	—	—	—	—	—	120,000
	TOTALS	$2,271,975		$2,271,975	$241,975	$885,000	$290,000	$300,000	$250,000	$305,000

* RUT = Road Use Tax
PC = Private Contributions
FG-USTEP = Federal Grants—Urban-State Traffic Engineering Program

GOB-TS = General Obligation Bonds—Tax Supported
FG-FAUS = Federal Grants—Federal Aid to Urban Systems

sites; and urban renewal all may require a consistent application of effort over a span of years. Consequently, administrators need to present to the legislative branch and to the public a multiyear capital improvements program, as well as the budget for revenues, operating expenditures, and capital outlays requested for the forthcoming year. Illustration 16–9 shows one such presentation that combines the projection of recommended improvements for five years beyond the forthcoming budget year with the proposed means of financing them.

Effective financial management also requires nonfinancial information such as physical measures of capital assets, their service condition, and their estimated replacement cost. Nonfinancial information of these types is useful for purposes of forecasting future asset repair and replacement schedules, repair and replacement costs, and financing requirements. Illustrations 16–10, 16–11, and 16–12

ILLUSTRATION 16–10   City of Dayton Inventory Summary

Program	Inventory		Replacement Cost
1. Street system	Thoroughfares:	613 lane miles	$ 110,000,000
	Residentials:	1,206 lane miles	
2. City bridges		158 bridges	277,000,000
3. Traffic signal controllers		325 controllers	7,608,000
4. Railroad crossings		123 crossings	2,460,000
5. Sidewalks and curbs		700 linear miles (est.)	90,500,000
6. Alleys		287 lane miles	10,300,000
7. Municipal buildings		22 buildings	51,231,000
8. Fire facilities		17 buildings	12,014,000
9. Human rehabilitation center		14 buildings	7,609,000
10. Recreation and parks		70 facilities	101,415,000
11. Air transportation	Buildings:	24	30,000,000
	Runways:	197 lane miles	82,400,000
	Roadways:	22.5 lane miles	1,700,000
	Land:	3,309 acres	31,472,000
12. Water supply and treatment	Treatment plants:	2	62,000,000
	Lime plant:	1	9,000,000
	Wells:	76	9,250,000
	Recharge facilities:	2	4,250,000
13. Water distribution	Pumping facilities:	14	10,000,000
	Storage facilities:	11	26,000,000
	Water mains:	719.9 linear miles	173,200,000
	Water meters:	95,391	3,825,000
14. Sewer system	Sanitary sewers:	593 linear miles	383,000,000
	Storm sewers:	387 linear miles	353,000,000
	Pumping stations:	25	7,900,000
	Valves and gates:	112	—
15. Wastewater treatment		51 facilities	79,700,000
Total			$1,936,834,000

SOURCE: Timothy H. Riordan, Maria E. Oria, and Joseph P. Tuss, "The Bridge from Dreams to Realities: Dayton's Capital Allocation Process," *Government Finance Review*, April 1987, p. 9. Reprinted with permission of the Government Finance Officers Association.

ILLUSTRATION 16–11   City Bridges Capital Program

Section I. Repair/replacement policy

The city's bridge repair/replacement schedule is developed in four steps. First, the engineering staff inspects each bridge and assigns a condition rating. Second, the engineering and street maintenance staffs review the condition ratings and develop a list of bridges with major deficiencies and a three-year work plan. Third, engineering, street maintenance and OMB meet to develop a three-year program based on the work plan and the projected funds available. Fourth, the three-year repair/replacement schedule is submitted to the Capital Investment Committee for review and adoption. The three-year program is developed using four criteria:

1. Repairs that upgrade a bridge to good structural condition are given priority.
2. No major repairs will be done to bridges that are candidates for total replacement.
3. Street maintenance bridge crews will do one major rehabilitation project annually.
4. All metal surfaces on bridges should be painted.

The repair/replacement schedule guarantees that bridges will be maintained in good condition. Major repair or replacement projects are considered as funds becomes available. Currently, there are three bridges with major deficiencies that are under consideration for replacement: Wagoner Ford over the Miami River, Rip Rap over the Miami River, and the Miller (Bridge Street) Bridge. All other bridges rated 4 (marginal) will be repaired as part of the three-year repair/replacement schedules.

As part of the repair/replacement program the city has begun testing concrete bridge decks with asphalt wearing surfaces. These decks cannot be visually assessed because of the overlay. The testing will allow engineering to better evaluate the condition of these bridges and identify any necessary repairs.

The city maintains a seven-year painting cycle for all metal surfaces on bridges. The schedule is developed each year by engineering based on the results of the annual inspection.

SOURCE: Timothy H. Riordan, Maria E. Oria, and Joseph P. Tuss, "The Bridge from Dreams to Realities: Dayton's Capital Allocation Process," *Government Finance Review,* April 1987, p. 9. Reprinted with permission of the Government Finance Officers Association.

show a capital infrastructure inventory, a statement of repair/replacement policy for city bridges, and a bridge inspection report for the city of Dayton, Ohio. GASB has established a project on nonfinancial service condition reporting for governmental capital assets and may prescribe disclosures similar to those illustrated for the City of Dayton in the future.

ILLUSTRATION 16–12   Bridge Inspection: Bridges Rated 4 (major deficiencies)

Bridge	Repair Needed	Year Repaired
1. Main over Great Miami	Repair backwalls and expansion joints.	1986
2. Wagoner Ford over Great Miami	Abutment seats, beams, joints, bearings, and expansion joints.	1986a
3. Rip Rap over Great Miami	Beams, joints, bearings and expansion joints.	
4. Findlay over Mad River	Expansion joints, general spalling.	1985
5. Shoup Mill over Stillwater	Deck	1987
6. Williams over Wolf Creek	General spalling, expansion joint.	1985
7. Broadway over Wolf Creek	General spalling	1985
8. Miller over Wolf Creek	Deck, beams, stringers, walk supports.	1985b
9. Goodlow over Guenther Ditch	Abutments	1988
10. I-75 and Ramp 37 over Conrail	Deck	1985c

Note: *a.* The west abutment will be repaired by contract.
   b. The walk supports are being repaired by maintenance.
   c. The I-75 bridge deck is being replaced as part of the I-75 upgrade projects.

SOURCE: Timothy H. Riordan, Maria E. Oria, and Joseph P. Tuss, "The Bridge from Dreams to Realities: Dayton's Capital Allocation Process," *Government Finance Review,* April 1987, p. 9. Reprinted with permission of the Government Finance Officers Association.

Budgeting for Performance

During the 1980s, growth in service demands and cutbacks in unrestricted federal funding forced numerous state and local governments to increase taxes and user fees. Meanwhile, taxpayers have become increasingly more frustrated with paying higher taxes for what they perceive as bloated, inefficient government bureaucracies. Fiscal reform has thus become a popular platform for politicians aspiring to key elective offices. Even though, as discussed previously in this chapter, many governments have experimented with so-called rational budgeting approaches (performance budgeting, program budgeting, PPBS, and ZBB), most of these experiments seem to have had little real impact on improving the efficiency and effectiveness of service delivery. Given their limited success with prior budgeting approaches, political leaders have had little choice but to experiment with recent management innovations in the private sector that might improve the efficiency of government operations and reduce the need for higher taxes. One such innovation being embraced by many governments is **total quality management (TQM).**[3]

---

[3] A recent survey by the National Governors Association found that 37 states are using some form of TQM, although most are initiatives of individual state agencies. Only in 13 states are there general TQM programs headed by a central steering group to guide TQM development within the state.

SOURCE: News Briefs, "States Using TQM," *Government Finance Review*, December 1992, p. 4.

TQM is attractive to many government officials because it links customer (taxpayer and other) satisfaction to improvements in the operating systems and processes used to provide goods and services. TQM seeks to continuously improve the government's ability to meet or exceed customer demands, where the customer might be external, such as taxpayers and service recipients, or internal, such as the customers of an internal service fund.[4] Central to TQM is using customer data to identify and correct problems. Individual governments have tailored their TQM structures to meet their unique requirements, but most incorporate a majority of the following elements:[5]

1. Support and commitment of top-level officials.
2. Customer orientation.
3. Employee involvement in productivity and quality improvement efforts.
4. Employees rewarded for quality and productivity achievement.
5. Training provided to employees in methods for improving productivity and quality.
6. Reduction of barriers to productivity and quality improvement.
7. Productivity and quality measures and standards that are meaningful to the governmental unit.
8. Written vision or mission statements which are linked directly to team-established targets or goals.

The elements of TQM are obviously consistent with those of the rational budgeting approaches (particularly PPBS) previously discussed. Thus governments which have previously implemented one of the rational budgeting approaches, or a mixed approach, may find it less costly to implement a TQM structure. On the other hand, few governments possess adequate data on customer satisfaction. Moreover, the traditional emphases of government on line-item budgeting, rigid personnel classifications, restrictive procurement regulations, etc., tend to reduce management autonomy, and thus may be inconsistent with the need under TQM to empower employees to be "entrepreneurial" in improving processes and meeting customer demand. It should also be noted that the objective of TQM is not necessarily to reduce cost but rather to increase "value for the dollar." Insofar as a TQM program successfully adds value, it has the potential to improve the public perception of government, in addition, of course, to improving service delivery.

Element 7 from the preceding list of TQM elements requires that the governmental unit develop meaningful standards for and measures of performance in terms of productivity and quality. In the government and nonprofit context, the analogous performance terms more typically used, are *efficiency* and *effective-*

---

[4] Adapted from James J. Kline. "Total Quality Management in Local Government," *Government Finance Review*, August 1992, p. 7.

[5] Ibid, p. 7.

ness, the former relating efforts (resource inputs) to outputs of a service process and the latter relating efforts to outcomes or the results produced by service (see the discussion in Chapter 13 on service efforts and accomplishments—SEA). Because of growing public demand for greater accountabilty, a number of governments currently report some SEA measures for selected service functions, although there are no generally accepted standards to guide selection of the measures to report. GASB has conducted and commissioned research into appropriate SEA measures for a variety of service functions, including, among others, police departments, fire departments, mass transit, public assistance programs, road maintenance, and colleges and universities.[6]

As discussed in Chapter 13, SEA measures fall into three broad categories: (1) service efforts (resources used), (2) service accomplishments (outputs and outcomes), and (3) those that relate service efforts to service accomplishments. An example of all three types of measures is presented in Illustration 16–13. These indicators, based on a GASB survey of police departments, are intended to be illustrative rather than exhaustive of all indicators that could be reported. As shown in Illustration 16–13 the input measures indicate quantities and dollar amounts of resources used in providing police services. The output and outcome indicators collectively indicate service accomplishments, where outputs indicate quantities of work done on particular activities (such as patrol, responding to calls, and investigations) and outcomes indicate the results of activities in achieving desired objectives (such as reduction of deaths, bodily injury, and property loss). SEA measures for key programs or service functions are essential for measuring entity performance and can provide much of the data needed for implementation of a TQM system.

Finally, development of sophisticated rational budgeting approaches and TQM systems requires sophisticated cost accounting systems to determine the full cost of programs or functions. Better managed state and local governmental units are therefore actively developing improved cost accounting systems. One innovative costing approach being implemented by some governments, which can be implemented in tandem with TQM or other performance measurement systems, is activity-based costing (ABC), discussed in Chapter 18.

If government is to be reinvented, then budgeting may also need to be reinvented. Specifically, the authors believe that, at a minimum, budgeting will need to: (1) become an integrated part of a multiple-year strategic plan, (2) be focused on program objectives (including customer-driven objectives if TQM is used), and (3) utilize data structures consistent with measuring and reporting service efforts and accomplishments, or whatever performance evaluation system is used. Accrual-based budgeting may be needed to develop the full costs of providing services so that management can evaluate the efficiency of providing those services, and whether they should be provided by the government or privatized. In

---

[6] Governmental Accounting Standards Board. Research Report, *Service Efforts and Accomplishments Reporting: Its Time Has Come* (Norwalk, Conn., GASB, 1990).

order to achieve needed budgeting reforms, would-be reformers must concern themselves not only with improving budgeting procedures and information systems but also with the reality that some politicians and bureaucrats will prefer to maintain their present budgeting methods, specifically because present systems often obscure detection of substandard performance. Even though the prospects

---

ILLUSTRATION 16–13   Recommended SEA Indicators for Police Departments*

Indicator	*Rationale for Selecting Indicator*
Inputs:	
Budget expenditures	To provide a measure of financial resources used to provide services.
Equipment, facilities, vehicles	To provide a measure of nonpersonnel resources used to provide services.
Number of personnel or hours expended	To provide a measure of the size of the organization and the human resources used to provide services.
Outputs:	
Hours of patrol	To provide a measure of the quantity of patrol service provided; patrol is generally regarded as a primary product of police efforts.
Responses to calls for service	To provide a measure of the quantity of response service provided.
Crimes investigated	To provide a measure of the quantity of services provided by investigation units.
Number of arrests	To provide a measure of the success of police efforts in apprehending criminal offenders.
Persons participating in crime-prevention activities	To provide a measure of the quantity of service provided by crime-prevention units.
Outcomes:	
Deaths and bodily injury resulting from crime	To provide a measure of the effectiveness of police efforts in reducing the incidence of personal harm attributed to criminal activity.
Value of property lost due to crime	To provide a measure of the effectiveness of police efforts in reducing the incidence of property loss due to criminal activity.
Crimes committed per 100,000 population	To provide a measure of the effectiveness of police efforts in reducing criminal activity.
Percentage of crimes cleared	To provide a measure of the effectiveness of police efforts in detection of criminal activity and apprehension of criminal offenders.
Response time	To provide a measure of the quality of police response to calls.
Citizen satisfaction	To provide a measure of the overall effectiveness of police efforts in meeting citizen needs.
Efficiency:	
Cost per case assigned; cost per crime cleared	To provide an indication of the cost efficiency of police efforts.
Personnel-hours per crime cleared	To provide an indication of the productivity of personnel in providing police services.

ILLUSTRATION 16–13 (*concluded*)

Indicator	Rationale for Selecting Indicator
Explanatory variables: Population by age-group; Unemployment rate; Number of households; number of business firm; Percentage of population below poverty level; Land area; Dollar value of property within jurisdiction; Demand — Calls for service, Cases assigned	To provide information on factors that are likely to affect the incidence and effects of criminal activity so that measures of output, outcome, and efficiency may be viewed in proper context.

* The recommended indicators presented in this exhibit are illustrative. They are intended to serve as a starting point for use in the development of a comprehensive set of SEA indicators for external reporting of an entity's results of operation.

This exhibit does not provide illustrations of indicator disaggregation or of comparison data such as trends, targets, or other comparable entities. Both disaggregation and comparison data are important aspects of SEA reporting. They are discussed in the chapter and in the Overview.

SOURCE: Governmental Accounting Standards Board. Research Report. *Service Efforts and Accomplishments Reporting: Its Time Has Come* (Norwalk, Conn.; GASB, 1990), Exhibit 8–1.

for current reform efforts are uncertain, improvements in budgeting could make an important contribution to more efficient and accountable government.

Fortunately, many governments have improved their budgeting practices over the past decade. A major impetus for this improvement has been the Government Finance Officers Association's Distinguished Budget Presentation Awards Program. Voluntary applications for this award increased from 113 in 1984, the year the program was initiated, to 691 in 1993. About 80 percent of the applicants have received the award and many of the unsuccessful applicants received confidential reviewer suggestions that permitted them to subsequently qualify for the award. Program improvements made in 1994 are expected to further enhance the effectiveness of this program.

Selected References

American Institute of Certified Public Accountants. *Audit and Accounting Guide. Audits of State and Local Governmental Units*. Revised. New York, 1993.

Fernandes, Peter P., and Myriam P. Laberge. "Setting Local Government Priorities through the Budget Process." *Government Finance Review* April 1986, pp. 21–27.

Governmental Accounting Standards Board. *Codification of Governmental Accounting and Financial Reporting Standards as of June 30, 1993*. Norwalk, Conn., 1993.

Kline, James J. "Total Quality Management in Local Government." *Government Finance Review*. August 1992, pp. 7–11.

Lee, Robert D. Jr. "Developments in State Budgeting: Trends of Two Decades." *Public Administration Review*. May/June 1991, pp. 254–62.

O'Toole, Daniel E., and Brian Stipak. "Patterns and Trends in Budget Format Innovation among Local Governments." *Public Budgeting and Finance* 4, no. 2 (Summer 1992), pp. 287–309.

Riordan, Timothy H., Maria E. Oria, and Joseph P. Tuss. "The Bridge from Dreams to Realities: Dayton's Capital Allocation Process." *Government Finance Review*, April 1987, pp. 7–13.

Robinson, Ann, and Bengt-Christer Ysander. "Re-Establishing Budgetary Flexibility." *Public Budgeting and Finance* 2, no. 3 (Autumn 1982), pp. 21–34.

Questions

16–1. "If a governmental unit is required by state law to prepare an annual budget for its General Fund, for all of its special revenue funds, and, after following all procedures required by laws, enact the budget as legally binding on administrators of the governmental unit, the administrators should use the legally enacted budget for all management purposes." Do you agree? Explain your answer.

16–2. Explain the interrelation among the processes of policy setting, service delivery, evaluation, and budgeting that should exist in a governmental unit.

16–3. If governmental budgets should be prepared to facilitate management of resources, why should the budget documents be subjected to study by individual taxpayers, reporters, and public interest groups, as well as by legislative bodies?

16–4. Explain the costs and benefits of performance budgeting compared with incremental budgeting.

16–5. Explain the costs and benefits of a planning-programming-budgeting system (PPBS) compared with performance budgeting.

16–6. "Every rational budgeting approach that has been experimented with by governments has been a failure." Do you agree or disagree with this statement? Explain fully.

16–7. What advantages does total quality management (TQM) offer compared with rational budgeting approaches? Is it fundamentally a budgeting approach?

16–8. What are some of the factors to be taken into account in preparing revenue estimates for inclusion in a budget?

16–9. Why should budgets for capital expenditures be prepared for several years beyond the operating budget year, even though the total amount is not to be appropriated for the operating budget year?

16–10. Some cities include in their capital budgets nonfinancial information on capital assets such as physical measures, the service condition of capital assets, and estimated repair and replacement schedules. For what purposes is such information useful?

16–11. Assuming the typical governmental budget is a collection of departmental budgets, each of which shows only the department's requested appropriation for personal services, materials and supplies, and capital outlays, specify the advantages and disadvantages each of the following groups should find if a city were to convert to a program budget:

    a. The city's central administration.

    b. The city's departmental administrators.

    c. The city's legislative body.

    d. The city's taxpayers.

16–12. Why is a good cost accounting system an important component of rational budgeting?

Exercises and Problems

16–1. Obtain a copy of a recent operating budget document of a governmental unit.* Follow the instructions below.

    a. Familiarize yourself with the organization of the operating budget document; read the letter of transmittal or any narrative that accompanies the budgets.

        Budgetary practices may differ from the GAAP reporting model as to *basis, timing, perspective, and entity*. GASB standards (Codification Section 2400.113–.122) define these differences as:

Basis differences arising through the employment of a basis of accounting for budgetary purposes that differs from the basis of accounting applicable to the fund type when reporting on the operations in accordance with GAAP.

Timing differences that can result in significant variances between budgetary practices and GAAP may include continuing appropriations, project appropriations, automatic reappropriations, and biennial budgeting.

Perspective differences resulting from the structure of financial information for budgetary purposes. The perspectives used for budgetary purposes include fund structure, and organizational structure, or program structure. In addition, some subsidiary perspective, such as nature of revenue source, special projects, or capital and operating budgets, may also be used. The fund structure and individual fund definitions establish which assets, liabilities, equities, and revenue and expenditure/expense flows are accounted for in a fund. In the traditional view, budgeting, accounting, financial reporting, and auditing would follow the fund perspective.

Entity differences are the fourth possible type of difference. Frequently, an "appropriated budget" may either include or exclude organizations, programs, activities, and functions that may or may not be compatible with the criteria defining the governmental reporting entity.

    Answer the following questions, which aid in assessing the quality of the budget document you are reviewing.†

    Policy Document: Does the operating budget you are reviewing include a coherent statement of organizationwide financial and programmatic policies and goals that address

---

* The footnote of Exercise 1–1 suggested that you attempt to obtain an operating budget document from the entity whose CAFR you analyzed for Exercises 1–1 through 13–1. If this was not possible, write the Budget Officer of the city, town, or county of your choice and request a copy of the most recent available operating budget document.

† These questions are paraphrased from the awards criteria established by the Government Finance Officers Association for its Distinguished Budget Presentation Awards Program. Questions are arranged under the four key categories included in the award criteria: **Policy Document, Financial Plan, Operations Guide,** and **Communication Device.**

long-term concerns and issues? Does the operating budget document describe the organization's short-term financial and operational policies that guide budget development for the upcoming year? Does the budget document include a coherent statement of goals and objectives of organizational units (e.g., departments, divisions, offices, or programs)? Does the document include a budget message that articulates priorities and issues for the budget for the new year and describes significant changes in priorities from the current year, and the factors producing those changes?

Financial Plan: Does the operating budget document include and describe all funds that are subject to appropriation? Does the document present a summary of major revenues and expenditures, as well as other financing sources and uses? Does the document include summaries of revenues, and other resources, and of expenditures for prior-year actual, current-year budget and/or estimated current-year actual, and proposed budget year? Are major revenue sources described? Are the underlying assumptions for revenue estimates and significant revenue trends explained? Does the document include projected changes in fund balances for governmental funds included in the budget presentation, including all balances potentially available for appropriation?

Does the budget document include budgeted capital expenditures and a list of major capital projects (even if these are authorized in a separate capital budget)? Does the document describe if, and to what extent, capital improvements or other major capital spending will impact the entity's current and future operating budget? Are financial data on current debt obligations provided, describing the relationship between current debt levels and legal debt limits, and explaining the effects of existing debt levels on current and future operations. Is the basis of budgeting explained for all funds, whether GAAP, cash, modified accrual, or some other basis?

Operations Guide: Does the operating budget document describe activities, services, or functions carried out by organizational units? Are objective methods (quantitative and/or qualitative) of measurement of results provided by unit or program? (Information on results should be provided for prior-year actual, current-year budget, and/or estimate, and budget year.) Does the budget document include an organizational chart for the entire organization? Is a schedule(s) or summary table(s) provided giving personnel or position counts for prior, current, and budget years, including descriptions of significant changes in levels of staffing or reorganizations planned for the budget year?

Communication Device: Does the operating budget document provide summary information, including an overview of significant budgetary issues, trends, and resource choices? Does the budget document explain the effect, if any, of other planning processes (e.g., strategic plans, long-range plans, capital improvement plans) upon the budget and budget process? Is the process used to prepare, review, adopt, and amend the budget explained? If a separate capital budget is prepared, is a description provided of the process by which it is prepared and how it relates to the operating budget? Are charts and graphs used, where appropriate, to highlight financial and statistical information? Is narrative information provided when the messages conveyed by the charts and graphs are not self-evident? Does the document provide narrative, tables, schedules, crosswalks or matrices to show the relationship between different revenue and expenditure classifications (e.g., funds, programs, organization units)? Is a table of contents provided to make it easy to locate information in the document? Is there a glossary to define terms (including abbreviations and acronyms) that are not readily understood by a reasonably informed lay reader? Does the document include statistical and supplemental data that describe the organization and the community of population it serves, and provide other pertinent background information related to services provided? Finally, is the document printed and formatted in such a way to enhance understanding and utility of the document to a lay reader? Is it attractive, consistent, and oriented to the reader's needs?

16–2. Write the numbers 1 through 10 on a sheet of paper. Beside each number write the letter corresponding with the best answer to each of the following questions.

1. The GASB *Budgeting, Budgetary Control, and Budgetary Reporting* Principle provides that:
   a. An annual budget should be adopted for every *governmental* fund type of a governmental unit.
   b. An annual budget should be adopted by every governmental unit.
   c. Budgetary comparisons should be included in the appropriate financial statements and schedules for governmental funds for which an annual budget has been adopted.
   d. Both *b* and *c* are correct.

2. Which of the following is *not* considered a "rational" budgeting approach?
   a. Incremental budgeting.
   b. Performance budgeting.
   c. Progam budgeting.
   d. PPBS.

3. Which of the following budgeting approaches focuses mainly on relating work activity outputs to resource inputs?
   a. Incremental (line-item) budgeting.
   b. Performance budgeting.
   c. Program budgeting.
   d. PPBS.

4. Which of the following budgeting approaches requires formulation of the governmental unit's fundamental objectives and identification and evaluation of alternative ways of achieving objectives?
   a. Incremental (line-item) budgeting.
   b. Performance budgeting.
   c. Program budgeting.
   d. PPBS.

5. Which of the following steps would *not* usually be part of the budgeting process?
   a. Heads of operating departments prepare budget requests.
   b. Budget officer and other central administrators review and make adjustments to departmental requests.
   c. One or more public budget hearings are held.
   d. The Chief Executive (Mayor or City Manager, as appropriate) formally adopts the budget, thus giving it the force of law.

6. Which of the following kinds of information is useful for effective capital budgeting?
   a. A multiple-year forecast of needed capital improvements and proposed means of financing them.
   b. Physical measures of the service condition of plant assets.
   c. Estimated replacement costs to replace plant assets.
   d. All of the above are useful for capital budgeting.

7. Which of the following budgeting approaches is most consistent with total quality management (TQM)?
   a. Incremental (line-item) budgeting.
   b. Performance budgeting.
   c. Program budgeting.
   d. PPBS.

8. Measurement of *efficiency* requires that:
   a. Inputs be related to outputs.
   b. Inputs be related to outcomes.
   c. Outputs be related to outcomes.
   d. Dollar cost of inputs be related to quantities of inputs.

9. Which of the following is the central focus of a TQM system?
   a. Measuring productivity and quality improvement.
   b. Rewarding employees for productivity and quality achievement.
   c. Obtaining the support and commitment of top-level officials.
   d. Continuously meeting or exceeding customer expectations.

10. Measures of service accomplishments include:
    a. Input measures.
    b. Output measures.
    c. Outcome measures.
    d. Both *b* and *c*.

16–3. A portion of the General Fund operating budget for the City of Belton, Texas, Street Department is shown below and on the following two pages.

Required   After reading and evaluating the budget information for the Street Department of the City of Belton, answer the following questions:

1. Does the City of Belton appear to be using program budgeting? If not, what form of budgeting is the City using?
2. Does the budget provide information useful for evaluating the performance of the Street Department's management?
3. Do the goals established for the Street Department appear appropriate? How could they be improved?

CITY OF BELTON   GENERAL FUND
ANNUAL BUDGET   DESCRIPTION
FY 1992–1993   STREETS

DEPARTMENT DESCRIPTION
The Street Department is responsible for maintaining all City owned streets, alleys and parking lots, keeping them in serviceable condition to ensure the safety and welfare of the public. Activities include repairing damage caused by waterline breaks; repairing potholes and patching utility cuts; repairing base failures; preparing street driving surfaces for annual seal coating program; reconstructing streets to upgrade driving surface and drainage to meet increased traffic volumes; cleaning and repairing drainage ditches and structures; inspecting and making repairs to City bridges and sidewalks; performing annual crack sealing to prevent water damage to driving surface of streets; performing traffic counts on an as-needed basis; installing and maintaining traffic control signs and paving markings; responding to emergency conditions by barricading, sandbagging, clearing of fallen trees and debris from streets and drainage structures, and sanding of streets during icing conditions; mowing rights-of-way and maintaining street and alley shoulders; installing and maintaining street name signs; and assisting other departments as needed.

CITY OF BELTON
ANNUAL BUDGET
FY 1992–1993 *(continued)*

GENERAL FUND
DEPARTMENTAL GOALS
STREETS

Expenditure Summary

Classification	90–91 Actual	91–92 Budget	91–92 Estimated	92–93 Budget
Personnel	$208,023	$226,748	$221,648	$212,959
Supplies	12,161	11,714	11,740	12,100
Maintenance	30,687	77,686	77,374	71,925
Services	87,961	81,145	79,967	65,115
Special Services	0	0	0	0
Capital Outlay	31,927	2,500	34,309	2,500
Total	$370,759	$399,793	$425,038	$364,599

Staffing

Position	Number
Superintendent	1
Assistant superintendent	1
Crew leader	1
Equipment operator	3
Equipment operator	2
Total	8

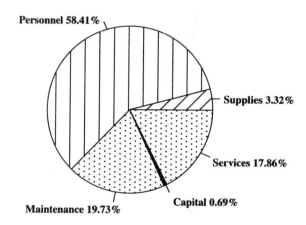

Personnel 58.41%
Supplies 3.32%
Services 17.86%
Capital 0.69%
Maintenance 19.73%

Department Goals

Increase the number of repairs for old utility cuts, upgrade the street driving surface, and prevent future water damage.

Pursue an aggressive weed and grass control program within street gutters, rights-of-way, and behind curbs.

Increase miles of street shoulder repairs to prevent pavement breaking and erosion.

Replace existing noncompliance yield signs with stop signs.

Increase work-hours spent on trimming overhanging limbs and brush in and over streets.

Indicators

Measurement	90–91 Actual	91–92 Estimated	92–93 Proposed
Traffic and street signs	84	159	175
Miles of streets maintained	66	70	70
Square yards of seal coating	42,500	44,800	42,500
Number of utility cuts	136	155	250
Miles of R.O.W. mowing	34	172	172
Tons of asphalt for potholes	84	102	175
Tons of asphalt for street leveling	66	40	100

CITY OF BELTON
ANNUAL BUDGET
FY 1992–1993 (*concluded*)

GENERAL FUND
EXPENDITURES
STREETS

Measurement	90–91 Actual	91–92 Estimated	92–93 Proposed
Feet of drainage ditches cleared	3,350	3,750	4,250
Feet of street shoulder bladed	4,150	5,275	6,000
Square yards of sidewalks repaired	40	65	150
Feet of weed control on streets	12,500	16,750	18,000
Miles of streets cleaned	10	19	76

Streets

Account Number	Account Description	FY 90–91 Actual	FY 91–92 Budget	FY 91–92 Estimated	FY 92–93 Budget
01-08-00-0101	Salaries—Administrative	$ 4,827.90	$ 4,910.00	$ 4,910.00	$ 4,910.00
01-08-00-0102	Salaries—Division and operations	29,333.37	29,834.00	29,834.00	36,617.00
01-08-00-0103	Salaries—Supervisory	67,951.32	70,081.00	53,606.00	35,566.00
01-08-00-0104	Salaries—Skilled and craft	42,957.99	42,944.00	55,175.00	69,443.00
01-08-00-0107	Salaries—OVERTIME	6,584.77	6,854.00	7,604.00	6,500.00
01-08-00-0108	Part-time and hourly	0	1,800.00	0	0
01-08-00-0116	TMRS retirement	12,159.21	11,847.00	12,169.00	11,665.00
01-08-00-0117	Employer's FICA	11,249.99	11,581.00	11,208.00	11,707.00
01-08-00-0118	Hospitalization insurance	12,203.21	13,532.00	13,090.00	15,544.00
01-08-00-0119	Workmen's compensation insurance	20,351.76	32,987.00	33,941.00	19,911.00
01-08-00-0120	Unemployment Compensation	403.38	378.00	111.00	1,096.00
	Total Personnel	**$208,022.90**	**$226,748.00**	**$221,648.00**	**$212,959.00**
01-08-00-0210	Chemical supplies	$ 760.95	$ 250.00	$ 0	$ 1,500.00
01-08-00-0220	Clothing supplies	1,638.28	2,164.00	1,520.00	1,600.00
01-08-00-0260	General office supplies	14.79	50.00	6.00	25.00
01-08-00-0270	Janitorial supplies	143.43	50.00	72.00	75.00
01-08-00-0280	Minor tools	609.32	300.00	496.00	400.00
01-08-00-0285	Fuel and vehicle supplies	8,450.60	8,500.00	8,783.00	8,000.00
01-08-00-0290	Other supplies	543.74	400.00	863.00	500.00
	Total Supplies	**$ 12,161.11**	**$ 11,714.00**	**$ 11,740.00**	**$ 12,100.00**
01-08-00-0302	Building maintenance	$ 0	$ 50.00	$ 93.00	$ 50.00
01-08-00-0304	Street maintenance	17,520.75	20,950.00	20,950.00	18,950.00
01-08-00-0305	Seal coating and overlays	0	35,488.00	35,488.00	35,275.00
01-08-00-0306	Sidewalks	5,085.75	1,048.00	1,048.00	1,000.00
01-08-00-0307	Street sweeping	0	10,500.00	10,500.00	8,500.00
01-08-00-0401	Heating and air conditioning maintenance	60.00	50.00	225.00	50.00
01-08-00-0420	Machine tools, etc. maintenance	1,928.05	1,500.00	1,978.00	1,500.00
01-08-00-0430	Motor vehicle maintenance	2,519.91	5,000.00	5,000.00	3,500.00
01-08-00-0460	Radio maintenance	0	100.00	0	100.00
01-08-00-0480	Signs	3,572.24	3,000.00	2,092.00	3,000.00
	Total Maintenance	**$ 30,686.70**	**$ 77,686.00**	**$ 77,374.00**	**$ 71,925.00**

16–4. The budget for the State's Attorney's Office of an urban county consists of two portions, reproduced below and on the following page: the Program and Performance section and the Program Appropriation Statement.

Required Assume you are a member of the County legislative body who is reviewing the budget in order to determine whether you will vote for or against its adoption. In what respects is the presentation helpful to you? What additional information or alternative presentation, if any, would you want before you voted? Why?

CRIMINAL PROSECUTION   STATE'S ATTORNEY
09 01

Program and Performance: This program includes the Circuit Court, District Court, Felony Complaint Investigation, Victim/Witness, and Juvenile Divisions of the State's Attorney's Office, which investigate, screen, prepare charging documents, and prepare and prosecute all felony, misdemeanor and juvenile cases before the Circuit Court and District Courts of _____ County. This includes presentation of cases to the Grand Jury and representing the State in bail hearings, writs of habeas corpus, post-convictions, violations of probation, extraditions, and related matters in _____ County. It also includes coordination with State's witnesses through the Victim/Witness Unit.

Workload figures are as follows:

	Actual FY 19x5	*Current FY 19x6*	*Projected FY 19x7*
Circuit court defendants disposed	3,518	4,200	5,000
District court defendants disposed	16,584	17,000	18,000
Juvenile respondents disposed	1,493	1,700	1,800
Felonies screened	1,980	2,250	2,500

Personnel Summary	*Actual FY 19x5*	*Appropriated FY 19x6*	*Budget FY 19x7*
Authorized Positions—Full Time	60	63	64
Authorized Positions—Part Time/Temporary	—	—	—
Man-Years of Performance	60	62³/12	63⁹/12

Appropriation Ordinance Text: Criminal Prosecution
01 09 01 General Fund Appropriation $1,868,020

PROGRAM APPROPRIATION STATEMENT

09-01   STATE'S ATTORNEY   CRIMINAL PROSECUTION

	Description	Actual FY 19x5	Appropriated FY 19x6	Budget FY 19x7
01	Personal Services	$1,444,873	$1,581,952	$1,736,967
02	Travel	32,999	35,586	39,586
03	Contractual Services	4,929	7,035	10,740
04	Rents and Utilities	21,076	20,800	25,180
05	Supplies and Materials	21,540	17,758	20,200
06	Equipment Maintenance	5,352	5,689	6,095
08	Other Charges	9,216	15,112	16,112
10	Equipment Replacement	4,021	2,297	—
11	Equipment Additional	14,955	2,760	13,140
	Expenditure Totals	$1,558,961	$1,688,989	$1,868,020
	Original General Fund Appropriation	$1,580,217	$1,688,989	$1,868,020
	General Fund Appropriation Transfer Supplement	−7,000	—	—
	Adjusted General Fund Appropriation	1,573,217	1,688,989	1,868,020
	Total Expenditure Authorization	1,573,217	1,688,989	1,868,020
	Less: Unexpended Balance	−14,256	—	—
	Expenditure Totals	$1,558,961	$1,688,989	$1,868,020

16–5. The budget for the General Fund of a small city contains several pages which present the budget for each program of the fire department: fire administration, fire equipment maintenance, fire prevention, fire suppression, and fire communication. The section presenting the budget for the fire suppression program is shown below. All other sections for the fire department—and all other departments whose activities are budgeted for by the General Fund—are similar in format and content.

Required   Assume that you are a member of the City Council who is reviewing the budget in order to determine whether you will vote for or against its adoption. In what respects is the presentation helpful to you? What additional information or alternative presentation, if any, would you want before you voted? Why?

FIRE SUPPRESSION

Goal:
To have available fully trained emergency crews who are able to respond quickly to any area in the City. Major activities include:

1. Active fire suppression.
2. Emergency situation response.
3. Training.

Objectives:
1. Maintain response time to any area in the City at three minutes.
2. Respond to an anticipated 3,800 emergency calls.
3. Improve personnel proficiency by increasing training from two to four hours per shift.

Resource summary:

	Budgeted 19x5	Requested 19x6	Approved 19x6
Salaries	$3,631,343	$3,663,132	$3,892,898
Operating expenses	87,629	89,989	89,589
Capital outlay	24,500	50,495	30,455
Total Program Resources	$3,743,472	$3,803,616	$4,012,942
Department Total	4,334,190	4,502,123	4,671,593
Permanent employees	124	124	124
Uniformed	124	124	124
Civilian	0	0	0

Program Review:

Approved capital outlay consists of general replacement, training items, and emergency equipment such as resuscitators and Laerdal bag masks.

16–6. The police chief of the Town of Parkridge submitted the following budget request for the Police Department for the forthcoming budget year 19x4–x5.

Item	Actual 19x2–x3	Budget 19x3–x4	Forecast 19x3–x4	Budget 19x4–x5
Personnel	$1,051,938	$1,098,245	$1,112,601	$1,182,175
Supplies	44,442	61,971	60,643	64,450
Maintenance	47,163	45,310	46,139	47,422
Miscellaneous	34,213	36,272	32,198	37,723
Capital outlay	65,788	69,433	67,371	102,210
Totals	$1,243,544	$1,311,231	$1,318,952	$1,433,980

Upon questioning by the newly appointed Town Manager, a recent Masters of Public Administration graduate from a nearby university, the Police Chief explained that he had determined the amounts in the budget request by multiplying the prior year's budget amount by 1.04 (to allow for the expected inflation rate of 4 percent). In addition, the personnel category includes a request for a new uniformed officer at an estimated $40,000 for salary, payroll expenses, and fringe benefits. Capital outlay includes a request for a new patrol vehicle at an estimated cost of $30,000. The amount of $300 was added to the Maintenance category for estimated maintenance on the new vehicle. The Police Chief is strongly resisting instructions from the Town Manager that he justify not only the need for the new uniformed position and additional vehicle but also the need for the *existing* level of resources in each category. The Town Manager has stated he will not request any increase in the Police Department's budget unless adequate justification is provided.

Required

1. Evaluate the strengths and weaknesses of the Police Chief's argument that his budget request is reasonable.
2. Are the Town Manager's instructions reasonable? Explain.
3. Would the Town Council likely support the Town Manager or the Police Chief in this dispute, assuming the Police Chief might take his case directly to the Town Council?
4. What other improvements could be made to the Town's budgeting procedures?

Continuous Problems

16–L. There is no City of Bingham problem for this chapter.

16–S. The following budget for the General Fund of the City of Smithville was legally adopted for the calendar year 19y1.

Appropriations:	
General Government	$ 326,000
Public Safety:	
Police	624,200
Fire	609,800
Building Safety	57,600
Public Works	501,400
Health and Welfare	353,500
Parks and Recreation	270,000
Contributions	278,000
Miscellaneous	39,500
Total Appropriations	$3,060,000

The City of Smithville's Director of Finance wishes to develop a program budget for internal management purposes. The following program categories and subcategories are to be used:

1000 Transportation
  1100 Planning
  1200 Street Construction and
      Maintenance
  1300 Parking
  1400 Sidewalks
  1500 Traffic Control

2000 Physical Environment and
      Economic Base
  2100 Planning and Design
  2200 Landscaping
  2300 Noise Abatement

3000 Health, Safety, and General
      Well-Being
  3100 Public Health
  3200 Animal Control
  3300 Crime Prevention
  3400 Building and Housing
      Inspection
  3500 Ambulance Service and
      Rescue Calls
  3600 Aids to Individuals and
      Groups

4000 Cultural and Recreational
  4100 Parks Maintenance
  4200 Swimming Pools
  4300 Tennis
  4400 Baseball
  4500 Other Group Programs

5000 Services to Property
  5100 Fire Protection
  5200 Theft and Vandalism Protection
  5300 Water Supply and Treatment
  5400 Water Distribution
  5500 Sanitary Sewer Collection and
      Treatment
  5600 Solid Waste Collection and
      Disposal

6000 General Management and Support
  6100 Legislative and Legal
  6200 Administration
  6300 Accounting and Budget
  6400 Personnel
  6500 Data Processing
  6600 Purchasing

Analysis of departmental budgets, and consultations with department heads, indicate the departmental appropriations budgets should be charged to program subcategories as shown below. Before distributing any departmental budget to program subcategories, distribute the Contributions appropriation to the departments in the following percentages:

Department	Percentage
General Government	15
Public Safety—Police	32
Public Safety—Fire	29
Public Safety—Building Safety	3
Public Works	16
Health and Welfare	3
Parks and Recreation	2

Distribution of departmental budgets to program subcategories:

General Government

Program	Percentage
1100	5
2100	5
2300	3
6100	15
6200	30
6300	18
6400	9
6500	10
6600	5

Public Works

Program	Percentage
1100	1
1200	70
1300	1
1400	2
2100	1
2200	15
5600	10

Public Safety—Police

Program	Percentage
1300	2
1500	43
3300	25
5100	3
5200	27

Public Safety—Fire

Program	Percentage
3500	5
5100	95

Parks and Recreation

Program	Percentage
2200	5
4100	40
4200	15
4300	5
4400	5
4500	30

Health and Welfare

Program	Percentage
3100	30
3200	10
3500	10
3600	50

Public Safety—Building Safety

Program	Percentage
3400	100

Miscellaneous

Program	Percentage
1100	10
2100	10
2300	10
5600	10
6100	10
6200	50

You are required to determine the budget for the Physical Environment and Economic Base program; show the budget for each of the subcategories within that program.

CHAPTER 17

Planning and Control of Cash and Temporary Investments

The evolution of rational budgeting approaches and, more recently, governments' experimentation with total quality management (TQM) and service efforts and accomplishments (SEA) reporting, were discussed in Chapter 16. Motivating these experiments, of course, is the objective of improving government performance through better management of resources. Efficient and effective management of cash and investments is an important aspect of improving overall resource management. Sound cash management ensures maximum availability of cash to meet operating liquidity needs and reduces the need for short-term borrowing. Sound management of temporary investments maximizes investment yield consistent with acceptable risk. Cash management and investment management are closely related activities, with cash representing both the input and output of the investment process. Both activities involve considerable risks that require well-designed policies and operating procedures to safeguard and protect cash and investments. Key aspects of managing cash and temporary investments, as well as internal control procedures for safeguarding cash and investments, are discussed in this chapter.

Cash Management

Cash flows of a governmental entity arise from its operating activities and from borrowing, grants and other intergovernmental transfers, private gifts, and sale of investments and other assets. This chapter focuses mainly on the government's operating activities, represented by its **operating cycle.** As shown in Illustration 17–1, the operating cycle involves forecasts of cash flows, collection of revenues, investment of excess cash, tracking the performance and security of investments, making disbursements for various purposes, and monitoring, evaluating, and auditing cash flows.

The cash management system should be designed to operate within the context of the overall financial management and operating systems of the government. As such, objectives for the cash management system should be consistent

ILLUSTRATION 17–1   The Cash Management Process

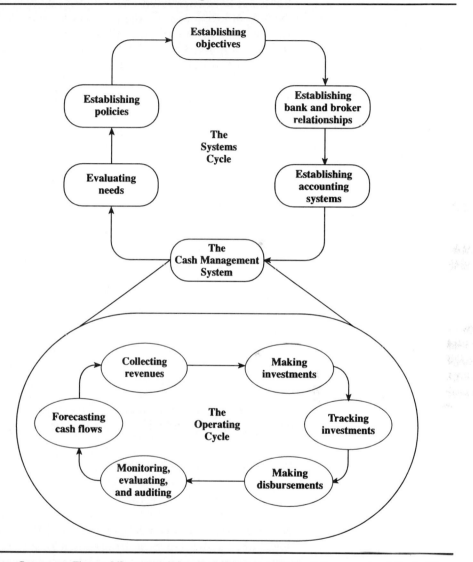

SOURCE: Government Finance Officers Association, *Cash Management for Small Governments*, ed. Ian J. Allan (Chicago: GFOA, 1989), Exhibit 1–4. Reprinted with permission of the Government Finance Officers Association.

with program objectives and contribute to their attainment. Objectives for cash management are usually stated in terms of availability of minimum balances to meet liquidity needs, yield, or return on investments of idle cash, and timing of collections and disbursements. Availability of minimum balances may be expressed as average days of cash on hand or percentage of budgeted cash outflows for a period such as a month. Expected or budgeted yield or return on investments of idle cash is determined, in part, by the governmental entity's policies for short-term investment of idle cash and its contractual arrangements with depository financial institutions (see Illustration 17–1). Actual yields for a period may be contractually fixed for investments such as deposits with depository institutions and repurchase agreements, but vary with market yields for other investments such as U.S. Government securities. Finally, effective policies for cash collections and disbursements are required to ensure revenues and other monies are collected as quickly as legally permissible and that obligations are paid when due but not before that date, except to take advantage of cash discounts for early payment.

Cash Planning and Budgeting

In Chapters 3, 4, and 16, it was assumed that, for the purposes described, Revenues and Expenditures budgets would best be prepared on the same basis as the accounts and financial reports: modified accrual, in the case of governmental funds—particularly general funds and special revenue funds. Although it is highly desirable for persons concerned with the financial management of governmental units (or any other organization) to foresee the effects of operating plans and capital improvement plans on receivables, payables, inventories, and facilities, it is absolutely necessary to foresee the effects on cash. An organization must have sufficient cash to pay employees, suppliers, and creditors amounts due at the times due, or it risks labor troubles, an unsatisfactory credit rating, and consequent difficulties in maintaining its capacity to render services at acceptable levels to its residents. An organization that maintains cash balances in excess of needs fails to earn interest on temporary investments; therefore, it is raising more revenues than would otherwise be needed, or failing to offer services.

Cash Receipts Budgeting

In Chapter 4 it was noted, that in a typical governmental unit, cash receipts from major sources of revenues of general funds and special revenue funds are concentrated in a few months of each fiscal year, whereas cash disbursements tend to be approximately level month by month. Under the heading "Tax Anticipation Notes Payable" in Chapter 4, reference is made to cash forecasting done by the Treasurer of the Town of Brighton in order to determine the amount of tax anticipation notes to be issued. The cash forecasting method illustrated in that chapter is quite crude but often reasonably effective if done by experienced persons. Sophisticated cash budgeting methods used in well-managed governmental units require additional data, such as historical records of monthly collections from each revenue source including percentage of billings, where applicable. In addition to the historical record of collections, the budget files should contain analyses of the factors affecting the collections from each source, so that adjustments to historical patterns may be made, if needed, for the budget year. For example, in the Town of Brighton illustrative case in Chapter 4, the revenue budget of the General Fund for 19y1 is:

Property taxes	$2,600,000
Interest and penalties on delinquent taxes	13,000
Sales taxes	480,000
Licenses and permits	220,000
Fines and forfeits	308,000
Intergovernmental revenue	280,000
Charges for services	70,000
Miscellaneous revenues	15,000
Total	$3,986,000

As illustrated in Chapter 4, the revenues budget is currently prepared on the modified accrual basis: those revenues susceptible to accrual are budgeted on the accrual basis. Property taxes, interest and penalties on delinquent taxes, and some items in the miscellaneous category are to be recognized as revenue when billed; the same would be true (although not specifically illustrated in Chapter 4) of regularly billed charges for inspection or other routinely provided services. Most intergovernmental revenues also may become measurable and available prior to collection; therefore, they may be accrued. Sales taxes and income taxes also may be accrued in instances in which taxpayer liability has been established and collectibility can be estimated with reasonable accuracy. Revenues expected from licenses and permits, fines and forfeits, charges for services, and items in the miscellaneous revenue category are usually budgeted (and recognized as revenue during the year) on the cash basis because the items ordinarily are not measurable in advance of collection. The only problem presented by the latter group of revenue sources in converting the revenues budget to a cash receipts budget is the forecast of how much revenue from each source will be collected during each month of the budget year. That is the primary problem, also, presented by converting the accrual-based estimated revenues to the cash basis for cash budgeting purposes.

Additional problems arise of forecasting how much of the billed receivables will be collected in the year(s) following the one in which they are to be recognized as revenue, and how much of the billed receivables will probably never be collected. For example, in Chapter 4 (see Transaction 7) it is estimated that 4 percent of the property taxes billed will never be collected; therefore, in order to realize revenue of $2,600,000 it is necessary to levy taxes totaling $2,708,333. Assuming the tax bills are mailed to the taxpayers in March of each year, and taxpayers are required to pay half of their taxes no later than the first Monday in May and the remaining half no later than the first Monday in November, the historical collection experience, adjusted for economic conditions expected to affect owners of property in the Town of Brighton in 19y1, gives the following expected pattern of collection of taxes billed in 19y1 (note that approximately 1 percent of the tax bills are paid in February before the bills are prepared and mailed; it is common for a few people who expect to be out of town during the late spring to have the

Treasurer compute their bills early so they can pay their taxes before they leave):

January 19y1	0.0%	August 19y1	1.5%
February 19y1	1.0	September 19y1	1.5
March 19y1	2.0	October 19y1	5.0
April 19y1	10.0	November 19y1	22.0
May 19y1	30.0	December 19y1	3.0
June 19y1	1.0	January 19y2 and later	18.0
July 19y1	1.0	Uncollectible	4.0

In accord with the above schedule, collections from the gross levy of $2,708,333 would be budgeted as (rounded to the nearest hundred dollars):

January 19y1	$ 0	August 19y1	$ 40,600
February 19y1	27,100	September 19y1	40,600
March 19y1	54,200	October 19y1	135,400
April 19y1	270,800	November 19y1	595,800
May 19y1	812,500	December 19y1	81,200
June 19y1	27,100	January 19y2 and later	487,600
July 19y1	27,100	Total collectible	$2,600,000

In addition to collections of 19y1 revenues, the monthly cash budget of the Town of Brighton should include anticipated collections of receivables existing at the beginning of 19y1 (Taxes Receivable—Delinquent, $660,000, and Interest and Penalties Receivable on Taxes, $13,200). Therefore, the total monthly Cash Receipts budget would be the sum of the amount expected to be collected each month from receivables as of the beginning of the year, revenues budgeted on the accrual basis, and revenues budgeted on the cash basis.

Cash Disbursements Budgeting

Except for special provisions regarding expenditures of debt service funds, the expenditures of all other governmental funds (and of all proprietary funds) are to be recognized and budgeted on the full accrual basis. Therefore, the conversion of the approved appropriations budget (which is the legal authorization to incur liabilities for purposes and amounts specified in the appropriations bill or ordinance) into a cash disbursements budget involves a knowledge of personnel policies, purchasing policies, and operating policies and plans, which should govern the timing of expenditures of appropriations, and the consequent payment of liabilities. Information as to current and previous typical time intervals between the ordering of goods and contractual services, their receipt, and the related disbursements should be available from the appropriation expenditures ledgers and cash disbursement records. In the case of salaries and wages of governmental employees, the cash disbursements budget for each month is affected by the number of paydays that fall in the month, rather than the number of working days in the month.

As an example of cash disbursements budgeting, in the Town of Brighton illustrative case in Chapter 4 the 19y1 appropriation for Public Safety is $1,240,000. No further detail is given in Chapter 4 as to the organization units, functions, activities, or other classifications of expenditures authorized under the Public Safety heading. Assume detail provided in the appropriation ordinance includes the Fire Department under the Public Safety heading and specifically authorizes the Fire Department to incur expenditures in 19y1 for the following object classes in the amounts given:

	Budget for 19y1
Personal services	$408,960
Contractual services	44,400
Supplies	36,720
Capital outlays	118,640
Total Fire Department	$608,720

The appropriations budget may have provided for additional personnel to be added on completion of a new fire station, or on some other event expected to occur during the budget year, for promotions, retirements, changes in base pay, or a number of other events that need to be provided for in the legal appropriations but may not actually cause cash outlays during the budget year in the authorized amounts. The cash disbursements budget is a management tool, not a legal document; therefore, it should be prepared on the basis of what is actually expected to happen. If the Town of Brighton Fire Department is expected to be fully staffed with persons at the ranks and salaries specified in the appropriation, and if the personnel are paid every two weeks (26 paydays per year), the monthly cash disbursements for personal services would be $31,460 for each month in which two paydays occur, but $47,190 for each month in which three paydays occur—ignoring such real-world complications as the fact that withholding taxes and other deductions from gross pay may not need to be remitted to the state and federal government in the same months in which paychecks are issued.

The cash disbursements budgets for contractual services, supplies, and capital outlays for the Town of Brighton Fire Department depend on when goods, services, and equipment are expected to be ordered, received, and paid for. Assume the plans of the Department, purchasing agents, and others concerned produce the following pattern of disbursements, in total, for the remaining three object classes of the Fire Department appropriation (contractual services, supplies, and capital outlays):

	Total		*Total*
January 19y1	$ 6,400	July 19y1	$ 5,300
February	5,600	August	6,300
March	5,800	September	114,200
April	7,200	October	5,400
May	16,460	November	6,200
June	5,300	December	6,600

Cash disbursements budgets must, of course, allow for the provision of cash required to pay liabilities expected to exist at the beginning of the budget year that will mature during the year; offsetting the payment of liabilities incurred prior to the budget year is the fact that not all goods and services ordered in the budget year will be received during that year, and some of those received are purchased under terms that will not require payment until the year following the budget year.

Forecasting Monthly Cash Surplus or Deficits

After monthly cash receipts budgets are prepared for all sources of revenues of each fund and cash disbursements budgets are prepared for all organization units, and so forth, it is possible, and desirable, to match the two in order to determine when and for how long cash balances will rise to unnecessarily high levels, or fall to levels below those prudent management would require (or even to overdraft positions). Note the preceding sentence is concerned with cash receipts and disbursements of all funds of a governmental unit, not a single fund. There is no reason for bank accounts and fund cash accounts to agree, except in total. Effective cash planning and control suggests that **all** cash be put under control of the Treasurer of the governmental unit. To illustrate this cash management concept, assume cash budgets of all funds of the Town of Brighton indicate that receipts and disbursements of 19y1 may be expected to have the relationships shown in Illustration 17–2, which appear to be self-explanatory. The operation of cash and investment pools is discussed in detail in Chapter 11.

Keeping the Cash Budget Realistic

In the preceding sections of this chapter, the illustrations are based on the assumption that cash receipts and cash disbursements should be budgeted for each month of the budget year. A very small governmental unit that has few receipts and infrequent disbursements may be able to plan temporary investments and short-term borrowings on the basis of cash budgets for periods longer than one month, perhaps quarterly or semiannually. Conversely, a governmental unit with considerable cash activity involving large sums might need to budget cash receipts and cash disbursements on a daily basis to maintain adequate, but not excessive, cash balances.

Budgeting, by definition, involves planning on the basis of assumptions about economic conditions, salary levels, numbers of employees at each salary level, prices of supplies and capital acquisitions, and other factors that cannot be foreseen with great accuracy. Accordingly, it is necessary at intervals throughout the year to compare actual receipts with budgeted receipts, source by source; and actual disbursements with budgeted disbursements for each organizational unit, function, and object; not only for the sake of control (cash control is discussed in the next section of this chapter) but for the sake of evaluating the budget and, if necessary, revising the budget in light of new knowledge about economic conditions, salary, and price levels, and other factors affecting collections and disbursements.

Cash Control

Because of its high state of liquidity and ease of transfer, cash occupies a preeminent position in the attention of accountants and auditors. Its usefulness to the rightful owners and its attractiveness to others cause it to be widely sought by means usually fair but sometimes foul. Furthermore, possibilities for honest mistakes are numerous in the receipt, custody, and disbursement of cash. Administrators, accountants, and auditors must be constantly alert in their endeavors that only fair or legal methods be used and that loss through error be reduced to a

ILLUSTRATION 17–2

TOWN OF BRIGHTON
Budgeted Cash Receipts and Disbursements for 19y1
(000 omitted)

	January	February	March	April	May	June	July	August	September	October	November	December
Balance, first of month	$ 610	$425	$435	$ 500	$ 695	$665	$479	$251	$296	$266	$ 201	$611
Expected receipts during month	165	250	295	570	1,096	134	280	370	285	270	892	116
Cash available	775	675	730	1,070	1,791	799	759	621	581	536	1,093	727
Expected disbursements during month	1,050	240	280	325	320	320	508	325	315	335	320	455
Provisional balance at end of month	(275)	435	450	745	1,471	479	251	296	266	201	773	272
Less: Temporary investments purchased	—	—	—	—	106	—	—	—	—	—	162	—
Less: Repayment of short-term borrowings	—	—	—	50	700	—	—	—	—	—	—	—
Add: Temporary investments sold	—	—	—	—	—	—	—	—	—	—	—	—
Add: Short-term borrowings	700	—	50	—	—	—	—	—	—	—	—	268
Balance at end of month	$ 425	$435	$500	$ 695	$ 665	$479	$251	$296	$266	$201	$ 611	$540

551

minimum. These observations are no less true of governmental cash than of that belonging to private individuals or enterprises. In fact, the greater separation in government of the ones who pay and the ones who spend, and the need for protection of those by whom government is financed, may constitute an even greater obligation for safeguarding public cash. Although parts of the following discussion are applicable to cash in general, special reference is intended to cash of governments.

Requirements for Adequate Cash Accounting

Some elements of desirable cash procedure pertain strictly to cash in one or another of its forms. Other elements may relate not only to cash but also to other financial aspects of the governmental unit concerned. As one example, some cash accounting procedures are closely related to accounting for revenue and expenditures, others to the reduction of noncash assets. It may be said that, in general, adequate cash control procedures must include the following:

1. Provision for determining, insofar as is reasonably possible, that the government receives all the cash to which it is legally entitled.
2. Accurate and complete accounting for cash received.
3. Adequate protection of cash between the time of receipt and the time of disbursement.
4. Provision for determining that the government disburses cash for all just debts when due.
5. Accurate and complete accounting for cash disbursed.

An indispensable element of good cash procedure, whatever other safeguards may exist, is a carefully planned and diligently applied system of internal control of the kind discussed in earlier chapters. In addition to the main scheme of internal control, numerous other techniques—such as the bonding of all employees handling cash and regular annual audits—serve to prevent or reveal irregularities; but detailed discussion of these precautions is not appropriate here.

Determining Whether All Cash that Ought to Be Received Is Received

One situation permitting a definite, clear-cut comparison between cash that should be received and cash actually received is found in the case of certain governmental revenue accounted for on the accrual basis. If one or more units or departments of government are charged with ascertaining and billing a given kind of revenue, whereas another department accounts for collection, the division of labor represents a very desirable form of control over cash. The best illustration of a situation such as the one described above is the prevailing practice and plan of handling the assessment, billing, and collection of property taxes. In one state, for example, assessing and billing are functions of the assessors' and auditors' offices, and collection rests with the treasurer. Because of direct and indirect checks on taxes reported as unpaid, the possibilities for the diversion of cash collected from taxpayers, without disclosure, is reduced to a minimum. Unfortunately, this control device cannot overcome defects in the assessment procedure that may undervalue property or entirely omit it from the basic inventory. However, this latter deficiency is more of a revenue problem than a cash problem.

Other forms of governmental revenue activity that lend themselves to the use of an accrual or semiaccrual basis are utility services, some kinds of licenses and permits, revenue from the use of money and property, and revenue from other agencies. Utility services are furnished on a contractual basis; and with the proper use of service, billing, and collection forms, a close degree of correlation between the amount due and the amount received is possible. Many kinds of licenses and permits are granted for privileges to operate at specified locations or within given areas, and failure to obtain a license or permit is readily ascertainable. Assuring that fees arising from licenses and permits will be accounted for is largely a matter of using prenumbered authorization forms, for which strict accounting must be made. Money and property are of such tangible nature that accrual of income for their use and receipt of cash from that source are readily ascertainable through record-keeping and the exercise of reasonable care. Also subject to exact verification are receipts from the sale of bonds, from the issuance of notes, and from special assessment levies.

Some forms of revenue do not lend themselves to the use of accrual accounting; but once having reached the realization stage, accurate accounting for the cash to be received is largely a matter of well-organized and well-administered procedures. Thus it is not possible to determine accurately the amounts of income or gross receipts taxes that each taxpayer should pay; but once the taxpayer has acknowledged his liability by filing a return, or his employer has filed an information return, there can be close correlation between amounts of cash that should be received and amounts actually finding their way into the treasury. On the local governmental level, there is no practicable way of accruing revenue from parking meters; but once the money has been placed in the meter, determination of whether it gets into the bank account is a matter of establishing recognized safeguards around its movement from meter to bank account, that is, at least one control procedure at every stage.

The nature of some kinds of revenue or receipts and the manner of collecting them almost defy conclusive accounting for the proceeds. Not only do they not lend themselves to accrual accounting but for some it is difficult to determine whether they have been collected and, if so, in what amount. In this category are fines, forfeitures, and penalties, some kinds of fees, refunds on disbursements, collection of receivables previously written off, and miscellaneous transactions not formally recorded until cash is received. Advance determination of amounts that should be received from each major revenue source, as discussed in the cash receipts budgeting section of this chapter, provides a basis for determining the reasonableness of amounts actually reported as collected.

In summary, to ensure that cash collected will be fully accounted for:

1. The accrual basis of accounting should be used wherever possible in order to establish liability of some employee or department to account formally for realization into cash of the asset recorded by the accrual.

2. Wherever possible, prenumbered forms should be used as a sort of receipt to be issued to the payer; every one of the numbered forms should be strictly accounted for; and payers should be encouraged to demand a formal, written receipt.
3. A system of internal control or check should be developed with the smallest possible number of weaknesses under the prevailing conditions and circumstances.
4. Cash receipts from all major revenue sources should be budgeted for each month of the fiscal year; actual collections should be compared with budgeted collections; and significant differences investigated.

After receipt of cash has been made a matter of record, the next step is proper and complete reporting. Since a governmental unit usually operates several funds, it is important to determine with certainty and to report the one to which each receipt belongs. Ownership of most cash is ascertainable without difficulty, but some collections may be of such miscellaneous nature that their classification should be settled by someone with recognized authority to decide doubtful cases. Within each fund, it is imperative to indicate the exact credit to be reported for the cash received. These credits may be to receivables, to revenue accounts for income not previously accrued, to liability accounts, to asset accounts for investments or properties sold, to expenditures accounts for refunds, and to others. Reporting of collections should be done in some prescribed form with supporting documents arranged in a predetermined manner, the entire arrangement devised to accomplish accurate and speedy recording of the transactions represented. Cash receipts should be delivered or deposited in total, without reductions for disbursements; but this admonition is sometimes ignored for convenience.

Classification by Fund

Techniques and rules for recording cash received by a governmental unit are primarily responsibilities of the accounting department. It is charged with ensuring that receipts are distributed to the various funds or activities to which they pertain. This means the accounting department must see that each fund or activity gets the cash to which it is rightfully entitled. Concerning the other side of the transaction, the sources from which cash is received must be recorded with accuracy. If it came from individuals or others to whom some charge had been made on a prior occasion, its recording must provide for properly crediting the accounts of those who had previously been charged. If no formal charge had been made, the credit will indicate the revenue or other source from which the collection originated, in order that statements and other financial reports may be prepared.

Media for the recording of cash receipts by the accounting department will normally consist of duplicate copies of receipts, stubs of licenses, and so forth, issued, but sometimes they will consist of only classified summaries of departmental collections. These media may originate in departments, in special cashiers' offices, or in the main office of the treasury itself. Preferably, media and records for cash collections submitted to the accounting department should include not only copies or portions of the underlying document for each transaction but also a formal summarization showing sources and ownership of cash collected. These evidences may be accompanied by one or more copies of a bank deposit slip if the collection was deposited directly by the collecting agency, or by the collectors themselves.

Going a step further in control, some procedures may require formal permission by the controller before the collections may be presented to the treasurer. This permission may be in the form of a document known as a **deposit warrant, pay-in warrant,** or order, which is basically a formal acknowledgment that the collections and records thereof are accepted and an authorization to the treasury to receive them.

Custody and Protection of Cash

As mentioned previously, one device used to protect against loss is the bonding of all employees entrusted with handling cash. To make this safeguard protective to the fullest extent, daily or other frequent checks must be made on cash in the custody of the individuals bonded. A common practice contributing to this end is the preparation of daily or other periodic cash statements accounting for beginning balances, increases, decreases, and ending balances. Wherever possible, increase and decrease totals should be properly substantiated by documentary evidence—for example, copies of paid **warrants for disbursements.** A disbursement warrant is essentially a formal certification of the validity of a debt, with authorization or direction to a financial agent to pay the debt. A warrant, therefore, advances a claim one step beyond a voucher in the payment process.

Under some circumstances, variations may exist between cash as shown by the accounting department and cash according to the treasurer's records. Certain transactions may have been recorded by one and not by the other. Accounting for warrants payable is a common source of difference between the two sets of records. Assume the accounting department credits Cash to record warrants drawn on the treasury, whereas the treasurer credits Cash only when a check is issued or when the warrant is countersigned and issued, if the warrant serves as a bill of exchange after signature by the treasurer. At a given time, warrants issued by the accounting department but not yet covered by payments in the treasurer's office would cause the records of cash in the two offices to differ. On the other hand, the accounting department may treat warrants as liability instruments and not credit Cash (and debit Warrants Payable) until evidence of disbursement has been received from the treasurer's office. In this event, warrant payments that have not yet been taken up on the controller's books would cause variance between the two Cash accounts. Thus, in governmental accounting, cash reconciliations must recognize not only deposits in transit, outstanding checks, and other similar causes of difference found in reconciling individual and commercial bank accounts, but also another set of differences in the form of variances between accounting and treasury records. To be complete, governmental cash reconciliations must be extended to incorporate both sets of variations.

The selection of depositories of public funds must be made with extreme care to provide a maximum of safety. Some states, if not all, have enacted statutes more or less regulating deposits of public funds. In some states, public funds are given priority of settlement over private deposits in the liquidation of banks. In others, certain standards of safety are prescribed, such as classification as a national bank or protection by the Federal Deposit Insurance Corporation, or both. However, the maximum direct insurance provided by FDIC protection is only $100,000 except for some very special types of trust funds in the custody of the governmental unit. Another common form of protection is the requirement that the depository of public funds must give security in excess of the amount of deposits of public funds that it holds. At least one state requires banks to enter into a formal contract with the governmental unit to cover their extra liability as public depositories. Recall that GASB standards require disclosure in the Notes to the Financial Statements of the types of deposits authorized by legal and contractual provisions, as discussed later in this chapter and also in Chapter 7.

Corollary to the protection of cash is the question of investing temporary excess funds in readily marketable securities. Any supplementary revenue that may be earned by a governmental unit reduces by that much the burden on taxpayers; but it should be borne in mind that safety is of paramount importance in handling public money, which limits the investment field to items of gilt-edge quality.

How many bank accounts should a governmental unit maintain? Should it have a separate bank account (not necessarily in separate banks) for each fund, bearing in mind that some states and local governments may have a multiplicity of funds? To this question no one answer will satisfactorily cover all situations. One argument favoring numerous bank accounts is that it is thus simpler to correlate the cash of each fund with the bank balance that belongs to it than if cash of several funds is mingled in one account. A second argument favoring separate bank accounts for each fund is that unauthorized interfund borrowing through fund overdrafts is made more difficult. If cash of two or more funds is deposited in one bank account, the cash of one fund may be overdrawn without showing as a bank overdraft, because of being covered by cash belonging to the other fund. Favoring a limited number of bank accounts are the arguments that fewer bank reconciliations are necessary at the end of each month and that consolidation of fund cash into a small number of accounts gives more substantial balances, minimizes overdrafts and service charges that might result from numerous small balances, and facilitates investment of amounts of cash not needed for disbursement. Also, as discussed in Chapter 11, pooling of cash and investments helps achieve improved investment of idle cash balances and contributes to improved cash management as well.

In determining the number of bank accounts to be used, convenience and details of the situation must be weighed carefully before making a decision. If only a few funds exist, a separate bank account for each one may be desirable and feasible. If the governmental unit has many funds, some consolidation would probably be advisable or even necessary.

Large cities and states have the problem of accounting for cash that is collected in regional, district, or departmental offices and that cannot well be delivered to the main treasury for acknowledgment and deposit. A sound and convenient method for handling such collections is to require them to be deposited daily to the credit of the governmental unit to which they belong. This reduces the danger of loss and also makes the collection promptly available for use by the fund to which it belongs.

Cash Records

As suggested elsewhere, the form of records used to account for cash in the control of a governmental finance officer is subject to numerous variations; however, at least two requirements are fundamental:

1. The finance officer's (treasurer's) records must show exactly the amount of cash in his custody. This must include both bank balances and undeposited receipts.
2. The finance officer's records must show the ownership of all the cash in his custody: that is, the amount belonging to each fund and organizational unit.

Charges to the finance officer's cash accounts and credits to his equity accounts will derive largely from collections turned over for the credit of the funds. Credits to his cash accounts and charges to equity accounts will derive principally from disbursement documents, probably either a warrant for payment presented by the controller, countersigned by the treasurer, and issued to the creditor, or a check based on a warrant presented by the controller. Another type of charge may be an interfund transfer based on a transfer warrant and not requiring a disbursement document; however, some governmental units require even interfund settlements to be accomplished by a disbursement warrant or check. Although records of the treasurer's office are likely to be more or less simple in form, they must provide for the ultimate in accuracy and be of such nature as to facilitate frequent proving and reporting of funds on hand.

Two kinds of situations may complicate record-keeping for the treasury. One of these is the receipt of uncollectible checks and counterfeit money, and the other is shortages and overages. To provide a measure of protection against uncollectible checks, some governmental units require a notation on each check to show the number of the receipt or other document issued for the check. This facilitates correlating the check with the transaction and allows it to be charged back, sometimes with an additional penalty charge, if it was for payment of a receivable, or allows cancellation of the license, permit, or other privilege represented. To minimize the danger of loss from accepting counterfeit money, special memoranda, usually involving identification of the payer, may be required on all currency exceeding a given denomination. Cashiers or other collecting agents may be held chargeable for counterfeits accepted. To reduce disruption of regular procedures on account of uncollectible checks, some governmental units operate a special cash revolving fund from which to finance uncollectible checks. Exact details of this plan may vary, but one common characteristic is that restitution is made directly to the revolving fund when the delayed item is collected.

Cash shortages and overages are unavoidable in handling large amounts of cash. Practices in accounting for these conditions vary extensively in the field of governmental accounting. Every reasonable effort should be made to determine the cause of each shortage and to correct it. If the effort is unsuccessful, the responsible cashier may be charged with the amount of the shortage; or it may be classified and accounted for as an additional disbursement. Shortages of large amounts that arise from misappropriation or other gross irregularities should be recovered from the cashier's bondsman. Causes of overages, likewise, should be carefully investigated and corrections made, if possible. Unadjusted overages should be credited to a revenue or other balance account. Some governmental units operate a Cash Short or Over account for recording shortages and overages for which adjustments or corrections have not been possible. One thoroughly reprehensible practice in handling cash overages and shortages is to make no record of them but to operate an unofficial fund into which overages are placed and from which shortages are made up. On the contrary, every individual overage and shortage should be made a matter of record, for administrative use. Employees experiencing a high frequency of shortages and overages should be relieved of cashier duties.

Accounting for Disbursements

Although custody of governmental cash is primarily a responsibility of the finance officer, general accounting for disbursements, as well as for collections, may be principally a duty of the chief accountant. In addition to making sure that all disbursements are properly classified as to the account or accounts to be charged, he must also be on guard that only legal, authorized purposes shall be served; that all laws, rules, and regulations governing the form, manner, and method of disbursing have been complied with; and that the amount and timing of payments are correct. Use of a well-developed voucher system is one of the best ways of making sure that a claim for payment receives regular, methodical scrutiny before final approval. Having been approved for payment, and a full record of the liability and related accounting facts having been made, the liability is passed to the finance officer in the form of a warrant or order for payment. Unlike the related voucher, the payment warrant will ordinarily cover only a few points, although an extra copy of the voucher might be utilized as a warrant. Among those points are the name of the fund to which the payment is to be charged; the amount ordered to be paid; identification of the claim, preferably by number, to which the warrant pertains; and authentication by the accounting officer. Payment warrants are of two general types. If the document is to be exclusively an order to pay, the actual disbursement still requires the writing of a check in many systems; however, a rapidly increasing number of governments are moving toward a sharp reduction in the amount of paper used by means of electronic funds transfers directly to banks.

If prescribed accounting procedures entail some delay between the issuance and payment of warrants, they may require accounting recognition as very current liabilities during the interval. Vouchers Payable would be debited and Warrants Payable credited by the accounting department to record this advancement of the claim toward payment. On receipt of official advice that payment has been made, Warrants Payable would be debited. If payment of the warrant promptly follows presentation to the finance department, it may be the practice to classify the issuance as a disbursement, with a debit to the liability account and a credit to Cash. Because of these variances in practice, a warrant is sometimes merely a form of liability and at other times a cash disbursement medium.

Cash Statements

Some cash statements serve the primary purpose of internal control, whereas others are chiefly instruments for general administration and guidance. In the former category are daily cash statements and periodic reconciliations, to mention the more common ones. In the latter are periodic statements setting forth receipts and disbursements by source and purpose and by funds, or in some less detailed form; detailed statements along other lines for individual funds or groups of funds; statements for a year to date, with projection into the future to forecast the probability of having to borrow; and others.

Treasurer's Daily Cash Statement

Statements of this type may serve two purposes:

1. They provide a constant check on the treasurer's records as a means of detecting irregularities and normal errors.
2. They provide daily information on the amount of money available for use.

If some collections and disbursements are handled outside the main offices, the validity of the treasurer's daily statements requires immediate reports of these extramural transactions in order that they may be incorporated in the summary report without undue delay to its preparation and issuance. Insofar as possible, the treasurer's daily report (see Illustration 17–3) should be supported by documentary evidence of changes included therein.

At the end of each month, daily cash reports may be recapitulated in a monthly cash report of the same form. Daily cash reports aid the treasurer in detecting irregularities that may have occurred in his department, either in handling or in reporting cash; and they are useful also to the controller as a constant

---

ILLUSTRATION 17–3

COUNTY OF RANDOLPH
All Funds
Treasurer's Daily Report
December 18, 19x9

Explanation	General Fund	Library Fund	Trust Funds	Agency Funds	Total
Balance, preceding day	$15,000	$9,000	$82,000	$13,000	$119,000
Receipts for today	4,200	160		4,100	8,460
Total	19,200	9,160	82,000	17,100	127,460
Disbursements for today	14,300	6,280		600	21,180
Closing balance, today	$ 4,900	$2,880	$82,000	$16,500	$106,280

check on the treasurer's activity. Both daily and monthly reports may be expanded to show transfers in and transfers out, or any other form of information that may contribute to more effective control. Whether subsidiary to the daily cash report shown in Illustration 17–3 or in addition to it, the treasurer may be required to submit a daily list of disbursements.

Other Cash Reports   At the end of each month, the treasurer may be called on to submit, in addition to the summary described above, an analysis of cash balances, including both bank deposits and actual cash, subdivided by funds—that is, a simple cash balance sheet for each fund.

For inclusion in the published annual report, it may be desirable to provide a somewhat more elaborate statement, including the following:

1. A summary of cash transactions by funds for the year, with an indication of fund equities in the closing balances.
2. A statement showing the composition of the total ending balance.
3. The treasurer's certification.

It is desirable that summaries of bank balances be supplemented by information to indicate that these balances are fully protected in the event the depository should experience financial difficulty. The information may be given in various forms.

The last treasurer's statement to be mentioned here is a bank reconciliation in which the treasurer accounts for differences between ending bank balances per his records and ending bank balances per bank statements. This statement has the usual purposes of bank reconciliations: first, to explain normal differences between the two sets of figures; and second, to bring to light possible variances

---

ILLUSTRATION 17–4

CITY OF SPRINGDALE
**Reconciliation of Bank Statements, Treasurer's Books, and
Controller's Books with Actual Cash Balances
May 31, 19—**

	Bank	Treasurer	Controller
Balances, per books	$117,131	$115,260	$112,600
Add: Unrecorded deposits	3,200		
Interest credited by bank		903	903
Warrants not countersigned			2,660
Totals	120,331	116,163	116,163
Deduct: Outstanding warrants	4,186		
Bank charges		18	18
Actual cash balance	$116,145	$116,145	$116,145

requiring investigation and possibly other action, such as corrections or adjustments.

Cash reconciliations should also be prepared by the controller. Prior to preparation of his own reconciliations, the controller should be provided with a copy of the treasurer's reconciliation and with reports of bank balances obtained directly from the depositories themselves. A standard certificate form may be furnished the banks for supplying this information, or copies of bank statements in the conventional form may be utilized. Reconciliations by the controller will likely be somewhat more complex than those prepared by the treasurer because the former must bring into agreement not two balances but three; his own, the treasurer's, and the bank's. Illustration 17–4 is an example of a statement reconciling bank balances with balances per controller's records and per treasurer's records.

Management of Cash Transfers between the Federal and State Governments

Annual cash transfers between the federal and state governments amount to nearly $150 billion. Dating back to the rapid expansion of federally funded programs during the 1960s, federal agencies have voiced concern that the federal government is losing interest earnings because states frequently "draw down" federal monies in advance of the time they are needed for program purposes. States, on the other hand, have complained about losing interest earnings from having to use their own funds for federal program purposes pending reimbursement by the federal government. To ensure greater efficiency, effectiveness, and equity in the exchange of monies between the federal government and the states, the U.S. Congress passed Public Law 101–453 known as the **Cash Management Improvement Act (CMIA) of 1990.** The Act, which became effective on October 24, 1992, requires the Secretary of the Treasury to regulate and enforce timely disbursement by federal agencies and to negotiate and monitor agreements with the states to achieve the efficient transfer of monies. CMIA's provisions apply as well to state-chartered colleges and universities, and all other organizations included within the GAAP definition of the state's reporting entity.

CMIA requires states to pay interest on federal monies received in advance of need when paying such interest is not inconsistent with program purposes. Exceptions are provided for programs which are below the "major program" threshold (see Chapter 14 for definition) or when interest earned is authorized to be spent for program purposes, or the state is legally required to retain the interest. Even in these exceptional cases, CMIA provides that state and federal agencies must minimize the time between the transfer of monies from the U.S. Treasury and the time the monies are needed for program purposes. A negotiated periodic transfer schedule method, such as monthly or bimonthly, is acceptable for certain programs. An example of the latter is block grants for which no matching requirements exist.

CMIA generally requires electronic funds transfer (EFT) of monies from the federal government to state governments. Several funding techniques may be or have been used in practice:

1. *Zero Balance Accounting.* Federal monies are transferred to a state on the basis of cash paid each day following program disbursements (e.g., several days may elapse between the time checks are issued to program recipients and the time the checks are presented to a bank for payment). The state shall request monies the same day it pays out monies, and the applicable federal agency shall deposit monies in the state's account the same day it receives a request.

2. *Estimated Clearance.* Federal monies are transferred to a state on the basis of *estimated* cash payments each day for program disbursements. The state shall request monies one business day prior to the day it expects to pay out monies, and the applicable federal agency shall deposit monies in the state's account the next day after it receives a request.

3. *Average Clearance.* Federal monies are transferred to a state on the basis of the dollar-weighted average number of days required for cash to be paid for program disbursements made by the state each day. The state shall request monies one business day prior to the dollar-weighted average number of days required for cash to be paid out following disbursements. The applicable federal agency shall deposit monies in the state's account the next day after it receives a request.

4. *Pre-issuance Funding.* Federal monies are transferred to a state on the day prior to the day checks are issued or EFT is initiated by the state. The state shall request monies one business day prior to the day it expects to pay out monies, and the applicable federal agency shall deposit monies in the state's account the next day after it receives a request.

5. *Reimbursable Funding.* Federal monies are transferred to a state after the state has paid out its own funds for program purposes. The federal agency shall deposit monies in the state's account the next business day after it receives a request. Though used extensively in the past, this funding technique is now prohibited, except where mandated by federal law. It is expected that this technique will be rarely used, if ever.

When funding techniques (1) through (3) above are properly applied neither the federal government nor the state will incur an interest liability to the other. In the case of pre-issuance funding (item 4), however, the state will incur an interest liability to the federal government from the day the funds are credited to the state's account until the day the state pays out cash for program purposes. In the case of reimbursable funding (item 5), if a federal agency requires a state to use reimbursable funding (in violation of CMIA), then the federal government will incur an interest liability to the state. The final Department of Treasury rules for CMIA state that there is no known federal law at this time that requires the use of reimbursable funding.

CMIA also provides alternatives for funding of indirect costs and administrative cost grants. For administrative cost grants (those strictly intended to cover the costs of administering a federal program rather than monies intended to benefit recipients), a state is permitted to draw down a prorated amount on each payday (e.g., one-third of a quarterly grant amount if payroll is monthly, or one-sixth if the payroll is semimonthly). For indirect costs (see Chapter 18 for definition), either a negotiated indirect cost rate is applied to each drawdown of cash or the costs are allocated pursuant to an approved allocation plan.

The preceding description of CMIA covers most but not all of its provisions. CMIA also requires each state to prepare an annual report for submission to the Financial Management Services Agency within the U.S. Department of the Treasury. The annual report must include, at a minimum, the federal interest liability for each program and in total for all programs administered by the state, the state interest liability for each program and in total for all programs, the net total interest owed by the state or federal government, and, for information purposes only, the actual interest earnings on and the related banking costs for all monies drawn from the state's account with the Unemployment Trust Fund. The net interest payable to or by a state for its most recently completed fiscal year will be paid no later than March 1.

Obviously, CMIA represents a major step forward in the management of cash flows between the federal and state governments. It consummates many years of joint efforts by federal and state officials to improve the efficiency, effectiveness, and equity of cash transfers between governments. As such it serves as a good example of how taxpayers can benefit from better intergovernmental cooperation. Conceivably, this program could serve as a model for future improvements in the management of cash transfers between the federal government and local governments or between state and local governments.

Management of Deposits and Temporary Investments

Management of cash resources, as discussed previously in this chapter, requires that cash be deposited with designated financial institutions to meet payrolls and other obligations of the government. In addition, legal and contractual provisions, as well as sound financial management, dictate investment of cash to meet various objectives. Investment activities of governmental entities range from overnight investments of idle cash to long-term investment of pension and sinking fund assets. Regardless of the type of deposit or investment, it is imperative that they be made and managed in conformity with applicable statutes, ordinances, local policies, and contractual agreements. Even without legal or contractual restrictions, however, a prudent policy for deposits and investments should be followed. Such a policy would include, at a minimum, the following items:[1]

1. A written policy approved by the governing board.
2. Knowledge of and compliance with legal authority.

---

[1] The following list is adapted from Judith K. Welch, and J. Dwight Hadley, "Cash and Investment Management," in *Handbook of Governmental Accounting & Finance*, ed. Nicholas G. Apostolou and D. Larry Crumbley, 2nd ed. (New York: John Wiley & Sons, 1992), p. 18.10.

3. Proper organization structure and effective internal controls.
4. A written procedures manual for managing deposits and investments.
5. Skilled, trained staff.
6. An up-to-date cash budget.
7. Consideration of the security for each investment and collateral for deposits.
8. Analyses of risks and rewards (returns or yields).
9. Well-maintained records and documentation.
10. Careful monitoring of portfolio performance.
11. Periodic reporting to management and elected officials.
12. Internal and external audits.

Generally speaking, sound management of deposits and investments requires close attention to the security of the deposits and investments, meeting liquidity needs, and achieving target rates of return or yield consistent with an acceptable level of risk. Although there are several types of risk that affect deposits and investments, the two major risks are **credit risk** and **market risk**.[2] Credit risk relates to the probability of loss due to nonpayment of principal or interest, either on investment securities or on securities pledged as collateral. Thus, credit risk relates to the financial viability and dependability of issuers of securities, depository financial institutions, and custodians of securities or collateral. Market risk is the risk of loss arising from increases in market rates of interest or other factors that reduce market value of securities. Market risk can be managed by careful attention to the average term to maturity of debt securities and matching maturities to forecasted liquidity needs. Credit risk is the primary concern of statutory provisions, and the main focus of the following section.

Security of Deposits and Temporary Investments

Statutes often impose restrictions on the governmental entity's deposit and investment procedures. Such laws, policies, and agreements usually prescribe permissible types of deposits and investments, methods for selecting depository financial institutions, minimum balances in liquid deposits and investments, and security requirements in terms of collateral for deposits. Restrictions such as these are intended to limit the level of risk to which public deposits and investments are exposed.

Deposits.   Demand deposits (checking) and time deposits (savings accounts, certificates of deposits, money market accounts, etc.), as noted previously in this chapter, are generally insured by the Federal Deposit Insurance Corporation (FDIC) up to $100,000 for each governmental entity. Statutes typically require that deposits in excess of FDIC insurance coverage be collateralized, either partially or fully, by low-risk securities. Qualifying securities that may be pledged

---

[2] GASB Codification Sec. 150.113.

ordinarily include obligations of the federal government, the state, or local governments or political subdivisions within the state.[3] The credit risk associated with such collateral depends on who is holding the security, in whose name the collateral is being held, the depositor's access to the collateral, and the depositor's rights to the collateral in the event the financial institution defaults.[4] The level of credit risk is lower if collateral is being held by the depositor or an independent third-party agent rather than by the financial institution or its agent. Similarly, the risk is lower if the collateral is held by the pledging financial institution, or by a trust department or agent of the institution, in the name of the depositor government rather than not in the depositor's name. Finally, if the depositor holds a *perfected security interest* (pursuant to the Uniform Commercial Code) in the collateral, risk is lower than if no perfected security interest is held in the collateral.

Investments. Governmental entities can choose from a wide array of investments. The nature of the investment chosen will depend on what is allowable under state and local law, specific investment objectives, liquidity needs, market conditions, experience of the chief financial officer, past practices, and other factors. Among the most commonly used investment securities are obligations of the federal government and its agencies or instrumentalities (e.g., U.S. Treasury bills, bonds, and notes, and obligations issued by the Farmers Home Administration), **certificate of deposits, repurchase agreements, bankers' acceptances, commercial paper, money market funds,** and state and local bonds and **investment pools.** Pension fund assets are often invested in corporate debt and securities, and even foreign debt and equity securities, as well as U.S. government securities.

Of the investments listed above, repurchase agreements, or repos as they are often called, have been both the most popular and the most risky. Repos involve the transfer of excess cash by a governmental entity (buyer-lender) to a financial institution or broker-dealer (seller-borrower) in exchange for U.S. government or other securities. The seller-borrower promises to repay the cash, with interest, in exchange for the *same* securities.[5] Repos provide a flexible, relatively high-yield investment, ostensibly backed by high-quality U.S. government securities. Unfortunately, repos can also have very high-credit risk, as explained in a cash management publication of the Government Finance Officers Association (GFOA):[6]

> Throughout the 1970s and 1980s repos revolutionized the world of local government finance. Even small jurisdictions found it possible to obtain high overnight rates of return using instruments that were secured by government securities. For ten years, the repo instrument was used without incident, and helped banks to avoid reserve requirements which detracted from their earnings and yields. Likewise, government

---

[3] Welch and Hadley, "Cash and Investment Management," p. 18.13.

[4] GASB Codification Sec. I50.119.

[5] GASB Codification Sec. I50.131.

[6] Government Finance Officers Association, *Cash Management for Small Governments*, ed. Ian J. Allen (Chicago: GFOA, 1989), p. 131.

securities dealers found repos an attractive way to finance their growing inventories of government securities. Meanwhile, local governments earned attractive interest rates and maintained considerable liquidity. Unfortunately, the collapse of several government securities dealers in the early and mid-1980s stunned the public markets and left numerous municipalities holding worthless paper.

As a result of the collapse of the repos market, numerous reforms have been implemented to avoid similar problems in the future, including[7]:

1. Thorough investigation of the counterparty bank or security dealer's creditworthiness.
2. Use of an independent custodian to hold collateral securities.
3. Adoption of the delivery versus payment procedure for settling repo transactions.
4. Marking collateral to market daily, so that price fluctuations do not undermine the value of the protective collateral.
5. Overcollateralization to provide a safe margin for error and possible price fluctuation.

Governments that continue to use repos should be advised to use a master repo agreement detailing the responsibilities of all parties, and to follow the steps listed above.

Required Financial Statement Disclosures

To assist users of financial statements in assessing the risks of a governmental entity's deposits and investments, GASB standards require the following disclosures in the Notes to the Financial Statements.[8]

1. A description of the types of investments authorized by legal or contractual provisions. Material differences between the authorized investments of specific funds, fund types, or component units and those of the combined entity should be disclosed.
2. Significant violations of legal or contractual provisions for deposits and investments.
3. Whether or not the bank balances of deposits as of the balance sheet date are entirely insured or collateralized with securities held by the entity or by its agent in the entity's name. If not, the following disclosures should be made:
   a. Carrying amount of total deposits, if not separately displayed on the balance sheet.
   b. Total bank balance classified in the following categories of credit risk:
      (1) Insured or collateralized with securities held by the entity or by its agent in the entity's name.

---

[7] Ibid.
[8] GASB Codification Sec. I50.159–172.

(2) Collateralized with securities held by the pledging financial institution's trust department or agent in the entity's name.

(3) Uncollateralized, including collateralized with securities held by the pledging financial institution's trust department or agent but *not* in the entity's name.

4. Carrying amount and market value of *investments* (including repurchase agreements) as of the balance sheet date, in total and for each type of investment, classified in the following three categories of credit risk:

   a. Insured or registered, or securities held by the entity or its agent in the entity's name.

   b. Uninsured or unregistered, with securities held by the counterparty's trust department or agent in the entity's name.

   c. Uninsured or unregistered, with securities held by the counterparty or its trust department or agent, but *not* in the entity's name.

5. The types of investments made during the period but not owned as of the balance sheet date.

6. Losses recognized during the period due to default by counterparties to deposit or investment transactions and amounts recovered from prior-period losses if not separately displayed on the operating statement.

Disclosures for certain specialized investment transactions are not included in the preceding list of disclosures. The term *securities* as used in item (4) above includes both securities held as investments and securities underlying repurchase agreements.

A good example of the required disclosures for deposits and investments is provided in Illustration 17–5, which presents the disclosures from the Notes to the Financial Statements of the City of Seattle, Washington. According to Illustration 17–5, deposits in excess of FDIC insurance are collateralized by a multiple financial institution collateral pool administered by the Public Deposit Protection Commission (PDPC). At the balance sheet date, only about 32 percent of the City of Seattle's deposits were collateralized. The City of Seattle's investments are classified into the three categories specified by GASB standards. As shown in Illustration 17–5, approximately 93 percent of the market value of the City's investments are held by the City's agents in the City's name, and are classified in category 1, the lowest of the three risk categories. Thus, the City of Seattle's investments appear quite safe, although financial statement users may want to know more about the riskiness of some investments, such as the repurchase agreements, reverse repurchase agreements, bankers' acceptances, and foreign entity securities. The City's disclosures for deposits and investments appear to conform to those required by GASB standards.

Other Considerations in Investment Management

As discussed briefly in Chapter 5, the Internal Revenue Code, particularly after the Tax Reform Act of 1986, significantly limits the ability of a governmental entity to realize "arbitrage earnings" by investing tax-exempt bond proceeds in

ILLUSTRATION 17–5

CITY OF SEATTLE, WASHINGTON
Note Disclosures for Cash and Investments
For Year Ended December 31, 1992

The FDIC insures the City's deposits up to $100,000. All deposits not covered by Federal Depository insurance are covered by the Public Deposit Protection Commission of the State of Washington (PDPC). The PDPC is a statutory authority established under Chapter 39.58 of the Revised Code of Washington. It constitutes a multiple financial institution collateral pool. In the case of a loss by any public depository in the state, each public depository is liable up to 10 percent of its public deposits. There is no provision for PDPC to make additional pro rata assessments if needed to cover a loss. Therefore, PDPC protection is of the nature of collateral, not insurance. At the end of 1992, approximately 32 percent of the City's deposits would have been covered by this collateral.

Note 1 describes the investment policies of the City. The City classifies time deposits as investments. Banks or trust companies acting as the City's agents hold most of the City's investments in the City's name. These investments are classified risk category 1. In some cases, the trust department of the City's depository bank holds City investments in the City's name. These investments are classified risk category 2. Certain investments are uninsured and held by the trust department of the City's agent in the agent's name. These are classified risk category 3.

Investments by Risk Category and Type

	Book	Market
Investments in the City's Name:		
Treasury Residual Investments:		
Bankers' acceptances	$ 56,555,546	$ $56,564,083
Treasuries	80,937,248	81,334,375
Agencies	80,760,822	80,369,063
Repurchase agreements	4,900,000	4,900,000
Reverse repurchase agreements	(30,100,000)	(30,100,000)
	193,053,616	193,067,521
Securities Held by Dedicated Funds:		
Bankers' acceptances	115,870,564	115,907,293
Treasuries	34,498,363	37,128,258
Agencies	77,800,931	80,259,080
	228,169,858	233,294,631
Employees' Retirement System Investments:		
U.S. Government bonds	116,043,673	123,189,384
Foreign government bonds	65,650,000	65,795,362
Corporate bonds	90,090,010	92,223,701
Common stock	111,261,757	221,935,629
International equities	93,304,714	90,592,712
	476,350,154	593,736,788
TOTAL INVESTMENTS IN RISK CATEGORY 1	897,573,628	1,020,098,940
Employees' Retirement System investments in Bank of New York—Negotiable CD's	12,307,849	12,307,849
TOTAL INVESTMENTS IN RISK CATEGORY 3	12,307,849	12,307,849

ILLUSTRATION 17–5   (*concluded*)

	Book	Market
Uncategorized investments		
Mortgages	29,016,416	31,048,255
Realty Equities	20,793,000	22,209,870
Venture Capital	3,250,000	4,473,545
TOTAL INVESTMENTS IN THE CITY'S NAME	$962,940,893	$1,090,138,459
Investment's Not in the City's Name:		
Museum Development Authority Investments (6-30-92):		
Money market fund	$ 313,402	$ 313,402
Agencies	3,010,772	3,348,812
Repurchase agreements	2,400,000	2,400,000
	5,724,174	6,062,214
TOTAL INVESTMENTS	$968,665,067	$1,096,200,673
Exhibit 1—Combined Balance Sheet:		
Cash and equity in pooled investments		$ 188,279,925
Cash with fiscal agent		3,108,602
Restricted cash and equity in pooled investments:		
Revenue bond reserve accounts		2,003,019
Construction accounts		13,391,935
Customer deposits		475,670
TOTAL—December 31, 1992		$ 207,259,151
Composition:		
Cash in banks		$ (16,855,335)
Cash held by Treasurer		160,753
Warrant clearing account		2,100,000
Cash in Transit on 12/31/92		
Receipts accrued as Revenues and Receivables		(10,375,463)
Other Reconciling Items		(1,009,523)
Residual investments—at amortized cost		193,053,616
Investments held by broker-dealers under reverse		
repurchase agreement obligations of $29,992,294		30,100,000
TOTAL TREASURER'S CASH AND		
INVESTMENTS		197,174,048
Cash with fiscal agent		3,108,602
Trustee accounts		
Municipal Courts		1,109,147
Community Development Revenue Sharing		31,662
Retainages on public works contracts in escrow		6,631,399
Less: Retainages not booked at 12/31/92		(886,639)
Cash deposited in the name of Museum Development		
Authority		6,319
Petty cash and revolving funds held by departments		84,612
TOTAL CASH AND EQUITY IN POOLED		
INVESTMENTS		$ 207,259,150

higher yielding taxable securities. Interest earnings in excess of those permitted by current federal tax regulations must be rebated to the federal government. The rules governing arbitrage are exceedingly complex and thus are beyond the scope of this text. Nevertheless, arbitrage considerations should be a standard part of investment policy for temporary investments of bond proceeds.

Proper accounting procedures are also a necessary aspect of investment management. Accounting procedures depend on the type of securities in which invested and the expected length of time the investments will be held. For long-term investments in bonds, premiums or discounts should be amortized over the life of the bonds, with appropriate adjustment of interest income. Detailed accounting guidance for long-term investments is provided in most intermediate accounting texts and Appendix 2 of this text.

It should be apparent that the increasing professionalism of investment management in government has been a double-edged sword. Although many governmental entities have benefited from the use of new and innovative investment instruments, some instruments (e.g., repurchase agreements) have exposed the governmental entity to added credit risk. GASB standards require that the entity specifically evaluate those risks and communicate them to interested financial statement users.

Summary

Efficient and effective management of cash, deposits, and temporary investments is an important aspect of improving the overall performance of government. This chapter discusses the processes by which sound cash and investment management can be achieved. By their nature, cash and investments require special attention to ensure public monies are protected and safeguarded. Thus, the emphasis in this chapter was on cash planning, well-designed operating procedures, and effective internal controls. Similarly, the primary focus of the discussion on management of deposits and investments was on assessing and reporting credit risks and compliance with legal and contractual requirements. Nevertheless, it is management's responsibility to invest all idle cash and to achieve the highest rate of return consistent with an acceptable level of risk. As new and innovative financial instruments continue to evolve, assessment and management of credit and market risk are likely to become more and more challenging.

Selected References

Bruebaker, Gary, and Jack Kiley. "Cash Management Improvement Act of 1990." *Government Finance Review*, October 1992, pp. 29–31.

Governmental Accounting Standards Board. *Codification of Governmental Accounting and Financial Reporting Standards as of June 30, 1993*. Norwalk, Conn.: 1993.

Government Finance Officers Association. *Cash Management for Small Governments*. Edited by Ian J. Allan. Chicago: GFOA, 1989.

Welch, Judith K., and J. Dwight Hadley. "Cash and Investment Management." In *Handbook of Governmental Accounting & Finance*. 2nd ed. Ed. Nicholas G. Apostolou and D. Larry Crumbley. New York: John Wiley & Sons, 1992, chap. 18.

Questions

17–1. How does cash and investment management contribute to improving overall resource management?

17–2. Explain what is meant by the "operating cycle" and how it relates to the cash management system

17–3. "The purpose of budgeting cash receipts month by month is to provide a means for determining that the government receives all the cash to which it is legally entitled." Do you agree? Why or why not?

17–4. Describe briefly the relationship between budgeting cash receipts and disbursements and planning short-term borrowing and/or temporary investments.

17–5. Sometimes a governmental unit with a limited amount of cash will endeavor to "window-dress" its liabilities at the end of the fiscal period by writing and recording checks in payment of the liabilities, but holding the checks until a later date, thus avoiding a bank overdraft. Would you consider such checks as outstanding in preparing a bank reconciliation? If you were an outside auditor charged with preparing correct financial statements of the governmental unit, what would you do about the situation described?

17–6. What are the objectives of the Cash Management Improvement Act of 1990?

17–7. Describe the alternative funding techniques that may be used under the Cash Management Improvement Act of 1990. Which of these techniques contributes to the most efficient cash management?

17–8. What is required, at a minimum, for a prudent management policy for deposits with financial institutions and investments?

17–9. What are the two major risks that affect the security of deposits and investments? Briefly define each of the two risks.

17–10. Explain the three risk categories into which a governmental entity's investments must be classified for financial reporting purposes.

Exercises and Problems

17–1. Write the numbers 1 through 10 on a sheet of paper. Beside each number write the letter corresponding with the best answer to each of the following questions:

1. Which of the following is *not* a universal rule for achieving strong internal control over cash?
   a. Separate the cash-handling and record-keeping functions.
   b. Have bank reconciliations performed by employees independent with respect to handling cash.
   c. Deposit each day's cash receipts by the end of the day.
   d. Decentralize the receiving of cash as much as possible.

2. Under which of the following circumstances would an auditor be most likely to intensify an examination of a $500 imprest petty cash fund?
   a. Reimbursement vouchers are *not* prenumbered.
   b. Reimbursement occurs twice each week.
   c. The custodian occasionally uses the cash fund to cash employee checks.
   d. The custodian endorses reimbursement checks.

3. An unrecorded check issued during the last week of the year would most likely be discovered by the auditor when the:

    a. Check register for the last month is reviewed.

    b. Cut-off bank statement is reconciled.

    c. Bank confirmation is reviewed.

    d. Search for unrecorded liabilities is performed.

4. The auditor's count of the client's cash should be coordinated to coincide with the:

    a. Study of the system of internal controls with respect to cash.

    b. Close of business on the balance sheet date.

    c. Count of marketable securities.

    d. Count of inventories.

5. When counting cash on hand, the auditor must exercise control over all cash and other negotiable assets to prevent:

    a. Theft.

    b. Irregular endorsement.

    c. Substitution.

    d. Deposits-in-transit.

6. Which one of the following would the auditor consider an incompatible operation if the cashier received remittances from the mailroom?

    a. The cashier posts the receipts to the accounts receivable subsidiary ledger cards.

    b. The cashier makes the daily deposit at a local bank.

    c. The cashier prepares the daily deposit.

    d. The cashier endorses the checks.

7. Which of the following statements regarding the Cash Management Improvement Act of 1990 is *not* true?

    a. For all federal assistance programs (major and minor), state governments are required to pay interest to the federal government if federal monies are received in advance of need.

    b. For *major* federal assistance programs only, state governments are required to pay interest to the federal government if federal monies are received in advance of need.

    c. If a federal agency requires a state government to use state monies for federal program purposes and request subsequent reimbursement, the federal government must pay interest to the state government.

    d. The net interest payable to or by a state for its most recently completed fiscal year must be paid no later than March 1.

8. Which of the following organizational units would be subject to the provisions of the Cash Management Improvement Act of 1990?

    a. State governments.

    b. A mental hospital supported by state appropriations.

    c. A state-chartered public college or university.

    d. All of the above.

9. The risk of loss from the insolvency of a financial institution acting as custodian of a local government's cash deposits is properly termed:

    a. Market risk.

    b. Call risk.

    c. Credit risk.

    d. Depositor's risk.

10. Which of the following risk categories represents the *least* amount of risk to a governmental depositor?
    a. Deposits insured or collateralized with securities held by the entity or by its agent in the entity's name.
    b. Deposits collateralized with securities held by the pledging financial institution's trust department or agent in the entity's name.
    c. Uncollateralized, including collateralized with securities held by the pledging financial institution's trust department or agent but not in the entity's name.
    d. A checking account with overdraft protection.

(Items 1 through 6, AICPA)

17–2. Given the following information about the City of Dalton General Fund, prepare a Cash Receipts budget for each month of fiscal year 19x6. Round each calculation to the nearest $1,000.

The following are balances expected as of the end of the fiscal year 19x5:

Taxes receivable—delinquent	$360,000
Interest and penalties receivable on taxes	40,000
Due from other funds	25,000
Due from state government	450,000

The Estimated Revenues budget for 19x6 consisted of:

Property taxes	$1,600,000
Licenses and permits	300,000
Fines and forfeits	200,000
Intergovernmental revenue	400,000

Additional information

1. Delinquent taxes and interest and penalties on taxes are expected to be collected as follows (for purposes of cash budgeting, the two items may be added together):

January 19x6	5%	August 19x6	2%
February	10	September	2
March	35	October	10
April	5	November	5
May	2	December	5
June	2	In following years	5
July	2	Uncollectible	10

2. The amount due from other funds is expected to be collected in full in January 19x6; the amount due from the state is expected to be collected in full in February 19x6.

3. Property taxes budgeted for 19x6 are expected to be collected as follows:

January 19x6	0%	August 19x6	2%
February	0	September	2
March	2	October	30
April	10	November	5
May	30	December	2
June	5	In following years	8
July	2	Uncollectible	2

4. Licenses and permits, and fines and forfeits budgeted for 19x6 are expected to be

collected as follows (for purposes of cash budgeting, the two items may be added together):

January 19x6	8%	July 19x6	8%
February	8	August	8
March	8	September	8
April	8	October	8
May	10	November	8
June	10	December	8

5. Intergovernmental revenue budgeted for 19x6 is expected to be collected as follows:

March 19x6	25%	September 19x6	25%
June	25	December	25

17–3. Given the following information about the City of Dalton's General Fund, prepare a Cash Disbursements budget for each month of fiscal year 19x6.

The following are balances expected as of the end of fiscal year 19x5:

Vouchers Payable	$360,000
Tax anticipation notes payable	280,000
Due to other funds	40,000

The Appropriations budget for 19x6 consisted of:

	Personal Services	Supplies	Capital Outlays
General government	$ 240,000	$ 25,000	$ 20,000
Public safety	510,000	70,000	120,000
Public works	400,000	100,000	60,000
Health, welfare, and recreation	670,000	150,000	40,000
Totals	$1,820,000	$345,000	$240,000

Additional information

1. Vouchers payable and the amount due to other funds on December 31, 19x5, are to be paid in full in January 19x6.

2. Tax anticipation notes as of December 31, 19x5, plus interest of $22,000, are to be paid in February 19x6.

3. The City of Dalton pays all employees every two weeks. Each month in 19x6 will have two paydays, except June and December will have three paydays. You may assume all items included in the Personal Services budget are paid by the General Fund on paydays.

4. Items included in the Supplies budget are expected to result in cash disbursements in the following months:

January 19x6	$12,000	July 19x6	$36,000
February	25,000	August	30,000
March	32,000	September	25,000
April	31,000	October	22,000
May	32,000	November	18,000
June	36,000	December	17,000
		Unpaid	29,000

5. Items included in the Capital Outlays budget are expected to result in cash disbursements in the following months:

February 19x6	$ 8,000	June 19x6	$60,000
April	48,000	September	50,000
May	52,000	December	22,000

17–4. From your solutions to Problems 17–2 and 17–3, prepare a Statement of Budgeted Cash Receipts and Disbursements for fiscal year 19x6 for the City of Dalton's General Fund. It is suggested that you follow the format in Illustration 17–2.

The cash balance on January 1, 19x6, is expected to be $80,000. The policy of the City Treasury is to issue 60-day tax anticipation notes in amounts of $100,000 or multiples thereof, as needed, in any month in which the provisional balance is expected to be negative. The notes bear interest at the rate of 1 percent per month. If payment of notes and interest could cause a negative cash balance, the policy is to issue a refunding note with the same terms as described.

17–5. The Town of Mount Vernon had poor internal control over its cash transactions. The facts about its cash position at November 30, 19x4, were as follows:

The cash books showed a balance of $19,101.62, which included cash on hand. A credit of $200 on the bank's record did not appear on the books of the town. The balance per the bank statement was $15,750; and outstanding checks were No. 62 for $116.25, No. 183 for $150, No. 284 for $253.25, No. 8621 for $190.71, No. 8623 for $206.80, and No. 8632 for $145.28.

The Treasurer removed all the cash on hand in excess of $3,794.41 and then prepared the following reconciliation:

Balance per books, November 30, 19x4		$19,101.62
Add: Outstanding checks:		
No. 8621	$190.71	
No. 8623	206.80	
No. 8632	145.28	442.79
		19,544.41
Deduct: Cash on hand		3,794.41
Balance per bank, November 30, 19x4		15,750.00
Deduct: Unrecorded credit		200.00
True cash, November 30, 19x4		$15,550.00

Required

a. How much did the Treasurer remove, and how did he attempt to conceal his theft?

b. Taking only the information given, name two specific features of internal control that were apparently missing.

c. If the Treasurer's October 31 reconciliation is known to be in order and the audit is started on December 5 for the year ended November 30, what procedures would uncover the fraud?

(AICPA, adapted)

17–6. Two sets of cash records are kept for the City of Fordham Recreation Center, one by the County Treasurer and one by the Director of the center.

The cash balance on the Treasurer's books at January 1, 19x6, was $5,060. The Director's books showed $3,040. The difference was due to a payment received from a state agency on December 31, 19x5, and recorded by the Treasurer on that date but not recorded by the Director until the next year.

On the Director's record, 19x6 receipts totals were $179,940, and total disbursements were $172,440. Among the receipts were $360 from the sale of certain recreational items that had not been reported to the City Treasurer by the end of the year. The sum of $1,600 cash contributed to the center by an anonymous donor was first reported to the City Treasurer in January 19x7. Disbursements not of record on the Treasurer's books until 19x7 were $610 paid by the Director for Christmas presents for underprivileged children and $500 for a Christmas party. Another cause of difference was $200 underfooting of disbursements by the Director.

At the end of December, the Treasurer had paid $100 for supplies and paid $1,040 for recreational equipment, neither of which was reported to the Director until the next month. The Treasurer showed a December receipt of $2,800 for the facility from a state agency, but this was not entered in the Director's records until the following month. As of December 31, 19x6, the Treasurer's books showed a balance of $11,150.

Required

    a. Determine the cash balance shown on the Director's books as of December 31, 19x6.

    b. Determine the correct cash balance as of December 31, 19x6.

    c. Prepare any correcting or adjusting entries the Treasurer would need to make as of December 31, 19x6.

17–7. All disbursements of the Village of Yarbey are made on the authority of warrants issued by the Controller and countersigned by the Treasurer. The Controller records all disbursements as credits to Cash at the time the warrants are issued. Since the warrants become bills of exchange on being countersigned, the Treasurer records cash disbursements as such at the time she countersigns the warrants.

On June 30, 19y4, the Treasurer's books showed the following balances:

Explanation	*First National Bank*
General Fund	$115,260
Internal Service Fund	11,462
Capital Projects Fund	98,327
Debt Service Fund	13,500

The balances according to the Controller's books were as follows:

General Fund	$110,480
Internal Service Fund	11,300
Capital Projects Fund	94,300
Debt Service Fund	13,500

One bank account is kept for all funds. The bank statement showed the following balance on June 30:

First National Bank	$250,387

The following deposits, made on June 30, did not appear on the bank statement:

General Fund	$3,200
Debt Service Fund	2,000

The Treasurer reports that the following countersigned warrants have not been returned by the bank:

Explanation	First National Bank	
General Fund:		
No. 1702	$ 937	
1712	489	
1714	1,825	
1717	715	
1718	220	
Total		$ 4,186
Internal Service Fund:		
No. 2431	42	
2440	125	
2442	283	
2443	94	
Total		544
Capital Projects Fund:		
No. 3674	3,500	
3680	740	
3684	1,285	
3686	375	
3687	1,460	
Total		7,360
Debt Service Fund:		
No. 4128	820	
4131	392	
4133	540	
4134	260	
Total		2,012
Grand Total		$14,102

The following warrants have been issued by the Controller but have not been countersigned by the Treasurer:

General Fund:		
No. 1720	$3,800	
1721	900	
1722	80	
Total		$4,780
Internal Service Fund:		
No. 2444	75	
2445	87	
Total		162
Capital Projects Fund:		
No. 3688	1,450	
3689	870	
3690	1,707	
Total		4,027
Grand Total		$8,969

An interest credit in the amount of $2,964 on the bank statement had not been recorded on the books; bank charges in the amount of $28 on the bank statement had not been recorded on the books. The Treasurer and Controller agreed that these amounts should be allocated to the funds as follows:

Explanation	First National Bank
Interest credited by the bank:	
General Fund	$1,450
Internal Service Fund	135
Capital Projects Fund	1,224
Debt Service Fund	155
Bank charges:	
General Fund	21
Internal Service Fund	7

Required

a. Reconcile the balance per Treasurer's books for each fund to the actual cash balance for each fund. Reconcile the balance per Controller's books for each fund to the actual cash balance for each fund.

b. Reconcile the balance per bank statement to the total actual cash balance of all funds.

17–8. The State Department of Corrections of a midwest state is responsible for administering the state's penal system and its parole board and probation network. The Department of Corrections has developed an unusually effective rehabilitation system for youthful offenders which is based on the military "bootcamp" concept. The major source of funding for the Youth Rehabilitation Program (YRP) is a grant from the Federal Department of Justice. For the year ended June 30, 19y2, which was prior to implementation of the Cash Management Improvement Act, the YRP received a special grant in the amount of $500,000 for purchase of military-style clothing for program participants. The $500,000 was received in cash during January 19y2, but, as of June 30, 19y2, only $150,000 of this amount had been expended. The unspent portion has been invested in the state's cash and investment pool where it has earned interest at 7 percent per annum.

In addition to the $500,000 for uniforms, the YRP received a grant for operations from the Department of Justice in the amount of $4,000,000. However, cash can only be drawn against this amount at the end of each month, after filing the required documentation showing amounts expended during the month for allowable purposes.

Required Answer the following questions and explain your answers fully.

1. In what respects are these grants inequitable to:
   a. The Federal Government?
   b. The State Government?
2. How would the Cash Management Improvement Act improve the efficiency and equity of cash flows between the federal government and the Youth Rehabilitation Program?

17–9. Note 4 from the Notes to the Financial Statements for the City of Eugene, Oregon, for the year ended June 30, 1992, is provided below.

Required Evaluate the City of Eugene, Oregon's note disclosure for cash and investments and comment on the extent to which it conforms or does not conform to GASB standards.

CITY OF EUGENE, OREGON
Notes to Combined Financial Statements

(4) Cash and Investments

Deposits

At June 30, 1992, the City's deposits with various financial institutions presented in the accompanying combined financial statements were as follows:

	Carrying Amount	Bank Value
Demand deposits (overdraft)	$(178,317)	1,336,951
Money market	3,148	3,148
Total deposits (overdraft)	$(175,169)	1,340,099

The city also had cash on hand of $55,190. Of the bank deposits, $200,000 was covered by federal depository insurance. The remaining $1,140,099 is uncollateralized per GASB Statement No. 3, as it is collateralized with securities held by the pledging financial institution but not in the City's name, although balances so collateralized meet the requirements of state law.

Investments

The City's investments are categorized to give an indication of the level of risk assumed by the City at year end. Category 1 includes investments that are insured or registered or for which the securities are held by the City or its agent in the City's name. Category 2 includes uninsured and unregistered investments for which the securities are held by the counterparty's trust department or agent in the City's name. Category 3 includes uninsured and unregistered investments for which the securities are held by the counterparty, or by its trust department or agent but not in the City's name. The following investments, except for the investment in Oregon State Treasurer's Investment Pool, are held in safekeeping by the financial institution counterparty in the financial institution's general customer account name and are considered to be Category 3 investments.

	Carrying Amount	Market Value
Repurchase agreements	$ 145,359	145,359
U.S. agency notes	31,369,428	31,522,333
Bankers' acceptances	17,584,463	17,588,371
Commercial paper	25,501,501	25,502,936
Investment in Oregon State Treasurer's Investment Pool	19,228,461	19,228,461
Total investments	$93,829,212	93,987,460

Cost Determination for Governmental and Nonprofit Entities

Cost accounting, as discussed in standard college texts, is generally applicable to business operations of governmental units. It is less immediately obvious that cost accounting concepts are applicable to governmental activities of a nonbusiness nature and to hospitals and other health care providers, universities, and other nonprofit entities. Yet, almost without exception in the case of hospitals, and in many instances in the case of governmental units and universities, the explosive increase in demand for services, relative to the increase in resources, has forced the adoption of the techniques of good financial management, including cost accounting. The use of cost as a measure of the input of resources into a program is discussed in Chapter 16 of this text, as are other uses of cost data in budgeting for improved financial management.

Cost accounting, in the sense of the routine collection of data concerning the costs of departments, programs, or products, through the mechanism of a double-entry bookkeeping system, is not as frequently found in governmental and non-profit entities as is cost **determination,** or the recasting of data derived from the fund accounts described in preceding chapters to obtain desired cost information. Cost determination procedures may be considered statistical, since they are done apart from the bookkeeping system and may be done at regular intervals or only on a special study basis. Nevertheless, general ledger-based cost accounting systems are likely to become more common given recent developments in governmental performance measurement systems (see Chapter 16). Further, as discussed in this chapter, some governments have adopted activity-based costing as a key element of their performance evaluation systems. Such systems are enhanced by designing accounting systems to provide as much activity-based cost data as possible, even though the need for some statistical cost data outside of the accounting system is inevitable.

Determination of Costs Applicable to Grants and Contracts

State and local governmental units and nonprofit entities, particularly colleges and universities, have found grants from and contracts with the federal government important, although diminishing, sources of financing. The United States Office of Management and Budget has issued a series of Circulars to set forth "cost principles" to govern payments by the federal government under grant programs, contracts, and other agreements, to state and local governments (OMB *Circular A-87*), educational institutions (OMB *Circular A-21*), and other nonprofit organizations (OMB *Circular A-122*). The wording of all three Circulars is similar in many respects. They provide that the total cost of a program or contract is the sum of the allowable direct costs incident to its performance, plus its allocable portion of allowable indirect costs, less applicable credits. The terms *allowable costs, direct costs,* and *indirect costs,* among others, are defined in the Circulars.

Allowable Costs

To be "allowable," costs must meet the following general criteria:

a. Be necessary and reasonable for proper and efficient performance and administration of the federal financial assistance (FFA) programs and be allocable thereto. (A cost is reasonable if it does not exceed that which would be incurred by a prudent person under the circumstances prevailing at the time the decision was made to incur the cost.)

b. Be authorized or not prohibited under state or local laws or regulations.

c. Conform to any limitations or exclusions, federal laws, terms and conditions of the federal financial assistance award and program, or other governing regulations as to types or amounts of cost items.

d. Be consistent with policies, regulations, and procedures that apply uniformly to both federally assisted and other activities of the governmental unit.

e. Be accorded consistent treatment. Consequently, a cost may not be assigned to a federal financial assistance program as a direct cost if any other cost incurred for the same purpose has been allocated to federal financial assistance program as an indirect cost.

f. Except as otherwise provided for, be determined in accordance with generally accepted accounting principles.

g. Not be included as a cost or used to meet cost sharing or matching requirements of any other federally supported activity in either the current or a prior period except as specifically provided by federal law.

h. Be determined net of all applicable credits (e.g., purchase discounts; rebates or allowances; recoveries or indemnities on losses; sale of publications and scrap; income from personal or incidental services; insurance refunds or rebates; earnings or imputed earnings on reserves; and adjustments of overpayments or erroneous charges).

i. Be adequately documented.[1]

---

[1] The foregoing criteria for allowable costs and the following discussion of cost items are based on an exposure draft (ED) of a revised *Circular A-87* "Cost Principles for State and Local Government," released August 19, 1993. These criteria and cost items are similar to those contained in *Circular A-21*, but the final version may change in some respects in response to comments received by the OMB on the ED. Executive Office of the President, Office of Management and Budget, Exposure Draft, *Circular A-87*, "Cost Principles for State and Local Governments, Attachment A," August 1993.

Each Circular provides standards for determining the allowability of selected items of cost. Certain items of cost are generally allowable whether or not mentioned specifically in a grant, contract, or other agreement document. Certain other cost items are allowable only if specifically approved by the grantor agency, and certain other cost items are unallowable. *Circular A-87* lists 42 cost items ranging alphabetically from Accounting to Underrecovery of Costs under Federal Agreements. Of the 42 cost items, 31 are allowable whether direct or indirect to the extent they pertain to specific grants or to the overall management of all grant programs. Depreciation and use allowances are included in the 31 allowable cost items. As explained in Chapter 6, even though governmental funds do not record depreciation expense, depreciation can be computed for purposes of claiming it as an allowable cost under federal grants and contracts. Similarly, public (governmentally owned) colleges and universities ordinarily do not record depreciation in their Current Funds for buildings and equipment, although private colleges and universities are required to do so by Financial Accounting Standards Board (FASB) standards. Public colleges and universities may find it useful, however, to report depreciation in Plant Fund accounts in order to compute depreciation charges for work under federal grants and contracts.

Costs Allowable under Some Circumstances and Unallowable Costs.   Several of the 31 allowable items are allowable under highly restrictive conditions, and generally require the explicit approval of the grantor agency. An example is advertising costs that are allowable only for such items as recruitment of personnel, procurement of goods and services, and disposal of scrap or surplus materials related to the performance of federal assistance programs. Eleven of the 42 cost items are **unallowable,** including such items as alcoholic beverages, bad debt expenses, contributions and donations, fund-raising and investment management costs, entertainment, general expenses of the state or local government (e.g., salaries of the chief executive, legislatures, judicial department officials, etc.), and lobbying. Similar prohibitions apply to colleges and universities under the provisions of *Circular A-21*.

Direct Costs

Direct costs are those that can be identified specifically with a particular **cost objective.** A cost objective, in federal terminology, is an organizational unit, function, activity, project, cost center, or pool established for the accumulation of costs. A **final,** or ultimate, cost objective is a specific grant, project, contract, or other activity (presumably one of interest to the federal agency that provides resources for the activity under a grant, contract, or other agreement). A cost may be direct with respect to a given function or activity but indirect with respect to the grant or other final cost objective of interest to the grantor or contractor. Typical direct costs chargeable to grant programs include compensation of employees for the time and efforts devoted specifically to the execution of grant programs; cost of materials acquired, consumed, or expended specifically for the purpose of the grant; and other items of expense incurred specifically to carry out the grant agreement. If approved by the grantor agency, equipment purchased and other capital expenditures incurred for a certain grant or other final cost objective would be considered direct costs.

Indirect Costs

Indirect costs, according to *Circular A-87,* are those *(a)* incurred for a common or joint purpose benefiting more than one cost objective, and *(b)* not readily assignable to the cost objectives specifically benefited, without effort disproportionate to the results' achieved. The term *indirect costs* applies to costs originating in the grantee department, as well as to those incurred by other departments in supplying goods, services, and facilities to the grantee department. To facilitate equitable distribution of indirect expenses to the cost objectives served, it may be necessary to establish a number of "pools" of indirect cost within the grantee department. Indirect cost pools should be distributed to benefited cost objectives on bases that produce an equitable result in consideration of relative benefits derived. In certain instances, grantees may negotiate annually with the grantor a predetermined fixed rate for computing indirect costs applicable to a grant, or a lump-sum allowance for indirect costs, but generally grantees must prepare a cost allocation plan that conforms with instructions issued by the U.S. Department of Health and Human Services. Cost allocation plans of local governments will be retained for audit by a designated federal agency. (Audit of federal grants is discussed in some detail in Chapter 14 of this text.) Some of the essential features of a cost allocation plan may best be illustrated here in the context of an example of cost determination for hospital services.

Cost Determination— A Hospital Example

Even though hospitals are presently paid by Medicare on a **prospective** basis (as discussed in Chapter 20), they need to determine the relationship between amounts they have received and the actual cost of rendering the services. In this chapter we are concerned with cost determination. Three terms are particularly important in the present discussion: direct cost, indirect cost, and full cost. A **direct cost** of a certain department is a cost incurred because of some definite action by or for the department (or program or project). Thus, in a hospital, the salary of the pharmacist is a direct cost of the pharmacy department. A hospital pharmacy exists to serve the patients of the hospital, however, so from the viewpoint of an inpatient nursing station the pharmacist's salary is an **indirect** cost. Likewise, the direct costs of all departments that exist to facilitate the work of the nursing station are indirect costs from the viewpoint of the nursing station.

In order to determine the total cost, or **full cost,** of serving the patient, it is necessary to add the indirect costs to the direct costs. Although the process of cost allocation is illustrated here in relation to a hospital, it underlies all cost accounting and cost determination systems, and some adaptation of one of the methods discussed below is used in every business and every nonprofit entity that attempts to determine costs (even if a "direct costing" system is used). A brief description of two basic methods of distributing the costs of service departments is:

Step-down: Costs of nonrevenue-producing departments are allocated in sequence to departments they serve, whether or not these produce revenue. Once the costs of a department have been allocated, the costing process for that department is closed, and it receives no further charges.

Multiple distribution: Costs of nonrevenue-producing departments are allocated to **all** departments they serve. In a computerized system, using a process of successive iterations, the amounts of cost allocated to nonrevenue-producing departments may be reduced to insignificant amounts, which may then be closed to revenue-producing departments. In a noncomputerized system, the number of iterations is generally reduced to two.

Although administrators of hospitals and other health care providers need to know the costs of services rendered in order to keep costs in line with payments by Medicare and other third-party payers, in order to measure the effectiveness of departmental supervisors, and in order to have a realistic basis for budgets, the primary reason why many hospitals have been concerned with cost determination is that a very large proportion of charges for services rendered to patients are paid by third-party payers. Third-party payers generally require hospitals to report cost information periodically in a specified form, either prospectively or retrospectively. The multiple distribution method is used in some cases because of the requirements of contract purchasers. The step-down method is also an accepted method.

Under the step-down method, departmental costs are allocated in sequence. It is important that the departments be ranked so that the cost of the one that renders service to the greatest number of other departments, while receiving benefits from the least number of departments, is allocated first; and the cost of the one rendering service to the least number of other departments, while receiving benefits from the greatest number, is allocated last. Practical application of this theory often requires arbitrary decisions as to the sequence in which departmental costs are closed. A further problem in cost allocation is the choice of bases. The base selected for the allocation of the expense of each department should meet two criteria:

1. It should result in an allocation that is fair to all departments concerned.
2. The application of the base should be clerically feasible.

An example of the application of the step-down method of allocating costs of nonrevenue-producing departments of the Frumerville Hospital is presented in Illustration 18–1. A glance at the worksheet shows that the method is aptly named, since the sequential closing of accounts gives the money columns the appearance of a series of steps. The worksheet technique here illustrated provides for the vertical distribution of general service department direct and allocated expenses. For example, the total direct expenses of the first department listed, Maintenance of Plant, are entered as negative figures (indicated by the parentheses enclosing the figures) on the first line in the second money column from the left. The amount of maintenance of plant expense allocated to each department served is entered on the appropriate line under the negative amount; that is,

ILLUSTRATION 18–1

FRUMERVILLE HOSPITAL
Step-Down Method—Expense Distribution
Year Ended April 30, 19—

	Direct Costs	Maintenance of Plant	Operation of Plant	Housekeeping	Laundry and Linen	Cafeteria	Administration	Medical Supplies	Medical Records	Nursing Service	Dietary	Total Costs
General Services:												
Maintenance of plant	$ 252,000	(252,000)	—	—	—	—	—	—	—	—	—	—
Operation of plant	354,600	113,400	(468,000)	—	—	—	—	—	—	—	—	—
Housekeeping	357,000	2,520	2,340	(361,860)	—	—	—	—	—	—	—	—
Laundry and linen service	216,000	10,080	16,848	7,236	(250,164)	—	—	—	—	—	—	—
Cafeteria	23,640	756	14,508	7,236	1,251	(47,391)	—	—	—	—	—	—
Administration	844,800	7,560	28,548	25,332	249	6,918	(913,407)	—	—	—	—	—
Medical supplies	480,000	2,520	6,084	1,809	501	1,707	39,276	(531,897)	—	—	—	—
Medical records	132,000	2,520	4,680	10,857	—	1,137	25,575	—	(176,769)	—	—	—
Nursing service	1,800,000	1,764	7,020	2,532	6,504	20,709	466,752	—	—	(2,305,281)	—	—
Dietary	657,000	10,080	19,188	10,857	3,003	4,596	103,215	—	—	—	(807,939)	—
Special Services:												
Operating rooms	482,460	25,200	28,548	3,618	41,778	3,459	77,640	79,785	—	—	—	742,488
Delivery rooms	141,000	15,120	14,508	10,857	21,015	1,422	31,968	53,190	—	—	—	289,080
Radiology	300,000	10,080	14,508	14,475	3,003	1,707	29,276	—	—	—	—	383,049
Laboratory	381,000	7,560	16,848	14,475	3,003	3,459	77,640	—	—	—	—	503,985
Blood bank	219,000	2,016	3,744	5,427	249	570	12,789	—	—	—	—	243,795
Cost of medical supplies sold	—	—	—	—	—	—	—	265,947	—	—	—	265,947
Routine Services:												
Medical and surgical	144,000	25,200	219,024	218,202	138,339	—	—	79,785	137,880	1,959,489	807,939	3,729,858
Nursery	13,500	3,024	23,868	7,236	18,762	—	—	26,595	8,838	345,792	—	447,615
Outpatient clinic	192,000	12,600	47,736	21,711	12,507	1,707	39,276	26,595	30,051	—	—	384,183
Totals	$6,990,000	0	0	0	0	0	0	0	0	0	0	$6,990,000

$113,400 of the $252,000 maintenance of plant expense was allocated to the Operation of Plant department. Inasmuch as the additions to other departments total the amount distributed, the column total is zero. Likewise, the Operation of Plant expense is allocated to departments served. In this case, the expense to be allocated is $468,000; the total of the direct expenses, $354,600; and the allocation of Maintenance of Plant expense, $113,400. Illustration 18–1 also shows that this method of cost analysis does not produce total cost figures for the nonrevenue-producing or "general services" departments. Many accountants feel direct departmental costs are more useful for managerial purposes than total costs (which include indirect costs charged to the department on the basis of many assumptions). Total cost figures are necessary, however, for determination that departmental revenues bear a reasonable relation to costs of the same department. Hospitals must cover the costs of departments that serve other hospital departments as well as the costs of the departments that serve patients directly.

Departmental costs, as determined in Illustration 18–1 (see the right-hand column), may be used in further allocations to determine costs of programs supported by grants, and to determine total costs of rendering services to inpatients (or to any given "diagnosis-related group" of patients). Bases for such an allocation must be chosen in accord with the same criteria as govern the choice of bases for the allocation of nonrevenue-producing departments.

For managerial purposes—and in some cases, for reimbursement purposes—it is desirable to compute unit costs of services rendered by special service departments. In the Frumerville Hospital, to continue the same example, records indicate 1,200,000 radiologic service units were rendered during the year (the Radiologic Section of the Connecticut State Medical Society, in cooperation with the Connecticut Hospital Cost Commission, has issued a table of such units, reflecting the relative complexity and time consumption of various services). The total of direct and allocated costs of the Radiology department of Frumerville Hospital was $383,049 (see Illustration 18–1); therefore, the cost per radiologic service unit is $383,049 ÷ 1,200,000, or 31.92 cents.

Cost Accounting

Job Order Cost Accounting. In order to record the costs chargeable to specific grants, programs, projects, activities, or departments in a systematic manner, the form of cost accounting described in collegiate cost accounting texts as **job order cost accounting** may be used. In brief, the essential characteristic of a job order system is the routine identification of each element of the direct cost of a given grant, etc., and the periodic allocation to the grant of an equitable portion of the indirect costs incurred to make it possible to perform the given grant and other grants. Indirect costs are often referred to as "overhead." Ordinarily, overhead is allocated on the basis of a predetermined rate.

Process Cost Accounting. Some activities of governmental units, health care entities, and universities are manufacturing activities operated as a continuous process and are appropriately accounted for by use of the form of cost accounting described in collegiate cost accounting texts as **process cost accounting.** In contrast with a job order system, which focuses on the accumulation of costs on a project basis, a process system focuses on the accumulation of costs on a time period basis. For example, the wages of workers assigned to the asphalt plant would be charged to an account for that activity; raw materials used in that activity and overhead allocable to that activity would be charged to the same account. The total costs incurred for the asphalt plant during a time period may be divided by the production of asphalt during that period to determine the average cost of the product for that period.

Activity-Based Costing

Activity-based costing (ABC) was developed for use by manufacturing companies when it became apparent that traditional cost accounting systems were producing distorted product costs. Thus, some products which were thought to be profitable were, on closer inspection, found to be unprofitable, and vice versa. Two Harvard University professors, Robin Cooper and Robert S. Kaplan, made convincing arguments that typical cost accounting systems often understate profits on high-volume products and overstate profits on low-volume specialty items.[2] This problem is attributable, in part, to greater product diversity, shorter product life cycles, shift in production technology from labor to automation, more diverse distribution channels, and greater quality demands, all of which are driven by need to more effectively compete in the global marketplace. The net effect of these trends (which are also applicable to government, at least to some extent) is to create a larger infrastructure of "production support" activities, and thus to shift costs from direct cost categories to indirect cost, or overhead, categories. As a larger proportion of these costs is allocated to products, product cost distortions become a larger problem and may result in poor product decisions.

ABC essentially attempts to determine the cost of specific process-related activities, the "drivers" of those costs (e.g., labor-hours, machine-hours, or units of material), and the consumption of cost drivers in producing outputs of goods or services. Emphasis is placed on tracing the specific activities performed to specific outputs of goods or services, rather than on allocating average costs to units of output as done in conventional cost accounting systems. A recent publication of the Institute of Management Accountants explains the advantage of the ABC approach relative to traditional cost accounting allocations:[3]

> In traditional systems, financial controllers usually create elaborate, step-down, sequential allocations that distribute service department cost to production work centers based on percentage estimates. These allocations are often flawed because they assume arbitrary relationships; for example, using square feet or head count. These

---

[2] Robin Cooper and Robert S. Kaplan, "Measure Costs Right: Make the Right Decisions," *Harvard Business Review*, September–October 1988, pp. 96–103.

[3] Gary Cokins; Alan Stratton; and Jack Helbling, *An ABC Manager's Primer: Straight Talk on Activity-Based Costing* (Montvale, N.J.: Institute of Management Accountants, 1993).

measures do not reflect disproportionate resource consumption. Such burden-averaging techniques are convenient for accountants but are not of service to users of information.

With ABC, resource cost drivers replace the step-down allocations with cause-and-effect relationships at the activity level. (p. 13)

Determining the amount of each activity that is consumed in each product or service utilizes materials usage records, observation, and timekeeping systems, but is often augmented with estimates obtained through employee interviews and other means. The cost of designing a system that totally eliminates the need for overhead allocation is likely to be prohibitive. If allocation of "residual" unassigned costs is not potentially distortive, it may be more cost effective to focus ABC design on major activities and cost drivers, and then allocate remaining costs on an appropriate basis.

As discussed in Chapter 16, many governments are implementing state-of-the-art approaches such as total quality management (TQM) and service efforts and accomplishments (SEA) measures to improve performance. Either approach requires timely information on the full cost of resources consumed in providing service outputs. To calculate the full cost of services, however, requires careful allocation of indirect costs such as the clerical and administrative costs of general government functions (e.g., chief executive's office, finance department, legal department, etc.). The use of inappropriate allocation bases may produce distorted cost estimates for some service outputs in much the same manner that conventional cost systems produce distorted product costs. It is not surprising then that some governments have adopted ABC for key service functions. A recent article by Bridget Anderson explains the objectives of ABC in a governmental environment as follows:[4]

The objectives of ABC are to preserve, at a minimum, the present quality and availability of core services but to acknowledge that some of the forces for greater expenditures have not been controlled. It seeks to reduce the costs of service outcomes by:

- reducing the number of service units through program redesign,
- finding lower cost alternatives,
- making volume increases dependent on cost reductions, and
- understanding and controlling the delivery/program design interaction.

A simplified diagram of an ABC cost model used by the City of Indianapolis to identify activity-based costs for snow control and patching chuckholes is shown in Illustration 18–2. Total activities cost for one particular district of the City for the two functions (snow control and chuckhole patching) is $2,600 as displayed in the leftmost table of Illustration 18–2. The five activities identified are C labor, D labor, salt, SAD (a type of truck), and central service overhead. The drivers identified in Illustration 18–2 are direct labor-hours of C and D labor, tons of salt,

---

[4] Bridget M. Anderson, "Using Activity-Based Costing for Efficiency and Quality," *Government Finance Review*, June 1993, pp. 7–9.

ILLUSTRATION 18–2   Identification of Activity-Based Costs

Activities

Activity Name	Total Dollars
C labor	$1,000
D labor	600
Salt	400
SAD truck	400
Central serv O/H	200
Total	**$2,600**

Activities and Related Drivers

Activity Name	Driver
C labor	C hours
D labor	D hours
Salt	Tons of salt
SAD truck	SAD hours
Central serv O/H	Total labor hours

Consumption

Drivers	Snow Control	Patch Chuckhole	Total
C hours	50	50	100
D hours	10	20	30
Tons of salt	500	.0	500
SAD hours	80	70	150
Total labor hours	60	70	130

Cost per Output

Activities	Snow Control	Patch Chuckhole	Total
C labor	$ 500	$ 500	$1,000
D labor	200	400	600
Salt	400	0	400
SAD truck	213	187	400
Central serv O/H	92	108	200
Total	**$1,405**	**$1,195**	**$2,600**

12 miles of road	$117.08	
14 tons of mix		$85.36

SOURCE: Bridget M. Anderson, "Using Activity-Based Costing for Efficiency and Quality," *Government Finance Review*, June 1993, p. 8. Reprinted with permission of the Government Finance Officers Association.

SAD (vehicle usage) hours, and total labor-hours for C and D combined to allocate overhead to units of output. The Consumption table shows the driver units of each activity that were consumed for each of the two service functions. Finally, as shown in the Cost per Output table, driver units consumed are multiplied by cost per driver unit and aggregated to determine the total cost of providing snow control and patching chuckholes. The cost for the current period for clearing snow from 12 miles of road was $1,405 or $117.08 per mile. Similarly, the cost of 14 tons of mix for patching chuckholes was $1,195 or $85.36 per ton.

Actual snow removal costs per mile for five geographic cost centers of the City of Indianapolis are presented in Illustration 18–3. As shown in this illustration, the cost per mile for snow removal ranged from $39.96 for 1,646 miles of road in the Southeast cost center to $117.59 for 1,000 miles of road in the Southwest cost center. Subsequent analysis by the City's Department of Transportation revealed that the Southwest cost center was using excessive amounts of salt per mile and was not using an optimal mix of equipment. The Center geographic cost center was using excessive labor. This analysis led to reallocation of both personnel and equipment between cost centers thus resulting in improved efficiency without loss of quality.[5]

---

[5] Ibid, p. 8.

ILLUSTRATION 18–3   Cost Analysis of Snow Removal

Activity	Geographic Cost Center				
	Northwest	**Northeast**	**Center**	**Southwest**	**Southeast**
C labor	0.89	1.19	3.08	0.14	0.42
D labor	7.27	11.76	25.29	13.21	7.73
E labor	5.09	5.84	5.59	2.77	1.17
Supervisors	2.27	2.69	3.81	6.10	1.81
T supervisors	2.60	5.10	2.13	2.06	2.08
Personnel Costs	**18.12**	**26.58**	**39.90**	**24.28**	**13.21**
Calcium	0.86			4.86	
Salt	36.18	9.25	20.78	43.96	5.24
Sand				0.14	
Direct Materials Costs	**37.04**	**9.25**	**20.78**	**48.96**	**5.24**
Central Services	9.35	13.29	19.74	18.63	7.47
Facilities	1.84	3.81	0.94	0.59	0.66
Fixed assets	0.14	0.08	0.05	0.07	0.05
Administration	3.18	4.30	4.98	3.77	2.34
Overhead Costs	**14.51**	**21.48**	**25.71**	**23.06**	**10.52**
Crewcab pickup	0.01				
Loader	8.24	3.83	1.43	4.25	0.77
Mini pickup	6.11				
SAD 90	6.24	6.12	0.50	6.51	2.73
SADA 85	1.17	1.93	0.88	4.02	1.67
Sedan	3.31				
TAD 90	2.87	0.79	3.72	2.98	1.89
TADA	10.41	4.25	1.73	2.98	2.85
Dump truck	0.01	0.02			
Unused equipment	0.48	0.55	0.13	0.55	1.08
Rolling Stock Costs	**38.85**	**17.49**	**8.39**	**21.29**	**10.99**
TOTAL	**$108.52**	**$74.80**	**$94.78**	**$117.59**	**$39.96**
Miles plowed	1,100	1,000	900	1,000	1,846

SOURCE: Bridget M. Anderson, "Using Activity-Based Costing for Efficiency and Quality," *Government Finance Review*, June 1993, p. 9. Reprinted with permission of the Government Finance Officers Association.

Clerical and Administrative Costs

A very large part of governmental expenditures are incurred for services of a general nature (such as the costs of the chief executive's office, costs of accounting and auditing, or costs of boards and commissions), which are somewhat remote from the results any given subdivision is expected to accomplish. Furthermore, in smaller units of government, many offices or departments perform such a variety of services that separating their costs is practically impossible under their present schemes of organization.

Given the importance and magnitude of key administrative offices, government officials should attempt to measure the efficiency and effectiveness of the activities of these offices just as it would other service activities. The primary difference is that many of these activities, such as those of the finance and legal departments for example, mainly serve customers within the government rather than the general public. Activity-based costing would seem to be a useful tool for measuring the cost of such activities. Possible activities and cost drivers for selected offices are provided below.

Office	Activities	Cost Drivers
Tax Collector	Preparing tax bills.	Number of bills prepared.
	Collecting tax bills.	Number of bills collected.
	Preparing receipts.	Number of receipts prepared.
	Mailing receipts.	Number of receipts mailed.
	Preparing deposits.	Number of deposits prepared.
Accounting	Recording revenues.	Number of revenue transactions.
	Recording expenditures.	Number of expenditure transactions.
	Processing payroll.	Number of employees.
	Recording purchase orders.	Number of orders.
Public Recorder	Recording documents.	Number of documents or number of lines.

This table is intended to be illustrative of the kinds of activities and cost drivers that might apply to certain administrative offices. Obviously, the list is incomplete, but, insofar as the activities and drivers are appropriate for a particular office, costs accumulated by activity could be useful both for internal performance review and pricing services to other offices. As an example of pricing services rendered, the costs of accounting activities could be priced to other departments on the basis of the amount of accounting activities they consume. For example, assume that the Public Works Department generates 30 percent of all purchase requisitions processed by the Accounting Department. Arguably, it should then be charged for 30 percent of the total cost of recording purchase orders in the accounting function. Similarly, the costs of recording expenditures could be charged to departments proportionate to the expenditures they make. Although an activity-based costing approach to costing central services seems technologically feasible, much additional research is needed to determine whether the benefits would warrant the considerable costs involved.

Limitations on the Use of Unit Costs

It has been said that **no** unit costs are better than inaccurate ones, the reason being that unless they are reliable they may lead to unwarranted and erroneous conclusions on the part of administrators, taxpayers, and the public, generally. Corollary to this, it may be said that crude unit costs, although both theoretically and technically correct, may be almost as misleading as inaccurate ones. No unit cost figure, especially in government, should be used as the basis for decisive action or opinions without careful evaluation in light of all pertinent facts. Such influences as regional variations in personnel costs, differences in climate and other physiographic conditions, size of the organization represented, and density of population in the area served are some of the factors that must be recognized if they are present and given due weight in appraising differences in unit costs. The establishment of standard costs that take into account all local circumstances and conditions has been recommended as one method for obviating the effect of comparisons with figures that are not entirely analogous. Historical costs compiled by other governmental units may not be entirely acceptable as a standard of comparison. This is true because one or more factors that affect costs in one jurisdiction may be decidedly more or less influential, or even not present. Finally, the quality of service represented by the unit of product must never be lost sight of in reaching a judgment as to the reasonableness of unit costs. Even such objective units as gallons of water and kilowatts of electricity have intangible qualities such as purity, taste, pressure, reliability, attention to complaints, and other service factors. For administrative government, on the other extreme, the possibilities for variance are far greater. At best, therefore, unit cost accounting in government and nonprofit entities is not an automatic process for turning out a standardized product, but only a means for helping to accomplish a desired end. Activity-based costing, discussed earlier in this chapter, can also help minimize problems arising from the use of unit costs for decision making.

Interrelation of Budgeting and Cost Accounting

Predetermination of overhead rates, whether for full standard cost accounting, process cost accounting, or job order cost accounting, involves budgeting the overhead costs that should be incurred at the level of activity chosen as a basis for determination of the rate. Thus, if the budgeting process that is required for reasons discussed at length in Chapters 3 and 16 is carefully structured, much of the work necessary for the operation of a cost accounting system is accomplished in the preparation of the budget. Since it is not possible to foresee the level of activity that any given department will be called upon to work, it is desirable to budget costs that should be incurred at several different levels of activity. This form of budget preparation is known as **flexible budgeting.** It allows managers to match costs that were actually incurred in a period with costs that should have been incurred to achieve the output that was actually achieved.

Cost Accounting and Expenditure Accounting

Accounting for proprietary funds and nonexpendable trust funds of state and local governments, and for health care and many kinds of nonprofit entities, focuses on costs and expenses, as business accounting does; therefore, a cost accounting system is relatively easily installed. Accounting for "governmental funds" of state and local governments, and for colleges and universities, however, focuses on expenditures rather than on costs and expenses, and it is necessary to translate the legalistic concept of expenditures into the business concept of cost before a cost accounting system can be implemented.

Translating Expenditures into Costs

Expenditures for Materials or Supplies.   An expenditure occurs when a liability is created. Since a liability is created when personal or contractual services are received, expenditures for service fit the accrual definition of cost. However, when materials or supplies are received, an appropriation is expended, but there is no "cost" until the materials or supplies are used. If the inventory of materials or supplies at the end of a period is approximately the same as at the beginning of a period, expenditures for these items during the period may be a reasonably close approximation of cost during the period. Although reasonably level inventories in total may be common, there is no assurance that the usage of supplies for each program, or grant, during a period corresponds to expenditures for supplies for each program, or grant, during that period. If the supply cost of a given program is small in relation to total costs of that program, again expenditure accounting may provide a reasonable approximation of cost. If inventories fluctuate widely, or if some programs are heavy users of expensive supplies while other programs are light users of inexpensive supplies, accounting for governmental funds (which provides for the use of inventory accounts) must be supplemented by a system to provide for routine reporting of supply usage by programs.

Depreciation.   As is true in the case of the purchase of materials and supplies, an appropriation is expended when a capital asset is acquired or constructed. By definition, a capital asset has a service life expected to extend over more than one fiscal period. The process of allocating the cost of a capital asset to the periods during which the asset is used is called **depreciation** accounting. The basis of accounting presently required by the GASB does not allow for the recording of depreciation of general fixed assets as an expense of the governmental fund that finances the department using the fixed asset (although the standards specifically provide for recording of depreciation by enterprise funds and other businesslike activities). The GASB standards further complicate the determination of depreciation expense by programs in that they require general fixed assets to be accounted for by the General Fixed Assets Account Group (GFAAG), not by the fund entity that accounts for the operations of the department or activity using the long-lived assets in the provision of services (nor even the fund entity that expended an appropriation in order to acquire the asset).

Recommended records of the General Fixed Assets Account Group provide enough information (cost of each asset, its estimated useful life, its location, or the department to which it is assigned) to enable depreciation to be computed in a system divorced from the currently recommended accounting system. The cost system may selectively focus only on those programs or activities, or grants, for which depreciation would be a significant element of cost.

It is fairly apparent that the assignment of depreciation expense as a program, activity, or grant cost is not difficult if the asset being depreciated is used for only one program, activity, or grant. If an asset benefits more than one program or activity (such as a building occupied by several departments), an equitable and clerically feasible basis for allocation of the total depreciation expense must be found. Presently recommended records of the General Fixed Assets Account Group would not necessarily provide the appropriate information, but it would not be difficult to supplement existing records by statistical studies and Bayesian estimates of knowledgeable personnel to provide depreciation expense chargeable to each program or activity in all instances in which depreciation is a significant element of cost. (The designers of accounting systems for agencies of the federal government of the United States have provided for routine recording of depreciation expense and other program expenses as well as the recording of appropriation expenditures, as explained in Chapter 15.)

Measurement of Costs *Ex* Ante

Underlying the discussion in the preceding section on translating expenditures into costs is the assumption that cost is being measured *ex post* (after the fact). The observations in that section would hold true in developing program costs *ex ante* (before the fact), but only in the rather near future for which costs will result from activities that may be planned with a reasonable degree of certainty. The costs of proposed programs, however, must often be projected for many years into the future (as much as 100 years in the case of natural resources programs). Capital budgeting techniques widely advocated for use by both profit-seeking businesses and governmental bodies—and actually used to some extent by both—provide for discounting future costs to their value at the time the decision to accept or reject the project is to be made. Economists argue among themselves as to the correct discount rate to use in these computations. The answer is probably easier for state and local governmental projects than for projects proposed for the federal government; at least there appears to be some agreement that the rate paid on tax-exempt state and local governmental bonds would be appropriate. This conclusion is an oversimplification, however, because it is logical to allow for opportunity costs and political and social costs as well as accounting costs, that is: (1) If available general obligation bonding power is used to finance one given proposed project, no general obligation bonding power would be available for present alternative projects or for future alternative projects until the growth of assessed valuation and the retirement of debt allowed new bond issues; therefore, other financing sources, probably bearing higher rates, would have to be used. So, should all projects be discounted at the higher rates? (2) If the proposed construction of new freeways would split neighborhoods, isolating people from accustomed schools, churches, or shopping centers, as well as cause the condemnation of homes and the forced relocation of numerous residents (who also need to be thought of as voters), what **are** the costs that should be charged to the project? Even if the cost factors can be identified, with what degree of certainty can they be measured?

Measurement of Benefits

In contrast to the problem of measurement of costs of governmental programs, which can be solved *ex post* at least by a reorientation of traditional accounting and the supplementation of it by additional statistical data, traditional government accounting offers little help in the solution of the problem of measurement of benefits. Nor does traditional business accounting offer much help. Determination of the existence or absence of a benefit of a governmental program is a subjective matter rather than the objective one faced by businesses, which can define a benefit in terms of earnings. Both direct benefits and spillover benefits may be claimed by proponents of a proposed program. Some benefits, of both categories, may be measurable in monetary units; some may be quantifiable but not in monetary terms; and some may be expressed in terms of increased cultural or recreational opportunities or other values of doubtful quantifiability. Further, each of the above categories can be subdivided on the basis of the expected timing of the occurrence of benefits (the range is from immediately on approval of the project to possibly 100 years in the future); on the basis of the degree of certainty of the occurrence of the benefits (ranging from reasonably certain to highly conjectural); and on the basis of dependence of the occurrence of the benefits on events external to the program under consideration (the range is from independent to highly dependent; the occurrence of the external events themselves may be of varying probabilities). Nonetheless, in spite of all the difficulties, rational allocation of resources requires the best available information as to benefits expected to result from a proposed program to be matched with the best available information as to costs of the same program. Before a purported benefit can be identified as a true benefit, the objectives of the government and the objectives of the proposed program must be identified. Relative to this, Hinrichs points out:

> . . . the student of government decision making must not always assume that obscure and obfuscated objectives are totally lacking in function. Many times objectives are uncertain, changing, conflicting; this may not be the time for total inaction but instead a time of discovering and discussing objectives in the very process of moving in a general direction. Objectives often are a result of a feed-back process in getting the job underway and in working toward broader goals.[6]

Equally pragmatic, and equally relevant to the present discussion, is a comment by Hatry on the problem of expressing benefits in monetary items:

> Realistically most governmental problems involve major objectives of a nondollar nature. Not only is it very difficult for analysts to assign dollar "values" to such nondollar objectives, but it is also questionable whether it would be desirable even if it could be done. Thus, questions of the value of such effects as reducing death rates, reducing illness incidences and severities, improving housing conditions, and increasing recreational opportunities should not become simply a problem of estimating the dollar values of these things.
>
> The analysts should rather concentrate upon the estimation and presentation, for each alternative, of full information as the actual dollar effects and the effects upon the nonmonetary criteria. *This is the primary function of program analysis.*[7] [Emphasis added]

If the anticipated benefits from a program cannot be stated in quantitative terms, they must be stated verbally. In order to be of value in the management process, the statement must be explicit and in operational terms, not "God and Motherhood" generalities.

---

[6] Harley M. Hinrichs and Graeme M. Taylor, *Program Budgeting and Benefit-Cost Analysis* (Santa Monica, Calif.: Goodyear Publishing, 1969), p. 13.

[7] Ibid., p. 101.

Relation of
Long-Term
Benefit/Cost Analysis
to Planning

The statement of anticipated benefits from a proposed program, activity, or grant should follow from a statement of objectives for it. The statement of objectives should be expanded into a plan of action to achieve the objectives, which in turn serves as a basis for planning costs to be incurred. Unless this course is followed, administrators and legislators will not be able to allocate resources of the governmental unit wisely, nor will administrators be able to manage resources committed to approved programs. Legislators and the public have a right to expect this integration of long-range analysis and fiscal period planning, so that they may evaluate the actions of the administrators in following the plan as well as the success of the programs in achieving the stated objectives.

Conclusion

Chapters 2 through 13 were concerned with accounting and financial reporting standards established by the Governmental Accounting Standards Board. These standards pertain primarily to general purpose external financial reports of state and local governments. Chapter 1 deals with the objectives of accounting and financial reporting for governmental units and nonprofit organizations set forth in GASB *Concepts Statement No. 1,* "Objectives of Financial Reporting," and in the FASB's *Statements of Financial Accounting Concepts.* As indicated in Chapter 1, financial reporting should address the needs of all persons concerned with decision making for governmental and nonprofit organizations. Chapter 16 introduced the subject of budgeting for resource management. Chapter 18 presents a brief statement of cost determination and cost accounting, indicates the interrelations of cost accounting and budgeting, and suggests the need for translating expenditure accounting and budgeting into cost accounting for long-term budgeting. Activity-based costing appears to be particularly useful in facilitating performance measurement systems such as total quality management and service efforts and accomplishments measures.

Selected References

Anderson, Bridget M. "Using Activity-Based Costing for Efficiency and Quality." *Government Finance Review* 9, no. 3 (June 1993), pp. 7–9.

Cokins, Gary; Alan Stratton; and Jack Helbling. *An ABC Manager's Primer: Straight Talk on Activity-Based Costing.* Montvale, N.J.: Institute of Management Accountants, 1993.

Cooper, Robin, and Robert S. Kaplan. "Measure Costs Right: Make the Right Decisions." *Harvard Business Review*, September–October 1988, pp. 96–103.

Hinrichs, Harley H., and Graeme M. Taylor. *Program Budgeting and Benefit-Cost Analysis.* Santa Monica, Calif.: Goodyear Publishing, 1969.

Office of Management and Budget. *Circular A-21, Cost Principles for Educational Institutions.* Washington, D.C.: Superintendent of Documents, U.S. Government Printing Office.

————. *Circular A-87, Cost Principles for State and Local Governments.* Washington, D.C.: Superintendent of Documents, U.S. Government Printing Office.

————. *Circular A-122, Cost Principles for Nonprofit Organizations.* Washington, D.C.: Superintendent of Documents, U.S. Government Printing Office.

Questions

18–1. If governmental units, educational institutions, and health care entities are interested in cost determination, does this imply that their accounting systems should conform with standards set by the FASB for business organizations? Explain your answer.

18–2. If governmental units, educational institutions, and nonprofit health care entities exist in order to provide services needed by the public, or a segment of the public, and are not concerned with the generation of net income, why should they be interested in the determination of costs? Explain your answer.

18–3. The Finance Officer of a small city has heard that certain items of cost may be allowable under federal grants and contracts, even though they were not incurred specifically for the grant or contract. To what source could the Finance Officer go to determine what costs are allowable under federal grants and contracts?

18–4. Explain in your own words what a cost objective is. What is the relationship of direct costs to a cost objective? If a governmental unit or nonprofit organization has no grants from the federal government, is there any reason for its accountants to identify direct costs?

18–5. Explain in your own words what indirect costs are. For what reason would the administrator of a governmental unit or nonprofit organization want indirect costs allocated to cost objectives?

18–6. What criteria should be applied to the selection of a basis for the allocation of indirect expenses? Explain.

18–7. Below are listed a number of activities and work units often used in measuring output of the activities for purposes of relating cost to output or determining unit costs. For each one, state one or more factors that might make it difficult to evaluate performance of the activity.

Street cleaning—linear mile	Servicing of parking meters—each
Sweeping and collection of leaves—square yard	School bus operation—student-day
Earth excavation—cubic yard	Billing of taxes—bill
Snow and ice removal—cubic yard	Solid waste collection—ton
Laying of mains—linear foot	Recording documents—document

18–8. What is the relationship between cost determination, as discussed in Chapter 18, and budget preparation, as discussed in Chapters 3 and 16 of this text?

18–9. Explain why conventional cost accounting systems have become less useful in both the business and government setting. How does **activity-based costing** (ABC) reduce the problems created by conventional cost accounting systems?

18–10. What is the role of **cost drivers** in an activity-based cost system? Explain how analysis of cost drivers can be useful in identifying inefficient activities and the cause(s) of the inefficiency.

Exercises and Problems

18–1. Write the numbers 1 through 10 on a sheet of paper. Beside each number write the letter corresponding with the best answer to each of the following questions:

1. Cost principles established by the federal Office of Management and Budget (OMB) apply to which of the following types of entities?

a. State and local governments.

b. Colleges and universities.

c. Nonprofit organizations such as museums.

d. All of the above.

2. Which of the following is *not* a general criterion for a cost item to be an "allowable" cost?

a. Be necessary and reasonable for proper and efficient performance and administration of the federal financial assistance program.

b. Be approved by the Cost Accounting Standards Board.

c. Be determined in accordance with generally acceptable accounting principles.

d. Be authorized or not prohibited under state or local regulations.

3. Which of the following is an example of an **applicable credit?**

a. Purchase discount.

b. Advertising expense.

c. A fund equity item that is reserved for capital construction with the permission of the grantor agency.

d. All of the above.

4. Which of the following cost items would be **unallowable** by a federal grantor agency?

a. Depreciation on buildings and equipment.

b. Advertising expense.

c. Alcoholic beverages for a Christmas party.

d. All of the above.

5. Which of the following ordinarily would *not* be classified as a **direct cost** of a particular grant?

a. Depreciation on buildings and equipment.

b. Compensation of employees for time spent working on the specific federal assistance programs.

c. Materials consumed in performance of the specific federal assistance programs.

d. None of the above.

6. Costs that are incurred for a common or joint purpose benefiting more than one cost objective and that are not readily assignable to the cost objectives specifically benefited, without effort disproportionate to the results achieved, are referred to as:

a. Pseudo costs.   c. Direct costs.

b. Indirect costs.   d. Activity-based costs.

7. Which of the following statements about **activity-based costing** is true?

a. It is intended to reduce the probability of distorted unit costs that may adversely affect management decisions.

b. It eliminates the need for allocation of indirect costs.

c. It permits measuring the true cost of every unit of output; cost measures that are free from subjective estimates.

d. All of the above.

8. In activity-based costing, the amount of activity-related cost that is consumed in producing goods or service is measured by the consumption of units of particular allocation bases referred to as:

   a. Activities.   *c.* Activity cost drivers.

   b. Cost objects.   *d.* Unit costs.

9. A good cost accounting system facilitates a kind of budgeting in which the costs associated with different levels of activity are planned for. Such a form of budget is referred to as:

   a. Incremental budgeting.

   b. Fixed budgeting.

   c. Rational budgeting.

   d. Flexible budgeting.

10. Determining the cost of depreciation related to the general fixed assets of a governmental unit for purposes of charging the cost to a federal grant, or for internal costing of services, is complicated by which of the following factors?

   a. The method of depreciation used does not correspond with actual patterns of asset consumption.

   b. Some fixed assets are used for many activities and typically no records of such use are maintained.

   c. Depreciation is not recorded in any fund for such assets, nor is depreciation usually recorded in the General Fixed Assets Account Group.

   d. Both *b* and *c* are correct.

18–2. Compensation for personal services rendered during the period of performance under the grant agreement is an allowable cost under OMB *Circular A-87,* as are employee benefits such as vacation leave, sick leave, or employers' contributions to retirement and health plans, etc., if "the cost thereof is equitably allocated to all related activities, including grant programs."

    During 19x7, Bill Jamison, an employee of the City of Caron, was paid an annual salary of $56,000. He took three weeks' paid vacation plus one-week paid sick leave. The employer's contributions to retirement and health plans amounted to 25 percent of Jamison's annual salary. During 19x7, Jamison worked 12 weeks on HHS Grant No. 9227. Compute the appropriate charge to that grant for Jamison's salary and fringe benefits (round to the nearest dollar).

18–3. On the basis of the following data, prepare a statement for the Town of Navaho for the year ended June 30, 19y5, showing the total cost of solid waste removal and the cost per ton of residential solid waste removed, or cubic yard of commercial solid waste removed (carry unit costs to three decimal places).

	Residential	Commercial
By town employees:		
Salaries and wages	$696,000	$467,000
Materials and supplies	$ 39,000	$ 36,090
Equipment use	$300,840	$201,470
Tons collected	165,000	—
Cubic yards collected	—	248,000
Labor-hours	90,000	68,000
By contractors:		
Cost	$ 78,900	$ 48,000
Tons collected	23,000	—
Cubic yards collected	—	30,000

Overhead for town force collection of residential solid waste is $0.948 per labor-hour; for commercial solid waste collection, $0.924 per labor-hour. Overhead for contract residential solid waste collection, 20 percent of cost (exclusive of overhead); for commercial solid waste collection, 15 percent of cost (exclusive of overhead).

18–4. The City of Bentonville operates a Shop and Maintenance Department and accounts for its activities by means of an internal service fund. In order to charge the using departments on an equitable basis for work orders filled, the Shop and Maintenance Department uses job order costing. Direct labor, materials used, and any other costs readily identifiable with a specific work order are charged to that work order, and overhead is allocated to each work order at the predetermined rate of 50 percent of direct labor dollars charged to the work order.

As of the end of fiscal year 19x7, four work orders were being worked on; costs charged to each during 19x7 were:

Work Order No.	Direct Labor	Direct Materials	Overhead	Total
871	$1,720	$ 770	$ 860	$3,350
875	240	660	120	1,020
876	860	750	430	2,040
877	380	630	190	1,200
Totals	$3,200	$2,810	$1,600	$7,610

During January 19x8, direct labor cost was incurred for the following orders in the amount shown:

Work Order No.	Amount
871	$1,200
875	3,600
876	4,400
877	700
878	800
879	1,280
880	360
881	540

During January 19x8, materials were used for the following orders in the dollar amounts shown:

Work Order No.	Amount
875	$2,600
876	570
877	120
878	440
879	680
880	600
881	1,210
882	80
883	120

The following orders were completed during January for departments accounted for by the funds shown:

Work Order No.	Fund
871	Capital Projects Fund
875	General Fund
876	Enterprise Fund
878	Special Revenue Fund

Required

a. Show in good form your computation of the total costs charged to each work order completed in January 19x8.

b. Assuming the department requesting work order 875 had estimated the cost to be $8,500, and the department requesting work order 876 had estimated the cost to be $9,000, show the entries each of these funds should make to record the approval of the invoice received from the Shop and Maintenance Department for the completed work order.

18–5. The Public Works Department of Parker City has an agreement with the city-owned electric utility whereby street lighting is charged to the Public Works Department at the cost of generation, transmission, and distribution.

The total cost of generating, transmitting, and distributing electricity, exclusive of charges for the use of equipment, was $5,288,000 in a certain period. The Public Works Department charges the utility for the use of City equipment, such charges being based on the actual cost of operation to the department. During the period, equipment units Nos. 4, 7, and 11 worked part of the time for the utility. Data regarding the number of hours operated and costs of operation are as follows:

Equipment Unit No.	Cost of Operation	Total Hours Operated	Hours Operated for Utility
4	$45,000	15,000	10,000
7	28,800	4,500	3,000
11	18,000	3,000	2,800

The utility generated a total of 61,712,000 kwhr. (kilowatt-hours), which were disposed as follows:

Used by utility itself	4,670,000 kwhr.
Sales to Public Works Department	1,567,000
Sales to other consumers	49,675,000
Lost and unaccounted for	5,800,000
Total	61,712,000

Prepare a statement for the electric utility of Parker City showing the cost of electricity furnished to the Public Works Department for street lighting during the year ended December 31.

18–6. The cost allocation plan for the urban campus of Midwest University is shown on pages 602–03. After reviewing this plan, answer the following questions:

1. What method is being used to distribute the costs of service departments or centers to programs?
2. Identify the service departments or centers whose costs are being distributed.
3. Discuss some of the potential pitfalls of this allocation method and suggest an alternative approach that might be better. Explain fully.

MIDWEST UNIVERSITY—URBAN CAMPUS
Summary of Statement of Operating Expenses and Overhead Rate Determination
Fiscal Year Ended June 30, 19x4

	TOTAL COSTS	LESS NON-APPLI-CABLE COSTS	APPLICABLE COSTS	ORGANIZED RESEARCH		EXTENSION & PUBLIC SERVICE	
				TOTAL COSTS	INDIRECT EXPENSES	TOTAL COSTS	INDIRECT EXPENSES
INSTRUCTION	34,821,748	933,971	33,887,776	583		1,773,745	
RESEARCH	1,174,538	25,847	1,148,691	1,004,982		4,827	
PUBLIC SERVICE	2,096,192	473,919	1,622,273			1,622,273	
ACADEMIC SUPPORT	7,078,180	559,464	6,518,715	10,897		15,133	
STUDENT SERVICES	3,249,331	703,826	2,545,505				
INSTITUTIONAL SUPPORT	5,682,397	869,331	4,813,066				
OPERATION & MAINTENANCE OF PLANT	6,232,056	33,599	6,198,488				
SCHOLARSHIPS & FELLOWSHIPS	4,548,453	4,535,044	13,409				
AUXILIARY ENTERPRISES	5,505,232	5,505,232	0				
TOTAL CURRENT FUND	70,388,127	13,640,233	56,747,923	1,016,462	0	3,415,978	0
LESS APPLICABLE CREDITS:							
OTHER MISCELLANEOUS INCOME			12,794				
ALLOCATIONS FROM CENTRAL ADMIN.							
(GRANT & CONTRACT FUNCTIONS)			32,994				
NET CURRENT FUNDS			56,793,711	1,016,462	0	3,415,978	0
EQUIPMENT USE CHARGES			479,502		5,005		21,265
IMPROVEMENTS OTHER THAN BUILDING CHARGES			31,727		1,201		348
BUILDING USE CHARGES			905,888		34,285		9,923
CAMPUS SHARE OF CENTRAL ADMIN. GENERAL AND ADMINISTRATIVE, LIBRARIES, & STUDENT SERVICES			1,443,969				
ALLOCATION OF OPERATION & MAINTENANCE OF PHYSICAL PLANT					283,900		88,849
ALLOCATION OF GENERAL & ADMINISTRATIVE			*		126,146		423,932
ALLOCATION OF LIBRARIES EXPENSE					4,658		0
ALLOCATION OF STUDENT SERVICE EXPENSE							
ALLOCATION OF DEPARTMENTAL OR DIVISIONAL ADMIN.			*		64,863		367,887
ALLOCATION OF DEPARTMENTAL ADMIN. SEPARATELY BUDGETED RESEARCH DEPARTMENTS			*		19,642		37,584
ALLOCATION OF SPONSORED PROJECTS ADMINISTRATION			*		38,199		29,178
			59,654,797	1,016,462	577,899	3,415,978	978,966
CAMPUS SHARE OF CENTRAL ADMINISTRATIONS INDIRECT				45,947	20,880	35,711	11,114
COST POOLS AND BASE TOTALS				1,062,409	598,779	3,451,689	990,080
LESS PORTION OF BASE APPLICABLE ONLY TO OFF CAMPUS ACTIVITIES				76,320		0	
TOTALS				986,089	598,779	3,451,689	990,080
ON CAMPUS RATES				0.5991		0.2868	

Note: The development of off-campus rates includes central administration pool costs from the same pools that are identified above by an asterisk. The amounts are as follows:

ORGANIZED RESEARCH	9,718
INSTRUCTION	12,523
EXTENSION AND PUBLIC SERVICE	7,039

INSTRUCTION		OTHER SPONSORED PROGRAMS	OTHER INSTITUTIONAL ACTIVITIES	SPONSORED PROJECTS ADMINISTRATION	DEPARTMENTAL ADMINISTRATION SEPARATELY BUDGETED RESEARCH DEPTS.	DEPARTMENTAL OR DIVISIONAL ADMINISTRATION	STUDENT SERVICES	LIBRARIES	GENERAL & ADMINISTRATIVE	OPERATION & MAINTENANCE OF PHYSICAL PLANT
TOTAL COSTS	INDIRECT EXPENSES									
30,622,756		(860)				1,380,201	(10,983)		122,336	
					25,390				113,491	
2,050,821		61,618	28,374		64,689	1,219,066		2,422,619	645,500	
		153,822	346,985				2,045,499			
		128,170	885,771	77,045			263,485		2,648,822	809,773
242,220									29,212	5,927,025
		(10,803)	24,212							
32,915,797	0	332,001	1,285,342	77,045	90,079	2,599,267	2,298,001	2,422,619	3,559,361	6,736,798
10,704										2,090
				32,994						
32,905,093	0	332,001	1,285,342	110,039	90,079	2,599,267	2,298,001	2,422,619	3,559,361	6,734,708
	281,731	1,114	48,788	0	757	24,027	17,422	9,223	42,104	28,067
	18,507	57	3,651	0	0	1,178	345	3,590	1,211	1,640
	528,418	1,629	104,254	0	0	33,648	9,845	102,489	34,583	46,814
							29,004	187,336	1,227,630	
	3,897,311	24,965	304,540	0	0	295,238	164,615	849,143	902,669	(6,811,229)
	4,083,614	41,096	159,514	13,656	11,179	322,576	285,188	300,654	(5,767,558)	
	3,052,768	0	817,636					(3,875,054)		
	2,804,420						(2,804,420)			
	2,836,631	6,552				(3,275,934)				
	44,789	0			(102,015)					
	63,381	1,016		(123,695)						
32,905,093	17,611,570	408,430	2,723,725	0	0	0	0	0	0	0
95,094	26,071									
33,000,186	17,637,641									
281,795										
32,718,392	17,637,641									
0.5391										

18–7. When the County Commission of Cooper County questioned the County Treasurer about his request for additional appropriations, he claimed the large number of tax bills prepared and collected was responsible for the heavy expenses of his office. Since the duties of the Treasurer's office are rather uniform and of limited range, it was decided to attempt a cost study in an effort to determine the reasonableness of the Treasurer's request. As tax bills are numbered serially, it is possible to determine accurately the number prepared and collected. It was decided to divide the activities of the office into general administration, billing, and collecting. General administration consists of supervising the office and providing information to taxpayers, attorneys, and others. It would be measured on the basis of thousands of dollars of collections. Preparing bills and collecting would be measured on the basis of numbers of bills prepared and collected, respectively. The following information is available about the costs of the office:

1. The salary of the Treasurer is $3,000 per month. His time is devoted to general administration, except that during approximately three months of each year he spends practically all his time on collections.

2. Two regular deputies each receive $1,800 per month. Their time is divided approximately four months to billing, four months to collections, and the remainder to general administration.

3. During the year, the office spent $12,000 for extra help, of which two thirds was chargeable to billing and one third to collecting.

4. The office collected $240,000 of delinquent taxes, interest, and penalties during the year, of which the Treasurer retained 4 percent, to be credited equally to administration and collection.

5. Utility bills, stationery and stamps, repairs to office equipment, and retirement contributions, etc., totaled $81,480 for the year. This was distributed to administration, billing, and collection on the basis of total salaries chargeable to those operations, except $20,600 spent for stamped envelopes was chargeable in total to collections.

6. The number of tax bills prepared during the year was 51,280, of which 740 were unpaid at the end of the year. The $240,000 of delinquent taxes collected during the year was on 625 bills.

7. Collection of current taxes during the year amounted to $3,000,000.

Required

a. Prepare a schedule to show the allocation of the Treasurer's office costs to general administration, billing, and collecting.

b. Prepare a schedule to show the computation of the unit costs for each activity. (The basis for measuring each activity is given above. Carry unit costs to the third decimal place.)

18–8. The administrator of Memorial Hospital feels radiology revenue may be considerably less than total radiology cost. For a month considered typical in terms of services performed by radiology, direct expenses incurred by the departments of Memorial Hospital were:

General service departments:		
Administration	$ 81,900	
Dietary	252,940	
Housekeeping	47,320	
Laundry	29,660	
Plant operation and maintenance	112,300	$ 524,120

"Revenue-producing" departments:

Inpatient medical and nursing	272,380	
Operating room	55,000	
Radiology	46,000	
Laboratory	45,000	
Outpatient direct expense	57,500	475,880
Total direct expenses		$1,000,000

Required

a. Compute the total Radiology cost using the step-down method to allocate indirect costs. Plant Operation and Maintenance should be allocated first; Laundry, second; Housekeeping, third; Administration, fourth; and Dietary, last. The only data available to serve as bases for cost allocation are shown below. Memorial Hospital decides to use "number of square feet" as the basis for allocation of Plant Operation and Maintenance expense and as the basis for allocation of Housekeeping expense. Number of pounds of laundry is to be used as the basis for allocation of Laundry expense, and number of employees is to be used as the basis for allocating Administration expense. Dietary expense is allocated entirely to Inpatients. Do *not* allocate any expenses to the department whose costs are being allocated, or to any department whose costs you have already allocated. A summary of the statistical bases follows:

Department	No. Employees	No. Sq. Ft.	No. Lbs. Laundry
Administration	12	3,000	3,000
Dietary	92	11,000	220,000
Housekeeping	38	500	9,000
Laundry	13	6,000	3,000
Plant operation and maintenance	18	5,000	2,500
Inpatient medical and nursing	103	50,500	1,198,000
Operating room	14	6,000	44,000
Radiology	2	1,500	2,000
Laboratory	12	2,000	2,000
Outpatient	3	1,000	6,000
Total	307	86,500	1,489,500

b. If revenue from radiology for the typical month was $49,000, what percentage of increase could be made in radiology charges without charging for the service in excess of cost?

18–9. Activity-based costing data for various activities relating to signs, one of many responsibilities of the Department of Transportation for the City of Indianapolis, is provided on the following pages. Pages 606–08 provide cost data relating to manufacturing, installation, removal, and other activities pertaining to highway signs and also show the level of accomplishment in term of labor-hours expended for each activity and the total number of signs for each type of activity.

Required

1. How does this method of accumulating costs compare with a typical cost accounting system that allocates many indirect costs on a predetermined overhead rate basis? Have you learned anything from this data that would not have been provided by a conventional costing system? Explain fully.

2. Can you envision any problems with the ABC approach used here in terms of cost versus benefit analysis?

3. Name some additional service programs that might benefit from a similar costing approach.

Total Costs for Signs

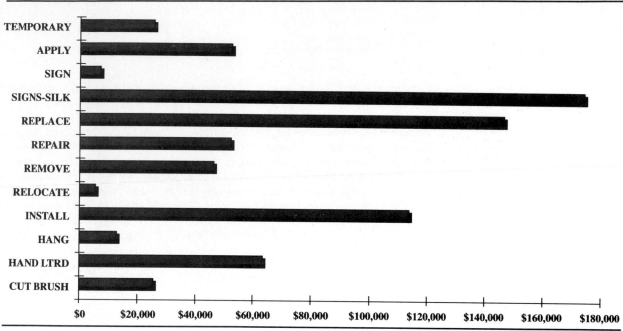

Total Costs for Signs (concluded)

Activity	Cut Brush	Hand-Lettered Signs	Hang Banners	Install Signs	Relocate Signs	Remove Signs	Repair Signs	Replace Signs	Signs—Silk Screen	Sign Cover	Apply Sign Face	Temporary Installation	Total
Operations administration	735	3,923	538	2,882	339	1,473	1,787	4,002	5,560	478	2,295	1,077	25,089
Section administration	627	3,348	459	2,460	290	1,257	1,525	3,416	4,746	408	1,959	919	21,416
Section admiritration OT	3	16	2	12	1	6	7	16	23	2	9	4	103
Sign installation TECH I	2,871	0	838	9,310	0	3,684	5,817	13,286	0	0	0	2,363	38,169
Sign installation TECH II	7,364	0	1,866	26,707	0	12,836	14,173	38,711	0	0	0	8,423	110,080
Sign manufacturer	0	20,965	0	0	0	0	0	0	30,547	814	11,442	0	63,768
Warehouse	0	2,304	2,304	2,304	2,304	2,304	2,304	2,304	2,304	2,304	2,304	2,304	25,344
Personnel Costs	11,600	30,556	6,008	43,676	2,934	21,560	25,614	61,735	43,181	4,006	18,009	15,091	283,969
Aluminum blank signs	0	0	0	0	0	0	0	0	0	0	7,072	0	7,072
Aluminum	0	4,290	0	0	0	0	0	0	35,450	0	0	0	39,739
Black ink	0	4	0	0	0	0	0	0	85	0	0	0	88
Face cover	0	0	0	0	0	0	0	0	0	0	13,559	0	13,559
Lettering	0	141	0	0	0	0	0	0	218	0	0	0	360
Red ink	0	15	0	0	0	0	0	0	44	0	0	0	59
Sheeting—ENG	0	2,193	0	0	0	0	0	0	10,132	0	0	0	12,324
Sheeting—HI	0	1,625	0	0	0	0	0	0	51,699	0	0	0	53,324
U iron	0	0	0	16,105	0	0	0	16,937	0	0	0	0	33,042
Direct Material Costs	0	8,267	0	16,105	0	0	0	16,937	97,628	0	20,630	0	159,567
Facility	2,138	0	543	7,769	0	3,734	4,123	11,264	0	0	0	2,450	32,021
Fixed assets	403	0	102	1,463	0	703	777	2,122	0	0	0	462	6,032
Central services	1,348	7,191	986	5,284	622	2,701	3,276	7,337	10,194	877	4,207	1,975	45,996
Supplies	3,184	16,989	2,330	12,484	1,469	5,380	7,738	17,333	24,082	2,071	9,939	4,665	108,664
Overhead Costs	7,073	24,180	3,961	27,000	2,091	13,518	15,913	38,056	34,276	2,948	14,146	9,552	192,713
Unused equipment	477	0	121	1,733	0	833	920	2,513	0	0	0	547	7,145
Aerial van 28	883	0	1,980	6,931	0	2,060	1,124	6,850	0	0	0	642	20,471
Crewcab	0	0	0	1,555	0	11	0	0	0	0	0	0	1,566
Double bucket	0	0	0	0	0	0	0	0	0	0	0	797	797
Sign truck	4,171	0	0	10,948	0	6,801	8,334	20,549	0	0	0	3,905	54,709
VL aerial truck	0	0	0	5,664	0	1,122	393	673	0	0	0	1,346	9,197
Rolling Stock Costs	5,531	0	2,101	26,831	0	10,827	10,771	30,586	0	0	0	7,236	93,884
Total	$24,204	$63,003	$12,070	$113,611	$5,025	$45,906	$52,298	$147,315	$175,084	$6,954	$52,785	$31,879	$730,133

Signs

Activity	Cut Brush	Hand-Lettered Signs	Hang Banners	Install Signs	Relocate Signs	Remove Signs	Repair Signs	Replace Signs	Signs—Silk Screen	Sign Cover	Apply Sign Face	Temporary Installation	Total
Operations administration	1.42	1.60	1.42	0.75	1.42	1.42	1.42	0.89	0.99	1.42	1.86	1.42	16.03
Section administration	1.21	1.37	1.21	0.64	1.21	1.21	1.21	0.76	0.84	1.21	1.59	1.21	13.68
Section administration OT	0.01	0.01	0.01	0.01	0.01	0.01	0.01	0.00	0.00	0.01	0.01	0.01	0.07
Sign installation TECH I	5.54	0.00	2.21	2.43	0.00	3.55	4.62	2.94	0.00	0.00	0.00	3.11	24.41
Sign installation TECH II	14.22	0.00	4.92	6.97	0.00	12.37	11.26	8.57	0.00	0.00	0.00	11.10	69.40
Sign manufacturer	0.00	8.57	0.00	0.00	0.00	0.00	0.00	0.00	5.43	2.41	9.29	0.00	25.70
Warehouse	0.00	0.94	6.08	0.60	9.64	2.22	1.83	0.51	0.41	6.84	1.87	3.04	33.97
Personnel Costs	22.40	12.49	15.85	11.40	12.28	20.76	20.35	13.67	7.67	11.89	14.62	19.89	183.26
Aluminum blank signs	0.00	0.00	0.00	0.00	0.00	0.00	0.00	0.00	0.00	0.00	5.74	0.00	5.74
Aluminum	0.00	1.75	0.00	0.00	0.00	0.00	0.00	0.00	6.30	0.00	0.00	0.00	8.05
Black ink	0.00	0.01	0.00	0.00	0.00	0.00	0.00	0.00	0.02	0.00	0.00	0.00	0.03
Face cover	0.00	0.00	0.00	0.00	0.00	0.00	0.00	0.00	0.00	0.00	11.01	0.00	11.01
Lettering	0.00	0.06	0.00	0.00	0.00	0.00	0.00	0.00	0.04	0.00	0.00	0.00	0.10
Red ink	0.00	0.01	0.00	0.00	0.00	0.00	0.00	0.00	0.01	0.00	0.00	0.00	0.01
Sheeting—ENG	0.00	0.90	0.00	0.00	0.00	0.00	0.00	0.00	1.80	0.00	0.00	0.00	2.70
Sheeting—HI	0.00	0.66	0.00	0.00	0.00	0.00	0.00	0.00	9.19	0.00	0.00	0.00	9.85
U iron	0.00	0.00	0.00	4.20	0.00	0.00	0.00	3.75	0.00	0.00	0.00	0.00	7.95
Direct Material Costs	0.00	3.39	0.00	4.20	0.00	0.00	0.00	3.75	17.36	0.00	16.75	0.00	45.44
Facility	1.81	2.05	1.81	0.96	1.81	1.81	1.81	1.13	1.26	1.81	2.38	1.81	20.45
Fixed assets	0.34	0.39	0.34	0.18	0.34	0.34	0.34	0.21	0.24	0.34	0.45	0.34	3.86
Central services	2.60	2.94	2.60	1.38	2.60	2.60	2.60	1.62	1.81	2.60	3.41	2.60	29.38
Supplies	6.15	6.95	6.15	3.26	6.15	6.15	6.15	3.84	4.28	6.15	8.07	6.15	69.41
Overhead Costs	10.90	12.33	10.90	5.78	10.90	10.90	10.90	6.80	7.59	10.90	14.31	10.90	123.10
Unused equipment	0.92	0.00	0.32	0.45	0.00	0.80	0.73	0.56	0.00	0.00	0.00	0.72	4.50
Aerial van 28	1.70	0.00	5.22	1.81	0.00	1.99	0.89	1.52	0.00	0.00	0.00	0.85	13.98
Crewcab	0.00	0.00	0.00	0.41	0.00	0.01	0.00	0.00	0.00	0.00	0.00	0.00	0.42
Double bucket	0.00	0.00	0.00	0.00	0.00	0.00	0.00	0.00	0.00	0.00	0.00	1.05	1.05
Sign truck	8.05	0.00	0.00	2.86	0.00	6.55	6.62	4.55	0.00	0.00	0.00	5.14	33.78
VL aerial truck	0.00	0.00	0.00	1.48	0.00	1.08	0.31	0.15	0.00	0.00	0.00	1.77	4.79
Rolling Stock Costs	10.67	0.00	5.54	7.01	0.00	10.43	8.55	6.78	0.00	0.00	0.00	9.53	58.52
Total	43.97	28.21	32.29	28.39	23.18	42.09	39.81	31.00	32.62	22.79	45.67	40.33	
Accomplishment	518 hours	2,446 signs	379 hours	3,832 signs	239 hours	1,038 hours	1,259 hours	4,517 signs	5,628 signs	337 hours	1,232 signs	759 hours	

CHAPTER
19

College and University Accounting

Accounting and financial reporting standards set by the Governmental Accounting Standards Board (GASB) have been cited in Chapters 2 through 13 as authoritative guidance for state and local governmental units and for public schools. The GASB also has jurisdiction over accounting and financial reporting standards for all other organizations, including colleges and universities, that are governmentally owned. The Financial Accounting Standards Board (FASB) has jurisdiction over accounting and financial reporting standards for business organizations and for nongovernmental not-for-profit organizations (which include many colleges and universities). The FASB is following the procedure of setting standards for certain selected financial reporting issues for *all* not-for-profit organizations under its jurisdiction. The GASB is following the approach of studying possible changes in existing standards for each category of governmentally related organization in the not-for-profit category. It is generally agreed that it is desirable for all colleges and universities to follow the same set of financial reporting standards. However, the present jurisdictional split between GASB and FASB for colleges and universities is likely to continue for the foreseeable future. Current differences between GASB and FASB standards are substantial and are noted at appropriate points throughout this chapter (and throughout Chapters 20 and 21, which deal with health care institutions, voluntary health and welfare organizations, and other not-for-profit entities).

Accounting and Financial Reporting Standards

Prior to the formation of the GASB in 1984, and, for practical purposes, until the issuance of FASB *Statements Nos. 116* and *117* in 1993, there had been a single set of accounting and financial reporting standards applicable to all colleges and universities, without regard to their ownership or sources of financing.[1] The standards were set by the American Institute of Certified Public Accountants (AICPA) in cooperation with committees of the National Association of College and University Business Officers (NACUBO) and task forces of groups related to the U.S. Department of Education. As noted in the preceding paragraph, however, the jurisdictional split for standards-setting between the GASB and the FASB has resulted in different accounting and financial reporting standards for governmentally owned and private colleges and universities. Standards and the fund structure applicable to *governmental* colleges and universities are discussed next, including a presentation of illustrative transactions and financial statements. Standards and financial reporting requirements unique to private colleges and universities are discussed later in this chapter.

Governmentally Owned (Public) Colleges and Universities

GASB has not yet established a comprehensive accounting and financial reporting model for governmentally owned colleges and universities, and is not likely to do so until its reporting model project for state and local governments is completed. In the interim, GASB standards permit governmentally owned colleges and universities to use either the traditional AICPA model or the governmental model (the same model used by state and local governmental units, as covered in Chapters 1–13). Colleges and universities with characteristics similar to governmental units (e.g., two-year institutions with taxing authority) typically have used the governmental accounting model and may continue to do so until GASB has completed its reporting model project for colleges and universities. Most governmentally owned colleges and universities, however, use the AICPA model. A discussion of the AICPA model follows.

The fund structure and accounting principles applicable to the AICPA model are set forth in the AICPA audit guide, *Audits of Colleges and Universities*, and in the NACUBO publications, *College and University Business Administration* (CUBA) and *Financial Accounting and Reporting Manual for Higher Education*. The audit guide was issued for the use of Certified Public Accountants who audit colleges and universities whereas the NACUBO publications are intended to provide guidance for accountants, managers, and others who work for colleges and universities. Fund categories generally needed by colleges and universities are:

- Currents funds (unrestricted and restricted)
- Loan funds
- Endowment and similar funds

---

[1] These FASB standards provide guidance for all *nongovernmental* not-for-profit organizations, including private colleges and universities, on accounting for contributions and financial statement display. The provisions of these standards are discussed later in this chapter, as well as in Chapter 20 on health care entities and Chapter 21 on voluntary health and welfare and other not-for-profit organizations. Financial Accounting Standards Board, *Statement of Financial Accounting Standards No. 116,* "Accounting for Contributions Received and Contributions Made" (Norwalk, Conn., 1993); and *Statement of Financial Accounting Standards No. 117,* "Financial Statements of Not-for-Profit Organizations," (Norwalk, Conn., 1993).

- Annuity and life income funds
- Agency funds
- Plant funds

Current Funds

Current resources available for use in carrying out operations directly related to the institution's educational objectives are accounted for in the Current Funds category. "Directly related" operations include residence halls, food services, intercollegiate athletics, student stores, and other auxiliary enterprises, as well as the instruction, research, and public service activities of the college or university. In NACUBO terminology, Current Funds is referred to as a "fund group" because it includes two "subgroups": Unrestricted Current Funds and Restricted Current Funds. (The association of the word *group* with the word *fund* will seem strange to the reader who is familiar with the distinction made between the two terms in state and local governmental accounting, discussed in the first 13 chapters of this text. The confusion may be clarified by reference to the practice discussed in Chapter 10 of maintaining a number of subfunds within an enterprise fund of a governmental unit.) *Assets that are available for all purposes of the institution at the discretion of the governing board are* **unrestricted.** *Assets that are available for current operating purposes subject to limitations placed on them by persons or organizations outside the institution are* **restricted.** For financial reporting purposes, unrestricted assets and related liabilities and fund balances should be reported separately from restricted assets, liabilities, and fund balances. In addition, revenues, expenditures, and transfers must be classified as being related to restricted or unrestricted current funds. It might be helpful at this point, and periodically during the discussion of the other fund groups, to refer to the illustrative financial statements for Midwest University presented later in this chapter. These statements are formatted as recommended by NACUBO and the AICPA. The three required financial statements are a Balance Sheet (Illustration 19–1), a Statement of Current Funds Revenues, Expenditures, and Other Changes (Illustration 19–2), and a Statement of Changes in Fund Balances (Illustration 19–3).

Current Funds Revenues. Governmentally owned colleges and universities should recognize revenues of **unrestricted** current funds on the accrual basis to the extent practicable. **Restricted** assets are **not** considered **earned until all of the terms of the agreement under which they were given to the institution have been met;** authoritative bodies agree that the terms are met only when the monies are expended in accordance with the donor's restrictions. For that reason, restricted assets are initially reported as **additions** in the Statement of Changes in Fund Balances when they are received and are recognized as revenues in the periods when required expenditures are made and in amounts equal to the expenditures. It may be observed that the recognition of Restricted Current Funds revenue in the amount of donor- and grantor-specified expenditures and in the fiscal period in which those expenditures take place is conceptually similar to the use of the

ILLUSTRATION 19–1

MIDWEST UNIVERSITY
Balance Sheet
June 30, 19y1
(with comparative figures at June 30, 19y0)

Assets

	Current Year	Prior Year
Current funds		
Unrestricted		
Cash	$ 150,000	$ 60,000
Investments	428,000	300,000
Accounts receivable, less allowance of $18,000 both years	87,000	130,000
Inventories, at lower of cost (first-in, first-out basis) or market	95,000	80,000
Prepaid expenses and deferred charges	29,000	20,000
Total unrestricted	$ 789,000	$ 590,000
Restricted		
Cash	161,000	90,000
Investments	265,000	250,000
Accounts receivable	23,000	50,000
Total restricted	449,000	390,000
Total current funds	$ 1,238,000	$ 980,000
Loan funds		
Cash	$ 43,000	$ 20,000
Investments	98,000	98,000
Loans to students, faculty, and staff, less allowance of $12,000 current year and $10,000 prior year	613,000	450,000
Total loan funds	$ 754,000	$ 568,000
Endowment and similar funds		
Cash	$ 46,000	$ 60,000
Investments	10,450,000	8,250,000
Total endowment and similar funds	$10,496,000	$ 8,310,000

Liabilities and Fund Balances

	Current Year	Prior Year
Current funds		
Unrestricted		
Accounts payable	$ 217,000	$ 100,000
Accrued liabilities	7,000	15,000
Students deposits	30,000	35,000
Deferred revenues	35,000	20,000
Fund balance	500,000	420,000
Total unrestricted	$ 789,000	$ 590,000
Restricted		
Accounts payable	50,000	40,000
Fund balances	399,000	350,000
Total restricted	449,000	390,000
Total current funds	$ 1,238,000	$ 980,000
Loan funds		
Fund balances		
U.S. government grants refundable	$ 218,000	$ 205,000
University funds		
Restricted	168,000	38,000
Unrestricted	368,000	325,000
Total loan funds	$ 754,000	$ 568,000
Endowment and similar funds		
Fund balances		
Endowment	$ 7,349,000	$ 6,150,000
Term endowment	1,632,000	1,180,000
Quasi-endowment–unrestricted	1,165,000	630,000
Quasi-endowment–restricted	350,000	350,000
Total endowment and similar funds	$10,496,000	$ 8,310,000

Annuity and life income funds — Assets

Annuity and life income funds		
Annuity funds		
Cash	$ 52,000	$ 40,000
Investments	2,825,000	2,600,000
Total annuity funds	2,877,000	2,640,000
Life income funds		
Cash	30,000	30,000
Investments	2,365,000	2,040,000
Total life income funds	2,395,000	2,070,000
Total annuity and life income funds	$ 5,272,000	$ 4,710,000
Plant funds		
Unexpended		
Cash	$ 298,000	$ 250,000
Investments	1,070,000	1,400,000
Total unexpended	1,368,000	1,650,000
Renewals and replacements		
Cash	60,000	10,000
Investments	160,000	305,000
Total renewals and replacements	220,000	315,000
Retirement of indebtedness		
Cash	37,000	35,000
Deposits with trustees	373,000	350,000
Total retirement of indebtedness	410,000	385,000
Investment in plant		
Land	650,000	650,000
Land improvements	1,190,000	1,300,000
Buildings	51,200,000	50,000,000
Equipment	11,150,000	11,000,000
Library books	2,040,000	2,000,000
Total investment in plant	66,230,000	64,950,000
Total plant funds	$68,228,000	$67,300,000
Agency funds		
Cash	40,000	80,000
Investments	280,000	220,000
Total agency funds	$ 320,000	$ 300,000

Liabilities and fund balances

Annuity and life income funds		
Annuity funds		
Annuities payable	$ 1,835,000	$ 1,700,000
Fund balances	1,042,000	940,000
Total annuity funds	2,877,000	2,640,000
Life income funds		
Income payable	20,000	20,000
Fund balances	2,375,000	2,050,000
Total life income funds	2,395,000	2,070,000
Total annuity and life income funds	$ 5,272,000	$ 4,710,000
Plant funds		
Unexpended		
Fund balances		
Restricted	$ 1,188,000	$ 1,300,000
Unrestricted	180,000	350,000
Total unexpended	1,368,000	1,650,000
Renewals and replacements		
Fund balances		
Restricted	180,000	275,000
Unrestricted	40,000	40,000
Total renewals and replacements	220,000	315,000
Retirement of indebtedness		
Fund balances		
Restricted	375,000	300,000
Unrestricted	35,000	85,000
Total retirement of indebtedness	410,000	385,000
Investment in plant		
Notes payable	650,000	700,000
Bonds payable	25,000,000	25,000,000
Net investment in plant	40,580,000	39,250,000
Total investment in plant	66,230,000	64,950,000
Total plant funds	$68,228,000	$67,300,000
Agency funds		
Deposits held in custody for others	320,000	300,000
Total agency funds	$ 320,000	$ 300,000

''measurable and available'' criterion currently used for the recognition of revenue by governmental fund types of state and local governments.

The term *revenues is properly used only in relation to Current Funds* and not in relation to any of the other categories of funds utilized by colleges and universities. Increases in the fund balances of all funds other than Current Funds are considered ''additions'' rather than ''revenues.''

Current funds revenues accounts provided in the NACUBO chart of accounts include Tuition and Fees; Federal Appropriations; State Appropriations; Local Appropriations; Federal Grants and Contracts; State Grants and Contracts; Local Grants and Contracts; Private Gifts, Grants, and Contracts; Endowment Income; Sales and Services of Educational Activities; Sales and Services of Auxiliary Enterprises; Sales and Services of Hospitals; Other Sources; and Independent Operations. All of the account titles listed are control accounts and should be supported by appropriately named subsidiary accounts. For example, Tuition and Fees may be supported by subsidiary accounts for the regular session, summer school, extension, continuing education, and any other accounts providing useful information for a given educational institution. Gross tuition and fees should be recorded as a revenue even though some will be offset by fee remissions, scholarships, and fellowships. Actual refunds should be charged to the Tuition and Fees account, but remissions, scholarships, and fellowships should be recorded as Expenditures. Also in regard to Tuition and Fees, it should be noted that because college fiscal years and academic years rarely coincide, it is common for tuition and fees collected near the end of a fiscal year to relate in large portion to services to be rendered by the institution during the ensuing fiscal year. Current recommendations of the AICPA and NACUBO indicate that revenues and related expenditures that apply to an academic term encompassing two fiscal years should be recognized totally within the fiscal year in which the term is predominantly conducted.[2] At the end of the year in which revenue is received but not earned, it is reported in the year-end balance sheet as *Deferred Revenue*.

Current Funds Expenditures and Transfers.   The term *expenditures is properly used only in relation to Current Funds*. Current funds expenditures should be recognized on a full accrual basis. Expenditures accounts may be identified as to program functions, organizational units, projects, and object classes. Functional classifications provided in the NACUBO chart of accounts for educational and general expenditures include Instruction, Research, Public Service, Academic Support, Student Services, Institutional Support, Operation and Maintenance of Plant, and Scholarships and Fellowships. Functional expenditure accounts are also provided for auxiliary enterprises, hospitals, and independent operations. Transfers between Current Funds and other funds of the college or university are recorded and reported separately from expenditures, but since transfers out of

---

[2] NACUBO, *Financial Accounting and Reporting Manual for Higher Education*, ¶311; Published in loose-leaf form with bimonthly updates. Also AICPA, *Audits of Colleges and Universities*, 2nd ed. (New York, 1975), p. 7.

Current Funds are expected to exceed transfers into Current Funds, the major heading in the operating statement is "Expenditures and Transfers." Note that in college and university financial reporting, a distinction is made between **mandatory** transfers and **nonmandatory** transfers rather than between operating transfers and equity transfers, as is the case in governmental financial reports. Mandatory transfers are transfers made from one fund to another in order to comply with legally enforceable agreements, such as bond indentures and grant agreements. Nonmandatory transfers are made at the discretion of the governing board to serve whatever purpose the board agrees is desirable.

Within each of the functional expenditure account categories listed above, accounts are kept by organizational unit, project, or other classification that provides useful information for internal or external users of the financial statements. A third level of analysis of expenditures is provided by an object classification—personnel compensation, supplies and expense, and capital expenditures are suggested as object classifications in the NACUBO chart of accounts. Further detail under each of these object classifications is usually kept to facilitate planning and control. For example, "personnel compensation" may be subdivided into "salaries," "other personnel services," and "personnel benefits," with each of these further subdivided as desired by the administrators of a given college or university.

Assets, Liabilities, and Fund Balances. Asset and liability accounts in both the unrestricted and restricted Current Funds groups are similar to those discussed in relation to the general funds of state and local governmental units and public schools; the most significant difference is that current funds of colleges and universities include prepaid expenses and deferred charges as assets, and include deferred revenues as liabilities, as is done by enterprise funds of governmental units. An additional difference may be encountered in the financial statements of governmentally owned colleges and universities that take advantage of the provision in the AICPA audit guide, *Audits of Colleges and Universities,* which permits these institutions to carry investments at market value, or fair value, rather than cost, provided the same basis is used for all investments of all funds.

Also similar to the practice of governmental enterprise funds is the provision in the NACUBO chart of accounts for the segregation of fund balances into Fund Balances—Allocated and Fund Balances—Unallocated. Allocated fund balances include the equity in auxiliary enterprises, the Reserve for Encumbrances, and any other reserves established in accord with the action of the governing board (for Unrestricted Current Funds) or in accord with the requirements of external agencies (for Restricted Current Funds).

Loan Funds

Assets that are loanable to students, faculty, and staff of an educational institution are provided by gifts, by grants, by income from endowment funds, by transfers from other funds, and, in some cases, from loans made to the institution for that purpose. The intent is that the loan fund be operated on a revolving basis: Repayment of loans and interest received on the loans are deposited in the loan fund and are then available for lending to other eligible persons. Interest earned on loans and interest earned on temporary investments of loan fund cash are expected to offset wholly or partially the cost of administration of the loan fund and the loss from uncollectible loans.

Assets may be given to the institution under very specific restrictions as to who may receive loans; other assets may be used in accord with policies set by the governing board of the institution. Loan funds of the first kind are **restricted;** loan funds of the second kind are **unrestricted.** In each case, accounts and reports must be in detail sufficient to demonstrate that the donor's restrictions and board policies are being adhered to. Accordingly, separate fund balance accounts should be kept to show the amounts the loan funds have received from the various sources. Interest on loans should be credited on the full accrual basis to appropriate specific fund balance accounts. Costs of administration of the loan funds, losses on investments of loan funds, and provision for losses on loans (either estimated or actual) should be reported as deductions from loan funds fund balances. Some institutions utilize income and expense accounts to facilitate management of the loan funds, but ultimately these items are reported as additions to and deductions from loan fund balances and are reported in the Statement of Changes in Fund Balances because the terms *revenues* and *expenditures* pertain only to Current Funds.

Endowment and Similar Funds

Funds whose principal is nonexpendable as of the date of reporting and is invested, or is available for investment, for the purpose of producing income are classified as "endowment and similar funds." Endowment funds are defined by NACUBO as funds for which donors or other external agencies have stipulated, as a condition of the gift, that the principal is to be maintained intact. The principal is invested in order to earn income. The use of the income may be restricted by the donor; if so, the income is considered as an addition to the fund balance of the appropriate restricted fund. If the use of the income is unrestricted, the income is considered to be revenue of the Unrestricted Current Funds.

"And similar" in the fund title refers to term endowment funds and quasi-endowment funds. **Term endowment funds** are defined in the same manner as endowment funds, with the exception that the conditions of the gift provide that the assets are released from inviolability to permit all or a part of them to be expended on the happening of a particular event or the passage of a stated period of time. **Quasi-endowment funds** are sometimes called "funds functioning as endowments"; they are funds established by the governing board of the institution to account for assets to be retained and invested. Since they are board-designated funds, the principal as well as the income may be utilized at the discretion of the board; therefore, the quasi-endowment funds generally are **unrestricted.** (In the event the assets of a quasi-endowment fund are taken from restricted funds, the quasi-endowment fund is **restricted.**)

Accounts and reports of endowment and similar funds should disclose separately each subgroup within the category, as is done in Illustration 19–1. Reports should disclose funds in this category for which the income is unrestricted in use and those for which the income is restricted to specific uses if the distinction exists in a given situation.

Earlier in this chapter, under the heading "Current Funds Revenues," *Endowment Income* is listed as one of the current funds revenues control accounts. Endowment fund income that may be expended at the discretion of the governing board of the college or university is credited on the accrual basis to the Endowment Income account of the Unrestricted Current Funds. Endowment income that may be expended only for purposes specified by donors is initially reported under the caption "Additions" in the Restricted Current Funds column of the Statement of Changes in Fund Balances. Amounts expended from restricted endowment income are credited to the Endowment Income account of Restricted Current Funds in the period when the expenditures are made; amounts of unexpended restricted endowment income remain in the restricted current fund Fund Balance until the period when they are expended. Note that endowment income is recognized as an addition to the endowment fund balance only if the provisions of the gift require the addition of the income to the principal.

Problems encountered in accounting for endowment and similar funds of educational institutions are much like those discussed in Chapter 12 of this text in relation to nonexpendable trust funds of a governmental unit. Accounting for investments of endowment and other funds is discussed in detail in Appendix 2. Statements and schedules illustrated in Chapter 12 and in Appendix 2 are appropriate for use in reporting the condition and results of operations of endowment and similar funds of educational institutions.

Traditionally, the investment objective of most educational institutions has been the preservation of principal and the production of dividend and interest income. More recently, a broadened concept of return on investments has developed which assumes that changes in market value of portfolio securities are also a part of return on assets. This concept is known as *total return,* the sum of net realized and unrealized appreciation or shrinkage in portfolio value plus dividend and interest yield. Total return has another aspect; this is the determination of "spending rate," the proportion of total return that may prudently be used by an institution for current operating purposes. The adoption of total return as a policy requires the approval of legal counsel and formal approval of its governing board. The total return concept appears to be used by an increasing number of colleges and universities, although the AICPA model followed by most public colleges and universities presently does not consider total return to be in conformity with GAAP. The AICPA audit guide does, however, permit use of the total return concept, provided that gains included in spendable return are reported as a nonmandatory transfer rather than endowment income. FASB *Statement No. 117* permits **private** colleges and universities to report unrealized gains on investments as unrestricted income if there are no donor stipulations to the contrary, no statutory prohibitions, and if approved by the institution's governing board.

In terms of balance sheet valuation, public colleges and universities that follow the AICPA audit guide are required to report investments of all funds on the same basis. Either cost or fair value may be used, but the same valuation must be used consistently. Private colleges and universities, as well as all other not-for-profit organizations, are exempted from the requirements of FASB *Statement No. 115*, which requires for-profit entities to report temporary investments, and long-term investments other than investments in debt securities held to maturity, at fair value; debt securities held to maturity are reported at amortized cost. Thus, since private colleges and universities are exempted from *Statement No. 115*, they are presumed to follow the guidance in the AICPA audit guide for valuation of their investments.

Annuity and Life Income Funds

The Annuity and Life Income Funds category consists of the Annuity Funds subcategory and the Life Income Funds subcategory. **Annuity** funds are used to account for assets given to an institution under agreements binding the institution to pay **stipulated amounts** periodically to the donors, or other designated individuals, for a period of time specified in the agreements, or for the lifetime of the donor or other designated individual. **Life income** funds are used to account for assets given to an institution under agreements that bind the institution to pay periodically to the donors, or other designated individuals, the total **income earned** by the donated assets for a period of time, usually the lifetimes of the income beneficiaries.

Annuity Funds.   The acceptance of annuity funds by a nonprofit organization is subject to regulation by the Internal Revenue Service and, in many jurisdictions, by agencies of the appropriate state government. The Internal Revenue Code and Regulations state the conditions under which (for IRS purposes) an annuity trust may be established and administered. State agencies may specify the types of investments that may be made by annuity funds. Investments received by the institution as a part of the principal of an annuity fund should be recorded at fair value as of the date of receipt; any assets acquired subsequently by purchase should, of course, be recorded by the annuity fund at cost. Liabilities of the fund would include any indebtedness against the assets and also the present value of "all expected annuity payments using appropriate actuarial assumptions."[3] If the liabilities recorded in this manner exceed the initial assets of the annuity fund, it will start operations with a deficit Fund Balance; if the initial assets exceed the liabilities to the annuitants, the annuity fund will have a positive Fund Balance. Accepting an annuity fund that would have an initial deficit Fund Balance would not appear to be in the institution's best interests. Agreements with potential donors of annuity funds should be carefully drawn by competent attorneys in consultation with competent accountants and investment managers in order to protect the interests of the receiving institution as well as the donor. The definition of "income" is one of the matters needing most careful attention. From the accounting point of view, income should be defined in accrual terms so that the principal of the gift will not be eroded by failure to deduct appropriate depreciation and amortization charges. It is also in the interest of the institution that an

---

[3] Ibid., ¶366.

equitable allocation of indirect administrative expenses be permitted, as well as a deduction for direct expenses of administering each annuity fund. Definitions and discussion of direct and indirect costs, and methods for assigning them, are covered in Chapter 18 of this text.

Annuity payments are charged to the liability account. Periodically, an adjustment is made between the liability and Fund Balance to record the actuarial gain or loss due to recomputation of the liability based on revised life expectancy and anticipated return on investments. On termination of an annuity agreement, the principal of the annuity fund is transferred to the fund category specified in the agreement; if the agreement is silent on the point, the principal of the terminated annuity fund should be transferred to Unrestricted Current Funds and identified so readers of the financial statements will not infer that a new gift has been received.

Life Income Funds. Life income funds differ from annuity funds principally in that the life income fund agreement provides that the income earned by the assets donated will be paid to the donors over the specified period, rather than a stipulated amount. Since the amount to be paid periodically by a life income fund will vary from period to period as the income of the fund varies, it is not practicable or necessary to compute the present value of the stream of unknown future payments. Accordingly, the liabilities of life income funds consist of life income payments currently due, amounts due to other funds for advances to income beneficiaries, and any indebtedness against the fund assets. Assets are recorded on the basis of fair market value on the date of receipt of donated assets, or cost, in the case of purchased assets. The amount credited to Fund Balance initially is, of course, the difference between the amount recorded for the assets and the amount recorded for the liabilities when the fund is established. Income from investments, computed as defined in the agreement under which the fund was established, should be credited to liability accounts during the term of the agreement. Gains and losses on sales of investments, however, are considered changes in Fund Balance unless the agreement with the donor provides differently. On termination of a life income agreement, the principal of the fund is handled in the manner described for terminated annuity funds.

The Internal Revenue Code and regulations provide for three variations of the life income "unitrust"—straight, net income, and net plus makeup. The technicalities of income tax law must be complied with by educational institutions with life income agreements in order to qualify for and maintain tax-exempt status. It is not possible in this brief treatment of life income funds to do more than alert the interested reader to the existence of IRS requirements.

Financial Statement Presentation. Each annuity fund and each life income fund should be accounted for separately to the extent required to enable the college or university to be able to demonstrate that it is in compliance with each annuity agreement and each life income agreement. In practice, good investment management would often dictate that assets of the individual funds be pooled for investment purposes. (Accounting for pooled investments is discussed and illustrated in

Chapter 11 in the context of state and local government investment pools.) Although each of the annuity and life income funds should be accounted for separately, all of the funds should be combined for balance sheet presentation in the Annuity and Life Income Funds category, as shown earlier in Illustration 19–1. If the combined total of annuity and life income funds is not material, this category may be further combined with the funds in the Endowment and Similar Funds category.

If operations of annuity and life income funds involve businesses or firms, it is appropriate that income statements be prepared. If operations of these funds are less complex, a Statement of Changes in Fund Balances, supported by appropriate schedules, may provide adequate disclosure.

Agency Funds

As is true of general governmental units and public schools, colleges and universities often act as agents of others for the collection, custodianship, and disbursement of assets. If agency assets are immaterial in amount, the assets and liabilities may be reported as assets and liabilities of the Current Funds. If they are material, however, they should be accounted for in separate agency funds. Inasmuch as assets are commonly held in a college agency fund for longer periods of time than is true of general governmental agency funds, assets may include temporary investments, as well as cash, receivables, and amounts due other fund categories, and amounts due individuals and organizations for which the institution is acting as fiscal agent, custodian, or depository. Earnings on temporary investments are added to the appropriate liability accounts. Total liabilities, therefore, equal total assets, and no Fund Balance exists.

Agency funds assets and liabilities are reported to the public and the college or university governing board in the balance sheet. Since there are no Fund Balances of funds in the agency category, present generally accepted accounting principles indicate it is not proper to report additions and deductions to agency funds during a fiscal period in the Statement of Changes in Fund Balances.[4] Accordingly, the changes in agency funds during a fiscal period are not reported in any of the basic financial statements; this is considered adequate disclosure because agency funds do not "belong" to the educational institution. Special periodic reports should be prepared for each agency fund for submission to individuals or organizations owning the assets in custody of the institution so that transactions and balances are disclosed to parties with a legitimate interest.

Plant Funds

The **Plant Funds Group** consists of four self-balancing subgroups:

1. **Unexpended Plant Funds.** The assets of this subgroup are set aside for the acquisition of long-lived assets for institutional purposes.

---

[4] AICPA, *Audits of Colleges and Universities*, pp. 53–54.

2. **Funds for Renewals and Replacements.** The assets of this subgroup are set aside for the renewal and replacement of existing institutional properties.
3. **Funds for Retirement of Indebtedness.** This is a subgroup similar to Debt Service Funds of state and local governmental units.
4. **Investment in Plant.** This is a subgroup that accounts for all property, plant, and equipment utilized by the college or university, except when the accounts are held as investments by endowment and similar funds and annuity and life income funds.

Although authoritative publications agree that the Plant Funds Group consists of the four subgroups itemized above, they also agree the assets and liabilities of the four subgroups may be combined in the balance sheet as long as separate Fund Balance accounts are reported for each subgroup. An additional alternative that is considered to be acceptable is the combination of the assets and of the liabilities of the first three subgroups (i.e., **Unexpended Plant Funds, Funds for Renewals and Replacements,** and **Funds for Retirement of Indebtedness**), and the reporting of each of the Fund Balance accounts pertaining to the three subgroups. Under the latter alternative, the **Investment in Plant** subgroup is presented separately in the balance sheet. A third acceptable alternative is to present each subgroup separately.

Authoritative publications are also ambivalent as to accounting for construction in progress; both the AICPA and NACUBO provide explicitly that the Construction in Progress account may be carried in either the Unexpended Plant Funds or the Investment in Plant subgroups. The NACUBO *Financial Accounting and Reporting Manual* also states that the Construction in Progress account may be carried in the Funds for Renewals and Replacements subgroup, but implies a preference for reporting all Construction in Progress in the Investment in Plant subgroup.[5]

Sources of Assets. The general sources of assets of Unexpended Plant Funds, Funds for Renewals and Replacements, and Funds for Retirement of Indebtedness are:

1. Funds from external agencies.
2. Student fees and assessments for debt service or other plant purposes, which create an obligation equivalent to an externally imposed restriction and which are not subject to the discretionary right of the governing board to use for other purposes.
3. Transfers, both mandatory and nonmandatory, from other fund groups.
4. Borrowings from external sources for plant purposes.

---

[5] NACUBO, *Financial Accounting and Reporting Manual for Higher Education*, ¶382 and 383.

5. Borrowings by advances from other fund groups.
6. Income and net gains from investments in the unrestricted and restricted elements of each of the subgroups.[6]

Liquid assets restricted by donors and other outside individuals and agencies for plant purposes, including student fees of the nature specified in the second item listed above, should be recorded directly in the proper Plant Funds subgroup and should not be passed through the Current Funds. Liquid assets transferred to Plant Funds for purposes designated by the governing board of the institution are considered **unrestricted**, because the board may change the designated purposes or transfer the assets to another fund category at its pleasure. The distinction between restricted and unrestricted assets should be maintained in the accounts of the Plant Funds so that appropriate disposition may be made of any portion of assets received in excess of the amount needed to accomplish a specified purpose. Some authorities consider that the restrictions under which liquid assets are received may be so binding as to apply to the proceeds from the eventual disposition of plant assets acquired from restricted sources. *Audits of Colleges and Universities* suggests that "the educational institution should consider obtaining a legal opinion" in regard to the proper accounting for the proceeds from the disposition of plant assets acquired from restricted sources.[7]

Unexpended Plant Funds.   Assets of the Unexpended Plant Funds subgroup may consist of cash, investments, receivables, and construction in progress. Liabilities may consist of accounts payable; and bonds, notes, mortgages, leaseholds, and any other payables issued to finance the acquisition of long-lived assets. Separate Fund Balance accounts should be maintained to indicate equity attributable to restricted sources and equity attributable to unrestricted sources.

If construction activities are accounted for within this subgroup rather than within the Investment in Plant subgroup, encumbrances outstanding at the end of a fiscal period may be reported as allocations of the appropriate Fund Balance; or, alternatively, disclosure may be made in the Notes to the Financial Statements. Subsidiary records should be kept for each project in order to accumulate project costs for accounting and control purposes. Capital expenditures and related liabilities and fund balances preferably are transferred to the Investment in Plant subgroup at the end of each fiscal period, although it is allowable for the transfer to take place on completion of the project. If any project expenditures are not to be capitalized, they should be written off against the Fund Balance of the Unexpended Plant Funds subgroup; any related liabilities should be transferred to the Investment in Plant subgroup. Readers may recall that liabilities are accounted for in the same fund as the related assets in trust funds and enterprise funds of state and local governmental units, but not in other funds of governmental units.

[6] Ibid, ¶381.
[7] AICPA, *Audits of Colleges and Universities*, p. 44.

Funds for Renewals and Replacements. The distinction between additions and improvements (accounted for in Unexpended Plant Funds) and renewal and replacement of plant fund assets (accounted for in Funds for Renewals and Replacements) is obvious in some cases but nebulous in others. Some portion of renewals and replacements may be capitalized as additions to plant. A thorough treatment of all these distinctions is found in intermediate accounting texts and need not be reproduced here. The discussion of assets, liabilities, fund balances, construction in progress, and encumbrances of Unexpended Plant Funds is also applicable to Funds for Renewals and Replacements.

Funds for Retirement of Indebtedness. Assets of this subgroup of Plant Funds may include cash, investments, deposits with fiscal agents, accounts and notes receivable, and amounts due from other funds, all of which are restricted or designated for the purpose of servicing plant fund indebtedness. Liabilities consist of accruals and accounts payable for fiscal agents' fees and other debt service charges, as well as amounts due to other funds. Fund balances should be designated as **restricted** or as **unrestricted** for reasons previously discussed. Expenditures of this subgroup that reduce debt principal represent an increase in the institution's investment in plant and will require recognition in the Investment in Plant subgroup as a reduction in the liability accounts of that subgroup and as an increase in the Net Investment in Plant (or Fund Balance of the Investment in Plant subgroup).

Investment in Plant. The Investment in Plant subgroup accounts for all property, plant, and equipment except that held by endowment and similar funds, and by annuity and life income funds as investments. Long-lived assets are carried at cost, or at fair value at date of acquisition in the case of assets acquired by gift. In the absence of historical cost records, the assets may be stated at historically based appraised values. The basis of valuation should be disclosed in the financial statements or in the Notes to the Financial Statements. As discussed later in this chapter, FASB *Statement No. 93* requires all not-for-profit organizations subject to its jurisdiction to recognize in general purpose financial statements depreciation of long-lived tangible assets. The GASB Codification Section Co5.102 provides that government-related colleges and universities should not change their accounting and reporting as a result of FASB *Statement No. 93,* since the GASB has projects under way that may affect reporting of depreciation by public colleges and universities. The "AICPA model" and "governmental model" (either of which remains effective for government-related colleges and universities until superseded by some future GASB pronouncement) do not require the computation of depreciation for plant assets of the college or university. However, the governmental model may result in depreciation being recorded on the fixed assets of auxiliary enterprises, whereas even the latter assets are not required to be depreciated under the AICPA model. The AICPA model does allow annual depreciation charges to be debited to the Net Investment in Plant account and credited to appropriate Allowance for Depreciation accounts of the Investment in Plant subgroup. Liability accounts of this subgroup may consist of all liabilities related to the fixed assets: accounts, bonds, notes, mortgages, and leaseholds payable, and amounts due other funds if associated with the acquisition, renewal, or replacement of plant assets. Net Investment in Plant instead of Fund Balance is the account title recommended for use in this subgroup to record the excess of the carrying value of plant assets over associated liabilities. The Net Investment in Plant account may be subdivided to show the sources from which plant assets were acquired, such as appropriations and gifts.

Transactions involving the fund groups used by Midwest University are illustrated in the next section of this chapter.

Illustrative Transactions (AICPA Model)

This section presents for each fund group a beginning trial balance, followed by journal entries for selected illustrative transactions for the fiscal year ending June 30, 19y1. This information is then summarized in the financial statements presented in Illustrations 19–1, 19–2, and 19–3.

Unrestricted Current Funds

Account balances for the Unrestricted Current Funds of Midwest University as of July 1, 19y0, are given as follows:

	Debits	Credits
Cash	$ 60,000	
Investments	300,000	
Accounts Receivable	148,000	
Allowance for Doubtful Accounts		$ 18,000
Inventories	80,000	
Prepaid Expenses and Deferred Charges	20,000	
Accounts Payable		100,000
Accrued Liabilities		15,000
Students Deposits		35,000
Deferred Revenues		20,000
Fund Balance		420,000
	$608,000	$608,000

During the fiscal year ended June 30, 19y1, Accounts Receivable were recorded for the following revenue items:

Tuition and Fees	$2,670,000
Federal Appropriations	230,000
State Appropriations	2,150,000
Federal Grants and Contracts	35,000
Private Gifts, Grants, and Contracts	40,000
Endowment Income	880,000
Sales and Services of Auxiliary Enterprises	2,300,000
Total	$8,305,000

In addition, Deferred Revenues in the amount of $20,000 reported in the beginning trial balance is reclassified as Revenues—Tuition and Fees, as that amount was collected in the preceding year from students for summer classes offered predominantly in the current year.

Entry 1 records the total amount of $8,325,000 to the Revenues control account, assuming that the existing balance of Allowance for Doubtful Accounts is adequate to cover the estimated uncollectibles. In addition, a subsidiary ledger, as explained in Chapters 3 and 4, should be used to record the detail of each revenue type. Alternatively, the detail of revenues could be recorded in general ledger accounts, or several Revenues control accounts could be used, along with a subsidiary ledger for as much detail as needed.

1.	Accounts Receivable	8,305,000	
	Deferred Revenues	20,000	
	Revenues		8,325,000

Entry 2 records the collections of cash for accounts receivable amounting to $8,348,000 during the current year.

2.	Cash	8,348,000	
	Accounts Receivable		8,348,000

Entry 3 records the incurring of expenditures of Unrestricted Current Funds. This entry illustrates the use of two Expenditures control accounts; the necessary detail for the functional, organizational unit, and object subclassifications, described earlier in this chapter, could be recorded in general ledger accounts or in subsidiary ledger accounts. Although the expenditure detail is omitted here for simplicity, it is included, for illustrative purposes, in the Statement of Current Funds Revenues, Expenditures, and Other Changes presented at the end of this section as Illustration 19–2.

3.	Expenditures—Educational and General	5,100,000	
	Expenditures—Auxiliary Enterprises	2,022,000	
	Accounts Payable		7,122,000

Mandatory transfers from Unrestricted Current Funds to other funds are recorded by Entry 4a; nonmandatory transfers from Unrestricted Current Funds to other funds by Entry 4b; and nonmandatory transfers to Unrestricted Current Funds by Entry 4c. Entry 4d records the accompanying transfer of cash from and to Unrestricted Current Funds arising from these transfers. Again, subsidiary ledger accounts should be used to record the detail necessary for internal management and financial reporting. Illustration 19–2, near the end of this section, provides additional detail on both mandatory and nonmandatory transfers. For example, mandatory transfers in the Educational and General category are reported separately from those in the Auxiliary Enterprises category.

4a.	Mandatory Transfers—Principal and Interest	360,000	
	Mandatory Transfers—Renewals and Replacements	185,000	
	Mandatory Transfers—Loan Fund		
	Matching Grant	3,000	
	Due to Funds for Retirement of Indebtedness		360,000
	Due to Funds for Renewals and Replacements		185,000
	Due to Loan Funds		3,000

4b. Nonmandatory Transfers—Unrestricted Gifts Allocated to
Other Funds 580,000

    Due to Loan Funds.................................... 40,000

    Due to Endowment and Similar Funds.................. 510,000

    Due to Unexpended Plant Funds 30,000

4c. Due from Endowment and Similar Funds 25,000

    Nonmandatory Transfers—Quasi-Endowment Gains
Appropriated....................................... 25,000

4d. Due to Funds for the Retirement of Indebtedness 360,000

Due to Funds for Renewals and
Replacements 185,000

Due to Loan Funds...................................... 43,000

Due to Endowment and Similar Funds.................... 510,000

Due to Unexpended Plant Funds 30,000

    Due from Endowment and Similar Funds 25,000

    Cash 1,103,000

Accounts payable and accrued liabilities were paid in the amounts of
$7,070,000 and $15,000, respectively. Refunds of students' deposits amounted to
$5,000.

5. Accounts Payable 7,070,000

Accrued Liabilities 15,000

Students' Deposits...................................... 5,000

    Cash 7,090,000

Inventories and prepaid expenses and deferred charges for Unrestricted Current Funds increased during the year in the amounts shown in Entry 6. These
increases reduced Expenditures as shown.

6. Inventories 15,000

Prepaid Expenses and Deferred Charges 9,000

    Expenditures—Educational and
General 16,000

    Expenditures—Auxiliary Enterprises 8,000

Investments in the amount of $100,000 were purchased during the year. The
Investments account was increased by an additional $28,000 for interest earnings
accrued at June 30, 19y1 (note that the interest earnings is reported as revenues
from "other sources" in the Statement of Current Funds Revenues, Expenditures, and Other Changes presented in Illustration 19–2).

7. Investments... 128,000

    Cash 100,000

    Revenues.. 28,000

Entry 8 records the accrual of educational and general expenditures, $51,000,
and auxiliary enterprises expenditures, $21,000, at June 30, 19y1.

8. Expenditures—Educational and General 51,000

Expenditures—Auxiliary Enterprises 21,000

    Accounts Payable 65,000

    Accrued Liabilities 7,000

Near the end of the current year, the university collected tuition and fees in the amount of $35,000 for classes to be offered in a term to be held predominantly in the following year. In conformity with present standards, the university recognizes a liability of $35,000 and will recognize the entire amount as revenue in the following year.

9.	Cash	35,000	
	Deferred Revenues		35,000

Revenues, Expenditures, and Transfers accounts were closed.

10.	Revenues	8,353,000	
	Nonmandatory Transfers—Quasi-		
	Endowment Gains Appropriated	25,000	
	Expenditures—Educational and General		5,135,000
	Expenditures—Auxiliary Enterprises		2,035,000
	Mandatory Transfers—Principal and Interest		360,000
	Mandatory Transfers—Renewals and Replacements		185,000
	Mandatory Transfers—Loan Fund Matching Grant		3,000
	Nonmandatory Transfers—Unrestricted Gifts Allocated		
	to Other Funds		580,000
	Fund Balance		80,000

Restricted Current Funds

Since Restricted Current Funds revenues are not considered to be earned until authorized expenditures take place, increases in assets of Restricted Current Funds are recorded as additions to the Fund Balance account. In order that the accounting system provide detail needed for the Statement of Changes in Fund Balances (shown in Illustration 19–3), it is desirable to maintain a Fund Balance subsidiary ledger for all college and university funds except Unrestricted Current Funds (that recognizes revenues and expenditures on the accrual basis). The Restricted Current Funds had the following account balances as of July 1, 19y0:

	Debits	Credits
Cash	$ 90,000	
Investments	250,000	
Accounts Receivable	50,000	
Accounts Payable		$ 40,000
Fund Balances		350,000
	$390,000	$390,000

Entry 11 records the additions to the Restricted Current Funds that occurred during the current year. (Only the general ledger accounts, assuming the use of a Fund Balances control account, are shown here and in the subsequent entries for the remaining fund groups; subsidiary ledger accounts should be used to record the details of fund balance additions and deductions needed for internal management and financial reporting. For the fund groups that have both restricted and unrestricted fund balances, two control accounts are used: Fund Balances—Restricted and Fund Balances—Unrestricted. The Statement of Changes in Fund Balances presented in Illustration 19–3 illustrates the level of detail typically reported for fund balance changes of all funds.)

11. Cash	1,034,000	
Accounts Receivable	75,000	
Fund Balances		1,109,000

Expenditures for authorized purposes during the period amounted to $1,025,000.

12. Expenditures—Educational and General	1,025,000	
Accounts Payable		10,000
Cash		1,015,000

As noted previously, when expenditures of Restricted Current Funds are incurred for purposes specified by donors and grantors, revenue is considered earned in an equal amount. Entry 13 records the earned revenues.

| 13. Fund Balances | 1,025,000 | |
| Revenues | | 1,025,000 |

Many granting agencies, including the federal government, allow colleges and universities to include overhead charges, including depreciation, as a part of grant expenditures. In this example, $35,000 has been allowed as indirect cost recoveries. Since that amount is now available for unrestricted purposes (this amount corresponds to the $35,000 unrestricted revenues from Federal Grants and Contracts included in Entry 1), the entry in the Restricted Current Funds would be:

| 14. Fund Balances | 35,000 | |
| Cash | | 35,000 |

Cash was received in the amount of $102,000 from various grantors, including the $55,000 billed in the previous year.

| 15. Cash | 102,000 | |
| Accounts Receivable | | 102,000 |

Investments were purchased in the amount of $15,000:

| 16. Investments | 15,000 | |
| Cash | | 15,000 |

Revenues and Expenditures were closed as shown in Entry 17.

| 17. Revenues | 1,025,000 | |
| Expenditures—Educational and General | | 1,025,000 |

Loan Funds

Loan funds assets consist primarily of cash, investments, and receivables resulting from loans to students, faculty, and staff. Fund balances are assumed to relate to refundable grants from the federal government and to university funds both restricted and unrestricted. Loan Fund account balances for Midwest University as of July 1, 19y0, are as follows:

	Debits	*Credits*
Cash	$ 20,000	
Investments	98,000	
Loans to Students, Faculty, and Staff	460,000	
Allowance for Uncollectible Loans		$ 10,000
Fund Balances:		
University Funds—Restricted		38,000
University Funds—Unrestricted		325,000
U.S. Government Grants Refundable		205,000
	$578,000	$578,000

Entry 18 records the additions to the Loan Funds Fund Balances accounts, including the transfers from the Unrestricted Current Funds.

18.	Cash	208,000	
	Fund Balances—University Funds—Restricted		130,000
	Fund Balances—University Funds—Unrestricted		43,000
	Fund Balances—U.S. Government Grants Refundable		35,000

Separate subsidiary Fund Balances accounts should be kept for the individual restricted loan funds in order to facilitate the preparation of periodic reports to the grantors, and to provide for appropriate compliance audits.

Deductions from the Fund Balances accounts of the loan funds for amounts refunded to grantors are summarized in the following entry:

19.	Fund Balances—US. Government Grants Refundable	20,000	
	Cash		20,000

Loans were made during the year in the amount of $260,000, and other loans were repaid in the amount of $95,000. Additionally, a year-end adjusting entry was made to increase the Allowance for Uncollectible Loans for expected write-offs in the amount of $2,000. These transactions and events are recorded by Entries 20a, 20b, and 20c.

20a.	Loans to Students, Faculty, and Staff	260,000	
	Cash		260,000
20b.	Cash	95,000	
	Loans to Students, Faculty, and Staff		95,000
20c.	Fund Balances—U.S. Government Grants Refundable	2,000	
	Allowance for Uncollectible Loans		2,000

Endowment and Similar Funds

Midwest University records and reports separately the Fund Balances for Endowment, Term Endowment, Quasi-Endowment—Unrestricted, and Quasi-Endowment—Restricted funds in the endowment and similar funds category. Each category of Fund Balance should, of course, be supported by subsidiary records to show the balance for each individual endowment. The account balances of Midwest University's endowment and similar funds as of July 1, 19y0, are as follows:

	Debits	Credits
Cash	$ 60,000	
Investments	8,250,000	
Fund Balances—Endowment		$6,150,000
Fund Balances—Term Endowment		1,180,000
Fund Balances—Quasi-Endowment—Restricted		350,000
Fund Balances—Quasi-Endowment—Unrestricted		630,000
	$8,310,000	$8,310,000

The additions to the Fund Balances of this fund group and unrestricted transfers to the group are summarized by the following entries.

21.	Cash	2,150,000	
	Fund Balances—Endowment		1,090,000
	Fund Balances—Term Endowment		550,000
	Fund Balances—Quasi-Endowment—Unrestricted		510,000

Fund Balances—Term Endowment was reduced in the amount of $98,000 for an expired term endowment restricted for use in the Unexpended Plant Funds. The effect of this transaction is shown in Entry 32 under Unexpended Plant Funds.

22.	Fund Balances—Term Endowment	98,000	
	Cash		98,000

Investments in the amount of $2,000,000 were sold for $2,159,000; the realized gain was allocated $109,000 to Fund Balances—Endowment and $50,000 to Fund Balances—Quasi-Endowment—Unrestricted. Of the latter amount, $25,000 was appropriated for use in Unrestricted Current Funds. Investments costing $4,200,000 were purchased:

23a.	Cash	2,159,000	
	Fund Balances—Endowment		109,000
	Fund Balances—Quasi-Endowment—Unrestricted		50,000
	Investments		2,000,000
23b.	Fund Balances—Quasi-Endowment—Unrestricted	25,000	
	Cash		25,000
23c.	Investments	4,200,000	
	Cash		4,200,000

It should be noted that many public universities maintain separate foundations that have the objective of obtaining contributions and endowments. In those cases, note disclosure should disclose the existence of those foundations, and the amount of investment income or other monies received from them.

Annuity and Life Income Funds

The annuity and life income funds had the following account balances as of July 1, 19y0:

	Debits	*Credits*
Annuity Funds:		
Cash	$ 40,000	
Investments	2,600,000	
Annuities Payable		$1,700,000
Fund Balances		940,000
Life Income Funds:		
Cash	30,000	
Investments	2,040,000	
Income Payable		20,000
Fund Balances		2,050,000
	$4,710,000	$4,710,000

Note that Midwest University's annuity funds have a large balance in the Annuities Payable account. That amount represents the present value of future payments due under the annuity agreements. The liability in the life income funds reflects only the currently unpaid portion of income due contributors, as explained in a previous section. During the fiscal year ended June 30, 19y1, cash in the amount of $487,000 was received from new annuity fund contributors. The actuarial annuities payable relating to these annuities were $385,000; the remainder added to Fund Balance. Also, during the year, annuitants were paid $250,000 and additional investments were purchased in the amount of $225,000. The effects of these transactions are summarized by the following entries.

24.	Cash—Annuity Funds	487,000	
	Annuities Payable		385,000
	Fund Balances—Annuity Funds		102,000
25.	Annuities Payable	250,000	
	Cash—Annuity Funds		250,000
26.	Investments...	225,000	
	Cash—Annuity Funds		225,000

Transactions for the life income funds are summarized by the following entries:

27.	Cash—Life Income Funds...............·..............	325,000	
	Fund Balances—Life Income Funds....................		325,000
28.	Investments...	325,000	
	Cash—Life Income Funds............................		325,000

Additional entries would be required for the receipt of investment income and the simultaneous recording of liabilities to the life income recipients. These transactions do not flow through the Statement of Changes in Fund Balances because the income is a liability, not a resource of the fund.

Plant Funds

Recall that the Plant Funds group consists of four distinct subgroups: (1) Unexpended Plant Funds, (2) Funds for Renewals and Replacements, (3) Funds for

Retirement of Indebtedness, and (4) Investment in Plant. Account balances for the four plant fund subgroups as of July 1, 19y0, are as follows:

	Debits	Credits
Unexpended Plant Funds:		
Cash	$ 250,000	
Investments	1,400,000	
Fund Balances—Restricted		$ 1,300,000
Fund Balances—Unrestricted		350,000
	$ 1,650,000	$ 1,650,000
Funds for Renewals and Replacements:		
Cash	$ 10,000	
Investments	305,000	
Fund Balances—Restricted		$ 275,000
Fund Balances—Unrestricted		40,000
	$ 315,000	$ 315,000
Funds for Retirement of Indebtedness:		
Cash	$ 35,000	
Deposits with Trustees	350,000	
Fund Balances—Restricted		$ 300,000
Fund Balances—Unrestricted		85,000
	$ 385,000	$ 385,000
Investment in Plant:		
Land	$ 650,000	
Land Improvements	1,300,000	
Buildings	50,000,000	
Equipment	11,000,000	
Library Books	2,000,000	
Notes Payable		$ 700,000
Bonds Payable		25,000,000
Net Investment in Plant		39,250,000
	$64,950,000	$64,950,000

Unexpended Plant Funds account for assets held for the acquisition or construction of property, plant, and equipment. Although the beginning trial balance does not show the account Construction in Progress in either the Unexpended Plant Funds or the Investment in Plant Funds, financial reporting standards allow it to be reported in either. Entries relating to transactions of the Unexpended Plant Funds are as follows:

Cash for construction of a new laboratory building was received from a state grant in the amount of $220,000, a nonmandatory transfer from Unrestricted Current Funds in the amount of $30,000, and issuance of 8 percent term bonds maturing in five years in the amount of $500,000.

29. Cash	750,000	
Fund Balances—Restricted		220,000
Fund Balances—Unrestricted		30,000
Bonds Payable		500,000

Investments costing $330,000 were sold for $350,000. These investments had been purchased with restricted cash.

30.	Cash	350,000	
	Investments..		330,000
	Fund Balances—Restricted.............................		20,000

Investment income received in cash was added to the restricted fund balance in the amount of $50,000.

31.	Cash	50,000	
	Fund Balances—Restricted.............................		50,000

A term endowment expired in the amount of $98,000 which specified use in the Unexpended Plant Funds.

32.	Cash	98,000	
	Fund Balances—Restricted.............................		98,000

During the year, construction expenditures for the laboratory building and other projects amounted to $1,200,000.

33.	Construction in Progress	1,200,000	
	Cash		1,200,000

The projects accounted for in Entry 33 were completed at year-end, and the related asset, liability, and Fund Balance accounts were closed in order to transfer accountability for the asset and liability to the Investment in Plant Funds.

34.	Fund Balances—Restricted...............................	500,000	
	Fund Balances—Unrestricted.............................	200,000	
	Bonds Payable	500,000	
	Construction in Progress		1,200,000

Funds for Renewals and Replacements exist to provide a mechanism to accumulate resources for rehabilitation and replacement of existing facilities. Often, in practice, this subgroup is used to account for construction (mainly remodeling) activities, as is the case for Midwest University in the transactions recorded below.

Investment income in the amount of $10,000 and a mandatory transfer from the Unrestricted Current Funds (see Entry 4a) in the amount of $185,000 were received and added to Fund Balances—Restricted.

35.	Cash	195,000	
	Fund Balances—Restricted.............................		195,000

Restricted investments costing $145,000 were sold for $155,000.

36.	Cash	155,000	
	Investments..		145,000
	Fund Balances—Restricted.............................		10,000

Restricted fund balances used for renovations and replacements totaled $300,000; none of this amount was capitalized.

37.	Fund Balances—Restricted	300,000	
	Cash		300,000

Funds for Retirement of Indebtedness are accounted for in a manner similar to debt service funds of state and local governmental units (except that resource inflows and outflows are additions to and deductions from fund balance rather than revenues and expenditures). Midwest University deposits investments of this subgroup with trustees. The following entries summarize the activities of this subgroup:

Cash in the amount of $2,065,000 was received from a state appropriation, a private gift, investment earnings, and in the amount of $360,000 from a mandatory transfer from the Unrestricted Current Funds. The total amount was added to Fund Balances—Restricted.

38.	Cash	2,425,000	
	Fund Balances—Restricted		2,425,000

Interest and principal payments were made on notes and bonds payable; $50,000 was from previously accumulated unrestricted funds. (See Entry 42 for the related effect on bond principal in the Investment in Plant Funds.)

39.	Fund Balances—Restricted	2,350,000	
	Fund Balances—Unrestricted	50,000	
	Cash		2,400,000

During the year, there was a net increase in cash deposited with trustees in the amount of $23,000.

40.	Deposits with Trustees	23,000	
	Cash		23,000

The **Investment in Plant** subgroup of plant funds consists of fixed asset accounts; debt related to the fixed assets; and an equity account, "Net Investment in Plant." As mentioned earlier in this chapter, governmentally owned colleges and universities may choose, under GASB standards, either to record, or not to record, depreciation. FASB standards, on the other hand, require nongovernmentally owned colleges and universities to record depreciation on fixed assets. Governmentally owned colleges and universities that opt to record depreciation will make the entry in the Investment in Plant subgroup as follows:

Net Investment in Plant	xx,xxx	
Allowance for Depreciation		xx,xxx

Midwest University is a state university and chooses not to record depreciation. The entries below record transactions affecting the Investment in Plant subgroup.

During the year, the following plant acquisitions were made from all funds, including current funds acquisition of equipment, library books, and so on. Note the additions to the Buildings and Bonds Payable accounts related to completion of the projects in Entry 34. The $250,000 for equipment and $40,000 for library books shown in the following entry were included in Entries 3 and 8 of the Unrestricted Current Funds.

41.	Buildings 1,200,000	
	Equipment.. 250,000	
	Library Books 40,000	
	Bonds Payable	500,000
	Net Investment in Plant	990,000

Principal was paid on notes and bonds as shown in Entry 39. This action increases the equity account.

42.	Notes Payable.. 50,000	
	Bonds Payable 500,000	
	Net Investment in Plant	550,000

Certain facilities were scrapped or sold:

43.	Net Investment in Plant 210,000	
	Land Improvements	110,000
	Equipment...	100,000

It should be emphasized that, unlike state and local governments in which proprietary fund fixed assets and long-term debt are accounted for differently from general fixed assets and long-term debt, college and university accounting, under the AICPA model, does not distinguish between the fixed assets and related long-term debt of auxiliary enterprises and those of educational and general activities; both are accounted for in the same manner in the Investment in Plant subgroup.

Agency Funds

Agency funds do not have fund balance accounts; therefore, additions to and deductions from agency funds should not be reported in the Statement of Changes in Fund Balances. A Statement of Changes in Assets and Liabilities of Agency Funds could be reported, as illustrated in Chapter 11 (Illustration 11–3), but this is not generally done by colleges and universities. Assets and offsetting liabilities of Agency Funds are reported in the Balance Sheet (see Illustration 19–1) as a matter of disclosure of the existence of the agency relationship. Account balances for the agency funds as of July 1, 19y0, were as follows:

	Debits	*Credits*
Cash	$ 80,000	
Investments	220,000	
Deposits Held in Custody for Others.........		$300,000
	$300,000	$300,000

Assume student groups and others deposited $130,000; $110,000 in withdrawals were made; and $60,000 in cash was invested:

44.	Cash 130,000	
	Deposits Held in Custody for Others	130,000

45. Deposits Held in Custody for Others	110,000	
Cash		110,000
46. Investments...	60,000	
Cash		60,000

Detailed records should be kept for each student group and for others for which the college or university is acting as agent.

Illustrative Financial Statements (AICPA Model)

Illustration 19–1 (shown earlier in this chapter) and Illustrations 19–2 and 19–3 (shown on the next two pages) present the three required financial statements for governmentally owned colleges and universities that follow the AICPA model.

The **Balance Sheet** (Illustration 19–1) was presented with funds arranged sequentially in vertical order ("pancake" format), although a columnar approach may be used. Note that in all cases, restricted and unrestricted fund balance accounts are disclosed separately. Some colleges and universities choose, as permitted by current standards, to present combined information for the Plant Funds group, with separate disclosure of the Fund Balance amounts for the four subgroups.

The **Statement of Current Funds Revenues, Expenditures, and Other Changes** (Illustration 19–2) presents those revenues and expenditures that have been recognized, as well as other Fund Balance changes, separately, for the unrestricted and restricted portions. Note that the revenues equal the expenditures for the Restricted Current Funds; remember that revenues are recognized only after the expenditures are recognized. The $49,000 "Excess of Restricted Receipts over Transfers to Revenues" represents the total additions to Fund Balance (see Illustration 19–3) of $1,109,000 less the indirect cost recoveries of $35,000 less the revenues recognized of $1,025,000. Note also that Mandatory Transfers are reported together with Expenditures, while "other changes" are reported separately.

The **Statement of Changes in Fund Balances** (Illustration 19–3) presents **all** of the changes in the Fund Balance accounts of all except the agency funds. The only "Revenues" in this statement are reported in the Unrestricted Current Funds. All other amounts represent direct credits to the Fund Balance accounts. Similarly, the only "Expenditures" in this statement are reported in the Current Funds, both Unrestricted and Restricted. All other amounts represent direct debits to Fund Balances, as described in this chapter. Students should compare how the net increases in Fund Balance for the current funds are presented in Illustrations 19–2 and 19–3.

Nongovernmentally Owned (Private) Colleges and Universities

Setting accounting and financial reporting standards for private colleges and universities, as noted at the beginning of this chapter, is the responsibility of the FASB. Until 1993, with the exception that private colleges and universities were required by FASB *Statement No. 93* to report depreciation of their plant assets,

ILLUSTRATION 19–2

MIDWEST UNIVERSITY
Statement of Current Funds Revenues, Expenditures, and Other Changes
Year Ended June 30, 19y1

	Current Year			Prior
	Unrestricted	*Restricted*	*Total*	*Year Total*
Revenues:				
Tuition and fees	$2,690,000		$2,690,000	$2,300,000
Federal appropriations	230,000		230,000	200,000
State appropriations	2,150,000		2,150,000	2,050,000
Federal grants and contracts	35,000	$ 400,000	435,000	430,000
Private gifts, grants, and contracts	40,000	410,000	450,000	445,000
Endowment income	880,000	215,000	1,095,000	950,000
Sales and services of auxiliary enterprises	2,300,000		2,300,000	1,975,000
Other sources	28,000		28,000	23,000
Total current revenues	8,353,000	1,025,000	9,378,000	8,373,000
Expenditures and mandatory transfers:				
Educational and general:				
Instruction	3,298,000	496,000	3,794,000	3,282,000
Research	220,000	404,000	624,000	701,000
Public service	146,000	25,000	171,000	180,000
Academic support	232,000		232,000	231,000
Student services	207,000		207,000	204,000
Institutional support	425,000		425,000	410,000
Operation and maintenance of plant	230,000		230,000	227,000
Scholarships and fellowships	377,000	100,000	477,000	456,000
Educational and general expenditures	5,135,000	1,025,000	6,160,000	5,691,000
Mandatory transfers for:				
Principal and interest	120,000		120,000	116,000
Renewals and replacements	100,000		100,000	97,000
Loan fund matching grant	3,000		3,000	2,000
Total educational and general	5,358,000	1,025,000	6,383,000	5,906,000
Auxiliary enterprises:				
Expenditures	2,035,000		2,035,000	1,698,000
Mandatory transfers for:				
Principal and interest	240,000		240,000	246,000
Renewals and replacements	85,000		85,000	85,000
Total auxiliary enterprises	2,360,000		2,360,000	2,029,000
Total expenditures and mandatory transfers	7,718,000	1,025,000	8,743,000	7,935,000
Other transfers and additions (deductions):				
Excess of restricted receipts over transfers to revenues		49,000	49,000	40,000
Unrestricted gifts allocated to other funds	(580,000)		(580,000)	(400,000)
Portion of quasi-endowment gains appropriated	25,000		25,000	
Net increase in fund balances	$ 80,000	$ 49,000	$ 129,000	$ 78,000

ILLUSTRATION 19–3

638

MIDWEST UNIVERSITY
Statement of Changes in Fund Balances
Year Ended June 30, 19y1

	Current Funds		Loan Funds	Endowment and Similar Funds	Annuity and Life Income Funds	Plant Funds			
	Unrestricted	Restricted				Unexpended	Renewals and Replacements	Retirement of Indebtedness	Investment in Plant
Revenues and other additions:									
Unrestricted current fund revenues	$8,353,000								
Expired term endowment—restricted						$ 98,000			
State appropriations—restricted								$1,800,000	
Federal grants and contracts—restricted		$ 525,000							
State grants and contracts—restricted						220,000			
Private gifts, grants, and contracts—restricted		400,000	$115,000	$1,640,000	$ 427,000		$ 10,000	260,000	
Investment income—restricted		184,000	8,000			50,000		5,000	
Realized gains on investments—unrestricted				50,000					
Realized gains on investments—restricted				109,000		20,000	10,000		
Interest on loans receivable			7,000						
U.S. government advances			35,000						
Expended for plant facilities (including $290,000 charged to current funds expenditures)									$ 990,000
Retirement of indebtedness									550,000
Total revenues and other additions	8,353,000	1,109,000	165,000	1,799,000	427,000	388,000	20,000	2,065,000	1,540,000
Expenditures and other deductions:									
Educational and general expenditures	$5,135,000	$1,025,000							
Auxiliary enterprises	2,035,000								
Indirect costs recovered		35,000							
Refunded to grantors			$ 20,000						
Loan cancellations and write-offs			2,000						
Expended for plant facilities (including noncapitalized expenditures of $300,000)						$ 700,000	$300,000		
Retirement of indebtedness								$ 550,000	
Interest on indebtedness								1,850,000	
Disposal of plant facilities									$ 210,000
Expired term endowments ($98,000 restricted to plant)				$ 98,000					
Total expenditures and other deductions	7,170,000	1,060,000	22,000	98,000		700,000	300,000	2,400,000	210,000
Transfers among funds—additions (deductions):									
Mandatory:									
Principal and interest	(360,000)							360,000	
Renewals and replacements	(185,000)						185,000		
Loan fund matching grant	(3,000)		3,000						
Unrestricted gifts allocated	(580,000)		40,000	510,000		30,000			
Portion of unrestricted quasi-endowment funds investment gains appropriated	25,000			(25,000)					
Total transfers	(1,103,000)		43,000	485,000		30,000	185,000	360,000	
Net increase (decrease) for the year	80,000	49,000	186,000	2,186,000	427,000	(282,000)	(95,000)	25,000	1,330,000
Fund balance at beginning of year	420,000	350,000	568,000	8,310,000	2,990,000	1,650,000	315,000	385,000	39,250,000
Fund balance at end of year	$ 500,000	$ 399,000	$754,000	$10,496,000	$3,417,000	$1,368,000	$220,000	$ 410,000	$40,580,000

most colleges and universities, both public and private, used what the GASB refers to as the "AICPA College Guide model"—the model for which illustrative transactions and financial statements have been provided in this chapter. The issuance of FASB *Statement 116,* "Accounting for Contributions Received and Contributions Made," and FASB *Statement No. 117,* "Financial Statements of Not-for-Profit Organizations," in 1993, marked a significant divergence in the accounting and reporting standards applicable to public and private colleges and universities. The FASB statements apply to all *nongovernmentally owned* not-for-profit organizations, not just private colleges and universities, and are effective for fiscal years beginning after December 15, 1994. The effective date is extended by one year for smaller entities having less than $5 million in total assets and less than $1 million in annual expenses. A brief overview of each of these standards follows:

Accounting for Contributions

Colleges and universities have traditionally accounted for their gifts, bequests, and grants according to the restrictions, if any, placed on their use by donors and the expected timing of receipt. Unrestricted gifts, bequests, and grants (contributions) have been accounted for in the Unrestricted Current Funds (but often were transferred to other fund groups), whereas restricted gifts and contracts were accounted for in the Restricted Current Funds, Endowment and Similar Funds, Annuity and Life Income Funds, Loan Funds, or Plant Funds, as appropriate. As discussed in a previous section, revenues for restricted gifts and grants accounted for in the Restricted Current Funds have been recognized only when earned; that is, in the same amount as expenditures for the period. Restricted amounts accounted for in fund groups other than the Restricted Current Funds have been recorded as Fund Balance additions, generally in the period received.

The AICPA audit guide for colleges and universities requires that pledges from donors for future contributions be disclosed in the Notes to the Financial Statements or, optionally, reported as a receivable on the balance sheet, offset by an appropriate allowance for estimated uncollectible pledges. A majority of colleges and universities have opted for note disclosure on the theory that it is difficult to determine an estimated net realizable value for pledges. Except for specialized GASB guidance on accounting for Pell Grants, most public colleges and universities will continue for the foreseeable future to follow the AICPA model requirements for accounting for gifts, bequests, and grants. Private colleges and universities, on the other hand, are required to modify their accounting practices in this area to conform with the requirements of FASB *Statement No. 116.*

FASB *Statement No. 116* provides guidance for recognition of revenues (expenses) for contributions received (made) and for reporting of such contributions in the financial statements of not-for-profit organizations. The statement defines several terms whose definitions are important in understanding and applying the standard, including the following:[8]

---

[8] FASB *Statement No. 116,* Appendix D.

1. **Collections.** Works of art, historical treasures, or similar assets that are:
   (a) Held for public exhibition, education, or research in furtherance of public service rather than financial gain.
   (b) Protected, kept unencumbered, cared for, and preserved.
   (c) Subject to an organizational policy that requires the proceeds of items that are sold to be used to acquire other items for collections.
2. **Conditional Promise to Give.** A promise to give that depends on the occurrence of a specified future and uncertain event to bind the promisor.
3. **Contribution.** An unconditional transfer of cash or other assets to an entity or a settlement or cancellation of its liabilities in a voluntary nonreciprocal transfer by another entity acting other than as an owner.
4. **Donor-Imposed Condition.** A donor stipulation that specifies a future and uncertain event whose occurrence or failure to occur gives the promisor a right of return of the assets it has transferred or releases the promisor from its obligation to transfer its assets.
5. **Donor-Imposed Restriction.** A donor stipulation that specifies a use for the contributed asset that is more specific than broad limits resulting from the nature of the organization, the environment in which it operates, and the purposes specified in its articles of incorporation or bylaws or comparable documents for an unincorporated association. A restriction on an organization's use of the asset contributed may be temporary or permanent.
6. **Nonreciprocal Transfer.** A transaction in which an entity incurs a liability or transfers an asset to another entity (or receives an asset or cancellation of a liability) without directly receiving (or giving) value in exchange.
7. **Promise to Give.** A written or oral agreement to contribute cash or other assets to another entity. A promise to give may be either conditional or unconditional.
8. **Unconditional Promise to Give.** A promise to give that depends only on passage of time or demand by the promisee for performance.

Statement No. 116 requires all private colleges and universities (and, as discussed in Chapters 20 and 21, all other nongovernmentally owned not-for-profit organizations) to **recognize contributions received and unconditional promises to give as revenues or gains in the period received** and as assets, decreases in liabilities, or expenses depending on the form of the benefits received. Contributions should be measured at their fair value when received. Quoted market prices should be used to measure fair value, when available. Otherwise, estimates based on quoted market prices for similar assets, independent appraisals, or other accepted valuation techniques should be used. **Conditional promises to give,** however, **are not recognized as a revenue or gain until the conditions on which they**

depend are substantially met, but the estimated amounts of such promises must be disclosed in the Notes to the Financial Statements. For private colleges and universities bequests are the most common occurrence of a conditional promise to give.

Under FASB *Statement No. 116,* private colleges and universities can **no longer defer recognition of restricted operating monies (e.g., research grants) until the period expenditures have been incurred for the restricted purposes.** Indeed, donor-imposed restrictions have no bearing whatsoever on the *period* in which contributions are recognized. Rather these restrictions affect the *manner of reporting* contributions and the related assets. Specifically, the college or university shall report all contributions received or unconditional promises by donors in the period received as increases in the appropriate category of net assets: **unrestricted net assets, temporarily restricted net assets,** or **permanently restricted net assets.** These are also the reporting categories specified in FASB *Statement No. 117,* discussed in the next section.

Unconditional promises to give that will not be paid by donors until future periods must be reported among the temporarily restricted net assets unless explicit donor stipulations or the circumstances surrounding the promise make it clear that the donor intended the contribution to support activities of the current period. In the latter case such contributions should be reported, wholly or partially, as an increase in unrestricted net assets. Private colleges and universities should recognize expirations of temporary restrictions on gifts or grants in the period expenses are incurred for the restricted purpose or, if restricted for acquisition of long-lived assets, in the period the long-lived assets are acquired. Gifts of long-lived assets should be reported in unrestricted net assets unless the donor stipulates a time restriction on how long the college or university must use the asset, or the institution itself has an accounting policy imposing a time restriction that expires over the life of the asset.

Many colleges and universities have historical archives, libraries, and museums containing valuable works of art, historical treasures, and similar assets. As is the case under the AICPA model, FASB *Statement No. 116* provides for note disclosure of such assets rather than reporting them on the balance sheet; however, *Statement No. 116* permits nonrecognition only if the donated items are added to collections that meet the conditions given under the definition of **collections** provided above, and:

a. Are held for public exhibition, education, or research in furtherance of public service rather than financial gain.

b. Are protected, kept unencumbered, cared for, and preserved.

c. Are subject to an organizational policy that requires the proceeds from sales of collection items to be used to acquire other items for collections.

The clear intent of the *Statement No. 116* criteria is to permit nonrecognition of contributions of valuable collections *only* if the collection is to be maintained to serve the public interest rather than to achieve financial gain from trading in collectible items.

A final form of contributions covered by FASB *Statement No. 116* is contributions of services. Although contributed service by unpaid volunteers is generally less important for colleges and universities than for other not-for-profit organizations, such as community service organizations and churches, some colleges and universities do utilize volunteers extensively for fund-raising and other activities. *Statement No. 116* permits recognition of contributed services at their fair value if the services received, *(a)* create or enhance nonfinancial assets (e.g., construction of a building) or *(b)* require specialized skill, are provided by individuals possessing those skills, and typically would need to be purchased if not provided by donation. These restrictive criteria make it unlikely that most private colleges and universities will recognize such contributions in their financial statements. Note disclosure of the fair value of contributed services is encouraged, if practicable.

Financial Reporting Requirements

Not-for-profit organizations exist in a variety of forms including colleges and universities, health care entities, voluntary health and welfare organizations (VHWOs), and other not-for-profit organizations (ONPOs). Different fund accounting structures and financial statement formats have evolved over time for these various forms of entities, as codified in AICPA audit guides. The AICPA model fund accounting structures and financial reporting requirements for these organizations are covered in this chapter for colleges and universities, in Chapter 20 for health care entities, and in Chapter 21 for VHWOs and ONPOs. It is still necessary to study the present fund structure and reporting requirements unique to each type of entity until such time when GASB has issued definitive guidance for *governmentally owned* organizations of each type.[9]

Nongovernmentally owned not-for-profit organizations, on the other hand, including private colleges and universities, must follow the general purpose external financial reporting requirements of FASB *Statement No. 117*. FASB's stated objective in issuing *Statement No. 117* was "to enhance the relevance, understandability, and comparability of financial statements by [not-for-profit] organizations."[10]

A complete set of financial statements for all nongovernmentally owned not-for-profit organizations must include a Statement of Financial Position (Balance Sheet), a Statement of Activities, and a Statement of Cash Flows. These statements are prepared on an entitywide aggregated basis rather than separately reporting data for each fund group. However, *Statement No. 117* does not prohibit the use of fund accounting for internal entity management, or even for supplemen-

---

[9] As GASB provides final standards or further guidance on accounting and financial reporting for governmentally owned not-for-profit organizations, the publisher will provide timely updates to adopters of the Tenth Edition of this text.

[10] FASB *Statement No. 117,* Summary.

tal external financial reporting, if desired. The authors expect that, given their substantial investment in their present accounting system, many nongovernmentally owned not-for-profit organizations will continue to maintain their accounting systems on a fund accounting basis for internal management purposes, but to prepare their general purpose financial statements on the required aggregated basis.

Illustrations 19–4, 19–5, and 19–6 present the Statement of Financial Position, Statement of Activities, and Statement of Cash Flows, respectively, for

ILLUSTRATION 19–4

VALLEY COLLEGE
Statement of Financial Position
June 30, 19y4

Assets:

Cash and cash equivalents	$ 1,590,953
Accrued interest on investments	1,344,201
Accounts receivable, less allowance for doubtful accounts of $8,833	588,840
Inventories, at average cost	969,287
Prepaid expenses	415,556
Loans receivable, less allowance for doubtful loans of $52,600	1,906,535
Pledges receivable, less allowance for doubtful pledges of $50,000	5,550,000
Long-term investments, at market, cost of $150,645,430	161,785,400
Property, Plant, and Equipment, net of accumulated depreciation of $10,174,082	23,417,628
Total Assets	$197,568,400

Liabilities and Net Assets:

Liabilities:

Accounts payable and accrued expenses	$ 1,481,908
Deposits and agency funds	385,476
Annuities payable	1,408,550
Deferred revenue	62,237
Advances from federal government for student loans	124,557
Notes payable	889,934
Bonds payable	5,500,000
Total Liabilities	9,852,662

Net Assets:

Unrestricted	73,690,687
Temporarily restricted	23,279,442
Permanently restricted	90,745,609
Total Net Assets	187,715,738
Total Liabilities and Net Assets	$197,568,400

ILLUSTRATION 19–5

VALLEY COLLEGE
Statement of Activities
Year Ended June 30, 19y4

	Unrestricted	Temporarily Restricted	Permanently Restricted	Total
Operating Revenues and Gains:				
Student tuition and fees	$ 1,348,685	$ —	$ —	$ 1,348,685
Government grants for student aid	1,166,566	—	—	1,166,566
Endowment income	6,112,895	—	—	6,112,895
Gifts and donations	2,341,276	—	—	2,341,276
Sales and services of auxiliary enterprises	7,440,722	—	—	7,440,722
Capital gains on investments utilized	258,002	—	—	258,002
Net assets released from restriction	756,194	(756,194)	—	—
Total operating revenues and gains	19,424,340	(756,194)		18,668,146
Operating Expenses and Losses:				
Educational and general expense:				
Instruction	3,478,676	—	—	3,478,676
Public service	938,714	—	—	938,714
Academic support	113,256	—	—	113,256
Student services	2,149,120	—	—	2,149,120
Institutional support	2,312,635	—	—	2,312,635
Operation and maintenance of plant	2,850,563	—	—	2,850,563
Total educational and general expense	11,842,964			11,842,964
Auxiliary enterprises	7,435,036	—	—	7,435,036
Annuity and life income payments	412,648	—	—	412,648
Total operating expenses and losses	19,690,648			19,690,648
Excess of operating expenses and losses over operating revenues and gains	(266,308)	(756,194)		(1,022,502)
Nonoperating Activities:				
Gifts and bequests	2,255,736	1,247,639	892,464	4,395,839
Investment income	587,223	407,481	110,515	1,105,219
Capital gains utilized	3,717,237	173,025	5,389,703	9,279,965
Net assets reclassified from temporarily restricted net assets	—	(28,741)	28,741	—
Matured annuity and life income funds	21,746	(57,346)	35,600	—
Refunds to federal government	—	—	(10,458)	(10,458)
Change in net assets from nonoperating activities	6,581,942	1,742,058	6,446,565	14,770,565
Total change in net assets	6,315,634	985,864	6,446,565	13,748,063
Net assets at beginning of year	67,375,053	22,293,578	84,299,044	173,967,675
Net assets at end of year	$73,690,687	$23,279,442	$90,745,609	$187,715,738

ILLUSTRATION 19–6

VALLEY COLLEGE
Statement of Cash Flows
Year Ended June 30, 19y4

CASH FLOWS FROM OPERATING ACTIVITIES:

Increase in net assets	$13,748,063
Adjustments to reconcile increase in net assets to net cash provided by operating activities:	
Depreciation	878,843
Decrease in pledges receivable	207,500
Decrease in accounts receivable	52,701
Increase in accounts payable and accrued expenses	110,987
Increase in deposits and agency funds	22,366
Increase in annuities payable	355,300
Decrease in deferred revenue	(10,621)
Decrease in advances from federal government	(15,177)
Increase in accrued interest receivable	(922,455)
Increase in prepaid expenses	(161,492)
Increase in inventories	(60,534)
Net capital gains used	(9,537,967)
Interest and dividends restricted for long-term investment	(804,467)
Contributions restricted for long-term investment	(4,603,338)
Adjustment of actuarial liability for annuities payable	(25,395)
Net cash used for operating activities	(765,686)

CASH FLOWS FROM INVESTING ACTIVITIES:

Proceeds from sale of investments	136,802,105
Purchases of investments	(141,199,838)
Purchases of property, plant, and equipment	(1,380,016)
Loans to students and faculty	(283,781)
Collections of loans to students and faculty	132,725
Net cash used for investing activities	(5,928,805)

CASH FLOWS FROM FINANCING ACTIVITIES:

Proceeds from contributions restricted for long-term investment	4,603,338
Issuance of long-term debt	3,000,000
Repayment of long-term debt	(3,021,687)
Interest and dividends restricted for long-term investment	804,467
Increase in long-term loans receivable	(151,043)
Net cash provided by financing activities	5,235,075
Net increase in cash and cash equivalents	(1,459,416)
Cash and cash equivalents, beginning of year	3,050,369
Cash and cash equivalents, end of year	$ 1,590,953

Valley College, a hypothetical private not-for-profit college.[11] As shown in Illustration 19–4, the difference between assets and liabilities is termed "net assets." Net Assets, as explained in the previous discussion on contributions, are segregated into three groups: unrestricted, temporarily restricted, and permanently restricted. The amount shown for Valley College as permanently restricted assets, $90,745,609, represents the net assets of certain loan funds and endowment funds. Net assets which are temporarily restricted by donor stipulation or for the passage of time amount to $23,279,442. This amount includes the net assets of Restricted Current Funds, Annuity and Life Income Funds, Term Endowment Funds, and restricted Plant Funds. Unrestricted net assets, shown in the amount of $73,690,687, includes the net assets of Unrestricted Current Funds and "funds functioning as endowment" (quasi-endowment) and unrestricted Loan Fund and Plant Fund assets, since the latter items are not restricted by external donors. *Statement No. 117* does not require that comparative amounts for the preceding fiscal year be provided, although comparative financial statements are recommended. Comparative amounts have been omitted from the financial statements shown in Illustrations 19–4, 19–5, and 19–6 for simplicity.

Illustration 19–5 presents the Statement of Activities for Valley College, which uses one of three alternative formats illustrated in *Statement No. 117*. The format shown utilizes separate columns for the three categories of net assets: unrestricted, temporarily restricted, and permanently restricted. The revenue and expense classifications are essentially the same as those shown for the Current Funds operating statement shown in Illustration 19–2, except that the AICPA model operating statement reports expenditures rather than expenses. Among the obvious differences between the Statement of Activities shown in Illustration 19–5 and the reporting requirements discussed previously for public colleges and universities is that the latter present an operating statement for the Current Funds only (Illustration 19–2) and a separate Statement of Changes in Fund Balances displaying fund balance additions and deductions for all fund groups (Illustration 19–3). Another difference is that the Statement of Activities reports, as required by FASB *Statement No. 93,* depreciation expense as part of the functional expense classifications, whereas if a public college or university opts to report depreciation it will do so in the Investment in Plant Fund.

The Statement of Cash Flows required by FASB *Statement No. 117* is shown in Illustration 19–6. Note that the format and terminology used for the cash flow statement prepared in conformity with FASB *Statement No. 95* are somewhat different than those for the cash flow statements for governmental proprietary and

---

[11] *Statement No. 117* allows the entity considerable discretion as to the format and the level of aggregation to be used in preparing the financial statements. As of mid-1994, however, there has not yet been sufficient reporting to determine what formats and levels of aggregation most private colleges and universities will prefer. The illustrative financial statements shown in Illustrations 19–4, 19–5, and 19–6 are based on general examples provided in *Statement No. 117* and are adapted from actual prototype financial statements of two institutions of higher learning that participated in a field test of the proposed standard before its final issuance.

fiduciary funds, illustrated previously in Chapters 9, 10, and 12. These differences are discussed more fully in Chapter 20 on health care entities.

The information needed to prepare the Statement of Cash Flows shown in Illustration 19–6 is assumed, since comparative balance sheets were not presented. In general, one should follow a worksheet approach or T-account analysis described in most intermediate financial accounting texts to prepare the cash flow statement.

Statement No. 117 permits the use of either the direct or the indirect method for displaying the cash flows from operating activities. The cash flow statement shown in Illustration 19–6 uses the indirect method in which adjustments are made to reconcile change in net assets with cash flows from operating activities. Since both operating and nonoperating transactions are reflected in change in net assets (see Illustration 19–5), nonoperating items such as contributions and interest or dividends reinvested in long-term investments must be deducted in computing cash flows from operating activities, and reported instead as "cash flows from financing activities." Items such as net capital gains/losses (both realized and unrealized) may be included in changes in net assets if investments are managed using the total return approach, discussed earlier in this chapter. Unrealized capital gains used (recognized) add to net assets but do not provide cash. Realized capital gains increase both net assets and cash, but the cash provided should be reported as part of the proceeds from sale of investments in the cash flows from financing activities section of the cash flow statement rather than the cash flows from operating activities section. Thus, both unrealized and realized capital gains should be deducted from changes in net assets in computing cash flows from *operating* activities. Finally, changes in actuarial estimates of the liability for annuities payable affect net assets but do not increase or decrease cash in the current period. Thus, the increase in net assets due to adjustment of actuarial liability is shown in Illustration 19–6 as a deduction in computing cash flows from operating activities. Most other items in the cash flow statement are similar to those discussed in intermediate accounting texts for corporate cash flow statements reported in the same format.

Finally, it should be noted that FASB *Statement No. 117* does not provide guidance on **measurement** of financial statement elements (i.e., assets, liabilities, net assets, revenues, gains, expenses, losses, etc.); it provides **display standards** for the required financial statements and what should be reported in the financial statements. Although it does not specify a basis of accounting, its use of the term "expenses" rather than "expenditures," together with required depreciation reporting, essentially describes the full accrual basis of accounting.

Auditing of Colleges and Universities

Most colleges and universities, whether private or public, publish audited financial statements. At a minimum, audits of colleges and universities will be performed in conformity with the generally accepted auditing standards (GAAS) promulgated by the AICPA, as discussed in Chapter 14. Additionally, many colleges and universities, as a condition of accepting federal financial awards, are audited under the auditing standards established by the U.S. General Accounting Office in its publication *Government Auditing Standards* (GAS), also known as the "yellow book," as discussed in Chapter 14. Specifically, if a college or university receives $100,000 or more in federal awards in a given fiscal year, it must have a "single audit" in accordance with the provisions of Office of Management and Budget (OMB) *Circular A-133*, "Audits of Institutions of Higher Education and Other Nonprofit Institutions." *Circular A-133* audit requirements agree in all major respects with those for *Circular A-128* single audits of state and local governmental units. In lieu of a *Circular A-133* audit, some *governmentally owned* colleges and universities may opt to be audited under *Circular A-128* rules as part of the audit of the primary government. Since the audit requirements for the single audit are described in considerable detail in Chapter 14, they need not be reiterated here.

An item of special emphasis in auditing colleges and universities is to ensure that costs that are unallowable under OMB *Circular A-21*, "Cost Principles for Educational Institutions," are not charged, either as direct costs or indirect costs, to federal grants or contracts. As with single audits of state and local governments, *Circular A-133* audits place heavy emphasis on evaluating the system of internal controls and compliance with applicable laws and regulations, in addition to the traditional audit of the financial statements.

Similar Standards for Similar Entities?

By issuing *Statement No. 116* and *Statement No. 117*, FASB requires *nongovernmentally owned* not-for-profit organizations, including private colleges and universities, to prepare their financial statements in a manner similar to commercial entities. In contrast, most *governmentally owned* not-for-profit organizations are expected to continue to follow their present reporting model until GASB has provided financial reporting standards, or other guidance, for each entity. GASB has a variety of options it could consider. These options include:

1. Retain the present "AICPA model" for each type of entity.
2. Require the use of the governmental model.
3. Require the use of the FASB *Statement No. 117* model.
4. Require the use of the commercial model.
5. Develop a new reporting model applicable to *all* governmental not-for-profit organizations.
6. Develop a new reporting model for *each* type of entity.

Some governmentally owned not-for-profit organizations that use proprietary fund accounting (particularly health care entities as discussed in Chapter 20) may opt, as permitted under GASB standards, to follow FASB *Statement No. 116* for recognition of contributions, and to follow the financial reporting requirements of *Statement No. 117,* to the extent they do not conflict with GASB reporting requirements. Some governmentally owned (or affiliated) not-for-profit organizations, such as museums and community service organizations, could consider adopting the governmental model. In the interest of reestablishing similar financial reporting for similar entities, the authors believe the GASB should consider requiring all stand-alone governmentally owned not-for-profit entities to use proprietary fund (i.e., full accrual) accounting, and to use standards consistent with those of FASB for their separately issued financial statements. Such a requirement would not only enhance comparability among similar entities, but would also help measure the full cost of entity programs and contribute to service efforts and accomplishments reporting, as discussed in Chapter 16.

Selected References

American Institute of Certified Public Accountants. *Audits of Colleges and Universities.* 2nd ed. New York, 1975.

_____. *Statement of Position 74-8.* New York, 1974.

Financial Accounting Standards Board. *Statement of Financial Accounting Standards No. 93. Recognition of Depreciation by Not-for-Profit Organizations.* Norwalk, Conn., 1987.

_____. *Statement of Financial Accounting Standards No. 116. Accounting for Contributions Received and Contributions Made.* Norwalk, Conn., 1993.

_____. *Statement of Financial Accounting Standards No. 117. Financial Statements of Not-for-Profit Organizations.* Norwalk, Conn., 1993.

Governmental Accounting Standards Board. *Codification of Governmental Accounting and Financial Reporting Standards as of June 30, 1993,* Norwalk, Conn., 1993.

National Association of College and University Business Officers. *College & University Business Administration: Administrative Service.* Washington, D.C. In loose-leaf form with periodic changes and supplements.

_____. *Financial Accounting and Reporting Manual for Higher Education.* Washington, D.C. In loose-leaf form with bimonthly updates.

National Center for Higher Education Management Systems. *Higher Education Finance Manual.* Washington, D.C.: U.S. Government Printing Office, 1980.

Questions

19–1. Many colleges and universities are governmentally owned; others are privately supported not-for-profit organizations. What bearing does this situation have on the determination of authoritative financial reporting standards for colleges and universities?

19–2. Explain how restricted gifts and grants are accounted for in the Current Funds group of a public college or university that follows the AICPA model. How would such restricted gifts and grants be accounted for and reported by a private college or university that follows FASB *Statement Nos. 116* and *117*?

19–3. "Since revenues and expenditures should not be recognized in Restricted Current Funds, resource inflows and outflows should be accounted for as additions to and deductions from Fund Balance—Restricted." Do you agree? Why or why not?

19–4. Distinguish between expenditures and transfers. How do mandatory transfers differ from nonmandatory transfers?

19–5. "Colleges and universities are deemed to be presenting financial statements in conformity with GAAP if they report temporary investments of Current Funds at market value and long-term investments of Endowment Funds at cost or amortized cost." Do you agree? Why or why not?

19–6. "Endowment funds of public colleges and universities should be accounted for in the same manner as nonexpendable trust funds of state and local governments." Do you agree? Why or why not?

19–7. Explain the primary distinction between an Annuity Fund and a Life Income Fund.

19–8. Explain fully how the plant fund accounts of a public college or university differ from the General Fixed Assets Account Group of a state or local government.

19–9. "Under FASB standards applicable to private colleges and universities, *all* contributions must be recognized as revenues or gains in the period received." Do you agree? Why or why not?

19–10. Explain the conditions that must exist for a private college or university to avoid accounting recognition of the value of its valuable collections of art, historical treasures, and similar assets.

19–11. Contrast and compare the financial statements required by the FASB for private colleges and universities with those required for public colleges and universities that follow the AICPA model.

Exercises and Problems	**19–1.** Write the numbers 1 through 10 on a sheet of paper. Beside each number, write the letter corresponding with the best answer to each of the following questions:

1. Funds that the governing board of a public university, rather than a donor or other outside agency, has determined are to be retained and invested for purposes other than loan or plant would be accounted for in the:
   a. Quasi-Endowment Fund.
   b. Endowment Fund.
   c. Agency Fund.
   d. Restricted Current Fund.

2. Which of the following is utilized for current expenditures by a public university?

	Unrestricted Current Funds	*Restricted Current Funds*
a.	No	No
b.	No	Yes
c.	Yes	No
d.	Yes	Yes

3. Clarkeville College, a public college, has a 10-week summer session that starts on June 15. During the fiscal year ending June 30, 19x1, tuition and fees in the amount of $750,000 were collected from students for classes to be conducted in this session. What amount should Clarkville College recognize as Unrestricted Current Funds Revenue in each of the years ended June 30, 19x1, and June 30, 19x2?

	Year Ended June 30, 19x1	Year Ended June 30, 19x2
a.	$150,000	$600,000
b.	$750,000	$ 0
c.	$ 0	$750,000

d. Either *a* or *c* is allowed, provided the same pattern of recognition is applied consistently in successive years.

4. Tuition waivers for which there is *no* intention of collection from the student should be classified by a not-for-profit university as

	Revenues	Expenditures
a.	No	No
b.	No	Yes
c.	Yes	Yes
d.	Yes	No

5. An alumnus donates securities to Rex College and stipulates that the principal be held in perpetuity and income from the securities be used for faculty travel. Dividends received from the securities should be recognized as revenues in:
   a. Endowment Funds.
   b. Quasi-Endowment Funds.
   c. Restricted Current Funds.
   d. Unrestricted Current Funds.

6. During the years ended June 30, 19x1, and 19x2, Sonata University, a public university, conducted a cancer research project financed by a $2,000,000 gift from an alumnus. This entire amount was pledged by the donor on July 10, 19x0, although he paid only $500,000 at that date. The gift was restricted to the financing of this particular research project. During the two-year research period, Sonata's related gift receipts and research expenditures were as follows:

	Year Ended June 30	
	19x1	*19x2*
Gift receipts	$1,200,000	$ 800,000
Cancer research expenditures	900,000	1,100,000

How much gift revenue should Sonata report in the restricted column of its Statement of Current Funds Revenues, Expenditures, and Other Changes for the year ended June 30, 19x2?
   a. $0.
   b. $800,000.
   c. $1,100,000.
   d. $2,000,000.

7. Are public and private colleges and universities required to report depreciation expense in their financial statements?

	Public	Private
a.	No	No
b.	No	Yes
c.	Yes	Yes
d.	Yes	No

8. During the year ended June 30, 19x2, Clarion College, a private college, received a federal government grant of $500,000 for research on the aged. Expenditures for this research amounted to $350,000 during the same year. Under applicable FASB standards, Clarion College would report what amount(s) as revenues or support for the year ended June 30, 19x2?

	Unrestricted	Temporarily Restricted	Permanently Restricted
a.	$0	$350,000	$0
b.	$0	$350,000	$150,000
c.	$350,000	$150,000	$0
d.	$500,000	$0	$0

9. Which of the following is *not* a condition that would permit a private college or university to avoid accounting recognition of the value of its valuable collections of art, historical treasures, and similar assets?
   a. The assets are held for public exhibition, education, or research in furtherance of public service rather than financial gain.
   b. The assets are protected, kept unencumbered, cared for, and preserved.
   c. The assets are subject to an organizational policy that ensures the proceeds of sales of collectible assets are used for operations of the organization.
   d. None of above; all three items are conditions that will avoid accounting recognition.

10. Which of the following is required as part of a complete set of financial statements for a private college or university?
    a. Statement of Activities.
    b. Statement of Current Funds Revenues, Expenditures, and Other Changes.
    c. Statement of Changes in Fund Balances.
    d. Statement of Changes in Financial Position.

(Items 1–7, AICPA, adapted)

19–2. The Balance Sheet for Mozark College as of June 30, 19x5, is shown below. Mozark College is a state-supported institution which follows the AICPA model for accounting and financial reporting purposes. Current Funds transactions during the year 19x5–x6 are given below. You are required to prepare journal entries for the transactions given and to prepare a Current Funds Balance Sheet as of June 30, 19x6. For each entry, indicate whether it affects Unrestricted Current Funds or Restricted Current Funds.

MOZARK COLLEGE
Balance Sheet
June 30, 19x5

Assets

Current funds:		
Unrestricted:		
Cash		$ 70,000
Accounts receivable—student fees	$25,000	
Less: Allowance for doubtful accounts	1,000	24,000
Due from restricted funds		8,000
State appropriation receivable		182,000
Inventory, at cost		14,000
Total Unrestricted		298,000

Restricted:		
Cash	3,000	
Investments, at cost	24,000	
Total Restricted		27,000
Total Current Funds		$325,000

Liabilities and Fund Balances

Current funds:		
Unrestricted:		
Accounts payable		$ 20,000
Deferred revenue		148,000
Fund balance		130,000
Total Unrestricted		298,000
Restricted:		
Due to unrestricted funds	$ 8,000	
Fund balance	19,000	
Total Restricted		27,000
Total Current Funds		$325,000

1. Fees charged to students for the fall and spring semesters of fiscal 19x5–x6 totaled $2,200,000 of which $2,100,000 was collected in cash. The Allowance for Doubtful Accounts was increased by $4,000.

2. Collections of accounts receivable totaled $20,000. Accounts amounting to $1,000 were written off.

3. The Deferred Revenue of $148,000 shown in the Balance Sheet resulted from student fees charged for the summer term which began in fiscal 19x4–x5 but was predominantly conducted in 19x5–x6.

4. Fees charged to students for summer school totaled $144,000, all of which was collected in cash. The summer term will be predominantly conducted in fiscal 19x6–x7.

5. Temporary investments in the amount of $10,000 held at the beginning of the year were sold for $10,500. Restricted current funds cash spent for authorized purposes amounted to $2,500; an additional $8,000 was transferred to unrestricted funds in payment of the liability existing on June 30, 19x5.

6. During the year, accounts payable for purchases, salaries and wages, utility bills, and other expenditures totaling $1,750,000 were recorded. Accounts payable at the end of the year amounted to $70,000.

7. Supplies inventory at the end of the year amounted to $25,000, according to physical count.

8. During the year, the state appropriation of $182,000 was received. A further appropriation for current general purposes of $192,000 was made by the state but had not been paid to the college by year-end.

9. Unrestricted fund cash in the amount of $160,000 was transferred to Funds for Retirement of Debt, and $500,000 of unrestricted fund cash was invested in short-term U.S. Treasury notes.

10. Income received in cash from investments of restricted current funds amounted to $1,050; an additional $160 interest was accrued at year-end.

11. All nominal accounts were closed.

19–3. A partial Balance Sheet of Rapapo State University as of the end of its fiscal year ended July 31, 19x2, is presented below:

RAPAPO STATE UNIVERSITY
Current Funds Balance Sheet
July 31, 19x2

Assets			*Liabilities and Fund Balances*	
Unrestricted:			Unrestricted:	
Cash	$200,000		Accounts payable	$100,000
Accounts receivable—tuition and			Due to other funds	40,000
fees, less allowance for doubtful			Deferred revenue—tuition and	
accounts of $15,000	370,000		fees	25,000
Prepaid expenses	40,000		Fund balance	445,000
Total unrestricted	610,000		Total unrestricted	610,000
Restricted:			Restricted:	
Cash	10,000		Accounts payable	5,000
Investments	210,000		Fund balance	215,000
Total restricted	220,000		Total restricted	220,000
Total current funds	$830,000		Total current funds	$830,000

The following information pertains to the year ended July 31, 19x3:

1. Cash collected from students' tuition totaled $3,000,000. Of this $3,000,000, $362,000 represented accounts receivable outstanding at July 31, 19x2; $2,500,000 was for current-year tuition; and $138,000 was for tuition applicable to the semester beginning in August 19x3.

2. Deferred revenue at July 31, 19x2, was earned during the year ended July 31, 19x3.

3. Accounts receivable in the amount of $13,000 were determined uncollectible and were written off against the allowance account. At July 31, 19x3, the allowance account was estimated at $10,000.

4. During the year, an unrestricted appropriation of $60,000 was made by the state. This state appropriation was to be paid to Rapapo sometime in August 19x3.

5. During the year, unrestricted cash gifts of $80,000 were received from alumni. Rapapo's board of trustees allocated $30,000 of these gifts to the student loan fund.

6. During the year, investments costing $25,000 were sold for $31,000. Restricted fund investments were purchased at a cost of $40,000. Investment income of $18,000 was earned and collected during the year.

7. Unrestricted general expenses of $2,500,000 were recorded in the voucher system. At July 31, 19x3, the unrestricted accounts payable balance was $75,000.

8. The restricted accounts payable balance at July 31, 19x2, was paid.

9. The $40,000 due to other funds at July 31, 19x2, was paid to the plant fund as required.

10. One quarter of the prepaid expenses at July 31, 19x2, expired during the current year, and pertained to general education expense. There was no addition to prepaid expenses during the year.

Required *a.* Prepare journal entries in summary form to record the foregoing transactions for the year ended July 31, 19x3, assuming Rapapo State University is a public university. Number each entry to correspond with the number indicated in the description of its respective transaction. Your answer sheet should be organized as follows:

		Current Funds			
		Unrestricted		Restricted	
Entry No.	Accounts	Debits	Credits	Debits	Credits

b. Prepare a statement of changes in fund balances for the year ended July 31, 19x3.

(AICPA, adapted)

19–4. The Balance Sheet of Razorback University as of June 30, 19x5, indicated the following with respect to the loan funds:

Loan Funds:			
Cash		$15,000	
Investments		30,000	
Loans to Students, Faculty and Staff	$100,000		
Accrued Interest Receivable	1,000		
	101,000		
Less: Allowance for Doubtful Loans and Interest	2,000	99,000	
Total Loan Funds			$144,000
Loan Funds:			
Fund Balances—Unrestricted			$144,000
Total Loan Funds			$144,000

You are required to prepare loan funds journal entries for the following transactions, which occurred in the year 19x5–x6. You are also required to prepare a loan funds Balance Sheet as of June 30, 19x6, assuming that Razorback University is a public university.

1. A bequest of $32,000 in securities was received by Razorback University. The decedent specified that both principal and interest were to be used for student loans.
2. Loans receivable of prior years in the amount of $31,000 were collected during the year. Interest collected on loans receivable in cash during the year amounted to $4,150, $900 of which was accrued at June 30, 19x5, and $3,250 of which was earned in 19x5–x6.
3. One loan of $600 and accrued interest of $50 (as of balance sheet date) was written off as uncollectible.
4. Loans made to students during the year totaled $42,000. All loans were secured by notes; repayments on these loans during the year amounted to $4,100 ($4,000 principal and $100 interest).
5. Dividends and interest on loan fund investments collected in cash during the year amounted to $2,150. Accrued interest receivable at the end of the year amounted to $640. The Allowance for Doubtful Loans and Interest was increased to $1,900.

19–5. The Balance Sheet of Longhorn University as of June 30, 19x5, indicated the following with respect to endowment and similar funds:

Endowment and similar funds:

Cash	$ 30,000
Securities (at cost)	800,000
Real estate	270,000
Cash held by trustee	100,000
Total Endowment and Similar Funds	$1,200,000

Endowment and similar funds:

Accounts Payable	$ 20,000
Endowment fund balances:	
Reserve for replacement of real estate	120,000
Fund balances—income unrestricted	750,000
Fund balances—income restricted	200,000
Quasi-endowment funds balances	110,000
Total Endowment and Similar Funds	$1,200,000

You are required to prepare journal entries to record the following transactions, which relate to the fiscal year 19x5–x6; you are also required to prepare a Balance Sheet as of June 30, 19x6, assuming Longhorn University is a public university.

1. Cash held by the trustee in the amount of $25,000 was transferred by the trustee to the Endowment Fund Cash Account.
2. Accounts payable on June 30, 19x5, were paid.
3. Securities of quasi-endowment funds carried at $55,000 were sold for $53,000 and the proceeds reinvested in other securities.
4. The Reserve for Replacement of Real Estate was increased by $10,000; cash in this amount was received from Unrestricted Current Funds.

19–6. The Balance Sheet of Cougar University as of June 30, 19x5, indicated the following with respect to annuity and life income funds. From the transactions that follow, prepare journal entries and a Balance Sheet as of June 30, 19x6, assuming Cougar University is a public university.

Annuity and life income funds:

Cash	$ 30,000	
Investments	135,000	
Total Annuity and Life Income Funds		$165,000

Annuity and life income funds:

Annuity funds:		
Annuities payable	$ 62,000	
Fund balances	30,000	$ 92,000
Life income funds:		
Fund balances		73,000
Total Annuity and Life Income Funds		$165,000

1. On August 1, 19x5, a tract of land with fair market value of $600,000 was received under an agreement that Cougar University would pay the donor $30,000 each year on the anniversary date of the agreement as long as the donor lived. No restrictions were placed on the use of the principal of the fund or any income in excess of $30,000 per year. The present value of the liability to the annuitant is $342,000.

2. Cash income received from annuity fund investments during the year totaled $34,000, of which $11,400 was disbursed to annuitant during the year.

3. During the year, one life income recipient died, her contribution, $42,000 in investments, was transferred to the loan funds.

19–7. The Balance Sheet of Mustang University as of June 30, 19x5, indicated the following with respect to plant funds. From the transactions given below, prepare journal entries and a Plant Funds Balance Sheet as of the end of the year, using subgroups shown below and assuming Mustang University is a public university.

Plant funds:		
Unexpended:		
Cash	$ 20,000	
Investments	276,000	
Due from other funds	4,000	
Total Unexpended Plant Funds		$ 300,000
Retirement of indebtedness:		
Cash	5,000	
Investments	125,000	
Total Retirement of Indebtedness		130,000
Investment in plant:		
Land	115,000	
Buildings	5,260,000	
Equipment	983,000	
Construction in progress	212,000	
Total Investment in Plant		6,570,000
Total Plant Funds		$7,000,000
Plant funds:		
Unexpended:		
Accounts payable	82,000	
Fund balance	218,000	
Total Unexpended Plant Funds		$ 300,000
Retirement of indebtedness:		
Fund balance—unrestricted		130,000
Investment in plant:		
Bonds payable	260,000	
Investment in plant:		
From operations	3,075,000	
From gifts	1,410,000	
From governmental appropriations	1,825,000	
Total Investment in Plant		6,570,000
Total Plant Funds		$7,000,000

Transactions during the fiscal year ended June 30, 19x6, were:

1. Retirement of Indebtedness Fund investments costing $125,000 were sold for $127,000 cash; bonds payable of the plant funds in the amount of $130,000 were retired by use of Retirement of Indebtedness Fund cash.

2. The amount due Unexpended Plant Funds from other funds at the beginning of the year was received.

3. A grant of $800,000 was made to Mustang University by the Mustang Foundation to be used for the acquisition of buildings and equipment. The grant was to be paid to the university in equal installments over an eight-year period; the sum for the current year was received in cash.

4. Invoices and payrolls amounting to $50,000 for the construction in progress were recorded as accounts payable. Accounts payable in the amount of $102,000 were paid during the year. The assets of the Unexpended Plant Funds had been obtained from gifts.

5. The construction in progress, an addition to the School of Business building, was considered completed. It was determined that 80 percent of the total cost was to be charged to Buildings and 20 percent to Equipment.

6. A firm of architects engaged to prepare plans for a new residence hall submitted an invoice for $40,000 for services performed by them this year. (You may credit Accounts Payable.)

7. Unrestricted Current Funds transferred $65,000 cash to the Retirement of Indebtedness Fund. The latter fund invested that amount in certificates of deposit.

19–8. Zenith College had always kept its accounts on a so-called commercial basis and not in the form ordinarily used by educational institutions. The Balance Sheet of June 30, 19x4, and the related statements of income and expenses for the year ended on that date were made up as follows:

Balance Sheet
June 30, 19x4

Assets

Current assets:		
Cash	$ 1,180	
Tuition fees receivable	8,000	
Inventory of supplies	2,000	$ 11,180
Endowment fund investments:		
Rented real estate—at cost	75,000	
Less: Allowance for depreciation	15,000	
	60,000	
Mortgages, 7 percent—at cost	145,000	
5 percent public utility bonds—at cost (market value $202,000)	220,000	425,000
Plant and equipment, net of allowance for depreciation of $166,000		830,000
		$1,266,180

Liabilities

Current liabilities:		
Bank loans	$ 15,000	
Accounts payable	9,000	$ 24,000
First-mortgage bonds, 7 percent, maturing at the rate of $15,000 semiannually on June 30 and December 31 of each year		300,000
Endowment fund balance		540,000
Capital:		
Balance at July 1, 19x3	400,000	
Excess of income over expenses for the year ended June 30, 19x4, per annexed statement	2,180	402,180
		$1,266,180

Statement of Revenues and Expenses
For the Year Ended June 30, 19x4

Revenues:

Tuition		$ 230,000
Endowment income:		
Rentals	$ 8,100	
Mortgage interest	10,150	
Bond interest	10,500	28,750
Income from auxiliary enterprises		65,000
Unrestricted donations		33,000
Miscellaneous		4,000
Total Revenues		360,750

Expenses:

Instruction and research	165,200	
Expenses of auxiliary enterprises	80,000	
Administration	34,000	
Operation and maintenance	35,375	
Depreciation of rented real estate	1,500	
Depreciation of plant and equipment	19,920	
Bond interest	22,575	358,570
Excess of Revenues over Expenses		$ 2,180

An examination of the books and records brought out the following additional information:

The original college property was completed 10 years ago at a cost of $916,000. It was financed by a 7 percent bond issue of $600,000 and by $316,000 appropriated from unrestricted gifts received at the time of organization of the college. Additions costing $80,000 have since been made from current funds, of which $10,000 was spent in the year ended June 30, 19x4.

The endowment funds are restricted with respect to principal to their investment in marketable securities and other income-producing properties. Income from the investments can be used for any purpose. The endowment fund assets are less than the endowment fund balance because investments had been sold from time to time when cash was needed to pay expenses; the total amount of investments sold for that purpose was $100,000.

Rentals and mortgage interest had been received regularly at the end of every month or quarter; and also the June 30, 19x4, interest on the public utility bonds had been collected on that date, so that no revenue other than the $8,000 of tuition fees was receivable as of June 30, 19x4.

The trustees adopted a policy of charging depreciation on income-producing properties so as to provide a reserve for their ultimate replacement. Assets are to be held in the Endowment Fund in the amount of accumulated depreciation. The public utility bonds have a face value of $210,000 and were purchased five years before balance sheet date at a cost of $220,000 and will mature on June 30, 19x9. Assets are to be held in the Endowment Fund in the amount of bond premium amortized.

The "capital" of June 30, 19x4, is made up as follows:

Unrestricted gifts at organization	$350,000
Excess of income over expenditures	57,000
	$407,000

Required   Prepare a written report for the Controller of Zenith College to set forth the changes that must be made to bring the College's financial statements into conformity with FASB financial reporting standards for a private college, as described in Chapter 19.

(AICPA, adapted)

19–9. Utilizing the information given in the financial statements of Zenith College (see Problem 19–8), and the additional information given following those statements and provided below, prepare a Statement of Financial Position and a Statement of Activities for Zenith College, as of June 30, 19x4, in conformity with FASB financial reporting standards for a private college. Use the format for these statements shown in Illustrations 19–4 and 19–5 earlier in this chapter.

   In preparing the financial statements, you may assume that unrestricted net assets as of July 1, 19x3 amounted to $499,500 and permanently restricted net assets (endowment fund) amounted to $540,000. The beginning balance of unrestricted net assets must be adjusted by deducting an amount of $117,500 for prior years' borrowing of endowment fund assets ($100,000), failure to record amortization of premium on endowment investments ($4,000), and failure to fund depreciation of rented endowment real estate ($13,500). The effects of current year premium amortization of endowment fund investments ($1,000) and current year depreciation of rented endowment real estate ($1,500) should be reflected in change in net assets for the period.

Accounting for Health Care Entities

Generally accepted accounting principles (GAAP) for hospitals and other health care organizations have evolved through the efforts of the American Hospital Association (AHA), the Healthcare Financial Management Association (HFMA), and the American Institute of Certified Public Accountants (AICPA). The AICPA *Audits of Providers of Health Care Services* applies to hospitals and a variety of other organizations that have become important providers of health care services.[1] These include:

1. Clinics, medical group practices, individual practice associations, individual practitioners, and other ambulatory care organizations.
2. Continuing care retirement communities.
3. Health maintenance organizations and similar prepaid health care plans.
4. Home health agencies.
5. Nursing homes that provide skilled, intermediate, and less intensive levels of health care.
6. Organizations whose primary activities are the planning, organization, and oversight of entities providing health care services.

The audit and accounting guide applies to the separate financial statements of investor-owned and nongovernmentally owned not-for-profit health care entities, and to state and local governmentally owned health care entities that use enterprise fund accounting and reporting.[2] It applies both to hospitals and the other

---

[1] American Institute of Certified Public Accountants, *Audit and Accounting Guide, Audits of Providers of Health Care Services* (New York, 1990).

[2] Governmentally owned and operated hospitals for the insane, and for certain other categories of patients, which are financed primarily from appropriations rather than from user charges, are, of course, accounted for as a General Fund or a special revenue fund department, and the accounting and financial reporting standards discussed in Chapters 3 and 4, not the standards discussed in this chapter, are applicable to hospitals of that nature.

forms of health care entities listed above. Although the audit and accounting guide is intended primarily to provide guidance for independent auditors who audit and report on the financial statements of health care entities, it is also a principal source of generally accepted accounting principles for health care entities. However, as discussed at length in Chapter 19 on colleges and universities, responsibility for setting accounting and financial reporting standards rests formally with the FASB for investor-owned and nongovernmentally owned not-for-profit health care entities and with the GASB for state and local governmentally owned health care entities.[3]

Until 1993, when the FASB issued *Statement 116,* "Accounting for Contributions Received and Contributions Made," and FASB *Statement No. 117,* "Financial Statements of Not-for-Profit Organizations," most health care entities relied on the AICPA audit and accounting guide as their primary source of GAAP. Although, as discussed in Chapter 19, the FASB statements create a substantial divergence in the accounting and financial reporting standards applicable to public (governmental) and private (nongovernmental) colleges and universities, they have much less impact on standards for health care entities. There are several reasons for the lesser impact of these statements on nongovernmentally owned not-for-profit health care entities. First, contributions, though perhaps significant, are generally not as important to the operations of health care entities as to the operations of colleges and universities (or the not-for-profit organizations discussed in Chapter 21). Second, GAAP for health care entities specifies the use of the accrual basis of accounting, including reporting of depreciation expense. Third, the financial reporting principles contained in the AICPA audit and accounting guide are similar to those in FASB *Statement No. 117,* particularly if an entity elects to prepare the optional "aggregated" rather than "layered," or fund-based, balance sheet permitted in the AICPA guide. Finally, both the audit and accounting guide and *Statement No. 117* require that net assets be classified as unrestricted, temporarily restricted by donors, and permanently restricted by donors.

Chapter 19 presents a full discussion of the requirements of FASB *Statement Nos. 116* and *117.* Since the differences in requirements between the FASB statements and those of the AICPA audit and accounting guide are modest for health care entities, the illustrative transactions discussed in this chapter are those that conform with the audit and accounting guide.[4] Appropriate explanations are pro-

---

[3] GASB *Statement No. 20,* "Accounting and Financial Reporting for Proprietary Funds and Other Governmental Entities That Use Proprietary Fund Accounting," gives governmental health care entities that use proprietary fund accounting the option of following all applicable FASB pronouncements (which would include FASB *Statement Nos. 116* and *117*) unless they conflict with GASB pronouncements. Thus, in this chapter, all discussion of FASB standards that are applicable to nongovernmentally owned health care entities will be understood to apply also to those governmentally owned entities that choose to follow all applicable FASB pronouncements.

[4] At this writing, a committee of the AICPA was preparing a revised audit and accounting guide for health care entities that likely will conform more closely with the requirements of FASB *Statement Nos. 116* and *117.* When the revised audit and accounting guide has been issued, the publisher will provide an update bulletin to adopters of the Tenth Edition of this text.

vided in the text at points where the FASB guidance differs from the audit and accounting guide. Additional financial statements are provided in the latter part of the chapter to illustrate those required by FASB *Statement No. 117.*

Fund Structure for Health Care Entities

Like organizations discussed in preceding chapters, health care entities *may* use a fund structure to facilitate reporting on the use of assets held under external restrictions versus assets available for use at the discretion of the governing board. As noted in the introduction to this chapter, the AICPA guide applies to a variety of health care entities, some of which may not find it necessary to use a fund structure for accounting and financial reporting. Generally, hospitals and certain other health care entities use the fund structure described in the AICPA guide. Unlike colleges and universities, all unrestricted resources of health care entities that use fund accounting are accounted for in the General Funds. The fund structure set forth in the AICPA audit and accounting guide is as follows:

A. General Funds.
B. Donor-Restricted Funds.
   1. Specific Purpose Funds.
   2. Plant Replacement and Expansion Funds.
   3. Endowment Funds.

General Funds

The AICPA's audit and accounting guide describes the function of General Funds as follows:[5]

> General Funds are used to account for resources not restricted for identified purposes by donors and grantors. They account for all resources and obligations not recorded in donor-restricted funds, including assets whose use is limited, agency funds, and property and equipment related to the general operations of the entity.

Although health care entities that use fund accounting need only one fund to account for all unrestricted assets and related liabilities, the AICPA guide uses the plural: General Funds. Property, plant, and equipment used in rendering health services are accounted for in the General Funds, and depreciation is recognized as a General Funds expense. Long-term debt, except that related to assets of endowment funds, is accounted for in the General Funds.

Health care entities that follow the AICPA audit and accounting guide (investor-owned health care entities and some governmentally owned health care entities that use proprietary fund accounting) report all revenues and expenses (not expenditures) in the General Funds. In a manner similar to colleges and universities, these health care entities report additions to and deductions from restricted funds in the Statement of Changes in Fund Balances rather than in the Statement of Revenues and Expenses. As explained in Chapter 19, however, FASB *Statement No. 116* requires all *nongovernmentally owned* and some governmentally

---

[5] *AICPA, Audits of Providers of Health Care Services*, p. 18.

owned health care entities (see footnote 3), to recognize contributions received and unconditional promises to give as revenues or gains in the period received, regardless of which fund, if any, is used to account for the contribution. Thus, unlike health care entities that follow the AICPA guide, health care entities that follow FASB *Statement Nos. 116* and *117* will recognize donor-restricted revenues or gains when received rather than delaying until expenses have been incurred for the intended purpose.

The illustrative financial statements provided in the AICPA guide indicate that assets set aside by the governing board of a health care entity for identified purposes and assets whose use is limited under terms of debt indentures, trust agreements, third-party reimbursement arrangements, or other similar agreements should be reported in the General Funds section of the balance sheet as "Assets Whose Use Is Limited" rather than in a self-balancing board-designated fund. If liabilities exist that are to be paid from "Assets Whose Use Is Limited," it is proper to segregate those liabilities from liabilities to be paid from other assets of the General Funds; captions should be provided to explain the reason for segregation. If a relatively large proportion of General Funds assets has been placed in the Assets Whose Use Is Limited category, it is logical that Fund Balance be segregated correspondingly so that financial statement users are readily informed as to net assets whose use is limited versus net assets whose use is not limited. Nongovernmentally owned health care entities also may report Assets Whose Use is Limited, if desired, since FASB *Statement No. 117* neither requires nor prohibits the use of such disaggregations within the unrestricted net assets classification.

Previous authoritative guidance of the AICPA provided for agency funds to account for assets owned by others (e.g., patients, residents, physicians, and students) and held by health care entities under agency relationships. The current AICPA audit and accounting guide, however, includes agency funds in the General Funds, rather than as a separate fund grouping. Transactions involving the receipt and disbursement of agency funds are not included in the operating statement.

Donor-Restricted Funds

Donor-restricted funds are used to account for resources restricted by donors and grantors for specific operating purposes, additions to property and equipment, endowments, term endowments, and annuity and life income arrangements. For financial reporting purposes, the AICPA guide specifies that donor-restricted funds be grouped into *temporarily restricted funds* and *permanently restricted funds*. Temporarily restricted funds include specific purpose funds, plant replacement and expansion funds, and term endowment funds. In addition, this category may include annuity and life income funds. Permanently restricted funds consist of endowment funds whose principal is not expendable and must be maintained in perpetuity. These classifications are consistent with the three classifications required by FASB for net assets of nongovernmental not-for-profit health care entities. The fund groups included in each category are described as follows:

Temporarily Restricted Funds.   The **specific purpose fund** classification employed by health care entities that follow the AICPA audit and accounting guide is similar in nature to the Restricted Current Funds classification used by colleges and universities. Specific purpose funds record as additions to restricted fund balance the principal and income of assets that may be used only for purposes specified by donors or grantors (usually in the area of research and education). Because revenues and expenses are recognized only in the General Funds, not in any of the restricted funds, expenses incurred for donor-specified purposes must be recorded in the General Funds; specific purpose fund assets in amounts equal to such expenses then should be transferred to the General Funds as reimbursement. Specific purpose funds are not used to record cash, securities, and so forth, restricted for plant assets (because that function is performed by the plant replacement and expansion fund), or to account for gifts whose principal must be kept intact (because that is the function of endowment funds).

The **plant replacement and expansion fund** is created to account for resources given to a health care entity to use for acquisition of property, plant, or equipment; it is emphasized that this is a restricted fund because the hospital accepted the resources subject to restrictions established by donors of the resources. (Resources designated by the hospital governing board for plant acquisition purposes are accounted for in the General Funds as "Assets Whose Use Is Limited.") Resources received from donors and grantors are considered capital contributions and are reported as additions in the Statement of Changes in Fund Balances. When expenditures are made for purposes specified by donors, the assets and Fund Balance of the plant replacement and expansion fund are decreased; the fixed assets are recorded in the General Funds with an offsetting credit to the Transfers from Restricted Funds for Capital Outlays account. The latter account is closed to General Funds Fund Balance at year-end.

Term Endowment Funds of health care entities are similar to those of colleges and universities or state and local government. They are created to account for resources given to the health care entity to be set aside for a specified term, or until a specified event occurs. The use of income from endowment funds may be restricted by the donor or may be available for use at the discretion of the governing board after the donor-imposed time or other restrictions are satisfied. Restricted income from endowments should be transferred to a specific purpose fund or to the plant replacement and expansion fund, if it is not expended in the fiscal period when earned; income available for use at board discretion should be transferred to the General Funds. Similarly, the ultimate use of the assets of endowment funds established for a specified term or until a specified event occurs may or may not be restricted by the donor. If the use of assets is still restricted when the endowment fund terminates, the assets must be transferred to an appropriately named restricted fund. If the use of the assets is unrestricted, they should be transferred to the General Funds.

Permanently Restricted Funds.   This grouping consists of endowment funds whose principal is not expendable and must be maintained in perpetuity. As described above for term endowment funds, the donor may impose restrictions on how investment income is to be used, or it may be available for unrestricted use. Accounting and financial reporting procedures for permanently restricted endowment funds are the same as those described above for temporarily restricted endowment funds.

Financial Statements   The basic financial statements specified by the AICPA audit and accounting guide for health care entities include a Balance Sheet, a Statement of Revenues and Expenses of General Funds, a Statement of Changes in Fund Balances, and a Statement of Cash Flows of General Funds (and restricted funds of governmentally owned health care entities that use proprietary fund accounting).

Sample financial statements are shown in Illustrations 20–1 through Illustration 20–7, provided later in this chapter. For comparative purposes Illustrations are provided both for the "layered" form of balance sheet (Illustration 20–2) and the optional "aggregated" form (Illustration 20–3), either of which is acceptable for health care entities covered by the AICPA guide. The latter form of balance sheet does not provide information about the assets and liabilities, and fund balances of the separate fund groups, although the amounts of fund balances that are unrestricted, temporarily restricted by donors, and permanently restricted by donors are separately reported.

Governmentally owned health care entities that use proprietary fund accounting are required to follow GASB Codification Section 2450 in preparing their Statement of Cash Flows. Accordingly, an example of a Statement of Cash Flows prepared in conformity with GASB Standards is presented as Illustration 20–5. Although FASB *Statement No. 95,* "Statement of Cash Flows," specifically excludes not-for-profit organizations from its scope, the AICPA audit and accounting guide prescribes a Statement of Cash Flows prepared in conformity with FASB *Statement No. 95* for all nongovernmentally owned health care entities that follow the guide. FASB *Statement No. 117* added further diversity to health care cash flow reporting by expanding the coverage of *Statement No. 95* to nongovernmentally owned not-for-profit organizations, and specifying a cash flow statement format that these organizations should follow. Thus, even though most health care entities (all those except for governmentally owned health care entities that use governmental fund accounting) are now required to prepare a Statement of Cash Flows, three different formats apply, depending on ownership of the entity: governmentally owned health care entities that use proprietary fund accounting follow the GASB format; investor-owned health care entities follow *Statement No. 95,* but in the format prescribed by the AICPA audit and accounting guide; and nongovernmentally owned not-for-profit entities follow *Statement No. 95,* but in the format specified by *Statement No. 117.* Illustration 20–7 provides an example of the latter cash flow statement. The differences among the three cash flow statement requirements are described in a later section of this chapter.

In addition to prescribing a particular form of cash flow statement for nongovernmentally owned not-for-profit health care entities, *Statement No. 117* also requires these entities, and governmentally owned health care entities that choose to follow all applicable FASB pronouncements (see footnote 3) to prepare a Statement of Financial Position (e.g., Balance Sheet) and a Statement of Activities. Illustration 20–3 provides an example of an optional "aggregated" balance sheet for a hospital, which also appears in most respects to reflect *Statement No. 117* requirements for a Statement of Financial Position. An example of a Statement of Activities is provided in Illustration 20–6.

Illustrative Case

General Funds

The illustrative transactions provided in this section are for a hypothetical governmentally owned not-for-profit hospital—the Bloomfield Hospital. Hospitals continue to be the dominant form of health care organization and usually exhibit a greater range of operating activities and transactions than other forms of health care organizations. Also, governmentally owned and other hospitals typically use the fund structure recommended in the AICPA guide whereas other health care entities, such as health maintenance organizations, nursing homes, and home health care agencies, may find it unnecessary to use fund accounting. Typical hospital General Funds transactions are illustrated below, following the after-closing trial balance as of September 30, 19x0, for Bloomfield Hospital, the end of its fiscal year.

	Debits	Credits
Cash	$ 120,000	
Accounts and Notes Receivable	300,000	
Allowance for Uncollectible Receivables		$ 86,000
Inventory	80,000	
Prepaid Expenses	12,000	
Assets Whose Use Is Limited—Cash	6,500	
Assets Whose Use Is Limited—Investments	400,000	
Land	1,080,000	
Buildings	11,050,000	
Fixed Equipment	2,680,000	
Major Movable Equipment	1,410,000	
Minor Equipment	830,000	
Accumulated Depreciation—Buildings		1,050,000
Accumulated Depreciation—Equipment		770,000
Accumulated Depreciation—Major Movable Equipment		490,000
Accounts Payable		110,000
Accrued Expenses Payable		16,000
Mortgages Payable		6,400,000
Fund Balance—Undesignated		8,640,000
Fund Balance—Designated for Expansion of Facilities		406,500
	$17,968,500	$17,968,500

Recall that hospitals and other health care entities that follow the AICPA guide and use fund accounting recognize revenues and expenses *only* in the General Funds. During 19x1, the gross revenues for patient services from all responsibility centers totaled $9,261,000. It is the practice of Bloomfield Hospital to debit receivable accounts for the gross charges for all services rendered to patients, except for charity care patients; the AICPA audit and accounting guide requires that charity care services be excluded both from receivables and revenues. The following entry should be made:

1. Accounts and Notes Receivable................................	9,261,000	
Patient Service Revenues..................................		9,261,000

The preceding entry recorded the revenues the hospital would have earned if all services rendered to each patient (other than charity care patients) were to be collected from the patients, or from third-party payers, as billed. Customers of profit-seeking businesses do not all pay their bills in full, and neither do the hospital patients nor the patients' insurance companies. Hospital contracts with Medicare, Medicaid, Blue Cross plans, insurance companies, and state and local welfare agencies customarily provide for payment by the third-party payers according to allowable costs or a predetermined (prospective) contractual rate rather than paying the service rates billed by the health care provider. For example, under the Medicare's Prospective Payment System (PPS), payments are based on allowable service costs for medical procedures within the same diagnosis-related group (DRG) rather than on the length of the patient's hospital stay or actual cost of services rendered. The variety of third-party payment policies makes estimation of net patient service revenue difficult but obviously necessary for sound financial management and proper financial reporting. For the year 19x1, it is assumed the estimated provision for bad debts is $180,000 and actual contractual adjustments from third-party payers is $100,000. The entry to record this information is:

2. Provision for Bad Debts.....................................	180,000	
Contractual Adjustments	100,000	
Allowance for Uncollectible Receivables..................		180,000
Accounts and Notes Receivable..........................		100,000

Provision for Bad Debts is another name for Bad Debts Expense and is reported as an operating expense (see Illustration 20–1 later in this chapter). Contractual Adjustments, however, is deducted from Patient Service Revenue and only the net amount is reported as revenues of the period (see Illustration 20–1). In addition to revenues from patient services, hospitals and other health care entities may receive **other revenues** or **gains,** both operating and nonoperating. The AICPA guide follows the definitions of elements of financial statements provided in FASB *Concepts Statement No. 6* which associates **revenues** and **expenses** with activities related to the ongoing major or central operations of health care providers and associates **gains** and **losses** with the activities of a peripheral or incidental nature, or as stemming from environmental events largely beyond control of management. Gains and losses are usually classified as ''nonoperating'' gains or losses. Properly classifying revenues, expenses, gains, and losses as operating or nonoperating requires an element of judgment. The classifications used in the illustrative transactions and financial statements contained in this chapter appear appropriate for a hospital.

Examples of **other revenues** for hospitals include transfers from restricted funds to the General Funds in the amount of expenses incurred for research, education, or other operating activities eligible for support by a restricted fund; tuition from nursing students, interns, or residents; cafeteria and gift shop revenues; parking fees; fees for copies of medical records; and other activities related to the ongoing major or central operations of the hospital. Similarly, unrestricted gifts, grants, and endowment income restricted by donors to finance charity care would appropriately be classified as **other revenue** of a hospital. If a total of $48,800 was received in cash during 19x1 from sources classified as "other revenue," Entry 3 is appropriate:

3. Cash	48,800	
Other Revenue		48,800

Apart from items previously described, hospitals may receive unrestricted donations of money or services. Ordinarily, such donations should be classified as nonoperating gains rather than revenues. Hospitals often receive donated medicines and other materials. If such medicines and materials would otherwise have to be purchased, it is appropriate to record these donations at fair value as **other revenue.** Hospitals also routinely receive benefit from the services of volunteer workers; however, it is only rarely that the value of such services is recorded as a revenue or gain (and as an expense) since the restrictive conditions required by the AICPA audit and accounting guide for recognition are seldom met. (See related discussions in Chapters 19 and 21.) Generally, income and gains from general investments, unrestricted income from endowment funds, and transfer of endowment principal to the General Funds upon the occurrence of an event or the expiration of the endowment term are classified as **nonoperating gains** of a hospital. Assume total nonoperating gains were received in cash from unrestricted gifts, $297,900, and from unrestricted endowment income, $8,100.

4. Cash	306,000	
Nonoperating Gains—Unrestricted Gifts		297,900
Nonoperating Gains—Endowment Income		8,100

One piece of major movable equipment, which had a historical cost of $28,000 and a book value of $2,000 as of September 30, 19x0, was sold early in the 19x1 fiscal year for $500 cash. The entry to record the disposal of the asset at a loss is:

5. Cash	500	
Nonoperating Loss—Disposal of Equipment...................	1,500	
Accumulated Depreciation—Major Movable Equipment	26,000	
Major Movable Equipment		28,000

New fixed equipment costing $100,000 was purchased during 19x1 by the Bloomfield Hospital Plant Replacement and Expansion Fund. Entries in that fund are illustrated in a following section of this chapter. The entry in the General Funds should be:

6. Fixed Equipment	100,000	
Transfers from Restricted Funds for Capital Outlays		100,000

New major movable equipment was purchased from General Funds cash for $300,000:

```
7. Major Movable Equipment ................................  300,000
       Cash ................................................              300,000
```

During the year, the following items were recorded as Accounts Payable: the $16,000 accrued expenses payable as of September 30, 19x0; nursing services expenses, $4,026,000; other professional services expenses, $947,200; general services expenses, $1,650,000; fiscal and administrative services expenses, $1,124,000; and supplies added to inventory, $400,000. The following entry summarizes that activity:

```
8. Accrued Expenses Payable ...............................    16,000
    Nursing Services Expenses ...............................  4,026,000
    Other Professional Services Expenses .......................   947,200
    General Services Expenses ................................  1,650,000
    Fiscal and Administrative Services Expenses .................  1,124,000
    Inventory ............................................   400,000
       Accounts Payable ...................................            8,163,200
```

Collections on accounts and notes receivable during the year amounted to $8,842,000; accounts and notes receivable totaling $131,000 were written off:

```
9. Cash ...................................................  8,842,000
    Allowance for Uncollectible Receivables ....................   131,000
       Accounts and Notes Receivable .........................            8,973,000
```

The following cash disbursements were made by the General Funds during 19x1: Accounts Payable, $8,014,200; a principal payment in the amount of $400,000 was made to reduce the mortgage liability; and interest amounting to $160,000 on mortgages was paid:

```
10. Accounts Payable .......................................  8,014,200
    Mortgages Payable......................................   400,000
    Interest Expense .......................................   160,000
       Cash ...............................................            8,574,200
```

Supplies issued during the year cost $320,000 ($20,000 of the total was for use by fiscal and administrative services; $120,000 for use by general services; and the remainder by other professional services):

```
11. Other Professional Services Expenses .......................   180,000
    General Services Expenses ...............................   120,000
    Fiscal and Administrative Services Expenses .................    20,000
       Inventory...........................................              320,000
```

Accrued expenses as of September 30, 19x1, included $160,000 interest on mortgages; fiscal and administrative service expenses, $8,700; and other professional services expenses, $4,800. Prepaid expenses, consisting of general services expense items, declined $4,000 during the year:

12. Interest Expense	160,000	
Fiscal and Administrative Service Expenses	8,700	
Other Professional Services Expenses	4,800	
General Services Expenses	4,000	
Accrued Expenses Payable		173,500
Prepaid Expenses		4,000

Depreciation of plant and equipment for 19x1 was in the amounts shown in the following journal entry:

13. Depreciation Expense	783,000	
Accumulated Depreciation—Buildings		315,000
Accumulated Depreciation—Fixed Equipment		268,000
Accumulated Depreciation—Major Movable Equipment		200,000

Notice that in the preceding entry no depreciation is taken on Minor Equipment. Minor equipment is defined as equipment of relatively small size, not used in a fixed location, subject to requisition or use by various hospital departments, and having a useful life of three years or less. It is easy to see why it is considered more reasonable to inventory minor equipment periodically than to keep equipment records and to compute depreciation on it. It is assumed the Bloomfield Hospital inventory of minor equipment disclosed a shrinkage of $4,000, all chargeable to Nursing Services Expenses. Entry 14 records this fact:

14. Nursing Services Expenses	4,000	
Minor Equipment		4,000

The hospital received cash of $28,000 for interest on investments held in the Assets Whose Use Is Limited—Investments account. Entry 15 records the receipt of cash and the corresponding credit to Nonoperating Gains.

15. Cash	28,000	
Nonoperating Gains—Investment Income		28,000

The $28,000 received in cash for interest (see Entry 15) was reinvested in investments to be held for eventual use for expansion of facilities; the hospital governing board decided to purchase an additional $350,000 of investments for the same purpose. Entries 16a and 16b reflect the purchase of the investments and the increase in Designated Fund Balance.

16a. Assets Whose Life Is Limited—Investments	378,000	
Cash		378,000
16b. Fund Balance—Undesignated	378,000	
Fund Balance—Designated for Expansion of Facilities		378,000

After posting the entries for 19x1, the trial balance of the General Funds of Bloomfield Hospital would be:

BLOOMFIELD HOSPITAL
General Fund
Pre-Closing Trial Balance
As of September 30, 19x1

	Debits	Credits
Cash	$ 93,100	
Accounts and Notes Receivable	488,000	
Allowance for Uncollectible Receivables		$ 135,000
Inventory	160,000	
Prepaid Expenses	8,000	
Assets Whose Use Is Limited—Cash	6,500	
Assets Whose Use Is Limited—Investments	778,000	
Land	1,080,000	
Buildings	11,050,000	
Fixed Equipment	2,780,000	
Major Movable Equipment	1,682,000	
Minor Equipment	826,000	
Accumulated Depreciation—Buildings		1,365,000
Accumulated Depreciation—Fixed Equipment		1,038,000
Accumulated Depreciation—Major Movable Equipment		664,000
Accounts Payable		259,000
Accrued Expenses Payable		173,500
Mortgages Payable		6,000,000
Fund Balance—Undesignated		8,262,000
Fund Balance—Designated for Expansion of Facilities		784,500
Patient Service Revenues		9,261,000
Other Revenue		48,800
Provision for Bad Debts	180,000	
Contractual Adjustments	100,000	
Nursing Services Expenses	4,030,000	
Other Professional Services Expenses	1,132,000	
General Services Expenses	1,774,000	
Fiscal and Administrative Services Expenses	1,152,700	
Depreciation Expense	783,000	
Interest Expense	320,000	
Nonoperating Loss—Disposal of Equipment	1,500	
Nonoperating Gains—Unrestricted Gifts		297,900
Nonoperating Gains—Endowment Income		8,100
Nonoperating Gains—Investment Income		28,000
Transfers from Restricted Funds for Capital Outlays		100,000
	$28,424,800	$28,424,800

    Revenue, deductions from revenues, expense, and transfer accounts that pertain to 19x1 are closed to the Fund Balance—Undesignated account as shown below:

17. Patient Service Revenues	9,261,000	
Other Revenue	48,800	
Nonoperating Gains—Unrestricted Gifts	297,900	
Nonoperating Gains—Endowment Income	8,100	
Nonoperating Gains—Investment Income	28,000	
Transfers from Restricted Funds for Capital Outlays	100,000	

Provision for Bad Debts	180,000
Contractual Adjustments	100,000
Nursing Services Expenses	4,030,000
Other Professional Services Expenses	1,132,000
General Service Expenses	1,774,000
Fiscal and Administrative Services Expenses	1,152,700
Depreciation Expense	783,000
Nonoperating Loss—Disposal of Equipment	1,500
Interest Expense	320,000
Fund Balance—Undesignated	270,600

The September 30, 19x1, Balance Sheet of the General Funds of Bloomfield Hospital is shown in Illustration 20–2, combined with the balance sheets of the other funds of the hospital as of that date. Inasmuch as all revenue and expense accounts are considered to be General Funds accounts, the results of operations for 19x1, including transfers, are summarized as shown in Illustration 20–1. Notice that the balance of Contractual Adjustment, $100,000, is deducted from Patient Service Revenues, $9,261,000, and *net* patient service revenue is reported in the Statement of Revenues and Expenses of General Funds.

ILLUSTRATION 20–1

BLOOMFIELD HOSPITAL
Statement of Revenues and Expenses of General Funds
Year Ended September 30, 19x1

Net patient service revenue		$9,161,000
Other revenue		48,800
Total revenue		9,209,800
Expenses:		
Nursing services	$4,030,000	
Other professional services	1,132,000	
General services	1,774,000	
Fiscal and administrative services	1,152,700	
Depreciation expense	783,000	
Interest	320,000	
Provision for bad debts	180,000	
Total expenses		9,371,700
Income (loss) from operations		(161,900)
Nonoperating gains (losses):		
Unrestricted gifts	297,900	
Income on investments of endowment fund	8,100	
Income on investments whose use is limited by board for expansion of facilities	28,000	
Loss on disposal of equipment	(1,500)	
Total nonoperating gains (losses)		332,500
Revenues and gains in excess of expenses and losses		$ 170,600

Illustration 20–4 (later in this chapter) presents a combined Statement of Changes in Fund Balances of all funds of Bloomfield Hospital for the year ended September 30, 19x1.

Plant Replacement and Expansion Fund Transactions

Individual philanthropists and civic and charitable groups have donated money and securities to Bloomfield Hospital subject to the restriction that the assets may be utilized only for plant replacement and expansion. The trial balance of the Plant Replacement and Expansion Fund as of September 30, 19x0, is:

	Debits	Credits
Cash	$ 105,000	
Marketable Securities	980,000	
Accrued Interest Receivable	36,000	
Pledges Receivable	1,460,000	
Allowance for Uncollectible Pledges		$ 73,000
Fund Balance		2,508,000
	$2,581,000	$2,581,000

Entry 6 in the illustration of General Funds transactions was made to record the purchase of fixed equipment costing $100,000 by the Plant Replacement and Expansion Fund. The corresponding entry by the latter fund is:

1. Fund Balance—Transfers for Capital Outlay................. 100,000
   Cash 100,000

In Entry 1, and the entries that follow, it is assumed that "Fund Balance" is a general ledger control account and the titles after the dashes are subsidiary ledger accounts. Cash was received by the Plant Replacement and Expansion Fund during 19x1 from the following sources: Interest on marketable securities (including the amount accrued at the end of the 19x0 fiscal year), $69,000; collections of pledges receivable, $292,000:

2. Cash 361,000
   Pledges Receivable 292,000
   Accrued Interest Receivable 36,000
   Fund Balance—Investment Income...................... 33,000

Marketable securities carried in the accounts at cost, $85,000, were sold for $59,000; the loss must be absorbed by the Fund Balance. The proceeds were reinvested in marketable securities, and $300,000 additional marketable securities were purchased from cash received during the year:

3. Cash 59,000
   Fund Balance—Loss on Sale of Investments 26,000
   Marketable Securities 85,000

   Marketable Securities 359,000
   Cash 359,000

A review of pledges receivable indicated pledges in the amount of $25,000 should be written off, and the allowance for uncollectible pledges should be increased to a total of 10 percent of the outstanding pledges, or $114,300. (Computation: September 30, 19x0, balance, $1,460,000, less collections of $292,000 and write-offs of $25,000 = $1,143,000 balance at time of review.) The increase in the Allowance account must be absorbed by the Fund Balance.

4. Allowance for Uncollectible Pledges.......................... 25,000
     Pledges Receivable   25,000

Fund Balance—Provision for Uncollectible Pledges 66,300
     Allowance for Uncollectible Pledges......................   66,300

At the end of the 19x1 fiscal year, the amount of interest accrued on marketable securities of this fund is computed to be $44,000:

5. Accrued Interest Receivable 44,000
     Fund Balance—Investment Income......................   44,000

As a result of the events and transactions recorded for the year ended September 30, 19x1, the trial balance of the Plant Replacement and Expansion Fund, assuming that Fund Balance is a general ledger control account, is:

	Debits	Credits
Cash	$ 66,000	
Marketable Securities	1,254,000	
Accrued Interest Receivable	44,000	
Pledges Receivable	1,143,000	
Allowance for Uncollectible Pledges		$ 114,300
Fund Balance		2,392,700
	$2,507,000	$2,507,000

The Balance Sheet of the Plant Replacement and Expansion Fund as of September 30, 19x1, and the Statement of Changes in its Fund Balance are shown in the combined statements, Illustrations 20–2 and 20–4. As indicated earlier, Illustration 20–3 is provided to show an alternative format for the balance sheet. Although a portion of the change in the balance of this fund is the result of interest earned and a portion is the result of loss on the sale of marketable securities during the year, these items should be reflected in the Statement of Changes in Fund Balance, and not in the Statement of Revenues and Expenses of General Funds because the items pertain to a donor-restricted fund and have no effect on the General Funds of the hospital.

Specific Purpose Fund Transactions

Bloomfield Hospital did not have any restricted funds classifiable as specific purpose funds as of September 30, 19x0. In September 19x1, however, a civic organization donated $5,000 to the hospital to be used to augment the physician residency program. The organization pledged an additional sum of $20,000 to be paid at the rate of $5,000 per year for the same purpose.

The establishment of the Specific Purpose Fund is recorded by the following entry:

1. Cash	5,000	
Pledges Receivable	20,000	
Fund Balance—Gifts, Grants, and Bequests		25,000

The governing board and administration of Bloomfield Hospital expect the civic organization to honor its pledge; therefore, no Allowance for Uncollectible Pledges is created. Because the gift was received shortly before the end of fiscal 19x1, no expenditures for the program were made during that year. Thus, the trial balance of the Specific Purpose Fund as of September 30, 19x1, would be identical with Entry 1 above. The financial statements of the Specific Purpose Fund are combined with those of the other funds of Bloomfield Hospital in Illustrations 20–2 and 20–4.

When the hospital incurs expenses for the program specified by the donors of the Specific Purpose Fund, the expenses should be recorded in the General Funds. Assume that early in 19x2, $3,000 is expended by the General Funds for the program to be supported by the Specific Purpose Fund. Entries in each fund are necessary, as shown below:

General Funds:

Physician Residency Expense...	3,000	
Accounts Payable		3,000
Due from Other Funds	3,000	
Other Revenue		3,000

Specific Purpose Fund:

Fund Balance—Transfers to General Funds for Operating Purposes.........	3,000	
Due to Other Funds		3,000

Cash should be transferred from the Specific Purpose Fund to the General Funds in the amount of the interfund liability. When the transfer is made, each fund should record the transfer by the following entries:

General Funds:

Cash	3,000	
Due from Other Funds		3,000

Specific Purpose Fund:

Due to Other Funds	3,000	
Cash		3,000

The General Funds must, of course, pay the Accounts Payable; the entry for that transaction should be obvious.

Endowment Fund Transactions

The hospital endowment fund is used to account for donated assets, the principal of which must be retained intact. The income from hospital endowment fund assets is expendable as the donor directed—either for general operating purposes or for named items or projects. Thus, the hospital endowment fund is a trust fund, as discussed in Chapter 12. The discussion in that chapter concerning the problems involved in distinguishing between principal and income are relevant, also, to hospital endowment funds.

In order to be able to show that the terms of each endowment have been complied with, it is desirable to keep records for each separate endowment. Ordinarily, such records may be in memorandum form, or they may be kept as subsidiary accounts controlled by the balance sheet accounts provided for the Endowment Fund. Asset accounts often provided are cash, investments, and receivables. Donated securities and real estate are to be recorded in the Endowment Fund at fair market value at date of acquisition; investments purchased by the fund are to be recorded at cost. Separate accounts are provided for current liabilities and long-term liabilities; the latter consist mainly of mortgages outstanding against Endowment Fund real estate. The Endowment Fund Fund Balance account should be subdivided into two accounts: Endowment Fund Balance— Income Unrestricted and Endowment Fund Balance—Income Restricted.

As of September 30, 19x0, Bloomfield Hospital is assumed to have only one endowment fund. The income from the endowment is to be transferred to the General Funds for use at the discretion of the governing board. The trial balance of the **Endowment Fund** at that time is:

	Debits	Credits
Cash	$ 8,000	
Long-Term Investments	146,000	
Fund Balance—Income Unrestricted		$154,000
	$154,000	$154,000

During the 19x1 fiscal year, the hospital received marketable securities with a market value at date of the gift of $24,000. The securities are to be held for the production of income; the income from these securities is to be transferred to the General Funds for unrestricted use. The new endowment may be accounted for in the same fund as the endowment on hand at the end of fiscal 19x0, as shown in the following entry:

1. Marketable Securities	24,000	
Fund Balance—Income Unrestricted.....................		24,000

Income received in cash from long-term investments of the Endowment Fund totaled $7,300; income received in cash from the marketable securities of this fund amounted to $800 during 19x1:

2. Cash	8,100	
Due to Other Funds......................................		8,100

The amount due to other funds is transferred before the end of fiscal 19x1:

3. Due to Other Funds...	8,100	
Cash		8,100

ILLUSTRATION 20–2   Illustration of "Layered" Balance Sheet

BLOOMFIELD HOSPITAL
Balance Sheet
As of September 30, 19x1

General Funds

Assets

Current Assets:			
Cash			$ 488,000
Accounts and notes receivable	$ 488,000		
Less: Allowance for uncollectible receivables	135,000		353,000
Inventory			160,000
Prepaid expenses			8,000
Total Current Assets			614,100
Assets Whose Use Is Limited by Board for Expansion of Facilities			784,500
Property, Plant, and Equipment:			
Land			1,080,000
Buildings	11,050,000		
Less: Accumulated depreciation	1,365,000		9,685,000
Fixed equipment	2,780,000		
Less: Accumulated depreciation	1,038,000		1,742,000
Major movable equipment	1,682,000		
Less: Accumulated depreciation	664,000		1,018,000
Minor equipment			826,000
Total Property, Plant, and Equipment			14,351,000
Total General Funds			$15,749,600

Liabilities and Fund Balances

Current Liabilities:			
Accounts payable		$ 259,000	
Accrued expenses payable		173,500	
Total Current Liabilities			$ 432,500
Long-Term Debt:			
Mortgages payable			6,000,000
Total Liabilities			6,432,500
Fund Balance:			
Designated for expansion of facilities		784,500	
Undesignated		8,532,600	
Total			9,317,100
Total General Funds			$15,749,600

Donor-Restricted Funds

Plant Replacement and Expansion Fund

Cash			$ 66,000
Marketable securities			1,254,000
Accrued interest receivable			44,000
Pledges receivable		$ 1,143,000	
Less: Allowance for uncollectible pledges		114,300	1,028,700
Total Plant Replacement and Expansion Funds			$ 2,392,700

Fund balance		$ 2,392,700
Total Plant Replacement and Expansion Funds		$ 2,392,700

Specific Purpose Funds

Cash			$ 5,000
Pledges receivable			20,000
Total Specific Purpose Funds			$ 25,000

Fund balance		$ 25,000
Total Specific Purpose Funds		$ 25,000

Endowment Funds

Cash			$ 8,000
Marketable securities			24,000
Long-term investments			146,000
Total Endowment Funds			$ 178,000

Fund balance—Income unrestricted		$ 178,000
Total Endowment Funds		$ 178,000

BLOOMFIELD HOSPITAL
Balance Sheet
As of September 30, 19x1

Assets

Current Assets:		
Cash and cash equivalents		$ 93,100
Accounts and notes receivable, net of allowance for uncollectibles of $135,000		353,000
Inventory		160,000
Prepaid expenses		8,000
Total Current Assets		614,100
Assets Whose Use Is Limited:		
By Board for expansion of facilities		784,500
By donors for plant replacement and expansion		2,392,700
By donors for specific purposes		25,000
By donors for permanent endowment funds		178,000
Total Assets Whose Use Is Limited		3,380,200
Property, Plant, and Equipment:		
Land		1,080,000
Buildings, net of accumulated depreciation of $1,365,000		9,685,000
Fixed equipment, net of accumulated depreciation of $1,038,000		1,742,000
Major movable equipment, net of accumulated depreciation of $664,000		1,018,000
Minor equipment		826,000
Total Property, Plant, and Equipment		14,351,000
Total Assets		$18,345,300

Liabilities and Net Assets

Current Liabilities:		
Accounts payable		$ 259,000
Accrued expenses payable		173,500
Total Current Liabilities		432,500
Long-Term Debt:		
Mortgages payable		6,000,000
Total Liabilities		6,432,500
Net Assets:		
Unrestricted		9,317,100
Temporarily restricted by donors		2,417,700
Permanently restricted endowment funds		178,000
Total Net Assets		11,912,800
Total Liabilities and Net Assets		$18,345,300

ILLUSTRATION 20–4   **Illustration of Statement of Changes in Fund Balances**

BLOOMFIELD HOSPITAL
Statement of Changes in Fund Balances
Year Ended September 30, 19x1

| | General Funds | Donor-Restricted Funds | | |
		Specific Purpose Funds	Plant Replacement and Expansion Funds	Endowment Funds
Balances, September 30, 19x0	$9,046,500	$ –0–	$2,508,000	$154,000
Additions:				
Revenue and gains in excess of expenses	170,600			
Investment income			77,000	
Gifts, grants, and bequests		25,000		24,000
Transfer for capital outlay	100,000		(100,000)	
	270,600	25,000	(23,000)	24,000
Deductions:				
Provision for uncollectible pledges			66,300	
Net realized loss on sale of investments			26,000	
Balances, September 30, 19x1	$9,317,100	$25,000	$2,392,700	$178,000

The amount of $8,100 is included in the total $306,000 credited to Nonoperating Gains in Entry 4 in the illustration of General Funds transactions.

Assuming no additional Endowment Fund transactions occurred during 19x1, the trial balance at the end of that fiscal year is:

	Debits	Credits
Cash	$ 8,000	
Marketable Securities	24,000	
Long-Term Investments	146,000	
Fund Balance—Income Unrestricted		$178,000
Totals	$178,000	$178,000

The Endowment Fund Balance Sheet as of September 30, 19x1, is shown in Illustration 20–2 as part of the "layered" balance sheet presented separately for each fund group. Changes in the Endowment Fund Fund Balance and cash flows are presented in the Statement of Changes in Fund Balances (Illustration 20–4) and in the Statement of Cash Flows (GASB format; see Illustration 20–5).

ILLUSTRATION 20–5 **Illustration of Statement of Cash Flows—GASB Jurisdiction**

BLOOMFIELD HOSPITAL
Statement of Cash Flows
Year Ended September 30, 19x1

Cash flows from operating activities:	
Cash received from patients and third-party payers	$8,842,000
Cash paid to employees and suppliers	(8,014,200)
Other receipts from operations	48,800
Net cash provided by operating activities	876,600
Cash flows from noncapital financing activities:	
Unrestricted gifts and income from endowments	306,000
Gift restricted for future operations	5,000
Net cash provided by noncapital financing activities	311,000
Cash flows from capital and related financing activities:	
Purchase of property and equipment	(400,000)
Principal paid on mortgage	(400,000)
Interest paid	(160,000)
Collection of pledges receivable	292,000
Proceeds from sale of equipment	500
Net cash used for capital and related financing activities	(667,500)
Cash flows from investing activities:	
Proceeds from sale of securities	59,000
Interest received on assets whose use is limited	28,000
Interest received on donor-restricted assets	69,000
Cash invested in assets whose use is limited	(378,000)
Cash invested in donor-restricted assets	(359,000)
Net cash used by investing activities	(581,000)
Net increase (decrease) in cash and cash equivalents	(60,900)
Cash and cash equivalents, September 30, 19x0	239,500
Cash and cash equivalents, September 30, 19x1	$ 178,600

Reconciliation of Operating Income to Net Cash
Provided by Operating Activities

Operating income (loss)	$ (161,900)
Adjustments:	
Depreciation	783,000
Increase in patient accounts receivable, net	(139,000)
Increase in inventory	(80,000)
Increase in accounts payable	149,000
Increase in accrued expenses	157,500
Decrease in prepaid expenses	4,000
Decrease in minor equipment	4,000
Interest paid in cash (Note 1)	160,000
Net cash provided by operating activities and gains and losses	$ 876,600

Note 1: Interest was classified as an operating expense on the income statement but as cash flows from capital and related activities on the cash flows statement prepared in conformity with GASB standards.

Financial Reporting Requirements for Nongovernmentally Owned Not-for-Profit Health Care Entities

As discussed in Chapter 19 on colleges and universities, and earlier in this chapter, FASB *Statement No. 117* requires nongovernmentally owned not-for-profit organizations to prepare three general purpose financial statements for external reporting purposes: a **Statement of Financial Position** (Balance Sheet), a **Statement of Activities,** and a **Statement of Cash Flows.**[6] The Statement of Financial Position reports the *aggregated* financial position of the entity in a manner similar to the alternative aggregated balance sheet permitted by the AICPA audit guide (see Illustration 20–3). One substantive difference is that the aggregated Balance Sheet displayed in Illustration 20–3 combines unrestricted and restricted assets, whereas the Statement of Financial Position specified in FASB *Statement No. 117* recommends reporting assets restricted for plant or other purposes separately from unrestricted assets. The separate reporting would be similar to the asset section Assets Whose Use Is Limited shown in Illustration 20–3. It should be noted that *Statement No. 117* neither requires nor precludes segregation of Assets Whose Use Is Limited; such information can be reported if deemed useful.

The required Statement of Activities and Statement of Cash Flow for nongovernmentally owned not-for-profit health care entities are unique to those entities. Illustrations 20–6 and 20–7 provide examples of Bloomfield Hospital's Statement of Activities and Statement of Cash Flows under the independent assumption that it is a *nongovernmentally* owned not-for-profit hospital. This assumption provides a useful comparison of the operating statements and cash flow statements required for a governmentally owned versus a nongovernmentally owned not-for-profit hospital. Comparing the Statement of Revenues and Expenses of General Funds presented in Illustration 20–1 with the Statement of Activities provided in Illustration 20–6 reveals the following differences: (1) The Statement of Revenues and Expenses of General Funds is similar to an income statement for a business enterprise; it presents income from operations as well as a bottom line that is equivalent to net income. The Statement of Activities (Illustration 20–6), on the other hand, does not provide an amount for income from operations (although FASB standards permit such reporting, if desired) and the "bottom line" is **change in net assets** rather than net income. Change in net assets pertains to the entire entity and is reported separately for the three categories: **unrestricted, temporarily restricted,** and **permanently restricted.**

The Statement of Cash Flows—GASB Jurisdiction (Illustration 20–5) and the Statement of Cash Flows—FASB Jurisdiction (Illustration 20–7) are similar in some respects. Both, for example, present cash inflows, outflows, and net cash flows related to operating activities, investing activities, and financing activities, although financing activities in the GASB statement are subdivided into noncapital financing activities and capital and related financing activities. Also, both the GASB statement and the FASB statement can be prepared using either the direct

---

[6] As noted in footnote 3 of this chapter, governmentally owned health care entities may also choose to follow all applicable FASB pronouncements provided they do not conflict with GASB pronouncements. Those entities that so choose will prepare a Statement of Financial Position and a Statement of Activities in conformity with FASB *Statement No. 117*, but they will prepare their Statement of Cash Flows in conformity with GASB standards.

method or the indirect method. Illustrations 20–5 and 20–7 show the use of the direct method.

The statements differ primarily in terms of which cash flows are reported as part of each activity. In the GASB statement, interest paid and interest received are reported as investing activities, whereas the same items are reported as operating activities in the FASB statement, except for interest and dividend income added to temporarily or permanently restricted net assets. Such restricted income is reported in the FASB statement as a financing activity. Acquisitions of property and equipment are reported as capital and related financing activities in the GASB statement but as investing activities in the FASB statement. Unrestricted gifts are reported as cash flows from noncapital financing activities in the GASB statement but as cash flows from operating activities in the FASB statement. A final, and major, difference is that the reconciliation schedule in the GASB statement reconciles operating income (loss) to cash flows from operating activities, whereas in the FASB statement the schedule reconciles changes in net assets to cash flows from operating activities. In preparing either cash flow statement, the worksheet or T-account approaches explained in most intermediate accounting texts may be useful.

Budgets for Hospitals and Other Health Care Entities

Governmental and other not-for-profit hospitals and other health care entities, even though they are service institutions, must have an inflow of funds at least equal to their outflow of funds. Since this is the case, prudent management will attempt to forecast the outlays for a definite period and forecast the income for the same period. Equating anticipated income and outgo means future operations must be planned. "Planning future operations" is a phrase that defines budgeting as it is thought of today in successful businesses. Budgeting is not merely planning financial affairs, but developing an integrated plan for all phases of the operations of the organizations. If this is done properly, each department knows the objectives of the organization and has determined to what extent and in what manner the department will contribute to them. The predetermination of the role each department is to play in achieving the organization's objectives enables management to measure the success each department has in attaining its objectives. Frequent measurement helps keep each department on the proper path. Thus, budgeting is of considerable usefulness to management.

Some hospitals use comprehensive budgets for managerial purposes but do not incorporate the budgetary provision in the accounts. Other hospitals do record their budgets in the ledger.

It is possible to generalize that although every hospital and other health care entity should have an annual budget, it is important that the budget be administered intelligently. For a hospital, or for any other enterprise, good financial management requires outlays to be evaluated in terms of results achieved. Insistence on rigid adherence to a budget not related to actual workload (as is the case in some governmental agencies) tends to make the budget useless as a management tool. Thus, unless budgetary accounts are required by law, they may well be dispensed with.

ILLUSTRATION 20–6   Illustration of a Two-Part Statement of Activities

BLOOMFIELD HOSPITAL
Statement of Unrestricted Revenues, Expenses, and
Other Changes in Unrestricted Net Assets
Year Ended September 30, 19x1

Unrestricted revenues and gains:	
Net patient service revenue	$9,161,000
Other revenue	48,800
Gifts, grants, and bequests	297,900
Endowment income	8,100
Income on investments whose use is limited by board for expansion of facilities	28,000
Total unrestricted revenues and gains	9,543,800
Net assets released from restrictions:	
Satisfaction of equipment acquisition restrictions	100,000
Total unrestricted revenues, gains, and other support	9,643,800

Unrestricted expenses and losses:		
Nursing services	$4,030,000	
Other professional services	1,132,000	
General services	1,774,000	
Fiscal and administrative services	1,152,000	
Depreciation expense	783,000	
Interest	320,000	
Provision for bad debts	180,000	
Total expenses		9,371,700
Loss on disposal of equipment		1,500
Total unrestricted expenses and losses		9,373,200
Increase in unrestricted net assets		$ 270,600

Statement of Changes in Net Assets
Year Ended September 30, 19x1

Unrestricted net assets (see Part 1)	
Total unrestricted revenues and gains	$ 9,543,800
Net assets released from restrictions	100,000.
Total unrestricted expenses and losses	(9,373,200)
Increase in unrestricted net assets	270,600
Temporarily restricted net assets:	
Gifts, grants, and bequests	25,000
Investment income	77,000
Increase in provision for uncollectible pledges	(66,300)
Net realized loss on sale of investments	(26,000)
Net assets released from restrictions	(100,000)
Decrease in temporarily restricted net assets	(90,300)
Permanently restricted net assets:	
Gifts, grants, and bequests	24,000
Increase in permanently restricted net assets	24,000
Increase in net assets	204,300
Net assets at beginning of year	11,708,500
Net assets at end of year	$11,912,800

ILLUSTRATION 20–7   Illustration of Statement of Cash Flows—
FASB Jurisdiction*

BLOOMFIELD HOSPITAL
Statement of Cash Flows
Year Ended September 30, 19x1

Cash flows from operating activities:	
Cash received from patients and third-party payers	$8,842,000
Other receipts from operations	48,800
Interest received on assets whose use is limited	36,100
Receipts from unrestricted gifts	297,900
Cash paid to employees and suppliers	(8,014,200)
Interest paid	(160,000)
Net cash provided by operating activities	1,050,600
Cash flows from investing activities:	
Purchase of property and equipment	(400,000)
Purchase of long-term investments	(737,000)
Proceeds from sale of securities	59,000
Proceeds from sale of equipment	500
Net cash used by investing activities	(1,077,500)
Cash flows from financing activities:	
Proceeds from contributions restricted for:	
Investment in plant	292,000
Future operations	5,000
	297,000
Other financing activities:	
Interest and dividends restricted to endowment	69,000
Repayment of long-term debt	(400,000)
	(331,000)
Net cash used by financing activities	(34,000)
Net increase (decrease) in cash and cash equivalents	(60,900)
Cash and cash equivalents, September 30, 19x0	239,500
Cash and cash equivalents, September 30, 19x1	$ 178,600

Reconciliation of Changes in Net Assets to Net Cash
Provided by Operating Activities

Change in net assets	$ 204,300
Adjustments to reconcile change in net assets to net cash provided by operating activities:	
Depreciation and amortization	783,000
Loss on disposal of equipment	1,500
Increase in patient accounts receivable, net	(139,000)
Increase in supplies	(80,000)
Increase in accounts payable and accrued expenses	306,500
Decrease in prepaid expenses	4,000
Decrease in minor equipment	4,000
Gifts, grants, and bequests restricted for long-term investment	(49,000)
Interest restricted for long-term investment	(77,000)
Realized loss on long-term investment	26,000
Increase in provision for uncollectible pledges	66,300
Net cash provided by operating activities	$1,050,600

* In the format presented in FASB *Statement No. 117*, "Financial Statements of Not-for-Profit Organizations" (Norwalk, Conn., 1993).

Cost Accounting for Hospitals and Other Health Care Entities

This chapter is limited to a brief presentation of financial accounting and financial reporting for hospitals and other health care entities. Until very recent years, it was customary for the majority of hospitals to determine costs of services rendered during a fiscal year by rearranging financial accounting data generated during that year. Although never satisfactory for financial management purposes, the procedure for cost determination was acceptable for purposes of reporting costs to third-party payers, which reimbursed hospitals on a retrospective (after-the-fact) basis. Since 1983, however, the largest purchaser of hospital services, Medicare, in an attempt to establish better control over hospital costs, has utilized a system of prospective cost reimbursement. The Medicare system pays health care providers standardized rates for services rendered to patients in each "diagnosis-related group" (DRG). Health care providers, therefore, have an incentive to determine actual costs of services rendered, by DRG, in order to keep their costs commensurate with Medicare's payments for services rendered to Medicare patients. Although many relatively small hospitals do not as yet have adequate cost accounting systems, it is now common for large hospitals (600 beds or more) to have systems to capture costs by procedure or DRG.

Conclusion

A single chapter on accounting for health care entities can touch on only the most outstanding features. Variations in the operating and accounting procedures for individual health care entities exist because of the variety in the type and size of health care providers, the range of services offered, the dependence of these entities on third-party payers, and the financial sophistication of the governing board, administrator, and finance director. For further information, the references cited in the Selected References section are recommended.

Selected References

American Institute of Certified Public Accountants. *Audits of Providers of Health Care Services*. New York, 1990.

————. *Statement of Position 89–5*. "Financial Accounting and Reporting by Providers of Prepaid Health Care Services." New York, 1989.

Financial Accounting Standards Board. *Statement No. 116*. "Accounting for Contributions Received and Contributions Made." Norwalk, Conn., 1993.

————. *Statement No. 117*. "Financial Statements of Not-for-Profit Organizations." Norwalk, Conn., 1993.

Periodicals

Healthcare Financial Management. The journal of the Healthcare Financial Management Association, Oak Brook, Illinois.

Hospital Progress. The journal of the Catholic Hospital Association, St. Louis.

Hospitals. The journal of the American Hospital Association, Chicago.

Questions

20–1. "All providers of health care services must use fund accounting." True or false? Explain your answer.

20–2. Identify the fund structure set forth in the AICPA audit and accounting guide for providers of health care services that use fund accounting. Briefly explain the function of each fund group.

20–3. What are the major differences between the accounting treatment of hospital property, plant, and equipment used in rendering hospital services and the accounting treatment of general fixed assets of state and local governmental units?

20–4. How do the accounting treatments for charity services, patient discounts, contractual adjustments, and provision for bad debts differ in terms of their effects on patient service revenues and related receivables?

20–5. Why are assets designated by a hospital governing board for special purposes considered General Funds assets rather than Donor-Restricted Funds assets?

20–6. Are hospital *specific purpose funds* similar in nature and accounting treatment to any funds recommended for use by state and local governments? Colleges and universities?

20–7. Some hospital fixed assets, referred to as "minor equipment," are not depreciated. Additions and replacements are debited to the Minor Equipment account. At ends of fiscal periods, the aggregate of such equipment is inventoried, and the equipment account balance is reduced to the inventory value.

    a. Why is the method more suitable for the class of assets referred to than the conventional method?

    b. Assuming the Minor Equipment account has a balance of $830,000 at the end of the year, compared with a physical inventory of the equipment totaling $815,000, show in general journal form the necessary adjusting entry.

20–8. Breyer Memorial Hospital received a $100,000 gift that was restricted by the donor for heart research. At fiscal year-end Breyer had incurred $25,000 in expenses related to this project. Explain how these transactions would be reported in Breyer's balance sheet and operating statement under the independent assumptions that *(a)* Breyer is a governmentally owned not-for-profit hospital and (b) Breyer is a nongovernmentally owned not-for-profit hospital.

20–9. "FASB standards applicable to nongovernmentally owned not-for-profit health care entities preclude such entities from distinguishing 'Assets Whose Use Is Limited' from other unrestricted assets." Do you agree? Explain fully.

20–10. Identify the financial statements required to be provided by *(a)* investor-owned and governmentally owned health care entities that follow the AICPA audit and accounting guide, and *(b)* nongovernmentally owned not-for-profit health care entities subject to FASB *Statement No. 117.* Explain in what respects these two sets of financial statements are similar and in what respects they are different.

Exercises and Problems

20–1. Write the numbers 1 through 10 on a sheet of paper. Beside each number, write the letter corresponding with the best answer to each of the following questions:

1. Revenue from the gift shop of a hospital would normally be included in:
   a. Nonoperating gains.
   b. Other revenue.
   c. Patient service revenue.
   d. Professional services revenue.

2. Which of the following would generally be included in Other Revenue of a hospital?

	Revenue from Educational Programs	Unrestricted Gifts
a.	Yes	No
b.	Yes	Yes
c.	No	Yes
d.	No	No

3. Donated medicine that normally would be purchased by a hospital should be recorded at fair market value and should be credited directly to:
   a. Other Revenue.
   b. Nonoperating Gains.
   c. Fund Balance.
   d. Deferred Revenue.

4. In hospital accounting, restricted funds are:
   a. Not available unless the board of directors removes the restrictions.
   b. Restricted as to use only for board-designated purposes.
   c. Not available for current operating use; however, the income generated by the funds is available for current operating use.
   d. Restricted as to use by the donor, grantor, or other external source of the resources.

5. On July 1, 19y1, Lilydale Hospital's Board of Trustees designated $200,000 for expansion of outpatient facilities. The $200,000 is expected to be expended in the fiscal year ending June 30, 19y4. In Lilydale's balance sheet at June 30, 19y2, this cash should be classified as a $200,000:
   a. Restricted current asset.
   b. Restricted noncurrent asset.
   c. Unrestricted current asset.
   d. Unrestricted noncurrent asset.

6. The property, plant, and equipment of a governmentally owned hospital should be accounted for as part of:
   a. General Funds.
   b. Restricted Funds.
   c. Specific Purpose Funds.
   d. Other Nonoperating Funds.

7. Depreciation should be recognized in the financial statements of:
   a. Proprietary (for-profit) hospitals only.
   b. Both proprietary (for-profit) and not-for-profit hospitals.
   c. Both proprietary (for-profit) and not-for-profit hospitals, only when they are affiliated with a college or university.
   d. All hospitals, as a memorandum entry not affecting the statement of revenues and expenses.

8. A gift to a governmentally owned not-for-profit hospital that is *not* restricted by the donor should be credited directly to:
   a. Fund Balance.
   b. Deferred Revenue.
   c. Other Revenue.
   d. Nonoperating Gains.

9. Which of the following sets of financial statements is required by FASB standards for nongovernmentally owned hospitals?
   a. Balance Sheet, Statement of Revenues and Expenses of General Funds, and Statement of Changes in Fund Balances.
   b. Balance Sheet, Statement of Revenues and Expenses of General Funds, and Statement of Cash Flows.
   c. Statement of Financial Position, Statement of Changes in Fund Balances, and Statement of Cash Flows.
   d. Statement of Financial Position, Statement of Activities, and Statement of Cash Flows.

10. Which of the following is a correct statement about the FASB financial reporting standards applicable to *nongovernmental* not-for-profit organizations?
    a. Net assets in the Balance Sheet must be displayed in aggregate amount for the entity, segregated according to whether the net assets are unrestricted, temporarily restricted, or permanently restricted.
    b. Gifts restricted for a specified operating purpose are *not* reported as a revenue, gain, or support until expenses have been incurred for the intended purpose.
    c. The Statement of Activities must display operating income (loss), difference between revenues/gains and expenses/losses, and changes in net assets.
    d. All of the above are correct statements.

(Items 1 through 8, AICPA, adapted)

20–2. Carter County Hospital General Funds Balance Sheet as of December 31, 19x5, is presented on the next page.

CARTER COUNTY HOSPITAL
General Funds
Balance Sheet
December 31, 19x5

Assets			*Liabilities and Fund Balance*		
Current:			Current:		
Cash		$ 65,000	Accounts payable		$ 65,000
Accounts and notes			Accrued payroll		110,000
receivable	$ 140,000				
Less: Allowance for					
uncollectibles	12,000	128,000			
Inventory		71,000	Total Current		
Total Current Assets		264,000	Liabilities		175,000
Assets Whose Use Is Limited:					
Cash	11,500		Long-Term Debt:		
Investments	210,000		Mortgage payable		3,500,000
Total Assets Whose Use					
Is Limited		221,500	Total Liabilities		3,675,000
Property, Plant and Equipment:			Fund Balance:		
Land		208,000	Undesignated		1,782,000
Buildings, at cost	4,516,000		Designated for		
Less: Accumulated			Plant Replacements		221,500
depreciation	1,506,000	3,010,000	Total Fund		
Fixed equipment, at cost	1,440,000		Balance		2,003,500
Less: Accumulated					
depreciation	583,000	857,000			
Major movable equipment					
at cost	1,207,000				
Less: Accumulated					
depreciation	313,000	894,000			
Minor equipment		224,000			
Total Property, Plant					
and Equipment		5,193,000	Total Liabilities		
Total Assets		$5,678,500	and Fund Balance		$5,678,500

Required

a. Record in general journal form the effect of the following transactions during the fiscal year ended December 31, 19x6, on the General Funds.

(1) Summary of revenue journal:

Patient services revenue, gross	$3,497,500
Adjustments and allowances:	
Contracting agencies	122,600

(2) Summary of cash receipts journal:

Interest on Investments in Assets	
Whose Use is Limited	20,000
Unrestricted grant from United	
Fund	160,000
Collections of receivables	3,373,600

(3) Purchases journal:

Administration	163,900
General services expenses	176,800
Nursing services expenses	269,400
Other professional services expenses	256,600

(4) Payroll journal:

Administration	247,600
General services expenses	175,000
Nursing services expenses	540,300
Other professional services expenses	412,200

(5) Summary of cash payments journal:

Interest expense	280,000
Payment on mortgage principal	500,000
Accounts payable for purchases	839,500
Accrued payroll	1,370,000
Transfer to Assets Whose Use Is Limited	30,000

(6) Fixed equipment which cost $6,560, and for which accumulated depreciation totaled $4,920, was traded for similar new equipment costing $9,840; the payment in cash amounted to $8,800 (the cash was paid from Assets Whose Use Is Limited—Cash).

(7) Depreciation charges for the year amounted to $117,000 for the buildings; $58,000 for fixed equipment; and $70,500 for major movable equipment.

(8) Other information:

(a) Provision for uncollectible receivables, $29,000.

(b) Supplies inventory:

	12/31/x5	12/31/x6
Administration	$ 8,000	$ 7,300
General services expenses	8,700	9,000
Nursing services expenses	17,000	17,200
Other professional services expenses	37,300	40,000
Totals	$71,000	$73,500

(c) Portion of Mortgage Payable due within one year, $500,000.

(9) Nominal accounts were closed.

b. Prepare a General Funds Balance Sheet as of December 31, 19x6.

c. Prepare a Statement of Revenues and Expenses of General Funds for the year ended December 31, 19x6.

20–3. The following transactions occurred in the specific purpose funds of the Jackson County Hospital:

(1) Under the will of Samuel H. Samuels, a bequest of $100,000 was received for research on gerontology.

(2) Pending the need of the money for the designated purpose, part of it was invested in $95,000 of par value City of Jackson 6 percent bonds, at 103 and accrued interest of $823.

(3) An interest payment of $2,850 was received on the City of Jackson bonds.

(4) The bonds were sold at 104 and accrued interest of $443.

(5) The sum of $20,000 was transferred to the General Funds.

(6) The income transfer from the Samuels fund was used by the General Funds for the purpose designated.

Required   Make journal entries for the above transactions in *all* funds affected.

20–4. Below is given the trial balance of the Centerville City Hospital Plant Replacement and Expansion Funds as of December 31, 19x4:

	Debits	*Credits*
Cash	$ 16,000	
Investments	160,900	
Fund Balance		$176,900
Totals	$176,900	$176,900

During 19x5, the following transactions affecting the Plant Replacement and Expansion Fund occurred:

1. Cash of $15,000 was transferred to the General Funds, which invested that amount in minor equipment.

2. Investments costing $50,500 were sold for $51,000; the entire proceeds plus the amount of cash on hand was invested.

3. Interest income on investments amounting to $8,600 was received in cash; $340 additional interest income on these investments was accrued as of December 31, 19x5.

4. It was discovered through audit that the General Funds erroneously had spent $5,000 for minor equipment from General Funds cash, although purchase of the equipment was to have been made from Plant Replacement and Expansion Fund cash. Since the transfer could not be made until January 19x6, the latter fund recorded a liability to the General Funds for $5,000, and the General Funds recorded a receivable as of December 31, 19x5.

Required   *a.* Record the 19x5 transactions in general journal form in *all funds affected.*

b. Prepare a Plant Replacement and Expansion Fund Balance Sheet as of December 31, 19x5.

c. Prepare a Statement of Changes in Fund Balance for the Plant Replacement and Expansion Fund for 19x5.

20–5. The Dexter City Hospital Combined Balance Sheet as of December 31, 19x5, is shown below. The Controller asks you to recast the balance sheet so that it will be in accord with current financial reporting standards. You determine that (1) the cash and investments of the "Plant Fund" are restricted under the terms of several gifts to use for plant replacement or expansion; income from "Plant Fund" investments is restricted to the same purposes. (2) Income from "Endowment Fund" investments may be used at the discretion of the hospital governing board.

DEXTER CITY HOSPITAL
Balance Sheet
As of December 31, 19x5

Assets			*Liabilities and Fund Balances*		
		Operating Fund			
Cash		$ 20,000	Accounts payable		$ 16,000
Accounts receivable	$ 37,000		Accrued expense—payable		6,000
Less: Allowance for uncollectible accounts	7,000	30,000	Total Liabilities		22,000
Inventory of supplies		14,000	Fund balance		42,000
Total		$ 64,000	Total		$ 64,000
		Plant Fund			
Cash		$ 53,800	Mortgage bonds payable		$ 150,000
Investments		71,200			
Land		400,000			
Buildings	$1,750,000				
Less: Accumulated depreciation	430,000	1,320,000	Fund balance: Investment in plant		2,021,000
			Reserved for plant improvement and		
Equipment	680,000		replacement		220,000
Less: Accumulated depreciation	134,000	546,000			2,241,000
Total		$2,391,000	Total		$2,391,000
		Endowment Fund			
Cash		$ 6,000	Fund balance—income		
Investments		260,000	unrestricted		$ 266,000
Total		$ 266,000	Total		$ 266,000

20–6. During 19x6, the following events and transactions were recorded by Dexter City Hospital (see Problem 20–5). Show in general journal form the entries that should be made for each of the 12 transactions and the closing entries in accord with the standards discussed in this chapter. Group your entries by fund; number your entries to correspond with the transactions described below:

1. Gross charges for hospital services, all charged to accounts and notes receivable, were as follows:

   Patient service revenues $1,086,000

2. Additional information relating to current year receivables and revenues were as follows:

Contractual Adjustments	$30,000
Provision for bad debts	$15,000

3. The General Funds paid $18,000 to retire mortgage bonds payable with an equivalent face value.

4. During the year, the General Funds received in cash unrestricted contributions of $50,000 and income from Endowment Fund investments of $6,500.

5. New equipment costing $26,000 was acquired from donor-restricted cash. An X-ray machine that cost $24,000 and had an undepreciated cost of $2,400 was sold for $500 cash.

6. Vouchers totaling $1,191,000 were issued for the following items:

Fiscal and administrative services expenses	$215,000
General services expenses	225,000
Nursing services expenses	520,000
Other professional services expenses	165,000
Inventory	60,000
Expenses accrued at December 31, 19x5	6,000

7. Collections of accounts receivable totaled $985,000. Accounts written off as uncollectible amounted to $11,000.

8. Cash payments on vouchers payable (paid to employers and suppliers) during the year were $825,000.

9. Supplies of $37,000 were issued to nursing services.

10. On December 31, 19x6, accrued interest income on Plant Replacement and Expansion Fund investments was $800.

11. Depreciation of buildings and equipment was as follows:

Buildings	$44,000
Equipment	73,000

12. On December 31, 19x6, an accrual of $6,100 was made for interest on mortgage bonds payable.

13. On December 31, 19x6, closing entries were made in the General Funds general journal.

(AICPA, adapted)

20–7. Using the information given for Dexter City Hospital in Problems 20–5 and 20–6:

a. Prepare a Balance Sheet at December 31, 19x6, using the "layered" format shown in Illustration 20–2 of this chapter.

b. Prepare a Statement of Revenues and Expenses of General Funds for the year ended December 31, 19x6.

c. Prepare a Statement of Changes in Fund Balances for the year ended December 31, 19x6.

d. Prepare a Statement of Cash Flows using the GASB format shown in Illustration 20–5 of this chapter.

20–8. Assume that Dexter City Hospital (see Problems 20–5 and 20–6), despite its name, is a *nongovernmental* not-for-profit hospital and thus subject to FASB financial reporting standards. Using the information given for Dexter City Hospital in Problems 20–5 and 20–6:

a. Prepare a Statement of Financial Position at December 31, 19x6, using the "aggregated" format shown in Illustration 20–3 of this chapter.

b. Prepare a Statement of Activities, using the format shown in Illustration 20–6 of this chapter.

c. Prepare a Statement of Cash Flows using the FASB format shown in Illustration 20–7 of this chapter.

20–9. The following selected information was taken from the books and records of Glendora Hospital (a voluntary hospital) as of and for the year ended June 30, 19y2.

- Patient service revenue totaled $16,000,000, with the allowance for uncollectible accounts and contractual adjustments amounting to $1,800,000 and $1,600,000, respectively. Other revenue aggregated $346,000 and included $160,000 from specific purpose funds. Revenue of $6,000,000 recognized under cost-reimbursement agreements is subject to audit and retroactive adjustment by third-party payers (other than Medicare). Estimated retroactive adjustments under these agreements have been included in allowances.

- Unrestricted gifts and bequests of $410,000 were received.

- Unrestricted income from endowment funds totaled $160,000.

- Income from investments of the General Funds aggregated $82,000.

- Operating expenses totaled $13,370,000 and included $500,000 for depreciation computed on the straight-line basis. However, accelerated depreciation is used to determine reimbursable costs under certain third-party reimbursement agreements. Net cost reimbursement revenue amounting to $220,000, resulting from the difference in depreciation methods, was deferred to future years.

- Also included in operating expenses are pension costs of $100,000, in connection with a noncontributory pension plan covering substantially all of Glendora's employees. Accrued pension costs are funded currently. Prior service cost is being amortized over a period of 20 years. The actuarially computed value of vested and nonvested benefits at year-end amounted to $3,000,000 and $350,000, respectively. The assumed rate of return used in determining the actuarial present value of accumulated plan benefits was 8 percent. The plan's net assets available for benefits at year-end was $3,050,000.

- Gifts and bequests are recorded at fair market values when received.

- Patient service revenue is accounted for at established rates on the accrual basis.

Required

a. Prepare a formal statement of revenues and expenses for Glendora Hospital for the year ended June 30, 19y2.

b. Draft the appropriate disclosures in separate notes accompanying the statement of revenues and expenses of General Funds referencing each note to its respective item in the statement.

(AICPA, adapted)

20–10. Esperanza Hospital's post-closing trial balance at December 31, 19x6, appears on the next page.

ESPERANZA HOSPITAL
Trial Balance
December 31, 19x6

	Debits	Credits
Cash	$ 60,000	
Investment in U.S. Treasury Bills	400,000	
Investment in Corporate Bonds	500,000	
Interest Receivable	10,000	
Accounts Receivable	50,000	
Inventory	30,000	
Land	100,000	
Building	800,000	
Equipment	170,000	
Allowance for Depreciation		$ 410,000
Accounts Payable		20,000
Notes Payable		70,000
Endowment Fund Balance		520,000
Other Fund Balances		1,100,000
Totals	$2,120,000	$2,120,000

Esperanza, which is a governmentally affiliated nonprofit hospital, did not maintain its books in conformity with the principles of hospital fund accounting. Effective January 1, 19x7, Esperanza's Board of Trustees voted to adjust the December 31, 19x6, general ledger balances and to establish separate funds for the General Funds, the endowment fund, and the plant replacement and expansion fund.

Additional Account Information

• *Investment in corporate bonds* pertains to the amount required to be accumulated under a board policy to invest cash equal to accumulated depreciation until the funds are needed for asset replacement. The $500,000 balance at December 31, 19x6, is less than the full amount required because of errors in computation of building depreciation for past years. Included in the allowance for depreciation is a correctly computed amount of $90,000 applicable to equipment.

• *Endowment fund balance* has been credited with the following:

Donor's bequest of cash	$300,000
Gains on sales of securities	100,000
Interest and dividends earned in 19x4, 19x5, and 19x6	120,000
Total	$520,000

The terms of the bequest specify that the principal, plus all gains on sales of investments, is to remain fully invested in U.S. government or corporate securities. At December 31, 19x6, $400,000 was invested in U.S. Treasury bills. The bequest further specifies that interest and dividends earned on investments are to be used for payment of current operating expenses.

• *Land* comprises the following:

Donation of land in 19x0, at appraised value	$ 40,000
Appreciation in fair value of land as determined by independent appraiser in 19x6	60,000
Total	$100,000

• *Building* comprises the following:

Hospital building completed 40 years ago, when operations were started (estimated useful life, 50 years), at cost	$720,000
Installation of elevator 20 years ago (estimated useful life, 20 years), at cost	80,000
Total	$800,000

Required

a. Prepare in general journal form adjusting entries necessary to restate the accounts given in the trial balance properly. Show all supporting computations in good form.

b. Prepare in general journal form entries to distribute the adjusted account balances to funds Esperanza Hospital should report in financial statements prepared in conformity with generally accepted accounting principles as set forth in the *AICPA Audit and Accounting Guide*.

(AICPA, adapted)

Accounting for Voluntary Health and Welfare and Other Not-for-Profit Organizations

Not-for-profit organizations in the United States number in the hundreds of thousands and receive several hundred billions of dollars in revenues and support each year.[1] There are many kinds of not-for-profit organizations, including the two kinds discussed in the preceding two chapters: not-for-profit colleges and universities (Chapter 19) and not-for-profit health care entities (Chapter 20). This text follows the broad categories set forth in industry audit guides published by the American Institute of Certified Public Accountants (AICPA). The two audit guides corresponding to the title of this chapter are *Audits of Voluntary Health and Welfare Organizations* (VHWO) and *Audits of Certain Nonprofit Organizations* (ACNO). ACNO "wraps around" (i.e., includes and supplements) AICPA *Statement of Position 78-10*, which was issued to provide accounting and financial reporting guidance for the many kinds of not-for-profit organizations not covered in the audit guides on colleges and universities, health care entities, and voluntary health and welfare organizations (VHWOs). Among the diverse entities covered by ACNO (referred to in this chapter as "other not-for-profit organizations," or ONPOs) are cemetery organizations, civic organizations, fraternal organizations, labor unions, libraries, museums, other cultural institutions and performing art organizations, political parties, private schools, professional and trade associations, social and country clubs, research and scientific organizations, and religious organizations. Excluded from ACNO are organizations that operate essentially as commercial businesses for the direct benefit of members or stockholders (such as employee benefit and pension plans, mutual insurance companies, mutual banks, trusts, and farm cooperatives).

---

[1] The U.S. Bureau of the Census (*1987 Census of Service Organizations*, SC87A-52, Tables 1 and 2) reports that in 1987 there were 175,829 different tax-exempt service organizations with reported revenues of $267.5 billion. The same year, however, the IRS reported 881,019 tax-exempt organizations that filed with Internal Revenue Code 501(c) tax-exempt status. Gross, Warshauer, and Larkin estimate that there are more than one million not-for-profit organizations. See Malvern J. Gross, William Warshauer, Jr., and Richard F. Larkin, *Financial and Accounting Guide for Not-for-Profit Organizations*, 4th ed. (New York: John Wiley & Sons, 1991).

Readers should note that many cemeteries, libraries, museums, other cultural institutions, and performing arts organizations are supported by governmental units rather than by not-for-profit corporations; some receive support from both, as well as contributions from individuals and businesses. As noted in Chapters 1, 19, and 20, jurisdiction for setting accounting and financial reporting standards for not-for-profit organizations is split between the Financial Accounting Standards Board (FASB) for nongovernmental not-for-profit organizations and the Governmental Accounting Standards Board (GASB) for governmental not-for-profit organizations. Until recent years, neither FASB nor GASB had issued accounting and reporting standards specifically applicable to not-for-profit entities; therefore, the AICPA audit guides cited above were the primary sources of accounting guidance. FASB, however, has now issued three standards applicable to not-for-profit organizations under its jurisdiction. These standards cover recognition of depreciation, accounting for contributions, and financial statement display.[2]

FASB's requirement for depreciation reporting had little impact on VHWOs and ONPOs since the AICPA audit guides already required depreciation reporting. However, FASB's standard on contributions (*Statement No. 116*) has major impact on VHWOs and ONPOs since many of these organizations rely almost exclusively on voluntary contributions for their support. FASB *Statement No. 117* on financial statement display impacts VHWOs to a greater extent than ONPOs since VHWOs have traditionally prepared disaggregated fund-based financial statements. Many ONPOs, on the other hand, already provided financial statements that were similar in many respects to those now required by FASB. Some important differences do exist, however, between the FASB and AICPA audit guide financial statement requirements, as discussed later in this chapter.

GASB has not issued accounting and reporting standards for governmental not-for-profit organizations, other than general standards which apply to all government entities, or those that follow proprietary fund accounting. Current GASB projects are examining the accounting and financial reporting model for business-type activities of governmental units, which would include any governmental not-for-profit organizations that use proprietary fund accounting. Pending completion of research in this area, and possible issuance of new standards, GASB has provided interim guidance which permits proprietary funds, and governmental entities that use proprietary fund accounting, to choose one of two financial reporting approaches.[3] The first approach is to consistently apply GASB stan-

---

[2] Financial Accounting Standards Board, *Statement No. 93*, "Recognition of Depreciation by Not-for-Profit Organizations" (Norwalk, Conn.: FASB, 1987); *FASB, Statement No. 116*, "Accounting for Contributions Received and Made" (Norwalk, Conn.: 1993); *FASB, Statement No. 117*, "Financial Statements of Not-for-Profit Organizations" (Norwalk, Conn.: 1993).

[3] This guidance is provided in GASB *Statement No. 20*, "Accounting and Financial Reporting for Proprietary Funds and Other Governmental Entities That Use Proprietary Fund Accounting" (Norwalk, Conn.: 1993). This guidance was needed to clarify what constitutes generally accepted accounting principles under the GAAP hierarchy defined in the AICPA's *Statement on Auditing Standards (SAS) No. 69*, "The Meaning of Present Fairly in Conformity with Generally Accepted Accounting Principles in the Independent Auditor's Report" (New York, 1992).

dards and applicable standards issued by FASB and its predecessor bodies on or before November 30, 1989, provided the latter do not conflict with GASB standards. The second approach is to apply GASB standards and *all* applicable standards issued by FASB and its predecessor bodies (both those issued before and after November 30, 1993), provided they do not conflict with GASB standards. November 30, 1989, is the date the current agreement was reached regarding FASB and GASB standards setting jurisdiction. Alternatively, some governmental not-for-profit entities may be accounted for in the General Fund or a special revenue fund of a primary government, in which case the standards discussed in Chapters 1 to 13 of this text would apply.

Governmental not-for-profit entities that use proprietary fund accounting and choose the second approach described above will use essentially the same accounting and reporting practices as nongovernmental not-for-profit organizations. Thus, *FASB Statement No. 116* on contribution accounting would apply to such governmental entities, and *Statement No. 117* would largely apply, even though some modification of the financial statements would be required for component unit reporting in the primary government's comprehensive annual financial report (see discussion of "reporting entity" in Chapter 13).

Governmental not-for-profit entities that choose the first approach (follow only FASB standards issued on or before November 30, 1989), will not modify their accounting and financial reporting practices to conform to FASB *Statement Nos. 116* and *117*. Presumably, these entities will follow the present guidance in AICPA audit guides until new GASB standards have been issued.[4]

Illustration 21–1 provides a summary display of which accounting and reporting standards apply to VHWOs and other not-for-profit organizations (ONPOs) and at what point in time. As explained in note (b) of Illustration 21–1, the effective date for most not-for-profit organizations (other than some governmental not-for-profit organizations) to adopt FASB *Statement Nos. 116* and *117* is for fiscal years beginning after December 15, 1994. Early adoption is encouraged, as explained in note (c) of Illustration 21–1. Readers should note that most VHWOs, as implied by the word "voluntary," should be considered nongovernmental, even though many receive governmental support in the form of grants and other subsidies. The key information shown in Illustration 21–1 is that VHWOs and *nongovernmental* other not-for-profit organizations may follow the guidance of either the appropriate AICPA guide or FASB *Statement Nos. 116* and *117* in the transition period prior to the effective date of the FASB statements. After the effective date, however, *Statement Nos. 116* and *117* are the primary sources of GAAP for these organizations. Even after the effective date of FASB *Statement Nos. 116* and *117,* AICPA audit guides are expected to provide guidance on matters not covered by the FASB statements.

---

[4] As of mid-1994, an AICPA committee was preparing a revised audit guide for voluntary health and welfare and other not-for-profit organizations. When this audit guide is issued, the publisher will provide an update to adopters of the Tenth Edition of this text.

ILLUSTRATION 21–1   **Applicability of FASB and GASB Accounting and Financial Reporting Standards to Not-for-Profit Organizations**

	Source of Generally Accepted Accounting Principles		
Type of Organization	*AICPA Audit Guides[a]*	*FASB Statements 116 and 117*	*GASB Standards*
Prior to December 15, 1995:[b]			
Voluntary health and welfare organizations	XXX	XXX[c]	
Other not-for-profit organizations:			
Nongovernmental	XXX	XXX[c]	
Governmental	XXX	XXX[d]	XXX[e]
After December 15, 1995:[b]			
Voluntary health and welfare organizations	XXX	XXX	
Other not-for-profit organizations:			
Nongovernmental	XXX	XXX	
Governmental	XXX	XXX[d]	XXX[e]

NOTES:

[a] *Audits of Voluntary Health and Welfare Organizations* or *Audits of Certain Nonprofit Organizations*, as applicable. These audit guides, as currently being revised, are likely to continue to be used by VHWOs and ONPOs since they provide guidance on a variety of items not yet addressed by FASB and GASB standards.

[b] The effective date of FASB *Statement Nos. 116* and *117* is for fiscal years beginning after December 15, 1994, or *ending* after December 15, 1995. For smaller entities (those with less than $5 million in total assets and less than $1 million in operating expenses), the effective date is one year later.

[c] Early implementation of FASB *Statement Nos. 116* and *117* is encouraged. Thus, many organizations can be expected to adopt these standards prior to the effective date.

[d] As mentioned previously, if a governmental not-for-profit organization should follow proprietary fund accounting, it has the option of adopting all applicable FASB standards that do not conflict with GASB standards. Such an organization could also adopt FASB *Statement Nos. 116* and *117* early, as explained in note (c) above.

[e] All governmental not-for-profit organizations must follow applicable GASB standards. Some such organizations are accounted for in the governmental fund types of a primary government, as discussed previously in this chapter.

    Chapters 19 and 20 explain in some detail the accounting and financial reporting requirements of FASB *Statement Nos. 116* and *117*; therefore, a full discussion of these standards need not be presented in this chapter. As was assumed previously for colleges and universities (Chapter 19) and health care entities (Chapter 20), the authors expect that many VHWOs and some ONPOs will continue to use fund accounting, at least for internal management purposes. Thus, this chapter explains the traditional fund structure used by VHWOs and some ONPOs. However, since FASB *Statement No. 117* prescribes the type and nature of financial statements for not-for-profit organizations subject to its jurisdiction, the financial statements illustrated later in this chapter for VHWOs are those recommended in *Statement No. 117*. Differences between the FASB and audit guide requirements are explained at appropriate points in this chapter. The remainder of the chapter is subdivided between accounting and reporting requirements for VHWOs and other not-for-profit organizations.

Voluntary Health and Welfare Organizations

The term *voluntary health and welfare organizations* includes all not-for-profit organizations that derive their support primarily from voluntary contributions from the general public to be used for health, welfare, or community service activities. The term *human service organizations* is used as a synonym for voluntary health and welfare organizations. Accounting and financial reporting standards for organizations in this category have traditionally been set forth in the AICPA audit guide, *Audits of Voluntary Health and Welfare Organizations.* FASB *Statement Nos. 116* and *117* now apply to most of these organizations, however, as shown in Illustration 21–1. The National Assembly of National Voluntary Health and Social Welfare Organizations, Inc.; National Health Council, Inc.; and United Way of America participated in the preparation of a book, based on the audit guide and earlier publications of the three organizations, designed to be used by persons concerned with the administration of national and local voluntary health and welfare organizations. That book, *Standards of Accounting and Financial Reporting for Voluntary Health and Welfare Organizations,* 3rd ed. (known by the short title of *Standards*), presents a comprehensive description of accounting and financial reporting for organizations in this category.

Many local voluntary health and welfare organizations are affiliated with national organizations that have the same objectives. The relationship of the national organization to the local organization varies from close control over all activities to simply providing educational materials, public relations materials, technical resources, and fund-raising guidance. "Fund-raising," in the sense of conducting a campaign to secure contributions for the furtherance of the programs of the voluntary organization, has naturally led to fund accounting because it is common for donors to place restrictions on the use of their contributions by the recipient. *Standards* states, "One of the distinctive characteristics of a Fund is that it is established to relate to the wishes and restrictions of the contributor."[5] Fund categories illustrated in the AICPA's *Audits of Health and Welfare Organizations,* and in *Standards,* are:

Current Fund—Unrestricted
Current Funds—Restricted
Land, Building, and Equipment Fund
Endowment Funds
Custodian Funds

[5] National Health Council, Inc.; National Assembly of National Voluntary Health and Social Welfare Organizations, Inc.; and United Way of America, *Standards of Accounting and Financial Reporting for Voluntary Health and Welfare Organizations,* 3rd ed. (New York, 1988), p. 8.

The first four categories of funds are accounted for on the full accrual basis. The **current fund—unrestricted** is used to account for all current assets that may be used at the discretion of the governing board for carrying on the operations of the organization, including assets designated by the board for specific purposes. **Current funds—restricted** account for current assets that may be used for operations, but only in accord with stipulations of donors or grantors. Current liabilities to be paid from unrestricted current assets and current liabilities to be paid from restricted current assets are recorded in the appropriate fund.

Land, buildings, and equipment used by a voluntary health or welfare organization in the conduct of its operations; liabilities relating to the acquisition or improvement of plant assets; and cash, investments, or receivables contributed specifically for acquiring, replacing, or improving plant are all accounted for by a **land, building, and equipment fund.** The principal amounts of gifts and bequests that must, under the terms of agreements with donors, be maintained intact in perpetuity, or until the occurrence of a specified event, or for a specified time period, are to be accounted for as **endowment funds.**

Readers who have studied Chapter 19 will note that the four fund categories described briefly above are similar in nature and title to funds recommended for use by public colleges and universities. Aspects of accounting for these four fund categories that are characteristic of voluntary health and welfare organizations are discussed and illustrated in this chapter; aspects of accounting that are discussed fully in Chapter 19 are not repeated here.

Custodian funds of a voluntary health or welfare organization are comparable to **agency funds** of colleges and universities, although custodian funds are somewhat more narrowly defined: "**Custodian funds** are established to account for assets received by an organization to be held or disbursed only on instructions of the person or organization from whom they were received."[6] Assets accounted for by a custodian fund are assets of the donors, not assets of the organization; income generated from the assets is added to the appropriate liability account. For these reasons, neither the receipt of assets to be held in custody nor the receipt of income from those assets should be reported by the voluntary organization as revenue or support. Assets of custodian funds and the offsetting liabilities should be reported in the organization's balance sheet, but they should in no event be combined with assets and liabilities of other funds.

In relatively rare instances, voluntary health and welfare organizations may need to use other fund categories, such as loan funds or annuity funds; in such cases, accounting procedures described in Chapter 19 for funds of these categories are appropriate.

Voluntary health and welfare organizations that use fund accounting recognize revenues and expenses for all categories of funds except custodian funds. This feature makes it relatively easy for VHWOs to prepare the aggregated entity-wide financial statements required by FASB *Statement No. 117.* Recall that health

---

[6] American Institute of Certified Public Accountants, *Audits of Voluntary Health and Welfare Organizations* (New York, 1974), p. 3.

care entities that use fund accounting recognize revenues and expenses only in their General Funds (see Chapter 20) and colleges and universities that use fund accounting recognize revenues and *expenditures* only in their Current Funds category (see Chapter 19).

Financial statements required by FASB *Statement No. 117* are discussed later in this chapter. An illustrative Statement of Financial Position, Statement of Activities, and Statement of Cash Flows are provided as Illustrations 21–3, 21–4, and 21–5, respectively. *Statement No. 117* also requires that voluntary health and welfare organizations prepare a supplementary Statement of Functional Expenses, as shown in Illustration 21–6. It should also be noted that these financial statements are prepared on an entitywide aggregated basis rather than by fund group. Occasional reference to these financial statements may assist in understanding the following discussion of revenues, support, and expenses of voluntary health and welfare organizations.

Revenues, Gains, and Support

Voluntary health and welfare organizations have traditionally distinguished between **revenues** (and **gains**) and **support.** Revenues represent increases in net assets arising from bilateral transactions in which the other party to the transaction is presumed to receive direct tangible benefit commensurate with the resources provided. Examples are membership dues, program service fees, sales of supplies and services, and investment income. Gains, such as realized gains on investment transactions and gains on sale or disposal of equipment, are increases in net assets that relate to peripheral or incidental transactions of the entity and often are beyond the control of management. Support is an increase in net assets arising from contributions of resources and "include only amounts for which the donor derives no direct tangible benefits from the recipient agency."[7] Regardless of any distinctions made, all revenues, gains, and support should be recognized on the accrual basis.

Note that the Statement of Activities shown in Illustration 21–4 provides a caption for "revenues and gains" only, under which revenues, gains, and support (contributions) are reported. FASB *Statement Nos. 116* and *117*, however, both use the term "support" to refer to contributions. Further, the alternative formats for the Statements of Activities provided in *Statement No. 117* (illustrated in Chapters 19 and 20 of this text) provide a caption for "revenues, gains, and other support," rather than just "revenues and gains." The authors thus expect that VHWOs will continue to distinguish between revenues and support in their financial statements.

Contributions

Voluntary health and welfare organizations receive contributions in the form of pledges, securities, plant assets, materials, and services as well as cash.

---

[7] *Standards of Accounting and Financial Reporting for Voluntary Health and Welfare Organizations*, p. 26.

Receipt of cash contributions poses no accounting or reporting problems not previously discussed. Receipt of pledges—promises to contribute a certain amount to an organization—requires the establishment of an allowance for estimated uncollectible pledges, inasmuch as pledges may not be enforceable under law or under organization policy. For financial reporting purposes, the allowance for uncollectible pledges is deducted from total contributions, so the amount shown as public support is that which has been collected or is expected to be collectible.

Donated securities may be received for any purposes, although generally they are received as a part of the principal of endowment. All donated securities should be recorded at their fair value at date of the gift. The same valuation rule is applied to land, buildings, and equipment received either as a part of an endowment or for use in the operations of the organization. The receipt of donated materials and services presents enough complexity to merit separate discussion later in this section.

It should be noted that donors or grantors may restrict the year of use, as well as the category of use, of their support. Amounts received in one year but designated by donors or grantors as being for use in a subsequent year are credited to "Contributions Temporarily Restricted for Future Use," or some similar account title. Under the AICPA audit guide requirements, such items were reported as a deferred credit and reclassified as support or revenue in the year in which the donors or grantors permit use. FASB *Statement No. 116,* however, requires all not-for-profit organizations subject to its jurisdiction to **recognize contributions received and unconditional promises to give as revenue or gains in the period received** and as assets, decreases in liabilities, or expenses depending on the form of the benefits received. Contributions should be measured at their fair value when received. **Conditional promises to give,** however, **are not recognized as a revenue or gain until the conditions on which they depend are substantially met**, but the estimated amounts of such promises must be disclosed in the notes to the financial statements.

Thus, as noted previously in Chapter 19, not-for-profit organizations subject to FASB *Statement No. 116* can **no longer defer recognition of restricted operating monies until a future period stipulated by the donor or grantor.** Indeed, donor-imposed restrictions have no bearing whatsoever on the *period* in which contributions are recognized. Rather these restrictions affect the *manner of reporting* contributions and the related assets. Specifically, the organization must report all contributions received or unconditional promises to give in the period received as increases in the appropriate category of net assets: **unrestricted net assets, temporarily restricted assets,** or **permanently restricted assets.** These are also the reporting categories specified in FASB *Statement No. 117,* discussed later in this chapter.

Unconditional promises to give that will not be received until future periods must be reported among the **temporarily restricted net assets** unless explicit donor stipulations or the circumstances surrounding the promise make it clear that the donor intended the contribution to support activities of the current period. In the latter case such contributions should be reported, wholly or partially, as an increase in **unrestricted net assets.** Voluntary health and welfare and other not-for-profit organizations should recognize expirations of temporary restrictions on gifts or grants in the period expenses are incurred for the restricted purpose or, if restricted for acquisition of long-lived assets, in the period the long-lived assets are acquired. Gifts of long-lived assets should be reported in unrestricted net assets unless the donor stipulates a time restriction on how long the organization must use the asset, or the organization itself has an accounting policy imposing a time restriction that expires over the life of the asset.

Donated Materials.   One of the basic characteristics that distinguishes voluntary health and welfare organizations from commercial organizations is their reliance on noncash contributions. Sheltered workshops for handicapped persons often depend heavily on donations of clothing, furniture, and other household articles. Health agencies may obtain contributions of drugs from pharmaceutical houses. Office space may be furnished rent free, and office equipment may be received as a contribution. Television, radio, newspapers, and magazines may publicize fund drives, special events, or the general work of health and welfare organizations at no charge; and the services of unpaid workers may well make the difference between an effective organization and one that fails to achieve its objectives.

Statement No. 116 requires that all unconditional gifts, including material amounts of donated materials, be reported at fair value on the date of the gift. An objective, clearly measurable basis for fair value can be established by proceeds from resale by the organization, price lists, market quotations, or appraisals.[8] Donated materials used or consumed in rendering services should be reported as part of the cost of the services rendered.

Donated Services.   Voluntary health and welfare organizations typically rely on the efforts of volunteer workers to supplement the efforts of paid employees in the performance of program services, support services, and periodic fund-raising drives. *Statement No. 116* permits recognition of contributed services at their fair value if the services received:

1. Create or enhance nonfinancial assets, or;
2. Require specialized skill and are provided by individuals possessing those skills, and;
3. Typically would need to be purchased if not provided by donation.

The second and third FASB criteria appear quite restrictive and make it likely that some donated services that would formerly have been recognized under similar but less restrictive criteria provided in the AICPA audit guide will no longer be recognized. Although *Statement No. 116* does not provide an example of the first criterion, a logical example would be recognition of support for donated architec-

---

[8] FASB *Statement No. 116*, par. 19.

tural, legal, and carpentry services related to construction of a building addition (rather than for program support). In this example a capital asset account, rather than expense, would be debited. In general, nonfinancial assets are noncash assets and other assets not readily convertible into cash, such as consumable supplies and fixed assets.

Special Events

Special events are fund-raising activities in which "something of tangible value is offered to donor participants or designees for a payment which includes a contribution" adequate to yield revenue for the sponsoring agency over and above direct expenses.[9] Dinners, dances, bazaars, card parties, fashion shows, and sales of candy, cookies, cakes, or greeting cards are typical "special events." The special events category of support is reserved for those events sponsored by the voluntary organization or by an organization over which it has control. If a completely independent organization sponsors an event for the voluntary agency's benefit, the amount given to the agency should be reported as contributions.

Special events may give rise to incidental revenue, such as advertising of programs; incidental revenue is properly reported in the special events category of support. VHWOs have traditionally netted direct costs of special events (such as the cost of dinner, rental of ballroom, or cost of prizes) against the gross proceeds of the special event. FASB *Statement No. 117,* par. 138, requires that all special event revenue and direct costs, except those of a peripheral or incidental nature, be reported at their gross amounts. In the Statement of Activities presented in Illustration 21–4 later in this chapter, special events support is included as part of the "Contributions" reported in the amount of $388,196 rather than as a separate amount. If desired, VHWOs can provide more detailed reporting of support categories, either on the face of the Statement of Activities or in the Notes to the Financial Statements.

Expenses of promoting and conducting special events, such as expenses of printing tickets and posters, mailings, fees and expenses of public relations and fund-raising consultants, and salaries of employees of the voluntary agency attributable to planning, promoting, and conducting special events, are treated as fund-raising expenses and are not charged against special events support.

The Classification and Recording of Expenses

The Statement of Activities (Illustration 21–4) reports on the accrual basis expenses for a fiscal period for each program offered by the voluntary health and welfare organization and for supporting services and payments to affiliated organizations. In addition, the supplemental financial statement required by FASB standards to be prepared by VHWOs, the Statement of Functional Expenses (Illustration 21–6), presents the allocation of natural expense classifications (i.e., salaries, fringe benefits, professional fees, supplies expense, and depreciation), and all other natural expense accounts, to each program and to supporting services.

---

[9] *Standards of Accounting and Financial Reporting,* p. 27.

ILLUSTRATION 21–2   **Functional Basis Financial Package of a Not-for-Profit Human Service Organization**

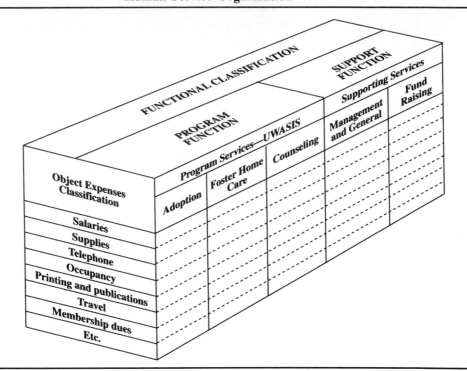

SOURCE: United Way of America, *Accounting and Financial Reporting: A Guide for United Ways and Not-for-Profit Human Service Organizations* (Alexandria, Va., 1989), p. 159.

Illustration 21–2 presents in schematic form the relation between expenses classified by nature or object and expenses classified by function.

Program Services Expenses

The objectives of a particular voluntary health or welfare organization will govern the nature of the programs it offers. The voluntary health and welfare service used as a basis for Illustrations 21–2, 21–4, and 21–6 has three basic programs, designated Counseling, Adoption, and Foster Home Care. A health organization might classify its programs as research, public health education, professional education and training, and community services. Other classifications are used as needed by voluntary organizations to describe services they render.

Direct costs attributable to programs should always be reported as program services expenses. Indirect costs readily allocable to programs should be allocated. For example, the costs of a public education program would generally include direct costs of meetings held to educate the public; salaries of employees while preparing, arranging for, and giving talks to groups; and costs of educational materials that give technical information or deal with a particular health or welfare problem.

Supporting Services Expenses

Supporting services expenses reported in a Statement of Functional Expenses are often summarized into two classes: "management and general" and "fund-raising." A local fund-raising organization, such as United Way, which is intended to allocate most of its inflows to participating agencies rather than to engage directly in offering program services to the public, may find it desirable to present a more detailed classification of supporting services. For example, a local fund-raising organization may report expenses of "allocating and agency relations," and "planning and evaluation," as well as fund-raising and management and general.

Expenses incurred for multiple purposes should be allocated to program services and to fund-raising, if allocation bases that are both equitable and clerically feasible are available. Illustration 21–6 shows that the majority of expenses are recorded in accounts that describe the nature, or the object, or the expense; the expenses are then allocated to program services and to fund-raising. The amounts shown in the Management and General column in Illustration 21–6 include both the amounts that were clearly incurred for general purposes and the residual amounts that were not reasonably allocable to program services or to fund-raising.

Management and general expenses include the cost of publicity and public relations activities designed to keep the organization's name before prospective contributors. Costs of informational materials that contain only general information regarding the health or welfare problem and the costs of informational materials distributed to potential contributors, but not as a part of a fund drive, are considered management and general expenses. The costs of budgeting, accounting, reporting, legal services, office management, purchasing, and similar activities are examples of expenses properly classifiable as management and general expenses.

Fund-raising expenses include the costs of television and radio announcements that request contributions, including the costs of preparing the announcements and purchasing or arranging for the time; the costs of postage, addressing, and maintenance of mailing lists and other fund drive records; the costs of preparing or purchasing fund-raising materials; the costs of public meetings to "kick off" a fund drive; and an appropriate portion of the salaries of personnel who supervise fund-raising activities or keep records of them.

Illustrative Transactions— Voluntary Health and Welfare Organizations

Preceding sections of this chapter point out the fact that there are many differences among VHWOs regarding the kinds of program services provided and in the sources of support and revenue utilized. Accordingly, the transactions and accounting entries presented in this section should be taken as illustrative of those considered appropriate for an organization that offers counseling, adoption, and foster home care, but not necessarily typical of an organization providing health, welfare, or community services of considerably different nature. The transactions illustrated in this section are assumed to pertain to the year 19x3 of a hypothetical organization called the Community Family Service Agency, Inc. Trial balances of all funds of the Community Family Service Agency, Inc., as of December 31, 19x2, are shown on the next page.

	Debits	Credits
Current Fund—Unrestricted:		
Cash	$ 52,814	
Short-Term Investments	22,000	
Accounts Receivable	2,485	
Allowance for Uncollectible		
Accounts Receivable		$ 135
Pledges Receivable	5,424	
Allowance for Uncollectible Pledges		259
Supplies Inventory	23,095	
Prepaid Expenses	3,917	
Long-Term Investments	17,000	
Accounts Payable and Accrued Expenses		25,911
Contributions Temporarily Restricted for Future Use		5,125
Fund Balance—Designated for Long-Term Investments		17,000
Fund Balance—Designated for Purchases of Equipment		9,200
Fund Balance—Designated for Special Outreach Project		30,000
Fund Balance—Undesignated		39,105
Totals	$126,735	$126,735
Current Funds—Restricted:		
Cash	$ 3,900	
Fund Balance—Restricted for Professional Education		$ 3,900
Totals	$ 3,900	$ 3,900
Land, Building, and Equipment Fund:		
Cash	$ 1,297	
Short-Term Investments	20,000	
Pledges Receivable	10,470	
Allowance for Uncollectible Pledges		$ 288
Land	16,900	
Building	58,000	
Allowance for Depreciation—Building		4,640
Furniture and Equipment	42,824	
Allowance for Depreciation—Furniture and Equipment		9,136
Mortgage Payable		55,000
Fund Balance—Expended		48,948
Fund Balance—Unexpended		31,479
Totals	$149,491	$149,491
Endowment Fund:		
Cash	$ 700	
Investments	230,000	
Fund Balance		$230,700
Totals	$230,700	$230,700

Notice that the fund equity of the Current Fund—Unrestricted in the trial balances shown above is reported as consisting of Fund Balance—Undesignated, Fund Balance—Designated for Long-Term Investments, Fund Balance—Designated for Purchases of Equipment, and Fund Balance—Designated for Special Outreach Project. By definition, all net assets of this fund are *unrestricted*—

available for use at the discretion of the governing board. However, amounts pledged or restricted by donors for unrestricted use in a future period would be reported as "temporarily restricted assets" in the financial statements illustrated in the next section. The governing board has the power to designate that certain assets be held for special purposes; if it does so, the designations should be disclosed by a corresponding segregation of Fund Balance, as shown in the Current Funds—Unrestricted trial balance. The trial balance of Current Funds—Restricted shows only one Fund Balance account; the title of this account discloses the nature of the restriction placed on the use of resources by the donors or grantors. Since all resources held for use only for those operating purposes specified by donors or grantors are accounted for in Current Funds—Restricted, as many Fund Balance accounts should be created as are necessary to disclose the nature of all restrictions.

Two Fund Balance accounts are shown in the trial balance of the Land, Building, and Equipment Fund: Fund Balance—Expended and Fund Balance—Unexpended. The former is similar to the Net Investment in Plant account used by colleges and universities (see Chapter 19) in that it represents the investment in land, buildings, and equipment that were contributed to the organization or financed from its operations; not financed by borrowing. In the trial balance (page 710), the total investment in plant, less allowances for depreciation, is $103,948 ($16,900 + $58,000 − $4,640 + $42,824 − $9,136). The total of Fund Balance—Expended ($48,948) and Mortgage Payable ($55,000) is also $103,948. As the principal of the mortgage is reduced, Fund Balance—Expended is correspondingly increased. As the depreciable assets are depreciated, Fund Balance—Expended is reduced. Since Cash, Short-Term Investments, and Pledges Receivable are held in this fund for acquisition, replacement, or improvement of fixed assets, the total of these items (net of Allowance for Uncollectible Pledges) will be reflected in the Fund Balance—Unexpended account until expenditures are made, at which time it is obviously appropriate to debit Fund Balance—Unexpended and credit Fund Balance—Expended.

Contributions received in 19x2, but specified by donors for unrestricted use in 19x3, were transferred from the temporarily restricted support and revenue category to the current category, as shown by Entry 1.

Current Fund—Unrestricted:

1.	Contributions Temporarily Restricted for Future Use	5,125	
	Net Assets Released from Restrictions—Satisfaction of Operating Requirements		5,125

Pledges receivable resulting from the 19x3 fund drive were recorded. Pledges of $69,500 were unrestricted; in addition, pledges of $16,500 were donor-restricted for a special outreach project to be undertaken in 19x3.

Current Fund—Unrestricted:

2a.	Pledges Receivable	69,500	
	Contributions		69,500

Current Funds—Restricted:

2b.	Pledges Receivable	16,500	
	Contributions		16,500

Cash collected for unrestricted pledges totaled $68,500; collection of accounts receivable amounted to $2,200. Cash collected for restricted pledges totaled $16,500. Cash in the amount of $9,200 was collected for pledges given during a building fund drive in a preceding year.

Current Fund—Unrestricted:

3a.	Cash	70,700	
	Pledges Receivable		68,500
	Accounts Receivable		2,200

Current Funds—Restricted:

3b.	Cash	16,500	
	Pledges Receivable		16,500

Land, Building, and Equipment Fund:

3c.	Cash	9,200	
	Pledges Receivable		9,200

The organization sponsored a bazaar to raise funds for the special outreach project. Direct costs of $3,000 incurred for this event were paid in cash; the event yielded payments and cash contributions of $10,000.

Current Funds—Restricted:

4a.	Cash	10,000	
	Special Events		10,000
4b.	Costs of Special Events	3,000	
	Cash		3,000

The 19x3 allocation from the United Way of Fairshare Bay amounted, in gross, to $317,000. Related fund-raising expenses to be borne by the Community Family Service Agency totaled $13,200; the net allocation was received in cash.

Current Fund—Unrestricted:

5.	Cash	303,800	
	United Way Fund-Raising Expense	13,200	
	Allocated by Federated Fund-Raising		
	Organization		317,000

Salaries expense for the year totaled $265,000; employee benefits expense totaled $51,000; and payroll taxes expense was $20,300. As of year-end, $15,100 of these expenses were unpaid; the balance had been paid from unrestricted cash.

Current Fund—Unrestricted:

6.	Salaries	265,000	
	Employee Benefits	51,000	
	Payroll Taxes	20,300	
	Cash		321,200
	Accounts Payable and Accrued		
	Expenses		15,100

Expenses incurred for the special outreach project were professional fees, $17,000; supplies, $4,500; and printing and publications, $1,600. All amounts were paid from restricted cash.

Current Funds—Restricted:

7.	Professional Fees	17,000	
	Supplies	4,500	
	Printing and Publications	1,600	
	Cash		23,100

Expenses for program services and supporting services financed by unrestricted current funds were professional fees, $43,000; supplies, $7,800; telephone, $9,800; postage and shipping, $7,800; occupancy, $23,900; rental and maintenance of equipment, $8,700; printing and publications, $7,900; travel, $22,000; conferences, conventions, and meetings, $13,800; specific assistance to individuals, $30,000; membership dues, $700; awards and grants to national headquarters, $5,500; costs of sales to public, $900; and miscellaneous, $4,200. All expenses were credited to Accounts Payable and Accrued Expenses.

Current Fund—Unrestricted:

8.	Professional Fees	43,000	
	Supplies	7,800	
	Telephone	9,800	
	Postage and Shipping	7,800	
	Occupancy	23,900	
	Rental and Maintenance of Equipment	8,700	
	Printing and Publications	7,900	
	Travel	22,000	
	Conferences, Conventions, and Meetings	13,800	
	Specific Assistance to Individuals	30,000	
	Membership Dues	700	
	Awards and Grants to National		
	Headquarters	5,500	
	Costs of Sales to Public	900	
	Miscellaneous	4,200	
	Accounts Payable and Accrued Expenses		186,000

Unrestricted current fund support and revenue were received in cash during 19x3 from the following sources: legacies and bequests, $15,000; membership dues—individuals, $1,000; program service fees, $55,000; net incidental revenue, $250; investment income, $2,900; and miscellaneous, $1,500.

Current Fund—Unrestricted:

9.	Cash	75,650	
	Legacies and Bequests		15,000
	Membership Dues—Individuals		1,000
	Program Service Fees		55,000
	Net Incidental Revenue		250
	Investment Income		2,900
	Miscellaneous Revenue		1,500

Sales to public amounted to $1,000 gross for the year. None of this amount was collected by year-end.

Current Fund—Unrestricted:

10.	Accounts Receivable	1,000	
	Sales to Public		1,000

Accounts payable and accrued expenses paid from unrestricted cash during 19x3 totaled $182,864.

Current Fund—Unrestricted:

11.	Accounts Payable and Accrued Expenses	182,864	
	Cash		182,864

Contributions received in cash in 19x3 but specified by donors for use in 19x4 amounted to $20,000. Of this total, $10,000 was unrestricted; $6,000 was for restricted operating purposes; and $4,000 was for the purchase of equipment.

Current Fund—Unrestricted:

12a.	Cash	10,000	
	Contributions Temporarily Restricted for Future Use		10,000

Current Funds—Restricted:

12b.	Cash	6,000	
	Contributions Temporarily Restricted for Future Use		6,000

Land, Building, and Equipment Fund:

12c.	Cash	4,000	
	Contributions Temporarily Restricted for Future Use		4,000

A physical count of supplies, valued at the lower of cost or market, indicated the proper balance sheet value should be $19,100. Prepaid expenses at year-end were $3,600; the decrease is chargeable to postage and shipping expense.

Current Fund—Unrestricted:

13.	Supplies	3,995	
	Postage and Shipping	317	
	Supplies Inventory		3,995
	Prepaid Expenses		317

The Land, Building, and Equipment Fund paid interest on the mortgage, $4,540; and $6,500 on the principal of the mortgage. Short-term investments of this fund were sold at par, $5,000; the proceeds were used to purchase equipment. Because the Fund Balance of this fund is segregated into Fund Balance—Expended and Fund Balance—Unexpended, it is necessary to transfer $5,000 from the latter to the former to record the fact that additional equipment has been purchased; similarly, because $6,500 of cash of this fund was used to reduce the mortgage payable, it is necessary to transfer $6,500 from Fund Balance—Unexpended to Fund Balance—Expended.

Land, Building, and Equipment Fund:

14a.	Miscellaneous Expense	4,540	
	Mortgage Payable	6,500	
	Cash		11,040
14b.	Cash	5,000	
	Short-Term Investments		5,000
14c.	Equipment	5,000	
	Cash		5,000
14d.	Fund Balance—Unexpended	11,500	
	Fund Balance—Expended		11,500

Depreciation on buildings, furniture, and equipment belonging to the Community Family Service Agency is recorded in the amounts shown in Entry 15a. Since the depreciation reduced the carrying value of the fixed assets, it is useful to transfer an amount equal to the annual depreciation charge from Fund Balance—Expended to Fund Balance—Unexpended, as shown in Entry 15b. This entry permits closing of all Land, Building, and Equipment Fund expenses, as reclassified in Entry 19, to Fund Balance—Unexpended (see Entry 26).

Land, Building, and Equipment Fund:

15a.	Depreciation of Buildings and Equipment	4,185	
	Allowance for Depreciation—Building		1,145
	Allowance for Depreciation—Furniture and Equipment		3,040
15b.	Fund Balance—Expended	4,185	
	Fund Balance—Unexpended		4,185

Interest received in cash on short-term investments of the Land, Building, and Equipment Fund amounted to $1,390. Interest received in cash on investments of endowment funds amounted to $12,780. This amount was available for unrestricted current use; therefore, it is recorded directly in the Current Fund—Unrestricted and is never recorded in the Endowment Fund.

Land, Building, and Equipment Fund:

16a.	Cash	1,390	
	Investment Income		1,390

Current Fund—Unrestricted:

16b.	Cash	12,780	
	Investment Income		12,780

The Community Family Service Agency paid its national affiliates in accord with the affiliation agreements; the amount of the payment in 19x3 was $8,574.

Current Fund—Unrestricted:

17.	Payments to Affiliated Organizations	8,574	
	Cash		8,574

An analysis of the receivables and investments accounts of all funds indicated the market value of all investments was equal to, or in excess of, costs; the allowance for uncollectible accounts receivable appeared adequate and not excessive; and the allowance for uncollectible unrestricted pledges should be increased by $104.

Current Fund—Unrestricted:

18.	Estimated Uncollectible Pledges	104	
	Allowance for Uncollectible Pledges		104

Miscellaneous expenses and depreciation expenses of the Land, Building, and Equipment Fund were allocated to program services and supporting services.
The allocation is assumed to be:

Land, Building, and Equipment Fund:

19.	Counseling	2,480	
	Adoption	990	
	Foster Home Care	2,510	
	Special Outreach Project	2,050	
	Management and General	530	
	Fund-Raising	165	
	Miscellaneous Expense		4,540
	Depreciation of Buildings and Equipment		4,185

Current Funds—Restricted expenses all pertained to the special outreach project. The following entry shows the reclassification.

Current Funds—Restricted:

20.	Special Outreach Project	23,100	
	Professional Fees		17,000
	Supplies		4,500
	Printing and Publications		1,600

Expenses of Current Fund—Unrestricted were allocated to program services and supporting services shown by the following entry.

Current Fund—Unrestricted:

21.	Counseling	183,033	
	Adoption	68,570	
	Foster Home Care	170,021	
	Special Outreach Project	37,720	
	Management and General	52,555	
	Fund-Raising	13,813	
	Salaries		265,000
	Employee Benefits		51,000
	Payroll Taxes		20,300
	Professional Fees		43,000
	Supplies		11,795
	Telephone		9,800
	Postage and Shipping		8,117
	Occupancy		23,900
	Rental and Maintenance of Equipment		8,700
	Printing and Publications		7,900
	Travel		22,000
	Conferences, Conventions, and Meetings		13,800
	Specific Assistance to Individuals		30,000
	Membership Dues		700
	Awards and Grants to National Headquarters		5,500
	Miscellaneous		4,200

Support and revenue for 19x3, less direct costs identified with raising specific classes of support and revenues, and less estimated uncollectible pledges, were closed to the Current Fund—Unrestricted Fund Balance—Undesignated.

Current Fund—Unrestricted:

22.	Contributions	74,625	
	Allocated by Federated Fund-Raising Organizations	317,000	
	Legacies and Bequests	15,000	
	Sales to Public	1,000	
	Membership Dues—Individuals	1,000	
	Program Service Fees	55,000	
	Net Incidental Revenue	250	
	Investment Income	15,680	
	Miscellaneous Revenue	1,500	
	United Way Fund-Raising Expense		13,200
	Cost of Sales to Public		900
	Estimated Uncollectible Pledges		104
	Fund Balance—Undesignated		466,851

Program service expenses, supporting service expenses, and payments to affiliated organizations were closed to Fund Balance—Undesignated of the unrestricted current fund.

Current Fund—Unrestricted:

23.	Fund Balance—Undesignated	534,286	
	Counseling		183,033
	Adoption		68,570
	Foster Home Care		170,021

Special Outreach Project	37,720
Management and General	52,555
Fund-Raising	13,813
Payments to Affiliated Organizations	8,574

The Fund Balance that had been designated in 19x2 by the governing board for the special outreach project to be conducted on an experimental basis during 19x3 was deemed no longer necessary; the board authorized the return of the amount, $30,000, to Fund Balance—Undesignated.

Current Fund—Unrestricted:

24.	Fund Balance—Designated for Special Outreach Project	30,000	
	Fund Balance—Undesignated		30,000

Items of support, revenue, and expense recorded in restricted current funds were closed to Fund Balance—Special Outreach Project.

Current Funds—Restricted:

25.	Contributions	16,500	
	Special Events	10,000	
	Cost of Special Events		3,000
	Special Outreach Project		23,100
	Fund Balance—Special Outreach Project		400

Investment income and program service and supporting service expenses of the Land, Building, and Equipment fund were closed to Fund Balance—Unexpended.

Land, Building, and Equipment Fund:

26.	Investment Income	1,390	
	Fund Balance—Unexpended	7,335	
	Counseling		2,480
	Adoption		990
	Foster Home Care		2,510
	Special Outreach Project		2,050
	Management and General		530
	Fund-Raising		165

Illustrative Financial Statements— Voluntary Health and Welfare Organizations

As noted in Chapters 19 and 20, and earlier in this chapter, FASB *Statement No. 117* requires nongovernmental not-for-profit organizations to prepare three financial statements—a Statement of Financial Position, a Statement of Activities, and a Statement of Cash Flows—as part of a complete set of general purpose financial statements. In addition, it requires VHWOs to continue to prepare the Statement of Functional Expenses long recommended by the AICPA and industry publications. Assuming in 19x3, there were no purchases or sales of investments held by endowment funds, or any additions to or deductions from the principal of endowment funds, and that there were no other transactions and events requiring journal entries except for those illustrated previously, the Statement of Financial Position as of December 31, 19x3, with comparative totals for 19x2, would be as shown in Illustration 21–3. This statement simply aggregates for the entity as a whole the data accumulated in the accounts on a fund basis. Three points are worth noting. First, assets restricted to investment (or likely to be invested) for nonoperating, temporarily and permanently restricted purposes (i.e., land, building, and equipment acquisition and endowment) are reported in a separate subsection of the Assets section of the statement. Second, FASB *Statement No. 117* requires that unconditional pledges received, which will not be collected until a future period, be reported as an increase in temporarily restricted net assets unless the donor

ILLUSTRATION 21–3

COMMUNITY FAMILY SERVICE AGENCY, INC.
Statement of Financial Position
December 31, 19x3, and 19x2

	19x3	*19x2*
Assets:		
Cash	$ 23,406	$ 56,714
Short-term investments, at market which approximates cost	22,000	22,000
Accounts receivable, less allowance for uncollectibles of $135 each year	1,150	2,350
Pledges receivable, less allowance for uncollectibles of $363 and $259	6,061	5,165
Supplies, at lower of cost or market	19,100	23,095
Prepaid expense	3,600	3,917
Assets restricted to investment:		
For land, buildings, and equipment:		
Cash	4,847	1,297
Investments, at market which approximates cost	15,000	20,000
Pledges receivable, less allowance of $288 each year	982	10,182
For endowment:		
Cash	700	700
Investments, at market which approximates cost	230,000	230,000
Land, buildings, and equipment, less allowance for accumulated depreciation of $17,961 and $13,776	104,763	103,948
Long-term investments	17,000	17,000
Total assets	$448,609	$496,368
Liabilities and net assets:		
Accounts payable and accrued expenses	$ 44,147	$ 25,911
8 1/4% mortgage payable, due 19z5	48,500	55,000
Total liabilities	92,647	80,911
Net assets:		
Unrestricted	84,133	144,253
Temporarily restricted	41,129	40,504
Permanently restricted	230,700	230,700
Total net assets	355,962	415,457
Total liabilities and net assets	$448,609	$496,368

explicitly intended the pledged amount to be used to cover current period expenses. In Illustration 21–3, it is assumed that all unrestricted pledges were intended to cover current period expenses. Moreover, the ending balance of unrestricted pledges receivable ($6,061—see Illustration 21–3) is relatively insignificant compared with the $69,500 of unrestricted pledges received during the year (see Entry 2a). Third, *net assets* are reported in three categories: unrestricted, temporarily restricted, and permanently restricted. Temporarily restricted net assets shown in the amount of $41,129 consist of the assets shown in Illustration 21–3 as restricted for land, buildings, and equipment ($20,829), plus $20,300 of cash for restricted operating purposes or support intended for future periods. Permanently restricted assets shown in the amount of $230,700 correspond to the amount restricted for endowment.

The Statement of Activities provided in Illustration 21–4 is prepared in one of the three formats illustrated in FASB *Statement No. 117*. Examples of the other two formats can be found in Chapter 19 for colleges and universities and Chapter 20 for health care entities. The Statement of Activities presents, in aggregated fashion, all increases and decreases in the three categories of net assets. It uses, of course, the term **net assets** rather than Fund Balance since the FASB-required Statement of Activities requires entitywide aggregation and does not assume (or preclude) that fund accounting is used. One key difference is that any temporarily restricted support reclassified to support in the current period is reported in the "Net assets released from restrictions" section of the statement, rather than on the Contributions line. Such treatment is appropriate given that the amount released was previously reported as "temporarily restricted net assets." In addition, as explained in Note B of Illustration 21–4, expenses incurred in Current Funds—Restricted, and depreciation and other expenses (e.g., interest expense) incurred in the Land, Building, and Equipment Fund, are reported in the "Net assets released from restrictions" section on the line titled "Satisfaction of operating restrictions." Purchasing land, buildings, and equipment releases donor-imposed restrictions on the use of such contributions, and thus should be reported in a manner similar to that shown in Illustration 21–4 as "Satisfaction of equipment acquisition restrictions."

A Statement of Cash Flows prepared in the format recommended in FASB *Statement No. 117* is presented in Illustration 21–5. This statement is similar to that required for commercial businesses by FASB *Statement No. 95* (that *Statement No. 117* now makes applicable to nongovernmental not-for-profit organizations). The information needed to prepare the cash flow statement is readily available from the other financial statements and the illustrative transactions provided in the chapter. As explained in Chapter 20 on health care entities, there are some unique aspects of this cash flow statement. First, contributions restricted for future operations and long-term investment are reported in the "Cash flows from financing activities" section. Second, in reconciling changes in net assets, any changes in net assets (such as from restricted contributions or restricted investment income) that do not affect cash flows from operating activities must be added to, or deducted from the change in net assets, as appropriate.

ILLUSTRATION 21–4

COMMUNITY FAMILY SERVICE AGENCY, INC.
Statement of Activities
Year Ended December 31, 19x3

Changes in unrestricted net assets:	
Revenues and gains:	
Contributions (Note A)	$388,196
Program service fees	55,250
Membership dues	1,000
Sales to public, net of direct expenses of $900	100
Investment income	15,680
Miscellaneous	1,500
Total unrestricted revenues and gains	461,726
Net assets released from restrictions:	
Satisfaction of operating requirements (Note B)	36,950
Satisfaction of equipment acquisition restrictions	7,315
Total net assets released from restrictions	44,265
Total unrestricted revenues, gains, and other support	505,991
Expenses and losses:	
Program services:	
Counseling	185,513
Adoption	69,560
Foster home care	172,531
Special outreach program	62,870
Total program services	490,474
Supporting services:	
Management and general	53,085
Fund-raising	13,978
Total supporting services	67,063
Payments to affiliated organizations	8,574
Total expenses and losses	566,111
Decrease in unrestricted net assets	(60,120)
Changes in temporarily restricted net assets:	
Contributions	43,500
Investment income	1,390
Net assets released from restrictions	(44,265)
Increase in temporarily restricted net assets	625
Change in permanently restricted net assets	–0–
Decrease in net assets	(59,495)
Net assets, December 31, 19x2	415,457
Net assets, December 31, 19x3	$355,962

NOTE A: Contributions of $393,321, less $5,125 (see Entry No. 1) reclassified from temporarily restricted support from prior year. This amount is included in "Net assets released from restrictions."

NOTE B: $5,125 of temporarily restricted support reclassified for unrestricted use (see Note A) + $23,100 of expenses incurred in Current—Restricted Fund + $8,725 of program and support expenses incurred in Land, Building, and Equipment Fund = $36,950.

ILLUSTRATION 21–5

COMMUNITY FAMILY SERVICE AGENCY, INC.
Statement of Cash Flows
Year Ended December 31, 19x3

Cash flows from operating activities:	
Cash received from contributors	$349,440
Cash collected on contributions receivable	68,500
Cash received from service recipients	57,200
Cash collected from members	1,000
Investment income	15,680
Miscellaneous receipts	1,750
Cash paid to employees and suppliers	(530,164)
Cash paid to affiliated organizations	(8,574)
Interest paid	(4,540)
Net cash used for operating activities	(49,708)
Cash flows from investing activities:	
Purchase of property and equipment	(5,000)
Proceeds from sale of securities	5,000
Net cash used by investing activities	–0–
Cash flows from financing activities:	
Proceeds from contributions restricted for:	
Investment in plant	8,660
Future operations	16,400
Other financing activities:	
Interest and dividends restricted for plant acquisition	1,390
Repayment of long-term debt	(6,500)
Net cash provided by financing activities	19,950
Net increase (decrease) in cash	(29,758)
Cash, December 31, 19x2	58,711
Cash, December 31, 19x3	$ 28,953
RECONCILIATION OF CHANGES IN NET ASSETS TO NET CASH USED FOR OPERATING ACTIVITIES:	
Change in net assets	$(59,495)
Adjustments to reconcile change in net assets to net cash provided by operating activities:	
Depreciation and amortization	4,185
Decrease in accounts receivable, net	1,200
Decrease in pledges receivable, net	8,304
Decrease in supplies	3,995
Decrease in prepaid expenses	317
Increase in accounts payable and accrued expenses	18,236
Gifts, grants, and bequests restricted for long-term investment	(25,060)
Interest restricted for long-term investment	(1,390)
Cash used for operating activities	$(49,708)

ILLUSTRATION 21–6

COMMUNITY FAMILY SERVICE AGENCY, INC.
Statement of Functional Expenses
Year Ended December 31, 19x3
(with comparative totals for 19x2)

	Program Services					Supporting Services			Total Program and Supporting Services Expenses	
	Counseling	Adoption	Foster Home Care	Special Outreach Project	Total	Management and General	Fund-Raising	Total	19x3	19x2
Salaries	$ 87,720	$36,559	$ 83,610	$13,738	$221,627	$35,153	$ 8,220	$43,373	$265,000	$232,170
Employee benefits	16,882	7,036	16,091	2,644	42,653	6,765	1,582	8,347	51,000	47,035
Payroll taxes	6,720	2,801	6,405	1,051	16,977	2,693	630	3,323	20,300	11,400
Total salaries and related expenses	111,322	46,396	106,106	17,433	281,257	44,611	10,432	55,043	336,300	290,605
Professional fees	25,107	3,929	11,643	18,143	58,822	1,178	—	1,178	60,000	54,600
Supplies	4,049	2,167	4,747	3,950	14,913	790	592	1,382	16,295	8,500
Telephone	3,897	1,430	3,350	190	8,867	600	333	933	9,800	9,610
Postage and shipping	2,840	1,073	2,402	908	7,223	684	210	894	8,117	6,750
Occupancy	8,772	1,415	8,078	2,586	20,851	2,468	581	3,049	23,900	24,600
Rental and maintenance of equipment	3,669	1,520	3,511	—	8,700	—	—	—	8,700	8,750
Printing and publications	2,761	1,420	1,352	1,462	6,995	940	1,565	2,505	9,500	7,200
Travel	7,700	1,500	7,500	5,000	21,700	300	—	300	22,000	24,000
Conferences, conventions, meetings	3,450	887	4,436	4,436	13,209	591	—	591	13,800	13,700
Specific assistance to individuals	9,000	1,000	16,100	3,900	30,000	—	—	—	30,000	28,500
Membership dues	234	187	93	93	607	93	—	93	700	677
Awards and grants—to National Headquarters	—	5,500	—	—	5,500	—	—	—	5,500	5,000
Miscellaneous	1,744	843	1,891	4,144	8,622	118	—	118	8,740	5,200
Total before depreciation	184,545	69,267	171,209	62,245	487,266	52,373	13,713	66,086	553,352	487,692
Depreciation of buildings and equipment	968	293	1,322	625	3,208	712	265	977	4,185	4,200
Total expenses	$185,513	$69,560	$172,531	$62,870	$490,474	$53,085	$13,978	$67,063	$557,537	$491,892

Illustration 21–6 presents the required supplemental Statement of Functional Expenses. The amounts shown in Illustration 21–6 are provided for illustrative purposes only and are not determinable from the limited transaction data provided in the illustrative journal entries shown in the preceding section.

Other Not-for-Profit Organizations

The large number and diversity of not-for-profit organizations were mentioned in the introduction to this chapter. It is apparent that accounting and reporting standards cannot comprehend fully the diversity of objectives, size, programs, and methods of operations that exist among these organizations. Therefore, both the AICPA audit guide, *Audits of Certain Nonprofit Organizations* (ACNO), and FASB *Statement No. 117* take the position that similar transactions should generally be reflected in financial statements in a similar manner by all not-for-profit organizations. In consideration of governmental not-for-profit organizations that continue to follow ACNO guidance, as well as nongovernmental not-for-profit organizations pending the effective date of *Statement Nos. 116* and *117* (see Illustration 21–1, note b), the following discussion is based primarily on the AICPA audit guide requirements, with differences in FASB guidance applicable to nongovernmental not-for-profit organizations noted where appropriate.

Fund Accounting and Reporting

Not-for-profit organizations that receive resources subject to donor restrictions generally account for restricted resources separately from unrestricted resources, ordinarily by using fund accounting as described in other chapters of this text. Similarly, to facilitate observance of limitations placed on the use of certain resources by the organization's governing board, funds may be established to account for acquisition and disposition of board-designated funds. Not-for-profit organizations that have no donor-restricted resources or board-designated resources may account for all activities within a single self-balancing set of accounts. If multiple funds are used for internal accounting and reporting purposes, funds that have similar characteristics should be combined for presentation in external general purpose financial reports. Financial statements should disclose all material externally imposed restrictions; resources whose use is limited by the organization's governing board are properly classified in financial statements as "unrestricted." In addition, not-for-profit organizations subject to FASB jurisdiction report separately net assets temporarily restricted by donors and those permanently restricted by donors.

Basic Financial Statements

Because of the diversity of organizations covered by *Audits of Certain Nonprofit Organizations,* specific titles or formats are not prescribed for the basic financial statements. In general, information customarily presented in balance sheets, operating statements, and cash flow statements should be included in financial reports intended for users external to the organization's management group.

Balance Sheets   Organizations that have only unrestricted resources should classify assets and liabilities as "current" and "fixed" or "long term." Current assets are defined as those realizable within one year, or within a normal operating cycle if the cycle is in excess of one year; current liabilities are those payable within one year. Board-designated funds should be reported as unrestricted funds, but it is considered proper to disclose amounts designated by the board for specific purposes.

ACNO standards applicable to governmental not-for-profit organizations require that current restricted resources and resources restricted for future acquisition of land, buildings, and equipment should be reported in the Balance Sheet as deferred revenue until the restrictions are met. FASB *Statement No. 116,* as discussed previously in this chapter, requires nongovernmental not-for-profit organizations to report all unconditional contributions received, including unconditional pledges, as "support" in the period received. Thus, these items are reported in the **Statement of Financial Position** (i.e., balance sheet) of nongovernmental not-for-profit organizations as part of *temporarily restricted net assets,* rather than as deferred revenue. ACNO requires other restricted resources such as endowment funds to be set forth separately in the Fund Equity section of the Balance Sheet. FASB standards require endowment funds to be reported as *permanently restricted net assets.* The nature of all restrictions should be described in the Notes to the Financial Statements.

Classification of Collectible Items.   Certain not-for-profit organizations, particularly museums and libraries, have significant holdings of valuable works of art, historical treasures, historical archives, and similar assets. As is the case under ACNO, FASB *Statement No. 116* provides for note disclosure of such assets rather than reporting them on the balance sheet; however, nonrecognition is permitted only if the donated items are added to collections that meet all of the following conditions (par. 11):

    a. Are held for public exhibition, education, or research in furtherance of public service rather than financial gain.

    b. Are protected, kept unencumbered, cared for, and preserved.

    c. Are subject to an organizational policy that requires the proceeds from sales of collection items to be used to acquire other items for collections.

The apparent intent of the *Statement No. 116* criteria is to permit nonrecognition of contributions of valuable collections *only* if the collection is to be maintained to serve the public interest rather than to achieve financial gain from trading in collectible items.

Statement of Activity   The Statement of Activity is the name given in *Audits of Certain Nonprofit Organizations* to the financial statement that reports the support, revenue, capital or nonexpendable additions, and functional expenses for a fiscal period. Its name and content are quite similar to the *Statement of Activities* required by FASB

Statement No. 117 to be prescribed for nongovernmental not-for-profit organizations. The latter statement, an example of which is shown in Illustration 21–4, reports all changes in unrestricted net assets, temporarily restricted net assets, and permanently restricted net assets. A statement of activity (or activities) is appropriate since no single format meets the needs of all categories of nonprofit organizations. For example, FASB *Statement No. 117* neither requires nor precludes reporting of operating income, although many not-for-profit organizations currently report operating income. Various formats are also permitted for the Statement of Activities, including the three alternative formats shown in *Statement No. 117*—all three of which have been illustrated in this text (see Chapters 19 and 20, and Illustration 21–4 in this chapter).

Donated Services. The criteria for recognition of donated services as contributions and expense presented in *Audits of Certain Nonprofit Organizations* agree with those in *Audits of Voluntary Health and Welfare Organizations,* with one further qualification. Not only must the donated services be (1) a normal part of the efforts of the organization that otherwise would be performed by salaried personnel, (2) under the control of the organization, and (3) have a clearly measurable basis for the amount to be recorded, but, in addition:

> The services of the reporting organization are not principally intended for the benefit of its members. Accordingly, donated and contributed services would not normally be recorded by organizations such as religious communities, professional and trade associations, labor unions, political parties, fraternal organizations, and social and country clubs.[10]

Illustration 21–8, located at the end of this chapter, shows a Statement of Activity for a fictitious performing arts organization. Capital additions, shown as a separate section in that statement, "include gifts, grants, and bequests to endowment, plant, and loan funds restricted either permanently or for a period of time by parties outside the organizations."[11] Capital additions also include investments that must be added to the principal of endowment, plant, and loan funds. It should be noted that Illustration 21–8 shows both the "Excess (deficiency) of support and revenue over expenses before capital additions" and the "Excess (deficiency) of support and revenue over expenses after capital additions." The former is considered an "important indicator of the financial health" of the nonprofit organization of interest to management, members of the governing board, donors, beneficiaries, and other users of the financial statements.[12] The second "Excess" figure is

---

[10] AICPA, *Audits of Certain Nonprofit Organizations*, p. 78. As noted previously, FASB *Statement No. 116* specifies a different—and more restrictive—set of criteria, applicable to nongovernmental not-for-profit organizations. These criteria are listed on page 706 of this chapter.

[11] Ibid., p. 68.

[12] Ibid., p. 69.

needed as an element in the reconciliation of the fund balances of the end of the period with the fund balances as of the beginning of the fiscal period.

Statement of Cash Flows

Audits of Certain Nonprofit Organizations and SOP 78–10 specify that a Statement of Changes in Financial Position should be presented by organizations covered by that audit guide and *SOP.* Guidance provided by ACNO in this instance has been effectively superseded by the Statement of Cash Flows required by FASB *Statement No. 117.* Further, governmental not-for-profit organizations that follow proprietary fund accounting are required to prepare a cash flow statement in the GASB format illustrated in Chapter 20 of this text. An illustrative Statement of Changes in Financial Position is not provided in this chapter since, after the effective date of FASB *Statement No. 117,* the requirement for such a statement has been eliminated.

Accounting for Investments and Investment Income

As a general rule, investments are initially recorded at cost, or in the case of donated investments, at fair value as of the balance sheet date. *Audits of Certain Nonprofit Organizations* permits either lower-of-cost-or-market accounting for marketable securities or market value accounting, even if market value is above original cost, provided the method used is followed consistently.

The concept of *total return,* which is discussed in Chapter 19 in the context of colleges and universities, has also been advocated for use by not-for-profit organizations covered by *Audits of Certain Nonprofit Organizations.* The audit guide, for reasons similar to those discussed in Chapter 19, does not encourage use of the total return concept but does not prohibit it. If an organization uses the total return procedure, any portion of the net gains of endowment investments made available as revenues must be reported in the Statement of Activity as a transfer from endowment funds to the recipient fund(s). To the extent that such gains are transferred to a restricted fund in which unexpended gifts and investment income are reported as deferred support and revenue, the gains should be transferred to deferred revenue. As noted in Chapter 19, FASB *Statement No. 117* does not preclude recognition of both unrealized and realized gains under the total return concept.

Illustrative Transactions

The diversity of organizations covered by the AICPA audit guide, *Audits of Certain Nonprofit Organizations,* precludes showing the range of transactions and financial statements encountered in practice. Illustrative transactions and journal entries are shown here for one example not-for-profit organization, the Sample Performing Arts Organization. It is assumed that Sample Performing Arts Organization follows the standards set forth in ACNO and uses unrestricted funds, a plant fund, and an endowment fund for accounting purposes, but combines the fund groups for financial reporting purposes. Beginning balances for all accounts are given in the following trial balance. The effects of the illustrative transactions are summarized in the financial statements provided in the next section.

SAMPLE PERFORMING ARTS ORGANIZATION
Post-Closing Trial Balance
June 30, 19x0

Account Title	Debits	Credits
Unrestricted Funds:		
Cash	$ 81,858	
Marketable Securities	20,467	
Accounts Receivable	28,685	
Allowance for Doubtful Accounts		$ 2,000
Grants Receivable	6,100	
Inventories	13,441	
Rent and Other Deposits	9,130	
Accounts Payable and Accrued Expenses		166,351
Deferred Revenues—Subscriptions		193,042
Entity Capital—Unrestricted Funds	201,712	
	$361,393	$361,393
Plant Fund:		
Cash	$ 87,608	
Marketable Securities	30,500	
Property and Equipment	51,426	
Accumulated Depreciation—Property and Equipment		$ 11,200
Current Portion of Long-Term Debt		50,000
Long-Term Debt		69,740
Entity Capital—Plant Fund		38,594
	$169,534	$169,534
Endowment Funds:		
Cash	$ 14,340	
Investments	242,308	
Entity Capital—Endowment Funds		$256,648
	$256,648	$256,648
Totals	$787,575	$787,575

Unrestricted Funds

During the year ended June 30, 19x1, Cash was received in the amount of $2,146,386 and accounts receivable increased in the amount of $52,488 from operating revenues (itemized in Entry 1) of Sample Performing Arts Organization. Of those amounts, $2,090,114 is recorded as current period revenues and $108,760 as Deferred Revenues—Subscriptions, a liability account:

1.	Cash	2,146,386	
	Accounts Receivable	52,488	
	Admissions		1,602,504
	Dividends		23,684
	Interest		37,485
	Tuition		279,389
	Concession and Other Support from Operations		147,052
	Deferred Revenues—Subscriptions		108,760

Marketable securities costing $10,200 were sold for $12,840. In addition, a gain of $52,060 realized on sale of Endowment Fund investments was recorded in the Unrestricted Funds per the endowment agreement (see Entry 9). These amounts and an additional $200,000 were reinvested in marketable securities:

2a.	Cash	64,900	
	Marketable Securities		10,200
	Realized Gain on Sale of Marketable Securities		2,640
	Realized Gain on Sale of Endowment Fund Investments		52,060
2b.	Marketable Securities	264,900	
	Cash		264,900

Unrestricted Cash of $985,600 was received from granting agencies in the amount of $750,000 and from a fund-raising activity in the amount of $235,600. Of the $750,000 received from granting agencies, $45,000 is designated by those agencies for use in a future period. In addition to those amounts, $6,100 reported as Grants Receivable at the end of the prior year was received in cash.

3.	Cash	991,700	
	Grants Receivable		6,100
	Grants		705,000
	Annual Giving		235,600
	Deferred Revenues—Grants		45,000

During the year $2,777,683 was paid for current expenses (itemized in Entry 4) and $166,351 was paid for accounts payable and other accrued expenses. In addition, $13,441 of inventories and $9,130 of rent and other deposits were recognized as expense.

4.	Accounts Payable and Accrued Expenses	166,351	
	Salaries, Payroll Taxes, and Employee Benefits	1,696,416	
	Professional Fees	27,712	
	Supplies	69,487	
	Telephone	12,118	
	Postage and Shipping	19,485	
	Occupancy	412,000	
	Rental and Maintenance of Equipment	68,000	
	Printing and Publications	10,800	
	Travel	8,467	
	Conferences, Conventions, and Meetings	2,843	
	Membership Dues	1,079	
	Scenery	196,488	
	Costumes	109,008	
	Cash		2,777,683
	Inventories		13,441
	Rent and Other Deposits		9,130

Supplies were received in the amount of $42,370. In addition, accrued payroll, including related payroll taxes and employee benefits, and accrued professional fees were recorded as liabilities at June 30, 19x1, in the amounts of $64,000 and $9,200, respectively.

5.	Inventories	42,370	
	Salaries, Payroll Taxes, and Employee Benefits	64,000	
	Professional Fees	9,200	
	Accounts Payable and Accrued Expenses		115,570

Prepaid rent on office space was recorded on June 30, 19x1, in the amount of $4,290. (The credit was to ''Occupancy.'')

| 6. | Rent and Other Deposits | 4,290 | |
| | Occupancy | | 4,290 |

Expenses for the period were reclassified in order to report by function. While, in practice, entries for expenses may record both object classes and functions, the classifications shown here accord with authoritative literature:

7.	Production Costs	505,027	
	Operating Expenses	845,274	
	Ballet School	502,030	
	Neighborhood Productions	401,314	
	General and Administrative Expenses	411,749	
	Fund-Raising	37,419	
	Salaries, Payroll Taxes, and Employee Benefits		1,760,416
	Professional Fees		36,912
	Supplies		69,487
	Telephone		12,118
	Postage and Shipping		19,485
	Occupancy		407,710
	Rental and Maintenance of Equipment		68,000
	Printing and Publications		10,800
	Travel		8,467
	Conferences, Conventions, and Meetings		2,843
	Membership Dues		1,079
	Scenery		196,488
	Costumes		109,008

The entry to close the accounts of the Unrestricted Funds would be:

8.	Admissions	1,602,504	
	Dividends	23,684	
	Interest	37,485	
	Tuition	279,389	
	Concessions and Other Support from Operations	147,052	
	Realized Gain on Sale of Marketable Securities	2,640	
	Realized Gain on Sale of Endowment Fund Investments	52,060	
	Annual Giving	235,600	
	Grants	705,000	
	Production Costs		505,027
	Operating Expenses		845,274
	Ballet School		502,030
	Neighborhood Productions		401,314
	General and Administrative Expenses		411,749
	Fund Raising		37,419
	Entity Capital—Unrestricted Funds		382,601

Endowment Funds   During the year, the Endowment Fund received a contribution in the amount of $20,000, which is to be invested and maintained in perpetuity. In addition, investments with a cost of $187,000 were sold for $239,060. Per the agreement with the donor, the $52,060 realized gain was recorded directly in the Unrestricted Funds (see Entry 2a). Cash in the amount of $220,000 was reinvested.

9.	Cash	20,000	
	Capital Additions		20,000
10.	Cash	187,000	
	Investments		187,000
11.	Investments	220,000	
	Cash		220,000

As shown in the Statement of Activity (see Illustration 21–8), "Capital Additions" are reported below the line "Excess from Current Endeavors" since, as discussed previously, the latter amount is considered important in evaluating the organization's financial viability. According to the Audit Guide, Capital Additions include: "Nonexpendable gifts, grants, and bequests restricted by the donor or grants for endowment, plant, or loan purposes, either permanently or for a period of time."[13] Capital Additions also include legally restricted investment income and gains and losses on investments held in such funds that must be added to the principal.

The following entry would be made to close the accounts of the Endowment Funds:

12.	Capital Additions	20,000	
	Entity Capital—Endowment Funds		20,000

Plant Funds

During the year, Sample Performing Arts Organization purchased equipment in the amount of $24,678, paying $9,038 in cash and signing a long-term note for the balance:

13.	Property and Equipment	24,678	
	Cash		9,038
	Long-Term Debt		15,640

The amount reported as "current portion of long-term debt" was paid early in the year. In addition, $30,000 of long-term debt due within the next year was recorded as a current liability.

14.	Current Portion of Long-Term Debt	50,000	
	Cash		50,000
15.	Long-Term Debt	30,000	
	Current Portion of Long-Term Debt		30,000

Depreciation is recorded in the amount of $6,270. Depreciation is allocated to the appropriate functional expense categories, in a manner similar to voluntary

---

[13] Ibid., p. 17.

health and welfare organizations:

16.	Depreciation and Amortization............................	6,270	
	Accumulated Depreciation—Property and Equipment		6,270

17.	Production Costs	1,247	
	Operating Expenses......................................	623	
	Ballet School...	680	
	Neighborhood Productions	340	
	General and Administrative Expenses......................	2,833	
	Fund-Raising..	547	
	Depreciation and Amortization...........................		6,270

The closing entry at year-end would be:

18.	Entity Capital—Plant Funds	6,270	
	Production Costs		1,247
	Operating Expenses......................................		623
	Ballet School...		680
	Neighborhood Productions		340
	General and Administrative Expenses......................		2,833
	Fund Raising...		547

Financial statements summarizing the effects of the foregoing transactions are presented in Illustrations 21–7, 21–8, and 21–9. The Balance Sheet (Illustration 21–7) and Statement of Activity (Illustration 21–8) were discussed earlier in this section. Both are adapted from ACNO and are similar to the aggregated Statement of Financial Position and Statement of Activities required by FASB *Statement No. 117,* examples of which were presented earlier for a VHWO (see Illustrations 21–3 and 21–4). The FASB-required statements focus on net assets and changes in net assets rather than entity capital. The Statement of Changes in Entity Capital shown in Illustration 21–9 is not required by any current reporting standards but is included in the illustrative statements provided in ACNO. Finally, Sample Performing Arts Organization would be required to prepare a Statement of Cash Flows. A cash flow statement for this organization would be quite similar to that shown in Illustration 21–5 for a VHWO. Thus, for the sake of brevity, it is not illustrated here.

Financially Interrelated Organizations

GASB standards for defining the governmental reporting entity, and for determining whether a potential component unit should be included in the reporting entity, are set forth in Chapter 13. Colleges and universities, hospitals, voluntary health and welfare organizations, and "other" not-for-profit organizations all may be "financially interrelated with," or "have control over," a fund-raising foundation or other entities. Until the GASB and the FASB set financial reporting standards for all these categories of not-for-profit organizations, the guidance found in AICPA audit guides and statements of position continues to be considered authoritative. Guidance provided in *Audits of Certain Nonprofit Organizations* is representative of that provided in other audit guides and SOPs referred to in Chapters

ILLUSTRATION 21–7

SAMPLE PERFORMING ARTS ORGANIZATION
Balance Sheet
June 30, 19x1, and 19x0

	19x1	19x0
Assets		
Current Assets:		
Cash	$ 270,831	$169,466
Marketable securities	305,667	50,967
Accounts receivable (net of allowance for doubtful accounts)	79,173	26,685
Grants receivable	—	6,100
Inventories	42,370	13,441
Total Current Assets	698,041	266,659
Noncurrent Assets:		
Investments and endowment funds cash	276,648	256,648
Property and equipment at cost (net of accumulated depreciation, $11,200 in 19x0 and $17,470 in 19x1)	58,634	40,226
Rent and other deposits	4,290	9,130
	$1,037,613	$572,663
Liabilities and Entity Capital		
Current Liabilities:		
Accounts payable and accrued expenses	$ 115,570	$166,351
Deferred revenues—subscriptions	301,802	193,042
Deferred revenues—grants	45,000	—
Current portion of long-term debt	30,000	50,000
Total Current Liabilities	492,372	409,393
Long-term debt	55,380	69,740
Entity Capital:		
Plant fund	32,324	38,594
Endowment funds	276,648	256,648
Unrestricted funds	180,889	(201,712)
	$1,037,613	$572,663

SOURCE: Adapted from AICPA, *Audits of Certain Nonprofit Organizations,* p. 132. Copyright © 1981 by the American Institute of Certified Public Accountants, Inc.

19 and 20 and earlier in this chapter. In essence, if a reporting organization controls another organization having a compatible purpose, combined financial statements are usually necessary for a fair presentation in conformity with generally accepted accounting principles. "*Control* means the direct or indirect ability to determine the direction of the management and policies through ownership, by contract, or otherwise."[14] In the case of financially interrelated not-for-profit organizations, combined financial statements would be presented when control

---

[14] AICPA, *Audits of Certain Nonprofit Organizations,* p. 71.

ILLUSTRATION 21–8

SAMPLE PERFORMING ARTS ORGANIZATION
Statement of Activity
Years Ended June 30, 19x1, and 19x0

	19x1	19x0
Revenues and Support from Operations:		
Admissions	$1,602,504	$1,287,564
Dividends and interest	61,169	2,430
Net realized gains and losses	54,700	18,300
Tuition	279,389	130,723
Concessions and other support	147,052	68,754
	2,144,814	1,507,771
Expenses:		
Production costs	506,274	427,754
Operating expenses	845,897	685,522
Ballet school	502,710	301,722
Neighborhood productions	401,654	81,326
General and administrative expense	414,582	469,891
	2,671,117	1,966,215
Deficiency from operations	(526,303)	(458,444)
Donated services, materials, and facilities	—	8,000
Annual giving	235,600	78,469
Grants	705,000	678,322
Fund-raising costs	(37,966)	(50,454)
	902,634	714,337
Excess from current endeavors	376,331	255,893
Capital additions	20,000	18,250
Total increase in entity capital	$ 396,331	$ 274,143

SOURCE: Adapted from AICPA, *Audits of Certain Nonprofit Organizations*, p. 133. Copyright © 1981 by the American Institute of Certified Public Accountants, Inc.

ILLUSTRATION 21–9

SAMPLE PERFORMING ARTS ORGANIZATION
Statement of Changes in Entity Capital
Years Ended June 30, 19x1, and 19x0

	Endowment Funds	Plant Fund	Unrestricted Funds	Total
Entity capital—June 30, 19x0	$256,648	$38,594	$(201,712)	$ 93,530
Excess from current endeavors	—	(6,270)	382,601	376,331
Capital additions	20,000	—	—	20,000
Entity capital—June 30, 19x1	$276,648	$32,324	$180,889	$489,861

SOURCE: Adapted from AICPA, *Audits of Certain Nonprofit Organizations*, p. 134. Copyright © 1981 by the American Institute of Certified Public Accountants, Inc.

exists and when *any* of the following circumstances exist:

> *a.* Separate entities solicit funds in the name of and with the expressed or implicit approval of the reporting organization, and substantially all of the funds solicited are intended by the contributor or are otherwise required to be transferred to the reporting organization or used at its discretion or direction.
> *b.* A reporting organization transfers some of its resources to another separate entity whose resources are held for the benefit of the reporting organization.
> *c.* A reporting organization assigns functions to a controlled entity whose funding is primarily derived from sources other than public contributions.[15]

If financial statements of two or more nonprofit organizations are combined, notes to the statements should disclose the basis for combination and the interrelationship of the combined organizations. The criteria for combination should not be interpreted so broadly that financial statements of organizations only loosely affiliated are combined. For example, if a national or international nonprofit organization has local organizations that determine their own program activities, are financially independent, and control their own assets, combined financial statements are not required. If affiliated organizations do not meet the combining criteria, the existence of affiliates and their relationships to the reporting organization should be disclosed in Notes to the Financial Statements.

FASB and GASB standards require disclosure of related party transactions. *Audits of Certain Nonprofit Organizations* provides the interpretation that contributions made to an organization by its governing board members, officers, or employees need not be disclosed if the contributors do not receive a reciprocal economic benefit in consideration for the contribution.[16] Reasonable amounts of salaries, wages, employee benefits, and reimbursement of expenses incurred in connection with a contributor's duties are not considered reciprocal benefits.

Funds Held in Trust by Others.   Funds held in trust by others under a legal trust instrument created by a donor to generate income for a nonprofit organization should not be included in the balance sheet of the nonprofit organization if it has no control over the actions of the trustee, and if the organization is not the remainderman under the trust. The existence of the trust may be disclosed either parenthetically in the endowment fund section of the balance sheet, or in Notes to the Financial Statements. Income from such trusts should be reported separately in the Statement of Activity, if the amount of the income is significant.

Selected References

American Institute of Certified Public Accountants. *Audits of Voluntary Health and Welfare Organizations*. New York, 1974.
_____. *Audits of Certain Nonprofit Organizations, including Statement of Position 78-10*. New York, 1981.

---

[15] Ibid., p. 72.
[16] Ibid., p. 73.

Financial Accounting Standards Board. *Statement of Financial Accounting Standards No. 93,* "Recognition of Depreciation by Not-for-Profit Organizations." Norwalk, Conn., 1987.

————. *Statement of Financial Accounting Standards No. 116,* "Accounting for Contributions Received and Made." Norwalk, Conn., 1993.

————. *Statement of Financial Accounting Standards No. 117,* "Financial Statements of Not-for-Profit Organizations." Norwalk, Conn., 1993.

Gross, Malvern J.; William Warshauer, Jr.; and Richard F. Larkin. *Financial and Accounting Guide for Not-for-Profit Organizations.* 4th ed. New York: John Wiley & Sons, 1991.

National Assembly of National Voluntary Health and Social Welfare Organizations, Inc.; National Health Council, Inc.; and United Way of America. *Standards of Accounting and Financial Reporting for Voluntary Health and Welfare Organizations.* 3rd ed. Alexandria, Va., 1988.

United Way of America. *Accounting & Financial Reporting: A Guide for United Ways and Not-for-Profit Human Service Organizations.* Alexandria, Va., 1989.

Questions

21-1. If the administrator of a local voluntary health organization wishes to make sure the financial statements of the organization are in accord with generally accepted accounting principles, to what sources of information would you direct her?

21-2. What categories of funds are recommended for use by voluntary health and welfare organizations? Are these categories similar to ones recommended for use by any other kinds of nonprofit organizations? Explain the reasons for your answer.

21-3. Distinguish between "Public Support" and "Revenue."

21-4. Health and welfare organizations typically rely heavily on the efforts of volunteer workers. Under what conditions should donated services be recognized in the financial statements as contributions and as expenses, assuming the organization is subject to FASB jurisdiction?

21-5. Distinguish between *program services* and *supporting services* as the terms are used in financial reports recommended for use by voluntary health and welfare organizations.

21-6. Why is a Statement of Functional Expenses considered an important financial statement for a voluntary health or welfare organization? How does a Statement of Functional Expenses relate to a Statement of Activities?

21-7. "The financial statements required for voluntary health and welfare organizations are (1) a Balance Sheet, (2) a Statement of Revenue and Expenses and Changes in Fund Balance, (3) a Statement of Functional Expenses, and (4) a Statement of Cash Flows." Do you agree or disagree? Explain.

21-8. "Responsibility for setting financial reporting standards for not-for-profit organizations is vested in the FASB." Do you agree or disagree? Explain.

21-9. "All not-for-profit organizations must use fund accounting to account for their activities." Do you agree or disagree? Why?

21-10. A privately endowed museum reports all investments at market, even if market is in excess of cost. As an independent CPA, would you be required to take exception to this practice?

21–11. Explain how FASB standards on recognition of contributions on which the donor has imposed time or use restrictions differ from those of the AICPA audit guides for voluntary health and welfare organizations and other not-for-profit organizations.

21–12. What financial statements must a not-for-profit performing arts association prepare if it is (*a*) a nongovernmental organization and (*b*) a governmental organization?

21–13. Explain the essential differences between (*a*) a statement of activity prepared in conformity with the AICPA's *Audits of Certain Nonprofit Organizations* (ACNO) and (*b*) a statement of activities prepared in conformity with FASB *Statement No. 117*.

Exercises and Problems

21–1. Write the numbers 1 through 10 on a sheet of paper. Beside each number, write the letter corresponding with the best answer to each of the following questions:

1. In a Statement of Activities of a voluntary health and welfare organization, depreciation expense should:
   a. Not be included.
   b. Be included as an element of support.
   c. Be included as an element of changes in fund balances.
   d. Be included as an element of expense.
2. Which of the following funds of a voluntary health and welfare organization does *not* have a counterpart *fund* in governmental accounting?
   a. Current Unrestricted.
   b. Land, Building, and Equipment.
   c. Custodian.
   d. Endowment.
3. Securities donated to voluntary health and welfare organizations should be recorded:
   a. At the donor's recorded amount.
   b. At fair market value at the date of the gift.
   c. At fair market value at the date of the gift, or the donor's recorded amount, whichever is lower.
   d. At fair market value at the date of the gift, or the donor's recorded amount, whichever is higher.
4. Fixed assets of a voluntary health and welfare organization should be reported:
   a. At historical cost.
   b. At historical cost less accumulated depreciation.
   c. At market value, even if market exceeds cost.
   d. Any of the above is permissible.

Items 5 and 6 are based on the following information pertaining to the sale of equipment by Nous Foundation, a voluntary health and welfare organization:

Sales Price	$12,000
Cost	14,000
Carrying amount	10,000

Nous made the correct entry to record the $2,000 gain on sale.

5. The additional entry that Nous should record in connection with this sale is:

	Debits	*Credits*
a.	Fund Balance—Expended	Fund Balance—Unexpended
b.	Fund Balance—Unexpended	Fund Balance—Expended
c.	Excess Revenues Control	Gain on Sale of Equipment
d.	Current Unrestricted Funds	Fund Balance—Undesignated

6. The amount that should be debited and credited for the additional entry in connection with this sale is:
   a. $ 2,000.
   b. $10,000.
   c. $12,000.
   d. $14,000.

Items 7 and 8 are based on the following information:
Expenditures incurred by a not-for-profit botanical society during 19x7 were as follows:

Printing of annual report	$10,000
Unsolicited merchandise sent to encourage contributions	$20,000

7. What amount should be classified as Fund-Raising Costs in the Society's Statement of Activity?
   a. $0.
   b. $10,000.
   c. $20,000.
   d. $30,000.

8. What amount should be classified as Supporting Services in the society's Statement of Activity?
   a. $0.
   b. $10,000.
   c. $20,000.
   d. $30,000.

9. Not-for-profit organizations covered by *Audits of Certain Nonprofit Organizations* may report their investments in marketable securities:
   a. At lower of cost or market value as of the balance sheet date.
   b. At cost as of the balance sheet date, regardless of market value.
   c. At market value as of the balance sheet date, regardless of cost.
   d. Either a or c is permissible.

10. Funds held in trust by others under a legal trust instrument created by a donor to generate income for a not-for-profit organization, and over which the not-for-profit organization has no control, should be:
    a. Included with the amounts reported in the Balance Sheet of the not-for-profit organization.
    b. Excluded from the amounts reported in the Balance Sheet of the not-for-profit organization.
    c. Disclosed either parenthetically in the endowment fund section of the Balance Sheet or in the Notes to the Financial Statements.
    d. Both b and c are correct.

(Items 1–3, 5–8, and 10, AICPA, adapted)

21–2. The characteristics of voluntary health and welfare organizations differ in certain respects from the characteristics of state or local governmental units. As an example, voluntary health and welfare organizations derive their revenues primarily from voluntary contributions from the general public, while governmental units derive their revenues from taxes and services provided to their jurisdictions.

Required

a. Describe fund accounting and discuss whether its use is consistent with the concept that an accounting entity is an economic unit that has control over resources, accepts responsibilities for making and carrying out commitments, and conducts economic activity.

b. Distinguish between accrual accounting as it should be applied to the recognition of revenues of a voluntary health and welfare organization and accrual accounting as it is applied to the recognition of governmental fund revenues.

c. Discuss how methods used to account for fixed assets differ between voluntary health and welfare organizations and governmental units.

(AICPA, adapted)

21–3. Listed below are four independent transactions or events that relate to a local government and to a voluntary health and welfare organization:

1. $25,000 was disbursed from the General Fund (or its equivalent) for the cash purchase of new equipment.
2. An unrestricted cash gift of $100,000 was received from a donor.
3. Listed common stocks with a total carrying value of $50,000, exclusive of any allowance, were sold by an endowment fund for $55,000, before any dividends were earned on these stocks. There are no restrictions on the gain.
4. $1,000,000 face amount of general obligation bonds payable were sold at par, with the proceeds required to be used solely for construction of a new building. This building was completed at a total cost of $1,000,000, and the total amount of bond issue proceeds was disbursed in connection therewith. Disregard interest capitalization.

Required

a. For each of the above-listed transactions or events, prepare journal entries, without explanations, specifying the affected funds and account groups, and showing how these transactions or events should be recorded by a local government whose debt is serviced by general tax revenues.

b. For each of the above-listed transactions or events, prepare journal entries, without explanations, specifying the affected funds, and showing how these transactions or events should be recorded by a voluntary health and welfare organization that maintains a separate plant fund.

(AICPA, adapted)

21–4. The Rural Human Services Association had the following expenses for the year ended September 30, 19x5.

Salaries and fringe benefits	$ 850,000
Professional fees and contract services	50,000
Supplies	38,000
Telephone	40,000
Postage and shipping	75,000
Occupancy costs	100,000
Travel and meetings	80,000
Printing and publications	100,000
Depreciation of buildings and equipment	17,000
Total expenses	$1,350,000

Required

a. The programs offered by this Association during that year were Counseling, Outreach, Meals, and Public Education. Supporting services were Management and General, and Fund-Raising. The governing board wants to know the cost of each program service and each supporting service for the year. After discussion with persons engaged in offering each service, and perusal of records of the Association, you determine that the following distribution would be reasonably realistic. Prepare a statement of functional expenses for the year.

	Program Services				Supporting Services	
	Counseling	*Outreach*	*Meals*	*Public Education*	*Management and General*	*Fund-Raising*
Salaries and fringes	20%	16%	3%	19%	22%	20%
Professional fees, etc.	10	10	20	20	10	30
Supplies	10	15	5	25	25	20
Telephone	10	20	5	20	15	30
Postage and shipping	5	23	15	15	7	35
Occupancy costs	20	10	10	20	20	20
Travel and meetings	25	10	15	15	25	10
Printing and publications	15	5	2	33	20	25
Depreciation	33	15	5	15	20	12

b. If the Rural Human Services Association approached you as a potential contributor, and presented the statement prepared as the solution to part *a* of this problem as evidence of its merit for your contribution, what would be your reaction and why?

21–5. Helping Hand Agency of America, Inc., was incorporated as a nongovernmental not-for-profit voluntary health and welfare organization on July 1, 19x3. During the fiscal year ended June 30, 19x4, the following transactions occurred:

1. A public-spirited citizen donated rent-free office space to the organization that would normally rent for $400 per month.
2. An administrator was hired to administer the program services and support services of the organization. The administrator is to be paid $50,000 for the year. Fringe benefits amount to 10 percent of the salary. The salary and the fringes are recorded as liabilities.
3. A fund drive raised $94,000 in cash and pledges of $196,000. Of the cash received, $10,000 was restricted by a donor for future construction of a building for the organization. This donor pledged to contribute $100,000 for this purpose, which was included in the $196,000 total pledges.
4. Furniture and office equipment were purchased for $3,000 in cash. The useful life of these items is estimated at 10 years.
5. Supplies were purchased on open account in the amount of $9,000. A periodic inventory at year-end showed supplies of $1,000 still on hand.
6. Pledges of $91,000 were collected in cash. Of this amount, $49,000 was from the pledge for future building construction. It was estimated that $9,000 of unrestricted pledges will not be collected.
7. All cash collected for future building construction was invested in low risk mutual funds.
8. Telephone and utilities expense for the year amounted to $5,200; $5,000 of this amount was paid in cash, and the remainder is recorded as a liability.

9. Postage and shipping expenses for the year amounted to $1,000, all paid in cash.
10. Printing and publications expense for the year totaled $15,000. This amount was paid in cash.
11. Liabilities for salaries and fringe benefits amounting to $55,000 and accounts payable in the amount of $8,000 were paid in cash. Part-time professional and clerical help received during the year amounted to $30,000; half of this amount was paid in cash, and the remainder was considered donated services in accord with agreements with the part-time volunteers.
12. Salaries, wages, and fringe benefits were allocated to program services and supporting services in the following percentages: public health education, 20 percent; professional education and training, 30 percent; community services, 10 percent; management and general, 15 percent; and fund-raising, 25 percent. All other expenses were allocated in the following percentages: public health education, 15 percent; professional education and training, 20 percent; community services, 10 percent; management and general, 35 percent; and fund-raising, 20 percent.
13. Income from mutual fund investments amounted to $2,100 during the year. This amount was added to the investment account balance.
14. Depreciation expense was recorded for a full year on the assets purchased in item 4. This expense was allocated to program services and supporting services in the same proportions shown in item 12 for all other expenses, except salaries, wages, and fringe benefits.
15. Nominal accounts for the year were closed to Fund Balance accounts.

Required

a. Record entries in general journal form in *all* funds affected by the preceding transactions for the year ended June 30, 19x4, assuming Helping Hand Agency uses fund accounting for internal management purposes.
b. Prepare a Statement of Financial Position, Statement of Activities, Statement of Cash Flows, and a Statement of Functional Expenses for Helping Hand Agency of America, Inc. as of and for the year ended June 30, 19x4.

21–6. The Professional Persons Association of Middleton is a not-for-profit organization subject to the provisions of *Audits of Certain Nonprofit Organizations*. The dues for members are $50 per year; the fiscal year ends on August 31. Prior to September 1, 19x0, 410 members had paid their dues for the year ended August 31, 19x1. Prior to September 1, 19x1, 457 members had paid their dues for the year ended August 31, 19x2; one of these died suddenly on August 30, 19x1, and the governing board decided to return his check to his widow. During the fiscal year ended on August 31, 19x1, 36 other members died; 15 members were dropped for nonpayment of dues; and one member was expelled—no dues refunds were made to the estates of the 36 decedents; a $25 refund was made to the person expelled. Offsetting these membership decreases, 123 new members joined in fiscal 19x1; membership as of September 1, 19x0, had been 2,980 persons. Members admitted during a year are charged dues for the full year.

The Association has reported membership dues revenue on the cash basis in prior years. You bring to the attention of the governing board the requirement that financial statements should be on the accrual basis, unless cash basis statements are not materially different. Since you are so knowledgeable, the board asks you to compute membership dues revenue for fiscal 19x1 on both the cash basis and on the accrual basis and to report to them the amount on each basis *and* your conclusion as to whether the difference between the two is material.

(AICPA, adapted)

21–7. A group of civic-minded merchants in Albury City organized the "Committee of 100" for the purpose of establishing the Community Sports Club, a not-for-profit sports organization for local youth. Each of the Committee's 100 members contributed $1,000 toward the Club's capital and in turn received a participation certificate. In addition, each participant agreed to pay dues of $200 a year for the Club's operations. All dues have been collected in full by the end of each fiscal year ending March 31. Members who have discontinued their participation have been replaced by an equal number of new members through transfer of the participation certificates from the former members to the new ones. Following is the Club's trial balance at April 1, 19x2:

	Debits	*Credits*
Cash	$ 9,000	
Investments (at market equal to cost)	58,000	
Inventories	5,000	
Land	10,000	
Building	164,000	
Accumulated Depreciation—Building		$130,000
Furniture and Equipment	54,000	
Accumulated Depreciation—Furniture and Equipment		46,000
Accounts Payable		12,000
Participation Certificates (100 at $1,000 each)		100,000
Cumulative Excess of Revenue over Expenses		12,000
	$300,000	$300,000

Transactions for the year ended March 31, 19x3, were as follows:

(1) Collections from participants for dues	$20,000
(2) Snack bar and soda fountain sales	28,000
(3) Interest and dividends received	6,000
(4) Additions to voucher register:	
House expenses	17,000
Snack bar and soda fountain	26,000
General and administrative	11,000
(5) Vouchers paid	55,000
(6) Assessments for capital improvements not yet incurred (assessed on March 20, 19x3; none collected by March 31, 19x3; deemed 100% collectible during year ending March 31, 19x4)	10,000
(7) Unrestricted bequest received	5,000

Adjustment data:

(1) Investments are valued at market, which amounted to $65,000 at March 31, 19x3. There were no investment transactions during the year.

(2) Depreciation for the year:	
Building	$ 4,000
Furniture and equipment	8,000
(3) Allocation of depreciation:	
House expenses	9,000
Snack bar and soda fountain	2,000
General and administrative	1,000

(4) Actual physical inventory at March 31, 19x3, was $1,000, and pertains to the snack bar and soda fountain.

Required On a functional basis:

    a. Record the transactions and adjustments in journal entry form for the year ended March 31, 19x3. Omit explanations.

    b. Prepare the activity statement illustrated in ACNO for the year ended March 31, 19x3.

(AICPA, adapted)

21–8. The University City Art League, Inc., is a governmentally affiliated not-for-profit organization dedicated to promotion of the arts within the community. The Art League conducts two programs: (1) Exhibition and sales of members' art (referred to as "Exhibition") and (2) Community Art Education. Activities of the Art League are administered by a full-time administrator, assisted by a secretary-bookkeeper, and several part-time volunteer receptionists. The volunteer receptionists greet visitors, monitor the security of the exhibit hall, and conduct sales of art to the public. Art on exhibit is considered the property of the member artists, not the Art League.

The post-closing trial balance for the University City Art League as of June 30, 19x3, the end of its fiscal year, is shown below.

UNIVERSITY CITY ART LEAGUE, INC.
Post-Closing Trial Balance
As of June 30, 19x3

Account Title

	Debits	*Credits*
Unrestricted Funds:		
Cash	$ 2,655	
Investments—Short-Term	9,462	
Grants Receivable	4,600	
Prepaid Expenses	1,060	
Accounts Payable		$ 1,893
Accrued Expenses		756
Deferred Revenues-Grants		2,800
Entity Capital		12,328
	$17,777	$17,777
Plant Fund:		
Cash	$ 164	
Investments—Long-Term	12,649	
Equipment	9,345	
Accumulated Depreciation—Equipment		$ 2,426
Long-Term Notes Payable		2,000
Entity Capital		17,732
	$22,158	$22,158
Endowment Fund:		
Cash	$ 1,196	
Investments—Long-Term	4,767	
Entity Capital		$ 5,963
	$ 5,963	$ 5,963
Totals	$45,898	$45,898

Following is information summarizing the transactions of the University City Art League, Inc., for the year ended June 30, 19x4.

1. During the year unrestricted cash was received from the following sources: grants, $11,600, of which $4,600 had been reported as receivable on June 30, 19x3; annual giving from fund drives and other unrestricted gifts, $13,861; membership dues, $16,285; sales of members' art, $12,010, of which 20 percent, or $2,402, represents commissions earned by the Art League; tuition and fees for educational courses and workshops, $6,974; and interest on unrestricted investments, $686. Grants reported as deferred revenue at the end of the previous year were reclassified as revenue of the current period. Grants receivable as of June 30, 19x4 totaled $5,020, of which $3,120 was recognized as current year revenue and $1,900 was reported as deferred revenue.

2. Investment earnings were received in cash in the amounts of $925 on plant fund investments and $344 on endowment fund investments. (These investment earnings are restricted as to use. Thus, "Capital Additions" should be credited in the Plant Fund and the Endowment Fund, respectively.)

3. Expenses incurred for activities of the unrestricted fund during the year were as follows: salaries and fringe benefits, $36,300; occupancy, $9,600; utilities, $2,680; postage and supplies, $2,313; and miscellaneous, $1,037. Included in miscellaneous was interest expense of $160 which was paid in cash during the year. As of June 30, 19x4, the balances of the following balance sheet accounts were: Prepaid Expenses, $970; Accounts Payable, $2,019; and Accrued Expenses, $727.

4. During the year $2,900 of matured CDs were sold from plant fund investments to purchase a new computer. The computer was purchased at a cost of $2,835.

5. In accordance with the terms of the Art League endowment, endowment fund cash in the amount of $825 was used to provide free art instruction for handicapped children. This amount was allocated $500 to Community Art Education and $325 to General and Administrative Expenses.

6. Unrestricted funds expenses for the year were allocated 20 percent to the Exhibition Program, 25 percent to the Community Art Education Program, 30 percent to General and Administrative Expenses, and 25 percent to Fund-Raising. (Round all amounts to the nearest whole dollar.)

7. Depreciation on equipment in the amount of $1,642 was recorded in the plant fund. This amount was allocated to programs, General and Administrative Expenses, and Fund-Raising in the same proportions as in item 6 above. (Round all amounts to the nearest whole dollar.)

8. $9,608, representing the proceeds of art sales, net of commissions, charged by the Art League, was paid to member artists during the year.

9. In order to prepare financial statements as of year-end, all temporary accounts were closed.

Required

    a. Prepare in general journal form all required journal entries to record the transactions summarized above for the year ending June 30, 19x4. Indicate clearly in which fund group each entry is being made.

    b. Prepare a Balance Sheet for University City Art League, Inc., as of June 30, 19x4, and a Statement of Activity for the year then ended, assuming all fund groups are combined for financial reporting purposes in the manner shown in Illustrations 21–7 and 21–8. Assume also that the Art League follows the AICPA's *Audits of Certain Nonprofit Organizations*.

    c. On the advice of their independent auditor, the Art League does not include support and expenses related to the value of services donated by their volunteer receptionists. Discuss the criteria for recognition of donated services and comment on the auditor's likely rationale for not recognizing them in this specific case.

21–9. Based on the post-closing trial balance provided in Problem 21–8 for University City Art League, Inc. as of June 30, 19x3 and its summarized transactions for the year ended June 30, 19x4, and assuming it is a *nongovernmental* not-for-profit organization:

    a. Prepare a Statement of Financial Position in the FASB *Statement No. 117* format shown in Illustration 21–3.

    b. Prepare a Statement of Activities in the FASB *Statement No. 117* format shown in Illustration 21–4.

    c. Prepare a Statement of Cash Flows in the FASB *Statement No. 117* format shown in Illustration 21–5.

APPENDIX 1 Governmental and Not-for-Profit Accounting Terminology*

Abatement A complete or partial cancellation of a levy imposed by a governmental unit. Abatements usually apply to tax levies, special assessments, and service charges.

ABC See Activity-Based Costing.

Account Group A self-balancing set of accounts, but not a fiscal entity; therefore not a *fund*. See General Fixed Assets Account Group, and General Long-Term Debt Account Group.

Accountability Being obliged to explain one's actions, to justify what one does; the requirement for government to answer to its citizenry—to justify the raising of public resources and expenditure of those resources. Also, in the GASB's view, includes the obligation to report whether the government operated within appropriate legal constraints; whether resources were used efficiently, economically, and effectively; whether current-year revenues were sufficient to pay for the services provided in the current year; and whether the burden for services previously provided will be shifted to future taxpayers.

Accounting Period A period at the end of which, and for which, financial statements are prepared. See also Fiscal Period.

Accounting System The total structure of records and procedures that discover, record, classify, and report information on the financial position and operations of a governmental unit or any of its funds, balanced account groups, and organizational components.

Accounts Receivable Amounts owing on open account from private persons, firms, or corporations for goods and services furnished by a governmental unit (but not including amounts due from other funds of the same governmental unit).

Note Although taxes and assessments receivable are covered by this term, they should each be recorded and reported separately in *Taxes Receivable* and *Special Assessments Receivable* accounts. Similarly, amounts due from other funds or from other governmental units should be reported separately.

Accrual Basis The basis of accounting under which revenues are recorded when earned and expenditures (or expenses) are recorded as soon as they result in liabilities for benefits received, notwithstanding that the receipt of cash or the payment of cash may take place, in whole or in part, in another accounting period. See also Accrue and Levy.

Accrue To record revenues when earned and to record expenditures (or expenses) as soon as they result in liabilities for benefits received, notwithstanding that the receipt of cash or payment of cash may take place, in whole or in part, in another accounting period. See also Accrual Basis, Accrued Expenses, and Accrued Revenue.

Accrued Expenses Expenses incurred during the current accounting period but not payable until a subsequent accounting period. See also Accrual Basis and Accrue.

Accrued Income See Accrued Revenue.

---

* Some of the definitions in this appendix were taken by permission from publications of the Government Finance Officers Association (formerly Municipal Finance Officers Association). Others were taken from specialized publications cited in the text; the remainder were supplied by the authors.

Accrued Interest on Investments Purchased Interest accrued on investments between the last interest payment date and the date of purchase.

Accrued Interest Payable A liability account that represents the amount of interest expense accrued at the balance sheet date but not due until a later date.

Accrued Revenue Revenue earned during the current accounting period but not to be collected until a subsequent accounting period. See also Accrual Basis and Accrue.

Accrued Taxes Payable A liability for taxes that have accrued since the last payment date.

Accrued Wages Payable A liability for wages earned by employees between the last payment date and the balance sheet date.

Accumulated Depreciation See Allowance for Depreciation.

Acquisition Adjustment Difference between amount paid by a utility for plant assets acquired from another utility and the original cost (q.v.)[1] of those assets less depreciation to date of acquisition. Similar to goodwill in nonmonopolistic enterprises.

Activity A specific and distinguishable line of work performed by one or more organizational components of a governmental unit for the purpose of accomplishing a function for which the governmental unit is responsible. For example, "Food Inspection" is an activity performed in the discharge of the "Health" function. See also Function, Subfunction, and Subactivity.

Activity-Based Costing A cost accounting system that identifies specific factors (cost drivers) that drive the costs of service or production activities, and tracks the consumption of cost drivers in producing outputs of goods or services. See also Cost Determination.

Activity Classification A grouping of expenditures on the basis of specific lines of work performed by organization units. For example, sewage treatment and disposal, solid waste collection, solid waste disposal, and street cleaning are activities performed in carrying out the function of sanitation, and the segregation of the expenditures made for each of these activities constitutes an activity classification.

Actuarial Basis A basis used in computing the amount of contributions to be made periodically to a fund so that the total contributions plus the compounded earnings thereon will equal the required payments to be made out of the fund. The factors taken into account in arriving at the amount of these contributions include the length of time over which each contribution is to be held and the rate of return compounded on such contribution over its life. A trust fund for a public employee retirement system is an example of a fund set up on an actuarial basis.

Ad Valorem In proportion to value. A basis for levy of taxes on property.

Advance Refunding The issuance of debt instruments to refund existing debt before the existing debt matures or is callable.

Agency Fund A fund consisting of resources received and held by the governmental unit as an agent for others; for example, taxes collected and held by a municipality for a school district.

Note Sometimes resources held by one fund of a governmental unit for other funds of the unit are handled through an agency fund known as "pass-through agency fund." An example would be taxes held by an agency fund for redistribution among other funds. See also Allocation.

Allocate To divide a lump-sum appropriation into parts that are designated for expenditure by specific organization units and/or for specific purposes, activities, or objects. See also Allocation.

Allocation A part of a lump-sum appropriation that is designated for expenditure by specific organization units and/or for special purposes, activities, or objects. In federal usage, a transfer of obligational authority from one agency to another. See also Allocate.

Allot To divide an appropriation into amounts that may be encumbered or expended during an allotment period. See also Allotment and Allotment Period.

Allotment A part of an appropriation (or, in federal usage, parts of an apportionment) that may be encumbered (obligated) or expended during an allotment period. See also Allot and Allotment Period.

Allotment Period A period of time less than one fiscal year in length during which an allotment is effective. Bimonthly and quarterly allotment periods are most common. See also Allot and Allotment.

Allotments Available for Commitment/Obligation The portion of a federal agency's allotments not yet obligated by issuance of purchase orders, contracts, or other evidence of commitment.

Allowance for Amortization The account in which are accumulated the amounts recorded as amortization of the intangible asset to which the allowance relates.

Allowance for Depreciation The account in which are accumulated the amounts of cost of the related asset that have been charged to expense.

---

[1] The letters "q.v." signify "which see."

Amortization (1) Gradual reduction, redemption, or liquidation of the balance of an account according to a specified schedule of times and amounts. (2) Provision for the extinguishment of a debt by means of a Debt Service Fund (q.v.).

Annuities Payable A liability account that records the amount of annuities due and payable to retired employees in a public employee retirement system.

Annuity A series of equal money payments made at equal intervals during a designated period of time. In governmental accounting, the most frequent annuities are accumulations of debt service funds for term bonds and payments to retired employees or their beneficiaries under public employee retirement systems.

Annuity, Amount of The total amount of money accumulated or paid during an annuity period from an annuity and compound interest at a designated rate.

Annuity Funds Funds established to account for assets given to an organization subject to an agreement that binds the organization to pay stipulated amounts periodically to the donor(s).

Annuity Period The designated length of time during which an amount of annuity is accumulated or paid.

Apportionment A distribution made of a federal appropriation by the Office of Management and Budget into amounts available for specified time periods, etc.

Appropriated Capital The equity of a federal agency provided by an appropriation which has not yet been expended.

Appropriated Capital Used An account used in federal government accounting to indicate resources provided by current or prior period appropriations that were consumed during the current fiscal period.

Appropriation An authorization granted by a legislative body to incur liabilities for purposes specified in the appropriation act (q.v.).

Note An appropriation is usually limited in amount and as to the time when it may be expended. See, however, Indeterminate Appropriation.

Appropriation Act, Bill, Ordinance, Resolution, or Order A legal action giving the administration of a governmental unit authorization to incur on behalf of the unit liabilities for the acquisition of goods, services, or facilities to be used for purposes specified in the act, ordinance, etc., in amounts not to exceed those specified for each purpose. The authorization usually expires at the end of a specified term, most often one year.

Appropriations Budget Appropriations requested by departments or by the central administration of a governmental unit for a budget period. When the Appropriations budget has been adopted in accord with procedures specified by relevant law, the budget becomes legally binding on the administration of the governmental unit for which the budget has been adopted.

Appropriation Expenditure See Expenditures.

Assess To value property officially for the purpose of taxation.

Note The term is also sometimes used to denote the levy of taxes, but such usage is not correct because it fails to distinguish between the valuation process and the tax levy process.

Assessed Valuation A valuation set on real estate or other property by a government as a basis for levying taxes.

Assessment (1) The process of making the official valuation of property for purposes of taxation. (2) The valuation placed on property as a result of this process.

Assets Probable future economic benefits obtained or controlled by a particular entity as a result of past transactions or events.

Audit The examination of documents, records, reports, systems of internal control, accounting and financial procedures, and other evidence for one or more of the following purposes:

a. To determine whether the financial statements, or other financial reports and related items, are fairly presented in accordance with generally accepted accounting principles or other established or stated criteria.

b. To determine whether the entity has complied with laws and regulations and other specific financial compliance requirements that may have a material effect on the financial statements, or that may affect other financial reports or the economy, efficiency, or effectiveness of program activities.

c. To determine whether the entity is acquiring, protecting, and using its resources economically and efficiently.

d. To determine whether the desired program results or benefits established by the legislature or other authorizing body are being achieved.

Auditor's Opinion, or Auditor's Report A statement signed by an auditor stating that he has examined the financial statements in accordance with generally accepted auditing standards (with exceptions, if any) and expressing his opinion on the financial condition and results of operations of some or all of the fund types and account groups of the reporting entity, as appropriate.

Authority A governmental unit or public agency created to perform a single function or a restricted group of related activities. Usually such units are financed from service charges, fees, and tolls, but in some instances they also have taxing powers. An authority may be completely independent of other governmental units, or in some cases it may be partially dependent on other governments for its creation, its financing, or the exercise of certain powers.

Authority Bonds Bonds payable from the revenues of a specific authority (q.v.). Since such authorities usually have no revenue other than charges for services, their bonds are ordinarily revenue bonds (q.v.).

Auxiliary Enterprises Activities of a college or university that furnish a service to students, faculty, or staff on a user-charge basis. The charge is directly related to, but not necessarily equal to, the cost of the service. Examples include college unions, residence halls, stores, faculty clubs, and intercollegiate athletics.

Balance Sheet A statement that discloses the assets, liabilities, reserves, and equities of a fund, governmental unit, or nonprofit entity at a specified date, properly classified to exhibit financial position of the fund or unit at that date.

Basis of Accounting The standard (or standards) used to determine the point in time when assets, liabilities, revenues, and expenses (expenditures) should be measured and recorded as such in the accounts of an entity. See Accrual Basis, Cash Basis, and Modified Accrual Basis.

Bearer Bond A bond which requires the holder to present matured interest coupons or matured bonds to the issuer or a designated paying agent for payment. Payments are made to the bearer since the issuer maintains no record of current bond ownership.

Note Federal law requires that all tax-exempt bonds issued since June 15, 1983 must be in registered form (see also Registered Bonds). However, many long-term bearer bonds remain outstanding.

Betterment An addition made to, or change made in, a fixed asset that is expected to prolong its life or to increase its efficiency over and above that arising from maintenance (q.v.) and the cost of which is therefore added to the book value of the asset.

Note The term is sometimes applied to sidewalks, sewers, and highways, but these should preferably be designated as "improvements" or "infrastructure assets" (q.v.).

Blended Presentation The method of reporting the financial data of a component unit in a manner similar to that in which the financial data of the primary government are presented. Under this method the component unit data are usually combined with the appropriate fund types of the primary government and reported in the same columns as the data for the primary government. See Discrete Presentation.

Board-Designated Funds Funds created to account for assets set aside by the governing board of an organization for specified purposes.

Bond A written promise to pay a specified sum of money, called the face value or principal amount, at a specified date or dates in the future, called the maturity date(s), together with periodic interest at a specified rate.

Note The difference between a note and a bond is that the latter runs for a longer period of time and requires greater legal formality.

Bond Anticipation Notes, or BANS Short-term interest-bearing notes issued by a governmental unit in anticipation of bonds to be issued at a later date. The notes are retired from proceeds of the bond issue to which they are related. See also Interim Borrowing.

Bond Discount The excess of the face value of a bond over the price for which it is acquired or sold.

Note The price does not include accrued interest at the date of acquisition or sale.

Bond Fund A fund formerly used to account for the proceeds of general obligation bond issues to be used for construction or acquisition of capital assets. Such proceeds are now accounted for in a Capital Projects Fund (q.v.).

Bond Indenture The contract between a corporation issuing bonds and the trustees or other body representing prospective and actual holders of the bonds.

Bond Ordinance or Resolution An ordinance (q.v.) or resolution (q.v.) authorizing a bond issue.

Bond Premium The excess of the price at which a bond is acquired or sold over its face value.

Note The price does not include accrued interest at the date of acquisition or sale.

Bonded Debt That portion of indebtedness represented by outstanding bonds. See Gross Bonded Debt and Net Bonded Debt.

Bonded Indebtedness See Bonded Debt.

Bonds Authorized and Unissued   Bonds that have been legally authorized but not issued and that can be issued and sold without further authorization.

Note   This term must not be confused with the terms *margin of borrowing power* or *legal debt margin,* either one of which represents the difference between the legal debt limit of a governmental unit and the debt outstanding against it.

Book Value   Value (q.v.) as shown by books of account.

Note   In the case of assets subject to reduction by valuation allowances, "book value" refers to cost or stated value less the appropriate allowance. Sometimes a distinction is made between "gross book value" and "net book value," the former designating value before deduction of related allowances and the latter after their deduction. In the absence of any modifier, however, the term *book value* is understood to be synonymous with *net book value.*

Budget   A plan of financial operation embodying an estimate of proposed expenditures for a given period and the proposed means of financing them. Used without any modifier, the term usually indicates a financial plan for a single fiscal year.

Budget Document   The instrument used by the budget-making authority to present a comprehensive financial program to the appropriating body. The budget document usually consists of three parts. The first part contains a message from the budget-making authority, together with a summary of the proposed expenditures and the means of financing them. The second consists of schedules supporting the summary. These schedules show in detail the information as to past years' actual revenues, expenditures, and other data used in making the estimates. The third part is composed of drafts of the appropriation, revenue, and borrowing measures necessary to put the budget into effect.

Budget Message   A general discussion of the proposed budget as presented in writing by the budget-making authority to the legislative body. The budget message should contain an explanation of the principal budget items, an outline of the governmental unit's experience during the past period and its financial status at the time of the message, and recommendations regarding the financial policy for the coming period.

Budgetary Accounts   Those accounts that reflect budgetary operations and condition, such as estimated revenues, appropriations, and encumbrances, as distinguished from proprietary accounts. See also Proprietary Accounts.

Budgetary Control   The control or management of a governmental unit or enterprise in accordance with an approved budget for the purpose of keeping expenditures within the limitations of available appropriations and available revenues.

Buildings   A fixed asset account that reflects the acquisition value of permanent structures used to house persons and property owned by a governmental unit. If buildings are purchased or constructed, this account includes the purchase or contract price of all permanent buildings and fixtures attached to and forming a permanent part of such buildings. If buildings are acquired by gift, the account reflects their appraised value at time of acquisition.

CAFR   See Comprehensive Annual Financial Report.

Callable Bond   A type of bond that permits the issuer to pay the obligation before the stated maturity date by giving notice of redemption in a manner specified in the bond contract. Synonym: Optional Bond.

Capital Assets   See Fixed Assets.

Capital Budget   A plan of proposed capital outlays and the means of financing them for the current fiscal period. It is usually a part of the current budget. If a Capital Program is in operation, it will be the first year thereof. A Capital Program is sometimes referred to as a Capital Budget. See also Capital Program.

Capital Expenditures   See Capital Outlays.

Capital Improvement Fund   A fund to accumulate revenues from current taxes levied for major repairs and maintenance to fixed assets of a nature not specified at the time the revenues are levied. Appropriations of this fund are made in accord with state law at the time specific projects become necessary.

Capital Lease   A lease that substantively transfers the benefits and risks of ownership of property to the lessee. Any lease that meets certain criteria specified in applicable accounting and reporting standards is a capital lease. See also Operating Lease.

Capital Outlays   Expenditures that result in the acquisition of or addition to fixed assets.

Capital Program   A plan for capital expenditures to be incurred each year over a fixed period of years to meet capital needs arising from the long-term work program or otherwise. It sets forth each project or other contemplated expenditure in which the government is to have a part and specifies the full resources estimated to be available to finance the projected expenditures.

Capital Projects Fund   A fund created to account for all resources to be used for the construction or acquisition of designated fixed assets by a governmental unit except those financed by proprietary or fiduciary funds. See also Bond Fund.

Cash Currency, coin, checks, money orders, and bankers' drafts on hand or on deposit with an official or agent designated as custodian of cash and bank deposits.

Note All cash must be accounted for as a part of the fund to which it belongs. Any restrictions or limitations as to its availability must be indicated in the records and statements. It is not necessary, however, to have a separate bank account for each fund unless required by law.

Cash Basis The basis of accounting under which revenues are recorded when received in cash and expenditures (or expenses) are recorded when cash is disbursed.

Cash Discount An allowance received or given if payment is completed within a stated period of time.

Cash Equivalent Short-term, highly liquid investments that are both readily convertible into known amounts of cash and so near their maturity that they present insignificant risk of changes in value due to changes in interest rates.

Certificate of Participation (COP). A long-term debt instrument authorized for construction of municipal facilities, typically issued by a quasi-independent authority but secured by a long-term lease with a general purpose local government.

Character A basis for distinguishing expenditures according to the periods they are presumed to benefit. See also Character Classification.

Character Classification A grouping of expenditures on the basis of the fiscal periods they are presumed to benefit. The three groupings are: (1) current expenditures, presumed to benefit the current fiscal period; (2) debt service, presumed to benefit prior fiscal periods primarily but also present and future periods; and (3) capital outlays, presumed to benefit the current and future fiscal periods. See also Activity, Activity Classification, Function, Functional Classification, Object, Object Classification, and Expenses.

Check A bill of exchange drawn on a bank and payable on demand; a written order on a bank to pay on demand a specified sum of money to a named person, to his order, or to bearer, out of money on deposit to the credit of the maker.

Note A check differs from a warrant in that the latter is not necessarily payable on demand and may not be negotiable. It differs from a voucher in that the latter is not an order to pay.

Clearing Account An account used to accumulate total charges or credits for the purpose of distributing them later among the accounts to which they are allocable or for the purpose of transferring the net differences to the proper account. Synonym for Suspense Account.

Combined Financial Statement A single financial statement that displays the combined financial data for various fund types and, if applicable, account groups and discretely presented component units in separate adjacent columns. See Combining Financial Statement.

Combining Financial Statement A financial statement that displays the financial data for each of the funds of a given fund type (e.g., special revenue funds) in separate adjacent columns. The totals reported for that fund type should agree with those reported in the column for that fund type in the combined financial statements. See Combined Financial Statement.

Commitments In federal government usage, a reservation of an agency's allotment in the estimated amount of orders for goods or services, prior to actually placing the orders. See also Obligations.

Compliance Audit An audit designed to provide reasonable assurance that a governmental entity has complied with applicable laws and regulations. Required for every audit performed in conformity with *Government Auditing Standards*.

Component Unit A separate governmental unit, agency, or nonprofit corporation which, pursuant to the criteria in the GASB Codification, Section 2100, is combined with other component units to constitute the reporting entity (q.v.).

Comprehensive Annual Financial Report (CAFR) A governmental unit's official annual report prepared and published as a matter of public record. In addition to the general purpose financial statements, the CAFR should contain introductory material, schedules to demonstrate legal compliance, and statistical tables specified in the GASB Codification.

Conscience Money Money received by governmental units in payment of previously undisclosed debts, usually based on embezzlement, tax evasion, or theft.

Construction Work in Progress The cost of construction work that has been started but not yet completed.

Contingent Fund Assets or other resources set aside to

provide for unforeseen expenditures or for anticipated expenditures of uncertain amount.

Contingent Liabilities Items that may become liabilities as a result of conditions undetermined at a given date, such as guarantees, pending lawsuits, judgments under appeal, unsettled disputed claims, unfilled purchase orders, and uncompleted contracts. Contingent liabilities of the latter two types are disclosed in balance sheets of governmental funds as Reserve for Encumbrances; other contingent liabilities are disclosed in notes to the financial statements.

Continuing Appropriation An appropriation that, once established, is automatically renewed without further legislative action, period after period, until altered or revoked.

Note The term should not be confused with Indeterminate Appropriation (q.v.).

Contributions Amounts given to an individual or to an organization for which the donor receives no direct private benefits. Contributions may be in the form of pledges, cash, securities, materials, services, or fixed assets.

Control Account An account in the general ledger in which are recorded the aggregate of debit and credit postings to a number of identical or related accounts called subsidiary accounts. For example, the Taxes Receivable account is a control account supported by the aggregate of individual balances in individual property taxpayers' accounts.

Cost The amount of money or money's worth exchanged for property or services.

Note Costs may be incurred even before money is paid; that is, as soon as a liability is incurred. Ultimately, however, money or money's worth must be given in exchange. Again, the cost of some property or service may, in turn, become a part of the cost of another property or service. For example, the cost of part or all of the materials purchased at a certain time will be reflected in the cost of articles made from such materials or in the cost of those services in the rendering of which the materials were used.

Cost Accounting That branch of accounting that provides for the assembling and recording of all the elements of cost incurred to accomplish a purpose, to carry on an activity or operation, or to complete a unit of work or a specific job.

Cost Determination The use of statistical procedures to determine or estimate the cost of goods or services, as opposed to accumulating such costs in a formal cost accounting system.

Cost Objective In federal terminology, is an organization unit, function, activity, project, cost center, or pool established for the accumulation of costs.

Cost Unit A term used in cost accounting to designate the unit of product or service whose cost is computed. These units are selected for the purpose of comparing the actual cost with a standard cost or with actual costs of units produced under different circumstances or at different places and times. See also Unit Cost and Work Unit.

Coupon Rate The interest rate specified on interest coupons attached to a bond. The term is synonymous with nominal interest rate (q.v.) for coupon bonds.

Credit Risk The risk that a debt issuer will not pay interest and principal when due. See also Default.

Current A term that, applied to budgeting and accounting, designates the operations of the present fiscal period as opposed to past or future periods.

Current Assets Those assets that are available or can be made readily available to meet the cost of operations or to pay current liabilities. Some examples are cash, temporary investments, and taxes receivable that will be collected within 60 days from the balance sheet date.

Current Fund In governmental accounting sometimes used as a synonym for General Fund.

Current Funds Funds the resources of which may be expended for operating purposes during the current fiscal period. Colleges and universities and voluntary health and welfare organizations use fund types called Current Fund—Unrestricted and Current Funds—Restricted, as explained in Chapters 19 and 21.

Current Liabilities Liabilities payable within a relatively short period of time, usually no longer than a year. See also Floating Debt.

Current Resources Resources (q.v.) to which recourse can be had to meet current obligations and expenditures. Examples are estimated revenues of a particular period not yet realized, transfers from other funds authorized but not received, and, in the case of certain funds, bonds authorized and unissued.

Current Revenue Revenues of a governmental unit available to meet expenditures of the current fiscal year. See Revenue.

Current Special Assessments (1) Special assessments levied and becoming due during the current fiscal period, from the date special assessment rolls are approved by the proper authority to the date on which a penalty for nonpayment is attached. (2) Special assessments levied in a prior fiscal period but becoming due in the current fiscal period, from the time they become due to the date on which a penalty for nonpayment is attached.

Current Taxes (1) Taxes levied and becoming due during the current fiscal period, from the time the amount of tax levy is first established to the date on which a penalty for nonpayment is attached. (2) Taxes levied in the preceding fiscal period but becoming due in the current fiscal period, from the time they become due until a penalty for nonpayment is attached.

Current-Year's Tax Levy Taxes levied for the current fiscal period.

Customer Advances for Construction Amounts required to be deposited by a customer for construction projects undertaken by the utility at the request of the customer.

Cycle Billing A practice followed by utilities, retail stores, and other organizations with a large number of credit customers of billing part of the customers each working day during a month, instead of billing all customers as of a certain day during the month.

Data Processing (1) The preparation and handling of information and data from source media through prescribed procedures to obtain such end results as classification, problem solution, summarization, and reports. (2) Preparation and handling of financial information wholly or partially by use of computers.

Debt A liability resulting from the borrowing of money or from the purchase of goods and services. Debts of governmental units include bonds, time warrants, notes, and floating debt. See also Bond, Notes Payable, Time Warrant, Floating Debt, Long-Term Debt, and General Long-Term Debt.

Debt Limit The maximum amount of gross or net debt that is legally permitted.

Debt Margin The difference between the amount of the debt limit (q.v.) and the net amount of outstanding indebtedness subject to the limitation.

Debt Service Fund A fund established to finance and account for the payment of interest and principal on all tax supported debt, serial and term, including that payable from special assessments.

Default Failure of a debtor to pay interest or repay the principal of debt when legally due.

Defeasance A transaction in which the liability for a debt is substantively settled, and the liability is removed from the accounts, even though the debt has not actually been paid. See also Legal Defeasance and In-Substance Defeasance.

Deferred Revenues or Deferred Credits In governmental accounting, items that may not be recognized as revenues of the period in which received because they are not "available" until a subsequent period.

Deferred Serial Bonds Serial bonds (q.v.) in which the first installment does not fall due for two or more years from the date of issue.

Deficiency A general term indicating the amount by which anything falls short of some requirement or expectation. The term should not be used without qualification.

Deficit (1) The excess of liabilities and reserved equity of a fund over its assets. (2) The excess of expenditures over revenues during an accounting period; or in the case of Enterprise and Internal Service Funds, the excess of expense over revenue during an accounting period.

Delinquent Special Assessments Special assessments remaining unpaid on and after the date on which a penalty for nonpayment is attached.

Delinquent Taxes Taxes remaining unpaid on and after the date on which a penalty for nonpayment is attached. Even though the penalty may be subsequently waived and a portion of the taxes may be abated or canceled, the unpaid balances continue to be delinquent taxes until abated, canceled, paid, or converted into tax liens.

Note The term is sometimes limited to taxes levied for the fiscal period or periods preceding the current one, but such usage is not entirely correct. See also Current Taxes, Current-Year's Tax Levy, and Prior-Years' Tax Levies.

Deposit Warrant A financial document prepared by a designated accounting or finance officer authorizing the treasurer of a governmental unit to accept for deposit sums of money collected by various departments and agencies of the governmental unit.

Depreciation (1) Expiration of the service life of fixed assets, other than wasting assets, attributable to wear and tear, deterioration, action of the physical elements, inadequacy, and obsolescence. (2) The portion of the cost of a fixed asset, other than a wasting asset, that is charged as an expense during a particular period.

Note In accounting for depreciation, the cost of a fixed asset, less any salvage value, is prorated over the estimated service life of such an asset, and each period is charged with a portion of such cost. Through this process, the cost of the asset less salvage value is ultimately charged off as an expense.

Designated Assets, or equity, set aside by action of the governing board are *designated;* as distinguished from assets or equity set aside in conformity with requirements of donors, grantors, or creditors, which are properly referred to as *restricted*.

Dimension Groupings of expenditure classifications specified by the National Center for Education Statistics (NCES) for public school accounting. Dimensions consist of two main groups: those essential for financial reporting to the federal government and those available optionally for management use.

Direct Cost A cost incurred because of some definite action by or for an organization unit, function, activity, project, cost center, or pool; a cost identified specifically with a cost objective (q.v.).

Direct Debt The debt that a governmental unit has incurred in its own name or assumed through the annexation of territory or consolidation with another governmental unit. See also Overlapping Debt.

Direct Expenses Those expenses that can be charged directly as a part of the cost of a product or service, or of a department or operating unit, as distinguished from overhead and other indirect costs that must be prorated among several products or services, departments, or operating units.

Disbursements Payments in cash.

Discrete Presentation The method of reporting financial data of component units in a column(s) separate from the financial data of the primary government.

Donated Assets Noncash contributions (q.v.). Donated assets may be in the form of securities, land, buildings, equipment, or materials. Proper accounting for donated assets is discussed in Chapter 21.

Donated Materials See Donated Assets.

Donated Services The services of volunteer workers who are unpaid, or who are paid less than the market value of their services. Accounting for donated services is discussed in Chapters 19, 20, and 21.

Double Entry A system of bookkeeping that requires, for every entry made to the debit side of an account or accounts, an entry for a corresponding amount or amounts to the credit side of another account or accounts.

Note Double-entry bookkeeping involves the maintaining of a balance between assets on the one hand and liabilities and fund equities on the other.

Earnings See Income and Revenue.

Effective Interest Rate The rate of earning on a bond investment based on the actual price paid for the bond, the maturity date, and the length of time between interest dates, in contrast with the nominal interest rate (q.v.)

Encumbrances An account used to record the estimated amount of purchase orders, contracts, or salary commitments chargeable to an appropriation. The account is credited when goods or services are received and the actual expenditure of the appropriation is known.

Endowment Fund A fund whose principal must be maintained inviolate but whose income may be expended.

Enterprise Debt Debt that is to be retired primarily from the earnings of governmentally owned and operated enterprises. See also Revenue Bonds.

Enterprise Fund A fund established to finance and account for the acquisition, operation, and maintenance of governmental facilities and services that are entirely or predominantly self-supporting by user charges; or where the governing body of the governmental unit has decided periodic determination of revenues earned, expenses incurred, and/or net income is appropriate. Government-owned utilities and hospitals are ordinarily accounted for by enterprise funds.

Entitlement The amount of payment to which a state or local government is entitled as determined by the federal government pursuant to an allocation formula contained in applicable statutes.

Entry (1) The record of a financial transaction in its appropriate book of account. (2) The act of recording a transaction in the books of account.

Equipment Tangible property of a more or less permanent nature (other than land, buildings, or improvements other than buildings) that is useful in carrying on operations. Examples are machinery, tools, trucks, cars, furniture, and furnishings.

Equity Transfer Nonrecurring or nonroutine transfers of equity between funds. Also referred to as Residual Equity Transfer (q.v.).

Escheat Property Private property that reverts to government ownership upon the death of the owner if there are no legal claimants or heirs.

Estimated Expenditures The estimated amounts of expenditures included in budgeted appropriations. See also Appropriations.

Estimated Other Financing Sources Amounts of financial resources estimated to be received or accrued during a period by a governmental or similar type fund from interfund transfers or from the proceeds of noncurrent debt issuances.

Estimated Other Financing Uses   Amounts of financial resources estimated to be disbursed or accrued during a period by a governmental or similar type fund for transfer to other funds.

Estimated Revenue   For revenue accounts kept on an accrual basis (q.v.), this term designates the amount of revenue estimated to accrue during a given period regardless of whether or not it is all to be collected during the period. For revenue accounts kept on a cash basis (q.v.), the term designates the amount of revenue estimated to be collected during a given period. Under the modified accrual basis (q.v.), estimated revenues include both cash and accrual basis revenues. See also Revenue, Revenue Receipts, Cash Basis, Accrual Basis, and Modified Accrual Basis.

Estimated Revenue Receipts   A term used synonymously with estimated revenue (q.v.) by some governmental units reporting their revenues on a cash basis. See also Revenue and Revenue Receipts.

Estimated Uncollectible Accounts Receivable (Credit) That portion of accounts receivable that it is estimated will never be collected. The account is deducted from the Accounts Receivable account on the balance sheet in order to arrive at the net amount of accounts receivable.

Estimated Uncollectible Current Taxes (Credit)   A provision out of tax revenues for that portion of current taxes receivable that is estimated will never be collected. The amount is shown on the balance sheet as a deduction from the Taxes Receivable—Current account in order to arrive at the net taxes receivable.

Estimated Uncollectible Delinquent Taxes (Credit)   That portion of delinquent taxes receivable that it is estimated will never be collected. The account is shown on the balance sheet as a deduction from the Taxes Receivable—Delinquent account to arrive at the net delinquent taxes receivable.

Estimated Uncollectible Interest and Penalties on Taxes (Credit)   That portion of interest and penalties receivable that it is estimated will never be collected. The account is shown as a deduction from the Interest and Penalties Receivable account on the balance sheet in order to arrive at the net interest and penalties receivable.

Estimated Uncollectible Tax Liens   That portion of tax liens receivable that it is estimated will never be collected. The account is shown as a deduction from the Tax Liens Receivable account on the balance sheet in order to arrive at the net amount of tax liens receivable.

Exemption   A statutory reduction in the assessed valuation of taxable property accorded to certain taxpayers. Typical examples are senior citizens and war veterans.

Exhibit   (1) A balance sheet or other principal financial statement. (2) Any statement or other document that accompanies or is a part of a financial or audit report. See also Schedules and Statements.

Expendable Fund   A fund whose assets and resources may be converted into cash and used in their entirety for purposes of the fund.

Expendable Trust Fund   A trust fund in which the fund balance can be expended for a purpose specified in the trust agreement. Typically used to account for the expendable income of a Nonexpendable Trust Fund (q.v.)

Expended Appropriation   A charge against an appropriation for the actual cost of items received; the appropriation is no longer available to acquire additional goods and services.

Expenditure Disbursements   A term sometimes used by governmental units operating on a cash basis (q.v.) as a synonym for expenditures (q.v.). It is not recommended terminology.

Expenditures   Expenditures are recorded when liabilities are incurred pursuant to authority given in an appropriation (q.v.). If the accounts are kept on the accrual basis (q.v.) or the modified accrual basis (q.v.), this term designates the cost of goods delivered or services rendered, whether paid or unpaid, including expenses, provision for debt retirement not reported as a liability of the fund from which retired, and capital outlays. Where the accounts are kept on the cash basis (q.v.), the term designates only actual cash disbursements for these purposes.

   Note   Encumbrances are not expenditures.

Expenditures Budget   See Appropriations Budget.

Expenses   Charges incurred, whether paid or unpaid, for operation, maintenance, interest, and other charges presumed to benefit the current fiscal period.

Face Value   As applied to securities, this term designates the amount of liability stated in the security document.

Federal Accounting Standards Advisory Board (FASAB) The nine-member standards setting body that *recommends* federal government accounting and financial reporting standards to the U.S. Comptroller General, Secretary of the Treasury, and Director of the Office of Management and Budget.

Fidelity Bond A written promise to indemnify against losses from theft, defalcation, and misappropriation of public finds by government officers and employees. See also Surety Bond.

Fiduciary Funds Any fund held by a governmental unit in a fiduciary capacity, ordinarily as agent or trustee. Also called Trust and Agency Funds.

Financial Accounting Standards Board (FASB) An independent seven-member standards setting body designated to set accounting and financial reporting standards for commercial entities and nongovernmentally affiliated not-for-profit entities.

Financial Accountability The obligation of government to justify the raising of public resources and what those resources were expended for. See Accountability.

Financial Audit One of the two major types of audits defined by the U.S. General Accounting Office (see Performance Audit for the other major type). A financial audit provides an auditor's opinion that financial statements present fairly an entity's financial position and results of operations in conformity with generally accepted accounting principles or that other financial reports comply with specified finance-related criteria.

Financial Condition The probability that a government will meet its financial obligations as they become due *and* its service obligations to constituencies, both currently and in the future. See Financial Position.

Financial Position The adequacy of cash and short-term claims to cash to meet current obligations and those expected in the near future. See Financial Condition.

Fiscal Agent A bank or other corporate fiduciary that performs the function of paying, on behalf of the governmental unit, or other debtor, interest on debt or principal of debt when due.

Fiscal Period Any period at the end of which a governmental unit determines its financial position and the results of its operations.

Fiscal Year A 12-month period of time to which the annual budget applies and at the end of which a governmental unit determines its financial position and the results of its operations.

Fixed Assets Assets of a long-term character that are intended to continue to be held or used, such as land, buildings, machinery, furniture, and other equipment.

Note The term does not indicate the immobility of an asset, which is the distinctive character of "fixture" (q.v.).

Fixed Charges Expenses (q.v.) the amount of which is set by agreement. Examples are interest, insurance, and contributions to pension funds.

Fixed Liabilities See Long-Term Debt.

Fixtures Attachments to buildings that are not intended to be removed and that cannot be removed without damage to the latter.

Note Those fixtures with a useful life presumed to be as long as that of the building itself are considered a part of such a building; all others are classed as equipment.

Floating Debt Liabilities other than bonded debt and time warrants that are payable on demand or at an early date. Examples are accounts payable, notes, and bank loans. See also Current Liabilities.

Forfeiture The automatic loss of cash or other property as a punishment for not complying with legal provisions and as compensation for the resulting damages or losses.

Note The term should not be confused with confiscation. The latter term designates the actual taking over of the forfeited property by the government. Even after property has been forfeited, it cannot be said to be confiscated until the governmental unit claims it.

Franchise A special privilege granted by a government permitting the continuing use of public property, such as city streets, and usually involving the elements of monopoly and regulation.

Full Cost The total cost of providing a service or producing a good; the sum of both direct costs (q.v.) and indirect costs (q.v.).

Full Faith and Credit A pledge of the general taxing power for the payment of debt obligations.

Note Bonds carrying such pledges are usually referred to as general obligation bonds.

Function A group of related activities aimed at accomplishing a major service or regulatory responsibility for which a governmental unit is responsible. For example, public health is a function. See also Subfunction, Activity, Character, and Object.

Functional Classification A grouping of expenditures on the basis of the principal purposes for which they are made. Examples are public safety, public health, public welfare, etc. See also Activity, Character, and Object Classification.

Fund A fiscal and accounting entity with a self-balancing set of accounts recording cash and other financial resources, together with all related liabilities, and residual equities or balances, and changes therein, which are segregated for the purpose of carrying on specific activities or attaining certain objectives in accordance with special regulations, restrictions, or limitations. See General Fixed Assets Account Group and General Long-Term Debt Account group.

Fund Accounting An accounting system organized on the basis of funds, each of which is considered a separate accounting entity. The operations of each fund are accounted for with a separate set of self-balancing accounts that comprise its assets, liabilities, fund equity, revenues, and expenditures, or expenses, as appropriate. Resources are allocated to and accounted for in individual funds based upon purposes for which they are to be spent and the means by which spending activities are controlled. Fund accounting is used by states and local governments and by not-for-profit organizations that need to account for resources the use of which is restricted by donors or grantors.

Fund Balance The portion of Fund Equity (q.v.) available for appropriation.

Fund Balance Sheet A balance sheet for a single fund. See Fund and Balance Sheet.

Fund Balance with Treasury An asset account of a federal agency representing cash balances held by the U.S. Treasury upon which the agency can draw. Treasury will disburse cash on behalf of and at the request of the agency to pay for authorized goods and services.

Fund Equity The excess of fund assets and resources over fund liabilities. A portion of the equity of a governmental fund may be reserved (q.v.) or designated (q.v.); the remainder is referred to as Fund Balance.

Fund Type A classification of funds that are similar in purpose and character. Fund types provided in GASB standards are explained in Chapters 1 through 13. Fund types recommended for use by nonprofit entities are explained in Chapters 19 through 21.

Funded Debt Same as Bonded Debt, which is the preferred term.

Funded Deficit A deficit eliminated through the sale of bonds issued for that purpose. See also Funding Bonds.

Funding The conversion of floating debt or time warrants into bonded debt (q.v.).

Funding Bonds See Refunding Bonds.

GASB See Governmental Accounting Standards Board.
General Fixed Assets Those fixed assets of a governmen-

tal unit that are not accounted for by a proprietary or fiduciary fund.

General Fixed Assets Account Group (GFAAG) A self-balancing group of accounts set up to account for the general fixed assets of a governmental unit. See General Fixed Assets.

General Fund A fund used to account for all transactions of a governmental unit that are not accounted for in another fund.

Note The General Fund is used to account for the ordinary operations of a governmental unit that are financed from taxes and other general revenues.

General Long-Term Debt Long-term debt legally payable from general revenues and backed by the full faith and credit of a governmental unit. See Long-Term Debt.

General Long-Term Debt Account Group (GLTDAG) A self-balancing group of accounts set up to account for the general long-term debt of a governmental unit. See General Long-Term Debt.

General Obligation Bonds Bonds for whose payment the full faith and credit of the issuing body is pledged. More commonly, but not necessarily, general obligation bonds are considered to be those payable from taxes and other general revenues. In some states, these bonds are called *tax supported bonds*. See also Full Faith and Credit.

General Obligation Special Assessment Bonds See Special Assessment Bonds.

General Purpose Financial Statements (GPFS) The five combined financial statements of a reporting entity that are required for conformity with generally accepted accounting principles.

General Revenue The revenues (q.v.) of a governmental unit other than those derived from and retained in an enterprise.

Note If a portion of the net income in an enterprise fund is contributed to another nonenterprise fund, such as the General Fund, the amounts transferred constitute general revenue of the governmental unit.

Generally Accepted Accounting Principles (GAAP) The body of accounting and financial reporting standards, conventions, and practices that have authoritative support from standards-setting bodies such as the Governmental Accounting Standards Board and the Financial Accounting Standards Board, or for which a degree of consensus exists among accounting professionals at a given point in time. Generally accepted accounting principles are continually evolving as changes occur in the reporting environment.

Generally Accepted Auditing Standards (GAAS) Standards prescribed by the American Institute of Certified Public Accountants to provide guidance for planning, conducting, and reporting on audits by Certified Public Accountants.

Generally Accepted Governmental Auditing Standards (GAGAS) Auditing standards set forth by the Comptroller General of the United States to provide guidance for federal auditors and state and local governmental auditors and public accountants who audit federal organizations, programs, activities, and functions.

GFOA See Government Finance Officers Association.

Government Auditing Standards (GAS) Auditing standards set forth by the Comptroller General of the United States to provide guidance for federal auditors, state and local governmental auditors, and public accountants who audit federal organizations, programs, activities, and functions. Also referred to as *generally accepted governmental auditing standards (GAGAS)*.

Government Finance Officers Association Formerly Municipal Finance Officers Association of the United States and Canada. Sponsored the National Council on Governmental Accounting (q.v.). Administers the Certificate of Achievement program and other programs to encourage excellence in financial reporting and budgeting by state and local governments.

Governmental Accounting The composite activity of analyzing, recording, summarizing, reporting, and interpreting the financial transactions of governmental units and agencies. The term generally is used to refer to accounting for state and local governments, rather than the U.S. federal government.

Governmental Accounting Standards Board The independent agency established under the Financial Accounting Foundation in 1984 as the official body designated to set accounting and financial reporting standards for state and local governments.

Governmental Funds A generic classification used by the GASB to refer to all funds other than proprietary and fiduciary funds. The General Fund, special revenue funds, capital projects funds, and debt service funds are the types of funds referred to as "governmental funds."

GPFS See General Purpose Financial Statements.

Grant A contribution by one governmental unit to another unit. The contribution is usually made to aid in the support of a specified function (for example, education), but it is sometimes also for general purposes, or for the acquisition or construction of fixed assets.

Grants-In-Aid See Grant.

Gross Bonded Debt The total amount of direct debt of a governmental unit represented by outstanding bonds before deduction of any assets available and earmarked for their retirement. See also Direct Debt.

Gross Revenue See Revenue.

Historical Cost The amount paid, or liability incurred, by an accounting entity to acquire an asset and make it ready to render the services for which it was acquired.

Improvements Buildings, other structures, and other attachments or annexations to land that are intended to remain so attached or annexed, such as sidewalks, trees, drives, tunnels, drains, and sewers.

Note Sidewalks, curbing, sewers, and highways are sometimes referred to as "betterments," but the term *improvements other than buildings* is preferred. Infrastructure Assets is a term also used.

Improvements Other than Buildings A fixed asset account that reflects the acquisition value of permanent improvements, other than buildings, that add value to land. Examples of such improvements are fences, retaining walls, sidewalks, pavements, gutters, tunnels, and bridges. If the improvements are purchased or constructed, this account contains the purchase or contract price. If improvements are obtained by gift, it reflects fair value at time of acquisition.

Income A term used in accounting for governmental enterprises to represent the excess of revenues earned over the expenses incurred in carrying on the enterprise's operations. It should not be used without an appropriate modifier, such as Operating, Nonoperating, or Net. See also Operating Income, Nonoperating Income, and Net Income.

Note The term Income should not be used in lieu of Revenue (q.v.) in nonenterprise funds.

Income Bonds See Revenue Bonds.

Indenture See Bond Indenture.

Indeterminate Appropriation An appropriation that is not limited either to any definite period of time or to any definite amount, or to both time and amount.

Note A distinction must be made between an indeterminate appropriation and a continuing appropriation. In the first place, whereas a continuing appropriation is indefinite only as to time, an indeterminate appropriation is indefinite as to both time and amount. In the second place, even indeterminate appropriations that are indefinite only as to time are to be distinguished from continuing appropriations in that such indeterminate appropriations may eventually lapse. For example, an appropriation to construct a building may be made to continue in effect until the building is constructed. Once the building is completed, however, the unexpended balance of the appropriation lapses. A continuing appropriation, on the other hand, may continue forever; it can only be abolished by specific action of the legislative body.

Indirect Charges   See Overhead.

Indirect Cost   A cost incurred which cannot be identified specifically with a cost objective (q.v.), but rather benefits multiple cost objectives (e.g., a hospital cafeteria, central data processing department, and general management costs).

Industrial Aid Bonds   Bonds issued by governmental units, the proceeds of which are used to construct plant facilities for private industrial concerns. Lease payments made by the industrial concern to the governmental unit are used to service the bonds. Such bonds may be in the form of general obligation bonds (q.v.) or revenue bonds (q.v.). Also called Industrial Development Bonds, or IDBs.

Infrastructure Assets   Roads, bridges, curbs and gutters, streets, sidewalks, drainage systems, and lighting systems installed for the common good.

In-Substance Defeasance   A transaction in which low risk U.S. Government securities are placed into an irrevocable trust for the benefit of debtholders, and the liability for the debt is removed from the accounts of the entity even though the debt has not been repaid. See Defeasance and Legal Defeasance.

Interest and Penalties Receivable on Taxes   The uncollected portion of interest and penalties receivable on taxes.

Interest Receivable on Investments   The amount of interest receivable on investments, exclusive of interest purchased. Interest purchased should be shown in a separate account.

Interest Receivable—Special Assessments   The amount of interest receivable on unpaid installments of special assessments.

Interfund Accounts   Accounts in which transactions between funds are reflected. See Interfund Transfers.

Interfund Loans   Loans made by one fund to another.

Interfund Transfers   Amounts transferred from one fund to another.

Intergovernmental Revenue   Revenue from other governments. Grants, shared revenues, and entitlements are types of intergovernmental revenue.

Interim Borrowing   (1) Short-term loans to be repaid from general revenues during the course of a fiscal year. (2) Short-term loans in anticipation of tax collections or bonds issuance. See Bond Anticipation Notes, Tax Anticipation Notes, and Revenue Anticipation Notes.

Interim Statement   A financial statement prepared before the end of the current fiscal year and covering only financial transactions during the current year to date. See also Statements.

Internal Control   A plan of organization under which employees' duties are so arranged and records and procedures so designed as to make it possible to exercise effective accounting control over assets, liabilities, revenues, and expenditures. Under such a system, the work of employees is subdivided so that no single employee performs a complete cycle of operations. Thus, for example, an employee handling cash would not post the accounts receivable records. Moreover, under such a system, the procedures to be followed are definitely laid down and require proper authorizations by designated officials for all actions to be taken.

Internal Service Fund   A fund established to finance and account for services and commodities furnished by a designated department or agency to other departments and agencies within a single governmental unit, or to other governmental units. Amounts expended by the fund are restored thereto either from operating earnings or by transfers from other funds, so that the original fund capital is kept intact. Formerly called a Working Capital Fund or Intragovernmental Service Fund.

Interperiod Equity   A term coined by the Governmental Accounting Standards Board indicating the extent to which current period revenues are adequate to pay for current period services.

Inventory   A detailed list showing quantities, descriptions, and values of property and frequently also units of measure and unit prices.

Invested Capital   The equity of a federal agency corresponding to the agency's investment in supplies and materials inventories and net property, plant, and equipment.

Investment in General Fixed Assets   An account in the general fixed assets group of accounts that represents the governmental unit's equity in general fixed assets (q.v.). The balance of this account is subdivided according to the source of funds that financed the asset acquisition, such as general fund revenues, special assessments, etc.

Investments   Securities and real estate held for the production of income in the form of interest, dividends, rentals, or lease payments. The term does not include fixed assets used in governmental operations.

Judgment   An amount to be paid or collected by a governmental unit as the result of a court decision, including a condemnation award in payment for private property taken for public use.

Judgment Bonds   Bonds issued to pay judgments (q.v.). See also Funding.

Judgments Payable   Amounts due to be paid by a governmental unit as the result of court decisions, including condemnation awards in payment for private property taken for public use.

Land   A fixed asset account that reflects the carrying value of land owned by a governmental unit. If land is purchased, this account shows the purchase price and costs such as legal fees, filling and excavation costs, and the like, that are incurred to put the land in condition for its intended use. If land is acquired by gift, the account reflects its appraised value at time of acquisition.

Lapse   (Verb) As applied to appropriations, this term denotes the automatic termination of an appropriation.

Note   Except for indeterminate appropriations (q.v.) and continuing appropriations (q.v.), an appropriation is made for a certain period of time. At the end of this period, any unexpended and unencumbered balance thereof lapses, unless otherwise provided by law.

Leasehold   The right to the use of real estate by virtue of a lease, usually for a specified term of years, for which a consideration is paid.

Legal Defeasance   A transaction in which debt is legally satisfied based on certain provisions in the debt instrument (e.g., third-party guarantor assumes the debt) even though the debt has not been repaid. See also Defeasance and In-Substance Defeasance.

Legal Investments   (1) Investments that public employee retirement systems, savings banks, insurance companies, trustees, and other fiduciaries (individual or corporate) are permitted to make by the laws of the state in which they are domiciled, or under the jurisdiction of which they operate or serve. The investments that meet the conditions imposed by law constitute the legal investment list. (2) Investments that governmental units are permitted to make by law.

Legal Opinion   (1) The opinion of an official authorized to render it, such as an attorney general or city attorney, as to legality. (2) In the case of municipal bonds, the opinion of a specialized bond attorney as to the legality of a bond issue.

Levy   (Verb) To impose taxes, special assessments, or service charges for the support of governmental activities. (Noun) The total amount of taxes, special assessments, or service charges imposed by a governmental unit.

Liabilities   Probable future sacrifices of economic benefits arising from present obligations of a particular entity to transfer assets or provide services to other entities in the future as a result of past transactions or events.

Note   The term does not include encumbrances (q.v.).

Life Income Funds   Funds, ordinarily of colleges and universities, established to account for assets given to the organization subject to an agreement to pay to the donor or designee the income earned by the assets over a specified period of time. See Chapter 19 for fuller explanation.

Limited Obligation Debt   Debt secured by a pledge of the collections of a certain specified tax (rather than by all general revenues).

Line Item Budget   A detailed expense or expenditure budget, generally classified by object within each organizational unit, and, often, classified within each object as to authorized number of employees at each salary level within each job classification, etc.

Loan Fund   A fund whose principal and/or interest is loaned to individuals in accordance with the legal requirements and agreements setting up the fund. Such a fund is accounted for as a trust fund. See also Trust Fund.

Loans Receivable   Amounts that have been loaned to persons or organizations, including notes taken as security for such loans.

Local Education Agency, or LEA   A broad term that is used to include school district, public school, intermediate education agency, and school system.

Local Improvement Fund   See Special Assessment Fund.

Local Improvement Tax   See Special Assessment.

Long-Term Budget   A budget prepared for a period longer than a fiscal year, or in the case of some state governments, a budget prepared for a period longer than a biennium. If the long-term budget is restricted to capital expenditures, it is called a Capital Program (q.v.) or a Capital Improvement Program.

Long-Term Debt Debt with a maturity of more than one year after the date of issuance.

Lump-Sum Appropriation An appropriation made for a stated purpose, or for a named department, without specifying further the amounts that may be spent for specific activities or for particular objects of expenditure. An example of such an appropriation would be one for the police department that does not specify the amount to be spent for uniform patrol, traffic control, etc., or for salaries and wages, materials and supplies, travel, etc.

Machinery and Equipment See Equipment.

Maintenance The upkeep of physical properties in condition for use or occupancy. Examples are the inspection of equipment to detect defects and the making of repairs.

Matured Bonds Payable Bonds that have reached their maturity date but remain unpaid.

Matured Interest Payable Interest on bonds that has reached the maturity date but remains unpaid.

Measurement Focus The nature of the resources, claims against resources, and flows of resources that are measured and reported by a fund or other entity. For example, governmental funds and certain fiduciary funds currently measure and report *available* financial resources, whereas proprietary and certain other fiduciary funds measure and report economic resources.

Modified Accrual Basis Under the modified accrual basis of accounting, required for use by governmental funds (q.v.), revenues are recognized in the period in which they become available and measurable, and expenditures are recognized at the time a liability is incurred pursuant to appropriation authority.

Modified Cash Basis Sometimes same as Modified Accrual Basis, sometimes a plan under which revenues are recognized on the cash basis, but expenditures are recognized on the accrual basis.

Mortgage Bonds Bonds secured by a mortgage against specific properties of a governmental unit, usually its public utilities or other enterprises. If primarily payable from enterprise revenues, they are also classed as revenue bonds. See also Revenue Bonds.

Municipal In its broadest sense, an adjective that denotes the state and all subordinate units of government. As defined for census statistics, the term denotes a city, town, or village as opposed to other units of local government.

Municipal Bond A bond (q.v.) issued by a state or local governmental unit.

Municipal Corporation A body politic and corporate established pursuant to state authorization for the purpose of providing governmental services and regulations for its inhabitants. A municipal corporation has defined boundaries and a population and is usually organized with the consent of its residents. It usually has a seal and may sue and be sued. Cities and towns are examples of municipal corporations. See also Quasi-Municipal Corporations.

Municipal Improvement Certificates Certificates issued in lieu of bonds for the financing of special improvements.

Note As a rule, these certificates are placed in the contractor's hands for collection from the special assessment payers.

National Council on Governmental Accounting The body that established accounting and financial reporting standards for state and local governments prior to the formation of the Governmental Accounting Standards Board.

NCGA See National Council on Governmental Accounting.

Net Assets The difference between total assets and total liabilities. Equivalent to the fund equity of a fund, the equity of a not-for-profit organization, or the owners' equity of a business.

Net Bonded Debt Gross bonded debt (q.v.) less any cash or other assets available and earmarked for its retirement.

Net Income A term used in accounting for governmental enterprises to designate the excess of total revenues (q.v.) over total expenses (q.v.) for an accounting period. See also Income, Operating Revenues, Operating Expenses, Nonoperating Income, and Nonoperating Expenses.

Net Profit See Net Income.

Net Revenue See Net Income.

Net Revenue Available for Debt Service Gross operating revenues of an enterprise less operating and maintenance expenses but exclusive of depreciation and bond interest. "Net Revenue" as thus defined is used to compute "coverage" of revenue bond issues.

Note Under the laws of some states and the provisions of some revenue bond indentures, net revenues used for computation of coverage are required to be on a cash basis rather than an accrual basis.

Nominal Interest Rate The contractual interest rate shown on the face and in the body of a bond and representing the amount of interest to be paid, in contrast to the effective interest rate (q.v.). See also Coupon Rate.

Nonexpendable Trust Fund A fund the principal, and sometimes also the earnings, of which may not be expended. See also Endowment Fund.

Nonexpenditure Disbursements Disbursements not chargeable as expenditures; for example, a disbursement made for the purpose of paying a liability previously recorded on the books.

Nonoperating Expenses Expenses (q.v.) incurred for nonoperating properties or in the performance of activities not directly related to supplying the basic service by a governmental enterprise. An example of a nonoperating expense is interest paid on outstanding revenue bonds. See also Nonoperating Properties.

Nonoperating Income Income of governmental enterprises that is not derived from the basic operations of such enterprises. An example is interest on investments or on bank time deposits.

Nonoperating Properties Properties owned by a governmental enterprise but not used in the provision of basic services for which the enterprise exists.

Nonrevenue Receipts Collections other than revenue (q.v.), such as receipts from loans where the liability is recorded in the fund in which the proceeds are placed and receipts on account of recoverable expenditures. See also Revenue Receipts.

Notes Payable In general, an unconditional written promise signed by the maker to pay a certain sum in money on demand or at a fixed or determinable time either to the bearer or to the order of a person designated therein. See also Temporary Loans.

Notes Receivable A note payable held by a governmental unit.

Object As used in expenditure classification, this term applies to the article purchased or the service obtained (as distinguished from the results obtained from expenditures). Examples are personal services, contractual services, materials, and supplies. See also Activity, Character, Function, and Object Classification.

Object Classification A grouping of expenditures on the basis of goods or services purchased; for example, personal services, materials, supplies, and equipment. See also Functional Classification, Activity Classification, and Character Classification.

Objects of Expenditure See Object.

Obligations Generally amounts that a governmental unit may be required legally to meet out of its resources. They include not only actual liabilities but also unliquidated encumbrances. In federal usage, *obligation* has essentially the same meaning as *encumbrance* in state and local government accounting.

Obsolescence The decrease in the value of fixed assets resulting from economic, social, technological, or legal changes.

Operating Budget A budget that applies to all outlays other than capital outlays. See Budget.

Operating Expenses (1) As used in the accounts of governmental enterprises, the term means those costs that are necessary to the maintenance of the enterprise, the rendering of services, the sale of merchandise, the production and disposition of commodities produced, and the collection of enterprise revenues. (2) The term is also sometimes used to describe expenses for general governmental purposes.

Operating Fund The title of the fund used to account for all assets and related liabilities used in the routine activities of a hospital. Also sometimes used by governmental units as a synonym for General Fund.

Operating Income Income of a governmental enterprise derived from the sale of its goods and/or services. For example, income from the sale of water by a municipal water utility is operating income. See also Operating Revenues.

Operating Lease A rental-type lease in which the risks and benefits of ownership are substantively retained by the lessor, and which does not meet the criteria defined in applicable accounting and reporting standards as a capital lease. See also Capital Lease.

Operating Revenues Revenues derived from the operation of governmental enterprises of a business character.

Operating Statement A statement summarizing the financial operations of a governmental unit for an accounting period as contrasted with a balance sheet (q.v.) that shows financial position at a given moment in time.

Operating Transfers Legally authorized interfund transfers (from a fund receiving revenue to the fund that is to make the expenditures). See also Residual Equity Transfer.

Order A formal legislative enactment by the governing body of certain local governmental units that has the full force and effect of law. For example, county governing bodies in some states pass "orders" rather than laws or ordinances.

Ordinance A formal legislative enactment by the council or governing body of a municipality. If it is not in conflict with any higher form of law, such as a state statute or constitutional provision, it has the full force and effect of law within the boundaries of the municipality to which it applies.

Note The difference between an ordinance and a resolution (q.v.) is that the latter requires less legal formality and has a lower legal status. Ordinarily, the statutes or charter will specify or imply those legislative actions that must be by ordinance and those that may be by resolution. Revenue-raising measures, such as the imposition of taxes, special assessments, and service charges, universally require ordinances.

Original Cost The total of assets given and/or liabilities assumed to acquire an asset. In utility accounting, the original cost is the cost to the first owner who dedicated the plant to service of the public.

Other Appropriations Realized A budgetary account used in federal government accounting to record an agency's basic operating appropriations for a fiscal period.

Other Financing Sources An operating statement classification in which financial inflows other than revenues are reported; for example, proceeds of long-term debt, operating transfers-in, etc.

Other Financing Uses An operating statement classification in which financial outflows other than expenditures are reported; for example, operating transfers-out.

Outlays Sometimes synonymous with disbursements. See also Capital Outlays.

Overdraft (1) The amount by which checks, drafts, or other demands for payment on the Treasury or on a bank exceed the amount of the credit against which they are drawn. (2) The amount by which requisitions, purchase orders, or audited vouchers exceed the appropriation or other credit to which they are chargeable.

Overhead Those elements of cost necessary in the production of an article or the performance of a service that are of such a nature that the amount applicable to the product or service cannot be determined accurately or readily. Usually they relate to those objects of expenditures that do not become an integral part of the finished product or ser-

vice, such as rent, heat, light, supplies, management, or supervision.

Overlapping Debt The proportionate share of the debts of local governmental units located wholly or in part within the limits of the government reporting entity that must be borne by property within each governmental unit.

Note Except for special assessment debt, the amount of debt of each unit applicable to the reporting unit is arrived at by (1) determining what percentage of the total assessed value of the overlapping jurisdiction lies within the limits of the reporting unit and (2) applying this percentage to the total debt of the overlapping jurisdiction. Special assessment debt is allocated on the basis of the ratio of assessments receivable in each jurisdiction that will be used wholly or in part to pay off the debt to total assessments receivable that will be used wholly or in part for this purpose.

Pay-As-You-Go-Basis A term used to describe the financial policy of a governmental unit that finances all of its capital outlays from current revenues rather than by borrowing. A governmental unit that pays for some improvements from current revenues and others by borrowing is said to be on a partial or modified pay-as-you-go basis.

Pay-In-Warrant See Deposit Warrant.

Payment Warrant See Warrant.

Pension Trust Fund See Public Employee Retirement Systems.

Performance Audit One of the two major types of audits defined by the U.S. General Accounting Office (see Financial Audit for the other type). A performance audit provides an auditor's independent determination (but not an opinion) of the extent to which government officials are efficiently, economically, and effectively carrying out their responsibilities.

Performance Budget A budget format that relates the input of resources and the output of services for each organizational unit individually. Sometimes used synonymously with program budget (q.v.)

Permanently Restricted Assets A term used in accounting for not-for-profit organizations indicating assets whose use is permanently restricted by an external donor. See Endowment Fund and Permanently Restricted Net Assets.

Permanently Restricted Net Assets A term used in accounting for not-for-profit organizations indicating the amount of *net* assets whose use is permanently restricted by an external donor. See Endowment Fund, Net Assets, and Permanently Restricted Assets.

Perpetual Inventory A system whereby the inventory of units of property at any date may be obtained directly from the records without resorting to an actual physical count. A record is provided for each item or group of items to be inventoried and is so divided as to provide a running record of goods ordered, received, and withdrawn, and the balance on hand, in units and frequently also in value.

PERS See Public Employee Retirement Systems.

Petty Cash A sum of money set aside for the purpose of making change or paying small obligations for which the issuance of a formal voucher and check would be too expensive and time consuming. Sometimes called a petty cash fund, with the term *fund* here being used in the commercial sense of earmarked liquid assets.

Plant Acquisition Adjustment See Acquisition Adjustment.

Plant Replacement and Expansion Fund A fund classification provided for hospitals to account for assets restricted by donors or grantors for plant replacement or expansion.

Pooled Investments In order to simplify portfolio management, obtain a greater degree of investment diversification for individual endowments or trusts, and reduce brokerage, taxes, and bookkeeping expenses, investments may be merged, or *pooled*. See Chapter 11 for further discussion and illustration of pooling of investments.

Postaudit An audit made after the transactions to be audited have taken place and have been recorded or have been approved for recording by designated officials if such approval is required. See also Preaudit.

Posting The act of transferring to an account in a ledger the data, either detailed or summarized, contained in a book or document of original entry.

Preaudit An examination for the purpose of determining the propriety of proposed financial transactions and financial transactions that have already taken place but have not yet been recorded; or, if such approval is required, before the approval of the financial transactions by designated officials for recording.

Prepaid Expenses Expenses entered in the accounts for benefits not yet received. Prepaid expenses differ from deferred charges in that they are spread over a shorter period of time than deferred charges and are regularly recurring costs of operations. Examples of prepaid expenses are prepaid rent, prepaid interest, and premiums on unexpired insurance.

Prepayment of Taxes The deposit of money with a governmental unit on condition that the amount deposited is to be applied against the tax liability of a designated taxpayer after the taxes have been levied and such liability has been established. See also Taxes Collected in Advance, also Deferred Revenues.

Primary Government A state government or general purpose local government. Also, a special purpose government that has a separately elected governing body, is legally separate, and is fiscally independent of other state or local governments.

Prior-Years' Encumbrances See Reserve for Encumbrances—Prior Year.

Prior-Years' Tax Levies Taxes levied for fiscal periods preceding the current one.

Private Trust Fund A trust fund (q.v.) that will ordinarily revert to private individuals or will be used for private purposes; for example, a fund that consists of guarantee deposits.

Pro Forma For form's sake; an indication of form; an example. The term is used in conjunction with a noun to denote merely a sample form, document, statement, certificate, or presentation, the contents of which may be either wholly or partially hypothetical, actual facts, estimates, or proposals.

Program Budget A budget wherein inputs of resources and outputs of services are identified by programs without regard to the number of organizational units involved in performing various aspects of the program. See also Performance Budget and Traditional Budget.

Project A plan of work, job, assignment, or task. Also used to refer to a job or task.

Property Taxes Taxes levied by a legislative body against agricultural, commercial, residential, or personal property pursuant to law and in proportion to the assessed valuation of said property, or other appropriate basis. See Ad Valorem.

Proprietary Accounts Those accounts that show actual financial position and operations, such as actual assets, liabilities, reserves, fund balances, revenues, and expenditures, as distinguished from budgetary accounts (q.v.).

Proprietary Fund Sometimes referred to as "income-determination" or "commercial-type" funds of a state or local governmental unit. Examples are enterprise funds and internal service funds.

Public Authority See Authority.

Public Corporation See Municipal Corporation and Quasi-Municipal Corporation.

Public Employee Retirement Systems The organizations that collect retirement and other employee benefit contributions from government employers and employees, manage assets, and make payments to qualified retirants, beneficiaries, and disabled employees.

Public Enterprise Fund See Enterprise Fund.

Public Improvement Fund See Special Assessment Fund.

Public Trust Fund A trust fund (q.v.) whose principal, earnings, or both, must be used for a public purpose; for example, a pension or retirement fund.

Purchase Order A document that authorizes the delivery of specified merchandise or the rendering of certain services and the making of a charge for them.

Quasi-Endowment Funds Funds established by a governing board of an institution to account for assets to be retained and invested as if they were endowments.

Quasi-external Transaction Transactions between funds that are similar to and accounted for the same as if the other party to the transaction had been an external entity. An example is the purchase of supplies by the General Fund from an internal service fund. This transaction results in an expenditure by the General Fund and a revenue to the internal service fund.

Quasi-Municipal Corporation An agency established by the state primarily for the purpose of helping to carry out its functions; for example, a county or school district.

Note Some counties and other agencies ordinarily classified as quasi-municipal corporations have been granted the powers of municipal corporations by the state in which they are located. See also Municipal Corporations.

Rate Base The value of utility property used in computing an authorized rate of return as authorized by law or a regulatory commission.

Realize To convert goods or services into cash or receivables. Also to exchange for property that is a current asset or can be converted immediately into a current asset. Sometimes applied to conversion of noncash assets into cash.

Rebates Abatements (q.v.) or refund (q.v.).

Receipts This term, unless otherwise qualified, means cash received.

Recoverable Expenditure An expenditure made for or on behalf of another governmental unit, fund, or department, or for a private individual, firm, or corporation, which will subsequently be recovered in cash or its equivalent.

Refund (Noun) An amount paid back or credit allowed because of an overcollection or on account of the return of an object sold. (Verb) To pay back or allow credit for an amount because of an overcollection or because of the return of an object sold. (Verb) To provide for the payment of a loan through cash or credit secured by a new loan.

Refunding Bonds Bonds issued to retire bonds already outstanding. The refunding bonds may be sold for cash and outstanding bonds redeemed in cash, or the refunding bonds may be exchanged with holders of outstanding bonds.

Registered Bond A bond the owner of which is registered with the issuing governmental unit, and which cannot be sold or exchanged without a change of registration. Such a bond may be registered as to principal and interest or as to principal only.

Registered Warrant A warrant that is registered by the paying officer for future payment on account of present lack of funds and that is to be paid in the order of its registration. In some cases, such warrants are registered when issued; in others, when first presented to the paying officer by the holders. See also Warrant.

Reimbursement Cash or other assets received as a repayment of the cost of work or services performed or of other expenditures made for or on behalf of another governmental unit or department or for an individual, firm, or corporation.

Replacement Cost The cost as of a certain date of a property that can render similar service (but need not be of the same structural form) as the property to be replaced. See also Reproduction Cost.

Reporting Entity The primary government and all related component units, if any, combined in accordance with GASB Codification Section 2100 constitute the governmental reporting entity.

Reproduction Cost The cost as of a certain date of reproducing an exactly similar property new in the same place.

Note Sometimes this term is designated as "reproduction cost new" to distinguish it from "depreciated reproduction cost," which is the reproduction cost of a given property less the estimated amount of accumulated depreciation applicable to it. In the absence of any modifier, however, the term *reproduction cost* is understood to be synonymous with *reproduction cost new*. See also Replacement Cost.

Repurchase Agreement   An agreement wherein a governmental unit transfers cash to a financial institution in exchange for U.S. government securities, and the financial institution agrees to repurchase the same securities at an agreed-upon price.

Requisition   A written demand or request, usually from one department to the purchasing officer or to another department, for specified articles or services.

Reserve   An account that records a portion of the fund equity that must be segregated for some future use and that is, therefore, not available for further appropriation or expenditure. See Reserve for Inventory or Reserve for Encumbrances.

Reserve for Advance to _____ Fund   A reserve that represents the segregation of a portion of a fund equity to indicate that assets equal to the amount of the reserve are invested in a long-term loan to another fund and are, therefore, not available for appropriation.

Reserve for Encumbrances   A segregation of a portion of fund equity in the amount of encumbrances outstanding. See also Reserve.

Reserve for Encumbrances—Prior Year   Encumbrances outstanding at the end of a fiscal year are designated as pertaining to appropriations of a year prior to the current year in order that related expenditures may be matched with the appropriations of the prior year rather than an appropriation of the current year.

Reserve for Inventory   A segregation of a portion of fund equity to indicate that assets equal to the amount of the reserve are invested in inventories and are, therefore, not available for appropriation.

Reserve for Realized Gains and Losses   An account used by a cash and investment pool to accumulate realized gains and losses on sales of investments pending distribution to pool participants. See Undistributed Earnings.

Reserve for Revenue Bond Contingency   A reserve in an Enterprise Fund that represents the segregation of a portion of retained earnings equal to current assets that are restricted for meeting various contingencies, as may be specified and defined in the revenue bond indenture.

Reserve for Revenue Bond Debt Service   A reserve in an Enterprise Fund that represents the segregation of a portion of retained earnings equal to current assets that are restricted to current servicing of revenue bonds in accordance with the terms of a bond indenture.

Reserve for Revenue Bond Retirement   A reserve in an Enterprise Fund that represents the segregation of a portion of retained earnings equal to current assets that are restricted for future servicing of revenue bonds in accordance with the terms of a bond indenture.

Reserve for Uncollected Taxes   A reserve equal to the amount of taxes receivable by a fund. The reserve is deducted from Taxes Receivable, thus effectively placing the fund on the cash basis of revenue recognition.

Residual Equity Transfer   Nonrecurring or nonroutine transfers of equity between funds (e.g., transfers of residual balances of discontinued funds to the General Fund or a Debt Service Fund). See also Equity Transfer.

Resolution   A special or temporary order of a legislative body; an order of a legislative body requiring less legal formality than an ordinance or statute. See also Ordinance.

Resources   Legally budgeted revenues of a state or local government that have not been recognized as revenues under the modified accrual basis of accounting as of the date of an interim balance sheet.

Restricted Assets   Assets (usually of an enterprise fund) that may not be used for normal operating purposes because of the requirements of regulatory authorities, provisions in bond indentures, or other legal agreements, but that need not be accounted for in a separate fund.

Restricted Fund   A fund established to account for assets the use of which is limited by the requirements of donors or grantors. Hospitals may have three types of restricted funds: specific purpose funds, endowment funds, and plant replacement and expansion funds. The governing body or administration cannot *restrict* the use of assets, they may only *designate* the use of assets. See Board-Designated Funds.

Retained Earnings   The accumulated earnings of an Enterprise or Internal Service Fund that have been retained in the fund and are not reserved for any specific purpose.

Retirement Allowances   Amounts paid to government employees who have retired from active service or to their survivors. See Annuity.

Retirement Fund   A fund out of which retirement annuities and/or other benefits are paid to authorized and designated public employees. A retirement fund is accounted for as a Trust Fund (q.v.).

Revenue   Additions to fund financial resources other than from interfund transfers (q.v.) and debt issue proceeds.

Revenue Anticipation Notes, or RANS   Notes issued in anticipation of the collection of revenues, usually from specified sources, and to be repaid upon the collection of the revenues.

Revenue Bonds   Bonds whose principal and interest are payable exclusively from earnings of a public enterprise. In addition to a pledge of revenues, such bonds sometimes contain a mortgage on the enterprise's property and are then known as mortgage revenue bonds.

Revenue Receipts   A term used synonymously with "revenue" (q.v.) by some governmental units that account for their revenues on a cash basis (q.v.). See also Nonrevenue Receipts.

Revenues Budget   A legally adopted budget authorizing the collection of revenues from specified sources and estimating the amounts to be collected during the period from each source.

Revenues Collected in Advance   A liability account that represents revenues collected before they become due.

Revolving Fund   See Internal Service Fund.

Schedules   (1) The explanatory or supplementary statements that accompany the balance sheet or other principal statements periodically prepared from the accounts. (2) The accountant's or auditor's principal work papers covering his examination of the books and accounts. (3) A written enumeration or detailed list in orderly form. See also Exhibit and Statements.

Scrip   An evidence of indebtedness, usually in small denomination, secured or unsecured, interest-bearing or non-interest-bearing, stating that the governmental unit, under conditions set forth, will pay the face value of the certificate or accept it in payment of certain obligations.

Securities   Bonds, notes, mortgages, or other forms of negotiable or nonnegotiable instruments. See also Investments.

Self-Supporting or Self-Liquidating Debt   Debt obligations whose principal and interest are payable solely from the earnings of the enterprise for the construction or improvement of which they were originally issued. See also Revenue Bonds.

Serial Annuity Bonds   Serial bonds in which the annual installments of bond principal are so arranged that the combined payments for principal and interest are approximately the same each year.

Serial Bonds   Bonds the principal of which is repaid in periodic installments over the life of the issue. See Serial Annuity Bonds and Deferred Serial Bonds.

Service Efforts and Accomplishments   A conceptualization of the resources consumed (inputs), tasks performed (outputs), and goals attained (outcomes), and the relationship among these items, in providing services in selected areas (e.g., police protection, solid waste garbage collection, and elementary and secondary education).

Shared Revenue   Revenue levied by one governmental unit but shared, usually on a predetermined basis, with another unit of government or class of governments.

Shared Tax   See Shared Revenue.

Short-Term Debt   Debt with a maturity of one year or less after the date of issuance. Short-term debt usually includes floating debt, bond anticipation notes, tax anticipation notes, and interim warrants.

Single Audit   An audit prescribed by federal law for state and local governmental units, colleges and universities, and not-for-profit organizations that receive federal financial assistance above a specified amount. Such an audit is to be conducted in conformity with Office of Management and Budget *Circular A-128* for state and local governments and *Circular A-133* for colleges and universities and other not-for-profit organizations. Such an audit is conducted on an organization-wide basis rather than on the former grant-by-grant basis. The Single Audit Act of 1984 and the two circulars cited above impose uniform, and rigorous, requirements for conducting and reporting on single audits.

Sinking Fund   See Debt Service Fund.

Sinking Fund Bonds   Bonds issued under an agreement that requires the governmental unit to set aside periodically out of its revenues a sum that, with compound earnings thereon, will be sufficient to redeem the bonds at their stated date of maturity. Sinking fund bonds are usually also term bonds (q.v.).

Special Assessment   A compulsory levy made against certain properties to defray part or all of the cost of a specific improvement or service that is presumed to be a general benefit to the public and of special benefit to such properties.

Special Assessment Bonds   Bonds payable from the proceeds of special assessments (q.v.). If the bonds are payable only from the collections of special assessments, they are known as "special-special assessment bonds." If, in addition to the assessments, the full faith and credit of the governmental unit is pledged, they are known as "general obligation special assessment bonds."

Special Assessment Fund A fund type no longer authorized for use in the GPFS.

Special Assessment Liens Receivable Claims that a governmental unit has on properties until special assessments (q.v.) levied against them have been paid. The term normally applies to those delinquent special assessments for the collection of which legal action has been taken through the filing of claims.

Special Assessment Roll The official list showing the amount of special assessments (q.v.) levied against each property presumed to be benefited by an improvement or service.

Special District An independent unit of local government organized to perform a single governmental function or a restricted number of related functions. Special districts usually have the power to incur debt and levy taxes; however, certain types of special districts are entirely dependent on enterprise earnings and cannot impose taxes. Examples of special districts are water districts, drainage districts, flood control districts, hospital districts, fire protection districts, transit authorities, port authorities, and electric power authorities.

Special District Bonds Bonds issued by a special district. See Special District.

Special Fund Any fund that must be devoted to some special use in accordance with specific regulations and restrictions. Generally, the term applies to all funds other than the General Fund (q.v.).

Special Revenue Fund A fund used to account for revenues from specific taxes or other earmarked revenue sources that by law are designated to finance particular functions or activities of government. After the fund is established, it usually continues year after year until discontinued or revised by properly legislative authority. An example is a motor fuel tax fund used to finance highway and road construction.

Special-Special Assessment Bonds See Special Assessment Bonds.

Specific Purpose Fund A fund classification provided for hospitals to record the principal and income of assets that may be used only for purposes specified by the donor. Distinctions among specific purpose funds, plant replacement and expansion funds, and endowment funds are presented in Chapter 20 of this text.

Statements (1) Used in a general sense, statements are all of those formal written presentations that set forth financial information. (2) In technical accounting usage, statements are those presentations of financial data that show the financial position and the results of financial operations of a fund, a group of accounts, or an entire governmental reporting entity, or component unit thereof, for a particular accounting period. See also Exhibit and Schedule.

Statute A written law enacted by a duly organized and constituted legislative body. See also Ordinance, Resolution, and Order.

Stores Materials and supplies on hand in storerooms, subject to requisition and use.

Straight Serial Bonds Serial bonds (q.v.) in which the annual installments of a bond principal are approximately equal.

Subactivity A specific line of work performed in carrying out a governmental activity. For example, replacing defective street lamps would be a subactivity under the activity of street light maintenance.

Subfunction A grouping of related activities within a particular governmental function. For example, "police" is a subfunction of the function "public safety."

Subsidiary Account One of a group of related accounts that support in detail the debit and credit summaries recorded in a control account. An example is the individual property taxpayers' accounts for taxes receivable in the general ledger. See also Control Account and Subsidiary Ledger.

Subsidiary Ledger A group of subsidiary accounts (q.v.) the sum of the balances of which is equal to the balance of the related control account. See also Control Account and Subsidiary Account.

Subvention A grant (q.v.).

Surety Bond A written promise to pay damages or to indemnify against losses caused by the party or parties named in the document, through nonperformance or through defalcation. An example is a surety bond given by a contractor or by an official handling cash or securities.

Surplus Now generally obsolete in accounting usage. See Fund Balance, Retained Earnings, and Investment in General Fixed Assets.

Surplus Receipts A term sometimes applied to receipts that increase the balance of a fund but are not a part of its normal revenue; for example, collection of accounts previously written off. Sometimes used as an account title.

Suspense Account An account that carries charges or credits temporarily, pending the determination of the proper account or accounts to which they are to be posted. See Suspense Fund, Clearing Account.

Suspense Fund   A fund established to account separately for certain receipts pending the distribution or disposal thereof. See also Agency Fund.

Syndicate, Underwriting   A group formed for the marketing of a given security issue too large for one member to handle expeditiously, after which the group is dissolved.

Tax Anticipation Notes, or TANS   Notes (sometimes called warrants) issued in anticipation of collection of taxes, usually retirable only from tax collections, and frequently only from the proceeds of the tax levy whose collection they anticipate.

Tax Anticipation Warrants   See Tax Anticipation Notes.

Tax Certificate   A certificate issued by a governmental unit as evidence of the conditional transfer of title to tax-delinquent property from the original owner to the holder of the certificate. If the owner does not pay the amount of the tax arrearage and other charges required by law during the special period of redemption, the holder can foreclose to obtain title. Also called tax sale certificate and tax lien certificate in some jurisdictions. See also Tax Deed.

Tax Deed   A written instrument by which title to property sold for taxes is transferred unconditionally to the purchaser. A tax deed is issued on foreclosure of the tax lien (q.v.) obtained by the purchaser at the tax sale. The tax lien cannot be foreclosed until the expiration of the period during which the owner may redeem his property through paying the delinquent taxes and other charges. See also Tax Certificate.

Tax Expenditure   A revenue loss attributable to provisions of federal tax laws that allow a special exclusion, exemption, or deduction from gross income, or which provide a special credit, a preferential rate of tax, or a deferral of tax liability.

Tax Increment Debt   Debt secured by an incremental tax earmarked for servicing the debt, such as a half-cent sales tax.

Tax Levy   See Levy.

Tax Levy Ordinance   An ordinance (q.v.) by means of which taxes are levied.

Tax Liens   Claims that governmental units have on properties until taxes levied against them have been paid.

   Note   The term is sometimes limited to those delinquent taxes for the collection of which legal action has been taken through the filing of liens.

Tax Liens Receivable   Legal claims against property that have been exercised because of nonpayment of delinquent taxes, interest, and penalties. The account includes delinquent taxes, interest, and penalties receivable up to the date the lien becomes effective, and the cost of holding the sale.

Tax Notes   See Tax Anticipation Notes.

Tax Rate   The amount of tax stated in terms of a unit of the tax base; for example, 25 mills per dollar of assessed valuation of taxable property.

Tax Rate Limit   The maximum rate at which a governmental unit may levy a tax. The limit may apply to taxes raised for a particular purpose, or to taxes imposed for all purposes; and may apply to a single government, to a class of governments, or to all governmental units operating in a particular area. Overall tax rate limits usually restrict levies for all purposes and of all governments, state and local, having jurisdiction in a given area.

Tax Roll   The official list showing the amount of taxes levied against each taxpayer or property. Frequently, the tax roll and the assessment roll are combined, but even in these cases the two can be distinguished.

Tax Sale Certificate   See Tax Certificate.

Tax Supplement   A tax levied by a local unit of government that has the same base as a similar tax levied by a higher level of government, such as a state or province. The local tax supplement is frequently administered by the higher level of government along with its own tax. A locally imposed, state-administered sales tax is an example of a tax supplement.

Tax-Supported Debt   All debt secured by pledges of tax revenues.

Tax Title Notes   Obligations secured by pledges of the governmental unit's interest in certain tax liens or tax titles.

Taxes   Compulsory charges levied by a governmental unit for the purpose of financing services performed for the common benefit.

   Note   The term does not include specific charges made against particular persons or property for current or permanent benefits such as special assessments. Neither does the term include charges for services rendered only to those paying such charges as, for example, sewer service charges.

Taxes Collected in Advance   A liability for taxes collected before the tax levy has been made or before the amount of taxpayer liability has been established.

Taxes Levied for Other Governmental Units   Taxes levied by the reporting governmental unit for other governmental units, which, when collected, are to be paid over to these units.

Taxes Paid in Advance Same as Taxes Collected in Advance. Also called Prepaid Taxes.

Taxes Receivable—Current The uncollected portion of taxes that a governmental unit has levied but that are not yet delinquent.

Taxes Receivable—Delinquent Taxes remaining unpaid on and after the date on which a penalty for nonpayment is attached. Even though the penalty may be subsequently waived and a portion of the taxes may be abated or canceled, the unpaid balances continue to be delinquent taxes until paid, abated, canceled, or converted into tax liens.

Temporarily Restricted Assets A term used in accounting for not-for-profit organizations indicating assets temporarily restricted by an external donor for use in a future period or for a particular purpose. See Temporarily Restricted Net Assets.

Temporarily Restricted Net Assets A term used in accounting for not-for-profit organizations indicating the amount of *net* assets temporarily restricted by an external donor for use in a future period or for a particular purpose. See Net Assets and Temporarily Restricted Assets.

Temporary Loans Short-term obligations representing amounts borrowed for short periods of time and usually evidenced by notes payable (q.v.) or warrants payable (q.v.). They may be unsecured, or secured by specific revenues to be collected. See also Tax Anticipation Notes.

Term Bonds Bonds the entire principal of which matures on one date.

Term Bonds Payable A liability account that records the face value of general obligation term bonds issued and outstanding.

Time Warrant A negotiable obligation of a governmental unit having a term shorter than bonds, and frequently tendered to individuals and firms in exchange for contractual services, capital acquisitions, or equipment purchases.

Time Warrants Payable The amount of time warrants outstanding and unpaid.

Total Quality Management (TQM) A management approach in which an organization seeks to continuously improve its ability to meet or exceed customer demands, where customer, in government or not-for-profit organization usage, may be broadly defined to include such parties as taxpayers, service recipients, students, members, etc.

TQM See Total Quality Management.

Traditional Budget A term sometimes applied to the budget of a governmental unit wherein appropriations are based entirely or primarily on objects of expenditure. The focus of a traditional budget is on input of resources, rather than on the relationship between input of resources and output of services. For budgets focusing on the latter, see Program Budget and Performance Budget.

Transfers See Operating Transfers and Residual Equity Transfers.

Trial Balance A list of the balances of the accounts in a ledger kept by double entry (q.v.), with the debit and credit balances shown in separate columns. If the totals of the debit and credit columns are equal or their net balance agrees with a control account, the ledger from which the figures are taken is said to be "in balance."

Trust Fund A fund consisting of resources received and held by the governmental unit as trustee, to be expended or invested in accordance with the conditions of the trust. See also Endowment Fund, Private Trust Fund, and Public Trust Fund.

Trust and Agency Funds See Agency Fund, Trust Fund, and Fiduciary Fund.

Unallotted Balance of Appropriation An appropriation balance available for allotment (q.v.).

Unamortized Discounts on Bonds Sold That portion of the excess of the face value of bonds over the amount received from their sale that remains to be written off periodically over the life of the bonds.

Unamortized Discounts on Investments That portion of the excess of the face value of securities over the amount paid for them that has not yet been written off.

Unamortized Premiums on Bonds Sold An account in an Enterprise Fund that represents that portion of the excess of bond proceeds over par value and that remains to be amortized over the remaining life of such bonds.

Unamortized Premiums on Investments That portion of the excess of the amount paid for securities over their face value that has not yet been amortized.

Unapportioned Authority The amount of a federal appropriation made by the Congress and approved by the president, but not yet apportioned by the Office of Management and Budget. See Other Appropriations Realized and Apportionments.

Unbilled Accounts Receivable An account that designates the estimated amount of accounts receivable for services or commodities sold but not billed. For example, if a utility bills its customers bimonthly but prepares monthly financial statements, the amount of services rendered or commodities sold during the first month of the bimonthly period would be reflected in the balance sheet under this account title.

Underwriting Syndicate   See Syndicate, Underwriting.

Undistributed Earnings   An account used by a cash and investment pool to accumulate investment earnings pending distribution to pool participants. See also Reserve for Realized Gains and Losses.

Unearned Income   See Deferred Revenues.

Unencumbered Allotment   That portion of an allotment not yet expended or encumbered.

Unencumbered Appropriation   That portion of an appropriation not yet expended or encumbered.

Unexpended Allotment   That portion of an allotment that has not been expended.

Unexpended Appropriation   That portion of an appropriation that has not been expended.

Unit Cost   A term used in cost accounting to denote the cost of producing a unit of product or rendering a unit of service; for example, the cost of treating and purifying a thousand gallons of sewage.

Unliquidated Encumbrances   Encumbrances outstanding.

Unrealized Revenue   See Accrued Revenue.

Unrestricted Assets   Assets that may be utilized at the discretion of the governing board of a nonprofit entity.

Unrestricted Funds   Funds established to account for assets or resources that may be utilized at the discretion of the governing board. Antonym of Restricted Funds.

Unrestricted Net Assets   The portion of the excess of total assets over total liabilities that may be utilized at the discretion of the governing board of a governmental or not-for-profit entity. See Net Assets, Temporarily Restricted Net Assets, and Permanently Restricted Net Assets.

User Charge   A charge levied against users of a service or purchasers of a product of an enterprise fund or an internal service fund.

Utility Fund   See Enterprise Fund.

Value   As used in governmental accounting, this term designates (1) the act of describing anything in terms of money or (2) the measure of a thing in terms of money. The term should not be used without further qualification. See also Book Value and Face Value.

Voucher   A written document that evidences the propri-

ety of transactions and usually indicates the accounts in which they are to be recorded.

Voucher Check   A document combining a check and a brief description of the transaction covered by the check.

Voucher System   A system that calls for the preparation of vouchers (q.v.) for transactions involving payments and for the recording of such vouchers in a special book of original entry (q.v.), known as a voucher register, in the order in which payment is approved.

Vouchers Payable   Liabilities for goods and services evidenced by vouchers that have been preaudited and approved for payment but not been paid.

Warrant   An order drawn by the legislative body or an officer of a governmental unit on its treasurer, directing the latter to pay a specified amount to the person named or to the bearer. It may be payable on demand, in which case it usually circulates the same as a bank check; or it may be payable only out of certain revenues when and if received, in which case it does not circulate as freely. See also Registered Warrant and Deposit Warrant.

Warrants Payable   The amount of warrants outstanding and unpaid.

Work Order   A written order authorizing and directing the performance of a certain task and issued to the person who is to direct the work. Among the items of information shown on the order are the nature and location of the job, specifications of the work to be performed, and a job number that is referred to in reporting the amount of labor, materials, and equipment used.

Work Program   A plan of work proposed to be done during a particular period by an administrative agency in carrying out its assigned activities.

Work Unit   A fixed quantity that will consistently measure work effort expended in the performance of an activity or the production of a commodity.

Working Capital Fund   See Internal Service Fund.

Yield Rate   See Effective Interest Rate.

Zero-Based Budget   A budget based on the concept that the very existence of each activity must be justified each year, as well as the amounts of resources requested to be allocated to each activity.

APPENDIX 2

Accounting for Investments

In governmental finance, investments consist of real estate, bonds, certificates of deposit, and other forms of indebtedness, stock, patents, royalties, and possibly other assets. Governmental resources may be converted to these forms of investments for one or the other of the two following reasons:

1. To make profitable use of cash that would otherwise be idle until needed for financing regular activities of the fund. These are called *short-term* or *temporary investments*. Since they must be readily marketable in order to make cash promptly available when needed, they should be well seasoned and subject to practically no market fluctuation. Otherwise, their quick sale may result in a loss. Any kind of fund having temporary excess cash may acquire short-term investments. Planning and budgeting of cash and short-term investments are discussed in Chapter 17.

2. To produce income on a permanent basis. These are characterized as long-term or permanent investments. They should combine the factors of safety and maximum income. Proclivity to market fluctuations is not particularly objectionable in this class of investments. This is true because any items chosen for sale may be disposed of in a more deliberate manner than if the proceeds are required for current expenditure, and a sizable portion of bond investments may even be held to maturity.

Since short-term investments represent employment of cash not immediately needed for normal purposes, they may conceivably be acquired by any fund of the seven standard types. Long-term investments, on the contrary, are peculiar to trust funds, debt service funds, and enterprise funds, with the greatest amount held by those of the first-named type.

From an accounting standpoint, the more difficult problems associated with fund investments are as follows:

1. Measuring and recording periodic income from investments.
2. Measuring and recording gain or loss on sale, or disposal in any other manner, of an investment.

In the next several paragraphs, these problems will be explored, first as they relate to permanent investments and afterward as they affect temporary investments.

Permanent Investments

Permanent investments should be recorded at cost.[1] This figure should include every outlay required to obtain clear title to the assets. Some of the more common elements of the cost of acquiring investments are purchase price, legal fees attendant on the acquisition, and taxes and commissions to which the transaction is subject. The difference between par value of an investment and the cost of the investment determines the amount of premium or discount. Acquisition of property by donation is not uncommon for some kinds of trust funds. There being no purchase price to use as a base, the gift should be recorded at fair value. Since the major problems of accounting for investments arise in connection with securities—that is, stocks, bonds, mortgages, etc.—subsequent discussion will be confined to them.

To illustrate some of the procedures recommended for recording acquisition of securities, a few suggested entries are given below:

1. An endowment fund receives as a gift 500 shares of no-par-value stock of the Rex Manufacturing Company, currently quoted at $61.20 per share. The entry in the endowment fund would be as follows:

Investments	30,600	
Endowment Fund Balance		30,600

2. Noninterest-bearing U.S. Treasury bills with a maturity value of $20,000 are bought as a short-term investment at "97⅝," which means at 97⅝ percent of face value.

Investments	19,525	
Cash		19,525

$20,000 × 97⅝% = 19,525.

3. Twenty-five bonds, par value $1,000 each, of Pacific City, were purchased at 96¼, with exchange fees and broker's commissions amounting to $105. The endowment fund entry would be as follows:

Investments	24,167.50	
Cash		24,167.50

---

[1] As discussed in Chapter 12, the FASB *Standards for Accounting for Investments of Defined Benefit Pension Plans* require the investments to be valued at market on each balance sheet date. Obviously, the discussion in this appendix of amortization of premium and discount does not apply to investments that are revalued to market periodically.

The cost of the 25 bonds was calculated by multiplying $25,000 by 96¼ percent, which gave a product of $24,062.50, and then adding the $105 cost of acquisition. If, instead of being acquired at a net discount (amount below per value) of $832.50, the bonds had cost a total premium (amount above par value) of that figure, the Investments account would have been debited for $25,832.50.

Except for perpetual bonds, which for practical purposes are nonexistent in the United States, all bonds, mortgages, notes, etc. (but not stock) have a maturity date, at which time holders of the bonds will receive the par value of their holdings. That is to say, as bonds approach the maturity date, whatever their values may have been or may now be, they approach par value. Thus, if the trust fund acquiring $25,000 par value of bonds for $24,167.50 holds them until maturity, it will gain $832.50. What is the proper distribution of this gain? Should it be recorded in the period in which the bonds were purchased or in the period in which they mature?

Had the discount been of small amount, either of the two periods, preferably the latter, could receive the credit without material distortion of results. However, if the amount is sizable, the preferred practice is to distribute it over the time the bonds are held. This method is preferred because it gives some part of the credit to each period and avoids distortion of income in any one period. The process of distributing total discount or premium over a number of periods is referred to as *amortization,* although, as applied to discount, it is sometimes described as *accumulation,* because reducing the discount builds up or accumulates the book value of the bond. If the bonds were acquired at a discount, the periodic amortization of discount is regarded as an addition to income for the period. It is not received in cash during the period but is represented by an increase in book value of the investment, subsequently to be realized in cash. Periodic amortization of premium is construed as a reduction of income, since it represents a decline in the investment's book value as compared with its purchase price. "Book" or "Carrying" value is cost plus discount amortized to date, or minus premium amortized to date.

The two most common methods of amortizing premium and discount are the straight-line and the effective interest methods. The former consists of allocating to each period during which the investment is owned an equal amount of premium or discount. Thus, if the Pacific City bonds were purchased at a discount of $832.50, 10 periods before their maturity date, the straight-line method would credit $83.25 of the discount amortization to each of the 10 periods. Use of the effective interest method, on the other hand, results in amortization at a regularly increasing amount, the first period receiving the smallest amount of credit, with the largest amount in the last period. Likewise, use of the straight-line method for amortizing premium gives equal distribution of amounts. However, amortizing premium by the effective interest method results in gradation of amounts, the first period being charged with the least, the last one with the most. The reason for the contrast in results from using the effective interest method for discount and premium is explained in a subsequent section of this appendix.

Before embarking on a detailed exposition of premium or discount amortization, a consideration of some general rules appears to be in order:

1. If investments having a designated maturity date are acquired as part of the original corpus of the trust, the older rule of law would not allow premium or discount amortization as adjustments of income. Gain or loss on disposal of such investments, by the same rule, is an adjustment of principal. Currently, it is widely accepted that income may be determined on the full accrual basis—after amortization—if specified by the trustor.

2. Circumstances may exist that minimize the importance of exact measurement of income in an accounting sense. Relatively small amounts of premium or discount on investments and absence of conflicting interests among beneficiaries are illustrations of such circumstances.

3. Because of probable changes in amounts of investments owned by long-term or large trusts, a **rate** of return is a more reliable **and** convenient criterion for judging efficiency of their management than is an **amount** of return. Use of the effective interest method of amortization (as compared with straight line) tends to produce a more uniform rate from period to period. This facilitates and fortifies comparisons.

Discussion of amortization in the next few pages will be predicated on the assumption that it is a function of income determination. No elaboration of the opposite situation is necessary. Under the latter concept, premium and discount transactions are regarded as adjustments of principal and affect the accounts only at the time of acquisition and disposal of the related investments.

Explanation of Straight-Line Amortization

Amortization of discount on bond investments over the life of the bonds has a twofold effect, as follows:

1. It adds periodically to the value of the investment as shown by the books, that is, "book value" or "carrying value." Current market value at any given time may be materially different than the book value. Ordinarily, this is of no importance to the trust fund that owns the bond, since the investment is a long-term commitment of earning power.

2. The increase in book value allotted to each period is an addition to the income on the investment for that period. Thus, if the nominal rate of interest on Pacific City bonds is 8 percent per annum, payable semiannually, the nominal interest per period is 4 percent times $25,000, or $1,000. The nominal rate of interest is the rate named in the bond, which the issuer covenants to pay on the par value of each bond. The effective interest on bonds acquired at a discount is the sum of the nominal interest plus the increase in the carrying value of the investment.

If bonds are acquired at a premium, their carrying value declines period by period. The effective interest on such bonds, therefore, is the remainder of nominal interest minus premium amortization.

From the foregoing statements, it is evident that the real earning on bonds bought at a discount or a premium is effective interest. Calculation of periodic effective income on a straight-line basis on $25,000 of par value bonds, nominal rate of interest 8 percent per annum, payable semiannually, may be illustrated as follows:

1. If purchased at a discount of $832.50, five years before maturity (10 *periods* before maturity):

$$(\$25,000 \times 4\%) + \frac{\$832.50}{10} = \$1,083.25 \text{ periodic effective interest}$$

2. If purchased at a premium of $832.50, five years before maturity (10 *periods* before maturity):

$$(\$25,000 \times 4\%) - \frac{\$832.50}{10} = \$916.75 \text{ periodic effective interest}$$

The process of discount amortization by the straight-line method may be represented by the schedule of amortization shown in Illustration 1.

A schedule of premium amortization can be constructed on the pattern of the discount amortization table in Illustration 1. A column labeled Premium Amortization would be substituted for Discount Amortization. Amounts in that column would be subtracted from, rather than added to, carrying value. Finally, carrying value at the end of Period 0 (same as beginning of Period 1) would be the sum of par value and premium.

Amortization schedules are not necessary if the straight-line basis is used. Periodic amortization is easily determined by simple arithmetic, and effective

---

ILLUSTRATION 1   Schedule of Discount Amortization—Straight-Line Method

Period	Nominal Interest (4 Percent)	Periodic Interest	Discount Amortization	Carrying Value of Investment at End of Period
0	—	—	—	$24,167.50
1	$1,000	$1,083.25	$83.25	24,250.75
2	1,000	1,083.25	83.25	24,334.00
3	1,000	1,083.25	83.25	24,417.25
4	1,000	1,083.25	83.25	24,500.50
5	1,000	1,083.25	83.25	24,583.75
6	1,000	1,083.25	83.25	24,667.00
7	1,000	1,083.25	83.25	24,750.25
8	1,000	1,083.25	83.25	24,883.50
9	1,000	1,083.25	83.25	24,916.75
10	1,000	1,083.25	83.25	25,000.00

interest is almost equally simple. The amounts and entries for nominal and effective interest are the same for each period.

Examination of the straight-line amortization table shown in Illustration 1 will reveal that although the investment carrying value increased periodically, the **amount** of effective interest for each of the 10 periods remained the same. This means the effective **rate** of interest, obtained as the quotient of effective interest divided by carrying value of investment, declines each period if discount is amortized equally by periods. Conversely, use of the straight-line method for amortizing premium would result in a periodically increasing effective rate of interest. Because of the importance of a regular rate of return in the management of investments, the straight-line basis for amortizing premium and discount is considered acceptable only if the difference between straight-line amortization and effective interest amortization has no material effect on financial statements.

Explanation of the Effective Interest Method of Amortization

The effective interest method of amortization utilizes actuarial tables to develop a schedule in which effective interest and the amount of amortization are adjusted periodically to produce a fixed **rate** of effective interest. That is, the effective interest for each period, divided by the carrying value of the investment for that period, gives the same quotient, which is the rate of interest. How the effective interest method operates will be demonstrated first as to bonds for which a premium was paid and then as to bonds acquired at a discount.

Referring to the Pacific City 8 percent bonds used as an example for straight-line amortization, suppose the safety factor of these bonds is such that they can command an effective rate of somewhat less than 4 percent semiannually. Further, assume the governing body of a trust fund decides that a semiannual yield of 3½ percent on these bonds is acceptable and accordingly decides to bid on $25,000 par value of them. What would be the bid price? It will depend on the time the bonds have yet to run, which for present purposes will be assumed as three years.

·What will the trust fund obtain if it becomes the successful bidder?

1. The right to receive $25,000 at the end of six periods.
2. The right to receive an interest payment of $1,000 at the end of each of the next six periods.

The series of interest payments is referred to as an "annuity," an annuity being defined as a series of equal payments, spaced at equal intervals of time. If each payment is made at the end of its respective period, the series is designated as an "ordinary annuity"; whereas if payments are made at the beginning of each period, the series becomes an "annuity due." Unless otherwise specified, "annuity" normally refers to the former.

Exact determination of the price that can be paid under the circumstances described, in order to obtain an effective yield rate of 3½ percent, consists of the following steps:

1. Determining the actuarial worth today, at 3½ percent discount of $25,000 for which the recipient will have to wait six periods.
2. Determining the actuarial worth today of an annuity of $1,000 at 3½ percent for six periods.

Both item 1 and item 2 require the use of mathematical tables giving various values of 1, or $1.00.

Reference to a table of present values of 1 (Table A at the end of this appendix) shows that the present value of 1 for six periods at 3½ percent is 0.81350. This means if an investor considers his money to be worth a return of 3½ percent per period, he could afford to give slightly more than $0.81 for the right to receive $1 at the end of six periods. Multiplying 0.81350 by $25,000 gives $20,337.50 as the present value of $25,000 discounted for six periods at 3½ percent.

A table of the present values of an annuity of 1 (Table B) shows the present value of an annuity of 1 at 3½ percent for six periods to be 5.32855, which would produce a value of $5,328.55 for an annuity of $1,000 under the same terms. Thus, it appears that for a return of 3½ percent semiannually on its investment, the trust fund management could bid the sum of $20,337.50 and $5,328.55, or $25,666.05, for the $25,000 of Pacific City bonds.

A schedule of effective interest and also of premium amortization on an effective interest basis for the above investment would appear as shown in Illustration 2.

To demonstrate the structure of a schedule for amortizing discount by the effective interest method, a table for that purpose is shown in Illustration 3. Without detailing the actuarial calculations involved, it will be assumed that a

---

ILLUSTRATION 2 **Schedule of Premium Amortization—$25,000 Par Value 8 Percent Bonds, Interest Payable Semiannually Acquired Three Years before Maturity, to Yield 3½ Percent Semiannually**

Period	Nominal Interest (4 Percent)	Effective Interest (3½ Percent)	Premium Amortization	Carrying Value at End of Period
0	—	—	—	$25,666.05
1	$1,000	$898.31	$101.69	25,564.36
2	1,000	894.75	105.25	25,459.11
3	1,000	891.07	108.93	25,350.18
4	1,000	887.26	112.74	25,237.44
5	1,000	883.31	116.69	25,120.75
6	1,000	879.25*	120.75	25,000.00

* This figure was "forced" from $879.23, the correct effective interest on $25,120.75 at 3½ percent, in order to give the required difference for premium amortization. The need for "forcing" was brought about by rounding each previous computation to the nearest cent.

ILLUSTRATION 3   **Schedule of Discount Amortization*—$25,000 Par Value 8 Percent Bonds, Interest Payable Semiannually Acquired Three Years before Maturity, to Yield 5 Percent Semiannually**

Period	Nominal Interest (4 Percent)	Effective Interest (5 Percent)	Discount Amortization	Carrying Value at End of Period
0	—	—	—	$23,731.19
1	$1,000	$1,186.56	$186.56	23,917.75
2	1,000	1,195.89	195.89	24,113.64
3	1,000	1,205.68	205.68	24,319.32
4	1,000	1,215.97	215.97	24,535.29
5	1,000	1,226.76	226.76	24,762.05
6	1,000	1,237.95†	237.95	25,000,00

* This might be called a "schedule of carrying value accumulation."
† This figure was "forced" in order to give the required difference for discount amortization. The need for "forcing" was brought about by rounding each previous computation to the nearest cent.

trust fund acquired the Pacific City 8 percent bonds on a 10 percent basis, that is, at a price to yield 5 percent semiannually. In order to obtain a semiannual yield rate of 5 percent on bonds paying a nominal rate of 4 percent on par value, the investment had to be bought at less than par. To obtain a yield rate of 5 percent for six periods on $25,000 par value of bonds would necessitate their purchase for $23,731.19. The purchase price equals the present worth of $25,000 for six periods at 5 percent ($18,655.50), plus the present worth of an annuity of $1,000 ($5,075.69) under the same terms.

An alternative method for determining what purchase price will yield a given rate is as follows:

1. Determine the periodic interest at the nominal rate on the par value of the proposed purchase.
2. Determine the periodic interest at the desired effective or yield rate on the par value of the proposed purchase.
3. Find the difference between item 1 and item 2.
4. Find the present value of an annuity of the amount of item 3 from time of purchase to maturity of the bonds, at the desired effective rate.
5. If the effective rate is higher, subtract the result in item 4 from the par value; if the nominal rate is higher, add the result of item 4 to the par value. The difference or sum will represent the cost that will yield the desired return.

Purchase between Interest Periods

In buying bonds, it is not usually practicable to make the purchase on the first day of an interest period. The question arises as to the determination of carrying value when bonds are bought, say, two months after an interest date, with interest payable semiannually. To explain the method of ascertaining the valuation between interest dates, it will be assumed the purchase occurred in the sixth semiannual period before maturity. Valuation will be calculated for the beginning of the sixth and fifth interest periods. Valuation at the interim date will be ascertained by the process of interpolation, which in this instance would consist of taking one third of the change from the sixth period before maturity and applying that to the valuation at the beginning of the sixth period. Thus, if the valuation at the beginning of the sixth period before maturity was $25,666.05, the premium amortization for that period was $101.69, and the interpolated valuation two months through the period would be $25,666.05 minus $101.69/3, or $25,632.15. It will be observed that the above interpolation was calculated on the basis of arithmetical progression. This is consistent if the straight-line basis of amortization is employed, but does not conform strictly with the effective interest basis, in which the amortization periodically increases.

Accounting for Income on Bonds—Straight-Line Amortization

As stated previously, when discount on bond investments is amortized, periodic earnings on the investments consist of the nominal interest, received in cash, and the increase in value of the investment during the period. Referring to the schedule of straight-line amortization of discount (Illustration 1), it is seen that total earnings for the first period were $1,083.25, consisting of $1,000 cash plus an $83.25 increase in the carrying value of the investment. In general journal entry form, the first-period earnings would be recorded as follows:

Cash..	1,000.00	
Investments	83.25	
Income on Bonds		1,083.25

By the nature of the straight-line method, the entry for each period's earnings would be the same.

Had the bonds been bought at a premium of $832.50, each period would have brought a reduction of $83.25 in the carrying value of the investment. The complete entry if premium amortization were involved would be as follows:

Cash..	1,000.00	
Investments		83.25
Income on Bonds		916.75

This entry is based on the logic that in each $1,000 interest payment the trust fund is recovering $83.25 of the amount paid out as premium, leaving a net earning of $916.75. It will be observed that amortization of either premium or discount will bring the investment carrying value to par value at the end of the last interest period.

Accounting for Income on Bonds—Effective Interest Method

Unlike entries for income on bonds by the straight-line method, those based on the effective interest method will not be the same in each period. If the bonds were acquired at a premium, for each period the premium amortization will be more, and the amount of effective interest less, than for the preceding period. If the bonds were acquired at a discount, both discount amortization and amount of effective interest will increase periodically.

The tabular summary of journal entries shown below portrays the change of amounts if the effective interest method is used:

Periodic Entries—Bonds Acquired at a Premium

Accounts	First Period	Second Period	Third Period	Fourth Period
Cash, Dr.	$1,000.00	$1,000.00	$1,000.00	$1,000.00
Investments, Cr.	101.69	105.25	108.93	112.74
Income on Bonds, Cr.	898.31	894.75	891.07	887.26

Periodic Entries—Bonds Acquired at a Discount

Accounts	First Period	Second Period	Third Period	Fourth Period
Cash, Dr.	$1,000.00	$1,000.00	$1,000.00	$1,000.00
Investments, Dr.	186.56	195.89	205.68	215.97
Income on Bonds, Cr.	1,186.56	1,195.89	1,205.68	1,215.97

Recording Discount and Premium Separately from Par Value

Thus far, discount and premium on bonds have been recorded in the same account with the par value of the bonds. That is, the purchase of $25,000 par value of bonds at a premium of $666.05 was recorded as a single debit, to Investments, of $25,666.05. The purchase of the securities at a discount of $1,268.81 was entered as a debit of $23,731.19. This practice is acceptable if the portfolio of investments includes only a few on which discount or premium must be amortized. However, as soon as bond investments reach any considerable proportions—say, at least 10 or 15—it becomes advantageous to record only par value in the Investments account, with supplementary accounts for premium and discount. Operation of supplementary accounts for premium and discount may be illustrated by the following entries for the purchase of $25,000 par value of bonds, first at $25,666.05 and then at $23,731.19:

Investments	25,000.00	
Unamortized Premium on Investments	666.05	
Cash		25,666.05
Investments	25,000.00	
Unamortized Discount on Investments		1,268.81
Cash		23,731.19

It will be noted that the carrying value is determined by adding unamortized premium to par value or subtracting unamortized discount from par value.

Separation of unamortized premium or discount from par value alters the form of entries for amortization. Instead of direct credits and debits to the Investments account, changes will be made in the supplementary accounts, as illustrated below, with amounts based on tables heretofore used.

1. For collection of interest on bonds bought at a premium, the following entry will be made:

Cash...	1,000.00	
Unamortized Premium on Investments................		101.69
Income on Bonds		898.31

2. For collection of interest on bonds bought at a discount, the entry will be as follows:

Cash...	1,000.00	
Unamortized Discount on Investments....................	186.56	
Income on Bonds		1,186.56

Insofar as amortization is concerned, the two entries above have the same effect on the carrying value as if Investments had been credited for \$101.69 in the first entry and debited for \$186.56 in the second. As Unamortized Premium on Investments is reduced by credits, it draws the carrying value nearer to par; as Unamortized Discount on Investments is reduced by debits, it draws the carrying value nearer to par.

All the preceding discussion of amortization has related to bonds owned as long-term investments. What about amortization of discount or premium on stock investments, or on bonds held as short-term commitments? Discount or premium on stock cannot be systematically amortized by any method because stock has no maturity date and there is no time basis for distributing the premium or discount, nor does stock necessarily tend to approach par value with the passing of time. Concerning short-term bond investments, since their holding is only temporary, their market value may trend even further away from par value during the period of ownership; so reducing book value by writing off discount or premium might be contradictory to facts.

Adjusting Entries to Income on Investments

Financial statements prepared in conformity with generally accepted accounting principles for funds owning long-term investments require adjusting entries for income earned but not received. If the holding of investments is small, or if the amount of accrued income at ends of periods is not material in amount, adjusting entries are frequently dispensed with for reasons of economy of time and effort.

Income earned but not received, in the form of real estate rentals, may be recorded in the following routine form for such an adjustment, using an assumed amount:

Accrued Rental Income...	320	
Rental Income		320

Dividends on stock investments are not earnings until the corporate board of directors has formally declared a dividend. This applies even though dividends on a certain stock have not been passed or omitted for many years. A trust fund closing its books on June 30 would violate accepted accounting practice to accrue one half of one year's dividends on stock of a corporation whose fiscal year coincides with the calendar year. However, if a dividend had been declared on June 20, payable to owners of record on July 10, the following entry, in an assumed amount, would be valid at June 30:

Dividends Receivable—Y Corporation Preferred
   Stock   400
      Dividend Income..   400

Accrual of income of investments in bonds, mortgages, and notes is sound because interest on such indebtedness of a corporation is a fixed charge, not contingent on approval by a board of directors. Calculating the amount of accrual on instruments of indebtedness such as those mentioned above is simple if they were acquired at par value. If acquired at a premium or discount that is being amortized, prorating of both nominal interest and amortization is necessary in the adjustment.

As an example of an adjusting entry for accrual of income on bonds purchased at a premium, figures will be taken from the table of premium amortization by the effective interest method (Illustration 2). Assume the interest dates on Pacific City bonds were May 1 and November 1,[2] and Period 3 in the table began on May 1. If the fiscal period of the trust fund owning these bonds ended on June 30, the accrual of effective interest at June 30 would be \$297.02, and amortization for the two months since May 1 would be \$36.31. The adjusting entry for June 30 would be as follows:

Accrued Interest on Bond Investments 333.33
   Investments (or Unamortized Premium
      on Investments)..   36.31
   Income on Bonds 297.02

An adjusting entry for accrued interest on bonds held at a discount may be framed on the basis of the above example.

The mission of some trust funds is to supply cash for more or less immediate purposes, such as tuition and other kinds of support or maintenance grants. Their primary interest is in periodical **spendable** income, which would exclude income accrued but not received and income based on amortization of discount. Amortization of discount adds to earnings only by adding to the carrying value of an investment (debit Unamortized Discount, credit Earnings). It is based on an expected **future** receipt of cash, at maturity of the investment.

Then why **do** funds record amortization of premium that **reduces** the showing of cash income of the present period (debit Earnings, credit Unamortized Premium)? The reason is that premium on investments represents part of the investment cost. That part of a periodic interest receipt that is attributed to premium amortization (debit Cash, credit Unamortized Premium, and credit Earnings) is actually a recovery of part of the **earning power** cost and not a part of earnings.

---

[2] Interest dates are sometimes indicated by the initial letters of the names of the months and the day date—for example, M and N1.

Eliminating accruals of income and amortization of discount on investments is important where emphasis is on periodic cash income. Where emphasis is on measurement of income over a long span of years, the accrual basis yields more precise measurement of results.

Purchase of Accrued Interest on Investments

The purchase of bonds or other interest-bearing securities between interest dates will include the purchase of accrued interest. That is, the purchaser of an interest-bearing security between interest dates obtains certain earning power, plus an amount of income already earned. A purchase, midway between interest dates, of $25,000 par value of Pacific City 8's, interest payable semiannually, acquires $500 accrued interest, plus the bonds. If the total purchase price was $26,115.20, the investment, or earning power, cost $25,615.20; the outlay for accrued interest will be recovered at the next interest date. Entries for the purchase and for the collection of interest at the next interest date would be as follows:

Investments	25,000.00	
Unamortized Premium on Investments	615.20	
Income on Bonds	500.00	
Cash		26,115.20
Cash	1,000.00	
Unamortized Premium on Investments		50.85
Income on Bonds		949.15

Amounts in the above explanation and entries are based on purchase of the bonds midway in Period 1 as represented in the schedule of effective interest amortization of premium (Illustration 2). Net income on bonds during the period of purchase was $949.15 less the $500 income purchased. This leaves a remainder of $449.15, which is one half the Period 1 effective interest as shown in the amortization schedule. When the accrued interest was purchased, a more accurate representation would have a debit to Accrued Bond Interest or Accrued Interest Purchased. Had either account title been used, when collection occurred, a split would have been necessary to credit the special title debited for the $500. Debiting the income account when interest is purchased is technically inaccurate; but when total income for the period is recorded, the adjustment for income purchased is automatic. The balance of the above account is $449.15, net income for the time the bonds were owned.

Income on Bonds			
Accrued interest purchased	$500.00	Credit at next interest date	$949.15

For reasons stated elsewhere, dividends on stock are not commonly accrued. However, owners of cumulative preferred stock sometimes calculate an accrual of dividend and add it to the price buyers must pay to get the stock. In preparing statements of cash receipts and disbursements for trusts and other funds that purchase accrued income, the outlay should be entitled Purchase of Accrued Interest on Investments or some similar name, regardless of the account debited for the acquisition.

Gain or Loss on Disposal of Investments

Investments may be disposed of by sale, through payment by the debtor at maturity of the debt, through liquidation of the debtor, and in a few other ways. Unless the transaction is consummated at exactly the book value of the investment at the time of disposal, there will be an accountable gain or loss. If a fund is nonexpendable as to both principal and income, obviously gain or loss, from whatever cause, is an adjustment of the Fund Balance. If the fund is expendable as to income but nonexpendable as to principal, accounting for gain or loss on disposal of investments will depend on whether such transactions are governed by specific instructions established by the trustor or by the older rule of law.[3] The individual or other authority establishing a trust has a legal right to specify whether such gains and losses are to be related to income or to principal. In the absence of such specific instructions, the older rule of law would operate and relate them to principal.

Every trust fund indenture should contain express provisions governing accounting for gains and losses on investments as well as other kinds of debatable transactions. If such is not the case, fund trustees should make the necessary decisions, with due regard for all pertinent law, and incorporate them in their minutes.

Measurement of gain or loss on disposal of investments consists of finding the difference between (1) the net amount realized from the investment and (2) the book value of the investment at the date of disposal. If gross receipts from the sale of investments include a charge for earnings accumulated since the interest or dividend date, the latter being very unusual, the amount thereof must be excluded from the selling price of the investment. Furthermore, brokerage or other fees incurred in consummating the sale must be deducted in finding the net selling price. In the discussion and examples to follow in this section, the decision as to whether gain or loss in each situation is chargeable to income or principal will be avoided by debiting Loss on Sale of Investments for all losses and crediting Gain on Sale of Investments for all gains. To illustrate accounting techniques for disposal of investments, it will be assumed, first, that the book value at the time of disposal is the same as the historical cost and, then, that the historical cost and the present book or carrying value are different.

The book value of investments at the time of disposal will be the same as the historical cost under the following general conditions:

1. If the investment is corporate stock, because premium and discount on stock investments are not amortized.[4]
2. If the investments are bonds acquired at par value.
3. If the investments are bonds acquired at a premium or discount, and none has been amortized.
4. If the investment consists of assets subject to depreciation or amortization, but none has been recorded in any way.

---

[3] As discussed in Chapter 12 (see footnote 1 of that chapter), there are signs that the rule is breaking down, particularly in respect to endowment funds of colleges and universities.

[4] If there has been a stock dividend or stock split on stock since it was acquired, the cost and book value *per share* will be lower.

Illustrative entries for the disposal of the above-named types of investments are as follows:

1. $5,000 par value of stock acquired for $5,125 was sold for $5,187.

Cash	5,187	
Investments.......................................		5,125
Gain on Sale of Investments		62

2. $2,000 par value of bonds purchased at par were sold for $1,793 and accrued interest of $25.

Cash	1,818	
Loss on Sale of Investments	207	
Investments..		2,000
Bond Interest Income		25

3. $3,000 par value of bonds acquired at a premium of $25, of which none had been amortized, were sold for $3,060 and accrued interest of $40.

Cash	3,100	
Investments..		3,025
Gain on Sale of Investments		35
Bond Interest Income		40

4. A building acquired for $27,000 and land that cost $1,000 were sold for $39,000. No depreciation had been recorded on the building.

Cash	39,000	
Buildings		27,000
Land		1,000
Gain on Sale Investments...............................		11,000

For at least two kinds of investments, the carrying value at the time of disposition will differ from the original cost. There are (1) depreciable fixed assets, ordinarily buildings, on which depreciation has been recorded; and (2) bonds bought for long-term investments, at either a premium or a discount, on which periodic amortization has been recorded. As to the bonds, if all the premium or discount has been written off, they will have been adjusted to par value. Accounting for proceeds at their maturity will be conducted as though they had been acquired at that figure. Disposal of a building for which an allowance for depreciation is carried, and disposal of bonds with a supplementary account for either premium or discount, will be alike in that book value of the investment is recorded in, and will have to be removed from, two accounts.

An additional complication arises when the disposal is made **during** a fiscal period, which is normal since such transactions are not ordinarily timed to coincide with the beginning or ending of a fiscal period. This means an adjustment must be made for depreciation or amortization since the last closing, in order to bring the book value up to date. The disposal of a building under such circumstances illustrates the principles involved. Assume a building acquired as an investment at a cost of $18,000 had been depreciated in the amount of $8,100 to the end of the preceding fiscal period, at an annual rate of $900. If disposal is made for

$10,000 net, three months after the last closing, the following entries might be made:

Depreciation—Buildings	225	
Allowance for Depreciation of Buildings		225
Cash	10,000	
Allowance for Depreciation of Buildings	8,325	
Investments		18,000
Gain on Sale of Investments		325

Correct accounting for disposal of bonds, the premium or discount on which is being amortized periodically, at a time between interest dates, requires the carrying value to be adjusted to the date of sale.

To illustrate the accounting entries involved, let the following assumptions be made about $25,000 par value of bonds.

Period Ending	Nominal Interest (4 Percent)	Effective Interest (3½ Percent)	Amortization for Period	Carrying Value at End of Period
December 31, 19x8.	$1,000	$891.07	$108.93	$25,350.18
June 30, 19x9......	1,000	887.26	112.74	25,237.44

Sale or other disposal of the bonds—say, on March 1, 19x9—would require carrying value to be brought one third of the way through the period ended on June 30, 19x9. Premium amortization for the two months since December 31, 19x8, is one third of $112.74, or $37.58, which would indicate a carrying value of $25,350.18 minus $37.58, or $25,312.60, for the investment at the interim date. The decrease in the carrying value may be recorded as follows:

Income on Bonds	37.58	
Unamortized Premium on Investments		37.58

Assuming the bonds were sold to net 100½ plus accrued interest, the transaction might be recorded by this entry:

Cash	25,458.33	
Loss on Sale of Investments	187.60	
Investments		25,000.00
Unamortized Premium on Investments		312.60
Income on Bonds		333.33

The amount of loss appearing in this entry is the difference between the carrying value of the investment at March 1, 19x9, which is $25,312.60, and the net selling price of the bonds ($25,000 times 100½, or $25,125). The two entries shown above might be condensed into one.

For the purpose of illustration, all gains on investments have been recorded as Gain on Sale of Investments; whereas all losses have been debited to Loss on Sale of Investments. In individual cases, it is necessary for the accountant to ascertain, in light of all pertinent information, whether such gains and losses are in fact operating transactions affecting net income, or are adjustments of fund principal and therefore to be credited or debited to the Fund Balance account or other account recording the fund equity.

TABLE A Present Value of $1 at Compound Interest: 0.5%–7% $P_{i,n} = \dfrac{1}{(1 + i)^n}$

Period	.5%	1%	1.5%	2%	2.5%	3%	3.5%	4%	4.5%	5%	5.5%	6%	6.5%	7%
1	0.99502	0.99010	0.98522	0.98039	0.97561	0.97087	0.96618	0.96154	0.95694	0.95238	0.94787	0.94340	0.93897	0.93458
2	0.99007	0.98030	0.97066	0.96117	0.95181	0.94260	0.93351	0.92456	0.91573	0.90703	0.89845	0.89000	0.88166	0.87344
3	0.98515	0.97059	0.95632	0.94232	0.92860	0.91514	0.90194	0.88900	0.87630	0.86384	0.85161	0.83962	0.82785	0.81630
4	0.98025	0.96098	0.94218	0.92385	0.90595	0.88849	0.87144	0.85480	0.83856	0.82270	0.80722	0.79209	0.77732	0.76290
5	0.97537	0.95147	0.92826	0.90573	0.88385	0.86261	0.84197	0.82193	0.80245	0.78353	0.76513	0.74726	0.72988	0.71299
6	0.97052	0.94205	0.91454	0.88797	0.86230	0.83748	0.81350	0.79031	0.76790	0.74622	0.72525	0.70496	0.68533	0.66634
7	0.96569	0.93272	0.90103	0.87056	0.84127	0.81309	0.78599	0.75992	0.73483	0.71068	0.68744	0.66506	0.64351	0.62275
8	0.96089	0.92348	0.88771	0.85349	0.82075	0.78941	0.75941	0.73069	0.70319	0.67684	0.65160	0.62741	0.60423	0.58201
9	0.95610	0.91434	0.87459	0.83676	0.80073	0.76642	0.73373	0.70259	0.67290	0.64461	0.61763	0.59190	0.56735	0.54393
10	0.95135	0.90529	0.86167	0.82035	0.78120	0.74409	0.70892	0.67556	0.64393	0.61391	0.58543	0.55839	0.53273	0.50835
11	0.94661	0.89632	0.84893	0.80426	0.76214	0.72242	0.68495	0.64958	0.61620	0.58468	0.55491	0.52679	0.50021	0.47509
12	0.94191	0.88745	0.83639	0.78849	0.74356	0.70138	0.66178	0.62460	0.58966	0.55684	0.52598	0.49697	0.46968	0.44401
13	0.93722	0.87866	0.82403	0.77303	0.72542	0.68095	0.63940	0.60057	0.56427	0.53032	0.49856	0.46884	0.44102	0.41496
14	0.93256	0.86996	0.81185	0.75788	0.70773	0.66112	0.61778	0.57748	0.53997	0.50507	0.47257	0.44230	0.41410	0.38782
15	0.92792	0.86135	0.79985	0.74301	0.69047	0.64186	0.59689	0.55526	0.51672	0.48102	0.44793	0.41727	0.38883	0.36245
16	0.92330	0.85282	0.78803	0.72845	0.67362	0.62317	0.57671	0.53391	0.49447	0.45811	0.42458	0.39365	0.36510	0.33873
17	0.91871	0.84438	0.77639	0.71416	0.65720	0.60502	0.55720	0.51337	0.47318	0.43630	0.40245	0.37136	0.34281	0.31657
18	0.91414	0.83602	0.76491	0.70016	0.64117	0.58739	0.53836	0.49363	0.45280	0.41552	0.38147	0.35034	0.32189	0.29586
19	0.90959	0.82774	0.75361	0.68643	0.62553	0.57029	0.52016	0.47464	0.43330	0.39573	0.36158	0.33051	0.30224	0.27651
20	0.90506	0.81954	0.74247	0.67297	0.61027	0.55368	0.50257	0.45639	0.41464	0.37689	0.34273	0.31180	0.28380	0.25842
21	0.90056	0.81143	0.73150	0.65978	0.59539	0.53755	0.48557	0.43883	0.39679	0.35894	0.32486	0.29416	0.26648	0.24151
22	0.89608	0.80340	0.72069	0.64684	0.58086	0.52189	0.46915	0.42196	0.37970	0.34185	0.30793	0.27751	0.25021	0.22571
23	0.89162	0.79544	0.71004	0.63416	0.56670	0.50669	0.45329	0.40573	0.36335	0.32557	0.29187	0.26180	0.23494	0.21095
24	0.88719	0.78757	0.69954	0.62172	0.55288	0.49193	0.43796	0.39012	0.34770	0.31007	0.27666	0.24698	0.22060	0.19715
25	0.88277	0.77977	0.68921	0.60953	0.53939	0.47761	0.42315	0.37512	0.33273	0.29530	0.26223	0.23300	0.20714	0.18425
26	0.87838	0.77205	0.67902	0.59758	0.52623	0.46369	0.40884	0.36069	0.31840	0.28124	0.24856	0.21981	0.19450	0.17220
27	0.87401	0.76440	0.66899	0.58586	0.51340	0.45019	0.39501	0.34682	0.30469	0.26785	0.23560	0.20737	0.18263	0.16093
28	0.86966	0.75684	0.65910	0.57437	0.50088	0.43708	0.38165	0.33348	0.29157	0.25509	0.22332	0.19563	0.17148	0.15040
29	0.86533	0.74934	0.64936	0.56311	0.48866	0.42435	0.36875	0.32065	0.27902	0.24295	0.21168	0.18456	0.16101	0.14056
30	0.86103	0.74192	0.63976	0.55207	0.47674	0.41199	0.35628	0.30832	0.26700	0.23138	0.20064	0.17411	0.15119	0.13137
31	0.85675	0.73458	0.63031	0.54125	0.46511	0.39999	0.34423	0.29646	0.25550	0.22036	0.19018	0.16425	0.14196	0.12277
32	0.85248	0.72730	0.62099	0.53063	0.45377	0.38834	0.33259	0.28506	0.24450	0.20987	0.18027	0.15496	0.13329	0.11474
33	0.84824	0.72010	0.61182	0.52023	0.44270	0.37703	0.32134	0.27409	0.23397	0.19987	0.17087	0.14619	0.12516	0.10723
34	0.84402	0.71297	0.60277	0.51003	0.43191	0.36604	0.31048	0.26355	0.22390	0.19035	0.16196	0.13791	0.11752	0.10022
35	0.83982	0.70591	0.59387	0.50003	0.42137	0.35538	0.29998	0.25342	0.21425	0.18129	0.15352	0.13011	0.11035	0.09366
36	0.83564	0.69892	0.58509	0.49022	0.41109	0.34503	0.28983	0.24367	0.20503	0.17266	0.14552	0.12274	0.10361	0.08754
37	0.83149	0.69200	0.57644	0.48061	0.40107	0.33498	0.28003	0.23430	0.19620	0.16444	0.13793	0.11579	0.09729	0.08181
38	0.82735	0.68515	0.56792	0.47119	0.39128	0.32523	0.27056	0.22529	0.18775	0.15661	0.13074	0.10924	0.09135	0.07646
39	0.82323	0.67837	0.55953	0.46195	0.38174	0.31575	0.26141	0.21662	0.17967	0.14915	0.12392	0.10306	0.08578	0.07146
40	0.81914	0.67165	0.55126	0.45289	0.37243	0.30656	0.25257	0.20829	0.17193	0.14205	0.11746	0.09722	0.08054	0.06678
41	0.81506	0.66500	0.54312	0.44401	0.36335	0.29763	0.24403	0.20028	0.16453	0.13528	0.11134	0.09172	0.07563	0.06241
42	0.81101	0.65842	0.53509	0.43530	0.35448	0.28896	0.23578	0.19257	0.15744	0.12884	0.10554	0.08653	0.07101	0.05833
43	0.80697	0.65190	0.52718	0.42677	0.34584	0.28054	0.22781	0.18517	0.15066	0.12270	0.10003	0.08163	0.06668	0.05451
44	0.80296	0.64545	0.51939	0.41840	0.33740	0.27237	0.22010	0.17805	0.14417	0.11686	0.09482	0.07701	0.06261	0.05095
45	0.79896	0.63905	0.51171	0.41020	0.32917	0.26444	0.21266	0.17120	0.13796	0.11130	0.08988	0.07265	0.05879	0.04761
46	0.79499	0.63273	0.50415	0.40215	0.32115	0.25674	0.20547	0.16461	0.13202	0.10600	0.08519	0.06854	0.05520	0.04450
47	0.79103	0.62646	0.49670	0.39427	0.31331	0.24926	0.19852	0.15828	0.12634	0.10095	0.08075	0.06466	0.05183	0.04159
48	0.78710	0.62026	0.48936	0.38654	0.30567	0.24200	0.19181	0.15219	0.12090	0.09614	0.07654	0.06100	0.04867	0.03887
49	0.78318	0.61412	0.48213	0.37896	0.29822	0.23495	0.18532	0.14634	0.11569	0.09156	0.07255	0.05755	0.04570	0.03632
50	0.77929	0.60804	0.47500	0.37153	0.29094	0.22811	0.17905	0.14071	0.11071	0.08720	0.06877	0.05429	0.04291	0.03395
51	0.77541	0.60202	0.46798	0.36424	0.28385	0.22146	0.17300	0.13530	0.10594	0.08305	0.06518	0.05122	0.04029	0.03173
52	0.77155	0.59606	0.46107	0.35710	0.27692	0.21501	0.16715	0.13010	0.10138	0.07910	0.06178	0.04832	0.03783	0.02965
53	0.76771	0.59016	0.45426	0.35010	0.27017	0.20875	0.16150	0.12509	0.09701	0.07533	0.05856	0.04558	0.03552	0.02771
54	0.76389	0.58431	0.44754	0.34323	0.26358	0.20267	0.15603	0.12028	0.09284	0.07174	0.05551	0.04300	0.03335	0.02590
55	0.76009	0.57853	0.44093	0.33650	0.25715	0.19677	0.15076	0.11566	0.08884	0.06833	0.05262	0.04057	0.03132	0.02420
56	0.75631	0.57280	0.43441	0.32991	0.25088	0.19104	0.14566	0.11121	0.08501	0.06507	0.04987	0.03827	0.02941	0.02262
57	0.75255	0.56713	0.42799	0.32344	0.24476	0.18547	0.14073	0.10693	0.08135	0.06197	0.04727	0.03610	0.02761	0.02114
58	0.74880	0.56151	0.42167	0.31710	0.23879	0.18007	0.13598	0.10282	0.07785	0.05902	0.04481	0.03406	0.02593	0.01976
59	0.74508	0.55595	0.41544	0.31088	0.23297	0.17483	0.13138	0.09886	0.07450	0.05621	0.04247	0.03213	0.02434	0.01847
60	0.74137	0.55045	0.40930	0.30478	0.22728	0.16973	0.12693	0.09506	0.07129	0.05354	0.04026	0.03031	0.02286	0.01726

Period	7.5%	8%	8.5%	9%	9.5%	10%	10.5%	11%	11.5%	12%	12.5%	13%	13.5%	14%
1 ...	0.93023	0.92593	0.92166	0.91743	0.91324	0.90909	0.90498	0.90090	0.89686	0.89286	0.88889	0.88496	0.88106	0.87719
2 ...	0.86533	0.85734	0.84946	0.84168	0.83401	0.82645	0.81898	0.81162	0.80436	0.79719	0.79012	0.78315	0.77626	0.76947
3 ...	0.80496	0.79383	0.78291	0.77218	0.76165	0.75131	0.74116	0.73119	0.72140	0.71178	0.70233	0.69305	0.68393	0.67497
4 ...	0.74880	0.73503	0.72157	0.70843	0.69557	0.68301	0.67073	0.65873	0.64699	0.63553	0.62430	0.61332	0.60258	0.59208
5 ...	0.69656	0.68058	0.66505	0.64993	0.63523	0.62092	0.60700	0.59345	0.58026	0.56743	0.55493	0.54276	0.53091	0.51937
6 ...	0.64796	0.63017	0.61295	0.59627	0.58012	0.56447	0.54932	0.53464	0.52042	0.50663	0.49327	0.48032	0.46776	0.45559
7 ...	0.60275	0.58349	0.56493	0.54703	0.52979	0.51316	0.49712	0.48166	0.46674	0.45235	0.43846	0.42506	0.41213	0.39964
8 ...	0.56070	0.54027	0.52067	0.50187	0.48382	0.46651	0.44989	0.43393	0.41860	0.40388	0.38974	0.37616	0.36311	0.35056
9 ...	0.52158	0.50025	0.47988	0.46043	0.44185	0.42410	0.40714	0.39092	0.37543	0.36061	0.34644	0.33288	0.31992	0.30751
10 ...	0.48519	0.46319	0.44229	0.42241	0.40351	0.38554	0.36845	0.35218	0.33671	0.32197	0.30795	0.29459	0.28187	0.26974
11 ...	0.45134	0.42888	0.40764	0.38753	0.36851	0.35049	0.33344	0.31728	0.30198	0.28748	0.27373	0.26070	0.24834	0.23662
12 ...	0.41985	0.39711	0.37570	0.35553	0.33654	0.31863	0.30175	0.28584	0.27083	0.25668	0.24332	0.23071	0.21880	0.20756
13 ...	0.39056	0.36770	0.34627	0.32618	0.30734	0.28966	0.27308	0.25751	0.24290	0.22917	0.21628	0.20416	0.19278	0.18207
14 ...	0.36331	0.34046	0.31914	0.29925	0.28067	0.26333	0.24713	0.23199	0.21785	0.20462	0.19225	0.18068	0.16985	0.15971
15 ...	0.33797	0.31524	0.29414	0.27454	0.25632	0.23939	0.22365	0.20900	0.19538	0.18270	0.17089	0.15989	0.14964	0.14010
16 ...	0.31439	0.29189	0.27110	0.25187	0.23409	0.21763	0.20240	0.18829	0.17523	0.16312	0.15190	0.14150	0.13185	0.12289
17 ...	0.29245	0.27027	0.24986	0.23107	0.21378	0.19784	0.18316	0.16963	0.15715	0.14564	0.13502	0.12522	0.11616	0.10780
18 ...	0.27205	0.25025	0.23028	0.21199	0.19523	0.17986	0.16576	0.15282	0.14095	0.13004	0.12002	0.11081	0.10235	0.09456
19 ...	0.25307	0.23171	0.21224	0.19449	0.17829	0.16351	0.15001	0.13768	0.12641	0.11611	0.10668	0.09806	0.09017	0.08295
20 ...	0.23541	0.21455	0.19562	0.17843	0.16282	0.14864	0.13575	0.12403	0.11337	0.10367	0.09483	0.08678	0.07945	0.07276
21 ...	0.21899	0.19866	0.18029	0.16370	0.14870	0.13513	0.12285	0.11174	0.10168	0.09256	0.08429	0.07680	0.07000	0.06383
22 ...	0.20371	0.18394	0.16617	0.15018	0.13580	0.12285	0.11118	0.10067	0.09119	0.08264	0.07493	0.06796	0.06167	0.05599
23 ...	0.18950	0.17032	0.15315	0.13778	0.12402	0.11168	0.10062	0.09069	0.08179	0.07379	0.06660	0.06014	0.05434	0.04911
24 ...	0.17628	0.15770	0.14115	0.12640	0.11326	0.10153	0.09106	0.08170	0.07335	0.06588	0.05920	0.05323	0.04787	0.04308
25 ...	0.16398	0.14602	0.13009	0.11597	0.10343	0.09230	0.08240	0.07361	0.06579	0.05882	0.05262	0.04710	0.04218	0.03779
26 ...	0.15254	0.13520	0.11990	0.10639	0.09446	0.08391	0.07457	0.06631	0.05900	0.05252	0.04678	0.04168	0.03716	0.03315
27 ...	0.14190	0.12519	0.11051	0.09761	0.08626	0.07628	0.06749	0.05974	0.05291	0.04689	0.04158	0.03689	0.03274	0.02908
28 ...	0.13200	0.11591	0.10185	0.08955	0.07878	0.06934	0.06107	0.05382	0.04746	0.04187	0.03696	0.03264	0.02885	0.02551
29 ...	0.12279	0.10733	0.09387	0.08215	0.07194	0.06304	0.05527	0.04849	0.04256	0.03738	0.03285	0.02889	0.02542	0.02237
30 ...	0.11422	0.09938	0.08652	0.07537	0.06570	0.05731	0.05002	0.04368	0.03817	0.03338	0.02920	0.02557	0.02239	0.01963
31 ...	0.10625	0.09202	0.07974	0.06915	0.06000	0.05210	0.04527	0.03935	0.03424	0.02980	0.02596	0.02262	0.01973	0.01722
32 ...	0.09884	0.08520	0.07349	0.06344	0.05480	0.04736	0.04096	0.03545	0.03070	0.02661	0.02307	0.02002	0.01738	0.01510
33 ...	0.09194	0.07889	0.06774	0.05820	0.05004	0.04306	0.03707	0.03194	0.02754	0.02376	0.02051	0.01772	0.01532	0.01325
34 ...	0.08553	0.07305	0.06243	0.05339	0.04570	0.03914	0.03355	0.02878	0.02470	0.02121	0.01823	0.01568	0.01349	0.01162
35 ...	0.07956	0.06763	0.05754	0.04899	0.04174	0.03558	0.03036	0.02592	0.02215	0.01894	0.01621	0.01388	0.01189	0.01019
36 ...	0.07401	0.06262	0.05303	0.04494	0.03811	0.03235	0.02748	0.02335	0.01987	0.01691	0.01440	0.01228	0.01047	0.00894
37 ...	0.06885	0.05799	0.04888	0.04123	0.03481	0.02941	0.02487	0.02104	0.01782	0.01510	0.01280	0.01087	0.00923	0.00784
38 ...	0.06404	0.05369	0.04505	0.03783	0.03179	0.02673	0.02250	0.01896	0.01598	0.01348	0.01138	0.00962	0.00813	0.00688
39 ...	0.05958	0.04971	0.04152	0.03470	0.02903	0.02430	0.02036	0.01708	0.01433	0.01204	0.01012	0.00851	0.00716	0.00604
40 ...	0.05542	0.04603	0.03827	0.03184	0.02651	0.02209	0.01843	0.01538	0.01285	0.01075	0.00899	0.00753	0.00631	0.00529
41 ...	0.05155	0.04262	0.03527	0.02921	0.02421	0.02009	0.01668	0.01386	0.01153	0.00960	0.00799	0.00666	0.00556	0.00464
42 ...	0.04796	0.03946	0.03251	0.02680	0.02211	0.01826	0.01509	0.01249	0.01034	0.00857	0.00711	0.00590	0.00490	0.00407
43 ...	0.04461	0.03654	0.02996	0.02458	0.02019	0.01660	0.01366	0.01125	0.00927	0.00765	0.00632	0.00522	0.00432	0.00357
44 ...	0.04150	0.03383	0.02761	0.02255	0.01844	0.01509	0.01236	0.01013	0.00832	0.00683	0.00561	0.00462	0.00380	0.00313
45 ...	0.03860	0.03133	0.02545	0.02069	0.01684	0.01372	0.01119	0.00913	0.00746	0.00610	0.00499	0.00409	0.00335	0.00275
46 ...	0.03591	0.02901	0.02345	0.01898	0.01538	0.01247	0.01012	0.00823	0.00669	0.00544	0.00444	0.00362	0.00295	0.00241
47 ...	0.03340	0.02686	0.02162	0.01742	0.01405	0.01134	0.00916	0.00741	0.00600	0.00486	0.00394	0.00320	0.00260	0.00212
48 ...	0.03107	0.02487	0.01992	0.01598	0.01283	0.01031	0.00829	0.00668	0.00538	0.00434	0.00350	0.00283	0.00229	0.00186
49 ...	0.02891	0.02303	0.01836	0.01466	0.01171	0.00937	0.00750	0.00601	0.00483	0.00388	0.00312	0.00251	0.00202	0.00163
50 ...	0.02689	0.02132	0.01692	0.01345	0.01070	0.00852	0.00679	0.00542	0.00433	0.00346	0.00277	0.00222	0.00178	0.00143
51 ...	0.02501	0.01974	0.01560	0.01234	0.00977	0.00774	0.00615	0.00488	0.00388	0.00309	0.00246	0.00196	0.00157	0.00125
52 ...	0.02327	0.01828	0.01438	0.01132	0.00892	0.00704	0.00556	0.00440	0.00348	0.00276	0.00219	0.00174	0.00138	0.00110
53 ...	0.02164	0.01693	0.01325	0.01038	0.00815	0.00640	0.00503	0.00396	0.00312	0.00246	0.00194	0.00154	0.00122	0.00096
54 ...	0.02013	0.01567	0.01221	0.00953	0.00744	0.00582	0.00455	0.00357	0.00280	0.00220	0.00173	0.00136	0.00107	0.00085
55 ...	0.01873	0.01451	0.01126	0.00874	0.00680	0.00529	0.00412	0.00322	0.00251	0.00196	0.00154	0.00120	0.00094	0.00074
56 ...	0.01742	0.01344	0.01037	0.00802	0.00621	0.00481	0.00373	0.00290	0.00225	0.00175	0.00137	0.00107	0.00083	0.00065
57 ...	0.01621	0.01244	0.00956	0.00736	0.00567	0.00437	0.00338	0.00261	0.00202	0.00157	0.00121	0.00094	0.00073	0.00057
58 ...	0.01508	0.01152	0.00881	0.00675	0.00518	0.00397	0.00305	0.00235	0.00181	0.00140	0.00108	0.00083	0.00065	0.00050
59 ...	0.01402	0.01067	0.00812	0.00619	0.00473	0.00361	0.00276	0.00212	0.00162	0.00125	0.00096	0.00074	0.00057	0.00044
60 ...	0.01305	0.00988	0.00749	0.00568	0.00432	0.00328	0.00250	0.00191	0.00146	0.00111	0.00085	0.00065	0.00050	0.00039

Period	14.5%	15%	15.5%	16%	16.5%	17%	17.5%	18%	18.5%	19%	19.5%	20%
1	0.87336	0.86957	0.86580	0.86207	0.85837	0.85470	0.85106	0.84746	0.84388	0.84034	0.83682	0.83333
2	0.76276	0.75614	0.74961	0.74316	0.73680	0.73051	0.72431	0.71818	0.71214	0.70616	0.70027	0.69444
3	0.66617	0.65752	0.64901	0.64066	0.63244	0.62437	0.61643	0.60863	0.60096	0.59342	0.58600	0.57870
4	0.58181	0.57175	0.56192	0.55229	0.54287	0.53365	0.52462	0.51579	0.50714	0.49867	0.49038	0.48225
5	0.50813	0.49718	0.48651	0.47611	0.46598	0.45611	0.44649	0.43711	0.42796	0.41905	0.41036	0.40188
6	0.44378	0.43233	0.42122	0.41044	0.39999	0.38984	0.37999	0.37043	0.36115	0.35214	0.34339	0.33490
7	0.38758	0.37594	0.36469	0.35383	0.34334	0.33320	0.32340	0.31393	0.30477	0.29592	0.28736	0.27908
8	0.33850	0.32690	0.31575	0.30503	0.29471	0.28478	0.27523	0.26604	0.25719	0.24867	0.24047	0.23257
9	0.29563	0.28426	0.27338	0.26295	0.25297	0.24340	0.23424	0.22546	0.21704	0.20897	0.20123	0.19381
10	0.25819	0.24718	0.23669	0.22668	0.21714	0.20804	0.19935	0.19106	0.18315	0.17560	0.16839	0.16151
11	0.22550	0.21494	0.20493	0.19542	0.18639	0.17781	0.16966	0.16192	0.15456	0.14757	0.14091	0.13459
12	0.19694	0.18691	0.17743	0.16846	0.15999	0.15197	0.14439	0.13722	0.13043	0.12400	0.11792	0.11216
13	0.17200	0.16253	0.15362	0.14523	0.13733	0.12989	0.12289	0.11629	0.11007	0.10421	0.09868	0.09346
14	0.15022	0.14133	0.13300	0.12520	0.11788	0.11102	0.10459	0.09855	0.09288	0.08757	0.08258	0.07789
15	0.13120	0.12289	0.11515	0.10793	0.10118	0.09489	0.08901	0.08352	0.07838	0.07359	0.06910	0.06491
16	0.11458	0.10686	0.09970	0.09304	0.08685	0.08110	0.07575	0.07078	.06615	0.06184	0.05782	0.05409
17	0.10007	0.09293	0.08632	0.08021	0.07455	0.06932	0.06447	0.05998	0.05582	0.05196	0.04839	0.04507
18	0.08740	0.04081	0.07474	0.06914	0.06399	0.05925	0.05487	0.05083	0.04711	0.04367	0.04049	0.03756
19	0.07633	0.07027	0.06471	0.05961	0.05493	0.05064	0.04670	0.04308	0.03975	0.03670	0.03389	0.03130
20	0.06666	0.06110	0.05602	0.05139	0.04715	0.04328	0.03974	0.03651	0.03355	0.03084	0.02836	0.02608
21	0.05822	0.05313	0.04850	0.04430	0.04047	0.03699	0.03382	0.03094	0.02831	0.02591	0.02373	0.02174
22	0.05085	0.04620	0.04199	0.03819	0.03474	0.03162	0.02879	0.02622	0.02389	0.02178	0.01986	0.01811
23	0.04441	0.04017	0.03636	0.03292	0.02982	0.02702	0.02450	0.02222	0.02016	0.01830	0.01662	0.01509
24	0.03879	0.03493	0.03148	0.02838	0.02560	0.02310	0.02085	0.01883	0.01701	0.01538	0.01390	0.01258
25	0.03387	0.03038	0.02726	0.02447	0.02197	0.01974	0.01774	0.01596	0.01436	0.01292	0.01164	0.01048
26	0.02958	0.02642	0.02360	0.02109	0.01886	0.01687	0.01510	0.01352	0.01211	0.01086	0.00974	0.00874
27	0.02584	0.02297	0.02043	0.01818	0.01619	0.01442	0.01285	0.01146	0.01022	0.00912	0.00815	0.00728
28	0.02257	0.01997	0.01769	0.01567	0.01390	0.01233	0.01094	0.00971	0.00863	0.00767	0.00682	0.00607
29	0.01971	0.01737	0.01532	0.01351	0.01193	0.01053	0.00931	0.00823	0.00728	0.00644	0.00571	0.00506
30	0.01721	0.01510	0.01326	0.01165	0.01024	0.00900	0.00792	0.00697	0.00614	0.00541	0.00477	0.00421
31	0.01503	0.01313	0.01148	0.01004	0.00879	0.00770	0.00674	0.00591	0.00518	0.00455	0.00400	0.00351
32	0.01313	0.01142	0.00994	0.00866	0.00754	0.00658	0.00574	0.00501	0.00438	0.00382	0.00334	0.00293
33	0.01147	0.00993	0.00861	0.00746	0.00648	0.00562	0.00488	0.00425	0.00369	0.00321	0.00280	0.00244
34	0.01001	0.00864	0.00745	0.00643	0.00556	0.00480	0.00416	0.00360	0.00312	0.00270	0.00234	0.00203
35	0.00875	0.00751	0.00645	0.00555	0.00477	0.00411	0.00354	0.00305	0.00263	0.00227	0.00196	0.00169
36	0.00764	0.00653	0.00559	0.00478	0.00410	0.00351	0.00301	0.00258	0.00222	0.00191	0.00164	0.00141
37	0.00667	0.00568	0.00484	0.00412	0.00352	0.00300	0.00256	0.00219	0.00187	0.00160	0.00137	0.00118
38	0.00583	0.00494	0.00419	0.00355	0.00302	0.00256	0.00218	0.00186	0.00158	0.00135	0.00115	0.00098
39	0.00509	0.00429	0.00362	0.00306	0.00259	0.00219	0.00186	0.00157	0.00133	0.00113	0.00096	0.00082
40	0.00444	0.00373	0.00314	0.00264	0.00222	0.00187	0.00158	0.00133	0.00113	0.00095	0.00080	0.00068
41	0.00388	0.00325	0.00272	0.00228	0.00191	0.00160	0.00134	0.00113	0.00095	0.00080	0.00067	0.00057
42	0.00339	0.00282	0.00235	0.00196	0.00164	0.00137	0.00114	0.00096	0.00080	0.00067	0.00056	0.00047
43	0.00296	0.00245	0.00204	0.00169	0.00141	0.00117	0.00097	0.00081	0.00068	0.00056	0.00047	0.00039
44	0.00259	0.00213	0.00176	0.00146	0.00121	0.00100	0.00083	0.00069	0.00057	0.00047	0.00039	0.00033
45	0.00226	0.00186	0.00153	0.00126	0.00104	0.00085	0.00071	0.00058	0.00048	0.00040	0.00033	0.00027
46	0.00197	0.00161	0.00132	0.00108	0.00089	0.00073	0.00060	0.00049	0.00041	0.00033	0.00028	0.00023
47	0.00172	0.00140	0.00114	0.00093	0.00076	0.00062	0.00051	0.00042	0.00034	0.00028	0.00023	0.00019
48	0.00150	0.00122	0.00099	0.00081	0.00066	0.00053	0.00043	0.00035	0.00029	0.00024	0.00019	0.00016
49	0.00131	0.00106	0.00086	0.00069	0.00056	0.00046	0.00037	0.00030	0.00024	0.00020	0.00016	0.00013
50	0.00115	0.00092	0.00074	0.00060	0.00048	0.00039	0.00031	0.00025	0.00021	0.00017	0.00014	0.00011
51	0.00100	0.00080	0.00064	0.00052	0.00041	0.00033	0.00027	0.00022	0.00017	0.00014	0.00011	0.00009
52	0.00088	0.00070	0.00056	0.00044	0.00036	0.00028	0.00023	0.00018	0.00015	0.00012	0.00009	0.00008
53	0.00076	0.00061	0.00048	0.00038	0.00031	0.00024	0.00019	0.00015	0.00012	0.00010	0.00008	0.00006
54	0.00067	0.00053	0.00042	0.00033	0.00026	0.00021	0.00017	0.00013	0.00010	0.00008	0.00007	0.00005
55	0.00058	0.00046	0.00036	0.00028	0.00022	0.00018	0.00014	0.00011	0.00009	0.00007	0.00006	0.00004
56	0.00051	0.00040	0.00031	0.00025	0.00019	0.00015	0.00012	0.00009	0.00007	0.00006	0.00005	0.00004
57	0.00044	0.00035	0.00027	0.00021	0.00017	0.00013	0.00010	0.00008	0.00006	0.00005	0.00004	0.00003
58	0.00039	0.00030	0.00023	0.00018	0.00014	0.00011	0.00009	0.00007	0.00005	0.00004	0.00003	0.00003
59	0.00034	0.00026	0.00020	0.00016	0.00012	0.00009	0.00007	0.00006	0.00004	0.00003	0.00003	0.00002
60	0.00030	0.00023	0.00018	0.00014	0.00010	0.00008	0.00006	0.00005	0.00004	0.00003	0.00002	0.00002

TABLE B Present Value of an Ordinary Annuity of $1 per Period: 0.5%–7%

$$P_{A_{i,n}} = \frac{1 - \dfrac{1}{(1 + i)^n}}{i}$$

Period	.5%	1%	1.5%	2%	2.5%	3%	3.5%	4%	4.5%	5%	5.5%	6%	6.5%	7%
1	0.99502	0.99010	0.98522	0.98039	0.97561	0.97087	0.96618	0.96154	0.95694	0.95238	0.94787	0.94340	0.93897	0.93458
2	1.98510	1.97040	1.95588	1.94156	1.92742	1.91347	1.89969	1.88609	1.87267	1.85941	1.84632	1.83339	1.82063	1.80802
3	2.97025	2.94099	2.91220	2.88388	2.85602	2.82861	2.80164	2.77509	2.74896	2.72325	2.69793	2.67301	2.64848	2.62432
4	3.95050	3.90197	3.85438	3.80773	3.76197	3.71710	3.67308	3.62990	3.58753	3.54595	3.50515	3.46511	3.42580	3.38721
5	4.92587	4.85343	4.78264	4.71346	4.64583	4.57971	4.51505	4.45182	4.38998	4.32948	4.27028	4.21236	4.15568	4.10020
6	5.89638	5.79548	5.69719	5.60143	5.50813	5.41719	5.32855	5.24214	5.15787	5.07569	4.99553	4.91732	4.84101	4.76654
7	6.86207	6.72819	6.59821	6.47199	6.34939	6.23028	6.11454	6.00205	5.89270	5.78637	5.68297	5.58238	5.48452	5.38929
8	7.82296	7.65168	7.48593	7.32548	7.17014	7.01969	6.87396	6.73274	6.59589	6.46321	6.33457	6.20979	6.08875	5.97130
9	8.77906	8.56602	8.36052	8.16224	7.97087	7.78611	7.60769	7.43533	7.26879	7.10782	6.95220	6.80169	6.65610	6.51523
10	9.73041	9.47130	9.22218	8.98259	8.75206	8.53020	8.31661	8.11090	7.91272	7.72173	7.53763	7.36009	7.18883	7.02358
11	10.67703	10.36763	10.07112	9.78685	9.51421	9.25262	9.00155	8.76048	8.52892	8.30641	8.09254	7.88687	7.68904	7.49867
12	11.61893	11.25508	10.90751	10.57534	10.25776	9.95400	9.66333	9.38507	9.11858	8.86325	8.61852	8.38384	8.15873	7.94269
13	12.55615	12.13374	11.73153	11.34837	10.98318	10.63496	10.30274	9.98565	9.68285	9.39357	9.11708	8.85268	8.59974	8.35765
14	13.48871	13.00370	12.54338	12.10625	11.69091	11.29607	10.92052	10.56312	10.22283	9.89864	9.58965	9.29498	9.01384	8.74547
15	14.41662	13.86505	13.34323	12.84926	12.38138	11.93794	11.51741	11.11839	10.73955	10.37966	10.03758	9.71225	9.40267	9.10791
16	15.33993	14.71787	14.13126	13.57771	13.05500	12.56110	12.09412	11.65230	11.23402	10.83777	10.46216	10.10590	9.76776	9.44665
17	16.25863	15.56225	14.90765	14.29187	13.71220	13.16612	12.65132	12.16567	11.70719	11.27407	10.86461	10.47726	10.11058	9.76322
18	17.17277	16.39827	15.67256	14.99203	14.35336	13.75351	13.18968	12.65930	12.15999	11.68959	11.24607	10.82760	10.43247	10.05909
19	18.08236	17.22601	16.42617	15.67846	14.97889	14.32380	13.70984	13.13394	12.59329	12.08532	11.60765	11.15812	10.73471	10.33560
20	18.98742	18.04555	17.16864	16.35143	15.58916	14.87747	14.21240	13.59033	13.00794	12.46221	11.95038	11.46992	11.01851	10.59401
21	19.88798	18.85698	17.90014	17.01121	16.18455	15.41502	14.69797	14.02916	13.40472	12.82115	12.27524	11.76408	11.28498	10.83553
22	20.78406	19.66038	18.62082	17.65805	16.76541	15.93692	15.16712	14.45112	13.78442	13.16300	12.58317	12.04158	11.53520	11.06124
23	21.67568	20.45582	19.33086	18.29220	17.33211	16.44361	15.62041	14.85684	14.14777	13.48857	12.87504	12.30338	11.77014	11.27219
24	22.56287	21.24339	20.03041	18.91393	17.88499	16.93554	16.05837	15.24696	14.49548	13.79864	13.15170	12.55036	11.99074	11.46933
25	23.44564	22.02316	20.71961	19.52346	18.42438	17.41315	16.48151	15.62208	14.82821	14.09394	13.41393	12.78336	12.19788	11.65358
26	24.32402	22.79520	21.39863	20.12104	18.95061	17.87684	16.89035	15.98277	15.14661	14.37519	13.66250	13.00317	12.39237	11.82578
27	25.19803	23.55961	22.06762	20.70690	19.46401	18.32703	17.28536	16.32959	15.45130	14.64303	13.89810	13.21053	12.57500	11.98671
28	26.06769	24.31644	22.72672	21.28127	19.95489	18.76411	17.66702	16.66306	15.74287	14.89813	14.12142	13.40616	12.74648	12.13711
29	26.93302	25.06579	23.37608	21.84438	20.45355	19.18845	18.03577	16.98371	16.02189	15.14107	14.33310	13.59072	12.90749	12.27767
30	27.79405	25.80771	24.01584	22.39646	20.93029	19.60044	18.39205	17.29203	16.28889	15.37245	14.53375	13.76483	13.05868	12.40904
31	28.65080	26.54229	24.64615	22.93770	21.39541	20.00043	18.73628	17.58849	16.54439	15.59281	14.72393	13.92909	13.20063	12.53181
32	29.50328	27.26959	25.26714	23.46833	21.84918	20.38877	19.06887	17.87355	16.78889	15.80268	14.90420	14.08404	13.33393	12.64656
33	30.35153	27.98969	25.87895	23.98856	22.29188	20.76579	19.39021	18.14765	17.02286	16.00255	15.07507	14.23023	13.45909	12.75379
34	31.19555	28.70267	26.48173	24.49859	22.72379	21.13184	19.70068	18.41120	17.24676	16.19290	15.23703	14.36814	13.57661	12.85401
35	32.03537	29.40858	27.07559	24.99862	23.14516	21.48722	20.00066	18.66461	17.46101	16.37419	15.39055	14.49825	13.68696	12.94767
36	32.87102	30.10751	27.66068	25.48884	23.55625	21.83225	20.29049	18.90828	17.66604	16.54685	15.53607	14.62099	13.79057	13.03521
37	33.70250	30.79951	28.23713	25.96945	23.95732	22.16724	20.57053	19.14258	17.86224	16.71129	15.67400	14.73678	13.88786	13.11702
38	34.52985	31.48466	28.80505	26.44064	24.34860	22.49246	20.84109	19.36786	18.04999	16.86789	15.80474	14.84602	13.97921	13.19347
39	35.35309	32.16303	29.36458	26.90259	24.73034	22.80822	21.10250	19.58448	18.22966	17.01704	15.92866	14.94907	14.06499	13.26493
40	36.17223	32.83469	29.91585	27.35548	25.10278	23.11477	21.35507	19.79277	18.40158	17.15909	16.04612	15.04630	14.14553	13.33171
41	36.98729	33.49969	30.45896	27.79949	25.46612	23.41240	21.59910	19.99305	18.56611	17.29437	16.15746	15.13802	14.22115	13.39412
42	37.79830	34.15811	30.99405	28.23479	25.82061	23.70136	21.83488	20.18563	18.72355	17.42321	16.26300	15.22454	14.29216	13.45245
43	38.60527	34.81001	31.52123	28.66156	26.16645	23.98190	22.06269	20.37079	18.87421	17.54591	16.36303	15.30617	14.35884	13.50696
44	39.40823	35.45545	32.04062	29.07996	26.50385	24.25427	22.28279	20.54884	19.01838	17.66277	16.45785	15.38318	14.42144	13.55791
45	40.20720	36.09451	32.55234	29.49016	26.83302	24.51871	22.49545	20.72004	19.15635	17.77407	16.54773	15.45583	14.48023	13.60552
46	41.00219	36.72724	33.05649	29.89231	27.15417	24.77545	22.70092	20.88465	19.28837	17.88007	16.63292	15.52437	14.53543	13.65002
47	41.79322	37.35370	33.55319	30.28658	27.46748	25.02471	22.89944	21.04294	19.41471	17.98102	16.71366	15.58903	14.58725	13.69161
48	42.58032	37.97396	34.04255	30.67312	27.77315	25.26671	23.09124	21.19513	19.53561	18.07716	16.79020	15.65003	14.63592	13.73047
49	43.36350	38.58808	34.52468	31.05208	28.07137	25.50166	23.27656	21.34147	19.65130	18.16872	16.86275	15.70757	14.68161	13.76680
50	44.14279	39.19612	34.99969	31.42361	28.36231	25.72976	23.45562	21.48218	19.76201	18.25593	16.93152	15.76186	14.72452	13.80075
51	44.91820	39.79814	35.46767	31.78785	28.64616	25.95123	23.62862	21.61749	19.86795	18.33898	16.99670	15.81308	14.76481	13.83247
52	45.68975	40.39419	35.92874	32.14495	28.92308	26.16624	23.79576	21.74758	19.96933	18.41807	17.05848	15.86139	14.80264	13.86212
53	46.45746	40.98435	36.38300	32.49505	29.19325	26.37499	23.95726	21.87267	20.06634	18.49340	17.11705	15.90697	14.83816	13.88964
54	47.22135	41.56866	36.83054	32.83828	29.45683	26.57766	24.11330	21.99296	20.15918	18.56515	17.17255	15.94998	14.87151	13.91573
55	47.98145	42.14719	37.27147	33.17479	29.71398	26.77443	24.26405	22.10861	20.24802	18.63347	17.22517	15.99054	14.90282	13.93994
56	48.73776	42.71999	37.70588	33.50469	29.96486	26.96546	24.40971	22.21982	20.33303	18.69854	17.27504	16.02881	14.93223	13.96256
57	49.49031	43.28712	38.13387	33.82813	30.20962	27.15094	24.55045	22.32675	20.41439	18.76052	17.32232	16.06492	14.95984	13.98370
58	50.23911	43.84863	38.55554	34.14523	30.44841	27.33101	24.68642	22.42957	20.49224	18.81954	17.36712	16.09898	14.98577	14.00346
59	50.98419	44.40459	38.97097	34.45610	30.68137	27.50583	24.81780	22.52843	20.56673	18.87575	17.40960	16.13111	15.01011	14.02192
60	51.72556	44.95504	39.38027	34.76089	30.90866	27.67556	24.94473	22.62349	20.63802	18.92929	17.44985	16.16143	15.03297	14.03918

TABLE B (*continued*)   Present Value of an Ordinary Annuity of $1 per Period: 7.5%–14%

Period	7.5%	8%	8.5%	9%	9.5%	10%	10.5%	11%	11.5%	12%	12.5%	13%	13.5%	14%
1	0.93023	0.92593	0.92166	0.91743	0.91324	0.90909	0.90498	0.90090	0.89686	0.89286	0.88889	0.88496	0.88106	0.87719
2	1.79557	1.78326	1.77111	1.75911	1.74725	1.73554	1.72396	1.71252	1.70122	1.69005	1.67901	1.66810	1.65732	1.64666
3	2.60053	2.57710	2.55402	2.53129	2.50891	2.48685	2.46512	2.44371	2.42262	2.40183	2.38134	2.36115	2.34125	2.32163
4	3.34933	3.31213	3.27560	3.23972	3.20448	3.16987	3.13586	3.10245	3.06961	3.03735	3.00564	2.97447	2.94383	2.91371
5	4.04588	3.99271	3.94064	3.88965	3.83971	3.79079	3.74286	3.69590	3.64988	3.60478	3.56057	3.51723	3.47474	3.43308
6	4.69385	4.62288	4.55359	4.48592	4.41983	4.35526	4.29218	4.23054	4.17029	4.11141	4.05384	3.99755	3.94250	3.88867
7	5.29660	5.20637	5.11851	5.03295	4.94961	4.86842	4.78930	4.71220	4.63704	4.56376	4.49230	4.42261	4.35463	4.28830
8	5.85730	5.74664	5.63918	5.53482	5.43344	5.33493	5.23919	5.14612	5.05564	4.96764	4.88205	4.79877	4.71774	4.63886
9	6.37889	6.24689	6.11906	5.99525	5.87528	5.75902	5.64632	5.53705	5.43106	5.32825	5.22848	5.13166	5.03765	4.94637
10	6.86408	6.71008	6.56135	6.41766	6.27880	6.14457	6.01477	5.88923	5.76777	5.65022	5.53643	5.42624	5.31952	5.21612
11	7.31542	7.13896	6.96898	6.80519	6.64730	6.49506	6.34821	6.20652	6.06975	5.93770	5.81016	5.68694	5.56786	5.45273
12	7.73528	7.53608	7.34469	7.16073	6.98384	6.81369	6.64996	6.49236	6.34058	6.19437	6.05348	5.91765	5.78666	5.66029
13	8.12584	7.90378	7.69095	7.48690	7.29118	7.10336	6.92304	6.74987	6.58348	6.42355	6.26976	6.12181	5.97943	5.84236
14	8.48915	8.24424	8.01010	7.78615	7.57185	7.36669	7.17018	6.98187	6.80133	6.62817	6.46201	6.30249	6.14928	6.00207
15	8.82712	8.55948	8.30424	8.06069	7.82818	7.60608	7.39382	7.19087	6.99671	6.81086	6.63289	6.46238	6.29893	6.14217
16	9.14151	8.85137	8.57533	8.31256	8.06226	7.82371	7.59622	7.37916	7.17194	6.97399	6.78479	6.60388	6.43077	6.26506
17	9.43396	9.12164	8.82519	8.54363	8.27604	8.02155	7.77939	7.54879	7.32909	7.11963	6.91982	6.72909	6.54694	6.37286
18	9.70601	9.37189	9.05548	8.75563	8.47127	8.20141	7.94515	7.70162	7.47004	7.24967	7.03984	6.83991	6.64928	6.46742
19	9.95908	9.60360	9.26772	8.95011	8.64956	8.36492	8.09515	7.83929	7.59644	7.36578	7.14652	6.93797	6.73946	6.55037
20	10.19449	9.81815	9.46334	9.12855	8.81238	8.51356	8.23091	7.96333	7.70982	7.46944	7.24135	7.02475	6.81890	6.62313
21	10.41348	10.01680	9.64363	9.29224	8.96108	8.64869	8.35376	8.07507	7.81149	7.56200	7.32565	7.10155	6.88890	6.68696
22	10.61719	10.20074	9.80980	9.44243	9.09688	8.77154	8.46494	8.17574	7.90269	7.64465	7.40058	7.16951	6.95057	6.74294
23	10.80669	10.37106	9.96295	9.58021	9.22089	8.88322	8.56556	8.26643	7.98447	7.71843	7.46718	7.22966	7.00491	6.79206
24	10.98297	10.52876	10.10410	9.70661	9.33415	8.98474	8.65662	8.34814	8.05782	7.78432	7.52638	7.28288	7.05279	6.83514
25	11.14695	10.67478	10.23419	9.82258	9.43758	9.07704	8.73902	8.42174	8.12361	7.84314	7.57901	7.32998	7.09497	6.87293
26	11.29948	10.80998	10.35409	9.92897	9.53203	9.16005	8.81359	8.48806	8.18261	7.89566	7.62578	7.37167	7.13213	6.90608
27	11.44138	10.93516	10.46460	10.02658	9.61830	9.23722	8.88108	8.54780	8.23552	7.94255	7.66736	7.40856	7.16487	6.93515
28	11.57338	11.05108	10.56645	10.11613	9.69707	9.30657	8.94215	8.60162	8.28298	7.98442	7.70432	7.44120	7.19372	6.96066
29	11.69617	11.15841	10.66033	10.19828	9.76902	9.36961	8.99742	8.65011	8.32554	8.02181	7.73717	7.47009	7.21914	6.98304
30	11.81039	11.25778	10.74684	10.27365	9.83472	9.42691	9.04744	8.69379	8.36371	8.05518	7.76638	7.49565	7.24153	7.00266
31	11.91664	11.34980	10.82658	10.34280	9.89472	9.47901	9.09271	8.73315	8.39795	8.08499	7.79234	7.51828	7.26126	7.01988
32	12.01548	11.43500	10.90008	10.40624	9.94952	9.52638	9.13367	8.76860	8.42866	8.11159	7.81541	7.53830	7.27864	7.03498
33	12.10742	11.51389	10.96781	10.46444	9.99956	9.56943	9.17074	8.80054	8.45619	8.13535	7.83592	7.55602	7.29396	7.04823
34	12.19295	11.58693	11.03024	10.51784	10.04526	9.60857	9.20429	8.82932	8.48089	8.15656	7.85415	7.57170	7.30745	7.05985
35	12.27251	11.65457	11.08778	10.56682	10.08699	9.64416	9.23465	8.85524	8.50304	8.17550	7.87036	7.58557	7.31934	7.07005
36	12.34652	11.71719	11.14081	10.61176	10.12511	9.67651	9.26213	8.87859	8.52291	8.19241	7.88476	7.59785	7.32982	7.07899
37	12.41537	11.77518	11.18969	10.65299	10.15992	9.70592	9.28700	8.89963	8.54072	8.20751	7.89757	7.60872	7.33904	7.08683
38	12.47941	11.82887	11.23474	10.69082	10.19171	9.73265	9.30950	8.91859	8.55670	8.22099	7.90895	7.61833	7.34718	7.09371
39	12.53899	11.87858	11.27625	10.72552	10.22074	9.75696	9.32986	8.93567	8.57103	8.23303	7.91906	7.62684	7.35434	7.09975
40	12.59441	11.92461	11.31452	10.75736	10.24725	9.77905	9.34829	8.95105	8.58389	8.24378	7.92806	7.63438	7.36065	7.10504
41	12.64596	11.96723	11.34979	10.78657	10.27146	9.79914	9.36497	8.96491	8.59541	8.25337	7.93605	7.64104	7.36621	7.10969
42	12.69392	12.00670	11.38229	10.81337	10.29357	9.81740	9.38006	8.97740	8.60575	8.26194	7.94316	7.64694	7.37111	7.11376
43	12.73853	12.04324	11.41225	10.83795	10.31376	9.83400	9.39372	8.98865	8.61502	8.26959	7.94947	7.65216	7.37543	7.11733
44	12.78003	12.07707	11.43986	10.86051	10.33220	9.84909	9.40608	8.99878	8.62334	8.27642	7.95509	7.65678	7.37923	7.12047
45	12.81863	12.10840	11.46531	10.88120	10.34904	9.86281	9.41727	9.00791	8.63080	8.28252	7.96008	7.66086	7.38258	7.12322
46	12.85454	12.13741	11.48877	10.90018	10.36442	9.87528	9.42739	9.01614	8.63749	8.28796	7.96451	7.66448	7.38554	7.12563
47	12.88794	12.16427	11.51038	10.91760	10.37847	9.88662	9.43656	9.02355	8.64349	8.29282	7.96846	7.66768	7.38814	7.12774
48	12.91902	12.18914	11.53031	10.93358	10.39130	9.89693	9.44485	9.03022	8.64887	8.29716	7.97196	7.67052	7.39043	7.12960
49	12.94792	12.21216	11.54867	10.94823	10.40301	9.90630	9.45235	9.03624	8.65369	8.30104	7.97508	7.67302	7.39245	7.13123
50	12.97481	12.23348	11.56560	10.96168	10.41371	9.91481	9.45914	9.04165	8.65802	8.30450	7.97785	7.67524	7.39423	7.13266
51	12.99982	12.25323	11.58119	10.97402	10.42348	9.92256	9.46529	9.04653	8.66190	8.30759	7.98031	7.67720	7.39580	7.13391
52	13.02309	12.27151	11.59557	10.98534	10.43240	9.92960	9.47085	9.05093	8.66538	8.31035	7.98250	7.67894	7.39718	7.13501
53	13.04474	12.28843	11.60882	10.99573	10.44055	9.93600	9.47588	9.05489	8.66850	8.31281	7.98444	7.68048	7.39839	7.13597
54	13.06487	12.30410	11.62103	11.00525	10.44799	9.94182	9.48043	9.05846	8.67130	8.31501	7.98617	7.68184	7.39947	7.13682
55	13.08360	12.31861	11.63229	11.01399	10.45478	9.94711	9.48456	9.06168	8.67382	8.31697	7.98771	7.68304	7.40041	7.13756
56	13.10103	12.33205	11.64266	11.02201	10.46099	9.95191	9.48829	9.06457	8.67607	8.31872	7.98907	7.68411	7.40124	7.13821
57	13.11723	12.34449	11.65222	11.02937	10.46666	9.95629	9.49166	9.06718	8.67809	8.32029	7.99029	7.68505	7.40198	7.13878
58	13.13231	12.35601	11.66104	11.03612	10.47183	9.96026	9.49472	9.06954	8.67990	8.32169	7.99137	7.68589	7.40262	7.13928
59	13.14633	12.36668	11.66916	11.04231	10.47656	9.96387	9.49748	9.07165	8.68152	8.32294	7.99232	7.68663	7.40319	7.13972
60	13.15938	12.37655	11.67664	11.04799	10.48088	9.96716	9.49998	9.07356	8.68298	8.32405	7.99318	7.68728	7.40369	7.14011

TABLE B (*concluded*)   Present Value of an Ordinary Annuity of $1 per Period: 14.5%–20%

Period	14.5%	15%	15.5%	16%	16.5%	17%	17.5%	18%	18.5%	19%	19.5%	20%
1	0.87336	0.86957	0.86580	0.86207	0.85837	0.85470	0.85106	0.84746	0.84388	0.84034	0.83682	0.83333
2	1.63612	1.62571	1.61541	1.60523	1.59517	1.58521	1.57537	1.56564	1.55602	1.54650	1.53709	1.52778
3	2.30229	2.28323	2.26443	2.24589	2.22761	2.20958	2.19181	2.17427	2.15698	2.13992	2.12309	2.10648
4	2.88410	2.85498	2.82634	2.79818	2.77048	2.74324	2.71643	2.69006	2.66412	2.63859	2.61346	2.58873
5	3.39223	3.35216	3.31285	3.27429	3.23646	3.19935	3.16292	3.12717	3.09208	3.05763	3.02382	2.99061
6	3.83600	3.78448	3.73407	3.68474	3.63645	3.58918	3.54291	3.49760	3.45323	3.40978	3.36721	3.32551
7	4.22358	4.16042	4.09876	4.03857	3.97979	3.92238	3.86631	3.81153	3.75800	3.70570	3.65457	3.60459
8	4.56208	4.48732	4.41451	4.34359	4.27449	4.20716	4.14154	4.07757	4.01519	3.95437	3.89504	3.83716
9	4.85771	4.77158	4.68789	4.60654	4.52746	4.45057	4.37578	3.30302	4.23223	4.16333	4.09627	4.03097
10	5.11591	5.01877	4.92458	4.83323	4.74460	4.65860	4.57513	4.49409	4.41538	4.33893	4.26466	4.19247
11	5.34140	5.23371	5.12951	5.02864	4.93099	4.83641	4.74479	4.65601	4.56994	4.48650	4.40557	4.32706
12	5.53834	5.42062	5.30693	5.19711	5.09098	4.98839	4.88918	4.79322	4.70037	4.61050	4.52349	4.43922
13	5.71034	5.58315	5.46055	5.34233	5.22831	5.11828	5.01207	4.90951	4.81044	4.71471	4.62217	4.53268
14	5.86056	5.72448	5.59355	5.46753	5.34619	5.22930	5.11666	5.00806	4.90333	4.80228	4.70474	4.61057
15	5.99176	5.84737	5.70870	5.57546	5.44747	5.32419	5.20567	5.09158	4.98171	4.87586	4.77384	4.67547
16	6.10634	5.95423	5.80840	5.66850	5.53422	5.40529	5.28142	5.16235	5.04786	4.93770	4.83167	4.72956
17	6.20641	6.04716	5.89472	5.74870	5.60878	5.47461	5.34589	5.22223	5.10368	4.98966	4.88006	4.77463
18	6.29381	6.12797	5.96945	5.81785	5.67277	5.53385	5.40075	5.27316	5.15078	5.03333	4.92055	4.81219
19	6.37014	6.19823	6.03416	5.87746	5.72770	5.58449	5.44745	5.31624	5.19053	5.07003	4.95443	4.84350
20	6.43680	6.25933	6.09018	5.92884	5.77485	5.62777	5.48719	5.35275	5.22408	5.10086	4.98279	4.86958
21	6.49502	6.31246	6.13868	5.97314	5.81532	5.66476	5.52101	5.38368	5.25239	5.12677	5.00652	4.89132
22	6.54587	6.35866	6.18568	6.01133	5.85006	5.69637	5.54980	5.40990	5.27628	5.14855	5.02638	4.90943
23	6.59028	6.39884	6.21704	6.04425	5.87988	5.72340	5.57430	5.43212	5.29644	5.16685	5.04299	4.92453
24	6.62907	6.43377	6.24852	6.07263	5.90548	5.74649	5.59515	5.45095	5.31345	5.18223	5.05690	4.93710
25	6.66294	6.46415	6.27577	6.09709	5.92745	5.76623	5.61289	5.46691	5.32780	5.19515	5.06853	4.94759
26	6.69252	6.49056	6.29937	6.11818	5.94631	5.78311	5.62799	5.48043	5.33992	5.20601	5.07827	4.95632
27	6.71836	6.51353	6.31980	6.13636	5.96250	5.79753	5.64084	5.49189	5.35014	5.21513	5.08642	4.96360
28	6.74093	6.53351	6.33749	6.15204	5.97639	5.80985	5.65178	5.50160	5.35877	5.22280	5.09324	4.96967
29	6.76064	6.55088	6.35281	6.16555	5.98832	5.82039	5.66109	5.50983	5.36605	5.22924	5.09894	4.97472
30	6.77785	6.56598	6.36607	6.17720	5.99856	5.82939	5.66901	5.51681	5.37219	5.23466	5.10372	4.97894
31	6.79288	6.57911	6.37755	6.18724	6.00734	5.83709	5.67576	5.52272	5.37738	5.23921	5.10771	4.98245
32	6.80601	6.59053	6.38749	6.19590	6.01489	5.84366	5.68150	5.52773	5.38175	5.24303	5.11106	4.98537
33	6.81747	6.60046	6.39609	6.20336	6.02136	5.84928	5.68638	5.53197	5.38545	5.24625	5.11386	4.98781
34	6.82749	6.60910	6.40354	6.20979	6.02692	5.85409	5.69054	5.53557	5.38856	5.24895	5.11620	4.98984
35	6.83623	6.61661	6.40999	6.21534	6.03169	5.85820	5.69407	5.53862	5.39119	5.25122	5.11816	4.99154
36	6.84387	6.62314	6.41558	6.22012	6.03579	5.86171	5.69708	5.54120	5.39341	5.25312	5.11980	4.99295
37	6.85054	6.62881	6.42041	6.22424	6.03930	5.86471	5.69965	5.54339	5.39528	5.25472	5.12117	4.99412
38	6.85637	6.63375	6.42460	6.22779	6.04232	5.86727	5.70183	5.54525	5.39686	5.25607	5.12232	4.99510
39	6.86146	6.63805	6.42823	6.23086	6.04491	5.86946	5.70368	5.54682	5.39820	5.25720	5.12328	4.99592
40	6.86590	6.64178	6.43136	6.23350	6.04713	5.87133	5.70526	5.54815	5.39932	5.25815	5.12408	4.99660
41	6.86978	6.64502	6.43408	6.23577	6.04904	5.87294	5.70660	5.54928	5.40027	5.25895	5.12475	4.99717
42	6.87317	6.64785	6.43643	6.23774	6.05068	5.87430	5.70775	5.55024	5.40107	5.25962	5.12532	4.99764
43	6.87613	6.65030	6.43847	6.23943	6.05208	5.87547	5.70872	5.55105	5.40175	5.26019	5.12579	4.99803
44	6.87872	6.65244	6.44024	6.24089	6.05329	5.87647	5.70955	5.55174	5.40232	5.26066	5.12618	4.99836
45	6.88098	6.65429	6.44176	6.24214	6.05433	5.87733	5.71026	5.55232	5.40280	5.26106	5.12651	4.99863
46	6.88295	6.65591	6.44308	6.24323	6.05522	5.87806	5.71086	5.55281	5.40321	5.26140	5.12679	4.99886
47	6.88467	6.65731	6.44423	6.24416	6.05598	5.87868	5.71137	5.55323	5.40355	5.26168	5.12702	4.99905
48	6.88618	6.65853	6.44522	6.24497	6.05664	5.87922	5.71180	5.55359	5.40384	5.26191	5.12721	4.99921
49	6.88749	6.65959	6.44608	6.24566	6.05720	5.87967	5.71217	5.55389	5.40409	5.26211	5.12738	4.99934
50	6.88864	6.66051	6.44682	6.24626	6.05768	5.88006	5.71249	5.55414	5.40429	5.26228	5.12751	4.99945
51	6.88964	6.66132	6.44746	6.24678	6.05809	5.88039	5.71275	5.55436	5.40447	5.26242	5.12762	4.99954
52	6.89052	6.66201	6.44802	6.24722	6.05845	5.88068	5.71298	5.55454	5.40461	5.26254	5.12772	4.99962
53	6.89128	6.66262	6.44850	6.24760	6.05876	5.88092	5.71318	5.55469	5.40474	5.26264	5.12780	4.99968
54	6.89195	6.66315	6.44892	6.24793	6.05902	5.88113	5.71334	5.55483	5.40484	5.26272	5.12786	4.99974
55	6.89253	6.66361	6.44928	6.24822	6.05924	5.88131	5.71348	5.55494	5.40493	5.26279	5.12792	4.99978
56	6.89304	6.66401	6.44959	6.24846	6.05944	5.88146	5.71360	5.55503	5.40500	5.26285	5.12797	4.99982
57	6.89348	6.66435	6.44987	6.24868	6.05960	5.88159	5.71370	5.55511	5.40507	5.26290	5.12801	4.99985
58	6.89387	6.66466	6.45010	6.24886	6.05974	5.88170	5.71379	5.55518	5.40512	5.26294	5.12804	4.99987
59	6.89421	6.66492	6.45030	6.24902	6.05987	5.88180	5.71386	5.55524	5.40516	5.26297	5.12807	4.99989
60	6.89451	6.66515	6.45048	6.24915	6.05997	5.88188	5.71393	5.55529	5.40520	5.26300	5.12809	4.99991

TABLE C Amount of 1 (at compound interest) $(1 + i)^n$

Periods	$\frac{1}{4}\%$	$\frac{1}{2}\%$	$\frac{3}{4}\%$	1%	$1\frac{1}{4}\%$	$1\frac{1}{2}\%$
1	1.0025 0000	1.0050 0000	1.0075	1.01	1.0125	1.015
2	1.0050 0625	1.0100 2500	1.0150 5625	1.0201	1.0251 5625	1.0302 25
3	1.0075 1877	1.0150 7513	1.0226 6917	1.0303 01	1.0379 7070	1.0456 7838
4	1.0100 3756	1.0201 5050	1.0303 3919	1.0406 0401	1.0509 4534	1.0613 6355
5	1.0125 6266	1.0252 5125	1.0380 6673	1.0510 1005	1.0640 8215	1.0772 8400
6	1.0150 9406	1.0303 7751	1.0458 5224	1.0615 2015	1.0773 8318	1.0934 4326
7	1.0176 3180	1.0355 2940	1.0536 9613	1.0721 3535	1.0908 5047	1.1098 4491
8	1.0201 7588	1.0407 0704	1.0615 9885	1.0828 5671	1.1044 8610	1.1264 9259
9	1.0227 2632	1.0459 1058	1.0695 6084	1.0936 8527	1.1182 9218	1.1433 8998
10	1.0252 8313	1.0511 4013	1.0775 8255	1.1046 2213	1.1322 7083	1.1605 4083
11	1.0278 4634	1.0563 9583	1.0856 6441	1.1156 6835	1.1464 2422	1.1779 4894
12	1.0304 1596	1.0616 7781	1.0938 0690	1.1268 2503	1.1607 5452	1.1956 1817
13	1.0329 9200	1.0669 8620	1.1020 1045	1.1380 9328	1.1752 6395	1.2135 5244
14	1.0355 7448	1.0723 2113	1.1102 7553	1.1494 7421	1.1899 5475	1.2317 5573
15	1.0381 6341	1.0776 8274	1.1186 0259	1.1609 6896	1.2048 2918	1.2502 3207
16	1.0407 5882	1.0830 7115	1.1269 9211	1.1725 7864	1.2198 8955	1.2689 8555
17	1.0433 6072	1.0884 8651	1.1354 4455	1.1843 0443	1.2351 3817	1.2880 2033
18	1.0459 6912	1.0939 2894	1.1439 6039	1.1961 4748	1.2505 7739	1.3073 4064
19	1.0485 8404	1.0993 9858	1.1525 4009	1.2081 0895	1.2662 0961	1.3269 5075
20	1.0512 0550	1.1048 9558	1.1611 8414	1.2201 9004	1.2820 3723	1.3468 5501
21	1.0538 3352	1.1104 2006	1.1698 9302	1.2323 9194	1.2980 6270	1.3670 5783
22	1.0564 6810	1.1159 7216	1.1786 6722	1.2447 1586	1.3142 8848	1.3875 6370
23	1.0591 0927	1.1215 5202	1.1875 0723	1.2571 6302	1.3307 1709	1.4083 7715
24	1.0617 5704	1.1271 5978	1.1964 1353	1.2697 3465	1.3473 5105	1.4295 0281
25	1.0644 1144	1.1327 9558	1.2053 8663	1.2824 3200	1.3641 9294	1.4509 4535
26	1.0670 7247	1.1384 5955	1.2144 2703	1.2952 5631	1.3812 4535	1.4727 0953
27	1.0697 4015	1.1441 5185	1.2235 3523	1.3082 0888	1.3985 1092	1.4948 0018
28	1.0724 1450	1.1498 7261	1.2327 1175	1.3212 9097	1.4159 9230	1.5172 2218
29	1.0750 9553	1.1556 2197	1.2419 5709	1.3345 0388	1.4336 9221	1.5399 8051
30	1.0777 8327	1.1614 0008	1.2512 7176	1.3478 4892	1.4516 1336	1.5630 8022
31	1.0804 7773	1.1672 0708	1.2606 5630	1.3613 2740	1.4697 5853	1.5865 2642
32	1.0831 7892	1.1730 4312	1.2701 1122	1.3749 4068	1.4881 3051	1.6103 2432
33	1.0858 8687	1.1789 0833	1.2796 3706	1.3886 9009	1.5067 3214	1.6344 7918
34	1.0886 0159	1.1848 0288	1.2892 3434	1.4025 7699	1.5255 6629	1.6589 9637
35	1.0913 2309	1.1907 2689	1.2989 0359	1.4166 0276	1.5446 3587	1.6838 8132
36	1.0940 5140	1.1966 8052	1.3086 4537	1.4307 6878	1.5639 4382	1.7091 3954
37	1.0967 8653	1.2026 6393	1.3184 6021	1.4450 7647	1.5834 9312	1.7347 7663
38	1.0995 2850	1.2086 7725	1.3283 4866	1.4595 2724	1.6032 8678	1.7607 9828
39	1.1022 7732	1.2147 2063	1.3383 1128	1.4741 2251	1.6233 2787	1.7872 1025
40	1.1050 3301	1.2207 9424	1.3483 4861	1.4888 6373	1.6436 1946	1.8140 1841

TABLE C *(concluded)*   Amount of 1 (at compound interest)

Periods	2%	2½%	3%	4%	5%	6%
1	1.02	1.025	1.03	1.04	1.05	1.06
2	1.0404	1.0506 25	1.0609	1.0816	1.1025	1.1236
3	1.0612 08	1.0768 9063	1.0927 27	1.1248 64	1.1576 25	1.1910 16
4	1.0824 3216	1.1038 1289	1.1255 0881	1.1698 5856	1.2155 0625	1.2624 7696
5	1.1040 8080	1.1314 0821	1.1592 7407	1.2166 5290	1.2762 8156	1.3382 2558
6	1.1261 6242	1.1596 9342	1.1940 5230	1.2653 1902	1.3400 9564	1.4185 1911
7	1.1486 8567	1.1886 8575	1.2298 7387	1.3159 3178	1.4071 0042	1.5036 3026
8	1.1716 5938	1.2184 0290	1.2667 7008	1.3685 6905	1.4774 5544	1.5938 4807
9	1.1950 9257	1.2488 6297	1.3047 7318	1.4233 1181	1.5513 2822	1.6894 7896
10	1.2189 9442	1.2800 8454	1.3439 1638	1.4802 4428	1.6288 9463	1.7908 4770
11	1.2433 7431	1.3120 8666	1.3842 3387	1.5394 5406	1.7103 3936	1.8982 9856
12	1.2682 4179	1.3448 8882	1.4257 6089	1.6010 3222	1.7958 5633	2.0121 9647
13	1.2936 0663	1.3785 1104	1.4685 3371	1.6650 7351	1.8856 4914	2.1329 2826
14	1.3194 7876	1.4129 7382	1.5125 8972	1.7316 7645	1.9799 3160	2.2609 0396
15	1.3458 6834	1.4482 9817	1.5579 6742	1.8009 4351	2.0789 2818	2.3965 5819
16	1.3727 8571	1.4845 0562	1.6047 0644	1.8729 8125	2.1828 7459	2.5403 5168
17	1.4002 4142	1.5216 1826	1.6528 4763	1.9479 0050	2.2920 1832	2.6927 7279
18	1.4282 4625	1.5596 5872	1.7024 3306	2.0258 1652	2.4066 1923	2.8543 3915
19	1.4568 1117	1.5986 5019	1.7535 0605	2.1068 4918	2.5269 5020	3.0255 9950
20	1.4859 4740	1.6386 1644	1.8061 1123	2.1911 2314	2.6532 9771	3.2071 3547
21	1.5156 6634	1.6795 8185	1.8602 9457	2.2787 6807	2.7859 6259	3.3995 6360
22	1.5459 7967	1.7215 7140	1.9161 0341	2.3699 1879	2.9252 6072	3.6035 3742
23	1.5768 9926	1.7646 1068	1.9735 8651	2.4647 1554	3.0715 2376	3.8197 4966
24	1.6084 3725	1.8087 2595	2.0327 9411	2.5633 0416	3.2250 9994	4.0489 3464
25	1.6406 0599	1.8539 4410	2.0937 7793	2.6658 3633	3.3863 5494	4.2918 7072
26	1.6734 1811	1.9002 9270	2.1565 9127	2.7724 6978	3.5556 7269	4.5493 8296
27	1.7068 8648	1.9478 0002	2.2212 8901	2.8833 6858	3.7334 5632	4.8223 4594
28	1.7410 2421	1.9964 9502	2.2879 2768	2.9987 0332	3.9201 2914	5.1116 8670
29	1.7758 4469	2.0464 0739	2.3565 6551	3.1186 5145	4.1161 3560	5.4183 8790
30	1.8113 6158	2.0975 6758	2.4272 6247	3.2433 9751	4.3219 4238	5.7434 9117
31	1.8475 8882	2.1500 0677	2.5000 8035	3.3731 3341	4.5380 3949	6.0881 0064
32	1.8845 4059	2.2037 5694	2.5750 8276	3.5080 5875	4.7649 4147	6.4533 8668
33	1.9222 3140	2.2588 5086	2.6523 3524	3.6483 8110	5.0031 8854	6.8405 8988
34	1.9606 7603	2.3153 2213	2.7319 0530	3.7943 1634	5.2533 4797	7.2510 2528
35	1.9998 8955	2.3732 0519	2.8138 6245	3.9460 8899	5.5160 1537	7.6860 8679
36	2.0398 8734	2.4325 3532	2.8982 7833	4.1039 3255	5.7918 1614	8.1472 5200
37	2.0806 8509	2.4933 4870	2.9852 2668	4.2680 8986	6.0814 0694	8.6360 8712
38	2.1222 9879	2.5556 8242	3.0747 8348	4.4388 1345	6.3854 7729	9.1542 5235
39	2.1647 4477	2.6195 7448	3.1670 2698	4.6163 6599	6.7047 5115	9.7035 0749
40	2.2080 3966	2.6850 6384	3.2620 3779	4.8010 2063	7.0399 8871	10.2857 1794

TABLE D Amount of an Annuity (if rent is 1) $\dfrac{(1 + i)^n - 1}{i}$

Periods	$\frac{1}{4}\%$	$\frac{1}{2}\%$	$\frac{3}{4}\%$	1%	$1\frac{1}{4}\%$	$1\frac{1}{2}\%$
1	1.000 0000	1.000 0000	1.000 0000	1.000 0000	1.000 0000	1.000 0000
2	2.002 5000	2.005 0000	2.007 5000	2.010 0000	2.012 5000	2.015 0000
3	3.007 5063	3.015 0250	3.022 5563	3.030 1000	3.037 6562	3.045 2250
4	4.015 0250	4.030 1001	4.045 2254	4.060 4010	4.075 6270	4.090 9034
5	5.025 0626	5.050 2506	5.075 5646	5.101 0050	5.126 5723	5.152 2669
6	6.037 6252	6.075 5019	6.113 6314	6.152 0151	6.190 6544	6.229 5509
7	7.052 7193	7.105 8794	7.159 4836	7.213 5352	7.268 0376	7.322 9942
8	8.070 3511	8.141 4088	8.213 1797	8.285 6706	8.358 8881	8.432 8391
9	9.090 5270	9.182 1158	9.274 7786	9.368 5273	9.463 3742	9.559 3317
10	10.113 2533	10.228 0264	10.344 3394	10.462 2125	10.581 6664	10.702 7217
11	11.138 5364	11.279 1665	11.421 9219	11.566 8347	11.713 9372	11.863 2625
12	12.166 3828	12.335 5624	12.507 5864	12.682 5030	12.860 3614	13.041 2114
13	13.196 7987	13.397 2402	13.601 3933	13.809 3280	14.021 1159	14.236 8296
14	14.229 7907	14.464 2264	14.703 4037	14.947 4213	15.196 3799	15.450 3821
15	15.265 3652	15.536 5475	15.813 6792	16.096 8955	16.386 3346	16.682 1378
16	16.303 5286	16.614 2303	16.932 2818	17.257 8645	17.591 1638	17.932 3698
17	17.344 2874	17.697 3014	18.059 2739	18.430 4431	18.811 0534	19.201 3554
18	18.387 6482	18.785 7879	19.194 7185	19.614 7476	20.046 1915	20.489 3757
19	19.433 6173	19.879 7168	20.338 6789	20.810 8950	21.296 7689	21.796 7164
20	20.482 2013	20.979 1154	21.491 2190	22.019 0040	22.562 9785	23.123 6671
21	21.533 4068	22.084 0110	22.652 4031	23.239 1940	23.845 0158	24.470 5221
22	22.587 2403	23.194 4311	23.822 2961	24.471 5860	25.143 0785	25.837 5799
23	23.643 7084	24.310 4032	25.000 9634	25.716 3018	26.457 3670	27.225 1436
24	24.702 8177	25.431 9552	26.188 4706	26.973 4648	27.788 0840	28.633 5208
25	25.764 5748	26.559 1150	27.384 8841	28.243 1995	29.135 4351	30.063 0236
26	26.828 9862	27.691 9106	28.590 2708	29.525 6315	30.499 6280	31.513 9690
27	27.896 0587	28.830 3702	29.804 6978	30.820 8878	31.880 8734	32.986 6785
28	28.965 7988	29.974 5220	31.028 2330	32.129 0967	33.279 3843	34.481 4787
29	30.038 2133	31.124 3946	32.260 9448	33.450 3877	34.695 3766	35.998 7009
30	31.113 3088	32.280 0166	33.502 9018	34.784 8915	36.129 0688	37.538 6814
31	32.191 0921	33.441 4167	34.754 1736	36.132 7404	37.580 6822	39.101 7616
32	33.271 5698	34.608 6238	36.014 8299	37.494 0678	39.050 4407	40.688 2880
33	34.354 7488	35.781 6669	37.284 9411	38.869 0085	40.538 5712	42.298 6123
34	35.440 6356	36.960 5752	38.564 5782	40.257 6986	42.045 3033	43.933 0915
35	36.529 2372	38.145 3781	39.853 8125	41.660 2756	43.570 8696	45.592 0879
36	37.620 5603	39.336 1050	41.152 7161	43.076 8784	45.115 5055	47.275 9692
37	38.714 6117	40.532 7855	42.461 3615	44.507 6471	46.679 4493	48.985 1087
38	39.811 3982	41.735 4494	43.779 8217	45.952 7236	48.262 9424	50.719 8854
39	40.910 9267	42.944 1267	45.108 1704	47.412 2508	49.866 2292	52.480 6837
40	42.013 2041	44.158 8473	46.446 4816	48.886 3734	51.489 5571	54.267 8939

TABLE D *(concluded)*   **Amount of an Annuity (if rent is 1)**

Periods	2%	2½%	3%	4%	5%	6%
1	1.000 0000	1.000 0000	1.000 0000	1.000 0000	1.000 0000	1.000 0000
2	2.020 0000	2.025 0000	2.030 0000	2.040 0000	2.050 0000	2.060 0000
3	3.060 4000	3.075 6250	3.090 9000	3.121 6000	3.152 5000	3.183 6000
4	4.121 6080	4.152 5156	4.183 6270	4.246 4640	4.310 1250	4.374 6160
5	5.204 0402	5.256 3285	5.309 1358	5.416 3226	5.525 6313	5.637 0930
6	6.308 1210	6.387 7367	6.468 4099	6.632 9755	6.801 9128	6.975 3185
7	7.434 2834	7.547 4302	7.662 4622	7.898 2945	8.142 0085	8.393 8377
8	8.582 9691	8.736 1159	8.892 3361	9.214 2263	9.549 1089	9.897 4679
9	9.754 6284	9.954 5188	10.159 1061	10.582 7953	11.026 5643	11.491 3160
10	10.949 7210	11.203 3818	11.463 8793	12.006 1071	12.577 8925	13.180 7949
11	12.168 7154	12.483 4663	12.807 7957	13.486 3514	14.206 7872	14.971 6426
12	13.412 0897	13.795 5530	14.192 0296	15.025 8055	15.917 1265	16.869 9412
13	14.680 3315	15.140 4418	15.617 7905	16.626 8377	17.712 9829	18.882 1377
14	15.973 9382	16.518 9528	17.086 3242	18.291 9112	19.598 6320	21.015 0659
15	17.293 4169	17.931 9267	18.598 9139	20.023 5876	21.578 5636	23.275 9699
16	18.639 2853	19.380 2248	20.156 8813	21.824 5311	23.657 4918	25.672 5281
17	20.012 0710	20.864 7305	21.761 5877	23.697 5124	25.840 3664	28.212 8798
18	21.412 3124	22.386 3487	23.414 4354	25.645 4129	28.132 3847	30.905 6526
19	22.840 5586	23.946 0074	25.116 8684	27.671 2294	30.539 0039	33.759 9917
20	24.297 3698	25.544 6576	26.870 3745	29.778 0786	33.065 9541	36.785 5912
21	25.783 3172	27.183 2741	28.676 4857	31.969 2017	35.719 2518	39.992 7267
22	27.298 9835	28.862 8559	30.536 7803	34.247 9698	38.505 2144	43.392 2903
23	28.844 9632	30.584 4273	32.452 8837	36.617 8886	41.430 4751	46.995 8277
24	30.421 8625	32.349 0380	34.426 4702	39.082 6041	44.501 9989	50.815 5774
25	32.030 2997	34.157 7639	36.459 2643	41.645 9083	47.727 0988	54.864 5120
26	33.670 9057	36.011 7080	38.553 0423	44.311 7446	51.113 4538	59.156 3827
27	35.344 3238	37.912 0007	40.709 6335	47.084 2144	54.669 1265	63.705 7657
28	37.051 2103	39.859 8008	42.930 9225	49.967 5830	58.402 5828	68.528 1116
29	38.792 2345	41.856 2958	45.218 8502	52.966 2863	62.322 7119	73.639 7983
30	40.568 0792	43.902 7032	47.575 4157	56.084 9378	66.438 8475	79.058 1862
31	42.379 4408	46.000 2707	50.002 6782	59.328 3353	70.760 7899	84.801 6774
32	44.227 0296	48.150 2775	52.502 7585	62.701 4687	75.298 8294	90.889 7780
33	46.111 5702	50.354 0345	55.077 8413	66.209 5274	80.063 7708	97.343 1647
34	48.033 8016	52.612 8853	57.730 1765	69.857 9085	85.066 9594	104.183 7546
35	49.994 4776	54.928 2074	60.462 0818	73.652 2249	90.320 3074	111.434 7799
36	51.994 3672	57.301 4126	63.275 9443	77.598 3139	95.836 3227	119.120 8667
37	54.034 2545	59.733 9479	66.174 2226	81.702 2464	101.628 1389	127.268 1187
38	56.114 9396	62.227 2966	69.159 4493	85.970 3363	107.709 5458	135.904 2058
39	58.237 2384	64.782 9791	72.234 2328	90.409 1497	114.095 0231	145.058 4581
40	60.401 9832	67.402 5535	75.401 2597	95.025 5157	120.799 7742	154.761 9656

Index